Lecture Notes of the Institute for Computer Sciences, Social Informatics and Telecommunications Engineering   164

More information about this series at http://www.springer.com/series/8197

Bhavani Thuraisingham · XiaoFeng Wang
Vinod Yegneswaran (Eds.)

Security and Privacy in Communication Networks

11th International Conference, SecureComm 2015
Dallas, TX, USA, October 26–29, 2015
Revised Selected Papers

 Springer

Editors
Bhavani Thuraisingham
The University of Texas at Dallas
Richardson, TX
USA

Vinod Yegneswaran
SRI International
Menlo Park, CA
USA

XiaoFeng Wang
Indiana University at Bloomington
Bloomington, IN
USA

ISSN 1867-8211 ISSN 1867-822X (electronic)
Lecture Notes of the Institute for Computer Sciences, Social Informatics
and Telecommunications Engineering
ISBN 978-3-319-28864-2 ISBN 978-3-319-28865-9 (eBook)
DOI 10.1007/978-3-319-28865-9

Library of Congress Control Number: 2015948705

Printed on acid-free paper

This Springer imprint is published by SpringerNature
The registered company is Springer International Publishing AG Switzerland

Preface

In the past 11 years, SecureComm has emerged as a leading international forum that covers all aspects of information and communications security with particular emphasis on security in communication and networking. SecureComm also serves as a venue for learning about the emerging trends in security and privacy research, giving participants the opportunity to network with experts in the field. The strategic objectives of SecureComm are to provide a common platform for security and privacy experts in academia, industry, and government as well as practitioners, standards developers, and policy makers to engage in discussions on the common goals in order to explore important research directions in the field.

For SecureComm 2015, 107 high-quality papers were submitted from all over the world. Unfortunately, the acceptance rate set for this conference did not allow us to accept all papers with relevant merits. In this respect, special thanks to the Technical Program Committee members for handling the challenging task and selecting 29 outstanding papers with a significant contribution to the field to be included in the proceedings. The 29 accepted papers can be broadly classified under the following themes:

- Mobile, System, and Software Security
- Cloud Security
- Privacy and Side Channels
- Web and Network Security
- Crypto, Protocol, and Models

Based on the submitted papers, we also extended invitations to the authors of 25 promising papers to be presented as posters, of whom 12 accepted. We awarded the Best Paper Award to the paper entitled "Enhancing Traffic Analysis Resistance for Tor Hidden Services with Multipath Routing" by Lei Yang and Fengjun Li.

In addition to the papers and posters presented at the conference, we also had two exciting keynote speakers:

- Engin Kirda, Northeastern University
- Joe St. Sauver, Farsight Security, Inc.

Finally, we are very grateful to the School of Computing and Informatics at the University of Indiana and the University of Texas at Dallas for their sponsorship, as well as the European Alliance for Innovation (EAI). We also thank the local Organizing Committee and its many members and volunteers for their support. A special thank goes to Anna Horvathova, EAI Conference Manager, and Rhonda Walls, Local Arrangements Coordinator, for their utmost professionalism in managing the administrative aspects of the conference. Last but not least, our gratitude goes to the Steering Committee members, in particular to Prof. Guofei Gu, whose continuous supervision helped make SecureComm a very successful event.

November 2015

Bhavani Thuraisingham
XiaoFeng Wang
Vinod Yegneswaran

Organization

General Chair

Bhavani Thuraisingham   The University of Texas at Dallas, USA

Technical Program Committee Chairs

XiaoFeng Wang   Indiana University at Bloomington, USA
Vinod Yegneswaran   SRI International, USA

Publications Chair

Yinzhi Cao   Lehigh University, USA

Local Arrangements Chairs

Latifur Khan   The University of Texas at Dallas, USA
Rhonda Walls   The University of Texas at Dallas, USA

Workshop Chair

Roberto Perdisci   University of Georgia, USA

Publicity Chairs

Damon McCoy   George Mason University, USA
Fabian Yamaguchi   University of Goettingen, Germany
Haixin Duan   Tsinghua University, China

Web Chair

Zhiqiang Lin   University of Texas at Dallas, USA

Program Committee

Prithvi Bisht   Adobe Research, USA
Yinzhi Cao   Lehigh University, USA
Kai Chen   Chinese Academy of Sciences, China
Yan Chen   Northwestern University, USA
Yangyi Chen   Google
Mihai Christodorescu   Qualcomm Research, USA

Contents

Privacy and Side Channels

Web and Network Security

Crypto, Protocol and Model

Poster Session

ATIS 2015: 6th International Workshop on Applications and Techniques in Information Security

Mobile, System and Software Security

FineDroid: Enforcing Permissions with System-Wide Application Execution Context

Yuan Zhang[1,2]([✉]), Min Yang[1,2], Guofei Gu[3], and Hao Chen[4]

[1] School of Computer Science, Fudan University, Shanghai, China
{yuanxzhang,m_yang}@fudan.edu.cn
[2] Shanghai Key Laboratory of Data Science, Fudan University, Shanghai, China
[3] SUCCESS Lab, Teax A&M University, College Station, USA
guofei@cse.tamu.edu
[4] University of California, Davis, USA
chen@ucdavis.edu

Abstract. To protect sensitive resources from unauthorized use, modern mobile systems, such as Android and iOS, design a permission-based access control model. However, current model could not enforce *fine-grained* control over the dynamic permission use contexts, causing two severe security problems. First, any code package in an application could use the granted permissions, inducing attackers to embed malicious payloads into benign apps. Second, the permissions granted to a benign application may be utilized by an attacker through vulnerable application interactions. Although ad hoc solutions have been proposed, none could systematically solve these two issues within a unified framework.

This paper presents the first such framework to provide context-sensitive permission enforcement that regulates permission use policies according to system-wide application contexts, which cover both *intra-application context* and *inter-application context*. We build a prototype system on Android, named *FineDroid*, to track such context during the application execution. To flexibly regulate context-sensitive permission rules, FineDroid features a policy framework that could express generic application contexts. We demonstrate the benefits of FineDroid by instantiating several security extensions based on the policy framework, for two potential users: administrators and developers. Furthermore, FineDroid is showed to introduce a minor overhead.

Keywords: Permission enforcement · Application context · Policy framework

1 Introduction

Modern mobile systems such as Android, iOS design a permission-based access control model to protect sensitive resources from unauthorized use. In this model, the accesses to protected resources without granted permissions would be denied

© Institute for Computer Sciences, Social Informatics and Telecommunications Engineering 2015
B. Thuraisingham et al. (Eds.): SecureComm 2015, LNICST 164, pp. 3–22, 2015.
DOI: 10.1007/978-3-319-28865-9_1

by the permission enforcement system. Ideally, the permission model should prevent malicious applications from abusing sensitive resources. However, the current permission model could not enforce a fine-grained control over permission use contexts (in this paper, when we say context we mean the application execution context). As a result, malicious entities could easily abuse permissions, leading to the explosion of Android malware these years [9] and the numerous reported application vulnerabilities [21,36].

Since Android has been expanding its market share rapidly as the most popular mobile platform [5], this paper mainly focuses on the permission model of Android. Currently, the coarse-grained permission enforcement mechanism is limited in the following two aspects.

- **Intra-application Context Insensitive.** Current permission model treats each application as a separate principal and permissions are granted at the granularity of application, thus all the code packages in the application could access the protected resources with the same granted permissions. In fact, not all the code packages in a single application come from a same origin.
- **Inter-application Context Insensitive.** Application interaction is a common characteristic of mobile applications. However, this new characteristic is transparent to the current coarse-grained permission enforcement mechanism, exposing a new attack surface, i.e., the permissions granted to a vulnerable application may be abused by an attacker application via inter-application communication.

Given these problems, plenty of extensions have been proposed to refine the Android permission model. Dr. Android and Mr. Hide framework [23] provides fine-grained semantics for serval permissions by adding a mediation layer. SEAndroid [33] hardens the permission enforcement system by introducing SELinux extensions to the Android middleware. FlaskDroid [15] extends the scope of current permission system by regulating resource accesses in Linux kernel and Android framework together within a unified policy language. Context-aware permission models [17,26,30,32] are proposed to support different permission policies according to external contexts, such as location, time of the day. However, these works still could not address the two limitations described above. There are also some work dedicated to reduce the risk of inter-application communication [12–14,18,20,26] or to isolate untrusted components inside an application [27,31,35,39]. However, none could achieve unified and flexible control according to the system-wide application context.

In this paper, we seek to fill the gap by bringing context-sensitive permission enforcement. We design a prototype, called FineDroid to provide fine-grained permission control over the application context. For example, if app A is allowed to use SEND_SMS permission in the context C, when app A requests SEND_SMS permission in another context C', it would be treated as a different request of SEND_SMS permission. In FineDroid, we consider both the *intra-application context* which represents the internal execution context of an application, and the *inter-application context* which reflects the IPC context of interacted applications. It is non-trivial to track such context in Android. FineDroid designs several techniques to automatically track such contexts along with the application execution. To ease the administration of permission control policies, FineDroid also features a policy framework which is general enough to express the rules for handling permission requests in a context-sensitive manner.

To demonstrate the benefits of FineDroid, we create two security extensions for administrators and developers. First, since permission leak vulnerability [20, 21, 24, 36] is very common and dangerous, we show how administrators could benefit from our system in transparently fixing these vulnerabilities without modifying vulnerable applications. Second, we provide application developers with the ability of restricting untrusted third-party SDK by declaring fine-grained permission specifications in the manifest file. All these security extensions can be easily built using policies.

We evaluate the effectiveness of our framework by measuring the effectiveness of the developed security extensions. For administrators, we show that FineDroid can easily fix permission leak vulnerabilities with context-sensitive permission control policies, and the policies could even be automatically generated by a vulnerability detector. For developers, we show that just several policies are enough to restrict the permissions that could be used by untrusted SDKs. It is worth noting that our system is not limited to support these two extensions. In addition, our system is showed to introduce minor performance overhead (less than 2%).

In this paper, we make the following contributions.

- We propose context-sensitive permission enforcement to deal with severe security problems of mobile systems. Considering the characteristics of mobile applications, it is important and necessary to take the application context into account when regulating permission requests.
- We design a novel context tracking technique to track *intra-application context* and *inter-application context* during the application execution.
- We design a new policy framework to flexibly and generally regulate permission requests with respect to the fine-grained application context.
- We demonstrate two security extensions based on the context-sensitive permission enforcement system, by just writing policies and sometimes a small number of auxiliary code.
- We evaluate the security benefits gained by the two security extensions and report the performance overhead.

2 Threat Model

This paper considers a strong threat model in which an attacker aims to gain and abuse sensitive resources stealthily. More specifically, this paper assumes an attacker could launch all kinds of *application-level* attacks, while the Linux kernel and `Android Runtime` are secure (not compromised). For the stealthiness, we mean an attacker tries to hide its identity in using permissions from the permission enforcement system. We consider these two kinds of attacks.

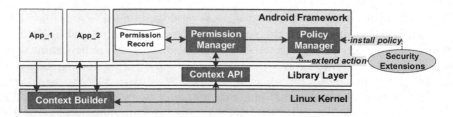

Fig. 1. Architecture of Context-Sensitive Permission Enforcement Framework.

Intra-application Attack. To hide the behavior of abusing permissions, an attacker could inject malicious payloads into a benign application (either before installation or during runtime). There are several ways for an attacker to infect benign apps. First, an attacker could actively embeds malicious payloads into popular benign apps and redistributes the repackaged version via third-party application markets. Second, an attacker could exploit code injection vulnerabilities (such as Man-in-the-Middle attack with dynamic class loading [28]) to inject malicious payloads. In addition, an attacker could also publish malicious SDKs, passively waiting for developers to include [1].

Inter-application Attack. The prevalent application interaction in the Android programming model may also be used by attackers to stealthily use permissions. This kind of attack has been verified in several forms, such as capability leak [20,21,36], component hijacking [24], content leak and pollution [41]. In these attacks, the permission enforcement system would see a permission request from a victim app which has a legitimate requirement for this privileged resource, while actually this permission is originally requested and utilized by an attacker app.

Note that our threat model does not consider other kinds of attacks such as privacy stealing, root exploits and colluding attacks, because they are not caused by the context-insensitive permission enforcement mechanism and have been well addressed by previous work [12,13,15,19,22].

3   Approach Overview

To defeat these attacks, we propose *context-sensitive* permission enforcement. The key idea is to construct a system-wide application context for each permission request and make granting decisions based on this context. Since the permission enforcement system could catch all the code packages and all the apps that participate in the permission request, an attacker could no longer stealthily abuse permissions.

The system-wide application context is composed of two parts: (1) **Intra-application Context** which represents the internal execution flow of an application, and (2) **Inter-application Context** which reflects the interaction flow among applications and system services. With these two kinds of contexts, our framework could accurately distinguish permission requests originated from different sources, thus achieving a fine-grained control over permission usage.

The overall architecture of FineDroid is presented in Figure 1. The rectangles filled with black color are new modules introduced by FineDroid. The core of our framework is the *Context Builder* module, which automatically tracks the application context along with the application execution. This module is placed in the Linux Kernel, so an attacker cannot escape from the context tracking. We also provide *Context API* at the library layer for applications and the Android framework to obtain the current application context from the *Context Builder* module.

Based on *Context API*, we design a context-sensitive permission enforcement system. To flexibly set context-sensitive permission control rules, FineDroid features a generic policy language. In FineDroid, all permission requests are intercepted by the *Permission Manager* module. To handle a permission request, the *Policy Manager* module examines all the polices in the system, and then *Permission Manager* could make a permission decision according to the action (e.g. allow or deny) specified in the match policy. Besides, our policy language is extensible for introducing new permission handling actions. To support building security extensions atop the policy framework, *Policy Manager* provides open interfaces for policy management and extension.

Next, we will detail the design of FineDroid. The application context tracking technique is presented in Section 4, and we describe the context-sensitive permission enforcement system in Section 5.

4   Application Context Tracking

Application context is the cornerstone of FineDroid, while it is not a primitive element yet in the Android system. Thus, we design *Context Builder* to automatically build the two kinds of application contexts. To prevent attackers from hiding their identities in the application context, we place the *Context Builder* in the Linux Kernel. However, the complexity of the Android programming model brings huge challenges in propagating application context along with the application execution. To deal with these complexities, we further introduce several techniques for context propagating. Next, we elaborate these techniques.

4.1   Intra-application Context Builder

Intra-application context is used to distinguish different execution flows inside an app. In FineDroid, the function calling context is used to abstract the internal execution context inside an app. However, it is too large to efficiently propagate and compare the complete calling context. Thus, we need to efficiently compute a birthmark for any given calling context.

PCC as Intra Context. We adopt a technique called *probabilistic calling context (PCC)* [11] to compute an integer birthmark based on all the functions in the flow. PCC can be efficiently calculated with a recursive expression

$pcc = 3 * pcc' + cs$ where pcc' is the PCC value of the caller and cs is a birthmark for the current call site. By applying this expression recursively from the leaf function on the stack to the root function, we could finally obtain a PCC value as the birthmark for the whole calling context. Note that PCC calculation is deterministic which means a given calling context would always get the same PCC value. As evaluated in millions of unique calling contexts [11], PCC is efficient and accurate for bug detection and intrusion detection in deployed software. Thus, PCC is very suitable to represent the internal execution context inside an app.

Call Site Birthmark. Since all Java code in an Android app is packed into a single DEX file, we use the relative offset of a call site in the DEX file as the birthmark of the call site (cs value). While at the first glance this solution may encounter problems with native code execution, it turns out that this solution could still calculate a PCC value for the Java functions invoked before the native code because native code could only be invoked from Java functions through Java Native Interface. It is worth noting that our solution does not need to calculate a PCC value for every function invocation. Instead, it just needs to compute PCC values for a small portion of calling contexts inside an application that may participate in a permission request, such as application interaction.

Implementation Issue. Since Java functions are executed in a dedicated Java stack by Dalvik virtual machine, *Context Builder* which lies in the Linux Kernel cannot recognize the user-space Java stack. To solve this problem, we instrument Dalvik virtual machine to register the base address of Java stack to the kernel whenever a Java thread is spawned. Thus, when *Context Builder* needs to calculate the PCC value for the current context, it could traverse all the Java functions in the execution flow by reconstructing the calling stack with the base Java stack address.

4.2   Inter-application Context Builder

Inter-application context reflects the IPC context among interacted applications. Since Binder IPC is the only way for an application to interact with other applications and system services, *Context Builder* extends Binder kernel module to keep the whole IPC call chain for every IPC invocation. As showed in Figure 2, the extended Binder driver allocates an array for each thread to record the application context in handling Binder communication. During each Binder IPC interaction, the driver would append caller's identity into caller's application context, and propagate it to the callee application as the callee's application context. The caller's identity is composed of two parts: assigned UID of the caller application and PCC value for the *intra-application context* inside the caller application when this interaction occurs.

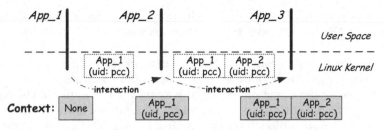

Fig. 2. Binder IPC Context Building.

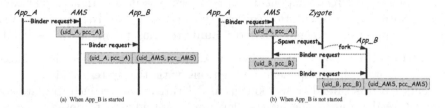

Fig. 3. Binder IPC Propagating Diagram in Component Interaction from App_A to App_B.

4.3 Context Propagating

Due to some unique features of Android, the built system-wide application context would be lost during normal execution. Thus, FineDroid further retrofits the `Android Runtime` which manages the application execution to propagate application context during the following interaction behaviors.

Component-Level Propagating. Component interaction is prevalent in Android apps. To initiate a component interaction, an application (named as A) first needs to send an `Intent` to the `ActivitManagerService` (referenced as AMS for short), then AMS would choose a target application (named as B) and route the `Intent` to B. Figure 3 (a) illustrates this process. Since the invocations from A to AMS and from AMS to B are all proceeded with Binder IPC, app B would get the application context as $[(uid_A, pcc_A), (uid_{AMS}, pcc_{AMS})]$ when receiving this `Intent`. During the component interaction, AMS plays as a mediator between the sender and the receiver. However, from the application context propagated to app B, AMS looks like a participator which is contrary to its actual role.

The problem would be even worse when the target application B has not been launched at the time of `Intent` delivery. Figure 3 (b) illustrates this scenario. When app B is chosen as the callee of this component interaction and AMS finds that app B has not been started. AMS would delay the `Intent` routing and notify `Zygote` (which is the application incubator in Android) to spawn a new process for app B. When B has been started, it would notify AMS and AMS would send the delayed `Intent` to B. The problem is that the `Intent` delivery from AMS to app B is performed in the context of receiving the start notification of app B, so the application context propagated to app B is $[(uid_B, pcc_B), (uid_{AMS}, pcc_{AMS})]$.

This problem is caused by that the application context for sending the `Intent` from app A to AMS has not been recovered in delivering the `Intent` from AMS to app B.

To solve the two problems, we design Intent-based component interaction tracking. The basic idea is that, we instrument AMS to annotate each `Intent` object with the sender's context, thus the context is propagated to the receiver together with the `Intent` object. When `Android Runtime` in the receiver application gets the `Intent` object from AMS, it first recovers the application context recorded in the `Intent` object and then triggers the invocation of the target component. Thus, the target component can be executed with the right application context. Note that the application context recovery in the receiver application is guaranteed by our instrumented `Android Runtime`, thus it could not be escaped.

Thread-Level Propagating. In each `Android Runtime`, there is a main thread to handle the component interactions with the system and dispatch UI events (so this thread is also known as UI thread). To reduce the latency of main thread in processing events, developers are advised to delegate time-consuming operations to worker threads. Android designs `Message` [4], `Handler` [3], `AsyncTask` [2] interfaces for developers to facilitate such workload migration and synchronization. However, since thread interaction is not proceeded via Binder IPC, the application context would be lost in the worker thread.

We design two countermeasures to propagate application contexts among thread interactions. First, during *thread creation*, we instrument the thread creation and initialization logic to propagate the application context of the creator thread to the new created thread and then recover the application context before the created thread is ready to run. Second, for *thread interaction*, we consider the message-based interaction mechanism in Android. Before a message is sent to a thread, the application context of the current thread is annotated to the `Message` object. Then before the target thread handles the `Message`, its application context is restored according to the one encapsulated in the `Message` object. It is worth noting that, our thread-level context tracking is transparently performed by our instrumented `Android Runtime`. Thus, this kind of tracking is mandatory without relying on any modification to the applications or cooperation with developers.

Event-Level Propagating. Callbacks are commonly used in Android to monitor system events. A typical use case is UI event handling. However, the event-based programming model also brings problems to application context tracking, because a callback may be executed in a future time by a thread which would have a different context to the one when the callback is registered. To deal with this problem, FineDroid annotates each callback with the application context when it is registered and recover the application context from the callback before it is triggered for execution. From Android documentation, we find more than 100 APIs that would register callbacks. We instrument each API to embed the registered callback into a wrapper which automatically records and recovers the context to/from the callback. Since only Android APIs are instrumented, this technique is also enforced transparently to the app.

5   Context-Sensitive Permission System

Based on the constructed system-wide application context, permission requests in FineDroid could be handled separately according to the concrete application context. To ease the regulation of permissions requests, FineDroid features a policy framework. Next, this framework is introduced in two parts.

5.1   Permission Manager

Permission Manager first needs to intercept all permission requests. As introduced in [35,40], two kinds of permission requests are intercepted: For KEPs (Kernel Enforced Permissions), we instrument the UID/GID isolation modules in the Linux Kernel to intercept all KEP permission requests and redirect them to *Permission Manager* in the Android framework for handling; For AEPs (Android Enforced Permissions), we instrument *PermissionController* service to redirect all permission requests to the *Permission Manager*.

To handle a permission request, *Permission Manager* first queries *Policy Manager* to select a policy which best matches the current application context. If no policy matches, *Permission Manager* would fall back to the original permission enforcement mode. In the original mode, permission requests are handled by querying the *Permission Record* (see Figure 1) to grant all the permissions declared in the application manifest file. When a matched policy is selected for the current permission request, *Permission Manager* just needs to follow the action (e.g. allow or deny) specified in the policy.

5.2   Policy Framework

FineDroid designs a declarative policy language to express the rules for handling permission requests in a context-sensitive manner. Basically, it states the handling action for a permission request from an app within a specified application context. Our policy is structured in XML format, with the following tags. (A sample policy can be found in Figure 4.)

- **policy** tag. It is the root tag for specifying a policy. Three attributes are required to designate the handling action (*action* attribute) when an app (*app* attribute) requests some permission (*permission* attribute). The expected application context for this policy can be figured by either a *context* attribute or child tags described below.
- **uid-selector** tag. It describes the composition relationship of several **uid-context** child tags. The *selector* attribute is mandatory to describe the composition relationship among the child tags. It supports 5 kinds of selectors: *"contains"*, *"startwith"*, *"endwith"*, *"strictcontains"* and *"fullymatch"*.

- **uid-context** tag. It describes context information for a single application participated in the inter-application communication. The _uid_ attribute is required to specify the identity of the application. Package name can also be used as the identity of the application. If the value of _uid_ attribute begins with "∧", it represents any application except the one specified by the _uid_ attribute. The intra-application context of the application can be described by either the _pcc_ attribute using the exact PCC value of the application, or detailed function call context information using a child **pcc-selector** tag.
- **pcc-selector** tag. It describes the composition relationship of several **method-sig** child tags. Just like **uid-selector** tag, it requires a _selector_ attribute which also supports 5 selectors.
- **method-sig** tag. It describes the signature for a method invoked in the calling context. Three attributes can be used for description: _className_, _methodName_, and _methodProto_.
- **or, and, not** tag. They describe the logic relationships among child tags. They are used to depict complex contexts which may be difficult to expressed only with **uid-selector** and **pcc-selector**. Meanwhile, these tags can be nested together.

Besides, the policy language supports using "*" as the wild card character in some attributes, such as _context_ attribute in **policy** tag, _pcc_ attribute in **uid-context** tag.

Policy Matching. To test whether a policy could match a permission request, _Policy Manager_ first checks the requested permission and the requestor application. When both attributes match, _Policy Manager_ further compares the application context. The application context matching is relatively slow, so we use a cache to remember the context matching results. If multiple policies are found to match, _Policy Manager_ would select the one that express the most fine-grained application context. _Policy Manager_ also supports adding and removing policies to/from the system, as well as registering new action types to extend the policy language. The next section will show how these policies can be used to refine current permission model.

6 Security Extensions

To demonstrate the effectiveness of context-sensitive permission enforcement, we create security extensions for administrators and developers. All these extensions are built upon the interfaces exposed by _Policy Manager_, without modifying other FineDroid modules.

6.1 For Administrator: Fixing Permission Leak Vulnerability

In the Android programming model, if a public component is not protected well, it may be misused to perform privileged actions by an attacker application. As demonstrated in [21,24,36], many high-risk permissions, such as SEND_SMS,

```
<policy action="deny" app="com.android.mms" permission="SEND_SMS" >
  <uid-selector selector="strictcontains" >
    <uid-context uid="^com.android.mms" pcc="*" />
    <uid-context uid="com.android.mms" />
      <pcc-selector selector="contains" >
        <method-sig className="com.android.mms.transaction.SmsReceiver"
                    methodName="beginStartingService" />
      </pcc-selector>
    </uid-context>
  </uid-selector>
</policy>
```

Fig. 4. Policy to fix SEND_SMS permission leak in *SmsReceiver*.

RECORD_AUDIO are found to be leaked in pre-installed apps and third-party apps. Next, we introduce how to use FineDroid to prevent permission leaks. Note that we do not want to prevent all kinds of component hijacking vulnerabilities, such as information leaks.

Leak Causes. There are two possible cases for the permission leak vulnerability. The first case is that some application-private components are mistakenly made publicly accessible. This may be caused by developer's lack of security awareness or insecure code generated by IDE. To fix such kind of leak, developers just need to mark these components as private ones in the manifest file. In Android, intra-application component interaction and the inter-application component interaction share the same communication channel [16]. Thus, a single component may be designed for two purposes: *internal use* and *public use*. The second case of permission leak is that developers do not perform enough security checks when an internal component is for *public use*. However, this case is quite difficult to handle, due to two levels of security requirements in a single component.

Our Solution. By tracking system-wide application context, FineDroid could be used to fix permission leak vulnerability. With *inter-application context*, we could find whether a component interaction is for *internal use* or for *public use*. With *intra-application context*, we could accurately specify the vulnerable flow inside the application. Combining *intra-application context* and *inter-application context* together, we could make a policy to prevent a vulnerable flow from using permissions when it is invoked from an external application. For example, the policy in Figure 4 denies the SEND_SMS permission request from the app *com.android.mms* when a foreign application participates in the interaction and the internal execution state of *com.android.mms* matches a vulnerable path (specified by the *<pcc-selector>* element).

The advantages of FineDroid in preventing permission leak vulnerabilities are that it requires no modification to the system nor the vulnerable applications and the policies are quite easy to write. In Section 7.1, we would evaluate the effectiveness of FineDroid in fixing real-world permission leak vulnerabilities, and show that how the policies could be automatically generated by enhancing a permission leak vulnerability detector.

```
...
<fine-permission android:package="com.flurry.android">
  <deny android:permission="android.permission.ACCESS_FINE_LOCATION" />
  <deny android:permission="android.permission.ACCESS_COARSE_LOCATION" />
</fine-permission>
...
```

Fig. 5. Policy to prevent Flurry Ads from requesting location permission.

6.2   For Developer: Fine-Grained Permission Specification

An Android application may contain many third-party code packages. For example, it is common for applications to embed an Ad library for fetching Ads, social network SDKs for publishing events, payment SDKs for financial charge, analytic SDKs for marketing. However, in this case multiple third-party SDKs from different origins (potentially with different trust levels) will share the same privileges as the host application, violating the principle of least privilege. Thus, a third-party SDK may abuse the permissions that granted to the host application. For example, a popular Ad library was found to collect text messages, contacts and call logs [1]. Unfortunately, developers have no way to restrict the permissions that are available to certain foreign packages.

Our Solution. By tracking *intra-application context*, FineDroid is capable of distinguishing the origins of permission requests inside an application. Thus, we could build a permission sandbox inside an application where code packages from different origins have different permission configurations. Based on the permission sandbox, developers could declare fine-grained permission specifications in the application manifest file to specify the permissions that could be used by each third-party SDK. Figure 5 shows the format of this kind of permission specification. The fine-grained permission specifications in the manifest file will be transformed to FineDroid policy by our enhanced *PackageManagerService* at the install-time and added to the *Policy Manager*. Note that application obfuscation [6] would not cause problems here, because developers could modify the manifest file after code obfuscation.

7   Prototype and Evaluation

We implement a prototype of FineDroid on Android 4.1.1 (Jelly Bean), running on both Google Nexus phones (Samsung I9250) and emulators. We also implement the two security extensions upon FineDroid. This section evaluates these extensions to demonstrate the effectiveness of our context-sensitive permission enforcement framework, as well as the performance overhead introduced by our framework.

7.1   Fixing Permission Leak Vulnerability

We evaluate the effectiveness of FineDroid in fixing permission leak vulnerabilities with two real-world vulnerabilities in Android AOSP apps: SEND_SMS

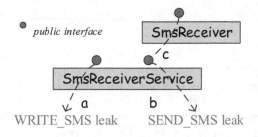

Fig. 6. Permission leak paths in Mms application.

leak [7] and WRITE_SMS leak [8]. These two vulnerabilities are both caused by the improper protection of public components exposed in the Mms application, which is the default message management app.

Vulnerability Analysis. There are two vulnerable components in the Mms application: *SmsReceiverService* which is a Service component and *SmsReceiver* which is a Broadcast Receiver component. Figure 6 illustrates the exploitable paths in this application. *SmsReceiverService* is intended for only *internal use* in the Mms application, while it is mistakenly exported to the public. Through sending a well-crafted Intent to *SmsReceiverService*, an attacker can drive the Mms application to fake the receiving of arbitrary SMS messages (WRITE_SMS leak, path *a*) or send arbitrary SMS messages (SEND_SMS leak, path *b*). *SmsReceiver* is designed for both *internal use* and *public use*. However, the functionality of sending arbitrary SMS messages which should only be used by private components is not protected properly, causing it to be exported to the public (SEND_SMS leak, path *c*).

Fixing the Vulnerability. Permission leak vulnerability is typically difficult to fix manually, because it requires enforcing multiple security requirements in a single component, such as SEND_SMS leak (path *c* in Figure 6) in *SmsReceiver*. Besides, even if carefully fixed, it also requires the re-distribution of the new application file. Based on FineDroid, we could easily prevent permission leaks by simply writing policies to deny the permission request occurred in the exploitable path without modifying the application. Figure 4 shows an example of how to prevent SEND_SMS leak (path *c* in Figure 6) in *SmsReceiver*. Similarly, we could fix the vulnerability of path *a* and *b*.

Effectiveness. We created three sample apps to exploit each vulnerable path mentioned above. The sample apps were first tested in our FineDroid prototype with no policies. The result shows that all the three apps successfully exploited the vulnerabilities in the Mms app. Then we added three policies (as showed in Figure 4) to our prototype to fix the three vulnerable paths. We also ran the same three sample apps to attack Mms again. We found that our security policies successfully prevented the permission re-delegation attacks this time, demonstrating the effectiveness of FineDroid in enforcing fine-grained permission use policies.

Policy Generation. The policies to fix permission-leak vulnerabilities rely on the precise understanding of vulnerable paths among component interactions. Thus the ideal scenario is to use together with an existing permission leakage vulnerability detector (such as CHEX [24]). Once a vulnerable path is detected, we can automatically generate a corresponding policy for FineDroid. Thus, the task of diagnosing vulnerable applications and writing policies can be greatly simplified. To demonstrate the feasibility of automatic policy generation to be used together with any vulnerability detector, we choose CHEX [24], a state-of-the-art tool in detecting permission leak vulnerability, in our evaluation. However, the source code of CHEX is not available, so we could not directly enhance CHEX for policy generation. Instead, the authors of CHEX provided us the output of CHEX in analyzing 20 vulnerable applications, among which 10 applications are vulnerable to INTERNET permission leak. By parsing the output files, we successfully extracted 414 vulnerable paths with detailed calling contexts. Based on the vulnerable paths (contexts), the automatic policy generation is quite straightforward. As showed in Figure 4, the generated policies could deny the permission request when the vulnerable path is exploited by a foreign application. Finally, for each vulnerable path detected by CHEX, a policy is automatically generated to fix it.

7.2   Fine-Grained Permission Specification

We evaluate the effectiveness of FineDroid in providing fine-grained permission specification by restricting the privileges of untrusted Ad libraries. In this experiment, we use an application named *Stock Watch* which embeds Flurry Ads for fetching and displaying advertisements. For demonstration purpose, we assume Flurry Ads is not trusted by *Stock Watch* developers, thus the developers want to restrict the permissions that could be used by Flurry Ads. Flurry Ads requests ACCESS_FINE_LOCATION permission during the execution, and we assume the developers think this is quite suspicious. With FineDroid, *Stock Watch* developers could easily prohibit Flurry Ads from using ACCESS_FINE_LOCATION permission. As Figure 5 shows, they just need to declare a fine-grained permission specification in the manifest file. During the installation, these specifications would be transformed to policies that could be added to FineDroid. Because we do not have the source code of the *Stock Watch* application, we mimic the behavior of *Stock Watch* developers by repackaging the application file to replace the manifest file. By running the new application, we could find the ACCESS_FINE_LOCATION permission requests from Flurry Ads are all denied by FineDroid, and this does not affect the normal operation of the *Stock Watch* application. Similar to *Stock Watch*, we also tested another 20 applications to restrict the permissions assigned to third-party libraries, including Google Ads, Tapjoy, Millennial Media. In all these cases, FineDroid provides strong enforcement of fine-grained permission specifications. We did encounter two cases that the applications crashed due to the denial of some permissions requested from the Ads library. Instead of considering it as the fault of FineDroid, we argue that developers of the Ads library should write more robust code to handle more necessary exceptions in the future.

7.3   Performance Overhead

We have conducted several experiments to measure the performance overhead caused by FineDroid. The experiments are performed on Google Nexus phones.

Overall Performance. We first use three performance benchmarks (Caffeine-Mark3, AnTuTu, and Linpack) to measure the overall overhead introduced by FineDroid. The results show that almost no noticeable performance overhead is observed, with the worst overhead case at 1.99% in the Linpack benchmark.

Permission Request Handling Performance. Most overhead of FineDroid is introduced when handling permission requests. We implement a test app that performs 10,000 times of permission requests to measure the average performance of FineDroid in handling a single permission request. We compare the performance of unmodified Android with FineDroid in two configurations. Context tracking is disabled in *FineDroid w/o Context*, where all overhead is caused by permission interception. In *FineDroid w/ Context*, context tracking is switched on and no policy is installed on the system. Table 1 shows the results.

FineDroid introduces an overhead of 2.02 ms per request in intercepting KEP permission requests, which is undoubtedly higher than the case of unmodified Andorid because in that case KEP request can be handled in the application process without communicating with *Permission Manager* in the system process. The overhead introduced by further application context tracking is very minor (0.02 ms per request). For AEP permissions, the interception overhead is quite minor because AEP is originally enforced in the system process, while the context tracking overhead is more significant because it needs to build intra- and inter-application contexts in several processes.

Table 1. Results on handling permission requests.

Permission Type	Original Android	FineDroid w/o Context	FineDroid w/ Context
Socket(KEP)	0.14ms	2.16ms Δ2.02ms	2.18ms Δ0.02ms
IMEI(AEP)	0.62ms	0.69ms Δ0.06ms	1.09ms Δ0.40ms

Policy Matching Performance. To test the overhead introduced by the policy matching, we add policies to the system to grant the permissions requested by the test app. Each policy is written with the same structure as Figure 4. Table 2 shows the overhead of policy matching.

Table 2. Results on policy matching.

Permission Type	FineDroid w/o Policy	FineDroid w/ Policy	Overhead
Socket(KEP)	2.18ms	3.06 ms	0.88ms
IMEI(AEP)	1.09ms	1.99ms	0.90ms

We believe the performance penalty introduced by FineDroid is acceptable because permission request (as well as policy matching) do not frequently occur in practice.

8 Discussion

To propagate application context, FineDroid relies on `Android Runtime` instance in each application to participate. Since `Android Runtime` is a user-space module in the application process, currently FineDroid cannot guarantee its integrity. Attackers may use Java Reflection to modify `Android Runtime`'s private data structures. To prevent such attacks, we instrument Reflection APIs to prevent manipulation of the private fields which are added by FineDroid to keep application context. Because these fields are unique to FineDroid, this kind of instrumentation would not break other legitimate use of Reflection. Besides, adversaries may also use native code to attack `Android Runtime`. Recent work on isolating native code in Android system [34] could be incorporated to our system to prevent native code attack.

Undesirable data flows among multiple permission requests are not considered in this paper. Actually, by providing fine-grained permission control to raise the bar for abusing permissions, FineDroid could also be used to prevent potential risky data flows.

9 Related Work

Permission System Extensions. Aurasium [37] provides time-of-use permission granting for legacy Android apps by automatically repackaging applications to attach user-level sandboxing code. Roesner et al. [29] introduced access control gadgets (ACGs) which embed permission-granting semantics in normal user actions. Dr. Android and Mr. Hide [23] provides finer semantics for coarse-grained permissions by rewriting privileged API invocations. Apex [25] introduces partial permission granting at installation time and runtime constraints over permission requests. SEAndroid [33] combines kernel-level MAC (SELinux) with several middleware MAC extensions to the Android permissions model, which could mitigate vulnerabilities in both system and application layer. FlaskDroid [15] extends kernel-level MAC to bring mandatory access control for all resources in Linux Kernel and Android framework. While these works refine or extend current permission system in some degree, they do not enforce fine-grained control over the permission use context, which is the focus of FineDroid.

Application Interaction Hardening. Felt et al. [20] proposed IPC inspection to prevent permission re-delegation attacks by intersecting the permissions of all the applications in the IPC call chain. However, this strategy is too rigid to allow intentional permission re-delegations. Quire [18] provides developers with new interfaces to acquire IPC call chain. Different from FineDroid, Quire relies on AIDL instrumentation to record the IPC call chain. However, the technique has several limitations: First, it could only track the IPC call chain during the invocation of AIDL-specified methods, while some system interfaces are not specified using AIDL such as `AcvitityManagerService`; Second, it is an opt-in option for developers to use these enhanced API proxies, thus an attacker application can easily escape.

TrustDroid [14] divides apps into two isolated domains: trusted and untrusted. However, communication problems inside a single domain are not considered. XManDroid [12,13] generally mitigates application-level privilege escalation attacks by prohibiting any application communication if the permission union of the two apps may pose a security risk. Saint [26] secures the application communication by providing developers with the ability to specify fine-grained requirements about the caller and callee. However, it could not improve the permission enforcement mechanism during the application communication.

AppSealer [38] is a tool to automatically fix component hijacking vulnerabilities by actively instrumenting vulnerable apps. Compared to AppSealer, our technique of fixing permission leak vulnerabilities does not require heavy application rewriting which is error-prone and needs redistribution of patched apps.

Similar to FineDroid, Scippa [10] also extends Binder driver and `Android Runtime` to provide IPC provenance. However, it does not cover *intra-application context* which is quite important for a unified fine-grained permission system. Moreover, the IPC context propagating technique in Scippa is quite simpler than the one designed in FineDroid which could systematically propagate IPC contexts at the level of component-interaction, thread creation/interaction, and events.

Application Internal Isolation. To isolate in-app Ads, a separate process is introduced by AFrame [39], AdDroid [27] and AdSplit [31] for running Ads libraries. By intersecting the permissions that can be used by different code packages in the same application, Compac [35] also provides fine-grained permission specification. However, without a systematic context tracking system and a generic policy framework, Compac could not flexibly handle permission requests that cross multiple code packages. Compared with FineDroid, these frameworks could not flexibly regulate permission use policies based on *intra-application* context.

Context-Aware Access Control. Recent works on context-aware access control model [17,26,30,32] also regulate access control rules based on context information. Different from the notion in FineDroid, these works mostly consider the external application context such as location, time of the day.

10 Conclusion

This paper presents FineDroid, which brings context-sensitive permission enforcement to Android. By associating each permission request with its application context, FineDroid provides a fine-grained permission control. The application context in FineDroid covers not only *intra-application context*, but also *inter-application context*. To automatically track such application context, Fine-Droid designs a new seamless context tracking technique. FineDroid also features a policy framework to flexibly regulate context-sensitive permission rules. This paper further demonstrates the effectiveness of FineDroid by creating two security extensions upon FineDroid for administrators and application developers. The performance evaluation shows that the overhead introduced by FineDroid is minor.

Acknowledgment. We thank the anonymous reviewers for their insightful comments. Yuan Zhang and Min Yang are funded in part by the National Program on Key Basic Research (NO. 2015CB358800), the National Natural Science Foundation of China (61300027), and the Science and Technology Commission of Shanghai Municipality (13511504402, 13JC1400800 and 15511103003). Guofei Gu is supported in part by the National Science Foundation (NSF) under Grant CNS-0954096. Any opinions, findings, and conclusions expressed in this material do not necessarily reflect the views of the funding agencies.

References

1. Ad vulna: A vulnaggressive (vulnerable & aggressive) adware threatening millions. http://www.fireeye.com/blog/technical/2013/10/ad-vulna-a-vulnaggressive-vulnerable-aggressive-adware-threatening-millions.html
2. Android asynctask class. http://developer.android.com/reference/android/os/AsyncTask.html
3. Android handler class. http://developer.android.com/reference/android/os/Handler.html
4. Android message class. http://developer.android.com/reference/android/os/Message.html
5. Android remains the leader in the smartphone operating system market. http://www.idc.com/getdoc.jsp?containerId=prUS24108913
6. Proguard. http://developer.android.com/tools/help/proguard.html
7. Send_sms capability leak in android open source project. http://www.csc.ncsu.edu/faculty/jiang/send_sms_leak.html
8. Smishing vulnerability in multiple android platforms. http://www.csc.ncsu.edu/faculty/jiang/smishing.html

9. Sophos security threat report (2013). http://www.sophos.com/en-us/security-news-trends/reports/security-threat-report/android-malware.aspx
10. Backes, M., Bugiel, S., Gerling, S.: Scippa: System-centric ipc provenance on android. In: Proc. ACSAC 2014 (2014)
11. Bond, M.D., Mckinley, K.S.: Probabilistic calling context. In: Proc. of OOPSLA 2007 (2007)
12. Bugiel, S., Davi, L., Dmitrienko, A., Fischer, T., Sadeghi, A.-R.: Xmandroid: A new android evolution to mitigate privilege escalation attacks. In: Technical report TR-2011-04, Technische Universität Darmstadt (2011)
13. Bugiel, S., Davi, L., Dmitrienko, A., Fischer, T., Sadeghi, A.-R., Shastry, B.: Towards taming privilege-escalation attacks on android. In: Proc. of NDSS 2012 (2012)
14. Bugiel, S., Davi, L., Dmitrienko, A., Heuser, S., Sadeghi, A.-R., Shastry, B.: Practical and lightweight domain isolation on android. In: Proc. of SPSM 2011 (2011)
15. Bugiel, S., Heuser, S., Sadeghi, A.-R.: Flexible and fine-grained mandatoryaccess control on android for diverse security and privacy policies. In: Proc. of USENIXSecurity 2013 (2013)
16. Chin, E., Felt, A.P., Greenwood, K., Wagner, D.: Analyzing inter-applicationcommunication in android. In: Proc. of MobiSys 2011 (2011)
17. Conti, M., Nguyen, V.T.N., Crispo, B.: Crepe: context-related policy enforcement for android. In: Proc. of ISC 2010 (2010)
18. Dietz, M., Shekhar, S., Pisetsky, Y., Shu, A., Wallach, D.S.: Quire:lightweight provenance for smart phone operating systems. In: Proc. of Security 2011 (2011)
19. Enck, W., Gilbert, P., Chun, B.-G., Cox, L.P., Jung, J., Mcdaniel, P., Sheth, A.N.: Taintdroid: an information-flow tracking system for realtime privacy monitoring on smartphones. In: Proc. of OSDI 2010 (2010)
20. Felt, A.P., Wang, H.J., Moshchuk, A., Hanna, S., Chin, E.: Permission redelegation: attacks and defenses. In: Proc. of USENIX Security 2011 (2011)
21. Grace, M., Zhou, Y., Wang, Z., Jiang, X.: Systematic detection of capabilityleaks in stock android smartphones. In: Proc. of NDSS 2012 (2012)
22. Hornyack, P., Han, S., Jung, J., Schechter, S., Wetherall, D.: These aren't the droids you're looking for: retrofitting android to protect data from imperious applications. In: Proc. of CCS 2011 (2011)
23. Jeon, J., Micinski, K.K., Vaughan, J.A., Fogel, A., Reddy, N., Foster, J.S., Millstein, T.: Dr. android and mr. hide: fine-grained permissions in androidapplications. In: Proc. of SPSM 2012 (2012)
24. Lu, L., Li, Z., Wu, Z., Lee, W., Jiang, G.: Chex: statically vetting android apps for component hijacking vulnerabilities. In: Proc. of CCS 2012 (2012)
25. Nauman, M., Khan, S., Zhang, X.: Apex: extending android permission mode-land enforcement with user-defined runtime constraints. In: Proc. of AsiaCCS 2010 (2010)
26. Ongtang, M., McLaughlin, S., Enck, W., McDaniel, P.: Semantically rich application-centric security in android. In: Proc. of ACSAC 2009 (2009)
27. Pearce, P., Felt, A.P., Nunez, G., Wagner, D.: Addroid: privilege separation forapplications and advertisers in android. In: Proc. of AsiaCCS 2012 (2012)
28. Poeplau, S., Fratantonio, Y., Bianchi, A., Kruegel, C., Vigna, G.: Executethis! analyzing unsafe and malicious dynamic code loading in android applications. In: Proc. of NDSS 2014 (2014)
29. Roesner, F., Kohno, T., Moshchuk, A., Parno, B., Wang, H., Cowan, C.: User-driven access control: rethinking permission granting in modern operating systems. In: Proc. of SP 2012 (2012)

30. Rohrer, F., Zhang, Y., Chitkushev, L., Zlateva, T.: Dr baca: dynamic role based access control for android. In: Prof. of ACSAC 2013 (2013)
31. Shekhar, S., Dietz, M., Wallach, D.S.: Adsplit: separating smartphoneadvertising from applications. In: Proc. of USENIX Security 2012 (2012)
32. Singh, K.: Practical context-aware permission control for hybrid mobile applications. In: Proc. of RAID 2013 (2013)
33. Smalley, S., Craig, R.: Security enhanced (se) android: bringing flexible mac toandroid. In: Proc. of NDSS 2013 (2013)
34. Sun, M., Tan, G.: Nativeguard: protecting android applications from third-party nativelibraries. In: Proc. of WiSec 2014 (2014)
35. Wang, Y., Hariharan, S., Zhao, C., Liu, J., Du, W.: Compac: enforcecomponent-level access control in android. In: Proc. of CODASPY 2014 (2014)
36. Wu, L., Grace, M., Zhou, Y., Wu, C., Jiang, X.: The impact of vendor customizations on android security. In: Proc. of CCS 2013 (2013)
37. Xu, R., Saidi, H., Anderson, R.: Aurasium: practical policy enforcement forandroid applications. In: Proc. of USENIX Security 2012 (2012)
38. Zhang, M., Yin, H.: AppSealer: automatic generation of vulnerability-specificpatches for preventing component hijacking attacks in android applications. In: Proc. ofNDSS 2014 (2014)
39. Zhang, X., Ahlawat, A., Du, W.: Aframe: isolating advertisements from mobile applications in android. In: Proc. of ACSAC 2013 (2013)
40. Zhang, Y., Yang, M., Xu, B., Yang, Z., Gu, G., Ning, P., Wang, X.S., Zang, B.: Vetting undesirable behaviors in android apps with permission use analysis. In: Proc. of CCS 2013 (2013)
41. Zhou, Y., Jiang, X.: Detecting passive content leaks and pollution in androidapplications. In: Proc. of NDSS 2013 (2013)

Detection, Classification and Characterization of Android Malware Using API Data Dependency

Yongfeng Li$^{(\boxtimes)}$, Tong Shen, Xin Sun, Xuerui Pan, and Bing Mao

State Key Laboratory for Novel Software Technology,
Department of Computer Science and Technology, Nanjing University,
Nanjing, China
{jsliyongfeng,shentongnju,sunxin508,xueruipan}@gmail.com,
maobing@nju.edu.cn

Abstract. With the popularity of Android devices, more and more Android malware are manufactured every year. How to filter out malicious app is a serious problem for app markets. In this paper, we propose DroidADDMiner, an efficient and precise system to detect, classify and characterize Android malware. DroidADDMiner is a machine learning based system that extracts features based on data dependency between sensitive APIs. It extracts API data dependence paths embedded in app to construct feature vectors for machine learning. While DroidSIFT [13] also attempts automated detection of Android applications according to data flow analysis, DroidADDMiner can not only reduce the run time but also characterize malware's behaviors automatically. We implement DroidADDMiner based on FlowDroid [14] and evaluate it using 5648 malware samples and 14280 benign apps. Experiments show that, for malware detection, DroidADDMiner achieves a 98% detection rate, with a 0.3% false positive rate. For malware classification, the accuracy of classifying malicious apps under their proper family labels is 96%. Although performing data flow analysis, most of the experimental samples can be examined in 60 seconds.

Keywords: Android malware · Machine learning · Data flow · Flowdroid

1 Introduction

Smartphone is performing a more and more important role in people's daily life. According to a recent study [1], in United States and Great Britain, Android has reached over 50% market share. Meanwhile, in China, the market share has exceeded 70%. There's no doubt that Android has become the most popular platform for smart phone today. This trend has attracted attention of attackers, more and more malicious applications emerged in the official and alternative Android marketplaces. As described in [2], over 150,000 malicious applications and 253 new malware families have been discovered in 2013 alone. In order to

© Institute for Computer Sciences, Social Informatics and Telecommunications Engineering 2015
B. Thuraisingham et al. (Eds.): SecureComm 2015, LNICST 164, pp. 23–40, 2015.
DOI: 10.1007/978-3-319-28865-9_2

maintain a healthy ecosystem for Android, robust malware detection techniques need to be designed.

Previously, many machine learning based approaches have been proposed to detect malware. Before utilizing machine learning algorithms, they use feature vectors to model the app's behaviors. Their main difference lies in how to extract feature vectors. Rather than in-depth understanding program semantics, Drebin [10] and DroidAPIMiner [20] extract features from application syntax like permissions listed in manifest file and API parameters used by application code. Malware and benign apps may use the same APIs and permissions, because some benign apps also need to access sensitive resources. So these approaches are not robust enough to model malware's behaviors. DroidMiner [11] focuses on the control flow of Android application, API sequences extracted from control flow graph are used to construct feature vectors. But it may miss important data flow information that can help build better behavior models which have effects on the detection rate.

For Android application, APIs can be invoked under two contexts: user interface and background callback. Malware always exploit background callbacks to launch malicious behaviors. Constant values like network address can also reveal a malware's intention when they are used as parameters of some APIs. Hence, DroidSIFT [13] adopts data flow analysis to construct weighted contextual API dependency graphs which contain data dependency, context and constant information. Their feature vectors are extracted based on similarity between weighted contextual API dependency graphs. Although DroidSIFT represents program semantics well, it cannot automatically generate malicious behavior characterization of malware. Moreover, DroidSIFT is time-consuming when analyzing large-scaled apps because it calculates all objects' point-to information during data flow analysis.

We present DroidADDMiner to automate the process of Android malware detection, classification and characterization. DroidADDMiner is a machine learning based system which extracts features on the basis of API data dependency and also considers context and constant information just like DroidSIFT. We define API data dependence path with context and constant information as *modality*. A modality repository is built by collecting all modalities extracted from malware samples. Feature vector is then generated according to whether the app's modalities are contained in modality repository. Finally, feature vectors are fed to machine learning techniques for detecting, classifying and characterizing malware.

Data flow analysis is the most important part of DroidADDMiner. Flowdroid [14][15] and Amandroid [17] are two state-of-the-art data flow analysis tools for Android. Like DroidSIFT [13], during data flow analysis, Amandriod calculates all objects' point-to information. Analyzing the same app, Flowdroid is quicker than Amandroid since it only focuses on objectes related to some specified sources and sinks. Using machine learning techniques needs to analyze abundant apps, so we choose to extend Flowdroid to build DroidADDMiner. We evaluate our system using 5648 malware samples and 14280 benign apps.

Experiments show that DroidADDMiner can achieve 98% accuracy in malware detection with 0.3% false positive rate, and it can label 96% malware instances to their right family. Although performing data flow analysis, for most of the experimental samples, DroidADDMiner can accomplish analysis in 60 seconds which leads us to believe that DroidADDMiner can handle large-scale applications.

To summarize, this paper makes the following contributions:

– We propose a semantic-based malware detection, classification and characterization approach. The program semantics of malware are modeled by API data dependence paths with context and constant information.
– We make an extension on Flowdroid [14]. Using the extended tool, we can perform API data dependence path construction, API context and constant analysis.
– We make an in-depth evaluation of DroidADDMiner. Experiments include run-time performance and efficacy in malware detection, family classification, and behavior characterization.

2   Motivation and System Goals

2.1   Motivation

We explain the motivation of our system design by introducing the inner working of a real-world malicious Android application. This malware sample (MD5: ecbbce17053d6eaf9bf9cb7c71d0af8d) belongs to the family of zitmo. The code of this malware is listed in Fig. 1. From the code snippet we can know that once a SMS is arrived, life cycle call `onReceive()` is invoked by Android system. Then `abortBroadcast()` is issued to abort current broadcast. In order to steal SMS message, an intent carries SMS message information is created to launch a background service (named "MainService"). Once the service is triggered, SMS message extracted from intent is stored in an object array named "pdus". Next, for extracting originating address (sender) and message body from this object array, `getOriginatingAddress()` and `getMessageBody()` are called. Now the address and message body are stored in String value "str1" and "str2" respectively. Meanwhile, after invoking `getDeviceId()`, the device id is stored in "str3". While malware gets all sensitive information it needs, these information are encoded into an `UrlEncodedFormEntity` object. Before sending these information through network, `HttpPost` object is created with a constant string "http://softthrifty.com/security.jsp" and then `setEntity()` is called to encode these information into a form that can be sent through network. Finally, `DefaultHttpClient.execute()` is issued to post data to remote server.

From the above description, we find an important design premise that when malware authors design malicious apps to achieve malicious behaviors, they always have to use some sensitive API calls like the APIs marked with red font in Fig. 1. DroidMiner [11] and DroidSIFT [13] is two state-of-the-art malware detection tools base on machine learning techniques. DroidMiner extracts API sequences according to control flow. For malware sample

```
 1:public class SmsReceiver extends BroadcastReceiver{
 2:  public void onReceive(Context pcontex,Intent pintent){
 3:   Bundle localBundle = pintent.getExtras();
 4:   if((localBundle != null)&&(localBundle. containsKey("pdus"))){
 5:     abortBroadcast();
 6:     Intent targetService = new Intent(pcontex, MainService.class);
 7:     targetService.putExtra("pdus", localBundle);
 8:     pcontex.startService(ts);
 9:   }
10: }
11:}
12:public class MainService extends Service{
13:  public int onStartCommand(Intent pintent,int pintent1,int pintent2){
14:   Bundle localBundle = pintent.getBundleExtra("pdus");
15:   Object[] pdus = (Object[])localBundle.get("pdus");
16:   ArrayList localAL = new ArrayList();
17:   SmsMessage localSMS = SmsMessage.createFromPdu(pdus);
18:   TelephonyManager localTM =  MainService.this.getSystemService("phone");
19:   String str1 = localSMS.getOriginatingAddress();
20:   String str2 = localSMS.getMessageBody();
21:   String str3 = localTM.getDeviceId();
22:   localAL.add(str1);localAL.add(str2);localAL.add(str3);
23:   postRequest(new UrlEncodedFormEntity(localAL));
24: }
25: public void postRequest(UrlEncodedFormEntity UEFE){
26:   String addr = "http://softthrifty.com/security.jsp";
27:   HttpPost localHP = new HttpPost(addr);
28:   localHP.setEntity(UEFE);
29:   BasicResponseHandler BRH = new BasicResponseHandler();
30:   DefaultHttpClient().execute(localHP, BRH));
31: }
32:}
```

Fig. 1. Example Malware

depicted in Fig. 1, it will extract a control flow sequence [`BroadcastReceiver`, `abortBroadcast()`, `setEntity()`, `execute()`] and sensitive resources "Vres" {`getOriginatingAddress()`, `getMessageBody()`, `getDeviceId()`}. DroidMinerthey does not analyze the data flow of sensitive data, they simply consider that there is an edge from the root "Vroot" (one component, in our example is BroadcastReceiver "SmsReceiver") to the resources "Vres". Actually, this is not precise. For example, in "SmsReceiver", the app invokes getOriginatingAddress(), getMessageBody() and getDeviceId() to obtain sensitive information, but if we change the sensitive information what we put into ArrayList "localAL" by Line 22, the malware's behaviors will be different. That's why analyzing data flow will get more precise behavior models which will affect the accuracy of identification process.

DroidSIFT [13] is another malware detection tool adopts machine learning techniques. During data flow analysis, it calculates all objects' point-to information, this is time consuming. Moreover, when DroidSIFT analyzes the demonstrated malware sample, it will construct a data dependence graph which is composed of red font marked API nodes list in Fig. 1. Because of utilizing the data dependence graph as an integrity to compute similarity related to base graphs in DroidSIFT's database, it loses the ability of digging out the relationships between APIs and malicious behaviors. So it cannot characterize a malware's behaviors automatically. In order to address this deficiency, we extract API data dependence paths embedded in known malware samples. Then mine out the relationships between API data dependence paths and malicious behaviors according to the malicious behaviors malware contain. We use these relationships to characterize a unknown malware's behaviors.

2.2   Goals and Assumption

DroidADDMiner is aimed to detect whether an app is malicious, label malware to correct family, and more specially, give a concise description of a malware's malicious behaviors. For example, given the app demonstrated in section 2.1, DroidADDMiner can know it is a malware, classify it to zitmo family, and find out that it can get SMS message, block SMS message, and send sensitive information to remote server. DroidADDMiner is built based on Flowdroid [14], so its data flow analysis has the same limits as Flowdroid.

3   System Design

We demonstrate DroidADDMiner's work flow in Fig. 2. As depicted in this figure, DroidADDMiner contains two phases: program analysis phase and machine learning phase.

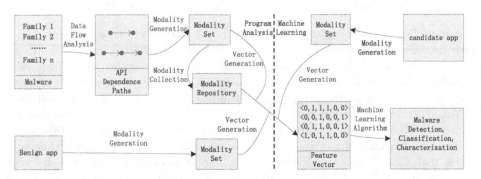

Fig. 2. System Architecture

The most important component of DroidADDMiner is program analysis. As described in section 2.1, we choose to use API data dependency, contex and constant information to represent the program semantics of malware. When performing data flow analysis, analyzing too much APIs will be very expensive. It is necessary to choose a set of APIs which can achieve computational efficiency and security analysis in the same time. So we leverage the API-permission mapping from Pscout [21] to conduct our data flow analysis.

We also need to know whether an API is activated from background callbacks, this is called context analysis. For context analysis, we select some background callbacks like `BroadcastReceiver$onReceive` and `GpsStatus$Listener`. Constant information of parameters of some sensitive APIs, like `exec()` are significant signature to identify malware. These parameters can decide an app's behavior significantly. Due to space limitations, we don't list all these callbacks and APIs in this paper. To extract API data dependence path and extract context and constant information, we extend Flowdroid [14], a detail description will be given in section 4.1.

After analyzing an app, DroidADDMiner will obtain some API data dependence paths with context and constant information. We define API data dependence path with context and constant information as *modality*. In this paper, we use following formula to represent *modality*:

$$S_1[constant; context] \rightarrow \cdots \rightarrow S_k[constant; context] \rightarrow \cdots$$

In this formula, S_k represents sensitive API. `'constant'` represents the constant information of sensitive API, for APIs whose constant information we don't analyze, `'constant'` value will be `'none'`. On the other hand, if we analyze an API's constant information, the value will be `'ture'` or `'false'` depends on whether the API's parameter contains constant value. `'context'` represents the context information, if the API is invoked under a background callback, `'context'` value will be this callback, otherwise the value will be `'none'`. For example, for the malware shown in section 2.1, one of its modalities is:

$$setEntity()[false; onReceive] \rightarrow execute()[true; onReceive]$$

The modality is made up of at least one node, each node is a sensitive API with its context and constant information. We show how to extract modalities from app in section 4.2. After analyzing all malware samples, we collect all modalities DroidADDMiner obtains, then build a modality repository. For the sake of performing machine learning techniques, we need to generate feature vector for every app. Those feature vectors can be calculated based on modality repository. The detail of how to generate feature vectors is shown in section 4.3. At machine learning phase, we use the classical algorithm to detect whether an app is malicious. If it is a malware, we can label it to correct family. Finally we use "Association Rule Mining" technique to characterize a malware's behaviors. This will be described in section 4.4.

4   Implementation

4.1   Extension of FlowDroid

In this section, we introduce how we extend FlowDorid [14] to extract API data dependence path with constant and context information.

In order to extract API data dependence path, for adopting FolwDroid, we need to solve two problems: First, in FlowDroid, all data dependencies are starting from source and ending at sink, but we need to extract API data dependence

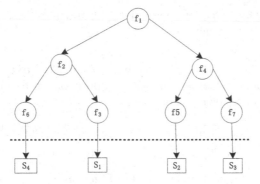

Fig. 3. An Example of Call Graph. Each circle vertex stands for a function, each rectangle vertex stands for a sensitive API

path, data dependency can start from or end at any sensitive API; Second, Flow-Droid can just output data dependency between every two API(source and sink), but the API data dependence path may contains more than two nodes. To solve the first problem, we modify FlowDroid to make it treat the sensitive APIs we specified as both source and sink. The data flow analysis start from a sensitive API, during taint propagation, if a tainted factor encounters a sensitive API, we will record it and stop propagate this factor. Because for every sensitive API, we'll also treat it as source and start taint propagation from it. In this way, we can get propagation path between every two sensitive APIs which have data dependency relationship. For the second problem, as we get data flow propagation path between every two sensitive APIs. To construct long API data dependence path, we use these propagation paths. For simplicity and time efficiency, when using these propagation paths, we only focus on their call context(function call sequence), so we modify FlowDroid to output these call context.

When analyzing an app, FlowDroid constructs an extended call graph. Any control flow transformation like lifecircle or callback method is modeled in this graph and this call graph has only one entry point. It means if one sensitive API data depends on the other sensitive API, the call graph must contains a fuction can reach both these two sensitive APIs. For example, in fig 3, if S_2 data depends on S_1, f_1 is the function which is able to reach both S_1 and S_2. More generally, if an app has an API data dependence path, there must exist a function in the call graph which can reach all sensitive APIs this API data dependence path contains. The API data dependence path with call context is defined as:

$$F_t\{\cdots \rightarrow (\dots, C_{k_m}, \dots, C_{S_j})S_i \rightarrow \cdots\}$$

F_t represents the function this API data dependence path happens. C_{k_m} represents call statement, k_m is a function. Statement sequence in parentheses is the call context of propagation path, the last call statement must call sensitive API. S_i represents sensitive API, and API data dependence path contains at least two nodes. Right arrow represents data dependence. The formula shows F_t can reach S_i through propagation path $(\ldots, C_{k_n}, \ldots, C_{S_j})$.

Short API Data Dependence Path with Call Context. To demonstrate the API data dependency path construction process, we assume that, for call graph in fig 3, we get following short paths

$$f_1\{(c[f_2], c[f_3], c[S_1])S_1 \rightarrow (c[f_4], c[f_5], c[S_2])S_2\} \tag{1}$$

$$f_4\{(c[f_5], c[S_2])S_2 \rightarrow (c[f_7], c[S_3])S_3\} \tag{2}$$

$c[F]$ denotes a call statement which invokes function or API.

Long API Data Dependence Path Construction. Before constructing long paths, we need to define what kind of paths can be assembled. Every path has at least two nodes, we call the first node start node and the last node end node. If two path can be assembled to construct a long path, this means the first path's end node is "equal" to the second path's start node. In this case, two nodes are "equal" does not mean they are identical. Every node in the API data dependence path has call context. During our path construction process, end node is "equal" to start node means their call context are identical or one's call context is the subsequence of the other one's. For example, $(c[f_5], c[S_2])S_2$ is subsequence of $(c[f_4], c[f_5], c[S_2])S_2$, so path (1) and path (2) can be assembled to a long path:

$$f_1\{(c[f_2], c[f_3], c[S_1])S_1 \rightarrow (c[f_4], c[f_5], c[S_2])S_2 \rightarrow (c[f_4], c[f_7], c[S_3])S_3\} \tag{3}$$

Context and Constant Analysis. After data flow analysis, we get all API data dependence paths embedded in an app. In this section, we demonstrate how to add context and constant information to API nodes in these API data dependence paths.

For constant analysis, APIs (such as `Runtime.exec()`) whose parameter have special meaning are selected. To perform constant analysis, starting from statements invoke these APIs, we backward search the control flow graph. Call context will be stored during this process. Hence, we can obtain sensitive APIs' constant information with call context. Just like path construction, using the call context, we can add constant information to nodes in API data dependence path. For example, if we get following constant information:

$$f_2\{(c[f_3], c[S_1])S_1[true; none]\}$$

$f_2\{(c[f_3], c[S_1])S_1$ is the subpath of $f_1\{(c[f_2], c[f_3], c[S_1])S_1$, so we can add this information to path (3), we'll get a new path:

$$f_1\{(c[f_2], c[f_3], c[S_1])S_1[true; none] \rightarrow (c[f_4], c[f_5], c[S_2])S_2$$
$$\rightarrow (c[f_4], c[f_7], c[S_3])S_3\} \tag{4}$$

For context analysis, we need to know whether a function is triggered in background. Among the code of an app, background callback is overridden to do some operations. In Flowdroid [14], all callback methods are modeled in a dummy method. This means if we perform a backward search on control flow graph, we can reach a single entry point. We know that every API data dependence path is happened in a function. For example, the path (4) is contained in function f_1. Starting from nodes in control flow graph which invoke f_1, we perform backward search. If we encounter a background callback method, record it. After the backward search, we can decide the context of f_1 based on the callback methods we record. But we can't directly apply the f_1's context to all nodes in path (4), because the nodes in this path also have call context. If a node's call context contains a background callback method, we specify this background callback method as the node's context. Otherwise, the node's context is decided by f_1's context. Using this approach, we can obtain context of all nodes in API data dependence path. For example, if our backward analysis find that f_1 is invoked under onRecieve, and $f_1, f_2, f_3, f_4, f_5, f_7$ are not background callback, we can get a new path with constant and context information:

$$f_1\{(c[f_2], c[f_3], c[S_1])S_1[true; onReceive] \rightarrow (c[f_4], c[f_5], c[S_2])S_2[none; onReceive]$$
$$\rightarrow (c[f_4], c[f_7], c[S_3])S_3[none; onReceive]\} \qquad (5)$$

Finally, we remove the call context information, and can get a API dependence path:

$$S_1[true; onReceive] \rightarrow S_2[none; onReceive] \rightarrow S_3[none; onReceive]\} \qquad (6)$$

4.2   Modality Generation

In section 3, we define *modality*. And in section 4.1, we demonstrate how to extract API data dependence path with constant and context information. For an API dependence path, we extract its subpaths, because these subpaths are both modalities. The length of these subpaths are not less than one. For path (6) obtained from section 4.1, we can get following subpaths:

$$S_1[true; onReceive] \qquad (7)$$
$$S_2[none; onReceive] \qquad (8)$$
$$S_3[none; onReceive] \qquad (9)$$
$$S_1[true; onReceive] \rightarrow S_2[none; onReceive] \qquad (10)$$
$$S_2[none; onReceive] \rightarrow S_3[none; onReceive] \qquad (11)$$

So, for Fig. 3, path (6)(7)(8)(9)(10)(11) are modalities. Through the approach, we collect modalities embeded in all malware samples to build a modality repository.

4.3   Feature Vector Construction

Before applying machine learning techniques, we need translating extracted information to mathematical form. For every app, we generate a feature vector. All app's feature vectors will be added to a data set used by machine learning algorithms. In section 4.2, we get a modality repository. For an app, we can extract the modalities embeded in it. The app's feature vector is constructed as a boolean vector $(B_1, B_2, ..., B_n)$: $B_i = 1$, if app??s modality set contains modality M_i in the modality repository. Otherwise, $B_i = 0$. Through this vector, all API data dependencies can be represented.

4.4   Malware Detection, Classification and Characterization

In this section, we introduce how to use app's feature vectors to achieve malware detection, classification and characterization:

Malware Detection. One application scene is to determine whether or not an Android app is malicious. This is not straightforward. Some benign apps also use sensitive APIs to accomplish some actions like sending SMS message and getting location information. So their feature vectors may contain some modalities mined from malware. However, usually, malicious behaviors are not launched by just a single modality. Multiple modalities are needed to achieve a malicious behavior. This observation makes us treat an app as malware only when its modalities exceed a threshold. In this paper, we use machine learning technique to automatically find the relationships between modalities and malware. Machine-learning classifier mines the relationships based on feature vectors extracted from known malware samples and benign apps, then unknown apps can be detected by this classifier.

Malware Classification. Another application scene is to label malware to a malware family which it actually belongs to. Generally, malware belong to the same family always share similar malicious behaviors. This leads to their modalities are similar. For us, we can use the similarity between malware's feature vectors to classify malware. Using the malware samples from known malware family, we can build a machine-learning classifier to classify unknown malware samples.

Malware Characterization. The last application scene is to automatically characterize the malicious behaviors a malware contains. In fact, to achieve a specified malicious behavior, malware always needs to invoke some sensitive APIs. Such as sending a SMS message needs `sendTextMessage()`, getting location information needs `getLastKnownLocation()`. It means there exist relationships between modalities and malicious behaviors. Our work is to dig out which modalities result a specific malicious behavior. This goal can be achieved by using a well-known machine learning technique called "Association Rule Mining". Malware from the same malware family share the similar malicious behavior, we can list malicious behaviors of a malware family from many sources [3][9]. Malware from a malware family may contains several malicious behaviors, like blocking SMS message, sending out phone id. We can use a boolean vector to represent a malware's behaviors according to whether it contains a specified malicious behavior. Then adding this vector to the end of malware's feature vector to construct a new vector. Feeding this vector to "Association Rule Mining" algorithm can mine out the relationships between modalities and malicious behaviors.

5   Evaluation

5.1   Dataset and Experiment Setup

We collect 6400 malware samples from the Android Malware Genome Project (AMGP) [9][22] and VirusShare project [5]. Then we submit these malware samples to VirusTotal [4]. For each malware, we get a VirusTotal report which lists the scan results of 57 different antivirus (AV) products. If a malware is labeled as malicious by more than 4 AVs, we add this malware to our malware dataset. Finally, we get a malware dataset contains 5648 malware samples. For malware classification, we need to know which malware family a malware belongs to. After we examine the scan results of AV products, we find Ad-Aware's [6] classification results are more approximate to the classification results of AMGP. So we chose the classification results of Ad-Aware to classify the malware. In order to construct a benign dataset, we crawls apps from two alternative Android markets(xiaomi [7] and anzhi [8]). We also upload crawled apps to VirusTotal. If an app passed all AVs, we add it to our benign dataset. In the end, we get 14280 benign apps. Finally, our dataset contains 5648 malware samples and 14280 benign apps.

We conduct experiments on a computer equipped with Intel(R) Core(TM) i7-4770k CPU(3.5GHz) and 16GB of physical memory. The operation system is Windows 7 and we utilize weka [25] as machine learning tool.

5.2   Summary of Modality Generation

The summary of Modality Generation is shown in Figure 4 and Figure 5. Among them, Figure 4 demonstrates the number of the modalities generated from both benign and malicious apps. As shown in this figure, for 94.3% of benign apps and 90.4% of malware samples, less than 20 modalities are extracted from an individual app. This is because the majority of apps don't invoke too many different sensitive APIs.

After analyzing 5648 malware samples, we obtain 4317 modalities. The length of modality is defined as the number of sensitive APIs it contains. Figure 5 illustrates the distribution of the length of modality. As shown in this figure, the longest modality is 7 and 87% of modalities carry less than 6 APIs.

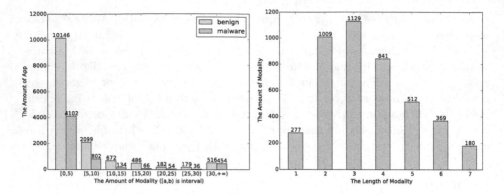

Fig. 4. Distribution of The Amount of Modality Extracted from Each App

Fig. 5. Distribution of The Length Modality

5.3 Malware Detection Result

As introduced in section 4.4, we use machine learning techniques to detect malware. In our experiment, we adopt NaiveBayes, SVM and Random Forest to conduct malware detection, and we use 10-fold cross validation to evaluate these machine learning approaches. The malicious apps and benign apps are both randomly split into 10 groups. In each time of 10 rounds, we select combination of one group of benign apps and malicious apps as testing dataset. The reminding groups are treated as training dataset. When using NaiveBayes, we can correctly identify 91.5% of experimental apps with a 0.8% false positive rate. This process can be completed in 30 seconds. For SVM algorithm, there are four kinds of kernel function in weka [25]: linear, polynomial, radial basis function and sigmid. After testing all these kernel functions, we find linear kernel can achieve 97.3% accuracy rate with a 1.6% false positive, the training and testing procedure can be finished in 3 minutes. We also evaluate the efficiency of using Random Forest, the experiment completes in 20 minutes and 98.5% of apps are correctly identified with a 0.3% false positive rate. For DroidMiner, it achieves 82.2%, 86.7% and 95.3% accuracy rate when using NaiveBayes, SVM and Random Forest respectively. This verify feature vectors extracted based on data flow is more efficient than control flow on modeling the program semantics of malware. The comparison is shown in Table 1.

5.4 Malware Classification Result

In this section, we evaluate the ability of DroidADDMiner [20] to label malware to its correct family. We select 1168 malware samples from 16 malware families. The number of samples selected from each family is listed in Table 2. For malware of each family, we divide them into training set and testing set. Training set contains 66% of malware samples and testing set contains 34% of

Table 1. Effectiveness of Malware Detection(DR denotes Detection Rate, FP denotes False Positive Rate)

Classifer	NaiveBayes		SVM		Random Forest	
Tool	DR	FR	DR	FR	DR	FR
DroidADDMiner	91.5%	0.8%	97.3%	1.6%	98.5%	0.4%
DroidMiner	82.2%	4.4%	86.7%	1.1%	95.3%	0.3%

malware samples. Then we use Random Forest as classifier for training and prediction. The experiments show the classifier can correctly label 96% of malware samples. We further examine 4% of the samples that are mislabeled. 7 samples from DroidDeluxe and GingerMaster are labeled as one another, DroidDeluxe and GingerMaster both root the phone and share some similar malicious behaviors, thus these mislabels are understandable. DroidKungFu4 is the variant of DroidKungFu2, so 4 samples belong to them are mislabeled as one another.

Table 2. Malware Samples Used for Classification

Ind	Family	Num	Ind	Family	Num
1	GingerMaster	42	9	DroidKungFu2	26
2	DroidDeluxe	22	10	DroidKungFu3	305
3	ADRD	27	11	DroidKungFu4	71
4	BaseBridge	114	12	Geinimi	67
5	AnserverBot	183	13	GoldDream	42
6	DroidDreamLight	46	14	KMin	71
7	DroidDream	21	15	Pjapps	44
8	DroidKungFu1	28	16	SmsSpy	59

5.5   Malware Characterization Result

As described in section 4.4, in order to characterize a malware's behaviors, we need to construct a boolean vector for each malware family to model its malicious behaviors. We use the malicious behavior characterization of malware family collected by DroidMiner [11], and also focus on following behaviors: stealing phone information (GetPho), Sending SMS (SdSMS), blocking SMS (BkSMS), communicating with a C&C (C&C), escalating root privilege (Root) and accessing geographical information (GetGeo). Then malicious behavior boolean vectors are generated for each malware family. Adding corresponding malicious behavior boolean vector to the end of a malware's feature vector, we can get new vector for Association Rule Mining.

We utilize Apriori algorithm [12] to mine the relationships between malicious behaviors and modalities. After mining, DroidADDMiner obtained 492 behavior

Table 3. Behaviors of 5 Test Malware Samples

MD5	Family	Behavior
3ae5c5ee6c118a3cdbf2c55132f55948	SmsSpy	BkSMS,C&C,SdSMS
156fdce65eb6e4287aed687a1c9c2589	GGTracker	BkSMS,C&C,GetPho,SdSMS
60ce9b29a6b9c7ee22604ed5e08e8d8a	Endofday	BkSMS,GetPho,SdSMS
e98791dffcc0a8579ae875149e3c8e5e	zitmo	BkSMS,SdSMS
de04914d84239fbd40aa470ad86e388c	DroidKungFuUpdate	Root,GetPho,C&C

Table 4. Representative Rules for Malicious Behavior Characterization

Index	Behavior	Rule
1	GetGeo	LocationManager.getBestProvider()[false;none] → Location.getLastKnownLocation()[false;none]
2	GetGeo	LocationManager.requestLocationUpdates()[true;none]
3	Root	Runtime.getRuntime()[false;none] → Runtime.exec()[true;none]
4	Root	Process.killProcess()[false;none]
5	C&C	ConnectivityManager.getActiveNetworkInfo()[false;none] → WifiManager.setWifiEnabled()[false;none]
6	C&C	URLConnection.openConnection()[false;none] → HttpURLConnection.connect()[false;none]
7	SdSMS	gsm.SmsManager.getDefault()[false;none] → gsm.SmsManager.sendTextMessage()[true;none]
8	SdSMS	SmsManager.getDefault()[false;none] → SmsManager.sendTextMessage()[true;none]
9	GetPho	TelephonyManager.getLine1Number()[false;none] → ConnectivityManager.getActiveNetworkInfo()[false;none]
10	GetPho	TelephonyManager.getDeviceId()[false;none] → HttpEntityEnclosingRequestBase.setEntity()[false;none]
11	BkSMS	ContentResolver.delete()[false;BroadcastReceiver$onReceive]
12	BkSMS	abortBroadcast()[false;BroadcastReceiver$onReceive]

association rules. Some representative rules are listed in Table 3. Then we use these mined rules to test malware samples which are not used in mining phase. The results show we can correctly characterize the malware's behaviors. We list the results in Table 4.

5.6   Runtime Performance

DroidADDMiner needs three steps to identify an app: modality generation, feature vector construction and machine learning. Compared with modality generation, the time of feature vector construction and machine learning are negligible. So we just focus on the time of modality generation. Fig. 6 illustrates the runtime performance of modality generation for benign apps and malware samples. As shown in this figure, because most of malware samples are very small, majority (91%) of malware samples are completed in 10 seconds. For 89% of benign apps and 95% malware samples, the process of modality generation can be completed in 1 minute. The average runtime of modality generation is 10 seconds. Droid-SIFT [13] also performs data flow analysis on Android app, as shown in Table 5, although their hardware is better than ours, its average runtime is 175.8 seconds. It's no doubt that when analyzing large-scaled apps, DroidADDMiner can vastly reduce the running time.

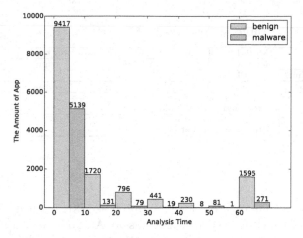

Fig. 6. Distribution of Modality Generation Time

Table 5. Runtime Performance of Malware Detection Tools

Tool	Average Performance	CPU	physical memory
DroidADDMiner	10s	Core(TM) i7-4770k	16G
DroidSIFT	175s	Xeon(R) E5-2650	128GB

6   Discussion

There is competition between defender and attacker, Android malware always evolutes itself to evade detection. DroidChameleon [23] and Adam [24] have demonstrated common malware transformation techniques like repackaging, changing field names could evade many existing commercial anti-malware tools. But for DroidADDMiner, it does not rely on external symptoms like package name, field name. So it's resilient to these common transformation attacks. Other transformation techniques like call indirections, code reordering and junk code insertion also can not evade DroidADDMiner. Because DroidADDMiner focuses on data flow between sensitive APIs, these transformation techniques do not change the data flow of sensitive APIs. To demonstrate it, we use Droid-Chameleon and Adam to obfuscate 100 malware samples selected from Droid-KungFu3 family. As expected, DroidADDMiner can label all these obfuscated samples to DroidKungFu3 family. But DroidADDminer also has some limitations. It does not take native code into consideration right now, so a malware can put malicious behaviors in native code to bypass detection of DroidAD-DMiner. And DroidADDMiner just performs a simple constant analysis, if malware author splits an string like "content://sms" into two parts, we can not get the original semantics of some APIs. These limitations are left for future work.

Table 6. Comparison of Different Tools

Tool	Modeling of App Behavior	Explanation of App Behavior
Dredin	permission, API, manifest file	support
DroidAPIMiner	API, parameters of API	-
DroidMiner	control flow of API	support
DroidSIFT	data flow of API context and constant information	-
DroidADDMiner	data flow of API context and constant information	support

7   Related Work

Static analysis techniques are widely adopted to extract features for using machine learning algorithm to detect and classify Android malware. We summarize the difference of exist tools in Table 6. We don't list the detection rate and time efficiency in this table, because these tools use different machine learning algorithms and hardwares. Drebin [10] proposes to detect Android malware by extracting feature vectors from application manifest file and app code. DroidAPIMiner [20] extracts features at API level, and they take some APIs' parameters into consideration. Despite the effectiveness, the extracted feature vectors of these approaches are related to application syntax instead of program semantics. The feature vectors they extract are not robust enough to reflect app's behaviors. DroidMiner [11] focuses on control flow, they select some sensitive APIs and specific resources as the nodes to construct control flow graph, node sequences are extracted from this graph to generate feature vectors. Missing of data flow information could affect its detection rate. DroidSIFT [13] performs data flow analysis on Android apps. For every app, it generats a weighted contextual API data dependence graph. Then similarities between graphs are calculated to construct feature vectors. Compared with DroidADDMiner, it not only lacks of the ability to automatically characterize the behaviors of malware but also needs more time to analyze an app.

CHEX [16], Flowdroid [14], AmanDroid [17] are three tools designed to deal with information leakage problem. CHEX [16] uses a ??spit?? based approach to perform data flow analysis, each program split includes code reachable from a single entry point. For every program split, a system dependence graph [18] will be generated. Sources and sinks connections are extracted from this graph. Amandroid [17] computes an inter-component data flow graph (IDFG) which contains all objects?? points-to information in a both flow and context-sensitive way. This IDFG can be used to solve security problems including information leakage problem. Flowdroid [14] is quite different from CHEX [16] and Amandroid [17], it models data flow analysis problem within the IFDS [19] framework for inter-procedural distributive subset problems. Flowdroid is faster than the other two tools, because when performing data flow analysis, it only focuses on the variables related to sources and sinks. DroidADDMiner is built based on Flowdroid, so it can benefit from Flowdroid.

8   Conclusion

In this paper, we propose a semantic-based approach which detects, classifies and characterizes Android malware via API data dependency. For each app, we extract API data dependence paths which we call modality embedded in the app. Feature vectors are constructed for every app according to these modalities. We present our prototype system, DroidADDMiner, extends FlowDroid [13]. We evaluate our system using 5648 malware samples and 14280 benign samples. Experiments show that DroidMiner can achieve 98% accuracy in malware detection, and it can label 96% malware instances to its right family. Although performing data flow analysis, for most of the experimental samples, DroidADDMiner can complete analysis in 60 seconds.

Acknowledgements. We would like to thank anonymous reviewers for their comments. This work was supported in part by grants from the Chinese National Natural Science Foundation (61272078, 61073027, 90818022, and 61321491), and the Chinese National 863 High-Tech Program (2011AA01A202).

References

1. iPhone market share shrinks as Android, Windows Phone grow. http://www.cnet.com/news/iphone-market-share-shrinks-as-android-windows-phone-grow/
2. Mobile threat report 2013 q3. F-Secure Response Labs (2013). https://www.f-secure.com/documents/996508/1030743/Mobile_Threat_Report_Q3_2013.pdf
3. Symantec   enterprise.   http://www.symantec.com/security_response/landing/azlisting.jsp
4. Virustotal. https://www.virustotal.com/
5. Virusshare. http://virusshare.com/
6. Ad-Aware. http://www.lavasoft.com/
7. Xiaomi android market. http://app.mi.com/
8. Anzhi Android market. http://www.anzhi.com/
9. Android malware genome project. http://www.malgenomeproject.org/
10. Arp, D., Spreitzenbarth, M., Hbner, M., Gascon, H., Rieck, K., Siemens, C.: Drebin: effective and explainable detection of android malware in your pocket. In: Proceedings of NDSS, February 2014
11. Yang, C., Xu, Z., Gu, G., Yegneswaran, V., Porras, P.: DroidMiner: automated mining and characterization of fine-grained malicious behaviors in android applications. In: Kutyłowski, M., Vaidya, J. (eds.) ICAIS 2014, Part I. LNCS, vol. 8712, pp. 163–182. Springer, Heidelberg (2014)
12. Agrawal, R., Srikant, R.: Fast algorithms for mining association rules in large databases. In: Proceedings of the 20th International Conference on Very Large Data Bases, pp. 641–644. Morgan Kaufmann Publishers Inc. (1994)
13. Zhang, M., Duan, Y., Yin, H., Zhao, Z.: Semantics-aware android malware classification using weighted contextual API dependency graphs. In: Proceedings of the 2014 ACM SIGSAC Conference on Computer and Communications Security, pp. 1105–1116. ACM, November 2014

14. Arzt, S., Rasthofer, S., Fritz, C., Bodden, E., Bartel, A., Klein, J., Le Traon, Y., Octeau, D., McDaniel, P.: Flowdroid: precise context, flow, field, object-sensitive and lifecycle-aware taint analysis for android apps. In: Proceedings of the 35th ACM SIGPLAN Conference on Programming Language Design and Implementation, pp. 29. ACM, June 2014
15. Fritz, C., Arzt, S., Rasthofer, S., Bodden, E., Bartel, A., Klein, J., Le Traon, Y., Octeau, D., McDaniel, P.: Highly precise taint analysis for Android applications. EC SPRIDE, TU Darmstadt, Tech. Rep. (2013)
16. Lu, L., Li, Z., Wu, Z., Lee, W., Jiang, G.: Chex: statically vetting android apps for component hijacking vulnerabilities. In: Proceedings of the 2012 ACM Conference on Computer and Communications Security, pp. 229–240. ACM, October 2012
17. Wei, F., Roy, S., Ou, X.: Amandroid: a precise and general inter-component data flow analysis framework for security vetting of android apps. In: Proceedings of the 2014 ACM SIGSAC Conference on Computer and Communications Security, pp. 1329–1341. ACM, November 2014
18. Horwitz, S., Reps, T., Binkley, D.: Interprocedural slicing using dependence graphs. ACM Transactions on Programming Languages and Systems (TOPLAS) 12(1), 26–60 (1990)
19. Reps, T., Horwitz, S., Sagiv, M.: Precise interprocedural dataflow analysis via graph reachability. In: Proceedings of the 22nd ACM SIGPLAN-SIGACT Symposium on Principles of Programming Languages, pp. 49–61. ACM, January 1995
20. Aafer, Y., Du, W., Yin, H.: DroidAPIMiner: mining API-level features for robust malware detection in android. In: Zia, T., Zomaya, A., Varadharajan, V., Mao, M. (eds.) SecureComm 2013. LNICST, vol. 127, pp. 86–103. Springer, Heidelberg (2013)
21. Au, K.W.Y., Zhou, Y.F., Huang, Z., Lie, D.: Pscout: analyzing the android permission specification. In: Proceedings of the 2012 ACM conference on Computer and communications security, pp. 217–228. ACM, October 2012
22. Zhou, Y., Jiang, X.: Dissecting android malware: characterization and evolution. In: 2012 IEEE Symposium on Security and Privacy (SP), pp. 95–109. IEEE, May 2012
23. Rastogi, V., Chen, Y., Jiang, X.: Droidchameleon: evaluating android anti-malware against transformation attacks. In: Proceedings of the 8th ACM SIGSAC Symposium on Information, Computer and Communications Security, pp. 329–334. ACM, May 2013
24. Zheng, M., Lee, P.P.C., Lui, J.C.S.: ADAM: an automatic and extensible platform to stress test android anti-virus systems. In: Flegel, U., Markatos, E., Robertson, W. (eds.) DIMVA 2012. LNCS, vol. 7591, pp. 82–101. Springer, Heidelberg (2013)
25. Hall, M., Frank, E., Holmes, G., Pfahringer, B., Reutemann, P., Witten, I.H.: The WEKA data mining software: an update. ACM SIGKDD Explorations Newsletter 11(1), 10–18 (2009)

KeyPocket - Improving Security and Usability for Provider Independent Login Architectures with Mobile Devices

André Ebert[1]([✉]), Chadly Marouane[2], Benno Rott[1,2], and Martin Werner[1,2]

[1] Mobile and Distributed Systems Group, Ludwig-Maximilians-University,
Oettingenstrasse 67, 80538 Munich, Germany
{andre.ebert,martin.werner}@ifi.lmu.de
[2] Virality GmbH, Rauchstrasse 7, 81679 Munich, Germany
{marouane,rott}@virality.de

Abstract. Nowadays, many daily duties being of a private as well as of a business nature are handled with the help of online services. Due to migrating formerly local desktop applications into clouds (e.g., Microsoft Office Online, etc.), services become available by logging in into a user account through a web browser. But possibilities for authenticating a user in a web browser are limited and employing a username with a password is still de facto standard, disregarding open security or usability issues. Notwithstanding new developments on that subject, there is no sufficient alternative available. In this paper, we specify the requirements for a secure, easy-to-use, and third-party-independent authentication architecture. Moreover, we present KeyPocket, a user-centric approach aligned to these requirements with the help of the user's smartphone. Subsequently, we present its state of implementation and discuss its individual capabilities and features.

Keywords: Multi-factor authentication · Mobile-based login architectures · Security · Usability

1 Introduction

Whether booking a journey, transferring money to a bank account, or reading the most recent news: Mobile devices with online capabilities are ubiquitous and their usage is common today [1]. But service providers insist on the user to create a user account, commonly secured by a username and a password, still. This leads to the dilemma of having a trade-off between security and usability. Short passwords, which do not contain special signs, numerics, or capital and lowercase letters are good to remember, but have a lack of security. In contrast, a complex password is hard to remember and users tend to write it down, which makes it accessible for possible attackers [2]. Even in the pre-smartphone era, users already had an average number of thirty user accounts and about 6.5 passwords to secure them [3]. This results in a multiple or combined usage of the same passwords for different services. But if one account is compromised, all accounts

© Institute for Computer Sciences, Social Informatics and Telecommunications Engineering 2015
B. Thuraisingham et al. (Eds.): SecureComm 2015, LNICST 164, pp. 41–57, 2015.
DOI: 10.1007/978-3-319-28865-9_3

secured with its credentials are also compromised [4]. Furthermore, complex passwords which have been robust against Brute-force attacks in the past, get stolen by Phishing or Keylogging mechanisms today [5]. Parwani et al. stated, that a huge number of private as well as of business accounts are accessed illegally every day, which results in great personal and financial damage [6]. Therefore, Bonneau et al. explored more than 35 different authentication approaches and claim that their security and usability is not suitable to substitute authentication systems based on usernames and passwords, yet [7]. Due to rapid development of smartphones and their capabilities to act as a mobile sensor, hardware tokens, or transmission systems, their inclusion in multi-factor authentication architectures is accelerated. Target is the improvement of usability and security in relation to conventional systems as well as the provision of a trustworthy and easy accessible platform for managing different credentials and identities for a user. Still, we are not aware of a login architecture which satisfies these needs concerning usability, security, data privacy, and service-independence.

In the following, we first present some fundamentals related to mobile authentication as well as a choice of current authentication concepts in order to explain their technical and architectural concepts in Section 2. The following section defines requirements for a login architecture as a function of usability, security, and technical as well as conceptual circumstances. Afterwards, we present Key-Pocket, a provider-independent, easy-accessible, and secured login architecture along with some of its unique features in Section 4. Furthermore, this section also deals with concrete insights into the system's implementation. Section 5 explores the mentioned concept in reference to the demanded requirements and discusses its features in respect of possible threats for mobile authentication. Afterwards, we summarize our findings and provide a glimpse towards open issues and future tasks.

2   Related Work

In this section, we present some security fundamentals in context of mobile authentication. Moreover, we provide a brief overview across recent mobile-device-based authentication architectures.

2.1   Secure Data Encryption and Transmission

Procedures for encryption are essential for the development of a authentication architecture based on a mobile device due to several reasons. On the one hand, it guarantees a secure data storage, on the other hand data integrity and confidence during a transmission process is ensured. Munro et al. proclaim, that it was difficult to encrypt data on Android smartphones, so far. Especially PIN-based encryption methods were susceptible for Brute-force attacks and did not provide adequate protection for sensible data [8]. But since the introduction of Android 5.0 Lollipop, hardware-based disk encryption is integrated into the operation system (OS). Therefore, a 128 bit Advanced Encryption Standard (AES) algorithm in combination with Cipher Block Chaining (CBC) is used. The master key also uses 128 bit AES encryption. For secure usage a key length of 256 bit is recommended [9]. Until now, we are not aware of any successful attacks onto recent Android versions. The procedure can currently be rated as secure for encrypting data on Android devices.

Apple iOS offers its Keychain feature for secure credential management, which was already part of Apples desktop operation system OS X. It realizes secure handling and inspection of certificates as well as of user credentials. There also occurred different security issues with the Keychain since its release, especially in combination with the processor architecture of some older iPhone models and jailbreaked devices. Referring to this issue, Heider et al. show that data can be stored in a save way on recent iOS-devices by using the Keychain, still [10].

The TLS encryption protocol, formerly known as Secure Sockets Layer (SSL), was originally developed for the combined usage with HTTPS in web browsers and is a de facto standard for secured end-to-end communication in networks. Therefore, the server provides a valid public key certificate (issued by a trustworthy Certification Authority (CA)) to the client during the handshake procedure, who is now able to validate it (e.g., period of validity, listed domain names, etc.) [11,12]. Due to security vulnerabilities, which emerged during the last years, there were doubts about the SSL technology's reliability. Despite that, Georgie et al. show that mainly inaccurate implementations (e.g., deactivated certificate validation) or poorly designed SSL libraries and not the protocol itself are responsible for these flaws [13]. An example for a security leak, which got a lot of attention during the last year was the Heartbleed bug. It was detected in the OpenSSL framework and facilitated the readout of 24 - 55% of the memory of popular HTTPS site's servers. However, the bug was fixed in version 1.0.1g [14,15]. In addition, Georgie et al. indicate that SSL can be used in a secure manner without any issues, as long as configuration parameters are set explicitly and development guidelines are followed. Irrespective of that, HTTPS and TLS/SSL do not protect the user from every kind of connection-aimed attacks. Callegati et al. indicate that even HTTPS connections are not immune against Man-in-the-Middle attacks (MitM) [16].

2.2 Smartphone-Based Login Architectures

Public-key-cryptography-based login architectures use encryption in order to protect the user's credentials from unauthorized access. In context of the chosen architectural concept, the used technologies, assigned roles and identified tasks are significantly dependent of the proposed system-design. All approaches introduced in the following integrate a smartphone into their authentication infrastructure. Its role differs in each individual concept (e.g., hardware token, data transmission, identity management, etc.).

Czeskis et al. proclaim an authentication system for opportunistically provided cryptographic identity assertion, called PhoneAuth [17]. The approach is called opportunistic because it is only used if the user fulfills the required system setup, consisting of a compatible web browser and a smartphone. In order to use PhoneAuth, the user first visits the web page he desires to log in to and enters his credentials. Subsequently, the browser redirects this data to the server, which creates a login ticket with a challenge for authentication. This ticket is sent back to the browser by using a TLS encrypted connection, which forwards it to the user's smartphone. The device functions as the second factor possession and is registered explicitly as belonging to the user. By signing the browsers public key contained by the login ticket with the user's private key on the smartphone, the user's identity can be proofed without doubt to the server. As soon as the user's identity is verified, the server sets a cookie which is channel-bound to the browser's key pair and the user becomes logged in. The authors state, that all MitM attacks are perceived by the usage of a TLS channel ID, which is unique for each communication partner. However, in its current state the system is not able to provide a reliable and usable management for complex passwords. They still need to be entered manually into the websites login form.

Based on the research of the university of Tübingen, Borchert et al. present a system for an indirect login under the usage of NFC [18]. For processing it, a smartphone and a NFC smartcard containing the user's asymmetric key material is needed. In order to conduct the indirect login the server generates a challenge, which is encoded together with the server's address in a two dimensional code (e.g., QR-Code) and shown at the login page. After scanning the code, the login address is presented to the user for confirmation. This allows the system to suspend MitM attacks. Subsequently, the user brings his smartcard near the smartphone and the challenge as well as the server's name are forwarded from the mobile device to the card via NFC. The smartcard now computes the response in terms of a private-key-signed challenge, which is sent back to the sever in combination with the original challenge and the username. Because of an in prior carried-out registration process, the user's public key is already known to the server, which is now able to verify the user's proclaimed identity. The authors do not make any specifications about the usage of the smartcard's PIN function. Furthermore, the smartphone's only functionality is being a relay between the smartcard and the server. The predecessor of the indirect NFC login called *ekaay* was also developed by Borchert et al. and is a one-factor possession architecture without the inclusion of a smartcard [19]. In this scenario, a new key pair is created on registration and the pre-shared public key is sent to the user. To proceed with the login, the user scans the shown QR-Code and signs the contained challenge, which enables the server to verify the users authorization permission. Because of the pre-shared key practice, this method is susceptible for MitM attacks. In addition, the key is no one-time key, which means that as soon as the system is compromised, a secure data exchange is not possible any more.

Van Rijswijk et al. present *tiqr*, a concept similar to ekaay which facilitates the binding of each service account to a unique key on its creation [20]. The tiqr architecture itself is similar to ekaay and needs to be implemented on the service provider's website. Each user account is bound to a unique key. A difference to ekaay is, that the key pair with the pre-shared public key is created locally on the user's device and subsequently transfered to the server. For the sake of login confirmation and protection from Phishing attacks, the user needs to check the login address and complete the procedure by entering his PIN. By binding accounts to individual keys as well as due to the constraint to implement tiqr on a service provider's server, the flexibility of the concept is weakened.

Snap2Pass also binds user accounts directly to a key and provides a symmetric as well as an asymmetric encryption mode [21]. Using the symmetric mode, a secret key is managed on the user's device for each server. A new account is created by scanning a QR-Code from the service provider's login page. The user provides only a username, the password is provided by the server in terms of a pre-shared secret. For logging in, the user again scans a QR-Code, which contains a challenge bound to the current browser session. The device computes the corresponding HMAC-SHA1-hash and sends the signed challenge together with the original challenge back to the server. The server now verifies both, the user and the browser session and completes the login procedure. In public key mode, a public key is generated on application startup on the user's device and is sent to the server, which now is able to verify the signed challenges. By using a pre-shared secret and storing it on the mobile device, the system is downgraded from the usage of two security factors (possession and knowledge) to one factor (possession).

The QR-Code based authentication concept propagated by *Galois Inc.* is similar to ekaay and tiqr, though it currently only exists as a loose concept without implementation and was published on the company's website [22]. For registration, a QR-Code containing a random secret, which is also saved in a session-bound cookie, must be scanned. In the following, either a username is entered by the user inside the corresponding smartphone application or a Unique-User-ID (UUID) is generated automatically. After sending the shared secret, the random secret, the session cookie and the UUID to the service provider, the registration process is completed. For logging in, the user scans a QR-Code containing a random secret and a session cookie. The smartphone's response contains the corresponding UUID and the appropriate random secret for the service's website. After reviewing the credentials the user becomes logged in automatically.

LastPass differs in multiple aspects from the systems mentioned above. It is a cloud-based SSO login architecture, which perches on the usage of a browser-plugin in order to communicate with the website of a service provider [23]. The user's inclusion into the LastPass system is carried out by using the corresponding authenticator application. To use LastPass, the user clicks a button in the browser to start the plugin. After entering his credentials, a one-time password is sent to the user's smartphone as a second authentication factor. This also needs to be entered into the browser-plugin, in order to complete the login process on the client's side. An advantage of this concept is its device independence due to storing and synchronizing user data in a cloud. By introducing the second factor possession, the system's security is increased. But in this case, the increased security also leads to a lack of usability, resulting in the login procedure becoming more complicated. Not only that the user needs to enter credentials for each login, additionally a one-time password is required, which results in multiple media breaks. Moreover, because of entering credentials in the browser-plugin the concept is vulnerable to Keylogging and Phishing attacks.

Besides smartphone-assisted login architectures without complex account or user management, there are also some commercially available architectures with extensive possibilities of managing personal data. Most of these do not use local, but cloud-based technologies to store user data, which leads to advantages regarding a provider's actionability, e.g., in case of device theft or loss. Otherwise, this also indicates privacy issues. Due to their proprietary architecture, the concepts presented in the following could not be evaluated completely in respect of their specific conceptual or technical details.

Click2Pass presents a login via smartphone application in combination with an own web API, which needs to be implemented on the provider's server [24]. Some PHP code fragments serve as an implementation guideline for developers, the comparatively protracted and complex registration process could discourage potential users.

MyDigipass provides a cloud-based two-factor authentication solution compatible with mobile applications as well as with websites. After the registration process, all personal data can be managed in a cloud. This offers a plus on usability,e.g., regarding data migration on device theft. Passwords are stored on a mobile device, which functions as a token. Currently, devices which are available as a token are Android and iOS smartphones and due to its eID function the Belgian identification card, among others. In order to log in, the user enters the MyDigipass launchpad where all registered services are listed. After choosing one service by a click on its icon, the user needs to enter a PIN code and after a successful verification he is redirected to the service's website or its mobile application.

LaunchKey and *Zapper* offer possibilities for multi-factor authentication based on a platform specific registration and implementation process [25,26]. LaunchKey in particular features a decentralized architecture where the entire authentication layer resides on the user's mobile device. Therefore, a cryptographic connection between the user and mobile device is initiated via SMS, QR-Code, email or manual entry. Due to a variable usage of fingerprints, geofencing, bluetooth device check, PINs, etc., the implementation of granular security levels is feasible. After the pairing and the security level setup, the reception of authentication and authorization requests is possible.

Clef supplies a smartphone-based login working with OAuth 2.0, which is also used by OpenID and Twitter [27,28]. A security enhancing feature of Clef is the usage of geolocations as well as the device's hardware information and usage data for fraud detection.

OneID also facilitates a cloud-based approach, where all user data is saved encrypted in order to enhance the users privacy [29]. For its transmission as well as its decryption, a pre-shared key is used, which is stored on the user's device.

Additionally an individual PIN can be set in order to secure this key. Even if a device gets lost, it is not possible to get access to the user's data itself due to its distributed storage in a cloud.

An authentication concept for Mac OS X based on BLE for an iPhone in combination with a MacBook is *Kocktounlock* [30]. As soon as the mobile phone is near the MacBook, it is prepared to become unlocked – only an additional knock onto the phone screen is needed as a signal of intent. Kocktounlock is not working anymore since Mac OS X Yosemite due to the lost feature of a MacBook to act as an iBeacon. Furthermore, the approach is not applicable to websites but only to unlock the OS' lock screen.

A generic, smartphone-based authentication solution which uses the smartphone as a key for vehicles and security doors or barriers is BlueID [31]. The communication between system components and the user's device is secured by an asymmetric public key infrastructure and the usage of certificates, which are issued by the system's own trust center. Data with login information is transferred optionally via WiFi, Bluetooth Smart, mobile network or NFC. For implementing the system on the service's side, a software development kit is provided.

3   Requirements of a Mobile-Based Login Architecture

In the context of developing an alternative login concept with the help of a mobile device, there is a rash of different requirements to be considered. Thus, we identified important basic points on basis of the concepts introduced before and by respecting the paradigms of usability.

1. **Security.** There are several security aspects to be kept in mind: a) the user's account and personal data must be protected under all circumstances and stay secret as well as with integrity, even in case of device theft or loss, b) it must be ensured that only the user alone has access to personal data, and c) all data transfer is secured and encrypted in order to eliminate all kind of unwanted manipulation.
2. **Usability.** The system's usage is as easy and its provided security as high as possible.
3. **Modularity, Compatibility and Scalability.** Existing as well as new service accounts can be integrated into the login architecture easily and without technical limitations.
4. **Privacy.** The user itself is the only person having access to user sensitive data.
5. **Third-Party-Independence.** The architecture is independent of implementations, limitations, and restrictions, stated by existing service architectures or foreign providers.
6. **Hardware Independence.** The hardware requirements are as little as possible; there is no need for additional hardware except the user's smartphone. All used devices are standard versions and commercially available.

4   KeyPocket - An Architecture for Secure and Usable Web Service Access

In the following we present KeyPocket, a user-centric, secured, and easy-accessible authentication architecture featuring multi-factor authentication as well as a decentralized identity management. The only precondition for usage is a smartphone and a computer with a compatible web browser. After highlighting its core concepts and main components, we also provide detailed information about its concrete implementation.

4.1   Architectural Concept

The KeyPocket architecture consists of three main components: 1) the user entity, which is constituted of the user and a mobile device, 2) the relay-server, and 3) a browser-plugin.

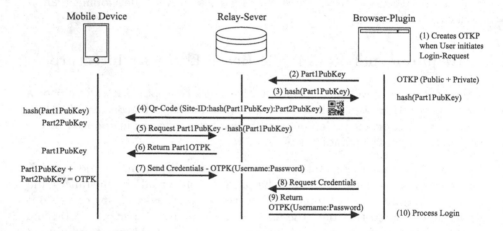

Fig. 1. Providing an overview across KeyPockets login process

Figure 1 illustrates the KeyPocket login concept in context of a flow chart. Core features of the architecture are its independence from third-parties, the decentralized user management as well as some unique security characteristics. E.g., the deployment of one-time key pairs and the commitment of a system for divided public key exchange. Instead of using a pre-shared key for encryption, an individual key pair is created on-demand for each login process. Multi-factor authentication becomes available due to knowledge (PIN), possession (the user's mobile device as a token) and being (e.g., analyzing the users fingerprint or voice). Another security factor is the proof of geographical proximity of the user to the device, which is about to become logged in due to QR-Code scanning. All network-based communication is secured by the usage of HTTPS and TLS.

4.2 Main Components

There are three main entities, which are essential for our architectural concept.

User-side Setup. On the one hand, the user's smartphone is used as a storage for credentials, on the other hand its camera is needed for optical data transmission and its network connection for transferring data to the relay-server. Before the smartphone is ready to use, the KeyPocket application must be installed. Afterwards, no further registration is needed. This enables the user to manage data completely autonomous and on-device; privacy issues due to third-parties can be suspended. To ensure the secure storage of data, it is encrypted before saving and only available by entering a password or providing the correct biometric information.

Browser-side Setup. The browser-plugin is the architecture's control unit. Here, required one-time key pairs (OTKP) are generated, encoded and provided to the user on-demand. Moreover, the plugin is frequently polling at the relay-server for requested user credentials. As soon as they are available at the plugin, they become decrypted and filled into the form on the service provider's website. After confirming these values, the process is completed. The correct form fields are identified by unique Cascading Style Sheet (CSS) selectors.

Relay-Server. The relay-server's main tasks are the forwarding of request and response calls (e.g., containing the users credentials) between the user's smartphone and the browser-plugin as well as the provision of a part of the one-time public key (OTPK). For realizing this connection, the relay-server supplies a Representational State Transfer (REST) interface.

4.3 Third-Party Independence and Privacy Enhancement

On the one hand, KeyPocket is a third-party independent system in terms of that there is no need to implement any code on the service provider's server. The service provider itself does not need to be aware of KeyPocket in order to make it work and due to its generic design it basically works with all web-based login sites without further conditions. On the other hand, the user downloads and installs the browser-plugin as well as the mobile application and is ready to use the architecture without any further registration processes. Moreover, no personal data, not even the user's email address for a registration is known to the KeyPocket infrastructure – all data is encrypted, managed and stored on-device. The relay-server only temporarily stores encrypted credentials until they are retrieved for processing a login.

4.4 Processing a Login

The following process is visualized in Figure 1. A login is initiated by the user opening a service's login page in the browser. After entering a login page, the user clicks the KeyPocket plugin symbol and the browser-plugin generates a new OTKP, containing a public key and a private key (1). A part of the public key (Part1PubKey) is forwarded to the relay-server (2). There it is stored temporarily and its hash is generated and sent back to the browser-plugin (3). There, a QR-Code is computed and shown for scanning by the user. The code contains three parameters: 1) the site ID, typically the domain name, 2) the hash of Part1PubKey and 3) the second part of the public key Part2PubKey (4). The smartphone now requests Part1PubKey from the relay-server (5). Due to the split public key system, it is impossible for attackers to obtain the complete public key and thereby is not able to channel malicious information into the system. Furthermore, a better readable and less granular QR-Code for easier scanning is created. As soon as the relay-server responds with Part1PubKey (6), the mobile device is able to merge the public key from its two fragments. By affirming the procedure due to provision of a password or a fingerprint, the user's credentials are decrypted from the device's storage. Subsequently, they become encrypted again with the one-time public key and transmitted to the relay-server (7). The browser-plugin frequently polls for the requested crendentials (8) and once they are available, they are transmitted to the plugin (9). The plugin encrypts the parameters with its private key, fills them into the designated form fields on the providers login page and confirms the procedure. If the user's data is valid, he is forwarded to the provider's individual welcome page. The presented approach is completely independent from third-party implementations and can generally be used for any kind of service.

4.5   On-Device Identity Management

In order to avoid privacy issues as well as attacks onto a central database containing sensible data, KeyPocket resigns a cloud-based management of user data. All user data is encrypted, respectively, is stored decentralized on-device. Depending on technical features of the used device, personal data is only available by entering a password or by providing biometric features. As soon as credentials become requested, the application searches for corresponding data on the user's device, encrypts them with the OTPK and returns them. If no suitable data is found, the user can enter new credentials or link already existing account information. Due to the fact that the user's device is the only place where private data is stored, the migration to other devices is feasible due to credential export and import via encrypted database files, e.g., KeyPass' .kdb. There is no data distributed on a web server that needs to be updated.

An issue which is still unsolved within the current concept is a homogeneous sync process for changing an existing account's password on the smartphone as well as in a service provider's database. Currently, this procedure needs to be done manually by the user. The use of background HTTP requests for posting a new password entered on the user's smartphone to the provider's corresponding website could be a solution. Still, this approach lacks of a generic potential due to the need of knowing individual server addresses and parameter names.

Therefore, this issue still needs to be addressed by further research in order to solve it sufficiently.

4.6   Implementation

The current version of KeyPocket is available for Google Android and Apple iOS – general as well as further information can be found on the project's website[1]. A second version with some major changes is about to be released within the forth quarterly period of 2015. Some conceptual characteristics, e.g., the export of user credentials via database file, are not featured by the current KeyPocket version, but will be part of the next release. The following implementation details are coined to the currently published version.

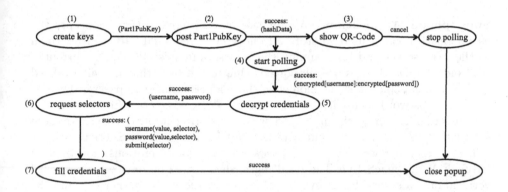

Fig. 2. Login process from the browser plugins point of view

Browser Plugin. Currently, browser-plugins for Google Chrome and Mozilla Firefox are provided. Both are implemented with JavaScript and individually optimized for the specific browsers. After their installation they are ready for usage without any further registration or setup process. The plugins' architecture is based on a message-oriented-architecture and Figure 4.6 shows the login process from a plugin's point of view. Therefore, an asymmetric key pair with a length of 2048 bit is created (1) with the Rivest Shamir Adleman (RSA) algorithm. In the following, the public key is split into two parts and one part is transferred to the relay server (2), which is responding with the corresponding hash of the public key part (3). The other part of the public key is shown to the user in the QR-Code. Subsequently, the plugin polls the server until it answers with the user's credentials or the login is terminated by the user (4). After the plugin has decrypted the credentials (5), it fills them into the selected login fields of a service's website (6,7). The identification of input fields is realized

---

[1] https://www.keypocket.de/

with the help of CSS selectors provided by an offline database. If a website's input fields are not registered in the database, the user is asked to mark the input fields manually with a mouse click. Unknown and new input fields become added automatically to the database after a successful login.

Relay Server. The relay-server is based on Java 1.8 and was implemented with the Play Framework[2]. It provides two REST interfaces, all data is JSON encoded and the connection is secured by TLS/HTTPS. The */pubkeys* interface is used to transfer one part of the public key to the server, which hashes the key and stores it temporarily in a database. The same interface also used for the data's retrieval. The */credentials* interface allows the temporarily storing and retrieval of the credentials, together with a corresponding hash. As soon as the credentials were transferred to the browser-plugin for the login, they become deleted automatically.

Smartphone Application. Within the current architectural concept, the user's smartphone is used to store all encrypted credentials, to transfer them to the relay server and for scanning the browser-plugin's QR-Code. Currently, Android and iOS devices are supported. Due to the fact, that not all Android devices are capable of using biometric data for securing the password vault, a master password is used as a fallback for devices without fingerprint sensor. In order to verify the password without storing it on device, a random salt with a size of 128 bit and SHA1PRNG is created first. Subsequently, it is hashed together with the user's password with 2000 iterations, 256 bit and PBKDF2WithHmacSHA1. The resulting hash is stored on device for password verification – a second hash key is created and stored with another salt and the users password, in order to use it for credential encryption. The credentials itself are encrypted with the AES algorithm with 256 bit in combination with HMAC. The creation of one hash key with $i = 1000$ iterations takes about $v = 0.15$ s, with $i = 2000$ iterations it takes about $v = 0.2$ s on a Samsung Galaxy S3 smartphone. The same amount of time is needed to decrypt the password later on for each decryption. This means, that even if an attacker had a CPU power of $f = 10000$ times faster than the user and the user's password an entropy of $n = 30$ bits, the attacker would still need about $\frac{v*2^{n-1}}{f} = 10.737$ hours to crack the password for $i = 2000$. In this context, the more iterations i are used, the more difficult it is for an attacker to learn a secret. On the other hand, especially due to limited resources on mobile devices it is necessary to find suitable parameters oriented on security as well as on usability.

For the iPhone implementation, we use the standard iOS Keychain in combination with a password or, if a fingerprint sensor is available, the user's fingerprint as a security feature.

---

[2] https://www.playframework.com/

5   Discussion

In this section we want to discuss the different features of the proposed Key-Pocket architecture on a qualitative basis. Therefore, we first match its security characteristics to threats relevant in this context. The qualitative requirements, which we identified in Section 3 are the system's usability, modularity, compatibility, scalability, security, privacy protection, and its independence from external hardware as well as from third-party providers. Finally, some general issues which occurred during the implementation phase are mentioned.

5.1   Threat Robustness

There are lots of different possibilities for attackers to compromise a user within the environment of mobile communication and authentication. In context of a **Man-in-the-Middle** attack, the attacker engages between two communicating parties and monitors their communication secretly. The so gained information can be modified, replaced or used for malicious purposes. Furthermore, the aggressor could disguise as the legitimate communication partner (e.g., a server) and response in this role to the other communication partner's requests in order thieve sensitive information [32]. Our application is not only robust to MitM attacks because of the usage of secured and fully encrypted communication channels. Furthermore, its split public key usage and the one-time key concept enhance the robustness significantly. Only in step (6) of Figure 1 an attacker is enabled to thieve a part of the key, which is useless without its counterpart. In general, **Brute-force** attacks can be aggrevated significantly by using sufficient passwords (e.g., sufficient length, special characters, capital and lowercase characters) [8]. Our architecture facilitates a completely user controlled data storing concept on the user's mobile device. Hence, the existing potential of Brute-force attacks is inevitable (e.g., on device theft). Nonetheless, as mentioned in Section 2, all data stored with the help of the iOS Keychain can be rated as relatively secure. For Android, we use a custom tailored encryption approach, which forces an attacker to invest several days or months in order to crack the user's password (accepting that the attacker has the CPU power of an up-to-date, high-end consumer machine and the user uses a password of sufficient complexity, see Section 4.6). After all, if no biometric sensor is available, the encryption security highly depends on the complexity of the user's password. The recording and readout of user input by the usage of malicious applications and without the user's knowledge is called **Keylogging** [33]. In general, our architecture offers no potential for Keylogging, because only the KeyPocket application is used for entering data. Still, if an attacker would be able to log the user's input while using KeyPocket (e.g., the OS security systems are compromised due to jail-breaking, rooting, etc.), the only potential for Keylogging attacks is present while the user enters his password or new account data. All already existing data is still safe due to its complete encryption. Furthermore, for doing harm with knowledge about the password, an attacker would still need the user's device. This also extends for **Shoulder-surfing** attacks, which means curious gazes across the user's shoulder without his knowledge and in order to peek passwords or other sensitive data. Within the scope of a classic **Phishing** attack, the user becomes redirected to a fake website, which is based on a brands website the user knows and trusts in. After entering his credentials into a faked website's login form and confirming it, the user is redirected to a site of the original provider and is probably not aware of the attack or the resulting leak of private data. There are only a few possibilities to take actions against these attacks on a technical basis. For the most part it is up to the user to verify the authenticity of a website [34]. Related to that, Phishing attacks are also a weakness of our proposed system, for it relies on the user to check service addresses manually. But, although we cannot force a user to carefully check an unknown server address, he still needs to take notice of it and to confirm it manually. In context of **Sweep attacks**, an attacker is able to steal multiple credentials at the same time due to the exploitation of a password manager's autofill functions [35]. This danger is suspended due to the hold out on a clear signal of intention by the user before filling in credentials into input fields.

5.2   Qualitative Requirements

In the following, we examine our architecture's features in respect of the requirements for an mobile-based authentication architecture. Concerning its **Usability**, KeyPocket offers an easy-to-use approach without ignoring the necessity for security standards – the only precondition for usage is the installation of the KeyPocket software. For logging in, there are only two steps: 1) scanning the QR-Code, and 2) confirming the login by providing a second security factor. Due to its need for only one password to be remembered by the user or the usage of biometric data for opening the credential's vault, the simplicity and usability is enhanced significantly for the user. In contrast to some of the approaches introduced in Section 2, KeyPocket facilitates no device pairing, which enables multi-device usage. Missing multi-device support is mostly related to the necessity for a registration process, an existing provider dependence, or pre-shared keys bound to a specific service or device. In order to guarantee **Modularity, Compatibility, and Scalability**, new and existing user accounts can be added to the application without restrictions and there are no limitations for their number or the assignment of accounts to domains and vice versa. A disadvantage of the KeyPocket architecture may be its need for a relay-server, which could be seen as a Single-point-of-failure or, in case of a large amount of login requests, could lead to scalability problems. Concerning **Hardware Independence**, there are no preconditions except the need for a smartphone with internet and a camera in order to use KeyPocket. Compared to other approaches, no additional tokens (e.g., Smartcards or ID cards) are used. As already mentioned, no cloud-systems or provider dependent storage is used in order to save and manage the user's credentials. There is no registration process and no information about the user within the system except the encrypted data on the smartphone and a temporary copy of credential pairs during the login process on the relay-server. But even this temporary copy is deleted after a few seconds. All of these routines and practices are strengthening the users **Privacy** significantly. Furthermore, **Third-Party Independence** is strengthened due to the fact that no service providers or third-parties are involved in the handling of confidential data and no registration process is needed. Furthermore, there is no code about to be deployed on the service provider's systems. The user solely decides, where and when to use the system without our or the service provider's knowledge.

5.3   General Notes

In the following, some specific details concerning KeyPocket are to be mentioned. Our generic plugin-based approach enables the adaptability for nearly each service provider featuring a website login without the providers inclusion. However, due to the necessity of using selectors for identifying form fields, the system's reliability can be weakened because of external influences (e.g., updates of provider sites, changes in technology, etc.). This may also lead to increased costs due to maintenance work. Nonetheless, this problem is addressed due to the feature of allowing users to mark unknown input fields manually and to use these information to update our database constantly. Furthermore, due to technical reasons the generation of on-demand key pairs took nearly 6 seconds with Google Chrome in a worst case scenario. This is way to much for a system with high usability requirements. In order to solve this problem, we changed our initial protocol for key creation and create the first key pair already on browser startup. Implying that the user is not logging in into different services with a frequency higher than each 6 seconds, we found this optimization to be sufficient. This pre-usage creation enables the system to simulate an on-demand usage experience.

6   Conclusion and Future Work

Within the scope of this paper, we provided a secured, and third-party independent platform for processing logins on websites under inclusion of the user's smartphone. The ability to manage digital identities without enforcing an additional registration process or effectuating privacy issues is provided to the user. Additionally, we introduced some unique features, namely the usage of a split one-time public key in combination with further security factors like possession, being and geographical proximity.

Another issue which is still unsolved is the development of a holistic process for updating and synchronizing account information automatically. Currently, it is the user's duty to do this manually.

Despite our efforts, there are still open issues as well as possibilities for extensions. For example, scanning of QR-Codes has performance issues due to technical reasons and furthermore, it lacks of user acceptance. It could be substituted with technologies featuring similar security aspects (e.g., geographical proximity, protection against eavesdropping, etc.) in this context, e.g., NFC or BLE. This could also increase the system's usability due to the disposal of the additional scanning interaction and is subject of our research for future KeyPocket versions.

References

1. Van Eimeren, B.: Always on - smartphone, tablet und co. als neue taktgeber im netz (ard/zdf). Media Perspektiven **7**(2013), 386–390 (2013)
2. Adams, A., Sasse, M.A.: Users are not the enemy. Communications of the ACM **42**(12), 40–46 (1999)
3. Florencio, D., Herley, C.: A large-scale study of web password habits. In: Proceedings of the 16th International Conference on World Wide Web, pp. 657–666. ACM (2007)
4. Gaw, S., Felten, E.W.: Password management strategies for online accounts. In: Proceedings of the Second Symposium on Usable Privacy and Security, pp. 44–55. ACM (2006)
5. Morris, R., Thompson, K.: Password security: A case history. Communications of the ACM **22**(11), 594–597 (1979)
6. Parwani, T., Kholoussi, R., Karras, P.: How to hack into facebook without being a hacker. In: Proceedings of the 22nd International Conference on World Wide Web Companion, pp. 751–754. International World Wide Web Conferences Steering Committee (2013)
7. Bonneau, J., Herley, C., Van Oorschot, P.C., Stajano, F.: The quest to replace passwords: a framework for comparative evaluation of web authentication schemes. In: 2012 IEEE Symposium on Security and Privacy (SP), pp. 553–567. IEEE (2012)
8. Munro, K.: Android scraping: accessing personal data on mobile devices. Network Security **2014**(11), 5–9 (2014)
9. Android 5.0 Encryption 2015. https://source.android.com/devices/tech/security/encryption/ (accessed January 20, 2015)
10. Heider, J., Boll, M.: iOS keychain weakness FAQ. Fraunhofer Institute for Secure Technology (2011)
11. Rescorla, E.: Rfc 2818: Http over tls. Internet Engineering Task Force (2000)
12. Myers, M., Ankney, R., Malpani, A., Galperin, S., Adams, C.: X. 509 internet public key infrastructure online certificate status protocol. IETF RFC2560, June 1999
13. Georgiev, M., Iyengar, S., Jana, S., Anubhai, R., Boneh, D., Shmatikov, V.: The most dangerous code in the world: validating ssl certificates in non-browser software. In: Proceedings of the 2012 ACM Conference on Computer and Communications Security, pp. 38–49. ACM (2012)
14. Durumeric, Z., Kasten, J., Adrian, D., Halderman, J.A., Bailey, M., Li, F., Weaver, N., Amann, J., Beekman, J., Payer, M., et al.: The matter of heartbleed. In: Proceedings of the 2014 Conference on Internet Measurement Conference, pp. 475–488. ACM (2014)
15. Tsoutsos, N.G., Maniatakos, M.: Trust no one: thwarting "heartbleed" attacks using privacy-preserving computation. In: 2014 IEEE Computer Society Annual Symposium on VLSI (ISVLSI), pp. 59–64. IEEE (2014)
16. Callegati, F., Cerroni, W., Ramilli, M.: Man-in-the-middle attack to the https protocol. IEEE Security and Privacy **7**(1), 78–81 (2009)
17. Czeskis, A., Dietz, M., Kohno, T., Wallach, D., Balfanz, D.: Strengthening user authentication through opportunistic cryptographic identity assertions. In: Proceedings of the 2012 ACM Conference on Computer and Communications Security, pp. 404–414. ACM (2012)
18. Borchert, B.: Ekaay-smart login (2013). http://www.ekaay.com/

19. eKaay Smart Login System (2015). http://www.ekaay.com/ (accessed January 14, 2015)
20. Van Rijswijk, R.M., Van Dijk, J.: Tiqr: a novel take on two-factor authentication. In: LISA (2011)
21. Dodson, B., Sengupta, D., Boneh, D., Lam, M.S.: Snap2pass: Consumer-friendly challenge-response authentication with a phone. Stanford University (2010)
22. Galois QR Authentication (2015). http://galois.com/blog/2011/01/quick-authentication-using-mobile-devices-and-qr-codes/ (accessed January 19, 2015)
23. Schieb, J.: Schieb. de Wissen—Das sichere Login: So haben Hacker keine Chance, vol. 1, pp. 42–44 (2014)
24. Click2Pass Handy statt Passwort (2015). http://www.click2pass.net/ (accessed January 14, 2015)
25. Next Authentication and Authorization Plattform (2015). https://launchkey.com/platform/mobile/ (accessed January 14, 2015)
26. Zapper (2015). https://www.zapper.com/about.php/ (accessed January 19, 2015)
27. CLEF Secure Two Factor Login (2015). https://getclef.com/features/ (accessed January 19, 2015)
28. Jones, M., Hardt, D.: The oauth 2.0 authorization framework: Bearer token usage. Technical report, RFC 6750, October 2012
29. OneID (2015). https://www.oneid.com/ (accessed September 03, 2015)
30. KnockToUnlock (2015). http://www.knocktounlock.com/ (accessed September 03, 2015)
31. BlueID (2015). https://www.blueid.net/ (accessed September 03, 2015)
32. Asokan, N., Niemi, V., Nyberg, K.: Man-in-the-middle in tunnelled authentication protocols. In: Christianson, B., Crispo, B., Malcolm, J.A., Roe, M. (eds.) Security Protocols 2003. LNCS, vol. 3364, pp. 28–41. Springer, Heidelberg (2005)
33. Felt, A.P., Finifter, M., Chin, E., Hanna, S., Wagner, D.: A survey of mobile malware in the wild. In: Proceedings of the 1st ACM Workshop on Security and Privacy in Smartphones and Mobile Devices, pp. 3–14. ACM (2011)
34. Hong, J.: The state of phishing attacks. Communications of the ACM **55**(1), 74–81 (2012)
35. Silver, D., Jana, S., Chen, E., Jackson, C., Boneh, D.: Password managers: attacks and defenses. In: Proceedings of the 23rd Usenix Security Symposium (2014)

Using Provenance Patterns to Vet Sensitive Behaviors in Android Apps

Chao Yang[1], Guangliang Yang[1], Ashish Gehani[2],
Vinod Yegneswaran[2(✉)], Dawood Tariq[2], and Guofei Gu[1]

[1] Texas A&M University, College Station, TX, USA
[2] SRI International, Menlo Park, CA, USA
vinod@csl.sri.com

Abstract. We propose Dagger, a lightweight system to dynamically vet sensitive behaviors in Android apps. Dagger avoids costly instrumentation of virtual machines or modifications to the Android kernel. Instead, Dagger reconstructs the program semantics by tracking provenance relationships and observing apps' runtime interactions with the phone platform. More specifically, Dagger uses three types of low-level execution information at runtime: system calls, Android Binder transactions, and app process details. System call collection is performed via Strace [7], a low-latency utility for Linux and other Unix-like systems. Binder transactions are recorded by accessing Binder module logs via *sysfs* [8]. App process details are extracted from the Android */proc* file system [6]. A data provenance graph is then built to record the interactions between the app and the phone system based on these three types of information. Dagger identifies behaviors by matching the provenance graph with the behavior graph patterns that are previously extracted from the internal working logic of the Android framework. We evaluate Dagger on both a set of over 1200 known malicious Android apps, and a second set of 1000 apps randomly selected from a corpus of over 18,000 Google Play apps. Our evaluation shows that Dagger can effectively vet sensitive behaviors in apps, especially for those using complex obfuscation techniques. We measured the overhead based on a representative benchmark app, and found that both the memory and CPU overhead are less than 10%. The runtime overhead is less than 63%, which is significantly lower than that of existing approaches.

1 Introduction

With the proliferation of Android smartphones and applications, there is a growing interest in scalable tools and techniques for blackbox testing of applications. Of specific interest are tools that enable screening for suspicious behavior patterns commonly exhibited by malware. While a rich body of prior work exists, contemporary static and dynamic analysis techniques fall short in many respects.

Static analysis techniques [48,55,56] analyze Android apps by disassembling them into Dalvik (or Java) source code, and further evaluating the permissions list, analyzing programming interfaces (i.e. Android APIs) and program logic used in the source. However, such approaches are unable to cope with complex code obfuscation techniques (e.g., source encryption, noise insertion, and use of Java reflection) or analyze code logic that uses the Android Native Development Kit (NDK)[1].

In contrast, dynamic analysis approaches monitor apps' behaviors by running them in real or emulated Android environments. Certain systems (e.g., [51]) rely on application source instrumentation to record API invocation details (e.g., API names and parameter values). However, such approaches are blind to malicious logic implemented using NDK. A few dynamic approaches [41,50] employ virtual machine introspection (VMI) techniques to gather the lower-level system information and thereby reconstruct high-level application semantics. Such approaches typically incur high performance overhead, especially when taint tracking is enabled. Thus, direct application of these approaches is impractical for analysis of a large corpus of apps.

We present Dagger as a lightweight system to dynamically vet sensitive behaviors in Android apps. Dagger avoids costly overheads and complexities associated with virtual machine instrumentation and modifications to the Android kernel. Instead, Dagger reconstructs the apps' semantics by tracking its runtime interactions with the phone platform and building provenance relationships. More specifically, at an app's runtime, Dagger uses the open source SPADE [26] provenance middleware to collect three types of low-level execution information, including Linux system calls, Android Binder transactions, and app process details. System call collection is done via Strace [7], a low-latency utility for Linux and other Unix-like systems. Binder activity is recorded by accessing transaction logs via *sysfs* [8]. App process details are extracted from the Android */proc* file system [6]. A data provenance graph is then built to record the interactions between the app and the phone system based on these three types of information. Dagger identifies behaviors by matching the provenance graph with a library of *sensitive provenance patterns* that have been previously extracted by carefully studying the inner workings of the Android framework.

We have built a prototype of Dagger, and evaluated both its effectiveness and efficiency. We first used Dagger to vet three representative Android malware families. These case studies demonstrate the effectiveness of Dagger in vetting sensitive behaviors that are implemented in more evasive ways (e.g., code obfuscation or encryption). Then, we evaluated Dagger on a large corpus of apps, which consists of over 1200 known malicious apps, and 1000 official apps randomly selected from a set of over 18,000 samples downloaded from Google Play. Our evaluation demonstrates that Dagger can effectively vet sensitive behaviors in a large scale of apps. To evaluate system efficiency, we used a popular benchmark app called AnTuTu (v 3.0.3) [1] that measures Android system overhead. We found both the memory and CPU overhead to be less than 10% and the runtime overhead to be less than 63%, which is significantly lower than that of

---

[1] The volume of apps involving native code has dramatically increased in recent years [33,53].

existing approaches that utilize VMI techniques (e.g., [50]). To summarize, the salient contributions of this paper include the following:

1. Design of a lightweight approach for runtime tracking of sensitive behavior that does not rely on the high overhead techniques of virtual machine introspection or Dalvik monitoring.
2. Development of the Dagger prototype that automates the abstraction of Android apps' runtime low-level execution information into high-level behavior semantics using the data-provenance approach.
3. Development of a library of sensitive provenance patterns for vetting Android apps.
4. Comprehensive system evaluation on a corpus of over 2200 benign and malicious applications that demonstrates how Dagger can be used to efficiently vet sensitive behaviors with minimal memory and runtime overhead.

2   Background And System Goals

The Android operating system is built on the top of the Linux kernel and organized in a layered architecture consisting of four layers: (*i*) the Linux kernel, (*ii*) Android's native system libraries and Dalvik virtual machine runtime, (*iii*) Android's application frameworks, and (*iv*) a collection of installed applications.

Linux Kernel: The bottom layer of the Android system is a customized Linux kernel. It provides services such as memory and process management, access control, and a driver framework. As the abstraction between the hardware and software, this layer provides generic services to the user space layer above while hiding the details of the hardware. Android also enhances the standard Linux kernel in several respects, including inter-application communication and power management. Android implements a custom inter-process communication (IPC) mechanism called Binder. Binder is used to mediate interactions between apps, as well as between apps and the operating system.

Android Libraries and Runtime: This layer contains two major parts: Android libraries and the Dalvik virtual machine runtime. The libraries consist of C and C++ code that compiles to the native binary format. The functionality in these libraries is exposed to applications from third party developers through the Android framework.

Android Framework: Many of the application-level functionalities for interacting with system resources are provided by the Android framework. It provides the interfaces (*Android Framework APIs*) to access the system apps; that is, components that provide indirect access to the underlying system resources (such as reading contacts, recording the current geographic location, or sending SMS messages) by invoking *system calls*, low-level interactions between app processes and GNU/Linux. For instance, the framework API of TelephonyManager.getDeviceId() provides the functionality of reading device ID; SmsManager.sendTextMessage() supports sending text messages. These framework APIs

Table 1. Malicious Android app behaviors targeted by prior work

Work	Type	Financial Charge				Privacy Leak		Remote Control	Rooting
System	Technique	Phone Call	Send SMS	Block SMS	Steal Contact	Track Location	Steal Phone Number	Net	Execute Shell
[54]	Static	✓	✓	✓			✓	✓	✓
[51]	Dynamic		✓	✓	✓	✓	✓		
[50]	Dynamic						✓	✓	✓

Table 2. Fined-grained sensitive behaviors associated with malicious behaviors

Index	Malicious Behaviors	Sensitive Behaviors	Index	Malicious Behaviors	Sensitive Behaviors
1	Phone Call	Phone Call	5	Steal Contact	Read Contact and Net
2	Send SMS	Send SMS	6	Track Location	Read Location and Net
3	Block SMS	Receive SMS, not Write SMSDB	7	Execute Shell	Execute Shell
4	Steal SMS	Read SMSDB and Net	8	Net	Net

essentially achieve the functionalities by invoking low-level system calls, e.g., open(), which opens file operators, and execve(), which executes shell commands. Thus, the usage of the low-level system calls and the access of Android resources in the runtime can indicate rich high-level behavior semantics.

Applications: Android distributions include a collection of system apps, including: one that provides the functionality of a phone, another that allows short message service (SMS) and multimedia message service (MMS) messages to be sent and received, an email client, a calendar, and a contact manager. The core set of applications also export services to third party applications through APIs in the Android application framework.

2.1   System Goals

Our objective is to design an effective and efficient system for vetting sensitive behaviors in Android apps that does not rely on VMI techniques or modifications to the operating system. In Table 1, we list a set of sensitive behavioral patterns in Android apps (Phone Call, Send SMS, Block SMS, Steal SMS, Steal Contact, Track Location, Steal Phone Number, Network Connection, and Execute Shell) that have been targeted by prior studies as indicators of malicious behavior.

Instead of focusing on such coarse-grained malicious behaviors, we designed Dagger to vet fine-grained sensitive behaviors that may be launched by both malicious and benign apps. As seen in Table 2, the aforementioned malicious functionalities can essentially be achieved by multiple fine-grained sensitive behaviors. In Table 2, we list 9 fine-grained sensitive behavioral patterns associated with the 8 malicious behaviors listed in Table 1. These are: Phone Call, Send SMS, Receive SMS, not Write SMSDB, Read SMSDB, Net, Read Contact, Read Location, and Execute Shell. (*Read SMSDB* and *Write SMSDB* refer to reads from and writes to the Android provider *content://sms/inbox/*.)

3   System Design

A rich body of prior work have attempted to vet the behavior of desktop applications by analyzing system call invocations. However, such approaches cannot be directly extended to vet the behavior on Android apps due to the unique aspects of the Android system. (1) Android apps access kernel resources through the Android application framework. Consequently, there is a semantic gap between low-level system call invocations and high-level Android-specific behavior. (2) Android apps interact with system services and the Android framework through the Binder IPC mechanism, which is unique to Android. Thus, vetting Android app behavior requires analysis of the Binder transactions that occur between apps and the system. (3) Android is an event-driven system; its multiple behavior patterns interweave together. Therefore, traditional temporal monitoring approaches are not effective during analysis of Android malware.

Dagger's design is motivated by the observations that an Android app's behaviors are achieved through (*i*) low-level interactions (system calls and Binder IPC) between app process and the Android kernel and (*ii*) accesses to underlying system resources (e.g., contacts, geo location, SMS messaging). Dagger uses data provenance analysis to first translate an app's runtime behaviors into a provenance graph that captures three types of low-level information: system call invocations, Binder IPC transaction logs, and process details. Essentially, the graph captures all interactions of the app with the Android application framework and the OS kernel. Dagger further identifies sensitive behaviors by matching the provenance graph with sensitive provenance patterns that have been extracted and developed through careful analysis of the inner workings of the Android framework.

To understand the internal logic of the Android framework, we ran Android apps with selected input that is known *a priori* to trigger sensitive behavior. We utilized two broad approaches for this investigation. In the first approach, we manually selected representative malware samples that belong to particular families with known sensitive behavior. We then used Androguard, a static analysis tool, to extract the relevant logic that would trigger sensitive behavior in each piece of malware. In a complementary approach, we triggered flows in synthetic apps that were developed to contain representative sensitive behavior.

3.1 Design Overview

Dagger is built on the open source SPADE provenance middleware [26]. Dagger is composed of five major components, as illustrated in Figure 1: AppExecutor, SysCall Collector, ProvEst Daemon, Graph Reporter, and Behavior Identifier. Sample apps are first loaded into the App Executor, which automatically executes the app in a sandbox Android runtime environment. Once the app is executed, SysCall Collector starts to collect the system call invocations, and ProvEst Daemon analyzes the binder transactions and collects more detailed information of the process in order to build the provenance relationships of the identities (e.g., processes and files) in the system call invocations. The Graph Reporter outputs the data provenance graph according to the provenance relationships established by the ProvEst Daemon. Finally, the Behavior Identifier detects sensitive behaviors from the provenance graph according to the working

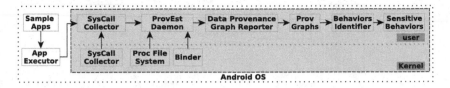

Fig. 1. Dagger takes a corpus of apps, runs each one, collects provenance records, and performs pattern matching to identify potentially sensitive behaviors.

mechanism of the Android system. Below, we discuss each component in greater detail.

1. App Executor is a Python script for controlling app execution. It first extracts the package and activity names (including the main activity) from the Android package (APK file), installs the package, and then automatically launches selected activities by using Android debugger adb commands.

App Executor uses MonkeyRunner [9] to drive the app with randomly generated events (such as pressing buttons or touching the screen). It first extracts the main activity of the app, and then sends an *intent* to initiate the activity. App Executor continues till it has generated at least 500 events or the app has run for at least three minutes.

2. SysCall Collector records low-level system call invocations (e.g., fork, read, write, setuid32) using the strace utility. Each system call invocation is internally recorded in the following format:

$[pid][timestamp][syscall(paramenters)] = [return]$

for example, "183 16:54:15.805684 open("/dev/binder", O_RDWR) = 9". The output of SysCall Collector is persisted in non-volatile storage. To avoid app-specific storage limits, the log is stored in the mobile device's Secure Digital (SD) card. The SysCall Collector functionality was developed by extending SPADE's *Strace Reporter* so it can run on Android (in addition to Linux).

3. ProvEst Daemon generates data provenance relationships by collecting system calls, Binder transactions, and process details. A data provenance record describes how a piece of information was derived, a historical approach which has been widely used in a variety of fields such as performance optimization, scientific computation, security verification, and policy validation. The data provenance graphs in Dagger conform to the Open Provenance Model [34] which has the following three types of elements, as illustrated in Figure 2. ProvEst leverages significant functionality from SPADE (that is summarized below), and augments the *Strace Reporter* with Android-specific details (from Binder transactions, for example).

Process Vertices. These are created to record dynamic entities; typically, these entities are operating system processes created by app execution. Each vertex contains a range of annotations, including the name of the process, the process identifier (pid), and the owner (uid) and group (gid). It also records the

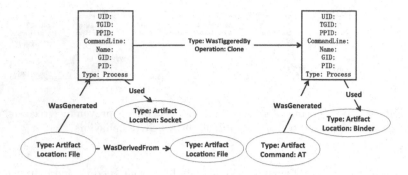

Fig. 2. Apps are represented with rectangular vertices, annotated with the properties of the executing process. Data artifacts, such as files and Binder transactions, are denoted with elliptical vertices. Edges have types define the operations being performed – for example, an artifact is related to a process with a *WasDerivedFrom* edge when it has been written to. In general, the types conform to the Open Provenance Model.

parent process, the command line with which it was invoked, and the values of environment variables.

Artifact Vertices. These are used to represent static elements that are consumed or produced by processes. There are four subtypes of such vertices: (*i*) *File Vertex*, which represents a file read or written by a process at a particular point in time; (*ii*) *Binder Vertex*, which denotes a Binder transaction that occurred between a pair of processes; (*iii*) *Socket Vertex*, which indicates a communication from or to a process through a socket; and (*iv*) *Command Vertex*, which records the details of high-level commands (e.g., AT commands, described in Section 3.2) issued by a process.

Edges. These are directed and used to represent the dependency between a pair of vertices. For example, an edge to a file vertex indicates that the file was read, and an edge from a file vertex indicates that the file had been modified. There are four types of edges: (*i*) *WasTriggeredBy*, from a process to another process; (*ii*) *WasGeneratedBy*, from an artifact to a process; (*iii*) *Used*, from a process to an artifact; and (*iv*) *WasDerivedFrom*, from an artifact to another artifact.

Given the design of the provenance graph, once a new entry is collected by the SysCall Collector, the ProvEst Daemon parses it to extract the *pid* of its process. Based on the *pid*, it further extracts its process details (e.g., process name, GID, UID, command line, etc.) from the "/proc" file system [6]. All these details are used to depict the process as a vertex in the graph. Every file, socket, and pipe that is accessed by the process is depicted as a single artifact vertex. Once the system call *ioctl()*, which leads to a Binder transaction, is invoked by one process, the Daemon inspects the Binder transaction log from *sysfs* [8], and extracts the communicated process in the transaction. Then, a directional edge is built from the request process to the response process. Edges are also generated to record accesses of sensitive system resources (e.g., read and write operations of content providers) from the app's process vertex to the resource artifact vertex.

4. Graph Reporter generates a provenance graph using Graphviz [2] and based on the low-level provenance relationships established by the ProvEst Daemon. Specific patterns can be further extracted from the graph by using our graph-based query service, which is implemented by Neo4j [4], an open-source graph-based database tool. This component uses SPADE's *Graphviz Reporter* to replay provenance records, sending them through SPADE's *Kernel*, and to its *Neo4 Storage*.

5. Behavior Identifier detects sensitive behaviors by using the provenance graphs output by the Graph Reporter. Intuitively, we abstract each sensitive behavior into a provenance graph pattern, according to the internal working logic in the Android platform to perform that behavior. We then identify an app's behaviors by mapping its provenance graph with these provenance graph patterns. Next, we elaborate on a few exemplar sensitive provenance patterns.

3.2   Exemplar Sensitive Provenance Patterns

We describe motivating examples, illustrated with figures that use a previously described [26] provenance data model.

Pattern 1: *Send SMS, Receive SMS and Phone Call.* Figure 3 illustrates the working logic of an app on the Android platform when sending an SMS, receiving an SMS, and making a phone call. When an app attempts to perform one of these three behaviors, it will first communicate with a process from the Telephony Manager Application Framework. The Telephony Manager will call the Radio Interface Layer (RIL) daemon in the Android's using sockets for communication. RIL is radio-agnostic and provides an abstraction layer between the Android Telephony Manager and the hardware. Once it receives communications from Android's Telephony Manager, the RIL daemon dynamically loads the Vendor RIL Library to dispatch the communications to the Vendor RIL. The radio-specific Vendor RIL processes communicate with radio hardware by using AT commands. The AT commands are used to control mobile modems in order to perform the specified functions. For example, the AT commands for sending an SMS, receiving an SMS and making phone calls are "AT+CMGS", "AT+CNMI", and "ATD+CLCC", respectively.

By exploiting an understanding of this functionality, the provenance patterns of these behaviors can be abstracted as Figure 4. From this figure, we can see that for each sensitive behavior, there is a provenance path from the app process to the final AT command with different command parameters.

Pattern 2: *Read Geolocation.* Figure 5 illustrates the system logic in the Android system that runs when an app gets the current location. Once an app attempts to read the geographic location, it will interact with the Location Manager Service, which will further request the location from the GpsLocationProvider. From this logic we can abstract the app's provenance pattern as Figure 6, which has a path from the process vertex to the GpsLocationProvider.

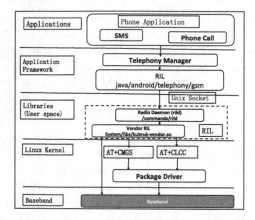

Fig. 3. Working logic of sending an SMS, receiving an SMS, and making a phone call.

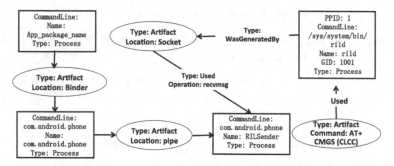

Fig. 4. Provenance pattern for sending an SMS, receiving an SMS, and making a phone call.

Pattern 3: *Read SMSDB and Write SMSDB.* The Android system work-flow dictates that once an app reads or writes the SMS database (i.e., the content provider of SMS inbox), it will first interact with the Telephony-Manager, and then read and write in the "/data/data/com.android.providers. telephony/database/" directory, to the "mmssms.db" file, in particular. The provenance pattern that results is illustrated in Figure 7.

Pattern 4: *Read Contact, Net, and Rooting.* On Android, the local Contacts resource is uniquely managed by the Acore process[2]. An app must interact with this process to read the contact list. If an app reads the contact, there is a path from the process of the app to the Acore process. Network usage can be identified by analyzing whether the process (or its descendants) makes system calls related to network sockets. Rooting behavior can be identified by analyzing whether the process (or a descendant) invokes the exeve("/system/bin/su") system call to attain root privilege. Since our data provenance graph will also record

---

[2] The process is identified as "com.android.acore".

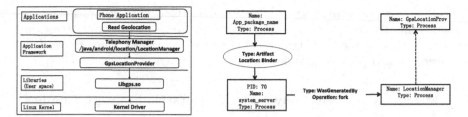

Fig. 5. Working logic of reading geo-location.

Fig. 6. Provenance pattern for reading geolocation.

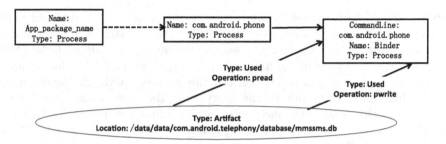

Fig. 7. Provenance pattern for reading from and writing to the SMS database.

the UID of the process, if the app successfully roots the phone, this behavior can be further identified by checking the change in UID from a non-zero value to zero.

After generating these provenance patterns, we can vet app behavior by matching these patterns in apps' provenance graphs as they are generated at runtime. Note that these provenance patterns are uniquely defined according to the working mechanism of the Android system, from the top layer to the bottom layer, and are more likely to remain unchanged than the source code is. Thus, our approach is more general than other approaches which rely on hooking specific APIs whose functions may be changed later. Also, since the patterns cover all the layers, our approach can identify those behaviors that are implemented by using both the Android SDK and NDK, as long as they follow the same workflow.

4   System Evaluation

Our prototype implementation of Dagger is capable of running on both Android phones and emulators. We evaluated the prototype implementation by running the app in a customized Android emulator and using it to extract provenance graphs with pre-settings of SMS inbox, contact list and geolocation information. Before each run, we restored the image to a clean snapshot to mitigate interference from other apps.

We evaluated the effectiveness of Dagger from the following three perspectives: (i) vetting real-world malware case studies, (ii) vetting Android Genome

Project malware, and (*iii*) vetting official market (Google Play) apps. Then, we evaluated the efficiency of Dagger by using a popular benchmark app to measure the performance overhead of Dagger including CPU overhead, memory overhead, I/O overhead and processing time.

4.1   Effectiveness Case Study on Representative Malware Families

To evaluate the effectiveness and demonstrate its unique advantages, we applied Dagger to vet sensitive behaviors on three representative real-world Android malware families: Gamex, Gone60 and Zsone.

Gamex: Code Encryption. Gamex, one of the most evasive Android malware, uses complex code obfuscation techniques. In an attempt to slow down discovery and detection, Gamex [5] uses encryption (byte XOR with 0x12) to hide a package in a fake image file named "assets/logos.png". When the malware is activated, it uses a decryption function to decrypt the file, and launch sensitive functions. Thus, due to the encryption, the static analysis will only find the paths that lead to the shell code execution function, instead of knowing specific malicious behaviors. Upon using Dagger to vet Gamex samples (MD5: 50836808a5fe7febb6ce8b2109d6c93a), we find shell code execution as well as hidden sensitive behaviors, including attempts to read contact list information and sensitive network communications, such as exfiltration of IMSI/IMEI numbers and malicious software downloads.

Gone60: Privacy Leakage. Gone60 steals private user information such as SMS messages, contact lists, recent call histories and browser-cached URLs by using the standard query API on the content providers of SMS inbox and browser. The app can access these content providers, which work as databases, by setting specific local URLs as the parameters. However, such parameters (i.e., strings) are easier for malware authors to obfuscate than Android framework APIs (e.g., by using complex string operations). Thus, simple approaches based on static analysis may fail to detect such malware. Upon using Dagger to vet a sample of Gone60 (MD5: 859cc9082b8475fe6102cd03d1df10e5), we successfully identified many sensitive behaviors exhibited by this malware, including reading of SMSDB and contact lists, as well as sensitive network communications. Moreover, since Dagger recognizes the access of content providers by checking the read operation of the file system instead of statically analyzing the parameters in the query function, it is more robust against string-obfuscating malware.

Zsone: SMS Service Usage. Dagger can also be used to vet the malicious behavior of blocking SMS by checking for the absence of a certain pattern in a specific event (i.e., receiving an SMS message but not writing to SMSDB). We applied Dagger to an exemplar Zsone malware sample (MD5: c0e6ba0e1b757e3c506a02282ffc5b4), which can both send and block SMS messages. In this experiment, we used Dagger to send the same pre-customized SMS to the phone in two situations: running without and alongside the malware sample. We found that while both receive the SMS message (observing the AT command "AT+CNMA=1"), the provenance graph in the first scenario includes the behavior pattern of writing SMSDB, while the second scenario does not. This validates that Dagger can be used to identify the blocking SMS behavioral pattern.

4.2   Measuring Effectiveness Using a Large App Corpus

We further evaluated the effectiveness of Dagger on a corpus of 1,260 real-world malware samples collected from the Genome Project [55], and another corpus of 1,000 apps that were randomly selected from 18,527 official market (Google Play) apps. For each app, to increase the code path execution coverage, we added 500 random UI events by using MonkeyRunner.

Table 3 shows the number of apps and corresponding malware families that perform each behaviors. Since there is no easy way to obtain complete ground truth about the sensitive behaviors found in these specific malware samples, we simply show the absolute number instead of the false positive/negative rate.

As summarized in the table, we find that Dagger can find sensitive behaviors from all malware families. Moreover, Dagger can successfully find all three types of sensitive behaviors (Send SMS, Net and Execute Shell) in the malware families that were reported by a prior measurement study on the same malware corpus [54].

After using Dagger to vet 1000 official apps from Google Play, we found the following. (*i*) One app reads SMSDB, which is a TV Channel client embedded with multiple advertisements, and reads users' SMS messages. (*ii*) Four apps have executed external/shell commands. After submitting them to VirusTotal, one app was recognized as malware belonging to Plankton. This malware dynamically downloads additional code from external server and executes it. The malware then executes shell commands (e.g., "/system/bin/cat /proc/cpuinfo") to get the system information. Two apps were recognized by VirusTotal as abusive adware. Both of them executed the shell commands to use the Logcat to obtain the system runtime log information. The fourth app was not recognized as malware by VirusTotal. However, it attempted to obtain root privilege by executing "su", which is recognized as a sensitive behavior by Dagger. (*iii*) Seven apps read users' geolocation information. More specifically, three apps use such geolocation information for the usage of maps; two apps are used for car rental guides; one app is for local shopping and another one is a photo editor app that can be used by users to share photos with geolocation information to their friends. Our findings confirm that our system has a low false positive rate, i.e., only a small number ($< 2\%$) of official apps are identified as performing sensitive behaviors, and the majority of these are related to known malware/adware families.

Analysis of False Positives and Negatives. Since it is very challenging to obtain a perfect ground truth for the Android malware dataset (i.e., knowing the exact sensitive behaviors of each malware sample we collect), we further evaluated the accuracy of Dagger by comparing it with other existing systems,

Table 3. Sensitive behaviors in different malware families identified by Dagger.

Family	Send SMS	Receive SMS	Read SMSDB	Write SMSDB	Read Contact	Read GeoLocation	Execute Shell	Net
ADRD	0	0	0	0	0	0	0	9
AnserverBot	0	7	3	3	3	2	61	78
Asroot	0	0	0	0	0	0	0	1
BaseBridge	0	1	1	1	1	0	16	37
BeanBot	0	0	0	0	0	0	0	1
Bgserv	0	1	0	0	0	1	0	3
CoinPirate	0	0	0	0	0	0	0	2
CruseWin	0	0	0	0	0	0	0	0
DogWars	0	0	0	0	0	0	0	0
DroidCoupon	0	0	0	0	0	0	0	0
DroidDeluxe	0	0	0	0	0	0	0	0
DroidDream	0	0	0	0	0	0	1	5
DroidDreamLight	0	0	0	0	3	1	1	9
DroidKungFu1	0	2	2	1	1	0	2	13
DroidKungFu2	0	1	1	0	1	0	5	8
DroidKungFu3	0	0	8	7	8	0	26	111
DroidKungFu4	0	4	5	3	4	2	7	47
DroidKungFuSapp	0	0	0	0	0	0	0	0
DroidKungFuUpdate	0	0	0	0	0	0	0	1
Endofday	0	0	0	0	0	0	0	0
FakeNetflix	0	0	0	0	0	0	0	0
FakePlayer	0	0	0	0	0	0	0	0
GamblerSMS	0	0	0	0	0	0	0	0
Geinimi	0	4	3	2	3	3	1	20
GGTracker	0	0	0	0	0	0	0	1
GingerMaster	0	0	0	0	0	0	0	2
GoldDream	0	1	1	1	1	2	0	20
Gone60	0	0	1	0	3	0	0	5
GPSSMSSpy	0	0	0	0	0	0	0	0
HippoSMS	0	0	0	0	0	0	0	3
Jifake	0	0	0	0	0	0	0	0
jSMSHider	0	0	0	0	0	0	7	4
KMin	1	1	0	0	13	0	0	17
LoveTrap	0	0	0	0	0	0	0	1
NickyBot	0	0	0	0	0	0	0	0
NickySpy	0	0	0	0	0	0	0	1
Pjapps	0	0	0	0	1	0	0	28
Plankton	0	0	0	0	0	0	0	5
RogueLemon	0	0	0	0	0	0	0	0
RogueSPPush	0	0	0	0	0	0	0	9
SMSReplicator	0	0	0	0	0	0	0	0
SndApps	0	1	0	0	0	0	0	0
Spitmo	0	0	0	0	0	0	0	0
Tapsnake	0	0	0	0	0	0	0	0
Walkinwat	0	0	0	0	0	0	0	1
YZHC	0	1	1	1	1	0	0	0
zHash	0	0	0	0	0	0	0	0
Zitmo	0	0	0	0	0	0	0	0
Zsone	2	1	0	0	1	0	0	12

instead of claiming accurate value of the false positive and false negative rate. More specifically, we ran Dagger on 112 malware samples, which were randomly selected from the Genome malware dataset. The specific number of malware samples that perform each type of sensitive behaviors can be seen in Table 4.

To measure possible false positives, we examined those behaviors identified by Dagger, which are not reported by [54]. [54] reports possible sensitive behaviors of the malware samples in each family by statically extracting programming paths that may execute sensitive behaviors. We found that only two apps, Asroot and DroidKungFuUpdate, access the Internet but are not reported by [54]. We

Table 4. Dagger analysis summary for 112 randomly selected malware samples.

Send SMS	Block SMS	Read SMSDB	Write SMSDB	Read Contact	Read Location	Execute Shell	Net
9	19	1	0	2	3	17	60

Table 5. Dagger's performance overhead as measured using the AnTuTu benchmark app.

Metric	OffScore	OnScore	Overhead
CPU score	7,199	6,522	9.40%
RAM score	1,213	1,092	9.98%

manually examined these two apps, and found that they do indeed access the Internet to load advertisements when they are activated.

To measure possible false negatives, we compared our system with Copper-Droid. (Since CopperDroid is not open-source, we obtained its results by submitting apps to its public website.) Since CopperDroid instruments QEMU to intercept all instructions that are executed in the Android emulator, it can report most sensitive behaviors. Compared with CopperDroid, we find that Dagger misses one network behavior and 2 reading contact behaviors due to the failure of triggering the execution paths. We also tested these malware samples on TaintDroid, which only detects that 1 app reads location information, and 23 apps access the Internet.

4.3   Measuring System Performance Overhead

To evaluate the efficiency of Dagger, we tested the performance overhead of Dagger by using AnTuTu (v 3.0.3) [1]. AnTuTu is a popular Android benchmark app developed to test the performance of Android devices. We are mostly interested in the major performance benchmark metrics such as CPU score and RAM score. CPU score represents the computation ability of the current CPU status; a higher score implies the CPU has more free computation ability. RAM score reflects the real processing ability of RAM; a higher score implies more free space in RAM.

Table 5 shows the scores of each benchmark metric while turning Dagger off/on
(denoted as *OffScore* and *OnScore*, respectively). In this table, the overhead of each metric is calculated as: $Overhead = (OffScore - OnScore)/OffScore$.

From this table, we can find that the overheads of CPU and RAM after turning Dagger on are acceptable, which are less than 10%. This clearly indicates that Dagger is a lightweight vetting approach that consumes a very small number of resources, an advantage makes it attractive for practical use.

Besides the above metrics, we also measure the time overhead generated by Dagger. The time spent running the Antutu benchmark app on an unmodified system was 1.89 seconds. When Dagger was used, Antutu took 3.07 seconds to run. From this we can see that the time overhead is reasonably low: 62.43%. It is worth noting that in another representative approach based on system call tracing, DroidScope [50], the slowdown was around 11 to 34 times (with taint-tracking enabled). This experiment clearly demonstrates that Dagger is a very lightweight tool.

In comparison with existing work, we can find that though it requires neither instrumentation of the system nor modification the OS, Dagger can achieve significantly high accuracy with appreciably lower performance overhead. Note that queries are performed offline using an indexed graph database. This ensures that complex graph queries can scale to large data sets, limited only by the underlying database Neo4j (that is used in production environments).

5   Related Work

We broadly classify related work into four major categories: detection of Android malware, security analysis and defense of the Android platform, and analysis of behaviors in Android apps.

Detection of Android Malware: An extensive body of systems has been developed to detect Android malware by monitoring system calls [15,27,30,39, 42,43,46,50], analyzing the usage of Android permissions [11,23,24,38], analyzing the usage of Framework APIs [13,17,47,52,55,56], and extracting information from the *sysfs* pseudofilesystem [12]. The design of these detection systems requires deep domain knowledge about Android system and the development of Android malware. Most of them also require effective and robust disassemblers to disassemble the target apps into Dalvik bytecode. These static approaches achieve limited effectiveness when detecting more evasive malware that is implemented with complex obfuscation techniques (e.g, encrypting the source, inserting noisy code, using Java reflection) and NDK. In contrast, Dagger does not require robust (or any) disassembly or deobfuscation technology.

Android Security Analyses: A few existing studies focus on analyzing the security mechanism of the Android platform and its applications. Stowaway [24] is designed to find those over-privileged apps. SmartDroid [52] finds UI triggers that result in privacy leakage. DroidChameleon [40] demonstrates the vulnerability of existing android anti-malware tools. Other related studies include attempts to detect component-hijacking vulnerabilities [32], inter-app communication vulnerabilities [19], and capability leaks [16,25]. In contrast to these analyses which focus on the leakage of security privileges, we focus on the leakage of sensitive data.

Android Platform Defenses: A variety of techniques have been developed to extend the security policies that can be supported by Android. Quire [21] is designed to prevent confused deputy attacks. Bugiel [14] *et al.* proposed a framework to prevent collusion attacks with pre-defined security policies. Saint [37], Porscha [36], and CRepE [20] were developed to isolate apps by designing more fine-grained access control policies. AppFence [28] prevents privacy leaks by either feeding fake data or blocking the leakage path. Checking at install time,

Apex [35] allows for the selection of granted permissions, and Kirin [23] performs lightweight certification of applications. Paranoid Android [39], L4Android [31] and Cells [10] use virtualization as an isolation mechanism to manage the risk of running malicious applications on Android. A prototype implementation of SELinux on an Android [3] device[44] provides mandatory access control. Aurasium [49] protects the system by enforcing practical policies. Previous work that relies on extensive modifications to the operating system that is brittle in the face of evolving codebases. In contrast, we are able to support sensitive behavior monitoring without modifying apps, the Dalvik virtual machine, or the Linux kernel.

Behavioral Analysis of Android Apps: Besides detecting malware and enhancing security mechanism of the Android platform, a few studies focus on analyzing sensitive/malicious behaviors in Android apps.

Dalvik Monitoring. As summarized in table 6, TaintDroid [22] is one of the first few systems that are designed to track possible sensitive leak from Android apps. VetDroid [51] vets sensitive behaviors by checking the permission usage at runtime. It requires modification to both the Android Dalvik virtual machine to intercept API invocations, and the Android framework to monitor invocations of app callbacks. Since these two approaches achieve the goal by mainly monitoring the execution of the Java instructions in the Dalvik, they are not effective when applied to finding sensitive behaviors that are implemented by Native Code. In addition, depending on whether hooks in the source of Android OS are used, these approaches are limited to the periodical change of the Android OS.

Virtual Machine Instrumentation (VMI). DroidScope [50] is designed to vet behaviors in Android apps by reconstructing both OS-level and Java-level semantics. NDroid [18] is a supplementary of TaintDroid, which is aware of the JNI semantic to track the data flow in the native code. CopperDroid [41] reconstructs malware behaviors by monitoring the system calls and the binder. Since these approaches rely on instrumenting the Android emulator, which typically incurs high overheads, especially when taint tracking is enabled, their direct application to analysis of a large scale of Android apps is inefficient. In addition, similar to the emulation-resistant desktop malware, Android malware can evade such approaches by staying dormant or simply crashing themselves, once the malware identifies that it is running within an emulated environment [29,45].

Motivated by the limitations of these approaches, Dagger is designed as a complementary and lightweight system to effectively and efficiently vet sensitive behaviors in Android apps. Dagger fills the semantic gap by representing Android apps' interactions with the system in a data provenance graph, and further matching the provenance graph with a library of sensitive provenance patterns.

6   Limitations and Future Work

Since Dagger's approach relies on the analysis of the inner working flow of the Android system to vet sensitive behaviors, it has to be updated if the workflow

Table 6. Comparison of Dagger with alternative sensitive behavioral vetting approaches.

	TaintDroid	VetDroid	DroidScope	NDroid	CopperDroid	Dagger
Technique	Taint Analysis	Taint Analysis & Permission Analysis	Taint Analysis & VMI	Taint Analysis & VMI	VMI & Monitoring System Calls and Binder	Data Provenance Analyiss & Monitoring System Calls, Binder and Process
Runtime Modifications	Modifying Android OS	Modifying Android OS	Instrumenting QEMU	Instrumenting QEMU	Instrumenting QEMU	None
Native Code Support	No	No	Yes	Yes	Yes	Yes
Overhead	Medium	Medium	High	High	High	Medium

of the Android system is significantly altered. However, due to the practical implications of such design, e.g., changes on a huge system that is being used by millions of devices, we believe that such significant changes are likely to be infrequent.

In the current design of Dagger, failed system call invocations are not captured in its data provenance graph. Such failure information might be useful in capturing certain sensitive behaviors that are missed by the current system. In the future work, we plan to improve Dagger by incorporating these into our analyses.

A common limitation of dynamic analysis techniques is that an exhaustive search of the space of all possible behavior of a target piece of code requires an untenable amount of testing. Consequently, techniques such as "fuzz testing" use random inputs or other methods for selecting a sparse subset of the test space. While Dagger is able to trigger security-sensitive behavior that matches particular provenance patterns, it is not exhaustive.

Finally, Dagger requires some manual effort to fine-tune the extracted provenance patterns that are currently used in vetting sensitive behaviors. We plan to extend our system with a learning-based approach to automatically mine graph patterns from apps that share similar sensitive behaviors. Furthermore, Dagger's provenance pattern library may be easily extended with additional verified patterns.

7   Conclusion

This paper presents Dagger, a novel and lightweight approach to dynamically vet sensitive behaviors in Android apps without system instrumentation or OS modification. Dagger achieves its goals by collecting three types of lower-level information and summarizing the app's system interactions through a lightweight provenance graph. In addition, Dagger contains a library of sensitive provenance patterns that can be used to automatically identify sensitive behaviors embedded in Android apps. Our evaluation demonstrates that Dagger is able to quickly and effectively isolate sensitive behaviors across a large corpus of (benign and malicious) real-world apps, with significantly lower performance overhead than prior studies.

Acknowledgements. This work was partially funded by the U.S. Department of Homeland Security (DHS) Science and Technology Directorate under contract HSHQDC-10-C-00144, National Science Foundation (NSF) under Grants IIS-0905518 and IIS-1116414, and Air Force Office of Scientific Research (AFOSR) under Grant FA9550-13-1-0077. The views and conclusions contained herein are those of the authors and should not be interpreted as representing the official views of DHS, NSF, AFOSR, or the U.S. government.

References

1. Antutu benchmark. https://play.google.com/store/apps/details?id=com.antutu. ABenchMark&hl=en
2. Graphviz - graph visualization software. http://www.graphviz.org/
3. National security agency. security-enhanced linux. http://www.nsa.gov/research/selinux
4. Neo4j. http://www.neo4j.org/?gclid=CIXUs_D-xb0CFQaBfgodIAMARw
5. Obfuscating embedded malware on android. http://www.symantec.com/connect/blogs/obfuscating-embedded-malware-android
6. The proc filesystem. http://en.wikipedia.org/wiki/Procfs
7. Strace - trace system calls and signals. http://linux.die.net/man/1/strace
8. Sysfs. http://en.wikipedia.org/wiki/Sysfs
9. Ui/application exerciser monkey. http://developer.android.com/tools/help/monkey.html
10. Andrus, J., Dall, C., Hof, A.V., Laadan, O., Nieh, J.: Cells: a virtual mobile smartphone architecture. In: Proceedings of 23rd SOSP (2011)
11. Au, K., Zhou, Y., Huang, Z., Lie, D., Gong, X., Han, X., Zhou, W.: Pscout: analyzing the android permission specification. In: Proceedings of the 19th CCS (2012)
12. Backes, M., Bugiel, S., Gerling, S.: Scippa: system-centric IPC provenance on Android. In: 30th Annual Computer Security Applications Conference (2014)
13. Bose, A., Hu, X., Shin, K.G., Park, T.: Behavioral detection of malware on mobile handsets. In: Proceedings of the 6th MobiSys (2008)
14. Bugiel, S., Davi, L., Dmitrienko, A., Fischer, T., Sadeghi, A.-R., Shastry, B.: Towards taming privilege-escalation attacks on android. In: Proceedings of the 19th NDSS (2012)
15. Burguera, I., Zurutuza, U., Nadjm-Tehrani, S.: Crowdroid: behavior-based malware detection system for android. In: Proceedings of the 1st Workshop on CCSSPSM (2011)
16. Chan, P.P., Hui, L.C., Yiu, S.M.: Droidchecker: analyzing android applications for capability leak. In: Proceedings of the 5th ACM Conference on Security and Privacy in Wireless and Mobile Networks (2012)
17. Chen, K., Johnson, N., Silva, V., Dai, S., MacNamara, K., Magrino, T., Wu, E., Rinard, M., Song, D.: Contextual policy enforcement in android applications with permission event graphs. In: Proceedings of the NDSS (2013)
18. Chenxiong, Q., Xiapu, L., Yuru, S., Alvin, C.: Ndroid: on tracking information flows through jni in android applications. In: Proceedings of the 44th DSN (2014)
19. Chin, E., Felt, A.P., Greenwood, K., Wagner, D.: Analyzing inter-application communication in android. In: Proceedings of the 9th MobiSys (2011)
20. Conti, M., Nguyen, V.T.N., Crispo, B.: CRePE: context-related policy enforcement for Android. In: Burmester, M., Tsudik, G., Magliveras, S., Ilić, I. (eds.) ISC 2010. LNCS, vol. 6531, pp. 331–345. Springer, Heidelberg (2011)

21. Dietz, M., Shekhar, S., Pisetsky, Y., Shu, A., Wallach, D.S.: Quire: lightweight provenance for smart phone operating systems. In: Proceedings of the USENIX Security (2011)
22. Enck, W., Gilbert, P., Chun, B.G., Cox, L.P., Jung, J., Mc-Daniel, P., Sheth, A.N.: Taintdroid: an information-flow tracking system for realtime privacy monitoring on smartphones. In: Proceedings of the 9th OSDI (2010)
23. Enck, W., Ongtang, M., McDaniel, P.: On lightweight mobile phone application certification. In: Proceedings of the 16th CCS (2009)
24. Felt, A.P., Chin, E., Hanna, S., Song, D., Wagner, D.: Android permissions demystied. In: Proceedings of the 18th CCS (2011)
25. Felt, A.P., Wang, H.J., Moshchuk, A., Hanna, S., Chin, E.: Permission re-delegation: attacks and defenses. In: Proceedings of the USENIX Security (2011)
26. Tariq, D., Gehani, A.: SPADE: support for provenance auditing in distributed environments. In: Narasimhan, P., Triantafillou, P. (eds.) Middleware 2012. LNCS, vol. 7662, pp. 101–120. Springer, Heidelberg (2012)
27. Joung Ham, Y., Moon, D., Lee, H.-W., Deok Lim, J., Nyeo Kim, J.: Android mobile application system call event pattern analysis for determination of malicious attack. International Journal of Security and Its Applications **8**(1) (2014)
28. Hornyack, P., Han, S., Jung, J., Schechter, S., Wetherall, D.: These are not the droids you are looking for: retrofitting android to protect data from imperious applications. In: Proceedings of the 18th CCS (2011)
29. Jing, Y., Zhao, Z., Ahn, G., Hu, H.: Morpheus: automatically generating heuristics to detect Android emulators. In: Proceedings of ACSAC (2014)
30. Karami, M., Elsabagh, M., Najafiborazjani, P., Stavrou, A.: Behavioral analysis of Android applications using automated instrumentation. In: 7th International Conference on Software Security and Reliability Companion (2013)
31. Lange, M., Liebergeld, S., Lackorzynski, A., Warg, A., Peter, M.: L4android: a generic operating system framework for secure smartphones. In: Proceedings of the 1st Workshop on Security and Privacy in Smartphones and Mobile Devices (2011)
32. Lu, L., Li, Z., Wu, Z., Lee, W., Jiang, G.: Chex: statically vetting android apps for component hijacking vulnerablilities. In: Proceedings of the 19th CCS (2012)
33. Mengtao, S., Gang, T.: Nativeguard: protecting android applications from third-party native libraries. In: Proceedings of ACM Conference on Security and Privacy in Wireless & Mobile Networks (2014)
34. Moreau, L., Clifford, B., Freire, J., Futrelle, J., Gil, Y., Groth, P., Kwasnikowska, N., Miles, S., Missier, P., Myers, J., Plale, B., Simmhan, Y., Stephan, E., Van, J.: The open provenance model core specification (v1.1). In: Future Generation Computer Systems (2010)
35. Nauman, M., Khan, S., Zhang, X.: Apex: extending android permission model and enforcement with user-defined runtime constraints. In: Proceedings of the 5th ACM Symposium on ICCS (2010)
36. Ongtang, M., Butler, K., McDaniel, P.: Porscha: policy oriented secure content handling in android. In: Proceedings of the 26th ACSAC (2010)
37. Ongtang, M., McLaughlin, S., Enck, W., McDaniel, P.: Semantically rich application-centric security in android. In: Proceedings of the 25th ACSAC (2009)
38. Peng, H., Gates, C., Sarm, B., Li, N., Qi, Y., Potharaju, R., Nita-Rotaru, C., Molloy, I.: Using probabilistic generative models for ranking risks of android apps. In: Proceedings of the 19th CCS (2012)
39. Portokalidis, G., Homburg, P., Anagnostakis, K., Bos, H.: Paranoid Android: versatile protection for smartphones. In: Proceedings of the 26th ACSAC (2010)

40. Rastogi, V., Chen, Y., Jiang, X.: Droidchameleon: evaluating android anti-malware against transformation attacks. In: Proceedings of the 8th ICCS (2013)

41. Reina, A., Fattori, A., Cavallaro, L.: A system call-centric analysis and stimulation technique to automatically reconstruct android malware behaviors. In: Proceedings of the EUROSEC (2013)

42. Schmidt, A., Bye, R., Schmidt, H., Clausen, J., Kiraz, O., Yxksel, K., Camtepe, S., Sahin, A.: Static analysis of executables for collaborative malware detection on android. In: ICC Communication and Information Systems Security Symposium (2009)

43. Schmidt, A., Schmidt, H., Clausen, J., Yuksel, K., Kiraz, O., Sahin, A., Camtepe, S.: Enhancing security of linux-based android devices. In: Proceedings of 15th International Linux Kongress (2008)

44. Shabtai, A., Fledel, Y., Elovici, Y.: Securing android- powered mobile devices using selinux. In: Proceedings of 31th IEEE Security and Privacy (2010)

45. Vidas, T., Christin, N.: Evading Android runtime analysis via sandbox detection. In: Proceedings of ASIACCS (2014)

46. Wei, X., Gomez, L., Neamtiu, I., Faloutsos, M.: Profiledroid: multi-layer profiling of Android applications. In: 18th Annual International Conference on Mobile Computing and Networking (2012)

47. Wu, D., Mao, C., Wei, T., Lee, H., Wu, K.: Droidmat: Android malware detection through manifest and api calls tracing. In: Proceedings of the 7th Asia JCIS (2012)

48. Wu, L., Grace, M., Zhou, Y., Wu, C., Jiang, X.: The impact of vendor customizations on android security. In: Proceedings of the CCS (2013)

49. Xu, R., Saidi, H., Anderson, R.: Aurasium: practical policy enforcement for android applications. In: Proceedings of the USENIX Security Symposium (2012)

50. Yan, L., Yin, H.: Droidscope: seamlessly reconstructing the os and dalvik semantic views for dynamic android malware analysis. In: Proceedings of the 21st USENIX Security Symposium (2012)

51. Zhang, Y., Yang, M., Xu, B., Yang, Z., Gu, G., Ning, P., Wang, X., Zang, B.: Vetting undesirable behaviors in android apps with permission use analysis. In: Proceedings of CCS (2013)

52. Zheng, C., Zhu, S., Dai, S., Gu, G., Gong, X., Han, X., Zhou, W.: Smartdroid: an automatic system for revealing ui-based trigger conditions in android applications. In: Proceedings of the 2nd edn. ACM Workshop on Security and Privacy in Smartphones and Mobile Devices (2012)

53. Zhou, W., Zhou, Y., Jiang, X., Ning, P.: Detecting repackaged smartphone applications in third-party Android marketplaces. In: CODASPY (2012)

54. Zhou, Y., Jiang, X.: Dissecting android malware: characterization and evolution. In: Proceedings of the 2012 IEEE Symposium on Security and Privacy (2012)

55. Zhou, Y., Wang, Z., Zhou, W., Jiang, X.: Hey, you, get off of my market: detecting malicious apps in official and alternative android markets. In: Proceedings of the 19th NDSS (2012)

56. Zhou, Y., Zhang, Q., Zou, S., Jiang, X.: Riskranker: scalable and accurate zero-day android malware detection. In: Proceedings of the 10th MobiSys (2012)

SplitDroid: Isolated Execution of Sensitive Components for Mobile Applications

Lin Yan, Yao Guo$^{(\boxtimes)}$, and Xiangqun Chen

Key Laboratory of High Confidence Software Technologies (Ministry of Education),
Institute of Software, School of EECS, Peking University, Beijing, China
{yanlin10,yaoguo,cherry}@sei.pku.edu.cn

Abstract. Although many approaches have been proposed to protect mobile privacy through techniques such as isolated execution, existing mechanisms typically work at the app-level. As many apps themselves might contain vulnerability, it is desirable to split the execution of an app into normal components and sensitive components, such that the execution of sensitive components of an app can be isolated and their private data are protected from accesses by the normal components.

This paper proposes SplitDroid, an OS-level virtualization technique to support the split-execution of an app in order to isolate the execution of sensitive components and protect its private data. SplitDroid is enabled by porting the Linux Container to the Android environment and the ability to split Android apps through programming and runtime support. We also introduce a secure network channel to allow communication between the isolated component and normal Android apps, such that non-privacy-related information can be interchanged to ensure its correct execution. Finally, we demonstrate the feasibility and effectiveness of SplitDroid through a case study.

Keywords: Mobile security · Isolated execution · Privacy protection · OS-level virtualization

1 Introduction

As the development of mobile Internet and smartphones, more and more mobile applications (*apps* for short) have been developed to help people with their work, entertainment and daily life. Currently, both Google Play and App Store have over one million apps available for mobile users [2] to download.

As the number of mobile apps grows, people are storing more and more sensitive information on smartphones, such as passwords, credit card numbers, geo-locations, contacts information and even biometric information like fingerprints. Unfortunately, these sensitive data are vulnerable to various attacks from different malicious apps such as malware. For example, there are already a huge number of malware aiming at stealing user privacy on the Android OS [30].

As a result, many approaches have been proposed to protect sensitive data on smartphones based on various techniques, such as data encryption [9], data isolation [8, 13, 15, 17–19, 27] and isolated execution [14, 16]. In this paper, we focus

© Institute for Computer Sciences, Social Informatics and Telecommunications Engineering 2015
B. Thuraisingham et al. (Eds.): SecureComm 2015, LNICST 164, pp. 78–96, 2015.
DOI: 10.1007/978-3-319-28865-9_5

on approaches based on isolated execution because it is able to separate the execution of attackers and target apps into isolated environments, thus preventing sensitive data from being stolen from target apps.

Researchers have proposed several isolated execution approaches to protect mobile privacy. Solutions like L4Android [16] and Xen on ARM [14] support multiple virtual machines (VMs) containing Android OS running simultaneously on the same hardware. With bare-metal virtualization, these solutions provide strong isolation guarantee between VMs. However, they are too heavyweight to be used in smartphone environments considering the impact on memory usage, performance, and energy consumption. Other solutions aim at isolating confidential data at the app-level. For example, TrustDroid [6], MOSES [22] and AppCage [31] extend the Android framework to group apps into different domains and enforce access control among domains to protect user confidential data. These app-level solutions are lightweight in essence, but they assume that the middleware layer can be trusted, which is not always true in reality.

Recent approaches like Cells [4] and Airbag [25] achieve isolated execution by leveraging OS-level virtualization technologies. Both of them support multiple Android user spaces running simultaneously on the same Linux kernel. OS-level isolation provides strong albeit lightweight isolation guarantee between user spaces. However, these solutions typically protect each app as a whole, which might not be enough in many cases.

Based on our observation, privacy leakage often occurs within one app, where private data in one component may be leaked through another component in the same app. For example, many apps employ "social login" capabilities, which allow users to log in using popular third-party accounts such as Facebook or Weibo. This technique is similar to *single sign-on (SSO)*, and it allows users to log into different apps with one account such as Facebook. However, one of the potential vulnerabilities here is that, when a user logs into her Facebook account within a different app, the account and password information might be leaked through this app. In order to protect user information being leaked in these situations, we need an environment where sensitive components in an app can be executed in an isolated environment, for example, when a user enters her passwords. After successful login, the app will receive a "log in successful" message or an authentication token, but it cannot access the actual login credentials such as passwords.

In order to achieve this kind of fine-grained protection on sensitive data, this paper proposes SplitDroid, an OS-level virtualization technique to support the split-execution of a mobile app. We introduce the concept of separating privacy-related sensitive components from the rest of a mobile app and isolating the execution of them in a secure environment. By porting the Linux Container to Android, we build a trusted container with a separate Android runtime that runs sensitive components alone. We also provide developers the ability to split Android apps with dedicated programming and runtime support. We introduce a secure communication channel across containers for exchanging non-sensitive information with sensitive components from the normal Android environment.

As a result, our approach is lightweight since both containers share the same OS kernel, but it also provides strong protection with the Linux Container.

As a case study, we implement SplitDroid on a Nexus 5 smartphone and demonstrate its feasibility by enabling the split-execution of an app using social login. We also evaluate the performance overhead of SplitDroid to show its effectiveness.

This paper makes the following main contributions:

- We propose SplitDroid, a fine-grained privacy protection technique based on OS-level virtualization, which enables isolated execution of sensitive components in an app.
- We successfully port the Linux Container to Android and demonstrate that it is feasible to achieve execution isolation through OS-level virtualization.
- We introduce a mechanism to split the execution of an Android app through programming and runtime support. Based on the mechanism, we implement SplitDroid on Android and demonstrate its feasibility through a case study.

2   Preliminaries

In this section, we introduce some preliminaries to define the scope of our work. We start by presenting a running example to demonstrate the motivation for split execution of sensitive app components. Then we describe our design goals, assumptions and the adversary model.

2.1   A Running Example

Figure 1 depicts our motivation for fine-grained privacy protection by isolating the execution of sensitive app components. The execution overflow on the left side of Figure 1 shows a normal execution overflow of some mobile app A. App A requires user login before accessing its services. This feature is reflected in the execution of the "login" component in the normal execution overflow, which means a user needs to provide her account and password to the remote authentication server via the login UI in app A.

As app A runs in an open environment together with many other apps, malware may coexist with app A and steal the account and password combination during the login procedure. Researchers have proposed many solutions to prevent this kind of privacy leakage. An app can be easily isolated into a stand-alone environment of many types, such as bare-metal VM, OS-level containers and app-level sandboxes.

However, isolating the mobile app as a whole may not be enough to prevent privacy leakage. As depicted in Figure 1, login credentials may be leaked through another component in app A itself. For example, if app A provides the login feature by integrating social login components from popular social networking services such as Facebook, user's Facebook password may be leaked through vulnerabilities of components in app A.

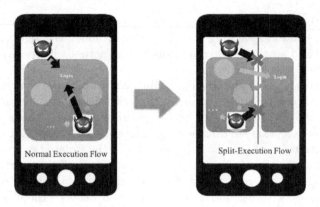

Note: Arrows among app components in this figure only denote the execution sequence, not data flow.

Fig. 1. A running example. *Left: an app containing a login component, in which the login credential might be stolen by adversaries; Right: the login component can be split and executed in an isolated environment, the original app has no access to login credentials.*

In order to prevent such kind of privacy leakage, we are motivated to build an isolated execution environment to confine the sensitive component that contains the private information. As depicted in the right side of Figure 1, software components with sensitive data (e.g., the "login" component in app A) can be split and executed in a fully-isolated environment. Threats on user privacy from both inside and outside app A will be blocked by the isolation mechanism.

2.2   Goals

In order to provide fine-grained protection on user privacy, we propose Split-Droid, which provides isolated execution of sensitive app components. Our design of SplitDroid aims to meet the following goals:

- **Privacy confinement.** As more and more sensitive data congregate on mobile devices, our work aims to confine user privacy by isolating the execution of software components that are related to the collection and transformation of these sensitive data. Isolated execution can be achieved by leveraging virtualization technologies, which could support multiple execution environments running simultaneously and provide strong isolation among them.
- **Ease of programming.** We want to minimize developer efforts to utilize the proposed mechanism to enable the spilt-execution of an app. The underlying mechanism that facilitates the isolated execution should not be exposed to developers. In other words, developers do not have to know how to construct and manage the isolated execution environment. Building a new app based on the SplitDroid should be as simple as building native Android apps with Java.
- **User transparency.** App users should not notice the existence of the split-execution in SplitDroid. For example, when a user clicks the "login" button in

an app and then types in "username" and "password", a user should not feel the action or delay of switching environments, although the login credentials collection UI and account authentication process actually happens in another isolated execution environment.

– **Low performance overhead.** The influence of isolated execution on system performance must be low. In order to meet this requirement, the performance overhead of the isolated execution environment must be low compared to the normal execution environment and the switch overhead between these two environments must also be kept low. Since the isolated execution environment is based on virtualization technologies and different virtualization technologies bring different performance overheads and trusted computing base(TCB) sizes, we must find a proper trade-off between them.

2.3   Assumptions

We make the following assumptions in our work.

– We assume that the isolated execution environment created by SplitDroid is fully trusted as sensitive user data are confined in it. The whole software stack within the isolated execution environment including the OS kernel, middlewares and applications are all assumed to be trustworthy.
– We assume that the OS kernel inside the normal execution environment is also trusted since we choose OS-level isolation to implement the isolated execution. In fact, the OS kernel is shared between the normal execution environment and the isolated execution environment.
– We assume that there exists a trusted communication channel between the normal and isolated execution environments. The communication channel is mainly used to exchange non-sensitive information such as "login successful" notifications and tokens which do not contain user credentials.
– We assume that the external parties communicating securely with the isolated execution environment can be trusted, such as login authentication servers, mobile banking services, etc.

2.4   Adversary Model

SplitDroid aims to protect user privacy against the following adversaries. In order to steal user's sensitive data, attackers can compromise any part of the user space in the normal execution environment and even gain access to the interface with APIs we propose to support isolated execution. The attacker may also have access to the persistent storage in the normal execution environment. Attackers can be any app in the normal execution environment or even the rest components of the same app, while the execution of its sensitive components can be isolated leveraging SplitDroid. However, we do not consider side-channel attacks or physical attacks in this paper.

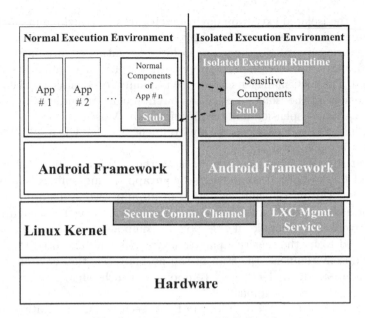

Fig. 2. Architecture of SplitDroid.

3 SplitDroid Design

In this section, we present the design of SplitDroid. We first give an overview of SplitDroid. Then we elaborate on its key functionalities and detailed design considerations.

3.1 Overview of SplitDroid

As depicted in Figure 2, SplitDroid separates the user space into two execution environments: a normal execution environment where an untrusted stack of software (middleware and most apps) runs, and an isolated execution environment created by SplitDroid where the trusted middleware and privacy-related app components run. By leveraging OS-level virtualization technology (Linux Container in our case), sensitive components running in the isolated execution environment is isolated from the untrusted code running in the normal execution environment. Besides, SplitDroid provides a secure communication channel between the two execution environments.

In order to leverage SplitDroid to protect privacy, a mobile app needs to be partitioned into two parts: one part consists of privacy-related component, and the other part consists of non-sensitive components. SplitDroid provides programming and runtime support for developers to develop and deploy the split-execution of mobile apps.

SplitDroid includes the following major components:

- **Isolated Execution Runtime.** First, the *isolated execution runtime* component in SplitDroid ensures the stand-alone execution of sensitive compo-

nents in the isolated execution environment. Its tasks include managing the
execution lifecycle and providing isolated storage for sensitive components.

- **LXC Management Service.** The isolated execution environment is implemented as a container enabled by porting the Linux Container (LXC) to
  Android. The LXC management service is mainly responsible for the lifecycle
  management of the isolated execution environment, including the initialization, creation, suspension and termination of it. Most importantly, the LXC
  management service performs the environment switches when split-execution
  happens in SplitDroid.
- **App Stubs.** We introduce *app stubs* as the proxies of the sensitive components to the normal components of an app during split execution, and
  vice versa. During the split execution of an app, two stubs are running in
  the normal execution environment and the isolated execution environment,
  respectively. For example, if the "login" components in a mobile app are
  considered to be the sensitive part that are split and executed the isolated
  execution environment, the stub in the normal execution environment will
  serve as an agent of the "login" component, which offers exactly the same
  interface as "login" components.
- **Secure Communication Channel.** A secure communication channel
  between two execution environments is constructed through the shared OS
  kernel. The communication channel is responsible to fulfill synchronization
  between the two parts of the mobile app running in different execution environments through trusted stubs. End-to-end security of the trusted communication channel can be achieved through encrypted communication between
  the app stubs.

3.2   The Isolated Execution Environment

SplitDroid creates an isolated execution environment to run sensitive app components separately. We introduce the isolated execution environment by adopting
OS-level virtualization. Compared to bare-metal virtualization, OS-level virtualization is lightweight since the OS kernel can be shared by VMs.

Overview of the Linux Container. SplitDroid adopts OS-level virtualization
to create the isolated execution environment. In particular, we use a container-
based lightweight virtualization framework in mainstream Linux kernel called
Linux Container [3], which enables multiple isolated user-space instances running
on a shared Linux kernel, thus offering OS-level virtualization. LXC relies on
several Linux kernel features, in which *Namespaces* and *Control Groups* are the
key enablers.

Porting LXC to Android. LXC was originally targeted at the X86 architecture for desktop Linux systems, so we need to port it to the ARM architecture
in order to support Android. Since the Linux kernel used in Android has been
optimized to support mobile environment, some kernel capabilities needed to

run LXC have been turned off and the standard GNU C library `libc` has been replaced by `bionic libc`. Thus, we first turn on those missing kernel capabilities and recompile the Android kernel. Missing kernel capabilities can be found by running the `lxc-checkconfig` script in the standard LXC-tools against the kernel config file of Android. After recompiling the Linux kernel, we cross compile and statically link all GNU `libc` independent libraries of LXC.

The most challenging part of constructing an isolated execution container is device virtualization which includes multiplexing the framebuffer and input devices.

In Android, all graphical contents shown on screen are updated by the screen updater to the *framebuffer* memory, which is mapped from kernel to user space. Since we have only one physical screen with two screen updaters from two VMs, we modify the framebuffer driver such that it will receive update requests from each container but will only allow the foreground VM to actually update the framebuffer. The other background container can still update its display data in a backend buffer, which will not be displayed until it switches to the foreground.

For input devices such as touch screen and physical buttons, we modify the device drivers only to respond to the requests from the foreground VM while input requests from the background container are discarded.

Resulting Environment. Based on LXC, SplitDroid creates a new container at system boot time. The new container is initialized with a clean copy of the same Android framework as the original Android running on the smartphone and relevant SplitDroid components. The new container is designed to serve as the isolated execution environment to confine the execution of sensitive components. LXC-tools are provided to enable on-demand switching between containers when the split execution of mobile apps starts. Two containers are configured to locate in the same virtual local network provided by LXC. SplitDroid also provides a secure communication channel between containers based on encrypted socket connection.

3.3   Split-Execution of Android Apps

SplitDroid introduces the concept of split execution of Android apps to protect user privacy. Specifically, an app can be split into sensitive components and normal components. By isolating the execution of sensitive components in a trusted environment, sensitive data can be protected from being leaked. Thus the goal of app split is to identify software components inside an app containing some specific sensitive data. In our current design, we provide app developer the ability to split the Android apps through programming support, which enables them to execute in a split manner with the provided runtime support. In the future, we plan to leverage static analysis techniques such as taint analysis to identify sensitive components automatically to help split Android app binaries.

App Split. Split execution of an Android app has been widely explored for various purposes such as computation offloading [7], where the computation-intensive components of an app can be executed on a remote environment such as a server or a cloud.

An Android app can be viewed as a state machine in which the states represent Android *Activities* and state transitions represent *Activity* switches. Each *Activity* corresponds to a Java class that inherits from the `ApplicationContext` class. Besides, an *Activity* may be related to other Java classes and string/img resources depending on its actual business logic. Throughout the generation, process and storage of sensitive data (e.g. passwords), one specific item of sensitive data relates to at least one *Activity* (e.g. "Login" *Activity*).

In our design, we split an Android app on the granularity of *Activities*. Given the sensitive data to be protected, all *Activities* inside an app will be analyzed to check if they are related to the sensitive data. After the app is analyzed, all privacy-related *Activities* (including the related classes and resources) will be extracted from the original app and packaged as sensitive components. A stub will be inserted in to the rest of the app to work as the interface proxy of the extracted sensitive components.

Runtime Support. The *isolated execution runtime* component inside Split-Droid provides runtime support for the split execution of Android apps. The first task of the isolated execution runtime is managing the code of sensitive components. In our design, there is a one-time configuration step to install the code of sensitive components into the isolated execution environment in parallel with the installation of normal components of an app into the normal execution environment. As there may exist more than one app needing split execution, the isolated execution runtime should not confuse among different sensitive components from different apps. To keep track of sensitive components from different apps, the isolated execution runtime maintains an identity table to enforce a signature-based check before isolated execution.

SplitDroid also provides runtime support to manage the lifecycle of isolated execution. Once receiving a request to run sensitive components from the normal execution environment, the isolated execution runtime starts a new service process to run the code. When sensitive components finish executing, the isolated execution runtime will terminate the service process and issue a notification to the normal execution environment through a callback function. To ensure isolation, SplitDroid only supports sensitive components from one app to run in the isolate execution environment at a given time.

Programming Support. SplitDroid provides programming support for developers to enable the split execution of Android apps. In order to enable isolated execution of the sensitive components, a developer should go through the following procedure.

1. **Define the interface for accessing the isolated components from the normal execution environment.** The first step towards developing an app with SplitDroid is to specify which part of the app is privacy-related. After figuring out privacy-related components, the developer must specify

an interface to access these isolated components from the normal execution environment. In the normal execution environment, the interface to access isolated components should inherit from an ITrustedStub interface.

2. **Implement the actual business logic running in the isolated execution environment.** The developer should provide the actual code to be executed in the isolated execution environment. There must be a core class in the business logic code that inherits the IsolatedExecution class since the *trusted runtime service* component in SplitDroid will search the core class to start isolated execution. Meanwhile, the core class has to implement the interface defined in the first step, which wires the interface in the *trusted stub* to the actual business logic.

3. **Interact with isolated components.** After defining the interface and implementation of isolated components, the developer can write code to start to run these software components in the isolated execution environment and interact with them at runtime. The first thing to start running isolated components is to create an instance of the IsolatedExeEnv class and pass an instance of the core class of the isolated components as parameter to the initialize function of the instance. Then the developer can write code to interact with isolated components using pre-defined interfaces from the normal execution environment.

3.4   Usage Scenarios

To illustrate the applicability of SplitDroid, we present two real-world usage scenarios: social login and mobile payment. The *confidentiality* and the *integrity* of user privacy can be guaranteed by adopting SplitDroid in both cases.

Social Login. Social login within mobile apps is a form of single sign-on (SSO), which enables a user logging into a third-party app with existing login information from social networking services such as Facebook and Weibo. Social login is beneficial to all parties involved.

However, malware in an untrusted environment or even malicious app components inside a third-party app that integrates Facebook social login service could steal user's login credentials. Once the login credentials of a popular social networking account get stolen, all related third-parties are in danger. As described in Section 2.1, SplitDroid can be used to eliminate this kind of privacy leakage by isolating the social login components in an isolated execution environment.

Mobile Payment. With the development of e-commerce and e-banking, more and more e-commerce services are moving to the mobile platform. While building one's own mobile payment system is expensive and insecure, many e-commerce apps choose to integrate third-party payment plugins such as PayPal and Alipay.

For example, when users place orders in an e-commerce app that integrates PayPal services. After adding desired products into her shopping-cart, a user can choose to check out with PayPal. By logging into PayPal and choosing a proper bank account, the user can successfully place her order. Convenient on one hand, this procedure contains potential risk of privacy leakage since PayPal login happens in an untrusted environment. The user's PayPal login credentials and related bank account information could be potentially leaked. With SplitDroid, we can prevent this from happening by isolating the software components of PayPal login and payment service.

4 Case Study

4.1 Goal

As a case study, we implement a prototype of SplitDroid to demonstrate its feasibility. Based on the prototype, we build a mobile app to show the effectiveness on privacy protection of SplitDroid. We also evaluate the performance of SplitDroid to show its practicality.

4.2 Implementation

Our implementation includes two parts: the prototype of SplitDroid and a mobile app based on the split-execution mechanism provided by SplitDroid.

SplitDroid Prototype. We implemented a prototype of SplitDroid based on CyanogenMod 11 (corresponds to Android 4.4) on a Nexus 5 smartphone. Then we port LXC 1.0 to Android and modify device drivers as we have described in Section 3.2. We use the same Android version for the runtime in both the normal execution environment (the host) and the isolate execution environment (the container created by LXC). We implement components in SplitDroid based on our design discussed in Section 3. We implement the programming support in SplitDroid by providing an SDK to app developers .

Mobile App Implementation. In a proof-of-concept implementation, we have implemented a simple app integrating social login services provided by Weibo. This usage scenario has been previously described in Section 2.1 and Section 3.4.

We implement the app by following the programming steps described in Section 3.3 . As shown in Code Example 1, the isolated sensitive components of Weibo social login function only has one interface, which is used to activate the `authorize` action.

Code Example 1. Declaring the interface for an SSO service.

```
public interface ISSOService extends ITrustedStub
{
  public void authorize(AuthListener authListener);
}
```

Code Example 2 presents the core class from the implementation of the actual business logic of Weibo social login service. The code example only shows some key steps to conduct the SSO authorization based on the Weibo SDK since the whole code base is relatively large and mostly irrelevant.

Code Example 2. Implementing the SSO service.

```
public class SSOService extends IsolatedExecution implements
    ISSOService
{
  public authorize(AuthListener authListener)
  {
    // Implements the authorize() function using the SSO SDK
    ......
    mAuthInfo = new AuthInfo(this, Constants.APP_KEY,
        Constants.REDIRECT_URL, Constants.SCOPE);
    mSsoHandler = new SsoHandler(WBAuthActivity.this,
        mAuthInfo);
    mSsoHandler.authorizeWeb(authListener);
    ......
  }
}
```

Code Example 3. The `AuthListener` Class.

```
class AuthListener implements WeiboAuthListener
{
  @Override
  public void onComplete(Bundle values)
  {
    // Parse login Token from Bundle
    mAccessToken = Oauth2AccessToken.parseAccessToken(values)
        ;
    if (mAccessToken.isSessionValid())
    {
      // Handle login information
      .........
    } else
    {
      // Handle error
      String code = values.getString("code", "");
      .........
    }
  }
}
```

Code Example 4. Calling the SSO service in Main Class.

```
IsolatedExeEnv isolatedExeEnv = IsolatedExeEnv.initialize(new
    SSOService);
ISSOService sSOService = (ISSOService) isolatedExeEnv.
    getTrustedStub();
sSOService.authorize(new AuthListener());
```

Code Example 4 shows how we interact with sensitive components running in the isolated execution environment. After initialization, the code running in the normal execution environment receives a reference of isolated components by calling the `getTrustedStub` function of the `IsolatedExeEnv` class instance. Then the `authorize` function of isolated Weibo social login components can be invoked directly through the definition of the `ISSOService` interface. Code Example 3 shows the implementation of a callback handler of SSO authorization, which is required as a parameter to call the Weibo social login Service.

4.3 Evaluation

To evaluate the effectiveness of our approach, we run the the mobile app we build in the SplitDroid environment. Figure 3 shows the screenshots of the whole split-execution process. The Weibo social login part of the app can be successfully isolated in a trusted environment.

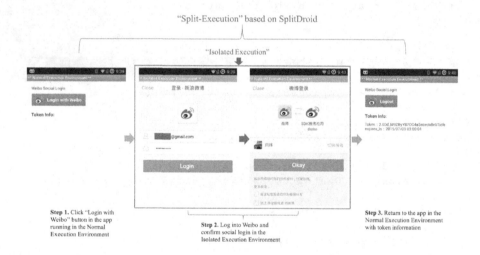

Fig. 3. Case Study: an Android app using the Weibo account login service.

To evaluate the performance impact of OS-level virtualization in SplitDroid, we first run the AnTuTu benchmark [1] with three different setups. "Baseline" means running AnTuTu in standard Android without SplitDroid. "NEE" means running AnTuTu in the normal execution environment of SplitDroid. "IEE" means running AnTuTu in the isolated execution environment created by Split-Droid. We can see from the results shown in Figure 4, the impact of the OS-level virtualization in SplitDroid on system performance is relatively low.

We then evaluated the performance of the mobile app running on SplitDroid by comparing the execution time of split-execution with the execution time of normal execution (normal app in standard Android environment) on the same Nexus 5 smartphone. The execution time is measured between clicking the "login

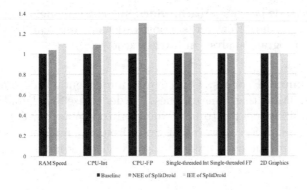

Fig. 4. Normalized performance impact of SplitDroid.

Table 1. Comparison of execution time (normal execution vs. split-execution).

	Execution time (ms)		
	Max.	Min.	Avg.
w/o SplitDroid	75	29	45
w/ SplitDroid	223	179	190

with weibo" button, which is shown as the first step in Figure 3, and switching back to the UI containing token information, which is shown as the last step in Figure 3. The input time of user login credentials and network communication time is subtracted to reflect only the overhead brought by SplitDroid. Results are shown in Table 1. We can see that although the average execution time of SplitDroid is more than three times of the normal Android, the worst execution time is roughly one fifth of a second, which should be acceptable to most mobile users.

5 Discussions

5.1 Limitations

Size of the Trusted Computing Base (TCB). The TCB size of a privacy protection solution has long been a major concern in the research community. People believe that smaller TCB will narrow the attack surface of the trusted software components and ease the formal verification efforts. Compared to solutions based bare-metal virtualization, SplitDroid has a larger TCB size due to the inclusion of the OS kernel and a trusted container. However, LXC is more lightweight than bare-metal virtualization to fit in the mobile environment. So it is a trade-off we make between practical security protections and the TCB size.

Lack of Support for Legacy Mobile Apps. Although SplitDroid can be used to isolate privacy-related sensitive components inside a mobile app, it still requires a source-code based approach, which means developers have to split the app manually in advance. However, support of legacy apps can be implemented with the help of program analysis in further studies.

Heavy Deployment Process. Our current implementation requires users to reinstall a new ROM on their smartphones in order to use SplitDroid. The reason is that the Android kernel has to be recompiled to support LXC by turning on several kernel capabilities. However, if SplitDroid is employed as a standard process in the future, the users do not to worry this any more.

5.2 Future Work

Automated App Split. The current way to support split-execution in Split-Droid relies on the efforts of developers to leverage our programming support. This would undermine the wide adoption of SplitDroid since it offers no support for existing mobile apps. One potential future direction is to find an automated way to split existing apps. This can be achieved by applying taint analysis on the data flow of sensitive data, thus identifying sensitive software components automatically.

SplitDroid Based on Cloud Services. Although SplitDroid can protect mobile privacy information from being leaked in a fine-grained level, sensitive data can still be retrieved by physical attacks of dumping memory or storage contents. As future work, we can investigate on building isolated execution environment with both container technology and cloud service such as storage service, which is similar to the idea of TinMan [26]. Sensitive data will never be leaked on the mobile devices by not appearing in the local environment. However, this requires a dedicated design on human computer interaction as the sensitive data can not be provided directly on mobile devices.

6   Related Work

6.1   Privacy Protection on Smartphones

Many approaches have been proposed to protect sensitive data on smartphones. Popular techniques include data encryption [9], data isolation [8,13,15,17–19,27] and isolated execution. Besides, TaintDroid [10] extends the Android platform to track the privacy data that flowing through third party applications. TaintDroid can be applied to monitor the system behaviors related to sensitive data on smartphones.

Our work focuses on isolated execution based privacy protection because it can separate the execution of attackers and target apps into isolated environments.

6.2   Isolated Execution Based Privacy Protection

Bare-Metal-Level Virtual Machines. Bare-metal virtualization provides a strong isolation guarantee to put different applications into separated VMs. Some efforts tried to improve the security of the Android platform by introducing platform virtualization [5,12,14,16]. However, platform virtualization is a heavyweight mechanism, which runs multiple software stacks in different virtual machines. It is usually neither necessary nor affordable in the current battery-powered mobile devices. Full platform virtualization requires the support of device virtualization to multiplex hardware to guest domains.

Application-Level Sandboxes. TrustDroid [6] introduces a lightweight isolation framework to protect apps in separate domains of different trust levels. TrustDroid can support the isolation between corporate applications and private applications. TrustDroid relies on the MAC mechanism to enforce the isolation policy of each domain. Meanwhile, TrustDroid also depends on the Android middleware to confine the inter-domain communication and data access. MOSES [22] also targets a similar usage scenario: company smartphones used by employees. MOSES introduces a policy-based framework to isolate apps with different security profiles on Android. AppCage [31] proposes two user-level sandboxes: dex sandbox and native sandbox to interpose and regulate an app's access to sensitive APIs. These app-level solutions all assume that the Android middleware is trusted, which is often not true in real cases.

OS-Level Containers. Cells [4] is a virtual mobile smartphone architecture by leveraging OS-level virtualization. It introduces a new device namespace mechanism and novel device proxies to multiplex a single set of phone hardware into multiple virtual phones (VPs). Airbag [25] adopts a similar container-based method to isolate suspicious apps. However, these work mainly focus on isolating the execution of a mobile app as a whole, which is not enough for real usage scenarios where software components from the same app can also steal sensitive data. SplitDroid adopts similar OS level virtualization technology while achieving more fine-grained privacy protection.

6.3   Split Execution of Mobile Apps

There are several attempts focusing on splitting the execution of some certain components inside mobile apps such as advertisement components [20,21,24]. These approaches mostly focus on isolating specific categories of untrusted components. However, our work aims to separate and protect trusted components with more strict isolation guarantee based on Linux Container.

Other previous work have investigated in split execution of applications such as Java or Android apps in order to provide features such as computation offloading [7]. These can be implemented by either splitting app binaries [7,11] or source code redevelopment [28,29]. TLR [23] proposes the split execution of .Net apps. Although the current design of SplitDroid requires developers to redesign the app to support split execution, it can also be implemented using an automated approach based on program analysis to split Android binaries.

7 Conclusion

Although isolated execution has been studied in smartphone environments such as Android, they typically isolate the apps as a whole. Since an app cannot always be trusted to handled all private information such as credentials in third-party login services, we introduce the concept of splitting the execution of an app into normal components and sensitive components, such that the execution of sensitive components of an app can be isolated and their private data is can be protected from being accessed by the normal components.

We have presented SplitDroid, an OS-level virtualization technique that supports the split-execution of an app. SplitDroid creates an isolated execution environment enabled by porting the Linux Container to the Android environment. SplitDroid also provides programming and runtime support for developer to fulfill the split-execution of mobile apps. We have demonstrated the feasibility and effectiveness of SplitDroid by building a prototype of SplitDroid and evaluation through a case study.

Acknowledgement. This work is supported in part by the High-Tech Research and Development Program of China under Grant No. 2013AA01A605 and the National Natural Science Foundation of China under Grant No. 61421091, No. 91118004, No. 61103026.

References

1. AnTuTu benchmark. http://www.antutu.com/
2. Google Play has more apps than apple now, but it's still behind in one key area. http://www.businessinsider.com/google-play-vs-apple-app-store-2015-2
3. Linux Container. http://lxc.sourceforge.net/
4. Andrus, J., Dall, C., Hof, A.V., Laadan, O., Nieh, J.: Cells: a virtual mobile smartphone architecture. In: Proceedings of the Twenty-Third ACM Symposium on Operating Systems Principles, pp. 173–187. ACM (2011)
5. Barr, K., Bungale, P., Deasy, S., Gyuris, V., Hung, P., Newell, C., Tuch, H., Zoppis, B.: The VMware mobile virtualization platform: is that a hypervisor in your pocket? ACM SIGOPS Operating Systems Review44(4), 124–135 (2010)
6. Bugiel, S., Davi, L., Dmitrienko, A., Heuser, S., Sadeghi, A.R., Shastry, B.: Practical and lightweight domain isolation on Android. In: Proceedings of the 1st ACM Workshop on Security and Privacy in Smartphones and Mobile Devices, pp. 51–62. ACM (2011)
7. Chun, B.G., Ihm, S., Maniatis, P., Naik, M., Patti, A.: CloneCloud: elastic execution between mobile device and cloud. In: Proceedings of the Sixth Conference on Computer Systems, EuroSys 2011, pp. 301–314 (2011)

8. Dam, M., Le Guernic, G., Lundblad, A.: TreeDroid: a tree automaton based app-roach to enforcing data processing policies. In: Proceedings of the 2012 ACM Conference on Computer and Communications Security, pp. 894–905. ACM (2012)
9. Diesburg, S.M., Wang, A.I.A.: A survey of confidential data storage and deletion methods. ACM Computing Surveys (CSUR)**43**(1), 2 (2010)
10. Enck, W., Gilbert, P., Han, S., Tendulkar, V., Chun, B.G., Cox, L.P., Jung, J., McDaniel, P., Sheth, A.N.: TaintDroid: an information-flow tracking system for realtime privacy monitoring on smartphones. ACM Transactions on Computer Systems (TOCS)**32**(2), 5 (2014)
11. Gordon, M.S., Jamshidi, D.A., Mahlke, S.A., Mao, Z.M., Chen, X.: COMET: code offload by migrating execution transparently. In: OSDI, pp. 93–106 (2012)
12. Heiser, G., Leslie, B.: The OKL4 microvisor: convergence point of microkernels and hypervisors. In: Proceedings of the First ACM Asia-Pacific Workshop on Workshop on Systems, pp. 19–24. ACM (2010)
13. Hornyack, P., Han, S., Jung, J., Schechter, S., Wetherall, D.: These aren't the droids you're looking for: retrofitting Android to protect data from imperious applications. In: Proceedings of the 18th ACM Conference on Computer and Communications Security, pp. 639–652. ACM (2011)
14. Hwang, J.Y., Suh, S.B., Heo, S.K., Park, C.J., Ryu, J.M., Park, S.Y., Kim, C.R.: Xen on ARM: system virtualization using Xen hypervisor for ARM-based secure mobile phones. In: 5th IEEE Consumer Communications and Networking Conference, CCNC 2008, pp. 257–261. IEEE (2008)
15. Kantola, D., Chin, E., He, W., Wagner, D.: Reducing attack surfaces for intra-application communication in Android. In: Proceedings of the Second ACM Workshop on Security and Privacy in Smartphones and Mobile Devices, pp. 69–80. ACM (2012)
16. Lange, M., Liebergeld, S., Lackorzynski, A., Warg, A., Peter, M.: L4Android: a generic operating system framework for secure smartphones. In: Proceedings of the 1st ACM Workshop on Security and Privacy in Smartphones and Mobile Devices, pp. 39–50. ACM (2011)
17. Li, X., Hu, H., Bai, G., Jia, Y., Liang, Z., Saxena, P.: DroidVault: a trusted data vault for Android devices. In: 2014 19th International Conference on Engineering of Complex Computer Systems (ICECCS), pp. 29–38. IEEE (2014)
18. Nauman, M., Khan, S., Zhang, X.: Apex: extending Android permission model and enforcement with user-defined runtime constraints. In: Proceedings of the 5th ACM Symposium on Information, Computer and Communications Security, pp. 328–332. ACM (2010)
19. Ongtang, M., McLaughlin, S., Enck, W., McDaniel, P.: Semantically rich application-centric security in Android. Security and Communication Networks**5**(6), 658–673 (2012)
20. Pearce, P., Felt, A.P., Nunez, G., Wagner, D.: AdDroid: privilege separation for applications and advertisers in Android. In: Proceedings of the 7th ACM Symposium on Information, Computer and Communications Security, ASIACCS 2012, Seoul, Korea (2012)
21. Roesner, F., Kohno, T.: Securing embedded user interfaces: Android and beyond. In: Presented as Part of the 22nd USENIX Security Symposium (USENIX Security 2013), Washington, D.C., pp. 97–112 (2013)
22. Russello, G., Conti, M., Crispo, B., Fernandes, E.: MOSES: supporting operation modes on smartphones. In: Proceedings of the 17th ACM Symposium on Access Control Models and Technologies, pp. 3–12. ACM (2012)

23. Santos, N., Raj, H., Saroiu, S., Wolman, A.: Trusted language runtime (TLR): enabling trusted applications on smartphones. In: Proceedings of the 12th Workshop on Mobile Computing Systems and Applications, pp. 21–26. ACM (2011)

24. Shekhar, S., Dietz, M., Wallach, D.S.: AdSplit: separating smartphone advertising from applications. In: Presented as Part of the 21st USENIX Security Symposium (USENIX Security 2012), Bellevue, WA, pp. 553–567 (2012)

25. Wu, C., Zhou, Y., Patel, K., Liang, Z., Jiang, X.: Airbag: boosting smartphone resistance to malware infection. In: Proceedings of the Network and Distributed System Security Symposium (2014)

26. Xia, Y., Liu, Y., Tan, C., Ma, M., Guan, H., Zang, B., Chen, H.: TinMan: eliminating confidential mobile data exposure with security oriented offloading. In: Proceedings of the Tenth European Conference on Computer Systems, pp. 27. ACM (2015)

27. Xu, R., Saïdi, H., Anderson, R.: Aurasium: practical policy enforcement for Android applications. In: USENIX Security Symposium, pp. 539–552 (2012)

28. Yuan, P., Guo, Y., Chen, X.: Uniport: a uniform programming support framework for mobile cloud computing. In: The 3rd IEEE International Conference on Mobile Cloud Computing, Services and Engineering, MobileCloud 2015 (2015)

29. Zhang, Y., Huang, G., Liu, X., Zhang, W., Mei, H., Yang, S.: Refactoring Android java code for on-demand computation offloading. In: OOPSLA 2012, pp. 233–248. ACM (2012)

30. Zhou, Y., Jiang, X.: Dissecting Android malware: characterization and evolution. In: IEEE S&P, pp. 95–109. IEEE (2012)

31. Zhou, Y., Patel, K., Wu, L., Wang, Z., Jiang, X.: Hybrid user-level sandboxing of third-party Android apps. In: Proceedings of the 10th ACM Symposium on Information, Computer and Communications Security, ASIA CCS 2015, Singapore, Republic of Singapore, pp. 19–30 (2015)

Intrinsic Code Attestation by Instruction Chaining for Embedded Devices

Oliver Stecklina[1]([⊠]), Peter Langendörfer[1], Frank Vater[1], Thorsten Kranz[2], and Gregor Leander[2]

[1] IHP, Im Technologiepark 25, 15236 Frankfurt (oder), Germany
{stecklina,langend,vater}@ihp-microelectronics.com
[2] Horst Görtz Institute for IT-Security (HGI), Ruhr-University Bochum, Bochum, Germany
{thorsten.kranz,gregor.leander}@rub.de

Abstract. In this paper we present a novel approach to ensure that no malicious code can be executed on resource constraint devices such as sensor nodes or embedded devices. The core idea is to encrypt the code and to decrypt it after reading it from the memory. Thus, if the code is not encrypted with the correct key it cannot be executed due the incorrect result of the decryption operation. A side effect of this is that the code is protected from being copied. In addition we propose to bind instructions to their predecessors by cryptographic approaches. This helps us to prevent attacks that reorder authorized code such as return-oriented programming attacks. We present a thorough security analysis of our approach as well as simulation results that prove the feasibility of our approach. The performance penalty as well as the area penalty depend mainly on the cipher algorithm used. The former can be as small as a single clock cycle if Prince a latency optimized block cipher is used, while the area overhead is 45 per cent for a commodity micro controller unit (MCU).

1 Introduction

Embedded devices especially when used in automation systems are becoming more and more often target of attacks. The modification of embedded systems software is extremely dangerous. Especially in cyber-physical systems (CPSs) such as energy distribution networks any penetration and modification can cause disasters. Common approaches cannot ensure that an embedded system runs the code that was initially deployed. Code injection attacks are feasible on any architecture. By using return-oriented programming (ROP) attacks [33] code can be injected even on Harvard architectures as shown in [17].

In order to prevent successful attacks and to detect alteration of the code deployed on the embedded devices quite some approaches have been researched in the last few years SWATT [32], SMART [15], etc. All these approaches share

The research leading to these results has received funding from the Federal Ministry of Education and Research (BMBF) under grant agreement No. 16 KIS0004.

© Institute for Computer Sciences, Social Informatics and Telecommunications Engineering 2015
B. Thuraisingham et al. (Eds.): SecureComm 2015, LNICST 164, pp. 97–115, 2015.
DOI: 10.1007/978-3-319-28865-9_6

a common drawback. They check whether the code originally deployed was changed or whether additional code was injected. Even if they work 100 per cent correct they cannot prevent malicious code from being executed, nor can they prevent ROP attacks. In this paper we present an approach we call intrinsic code attestation. The core idea is to execute encrypted instructions, so only instructions that are authorized can be executed. Consequently, no malicious code can be inserted. In addition we "chain" instructions so that a certain instruction can be executed only after its predecessor. This prevents ROP based attacks. As an important side effect enciphered code to be deployed on the embedded devices protects the code from being stolen by an adversary. We denote our approach as intrinsic code attestation (ICA). The main contributions of this paper are:

- Introduction of core principles of ICA, especially how chaining of instructions can be ensured for non-sequential program flows e.g. if jump instructions or branches are used.
- Discussion of simulation results that show on the one hand that our approach can be implemented with existing widely used micro controller unit (MCU) architectures and on the other hand that the performance penalty is a single clock cycle only.
- Thorough security analysis of the ICA approach including the discussion of collisions of the nonce used for instruction chaining in ICA and brute forcing encrypted instructions.

The rest of this paper is structured as follows. Section 2 details the ICA concept. Our security analysis is presented in section 3. The following section provides the implementation of ICA in an MSP430 simulation environment and for a 8-bit VLIW RISC processor. Related work is discussed in section 5, while section 6 and 7 present future work and conclusions, respectively.

2   Intrinsic Code Attestation

The core idea of intrinsic code attestation (ICA) is to ensure that only authorized instructions can be executed on a certain MCU and that also their sequence is fixed. The presented approach is based on a standard block cipher to provide a high security level. We use the block cipher in the counter mode (CTR) to overcome the block size limitation when encrypting sole instructions. The block cipher is parametrized by an individual program key (IPK) and an instruction individual key (IIK). The IPK guarantees that the program text cannot be read by an adversary to gather intellectual property (IP). The IIK is used to built an instruction chaining that ensures that instructions cannot be reordered or invoked from extrinsic program locations.

2.1   Instruction Chaining

Figure 1 illustrates the idea of a crypto-based instruction chaining. Information of instruction (n) are input of a cipher that decrypts instruction $(n + 1)$. In case of a manipulation of the program flow any out of order instruction is decrypted with wrong cipher inputs, which results in an illegal or at least an unpredictable instruction. Since an instruction chaining by using the instruction as input for the cipher strictly binds an instruction to its previous instruction, non-sequential program flows become infeasible. Due to such a restriction cannot be applied to real applications our chaining is based on additional information. Hence, we extended each instruction by an individual *nonce*, the IIK, that is encrypted in conjunction with the instruction. The nonce is used as input for the cipher to decrypt the succeeding instruction. Using individual nonces prevent a modification of the program flow similar to applying the instruction to cipher. However, in addition non-sequential program flows can be encrypted as well.

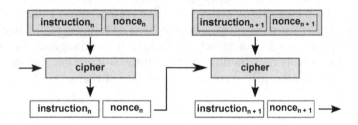

Fig. 1. An ICA can be enforced by a crypto-based instruction chaining so that an instruction cannot be decrypted without executing the previous one.

An insuperable program code encryption can only be guaranteed if the decryption unit is integrated in the processor's data path without any bypass. Hereby, each instruction must pass the decryption unit before its execution. Wrong key information will result in illegal or unpredictable instructions, which are passed to the instruction decoder and cause an illegal instruction trap or an unpredictable behavior. Therefore, the IPK and the IIK must be stored in a secure manner. The IPK storage will be illustrated in Section 4.3. The IIK is decrypted with an instruction and hold inside the decryption unit for decrypting the succeeding instruction. Any external access to the key is unnecessary and may not be implemented.

Conditional Jumps. A non-sequential program flow is generated by each conditional jump. As shown in Figure 2, a jump instruction has two possible successors. Due to dynamic program flow both predecessor instructions must be considered. Therefore, two identical IIKs are used to encrypt the jump instruction (*instrA*) and the instruction immediately before the jump target (*instrC*).

But by using two identical IIKs for one instruction a program flow modification becomes possible. It cannot be guaranteed that the program does not jump from instruction *instrC* to *instrB*. The remaining risk of such a modification is analyzed in Section 3.

Fig. 2. Conditional jumps require that both possible jump target (*instrB* and *instrD*) are encrypted with the same IIK (K_{instrB}).

Function Calls. Beside conditional jumps each function call generates a non-sequential code sequence as well. Figure 3 illustrates a call of a function by two different threads. Each caller attaches the nonce of the first callee instruction to its call instruction. This ensures that the considered function can only be called. Furthermore, each instruction just behind the call instruction must be encrypted by the nonce that is attached to the return of the callee. Although, this enforces that a return instruction cannot be used to jump to any instruction, as is used by ROP attacks, an attacker can modify the program flow to jump to any thread that calls the function. Although the instruction chaining reduces the attack vector significantly a remaining risk is still there.

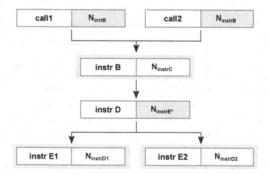

Fig. 3. Callers must attach the same nonce to the call instruction and instructions just after the call must be encrypted by a nonce attached to the return of the callee.

Strict binding of a callee to a caller makes dynamic function calls impossible. Therefore, function pointers and polymorphism cannot be used with ICA. However, this restriction can be mostly circumvented by using trampoline functions.

Asynchronous Events. On real processor the program execution flow can be interrupted by an asynchronous event. Such an event is a signal from a peripheral unit or an internal exception that needs immediate attention. Software includes service routines to deal with event. The interruption is temporary, the processor resumes to normal activity after finishing the service routine.

The ICA approach has to deal with asynchronous events to be suitable for real world applications. Due to that the asynchronous events can interrupt any instruction the nonce must be provided externally and the current nonce must be saved while handling the event. In case that nested events are allowed a nonce stack to store the current nonces is necessary. However, the maximum stack size is equal to the number of interrupts, which is usually small on embedded systems.

2.2   Instruction Key Expanding

Each instruction is encrypted with an individual nonce. Due to the fact that the suffix inflates the program size a minimal nonce must be chosen. But since the nonce is used as input of the block cipher it must be expanded to the size of the block cipher. In a simple way as shown in Figure 4 (a) the nonce can be padded to the block size with zeros.

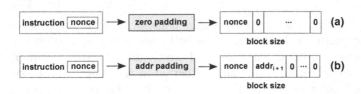

Fig. 4. IIK expanding by padding zeros to the nonce (a) or including the instruction address (b).

Since the nonce have no relation to the instruction address the enciphered program code can be used on any location. It can be circumvented by applying the instruction address to the cipher. Due to the decryption unit is integrated in the MCU's memory path the instruction address is available there. As shown in Figure 4 (b), the address can be appended to the nonce and only the remaining bits are padded by zeros. We discuss the advantage of such an instruction pinning in more detail in Section 3.

2.3   Instruction Size Fitting

Depending on the MCU's instruction set architecture (ISA) the block size of the chosen cipher does not need to be identical to the length of the instruction plus the nonce. Therefore, we use a symmetric block cipher in a CTR to generate a temporary instruction key (TIK) as shown in Figure 5. The XOR-operation uses the first n-bits of the TIK to decrypt the instruction and the nonce. Due to non-sequential code the counter is reseted with each instruction. Therefore, the TIK depends on the nonce and the address if used only.

If an instruction plus nonce is longer than a single cipher block the IIK is incremented to generate an additional TIK block. The cipher stream builds

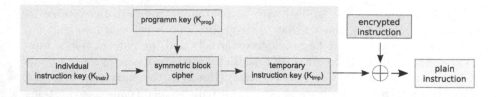

Fig. 5. Instructions are decrypted by using the CTR of a symmetric block cipher. The block cipher gets the IPK and a IIK to generate the TIK.

a TIK with a proper length. However, any additional block causes additional performance penalty, a block cipher should be chosen that has a suitable block size or encrypt speed.

3   Security Analysis

Due to it is difficult to quantify the security benefits of any given technology. The effects of unexploited vulnerabilities cannot be predicted and real-world attacks can be thwarted by trivial changes to those details. Therefore, our presented security argument is informal. A more substantial argument (or a proof) would require formal analysis and verification of the ICA hardware implementation. The security of the ICA approach is based on the following assertions:

A1 The TIK calculated by the memory decryption unit (MDU) cannot be forged. Since the TIK is the result of a strong block cipher with an adequate security level.
A2 The program key can be accessed only from within the MDU. This is guaranteed by the absence of physical lines to read the key outside.
A3 Physical and hardware-based attacks on the MDU are beyond the adversary's capabilities.
A4 The MDU cannot be bypassed since it decouples the instruction memory from the instruction decoder. All instructions must pass the MDU.
A5 The nonce cannot be replaced by a user defined value. The hardware guarantees that the nonce is directly read from the encrypted instruction memory.
A6 An instruction can be only decrypted with the correct nonce. The nonce and the instruction address are the initialization vector of the CTR block cipher.
A7 The program key update is forbidden or protected by a strong authentication scheme.
A8 Any erroneous decryption results in an unpredictable program behavior or leads to a hardware reset.
A9 The normal execution of an encrypted program should leak no information about the program key and the encrypted nonces.

Considering these assertions the system's security is mainly determined by the resources spent for the ICA implementation. Especially the nonce size and the ISA have a major impact on the remaining risk.

3.1   Remaining Risk

Due to our approach is mainly based on individual nonces, we focused our remaining risk analyze on attacks on the nonces as well as on the instruction chaining. We assume that a 16-bit nonce was chosen. It is a good compromise between minimal nonce size and memory overhead. In the following we discuss the effect of key collisions, brute-force attacks, and attacks based on ROP.

Instruction Key Collisions. In case of using all 16-bit nonces the number of TIKs is determined by the number of images of the block cipher function. When using the first 16-bit of a block cipher output with a block size larger than 16-bit the number of images is approximately $2^{16}(1 - e^{-1})$. Using the instruction address within that enlarges the input domain does not affect the number of images. Due to commodity 16-bit MCUs have an address space up to 22-bit TIK collisions cannot be avoided. On an architecture with 22-bit address space each TIK may be used up to 100 times.

However, from the perspective of security the reduced number of TIKs and their multiple used is harmless. Since an attacker does not know the IPK it cannot qualify the correct set of TIKs. The probability of guessing a precise nonce of an instruction remains 2^{-16}. Furthermore, in case of randomly spreading the nonces over all instructions the multiple use of a TIK does not increase the probability as well.

Cipher Instruction Search Attack. The idea behind a *cipher instruction search (CIS) attack* is presented by Kuhn [24]. It is based on a brute force attack on the enciphered machine instructions and then observing the CPU reaction. The adversary presents a large number of guessed encrypted machine instructions to the CPU to construct an enciphered program to gain more information or to provide cleartext access to the instruction memory.

For a CIS attack the target device must be connected to a programming device. We must assume that the device provides access to all processor registers except the MDU internal registers. Depending on the system architecture instruction memory may be non-volatile memory (flash) or RAM. Due to flash modifications are very complex and the low flash endurance, flash based attacks can be neglected. An architecture that executes instructions located in the RAM is much more vulnerable for CIS attacks. Depending on the speed of the programming device an attack can be done quite fast. At an MCU clock speed of 20 MHz a shot of a single instructions needs only few milliseconds. So brute forcing all 2^{16} alternatives takes only few seconds. Furthermore, the brute force strategy can applied to each instruction in the same way with the same effort. Hence, on a von-Neumann architecture with shared instruction and data memory, an enciphered program can be constructed in short time.

The success of a (CIS) attack can be significantly reduced on systems with larger instructions. Furthermore, adding the instruction address to the nonce pad prevents a copy of guessed program code and makes the reuse of an enciphered program code, which was constructed in a RAM, infeasible. Nevertheless, we assume that a gain or an update of the IPK is infeasible by guessing a program sequence if both are protected by additional schemes, which are not infected by that attack.

Multiple Return Points. The instruction chaining presented in Section 2 uses the nonce that was encrypted together with the previous instruction for decrypting the next instruction in a CTR wise fashion. Hence, for sequential code that does not include any branches, a unique nonce is used for encryption of each instruction. This uniqueness assures that only the legitimate previous instruction can be the predecessor of the current instruction. Any other instruction comes with a different nonce and will most likely propose a wrong TIK. That is because a good block cipher behaves similar to a random function. Since we use the first n bits of a block cipher output as the TIK, the probability that two given nonces propose the same TIK is approximately 2^{-n}. If a wrong TIK is used to decrypt an instruction this will result in an illegal or unpredictable instruction.

As soon as there are branches a nonce will be used multiple times, thus allowing an instruction to have multiple successors that can be decrypted with this nonce. This introduces the possibility of undesired modifications in the program flow: multiple instructions sharing a nonce are able to jump to each others successors. For example, in Figure 2 instruction *instrC* has a valid nonce for decrypting instruction *instrB*. Nevertheless, the number of instruction that might be jumped at is significantly reduced to the number of two.

A second risk occurs by legitimate jumps that might be taken when they are actually not allowed: the return instruction of a function might have multiple successors corresponding to multiple calling instructions. Although a jump to all these successors is legitimate in general, only one of these jumps should be taken at a certain point of time. Namely that one that returns to the instruction that was actually calling the function. The same obviously holds true for conditional jumps where both jumps are valid while only one of them should be taken at a certain point in time. Again, in both cases the attack vector is significantly reduced.

4   System Integration

To assess feasibility, practicality and impact of our approach we integrated it in the MSPsim. The MSPsim is a Java-based cycle accurate instruction set simulator (ISS) developed by the SICS [16]. It allows an execution of unmodified MSP430 firmwares. The ICA integration was done by implementing an additional Java module, which was bound to the instruction emulation module.

Beside the MSPsim extension we analyzed a more suitable tiny ISA and did deeper investigations on block ciphers and tool chains.

4.1   Secured MSP430

The MSP430 is a 16-bit MCU developed by Texas Instruments (TI). It uses a classical von-Neumann architecture with a shared data and program memory. The MCU is very popular in ultra low power applications and wireless sensor networks (WSNs). We used the MSP430 due to the availability of soft cores [20,28] and the MSPsim.

MSP430 Integration. All MSP430 instructions are structured in 16-bit words and the length of the instruction depends on the addressing mode. It differs from a single word up to four words. Therefore, the MSP430 instruction decoder performs multiple memory accesses within a single instruction. An integration of the MDU is shown in Figure 6. Each fetch is passed to the MDU and processed separately.

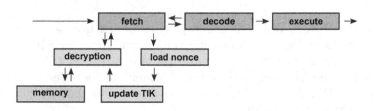

Fig. 6. The MSP430 performs multiple fetches within a single instruction, which must be separately decrypted. Finally the nonce is loaded and the TIK is updated.eps

The nonce is loaded automatically as an additional instruction word after loading all words of an instruction. We must only extend the instruction decoder to initiate the TIK update. The operation can be executed in parallel with the final instruction phases.

Instruction Encryption. Due to the variable instruction size the instruction encryption must be done in three steps. Listing 1 shows assembler text of a short loop program. The program starts at address 0x4000 and loops between the instructions at address 0x4006 and 0x4008. All instructions beside the move instruction use a single word.

```
00004000 <__ctors_end >:
    4000:  31 40 80 02   mov  #640,    r1
    4004:  02 43         clr  r2
00004006 <LOOP>:
    4006:  12 53         inc  r2
    4008:  fe 3f         jmp  \$−2
```

Listing 1. Assembler program of a simple loop implemented on an MSP430.

The Listing 2 shows the instructions of Listing 1 extended by the nonces. We chose 16-bit nonces driven by the architecture of the MSP430. Since each nonce consumes two bytes of the address space the instruction addresses were changed. Hence, the jump instruction at address 0x400e had to be adapted accordingly.

```
00004000 <__ctors_end >:
  4000: 31 40 80 02 00 01
  4006: 02 43 00 02
0000400a <LOOP>:
  400a: 12 53 00 03
  400e: fd 3f 00 04
```

Listing 2. Listing 1 extended by the nonce. Due to the new instruction length the jump instruction had to be adapted.

In a final step the program is encrypted. Due to the CTR the size of the instruction has not to be changed and the encrypted instructions can be placed at their origin addresses.

Interrupt Handling. When an interrupt is requested from a peripheral the MSP430 executes at least the following: the currently executed instruction is completed, the program counter (PC) and the status register (SR) are pushed onto the stack, the SR is cleared, and the content of the interrupt vector is loaded into the PC. The next instruction continues with the interrupt service routine (ISR) at the given address.

The interrupt processing is extended by storing the current nonce inside the MDU and providing a predefined ISR nonce. Afterwards, the TIK can go on similar to the normal program execution. The ISR terminates with the instruction *reti*, which restores the PC, the SR and the instruction nonce. Since the MSP430 does not feature an *in interrupt flag* the ICA needs to be fully integrated in the interrupt logic to detect interrupts.

For each interrupt a static nonce is needed. The current implementation uses a single nonce for all interrupts. The nonce is stored inside the MDU and update is handled similar to the IPK.

4.2   Secured tinyVLIW8

The tinyVLIW8 is a size-optimized soft-core processor for deeply embedded control tasks [36]. We analyzed the tinyVLIW8 soft-core processor in addition to the MSP430 to evaluate the suitability of our approach on different system architectures. In contrast to the MSP430 the tinyVLIW8 features a Reduced Instruction Set Computer (RISC) architecture with a uniform instruction format and a Harvard architecture with a dedicated instruction, data, and IO memory. The processor executes two 16-bit instructions coded in a single 32-bit instruction word in parallel. Each instruction address points to a 32-bit instruction word. Hence, the nonce can be easily added by widening the instruction memory. Any adaptations to instruction address are not necessary.

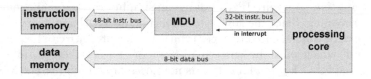

Fig. 7. The architecture of the tinyVLIW8 allows a placing of the MDU between the instruction memory and the processing core. Due to the dedicated data memory is not encrypted, it can be used unchanged.

Furthermore, due to the Harvard architecture a dedicated nonce load is not necessary. Instead the data bus can be split into a lower 32-bit bus for the processing core and additional n-bit bus for the nonce. Figure 7 shows a placement of the MDU. Only the instruction bus must be routed via the MDU. The data memory can be connected unchanged to the processing core. The interrupt handling of the tinyVLIW8 is similar to one of the MSP430. On an interrupt request the current instruction is completed and the PC is loaded from the interrupt vector table. But the processor provides an *in interrupt flag* that can be used to easily detect an interrupt service.

The fixed instruction size of the processor simplifies the integration of our approach in a significant manner. Furthermore, 32-bit instruction are much less vulnerable for CIS attacks. Without deeper investigations we are convinced that most of the RISC architectures with a uniform instruction length allow a similar integration. Possible candidates are the Leon2 or ARMv7 cores.

4.3   Secure Key Storage

The primary target of an attacker may be the program key of the device. Clearly, it cannot be stored in the systems memory, since malware code can easily access it and use it to encrypt additional malicious code. Therefore, the key is stored inside the MDU and readable from there only. However, installing new firmware images requires an export or import of the symmetric key. While a public key implementation could simplify the key management significantly, it comes with an unacceptable overhead. Hence, we propose three different approaches for management of a symmetric key: one-time programmable (OTP) memory, password protection, and physical unclonable function (PUF).

OTP Memory. An OTP memory is a memory where the setting of each bit is locked by a fuse or an antifuse. The memory can be written only once. It is possible after fabrication without any special equipment. Hence, the key can be set by the device owner before the first deployment. External read lines are not necessary, so that the key is only externally writable. But an OTP based key cannot be updated later. In case of a key revealing the device becomes insecure and must be replaced.

Password Protection. A secure IPK update can simplify the key management in case of a key revealing. Since the key is stored inside the MDU a memory mapped IO interface can be implemented to access the key. The interface can be protected by a password, which must be written in-front of the new key to unlock the memory mapped IO. A key read function is not necessary. Similar to the MSP430 boot-strap loader protection [38], the password can be stored within the firmware image. Because the firmware image is decrypted the password is protected by the current program key. A special protected memory is not necessary.

PUF. A very high security level can be provided by a local re-encryption of the firmware image. The firmware can be deployed with a shared program key, which can be stored inside the current firmware image similar to the password, described above. After deployment the image is re-encrypted with a device specific key on the device itself. Such a key can be based on a PUF, which provide true random numbers [21]. The PUF-based IPK must never leave the MDU. Such a re-encrypted firmware is bounded to the device, which prevents any firmware copy or off-line attacks on alternative devices.

4.4 Design Size and Speed Estimation

Due to using the block cipher in a CTR the instruction decryption works in two steps. First, the TIK must be generated by loading the nonce and running a block decryption. Second, the TIK is combined with the encrypted instruction by using an XOR-operation. As shown in Figure 8, the XOR-operation works in parallel with the data fetch and does not consume any additional clock cycles. However, the block cipher cannot be started before decoding the last instruction word and loading the nonce. Some cycles may run in parallel with block decryption, but the fetch of the next instruction must be delayed until the block decryption is finished. Hence, the instruction execution time is strongly coupled with the performance of block cipher.

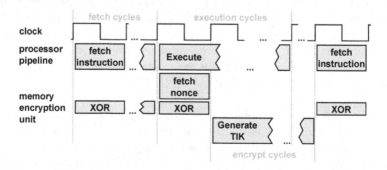

Fig. 8. The TIK can be generated in parallel with the execution phase of the processor's pipeline. But the fetch of the next instruction must be block until the TIK generation has been finished.

On the MSP430 few instruction are coded in four words. Hence, a 64-bit cipher needs two block operations for those instructions. Depending on the speed of the block cipher the instruction fetch may be interrupted twice. Therefore, on such a system the cipher speed becomes more significant.

We used the AES in the MSPsim extension. Therefore, we analyzed the AES algorithm as a candidate for a hardware implementation first. Table 1 gives an overview about the design size of the algorithm and the number of cycles for a single block decryption on a commodity FPGA. We analyzed a size-optimized and speed-optimized version. However, both were inadequate. The speed-optimized version need 12 clock cycles and is 8 times larger than our tinyVLIW8 processor (see Table 2). Therefore, we analyzed the PRINCE algorithm next [8]. The algorithm has a block size of 64 bits and is hardware-optimized. The size-optimized version needs 750 LCs only and is faster than the speed-optimized version of the AES. Furthermore, the PRINCE algorithm can be implemented in a fully unrolled version with a moderate design size enlargement. It needs 1.9 kLCs only and decrypts a block immediately. The maximum clock speed is limited by the longest logical path. In simulations we could measure a maximum end-to-end delay of 64,9 ns, which is equivalent to clock speed of 30.8 MHz.

Table 1. Design size of block ciphers (measured with Quartus II 11.0 Design Suite).

Cipher	Cycles	logical cells (LCs)	Regs	Fmax
AES [41]	60	2,403	428	53.7 MHz
AES [40]	12	8,855	792	104.9 MHz
PRINCE [8]	11	750	70	159.1 MHz
PRINCE (unrolled) [8]	0	1,875	0	30.8 MHz

Due to the power consumption is tightly coupled with the design size of the MCU the ICA extension must be based on a tiny cipher implementation. To evaluate the size impact of the block cipher, we analyzed soft-core MCUs on an FPGA. Table 2 gives an overview about the results. The larges MCU has a size less than 10 kLC and features a SPARC V8 ISA. The commodity MSP430 needs 2.8 kLC with a 16-bit ISA and 4.1 kLC with a 20-bit ISA. The size-optimized tinyVLIW8 soft-core needs around 1 kLC only.

We chose the tinyVLIW8 soft-core and the unrolled PRINCE version for a prototype implementation. Table 3 shows the sizes of the processor entities. The MDU entity includes the PRINCE implementation, the CTR, interrupt handling and the instruction decryption. Is quite smaller than the sole one, which is reasoned by absence of the external FPGA pins. Furthermore, we integrated a memory-mapped IO interface for a program key update. We can see, that the MDU overhead is 156 per cent for the tinyVLIW8 processor. A similar implementation for an MSP430 will result in an overhead of just about 44 per cent.

---

[1] The Leon2 design size could not be measured on Cyclone II, it was taken from [1].

Table 2. Design size of soft-core MCUs (measured with Quartus II 11.0 Design Suite).

Soft-core	LCs	FPGA
Leon2 [1]	9,299	Altera Cyclone[1].
openMSP [20]	2,841	Altera Cyclone II
IHP430X [28]	4,107	Altera Cyclone II
TinyVLIW8 [36]	1,162	Altera Cyclone II

The overhead is mainly driven by the cipher design size. The MDU, without cipher, needs only 126 LCs and 165 registers.

Table 3. Design size of tinyVLIW8 processor extended by the ICA approach (measured with Quartus II 11.0 Design Suite).

Entity	Design	Core	MDU	Peripherals	Dbg.-Inf.
LCs	2979	818	1817	234	110
Registers	558	224	165	113	56

4.5 Compiler Tool Chain Extension

The generation of an encrypted firmware is split in two steps. First, all instructions of the firmware are extended by the nonce. For this purpose the firmware must be analyzed to identify non-sequential instruction sequences. On an MSP430 furthermore, all jumps and calls must be adapted to new addresses. In a second step the instructions are encrypted.

The program analysis to identify non-sequential code can be done on the final firmware image or as an integrated step of the build process. Depending on the software and ICA the first approach could be complex. Therefore, we analyzed common build chains to identify possible candidates for an extension. The software of an MSP430 can be build with the GNU as well as the TI compiler. But both are not designed to be easy to extend. A more promising approach is to extent a modular build chain as provided by the LLVM project [25]. The LLVM tool chain splits the build process in a front-end step, an unrestricted number of optimization steps, and a back-end step. The two steps of the ICA encryption can be integrated as replacement of the origin back-end step.

A similar approach is provided by the CoMet tool [39]. CoMet uses any front-end compiler and can transform any intermediate code. In contrast to LLVM, based on intermediate codes a program can be simulated with the integrated simulator. Due to its flexibility and its simulation capability we decided to use it to generate the encrypted firmware.

5   Related Work

Approaches for a secure boot strap architectures to verify the program start [4] and stack protection schemes to prevent program flow modifications [18,34] work locally as well as with foresight, but leak a dynamic verification of the program code. An enforcement that a software follows a path determined ahead of time is provide in the work of Abadi et al. [2,3]. The control flow integrity (CFI) approach shares many ideas with methods that attempt to discern program execution deviation from a prescribed static control flow graph (CFG) [27,31,42]. While these works are focused on fault-tolerance, the CFI approached concerns with a persistent adversary that is able to change data memory, e.g. by exploiting program vulnerabilities. It ensures that an attacker can never execute instructions outside the legal CFG. But CFI inserts inlined labels and checks, which requires a program code modifications at run-time and does not provide any program code integrity. Furthermore, we are convinced that a secure approach must provide a dynamic program flow as well as a program code verification, which can be provided by none of these approaches.

Device attestation is the process of verifying the local state of a device. Previously proposed attestation techniques are mainly based on remote attestation protocols, where an external prover is used to verify the internal state of a device. These approaches can be differentiated in software-based [13,22,29,32], locally assisted by specialized secure hardware [15,30,35], and cluster-based protocols [23]. Though, the authors of software-based techniques argue that locally assisted approaches require specialized hardware, these approaches have been subject to successful attacks [10] and provide thus a disputable security level. Hardware-based approaches, such those based on local read-only memory [15,30], provide a secure anchor, which helps to overcome basic drawbacks of the software approaches. Beside binary attestation property-based attestation protocols are proposed [11,22]. These protocols are also assisted by specialized hardware and allow a blind verification and revocation of mappings between properties and configurations. Nevertheless, all these approaches work after the fact. If an adversary has successfully injected malicious code the victim operates out of its specification until a remote attestation detects the misbehavior.

Program code integrity and confidentiality is key in digital rights management and smartcard systems. Specialized processors with an integrated MDU are already state of the art. The DS5002FP and DS5240 secure microprocessors presented by Best [5–7] provide an execution of enciphered firmwares. But reasoned by the weakness of the used cipher the system can be broken by a CIS attack [24]. A security enhanced MMU (SMU) based on TDES is presented by Gilmont et al. [19]. In contrast to Best the approach uses the TDES cipher to encrypt the instruction memory. The work of Elbaz et al. gives an overview about hardware-based memory-bus encryption techniques [14]. It illustrates and compares the patent of Candelore [9], the SMU [19], the Xom approach of Lie et al. [26], and the AEGIS project [37]. The work of Chen et al. [12] presents a software-based approach, which uses a supervisor instance to decrypt instructions. But all these approaches are focused on memory encrypted to prevent illegal copies or modifications of the static program code image. Although most of these approaches include the instruction address none of them check the program flow. Therefore, ROP attacks at run-time are still possible and a secure program execution or a program code attestation are addressed by none of them.

6   Future Work

In a first prove of concept integration the tinyVLIW8 soft-core processor was extended by our approach. Since the processor is quite limited and not used in any common system an extension of the MSP430 is planned. Due to the von-Neumann architecture and the variable instruction format a more complex implementation of the MDU is necessary. Nevertheless, we are convinced that the logical overhead is quite moderate and the presented approach is still suitable.

Beside a hardware integration of our approach in an MSP430 soft-core an adaptation of the nonce will be investigated. The current approach causes a significant memory overhead on an MSP430. Each instruction expanded by a nonce gets an address of the limited address space. But a nonce is necessary for non-sequential instructions only. Therefore, we investigate the building of instruction blocks instead of single instruction as well as the usage of the instruction as nonce itself. But both approaches may have its own drawbacks and must be analyzed carefully.

In this paper we did not consider side-channel attacks, but they are highly interesting. Hence, we will investigate these effects on FPGA as well as on silicon devices with different MCU cores. Especially the current separation of the code execution and the block encryption may be an ideal entry point for side-channel attacks and must be analyzed.

7   Conclusion

In this paper we introduced the concept of intrinsic code attestation (ICA), shown its resistance against a wide variety of attacks and evaluated its overhead. ICA allows to execute encrypted instructions that are even depending on their predecessors. These features ensure that only authorized code can be executed. Decrypting non authorized instructions does not result in valid instructions. The chaining prevents reordering of instructions to implement an attack by "re-using" authorized instructions. These features allow a continuous protection of the devices, which sets our approach apart from earlier approaches that detect attacks only after the fact. Our simulations show that ICA comes at reasonable cost. The performance penalty can be as small as a single clock cycle. The related area overhead is then about 45 per cent for an MSP430 clone. The latter is somewhat significant if production cost is taken into account. But, if applications such automation control of energy distribution networks or similar sensitive applications are considered, the additional cost of the MCU are affordable and by far cheaper than costs resulting from a successful attack.

References

1. Running Leon2 on the Altera Nios Development Board, Cyclone Edition
2. Abadi, M., Budiu, M., Erlingsson, Ú., Ligatti, J.: Control-flow integrity. In: ACM Conference on Computer and Communication Security (CCS), number MSR-TR-2005-18, Alexandria, VA, pp. 340–353, November 2005
3. Abadi, M., Budiu, M., Erlingsson, Ú., Ligatti, J.: A theory of secure control flow. In: Lau, K.-K., Banach, R. (eds.) ICFEM 2005. LNCS, vol. 3785, pp. 111–124. Springer, Heidelberg (2005)
4. Arbaugh, W.A., Farber, D.J., Smith, J.M.: A secure and reliable bootstrap architecture. In: Proceedings of the IEEE Symposium on Security and Privacy, SP 1997, pp. 65. IEEE Computer Society, Washington, DC (1997)
5. Best, R.M.: Microprocessor for executing enciphered programs (1979)
6. Best, R.M.: Crypto microprocessor for executing enciphered programs (1981)
7. Best, R.M.: Crypto microprocessor that executes enciphered programs (2004)
8. Borghoff, J., et al.: PRINCE - a low-latency block cipher for pervasive computing applications - extended abstract. In: Wang, X., Sako, K. (eds.) Advances in Cryptology – ASIACRYPT 2012. LNCS, vol. 7658, pp. 208–225. Springer, Heidelberg (2012)
9. Candelore, B., Sprunk, E.: Secure processor with external memory using block chaining and block re-ordering (2000)
10. Castelluccia, C., Francillon, A., Perito, D., Soriente, C.: On the difficulty of software-based attestation of embedded devices. In: Proceedings of the 16th ACM Conference on Computer and Communications Security, CCS 2009, pp. 400–409. ACM, New York (2009)
11. Chen, L., Landfermann, R., Löhr, H., Rohe, M., Sadeghi, A.-R., Stüble, C.: A protocol for property-based attestation. In: Proceedings of the First ACM Workshop on Scalable Trusted Computing, STC 2006. ACM, New York (2006)
12. Chen, X. Dick, R.P., Choudhary, A.: Operating system controlled processor-memory bus encryption. In: Proceedings of the Conference on Design, Automation and Test in Europe, DATE 2008, pp. 1154–1159. ACM, New York (2008)
13. Deng, J., Han, R., Mishra, S.: Secure code distribution in dynamically programmable wireless sensor networks. In: Proceedings of the 5th International Conference on Information Processing in Sensor Networks, IPSN 2006, pp. 292–300. ACM, New York (2006)
14. Elbaz, R., Torres, L., Sassatelli, G., Guillemin, P., Anguille, C., Bardouillet, M., Buatois, C., Rigaud, J.B.: Hardware engines for bus encryption: a survey of existing techniques. IEEE (2005)
15. Eldefrawy, K., Francillon, A., Perito, D., Tsudik, G.: SMART: secure and minimal architecture for (establishing a dynamic) root of trust. In: Proceedings of 19th Annual Network and Distributed System Security Symposium, NDSS 2012, San Diego, CA, USA, February 2012
16. Eriksson, J., Dunkels, A., Finne, N., Österlind, F., Voigt, T., Tsiftes, N.: Demo abstract: MSPsim - an extensible simulator for MSP430-equipped sensor boards. In: Proceedings of the 5th European Conference on Wireless Sensor Networks (EWSN 2008), Bologna, Italy, January 2008
17. Francillon, A., Castelluccia, C.: Code injection attacks on harvard-architecture devices. In: Proceedings of the 15th ACM Conference on Computer and Communications Security, CCS 2008, pp. 15–26. ACM, New York (2008)

18. Francillon, A., Perito, D., Castelluccia, C.: Defending embedded systems against control flow attacks. In: Proceedings of the First ACM Workshop on Secure Execution of Untrusted Code, SecuCode 2009, pp. 19–26. ACM, New York (2009)
19. Gilmont, T., Legat, J.-D., Quisquater, J.-J.: Enhancing security in the memory management unit. In: Proceedings of the 25th EUROMICRO Conference, vol. 1, pp. 449–456. IEEE Computer Society (1999)
20. Girard, O.: openMSP:: Overview (2014)
21. Holcomb, D.E., Burleson, W.P., Fu, K.: Power-up sram state as an identifying fingerprint and source of true random numbers. IEEE Trans. Comput. **58**(9), 1198–1210 (2009)
22. Kil, C., Sezer, E., Azab, A., Ning, P., Zhang, X.: Remote attestation to dynamic system properties: towards providing complete system integrity evidence. In: IEEE/IFIP International Conference on Dependable Systems Networks, DSN 2009, pp. 115–124, June 2009
23. Krauß, C., Stumpf, F., Eckert, C.: Detecting node compromise in hybrid wireless sensor networks using attestation techniques. In: Stajano, F., Meadows, C., Capkun, S., Moore, T. (eds.) ESAS 2007. LNCS, vol. 4572, pp. 203–217. Springer, Heidelberg (2007)
24. Kuhn, M.G.: Instruction search attack on the bus-encryption security microcontroller ds5002fp. IEEE Transactions on Computer-Aided Design of Integrated Circuits and Systems **47**, 1153–1157 (1998)
25. Lattner, C., Adve, V.: LLVM: a compilation framework for lifelong program analysis and transformation. In: Proceedings of the International Symposium on Code Generation and Optimization: Feedback-directed and Runtime Optimization, CGO 2004, p. 75. IEEE Computer Society, Washington, DC (2004)
26. Lie, D.: Architectural support for copy and tamper resistant software. Architectural Support for Programming Languages and Operating Systems, November 2000
27. Oh, N., Shirvani, P.P., McCluskey, E.J.: Control-flow checking by software signatures. IEEE Transactions on Reliability **51**(1), 111–122 (2002)
28. Panic, G., Basmer, T., Schrape, O., Peter, S., Vater, F., Tittelbach-Helmrich, K.: Sensor node processor for security applications. In: Proceedings of 18th IEEE International Conference on Electronics, Circuits and Systems, ICECS 2011, Beirut, Lebanon, pp. 81–84, December 2011
29. Park, T., Shin, K.G.: Soft tamper-proofing via program integrity verification in wireless sensor networks. IEEE Trans. on Mobile Computing **4**(3), May 2005
30. Perito, D., Tsudik, G.: Secure code update for embedded devices via proofs of secure erasure. In: Gritzalis, D., Preneel, B., Theoharidou, M. (eds.) ESORICS 2010. LNCS, vol. 6345, pp. 643–662. Springer, Heidelberg (2010)
31. Reis, G.A., Chang, J., Vachharajani, N., Rangan, R., August, D.I.: Swift: software implemented fault tolerance. In: Proceedings of the International Symposium on Code Generation and Optimization, CGO 2005, pp. 243–254. IEEE Computer Society, Washington, DC (2005)
32. Seshadri, A., Perrig, A., Doorn, L.V., Khosla, P.: SWATT: SoftWare-based ATTestation for embedded devices. In: Proceedings of the IEEE Symposium on Security and Privacy, Oakland, CA, USA (2004)
33. Shacham, H.: The geometry of innocent flesh on the bone: return-into-libc without function calls (on the x86). In: Proceedings of the 14th ACM Conference on Computer and Communications Security, CCS 2007, New York, NY, USA (2007)

34. Shacham, H., Page, M., Pfaff, B., Goh, E.-J., Modadugu, N., Boneh, D.: On the effectiveness of address-space randomization. In: Proceedings of the 11th ACM Conference on Computer and Communications Security, CCS 2004, pp. 298–307. ACM, New York (2004)
35. Spinellis, D.: Reflection as a mechanism for software integrity verification. ACM Trans. Inf. Syst. Secur. **3**(1), 51–62 (2000)
36. Stecklina, O., Methfessel, M.: A tiny scale VLIW processor for real-time constrained embedded control tasks. In: Proceedings of the 17th Euromicro Conference on Digital Systems Design, DSD 2014, Verona, Italy, August 2014
37. Suh, G.E., O'Donnell, C.W., Sachdev, I., Devadas, S.: Design and implementation of the aegis singlechip secure processor using physical random functions. Technical report, MIT CSAIL, November 2004
38. Texas Instruments, Dallas, TX, USA. MSP430 Programming via the bootstrap loader (BSL), slau319l edition, September 2014
39. Urban, R., Schölzel, M., Vierhaus, H.T.: Entwicklungsumgebung fr den compilerzentrierten Mikroprozessorentwurf (CoMet). In: Tagungsband Dresdner Arbeitstagung Schaltungs- und Systementwurf, DASS 2014. Fraunhofer Verlag (2014)
40. Usselmann, R.: AES (Rijndael) IP Core:: Overview (2013)
41. Vater, F., Langendörfer, P.: An Area Efficient Realisation of AES for Wireless Devices. it - Information Technology **49**, 188–193 (2007)
42. Venkatasubramanian, R., Hayes, J., Murray, B.: Low-cost on-line fault detection using control flow assertions. In: Proceedings of the 9th IEEE Conference on On-Line Testing Symposium, IOLTS 2003, pp. 137–143, July 2003

Defeating Kernel Driver Purifier

Jidong Xiao[1]($\boxtimes$), Hai Huang[2], and Haining Wang[3]

[1] College of William and Mary, Williamsburg, VA 23185, USA
jxiao@email.wm.edu
[2] IBM T.J. Watson Research Center, Hawthorne, NY 10532, USA
[3] University of Delaware, Newark, DE 19716, USA

Abstract. Kernel driver purification is a technique used for detecting and eliminating malicious code embedded in kernel drivers. Ideally, only the benign functionalities remain after purification. As many kernel drivers are distributed in binary format, a kernel driver purifier is effective against existing kernel rootkits. However, in this paper, we demonstrate that an attacker is able to defeat such purification mechanisms through two different approaches: (1) by exploiting self-checksummed code or (2) by avoiding calling kernel APIs. Both approaches would allow arbitrary code to be injected into a kernel driver. Based on the two proposed offensive schemes, we implement prototypes of both types of rootkits and validate their efficacy through real experiments. Our evaluation results show that the proposed rootkits can defeat the current purification techniques. Moreover, these rootkits retain the same functionalities as those of real world rootkits, and only incur negligible performance overhead.

1 Introduction

Modern operating systems are often divided into a base kernel and various loadable kernel modules. Kernel drivers are often loaded into the kernel space as modules. The ability to quickly load and unload these modules makes driver upgrade effortless, as the new code can take an immediate effect without rebooting the machine. While the base kernel is trusted, kernel drivers are sometimes released by third-party vendors (i.e., untrusted) in binary format. This creates a problem as it is much more difficult to detect malicious code at the binary level than at the source level. Therefore, kernel drivers have been heavily exploited for hosting malicious code in the past. Sony's infamous XCP rootkit in 2005 [1,22] and its USB device driver rootkit in 2007 [18] have exemplified this risk. In addition, kernel drivers, which constitute 70% of modern operating system's code base [16],are a significant source of software bugs [7,10], making them substantially more vulnerable to various malicious attacks than the base kernel.

During an attack, once an attacker gains root access, rootkits are then installed to hide their track and provide backdoor access. Rootkits normally hook to the kernel and modify its data structures such as system call table, task list, interrupt descriptor table, and virtual file system handlers. Rootkits can be either installed as a separate kernel module, or injected into an existing kernel module. To protect against rootkits, different defense mechanisms have

© Institute for Computer Sciences, Social Informatics and Telecommunications Engineering 2015
B. Thuraisingham et al. (Eds.): SecureComm 2015, LNICST 164, pp. 116–134, 2015.
DOI: 10.1007/978-3-319-28865-9_7

been proposed and can be categorized into two basic approaches: kernel rootkit detection and kernel module isolation. In the former, various detection frameworks are created using either an extra device to monitor system memory [23] or virtual machine introspection techniques [9,15]. And in the latter, strict isolation techniques are introduced to further isolate kernel modules from the base kernel [5,30].

While the idea of enhancing the isolation of kernel drivers has been extensively studied in the past, it has not yet been widely adopted by mainstream operating systems. One of the key reasons is that it involves too much re-implementation effort. Instead of isolating kernel drivers, safeguarding a kernel driver itself looks more promising. As kernel drivers run at the same privilege level as the base kernel, one can achieve this goal by detecting and eliminating malicious code from kernel drivers before they are loaded into the kernel space. This technique is called kernel driver purification. Based on this design principle, Gu et al. [11] proposed and implemented a kernel driver purification framework, which aims to detect malicious/undesirable logic in a kernel driver and eliminate it without impairing the driver's normal functionalities. Their experimental results demonstrate that this technique can purify kernel drivers infected by various real world rootkits. However, we observe that there are two approaches which attackers can employ to defeat such a technique. The first approach uses self-checksum code to protect malicious kernel API calls, and the second approach is to simply avoid using kernel API calls altogether when writing a rootkit. We show that both approaches can effectively defeat current kernel driver purifiers.

The major contributions of our work are summarized as follows:

- We first present a self-checksum based rootkit that is able to evade the detection of current kernel driver purifiers. While self-checksum has long been proposed as a way to protect benign programs, as far as we know, we are the first to use it for hiding kernel rootkits. We also develop a compiler level tool, with which, attackers can automatically re-write existing rootkits and convert them into self-checksum based variants that are resistant to kernel driver purifiers.

- We present another approach of creating a more stealthy rootkit, which avoids using kernel API calls. While our first approach attempts to protect malicious kernel API calls from being removed by kernel driver purifiers, this new type of rootkit demonstrates that most kernel API calls can be avoided, and thus making the kernel driver purifier completely ineffective.

- We evaluate the functionality and performance of both rootkits. Our experimental results show that the presented rootkits maintain the same set of functionalities as most real world rootkits have and only incur minor performance overhead.

2   Background

Kernel drivers have always been a major source of kernel bugs and vulnerabilities, and improving their reliability has drawn significant attentions from the

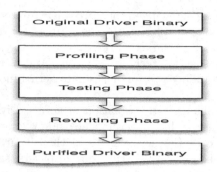

Fig. 1. Overview of kernel driver purification

research community. The kernel driver purification technique has been shown to effectively sanitize kernel drivers infected by existing rootkits. In this section, we present a brief overview of the kernel driver purification technique. The design principle of kernel driver purification is based on two observations. First, malicious/undesirable logic embedded within a kernel driver is normally orthogonal to the driver's base functionalities; second, its malicious goal is mainly achieved by interacting with the base kernel via kernel API invocations.

Figure 1 illustrates how a kernel driver purifier works at a high level with three different phases: profiling, testing, and rewriting.

- In the profiling phase, test cases are selected to exercise the common code paths of the kernel driver, where all kernel API invocations and return values are recorded. One key technique used in this phase is called driver-kernel interaction tracking. To record the kernel API invocations and return values, it is crucial to detect the transitions between the driver and the kernel code. This is achieved by monitoring the program counter: if the current basic block is within the driver's memory space but the previous basic block does not, it indicates that the control flow is transitioned from the kernel into the driver, and vice versa. Exploiting these observations, one can track all the transitions between the driver and the kernel code.

- In the testing phase, a subset of the kernel API invocations detected from the profiling phase are removed. If all the test cases complete successfully, these kernel API invocations can be viewed as not affecting the correct execution of the driver code, and therefore, they are marked as non-critical. If any test fails or the system crashes/halts/reboots, a divide-and-conquer approach is then used to narrow down the offending kernel API invocation. In the end, a list of non-critical kernel API invocations and their addresses are noted.

- In the rewriting phase, those non-critical kernel API invocations are removed from the binary kernel driver, and a new binary file, i.e., the purified driver binary file, is generated for use.

The above procedure ensures that malicious logic is removed while benign logic is maintained in the newly generated kernel driver. Although there are several limitations to this approach, including test coverage, false positives of the removed kernel API invocations, etc., the approach has been proven [11] to be very effective in purifying trojaned drivers that have been infected by various real world rootkits.

However, the two fundamental assumptions of this approach, i.e., (1) the removal of kernel API calls made by the malicious code will not affect the base functionality of the kernel driver and (2) rootkits have to call kernel APIs to achieve its malicious goals, are challengeable. Although they might be true for existing rootkits, we will show that generic enhancements to these rootkits will void these assumptions, and thus, rendering the purification process ineffective.

3   Attack Model

In this section, we present our attack methods for defeating kernel driver purifier. We will use KBeast [14] as an example as it has been widely used in case studies in the past [28,32]. KBeast is a Linux kernel rootkit that hijacks system calls, and it allows attackers to provide their own system call functions. By doing so, attackers can hide malicious kernel modules, files, directories, processes, sockets, and active network connections. Moreover, KBeast provides keystroke logging, anti-kill, anti-delete, and anti-remove functions.

Below we show a snippet of KBeast's code, which is the malicious version of the *unlink* system call. This function executes the real sys_unlink call when removing normal files and directories, but denies those requests that attempt to remove malicious files and directories.

```
1 asmlinkage int h4x_unlink(const char __user *pathname) {
2 int r;
3 char *kbuf=(char*)kmalloc(256,GFP_KERNEL);
4 copy_from_user(kbuf,pathname,255);
5 if(strstr(kbuf,_H4X0R_)||strstr(kbuf,KBEAST)){
6   kfree(kbuf);
7   return -EACCES;
8 }
9
10  r=(*o_unlink)(pathname);
11  kfree(kbuf);
12  return r;
}
```

The code above performs the following operations. Line 1: the start of the function definition. Line 2 to Line 4: allocate a memory buffer and use that memory buffer to store the pathname of a file. Line 5 to Line 8: compare the pathname with some predefined values to determine whether or not the file/directory in the request is malicious, and if so, return and release the memory buffer. Line 10: for any other ordinary files, invoke the original system call, i.e., sys_unlink. Line 11 to Line 12: free the memory buffer and return. A driver purifier would remove the kernel API calls such as kmalloc(), copy_from_user(), strstr(), and kfree() used by the malicious code. When these function calls are removed, the rootkit would lose its functionality partially or even completely. Therefore, from the attacker's perspective, it is important to protect these calls from being removed, or implement the rootkit without calling these kernel functions.

3.1 Self-Checksum Based Rootkit

We first present a self-checksum based approach to protect kernel API calls in a rootkit from being purified. To do so, there are at least two different strategies we can employ.

The first strategy is more straightforward, which is to add a conditional statement after each kernel API invocation. The conditional statement would test whether or not the preceding kernel API invocation is executed. It does nothing if the call is executed as expected. However, if the call is not executed (i.e., dynamically removed by a kernel driver purifier), it will trigger something abnormal, such as crashing the system or causing other types of failures that would result in the test cases to fail.

However, we found that it is very challenging to track whether or not a kernel API function is called. This is because a kernel driver purifier can store the return value of each kernel API invocation, and for each removed API function invocation, it could fill the stored return value in the EAX register as if the function was invoked and returned. Thus, we cannot determine if the function is really called by checking the return value.

The key idea of our proposed approach is that when a kernel module is loaded into the kernel, a special module initialization function will automatically get called, and within this function, we embed the checksum code that computes the checksum for each of the module's functions. The pre-computed checksums are then stored in memory. When a malicious function is invoked, we can re-calculate the checksum and compare it with the stored value. By doing so, any modification against h4x_unlink() will be detected, and we can trigger a system crash (or some other abnormal behaviors). One might think that this is a denial-of-service attack, but in fact, it is not. The reason is that this attack is only mounted at the testing phase of a kernel driver purifier tool, not at a real production scenario.

Using the approach we presented, the re-generated h4x_unlink() function looks like the following:

```
1 asmlinkage int h4x_unlink(const char __user *pathname) {
2   int r;
3   char *kbuf=(char*)kmalloc(256,GFP_KERNEL);
4   copy_from_user(kbuf,pathname,255);
5   if(strstr(kbuf,_H4X0R_)||strstr(kbuf,KBEAST)){
6       kfree(kbuf);
7       if(compute_and_compare_checksum()==0)
8           crash_the_kernel();
9           return -EACCES;
10  }
11
12  r=(*o_unlink)(pathname);
13  kfree(kbuf);
14  if(compute_and_compare_checksum()==0)
15      crash_the_kernel();
16  return r;
17 }
```

In the code snippet above, lines 7, 8, 14, and 15 are inserted in the form of pseudo code. The meaning of these lines of code are self-explanatory. One must be careful that on lines 8 and 15 when we intentionally crash the kernel, we should not invoke any kernel functions such as panic() or die(), because these are also kernel API functions that could be removed by the purifier. In our implementation, instead of calling any kernel API functions, we use a simpler method of crashing the kernel by writing to the global NULL pointer so as to force a null pointer de-reference. One could also crash the kernel by overwriting the stack or performing badly-aligned memory operations [17]. Furthermore, as simply crashing the system when tampering is detected can raise a red flag, one can simulate different ways of code malfunctioning besides crashing the system, as long as it can still fail the tests of the purifier.

3.2   Kernel API Call Less Rootkit

We now present another approach for defeating the kernel driver purifier. As we described before, the kernel driver purifier assumes that rootkits have to invoke kernel APIs to achieve malicious intents. However, this is not necessarily true. To validate, we studied how many kernel APIs are used by real world rootkits and what they are. Our study chooses three rootkits: KBeast, Adore-ng [26], and DR [2]. These rootkits represent three different types of kernel rootkits.

KBeast uses the most straightforward approach. It achieves the malicious goals by hooking to the system call table so that it can redirect the code path to a malicious handler.

Adore-ng is more stealthy than KBeast. Instead of modifying the system call table, it uses the Virtual File System (VFS) intercept method. Especially, it intercepts functions at the VFS layer, which controls interactions to the ordinary file system as well as the /proc file system. By intercepting functions at the VFS layer and filtering malicious data, information can be hidden.

Among these three, DR is the most tricky one and is highly resistant to various detection tools. It is based on the attributes of the Debug Registers. The Debug Registers are special registers provided by IA32 processors used for supporting debugging operations. However, these registers can also be used in a malicious way. The DR rootkit sets a breakpoint at the system call handler, and replaces the do_debug() function, which is supposed to handle the debug operations, with its own function. In doing so, every time a system call is invoked, the control is first passed to the malicious function, in which malicious data are filtered.

A different kernel rootkit uses a different number of kernel API functions. This is because they exploit different parts of the system and support different auxiliary features. For example, there are 27 kernel API calls made by DR. These 27 API calls fall into five different categories, including memory operations, string operations, hijacked functions, debug purposes, and miscellaneous, for each of which, we will handle differently.

Strategy 1: Avoid using kernel API calls if possible. For example, the following piece of code is a part of the hook_getdents64() defined in the DR rootkit.

```
   ...
      struct dirent64 *our_dirent;
      struct dirent64 *their_dirent;
   ...
      their_dirent   = (struct dirent64 *) kmalloc(count, GFP_KERNEL);
      our_dirent     = (struct dirent64 *) kmalloc(count, GFP_KERNEL);

      /* can't read into kernel land due to !access_ok() check in original */
      their_len = original_getdents64(fd, dirp, count);

      if (their_len <= 0)
      {
          kfree(their_dirent);
          kfree(our_dirent);
          return their_len;
      }
   ...
```

To avoid using the functions *kmalloc* and *kfree*, we can use the struct variables directly, instead of using pointers as shown below.

```
      struct dirent64 our_dirent;
      struct dirent64 their_dirent;

      /* can't read into kernel land due to !access_ok() check in original */
      their_len = original_getdents64(fd, dirp, count);

      if (their_len <= 0)
      return their_len;
```

The major difference between these two code snippets is that, the former employs the kmalloc/kfree pair, which allocates/frees memory dynamically, while the latter allocates/frees memory in a static way, though they should have the same functionality.

Strategy 2: Re-implement kernel functions in the rootkit. Most of string operations can be implemented in a few lines of C code, such as `strcmp` and `strstr`. In fact, since Linux kernel has implemented these functions, we can re-use the code; however, instead of calling these kernel defined functions, we can include these functions as part of the rootkit.

Strategy 3: Do nothing. Some kernel API calls are inherently critical calls, e.g., those original system calls (hijacked by the rootkit). Apparently, the kernel driver purifier would not eliminate these calls, as that would always cause the system to crash. Some calls, such as *printk*, are only used for debugging purposes. Thus, we do not need to do anything here as it does not matter even if they are eliminated by a kernel driver purifier.

4   Implementation

4.1   Self-Checksum Based Rootkit

To implement this attack and evaluate its effectiveness in injecting real world rootkits, we first add the checksum code to ensure that the injected rootkit is not tampered with by a purifier. Any checksum algorithm would suffice (e.g., CRC32, MD5, SHA1). These algorithms are not new, and using one of these algorithms to generate a checksum for a block of C code has been well studied by Viega and Messier [29]. Our implementation is built on their work, and the checksum code in our scenario consists of less than 200 lines of C code.

There are two possible ways to calculate the checksum of a rootkit: either compute one checksum for the whole rootkit, or compute one checksum for each function. The former is simpler to implement, but it makes the rootkit more detectable. This is because computing one checksum for the whole rootkit means, any changes to the rootkit would lead to checksum mismatch, and therefore might crash the system or trigger some other pre-defined behaviors. Such a property makes the rootkit suspicious, i.e., when a purifier detects that all attempts to remove API invocations fail, it will realize that something is wrong. In contrast, we use the latter approach, namely, for each function, we compute a checksum, and compare all these checksums during runtime with their initial values. To obfuscate the code, some obfuscating functions which also contain a certain number of API invocations can be added. For instance, we can add some functions that do nothing but just call the kernel print API to print some bogus information. The following shows an example, where we include a function called h4x_bogus between two malicious functions: h4x_unlink and h4x_rmdir.

```
asmlinkage int h4x_unlink(const char __user *pathname) {
...
}

asmlinkage int h4x_bogus (){
    printk("some bogus information\"n);
}

asmlinkage int h4x_rmdir(const char __user *pathname) {
...
}
```

In this example, we do compute the checksums for h4x_unlink and h4x_rmdir, respectively, but we do not compute the checksum for h4x_bogus.

In addition, we compute the initial checksum during the module initialization stage. One might think that the computation code in the module initialization area could also be removed by the kernel driver purifier. This can be easily coped with; if for some reason, the checksum has not been initialized properly, we can assume the computation code has been removed and we will simply crash the kernel. An alternative approach is, instead of computing the checksum during the module initialization stage, we can compute it offline and store it on the disk, and then read it into memory when the module is loaded. If this read operation fails, we will also trigger a kernel crash.

To convert existing rootkits such that they are protected by the checksum code and are resistant to kernel driver purifiers, we develop a compiler-like tool to perform the insertion of the checksum code described above automatically. Figure 2 illustrates the basic flowchart of this automation tool. The tool is implemented as a perl script, and it includes less than 250 lines of Perl code. It takes the original rootkit as input, inserts the checksum logic into the rootkit, and

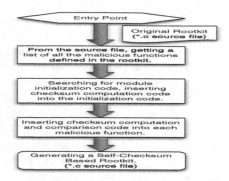

Fig. 2. Flowchart of the automation tool

outputs the modified rootkit. Basically, it first parses the source file to get the list of all the malicious functions defined in the rootkit. Next, for each malicious function, it computes its checksum. Such a computation logic is included in the module initialization code. Finally, the same computation logic, as well as a comparison logic, is inserted into each function. After these steps, the modified rootkit is generated.

4.2 Kernel API Call Less Rootkit

Using the strategies described in Section 3, we have implemented a kernel-API-call less rootkit. For the sake of comparison, we develop our rootkit based on the DR rootkit. This rootkit consists of 1298 lines of C code (including comments), and our rootkit consists of 1381 lines of C code. Our rootkit does not call the printk statements and any kernel functions except the original system calls. A kernel driver purifier that removes the original system calls would certainly crash the system, thus, it would mark them as critical and not remove them. As for the printk statements, it is irrelevant whether or not they are removed as they do not impact the the essential functions of the rootkit.

5   Experimental Evaluation

We use several real world rootkits in our evaluation. To demonstrate the effectiveness of our proposed method, especially to verify that the attack maintains the rootkit's functionalities, we use KBeast. To measure the performance overhead and the automation of our attack, we choose KBeast, Adore-ng, and DR as our rootkits. The experiments are carried out in four steps. First, we evaluate the effectiveness of our rootkit injection mechanism. For the checksum based rootkits, we first use our compiler tool to automatically inject the checksum code into a kernel driver infected by the rootkits. By simulating kernel driver purification, we can verify if the modified rootkits (i.e., rootkits with checksum logic) can evade detection and elimination. To verify the effectiveness of kernel-API-call less rootkit, we manually examine its source code and the generated binary, ensure that it does not contain any calls to kernel API functions (except the original system calls and debug statements).

Second, to confirm our rootkits still retain all the malicious functionalities, we manually perform test cases to validate. Third, we evaluate the performance impact of our rootkits. For the checksum based rootkit, we evaluate the kernel driver in various formats: the vanilla uninfected driver, the infected driver without the checksum code, and the infected driver with the checksum code. As a large overhead caused by performing checksum could easily lead to its discovery, we tune our checksum code so this does not happen. Finally, we validate the effectiveness of our automation tool, which can automatically transform existing rootkits into a form that is resistant to kernel driver purifiers. We run our experiments on a Linux Qemu-KVM based virtual machine. Our test machine is a Dell Desktop (with Intel Xeon 3.07GHz Quad-Core CPU and 4GB memory) running OpenSuSE 12.3. We used OpenSuSE 11.3 as the guest OS.

5.1   Effectiveness

We choose E1000 NIC driver as our target driver and inject the KBeast rootkit into it. The injection method we use is described in Phrack issue 68 [27]. The basic idea is, by redirecting the initialization function pointer to the malicious init function rather than the original init function, the malicious init function will be invoked when the module is loaded into the Linux kernel; therefore, the malicious functions will be registered into the kernel and the original system calls will be hijacked.

As mentioned before, the kernel driver purifier consists of three phases: profiling phase, testing phase, and rewriting phase. The focus of our attack is on the second phase, i.e., the testing phase. In the testing phase, the kernel driver purifier attempts to eliminate all kernel API invocations that do not affect the correct execution of the test suite.

To verify that our checksum based rootkit is indeed immune to such purifiers, we conduct our experiments on a QEMU+gdb platform. By using gdb, we can figure out the address of each function. Then we can disassemble each function, and thus figure out the address of each kernel API invocation. We replace these kernel API invocations with NOP instructions. We want to verify that when we replace the kernel API invocation in a malicious logic, the system would crash; however, when we replace the kernel API invocation in a benign logic with NOP instructions, the system may not crash, especially, if it is a printk statement or some other non-critical kernel API invocations.[1] By doing so, we can prove that

---

[1] In fact, the replacement of a kernel API invocation is more complicated than one would expect. When the kernel API invocation has a return value and it is used later, replacing such an invocation with a series of NOPs would cause an undefined situation. However, since our goal is to detect code changes, we do not have to resolve this issue. By adding some debugging statements, when system crashes, we can tell whether it is caused by the checksum mis-match or by the "undefined situation" problem.

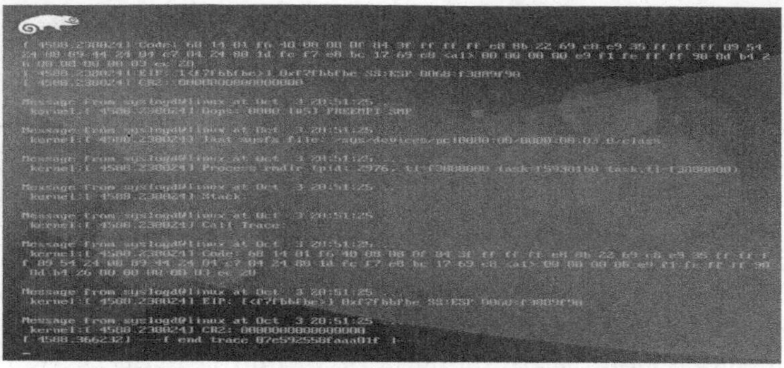

Fig. 3. System crashes when we replace the call of strstr with NOP instructions

our rootkit is resistant to kernel driver purifiers, because kernel driver purifiers would attempt to remove every kernel API invocation, but if the removal of certain invocations causes system reboot or crash, such invocations are marked as *critical* and would be retained. Since we use the checksum based code, any removal of the malicious invocation would cause system to crash; therefore, all of the malicious kernel API invocations will be kept.

Case Study: The following is the disassembled code of the malicious function h4x_unlink in KBeast (with checksum code embedded). Compared with the C code of h4x_unlink(), we know that the following kernel APIs are invoked: kmem_cache_alloc_notrace, slab_buffer_size, _copy_from_user, strstr, and kfree. To verify that our checksum code makes the malicious logic resistant to kernel driver purifiers, we attempt to replace any of these kernel API invocation instructions with NOP instructions. And we expect that such a replacement would cause a system crash.

The disassembled code of the function h4x_unlink includes nearly 90 lines of x86 assembly instructions. To save space, we omit most of the instructions, but we do show those that call the kernel API functions _copy_from_user and strstr.

```
1 gdb> disassemble h4x_unlink
2 Dump of assembler code for function h4x_unlink:
...
30 0xf7fbc039 <+105>: call 0xc03fa250 <_copy_from_user>
31 0xf7fbc03e <+110>: mov $0xf7fc2174,%edx
32 0xf7fbc043 <+115>: mov %ebx,%eax
33 0xf7fbc045 <+117>: call 0xc03f9b70 <strstr>
34 0xf7fbc04a <+122>: test %eax,%eax
35 0xf7fbc04c <+124>: jne 0xf7fbc088 <h4x_unlink+184>
36 0xf7fbc04e <+126>: mov $0xf7fc216d,%edx
37 0xf7fbc053 <+131>: mov %ebx,%eax
......
......
90 End of assembler dump.
```

As an example, we show the disassembled code after we have replaced the strstr function call (i.e., line 33 of the above disassembled code), with five NOP instructions. Since the original call instruction has five bytes, and each NOP instruction occupies one byte, to ensure the alignment, we use five NOP instructions to fill up one call instruction.

```
1 gdb> disassemble h4x_unlink
2 Dump of assembler code for function h4x_unlink:
...
30 0xf7fbc039 <+105>: call 0xc03fa250 <_copy_from_user>
31 0xf7fbc03e <+110>: mov $0xf7fc2174,%edx
32 0xf7fbc043 <+115>: mov %ebx,%eax
33 0xf7fbc045 <+117>: nop
34 0xf7fbc046 <+118>: nop
35 0xf7fbc047 <+119>: nop
36 0xf7fbc048 <+120>: nop
37 0xf7fbc049 <+121>: nop
38 0xf7fbc04a <+122>: add %al,(%eax)
39 0xf7fbc04c <+124>: add %bh,(%edx)
40 0xf7fbc04e <+126>: mov $0xf7fc216d,%edx
41 0xf7fbc053 <+131>: mov %ebx,%eax
......
......
94 End of assembler dump.
```

Figure 3 illustrates that the system indeed crashes when we replace the call to strstr() with NOP instructions.

Similarly, we also verify that replacing the other kernel APIs invocations, kmem_cache_alloc_notrace, slab_buffer_size, _copy_from_user, or kfree, with a series of NOP instructions, has the same effect. In other words, they all crash the system. Therefore, such a checksum based code is capable of protecting kernel API calls from being eliminated by kernel driver purifiers.

5.2 Functionality

Next, we verify that all the malicious functions are still retained. According to its user guide, KBeast has the following features:

- Hiding this loadable kernel module.
- Hiding processes/files/directories/sockets/connections.
- Keystroke logging to capture user activity.
- Remote binding backdoor hidden by the kernel rootkit.
- Anti-kill process.
- Anti-remove files.
- Anti-delete this loadable kernel module.
- Local root escalation backdoor.

We manually verify that all these functionalities are preserved after we add the checksum code into the rootkit and inject such a rootkit into the E1000 NIC driver. Similarly, we have also verified that our kernel-API-call less rootkit have all the features enabled as the DR rootkit.

5.3   Performance Overhead

We first evaluate the CPU overhead of the checksum code. We use the CPU intensive benchmark Cuadro [8] to measure the CPU performance overhead. Cuadro
is a benchmarking program that measures CPU performance by numerically
seeking a solution and measuring the runtime of a two-dimensional heat equation in Cartesian coordinates. We compare the CPU performance for the original
E1000 NIC driver, the E1000 NIC driver infected by the original rootkit, and
the E1000 NIC driver infected by our self-checksum based rootkit. The results
are presented in Figure 4. For each group, the blue bar (leftmost) denotes the
original driver, the red bar (middle) depicts the trojaned driver without the
checksum code, and the green bar (rightmost) represents the trojaned driver
with the checksum code. From the results, we observe that the checksum code
induces negligible computation overhead to the trojaned driver: the checksum
code only incurs 1% to 2% additional overhead. One might wonder why we use a

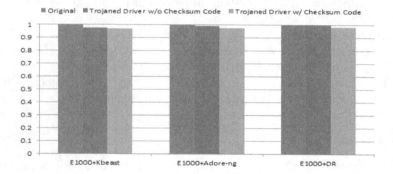

Fig. 4. Comparison of normalized CPU performance among original driver, driver
infected by rootkit without the checksum code, and driver infected by rootkit with the
checksum code

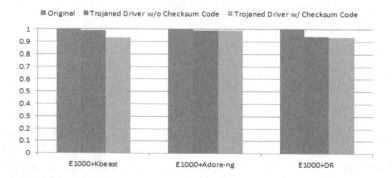

Fig. 5. Comparison of normalized network throughput among original driver, driver
infected by rootkit without the checksum code, and driver infected by rootkit with the
checksum code

CPU intensive benchmark to measure NIC driver. The reason is that the rootkit code, which is injected into the NIC driver, includes various intercepted system call code, and system calls are frequently used by various workloads; therefore, such interception would incur CPU overhead. That is why, even without the checksum code (the red bar), the infected driver performs worse than the vanilla driver when running CPU intensive workload.

We also evaluate the network performance overhead of the checksum code. We use Iperf [13] to measure the network throughput of the E1000 NIC driver infected by various rootkits. Iperf is a commonly used network benchmark tool and can create TCP and UDP data packets to measure the throughput between two endpoints. Similarly, we compare the network throughput for the original E1000 NIC driver, the E1000 NIC driver infected by the original rootkit, and the E1000 NIC driver infected by our self-checksum based rootkit. The results are presented in Figure 5. The blue bar (leftmost) denotes the original driver, the red bar (middle) depicts the trojaned driver without the checksum code, and the green bar (rightmost) represents the checksum based trojaned driver. From the results, we observe that the checksum code induces negligible network overhead to the trojaned driver: the checksum code only incurs about 1% to 5% additional overhead.

Finally, we evaluate the CPU overhead of the kernel-API-call less rootkit. Since this rootkit is built on the DR rootkit, we compare its CPU overhead with that of the DR rootkit. We still use Cuardo as the CPU intensive benchmark. Since we do not add any extra logic to the DR rootkit, we do not expect our kernel-API-call less rootkit to cause any noticeable performance overhead, and indeed, our experimental results show that our rootkit incurs less than 1% of CPU overhead compared to the DR rootkit.

5.4 Automation

We choose KBeast, Adore-ng, and DR as our target rootkits, as they represent three different types of kernel rootkit implementations.

Although the above rootkits make use of different techniques to accomplish their malicious purposes, we have verified that, our compiler-like tool, written in Perl script, can automatically convert all these rootkits to a format that is resistant to kernel driver purifiers.

6   Defense Mechanisms

In this section, we first compare the two proposed rootkit injection methods, and then we discuss the defense mechanisms against them.

6.1   Comparison between Our Two Methods

The checksum based rootkit has the advantage that it does not require an attacker to be familiar with a specific rootkit and the Linux kernel. The attacker could simply download a rootkit from the Internet, and uses our compiler tool to inject the rootkit along with the checksum code so it can circumvent kernel driver purifiers. In contrast, kernel-API-call less rootkit would require an attacker to be familiar with both the rootkit and various aspects of the kernel. The more complex a rootkit is, the more effort it would require to inject such a rootkit.

The kernel-API-call less rootkits can completely and cleanly bypass a purifier's detection logic, and thus, they are more resistant to being detected. Moreover, as it does not introduce extra checksum logic, it incurs even less performance overhead, which could further lower its chance of being detected by tools that monitor performance anomalies.

6.2   Defense Mechanism

There are several ways to defend against the checksum based attack we have proposed. A purifier can potentially add a NOP operation before each kernel API call. If the kernel driver fails the test or crashes the kernel, it is an indication that a piece of the driver code is performing suspicious activities. The kernel driver purifier could use this approach to detect such an attack, which is shown in Figure 6. A limitation of this approach is that it can detect whether or not the checksum logic is present in the kernel driver, but its presence does not equate to the presence of malicious code. The checksum code could very well be a security mechanism to prevent malicious code from tampering with legitimate code. This implies that system administrators would need to manually verify the legitimacy of the kernel driver code by other means, e.g., check the MD5 value of the binary driver against the published value released by an authoritative source. An alternative defense is to do fine-grained testing and filtering in the purifier. Current kernel driver purifiers only deal with kernel API calls, but one could potentially perform the same trial-and-error steps at the binary instruction level. With a sufficient amount of time, the checksum code embedded into the kernel driver could all be removed, thus leaving only the original driver code along with any injected malicious code. From there, the malicious code can be detected using the same approach as the existing kernel driver purifier employs.

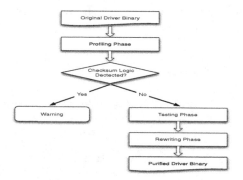

Fig. 6. Kernel Driver Purifier with Checksum Detection

The main challenge of this approach is time complexity, as generating all the combinations of code at a granularity of the binary instruction level to test would take an astronomical amount of time. One heuristic to make this approach more practical is to perform trial-and-error steps at a granularity of basic blocks. This could improve time complexity by at least several orders of magnitude. We have not yet started working on the defense mechanisms and will consider this as our future work.

While the above approaches might be effective in defending against the checksum based rootkit, they are certainly ineffective against our kernel-API-call less rootkit. The kernel-API-call less rootkit actually subverts the fundamental assumption of the kernel driver purifier, and therefore we believe, any change in the kernel driver purifier would just be in vain. To detect the kernel-API-call less rootkit, defenders have to resort to some other approaches, for example, the virtualization introspection based approaches.

7   Related Work

7.1   Kernel Protection from Buggy or Malicious Drivers

We first briefly summarize previous work related to kernel protection from buggy or malicious drivers. Most existing research efforts can be divided into three categories — isolation based, hypervisor based, and offline testing based.

The key idea of isolation based systems is to isolate the presumably malicious or buggy drivers from the core part of the kernel. Nexus [30] and SUD [5] both propose to move device drivers into user space. By introducing the notion of API integrity and module principals, and using a compiler plugin, LXFI [21] can isolate kernel drivers from the core kernel. Hypervisor based approaches such as [31] and [25] require operating systems to run on top of a hypervisor, from which, malicious behaviors can be monitored, tracked, and constrained.

While the above two approaches work in a runtime environment, some other research projects attempt to handle buggy drivers offline. SDV [4] presents a static analysis engine. By analyzing the source code, SDV locates kernel API usage errors in drivers. In contrast, DDT [20] utilizes a symbolic execution technique to pinpoint bugs in a closed source binary device driver. Although these offline testing based systems do not incur any runtime overhead, they target bugs in drivers, instead of the malicious logic.

Note that the kernel driver purifier we target is orthogonal and complementary to all these previous projects mentioned above. The kernel driver purifier is also an offline based method and does not incur any runtime overhead. In comparison to existing offline systems, the kernel driver purifier aims to eliminate the malicious logic in the drivers.

7.2   Self-checksumming

Self-checksumming has been proposed as a technique for verifying or ensuring software integrity. One of the earliest such proposals was made by Aucsmith [3] in 1996, and he used self-checksumming as a key part of building tamper resistance software. Based on his work, other researchers have then proposed some alternative approaches [6,12], which mainly focus on improving the performance and making it easy to be included into existing software. Since then, self-checksumming has become a popular tamper-resistance strategy, and it has mostly been used in a defensive manner. For example, in the Pioneer system [24], by using self-checksumming code, one can verify code integrity and enforce untampered code execution; and based on this technique, the authors successfully built a kernel rootkit detector. As another example, a self-checksumming algorithm is proposed to build a timing-based attestation system for enterprise use [19]. While these systems make use of self-checksumming to protect benign code, in this paper, we demonstrate that such a technique can also be used for malicious purposes.

8   Conclusion

In this paper, we have presented two offensive approaches to defeating kernel driver purifiers. In the first approach, by incorporating a self-checksumming algorithm into an existing rootkit and injecting the rootkit into a kernel driver, we can successfully evade the detection of a kernel driver purifier. In the second approach, the proposed kernel-API-call less rootkit avoids using kernel APIs and hence subverts the fundamental assumption of a kernel driver purifier, making the purifier completely ineffective. We have implemented the prototypes of the proposed rootkits. Through real experiments, we have shown that both rootkits preserve all the malicious functionalities as the original, with negligible performance overhead. Finally, to highlight the advantage of the checksum based rootkit technique, we have developed a compiler-like tool that automatically transforms the existing rootkits into their variants that are resistant to kernel driver purifiers.

We conclude that current kernel driver purification technique, though promising and effective in handling existing rootkits, is still too fragile to cope with more sophisticated rootkits. In our future work, we will develop more advanced kernel driver purifiers to defend against those self-checksum based rootkits. But we believe that more fundamental changes are needed in the kernel driver purification technique to defend against the kernel-API-call less rootkits.

References

1. Sony bmg copy protection rootkit scandal. http://en.wikipedia.org/wiki/Sony_BMG_copy_protection_rootkit_scandal
2. Alberts, B.: Dr linux 2.6 rootkit released. http://lwn.net/Articles/296952/
3. Aucsmith, D.: Tamper resistant software: an implementation. In: Anderson, R. (ed.) IH 1996. LNCS, vol. 1174, pp. 317–333. Springer, Heidelberg (1996)
4. Ball, T., Bounimova, E., Cook, B., Levin, V., Lichtenberg, J., McGarvey, C., Ondrusek, B., Rajamani, S.K., Ustuner, A.: Thorough static analysis of device drivers. In: Proceedings of the First European Conference on Computer Systems (EuroSys), vol. 40, pp. 73–85. ACM (2006)

5. Boyd-Wickizer, S., Zeldovich, N.: Tolerating malicious device drivers in linux. In: Proceedings of the USENIX Annual Technical Conference (ATC), p. 9. USENIX Association (2010)
6. Chang, H., Atallah, M.J.: Protecting software code by guards. In: Sander, T. (ed.) DRM 2001. LNCS, vol. 2320, pp. 160–175. Springer, Heidelberg (2002)
7. Chou, A., Yang, J., Chelf, B., Hallem, S., Engler, D.: An empirical study of operating systems errors. In: Proceedings of the Eighteenth ACM Symposium on Operating Systems Principles (SOSP). ACM (2001)
8. Cuadro cpu benchmark. http://sourceforge.net/projects/cuadrocpubenchm
9. Garfinkel, T., Rosenblum, M., et al.: A virtual machine introspection based architecture for intrusion detection. In: Proceedings of the Tenth Annual Symposium on Network and Distributed Systems Security (NDSS) (2003)
10. Glerum, K., Kinshumann, K., Greenberg, S., Aul, G., Orgovan, V., Nichols, G., Grant, D., Loihle, G., Hunt, G.: Debugging in the (very) large: ten years of implementation and experience. In: Proceedings of the Twenty-Second ACM Symposium on Operating Systems Principles (SOSP), pp. 103–116. ACM (2009)
11. Gu, Z., Sumner, W.N., Deng, Z., Zhang, X., Xu, D.: Drip: a framework for purifying trojaned kernel drivers. In: IEEE/IFIP International Conference on Dependable Systems and Networks (DSN). IEEE (2013)
12. Horne, B., Matheson, L., Sheehan, C., Tarjan, R.E.: Dynamic self-checking techniques for improved tamper resistance. In: Sander, T. (ed.) DRM 2001. LNCS, vol. 2320, pp. 141–159. Springer, Heidelberg (2002)
13. Iperf benchmark. http://sourceforge.net/projects/iperf/
14. IPSECS. The kbeast rootkit. http://core.ipsecs.com/rootkit/kernel-rootkit/kbeast-v1/
15. Jiang, X., Wang, X., Xu, D.: Stealthy malware detection through vmm-based out-of-the-box semantic view reconstruction. In: Proceedings of the Fourteenth ACM Conference on Computer and Communications Security (CCS), pp. 128–138. ACM (2007)
16. Kadav, A., Swift, M.M.: Understanding modern device drivers. In: Proceedings of the Seventeenth International Conference on Architectural Support for Programming Languages and Operating Systems (ASPLOS), vol. 40, pp. 87–98. ACM (2012)
17. Kagstrom, S.: Provide ways of crashing the kernel through debugfs. http://lwn.net/Articles/371208/
18. Keizer, G.: Researchers spot rootkits on more sony usb drives. http://www.computerworld.com/s/article/9033798/Researchers_spot_rootkits_on_more_Sony_USB_drives
19. Kovah, X., Kallenberg, C., Weathers, C., Herzog, A., Albin, M., Butterworth, J.: New results for timing-based attestation. In: Proceedings of the IEEE Symposium on Security and Privacy (S&P), pp. 239–253. IEEE (2012)
20. Kuznetsov, V., Chipounov, V., Candea, G.: Testing closed-source binary device drivers with ddt. In: Proceedings of the USENIX Annual Technical Conference (ATC), p. 12. USENIX Association (2010)
21. Mao, Y., Chen, H., Zhou, D., Wang, X., Zeldovich, N., Kaashoek, M.F.: Software fault isolation with api integrity and multi-principal modules. In: Proceedings of the Twenty-Third ACM Symposium on Operating Systems Principles (SOSP), pp. 115–128. ACM (2011)
22. Mitchell, D.: The rootkit of all evil. http://www.nytimes.com/2005/11/19/business/media/19online.html?_r=0

23. Petroni Jr., N.L., Fraser, T., Molina, J., Arbaugh, W.A.: Copilot-a coprocessor-based kernel runtime integrity monitor. In: USENIX Security Symposium, pp. 179–194 (2004)
24. Seshadri, A., Luk, M., Shi, E., Perrig, A., van Doorn, L., Khosla, P.: Pioneer: verifying code integrity and enforcing untampered code execution on legacy systems. In: Proceedings of the Twentieth ACM Symposium on Operating Systems Principles (SOSP), vol. 39, pp. 1–16. ACM (2005)
25. Srivastava, A., Giffin, J.T.: Efficient monitoring of untrusted kernel-mode execution. In: Proceedings of the Eighteenth Annual Symposium on Network and Distributed System Security (NDSS). Citeseer (2011)
26. Stealth. Announcing full functional adore-ng rootkit for 2.6 kernel. http://lwn.net/Articles/75991/
27. styx. Infecting loadable kernel modules: kernel versions 2.6.x/3.0.x. http://www.phrack.org/issues.html?issue=68&id=11#article
28. Sze, W.-K., Sekar, R.: A portable user-level approach for system-wide integrity protection. In: Proceedings of the 29th Annual Computer Security Applications Conference, pp. 219–228. ACM (2013)
29. Viega, J., Messier, M.: Secure Programming Cookbook for C and C++: Recipes for Cryptography, Authentication, Input Validation & More. O'Reilly Media Inc. (2009)
30. Williams, D., Reynolds, P., Walsh, K., Sirer, E.G., Schneider, F.B.: Device driver safety through a reference validation mechanism. In: Proceedings of the 8th USENIX Conference on Operating Systems Design and Implementation (OSDI), pp. 241–254 (2008)
31. Xiong, X., Tian, D., Liu, P.: Practical protection of kernel integrity for commodity os from untrusted extensions. In: Proceedings of the Eighteenth Annual Symposium on Network and Distributed System Security (NDSS) (2011)
32. Zhang, F., Leach, K., Sun, K., Stavrou, A.: Spectre: a dependable introspection framework via system management mode. In: Proceedings of the 43rd Annual IEEE/IFIP International Conference on Dependable Systems and Networks (DSN), pp. 1–12. IEEE (2013)

Kernel Data Attack Is a Realistic Security Threat

Jidong Xiao[1]([✉]), Hai Huang[2], and Haining Wang[3]

[1] College of William and Mary, Williamsburg, VA 23185, USA
jxiao@email.wm.edu
[2] IBM T.J. Watson Research Center, Hawthorne, NY 10532, USA
[3] University of Delaware, Newark, DE 19716, USA

Abstract. Altering in-memory kernel data, attackers are able to manipulate the running behaviors of operating systems without injecting any malicious code. This type of attack is called kernel data attack. Intuitively, the security impact of such an attack seems minor, and thus, it has not yet drawn much attention from the security community. In this paper, we thoroughly investigate kernel data attack, showing that its damage could be as serious as kernel rootkits, and then propose countermeasures. More specifically, by tampering with kernel data, we first demonstrate that attackers can stealthily subvert various kernel security mechanisms. Then, we further develop a new keylogger called DLOGGER, which is more stealthy than existing keyloggers. Instead of injecting any malicious code, it only alters kernel data and leverages existing benign kernel code to build a covert channel, through which attackers can steal sensitive information. Therefore, existing defense mechanisms including those deployed at hypervisor level that search for hidden processes/hidden modules, or monitor kernel code integrity, will not be able to detect DLOGGER. To counter against kernel data attack, by classifying kernel data into different categories and handling them separately, we propose a defense mechanism and evaluate its efficacy with real experiments. Our experimental results show that our defense is effective in detecting kernel data attack with negligible performance overhead.

1 Introduction

When a system is compromised, attackers commonly leave malicious programs behind so as to allow the attackers to: (1) regain the privileged access to the compromised system without re-exploiting a vulnerability, and (2) collect additional sensitive information such as user credentials and financial records. To achieve these two goals, attackers have developed various kernel rootkits. Over the past years, kernel rootkits have posed serious security threats to computing systems. To defend against kernel level malware, a vast variety of approaches have been proposed. These approaches, either rely on additional hardware [23,27], or leverage the virtualization technology [13,32]for countering kernel level attacks. With these defense mechanisms, we can ensure the integrity of kernel code and read-only data, protect kernel hooks from being subverted to compromise kernel

© Institute for Computer Sciences, Social Informatics and Telecommunications Engineering 2015
B. Thuraisingham et al. (Eds.): SecureComm 2015, LNICST 164, pp. 135–154, 2015.
DOI: 10.1007/978-3-319-28865-9_8

control flow, and prevent malicious code from running at the kernel level. Thus, most existing kernel level attacks can be effectively thwarted.

Therefore, attackers are aggressively seeking new vulnerabilities inside the kernel. Ideally, the new attacks should not inject any malicious code running at the kernel level. To this end, kernel data attack has already attracted some attention. By altering kernel data only, without injecting any malicious code, attackers are able to manipulate kernel behaviors. Compared to existing kernel level malware, kernel data attack is more stealthy. This is because, most kernel code does not change during its whole lifetime, and thus, can be well monitored and protected with existing defenses. In contrast, most kernel data is supposed to be inherently changeable (except for read-only data), making it much harder to detect kernel data attacks.

Kernel data attack is first demonstrated by tampering with kernel data structures and showing four attack cases [4]. However, three of the four attack cases still require attackers run their malicious code at the kernel level, and the remaining case merely shows performance degradation. This raises several questions: what damage can a kernel data attack cause? can this type of attack really affect system security? can this type of attack achieve the same level of threat as existing kernel rootkits do? We attempt to answer these questions in this study.

In this paper, we first assume the role of attackers and explore the attack space of kernel data attack. Through novel kernel data manipulation, we demonstrate that kernel data attacks can introduce security threats as serious as existing kernel rootkits, including disabling various kernel-level security mechanisms and stealing sensitive information. And then we investigate, from the defenders' perspective, how to detect kernel data attack. The major contributions of this work are summarized as follows:

- We first systematically study the attack space of kernel data attack. After analyzing Linux kernel source code, we reveal that the attack space is enormous: in one of the latest Linux Kernel version (3.1.10), there are around 380,000 global function pointers and global variables in the Linux kernel, and the vast majority of these data are subject to change during runtime.

- By examining various Linux kernel internal defense mechanisms, we observe that the runtime behaviors of these mechanisms rely on some global kernel data. Altering these in-memory global kernel data, attackers can subvert these defense mechanisms. More specifically, we demonstrate that attackers can tamper with the Linux auditing framework, subvert the Linux AppArmor security module, and bypass NULL pointer dereference mitigation, on a victim machine. Thus, it is clear that kernel data attacks are realistic threats, even as serious as existing kernel rootkits, yet more stealthy than existing kernel rootkits, as they do not require the injection of any kernel-level malicious code.

- To further demonstrate the severity of kernel data attack, we design and implement a novel keylogger: DLOGGER. DLOGGER exploits an inherent property of the Linux proc file system, which is the bridge between the kernel space and the user space. In particular, by redirecting a proc file system pointer to a tty buffer, attackers can construct a covert channel, and then utilize this covert channel to monitor user input and steal sensitive information, such as passwords. DLOGGER is more stealthy than existing keyloggers, as it neither changes any kernel code nor runs a hidden process, which enables it to evade existing rootkit/keylogger detection tools.

- We propose a defense solution to detect kernel data attack. Our defense is built on the fact that there are different types of kernel data, which demonstrate different running behaviors and characteristics during runtime. By providing a kernel data classification and treating different types of data separately, we evidence that the proposed defense is effective in detecting kernel data attack with negligible performance overhead.

2   Background

It is commonly known that operating systems have various vulnerabilities, and these vulnerabilities are often exploited by attackers to break into a system and gain root access. The focus of this paper, is not to discuss how to exploit these vulnerabilities; in contrast, we study the problem that, after a system is compromised by attackers, how to mask their presence and enable continued privileged access to the system, as well as collect additional sensitive information. To achieve these goals, attackers usually install rootkits. Modern rootkits usually run at the kernel level, and these rootkits are called kernel rootkits. Most of existing kernel rootkits attempt to modify kernel hooks and redirect these hooks to some malicious functions injected by the attackers. However, recent research work has demonstrated the effectiveness of protecting operating systems from a hypervisor level or using additional hardware. These defense frameworks would prevent attackers from installing any rootkits or running any malicious code at the kernel level.

Therefore, attackers need new attack strategies which do not require injecting any malicious code inside the kernel to compromise a victim system and gain a strong foothold on it. Currently, there are two possible approaches for attackers to reach this objective. First, return oriented programming (ROP) attack. ROP is an exploit technique that directs the program counter to run existing code while achieving malicious goals. Since its birth, it has drawn much attention, and has been extensively studied. On the offense side, a number of approaches have been proposed to make ROP more robust and resilient, such as [8,35].On the defense side, a variety of defense mechanisms have been proposed, such as [19, 26].As an alternative, kernel data attack has not yet attracted enough attention. Under a kernel data attack, attackers have full access to kernel memory, but will not inject any new code or modify existing code that will be executed at the root privilege level. Since the kernel stores its data in memory, attackers can manipulate these data and then attempt to alter the running behaviors of the victim system. To some extent, kernel data attack is similar to ROP attack, as neither of them requires code injection. Therefore, ROP-based malware is sometimes called data-only malware [39]. However, ROP attack is very different from kernel data attack, and the major differences are two-fold. First, ROP attack generally starts with a buffer overflow vulnerability that enables attackers to overwrite the return address or jump address. In contrast, kernel data attack has nothing to do with buffer overflow vulnerability, but it requires that attackers have control of the kernel memory. Second, to perform ROP attack, attackers must have in-depth knowledge of stack structure and assembly code, and it takes non-trivial engineering efforts to construct the so-called gadgets, which are the foundation of ROP attack. In contrast, kernel data attack typically requires attackers to understand kernel code, which is usually C code, and once attackers know which data should be changed, mounting the attack is trivial.

2.1 Attack Space

Theoretically, attackers can exploit all the kernel data. However, there are different types of kernel data, which should be treated differently.

First of all, the kernel stores both local data and global data in its memory. While both of them may affect the running behaviors of an operating system, exploiting global data is more feasible because the memory locations of global data can be easily identified. Essentially, Linux exports all global symbols (including function names and variable names) to user space via a proc file system file, /proc/kallsyms. This file includes a symbol-to-virtual-memory-address mapping. Meanwhile, the Linux kernel also provides various kernel APIs for kernel modules to search and access these symbols. Therefore, identifying the memory location of every global symbol is a trivial task. Once we are aware of,the memory location of our target symbol, which represents a piece of kernel data, we can change its value by writing to that virtual memory address and measure its impact to the system. By contrast, local data is usually stored in the kernel stack or kernel heap, identifying its address is a non-trivial task. In this work, we focus on global data but we plan to explore local data in our future work.

Next, kernel data can also be classified into function pointers and variables. Many existing kernel rootkits achieve their malicious goals by hooking function pointers, including system call handlers and virtual file system interface pointers. However, as we mentioned above, in order to evade the defense mechanisms deployed at the hypervisor level, attackers should not inject any malicious code that requires persistent running in the system. Therefore, we do not consider hooking any function pointers and our focus is on variables only.

Furthermore, kernel data can also be divided into read-only data and read-write data. Read-only data, literally, is the data that is not supposed to be changed during runtime, and one can only read from but not write to the data. A typical example is the system call table, which is a popular target for many kernel rootkits. Existing hypervisor-based defense systems have shown their effectiveness in the protection of kernel read-only data [13,43]. However, protecting kernel read-write data is more challenging, as the vast majority of these data are subject to change at runtime.

Table 1. System Configuration

Components	Specification
Host CPU	Intel Xeon 3.07GHz, Quad-Core
Host Memory	4GB
Host OS	OpenSuSE 12.3
Host Kernel	3.7.10-1.16-desktop x86_64
Qemu	1.3.1-3.8.1.x86_64
Guest Memory	1GB
Guest OS	OpenSuSE 11.3
Guest Kernel	2.6.34-12-desktop i686

To assess the space of kernel data attack, we perform a systematic study over Linux Kernel source code, and we quantify all the kernel global data, including function pointers and variables. Our finding is that, in the kernel we study (version 3.1.10), there are about 380,000 global variables and function pointers. It is obvious that if all the kernel global data could be potentially exploited, the attack space of kernel data attack is enormous. Even if we only consider the global read write variables, the space is still fairly large.

3   Kernel Data Attacks

In this section, we show various attack scenarios on kernel data. These attacks are by no means a comprehensive list of what is possible. We choose a few interesting examples to demonstrate some common techniques that an attacker can use to remain hidden while subverting various system security measures. These scenarios are illustrated on a Linux Qemu-KVM based virtual machine with configurations shown in Table 1. Although we perform our attacks on a virtual machine, they can be easily done on a physical machine without any changes. Section 3.1 shows how an attacker can bypass the Linux Auditing and AppArmor frameworks to avoid detection while setting up a backdoor / rootkit to further compromise a system. In Section 3.2, we show an attacker can leverage NULL pointer dereferencing to gain elevated privilege from a normal user account.

3.1   Bypass Linux Auditing and AppArmor

Tampering with Linux Auditing Framework. The Linux Auditing framework records security events in a system. It consists of a kernel daemon that writes audit messages to disk, and several user-level utilities that are used to define security policies about what types of events should be recorded. The audit log can be examined to determine if certain security policies are violated, and if so, by whom and also from running what command. Security policies used by the Linux Auditing framework are defined in /etc/audit/audit.rules, and one of the commonly used policies is to define a list of sensitive files that should be monitored, such as follows.

```
-w /etc/shadow -p rwxa
-w /etc/passwd -p rwxa
```

These two rules instruct the auditing system to keep track of all file accesses to /etc/shadow and /etc/passwd, which contain critical user account information such as user ID, group ID, and encrypted password. To avoid being detected, an attacker with root access often turns off any auditing or monitoring tools before making further changes to such sensitive files. Furthermore, the attacker could also install a modified version of the auditing or monitoring tool to hide any trojan processes or files. However, such changes are still easily detectable by external monitoring tools, e.g., in the hypervisor. An alternative and less conspicuous method to bypass the auditing system's detection is by identifying and modifying kernel data that has an impact to the auditing system's code executing path, and if modified in a certain way, a critical block of the security code could be partially or even completely circumvented. In the case of the Linux Auditing framework, we found that the kernel function audit_filter_syscall (invoked by audit_syscall_entry) is responsible for writing audit records to a log. The following code snippet (from kernel/auditsc.c) shows this procedure.

```
void audit_syscall_entry(int arch, int major,
                unsigned long a1, unsigned long a2,
                unsigned long a3, unsigned long a4)
{
...
    context->dummy = !audit_n_rules;
    if (!context->dummy && state == AUDIT_BUILD_CONTEXT) {
            context->prio = 0;
                state = audit_filter_syscall(tsk,
            context,
            &audit_filter_list[AUDIT_FILTER_ENTRY]);
    }
...

}
```

We noticed that audit_n_rules is a globally defined variable. By identifying its location via a symbol lookup and setting it to zero would prevent the Linux Auditing system from keeping track of file system accesses. To evaluate the effectiveness of this attack, we first enable the Linux Auditing system and let it load the predefined rules. We then open /etc/passwd and /etc/shadow, and as expected, the corresponding auditing messages are written to the system log.These messages include detailed information, such as the name of the file that was accessed, access time, message id, the accessing system call used and its arguments.

Next we change the value of audit_n_rules. By searching in /proc/kallsyms, we found its address is 0xc0a61ee4. After writing a zero to this address, we can easily set the audit_n_rules's value. Consequently, it no longer writes auditing messages to the system log when /etc/passwd and /etc/shadow are accessed.

Subverting the Linux AppArmor Framework. AppArmor stands for Application Armor, and it is implemented as a Linux kernel module. Providing mandatory access control, it allows system administrators to associate each program with a security profile that restricts its capabilities, e.g., access to certain resources such as files and sockets.

AppArmor supports three profile modes: enforce, complain, and kill. "Enforce" means the predefined policies will be enforced. "Complain" means AppArmor will only report violations but will not take any actions. And "kill" means a program that violates a predefined policy will be killed. In addition, AppArmor also supports auditing, and it implements five types of auditing services including: normal, quiet_denied, quiet, noquiet, and all.

To bypass Linux AppArmor, we manipulate two variables, which are g_profile_mode and g_apparmor_audit. Both of them are defined in apparmor/lsm.c as enum type variables. The variable of g_profile_mode controls the profile mode and g_apparmor_audit controls the auditing type. The values of g_profile_mode and g_apparmor_audit can be altered so that AppArmor is running at the complain profile mode and the quiet audit type to prevent policy violations from being reported.

To evaluate the effectiveness of this attack, we write a test program called TestApp. This program attempts to read, write, and access certain files. We then define a corresponding AppArmor policy for this program. The policy states that TestApp is not allowed to read or write to File A, and is allowed to read File B but not allowed to write to it. When TestApp runs, AppArmor correctly identifies access violations according to the defined policy. Access violations are prevented and also logged. However, after we set g_profile_mode to 1 and set g_apparmor_audit to 2 (corresponding to the "complain" profile mode and the "quiet" audit type) by directly altering their values in memory, AppAmor can no longer prevent access violation or report anything even if the policy is violated.

3.2 Bypass NULL Pointer Dereference Mitigation

A NULL pointer dereference happens when a program attempts to read from or write to an invalid (and more specifically, NULL) memory location. It is commonly caused by a software bug in the program. In user programs, it causes segmentation faults; and in kernel code, it could cause system crashes. It has been demonstrated in recent years how the behavior of kernel NULL pointer dereferencing can be exploited to facilitate privilege escalation [25,33,37]. As a matter of fact, 2009 has been proclaimed by some security researchers as "the year of the kernel NULL pointer dereference flaw" [10].

By default, a NULL pointer does not correspond to any valid memory address. To exploit the NULL pointer dereference vulnerability, an attacker maps the NULL page (i.e., page zero) with a mmap() system call, puts malicious shellcode into it, and then forces a NULL pointer dereference. If done correctly, this

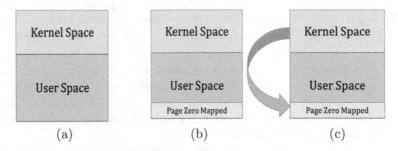

Fig. 1. Exploiting Kernel NULL Pointer Dereference

(a) Initial state; (b) Map page zero and put malicious shellcode in page zero; (c) Trigger kernel NULL pointer dereference

allows an attacker to gain root access with full control of the operating system [12,34]. Figure 1 depicts this procedure.

To mitigate this exploit, Linux introduces a variable called mmap_min_addr, which specifies the minimum virtual address that a process is allowed to map. It is set to be 4096 on x86 machines as default. By setting mmap_min_addr to 0, we can bypass this mitigation mechanism. Linux kernel actually exports mmap_min_addr to user space via the proc file system, so that system administrators can tune this variable. Consequently, any manipulation to this variable is noticeable by system administrators. To address this problem, we observe that for many proc file system entries, Linux kernel associates them with one variable and one pointer. While the variable is used by the core kernel, the pointer is used by the proc file system. In a healthy system, this pointer points to the memory location that stores this variable. Figure 2 shows this relationship. To avoid detection, we can redirect it to another memory location, which we call a *safe memory location*. A safe memory location refers to a memory address that is rarely or never used by the kernel. For example, we observe that there is a 4K gap between the end of the kernel read-only data section and the start of the kernel read-write data section, which can be used for this purpose as the kernel normally does not access any of these addresses. We also set the safe memory location's value as the default mmap_min_addr value, which is 4096. By doing so, we dissolve the connection between the pointer and the variable. This new relationship is illustrated in Figure 3. Any subsequent read or write access to /proc/sys/vm/mmap_min_addr would only access the safe memory location. This leaves the attacker free from changing the value of the corresponding kernel variable to anything he wishes without being detected by security tools that monitor abnormalities in the proc file system.

To evaluate the effectiveness of this attack, we write a C program that invokes the mmap() system call to map page zero. When mmap_min_addr is by default set to 4096, our program simply fails, and the mmap() system call returns EACCES (indicating permission denied). Next, we set the variable mmap_min_addr

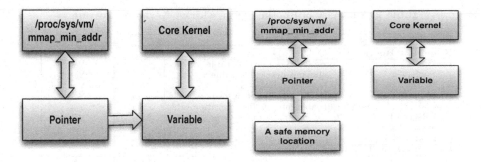

Fig. 2. Original Relationship   **Fig. 3.** After Manipulation

```
test@linux:~/test> id
uid=1001(test) gid=100(users) groups=33(video),100(users)
test@linux:~/test> whoami
test
test@linux:~/test> ./myexploit
[*] Resolving kernel addresses...
 [+] Resolved econet_ioctl to 0xf802cda8
 [+] Resolved econet_ops to 0xf802cfe4
 [+] Resolved commit_creds to 0xc104761b
 [+] Resolved prepare_kernel_cred to 0xc1047517
[*] Calculating target...
[*] Triggering payload...
[*] Got root!
linux:~/test> id
uid=0(root) gid=0(root)
linux:~/test> whoami
root
linux:~/test>
```

Fig. 4. Privilege Escalation Attack

to zero, and run the program again, this time the mmap() system call succeeds. Once this has been done, by exploiting the notorious sock_sendpage() NULL pointer dereference vulnerability (available since 2001 and was only discovered in 2009 [20]), we verified that a local unprivileged user can execute arbitrary code in kernel context and gain root privilege. This privilege escalation attack is shown in Figure 4.

4   Keylogger Design and Implementation

While the attacks we presented in Section 3 can passively bypass some of the existing security frameworks, we now demonstrate an active kernel data attack in the form of a keylogger. A keylogger is a type of surveillance software[1] that

---

[1] To be accurate, keyloggers can be classified into software and hardware types, but in this work, our focus is on software keyloggers, in particular, kernel level keyloggers.

Table 2. Summary of Rootkits with/without Keylogger Feature

Rootkit Name	Attack Vector	Keylogger	Code Injection
Complete Rootkits:			
Adore-ng-2.6	proc fs file operations table	No	Yes
SucKIT-2	interrupt descriptor table	No	Yes
DR	debug register	No	Yes
enyelkm v1.1	system call table, interrupt descriptor table	No	Yes
Knark 2.4.3	system call table, proc fs file operation table	No	Yes
KBeast-v1	system call table	Yes	Yes
Sebek 3.1.2b	system call table	Yes	Yes
Mood-nt 2.3	system call table	Yes	Yes
Demonstrates Key Logging Only:			
Linspy v2beta2	system call table	Yes	Yes
kkeylogger	system call table	Yes	Yes
vlogger	tty → ldisc.receive_buf	Yes	Yes

records the keystrokes typed by a user. Over the years, keyloggers have been demonstrated to be a tremendous threat in the real world. For example, in 2008, a keylogger harvested over 500,000 online banking and other account information [30]. And then in 2013, 2 million Facebook, Gmail, and Twitter passwords were compromised by a keylogger [1].

Keyloggers are commonly implemented as a part of kernel rootkits. Before we present the design of our keylogger, we first studied 10 existing rootkits, as shown in Table 2. Most of these rootkits were also studied by many recent research efforts [3,14,15,22,27,29].

From Table 2, we can see that among the 10 rootkits we have studied, six of them have a keylogging feature, including KBeast, Sebek, Mood-nt, Linspy, kkeylogger, and vlogger. Except for vlogger, the other five rootkits use similar techniques to record keyboard inputs, i.e., by intercepting read or write system calls. By contrast, vlogger [31] attempts to hijack the tty buffer processing function, instead of intercepting read/write system calls.

We can also see from Table 2 that, no matter which approach they use, existing keyloggers rely heavily on hooking kernel function pointers to interpose its own functions. As we described before, recent advances on the defense side have already demonstrated their effectiveness in defeating this type of attack, therefore, a new attack method is needed. In this work, we propose a new keylogger, called DLOGGER[2], which only relies on manipulating kernel data. The key idea behind DLOGGER is that, when the keyboard receives any input information, that piece of information must be transferred into the kernel (via the keyboard driver) and stored in a memory buffer. A keylogger should grab that information and pass it to the user space. Since we are not allowed to run our own code, we have to enable the kernel do the information passing, i.e., pass the data from the kernel into the user space. Fortunately, the Linux kernel does provide such an avenue, the proc file system (and also the sysfs file system), which bridges the kernel space and the user space. Thus, if we can direct the kernel to pass the information from its memory buffer into a proc file system buffer, or if we can

---

[2] DLOGGER, denotes Data only attack based keyLOGGER.

redirect a proc file system pointer to that memory buffer, then we can expect that, by reading from a file under the /proc directory, an ordinary user can collect that information.

The detailed explanation of our design is as follows. To receive user input, the Linux kernel emulates several terminal devices, called ttys, and the first emulated terminal device is referred to as tty1. For each emulated terminal device, the kernel would generate a file under the /dev directory, as the Linux system views every device as a file. So, /dev/tty1 represents the emulated terminal device tty1. The kernel defines a data structure called *struct tty_struct* (include/linux/tty.h), which refers to one tty terminal device. And *struct tty_struct* has a field called *char * read_buf*, which is exactly the memory buffer to accommodate the user input from that emulated terminal device. By opening the device file /dev/tty1, we can get its file descriptor, which has a pointer pointing to the *struct tty_struct*. Once we access the *struct tty_struct*, we can locate the address of its *read_buf*. Then we need to pick up a proc file system pointer, and let it point to this memory buffer. The selected proc file system pointer should represent a proc file that is rarely accessed by system administrators. Given the fact that there are a large number of files under a proc file system, a vast majority of files under /proc would rarely, if not never, be accessed. In our experiments, we choose /proc/sys/kernel/modprobe. In a healthy system, cat /proc/sys/kernel/-modprobe would display the path of the modprobe binary[3], which by default, is /sbin/modprobe. The kernel defines a char pointer called modprobe_path, which just points to the string "/sbin/modprobe". Consequently, if we set this char pointer to the tty_struct's read_buf, we can expect that any read to /proc/sys/kernel/modprobe would display the content of the tty read buffer, which should be the user input from keyboard.

Figures 5, 6, 7 illustrate how DLOGGER differs from existing keyloggers. Figure 5 shows the normal data flow, i.e., when there is no keylogger. Figure 6 shows the data flow of a traditional keylogger, and Figure 7 shows the data flow of DLOGGER. It can be seen from these figures, while existing keyloggers actually change the data flow, DLOGGER does not, instead, it creates a new branch to collect the information.

We then validate the efficacy of DLOGGER. After login as the root user from a tty terminal, we input our password, and type several commands. We then try to login remotely as an ordinary user, by reading the /proc/sys/kernel/modprobe file, we can see the information typed in the tty terminal.

5   Defense

In this section, we first present a defense mechanism to detect kernel data attacks by classifying kernel data into different types. Then, we evaluate the effectiveness of the proposed defense and measure its overhead in terms of CPU and memory usage.

---

[3] The modprobe binary is a program to add or remove loadable modules to/from the Linux kernel.

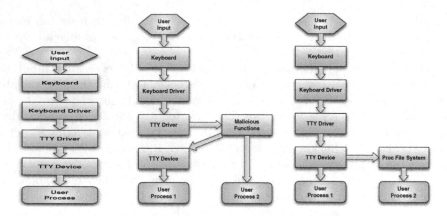

Fig. 5. Normal Data Flow **Fig. 6.** Data Flow in a Tra- **Fig. 7.** Data Flow in DLOG-
ditional Keylogger   GER

5.1 Defense Mechanism

We observe that kernel data can be classified into the following four types:

- Type 1: Read-only data.
- Type 2: Modifiable data that normally remains constant across different systems.
- Type 3: Modifiable data that normally does not change, but can differ from system to system.
- Type 4: Modifiable data that changes frequently.

The different types of data exhibit different runtime behavioral characteristics. An effective defense mechanism, thus, should be tailored to the characteristics of the different types. Our defense mechanism consists of two phases: splitting phase and monitoring phase.

Splitting Phase. In this phase, we split different types of data into different lists. To accomplish this, we first set up multiple identical virtual machines. In our experiment we used two VMs, which we observed were as good as if we had more VMs, VM1 and VM2. Algorithm 1 describes the subsequent splitting procedure. Essentially, we get all the variable symbols from /proc/kallsyms and put them into a list called ListAll. We then use List1, List2, List3, and List4 to represent the symbol lists for Type 1, Type 2, Type 3, and Type 4 data, respectively. The algorithm consists of three steps:

- The first step is to get List 1. It is rather straightforward, as these symbols are explicitly marked in the /proc/kallsyms with a "r" or "R". Therefore, we extract all these symbols and put them into List1, and leave the rest into ListRW (denoting a list of read-write symbols).

Algorithm 1. Get Type 1,2,3,4 symbols

Require: /proc/kallsyms, VM1, VM2
Ensure: VM1 and VM2 run the same OS, have the same configuration
   $ListAll \leftarrow Get$ all variable symbols from /proc/kallsyms
   $List1 \leftarrow Get$ all read only symbols from /proc/kallsyms
   $ListRW \leftarrow ListAll - List1$
   for each symbol in $ListRW$ **do**
      $var1 \leftarrow get$ its value from VM1
      $var2 \leftarrow get$ its value from VM2
      if $var1 = var2$ **then**
         $List2 \leftarrow insert$ symbol
      else
         $ListDiff \leftarrow insert$ symbol
      end if
   end for
   for each symbol in $ListDiff$ **do**
      $var0min \leftarrow get$ its value from VM1
      $ListPair0 \leftarrow insert$ (symbol,var)
   end for
   wait for a predefined time interval $T1$
   for each symbol in $ListDiff$ **do**
      $vartmin \leftarrow get$ its value from VM1
      $var0min \leftarrow get$ its value from $ListPair0$
      if $var0min = vartmin$ **then**
         $List3 \leftarrow insert$ symbol
      else
         $List4 \leftarrow insert$ symbol
      end if
   end for

- The next step is to extract List2 from ListRW. Since Type 2 data remain the same across VM1 and VM2, for the symbols in ListRW, we get their values from VM1 and VM2, identify those equivalent pairs, and put these symbols into List2, and leave the rest into ListDiff.
- The final step is to extract Type 3 and Type 4 data from ListDiff. Since data in Type 3 rarely change, for each symbol in ListDiff, we measure its value from VM1 at multiple points during a span of multiple days. If no changes were identified, we put it into List3; otherwise, we put it into List4. To avoid false positives in the later monitoring phase, this step should be run iteratively, so that we can ensure List 3 only contains data that rarely change or never change.

Monitoring Phase. After we have built List1, List2, List3, and List4, we can start the monitoring phase. Typically, an attack target falls into either Type 1, Type 2, or Type 3 categories. As for Type 4 data, they can be divided into six subtypes, which are shown in Table 3.

Type 4 data are very system-specific. An example of such data is jiffies, which is a global variable Linux kernel used to keep track of the number of ticks since the system last booted. It is highly unlikely that the jiffies values would be the same between two systems. We did not discover any Type 4 data that could have been attacked similarly to those we illustrated before, and thus, we focus on the other data types for building our defense mechanism. Type 1 data are

Algorithm 2. Monitor Type 2,3 symbols

Require: List2, List3, VM1, VM2
Ensure: VM1 and VM2 run the same OS, have the same configuration
  for each symbol in List3 **do**
    $varinit \leftarrow get$ its value from VM1
    $ListPair0 \leftarrow insert$ (symbol,$varinit$)
  end for
  loop
    for each symbol in List2 **do**
      $var1 \leftarrow get$ its value from VM1
      $var2 \leftarrow get$ its value from VM2
      if $var1 \neq var2$ **then**
        Raise Alarm: Symbol Value Changed
      end if
    end for
    wait for a predefined time interval $T2$
    for each symbol in List3 **do**
      $varrun \leftarrow get$ its value from VM1
      $varinit \leftarrow get$ its value from $ListPair0$
      if $varrun \neq varinit$ **then**
        Raise Alarm: Symbol Value Changed
      end if
    end for
  end loop

Table 3. Global Variables Belong to Type 4

Category	Example Variable	Meaning
Timing Related	jiffies	The number of clock ticks have occurred since the system booted
Random Numbers	skb_tx_hashrnd	A random hash value for socket buffer
Runtime Workload Related	nr_files	Number of opened files
Index Related	log_start	Index into log_buf
Cookies	fsnotify_sync_cookie	Cookies used by fsnotify to synchronize monitored events
Spinlocks and Semaphores	pidmap_lock	Spinlock for pidhash table

read-only, and prior works [13,43] have already demonstrated thoroughly how to defeat such attacks.

To detect attacks against Type 2 data, one can use an approach similar to PeerPressure [41], where collective information across peer machines dictates what is normal and what is abnormal for data values. For Type 3 data, as they normally do not change once initialized, one can record their initial values and periodically compare their current values against initial ones, similar to the Tripwire [17] approach. Algorithm 2 depicts this monitor procedure.

5.2   Defense Evaluation

To evaluate the effectiveness and performance overhead of our defense mechanism, we conducted several experiments on a hypervisor running two VMs. Based on Algorithm 2, we developed a tool that runs on the hypervisor level and monitors both Type 2 and Type 3 data. Any kernel data attacks (those described in Sections 3 and 4) can be easily detected. Naturally, the detection response time and performance overhead are mainly dependent on the time interval described in Algorithm 2. A shorter interval leads to a shorter response time but a higher performance overhead. However, since the tool is rather lightweight, we do not

Table 4. CPU Overhead (%)

Interval / Benchmark	1000ms	500ms	100ms	0ms
Cuadro	0.35	1.69	2.88	3.28
Kernel Decompression	0.70	1.87	3.10	4.06

expect it to cause any noticeable performance overhead. For example, when we set the time interval to 500 milliseconds, and we mounted the attacks presented in Sections 3 and 4, all the attacks can be detected in about 1 second. We measured the monitoring tool's performance overhead by using the cuadro benchmark [11], which shows the CPU overhead is less than 2% when the time interval is set to 500 milliseconds. We also run a Linux kernel decompression task, in which a standard Linux kernel source package linux-2.6.34.tar.bz2 is decompressed with the *tar* program. The result also shows that the monitor tools incurs less than 2% of runtime overhead when the time interval is set to 500 milliseconds. Table 4 lists these experimental results. We also observed that the memory usage of our defense is no more than 0.3%. Therefore, the performance overhead induced by our defense is negligible. Additionally, since we use an iterative approach in the splitting phase, we ensure only those data that never change are classified as Type 3, and thus, there is no false positive during the monitoring phase.

6   Discussion

In this section, we discuss the limitations and extensions of kernel data attack. While we have mainly demonstrated malicious exploits based on global variables, attackers can also potentially misuse local variables. Local variables are stored in kernel stacks or heaps. A sophisticated attacker can explore the kernel memory to identify the locations of any exploitable local variables. In fact, manipulating local variables could make the attack even more undetectable as knowing what is a good value of every local variable is almost impossible.

Linux kernel extensively uses linked list data structures. Many of these linked lists change frequently, e.g., the linked list representing the current running processes. An element is added to the list when a process is created, and is removed when the process exits. In a running system, as there are a lot of process creation and destroy events, this linked list changes almost constantly, which makes anomaly detection on the linked list a daunting task. A common attack many existing rootkits use is to remove certain elements from the process linked list (used by the *ps* command) to hide certain malicious processes. This works well due to the fact that the CPU scheduler uses another process linked list when scheduling processes. As stated earlier, it is becoming increasingly difficult to inject malicious code and launch malicious processes as it is easily detectable by many security tools. However, a similar attack can still be mounted, but in a reverse manner, i.e., by removing an element from the CPU scheduler linked list but keeping it in the *ps* linked list, an attacker can prevent a benign process (e.g., a process launched by a security tool) from being scheduled. Even if system administrators periodically check if this process is still running by using the *ps* command, they will be deceived to believe that the process is running normally.

A limitation of the kernel data attack is that it no longer works when the target system reboots as all the modified data are in memory. One could persist all the kernel data changes by modifying system initialization scripts, but this will render the attack more prone to be detected. However, as non-volatile memory technology is getting cheaper and denser, many researchers [2,7,21,38] believe that it will soon appear on the processor memory bus complementing the traditional memory. As non-volatile memory becomes more prevalent, it will make kernel data attack easier to be mounted and last longer. In addition, some of the global data can be accessed by multiple processes/threads, modifying these data might cause side effects. Therefore, how to ensure the safe execution of the OS kernel is something that attackers have to handle.

7   Related Work

Kernel Data Attack and Defense: Although kernel data consists of both function pointers and variables, most attacks against function pointers still require injecting new code. Therefore, we do not categorize these attacks as kernel data attacks. Also, defeating such an attack is straightforward, either by protecting function pointers [42] or monitoring system control flow integrity [29]. In contrast, kernel data attacks that only manipulate variables or variable pointers, instead of function pointers, are more stealthy and harder to defeat. This type of attack is defined by Chen et al. [9] as non-control-data attack. But they demonstrated the viability of such an attack at the application level rather than at the kernel level. The possibility of mounting this type of attack at the kernel level is first presented in [4]. However, among the four different attack cases shown in the work, three of them still require attackers run their own code at the kernel level; the remaining one merely degrades system performance by manipulating memory page related data.

To defend against non-control data attacks, Baliga et al. [3] proposed Gibraltar, which infers kernel invariants during the training stage and protects the integrity of these invariants at runtime. Petroni et al. [28] and Hofmann et al. [15] both proposed a specification based solution, which requires users manually specify integrity check policies. Although these solutions are effective in defeating several rootkits that manipulate non-control-data, they rely heavily on a prior knowledge of the attacks, which limits themselves to deal with existing rootkits only. As the space for kernel data attack is enormous, attackers have sufficient target data to exploit and bypass these defense tools. In addition, Bianchi et al. [6] designed Blacksheep, which aims to detect kernel data attack, but it ends up failing to do so. The main reason is that their approach is mainly through analyzing memory dump, which includes all kinds of kernel data. They computed a difference for all the data between multiple dump images, and a significant difference between them would raise an alarm. They finally conceded that their approach is not effective against kernel data attack, and they attributed it to that kernel data continues to change while taking memory dumps.

Keylogger: Keyloggers, including both software and hardware keyloggers, have been studied extensively over the past years. Compared with software keyloggers, hardware based keyloggers [5,18,40,46], either rely on an external device to collect the acoustic or electromagnetic emanations of the keyboard, or utilize a GPU to monitor the keyboard buffer. A common limitation of these hardware based keyloggers is that attackers must have physical access to the victim system, which to some extent, restricts the impact of this attack. In contrast, software based keyloggers do not have this limit. To defend against software based keyloggers, as well as other malware that collects user privacy information, a number of taint analysis based solutions have been proposed [16,24,44,45]. The key observation of these approaches is that keyloggers or malware usually incur suspicious access to sensitive information. By tracking the information flow, these tools are able to accurately detect privacy leakage. However, these approaches usually induce significant performance degradation, and thus might not be suitable for deploying in production systems. For instance, Panorama causes a system slowdown by a factor of 20. Moreover, Slowinska et al. [36] evaluated the practicality of taint analysis, and found that most of the existing solutions have serious drawbacks; finally, they concluded that taint analysis "may have some value in detecting memory corruption attacks, but it is fundamentally not suitable for automated detecting of privacy-breaching malware such as keyloggers".

8   Conclusion

Without injecting any kernel-level malicious code, attackers can launch a kernel data attack in a much more stealthy manner by merely altering kernel data. However, whether kernel data attack could cause serious security damage to a victim system is unanswered question. In this paper, we have demonstrated the severity of kernel data attack. In particular, we have shown that by altering in-memory global kernel data, attackers can bypass the Linux Auditing framework, the Linux Apparmor framework, and the NULL pointer dereference mitigation, which significantly facilitates malicious privilege escalation. To further demonstrate the security threat posed by kernel data attack, we have designed and implemented a new keylogger. Our keylogger is more stealthy than existing keyloggers and is able to evade the existing rootkit/keylogger detection tools, as it neither changes any kernel code nor requires running a hidden process. Therefore, we conclude that kernel data attacks are indeed realistic security threats. To counter against kernel data attacks, we have proposed a defense mechanism that classifies kernel data into four different types and handles these different types of kernel data separately. Our experimental results show that our proposed defense is very effective against kernel data attacks.

References

1. 2 million facebook, gmail and twitter passwords stolen in massive hack (2013). http://money.cnn.com/2013/12/04/technology/security/passwords-stolen/
2. Bailey, K., Ceze, L., Gribble, S. D., Levy, H. M.: Operating system implications of fast, cheap, non-volatile memory. In: Proceedings of the 13th USENIX Conference on Hot topics in Operating Systems (HotOS), pp. 2–7. USENIX Association (2011)
3. Baliga, A., Ganapathy, V., Iftode, L.: Automatic inference and enforcement of kernel data structure invariants. In: Annual Computer Security Applications Conference (ACSAC), pp. 77–86. IEEE (2008)
4. Baliga, A., Kamat, P., Iftode, L.: Lurking in the shadows: identifying systemic threats to kernel data. In: IEEE Symposium on Security and Privacy (SP), pp. 246–251. IEEE (2007)
5. Berger, Y., Wool, A., Yeredor, A.: Dictionary attacks using keyboard acoustic emanations. In: Proceedings of the 13th ACM Conference on Computer and Communications Security (CCS), pp. 245–254. ACM (2006)
6. Bianchi, A., Shoshitaishvili, Y., Kruegel, C., Vigna, G.: Blacksheep: detecting compromised hosts in homogeneous crowds. In: Proceedings of the ACM Conference on Computer and Communications Security (CCS), pp. 341–352. ACM (2012)
7. Caulfield, A.M., De, A., Coburn, J., Mollow, T.I., Gupta, R.K., Swanson, S.: Moneta: a high-performance storage array architecture for next-generation, non-volatile memories. In: Proceedings of the 43rd Annual IEEE/ACM International Symposium on Microarchitecture (MICRO), pp. 385–395. IEEE Computer Society (2010)
8. Checkoway, S., Davi, L., Dmitrienko, A., Sadeghi, A.-R., Shacham, H., Winandy, M.: Return-oriented programming without returns. In: Proceedings of the 17th ACM Conference on Computer and Communications Security (CCS), pp. 559–572. ACM (2010)
9. Chen, S., Xu, J., Sezer, E.C., Gauriar, P., Iyer, R.K.: Non-control-data attacks are realistic threats. In: Proceedings of the 14th Conference on USENIX Security Symposium, p. 12 (2005)
10. Cox, M.: Red hat's top 11 most serious flaw types for 2009 (2010). https://lwn.net/Articles/374752/
11. Cuadro cpu benchmark. http://sourceforge.net/projects/cuadrocpubenchm
12. Elhage, N.: Much ado about null: Exploiting a kernel null dereference. https://blogs.oracle.com/ksplice/entry/much_ado_about_null_exploiting1
13. Garfinkel, T., Rosenblum, M.: A virtual machine introspection based architecture for intrusion detection. In: Proceedings of the 10th Annual Symposium on Network and Distributed Systems Security (NDSS), pp. 191–206 (2003)
14. Gu, Z., Sumner, W.N., Deng, Z., Zhang, X., Drip, D.: A framework for purifying trojaned kernel drivers. In: Proceedings of the 43rd Annual IEEE/IFIP International Conference on Dependable Systems and Networks (DSN). IEEE (2013)
15. Hofmann, O., Dunn, A., Kim, S., Roy, I., Witchel, E.: Ensuring operating system kernel integrity with osck. In: Proceedings of the Sixteenth International Conference on Architectural Support for Programming Languages and Operating Systems (ASPLOS), pp. 279–290. ACM (2011)
16. Kang, M.G., McCamant, S., Poosankam, P., Song, D.: Dta++: dynamic taint analysis with targeted control-flow propagation. In: Proceedings of the 18th Annual Symposium on Network and Distributed Systems Security (NDSS) (2011)

17. Kim, G.H., Spafford, E.H.: The design, implementation of tripwire: a file system integrity checker. In: Proceedings of the 2nd ACM Conference on Computer and Communications Security (CCS), pp. 18–29. ACM (1994)
18. Ladakis, E., Koromilas, L., Vasiliadis, G., Polychronakis, M., Ioannidis, S.: You can type, but you can't hide: a stealthy gpu-based keylogger. In: Proceedings of the 6th European Workshop on System Security (EuroSec) (2013)
19. Li, J., Wang, Z., Jiang, X., Grace, M., Bahram, S.: Defeating return-oriented rootkits with return-less kernels. In: Proceedings of the 5th European Conference on Computer Systems (EuroSys), pp. 195–208. ACM (2010)
20. Linux kernel 'sock_sendpage()' null pointer dereference vulnerability. http://www.securityfocus.com/bid/36038
21. Liu, R., Shen, D., Yang, C., Yu, S., Wang, C.M.: Nvm duet: unified working memory and persistent store architecture. In: Proceedings of the 19th International Conference on Architectural Support for Programming Languages and Operating Systems (ASPLOS), pp. 455–470. ACM (2014)
22. Liu, Z., Lee, J., Zeng, J., Wen, Y., Lin, Z., Shi, W.: Cpu transparent protection of os kernel and hypervisor integrity with programmable dram. In: Proceedings of the 40th Annual International Symposium on Computer Architecture (ISCA), pp. 392–403. ACM/IEEE (2013)
23. Moon, H., Lee, H., Lee, J., Kim, K., Paek, Y., Kang, B.B.: Vigilare: toward snoop-based kernel integrity monitor. In: Proceedings of the ACM Conference on Computer and Communications Security (CCS), pp. 28–37. ACM (2012)
24. Newsome, J., Song, D.X.: Dynamic taint analysis for automatic detection, analysis, and signature generation of exploits on commodity software. In: Proceedings of the 13th Annual Symposium on Network and Distributed System Security Symposium (NDSS) (2005)
25. Ormandy, T.: Another kernel null pointer vulnerability. http://lwn.net/Articles/347006/
26. Pappas, V., Polychronakis, M., Keromytis, A.D.: Smashing the gadgets: hindering return-oriented programming using in-place code randomization. In: IEEE Symposium on Security and Privacy (SP), pp. 601–615. IEEE (2012)
27. Petroni, Jr., N.L., Fraser, T., Molina, J., Arbaugh, W.A.: Copilot-a coprocessor-based kernel runtime integrity monitor. In: Proceedings of the 13th Conference on USENIX Security Symposium, pp. 179–194 (2004)
28. Petroni, Jr., N.L., Fraser, T., Walters, A., Arbaugh, W.A.: An architecture for specification-based detection of semantic integrity violations in kernel dynamic data. In: Proceedings of the 15th Conference on USENIX Security Symposium, pp. 15–22 (2006)
29. Petroni, Jr., N.L., Hicks, M.: Automated detection of persistent kernel control-flow attacks. In: Proceedings of the 14th ACM Conference on Computer and Communications Security (CCS), pp. 103–115. ACM (2007)
30. Raywood, D.: Sinowal trojan steals data from around 500,000 cards and accounts. SC Magazine (2008)
31. rd. Writing linux kernel keylogger. https://www.thc.org/papers/writing-linux-kernel-keylogger.txt
32. Riley, R., Jiang, X., Xu, D.: Guest-transparent prevention of kernel rootkits with vmm-based memory shadowing. In: Lippmann, R., Kirda, E., Trachtenberg, A. (eds.) RAID 2008. LNCS, vol. 5230, pp. 1–20. Springer, Heidelberg (2008)
33. Rosenberg, D.: Interesting kernel exploit posted. https://lwn.net/Articles/419141/
34. Rosenberg, D.: Linux kernel <= 2.6.37 - local privilege escalation. http://www.exploit-db.com/exploits/15704/

35. Schwartz, E.J., Avgerinos, T., Brumley, D.: Q: exploit hardening made easy. In: Proceedings of the 20th Conference on USENIX Security Symposium (2011)
36. Slowinska, A., Bos, H.: Pointless tainting?: evaluating the practicality of pointer tainting. In: Proceedings of the 4th ACM European Conference on Computer systems (EuroSys), pp. 61–74. ACM (2009)
37. Spengler, B.: On exploiting null ptr derefs, disabling selinux, and silently fixedlinux vulns. http://seclists.org/dailydave/2007/q1/224
38. Venkataraman, S., Tolia, N., Ranganathan, P., Campbell, R.H., et al.: Consistent and durable data structures for non-volatile byte-addressable memory. In: Proceedings of the 9th USENIX Conference on File and Storage Technologies (FAST), pp. 61–75 (2011)
39. Vogl, S., Pfoh, J., Kittel, T., Eckert, C.: Persistent data-only malware: function hooks without code. In: Symposium on Network and Distributed System Security (NDSS) (2014)
40. Vuagnoux, M., Pasini, S.: Compromising electromagnetic emanations of wired and wireless keyboards. In: Proceedings of the 18th Conference on USENIX Security Symposium, pp. 1–16 (2009)
41. Wang, H.J., Platt, J.C., Chen, Y., Zhang, R., Wang, Y.-M.: Automatic misconfiguration troubleshooting with peerpressure. In: Proceedings of the 6th USENIX Conference on Operating Systems Design and Implementation (OSDI), vol. 4, pp. 245–257 (2004)
42. Wang, Z., Jiang, X., Cui, W., Ning, P.: Countering kernel rootkits with lightweight hook protection. In: Proceedings of the 16th ACM Conference on Computer and Communications Security (CCS), pp. 545–554. ACM (2009)
43. J. Xiao, Xu, Z., Huang, H., Wang, H.: Security implications of memory deduplication in a virtualized environment. In: Proceedings of the 43rd Annual IEEE/IFIP International Conference on Dependable Systems and Networks (DSN), pp. 1–12. IEEE (2013)
44. Yin, H., Liang, Z., Song, D.: HookFinder: identifying and understanding malware hooking behaviors. In: Proceedings of the 15th Annual Symposium on Network and Distributed Systems Security (NDSS) (2008)
45. Yin, H., Song, D., Egele, M., Kruegel, C., Kirda, E.: Panorama: capturing system-wide information flow for malware detection and analysis. In: Proceedings of the 14th ACM Conference on Computer and Communications Security (CCS), pp. 116–127. ACM (2007)
46. Zhuang, L., Zhou, F., Tygar, J.D.: Keyboard acoustic emanations revisited. In: Proceedings of the 12th ACM Conference on Computer and Communications Security (CCS), pp. 373–382. ACM (2005)

Cloud Security

RScam: Cloud-Based Anti-Malware via Reversible Sketch

Hao Sun[1](✉), Xiaofeng Wang[1], Jinshu Su[1,2], and Peixin Chen[1]

[1] College of Computer, National University of Defense Technology, Changsha, China
haosunlight@163.com
[2] National Key Laboratory for Parallel and Distributed Processing,
National University of Defense Technology, Changsha, China

Abstract. Cybercrime caused by malware becomes a persistent and damaging threat which makes the trusted security solution urgently demanded, especially for resource-constrained ends. The existing industry and academic approaches provide available anti-malware systems based on different perspectives. However, it is hard to achieve high performance detection and data privacy protection simultaneously. This paper proposes a cloud-based anti-malware system, called RScam, which provides fast and trusted security service for the resource-constrained ends. In RScam, we present suspicious bucket filtering, a novel signature-based detection mechanism based on the reversible sketch structure, which provides retrospective and accurate orientations of malicious signature fragments. Then we design a lightweight client which utilizes the digest of signature fragments to sharply reduce detection range. Finally, we design balanced interaction mechanism, which transmits sketch coordinates of suspicious file fragments and transformation of malicious signature fragments between the client and cloud server to protect data privacy and reduce traffic volume. We evaluate the performance of RScam with campus suspicious traffic and normal files. The results demonstrate validity and veracity of the proposed mechanism. Our system can outperform other existing systems with less time and traffic consumption.

Keywords: Reversible sketch · Suspicious bucket filtering · Signature-based · Anti-malware · Cloud-based

1 Introduction

Cybercrime caused by malicious software(malware) is a persistent and damaging threat looms over businesses and consumers. Targeted attacks increase every year and expose more interest in social media and mobile devices as they are continuing to work their ways deeper into our digital lives. In the year of 2014, 496,657 web attacks blocked per day, and of the 6.3 million apps analyzied, one million of these are classified as mobile malware [1]. The McAfee Labs indicate attacks on the Internet of Things devices will increase rapidly due to hypergrowth in the number of connected objects, poor security hygiene and the high value of

© Institute for Computer Sciences, Social Informatics and Telecommunications Engineering 2015
B. Thuraisingham et al. (Eds.): SecureComm 2015, LNICST 164, pp. 157–174, 2015.
DOI: 10.1007/978-3-319-28865-9_9

data on these devices [2]. Hence, it is urgent to provide a trusted and one-stop security solution to take care of data privacy in those resource-constrained ends.

To defend against various malware, signature-based detection approach still plays an important role and takes up a large proportion after decades of development in both industry and academic research. It is based on the theory that the crux of various malware, called signature, is generally unchangeable and can be detected at the early stage of propagation though the amount of malware samples is limited [3]. This approach is implemented by scanning and checking if a file contains the contents which match the known signatures. There are several commonly used and effective signature matching algorithms, such as Aho-Corasick [4] and Wu-Manber [5]. Besides, many heuristic and complex algorithms [21,22] are proposed for detecting unknown signatures. However, most of them consume a great mount of memory and time which is inapplicable for resource-constrained devices.

Two primary kinds of anti-malware systems with signature-based approach have been deployed according to their infrastructures in state-of-the-art technology. The first one is host-based systems which install detection agents in the users' devices and update the signature databases to ensure timely and complete security protection. ClamAV [6] is an open-source anti-virus system most widely used and many reformative works based on it are recently proposed, such as GrAVity [7]. However, these systems have become increasingly bloated with the development of malware attacks [8]. The problems mainly embody in the following two areas: (1) heavy resource consumption caused by the growing number of signatures, such as memory, time and network bandwidth; (2) system vulnerabilities are easy to be aimed due to their complexity.

The other solution is cloud-based security service [2] which places different types of detection agents over the cloud servers and offers security as a service. This newly developed framework is lenitive and cost-saving for resource-constrained ends. However, the existing cloud-based anti-malware technologies cannot address the following problems: (1) security vendors are designed to directly expose or deliver the signature databases to the clients which is unwillingness for the vendors and do not actually lighten the consumption of clients, such as SplitScreen [9]; (2) users have to upload the whole file contents which may result in some important information(e.g., location, password) leakage without realization, such as CloudAV [10]; (3) the optimization of traffic volume between the server and client is often neglected which is significant for the improvement of detection efficiency. Hence, it is hard to achieve high performance of security detection and data privacy protection simultaneously.

To overcome above shortcomings, we propose a cloud-based anti-malware system, called RScam, which provides fast and trusted security service for the resource-constrained ends. Specifically, we make the following contributions:

- We propose a novel signature-based detection mechanism, called suspicious bucket filtering, based on the structure of reversible sketch for cloud server. It can provide retrospective and accurate orientations of malicious signature fragments. As a result, the time and computation consumption in signature-based malware scanning are cut down. To the best of our knowledge, no previous work has implemented similar endeavor.

- We implement a lightweight client which utilizes the digest of signature fragments to rapidly classify the file contents into suspicious and clean parts. It can dramatically reduce the scanning range with slight adjustable false positive and further avoid the accurate matching of the whole file contents.
- To protect the data privacy and reduce the traffic volume, we design the balanced interaction mechanism. The client transmits the sketch coordinates of suspicious file segments, instead of the whole file content, to the cloud after fast matching. As for the cloud server, transformations of signature fragments are sent back to the client, rather than the signature database.

We analyze the accuracy of the proposed mechanism theoretically to prove its validity and veracity with appropriate parameters. Our implementation of RScam consists of roughly 2.5K lines of C/C++ code for client and 4.5K for server which makes it easily applied to the resource-constrained devices. In addition, we evaluate the system by normal files and suspicious traffic captured from campus network with the number of signatures ranges from 460000 to 3700000. Statistical results show that RScam can outperform ClamAV and SplitScreen with lower time consumption and smoother increment when scanning increasing number of samples. Moreover, the traffic volume in RScam is averagely 10 times smaller than that in SplitScreen.

The rest of this paper is organized as follows: Section 2 introduces related work about signature-based malware detection. Section 3 gives a detail description about the system architecture and signature-based detection mechanism, followed by discussion of the system in Section 4. Section 5 presents the experimental results and analysis. Finally, we conclude the paper in Section 6.

2   Related Work

Signature-based malware detection remains important and technically reliable after decades of development in anti-malware industry.

ClamAV [6] is the most widespread and representative open-source anti-malware system. The latest database(main v.55 and daily v.19688) approximately contains 3700000 signatures consist of MD5 and regular expression signatures. Input file contents are sequentially matched with the signature database when scanning. If a known signature is successfully matched, the file is claimed to be infected by malware. The matching algorithms adopted are primarily Aho-Corasick [3] and Wu-Manber [5].

Recently, several efforts to improve the detection performance based on host have been proposed. Hash-AV [11] proposes a malware scanning technique which aims to take advantage of improvements in CPU performance. It utilizes hashing functions that fit in L2 caches to speed up the exact pattern matching algorithms in ClamAV. GrAVity [7] is a massively parallel anti-malware engine which utilize the good performance of GPUs to accelerate the process of scanning. Hardware implementations provide better performance, but it is always impracticable for the resource-constrained devices, such as mobile phones and wearable devices. Deepak et al. [12] design a signature matching algorithm which is well suited in mobile device scanning, but its testing signatures are limited by fixed byte and the performance declines with the growth of signatures volume.

Cloud servers provide high-performance computation support to reduce the match consumption in malware scanning which is the main limitation of signature-based mechanism. Now it is attracting lots of security vendors to start to deploy their cloud solutions, like Trend Micro, Panda Security and Kaspersky Lab.

CloudAV [10] first puts forward the notion of cloud-based malware scanning in academic research and the authors apply their strategy to a mobile environment [13]. It runs a local cloud service consists of heterogeneous anti-virus engines running in parallel virtual machines and uses an end-user agent to transfer suspicious files to the cloud to be checked by all anti-virus engines. CloudAV achieves high detection rate, yet obviously, exposes the sensitive data which compromise users privacy. CloudSEC [14] achieves similar research which moves the analysis and correlation of network alerts into network cloud which also consists of plenty autonomous anti-malware agents, Jakobsson et al. [15] proposed a strategy for malware scanning which allows trusted cloud servers to look through the activity logs of clients in order to give timely monitoring and protection.

SplitScreen [9] designs a distributed anti-malware system based on ClamAV to speed up the malware scanning. SplitScreen designs its first scanning mechanism based on Bloom filter [16] to perform slight comparisons with file data and reduce the size to be accurately matched. However, bloom filter is not reversible which is similar to sketch data structure due to the multiple-to-one nature of hashing functions, so it does not store any information about the fragments. Actually the first scanning is so coarse-grained that the client still spends plenty of time and computation in exact pattern matching. Our study results show SplitScreen averagely spends 74.3 percent of its time in accurate pattern matching about 65 percent of pending files with small caches.

Our work is inspired by SplitScreen, but differs from it on two significant fronts. First, we employ reversible sketch structure with buckets containing suspicious signature fragments for malware detection. It is more efficient than Bloom filter structure because of needless to accurately match the whole contents of suspicious files. Second, we give consideration to the perspectives of both anti-malware vendors and end-users. Given the rapid incremental trend of signature volume and the security vendors unwillingness of directly exposing malware signature databases which are their core profit and competitiveness, the system opts to transmit the sketch coordinates of file fragments and transformation of malicious signature fragments between the client and cloud server which cut down the traffic volume simultaneously.

3   Design

In this section, we present a lightweight cloud-based anti-malware system called RScam, which can provide fast and trusted security protection for the resource-constrained ends. We first show the system architecture of RScam and then give a detail description about the signature-based detection mechanism via reversible sketch structure in the proposed system.

3.1   System Architecture

To break out of high time consumption, which is primarily caused by a vast sum of signatures, RScam adopts the reversible sketch structure for effective representation and orientations of signatures, while designing balanced interactive mechanism to protect the data privacy and reduce the traffic volume.

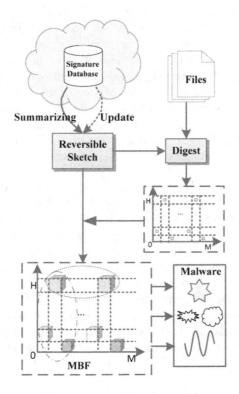

Fig. 1. The system architecture of RScam

We illustrate the system architecture of RScam in Fig. 1. The cloud server maintains the signature database, summarizes the signatures into the reversible sketch. Meanwhile, the cloud generates a digest of the sketch which represents the existence of signatures. The digest is stored in the client when RScam is firstly installed. The cloud updates the signature database and sketch periodically and sends the locations in the sketch where the changes take place to the client. The detail operations will be described in Section 3.3. As for file scanning, the client first initializes the file contents into the segments by the similarity method with the signatures(described in section 3.2), then sifts out the unmatched segments with the digest. The matched ones are suspicious and their sketch coordinates in the digest are sent to the cloud, rather than the whole file contents. We design the suspicious bucket filtering(SBF) mechanism for the cloud to locate the malicious signature fragments according to the sketch coordinates from the client. The results which consist of transformation of malicious signature fragments and short signatures are sent back to the client as a confirmed report according to which the client takes corresponding security measures.

3.2   Signature Initialization

Let DB be the signature database managed in the cloud. Considering signatures do not have uniform length generally, we set a sliding window with length w to scan the signatures in DB. For an arbitrary signature S of length l, there will be a set of segements with length $w\text{-}byte$ after initial scanning, namely, $S \rightarrow \{S_1, S_2, \ldots, S_{l-w+1}\}$. Moreover, we take account of the wildcards in specific signatures to map down multiple versions of a malware that originated from the same source. In a way, the initialization can be effective in handeling polymorphic malware caused by wildcards [11]. However, it is still impractical to deal with all possiblilties. In CloudEyes, the signatures with wildcard are roughly divided into two portions.

(1) Fixed-Size Wildcard: It denotes the wildcards which contains numbered probabilities. For example, $"?"$ matches any byte, $"a|b|c"$ matches $"a"$ or $"b"$ or $"c"$. We adapt modulo(q) in the wildcard signature initialization, which maps each string byte to a class between 0 to $q-1$(q is a random number smaller than 256), to support wildcard matching [17]. Therefore the matching space size is restricted because matching any value between the range of $[0,q-1]$, instead of all possible values between 0 to 255, means successful hit. For instance, suppose a signature $"abcd?efgh"$ is initialized with $q = 4$ and $w = 9$. The initialization is processed by constructing four segments:$"abcd0efgh"$,$"abcd1efgh"$,$"abcd2efgh"$ and $"abcd3efgh"$. Similarly, $"abcd(x|y|z)efgh"$ is classified into three substrings: $"abcd0efgh"$,$"abcd1efgh"$ and $"abcd2efgh"$ because character x would be mapped to class 0 as $ASCII(x) \bmod q = 0$.

(2) Variable-Size Wildcard: It denotes the wildcards with unfixed size, such as, $"*"$ matches any number of bytes, $"\{n\}"$ matches n bytes. Considering the large amount of probabilities lead to serious performance slowdown, we ignore these wilcards and initialize the rest part of signature. For instance, a signature $"abcdef*ghijkl"$ or $"abcdef\{200\}ghijkl"$ is initialized with $w = 6$, the corresponding substrings are $"abcdef"$ and $"ghijkl"$.

Additionally, if a signature does not contain a fixed fragment at least as long as the window size, the signature cannot be initialized. Small value of w cannot provide enough amount of unique fragments which raises the rate of collision to an unacceptable level during mapping. Alternatively, if the value is too large, there is not enough granularity to answer queries for smaller file fragments in detection. Study result of ClamAV's signature set for the 16-byte window size shows that the short-signature proportion is about 0.15% after initialization. This infrequence does not significantly reduce performance. For convenience, below we use X to represent a signature fragment after initialization.

3.3 Reversible Sketch Structure

Sketch structure is an aggregation method which maps diverse data streams into uniform vectors based on the Turnstile Model [18]. Let $I = \alpha_1, \alpha_2, \ldots,$ be a sequential input stream during a given time interval. Ecah item $\alpha = (\alpha_i, \mu_i)$ consists of a key $\alpha_i \in \{0, 1, \ldots, n-1\} \Leftrightarrow [n]$, and a value $\mu_i \in R$. The model assigns a time varying signal $T[\alpha_i]$ for each key $\alpha_i \in [n]$, and update $T[\alpha_i]$ with an increment of μ_i if a new item (α_i, μ_i) arrives. Most researches [19,20] based on sketch are applied to analysis of elements in flow, such as source and destination IP/Port, but rarely content. Our design is inspired by this structure whose properties can be applied in identifying malicious data fragments from large amount of suspicious data.

Reversible sketch(represented by RS) is based on the k-ary sketch data structure which H is the number of hash tables and m is the size of per hash table, i.e. $m = k$. In our design, each element of hash table consists of a container called $bucket(RB)$ which stores the information of signature and a bit called $digest(D)$ which stands for the bucket is empty or not, with the value 0 or 1 respectively. Let $h_1, h_2, \ldots, h_H$ be H functions randomly chosen from a class of 2-universal hash functions, each hash table adopts one independent function respectively. Assume an arbitrary signature X with length of w-byte, that is $X = \{x_1, x_2, \ldots, x_w\}$. As we adopt modulo($q$) to deal with the signature contain fixed-size wildcards initially, each byte of X(or file content) needs to do the same modulo arithmetic to avoid false negative rate in detection, although it will bring slight false positive rate. Hence the hashing result of X is $h_i(X) = h_i((x_1 \bmod q), (x_2 \bmod q), \ldots, (x_w \bmod q))$. Then we can use $L(X) = \{L_1(X), L_2(X), \ldots, L_H(X)\}$ which consists of $L_i(X) = (i, h_i(X))(1 \leq i \leq H)$ to be the sketch coordinate of X. When summarizing X into RS, $L_i(X)$ can be utilized to locate the corresponding reversible bucket $RB[i][j]$ and digest $D[i][j](j = h_i(X))$.

There are three operations related with RS:

(1) Insert(X,$L(X)$): Initially, RB contains no element and all the digests value is 0. For X which has not been mapped, $L(X)$ decides which buckets it belongs to. Then the sketch is updated as follows.

$$RB[i][j] \leftarrow RB[i][j] \bigcup \{X\}$$
$$D[i][j] \leftarrow 1, 1 \leq i \leq H$$

Fig. 2 illustrates the state of reversible sketch structure after inserting X_1, X_2 and X_3. The buckets labeled by coordinates mean each contains at least one signature and the rest stand for empties.

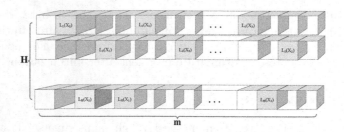

Fig. 2. Reversible Sketch Sturcture

(2) Delete(X,$L(X)$): For the signature X that is proved to be incorrect or reduplicate for malware description, the servers call delete operation to get rid of X from the sketch with following steps:

$$RB[i][j] \leftarrow RB[i][j] - \{X\}$$
$$D[i][j] \leftarrow 0, if\ RB[i][j] = \emptyset, 1 \leq i \leq H$$

(3) Update(Σ_X,Π_L,OP): The cloud needs to periodically update the signature database with the increment of signature quantity. $\Sigma_X = \{X_1, X_2, \ldots, X_n\}$ is the set of signatures need to be updated, $\Pi_L = \{L(X_1), L(X_2), \ldots, L(X_n)\}$ is the set of sketch coordinates to locate the signatures and OP is the set of operations(*Insert* or *Delete*) corresponding to each signature. After the *Update* operation, the RB and D complete the similar changes with the two operations described above.

After summarizing the signature database into the reversible sketch, fundamental scanning about the database can be approximately answered very quickly according to the previous work [20]. However, more information about signature should be stored in the structure in order to insure the scanning veracity without the accurate scanning process like SplitScreen. Generally speaking, the basic signature database contains plenty of two-tuples (*signature, malwarename*). Once a signature is matched, the comprehensible malware name is needed to show what kind of attack it is. So the malware name should be stored by certain format into the RS with corresponding signature segment. To balance memory consumption and searching speed in the implementation, we design the infrastructure based on red black tree for fast and dynamic operations. More theoretical analysis about the accuracy of reversible sketch structure is discussed in section 4 below and details about the performance are illuminated in section 5.

3.4   Matching Mechanism

The design of matching mechanism in RScam is inspired by two purposes we desired: (1) taking the demands of both security vendors and clients into account and (2) ensuring high performance in file scanning. Hence we divide the process of matching into two steps, fast matching and suspicious bucket filtering, for the client and cloud respectively. Detail descriptions are listed below:

(1) Fast Matching: In the RScam system, the reversible sketch structure, which contains the reversible buckets and digest, is designed to store the summarization of signature and service for matching. The digest is the crux of fast matching process which is stored in the client when the system is firstly installed. The files need to be initialized with w and q before scanning because of their diverse types and sizes, that is the file content should be incised into regular fragments and then do the modulo arithmetic. Let F be the set of file fragments after initialization, the purpose of fast matching is picking out the suspicious set of fragments F_{sus} and the corresponding set of sketch coordinates Π_{sus} with the digest D.

Algorithm 1 Fast Matching

Input: file fragments set F, digest D
Output: suspicious fragment set F_{sus} and sketch coordinate set Π_{sus}
  1: $F_{sus}, \Pi_{sus} = \emptyset$
  2: $clear = 0$
  3: **while** each $f \in F$ **do**
  4:      calculate $L(f)$;
  5:      **for** $i = 1$ to H **do**
  6:        **if** $D[i][h_i(f)] = 0$ **then**
  7:           $clear = 1$, **break**; $//f$ is not suspicious
  8:        **end if**
  9:      **end for**
 10:      **if** $clear = 0$ **then**
 11:        insert f into F_{sus} and $L(f)$ into Π_{sus}
 12:      **end if**
 13: **end while**

For each fragment in F, we calculate its sketch coordinate in the digest and check the corresponding value to estimate its existence. Only successful matching in all H hash tables make the fragment suspicious, the others are normal because the hash functions bring no false negative during signature summarization. Algorithm 1 presents details of fast matching mechanism. This process is easy to be applied in the client due to its lightweight and can largely reduce the number of file fragments to be further confirmed. Considering the privacy protection of client, we send the sketch coordinates of suspicious fragments to the cloud after fast matching, which also can cut down the communincation consumption for the client.

(2) Suspicious Bucket Filtering: This process aims at confirming the suspicion of the fast matching result. The basic idea is checking every reversible bucket according each sketch coordinate sent from the client to find the signature fragment which exists in all the H hash tables. As we describe above, different types of signature need to be initialized into regular segments. Let N_S

be the total number of signatures in the DB(including the signatures with wild-cards after initialized), and $\bar{l}$ be the average length of the signatures, w is the size of sliding window, m is the size of per hash table. So the number of segments after initialization is $(\bar{l} - w + 1) \cdot N_S$, and each bucket averagely contains $t = (\bar{l} - w + 1) \cdot N_S/m$ segments. One possible heuristic to find the target signature fragment is take the intersections of each bucket, nevertheless this can lead to a enormous amout of fragments output that do not match and needless computation which called Reverse Sketch Problem [20]. So we build another small red black tree T_{mal} as a filtering buffer which is indexed by the signature fragments stored in the bucket to count their times of appearance.

Algorithm 2 Suspicious Bucket Filtering

Input: Sketch coordinates Π_{sus},reversible bucket RB
Output: Set of malicious signature fragments R_{mal}
 1: $T_{mal}, R_{mal} = \emptyset$
 2: **while** each $L(f) \in \Pi_{sus}$ **do**
 3:     **for** $i = 1$ to H **do**
 4:         **if** $RB[i][h_i(f)] \neq \emptyset$ **then**
 5:             **for** $k = 1$ to t **do**
 6:                 insert $X_k \in RB[i][h_i(f)]$ into T_{mal}
 7:             **end for**
 8:         **end if**
 9:         **else** $T_{mal} = \emptyset$
10:     **end for**
11:     **for** each fragment $X \in T_{mal}$ **do**
12:         **if** count$(X) = H$ **then**
13:             insert X into R_{mal}
14:         **end if**
15:     **end for**
16: **end while**

Algorithm 2 shows the process of malicious bucket filtering. T_{mal} is a signature-fragment buffer for each sketch coordinate $L(f)$ in Π_{sus}. First, we pass over the $L(f)$ which any one of the corresponding reversible buckets is empty which is caused by the hashing collision. Then we insert all signature fragments contained in the targeted RB into T_{mal} and pick out the fragments whose count is H. The result R_{mal} consists of the confirmed signature fragments which can be utilized to claim the malice of file fragment in the client. The filtering shrinks the scope of malicious signature fragments in $O(H \cdot t)$ time at the price of slight memory cost. After suspicious bucket filtering, the cloud sends the result back to the client. The confirmed signature fragments and short signatures should be compared with the suspicious file fragments to make sure the veracity of matching mechanism. The cloud can take some simple transformation of the fragments to avoid direct exposure. This can be implemented by using a bijective reversible function from fragment space $[N]$ to $[N](N = 2^{8w})$. The security vendors can also choose some classical encryption algorithms to ensure the secure communication which is beyond the scope of this work. The client will take some security measures, such as deletion or isolation, with the infected files after validate the matching results.

4 Discussion

In this section, we discuss the accuracy of the reversible sketch structure which is measured based on the false negative and false positive rates generally. A false negative occurs when a fragment summarized into the RS earlier is asserted as clean when matching. While the false positive occurs when a query fragment not summarized into the RS is incorrectly stated as present. There are two types of false positives in RScam. The first one is caused by the hash functions employed in the RS, which is called *hashing false positive*. Secondly, the modulo arithmetic adopted in the initialization brings the possibility of collision between two different fragments and modular hashing of signature fragments adopted in the storage mechanism. Here we call it *fragment false positive*. In what follows we will conduct the theoretical and statistical analysis of these measurements.

4.1 Fasle Negative

The false negative is caused by the initialization based on fixed-size slide window, rather than the hash function. For example, suppose the signature $"abcdefg"$ has been summarized into RS with window size of 6, which means two signature fragments are constructed and mapped into the RS: $"abcdef"$ and $"bcdefg"$. Now if we scan the file content $"bcdef"$ will respond that the file was clean which is incorrect. It is remarkable that false negative in RScam would occur only for the short file content whose length is less than w bytes. So it greatly depends on the length of the scanning content. However, this situation is seldom in prevalent security detection because sizes of files to be scanned are always larger than w bytes which we set in the evalutaion(more details in Section 5.4). Hence we can adjust the value of w to minimize the false negatives and ensure the false positives acceptable. Therefore we put our focus on calculating the false positive rate in the rest of this section.

4.2 Hashing False Positive

The hash functions we use above are 2-universal which make the hash results are nearly randomized. Hence the principle and accuracy of summarization is similar with the Bloom Filter. This type of false positive comes from the hash collisions which may lead to the conclusion that a specific fragment is suspicious when it is not. Alternatively, the false negative will never exist. We learn about the probability of false positive in a bloom filter can be calculated with following relation.

$$FP = (1 - (1 - \frac{1}{m})^{kN})^k \tag{1}$$

where m is the length of bloom filter, k is the number of used hash functions and N is the amount of inserted elements. We can easily conduct the hashing false positive of a hash table in RS. As described earlier, each hash table uses only one hash function and $(\bar{l} - w + 1) \cdot N_S$ fragments are inserted into it. So the false positive of each hash table is:

$$\alpha = (1 - (1 - \frac{1}{m})^{(\bar{l}-w+1)\cdot N_S}) \tag{2}$$

There are H hash tables built in RS which makes the hashing false positive tenable if and only if collisions exist in all the H ones. According to the relation (2), let FP_h be the hashing false positive of RS that is

$$FP_h = (1 - (1 - \frac{1}{m})^{(\bar{l}-w+1)\cdot N_S})^H \tag{3}$$

4.3   Fragment False Positive

As we described in Section 3, the RScam system adopt the modulo arithmetic to deal with the wildcards in specific signatures. However, this will introduce collisions between different fragments. Specifically, there are two distinct scenarios lead to fragment collision discussed below.

(1) Collision Before Summarization: This scenario occurs between two unsummarized fragments, that is, the hashing value of them is uniform. Suppose that S and S' are two different strings(signatures or files) with same length of $\bar{l}$. Assume that $S = s_1 s_2 \ldots s_{\bar{l}}$ and $S' = s'_1 s'_2 \ldots s'_{\bar{l}}$, and the number of classes by q, then the collision happens if each byte of string belongs to same class after modulo. Let F_1 be the false positive before summarization, which is calculated by:

$$F_1 = (\frac{\lceil \frac{256}{q} \rceil}{256})^{\bar{l}} \leq (\frac{1}{q} + \frac{1}{256})^{\bar{l}} \tag{4}$$

(2) Collision After Summarization: This scenario occurs when the unsummarized file content is matched which is incorrect. Suppose that $S = s_1 s_2 \ldots s_{\bar{l}}$ is initialized with the window length of w. As noted earlier, the number of w-byte fragments after initialization is $(\bar{l} - w + 1)$. The collision happens when all these fragments are wrongly resulted in suspicion. Let F_2 be the false positive after summarization, we can conclude the relation below according relation (4):

$$F_2 = (\frac{\lceil \frac{256}{q} \rceil}{256})^{w \cdot (\bar{l}-w+1)} \leq (\frac{1}{q} + \frac{1}{256})^{w \cdot (\bar{l}-w+1)} \tag{5}$$

Consequently the probability of collisions are the sum of F_1 and F_2. However, we should negate the situation that all the bytes in the string are really equal.

Moreover, the collision is directly related to the number of signatures summarized into the RS. Let FP_f be the fragment false positive rate, then we have:

$$FP_f = [F_1 + F_2 - (\tfrac{1}{256})^{\bar{l}}] \cdot N_S$$
$$\leq [(\tfrac{1}{q} + \tfrac{1}{256})^{\bar{l}} + (\tfrac{1}{q} + \tfrac{1}{256})^{w \cdot (\bar{l} - w + 1)} - (\tfrac{1}{256})^{\bar{l}}] \cdot N_S \qquad (6)$$

In conclusion, the false positive of RScam can be computed by the summation of relations (3) and (6). As observed in Fig. 3, the hashing false positive, denoted by FP_h, is much larger than the fragment false positive, denoted by FP_f, with different number of signatures after initialization. So FP_f is negligible compared to FP_h. It is reasonable that FP_h grows close to 1 when the number of signatures grows close to the size of hash table because empty reversible buckets get rare.

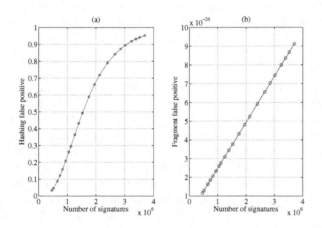

Fig. 3. Two types of false positive in RScam with $m = 2^{24}, w = 16, \bar{l} = 30, H = 4, q = 8$ and different number of signatures between 460000 to 3700000. (a) is hashing false positive and (b) is fragment false positive.

5   Evaluation

In this section, we evaluate the performance of the RScam system and make some comparison with the ClamAV and SplitScreen. We have implemented RScam based on the file and signature identification model of ClamAV with approximately 7K lines of C/C++ code which consist of 4.5K for cloud server and the rest for client. The signature databases which originate from the ClamAV open source platform contain two types of signatures: whole file or segment MD5 signatures and regular expression signatures. We employ several versions from Nov. 2008 to Nov. 2014, which the number of signatures ranges from 460000 to 3700000. If unspecified, we implement the evaluation with the latest database (main v.55 and daily v.19688) and show the average results over 20 runs. Our total 36GB suspicious data set consists of about 240000 unique samples by MD5

Table 1. Memory Cost

Memory	The number of signature					
	530K	860K	1M	2M	3M	3.7M
Cloud(MB)	110	198	274	642	1032	1500
Client(MB)	39	39	43	46	51	55
SplitScreen Client(MB)	58	63	67	74	78	84

hash, which are captured by specific IDS from the campus network. The experiments are performed on a CentOS 5.6 virtual cloud server(8 cores, 32-GB memory and 2.53 GHz) and a common open research network emulator based on OpenVZ which provides different types of virtual machines.

5.1 Memory Analysis

As described earlier, we adopt the reversible sketch structure in the cloud server. Each bucket averagely contains $t = (\bar{l} - w + 1) \cdot N_S/m$ signature segments, so the entire memory cost is $w \cdot t \cdot m \cdot H$ bytes theoretically. We utilize the dynamic red black tree structure to store these segments and prune the reduplicate ones after initialization. Meanwhile, we assign each malware name a unique number in advance to reduce the overhead. This process takes up a period of time, but we don't count it in the performance of RScam because it performs only once at the starting of evaluation. Unless otherwise specified, we use $w = 20, m = 2^{24}, q = 4, H = 2, \bar{l} = 20$ for the RS in our experiment. Table 1 lists the average memory cost of the cloud server and client with various number of signatures after we adjust from different versions when scanning 600MB suspicious samples. As observed, the memory cost of cloud server in RScam mounts up with the growth of signatures. However, it is acceptable for security vendors. In the side of client, the cost does not grow with the number of signatures. We also evaluate the memory cost of SplitScreen client and find our client appropriator less memory, which means RScam is more applicable than SpliltScreen because the latter calls the accurate scanning of ClamAV after its first scanning.

5.2 Time Analysis

We evaluate the time performance of the RScam system in the virtual machine as a resource-constrained client with 350MB memory, 256KB L2 cache and 1GHz CPU, and the bandwidth between the cloud and client is 1MB/s. The testing data are the samples randomly chosen from our data set. The average size of each sample is 2MB. Meanwhile, we make comparisons with the system of ClamAV and SplitScreen in the same environment. We implement this with 1MB signature database(main v.54 and daily v.13810) because ClamAV exhausts the system memory when running with larger signature databases. Fig. 4 shows the details of the time cost. RScam outperform the others with lower time consumption and smoother increment. We can conclude that small cache volume slows down the detecting speed of SplitScreen distinctly. In some condition, SplitScreen even runs slower than ClamAV.

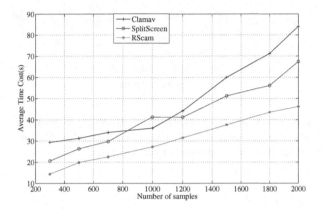

Fig. 4. Time performance of RScam, SplitScreen and ClamAV using different number of samples.

Moreover, we are concerned about the composing of the time cost illustrated in Fig. 5 which reveals the effect of our matching mechanism. The mean percentage of accurate scanning of SplitScreen is 74.3% while that of RScam is 16.4%. The fast matching takes account of all the file fragments which matched in the digest to avoid the accurate scanning of whole file content, while the fast scanning of SplitScreen only reserve the first matched file fragment to label the file to be accurately scanned. In this way, we cut down a mass of computation and time. Hence, we can confirm that the matching mechanism based on the reversible sketch structure can largely improve time performance.

5.3 Traffic Analysis

Another important inspiration of our design is data privacy protection with slight amount of traffic between the client and server. We achieve this through the communication mechanism labored above. The client sends the sketch coordinates of suspicious file fragments to the server and the server send the short signatures and transformation of malicious signature segments back to the client.

Fig. 6 illustrates the average traffic between the client and server with different number of signatures in RScam and SplitScreen when scanning 2GB suspicious samples. The experiment parameters are same with section 5.2, besides the client and server are connected with TCP protocol. As observed, the traffic in RScam is averagely 10 times smaller than that in SplitScreen, and stand

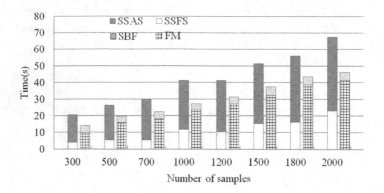

Fig. 5. The composing of time cost of RScam and SplitScreen. SSAS and SSFF stand for the accurate and first scanning of SplitScreen, respectively. SBF and FM stand for suspicious bucket filter and fast matching of RScam.

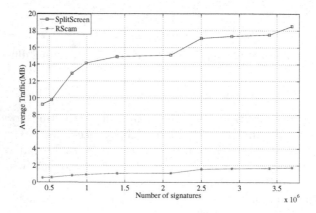

Fig. 6. The traffic between the client and server with different number of signatures.

smooth with the growth of signatures. The traffic of RScam during scanning is averagely 39.8 KB/S which is acceptable for the resource-constrained clients, such as mobile phones and pads.

5.4   Practical Accuracy

We discuss the accuracy of the reversible sketch structure in Section 4 and conclude that it can be measured primarily by hashing false positive. Moreover, we give a practical test of the accuracy in detecting 5972 clean PE files(totally 1.42GB) with different window size under the latest signatures database. Table 2 lists the details of the practical accuracy. The false positive of RScam is calculated by the number of suspicious file fragments divided by the total number of file fragments. For MD5 signatures, we fix the value of w to be 16, the other variable values are for regular expression signatures. The false negative is calculated by the number of short signatures divided by the total number of signatures. Small window size cannot provide enough possibilities for the large amount of signature fragments which caused high false positive. While large window size will produce more short signatures which bring higher false negative and not be fine-grained enough. Hence we can ensure the high accuracy of RScam with considered window size and 20 seems to be the moderatest value.

Table 2. Practical accuracy of RScam

Window size	Fasle Positive	Short Sigs	False Negative
$w = 12$	7.861%	3467	0.092%
$w = 16$	5.726%	5741	0.152%
$w = 20$	3.380%	7676	0.203%
$w = 24$	2.371%	10929	0.289%

6 Conclusion

In this paper, we proposed RScam, a cloud-based anti-malware system which provide fast and trusted security protection for resource-constrained clients. In RScam, we design a novel signature-based detection mechanism based on the reversible sketch structure which dramatically reduce the scanning range and provide retrospective and accurate orientations of malicious data fragments. Meanwhile, we design the balanced interaction mechanism to protect the data privacy and reduce the traffic volume for both the clients and security vendors. Evaluations with suspicious campus network and normal files show that the system is able to achieve fast and accurate malware detection with slight traffic and acceptable memory requirement. As part of our future work, we are planning to address several challenges. The memory cost in the cloud serve side can be reduced ulteriorly by modular hashing of the signature fragments before they are inserted into the buckets, and we are trying to enhance the detection performance by adopting multiple hashing in each hash table.

Acknowledgement. This research is supported in part by the program of Changjiang Scholars and Innovative Research Team in University (No. IRT1012); Science and Technology Innovative Research Team in Higher Educational Institutions of Hunan Province ('network technology').

References

1. Symantec Corporation Internet Security Threat Report 2015, vol. 20 (2015). http://www.symantec.com/security_response/publications/threatreport.jsp
2. McAfee threats report: fourth quarter (2014). http://www.mcafee.com/us/mcafee-labs.aspx

3. Chen, Z., Ji, C.: An information-theoretic view of network aware malware attacks. IEEE Transactions on Information Forensics and Security **4**(3), 530–541 (2009)

4. Aho, A.V., Corasick, M.J.: Efficient string matching: an aid to bibliographic search. Comm. of the ACM **18**, 333–340 (1975)

5. Wu, S., Manber, U.: A fast algorithm for multi-pattern searching. Technical Report TR-94-17, University of Arizona (1994)

6. Clamav. http://www.clamav.net

7. Vasiliadis, G., Ioannidis, S.: GrAVity: a massively parallel antivirus engine. In: Jha, S., Sommer, R., Kreibich, C. (eds.) RAID 2010. LNCS, vol. 6307, pp. 79–96. Springer, Heidelberg (2010)

8. AV-comparative.: On-demand detection of malicious software. Technical Report, AV-comparative (2010)

9. Cha, S.K., et al.: Splitscreen: enabling efficient, distributed malware detection. In: Proc. of NSDI, pp. 12–25 (2010)

10. Oberheide, J., Cooke, E., Jahanian, F.: CloudAV: N-version antivirus in the network cloud. In: Proc. of the 17th USENIX Security Symposium, pp. 91–106 (2008)

11. Erdogan, O., Cao, P.: Hash-AV: fast virus signature scanning by cache-resident filters. International Journal of Security and Networks **2**, 50–59 (2007)

12. Venugopal, D., Hu, G.: Efficient signature based malware detection on mobile devices. Mobile Information Systems **4**(1), 33–49 (2008)

13. Oberheide, J., Veeraraghavan, K., Cooke, E., Flinn, J., Jahanian, F.: Virtualized in-cloud security services for mobile devices. In: Proc. of the First Workshop on Virtualization in Mobile Computing, pp. 31–35 (2008)

14. Xu, J., Yan, J., He, L., Su, P., Feng, D.: CloudSEC: a cloud architecture for composing collaborative security services. In: 2nd IEEE International Conference on Cloud Computing Technology and Science, pp. 703–711 (2010)

15. Jakobsson, M., Juels, A.: Server-side detection of malware infection. In: Proceedings of the 2009 Workshop on New Security Paradigms Workshop, pp. 11–22. ACM (2009)

16. Bloom, B.H.: Space/Time Trade-offs in Hash Coding with Allowable Errors. Comm. of the ACM **13**, 422–426 (1970)

17. Haghighat, M.H., Tavakoli, M., Kharrazi, M.: Payload Attribution via Character Dependent Multi-Bloom Filters. IEEE Transactions on Information Forensics and Security **8**(5), 705–716 (2013)

18. Muthukrishnan, S.: Data streams: Algorithms and application. Foundations and Trends in Theoretical Computer Science **1**(2) (2005)

19. Krishnamurthy, B., Sen, S., Zhang, Y., Chen, Y.: Sketch-based change detection: methods, evaluation, and applications. In: Proceeding of ACM SIGCOMM IMC, pp. 234–247 (2003)

20. Schweller, R., Li, Z., Chen, Y., Gao, Y., et al.: Reversible sketches: enabling monitoring and analysis over high-speed data streams. IEEE/ACM Transactions on Networking **15**(5), 1059–1072 (2007)

21. Tang, Y., Xiao, B., Lu, X.: Signature Tree Generation for Polymorphic Worms. IEEE Transactions on Computers **60**(4), 565–579 (2011)

22. He, M., Gong, Z., Chen, L.: Securing network coding against pollution attacks in P2P converged ubiquitous networks. Peer-to-Peer Networking and Applications **8**(4), 642–650 (2015)

TADOOP: Mining Network Traffic Anomalies with Hadoop

Geng Tian[1,3], Zhiliang Wang[2,3(✉)], Xia Yin[1,3], Zimu Li[2,3],
Xingang Shi[2,3], Ziyi Lu[4], Chao Zhou[4], Yang Yu[1,3], and Dan Wu[1,3]

[1] Department of Computer Science and Technology,
Tsinghua University, Beijing, China
[2] Institute for Network Sciences and Cyberspace,
Tsinghua University, Beijing, China
wzl@cernet.edu.cn
[3] Tsinghua National Laboratory for Information
Science and Technology (TNList), Beijing, China
[4] Cisco Systems, Inc., Shanghai, China

Abstract. Today, various anomalies and large number of flows in a network make traffic anomaly detection a big challenge. In this paper, we propose **DTE-FP** (**D**ual q **T**sallis **E**ntropy for flow **F**eature with **P**roperties), a more efficient method for traffic anomaly detection. To handle huge amount of traffic, based on Hadoop, we implement a network traffic anomaly detection system named TADOOP, which supports semi-automatic training and both offline and online traffic anomaly detection. TADOOP with a cluster of five servers has been deployed in Tsinghua University Campus Network. Furthermore, we compare DTE-FP with Tsallis entropy, and the experimental results show that DTE-FP has much better detection capability than Tsallis entropy.

Keywords: Tsallis entropy · Traffic anomaly detection · Hadoop · Big data · MapReduce

1 Introduction

Today the explosive growth of network size, users and applications generates huge amount of traffic in the Internet. The obvious network traffic fluctuation also reduces the efficiency in traffic anomaly detection. Besides, it is very difficult to use one way to detect all network anomalies, including both known and unknown ones. All of the above make traffic anomaly detection in a network still be a big challenge.

Entropy has been proved to be an effective metric on network traffic anomaly detection [1], [2], [3], and entropy-based methods can detect both known and unknown traffic anomalies. A typical method of entropy-based traffic anomaly detection is to split the traffic into several time bins and compute the entropy value of each time bin for anomaly detection. In recent years, Tellenbach et al. [4] have presented a Traffic Entropy Spectrum (TES) to reveal traffic anomalies.

© Institute for Computer Sciences, Social Informatics and Telecommunications Engineering 2015
B. Thuraisingham et al. (Eds.): SecureComm 2015, LNICST 164, pp. 175–192, 2015.
DOI: 10.1007/978-3-319-28865-9_10

The basic idea is using several different Tsallis entropy values corresponding to different parameters to form TES. Berezinski et al. [5] have shown that Tsallis entropy has better performance than Renyi entropy and Shannon entropy. In order to find an easy and efficient method to detect traffic anomalies, we analyze the characteristics of Tsallis entropy for flow feature distributions, and propose **DTE-FP** (**D**ual q **T**sallis **E**ntropy for flow **F**eature with **P**roperties), a new method for anomaly detection. The basic insight is to use the two most efficient q values for highlighting high and low probability feature distributions respectively, which usually imply anomalies in network traffic. DTE-FP contains two parts: DTE and FP. On one hand, we introduce DTE to reveal the high and low probability events in a network. On the other hand, we calculate entropy value for each flow feature with properties (FP). In this way, we can obtain both more concise detection results and more details of the anomalies.

In order to process huge amount of flow data, big data analytics has been widely used to process large scale data set in recent years. An increasing number of people have leveraged MapReduce [6] and Hadoop [7] to mine network traffic anomalies [8], [9], [10]. Zhang et al. [9] have implemented a Shannon entropy based system with Mapreduce. Hodge et al. [10] have proposed a Hadoop based framework for parallel and distributed feature selection. In this paper, we have implemented **TADOOP**, a network **T**raffic **A**nomaly **D**etection system based on had**OOP**, to detect flow-level traffic anomalies. Finally, We have deployed TADOOP with a cluster of five servers in Tsinghua University Campus Network. The experimental results show that our system has strong capability in traffic anomaly detection.

The key contributions of this paper are described as follows:

- First, we analyze the characteristics of Tsallis entropy for flow feature distributions, and present a new traffic anomaly detection method DTE-FP.
- Second, we implement TADOOP, which supports semi-automatic training, offline detection and online detection, deploy our system with a cluster of five servers in Tsinghua University Campus Network.
- Third, we compare DTE-FP with Tsallis entropy, and the results show that DTE-FP performs much better than Tsallis entropy in traffic anomaly detection.

The paper is organized as follows. Section 2 introduces the related work. In Section 3, we analyze the characteristics of Tsallis entropy for network traffic anomaly detection, and describe the details of DTE-FP. In Section 4, we describe the implementation of TADOOP. Then the experimental results are presented in Section 5. In Section 6, we emphasis on which kinds of anomalies can be detected. Finally, Section 7 concludes this paper.

2   Related Work

Nowadays, network traffic anomaly detection [11] is still a big challenge for the explosive growth of network traffic, so that big data analytics is very necessary for network traffic analysis because of their online and offline detection capability. There are several studies on network traffic analysis based on big data analytics, e.g. [8], [12]. Till now, MapReduce [6] and its open source implementation Hadoop [7] are still the most popular big data programming model and platform used in network traffic analysis. As a representative work of network traffic analysis with Hadoop, Lee et al. [8] presented a Hadoop-based traffic monitoring system that can perform network traffic analysis of both packet-level and flow-level. However, this work was limited to simple IP packet statistics of the traffic with Hadoop.

Shannon entropy has been proved as a good metric in network traffic anomaly detection [1], [13], [4], [3], [14], and has shown stronger anomaly detection capability than volume-based methods [1]. Zhang et al. [9] implemented a Shannon entropy based system with MapReduce. Besides Shannon entropy, Tsallis proposed and analyzed Tsallis entropy in their works [15], [16], [17]. However, the first work for using Tsallis entropy in anomaly detection was introduced in 2007 [13]. After that, Tellenbach et al. [4] proposed a Traffic Entropy Spectrum (TES) method, in which different entropy values corresponding to different parameters are used to form TES to reveal anomalies. Berezinski et al. [5] presented that Tsallis entropy had better performance than Renyi entropy and Shannon entropy.

Entropy based detection method usually splits time into several time bins, and calculates entropy values for flow feature distributions in each time bin [1]. Lakhina et al. used entropy values of source IP address/port and destination IP/port for traffic anomaly detection [1]. Besides above feature distributions, Nychis et al. employed Shannon entropy for in-degree, out-degree and flow size distribution (FSD) to mine more anomalies [3]. In this paper, besides source IP/port and destination IP/port, we not only introduce flow byte for traffic anomaly detection, but also use flow feature with properties instead of one single feature. For example, we use source IP as the main flow feature, and use flow direction, protocol and TCP control bit as its properties.

3 DTE-FP

Entropy has been proved to be an efficient matric for traffic anomaly detection, and widely used in anomaly detection systems. A typical mode of entropy-based traffic anomaly detection is to split the traffic into several time bins and compute the entropy values of flow feature distributions for all time bins. Finally, we can find out the anomalous time bins, in which their entropy values deviate much from the normal ones. In this section, we propose a new Tsallis entropy based method for traffic anomaly detection.

3.1 Tsallis Entropy Characteristics for Anomaly Detection

Tsallis entropy $S_{Ts} = \frac{k}{q-1}(1 - \sum_{i=1}^n p_i^q)$ performs well in traffic anomaly detection. The parameter q means different sensitivity for different probability events, which makes Tsallis entropy flexible and efficient for traffic anomaly detection. We will illustrate its characteristics from two aspects: stability for normal flows and sensitivity for anomalous flows.

Stability for Normal Flows. The flow numbers in a network change all the time, especially between day and night, which makes Tsallis entropy values change with the flow numbers. In order to know the effect of flow numbers in a whole day, we analyze the flow data with few anomalies for the period 0:00 to 24:00. We divide the whole time into 8640 time bins by using 10s as the time interval. We then obtain Tsallis entropy values with different q values, such as $q = 2.5, 1.5, 0.5, -0.5, -1.5$, because the work of Tellenbach et al. finds that the selection $q = 2, 1.75, ..., -1.75, -2$ gives sufficient information to detect network anomalies [4]. We normalize Tsallis entropy values by dividing by the max entropy value for each feature. As shown in Fig. 1, we can find that the flow numbers obviously decrease in the night while increase during the daytime. The corresponding Tsallis entropy values for source IP address decrease when there are few flows in the night, and increase when there are many flows in the day. Furthermore, Fig. 1 also shows that Tsallis entropy with a bigger q value is more stable and less effected by flow numbers.

Sensitivity for Anomalous Flows. In order to test the sensitivity of Tsallis entropy for different q values, we randomly select a normal data with 60 time tins. We inject a DDoS attack of 20k flows into time bin #30. In this attack, a large number of source IP addresses and ports launch a SYN flood to a same destination IP and port. As shown in Fig. 2, we can find that a small q value results in an obvious fluctuation of entropy values, while a bigger q means a more steady entropy value. We can also find that the Tsallis entropy value of destination IP address will decrease sharply when $q > 1$, while the entropy value for source IP address has no obvious increase. We thus observe that Tsallis entropy is sensitive to high probability elements but insensitive to low probability elements when $q > 1$. Furthermore,

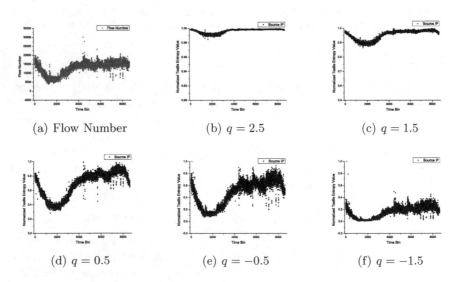

(a) Flow Number   (b) $q = 2.5$ (c) $q = 1.5$

(d) $q = 0.5$ (e) $q = -0.5$ (f) $q = -1.5$

Fig. 1. Stability for Normal Flows

the Tsallis entropy value for source IP address increases sharply, while the entropy value for destination IP address decreases smaller, even increases when $q < 1$. The situation above means Tsallis entropy is sensitive to low probability elements but insensitive to high probability elements when $q < 1$.

Therefore, the characteristic of Tsallis entropy can be summarized into following points: (1) A bigger q value is less effected by total normal flow numbers when $q > 1$. (2) Tsallis entropy is sensitive to high probability elements when $q > 1$, and sensitive to low probability elements when $q < 1$.

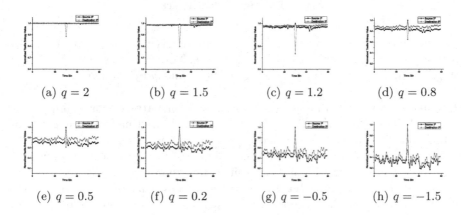

(a) $q = 2$ (b) $q = 1.5$ (c) $q = 1.2$ (d) $q = 0.8$

(e) $q = 0.5$ (f) $q = 0.2$ (g) $q = -0.5$ (h) $q = -1.5$

Fig. 2. Sensitivity of Tsallis Entropy for The DDoS Attack

3.2 DTE-FP

According to the characteristic of Tsallis entropy for the normal flows and anomalous flows, we propose DTE-FP, a new method for traffic anomaly detection. The basic insight is to use the two most efficient q values for highlighting high and low probability feature distributions respectively, which usually imply anomalies in network traffic. DTE-FP contains two aspects: DTE and FP. For one thing, we present dual q Tsallis entropy (DTE), whose definition is shown in Definition 1. For another, we calculate entropy for each flow feature with properties (FP).

Definition 1.

$$S_{DTE} = < S_L, S_H >, where$$

$$\begin{cases} S_L = \frac{k}{q_l - 1}(1 - \sum_{i=1}^{n} p_i^{q_l}), (q_l < 1) \\ S_H = \frac{k}{q_h - 1}(1 - \sum_{i=1}^{n} p_i^{q_h}), (q_h > 1) \end{cases} \tag{1}$$

DTE for Detection. In DTE, a pair of q value $< q_h, q_l >$ is employed for different anomalies. We use q_h and q_l to detect the anomalies with high and low probability feature distribution respectively. As shown in Fig. 3, if a DDoS attack happens in time bin #30, we can find the entropy value for source IP address exceeds its

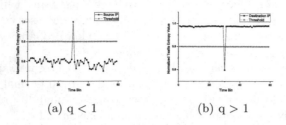

(a) q < 1   (b) q > 1

Fig. 3. DTE for DDoS Attack

upper threshold, and the entropy value for destination is below its lower threshold. Therefore, a suitable q could find more anomalies. Note that we should guarantee that $q_h > 1$ and $q_l < 1$. Normally, we can select q_h and q_l by training.

FP. Usually, the flows of an attack have the similar pattern. For example, the flows of a DDoS attack have the same destination IP, destination port, protocol number and TCP control bit. However, we cannot use each traffic feature to compute entropy values, such as protocol numbers, because the entropy values for protocol number distributions have little information, and they can hardly help us to detect anomalies. But if we select some flow features as main features and other features as their properties, we will obtain more precise results. As shown in Fig. 4, we choose source IP/port, destination IP/port, and flow byte as the main features, and use time bin of flow, flow direction, protocol number and TCP control bit as the properties of main features. We use the time bin and flow direction to divide the traffic into different feature distributions. Protocol number and TCP control bit help to compute entropy value for each feature distribution. FP will not only help to obtain more concise results, but also provide more details of the anomalies for more detailed classification.

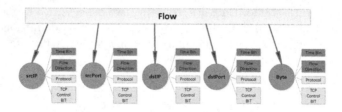

Fig. 4. Flow Feature with Properties

3.3   Detection for Common Attacks

DDoS. As shown in Fig. 5, in time bin #30, we inject a DDoS attack of 20k flows, in which a large number of source IP addresses and ports launch a SYN

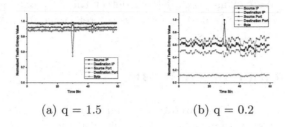

(a) q = 1.5   (b) q = 0.2

Fig. 5. DDoS Attack

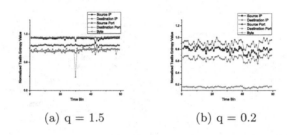

(a) q = 1.5   (b) q = 0.2

Fig. 6. Spam

Table 1. Relationships between DTE-FP and Typical Traffic Anomalies

Anomaly	q < 1				q > 1					Protocol	TCPctrlBit
	sIp	sPt	dIp	dPt	sIp	sPt	dIp	dPt	byte		
DoS: SYN flood					↓		↓	↓		6	2
DoS: ACK flood					↓		↓	↓		6	18
DoS: UDP flood					↓		↓	↓		17	0
DoS: ICMP flood					↓		↓	↓		1	0
DDoS: SYN flood	↑						↓	↓		6	2
DDoS: ACK flood	↑						↓	↓		6	18
DDoS: UDP flood	↑						↓	↓		17	0
DDoS: ICMP flood	↑						↓	↓		1	0
DRDoS		↑	↑	↓	↓					6	2
PortScan1		↑		↓				↓		1/6/17	0/2/0
PortScan2			↑	↓			↓			1/6/17	0/2/0
Spam								↓		6	-
Worm							↓	↓		6/17	-

flood to a same destination IP and port. Then we can find the entropy value for
source IP address in this time bin sharply increases when $q < 1$, and entropy
value for destination IP address and port obviously decreases when $q > 1$.

Spam. As shown in Fig. 6, if a spam of 2k flows happens in time bin #30, the
Tsallis entropy value for the flow byte feature will decrease sharply.

Other Attacks. We can use DTE-FP to detect the anomalies which deviate from the normal situation. Table 1 introduces the relationships between entropy and the typical traffic anomalies.

4   Implementation of TADOOP

In this section, we describe the architecture and implementation of TADOOP. As shown in Fig. 7, our system consists of a traffic collector, a entropy calculation module, a training module, a detection module and a web-based interface.

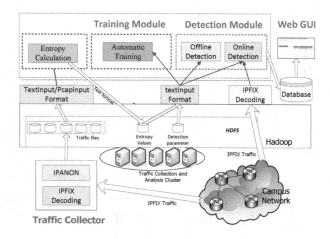

Fig. 7. Architecture of TADOOP

4.1   Traffic Collector

The traffic collector receives NetFlow packets from the edge routers of an AS or edge network, and supports NetFlow v5 and IPFIX format flow data. We leverage "libipfix" [18] to decode IPFIX format data and use "p3" [8] to decode NetFlow v5 format data. Besides, we anonymize all IP addresses by "IPANON".

4.2   Entropy Calculation Module

Entropy calculation module aims at computing Tsallis entropy value pairs for each flow feature distribution. We implement this module in MapReduce framework. In our system, we use one-round MapReduce to achieve above function. Algorithm *Tsallis.map* aims to extract and transform flow information. First, it extracts flow features from each flow (line 2), and obtains flow direction and time bin value (line 3-4), then outputs the final flow features with properties (line 5-20). We divide all flows into outside flows, incoming flows, outgoing flows

---

Algorithm 1. Tsallis.map

Input: The set of flow records decoded from NetFlow file (FR), the length of each time bin (L), the set of owner As numbers (AS)

Output: The set of new $< key, value >$ pairs (MS)

1 **foreach** $flow \ f \in FR$ **do**
2 | $Extract(sIp, sPt, dIp, dPt, Bt, srcAs, dstAs, pro, bit, endTime)$ from flow f;
3 | $fD \leftarrow flowDirection(srcAs, dstAs, AS)$;
4 | $tNum \leftarrow endTime/L$;
5 | %form new flow feature with property $newSrcIp \leftarrow fD + tNum$;
6 | $newSrcIpVal \leftarrow$ "sIp" $+ sIp + pro + bit + 1$;
7 | $newSrcPt \leftarrow fD + tNum$;
8 | $newSrcPtVal \leftarrow$ "sPt" $+ sPt + pro + bit + 1$;
9 | $newDstIp \leftarrow fD + tNum$;
10 | $newDstIpVal \leftarrow$ "dIp" $+ dIp + pro + bit + 1$;
11 | $newDstPt \leftarrow fD + tNum$;
12 | $newDstPtVal \leftarrow$ "dPt" $+ dPt + pro + bit + 1$;
13 | **if** $bit == 19 || bit == 27 || bit == 31$ **then**
14 | | $newByte \leftarrow fD + tNum$;
15 | | $newByteVal \leftarrow$ "Bt" $+ Bt + pro + bit + 1$;
16 | | $MS \leftarrow MS \ \cup \ < newByte, newByteVal >$;
17 | $MS \leftarrow MS \ \cup \ < newSrcIp, newSrcIpVal >$;
18 | $MS \leftarrow MS \ \cup \ < newSrcPt, newSrcPtVal >$;
19 | $MS \leftarrow MS \ \cup \ < newDstIp, newDstIpVal >$;
20 | $MS \leftarrow MS \ \cup \ < newDstPt, newDstPtVal >$;

---

and inner flows. For example, if both the source and destination AS number belongs to the network, the flow is inner flow.

Algorithm $Tsallis.reduce$ is in charge of obtaining the final Tsallis entropy value pairs for each flow feature distribution. First, it classifies all flow features into five hash maps for source IP address, source port, destination IP address, destination port and flow byte. It then employs function $update\_hm$ to compute the occurrence number of the same flow features and combine them into one $< key, value >$ pair (line 2-14). Second, it uses function $TsallisEn$ to calculate Tsallis entropy value pairs for all flow features in each time bin (line 16-18). At last, it outputs the results (line 20-25).

4.3 Semi-automatic Training Module

Training module helps us to obtain the detection thresholds for all flow feature distributions. First of all, we select a long time flow data for training, and mark anomalous time bin for each flow feature. We then use Algorithm $AutoTrain$ to obtain the final threshold pair for each feature distribution. As described in Algorithm 4 $AutoTrain$, we employ a while-loop to obtain the fine threshold pairs step by step. We set the max false positive rate (MFPR) as the termination condition. If the current false positive rate $fp1$ or $fp2$ is smaller than MFPR,

---

Algorithm 2. Tsallis.reduce

Input: The set of $< key, value - list >$ pairs (MS), q_l, q_h
Output: Tsallis entropy file EF

1 **foreach** $< key, value - list > \in MS$ **do**
2   create $HashMap < String, int >$ set (HS) from hm_1 to hm_5;
3   **foreach** $val \in value - list$ **do**
4          $< flowObj, sum > \leftarrow split(val)$;
5   **if** $flowObj.contains("sIp")$ **then**
6             $update\_hm(flowObj, hm\_1)$;

7   **else if** $flowObj.contains("sPt")$ **then**
8             $update\_hm(flowObj, hm\_2)$;
9   **else if** $flowObj.contains("dIp")$ **then**
10             $update\_hm(flowObj, hm\_3)$;
11   **else if** $flowObj.contains("dPt")$ **then**
12             $update\_hm(flowObj, hm\_4)$;

13   **else if** $flowObj.contains("Bt")$ **then**
14             $update\_hm(flowObj, hm\_5)$;

15   % compute Tsallis entropy;
16   **foreach** $hm\_i \in HS$ **do**
17          $S_{q_l\_i} \leftarrow TsallisEn(hm\_i, q_l)$;
18          $S_{q_h\_i} \leftarrow TsallisEn(hm\_i, q_h)$;

19   % output Tsallis entropy;
20      $srcIpEntro \leftarrow < S_{q_l\_1}, S_{q_h\_1} >$;
21      $srcPtEntro \leftarrow < S_{q_l\_2}, S_{q_h\_2} >$;
22      $dstIpEntro \leftarrow < S_{q_l\_3}, S_{q_h\_3} >$;
23      $dstPtEntro \leftarrow < S_{q_l\_4}, S_{q_h\_4} >$;
24      $byteEntro \leftarrow < S_{q_l\_5}, S_{q_h\_5} >$;
25      $entropy \leftarrow srcIpEntro + srcPtEntro + dstIpEntro + dstPtEntro$
         $EF \leftarrow EF \cup < key, entropy >$;

Threshold T_{q_l} minuses δ or T_{q_h} pluses δ. We obtain the final results when the while-loop is over.

4.4 Detection Module

The detection module includes both an offline detection module and an online detection module. The offline detection module is running on the whole Hadoop platform, while the online detection module is running on a single node.

Offline Detection Module. Offline detection module can detect all the historical data and find the anomalies. It calls the entropy calculation module to compute the entropy values for all time bins, then uses the thresholds obtained from training to detect anomalies.

Algorithm 3. TsallisEn

Input: HS, k, q_l, q_h
Output: $< S_{q_l}, S_{q_h} >$ value pairs

1 **foreach** $hm_i \in HS$ **do**
2      $total \leftarrow 0$;
3   **foreach** $val \in hm_i$ **do**
4          $total \leftarrow total + sum$;
5   List $lst \leftarrow val$;
6      $total1 \leftarrow 0$;
7      $total2 \leftarrow 0$;
8   **foreach** $val \in lst$ **do**
9          $sum1 \leftarrow sum1 + (\frac{val}{total})^{q_l}$;
10         $sum2 \leftarrow sum2 + (\frac{val}{total})^{q_h}$;
11     $S_{q1} \leftarrow \frac{k}{q1-1} \times (1 - sum1)$;
12     $S_{q2} \leftarrow \frac{k}{q2-1} \times (1 - sum2)$;
13   Output $< S_{q1}, S_{q2} >$ value pair

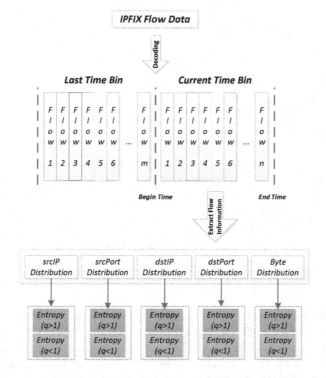

Fig. 8. Entropy Calculation for Online Detection

Algorithm 4. AutoTrain

Input: Entropy value file $eFile$, time bin list for all flow features (LST), the max false positive rate $MFPR$, increase/decrease degree δ, q_l, q_h

Output: Threshold T_{q_l}, T_{q_h}, false positive rate pair $< fp1, fp2 >$, false negative rate pair $< fn1, fn2 >$

1 % obtain initial threshold value;
2 $T_{q_h} \leftarrow 0$;
3 $T_{q_l} \leftarrow 1$;
4 **foreach** *flow feature i* **do**
5     $runFlag1 \leftarrow true$;
6     $runFlag2 \leftarrow true$;
7   **while** $runFlag1 \| runFlag2$ **do**
8   **foreach** $line \in eFile$ **do**
9           $< timeBin, S_{q_l}, S_{q_h} > \leftarrow readEntro(line, i)$;
10   **if** $(S_{q_l} > T_{q_l})\& runFlag1$ **then**
11              $list1.add(timeBin)$;
12   **if** $(S_{q_h} < T_{q_h})\& runFlag2$ **then**
13              $list2.add(timeBin)$;
14        $< fp1\_i, fn1\_i > \leftarrow compare(list1, LST)$;
15        $< fp2\_i, fn2\_i > \leftarrow compare(list2, LST)$;
16   **if** $fp1 < MFPR$ **then**
17           $T_{q_l}\_i \leftarrow T_{q_l}\_i - \delta$;
18   **else**
19           $break$;
20           $T_{q_l}\_i \leftarrow T_{q_l}\_i + \delta$;
21           $runFlag1 \leftarrow false$;
22   **if** $fp2 < MFPR$ **then**
23           $T_{q2}\_i \leftarrow T_{q2}\_i + \delta$;
24   **else**
25           $break$;
26           $T_{q2}\_i \leftarrow T_{q2}\_i - \delta$;
27           $runFlag2 \leftarrow false$;
28   **if** $!(runFlag1 \| runFlag2)$ **then**
29   Output $< T_{q_l}\_i, T_{q_h}\_i, fp1\_i, fn1\_i, fp2\_i, fn2\_i >$;

Online Detection Module. Online detection module achieves online detection without employing a distributed processing. It consists of two parts: entropy calculation and anomaly detection. The entropy calculation part aims to calculate entropy values for the current time bin. As shown in Fig. 8, after decoding the NetFlow format data into text format flow information, the online detection module extracts flow features with properties between the begin time and the end time, and calculates entropy values for all flow features in this time bin after the end time. Finally, we obtain the detection results by comparing with the thresholds, and show them on web page.

5   Experiments

5.1   Experiment Environment

We have deployed TADOOP with a cluster of five servers in Tsinghua University Campus Network. Each server integrates two 2.60 GHz Intel Xeon E5-2630 CPU with 12 cores, 32G memory and 9T hard disk. The five servers are connected with a Gigabit Ethernet switch.

5.2   Data

We study the proposed anomaly detection methods using 1.3T IPFIX format flow data collected from one edge router of Tsinghua University Campus Network for the period from 2014-3-2 23:39:20 to 2014-3-11 13:03:00. The sampling ratio is 1:1. For our experiment, we use the data of the period from 2014-3-2 23:39:20 to 2014-3-6 10:58:00 for training, and use the rest data to detect traffic anomalies.

5.3   Detection in Tsinghua University Campus Network

In order to make comparisons, we leverage both Tsallis entropy and DTE-FP to detect anomalies of incoming flows, in which only the destination IP addresses belong to Tsinghua University.

Training for Detection Parameters. Before actual detection, the detection parameters and thresholds should be obtained by the training module. Therefore, we must obtain a fixed time interval, a suitable $< q_h, q_l >$ value pair and all thresholds for the used flow features in the training phase.

Tian et al. [19] shows that a smaller time interval is more sensitive for detecting traffic anomalies by Shannon entropy, because there are less flows in a time bin, and it is more likely for us to find the anomalies of a certain scale. Additionally, we also find that, in a time bin of too many flows, some traffic anomalies will be masked in our Tsallis entropy based method too. Therefore, we refer to the experiment parameter in [19] and set 10s as our time interval.

The work of Tellenbach et al. finds that the selection $q = 2, ..., -2$ gives sufficient information to detect network anomalies [4]. According to the experiments shown in Fig. 1 and Fig. 2, we also find that the q of a too big or small value will not results in a good detection result. Therefore, we select $q = 1.5, 1.1, 0.8, 0.2, -0.5$ as q value candidates for DTE-FP, and use these q values to calculate Tsallis entropy values for each flow feature. For calculating the actual false positive rate, we analyze the whole training data, and both find out and label all anomalous time bins for each feature. In order to obtain good detection results, we ignore the time bins whose flow numbers is under 2k in training and detection, because it is likely that a lot of flows which should be in these time bins were lost in the collection process.

After that, we set MFPR as 0%, 1%, 2% and 5% respectively, and employ Algorithm 4 *AutoTrain* to obtain the upper threshold (UT) and lower threshold (LT) for each feature. Table 2 shows the detection thresholds, anomaly number (AN) and false positive number (FPN) for the training data. From this table, for all MFPR values, we can clearly find that the detection capability for the lower thresholds decrease obviously when q value becomes smaller from 1.5 to -0.5, and we even cannot detect any anomaly by the lower threshold when $q = -0.5$. However, the detection capability for the upper threshold becomes stronger when q changes from 1.5 to 0.2, and it has the best detection capability when $q = 0.2$. Therefore, we can use both the best q value for upper thresholds $q = 0.2$ and the best q value for lower thresholds $q = 1.5$ to form the $< q_h, q_l >$ value pair of DTE-FP.

Detection Capability Comparison. After training, we can mine traffic anomalies from the flow data for detection, Fig. 9 shows the detection results by DTE-FP when $MFPR = 5\%$, and all results are summarised in Table 3.

Table 2. Detection Thresholds and Capability in Training

FP	q	Lower Threshold (LT) & Upper Threshold (UT)					AN & FPN		
		sicip	srcpt	dstip	dstpt	byte	LT	UT	both
0%	1.5	0.625,0.965	0.329,0.988	0.891,0.994	0.732,0.979	0.597,1	1860,0	36,0	1860,0
	1.1	0.488,0.999	0.233,0.955	0.573,0.967	0.500,0.984	0.421,1	1243,0	73,0	1245,0
	0.8	0.327,0.968	0.107,0.862	0.235,0.869	0.234,0.877	0.019,1	652,0	95,0	678,0
	0.2	0.081,0.862	0.023,0.618	0.026,0.604	0.027,0.581	0.008,1	43,0	303,0	332,0
	-0.5	0,1.000	0,0.578	0,0.392	0,0.515	0,1	11,0	123,0	134,0
	DTE	0.625,0.862	0.329,0.618	0.891,0.604	0.732,0.581	0.597,1	1860,0	303,0	2003,0
1%	1.5	0.631,0.965	0.330,0.988	0.892,0.994	0.743,0.979	0.597,1	1862,1	36,0	1862,1
	1.1	0.493,0.999	0.233,0.955	0.573,0.967	0.512,0.984	0.421,1	1392,2	73,0	1394,2
	0.8	0.330,0.968	0.235,0.862	0.107,0.869	0.239,0.877	0.019,1	668,2	95,0	693,2
	0.2	0.330,0.861	0.107,0.618	0.235,0.603	0.239,0.581	0.019,1	43,0	311,0	340,0
	-0.5	0,1.000	0,0.578	0,0.391	0, 0.515	0, 1	11,0	125,0	136,0
	DTE	0.631,0.861	0.329,0.618	0.891,0.603	0.732,0.581	0.597,1	1862,1	311,0	2011,1
2%	1.5	0.638,0.965	0.331,0.988	0.893,0.993	0.750,0.979	0.597,1	2112,3	58,0	2112,3
	1.1	0.500,0.999	0.234,0.955	0.573,0.966	0.522,0.984	0.421,1	1495,3	76,0	1497,3
	0.8	0.335,0.968	0.108,0.862	0.235,0.868	0.243,0.877	0.019,1	753,3	97,0	778,3
	0.2	0.081,0.861	0.023,0.617	0.026,0.602	0.027,0.581	0.008,1	43,0	313,0	342,0
	-0.5	0,1.000	0, 0.578	0, 0.390	0, 0.515	0, 1	11,0	126,0	137,0
	DTE	0.638,0.877	0.331,0.613	0.893,0.599	0.750,0.580	0.597,1	2112,3	313,0	2256,3
5%	1.5	0.667,0.965	0.334,0.988	0.893,0.991	0.765,0.979	0.597,1	2344,4	130,0	2344,4
	1.1	0.525,0.999	0.235,0.954	0.573,0.964	0.536,0.984	0.421,1	1665,5	88,0	1668,5
	0.8	0.350,0.968	0.110,0.861	0.235,0.866	0.252,0.877	0.019,1	891,5	102,0	915,5
	0.2	0.082,0.859	0.023,0.615	0.026,0.598	0.028,0.580	0.008,1	44,1	333,0	363,1
	-0.5	0,1.000	0, 0.577	0, 0.385	0, 0.515	0, 1	11,0	131,0	142,0
	DTE	0.667,0.859	0.334,0.615	0.893,0.598	0.765,0.580	0.597,1	2344,4	333,0	2502,4

From this table, we can find that DTE-FP has better detection capability than any single Tsallis entropy. If a bigger MFPR is selected, more anomalies will be detected. We validate the anomalous time bins by using automatic and manual check. If a time bin has obvious heavy hitters, we mark it as anomalous time bin. For the rest detected ones, we manually check them by flow feature distribution. For example, as shown in Fig. 10(a), by checking the heavy hitters for source IP, source port and destination port in time bin 1, we find the source IP address 241.119.171.133 used 8534 flows to scan No.1443 port of a large number of hosts. The same, we also find there was a port scan attack that scaned different ports of 88.15.139.82 in time bin 2. Note that the IP addresses are anonymized by our system.

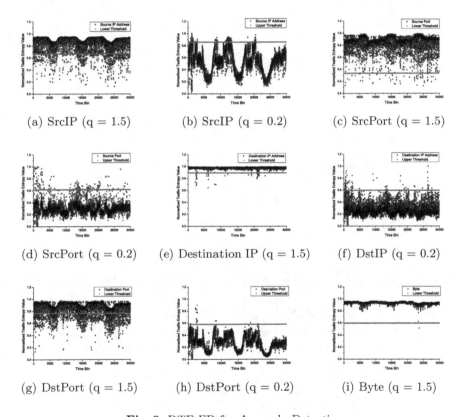

(a) SrcIP (q = 1.5)   (b) SrcIP (q = 0.2)   (c) SrcPort (q = 1.5)

(d) SrcPort (q = 0.2)   (e) Destination IP (q = 1.5)   (f) DstIP (q = 0.2)

(g) DstPort (q = 1.5)   (h) DstPort (q = 0.2)   (i) Byte (q = 1.5)

Fig. 9. DTE-FP for Anomaly Detection

Anomaly Classification. We can classify the detection results by different flow features. As shown in TABLE 4, we find 13 kinds of entropy patterns when we detect anomalies by the thresholds of DTE-FP when $MFPR = 5\%$.

Table 3. Detection Capability

q	MFPR=0%			MFPR=1%			MFPR=2%			MFPR=5%		
	LT	UT	both	LT	UT	both	LT	UT	both	LT	UT	both
1.5	659,0	4,0	**659,0**	721,0	4,0	**721,0**	756,0	6,0	**756,0**	841,0	23,0	**841,0**
1.1	299,0	18,0	**301,0**	348,0	18,0	**350,0**	387,0	20,0	**389,0**	445,0	23,0	**448,0**
0.8	81,0	74,1	**146,1**	87,0	74,1	**152,1**	94,0	75,1	**160,1**	102,0	75,1	**168,1**
0.2	0,0	415,0	**415,0**	0,0	423,0	**423,0**	0,0	425,0	**425,0**	0,0	445,0	**445,0**
-0.5	0,0	98,0	**98,0**	0,0	101,0	**101,0**	0,0	101,0	**101,0**	0,0	105,0	**105,0**
DTE	659,0	415,0	**949,0**	721,0	423,0	**957,0**	756,0	425,0	**1047,0**	841,0	445,0	**1148,0**

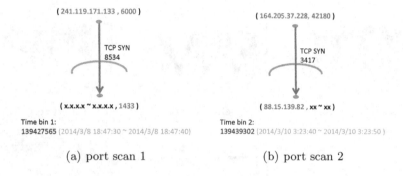

(a) port scan 1   (b) port scan 2

Fig. 10. Examples for Anomaly Validation

Table 4. Anomaly Classification

Feature					Anomaly Number
sicip	srcpt	dstip	dstpt	byte	DTE-FP
			√		474
		√			10
		√	√		52
	√				10
	√		√		22
	√	√	√		8
√					365
√			√		122
√		√			3
√		√	√		8
√	√				16
√	√		√		31
√	√	√	√		27
Total Anomaly Number					1148

6 Discussion

DTE-FP is only used to detect the flow-level traffic anomalies with a certain scale, such as DoS, DDoS, port scan, network scan, worm and spam. However, it doesn't care about other kinds of anomalies without flow-level feature deviation, e.g. virus and Trojan.

In this paper, in order to make comparisons between DTE-FP and Tsallis entropy, we use a constant threshold for entropy value to detect traffic anomalies. But DTE-FP is independent of detection algorithm. We can use other detection algorithms, such as a change-based algorithm for entropy, to detect anomalies.

7 Conclusion and Future Work

In this paper, we analyze the characteristics of Tsallis entropy for flow-level network traffic anomaly detection, and propose a new traffic anomaly detection method DTE-FP. Additionally, we implement a Hadoop-based system named TADOOP, which supports semi-automatic training, offline detection and online detection. finally, we deploy our system in Tsinghua University Campus Network, and use it to mine traffic anomalies. The experiment results reveal that DTE-FP performs much better than Tsallis entropy and TADOOP plays a good role in traffic anomaly detection. In our future work, we plan to use a change-based algorithm for entropy to detect traffic anomalies, and make comparisons between the two methods.

Acknowledgement. We thank for the support of Cisco-Tsinghua Joint Lab Research Project Funding and the helpful comments of our shepherd Mohan Dhawan. This work is also partially supported by the National High Technology Research and Development Program of China (863 Program) No. 2015AA016105, the National Natural Science Foundation of China (Grant No. 61202357, 61402253), and the Project for 2012 Next Generation Internet technology research and development, industrialization, and large scale commercial application of China (No. 2012 1763).

References

1. Lakhina, A., Crovella, M., Diot, C.: Mining anomalies using traffic feature distributions. In: Proceedings of the 2005 Conference on Applications, Technologies, Architectures, and Protocols for Computer Communications (SIGCOMM 2005), pp. 217–228. ACM, New York (2005)
2. Gu, Y., McCallum, A., Towsley, D.: Detecting anomalies in network traffic using maximum entropy estimation. In: Proceedings of the 5th ACM SIGCOMM Conference on Internet Measurement, IMC 2005, pp. 32–32. USENIX Association, Berkeley (2005)
3. Nychis, G., Sekar, V., Andersen, D.G., Kim, H., Zhang, H.: An empirical evaluation of entropy-based traffic anomaly detection. In: Proceedings of the 8th ACM SIGCOMM Conference on Internet Measurement, pp. 151–156. ACM (2008)

4. Tellenbach, B., Burkhart, M., Sornette, D., Maillart, T.: Beyond shannon: characterizing internet traffic with generalized entropy metrics. In: Moon, S.B., Teixeira, R., Uhlig, S. (eds.) PAM 2009. LNCS, vol. 5448, pp. 239–248. Springer, Heidelberg (2009)
5. Bereziński, P., Szpyrka, M., Jasiul, B., Mazur, M.: Network anomaly detection using parameterized entropy. In: Saeed, K., Snášel, V. (eds.) CISIM 2014. LNCS, vol. 8838, pp. 465–478. Springer, Heidelberg (2014)
6. Dean, J., Ghemawat, S.: Mapreduce: Simplified data processing on large clusters. Commun. ACM **51**(1), 107–113 (2008)
7. Apache hadoop (2014). http://hadoop.apache.org
8. Lee, Y., Lee, Y.: Toward scalable internet traffic measurement and analysis with hadoop. SIGCOMM Comput. Commun. Rev. **43**(1), 5–13 (2013)
9. Zhang, L., Wang, J., Lin, S.: Design of the network traffic anomaly detection system in cloud computing environment. In: 2012 International Symposium on Information Science and Engineering (ISISE), pp. 16–19. IEEE (2012)
10. Hodge, V.J., Jackson, T., Austin, J.: A hadoop-based framework for parallel and distributed feature selection (2013)
11. Bhuyan, M., Bhattacharyya, D., Kalita, J.: Network anomaly detection: Methods, systems and tools. IEEE Communications Surveys Tutorials **16**(1), 303–336 (2014)
12. Fontugne, R., Mazel, J., Fukuda, K.: Hashdoop: a mapreduce framework for network anomaly detection. In: 2014 IEEE Conference on Computer Communications Workshops (INFOCOM WKSHPS), pp. 494–499, April 2014
13. Ziviani, A., Gomes, A.T.A., Monsores, M., Rodrigues, P.: Network anomaly detection using nonextensive entropy. IEEE Communications Letters **11**(12), 1034–1036 (2007)
14. Wang, Z., Yang, J., Li, F.: An on-line anomaly detection method based on a new stationary metric-entropy-ratio. In: 2014 IEEE 13th International Conference on Trust, Security and Privacy in Computing and Communications (TrustCom), pp. 90–97. IEEE (2014)
15. Tsallis, C.: Possible generalization of boltzmann-gibbs statistics. Journal of Statistical Physics **52**(1–2), 479–487 (1988)
16. Tsallis, C.: Nonextensive statistics: theoretical, experimental and computational evidences and connections. Brazilian Journal of Physics **29**(1), 1–35 (1999)
17. Tsallis, C.: Entropic nonextensivity: a possible measure of complexity. Chaos, Solitons & Fractals **13**(3), 371–391 (2002)
18. IPFIX library (2014). http://libipfix.sourceforge.net/
19. Tian, G., Wang, Z., Yin, X., Li, Z., Shi, X., Lu, Z., Zhou, C., Yu, Y., Guo, Y.: Mining network traffic anomaly based on adjustable piecewise entropy. In: IEEE/ACM International Symposium on Quality of Service (IWQoS), June 2015

SuperCall: A Secure Interface for Isolated Execution Environment to Dynamically Use External Services

Yueqiang Cheng[1]([⊠]), Qing Li[2], Miao Yu[1], Xuhua Ding[3], and Qingni Shen[2]

[1] CyLab, Carnegie Mellon University, Pittsburgh, USA
{yueqiang,miaoy1}@andrew.cmu.edu
[2] Department of Information Security, School of Software and Electronics,
Peking University, Beijing, China
qingli@pku.edu.cn, qingnishen@ss.pku.edu.cn
[3] School of Information Systems, Singapore Management University,
Singapore, Singapore
xhding@smu.edu.sg

Abstract. Recent years have seen many virtualization-based Isolated Execution Environments (IEE) proposed in the literature to protect a Piece of Application Logic (PAL) against attacks from an untrusted guest kernel. A prerequisite of these IEE system is that the PAL is small and self-contained. Therefore, a PAL is deprived of channels to interact with the external execution environment including the kernel and application libraries. As a result, the PAL can only perform limited tasks such as memory-resident computation with inflexible utilization of system resources. To protect more sophisticated tasks, the application developer has to segment it into numerous PALs satisfying the IEE prerequisite, which inevitably lead to development inefficiency and more erroneous code. In this paper, we propose SuperCall, a new function call interface for a PAL to safely and efficiently call *external* untrusted code in both the kernel and user spaces. It not only allows flexible interactions between a PAL and untrusted environments, but also improved the utilization of resources, without compromising the security of the PAL. We have implemented SuperCall on top of a tiny hypervisor. To demonstrate and evaluate SuperCall, we use it to build a PAL as part of a password checking program. The experiment results show that SuperCall improves the development efficiency and incurs insignificant performance overhead.

1 Introduction

Numerous Isolated Execution Environments (IEE) [4,8,11,17,20,23] have been proposed using virtualization techniques to tackle attacks from both the user and kernel spaces. An IEE separates a Piece of Application Logic (PAL)'s execution from the rest of the platform, including the operating system, so as to protect its execution integrity as well as data secrecy. An indispensable prerequisite of

© Institute for Computer Sciences, Social Informatics and Telecommunications Engineering 2015
B. Thuraisingham et al. (Eds.): SecureComm 2015, LNICST 164, pp. 193–211, 2015.
DOI: 10.1007/978-3-319-28865-9_11

an IEE's protection over a PAL is the *self-contained* property stating that the execution flow does not leave the PAL's code, which implies no function calls to external code including the kernel code. The reason of this restriction is that sharing the same execution flow jeopardizes the security of the PAL and IEE.

One limitation of PAL-based IEE is its impact on the utilization of system resources. Without dynamically resource (e.g., memory) allocation and deallocation services, the PAL has to acquire all needed resources before execution and hold them till the end. For instance, the OS allocates to the PAL a bulky memory region with the maximum size in estimation. Such resource usage strategy is obviously not efficient. Moreover, the self-contained property requires the PAL to assemble all needed inputs before its execution. Dynamic data or events generated at runtime cannot be used as an input, which significantly limits the PAL's functionality. At last, the PAL based IEE also introduces great efforts into the development of PAL. For instance, developers have to carefully write their PAL code to avoid invoking library function calls. As a result, the PAL capable of running within an IEE is either small with limited functionality (e.g., computation only), or cumbersome with a higher chance of harboring vulnerabilities.

In this work, we propose a novel interface for a PAL inside an IEE to safely utilize external functions and system calls, e.g., to allocate/deallocate memory buffers and to load encrypted files. It dismisses the self-contained PAL prerequisite and allows the PAL developers to code PALs like a normal program. Our new mechanism is called *SuperCall* as depicted in Figure 1. SuperCall separates the execution flow of the external code from the isolated one, and ensures that the invocation and return procedures always go through the predefined out-and-back gates. Out gates are for safely switching isolation spaces (i.e., from IEE space to non-IEE space) and facilitating call invocations, and back gates are for securely resuming IEE's execution flow, e.g., restoring execution context as well as sanitizing and validating inputs (i.e., return values). Due to the non-bypassable verifications in the back gates and the secure space switches, SuperCall is able to defend against Iago attacks [5] and code reuse attacks [3], and keep other desired security properties, e.g., code and data integrity, data secrecy and control flow integrity.

SuperCall is a new interface, allowing existing IEEs to actively and securely invoke external services. It is similar to upcall [16] that allows the hypervisor to actively invoke guest services. Due to SuperCall needs to validate all inputs of the back gates, developers should carefully select the external services to minimize the validation costs. If the cost is quite high, e.g., requiring numerous code or a long execution, we suggest to reconsider about the possibility of adding the external service into the PAL. There are two typical scenarios for SuperCall. One is to dynamically update resources (e.g., memory can be dynamically allocated/released by malloc-like functions), providing flexible usage model, instead of preserving them in a maximum estimation. The second one is to do securely data exchange with untrusted environments, e.g., saving or reading encrypted files. To demonstrate these two typical scenarios, we have implemented a

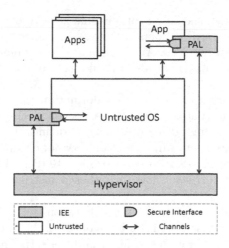

Fig. 1. PALs within IEEs on virtualization-based system. PALs can securely communicate with untrusted applications/OS functions via the SuperCall interface.

password authentication scheme called PwdChecker which is a secure login console in a multi-user system and uses passwords to authenticate users with secret questions as a back-up means. It uses SuperCall to dynamically request memory, load an encrypted database (i.e., secure questions and answers) and get user secure answers. Moreover, this case study also demonstrates that the development efforts of PAL are much reduced. We have conducted performance evaluation of SuperCall by using micro-benchmark tools. The results indicate that the performance overhead of SuperCall is reasonably small.

ORGANIZATION In the next section, we explain the background and the setting of the problem we undertake to resolve, and present the overall design of SuperCall. Then we describe the typical execution flow and a SuperCall and present the typical application scenarios in Section 3 and Section 4. In Section 5, we use a case to demonstrate the benefits of using SuperCall, and further evaluate the incurred cost. We discuss the related work in Section 6. Section 7 concludes the paper.

2   The Problem Definition and Design Overall

In this section, we first explain the background of the PAL in existing literature, and then highlight our goals followed by a description of the security assumptions. At last, we generally describe how a SuperCall works.

2.1   Piece of Application Logic (PAL)

As shown in [23], PALs in various isolation systems share a common layout consisting of three sections depicted in Figure 2(a). The *private* section contains the security related data, such as cryptographic keys, and other sensitive information, such as credit card numbers. Accesses to the private section are only allowed if they are from the PAL. Any external access is blocked. Note that the PAL's stack and heap regions are also in this section and they are not shared with untrusted code.

The *public* section contains *read-only* information shared between the PAL and untrusted code. It contains the PAL's code and constant data, such as constant numbers and strings. The public section defines the entry point address for the PAL to start execution. Any execution flow not originating from the entry point is not allowed by the IEE, so as to prevent ROP [3] like attacks whereby the adversary twists the control flow to a chosen instruction for a malevolent purpose.

The *shared* section is for data exchange between the PAL and the external environment. Although it is writable for both of them, their accesses are exclusive to each other. This is to deal with the Time-Of-Check-To-Time-Of-Use (TOCT-TOU) attack which alters the data when the PAL is about to use sanitized data in the section. Note that this section could be dynamically allocated at runtime (Figure 2(b)).

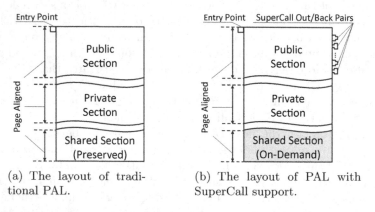

(a) The layout of traditional PAL.

(b) The layout of PAL with SuperCall support.

Fig. 2. The layout of PAL. The shared section (shaded region) could be dynamically allocated for PALs with SuperCall support.

2.2 Desired Security Properties

We consider a PAL under the protection of the SuperCall. Specifically, the hypervisor maintains a table for a pre-registered PAL's section information as well as the entry points. It checks the initial integrity of the PAL's public and private sections and ensures that their memory pages are exclusively occupied by the PAL. Upon this, SuperCall is able to ensure address space isolation and execution integrity of a PAL.

Address Space Isolation. Address space isolation implies code integrity, data integrity and secrecy. Various isolation mechanisms have been proposed [8, 11, 17, 23] which leverage the processor virtualization to prevent illicit software accesses. Specifically, the hypervisor controls the attribute bits of the Extended Page Table (EPT)[1] entries to specify the desired access control permissions according to the entity occupying the CPU. To prevent malware from making DMA access to unauthorized memory regions, the hypervisor leverages device virtualization to block illicit DMA accesses by configuring the IOMMU page table in the same way as the EPT entries. Note that since all memory resources are allocated before PAL execution, the address mapping is never changed during PAL execution. Thus, the hypervisor can enforce the isolation in the beginning of the PAL and freeze the address mapping until the PAL exits.

Execution Integrity. Execution integrity refers to the property that PAL actually executes with inputs P_ins and produces outputs P_outs. It implies control flow integrity (CFI), code and data integrity. The hypervisor enforces that the execution flow of PAL always starts to run from a pre-defined entry point, e.g., a back gate or the entry point. At runtime, hypervisor isolates the entire execution environment of the PAL from the rest of the platform without allowing any intervention, so that the PAL's context and control flow are not exposed to any untrusted code.

2.3 Design Goals

We aim to design the SuperCall mechanism for the PAL to securely call external (untrusted) code without undermining the aforementioned security properties. Through SuperCall, a PAL can efficiently invoke system calls and library functions, e.g., invoking *malloc* to allocate memory buffers or issuing *mmap2* for a file reading.

To make SuperCall secure, efficient and practical, we use the following criteria to guide our design.

- **Small TCB.** The TCB of SuperCall should be small and simple. It minimizes the risk of subverting the TCB and allow for formal verification [12]. This property implies that the size expansion and complexity increasing of the hypervisor should be minimum.
- **High Efficiency.** The SuperCall interface should have minimum performance impact on the PAL execution, the IEE protection and the platform as a whole. In addition, SuperCall should minimize the latency for one invocation by reducing unnecessary operations and simplifying interactions.
- **Easy to Use.** The APIs of SuperCall should be easy to use. Thus, the calling convention of SuperCall is the same as regular system calls. SuperCall provides a routine as a wrapper to handle the minor differences which is therefore transparent for PAL developers.

---

[1] In AMD's virtualization terminology, the Nested Page Table plays the same role as Intel's EPT.

– **Well Defined Entry Points.** The entry point for the SuperCall should
be well defined, and the inputs of each entry point should be sanitized and
validated before using them, which aim to defend against Iago attack [5].

2.4   Assumptions

We consider a subverted commodity OS as the adversary. This is a realistic
threat, since the legacy OS usually has a large code base and a broad attack surface. After gaining the root privilege, the adversary can launch arbitrary code
and DMA operations to access or even modify any memory regions and other
system resources, e.g., Model Specific Registers (MSRs). The purpose of the
adversary is to compromise the security properties of the PAL, for example, to
tamper with the PAL's private data and/or to manipulate it execution logic.
SuperCall requires that the underlying platform supports hardware-assisted virtualization techniques, and the hypervisor is trusted. We also assume all the
I/O devices are trusted and always behave according to their hardware specifications. In this paper, we do not consider attacks that involve physical control
of the platform. In addition, we do not consider side channel attacks.

2.5   Overview of SuperCall

The semantics of SuperCall is the same as a function call as shown in Figure 3
where the control flow transfers from the caller (X) to the callee (Y), and returns
back after the end of the execution of Y. During the development of a PAL, people could simply replace the function with a SuperCall and add the corresponding
out and back gates/interfaces for parameter marshaling and inputs validation
(e.g., defending against Iago attack [5]).

Specifically, when caller X attempts to invoke callee Y through a SuperCall,
the PAL firstly transfers the control flow to the corresponding *out gate*. The
out gate prepares the stack frame needed by the called function (Y) and do
the parameter marshalling. The hypervisor saves the context of PAL, and isolates the PAL by manipulating the guest context and transfers the execution
flow to the callee function. In SuperCall, this request is issued through a dedicated hypercall, named as *SuperEnter*. When returns, the callee function[2] issues
another hypercall, *SuperExit*, to notify the hypervisor return to the corresponding *back gate*. In the back gate, all returns should be sanitized and validated
before they are used. The SuperEnter and SuperExit together indicate the start
and the end of a SuperCall. Their working style is similar to fast-system-call
instruction pair SYSENTER and SYSEXIT [14].

---

[2] In the implementation, an inserted code issues the SuperExit hypercall for the callee
function (details in Figure 4).

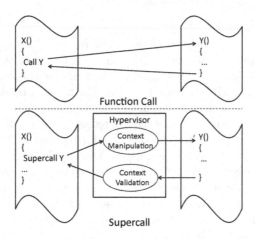

Fig. 3. The SuperCall mechanism. a SuperCall is quite similar to a traditional function call, but it always go through well-defined interfaces and invoke the hypervisor to protect the control flow transitions.

3   Typical Control Flow of SuperCall

A typical control flow of a SuperCall is also similar but relatively complex comparing to the control flow of the traditional function call. It always starts from an out gate and ends with a back gate, involving two space switches driven by a SuperEnter and a SuperExit respectively, as despited in Figure 4.

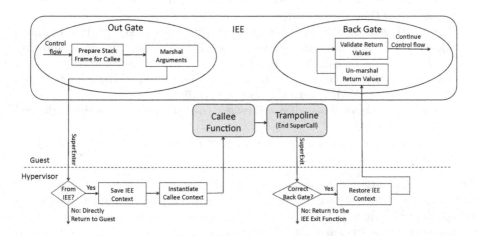

Fig. 4. The execution path of the SuperCall interface. The shaded operations are executed in the untrusted guest environment. Other operations are trusted and executed either in the PAL or in the hypervisor.

3.1   Out Gate

The out gate that is like a wrapper of the callee function shares the same calling conversion and the same parameters with the callee function. After doing several pre-processing operations, the out gate would transfer the control flow to the callee function. Specifically, it does two main tasks: 1) prepare a stack frame for the callee function, and 2) do argument marshalling. It is relatively easy to finish the first task, as the out gate could reuse the stack frame prepared by its caller. The only update is for the return address, which should point to the entry of the prepared trampoline (Figure 4). During the argument marshalling, all non-pointer arguments are kept the same in the stack frame. For pointer arguments, the out gate will move the pointed data, e.g., structures or buffers, into the shared section, and update the pointers to point to the new copies. After these two tasks, the out gate will issue a SuperEnter to inform the hypervisor to transfer the control flow to the callee function.

3.2   SuperEnter

The SuperEnter has two main purposes: 1) functional purpose which aims to achieve the control flow transferring like the traditional function call (i.e., transferring the control flow from the caller to the callee), and 2) security purpose that aims to keep the desired security properties of PALs.

Functional Requirement. SuperCall should be able to transfer the execution flow to the callee function, and let the callee function execute as normal. To achieve these, the following information should be provided and set properly:

- The arguments needed by the callee function. They are necessary for the execution of the callee function.
- The starting address of the callee function. SuperEnter requires it to continue the execution flow from an address specified by the caller function, and that address can not be calculated in advance.
- The stack used by the callee function. Its stack should be different from the one used by the PAL due to the security requirement.
- The return address: The callee will return to this address to indicate the end of its execution flow.
- The entry point of a back gate: The control flow of the PAL will restart from the specific back gate.

All stack-based arguments are handled by the out gate. Thus, the SuperEnter only ask the hypervisor to handle the arguments that are passed through registers. Note that it is not safe that the out gate in the PAL space to directly set those registers, because the values in some or all of them would be flushed or replaced by the hypervisor during its execution for serving the *SuperEnter* request.

Besides these arguments, the SuperEnter has to prepare some additional information to smoothly transfer the control flow. In particular, the entry of the callee function and the callee's stack should be provided. In addition, to make the control flow correctly resume, the entry of the corresponding back gate should be also specified. The provided information as well as the identity of the PAL is safely saved in a dedicated list within the hypervisor space, which is always inaccessible for the untrusted execution environment. Note that the saved record will be used for the validation of the return flow, as well as the context restoration.

Context Manipulation. After getting such information, the hypervisor needs to manipulate the context to let the callee function execute as normal. The hypervisor achieves it by leveraging the processor virtualization technique. Specifically, in hardware-assisted virtualization, almost all guest context information is automatically stored in a dedicated control structure, named as the Virtual Machine Control Structure (VMCS) in Intel VT-x [14]. Only the general registers are manually saved by the hypervisor. The hypervisor is able to read and write the VMCS and the saved general registers. Thus, it manipulates the values of the corresponding registers before the processor enters the guest domain using VM-entry instructions (i.e., $VMLAUNCH$ and $VMRESUME$). More specifically, the hypervisor can modify the IP value to let the guest start the execution from the called starting address, and change the stack pointer SP to assign the top of the stack for the callee function.

Security Requirement. The two basic security properties (i.e., address space isolation and execution integrity) of the PAL should be guaranteed by the hypervisor during the SuperCall process. Specifically, the hypervisor should protect both memory regions occupied by the PAL and the context registers temporally used by the PAL. The private data and all code of the PAL are located in the PAL memory regions. Any malicious modifications and/or illicit reads are possibly lead to the integrity breaking and/or the leakage of the sensitive information. Even worse, the modifications of control data (e.g., function pointer) will subvert the control flow integrity. The context registers can contain temporal data relevant to the private data or even the cryptographic keys. Moreover, a smarter attacker is able to infer more sensitive information from the leaked seed-data. Some registers can also impose the execution behaviors of the PAL, e.g., if the stack pointer SP is illicitly modified, the PAL will fetch wrong local variables or even use incorrect return address, violating the control flow integrity.

To protect the memory regions, the hypervisor could prepare two EPTs/NPTs. One EPT_{iee} is for the PAL, where the memory regions occupied by the PAL are accessible, and another one EPT_{others} is for the untrusted code, where all PAL memory regions are completely inaccessible. When the PAL occupies the CPU, the hypervisor installs the EPT_{iee}. When the PAL invokes the SuperCall to transfer the control flow to an external function, the hypervisor switches to another one EPT_{others}. In this way, the untrusted code occupying the CPU still can not access the memory regions of the PAL.

To protect the context information in the processor registers, the hypervisor should save them before passing the control to the untrusted code, and restore them after the execution flow returns. Specifically, the guest context includes the general registers, flag registers, stack pointer, instruction pointer, as well as the segment descriptors and selectors. After the backup, the hypervisor clears the values of general registers, flags register, stack pointer, instruction pointer and segment descriptors/selectors to avoid the potential data leakage. Note that the stack pointer, instruction pointer and/or general registers will be set for the callee function according to the request of the caller. Note that the SuperCall states are maintained in PAL granularity and saved separately. Thus, those states would not intervene with each other.

3.3   SuperExit

Similar to SuperEnter, the functionalities of SuperExit are also separated into functional and security aspects. For the functional support, SuperExit is to inform the exit of the previous SuperCall. Specifically, the caller function prepares the return address for the callee function. When the callee function finishes and returns, the processor automatically loads the prepared return address into instruction pointer (IP), and jumps to the specific address to continue the execution. The specific address is a prepared trampoline, which can be located in the PAL public section or a pre-defined address (similar to the *vdso* on Linux platform for assisting system calls [19]). Note that the data in the Private section, before the SuperCall returns, is inaccessible. In order to allow the PAL to perform full operations (e.g., accessing the private data), the SuperExit is non-bypassable. This exit request is sent through a dedicated hypercall - SuperExit. More specifically, we put a SuperExit at the very beginning of the prepared trampoline, which is able to guarantee that the processor immediately perform the $VMCALL$ instruction.

Context Validation.   The primary purpose of the context validation is to guarantee that the resumed control flow is correct. Recall that the hypervisor saves the PAL and the entry of the back gate during the invocation of the SuperEnter. Thus, the hypervisor will attempt to locate the record by searching in the saved items. If there is one record matched, the hypervisor will remove the record and close this temporal entry point from this PAL before returning to the PAL. Otherwise, there must be something wrong in the current guest execution flow. For such cases, the hypervisor can either inform the guest using an error code or directly terminate the PAL with a fatal error.

The last task of the context validation is to restore the original context of PAL. The unrelated registers, such as ESP and EBP, will be overwritten by previously saved PAL's context. If the hypervisor misses this step and directly reuse the untrusted context left by the SuperExit, the execution integrity is likely to be broken. Note that the hypervisor needs switching back to EPT_{iee} to allow the PAL to access its private data. At the same time, the hypervisor has to restore the context of the PAL, as the context used by the SuperExit is not trusted. If the hypervisor reuse the context left by the SuperExit, the execution integrity is likely to be broken, e.g., the start point of the resumed control flow could be wrong.

3.4 Back Gate

When the callee function finishes and the execution flow returns to the PAL, a *SuperExit* is immediately issued to indicate the end of the SuperCall. From that time, the hypervisor isolates the PAL and restores the control flow. The following work for the *back gate* is to un-marshal and validate the return values, and continue the original execution flow. Unmarshalling return values is the reverse operation of the parameter marshaling. If the return values are non-pointer values, PAL could directly use them. If the return values are pointer values, the back gate should move the pointed data into the private section, and update the pointer accordingly.

After the unmarshalling of return values, the control flow will move to the return validation procedure. In our SuperCall design, each back gate has its own validation procedure, and guarantees that the control flow always goes through the validation procedure before resuming the original control flow. The validation code for a specific input is usually small and simple. Thus, the IEE developers could manually verify its correctness. In addition, it is highly possible to formally verified using certain formal verification methods [12]. As all inputs of back gates are sanitized and validated, an adversary cannot bypass the verification to launch Iago attacks [5] or code reuse attacks.

4 Typical Scenarios

There are two main scenarios for PALs to invoke external functions: 1) update (i.e., allocate/release) memory resources (e.g., main memory and I/O ports), such as allocating/deallocating memory, and 2) exchange data with outside, such as getting file/socket content, reading the inputs of peripheral devices (e.g., user passwords, biometric information), or processing data instead of PALs (e.g., sorting data).

4.1 Resource Update

The first typical scenario is to update memory resource. In the real cases, a PAL usually need extra memory for new inputs or generated data. For a PAL without SuperCall support, it has to allocate a bulky memory with the maximum size in estimation. Obviously the resource usage is not efficient in this situation. With SuperCall support, a PAL does not need to do pre-allocation, instead it could dynamically allocate memory according to the real demand.

To securely use the dynamically allocated memory, the PAL has to trace the memory boundary and requires the protection from the hypervisor. Specifically, in the validation step of the back gate, the PAL gets the boundary (i.e., the start address and the length) of the newly allocated memory resource. Once it is done, the PAL issues a hypercall to the hypervisor to mark the occupied physical memory into its own address space. If the memory is PAL's private resource, it will be marked into the private section. If it is for sharing with others, it will be put into the shared region. Once the newly allocated memory resource is moved into the PAL's address space, the hypervisor will set proper access permissions to grant legal PAL accesses and prevent illicit accesses that are originated from outside of the PAL.

When the allocated memory is not needed, the PAL will release it for maximizing resource utilization. In such cases, the PAL needs to inform the hypervisor to remove the resource from its address space. In particular, the out gate of the PAL collects the memory boundary of the memory resource and issues a hypercall to inform hypervisor that it does not exclusively occupy this memory resource. Note that there would be some problems if the releasing notification to the hypervisor is done in the back gate, because the released memory could be immediately reused by others, before the execution flow returns. In this case, there will be exception to indicate the access violation. If it happens in the user space, the corresponding process would be killed. If it is in the kernel space, it could lead to unrecoverable events, such as system shutdown or rebooting.

4.2   Data Exchange with Outside

Another typical scenario of using SuperCall is to exchange data. In the real cases, a PAL usually needs to exchange data with outside, such as sending dynamic output data (e.g., log file, warning messages) or receiving dynamic input data (e.g., user name, password and PIN number). In the PAL without SuperCall support, it has to get all possible inputs at the very beginning and send all output data at the final end. In this case, the developers have to predict all possible inputs needed by the PAL. In certain extreme cases, the number of the possible combination is extremely large, and consequently the needed memory region is huge. In addition, the generated output data could also occupy a large number of memory regions. If one of these two extreme cases happens, the PAL has to be totally redesigned or divided into many smaller pieces. All these cases imply the impracticality and inflexibility of the traditional PAL design. With the help of SuperCall, the PAL could dynamically receive the inputs according to the real demand. In addition, the PAL also does not need to hold the generated output data to the end of the whole control flow, it could send output data as normal.

To securely send the output data, the PAL has to prepare the data in its private section or the shared section. For the common cases, the out gate could handle them automatically, such as sending a string message or a binary stream. For certain cases, the related data structures could be extremely complex. Facing such conditions, SuperCall has to rely on the developers to manually handle those output data. To facilitate the implementation of SuperCall and allow SuperCall to automatically handle the output data, we recommend that all output data are processed into a string or a binary stream.

In addition, all I/O data could be selectively encrypted according to the requirement of the PAL, achieving secure I/O. The encryption key will be provided by the hypervisor. As the hypervisor space is inaccessible for the untrusted guest environment, the key generation process done by the hypervisor is secure. The encrypted data could be safely stored in the hard drive or send to the remote cloud server.

5   Evaluation

To evaluate SuperCall, we have implemented an exemplary application to use SuperCall, and then measured its performance using several benchmark tools.

5.1   Case Study: PwdChecker

To conduct the case study, we develop an application called PwdChecker which performs the back-end authentication of a remote server. The logic of Pwd-Checker is as follows. It first loads user password file and the secure question database from the disk to the main memory. It then accepts user inputs including user name and password. If the password is incorrect, PwdChecker allows the user to have another try and increases the login-attempt counter accordingly. When the counter is more than three, it challenges the user with a predefined question. The user has the last chance to get authenticated by supplying the correct answers.

The details of the workflow is depicted in Figure 5 which shows runtime inputs are fed in different stages. There are three dynamic inputs and one static inputs. The static inputs are the inputs passed as parameters (i.e., username and password), while the dynamic inputs are dynamically got at runtime according to

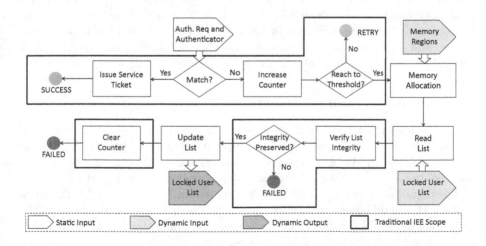

Fig. 5. The work flow of PwdChecker.

the demands (e.g., user answers). It is noteworthy that the dynamic inputs could be passed as the static inputs through carefully modifying the code or even the algorithm logic, e.g., the database containing the secure questions and answers can be passed as a static input. However, it will lead to a waste of memory, e.g., the database occupies many memory pages but it may not be used in most cases.

According to this logic, PwdChecker makes at least three types of system calls in order to acquire the needed resources and inputs during runtime.

- Memory allocation. It needs memory buffers to hold data, e.g, the secure questions and answers.
- File operation. It needs to load the database which encloses user authentication related information.
- I/O operation. It needs to read from the device (e.g., a keyboard) the user's inputs, such as user name and passwords.

5.2   PwdChecker without SuperCall

We select the PwdChecker as a representative example to discuss the PAL development, and SuperCall in particular, when considered in comparison with the two alternatives available at current. The first alternative is to put everything inside a single PAL. As a result, it needs great engineering effort to write their own code or customize existing code, e.g., adding a memory management in the PAL. This design will lower PAL's security level because the size of PAL will be dramatically enlarged. The other solution is to separate PwdChecker logic in multiple PALs in order to maintain the self-contain property for each PAL. As shown in Figure 5, PwdChecker is divided into three PALs. With this design, all the three PALs are self-contained and isolated from each other, and the dynamic inputs are now static inputs for each of them. However, this design is likely to introduce the following issues: 1) it breaks the original logic into multiple pieces, which may not be easily divided in most cases; 2) it would lead to a waste of resource, e.g., the PALs will need to reserve the memory with the highest estimation; and 3) it will increase the size and the complexity to manage shared global states and the communication channels.

5.3   PwdChecker with SuperCall

With the support of SuperCall, developers can easily build a PAL with the similar logic to the traditional insecure implementation, as well as the flexible resource utilization. We only describe the additional operations to demonstrate how easy to convert traditional code into self-contained with SuperCall.

The first operation is the stack switch. As introduced in Section 2.1, the stack for the PAL should be separated with the one for the untrusted code. Thus, in the entry point of the PAL, it immediately backups the untrusted stack and switches to its private stack. Before exiting the execution, it switches the stack back to prevent information leakage. To facilitate this step, we introduce two macros with 6 SloC to perform all these backup, switch and restoration operations. The second operation is to prepare stack frame and marshal the arguments for the untrusted callee function. Traditionally, the compiler generates suitable assembly code to implicitly complete these operations. But now we must explicitly do such operations via a dedicated function (i.e., the out gate). The out gate works like a wrapper of the callee function. The caller function firstly invokes the out gate as normal. In the out gate, it copies the arguments into the untrusted stack, and adjusts the top of the untrusted stack. If there are pointers in the arguments, the out gate must copy the content into the shared memory and update the corresponding pointers to keep semantic consistency. SuperCall adds *12 SLOC* to achieve all these goals. The operations in the back gate are case by case due to the return validation processes are different. However, the basic frame is the same. Thus, we insert a framework for each back gate. The left things are to fill the validation operations accordingly. The verification of the encrypted database is to decrypt the ciphered database, re-calculate and compare the hash value with the trusted one. As the memory allocation and deallocation are common in the real cases, we summarize their verification operations into macros. Later, developers could reuse the Macos to further simplify the development.

Although the out and back gates are manually added, we believe that all code could be automatically generated. Even for pointer arguments, it is still possible once the type and the size of the pointed data structure are collected, e.g. from the data structure definitions and/or the runtime parameters.

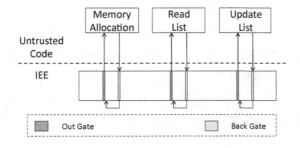

Fig. 6. External function invocations in PwdChecker based on SuperCall.

5.4   Performance Evaluation

We evaluated the performance of our SuperCall implementation and the example app PwdChecker on Ubuntu 10.04 LTS with the Linux kernel 2.6.32.59. These tests were run on a machine with Intel i5-670 CPU (3.47GHZ) and 4GB memory. SuperCall is built upon the Guardian hypervisor [7]. The original Guardian is about $25K$ SLOC, and the SuperCall service adds about 145 SLOC[3].

Firstly, we measure the performance cost of an empty hypercall. It is the baseline to launch a hypercall. This cost can be used later to evaluate the costs of SuperEnter and SuperExit. We create an empty hypercall, and call it from

---

[3] We use the tool *sloccount* [22] to calculate the source code.

Table 1. The time cost of SuperCall.

Operations	CPU Cycles	Time (μs)
An Empty Hypercall	3879	1.12
SuperEnter	13794	3.98
SuperExit	13438	3.87
SuperCall	27232	7.85

the guest domain. We treat the hypercall as a whole, and measure the round time from issuing the hypercall to its returning (i.e., from guest domain to guest domain via the hypervisor). The time cost (i.e., $1.12\mu s$ on average) demonstrate the basic cost of a hypercall. Based on this, we can evaluate the extra cost added in SuperEnter and SuperExit. The measurement results of SuperEnter and SuperExit are listed in Table 1. Because an empty SuperCall contains one SuperEnter and one SuperExit only, the total round-trip time on a SuperCall is about $7.85\mu s$. To further demonstrate the performance cost, we also measure the time cost in the PwdChecker example. The results in Table 2 show that the performance overhead is small that is roughly the cost of one SuperCall. We do not measure the third SuperCall due to the instability of typing answers through keyboard.

Table 2. The measurement results of PwdChecker.

Operations	Time (μs)	Overhead (μs)
Original Malloc	0.08	8.33
Malloc with SuperCall	8.41	
Original LoadDB	30.69	9.45
LoadDB with SuperCall	40.14	

The code expansion is limited due to the support of SuperCall. In the PwdChecker example, there are three out and back gates. All of them together need 180 SLoC in total, which is even far less than the memory allocation function (e.g., `malloc`).

6   Related Work

PAL Protection.   There are many existing schemes to protect a PAL [4,17, 18,23]. The Flicker [18] system aims to put a PAL into the isolated environment protected by the DRTM technique [9]. Due to the high latency and the poor communication channel, many virtualization-based schemes proposed [4,17,23]. However, in all of them a PAL still has only limited functionalities, without a secure interface to invoke untrusted services. This gap is addressed by our scheme. In addition, many virtualization-based schemes [6,10,13] aim to protect a whole high-insurance application, rather than a PAL. For all of them, the interaction interfaces are system calls that are not well-defined, and therefore surfer from the Iago [5] attack. In our scheme, back gates explicitly sanitize and validate all inputs, with the purpose to defend against Iago attack. The Intel SGX technique [15] and a similar architecture [21] are also promising techniques to protect a PAL or a whole application [2]. Similar to SuperCall, both also require adding specific well-defined interfaces for PALs.

Hypercall. Traditionally, a PAL has only one communication channel, through which the PAL can issue hypercalls to ask for services from the hypervisor. But it now has another new channel, allowing it to communicate with the untrusted code without losing the security properties. The virtualization technique provides hypercall, a communication channel for guest to actively communicate with the hypervisor. In paravirtualization, the hypercall is implemented as an interrupt, e.g., int $0x82$ on Xen [1], similar to the traditional system call mechanism. In the hardware-assisted virtualization, the processor is extended to support a series of virtualization instructions [14], and one of them is to launch a hypercall. In the original design of hypervisor, the return address of a hypercall is always the next instruction of the hypercall instruction. But in SuperCall technique, we reuse the virtualization instructions, and change the return behaviors of hypercalls. Specifically, the SuperEnter returns to the specified callee function, instead of the next instruction. The new return behavior (i.e., SuperExit) is similar to the *SymCall* mechanism [16], but not the same.

Upcall. The SymCall [16] provides a synchronous way (upcall) to invoke a function in a running guest environment. It provides a shared structure between the hypervisor and the guest domain. Through the shared structure, the hypervisor is able to enumerate the available functions (like system calls in syscall table). The guest and the hypervisor can directly read/write to this memory regions without triggering any vm_exit or protection violation. In our SuperCall design, we choose the synchronous way, but do not use the shared structure, because the hypervisor does not need to know the callee functions in advance. Dynamically updating function information to the hypervisor increases the flexibility of SuperCall. The direct benefit is that PAL can freely decide to use which function at runtime, without needing the registration procedure to register to the hypervisor. Another benefit is saving memory and the corresponding maintain cost. If a large number of PALs attempt to use many different functions, the size of the shared structure will be dramatically enlarged in SymCall setting, while in our design, the hypervisor only temporally maintains the function information and throws it away after the end of the execution.

7   Conclusion

In this paper, we introduced SuperCall as a new interface, through which a PAL could securely and efficiently invoke untrusted external functions, increasing the flexibility of interactions and improving the utilization rate of resources. The control flow is escorted by the hypervisor and all inputs of the SuperCall interfaces are sanitized and validated, and therefore Iago attacks and code reuse attacks do not work here. We implemented and evaluated a prototype of SuperCall on Guardian hypervisor by adding 145 SLOC. The experiment results indicated that SuperCall improved the development efficiency with insignificant performance overhead.

Acknowledgments. We are grateful to the anonymous reviewers for their useful comments and suggestions. This research was supported in part by the National Natural Science Foundation of China under Grant No. 61232005.

References

1. Barham, P., Dragovic, B., Fraser, K., Hand, S., Harris, T., Ho, A., Neugebauer, R., Pratt, I., Warfield, A.: Xen and the art of virtualization. In: SOSP 2003: Proceedings of the Nineteenth ACM Symposium on Operating Systems Principles, pp. 164–177. ACM, New York (2003)
2. Baumann, A., Peinado, M., Hunt, G.: Shielding applications from an untrusted cloud with haven. In: Proceedings of the 11th USENIX Conference on Operating Systems Design and Implementation, OSDI 2014, pp. 267–283. USENIX Association, Berkeley (2014)
3. Buchanan, E., Roemer, R., Shacham, H., Savage, S.: When good instructions go bad: generalizing return-oriented programming to RISC. In: Syverson, P., Jha, S. (eds.), Proceedings of CCS 2008, pp. 27–38. ACM Press, October 2008
4. Champagne, D., Lee, R.B.: Scalable architectural support for trusted software, Bangalore, India, January 9–14, 2010. Nominated for Best Paper Award (2010)
5. Checkoway, S., Shacham, H.: Iago attacks: why the system call api is a bad untrusted rpc interface. In: Proceedings of the Eighteenth International Conference on Architectural Support for Programming Languages and Operating Systems, ASPLOS 2013, pp. 253–264. ACM, New York (2013)
6. Chen, X., Garfinkel, T., Lewis, E.C., Subrahmanyam, P., Waldspurger, C.A., Boneh, D., Dwoskin, J., Ports, D.R.K.: Overshadow: a virtualization-based approach to retrofitting protection in commodity operating systems. In: Proceedings of the 13th International Conference on Architectural Support for Programming Languages and Operating Systems, ASPLOS XIII, pp. 2–13. ACM, New York (2008)
7. Cheng, Y., Ding, X.: Guardian: hypervisor as security foothold for personal computers. In: Huth, M., Asokan, N., Čapkun, S., Flechais, I., Coles-Kemp, L. (eds.) Trust and Trustworthy Computing. LNCS, vol. 7904, pp. 19–36. Springer, Heidelberg (2013)
8. Cheng, Y., Ding, X., Deng, R.H.: Driverguard: Virtualization-based fine-grained protection on i/o flows. ACM Trans. Inf. Syst. Secur. **16**(2), 6:1–6:30 (2013)

9. INTEL CORPORATION. Intel trusted execution technology (intel txt) c software development guide, December 2009

10. Criswell, J., Dautenhahn, N., Adve, V.: Virtual ghost: protecting applications from hostile operating systems. In: Proceedings of the 19th International Conference on Architectural Support for Programming Languages and Operating Systems, ASPLOS 2014, pp. 81–96. ACM, New York (2014)

11. Dinaburg, A., Royal, P., Sharif, M., Lee, W.: Ether: malware analysis via hardware virtualization extensions. In: Proceedings of the 15th ACM Conference on Computer and Communications Security, CCS 2008, pp. 51–62. ACM, New York (2008)

12. Heitmeyer, C.L., Archer, M., Leonard, E.I., McLean, J.: Formal specification and verification of data separation in a separation kernel for an embedded system. In: Proceedings of the 13th ACM Conference on Computer and Communications Security, CCS 2006, pp. 346–355. ACM, New York (2006)

13. Hofmann, O.S., Kim, S., Dunn, A.M., Lee, M.Z., Witchel, E.: Inktag: secure applications on an untrusted operating system. In: Proceedings of the Eighteenth International Conference on Architectural Support for Programming Languages and Operating Systems, ASPLOS 2013, pp. 265–278. ACM, New York (2013)

14. Intel. Intel 64 and IA-32 architectures software developer's manual combined volumes: 1, 2a, 2b, 2c, 3a, 3b and 3c, October 2011

15. Intel. Software guard extensions programming reference, September 2013

16. Lange, J.R., Dinda, P.: Symcall: symbiotic virtualization through vmm-to-guest upcalls. In: Proceedings of the 7th ACM SIGPLAN/SIGOPS International Conference on Virtual Execution Environments, VEE 2011, pp. 193–204. ACM, New York (2011)

17. McCune, J.M., Li, Y., Qu, N., Zhou, Z., Datta, A., Gligor, V., Perrig, A.: Trustvisor: efficient tcb reduction and attestation. In: Proceedings of the 2010 IEEE Symposium on Security and Privacy, SP 2010, pp. 143–158. IEEE Computer Society, Washington, DC (2010)

18. McCune, J.M., Parno, B.J., Perrig, A., Reiter, M.K., Isozaki, H.: Flicker: an execution infrastructure for tcb minimization. In: Proceedings of the 3rd ACM SIGOPS/EuroSys European Conference on Computer Systems, Eurosys 2008, pp. 315–328. ACM, New York (2008)

19. nixCraft. Explains: Linux linux-gate.so.1 Library / Dynamic Shared Object [vdso]. http://www.cyberciti.biz/faq/linux-linux-gate-so-1-library-dynamic-shared-object-vdso/

20. Payne, B.D., Carbone, M., Sharif, M., Lee, W.: Lares: an architecture for secure active monitoring using virtualization. In: Proceedings of the 2008 IEEE Symposium on Security and Privacy, SP 2008, pp. 233–247. IEEE Computer Society, Washington, DC (2008)

21. Shinde, S., Tople, S., Kathayat, D., Saxena, P.: PodArch: Protecting Legacy Applications with a Purely Hardware TCB. Technical Report NUS-SL-TR-15-01, School of Computing, National University of Singapore, February 2015

22. Spillner, J.: Sloccount. http://www.dwheeler.com/sloccount/

23. Strackx, R., Piessens, F.: Fides: selectively hardening software application components against kernel-level or process-level malware. In: Proceedings of the 2012 ACM Conference on Computer and Communications Security, CCS 2012, pp. 2–13. ACM, New York (2012)

Authenticating Top-k Results of Secure Multi-keyword Search in Cloud Computing

Xiaojun Xiao[1], Yaping Lin[1(✉)], Wei Zhang[1], Xin Yao[1], and Qi Gu[2]

[1] College of Computer Science and Electronic Engineering, Hunan University,
Changsha 410082, China
{S1324W1015,yplin,zhangweidoc,xinyao}@hnu.edu.cn
[2] Google Inc., California, USA
qig@google.com

Abstract. Cloud computing brings abundant benefits to our lives nowadays, including easy data access, flexible management, and cost saving. However, due to the concern for privacy, most of us are reluctant to use it. To protect privacy while making full use of cloud data, secure keyword search is proposed and attracts many researchers' interests. However, all of the previous researches are based on a weak threat model, i.e., they all assume the cloud to be "curious but honest". Different from the previous works, in this paper, we consider a more challenging model where the cloud server would probably be compromised. To achieve a privacy preserving and personalized multi-keyword search, we first formulate different users' preference with a preference vector, and then adopt the secure k nearest neighbor (KNN) technique to find the most relevant files corresponding to the personalized search request. To verify the dynamic top-k search results, we design a novel Multi-Attribute Authentication Tree (MAAT). In particular, we propose an optimization scheme to reduce the size of verification objects so that the communication cost between the cloud and data users is tunable. Finally, by doing extensive experiments, we confirm that our proposed schemes can work efficiently.

Keywords: Cloud computing · Privacy preserving · Personalized multi-keyword search · Multi-Attribute Authentication Tree (MAAT) · Optimization

1 Introduction

Cloud computing brings abundant benefits to our lives nowadays, including easy data access, flexible management, and cost saving. It becomes critically important for data owners to outsource their data to the public cloud server while allowing data users to retrieve them [1].

However, most of us are reluctant to use it. One of the most important reasons is the concern for privacy. Data encryption would be an alternative way to reduce the data leakage. However, data encryption obviously prevents the plain-text based keyword search techniques. A trivial solution is downloading

© Institute for Computer Sciences, Social Informatics and Telecommunications Engineering 2015
B. Thuraisingham et al. (Eds.): SecureComm 2015, LNICST 164, pp. 212–229, 2015.
DOI: 10.1007/978-3-319-28865-9_12

all the encrypted data and decrypting them locally. But this is also impractical because of the huge amount of communication cost. Therefore devising a secure keyword search protocol is imperative.

Secure keyword search over encrypted cloud data has attracted several researchers' interests recently. Song et al. [2] first propose the notion of searchable encryption, which is further developed by [3], [7]. However, extending these researches to large scale cloud data will bring heavy computation and storage overhead. Wang et al. [8] first consider the secure keyword search over encrypted cloud data, which is followed by [9], [10], [11], [12]. These researchers not only enrich the search capabilities, but also reduce the computation and storage cost.

However, all these schemes are based on the ideal assumption that the cloud server is "curious but honest". Unfortunately, in practical applications, the cloud server may behave dishonestly with a lot of motivations, which mainly include:

- The cloud server may return forged search results. For example, an advertisement may be ranked higher than his competitors since the cloud server provider may earn profits from that advertising company.
- The cloud server may return incomplete search results in peak hours to avoid suffering from performance bottlenecks.

Therefore, enabling authorized data users to authenticate the search results would be significant. Additionally, a user-friendly system should enable data users to achieve a personalized multi-keyword search. To verify the search results, conventional solutions (including linked signature chaining [13] and the Merkle hash tree [14]) need the data owners to pre-know the order of search results. However, to enable personalized keyword search, search results have to be computed on the cloud server according to different data users' preferences, where data owners cannot pre-know the order of search results. An example is illustrated in Fig. 1. As we can see, data owner has four files (F_1, F_2, F_3, F_4), each file is attached with a file vector (each attribute in a file vector is a relevance score between a keyword and a file). Given different search vectors (Q_1, Q_2, Q_3, Q_4) (the order of search results is ranked by the inner product of the search vector and the file vectors), the order of search results are totally different.

In this paper, we consider a more challenging model where the cloud server would probably be compromised. A compromised cloud server would not only reveal sensitive data but also return forged or incomplete search results. To achieve a privacy-preserving personalized multi-keyword search, we first formulate different users' preference into a preference vector, and then adopt the secure k nearest neighbor (KNN) technique to find the most relevant files corresponding to the personalized search request. To preserve the relevance scores between keywords and files, we use an order and privacy preserving function. Additionally, we propose a novel Multi-Attribute Authentication Tree (MAAT) to authenticate the dynamic top-k search results. In particular, to reduce the size of verification objects, we propose an optimization scheme so that the communication cost between the cloud and data users is tunable. Finally, we conduct extensive experiments on real-world datasets which confirms that our proposed schemes work efficiently.

File Vectors	Search Vectors	Order of Results
F_1: (0.82,0.63,0.28)	Q_1: (0.1, 0.2, 0.7)	F_4, F_3, F_2, F_1
F_2: (0.92,0.54,0.43)	Q_2: (0.2, 0.3, 0.5)	F_4, F_2, F_3, F_1
F_3: (0.52,0.45,0.62)	Q_3: (0.5, 0.4, 0.1)	F_2, F_1, F_3, F_4
F_4: (0.25,0.62,0.68)	Q_4: (0.4, 0.6, 0.0)	F_1, F_2, F_3, F_4

Fig. 1. An example of dynamic order of search results corresponding to different search vectors

The main contributions of this paper are as follows:

- We consider a more challenging threat model where the cloud server would behave dishonestly. Based on this model, we solve the privacy preserving personalized multi-keyword search and dynamic top-k search results authentication.
- We propose a novel Multi-Attribute Authentication Tree (MAAT) to authenticate the dynamic top-k search results.
- We propose an optimization scheme to reduce the size of verification objects so that the communication cost between the cloud and data users is tunable.
- We analyze security properties and conduct extensive performance experiments for our proposed schemes.

The rest of this paper is organized as follows. Section 2 reviews the related works. Section 3 formulates the problem and introduces notations used in later discussions. Section 4 describes the secure search schemes and Section 5 introduces the authentication schemes. In Section 6, we introduce how to optimize the parameters. In Section 7 and 8, we presents security analysis and performance evaluation of our proposed schemes respectively. In Section 9, we conclude the paper.

2   Related Work

2.1   Traditional Searchable Encryption

Encrypted data search has been studied extensively in the literature. Song et al. [2] first defined the conception of searching on encrypted, proposed the cryptographic schemes for the problem of searching on encrypted data, and proved the security of their scheme. Goh et al. [3] defined a secure index to accelerate the search operation. Chang et al. [7] proposed a privacy preserving keyword search scheme, which not only enables data user to perform a keyword search over encrypted data, but also prevent from leaking the data privacy. The researches [4], [5], [6] further enhanced the search capabilities. But most of these works only support the search of single or boolean keyword, extending these techniques to large scale cloud data will bring heavy computation and storage overhead.

2.2   Secure Keyword Search in Cloud Computing

Secure keyword search in cloud computing has attracted many interests. Wang et al. [8] first defined the problem of secure ranked keyword search over encrypted cloud data. Cao et al. [9], Xu et al. [12] and Wen et al. [15] proposed to address the privacy preserving multi-keyword search over encrypted cloud data. To accelerate the search process, Hore et al. [11] proposed to adopt a set of colors to encode the presence of the keywords and create a search index. To enrich search functionality, Li et al. [10] proposed fuzzy keyword search over encrypted cloud data, respectively. To support multiple data owners to search over large scale cloud data, Sun et al. [16] proposed secure attribute-based keyword search schemes. Zhang et al. proposed to ensure secure ranked multi-keyword search to support multiple data owners in [17], [18], [19], and achieve secure distributed keyword search in geo-distributed clouds in [20], respectively.

However, all these schemes assume the cloud server to be "curious but honest". Different from these schemes, in this paper, we assume the cloud server would be compromised, under this assumption, we propose to securely authenticate the dynamic top-k search results.

2.3   Authenticating the Search Results

Methods used in authentication can be classified into two categories: the linked signature chaining, and the Merkle hash tree.

The linked signature chaining schemes [13], [21], require to pre-know the order of search result, so that the data owner can obtain an ordered link, and sign for the consecutive data in the link, which forms the linked signature chaining. Consequently, any data forging or deletion will be easily discovered once the signature chaining is incomplete. However, as illustrated in [22], the linked signature chaining will lead to very high computational cost, storage overhead, and user-side verification cost.

The Merkle hash tree proposed in [14], [23], [24] is proposed to verify the integrity of a very large data set. The merkle hash tree also require to pre-know the order of search results. The data owner constructs the merkle hash tree and signs for the root. Data users re-construct the merkle hash tree, and compare the computed root with the returned root. Therefore, any data forging or deletion will lead to the inconsistency of the comparison. However, as illustrated in Fig. 1, for the personalized keyword search, data owners cannot know the order of search results in advance, we cannot use the existed authentication method here. In this paper, we propose to construct a novel Multi-Attribute Authentication Tree (MAAT) to authenticate the dynamic top-k search results.

3   Problem Formulation

3.1   System Model

There are three entities involved in our system model, as illustrated in Fig. 2, they are data owner, cloud server and data users. The data owner has a collection of files $\mathcal{F}$. To enable search operation on these files which will be encrypted,

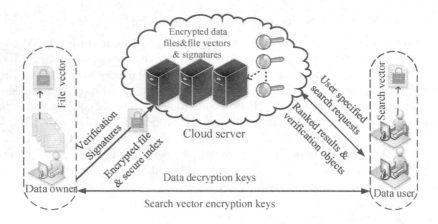

Fig. 2. Architecture of secure keyword search in cloud computing

the data owner performs some operations in advance which includes extracting a keyword set $\mathcal{W}$ from $\mathcal{F}$, computing relevance scores between keywords and files, constructing and signing a multi-attribute authentication tree. Then the data owner outsources all the encrypted data files, file vectors and signatures to the cloud server. Once an authorized data user wants to perform a secure keyword search over these encrypted files based on his preference, he first generates his trapdoor $\widetilde{Q}$ (encrypted query vector) and submits it to the cloud server. Upon receiving the trapdoor $\widetilde{Q}$, the cloud server first searches over the encrypted file vectors stored on it, then it returns the top-k relevant data files and corresponding verification objects. The authorized data user further verifies the integrity of returned search results. If the search results pass the verification, data user decrypts and obtains satisfied data files. Otherwise the search results are considered as contaminated and abandoned.

3.2 Threat Model

In our threat model, both data owner and authorized data users are trusted, however, different from previous works [8], [9], [12], the cloud server is not trusted and would be compromised, which is more challenging and takes a firm step towards practical application. Specifically, the cloud server not only aims at revealing the contents of encrypted files, keywords and relevance scores, but also tends to return forged or incomplete data. Note that how to authorize a data user is out of the scope of this paper, an outstanding example can be found in [25].

3.3 Design Goals

Our system design should simultaneously satisfy security and performance goals illustrated as follows:

- **Ranked multi-keyword search:** The proposed scheme should enable personalized and ranked multi-keyword search. Specifically, a data user constructs the personalized search vector, and submits its encryption to the cloud server. The cloud server returns the most relevant top-k results based on the personalized search vector.
- **Privacy preserving:** The proposed scheme should prevent the cloud server from learning the actual data of encrypted files, indexes, and signatures.
- **Authenticating the integrity of result:** When the cloud server behaves dishonestly, i.e., cloud server returns forged or incomplete search results, data user can discover the misbehavior.
- **Efficiency:** All the above goals should be achieved with low computation and communication overhead.

3.4 Notations

- $\mathcal{F}$: the plaintext file collection.
- $\mathcal{C}$: the ciphertext file collection of $\mathcal{F}$.
- $\mathcal{W}$: the keyword dictionary.
- P: each file vector P_i corresponds to the file F_i.
- $\widetilde{P}$: the encrypted file vectors of P.
- $\widehat{P}$: the encoded file vectors of P.
- Q: the search vectors issued by data users.
- $\widetilde{Q}$: the encrypted search vectors of Q.
- H: a one-way hash function.

4 Privacy-Preserving and User-Specified Ranked Multi-keyword Search

Since different data users may have different personal preferences. Additionally, huge amount of files are stored on cloud servers, we cannot simply return indifferential files to data users for two reasons. First, returning all satisfied files would cause tremendous communication overhead for the whole system. Second, data users would only concern top-k relevant files corresponding to their queries. So our scheme should also achieve ranked multi-keyword search.

Motivated by the secure k-nearest neighbor scheme proposed in [9] and [26], we use the inner product of a file vector P and a search vector Q, i.e., $P \cdot Q$, to quantitatively evaluate the similarity of a file and a query. A file corresponding to a higher value of the inner product will have higher probability to be returned. The file vector is assembled according to the following principle: the ith data item in the jth file vector is the relevance score between the ith keyword in the keyword set $\mathcal{W}$ and the jth file in the file set. Meanwhile, the search vector is formalized according to user's preference. For example, data user wants to search the ith and i'th keyword in the keyword set $\mathcal{W}$, since he thinks the ith keyword is more important than the i'th keyword, he gives each keyword a weight, say

0.8 and 0.2. Then the ith data item in the search vector is assembled with 0.8, and the i'th data item is assembled with 0.2.

Given a file vector P_i and a search vector Q_j, we use the encryption method proposed in [9] to encrypt them. Specifically, the data owner uses three secret keys to encrypt them, i.e., a vector split indicator S, two invertible matrixes M_1 and M_2. The encryption process is divided into two phases. First, data owner splits P_i into $P_{i'}, P_{i''}$ and Q_j into $Q_{j'}, Q_{j''}$ as follows, if the kth bit of S is 0, then $P_{i'}$ and $P_{i''}$ are set the same as P_i, while $Q_{j'}$ and $Q_{j''}$ are randomly set so that their sum are equal to Q_j. If the kth bit of S is 1, then $P_{i'}$ and $P_{i''}$ are randomly set so that their sum are equal to P_i while $Q_{j'}$ and $Q_{j''}$ are set the same as Q_j. Second, data owner encrypts $\{P_{i'}, P_{i''}\}$ as $\widetilde{P}_i = \{M_1^T \cdot P_{i'}, M_2^T \cdot P_{i''}\}$, and $\{Q_{j'}, Q_{j''}\}$ as $\widetilde{Q}_j = \{M_1^{-1} \cdot Q_{j'}, M_2^{-1} \cdot Q_{j''}\}$. Therefore,

$$\widetilde{P}_i \cdot \widetilde{Q}_j = \{M_1^T \cdot P_{i'}, M_2^T \cdot P_{i''}\} \cdot \{M_1^{-1} \cdot Q_{j'}, M_2^{-1} \cdot Q_{j''}\} = P_i \cdot Q_j \qquad (1)$$

Finally, the cloud server returns the top-k relevant search results to the data user according to the rank of $\widetilde{P}_i \cdot \widetilde{Q}_j$. For more rigorous security requirement, we can use the techniques proposed in [9].

5 Dynamic Top-k Results Authentication

In the aforementioned section, we introduce how to achieve privacy preserving and personalized ranked multi-keyword search in cloud computing. When the cloud server behaves dishonestly, we need to verify whether there are false search results corresponding to different users' preference. In this section, we first introduce the privacy preserving function [27], which will be used to protect the privacy of relevance scores between keywords and files. Then we elaborate on how to construct our proposed Multi-Attribute Authentication Tree (MAAT). Finally, we describe how to authenticate the integrity of the dynamic top-k search results with the proposed MAAT.

5.1 Privacy Preserving Function

The privacy preserving function $F(x)$ is composed of a data processing part $f(x)$ and a disturbing part r_f. The data processing part preserves the order of x while the disturbing part r_f prevents cloud server from revealing $F(x)$. Therefore, $F(x) = f(x) + r_f$ and the $f(x)$ is defined as follows:

$$f(x) = \sum_{0 \le j \le \tau} A_j \cdot m^2(x, j) \qquad (2)$$

where τ denotes the degree of $f(x)$ and A_j denotes the coefficients of $m^2(x, j)$.

The $m(x, j)$ is defined as follows: 1) $j = 0$, $m(x, j) = 1$; 2) $j = 1$, $m(x, j) = x + 1$; 3) $j > 1$, $m(x, j) = \lfloor (m(x, j-1) + \alpha) \cdot (1 + \lambda \cdot x) \rfloor$, where α and λ are two constant numbers.

$\forall x_1 \geq x_2$, where x_1 and x_2 are positive integer numbers,

$$
\begin{aligned}
& f(x_1) - f(x_2) \\
= {} & \sum_{0 \leq j \leq \tau} A_j \cdot \left(m^2(x_1, j) - m^2(x_2, j) \right) \\
= {} & \sum_{0 \leq j \leq \tau} A_j \cdot (m(x_1, j) + m(x_2, j)) \\
& \qquad \cdot (m(x_1, j) - m(x_2, j)) \\
\geq {} & \sum_{0 \leq j \leq \tau} A_j \cdot \lambda \cdot (x_1 - x_2) \cdot m(x_2, j-1) \\
& \qquad \cdot (m(x_1, j) + m(x_2, j)) \\
\geq {} & \lambda \cdot \alpha^2 \cdot \sum_{0 \leq j \leq \tau} A_j
\end{aligned}
\tag{3}
$$

Obviously, $\forall x_1 > x_2$, we have $f(x_1) > f(x_2)$. Let ϵ be a system parameter such that $2^\epsilon \leq \lambda \cdot \alpha^2 \cdot \sum_{0 \leq j \leq \tau} A_j$, then the disturbing part r_f of $F(x)$ is set to $2^\epsilon - 1$.

5.2 Multi-Attribute Authentication Tree

Definition 1. *If each element (relevance score) in a file vector P_i is not smaller than that in P_j, i.e, $\forall k \in [1, n], P_{i,k} \geq P_{j,k}$, and at least one element in P_i is greater than that in P_j, i.e., $\exists k \in [1, n], P_{i,k} > P_{j,k}$. Then we define P_i dominates P_j, and P_j is dominated by P_i.*

Definition 2. *If the first k $(k = 0, 1, \cdots, n-1)$ elements in P_i are equal to that in P_j (i.e., $P_{i,0} = P_{j,0}, P_{i,1} = P_{j,1}, \cdots, P_{i,k} = P_{j,k}$), for the $(k+1)$th element, if $P_{i,k+1} > P_{j,k+1}$, then we define $P_i > P_j$.*

Algorithm 1 illustrates the process of constructing MAAT, which is composed of two phases, i.e., generating the framework of MAAT, and aggregating the hash value of MAAT. The first phase is divided into three steps described as follows: first of all, sorting all encoded vectors in descending order according to the comparison method defined in Definition 2. Second, initializing the root of MAAT, i.e., the value of each item in the vector is a pre-defined maximum number. Finally, inserting the sorted vectors into the MAAT one by one. Specifically, given $\widehat{P}_i$, the algorithm inserts $\widehat{P}_i$ as follows: each time the algorithm traverses from the root node, if the visited node $\widehat{P}_j$ dominates $\widehat{P}_i$, then the algorithm sets $\widehat{P}_i$'s parent node to be $\widehat{P}_j$, if $\widehat{P}_j$ has no child node, the algorithm finishes inserting $\widehat{P}_i$. If $\widehat{P}_j$ has child node, the algorithm visits $\widehat{P}_i$'s whole child nodes, if no child nodes of $\widehat{P}_j$ dominate $\widehat{P}_i$, the algorithm finishes inserting $\widehat{P}_i$, otherwise, if $\widehat{P}_j$'s child node $\widehat{P}_c$ dominates $\widehat{P}_i$, the algorithm sets $\widehat{P}_i$'s parent node to be $\widehat{P}_c$, and conducts the insertion recursively. The MAAT framework is constructed when all encoded vectors are inserted. The second phase is aggregating the hash value of MAAT from the leaf nodes to the root node. Specifically, for a leaf node, the algorithm only computes its hash value. For a non-leaf node, the algorithm computes its hash value, conducts exclusive or operation on the hash value of all its children, and combines them as its hash values.

Algorithm 1.. The MAAT construction algorithm

Input:

Encoded file vectors $\widehat{P}$ and ciphertext of file vectors $\widetilde{P}$

Output:

MAAT

Step1: generate the framework of MAAT

1: Sort $\widehat{P}$ on their first encoded attribute.

2: root=$\{\widehat{P}_{max}\}$ //initialize the MAAT

3: **for** i=1 to m **do**

4:     $\widehat{P}_t = root$

5:     **if** $\widehat{P}_t$ has no child **then**

6:         add $\widehat{P}_i$ to the child set of $\widehat{P}_t$

7:         continue

8:     **else**

9:         **for** each child $\widehat{P}_j$ of $\widehat{P}_t$ **do**

10:             **if** $\widehat{P}_i$ is dominated by $\widehat{P}_j$ **then**

11:                 $\widehat{P}_t = \widehat{P}_j$

12:                 goto step 5

13:     add $\widehat{P}_i$ to the child set of $\widehat{P}_t$

14: **for** each node $\widehat{P}_i$ in the MAAT **do**

15:     add $\widetilde{P}_i$ to $\widehat{P}_i$

Step2: aggregate the hash value of MAAT

16: **for** each node in the MAAT **do**

17:     **if** node $\widehat{P}_i$ is a leaf node **then**

18:         $\widehat{P}_i$ submits $hash(\widehat{P}_i||\widetilde{P}_i)$ to its parent node

19:     **else**

20:         **if** $\widehat{P}_i$ has only one child **then**

21:             $\widehat{P}_i$ set the received value as H_i and submits $hash(\widehat{P}_i||\widetilde{P}_i||H_i)$ to its parent node.

22:         **else**

23:             $\widehat{P}_i$ first aggregates the hash value to H_i by doing XOR operation on received data from different child nodes and submits $hash(\widehat{P}_i||\widetilde{P}_i||H_i)$ to its parent node

24: **return** root

Now we give an example of constructing MAAT in Fig. 3, there are 10 encoded vectors, each vector includes four attributes. First, the algorithm sorts the 10 encoded vectors and gets $\{\widehat{P}_2, \widehat{P}_1, \widehat{P}_5, \widehat{P}_4, \widehat{P}_9, \widehat{P}_3, \widehat{P}_8, \widehat{P}_7, \widehat{P}_6\}$. Then the algorithm initializes the root of MAAT to be $\widehat{P}_{max}$, where the value of each attribute in $\widehat{P}_{max}$ is set to be maximal. Further, $\{\widehat{P}_2, \widehat{P}_1, \widehat{P}_5, \widehat{P}_4, \widehat{P}_9, \widehat{P}_3, \widehat{P}_8, \widehat{P}_7, \widehat{P}_6\}$ are inserted into MAAT subsequently. Finally, the algorithm computes the hash value. Specifically, $H_3 = hash(\widehat{P}_8||\widetilde{P}_8)$, $H_1 = hash(\widehat{P}_3||\widetilde{P}_3||H_3)$, and $H_2 = hash(\widehat{P}_1||\widetilde{P}_1||H_1) \oplus hash(\widehat{P}_9||\widetilde{P}_9)$.

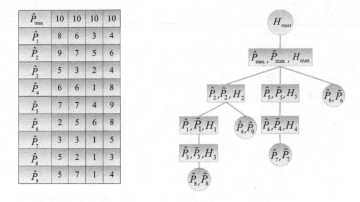

Fig. 3. An example of constructing MAAT

5.3   Authenticating Integrity of the Dynamic Top-k Search Results

In this subsection, we will introduce how to verify the integrity of ranked top-k search results based on MAAT. To enable the authorized data users to verify the dynamic top-k search results, the data owner processes his data as follows: first, the data owner extracts the file vectors from all of his files. Then, he encodes these file vectors with the privacy and order preserving function. Further, the data owner constructs the MAAT with the encoded file vectors. Finally, the data owner outsources encrypted vectors, encoded vectors, $sign(H_{root})$ (signature of the root of MAAT), and encrypted files to the cloud server. Once the cloud server finds the encrypted search results $\{C_{i1}, C_{i2}, \cdots, C_{im}\}$, it further prepares the authentication data with the following steps: first of all, the cloud server adds the nodes corresponding to $\{C_{i1}, C_{i2}, \cdots, C_{im}\}$ in MAAT to a node set S. Then it adds all the ancestors of these nodes to S. Further, it finds all the sibling nodes of nodes in S and adds them to S. Finally, together with $sign(H_{root})$, the encoded vector and encrypted vector corresponding to nodes in S are returned as authentication data. For example, given the search results $\{F_1, F_2\}$, the corresponding authentication data would be $\{\widehat{P}_1, \widehat{P}_2, \widehat{P}_5, \widehat{P}_6, \widehat{P}_9, \widetilde{P}_1, \widetilde{P}_2, \widetilde{P}_5, \widetilde{P}_6, \widetilde{P}_9, H_1, H_5, sign(H_{root})\}$. When the data user attains the returned result and authentication data, he verifies the results with the following steps: first of all, he reconstructs the MAAT with the corresponding encoded vectors. Then, he checks whether the computed root of MAAT is equal to H_{root}. If they are not equal, the results are contaminated and discarded. Finally, the data user checks whether the results are the most relative top-k files with the help of the decrypted file vectors. If any false results are detected during the process, the results are regarded as false and discarded.

6   MAAT Optimization

MAAT can achieve privacy preserving and dynamic top-k search results verification. However, when the keyword set is large, many encoded file vectors

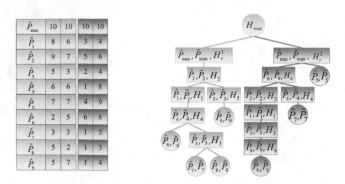

Fig. 4. An example of constructing optimized MAAT

would not be dominated by others. Consequently, the cloud server has to return numerous verification data for search results verification, which is obviously inapplicable. In the following subsection, we first introduce the scheme of optimizing the MAAT. Then we analyze the trade-off value between privacy and communication cost.

6.1 Optimizing Method

As we know, in real applications, when we want to perform a search, we often issue a few keywords. Therefore we can specify the cloud server to return verification data for these keywords. This can reduce a large number of verification data. Though telling cloud server which keywords we want to verify will bring the threat of privacy revealing, we can issue some dummy keywords to obfuscate the cloud server. The optimizing process is described as follows: first, we split each encoded vector into T encoded sub-vectors. Then we use these encoded sub-vectors to construct sub-MAAT. Finally, we combine the T sub-MAATs and get the optimized MAAT. Fig. 4 shows the optimized MAAT of the one in Fig. 3. As we can see, when $\{F_1, F_2\}$ are the search results, and the data user specifies to verify the first two attributes, the corresponding authentication data would be $\{\widehat{P}_1, \widehat{P}_2, \widehat{P}_5, \widetilde{P}_1, \widetilde{P}_2, \widetilde{P}_5, H_1, H_5, H_r^2, sign(H_{root})\}$. As we can see, compared with the former verification cost, the optimized one will obviously reduce verification cost.

6.2 Trade-off Between Privacy and Communication Cost

From the above discussion, when the number of items in each file vector is very large, the privacy is well preserved, while the communication cost spent on verification would be very large. On the other hand, when we split the file vector into very small sub-vectors, i.e., the number of items in each sub-vector is small, the communication cost would be reduced, while the privacy preservation would be weakened. Therefore, we need to find a trade-off between privacy and communication cost.

Recall that, to obfuscate the cloud server of which keywords are actually verified, we propose to add some dummy keywords in the specified keyword set. In this paper, we use entropy to evaluate the uncertainty of determining data user's verified keywords from all the candidate keywords. Without loss of generality, we define p_i to be the probability that a keyword is specified to be verified. For a sub-vector with d elements (keywords), the entropy of identifying an individual element in the sub-vector is defined as

$$H(d) = -\sum_{i=1}^{d} p_i \cdot log_2 p_i \tag{4}$$

Obviously, when all the keywords in the sub-vector shares the same probability to be verified, i.e., $p_i = 1/d$, the maximum entropy is achieved, that is $H(d) = log_2 d$. When the dimension (number of elements in the sub-vector) of sub-vector is D, i.e., $d = D$, we get the maximum entropy $log_2 D$.

Now we investigate the relationship between the dimension of sub-vectors and the communication cost of verification. To get this relationship, we conduct experiment on a real data set [28], and get the empirical result. We set the size of keyword set to be 64, and $k = 10$. Fig. 5(b) illustrates the relationship between the dimension of sub-vectors and the communication cost of verification. The corresponding fitting equation is $y = 0.015 \cdot d^2 + 0.219 \cdot d - 0.203$.

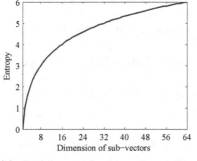

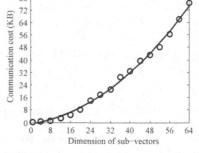

(a) Entropy with dimension of sub-vectors

(b) Communication cost with dimension of sub-vectors

Fig. 5. Entropy and communication cost with dimension of sub-vectors

As we can see from Fig. 5(a) and Fig. 5(b), the larger the dimension of sub-vectors is, the higher entropy we get, while the more communication cost is also caused. Therefore, we need to find an optimal dimension(number of elements in the sub-vector) of the sub-vector, so that we can maximize the entropy while minimize the communication cost. The key idea is described as follows: first of all, to allow consistent computation, we convert the data range of both entropy and communication cost to the same range, say, [0,1]. Second, we define the difference between entropy and communication cost as the optimization objective. Finally, we find the optimal dimension of sub-vector where the value of the difference is maximized. For example, we denote the relationship between the entropy and the dimension of sub-vector as $y_1 = log_2 x$, and the relationship between the communication cost and the dimension of sub-vector as $y_2 = 0.015 \cdot x^2 + 0.219 \cdot x - 0.203$. First of all, we encode them in the same range $[0,1]$, therefore, we get $y_1' = log_2 x/6$ and $y_2' = 1.994 \times 10^{-4} \cdot x^2 + 0.003 \cdot x - 0.002$. Then we define the optimization objective as: $f(x) = y_1' - y_2' = log_2 x/6 - 1.994 \times 10^{-4} \cdot x^2 - 0.003 \cdot x + 0.002$. Finally, we compute the optimal value of x. Obviously, when $x \in (0, 22]$, $f(x)$ keeps increasing, when $x \in (22, 64]$, $f(x)$ keeps decreasing. Therefore, we can easily conclude that when $x = 22$, $f(x)$ gets the maximum data, i.e., the optimal dimension of the sub-vector is $x=22$. To make the dimension (length) of the original file vector divisible by the dimension of sub-vector 22, we can pad 2 dummy attributes into the original file vector.

7   Security Analysis

In this section, we analyze the security of our proposed scheme from the following two aspects.

7.1   Privacy Preserving and User Specified Ranked Multi-keyword Search

In our scheme, we use the inner product on the file vector P and the search vector Q, i.e., $P \cdot Q$, to quantitatively evaluate the similarity between a file and a query. Since the vector encryption method has been proved to be secure in the known ciphertext model in [26], the privacy of both P and Q are well protected if the secret key $\{S, M_1, M_2\}$ are kept secret.

7.2   Authenticating Dynamic Top-k Results

For search results verification, the cloud server only operates on random cipher-text, and returns the encoded vector, encrypted vector, hash value and $sign(H_{root})$. The security of privacy and order preserving function is proved in [27], therefore, the encoded vector is secure. The security of encrypted vector is proved [26]. Additionally, we adopt the RSA to get the signature, whose security is also guaranteed. Therefore, the security of the verification scheme is assured.

8   Performance Evaluation

In this section, we demonstrate a thorough evaluation on the storage overhead, communication cost, and time cost of our proposed schemes.

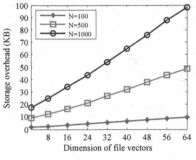
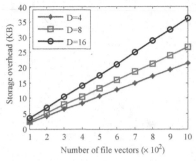

(a) Storage overhead with different dimension of file vectors

(b) Storage overhead with different number of file vectors

Fig. 6. Storage overhead of dimension of file vectors and number of file vectors

8.1   Experiment Settings

We conducted a performance evaluation on a real data set, i.e., US Census Data (1990) Data Set [28]. The data set has 2458285 census instances, where each data has 68 attributes. The data value of each attribute changes between 0 and 225. Our experiment is implemented with C++ on a PC with 3.40GHz Intel Core CPU and 4GB memory. We use RSA to sign the root node of MAAT with a 1024-bit key, and set the size of the hash digest to be 16 Bytes. Additionally, since the max attribute value is 225, we use 8 bits to represent each attribute. The performance of our scheme is evaluated regarding the effectiveness and efficiency of our proposed MAAT, including the storage overhead, the communication cost, and the construction time.

8.2   Experiment Results

Storage Overhead. Fig. 6(a) demonstrates the relationship between storage overhead and dimension of file vectors. As we can see, the storage overhead increases linearly with the dimension of file vectors increases. Additionally, the more file vectors we involve, the higher storage overhead is caused. The fundamental reason is that, the larger the dimension of file vectors is, the more storage overhead we spend to store the additional dimensions (attributes). Fig. 6(b) describes the relationship between the storage overhead and the number of file vectors. As we can see, the storage overhead also increases linearly and slowly with the number of file vectors. When $D=16$, and the number of file vectors changes from 100 to 1000, the storage overhead increases from 0.5 KB to 35 KB, which is acceptable.

Communication Cost. In our scheme, since the communication cost between the data owner and the cloud server is nearly the same with the storage overhead of the cloud server, we do not consider it here. Instead, we only consider the

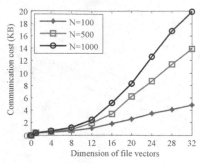
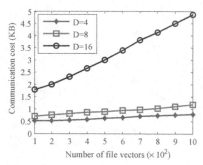
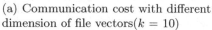

(a) Communication cost with different dimension of file vectors($k = 10$)

(b) Communication cost with different number of file vectors ($k =10$)

Fig. 7. Communication cost with number of file vectors and dimension of file vectors

communication cost between the cloud server and the data users. When the data users submit the query vector to the cloud server, the cloud server would not only return top-k search results, but also return verification data. Since different search requests will contribute to different size of verification data, we show the average communication cost here.

Fig. 7(a) demonstrates the relationship between the communication cost and dimension of file vectors. As we can see, when the dimension of file vectors increases from 1 to 12, the communication cost increases slowly. When $k=10$, $N=1000$, and the dimension of file vectors increases from 0 to 32, the communication cost increases from 0 KB to about 20 KB. Fig. 7(b) shows that the communication cost increases linearly with the number of file vectors. As we can see, when the dimension $D=4$ and $D=8$, their communication cost is relatively small. However, when the dimension is more than 16, the communication cost increases rapidly with the number of file vectors. As we can see, when the dimension of file vectors is 16, and the number of file vectors changes from 100 to 1000, the communication cost increases from 1.75 KB to 5 KB. In our optimized MAAT, we propose that splitting the large vector into small sub-vectors will help reduce, and control the communication cost, which is proved by the experiment.

Time Cost. In our scheme, we mainly consider the time cost caused by constructing MAAT and encrypting file vectors. Fig. 8(a) demonstrates that, the encryption time increases linearly with the number of file vectors. As we can see, when the dimension of file vectors is 16, and the number of file vectors increases from 1000 to 10000, the encryption time increases from 0.3s to 3.2s. Fig. 8(b) shows the time cost of constructing MAAT with different number of file vectors. The time cost increases linearly with the number of file vectors. As shown in Fig. 8(b), when the dimension of file vectors is 4, and the number of file vectors

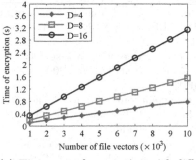
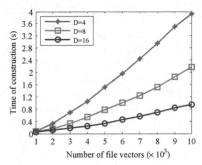

(a) Time cost of encryption with different number of file vectors

(b) Time cost of constructing MAAT with different number of files vectors

Fig. 8. Time of construction and encryption with different number of file vectors

increases from 1000 to 10000, the time spent on constructing MAAT increases from 0.1s to 4s, which is acceptable.

9 Conclusion

In this paper, for the first time, we consider a challenging security model where the cloud server would probably behave dishonestly. We first formalize different users' preferences and adopt the secure k nearest neighbor techniques to achieve privacy preserving personalized multi-keyword search. Then we use the order and privacy preserving function to preserve the relevance scores between keywords and files. Further, we propose a novel Multi-Attribute Authentication Tree (MAAT) to authenticate the dynamic top-k search results. In particular, we propose to optimize the MAAT, and compute the optimal parameter value to trade off the privacy and communication cost. Finally, we conduct extensive experiments on real-world datasets to confirm the efficacy and efficiency of our proposed schemes.

Acknowledgements. This work is supported in part by the National Natural Science Foundation of China (Project No. 61173038, 61472125).

References

1. Armbrust, M., Fox, A., Griffith, R., Joseph, A.D., Katz, R., Konwinski, A., Lee, G., Patterson, D., Rabkin, A., Stoica, I., Zaharia, V.: A View of Cloud Computing. Communications of the ACM **53**(4), 50–58 (2010)
2. Song, D., Wagner, D., Perrig, A.: Practical techniques for searches on encrypted data. In: Proceedings of the IEEE International Symposium on Security and Privacy (S&P00), pp. 44–55. IEEE, Nagoya (2000)

3. Goh, E.J.: Secure indexes. In: IACR Cryptology ePrint Archive, 216 (2003)
4. Boneh, D., Di Crescenzo, G., Ostrovsky, R., Persiano, G.: Public key encryption with keyword search. In: Cachin, C., Camenisch, J.L. (eds.) EUROCRYPT 2004. LNCS, vol. 3027, pp. 506–522. Springer, Heidelberg (2004)
5. Golle, P., Staddon, J., Waters, B.: Secure conjunctive keyword search over encrypted data. In: Jakobsson, M., Yung, M., Zhou, J. (eds.) ACNS 2004. LNCS, vol. 3089, pp. 31–45. Springer, Heidelberg (2004)
6. Ballard, L., Kamara, S., Monrose, F.: Achieving efficient conjunctive keyword searches over encrypted data. In: Qing, S., Mao, W., López, J., Wang, G. (eds.) ICICS 2005. LNCS, vol. 3783, pp. 414–426. Springer, Heidelberg (2005)
7. Chang, Y.-C., Mitzenmacher, M.: Privacy preserving keyword searches on remote encrypted data. In: Ioannidis, J., Keromytis, A.D., Yung, M. (eds.) ACNS 2005. LNCS, vol. 3531, pp. 442–455. Springer, Heidelberg (2005)
8. Wang, C., Cao, N., Li, J., Ren, K., Lou, W.: Secure ranked keyword search over encrypted cloud data. In: The 30th International Conference on Distributed Computing Systems, pp. 253–262. IEEE, Genoa (2010)
9. Cao, N., Wang, C., Li, M., Ren, K., Lou, W.: Privacy-preserving multi-keyword ranked search over encrypted cloud data. In: Proceedings of the 30th IEEE International Conference on Computer Communications, INFOCOM 2011, pp. 829–837. IEEE, Shanghai (2011)
10. Li, J., Wang, Q., Wang, C., Cao, N., Ren, K., Lou, W.: Fuzzy keyword search over encrypted data in cloud computing. In: Proceedings of the 29th IEEE International Conference on Computer Communications, INFOCOM 2010, pp. 1–5. IEEE, San Diego (2010)
11. Hore, B., Chang, E.-C., Diallo, M.H., Mehrotra, S.: Indexing encrypted documents for supporting efficient keyword search. In: Jonker, W., Petković, M. (eds.) SDM 2012. LNCS, vol. 7482, pp. 93–110. Springer, Heidelberg (2012)
12. Xu, Z., Kang, W., Li, R., Yow, K., Xu, C.Z.: Efficient multi-keyword ranked query on encrypted data in the cloud. In: The 18th IEEE International Conference on Parallel and Distributed Systems (ICPADS 2012), pp. 244–251. IEEE, Singapore (2012)
13. Pang, H., Jain, A., Ramamritham, K., Tan, K.L.: Verifying completeness of relational query results in data publishing. In: Proceedings of the 2005 ACM SIGMOD International Conference on Management of Data, pp. 407–418. ACM, New York (2005)
14. Merkle, R.C.: A certified digital signature. In: Brassard, G. (ed.) CRYPTO 1989. LNCS, vol. 435, pp. 218–238. Springer, Heidelberg (1990)
15. Sun, W., Wang, B., Cao, N., Li, M., Lou, W., Hou, Y.T., Li, H.: Privacy-preserving multi-keyword text search in the cloud supporting similarity-based ranking. In: Proceedings of the 8th ACM SIGSAC Symposium on Information, Computer and Communications Security, pp. 71–82. ACM, Hangzhou (2013)
16. Sun, W., Yu, S., Lou, W., Hou, Y.T., Li, H.: Protecting your right: attribute-based keyword search with fine-grained owner-enforced search authorization in the cloud. In: Proceedings of the 33nd IEEE International Conference on Computer Communications, INFOCOM 2014, pp. 226–234. IEEE, Toronto (2014)
17. Zhang, W., Xiao, S., Lin, Y., Zhou, T., Zhou, S.: Secure ranked multi-keyword search for multiple data owners in cloud computing. In: Proceedings of 44th Annual IEEE/IFIP International Conference on Dependable Systems and Networks (DSN 2014), pp. 276–286. IEEE, Atlanta (2014)

18. Zhang, W., Lin, Y., Xiao, S., Wu, J., Zhou, S.: Privacy preserving ranked multi-keyword search for multiple data owners in cloud computing. In: The IEEE Transactions on Computers. IEEE (2015)
19. Zhang, W., Lin, Y.: Catch you if you misbehave: ranked keyword search results verification in cloud computing. In: IEEE Transactions on Cloud Computing. IEEE (2015)
20. Zhang, W., Lin, Y., Xiao, S., Liu, Q., Zhou, T.: Secure distributed keyword search in multiple clouds. In: 2014 IEEE 22nd International Symposium on Quality of Service (IWQoS), pp. 370–379. IEEE, Hongkong (2014)
21. Narasimha, M., Tsudik, G.: DSAC: integrity for outsourced databases with signature aggregation and chaining. In: Proceedings of the 14th ACM International Conference on Information and Knowledge Management, pp. 235–236. ACM (2005)
22. Pang, H., Mouratidis, K.: Authenticating the query results of text search engines. Proceedings of the VLDB Endowment 1(1), 126–137 (2008). ACM
23. Li, F., Hadjieleftheriou, M., Kollios, G., Reyzin, L.: Dynamic authenticated index structures for outsourced databases. In: Proceedings of the 2006 ACM SIGMOD International Conference on Management of Data, pp. 121–132. ACM, Chicago (2006)
24. Sun, W., Wang, B., Cao, N., Li, M., Lou, W., Hou, Y.T., Li, H.: Verifiable privacy-preserving multi-keyword text search in the cloud supporting similarity-based ranking. IEEE Transactions on Parallel and Distributed Systems 52(11), 3025–3035 (2013). IEEE
25. Jung, T., Li, X.Y., Wan, Z., Wan, M.: Privacy preserving cloud data access with multi-authorities. In: Proceedings of the 32nd IEEE International Conference on Computer Communications, INFOCOM 2013, pp. 2625–2633. IEEE, Turin (2013)
26. Wong, W.K., Cheung, D.W.L., Kao, B., Mamoulis, N.: Secure knn computation on encrypted databases. In: Proceedings of the 2009 ACM SIGMOD International Conference on Management of data, pp. 139–152. ACM, Paris (2009)
27. Yi, Y., Li, R., Chen, F., Liu, A.X., Lin, Y.: A digital watermarking approach to secure and precise range query processing in sensor networks. In: Proceedings of the 32nd IEEE International Conference on Computer Communications, INFOCOM 2013, pp. 1950–1958. IEEE, Turin (2013)
28. US Census Data (1990) Data Set. https://archive.ics.uci.edu/ml/datasets/US+Census+Data+ (1990)

Privacy and Side Channels

Resource Efficient Privacy Preservation of Online Social Media Conversations

Indrajeet Singh[1], Masoud Akhoondi[1], Mustafa Y. Arslan[2],
Harsha V. Madhyastha[3], and Srikanth V. Krishnamurthy[1(✉)]

[1] UC Riverside, Riverside, USA
{singhi,makho001,krish}@cs.ucr.edu
[2] NEC Labs, 4 Independence Way, Suite 200, Princeton, NJ, USA
marslan@nec-labs.com
[3] University of Michigan, Ann Arbor, USA
harshavm@umich.edu

Abstract. On today's online social networks (OSNs), users need to reveal their content and their sharing patterns to a central provider. Though there are proposals for decentralized OSNs to protect user privacy, they have paid scant attention to optimizing the cost borne by users or hiding their sharing patterns. In this paper, we present *Hermes*, a decentralized OSN architecture, designed explicitly with the goal of hiding sharing patterns while minimizing users' costs. In doing so, *Hermes* tackles three key challenges: 1) it enables timely and consistent sharing of content, 2) it guarantees the confidentiality of posted private content, and 3) it hides sharing patterns from untrusted cloud service providers and users outside a private group. With extensive analyses of *Hermes* using traces of shared content on Facebook, we estimate that the cost borne per user will be less than \$5 per month for over 90% of users. Our prototype implementation of *Hermes* demonstrates that it only adds minimal overhead to content sharing.

1 Introduction

Today, leakage of information from OSN servers [5,6], coupled with the need for OSN providers to mine user data (e.g., for targeted advertisements), have concerned users [12]. While posting encrypted data on OSNs [15,23] can work in theory, it compromises the profit motives of an OSN if done at scale. Alternatively, one could share private content with OSN friends by storing data outside the OSN provider's control. Prior works that follow this approach either store private content in the cloud [4,13,29] or across client machines [24,27]. The former simply leaks private information to the cloud providers in lieu of the OSN providers, and also increases user costs. The viability of an approach based on the latter depends on the availability of consistent access to client machines.

Our Contributions: In this paper, we design a decentralized OSN architecture, *Hermes*, with cost-effective privacy in mind. *Hermes* seeks to ensure that both the content shared by a user and her sharing habits are kept private from both the

© Institute for Computer Sciences, Social Informatics and Telecommunications Engineering 2015
B. Thuraisingham et al. (Eds.): SecureComm 2015, LNICST 164, pp. 233–255, 2015.
DOI: 10.1007/978-3-319-28865-9_13

OSN provider and undesired friends. In doing so, *Hermes* seeks to (i) minimize the costs borne by users, and (ii) preserve the interactive and chronologically consistent conversational structure offered by a centralized OSN.

Hermes uses three key techniques to meet these goals. First, it judiciously combines the use of compute and storage resources in the cloud to bootstrap conversations associated with newly shared content. This also supports the high availability of the content. Second, it employs a novel cost-effective message propagation mechanism to enable dissemination of comments in a timely and consistent manner. It identifies and purges (from cloud storage) content that has been accessed by all intended recipients. Lastly, but most importantly, *Hermes* carefully orchestrates how fake postings are included in order to hide sharing patterns from the untrusted cloud providers used to store and propagate content, while minimizing the additional costs incurred in doing so. A key feature of *Hermes* is its flexibility in deployment; it can either be implemented as a stand alone distributed OSN or as an add-on to today's OSNs like Facebook (while maintaining the decentralized nature of content sharing). To summarize, our contributions are:

Design of *Hermes*: As our primary contribution, we design *Hermes*. It utilizes extremely small amounts of storage, bandwidth, and computing on the cloud to facilitate real-time, consistent and anonymous exchange of private content. Importantly, *Hermes* ensures that cloud providers cannot discover the users involved in private conversations and is robust to the intersection attack [18].

Analyzing OSN Data to Determine Resource Requirements: Based on 1.8 million posts crawled from Facebook, we 1) perform an analysis to determine key parameters for implementing *Hermes*, and 2) conduct realistic simulations to show that (a) *Hermes* effectively anonymizes users' sharing patterns and (b) *Hermes*'s use of cloud resources is low enough to facilitate its practical deployment. Our analysis suggests that, for 90% of users, *Hermes* would typically require 1) cloud storage of much less than 5 MB, and 2) a compute instance on the cloud that is active for roughly 4 days every month. This corresponds to a monthly cost of less than $5 per user. With this budget, *Hermes* ensures that cloud service providers are unable to guess the members or the group size of any private conversation. If the cloud provider attempts to randomly guess the group members, it is correct less than 15% of the time.

Implementation and Evaluation: We implement a prototype of *Hermes* as a rudimentary add-on to Facebook. Our evaluations show that *Hermes* incurs low cost, and the user experience, in terms of delays, is similar to that with Facebook.

Scope: The privacy preserving features of *Hermes* can be used in conjunction with a centralized component that can be used for posts that are not intended to be private. In fact, our prototype of *Hermes* as an add on to Facebook achieves just that; private posts are directed to *Hermes* while other content is shared in the traditional way. We wish to also point out that we do not explicitly consider mobile users; however, *Hermes* can be used in such contexts, and across multiple devices.

2   Related Work

Improving Privacy in OSNs: Several systems propose to post encrypted content on OSNs to protect privacy (e.g., [15,16,21]). However, encryption precludes OSN providers from interpreting posted content and/or hides users' social connections from OSNs. These are not in the commercial interests of OSN providers, who may thus disallow such postings. *Hermes* does not post any encrypted content on an OSN; it uses either cloud storage or users' personal devices to do so. Further, it does not use a centralized OSN framework to inform users of new content; doing so also informs the OSN provider of the specifics of ongoing conversations.

Distributed OSNs: Other efforts propose storing private shared data on devices other than OSN servers [4,24,27,29]. However, unlike *Hermes*, they either expose user sharing patterns to cloud providers [4,29] or degrade user experience in terms of timely and consistent sharing. Systems that store private data in the cloud do not control either storage or bandwidth costs which increase over time as the volume of shared data grows. While other systems store the data on users' personal machines [24,27] to reduce costs, the low availability of these machines (they may be turned off when not used) reduces the timeliness of conversations and compromises data consistency. *Hermes* combines resources on cloud services (within limit) with that on users' personal machines to support cost-effective sharing that is held privy from cloud providers.

Priv.io [33] is a new decentralized OSN that aims to minimize the cost incurred for facilitating private content sharing. However, Priv.io critically relies on support for advanced messaging APIs from cloud services, which restricts the generality of Priv.io's architecture. In contrast, *Hermes* only requires cloud storage services to offer a minimal PUT, GET, DELETE interface. Most importantly, due to Priv.io's reliance on messaging APIs offered by cloud services, unlike *Hermes*, it does not attempt to hide sharing patterns (i.e., whom does a user share data with) from cloud providers.

Other Related Work: Efforts [21,22,30] that secure the data stored on untrusted servers or the cloud do not try to account for OSN-specific characteristics (e.g., hiding content sharing patterns). Unlike *Hermes*, these solutions would either significantly increase cost or degrade timeliness. Moreover, *Hermes* enables anonymity in OSN conversations without requiring all members of a conversation to be simultaneously online.

3   Goals and Threat Model

Goals and Challenges: Our over-arching goal is to design a decentralized, private OSN architecture. In doing so, we have the following three objectives.

- *High availability, timeliness, and consistency:* First, we seek to preserve the desirable properties enabled by a central provider. Specifically, (a) users should always be able to access content shared with them, (b) content shared by a user should be received by the intended recipients in a timely manner, so as to preserve the interactive comment "threads" associated with content shared on OSNs, and, (c) all users involved in a conversation should receive comments in the same causally consistent order. How do we preserve these desirable properties despite the fact that content is stored in a decentralized manner in *Hermes*?

- *Protect the privacy of content and sharing patterns:* While *Hermes* lacks any central OSN provider, cloud services used to store and disseminate content may be able to monitor conversations. How do we preserve the privacy of shared content from cloud providers and prevent them from discovering the participants in any conversation?

- *Minimize cost:* Finally, we seek to minimize the storage, bandwidth, and compute costs incurred by users in *Hermes*'s use of cloud services. This is made particularly challenging due to the previous two goals. For example, one could enable timely dissemination of comments if every user were to maintain her own compute instance in the cloud at all times. Similarly, the members of any particular conversation can be hidden from cloud providers by having all users constantly exchange fake comments with each other. However, such measures will result in high cost.

Threat Model: We assume that all service providers (of cloud services or of a centralized OSN) preserve the integrity and availability of the data that users store on them. This may be either in fear of bad publicity or because users pay for the service. However, we assume that all service providers may benefit from inferring information associated with private conversations. Thus, we treat all service providers as "curious but honest", as in [33]. Moreover, if cloud providers discover the members of private conversations, this information may leak. Therefore, we seek to ensure that, when a group of users are involved in a private conversation using *Hermes*, no one outside the group learns either the size or membership of this group. Here, we assume that cloud providers can perform network-level traffic analysis (e.g., a provider can map the IP addresses from which it is accessed, to user identities). The use of anonymity networks such as Tor [19] would not scale to meet the traffic demands of a large-scale OSN. Lastly, ensuring the privacy of a users' conversation group via fake messages (as in *Hermes*) requires that the user has a sufficiently large set of friends; if a user has very few friends (e.g, < 5), preserving the anonymity of a private conversation group is hard. We assume that users have friends of the order of hundreds, as is typical on OSNs [3]; however, we assume the sizes of private conversation groups to be much smaller.

4   Hermes Architecture

In this section, we describe the *Hermes* architecture with a simple running example.

Consider an OSN user (Alice), who wishes to share some content (say a photo) meant only for her friends Bob and Chloe. To ensure that neither the private content nor the intended recipients are exposed to anyone other than the

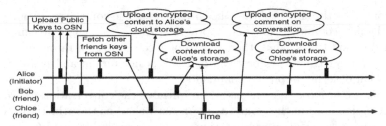

Fig. 1. Illustration of conversation timeline.

intended recipients, Alice encrypts the photo with an appropriate key (known only to Bob and Chloe) and shares it using resources in the cloud. There are four main issues that we need to address to enable this: 1) how do Bob and Chloe discover this content *and* the associated key to decrypt it?, 2) how can comments on the content, posted by Alice, Bob, and Chloe, be disseminated in a timely manner?, 3) how do we prevent the cloud provider from inferring the members of this private exchange?, and 4) how to minimize costs incurred by Alice, Bob, and Chloe? We next describe how *Hermes* tackles these questions.

Sharing New Content: As shown in Fig. 1, every user (including Alice) first posts her public key component to enable an ECDH key exchange (details of ECDH can be found in [25]) on her OSN profile[1], which is visible to all of her friends. Any user can thus, fetch the public key components from her friends' profiles and derive pairwise keys with any of her friends.

To share a photo, Alice's *Hermes* client chooses a new *group key* and creates two encrypted copies (using a cipher such as AES) of this key, one copy encrypted using her pairwise key with Bob and the other using her pairwise key with Chloe. Alice's client then stores these encrypted group key copies in Alice's cloud store. The client also puts the photo, encrypted with the group key (again using AES), in her cloud storage.

Bob's and Chloe's *Hermes* clients periodically check Alice's cloud store for new content shared with them. When new content exists, they fetch their respective encrypted group key copies from Alice's store (the process is discussed later) and extract it using their respective pairwise keys with Alice. Bob's and Chloe's clients then store the extracted group key locally on their personal devices. The clients can fetch and decrypt the photo using this group key.

Enabling OSN-Like Conversations: We next describe how *Hermes* enables OSN like conversations with low cost.

Disseminating Comments: After Bob and Chloe discover Alice's photo, the three of them may post comments on it. Our goal is to ensure that these comments are disseminated in a timely and consistent manner, as is the case with a centralized OSN. If all users involved in the conversation are always online, whenever a user posts a comment, that user's client can establish secure

---

[1] This could be on her favorite OSN or *Hermes*'s servers depending on the implementation.

connections with the clients of the other members of the conversation and inform them of the new comment. However, in practice, Alice, Bob, and Chloe may come online at different times. Thus, there has to be a common arbitrator that enables a user to discover comments posted when she is not online and facilitates the chronological ordering of posted comments.

For this, we propose that the user who initiates the conversation (Alice) uses a computing instance in the cloud to act on her behalf as the arbitrator. Today, there are many such online computation resources available (e.g., Google App Engine [7], Heroku [9], and Amazon EC2 [1]). Alice's instance acts as a proxy for her.

Reducing Compute Instance Costs for Alice: However, keeping the compute instance active at all times is not cost-effective for Alice. Thus, by default, Alice's *Hermes* client terminates her instance following a preset period after Alice has shared any new content (discussed later in Section 6). However, there may be users who come online much after the instance has been terminated. To deal with such cases, *Hermes* uses log files called *ufiles* (update files). Every user maintains a *ufile* in her cloud store for each friend; these *ufiles* are created and the location of the *ufiles* are exchanged between friends either when a user installs the *Hermes* client or when the user adds a friend. Thereafter, whenever a user (Alice) posts a new piece of content relevant to a specific friend (Chloe), Alice's *Hermes* client adds an entry to the *ufile* for Chloe. In all subsequent discussion, for the purposes of clarity, we only provide a high level description of how *ufiles* are used and defer a detailed description to an appendix.

If Bob comes online after Alice's compute instance has been terminated, his client retrieves her *ufile* for him and locates any new updates. This allows Bob to retrieve any content or comments shared by Alice. His client then indicates that the content has been retrieved in his own *ufile* for Alice. Upon checking this entry when Alice comes online, her *Hermes* client deletes the original entry in her *ufile* for Bob.

Note that *ufiles* also enable a user to discover comments without waiting for the initiator of a conversation to come online. For example, if Bob is also Chloe's friend, Bob's *ufile* for Chloe will indicate that he has commented on Alice's photo. Chloe can thus retrieve the comment and associate it with the original photo received from Alice (based on an associated conversation ID).

Ensuring Consistency of Comments with ufiles: The above framework allows a user who comes online after the instance is terminated to retrieve the object and reconstruct the conversation associated with it (i.e., put the comments in chronological order using vector timestamps [26]) as long as all the group members are his friends. However, if a group member (say Chloe) is not Bob's friend, Chloe is unable to read Bob's *ufiles*; in fact, such a file for Chloe will not exist in Bob's cloud storage, since *ufiles* are only maintained for friends. This violates the structure of an OSN conversation.

To deal with such cases, Alice relays the locations of the comments associated with her content via her own *ufiles* for each member of the conversation (who are her friends since she initially shared the content with them). Since there may be delays in relaying these locations (in rare cases where multiple users come online much after the compute instance is terminated), there may be temporary loss in the chronological consistency for a user who comes online at a late stage. There is an inherent trade-off here; the longer Alice's compute instance is active, the less likely is that there is such a loss in consistency. However, this will incur a higher cost.

Reducing Storage Costs: Finally, Alice cannot store her photo (or for that matter, Bob cannot store his comment) on the cloud forever. This would result in a monotonic growth in the consumed storage and thus, the associated cost. Instead, with *Hermes*, content is removed from cloud storage after a certain time (the duration can be set by Alice, but we discuss what might be appropriate in Section 6). A simple way of ensuring that all group members have seen the content before it is purged is for Alice to check if they have indicated this to be the case in their *ufiles* for her. If a user (say Bob) comes online after a prolonged absence (much after when the content was removed from the cloud), he may still learn of its existence via Alice's *ufile* meant for him. Via his own *ufile* for Alice, Bob's client then requests Alice for the purged content. When Alice comes online next, her client then copies the requested content back on to the cloud. In fact, Bob can request the purged content from any or all of the group members of that conversation (information on the group can be embedded as metadata in the encrypted content) to restore the content on the cloud for him. Once a group member (say Chloe) restores the content, Bob's *ufiles* can be updated to indicate that the content is no longer needed from other members.

This process increases the complexity of *Hermes*'s design, and thus, is not currently implemented in our prototype; however, as we show in Section 6, such cases are rare if one looks at typical content sharing on Facebook. Here, we also point out that *Hermes* enables users to access their content from multiple devices; however, we omit the details of how this is made possible due to space constraints.

5   Hiding Users' Sharing Patterns

Next, we discuss how *Hermes* ensures that cloud providers cannot determine any of the following: a) "when" a private conversation is occurring, b) the group size of any given conversation, and c) the individual members taking part in that conversation.

5.1   Hiding the Membership Information within Each Private Conversation

First, let us consider a single private conversation initiated by Alice. Our goal here is to ensure that the identities of the members of this private group and the size of the group are not exposed to anyone outside the group.

Strawman Approach: To hide the group members in a given conversation initiated by Alice, one simple approach is to make *ufiles* indistinguishable across all of Alice's friends. Whenever Alice's *Hermes* client needs to insert an entry into the *ufile* for a particular friend, it can also insert dummy entries into the *ufiles* for all of Alice's remaining friends; the entries in the *ufile* for any particular friend are encrypted with the shared pairwise key between Alice and that friend, thus preventing the cloud provider from inferring which entries are fake. Thus, based on the writes to and reads from the *ufiles* in Alice's cloud storage, the cloud provider will not be able to determine which subset of Alice's friends are involved in ongoing private conversations.

However, this simple approach has two limitations. First, it results in high storage, bandwidth, and operational query costs for Alice, because a large number of fake entries will need to be stored by Alice and accessed by Alice's friends. Second, the cloud provider may still be able to infer the members of Alice's private conversation by observing which of Alice's friends insert updates into the *ufiles* in their own storage space; group members will post comments, but friends who are not part of the group will not. We next discuss how we address both of these issues in *Hermes*.

Obfuscating Group Size: Instead of making the *ufiles* for all of Alice's friends indistinguishable, *Hermes* attempts to hide the group members ($\mathbb{G}$) among a subset of Alice's friends ($\mathbb{D}$), where $\mathbb{G}$ is a subset of $\mathbb{D}$ (referred to as the anonymity set). Whenever an entry has to be added to the *ufile* for any user in $\mathbb{G}$, dummy entries are also added to the *ufiles* for those users in ($\mathbb{D} - \mathbb{G}$). The number of users in ($\mathbb{D}-\mathbb{G}$) follows an exponential distribution, with its minimum, mean, and maximum values set to α, $|(\mathbb{N} - \mathbb{G})|/4$ (rationale in Section 6), and $|(\mathbb{N} - \mathbb{G})|^2$, where $\mathbb{N}$ contains all of Alice's friends. The parameter α allows us to handle small groups and is set to $\max(15, |\mathbb{G}|)$.

The effect of these parameters is that the size of the anonymity set is always at least double that of the private group. As a result, random guessing as to whether a particular user in the anonymity set is a member of the group will be correct with a probability of at most 50%. For small groups of size less than 15, randomly guessing as to whether a user in $\mathbb{D}$ is a group member succeeds with probability $|\mathbb{G}|/(|\mathbb{G}| + 15)$. In addition, the exponential distribution biases the anonymity set towards smaller sizes. This reduces the additional storage and bandwidth costs incurred for providing anonymity, as compared to a uniform distribution that chooses the size of the anonymity set at random from the range $[\alpha, |\mathbb{N} - \mathbb{G}|]$. Lastly, note that it is insufficient to determine the size of the anonymity set simply by inflating the group size by a fixed factor (since this clearly reveals the group size).

Preventing Inference of Group Membership Based on Comments: So far, Alice has been able to share content with $\mathbb{G}$ without revealing $\mathbb{G}$ or its size ($|\mathbb{G}|$). However, since only members of $\mathbb{G}$ will post comments on the shared content, the cloud provider will be able to distinguish the users in $\mathbb{G}$ from all those in $\mathbb{D}$. Thus, the additional fake members in $\mathbb{D}$ must also post fake comments

---

[2] Since private group sizes are typically small, we assume $|(\mathbb{N} - \mathbb{G})| > |\mathbb{G}|$.

as part of the conversation (these fake comments are discarded upon retrieval by group members).

A naive approach would require all the additional members in $\mathbb{D}$ to post as per either some random distribution or based on their previous posting habits. However, it is hard to provide any anonymity guarantees with such an approach. Moreover, since we assume that the source code for the *Hermes* client is publicly accessible, cloud service providers will have access to any distributions hard-coded into the client software.

Instead, our approach for posting of dummy comments works as follows. We divide time into slots, where all the members of a conversation can derive the slot boundaries based on the time at which the conversation was initiated (see Figure 2). We refer to each time slot as a round. In each round, every member of the conversation who is online during that period posts at least one comment, at a random point in time during that round. Those group members who have no real comments to post in a particular round—this includes both the users in $(\mathbb{D} - \mathbb{G})$ and the users in $\mathbb{G}$ who have no comments to post during that round— post at least one dummy comment during that round. All entries added to any $ufile$ are padded to a fixed size in order to hide the number of comments being posted by a user; this is necessary because a user who posts real comments may post multiple comments in a single round.

Importantly, every user in $\mathbb{D}$ posts either real or fake comments at only one particular time during each round. This ensures that the cloud provider cannot distinguish between users in $\mathbb{G}$ and those in $(\mathbb{D} - \mathbb{G})$, since it observes the same pattern of writing to and reading from $ufiles$ for all users in $\mathbb{D}$. Thus, when all users in $\mathbb{D}$ are online, the cloud provider has only a $\frac{\mathbb{G}}{\mathbb{D}}$ probability of correctly inferring whether a particular user in $\mathbb{D}$ is indeed a member of the private group $\mathbb{G}$.

Selecting the Length of a Round: A key design decision in instantiating the approach described above is to determine how time should be divided into rounds. Shorter rounds lead to more timely dissemination of comments. This is because when one user posts a comment in a particular round, another user can respond to this comment only in the next round; note that every user can post comments only once in each round. In contrast, longer rounds result in lower cost since fewer fake comments are posted, but compromise timeliness. Based on this trade-off, we split the timeline of a conversation into rounds as follows.

Our design is based on the observation that the commenting activity associated with most conversations is high when the conversation initially begins. After this initial period, the conversation goes stale and users may have few new comments.

Given this, to reduce the costs incurred to guarantee anonymity (hiding user sharing patterns), we partition any conversation into two phases. The first phase is when the conversation is fresh and one is likely to expect a comment in the near future. In this phase, the timeliness of comment dissemination is important, and therefore we keep a round's length short. Once several rounds with no real comments are observed, the conversation transitions to the second phase. The

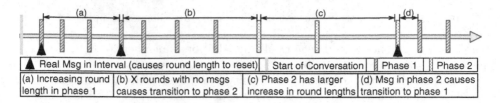

Fig. 2. Round structure in *Hermes*.

second phase aims to capture that phase of a conversation where no user has posted a comment for a while and there is a low probability of new comments. In this phase, we want to limit the cost associated with the conversation by minimizing the number of fake comments. The key property we exploit in this second phase is that, since the conversation is already stale, the timeliness of straggler comments posted during this period is not of concern.

In the first phase, all rounds are of equal length as long as at least one real comment is posted in each round. When there are no real comments in a particular round, we increase the length of the round by a multiplicative factor. The round length in the first phase is reset to its original value when a real comment is posted in the previous round. After a certain number of consecutive rounds with no real comments, the conversation transitions to the second phase. We model round durations in the second phase as a geometric series also, but use a larger multiplicative factor to increase round durations as compared to that used in the first phase. When a real comment is posted in the second phase, the conversation is reset to the first phase, but a fewer number of rounds of inactivity transitions the conversation back to the second phase in this case.

Note that the users who are in $\mathbb{D}$ but not in $\mathbb{G}$ cannot distinguish between real and fake comments; this is intentional, since we seek to hide group membership not only from cloud providers but also from users who are not in $\mathbb{G}$. Therefore, in every round, every user in $\mathbb{G}$ broadcasts to all of her friends who are also in $\mathbb{D}$ as to whether a real comment was posted in the previous round or not. Every user in $\mathbb{D} - \mathbb{G}$ who receives this notification relays this on to all of the user's friends who are in $\mathbb{D}$, exactly once. Thus, a user who receives a notification cannot distinguish between whether this was an original broadcast or a relayed broadcast. Once a user receives this information, she can independently determine what the length of the next round will be and when the transition between phases is triggered. Note that, from the cloud provider's perspective, these notification messages that convey whether a real comment was posted in a particular round are indistinguishable from real and fake comments. Moreover, though the cloud provider may be able to infer when real comments are posted based on when inter-comment spacings decrease, *no one other* than the users in $\mathbb{G}$ can determine *which* users posted the real comments.

5.2   Hiding Users' Conversation Patterns by Handling Intersection Attacks

Thus far, we have only considered hiding the identities of group members within a conversation. Unfortunately, the above approach is insufficient in completely hiding a users' sharing patterns across conversations. If fake users (in $\mathbb{D} - \mathbb{G}$) are chosen randomly from the user's friends ($\mathbb{N}$), the cloud provider can infer that users who appear repeatedly in different conversations are likely to indeed be real members of private groups.

To prevent such intersection attacks [18], we need to preserve anonymity *across* conversations. For this, we seek to ensure that a consistent group of $\mathbb{K}$ friends ($\mathbb{K} \subset \mathbb{N}$) appear across the conversations initiated by a user (Alice); we refer to this group as the Top $\mathbb{K}$ group. Thus, if a private, repetitive, group initiated by Alice is of size $\mathbb{G}$, the provider can only randomly guess if a user in the group of $\mathbb{K}$ friends ($\mathbb{K} >> \mathbb{G}$) is a true repetitive member with probability $\frac{\mathbb{G}}{\mathbb{K}}$. In essence, this provides $|\mathbb{K}|$-anonymity [31].

Our approach to form the Top $\mathbb{K}$ group (algorithmically depicted below) is to (1) tune the membership of $\mathbb{D}$ and (2) use fake conversations. We identify the friends with whom Alice consistently has private conversations (say $\mathbb{K}_1 \supset G$) and include them in the Top $\mathbb{K}$ group. We then fill the remainder of the Top $\mathbb{K}$ group with other friends with whom Alice rarely initiates private conversations (say $\mathbb{K}_2$).

Stage 1 Learn user habits

1: **for** Next M_1 conversations **do**
2:     $\{\forall x \in \mathbb{G} : x.count+ = 1\}$
3:     set $\mathbb{D} = \mathbb{N}$ and start conversation with entire friends list.
4: **end for**
5: Select $\mathbb{K}_1$ users with highest count values
6: Select $\mathbb{K}_2$ random friends s.t. $\{\forall x \in \mathbb{K}_2 : x \in \mathbb{N} \wedge x \notin \mathbb{K}_1\}$
7: reset count Values
8: **return** $\mathbb{K} = \mathbb{K}_1 \cup \mathbb{K}_2$

Stage 2 Use learned habits

1: **for** Next M_2 conversations **do**
2:     Select size for $|\mathbb{D}| = \alpha + Exp(\frac{|\mathbb{N}| - |\mathbb{G}|}{4})$
3:     $\forall x \in (\mathbb{N} - (\mathbb{G} \cup \mathbb{K})) : \mathbb{P}(x \in \mathbb{D}) = p$
4:     Fill $\mathbb{D}$ from $\mathbb{K} - \mathbb{G}$ with probability of $x \in \mathbb{D} \propto Max(c - x.count, delta)$, where $c = Max(\forall x \in \mathbb{K} : x.count)$
5:     $\forall x \in \mathbb{D} : x.count+=1$
6:     schedule $\lceil \frac{\mathbb{K} - \mathbb{D}}{\mathbb{D}} \rceil$ fake conversations with $\mathbb{G} = \emptyset$ in current M_2 conversations
7: **end for**

Tuning the Membership of $\mathbb{D}$: As the first step, we need to determine which of Alice's friends consistently belong in private conversations. While doing so, in order to preserve anonymity, we simply use the naive approach wherein all of her friends are included in all conversations. This is referred to as the *first stage* or the *learning stage* of anonymizing conversations (Stage 1). This stage is executed for M_1 (tunable parameter) conversations. During this stage, the *Hermes* client learns of the user's posting habits and with which friends the user is more likely to privately exchange information (set $\mathbb{K}_1$). It then forms the Top $\mathbb{K}$ group as described above.

In the second stage (Stage 2) which is then executed for the subsequent M_2 (tun able parameter) conversations, we reduce the total cost incurred by a user (Alice) by only consistently including the Top $\mathbb{K}$ group in private conversations. In each true conversation initiated by Alice, we now form the group $\mathbb{D}$ for that conversation as follows. First, all the user's friends that are neither part of the conversation group $\mathbb{G}$ nor the Top $\mathbb{K}$ group (determined in the first stage) are considered as candidates for inclusion in $\mathbb{D}$. Each of these candidates is included in $\mathbb{D}$ with a very small fixed probability p. This ensures that friends outside of Alice's Top $\mathbb{K}$ group, i.e., users with whom she rarely exchanges private content, are included with a small probability; this protects against the server correctly identifying true rare inclusions of such friends. Subsequently, Alice's friends that are part of her Top K group but not in $\mathbb{G}$, are considered for inclusion. The probability that a particular user (say Chloe) in the Top $\mathbb{K}$ group is selected is proportional to the difference between the maximum number of conversations any member of Top $\mathbb{K}$ group is involved in (both true or fake roles), and the number of conversations that Chloe is involved is involved in (both true or fake roles). This ensures that all of the members of the Top $\mathbb{K}$ group are consistently involved in conversations.

Using Fake Conversations: In spite of filling the groups as above, it is possible that real users appear more often than fake users. To address this, we schedule $\lceil \frac{K-\mathbb{D}}{\mathbb{D}} \rceil$ *fake* conversations (with fake comments) where $\mathbb{G} = \emptyset$ (since each real conversation already includes $\approx \mathbb{D}$ members from the Top $\mathbb{K}$ group). The groups, $\mathbb{D}$, for such fake conversations are filled exactly as the real conversations are filled. Together, the above two steps of stage two ensure that every member of the Top K group is in (approximately) the same number of conversations on average.

To cope with the dynamics of Alice's sharing behaviors (she could converse more often with Bob and Dave at some point in time, and at a different time, exchange more private content with Chloe and Eve), we return to the first stage periodically to recompute the Top $\mathbb{K}$ group. Here, we take care to ensure that only minimal changes are made to the group $\mathbb{K}_2$ to prevent the server from identifying these as fake users.

Finally, instead of using fake conversations, to reduce costs one can think of suppressing an initiator's conversations with particular users with whom she is conversing too frequently. We do not explore this option as it violates our goal of ensuring timely sharing as in a traditional OSN.

6   Quantifying Cost, Anonymity, and Timeliness Trade-offs

In order to tune *Hermes*'s configuration, we seek to understand the trade-offs between anonymity, timeliness, and cost. To do this, we crawl a large dataset

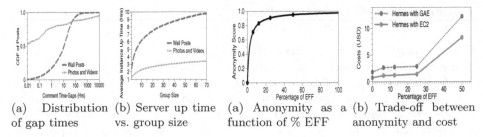

(a)   Distribution   (b) Server up time   (a) Anonymity as a   (b) Trade-off between
of gap times   vs. group size   function of % EFF   anonymity and cost

Fig. 3. Analyses with Facebook data   **Fig. 4.** Anonymity trade-offs per conversation

from Facebook, and use the posting habits seen to perform a trace-driven simulation of *Hermes*.

Understanding the Temporal Nature of Conversations: We first seek to understand how long a posting is likely to be of interest to a user's friends, in the common case. Our particular interest is the *time gap* between when specific content was posted by a user and when the friends of that user lose interest in viewing it (the interested friends have already viewed it with high probability). However, it is impossible to accurately determine this duration without access to Facebook's server-side logs. Therefore, we instead use users' comments on a post as a proxy for their interest in the post. Though all users who find a posting to be of interest may not comment on it, previous studies have shown that the number of friends that see a post and the number of friends commenting or liking it are positively correlated [17]. Thus, we ask the question: for those postings that have associated comments, what is the time gap between the instant when the posting was made and when the last associated comment was posted?

Due to the lack of a publicly available dataset on users' posting habits, we crawled the profiles of 68,863 Facebook users using a combination of FQL (Facebook query language) and RestFB. Our crawled dataset, which spans a month, roughly comprises 1) 1.8 million wall posts and associated comments, and 2) 40K posts of either photos or videos with ≈ 35K associated comments. Remarkably, 70% of the 1.8 million posts did not have any associated comments. Thus, we look at the other 30% and the photos/videos to determine the time-gap between when the initial content was posted and when the last associated comment was seen. Based on Fig. 3a, we set the duration for which a user caches data on her cloud storage to 3 days; 90% of posts do not receive new comments beyond this period. In outlier cases, where content is sought long after it was posted, we sacrifice timeliness for resource thriftiness as discussed earlier.

A Simulation of *Hermes*: Next, we build a simulator to capture user interactions with *Hermes* in a large-scale setting; the simulation provides both 1) an understanding of how *Hermes* may perform, and 2) a validation of *Hermes*'s ability to provide anonymity with limited resources (small volumes of storage and bandwidth, few operational queries, and short uptimes for a user's computing instance). To the best of our knowledge, there does not exist a simulator that mimics user interactions on an OSN.

Determining Simulation Parameters: The first input required by our simulator is a measurement of how often users come online. This dictates the expected time for disseminating content across *Hermes* clients, and thus, impacts how long the computing instance, or data stored on the cloud, will need to be active. Note that the *Hermes* client on a user's device does not need her to interact with it to fetch new content. Thus, the only time of interest is when the device is powered on and connected to the Internet. Here, we use data from [32], which provides the time per day for which users' devices are active. We assume that most powered on devices today are connected to the Internet. The weighted average of this time for desktops is 9.7 hours a day. The weighted average of online time for portable computers is comparable at 8.3 hours a day [32].

Second, to determine when a friend retrieves a private posting made by a user, we compute the relative time-gap between when the user is online and when the friend comes online later. We assume that users in similar time-zones are online during similar periods; if users are in time zones far apart, this time gap may be larger. Unfortunately, we were unable to access the location information of users in our data set; Facebook does not allow programmatic access to this information. Hence, we use two approximations to characterize the distribution of when the friends of a user come online. 1) We assume that users come online at random instances uniformly distributed over a 24 hour period, and stay online for a uniformly distributed period with an average of 9.7 hours; we believe that this model represents the likelihood that a user's friends are distributed all over the globe. 2) We consider a best case scenario wherein all of a user's friends are in her time-zone; here, we assume that the user and her friends come online within a 12 hour period. Again, the time at which the user comes online is uniformly distributed within this period, and the duration for which one stays online is chosen as before.

Third, to accurately represent a user's posting habits, we replay the posts in our Facebook data set. Since the posts we crawl are those shared by a user with all her friends, we obtain an estimate for the expected *private* group size from [20] and [3]; these studies suggest that while the social group size of a user is about 190, the more intimate size of a social group is 12. On this basis, we consider expected group sizes of 15, and use a uniform distribution with variance 10 (to cover group sizes from 5 to 25).

Selecting System Parameters: To simulate *Hermes*, we also need to choose the parameters that control how the system trades off timeliness for anonymity. The two phases of a conversation, as discussed in Section 5, depend on four factors, namely the initial length of a round (l), the multiplicative growth rate in phase one (A_1), the growth rate in phase two (A_2), and the number of rounds with no real comments in phase 1 (X), after which a conversation transitions to phase 2. To set X, we observe from the Facebook data that 95% of the time, the time gap between two consecutive comments is less than 24 hours. In other words, a conversation is unlikely to be of interest to friends if there are no comments for about 24 hours. Hence, we transition a conversation from the first to the second phase if we do not see a comment for 24 hours. Later we vary l and A_1 in our simulator and examine the effects on average cost and timeliness. For phase 2, we seek an exponential growth, but want to simultaneously keep in check the delay incurred in retrieving straggler comments; thus we set $A_2 = 2$.

Simulator Design: Our simulator captures all the features of *Hermes* described in Sections 4 and 5. In our simulation, every user initiates conversations and posts comments as per her posting activity on Facebook. For each private conversation initiated by a user, we select a randomly chosen subset of the user's friends based on her posting habits and the expected group size considered. We consider the size of every shared photo as 2 MB and the size of all other private posts as 0.5 KB (these numbers are much larger than what we got from our crawled data). Since a user's comments in our crawled data may be on posts made by users outside our crawled population, we post any comment by a user to a pre-existing randomly chosen conversation that she is involved in.

Results and Interpretations: Our metrics of interest are (i) the time for which a user's compute instance needs to be active, (ii) the anonymity (likelihood of guessing if a friend is a true group member) a conversational group is provided, (iii) the total cost incurred, and (iv) the loss of timeliness due to users receiving stale data.

Compute Costs: First, we seek to determine the time for which the instance associated with any object (post) needs to be active. Recall that a *Hermes* client of a group member obtains new content as soon as she comes online. Considering the two approximations discussed above for when users come online, Fig. 3b plots the distribution of the time it takes for all the members of a private group to access the object. This is the time for which the compute instance has to be up. To handle the common cases where the group size is small (< 15), the compute instance needs be up for 6–7 hours even if a user's friends are globally distributed; if the friends are all local, it needs to be up for ≈ 4 hours. One may expect that in a typical case (when a user has both global and local friends), the compute instance will have to be up for a duration somewhere in between 4 and 7 hours; we conservatively choose the duration to be 10 hours. In rare cases where not all members access a posted object within the 10 hours, we trade-off timeliness in serving the content for lower cost. Based on this, our simulations indicate that, for $\approx 90\%$ of the users, *Hermes* will need to keep their instances active for less than 100 hours (or 4 days) in a month, in order to privately exchange *all the Facebook data* that they shared in the entire month. In comparison, prior solutions for OSN privacy [4, 29] require every user to persistently have a compute presence in the cloud.

Quantifying Anonymity: Second, we seek to quantify the anonymity provided to a conversational group. First, we consider each conversation individually. We define the *anonymity score* to be the probability that the server is unable to correctly identify a group member as true or fake (as discussed in Section 5 this

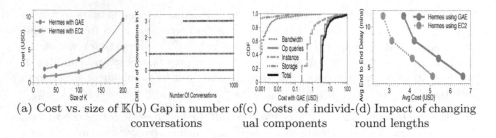

(a) Cost vs. size of $\mathbb{K}$ (b) Gap in number of (c) Costs of individ- (d) Impact of changing
conversations   ual components   round lengths

Fig. 5. Anonymity across conversations and system costs

is $(1 - \frac{|G|}{|D|}))$. In Figure 4a, we plot the anonymity score while varying the number
of fake group members. The x-axis represents the percentage of the initiator's
friends outside the group, who are added as fake members (denoted as external
fake friends or EFFs). Specifically, $\mathbb{D} = \mathbb{G} \cup EFF$ where, $EFF \subseteq \{\mathbb{N} - \mathbb{G}\}$. The
y-axis represents the anonymity score. Since the likelihood that the server is
able to guess correctly is approximately proportional to the ratio of the number
of true members (fixed) to the size of the composite group (with true and fake
members), the anonymity score steeply increases as the size of the composite
group increases initially. Beyond a certain point, we reach a point of diminishing
gains, wherein the increase in the anonymity score is less significant with an
increase in the composite group size. To achieve an anonymity score of about
0.9, we need to add 25% of the friends outside the true group as fake members
in each conversation.

Per Conversation Anonymity vs. Cost Trade-Off: Next, in Figure 4b, we depict
the expected (total) cost incurred as a function of the percentage of EFFs. We
obtain the per-resource costs for different contributing factors from [1,2,8], and
multiply this with the amount of resources consumed. For an anonymity score
of 0.9 (% of EFFs = 25), we see that the expected *total* monthly cost per user
is relatively low (< \$ 4) with both Google App Engine (GAE) and Amazon
EC2 (storage and computing are from the same provider). Thus, an EFF of 25%
(or $|\mathbb{N} - \mathbb{G}|/4$) presents the best trade-off between per conversation cost and
anonymity in *Hermes*.

Handling Intersection Attacks: In the scenario described above, we only considered the anonymity in a given conversation; the cost due to fake conversations
(included for protection against intersection attacks) was not considered. Next,
we present results that capture the effect of these conversations, which appear
at a rate of $\lceil \frac{K-D}{D} \rceil$ (recall Stage 2). The parameter $\mathbb{K}$ determines the level of
anonymity provided across conversations as discussed earlier. The value of $\mathbb{G}$ is
specific to each user and varies from 5 to 25; we fix an EFF of 25 % based on our
previous results. In Figure 5a, we change $\mathbb{K}$ by varying $\mathbb{K}_2$ ($\mathbb{K}_1$ is estimated in the
first stage of the process for each user as discussed in Section 5). We immediately
see that $\mathbb{K} \approx 150$ yields the highest anonymity at a reasonable cost. This is only
marginally higher than the value of $\mathbb{D}$ (with the chosen EFF value). This implies

Table 1. Cost for various values of A_1

A_1	Avg. Delay (min)	Avg. Ops Cost ($)
1.025	2.8867	5.13
1.05	3.096	2.80
1.10	22.52	2.32

Table 2. *Hermes*'s resource consumption on GAE

Operation	MS/Req	Bytes Rx	Bytes Sent
Posts links	130	78	4
Check and retrieve update	50	22	35
Add comment	45	42	2

that, on average, we need only one fake conversation for every real conversation in order to thwart the intersection attack. In Figure 5b, we plot the difference in the maximum and minimum number of conversations that the members of Top $\mathbb{K}$ group have participated in. We see that this difference is no greater than 3 at all times; this demonstrates the high degree of anonymity within the Top $\mathbb{K}$ group.

Cost Breakdown: Figure 5c shows the distribution (across users) of the total costs due to the various components required by *Hermes*, viz., storage, bandwidth, operational queries, and the computing instance, with GAE. We see that, for about 95% of the users, the total cost is $< \$10$ a month. In comparison, if a compute instance is always active, the cost of this alone would be $> \$60$ per month. We also see that the cost due to operational queries and the instance are the biggest contributors to the total cost. This is expected since storage and bandwidth are relatively cheap, especially since *Hermes* purges the cloud storage regularly. Operational costs are *relatively* high since storing, retrieving, or even checking for content, incurs a cost [2,8]. The total cost with EC2 is slightly lower than that with GAE ($< \$9$ for 95% of the users) but the trends in the cost components are similar; we do not plot the results here due to space considerations.

Timeliness vs. Cost: In Figure 5d, we plot the expected delay incurred in accessing posts (a measure of timeliness) versus the expected (total) cost. We again use GAE. If the length l of each round (recall Section 5) is reduced, the operational costs are increased, but the timeliness is improved as well. If instead, we increase l, the timeliness suffers but queries are made less often (to check for content) and thus, cost decreases. Even if the desired expected delay is as low as 5 minutes, the incurred cost with GAE is no more than $5 per month. With EC2, this cost is even lower ($3). These results demonstrate that good timeliness is possible with *Hermes*, with fairly low cost.

Timeliness vs. Anonymity: Next, we quantify the impact of varying A_1 on timeliness for a fixed l (set to 5 minutes for our experiments). We measure this impact in terms of average costs and the average delay over all conversations in the simulation. In Table 1 we show a representative subset of our results that is of interest. As evident, increasing A_1 decreases average cost but increases the average delay of message propagation. From the table we see that when A_1 is decreased to 1.05

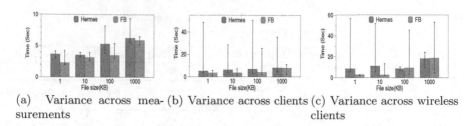

(a) Variance across measurements   (b) Variance across clients   (c) Variance across wireless clients

Fig. 6. End-to-end delays on *Hermes* and on Facebook

from 1.10, the marginal reduction in delay is significant; however, the additional reduction is marginal when A_1 is further reduced to 1.025. The cost growth is almost linear. These results suggest that setting A_1 (by default) to 1.05 provides the best trade-off between delay and cost.

7   Prototype Implementation and Evaluations

Implementation: We prototype *Hermes* in Java as an add-on to Facebook. We use the Facebook front end and a user's profile therein is used for making her public key component available. *Hermes* runs as a middleware and intercepts posts classified as private. Dropbox and Google App Engine (GAE) are used for storage and computation. Upon installation, the *Hermes* client requests OAuth 2.0 [10] access tokens from both Facebook and Dropbox and stores these locally for later use. The client crawls the list of the user's friends on Facebook and creates one *ufile* for each of them on Dropbox. The client also initializes a web-based application on GAE on behalf of the user.

The implementation of *Hermes* essentially follows the design as described in the previous sections. ECDH is used to establish pairwise keys between the initiator and each of her friends and these are then used to establish conversation specific group keys. Then, the *Hermes* client uploads the content encrypted with the group key, to the user's space on Dropbox and requests Dropbox for the public URLs for these files.[3] When the user shares content, the *Hermes* client also invokes a GAE instance and uses the GAE data store to save the encrypted public URL to the file on Dropbox. All communications with the instance are over HTTPS. For efficiency, the instance shuts itself down after a configurable time has elapsed after creation (10 hours by default).

Both true and fake members access content as described earlier. The client devices of fake users are provided with a group key whose prefix indicates that it is a fake member; the server cannot detect a fake member, since the fake group key is encrypted using the pairwise keys. The client of a fake member simply

---

[3] With typical file sharing on Dropbox, when Alice shares a file with Bob, the shared file is counted towards the storage capacity of both Alice and Bob. In our implementation, public links are simply pointers to Alice's files; the files are then directly accessed by Bob.

discards all content retrieved with respect to the conversation (both the original posting as well as comments).

Storage Overhead Associated with Shared Content: Our implementation uses AES (256 bit key) to encrypt data and ECDH to establish a symmetric key (using the P-256 curve defined in [11]). The parameters (such as the curve and p) are defined in P-256 and available to all users.

Hermes adds overhead to shared content in three ways. (1) As described in Section 4, each $ufile$ entry occupies 16 bytes for a hash value and ≈ 20 bytes for an encrypted URL on Dropbox. (2) Each $ufile$ entry also includes the group key encrypted with the pairwise key of the sender and its corresponding receiver, with information for associating the entry with the receiver and authenticating her. In our implementation, the size of each $password$ tuple is 62 bytes. (3) *Hermes* stores information about the uploaded files and the access tokens for writing to a user's Dropbox account on the user's GAE instance. In our implementation, every post accounts for 440 bytes of space on the GAE instance. In essence, (1) *Hermes*'s storage overhead is a few KB for sharing data of any size; as an illustration, storage overhead is 82, 820, and 1640 bytes for group sizes of 1, 10, and 20 members (including fake), and (2) storage overhead of *Hermes* increases linearly with the composite group size. Note that we expect private groups to be typically small [3, 20].

Efficiency of *Hermes*: We next evaluate our prototype by comparing the delay incurred in sharing data with *Hermes* to that with Facebook. We share files of different sizes and measure the total delay between when a user shares a file and when a recipient completes receiving that file. To mimic the overhead seen by real users, the receiver program contacts 250 compute instances (250 is the average number of friends on Facebook [14]) to check for new content.

Fig. 6a shows the variance in delays incurred (the minimum, median, and maximum values across 5 trials) in the above experiment. The overhead imposed by *Hermes* as compared to sharing and receiving data on Facebook, especially for delay-sensitive sharing of small files, is within reason (a few seconds). Delays on *Hermes* are higher than delays on Facebook because *Hermes* not only posts the shared content on Dropbox, but also sends the links to these files to the user's GAE instance. Furthermore, *Hermes* uploads and downloads $ufiles$ in addition to the content being shared.

We repeat the experiment on 6 PlanetLab [28] nodes, two on the US west and east coasts, and one each in Europe, Asia, Australia, and South America, and with 10 clients that access *Hermes* and Facebook via WiFi. Figs. 6b and 6c show the variance in median access times across the PlanetLab nodes and across the wireless clients. We see that the access times with *Hermes* are comparable to that of direct data sharing on Facebook.

Resource Usage: Next, we measure the compute and bandwidth resources consumed by the three *Hermes* client operations that require interactions with the compute instance: (i) post links to newly shared content to the instance, (ii) serve requests from friends who check if anything new has been shared with them (and download new comments, if any), and (iii) receive the link to a recipient's comment and post it to the conversation. We perform each operation 1000 times and examine GAE's reports for resource usage. Table. 2 shows that the compute time and incoming/outgoing network traffic incurred on average, for each operation is low.

8   Conclusions

We design and implement *Hermes*, a practical, cost-effective, OSN architecture for private content sharing. *Hermes* intelligently uses limited storage and computing resources on the cloud to facilitate timeliness and high availability, while minimizing resource usage. A key property of *Hermes* is that neither the cloud providers nor other friends of a user can infer the membership of a private group. Via an analysis of mined Facebook data and exhaustive simulations, we show that *Hermes* greatly reduces costs compared to alternative solutions while ensuring the anonymity of the private group.

Acknowledgement. This work was supported by Army Research Office grant 62954CSREP.

References

1. Amazon EC2 micro-instance. amzn.to/14fxKbM
2. Amazon S3 pricing. amzn.to/1dRGFuz
3. Anatomy of Facebook. on.fb.me/1az2axi
4. The Diaspora project. diasporaproject.org/
5. Facebook fixes security glitch after leak of Mark Zuckerberg photos. lat.ms/14fx4mC
6. Facebook says it fixed leak that opened info to third-parties. wapo.st/12UidOW
7. Google App Engine. bit.ly/117kPXo
8. Google App Engine Pricing. bit.ly/1cclPzm
9. Heroku. www.heroku.com/
10. OAuth. oauth.net/
11. Recommended elliptic curves for federal government use. 1.usa.gov/14fwPYI
12. Some quitting Facebook as privacy concerns escalate. bit.ly/15pqQmK
13. Syme. getsyme.com
14. Your Facebook friends have more friends than you. wapo.st/11I58Mj
15. Baden, R., Bender, A., Spring, N., Bhattacharjee, B., Starin, D.: Persona: an online socialnetwork with user-defined privacy. In: SIGCOMM 2009 (2009)
16. Beato, F., Kohlweiss, M., Wouters, K.: Scramble! your social network data. In: Fischer-Hübner, S., Hopper, N. (eds.) PETS 2011. LNCS, vol. 6794, pp. 211–255. Springer, Heidelberg (2011)
17. Bernstein, M.S., Bakshy, E., Burke, M., Karrer, B.: Quantifying the invisible audience insocial networks. In: CHI 2013 (2013)
18. Danezis, G., Serjantov, A.: Statistical disclosure or intersection attacks on anonymity systems. In: Fridrich, J. (ed.) IH 2004. LNCS, vol. 3200, pp. 293–308. Springer, Heidelberg (2005)

19. Dingledine, R., Mathewson, N., Syverson, P.: Tor: the second-generation onion router. In: Security 2004 (2004)
20. Dunbar, R.: The ultimate brain teaser. bit.ly/17Floky
21. Feldman, A.J., Blankstein, A., Freedman, M.J., Felten, E.W.: Social networking with frientegrity: privacy and integrity with an untrusted provider. In: Security 2012 (2012)
22. Feldman, A.J., Zeller, W.P., Freedman, M.J., Felten, E.W.: Sporc: group collaboration usinguntrusted cloud resources. In: OSDI 2010 (2010)
23. Guha, S., Tang, K., Francis, P.: Noyb: privacy in online social networks. In: WOSN 2008 (2008)
24. Jahid, S., Nilizadeh, S., Mittal, P., Borisov, N., Kapadia, A.: DECENT: a decentralized architecture for enforcing privacy in online social networks. In: IEEE SESOC 2012 (2012)
25. Koblitz, N., Menezes, A., Vanstone, S.: The state of elliptic curve cryptography. Designs, Codes and Cryptography (2000)
26. Lamport, L.: Time, clocks, and the ordering of events in a distributed system. Commun. ACM (1978)
27. Liu, D., Shakimov, A., Cáceres, R., Varshavsky, A., Cox, L.P.: Confidant: protecting OSN data without locking it up. In: Kon, F., Kermarrec, A.-M. (eds.) Middleware 2011. LNCS, pp. 61–80. Springer, Heidelberg (2011)
28. Peterson, L., Anderson, T., Culler, D., Roscoe, T.: A blueprint for introducing disruptivetechnology into the internet. In: HotNets 2002 (2002)
29. Shakimov, A., Lim, H., Caceres, R., Cox, L., Li, K., Liu, D., Varshavsky, A.: Vis-a-vis: privacy-preserving online social networking via virtual individual servers. In: COMSNETS 2011 (2011)
30. Stefanov, E., Shi, E., Song, D.X.: Towards practical oblivious ram. In: NDSS 2012 (2012)
31. Sweeney, L.: K-anonymity: A model for protecting privacy. Int. J. Uncertain. Fuzziness Knowl.-Based Syst. (2002)
32. Urban, B., Tiefenbeck, V., Roth, K.: Energy consumption of consumer electronics in US homes in 2010. bit.ly/10NMqOn
33. Zhang, L., Mislove, A.: Building confederated web-based services with priv.io. In: COSN 2013, New York, NY, USA (2013)

A   Propagating Updates via *ufiles*

The *ufile* contains tuples $< id, c_{url}, up, data >$, where *id* is a monotonically increasing counter (eventually wraps around), c_{url} is the unique URL pointing to the folder of the owner of conversation *c*, *up* indicates the type of update, and *data* is the data associated with a specific update status (explained later). A user's *Hermes* client creates a *ufile* for each of the user's friends when the user first begins using *Hermes* (and whenever the user adds a new friend thereafter). The first time that a pair of friends engage in a private conversation, they use the computing instance to exchange pointers to the *ufiles* they have created for each other. The links to the *ufiles* are then stored on their respective cloud storage permanently.

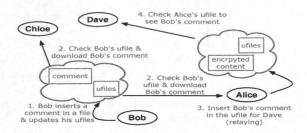

Fig. 7. Illustration of comment propagation in *Hermes*.

Consider a new bootstrapped conversation between Alice and all her friends. We consider the scenario where Bob wants to post a comment (or reply) to content that was originally shared by Alice.

Step 1: To comment on the content posted by Alice, Bob writes an update to the $ufiles$ that he maintains for his friends Alice and Chloe. Bob's *Hermes* client writes this update only to his $ufiles$ for Alice and Chloe, and not his other friends, since they are the members of the group. This update contains the tuple $< id, c_{url}, 1, link >$, where '1' is an integer code to indicate that a new comment in conversation c is in $link$,which is owned by Bob.

Step 2: When Alice and Chloe come online, they download their respective $ufiles$ from Bob's storage and learn of the new comment in c. They individually retrieve Bob's comment and create new tuples of the form $< id, c_{url}, 2, link >$ in their own $ufiles$ for Bob. Here, '2' is an integer code indicating that they have received the last comment made by Bob in conversation c.

Step 3: When Bob comes online again and his client downloads the corresponding $ufiles$ from Alice and Chloe, it realizes that all his relevant friends have read his latest comment. It then deletes the prior update $< id, c_{url}, 1, link >$ from his $ufiles$; it also purges the corresponding comment from his cloud storage. By doing this, the space occupied by the comment and $ufiles$ do not simply grow over time, thus drastically decreasing *Hermes*'s cloud storage requirements. Upon returning online, Alice and Chloe notice that Bob's original entry is deleted from his $ufiles$. This implicitly tells them that Bob has received their update and hence, they delete their update tuples from their $ufiles$ for Bob.

Step 4: While Alice and Chloe get Bob's comment, Dave is not Bob's friend and hence, does not receive it (Bob does not even maintain a $ufile$ for Dave). To allow Dave to see all the comments in a conversation he is part of (as with Facebook), *Hermes* leverages the fact that Alice is a friend to all group members and incorporates an additional step (shown in Fig. 7). When Alice notices Bob's update (step 2), she checks whether there exist group members who are not friends with him. For each such member (e.g., Dave), Alice inserts an update tuple $< id, c_{url}, 3, rc >$ in their respective $ufiles$; here '3' is a code for the relaying of a comment. rc refers to the relayed comment included in the tuple.

Upon coming online, Dave downloads Alice's $ufile$ for him, finds the comment, and notifies Alice of the receipt of this update. Alice and Dave then purge the associated updates from their respective $ufiles$ (steps 2-4 as before).

Note that the above scheme for distributing comments also works for other types of notifications (e.g., 'Likes' on Facebook) by simply having different update codes for different types of notifications.

Uranine: Real-time Privacy Leakage Monitoring without System Modification for Android

Vaibhav Rastogi[1,2]([✉]), Zhengyang Qu[3], Jedidiah McClurg[4], Yinzhi Cao[5], and Yan Chen[3]

[1] University of Wisconsin, Madison, USA
vrastogi@wisc.edu
[2] Pennsylvania State University, State College, USA
[3] Northwestern University, Evanston, USA
zhengyangqu2017@u.northwestern.edu, ychen@northwestern.edu
[4] University of Colorado Boulder, Boulder, USA
jedidiah.mcclurg@colorado.edu
[5] Lehigh University, Bethlehem, USA
yinzhi.cao@lehigh.edu

Abstract. Mobile devices are becoming increasingly popular. One reason for their popularity is the availability of a wide range of third-party applications, which enrich the environment and increase usability. There are however privacy concerns centered around these applications – users do not know what private data is leaked by the applications. Previous works to detect privacy leakages are either not accurate enough or require operating system changes, which may not be possible due to users' lack of skills or locked devices. We present Uranine (Uranine is a dye, which finds applications as a flow tracer in medicine and environmental studies.), a system that instruments Android applications to detect privacy leakages in real-time. Uranine does not require any platform modification nor does it need the application source code. We designed several mechanisms to overcome the challenges of tracking information flow across framework code, handling callback functions, and expressing all information-flow tracking at the bytecode level. Our evaluation of Uranine shows that it is accurate at detecting privacy leaks and has acceptable performance overhead.

1   Introduction

Privacy encompasses an individual's or a party's control of information concerning themselves. With the advent of smartphones and tablets, third party applications play an important role in the lives of individual consumers and in enterprise businesses by providing enriched functionality and enhanced user experience, but have simultaneously also led to privacy concerns. On the consumers' side, how third-party applications deal with the wealth of private data stored on mobile devices is not quite clear. Enterprises, on the other hand, need to protect sensitive business data. With the implementation of Bring Your Own Device (BYOD) policies to better accommodate the needs of employees, the

© Institute for Computer Sciences, Social Informatics and Telecommunications Engineering 2015
B. Thuraisingham et al. (Eds.): SecureComm 2015, LNICST 164, pp. 256–276, 2015.
DOI: 10.1007/978-3-319-28865-9_14

issue is further aggravated, as the business data is stored on devices that are not completely trusted. Leakage of business data to the Internet or from business applications to personal applications is an important concern. Some leakage of private data may be legitimate and even intended; yet, other leakages may be questionable. We therefore believe that information about the privacy leaks should be completely transparent and accessible to the user (or the IT administrator in case of enterprises). The user may then choose to allow or disallow the leaks either through real-time interaction with an on-device controller or through preset policies. In particular, apart from good accuracy and performance, the detection of privacy leaks should have the following requirements.

- *Real-time.* Real-time detection, or detection immediately when leaks happen, enables situationally-aware decision making. The situation (condition) under which a leak happens is important—a privacy leak may be user-intended, and in that case legitimate. For example, upload of a user's address book to a social network under user's consent is legitimate. Offline detection of leaks may be helpful, but does not usually identify the complete situation under which a leak happens.
- *No system modification.* Mobile devices typically come locked, and it is difficult for an average user to root or unlock them to install a custom firmware.
- *Easily configurable.* The user should be able to enable the privacy leak detection just for the apps she is concerned about. Other parts of the device such as system server processes and trusted apps from the device vendor should be able to run without overhead.
- *Portability.* The framework should work across different devices with potentially different architectures, e.g. ARM and x86, and with different runtimes, e.g. Dalvik and ART (a recently introduced Android runtime[1]), with little or no code modification.

There have been many earlier systems targeted at detecting privacy leaks, but all have some drawbacks with regards to the above characteristics. Taint-Droid [13] detects privacy leaks in real-time, but requires the installation of a custom Android firmware, which possibly limits its accessibility to expert users. Furthermore, TaintDroid's firmware code modifications must be adapted to different architectures and even different Android versions. Phosphor [4] is a dynamic taint tracking system for Java which can work on Android. It instruments the application and library code to detect privacy leaks in real-time. However, it requires modification of the bytecode of platform libraries, which again requires custom firmware and hinders wide-scale deployment. Static analysis systems [2,14] fail on the real-time requirement—inputs from the user or from the remote server may affect what is sent out of the device and thus the leak may or may not be considered legitimate.

In this paper we propose *Uranine*, a real-time system for monitoring privacy leaks in Android applications without the need for platform modification. The major challenge comes from the requirement of *no platform modification*,

---

[1] https://source.android.com/devices/tech/dalvik/art.html

Table 1. Uranine compared with dynamic approaches. $+$ is better, $-$ is worse.

	TaintDroid [13]	Phosphor [4]	Uranine
Real Time	Yes $(+)$	Yes $(+)$	Yes $(+)$
System Modification	Yes $(-)$	Yes $(-)$	No $(+)$
Configurability	Little $(-)$	Little $(-)$	High $(+)$
Accuracy	Good $(+)$	Good$(+)$	Good $(+)$
Performance (runtime)	Good $(+)$	Good$(+)$	Good $(+)$
Portable	No $(-)$	Yes$(+)$	Yes $(+)$

including being unable to instrument framework code:[2] we need to approximate flow through the framework code and for *callbacks*, i.e. application code called by the framework code. This is further complicated by the existence of heap objects, which often point to other heap objects and whose effects may easily lead to missing leaks if not handled carefully.

Uranine provides a framework for instrumenting stock Android applications without the need for the application source code. It begins by converting the application bytecode to an intermediate representation (IR), which it instruments employing the techniques presented in this paper. The instrumented IR is assembled back into a new application installable on an Android device. As the instrumented application runs, privacy leakages are automatically tracked.

Apart from being real-time and requiring no system modification, our approach also brings the added benefit of instrumenting only apps that the user is concerned about; the rest of the system, including the middleware and other apps, run without overhead. Finally, since we do not touch the Android middleware and the virtual machine runtime, our approach ensures portability. Table 1 summarizes the comparison between Uranine and other similar systems.

This paper makes the following contributions.

- We solve the problem of tracking private information through platform APIs and libraries without modifying the platform, by developing appropriate data structures and algorithms in Section 3.1.
- The Java language and especially the Android platform relies heavily on callbacks, i.e. functions in app code that are called by the platform libraries. We discuss the challenges of handling callbacks for real-time information flow tracking, and propose the first solution for this problem in Section 3.1.
- Aspects of Java, including reference semantics for objects and garbage collection, pose a problem with regards to developing a clean solution that does not interfere with the Java model. Our solution, centered on hashtables with weak references to hold necessary data-structures for different objects, solves this problem (Section 3.1).
- We have developed a system prototype called Uranine for real-time detection of privacy leakages in Android apps without system modification.

---

[2] Throughout the paper, *app code* refers to the code contained in the app; *framework code* refers to the code defined in the Android platform and may be called through Android APIs.

We evaluated (Section 5) a working prototype of Uranine on real-world applications from Google Play. The evaluation shows that Uranine is accurate in tracking information flows. Our evaluation of performance overhead shows that Uranine has acceptable overhead on real-world applications. We also note that it is possible to further reduce the performance overhead of Uranine by performing static analysis and instrumenting only paths along which private information flows can take place.

The rest of this paper is organized as follows. Section 2 gives the background and states our approach together with the challenges involved. A detailed description of the Uranine framework is covered in Section 3, while Section 4 covers the implementation aspects. Section 5 gives our evaluation of Uranine. We then present some relevant discussion in Section 6 and related work in Section 7. We finally conclude in Section 8.

2   Background and Problem Statement

2.1   Android Background

Android is an operating system for mobile devices such as smartphones and tablets. It is based on the Linux kernel and implements middleware for telephony, application management, window management, etc. Applications are typically written in Java and compiled to Dalvik bytecode, which can run on Android. The bytecode and virtual machine mostly comply with the Java Virtual Machine Specification.

Unlike the JVM, The Dalvik Virtual Machine is a register-based VM. Each method has its own set of registers (not overlapping with other methods). Instructions address these registers to perform operations on them.

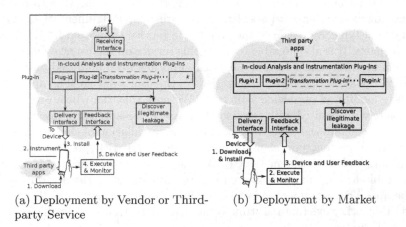

(a) Deployment by Vendor or Third-party Service   (b) Deployment by Market

Fig. 1. Deployment by Vendor or Third-party Service

2.2   Problem Statement

Static analysis has its own advantages for information flow tracking, but a dynamic information flow tracking solution may also be desirable for the following reasons: (a) Static analysis may only tell what may happen but cannot tell what actually happens. Runtime conditions, including inputs from the user and the server may influence what actually happens, meaning that any privacy leaks may be classified as legitimate or illegitimate. Even if a static analysis can detect user interaction, what exactly a user confirms is very difficult for it to capture. (b) Private sources in Android, which are based on URIs, such as contacts, cannot be soundly tracked by static analysis (unless it marks all database queries as possible private sources). Databases such as contacts are accessed through corresponding URIs, which are simply wrapped strings and may be obfuscated or inaccessible statically. Lastly, (c) static analysis is often conservative due to scalability reasons, and thus may have false positives. In the light of all these points, we focus on dynamic information flow tracking in this paper.

Previous dynamic analysis approaches on Android for tracking information flow have modified the Dalvik VM or the library code to propagate taints [4,13]. As this requires platform modification and thus limits the usability, it is reasonable to ask whether dynamic information flow tracking is possible without platform modification by rewriting the apps alone. Uranine answers this question positively. It accepts stock apps from the user, and returns a ready-to-run instrumented app enabled with information flow tracking.

Deployment Models. Figure 1 shows the two possible deployment models of our approach. The first model is suitable when there is no control on the source of apps. It is suitable for enterprise, third-party subscription services, individual users, and smartphone vendors and carriers. As the user downloads a third-party app, the downloaded app is passed to our system for instrumentation. Such a system would typically reside in the cloud as a service supported by the vendor or a third-party. It is also possible to place this service on the users' own personal computers or enterprise's servers. Once the app has been analyzed and instrumented by the system, the app is installed on the user's device. The app is then constantly monitored on-device as it runs. We note that the whole process may be completely automated with the use of an on-device app so the user needs to only confirm the removal of the original app and installation of the instrumented app. Furthermore, entry-level users may be provided with preset information flow tracking and enforcement policies. The second deployment model, which is more suitable for app markets and enterprise app stores, is slightly different in that the apps are instrumented before the user downloads and installs the app. We note that other existing real-time taint-tracking systems do not have similar deployment models.

Android apps are digitally signed by their developers, so instrumenting an app would require an application to be re-signed. The current app update system at Google Play (and possibly other Android markets) depends on apps' signatures. Deployment by third party services will therefore need to provide out-of-band mechanisms to notify users of available updates. This is however not much of a concern: mobile app management and app wrapping products such as Good [17] and MobileIron [22] already provide similar deployment models to enterprises in the context of API interposition similar to [9,35].

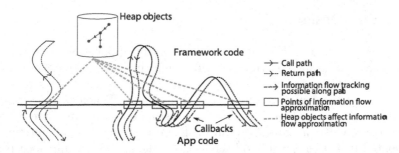

Fig. 2. A depiction of challenges C1 and C2 met in Uranine. There are paths between app code and framework code depicted as meandering function call paths and return paths, together with callbacks (the app code that is called by framework code). The left path results from ordinary calls while the right path includes callbacks. Information flow tracking can only be done for app code, requiring approximations for framework code. Callbacks must be handled soundly. Objects on the heap point to each other and their effect on information flow should be properly accounted for during approximations.

Challenges. Following are the challenges that we solve in creating Uranine.

C1 Framework code should not be modified, i.e. we cannot instrument framework code. We summarize the effect of framework APIs according to a custom policy, combined with manual summarization for a few special cases. Previous works on static or dynamic binary instrumentation [24,36,41] have needed to summarize system calls or very simple functions in low-level libraries like `libc`, which are much simpler. Static analysis works also typically use summarization [15,21] to achieve scalability. However, we show by example that in our context of dynamic analysis and complex framework with Java data structures in Android, summarization alone is not sufficient. Heap objects can be particularly challenging to handle, and we need additional techniques for effective taint propagation.

C2 The effect of callbacks should be accounted for. Callbacks are functions in app code that may be invoked by the framework code. Since framework code cannot be instrumented, we cannot do taint propagation when callbacks are invoked. We propose a technique which uses over-tainting to avoid false negatives.

C3 In the Java language model, objects follow reference semantics, so we must have a way to taint the locations referenced. Furthermore, objects are deallocated automatically by garbage collection, so our taint-tracking data structures should not interfere with garbage collection.

As noted above, there are trade-offs between system modification and detection accuracy. However, we note that even though we resort to over-tainting to solve some of the above challenges, our results demonstrate that a carefully conceived design may still have a low false positive rate in practice. We discuss our solutions in detail in the next section.

3 Uranine Design

Uranine offers a general framework for instrumenting applications statically and for providing information flow tracking, which may be used in a number of applications, including tracking privacy leaks and hardening applications against vulnerabilities. Figure 3 depicts the architecture of Uranine. When an app is given to Uranine, the app code is first converted to a custom intermediate representation (IR) that can be instrumented for taint propagation to happen at runtime. The instrumented IR is then converted back to bytecode and a new app is prepared. Since the framework code cannot be instrumented, we approximate the effects of framework code through a few general but customizable summarization rules. The rest of this section first describes our techniques for taint storage/propagation and the instrumentation details. The latter part of the section then describes our static analysis.

Fig. 3. Instrumentation flow in Uranine

3.1 Taint Storage and Propagation

The techniques for taint storage and propagation influence the accuracy and runtime performance of privacy leakage detection. Our techniques focus on providing privacy leakage detection without false negatives under the constraint that the platform not be modified. Much of the design for taint tracking here is fairly routine and may be found in previous work [4,13,30]. We describe the routine or obvious aspects very briefly and then discuss in detail the specific challenges and corresponding solutions in our work.

Each entity that may be tainted is associated with a taint tag, which identifies what kind of private information may be carried by the entity. In the Uranine model, taints are stored and propagated for local variables (i.e. method registers), fields, method parameters/returns, and objects. Different bytecode instructions handle different storage types (i.e. local variables, fields, etc.) and accordingly have different taint propagation rules. Additionally, in a complete system, IPC (inter-process communication) taints and file taints may be handled at a coarser granularity. For IPC, the entire message carries the same taint. Similarly, an entire file is assigned a single taint tag. In our design, tracking IPC and file taints requires communication with an on-phone Uranine app, which keeps track of all file taints and IPC taints from instrumented applications. This paper focuses on taint tracking within Java code (more specifically, Dalvik bytecode) and further discussion on IPC and file taints is out of the scope of this paper.

We next describe the taint propagation rules for the different situations. We begin our discussion by assuming that we can instrument all the code (including the framework) and then introduce changes that would be required to leave the framework code intact.

Method-Local Registers. For each register that may possibly be tainted, we introduce a shadow register that stores the taint for this register. Any move operations simply also move the shadow registers. The same also happens for unary operations, while for binary operations, we combine the taints of the operands, assigning this to the shadow register of the result. Instructions assigning constants or new object instances cause the taint of the registers to be zeroed.

Heap Objects. Heap objects include class objects containing fields, and arrays. For each field that may possibly be tainted, we insert an additional shadow taint field in the corresponding class. The load and store instructions for instance fields and static fields are instrumented to assign to or load from these taint fields to the local registers. We note that we may not insert additional fields into framework classes. In this case, we taint the entire object. How this is done and the effects of this will be discussed shortly.

In the case of arrays, each array is associated with only a single taint tag. If anything tainted is inserted into an array, the entire array becomes tainted. This policy is used for efficiency reasons, and has been also adopted by other works such as TaintDroid. We also support index-based tainting so that if there is an `array-get` (i.e. a load operation) with a tainted index, the retrieved value is tainted. We will discuss shortly how we associate taint with Array objects.

Method Parameters and Returns. Methods may be called with tainted parameters. In this case, we need to pass on the tainted information from the caller to the callee. We take a straightforward approach to achieve this—for each method parameter that may be tainted, we add an additional shadow parameter that carries the taint of the parameter. These shadow parameters may then convey the tainted information to the local registers. Method returns are trickier. Since we can return only one value, we instead introduce an additional parameter to carry the taint of the return value. In Java, we have call-by-value semantics only, so that making assignments to the parameter inside the callee will not be visible to the caller. We therefore pass an object as the parameter, which is intended to wrap the return taint. The caller can then use this object to see the return taint set by the callee.

Our next part of discussion relates to specific challenges discussed in Section 2 and mostly relates to the requirement of not changing the framework code.

Calls into the Framework (Challenge C1). Whereas the application code may be instrumented for taint propagation, we may only approximate the effects of calls into the framework code on taint propagation. We use a worst-case taint policy to propagate taints in this case:

- Static methods. For static methods with void return, we combine the taints of all the parameters and assign this to all the parameter taints. For static methods with non-void returns, the taints of all the parameters are combined and assigned to the taint of the register holding the return value.
- Non-static methods. Non-static methods often modify the receiver object (the object on which the method is invoked) in some way. Therefore, we combine the taints of all the non-receiver parameters; apart from its original taint, the receiver object is now additionally tainted with this combined taint. In case the method returns a value, the return taint is defined as the receiver taint.

Note that these rules are not enough to summarize the effects of framework code. Non-static methods often have arguments that are stored into some field of the receiver. Consider the following piece of code.

```
1   List list = new ArrayList();
2   StringBuffer sb = new StringBuffer();
3   list.add(sb);
4   sb.append(taintedString);
5   String ret = list.toString();
```

In this case, `sb` and `list` are untainted until line 4. Thereafter, `sb` is tainted and `ret` should be tainted because it will include the contents of `taintedString`. Our general solution is that when an object becomes tainted, any objects containing that should also become tainted. For every object o_1 that may be contained in another object o_2, we maintain a set of the containing objects. If the taint of o_1 ever changes, we propagate this taint to all the containing objects. The set of containing objects is updated whenever we have a framework method call $o_2.meth(.., o_1, ..)$, where $meth$ is a method on o_2 and possibly belongs to the framework code. This is a worst case solution; in certain cases, such a method would not lead o_1 to be contained in o_2. The update operation may be recursive, so that an update to taint of o_2 may lead to updating the taint of the objects containing o_2, and so on. Objects may point to (contain) each other and hence there may be cycles; the update operation will however achieve a fixed point eventually and then terminate.

Handling Callbacks (Challenge C2). A callback is a piece of code that is passed onto another code to be executed later on. In Java, these are represented as methods of objects that are passed as arguments to some code, and the code may later invoke methods on that object. These objects typically implement an interface (or extend a known class) so that code is aware which methods are available on the object.

Android makes an extensive use of callbacks, which often serve as entry points to the application. Examples of such callbacks are `Activity.onCreate()` and

`View.onClick()` when overridden by subclasses. Apart from these, callbacks may be found at other places as well. For example, `toString()` and `equals()` methods on objects are callbacks. Identifying callback methods correctly may be done using class hierarchy analysis. A class hierarchy analysis analyzes the inheritance relationships between different classes and, based on these results, the overriding relationships between different methods. The class hierarchy analysis acts as a guide to the rest of the instrumentation by defining how different methods are dealt with during instrumentation.

Since callback methods override methods in the framework code, their method signatures may not be changed to accommodate shadow taint parameters and returns, lest the overriding relationships are disturbed. For example, consider the following class.

```
1  class DeviceIdKeeper {
2    private String id;
3    public DeviceIdKeeper(TelephonyManager m) {
4      id = m.getDeviceId();
5    }
6    public toString() { return id; }
7  }
```

The app code may call `toString()` on a `DeviceIdKeeper` instance. Since the return here may not be instrumented to propagate taint, we may lose the taint here. Furthermore, it is also possible that this method is called at some point by the framework code.

Our Solution. In order to not lose taint in this case, our solution is to lift the return taints of all callback methods to the receiver objects. That is, in the instrumented callback method, the return taint is propagated to the receiver object taint. In case a possible callback method is called by app code with tainted parameters, we taint the receiver object with the taint of the parameters and then inside the method definition taint the parameter registers with the taint of the receiver. Since heap objects can carry taints in our model, such over-tainting needs to be done only in case of parameters of primitive types. With the parameter and return tainting in place, we may use the techniques described for calls into the framework (Section3.1) to summarize the effect of this call. The key to note here is that the receiver object of the callback serves as a convenient taint carrier and thus taint is not lost in both the cases: when the callback is called by an app method, and when it is called by the framework.

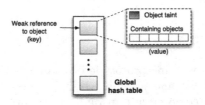

Fig. 4. Associating taint data-structures with objects

Taint Data-Structures (Challenge C3). From the above, it is quite clear that we need a way to taint objects. Java uses reference semantics to address objects. That is, object variables are pointers to object values on the heap and assignment for objects is only a pointer copy. Thus, we may have two types of tainting, either tainting the pointer, or tainting the object. Storing pointer taints is simple and has been discussed as storing taints for method-locals and fields. In addition, we also need to associate a set of containing objects with each object (Section 3.1).

Our Solution. In our solution, we use a global hashtable, in which the keys are objects and the values are records containing their taints and the set of containing objects. Any time the taints or containing objects needs to be accessed or updated, we access these records through the hashtable. Our hashtable uses weak references for keys to prevent interference with garbage collection. In Java, heap memory management is automatic; so we cannot know when an object gets garbage-collected. Weak references are references that do not prevent collection of objects and so are ideally suited for our applications. We further note that these data-structures should allow concurrent access as the instrumented app may have multiple threads running simultaneously. A schematic of our global hashtable is presented in Figure 4.

We considered but rejected an alternative method of keeping these data structures. With every object, we can possibly keep a shadow record, which is an object that stores the object taint and the set of containing objects in its fields. The instrumentation may then move this shadow record together with the main object through method-local moves, function calls and returns, and heap loads and stores. This technique however does not work well with the way we handle calls into the framework. Consider the following code fragment.

```
1    // list is a List
2    // obj is an object
3    list.add(obj);
4    obj2 = list.get(0);
```

In the above code, `obj` and `obj2` could be the same objects. However, since the loads/stores and moves inside the `List` methods are not visible to us, we cannot track the shadow record of `obj` there. The shadow record of `obj2` may at most depend on the record of `list`. Thus, there is no way to make the shadow records of `obj` and `obj2` the same, something that we achieve easily with our approach of weak hashtables.

4   Implementation

We have implemented a working prototype of Uranine. We use a library called `dexlib` [32] to disassemble and assemble Dalvik bytecode. The disassembled representation is converted to an intermediate representation (IR). In addition, we also use `apktool` [1] to disassemble the binary Android XML format (needed to discover entry points for static analysis) and other tools from the Android

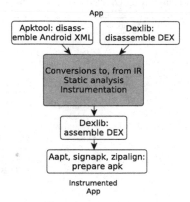

Fig. 5. Uranine implementation depicting the use of existing code (white boxes) and the features we implemented (gray, discussed in detail in Section 3).

SDK and elsewhere to prepare an instrumented app. Figure 5 provides these details graphically.

We choose to work on an IR very close to the bytecode, and do not require decompilation to either Java bytecode or the source code as some previous works have required. Since decompilation is not always successful, this approach improves the robustness of our system. The IR enables us to simplify the bytecode instruction set to a smaller instruction set containing only the details relevant to the rest of the analysis and instrumentation. Disregarding details like register widths, the Dalvik bytecode instructions[3] generally have a direct correspondence with the instructions in the IR. Similar instructions (such as all binary operations or all kinds of field accesses) are represented as variants of the same IR instruction. Range instructions (`invoke-*/range` and `filled-new-array-*/range`) access a variable number of registers; these are converted to the simple representations of `invoke-*` and `filled-new-array-*` instructions with a variable number of register arguments in the IR. Even though we use this IR for instrumentation, it is also suitable for performing static control flow and data flow analysis. In fact, the same IR is used as input to our class hierarchy analysis, the results of which then guide the instrumentation. The instrumented IR is then finally assembled back to Dalvik bytecode.

Most of our instrumentation code is written in Scala, with about a hundred lines of Python code. The taint-tracking data structures and related code is written in Java. The instrumentation adds a compiled version of this code to every app for runtime execution. The total Uranine codebase sizes to over 6,000 lines of code. We note that Scala allows for writing terse code; the equivalent Java or C++ code is usually two to three times as long.

---

[3] http://s.android.com/devices/tech/dalvik/dalvik-bytecode.html

Table 2. Accuracy evaluation of Uranine and comparison with TaintDroid

App	Uranine	TaintDroid	App	Uranine	TaintDroid
mobi.android-cloud.app.ptt.client	Contact	Contact	com.ama.lovetest.calculator	IMEI, Phone#	IMEI
com.enlightened.AndroidskyjewelsfreE	IMEI	None	com.flashlight.trefilm.coins	IMEI	IMEI
com.magmamobile.game.Slots	IMEI	None	com.silkenmermaid.gau.dldic	IMEI	IMEI
me.zed_0xff.android.alchemy	IMEI	None	com.gamevolution.MarbleMadnessPro	IMEI	IMEI
com.magmamobile.game.BubbleBlast2	IMEI	None	com.reverie.game.toiletpaper	IMEI	IMEI
com.rhs.wordhero	Loc	Loc	com.red.white.blue.free	IMEI	IMEI
com.rferl.almalence.staringcat	IMEI	IMEI	com.gameloft.android.ANMP.GloftGTFM	IMEI	IMEI
app.win.confor11	ICCID, IMEI, Phone#	None	com.alloright.trib	IMEI, Loc, Phone#	IMEI, Loc
com.anbgames.openthedoor.hoola2	IMEI	IMEI	com.euro2012.geekbeach.acquariusoft	IMEI	IMEI
com.aceviral.toptruckfree	IMEI	IMEI	com.fjj24512014.korea	IMEI	None
com.flirtalike.android	IMEI, ICCID	IMEI, ICCID	net.aaronsoft.poker.eva	IMEI	IMEI
com.keithe.lwp.aquarium	IMEI	IMEI	com.mobizi.scratchers	IMEI	None
com.androiminigsm.fscifree	Contact, IMEI	Contact, IMEI	sg.vinay.FourpicsOnewordcheatsanswers	IMEI, Phone#	None
mobi.jackd.android	Loc	Loc	com.electricpocket.ringo	Contact	Contact
com.topface.topface	IMEI	IMEI	com.keek	IMEI, ICCID	IMEI
com.pilotfishmediainc.happyfish	IMEI, Loc, Phone#	Loc	com.phantomefx.reeldeal	IMEI	IMEI

5   Evaluation

We evaluate Uranine on two aspects: accuracy and performance overhead. To perform accuracy evaluation, we configured Uranine to detect the leakage of location, phone identifiers (like IMEI and phone number), and contacts (address book). Our sinks include all APIs that send data to the network, write to the file system, or send SMS messages. We note that even though we restrict to a few relevant sources and sinks, we can easily extend the privacy leakage tracking by adding other private information sources and sinks as well.

Our app dataset consists of 1,490 apps randomly selected from Google Play. Apps are instrumented automatically and run with random inputs (fuzz testing) provided by the Android Monkey tool[4]. For understanding privacy leakage results, we also conducted manual tests for a smaller set of apps.

5.1   Accuracy

In this section we evaluate how Uranine performs in detecting privacy leaks. We use our dataset real-world applications from Google Play for the evaluation. We use TaintDroid results to compare with our results. Our methodology involves running Uranine-instrumented applications on a TaintDroid build, allowing us

---

[4] http://developer.android.com/tools/help/monkey.html

to generate both TaintDroid's and Uranine's results together in one run, and thus eliminating any differences that may arise because of random inputs or non-determinism in multiple runs.

Manual Tests. We conducted manual tests on a physical device (Samsung Nexus S) over a small random subset of apps. These results enable us to carefully study the differences between TaintDroid and Uranine. The results are depicted in Table 2. The results, where neither TaintDroid nor Uranine detected any leakage, are not shown in the table.

Our results show some disagreement with TaintDroid. We see that TaintDroid does not detect any phone number leaks that we detect; a look into TaintDroid code then revealed to us that TaintDroid has disabled tracking of phone numbers with the comment "causes overflow in logcat, disable for now" in source code. In all other cases of disagreement between Uranine and TaintDroid, we manually confirmed the correctness of Uranine. It turns out that in the cases where Uranine does detects an IMEI (or ICCID) leak while TaintDroid does not, there is some kind of hashing of the identifier involved, such as the calculation of MD5 or SHA1 digests. It appears that TaintDroid does not propagate taint across the functions that calculate these digests. This is also confirmed in AppsPlayground [26]. In conclusion, our results are generally consistent with TaintDroid. Any apparent inconsistencies result from implementation artifacts of taint tracking. It is worth emphasizing here that our contribution is not to show an improvement over other systems in terms of detecting more privacy leaks, but to do the detection without system modification.

Automatic Tests. We further conducted automatic, random testing on a bigger dataset of 1,490 apps. The tests were conducted on the Android emulator (provided with the Android SDK) running a TaintDroid image. Since the emulator does not provide most of the device identifiers (such as IMEI and phone number), we further added some code to our emulator image to provide real-looking identifiers on the respective APIs for accessing these identifiers. Because of these modifications, our emulator's TaintDroid can also detect phone number and IMSI leaks.

Our runs detected privacy leaks in a total of 360 apps; in the rest of the apps, no leak was detected either by TaintDroid or Uranine. The results for TaintDroid and Uranine differed for 177 apps. We have manually analyzed each of these cases, and have found that Uranine was accurate in most cases. Below, we detail our findings and bring out relevant insights.

For 92 apps where Uranine detected privacy leaks but TaintDroid did not— we confirmed that these were TaintDroid's false negatives. In all these cases, the apps leak the device identifiers after hashing (with, for example, MD5). In most cases, we were able to see the MD5 checksum of the device identifier being leaked (IMEI leaks were most frequent) in plaintext. Further, in other cases, these leaks were in ad libraries that are known to have the leaks flagged by Uranine. For example, our analysis of an older version of the Admob library shows that it leaks the MD5 of a string derived from the phone's IMEI number.

Uranine's detection of leakage in 4 apps is likely to be a false positive. In two apps, our logs reveal Uranine flags leakage when an empty string is being written to a file. In the other two cases, Uranine detects IMEI leakages on writing strings that look like base64 codes. Decoding those codes however does not reveal the IMEI number nor anything that looks like a hash of that. False positives are actually expected in Uranine, due to overtainting as part of our design. Considering this, 0.2% false positives are insignificant.

Table 3. Leaks detected in automatic tests

Leak type	Apps leaking	Leak type	Apps leaking
IMEI	310	IMSI	18
ICCID	16	Phone #	79
Location	107	Contacts	5

There was another set of 13 apps where Uranine flagged leakage but Taint-Droid did not. In all these cases, we can see strings looking like MD5 or SHA hashes being leaked, but were unable to derive them from known identifiers (perhaps they were mixed with some salt before hashing). Though we could not classify these cases, we believe them to be TaintDroid false negatives. Finally, we detected 14 cases that were false negatives for Uranine—we could however correct them by adding additional sinks that we missed earlier.

In summary, we found Uranine to be fairly accurate in detecting privacy leaks with few errors. Table 3 shows the privacy leaks detected by Uranine.

5.2   Performance

Measuring the runtime overhead of applications instrumented by Uranine is not trivial. First, there are no popular macrobenchmarks for Android. The DaCapo benchmarks [6], which are popular Java benchmarks, are not easily ported to Android (due to their use of Java-specific libraries and GUI) and moreover, may also differ from real-world application workloads on Android. Second, conventional microbenchmark suites for evaluating virtual machine performance may also give skewed results as we are instrumenting applications here rather than the virtual machine. A lot of the code for real applications runs in the framework, is not instrumented, and runs without overhead—a microbenchmark will thus misrepresent this situation.

We measure performance overhead using real-world Android applications. However, most applications are GUI-intensive and interactive in nature. Thus, one cannot simply run the benchmark application and obtain the results. We devise our own methodology of evaluating performance of Android applications in response to certain events. For our benchmarks, we select a total of six events from three very popular applications: BBC News, Last.fm (a music application with social networking features), and the stock Android application for managing contacts. For each application, we evaluate the time to launch the main activity of the application and the time to complete a click of a pre-selected feature on the application. The time to launch the main activity is as reported by the ActivityManager (part of the Android middleware). The time to complete a click is measured by instrumenting the click handler function to report the interval from its beginning to the point it returns.

Table 4. Macrobenchmark performance. The reported times (Original/Instrumented columns) are medians over five independent runs.

Benchmark	Event	Original (ms)	Instrumented (ms)	Overhead
BBC News (version 2.5.2 WW)	Launch	953	1418	49%
BBC News (version 2.5.2 WW)	Click ("Live BBC World Service")	450	434	-
Last.fm (version 1.9.9.2)	Launch	523	567	10%
Last.fm (version 1.9.9.2)	Click ("Sign up")	132	140	6%
Contacts (from AOSP 4.0.4)	Launch	580	645	11%
Contacts (from AOSP 4.0.4)	Click ("Done" after contact creation)	23	59	156%

Table 4 presents the comparison of the original applications and those instrumented for information flow-tracking. As can be seen from the table performance overhead is usually low, almost always within 50% and often around 10%. We attribute this to the fact that the Android framework does most of the heavy-lifting during runtime, from creating the UI to managing the data structures and data stores. Thus, even though we may expect a huge performance overhead because each instruction is instrumented, real-world application overhead appears quite low in comparison. Anecdotally, in our runs, we have seen noticeable performance overheads, but the overheads have never been intolerable. Furthermore, the performance of Uranine compares favorably with the reported performance of TaintDroid (15-30% overhead) and Phosphor (50% overhead).

Finally, we would like to reiterate that our approach is highly amenable to static analysis. We expect that in production, a tool such as Uranine will be guided by a static analysis, which will be able to identify that most paths cannot propagate the relevant information and thus do not need instrumentation.

6   Discussion

6.1   Static Analysis and Optimizations

We believe that Uranine has great potential for optimizations so that runtime overhead can be minimized. First, it is possible to tune the instrumentation, and perform constant propagation passes to reduce the instrumentation overhead. Second and more importantly, it is possible to perform a static information flow analysis that identifies the paths along which the relevant information flow could take place. Such paths are usually small in number, and if Uranine instruments those paths only, applications may run with negligible overhead. In fact, the implementation of Uranine already includes hooks to attach a static analysis, which can then guide the instrumentation. We have performed preliminary studies testing the use of static analysis to guide the instrumentation and a complete study is part of future work. Note that the use of static analysis does not obviate the need for a dynamic analysis system (Section 2.2).

We note that the opportunity for static analysis is present in our approach only, involving no platform modification. Previous works such as Phosphor [4] modify the platform libraries to track information flow and will therefore not benefit much from optimizing instrumentation by static analysis.

6.2 Limitations

We discuss here our limitations and avenues of future work. While Uranine is good for detecting privacy leaks in legitimate applications, a truly malicious app may be able to evade the system through some of these limitations.

Implicit Flows. A fundamental limitation of dynamic taint tracking is the inability to track implicit information flows via control flow [30]. Our work shares this limitation. Static analysis may be used to track control flow. However, this leads to the risk of severe over-tainting. Research is underway to make implicit flow tracking practical [19].

Native Code. We currently do not support taint tracking through native code, which some Android applications include in addition to bytecode. Previous works such as Phosphor and TaintDroid, as well as static analysis works on Android which only analyze bytecodes, all have this limitation.

Dynamic Aspects of Java. As a limitation of static instrumentation, the dynamic aspects of JVM, such as reflection and dynamic class loading (using `DexClassLoader` or similar features in Android) do not cleanly fit in. These may however be supported by our approach in the future. We may apply worst-case tainting for all method calls made by reflection as we do for other methods. Furthermore, we can instrument calls by reflection and alert the user if they do not pass certain security policies (such as restricting reflective calls to only certain APIs in the Android platform). Code loaded by dynamic class loading may also not be available during static instrumentation. In a deployment, it may be possible to prompt the user to allow re-analysis whenever dynamic code loading is detected, so that an instrumented version of the code being loaded can be created.

Incorrect Summarization. Policy-based summarization of framework code, as used in our work, not only has the problem of over-tainting, but could also result in under-tainting of data passing through APIs that do not fit within those policies. For example, some classes may update a global state when their methods are called. We are not aware of such a situation but such cases could be used to bypass the system. Manual summarization of known cases is obviously one solution. Automatic method summarization is an open research problem in static analysis, and any progress there will benefit our cause as well.

7   Related Work

Information Flow Tracking. The closest to our work are TaintDroid [13] and Phosphor [4]. The key advantage of our technique is that we do not require modification of the Android platform as these do.

Dynamic taint analysis has been employed in a variety of applications from vulnerability detection and preventing software attacks [24,25,33] and malware analysis [31,37] to preventing privacy exposures [10,41]. We present a general technique for taint tracking in this paper without modifying the Android platform. Our technique may be used for the above applications, especially when there is a constraint to run applications on an unmodified platform. There are also works doing taint tracking by bytecode instrumentation. Haldar et al. [18] implement taint tracking by instrumenting the Java String class. Chandra and Franz [8] instrument the Java bytecode for taint tracking. These works share the same limitation of Phosphor discussed earlier.

There are also a number of related works using static analysis. PiOS [11] uses it to detect privacy leaks on iOS apps. Enck et al. [14] and Gibler et al. [16] decompile Dalvik to Java bytecode and perform static analysis on that using existing tools for Java. FlowDroid [2] also converts Dalvik back to Java byte-code and builds on top of Soot[5] while adding in Android-specific requirements to the analysis. Chex converts Dalvik bytecode to the WALA[6] IR and then employs WALA for static analysis [21]. Cao et al. [7] automatically collected implicit control flow transitions through the Android framework code to assist static analysis tools. As discussed earlier, there are limitations of static analysis over real-time dynamic analysis. Xia et al. [34] eliminate some limitations by performing offline partial executions of apps after static analysis. However, they are still unable to handle situations with external input from users or servers, which is quite common.

Static Instrumentation. Static instrumentation has been used earlier for Android applications [9,35]. These works have focused on API interposition rather than tracking information flow; the latter is more challenging because of the need to instrument many instructions and to encode the semantics of information-flow tracking. AppSealer [38] statically instruments Android applications to repair component hijacking vulnerabilities. Capper [39] is a follow-up work that detects privacy leakages without platform modification. Both these works are similar to Uranine; however, their taint tracking will have false negatives: they try to address C1 but do not solve it adequately and do not even discuss C2 and C3. Instrumentation has been used in other applications as well, some of which even use static analysis to optimize it. Saxena et al. use static analysis to make their binary instrumentation efficient [28]. Xu et al. [36] instrument C sources for taint tracking and further optimize it using static analysis.

Other Related Work in Mobile Device Security. Kirin [12] defines security policies based on Android permissions. A number of works additionally prevent

---

[5] http://www.sable.mcgill.ca/soot/
[6] http://wala.sourceforge.net

access of private information or supply fake data to apps [5,23,40]. The above works enable access control while we provide information flow control. Another line of works [3,20] investigates user perceptions as related to mobile privacy. They conclude that users are often not aware of privacy leakages, and that proper awareness and usable controls can mitigate users' concerns about privacy. Rosen et al. [27] perform static analysis of Android applications and provide end-users with information about privacy-related behaviors of these applications. Our tool could easily supplement such works by providing real-time insights about the behaviors of these applications to the users. Finally, researchers have developed proof-of-concept malware utilizing side channels that cannot be detected by a traditional information-flow analysis such as ours [29].

8   Conclusion

This paper describes Uranine, a framework for dynamic privacy-leakage detection in Android applications without modifying the Android platform. To achieve this, Uranine statically instruments Android apps only, and does not need support for information flow tracking from the platform. We present a design and implementation of Uranine and evaluate its performance and accuracy. Our results show that Uranine provides good accuracy and incurs acceptable performance overhead compared to other approaches.

Acknowledgements. We thank our reviewers for their valuable comments. We also thank Peng Xu and Weiwu Zhu, who helped in the system implementation and evaluation. This paper was made possible by NPRP grant 6-1014-2-414 from the Qatar National Research Fund (a member of Qatar Foundation). The statements made herein are solely the responsibility of the authors.

References

1. Apktool. Android-apktool: A tool for reengineering Android apk files. http://code.google.com/p/android-apktool/
2. Arzt, S., Rasthofer, S., Fritz, C., Bodden, E., Bartel, A., Klein, J., Le Traon, Y., Octeau, D., McDaniel, P.: Flowdroid: precise context, flow, field, object-sensitive and lifecycle-aware taint analysis for android apps. In: ACM PLDI (2014)
3. Balebako, R., Jung, J., Lu, W., Cranor, L.F., Nguyen, C.: Little brothers watching you: raising awareness of data leaks on smartphones. In: Proceedings of the Ninth Symposium on Usable Privacy and Security, p. 12. ACM (2013)
4. Bell, J., Kaiser, G.E.: Phosphor: illuminating dynamic data flow in the jvm. In: OOPSLA (2014)
5. Beresford, A., Rice, A., Skehin, N., Sohan, R.: Mockdroid: trading privacy for application functionality on smartphones. In: HotMobile (2011)
6. Blackburn, S.M., Garner, R., Hoffmann, C., Khang, A.M., McKinley, K.S., Bentzur, R., Diwan, A., Feinberg, D. Frampton, S.Z., Guyer, et al. :The dacapo benchmarks: Java benchmarking development and analysis. In: ACM Sigplan Notices, vol. 41, pp. 169–190. ACM (2006)

7. Cao, Y., Fratantonio, Y., Bianchi, A., Egele, M., Kruegel, C., Vigna, G., Chen, Y.: Edgeminer: automatically detecting implicit control flow transitions through the android framework. In: Proceedings of the ISOC Network and Distributed System Security Symposium (NDSS) (2015)
8. Chandra, D., Franz, M.: Fine-grained information flow analysis and enforcement in a java virtual machine. In: ACSAC (2007)
9. Davis, B., Chen, H.: Retroskeleton: retrofitting android apps. In: Mobisys (2013)
10. Egele, M., Kruegel, C., Kirda, E., Yin, H., Song, D.: Dynamic spyware analysis. In: Usenix ATC (2007)
11. Egele, M., Kruegel, C., Kirda, E., Vigna, G.: Pios: detecting privacy leaks in ios applications. In: NDSS (2011)
12. Enck, W., Ongtang, M., McDaniel, P.: On lightweight mobile phone application certification. In: ACSAC (2009)
13. Enck, W., Gilbert, P., Chun, B., Cox, L., Jung, J., McDaniel, P., Sheth, A.: Taintdroid: an information-flow tracking system for realtime privacy monitoring on smartphones. In: OSDI (2010)
14. Enck, W., Octeau, D., McDaniel, P., Chaudhuri, S.: A study of android application security. In: USENIX Security (2011)
15. Fuchs, A., Chaudhuri, A., Foster, J.: Scandroid: Automated security certification of android applications. Manuscript, Univ. of Maryland (2009). http://www.cs.umd.edu/~avik/projects/scandroidascaa
16. Gibler, C., Crussell, J., Erickson, J., Chen, H.: Androidleaks: automatically detecting potential privacy leaks in android applications on a large scale. In: Katzenbeisser, S., Weippl, E., Camp, L.J., Volkamer, M., Reiter, M., Zhang, X. (eds.) Trust 2012. LNCS, vol. 7344, pp. 291–307. Springer, Heidelberg (2012)
17. Good. Mobile app containerization. http://www1.good.com/secure-mobility-solution/mobile-application-containerization
18. Haldar, V., Chandra, D., Franz, M.: Dynamic taint propagation for java. In: 21st Annual Computer Security Applications Conference (ACSAC). IEEE (2005)
19. Kang, M., McCamant, S., Poosankam, P., Song, D.: Dta++: dynamic taint analysis with targeted control-flow propagation. In: Proc. of NDSS (2011)
20. Lin, J., Amini, S., Hong, J.I., Sadeh, N., Lindqvist, J., Zhang, J.: Expectation and purpose: understanding users' mental models of mobile app privacy through crowd-sourcing. In: Proceedings of the 2012 ACM Conference on Ubiquitous Computing, pp. 501–510. ACM (2012)
21. Lu, L., Li, Z., Wu, Z., Lee, W., Jiang, G.: CHEX: statically vetting android apps for component hijacking vulnerabilities. In: ACM CCS (2012)
22. MobileIron. Appconnect. http://www.mobileiron.com/en/products/appconnect
23. Nauman, M., Khan, S., Zhang, X.: Apex: extending android permission model and enforcement with user-defined runtime constraints. In: ASIACCS (2010)
24. Newsome, J., Song, D.: Dynamic taint analysis for automatic detection, analysis, and signature generation of exploits on commodity software. In: NDSS (2005)
25. Qin, F., Wang, C., Li, Z., Kim, H., Zhou, Y., Wu, Y.: Lift: a low-overhead practical information flow tracking system for detecting security attacks. In: IEEE MICRO (2006)
26. Rastogi, V., Chen, Y., Enck, W.: AppsPlayground: automatic security analysis of smartphone applications. In: Proceedings of ACM CODASPY (2013)

27. Rosen, S., Qian, Z., Mao, Z.M.: Appprofiler: a flexible method of exposing privacy-related behavior in android applications to end users. In: Proceedings of the Third ACM Conference on Data and Application Security and Privacy, pp. 221–232. ACM (2013)
28. Saxena, P., Sekar, R., Puranik, V.: Efficient fine-grained binary instrumentation-with applications to taint-tracking. In: IEEE/ACM CGO (2008)
29. Schlegel, R., Zhang, K., Zhou, X.-Y., Intwala, M., Kapadia, A., Wang, X.: Soundcomber: a stealthy and context-aware sound trojan for smartphones. In: NDSS, vol. 11, pp. 17–33 (2011)
30. Schwartz, E., Avgerinos, T., Brumley, D.: All you ever wanted to know about dynamic taint analysis and forward symbolic execution (but might have been afraid to ask). In: IEEE SP (2010)
31. Sharif, M., Lanzi, A., Giffin, J., Lee, W.: Automatic reverse engineering of malware emulators. In: 2009 30th IEEE Symposium on Security and Privacy (2009)
32. smali. Smali: An assembler/disassembler for Android's dex format. http://code.google.com/p/smali/
33. Suh, G., Lee, J., Zhang, D., Devadas, S.: Secure program execution via dynamic information flow tracking. In: ACM SIGPLAN Notices, vol. 39, pp. 85–96 (2004)
34. Xia, M., Gong, L., Lyu, Y., Qi, Z., Liu, X.: Effective real-time android application auditing. In: IEEE S&P (2015)
35. Xu, R., Saïdi, H., Anderson, R.: Aurasium: practical policy enforcement for android applications. In: Proceedings of the 21st USENIX conference on Security (2012)
36. Xu, W., Bhatkar, S., Sekar, R.: Taint-enhanced policy enforcement: a practical approach to defeat a wide range of attacks. In: USENIX Security (2006)
37. Yin, H., Song, D., Egele, M., Kruegel, C., Kirda, E.: Panorama: capturing system-wide information flow for malware detection and analysis. In: ACM CCS (2007)
38. Zhang, M., Yin, H.: Appsealer: automatic generation of vulnerability-specific patches for preventing component hijacking attacks in android applications. In: NDSS (2014)
39. Zhang, M., Yin, H.: Efficient, context-aware privacy leakage confinement for android applications without firmware modding. In: ASIACCS (2014)
40. Zhou, Y., Zhang, X., Jiang, X., Freeh, V.W.: Taming information-stealing smartphone applications (on android). In: McCune, J.M., Balacheff, B., Perrig, A., Sadeghi, A.-R., Sasse, A., Beres, Y. (eds.) Trust 2011. LNCS, vol. 6740, pp. 93–107. Springer, Heidelberg (2011)
41. Zhu, D., Jung, J., Song, D., Kohno, T., Wetherall, D.: Tainteraser: protecting sensitive data leaks using application-level taint tracking. ACM SIGOPS Operating Systems Review **45**(1), 142–154 (2011)

Practicality of Using Side-Channel Analysis for Software Integrity Checking of Embedded Systems

Hong Liu, Hongmin Li, and Eugene Y. Vasserman[(✉)]

Department of Computing and Information Sciences,
Kansas State University, Manhattan, KS 66506, USA
{hongl,hongminli,eyv}@ksu.edu

Abstract. We explore practicality of using power consumption as a non-destructive non-interrupting method to check integrity of software in a microcontroller. We explore whether or not instructions can lead to consistently distinguishable side-channel information, and if so, how the side-channel characteristics differ. Our experiments show that data dependencies rather than instruction operation dependencies are dominant, and can be utilized to provide practical side-channel-based methods for software integrity checking. For a subset of the instruction set, we further show that the discovered data dependencies can guarantee transformation of a given input into a unique output, so that any tampering with the program by a side-channel-aware attacker can either be detected from power measurements, or lead to the same unique set of input and output.

Keywords: Side-channels · Power consumption · Software integrity · Security · Embedded systems

1 Introduction

Checking software integrity is a fundamental problem of system security. Given a device under test (DUT), a verifier tries to determines whether it runs the desired code or not. Developers traditionally focus on realizing functionality, while ignoring the fact that an attacker can change the behavior of the DUT by overwriting its program and/or data remotely [15,17,18,23] or locally [7,11,13,25].

Many approaches have been proposed to try to enforce that a device runs the original code. The approaches can be classified by where the verifier resides. An *internal* approach resides in the same device with the target software. Hypervisors [30,45], mandatory access control [1,42], and control flow integrity [14,19], are internal software-based approaches that aim to prevent "anomalous behavior" of programs that share the same hardware with the verifier. Watchdog coprocessors [33,38] and TPM [4,9] are internal hardware-based approaches that examine hardware status such as "signatures" of code that appear on buses or statistics of software and firmware to prevent deviations from the original design.

© Institute for Computer Sciences, Social Informatics and Telecommunications Engineering 2015
B. Thuraisingham et al. (Eds.): SecureComm 2015, LNICST 164, pp. 277–293, 2015.
DOI: 10.1007/978-3-319-28865-9_15

The verifier can also be outside of the DUT, leading to *external* verification. Software attestation [27,34,44] and remote attestation [21] are approaches in which a verifier external to the DUT asks the DUT to provide evidence of integrity from time to time and checks it against prior knowledge of hardware and software configuration and/or shared secrets.

Another promising external approach is to check evidence of integrity from side-channels. Unlike attestation, which communicates with the DUT explicitly and actively, this approach tries to identify tampering by analyzing passive information leakage from the DUT, such as timing of network traffic, power consumption, electromagnetic (EM) emissions, light emissions, vibrations, etc. [6,24,35–37]. These channels are "side" because they are unavoidable byproducts of implementing the desired functionality on a physical device. A side-channel approach has advantages over other approaches in that

1. It does not interfere with the normal execution of the DUT – the DUT does not even know about the existence of the verifier;
2. since the DUT does not have a verifier implemented, an attacker who successfully penetrates into the DUT still does not know about the existence or the implementation of the verifier;
3. verification instrumentation and algorithms can be easily updated;
4. it works with legacy devices that cannot implement modern integrity checking techniques;
5. it works with attacks against CAD tools which may tamper the debugging and programming traffic and therefore fail all internal protection mechanisms.

Previous research has been successful in using side-channels to check IC integrity [6,24,35]. By comparing side-channel information of the DUT to that of the "golden samples", researchers are able to find minimal differences that indicate tampering of the design. A great number of embedded systems, however, are based on general-purpose microcontrollers/microprocessors. Detailed hardware information about the microcontrollers (μCs) are in general not accessible to system developers. It is therefore hard to obtain "golden samples" for side-channel analysis (SCA).

Using side-channel information for integrity checking of μCs without detailed design information poses a great challenge. Given a set of samples of side-channel emissions, we need to extract instruction-level information about the running device. The sample is an aggregation of power consumption cost by reading memory, executing instructions, accessing peripherals, and noise. In the worst case the tampered code only gets executed once during sampling. The verifier therefore does not have the advantage of reducing noise in samples by averaging thousands of execution traces, as in DPA [26,28].

Previous attempts on instruction-level SCA have been focused on reverse engineering of instruction operations [16,20,39] by using either the power consumption or the EM side-channel, and have achieved different degrees of success. One recent work [31] proposed using instruction-level power consumption SCA for software integrity checking, yet was found not repeatable on a different (but simpler) μC [39].

Current trends in SCA demand more and more advanced acquisition equipment such as broadband high-sensitivity oscilloscopes, Picosecond Imaging Circuit Analysis [37], micro magnetic-field probes [40], etc. Occasions that need SCA-based checking for legacy or low-cost μCs are not always able to afford such equipment. Another major obstacle is noise both from the ambient environment and from the DUT. As shown by research on breaking cryptographic embedded systems [5], power consumption is mainly due to bus traffic as opposed to the smaller currents within a CPU.

In this work, we propose practical methods and results for power-based software integrity checking. Our contributions are:

– We point out pitfalls in previous work that an attacker will always try to replace instructions with those that have similar side-channel characteristics, and thus turns any ($< 100\%$) recognition rate on random code into near-0 on crafted code.
– We propose a systematic approach for SCA profiling which enables us to design experiments and analyze the effects of runtime status on power consumption efficiently.
– We show mechanisms that determine side-channel characteristics. The results have direct implications on using simple (versus differential) SCA for software integrity checking of embedded systems in practice.
– For a subset of the instruction set, we show that the data dependencies we have discovered are enough to guarantee unique transformations of input and output. So, the verifier can ensure that even if the program is altered by a side-channel-aware attacker, as long as the side-channel measurements are the same, the program still computes the same value.

2   Related Work and Pitfalls

Research on SCA is mostly focused on breaking cryptographic hardware, including general-propose μCs, FPGAs, and ASICs. The goal is to extract secret keys by analyzing several thousands of executions of cryptographic routines [22,26,28,35]. Cryptographic routines are in general publicly available. In our case, in contrast, only a single trace of side-channel emission is available, and we also need to derive runtime instructions from side-channel measurements. Techniques in breaking cryptographic hardware are therefore not directly applicable to SCA for software integrity checking.

SCA for IC integrity relies on full knowledge of the IC design. By scanning emissions of the IC for enough time, it is possible to detect untriggered trojan circuits [6,24,36,37]. For software-integrity checking of μCs, detailed knowledge of the IC design is not available. It is therefore not possible either to use simulation tools or to infer power consumption from the architecture design.

At the system level, SCA has been used to provide preliminary detection of abnormal behaviors such as malware and anomalous reboots. Yang et al. [43]

used external power measurements to distinguish between several categories of failures in remote high-end sensing systems. WattsUpDoc [12] applies machine learning to detect untargeted malware by monitoring system-wide AC (wall outlet) power consumption of medical devices and SCADA systems that run variants of the Windows operating system. WattsUpDoc specifically excludes malware that is designed to evade power analysis. While an aggressive malware may be visible at the system level through abnormal power consumption (e.g., by draining too much energy), a stealthy malware will hide itself in the noise introduced from multiple components that are running in parallel in a big system. Real malware detection requires instruction-level integrity checking techniques.

Previous work on instruction-level SCA uses random data input, PCA+LDA and template analysis [16,20,31,39]. In particular, [39] claims a relevant recognition rate of 96.24% on test data and 87.69% on real code by using multi-position localized EM emissions and semi-invasive access to the chip. In [31], a 100% classification rate was reported by using power measurements, However, neither [39] nor us succeeded in repeating the authors' results on a different (but simpler) μC.

There are two major shortcomings in all of the previous work. First, previous work has been focused on recovering the instruction operations. Data, including operands and values of registers are regarded as noise. Operands and other runtime status such as PC are therefore not known.

The more significant drawback of previous research, however, is that little is known about the reason for failure of recognition. Given any non-100% average recognition rate, an attacker will naturally try to write malware utilizing only the misclassified instructions to any extent possible, and therefore turns a high recognition rate on random code into 0 on crafted code, in a way similar to [29]. This problem is fatal both for reverse engineering and for software integrity checking. It is more demanding to discover whether instructions can lead to distinguishable side-channel information or not and, if so, how the side-channel characteristics differ.

3   A Systematic Approach for Instruction-level Side-channel Analysis

We use PIC16F687 as our DUT, because most previous research in this area has been performed on this IC [16,20,31,39]. We assume that the attacker is able to modify the software of the DUT, for instance by reprogramming the device or inserting trojans into the CAD software. The attacker is able to profile the side-channel emissions of the DUT and to modify the software in a fashion that minimizes side-channel deviations. The attacker is however unable to modify the hardware, including the IC design and the PCB on which the DUT is mounted.

PIC16F687 is a 8-bit RISC μC in Harvard architecture. It has a 14-bit program bus, which is connected to the program flash, and a 8-bit data bus, which is connected to RAM, EEPROM, PORTs, ADC, etc. The instruction set has 35 operations, all executed in single instruction cycle, except branches. The processor has a two-stage pipeline, therefore unconditional and conditional branches

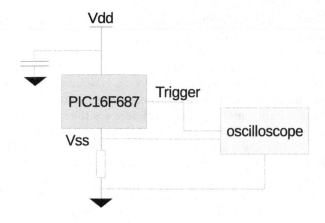

Fig. 1. Measurement setup

take two instruction cycles if a branch is taken. Each instruction execution is overlapped with the next instruction fetch. The working register is one of the two operands of the ALU. There is a 128-byte register file including general purpose registers and special function registers (SFRs).

Because there are so many factors that may affect power consumption, an ad hoc experiment will soon become unmanageable. We develop a systematic approach for instruction-level side-channel analysis:

- Build semantic models of the instruction set, using known architecture information.
- Generate random testing code that is long enough to execute each instruction operation many times.
- Calculate runtime status according to semantic models for each instruction.
- Cross-validate power consumption and the semantic models with respect to instruction operations and runtime status.

We use random instructions rather than real code in order to evenly sample the code space, avoiding overfitting to any specific code base. Potential high-order side-channel characteristics that exist only among some particular instruction pairs/blocks will be averaged out when using random code. While we may lose some information for particular instruction blocks, we retain side-channel properties that are applicable to arbitrary programs. It is therefore not necessary to reanalyze every new piece of software made to run on the target IC, as we are able to develop general protection mechanisms. See Section 5 for additional details.

Semantic models. Building semantic models of an instruction set includes elaborating the detailed operations, such as fetch, decode, and data read/write, that happen during an instruction execution. Because the known architecture information is not complete, our semantic models are only assumptions, which can be cross-validated with the side-channel measurements. This has numerous benefits. First, this is necessary for predicting branches during code generation. Second, analyzing the measurements with respect to the runtime status reveals effects of data versus those of processing. Third, waveforms can also be checked against the predicted runtime status in order to guarantee that the chip functions correctly. This is necessary because using a large shunt resistor (see below), introduces common impedance coupling and narrows the voltage drops between V_{DD} and V_{SS}, whereas a large enough shunt resistor eliminates amplification circuits which may introduce additional noise. Sanity checking of the waveform against the predicted status helps in choosing the right resistor value besides the bandwidth consideration.

Based on the limited architecture information described in the PIC16F687 datasheet [2,3], we deduce that potential data that may appear on buses, and therefore are likely to cause the major power consumption, include values of the program counter (PC), the operands and opcode of instructions, the working register, the selected file register, and the STATUS SFR. Then we generate random code traces and calculate bus traffic from instruction semantics.

Power traces are collected following the standard setup for power-based SCA, as shown in Figure 1. The ground pin of the DUT is connected to a 82Ω shunt resistor. Voltage drop across the shunt resistor is captured by the PicoScope 5444B 200MHz USB oscilloscope. The ground pin, instead of the power supply pin, is used due to limitations of the oscilloscope. To mitigate the low-pass filtering effects of the chip itself [28,32], we set the frequency to 125 kHz. The sample rate is 31.3 MS/s. Higher frequency settings suffers more from the low-pass filtering effects and do not work with the oscilloscope. The setup is low-cost and reflects a worse-case scenario from the verifier's perspectives.

To build side-channel models, the verifier needs to have access to the device. For integrity checking, it is reasonable to assume that the verifier has access to the exact DUT, thus to ignore small variations among chips of the same device model resulted from the process technology. In all the following experiments, tests are performed on the same device that is used to build the models.

3.1   Recognizing Operations Versus Recognizing Execution Instances

For our 2K-memory μC, we generate 1435 instructions, which are randomly selected from 29 instruction operations (excluding CALL, RETFIE, RETLW, RETURN, SLEEP, and CLRWDT). Operands are also random.[1] CALL, RETFIE, RETLW, and RETURN are manually inserted in multiple places so that the program can execute normally. 1020 power traces are collected, among which 50% are used for modeling and 50% are used for testing. A typical waveform is shown in Figure 2. PIC16F687 has an instruction cycle of four clock cycles, denoted as Q1 to Q4. The waveform exhibits sharp peaks at clock rising/falling edges, showing that

---

[1] To have enough samples per operation, file register access is limited to 12 general-purpose registers and the STATUS SFR.

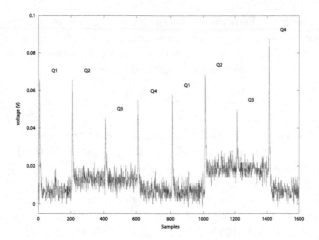

Fig. 2. Sample waveform of executing "MOVLW 0x69" and "ADDWF 0x40,F"

the low-pass effects are not prominent in our experiment setup. Samples are
time-aligned according to peak values.

We first build a model with respect to instruction operations, as in previous research [16,20,31,39]. Given a single trace of power samples of four clock
cycles, the verifier tries to recognize one out of 33 instruction operations, a typical
pattern recognition/classification problem. We apply various classifiers, including naive Bayes, kNN, SVM, Multilayer Perceptron, etc., together with/without
feature selection by PCA, mutual information, and LDA. The best recognition
rate is obtained by using template analysis [10,16]. The power consumption is
approximated as multi-variate Gaussian signals, which yields very good results in
recognition/classification and separability analysis. One template is built for each
instruction operation ω_i. When selecting l samples in one instruction cycle for
modeling, the templates are l-dimensional Gaussian distributions with parameters estimated from power consumption observations when executing ω_i.

$$p(\boldsymbol{x}|\omega_i) = \frac{1}{(2\pi)^{l/2}|\boldsymbol{\Sigma}_i|^{1/2}}\exp\Big(-\frac{1}{2}(\boldsymbol{x}-\boldsymbol{\mu}_i)^T\boldsymbol{\Sigma}_i^{-1}(\boldsymbol{x}-\boldsymbol{\mu}_i)\Big)$$

$$\boldsymbol{\mu}_i = \frac{1}{N_i}\sum_{j=1}^{N_i}\boldsymbol{x}_{ij}$$

$$\boldsymbol{\Sigma}_i = \frac{1}{N_i-1}\sum_{j=1}^{N_i}(\boldsymbol{x}_{ij}-\boldsymbol{\mu}_i)(\boldsymbol{x}_{ij}-\boldsymbol{\mu}_i)^T$$

where $\boldsymbol{x}_{ij}$ is an l-dimensional observation of executing operation ω_i in the modeling data, N_i is the number of such observations in the modeling data. When
given a new observation $\boldsymbol{x}$, the instruction operation is estimated by applying
the Bayes rule, which is the ω_i that gives the maximum a posteriori probability.

$$\hat{\omega} = \underset{\omega_i}{\operatorname{argmax}}\,p(\omega_i|\boldsymbol{x}) = \underset{\omega_i}{\operatorname{argmax}}\,p(\boldsymbol{x}|\omega_i)P(\omega_i)$$

For integrity checking, the a priori distribution $P(\omega_i)$ is meaningless, since the verifier is unlikely to know with which instruction the attacker may use to replace the original code. We therefore assume the a priori distribution is uniform, thus reduce Bayes rule to the maximum likelihood criterion.

$$\hat{\omega} = \underset{\omega_i}{\operatorname{argmax}}\, p(\boldsymbol{x}|\omega_i)$$

One template is built for each operation. For file-register operations, each template is built for writing to the file/working register. In total, 47 templates are built. The resulting average recognition rate is 45.6%, which is comparable to unoptimized results of [10,16] and the single-location result of [39]. While some operations still have acceptable recognition rates, such as CLRW (99.0% recognition rate), GOTO (97.8%), and COMF f,F (95.7%), other operations, such as CLRF, DECFSZ f,W and IORWF f,F, are almost always misclassified.

To explore the sources of recognition errors, we perform the same template analysis but now build one template for each instance of instruction execution. The models thus incorporate power consumption caused by execution with different operands and runtime status. For the same data, we build 1435 templates. Applying again the maximum likelihood criterion, the average recognition rate is surprisingly 99.90%, in contrast with 0.0678% for random guess.

3.2 Separability

The high recognition rate can be explained by the separability of templates. One measure of separability is the Bhattacharyya distance, which is related to the upper bound of the minimum attainable error of the Bayes classifier [41].

$$P_e \leq \epsilon_{CB} = \sqrt{P(\omega_i)P(\omega_j)} \int_{-\infty}^{\infty} \sqrt{p(\boldsymbol{x}|\omega_i)p(\boldsymbol{x}|\omega_j)} d\boldsymbol{x}$$

For multi-variate Gaussian,

$$\epsilon_{CB} = \sqrt{P(\omega_i)P(\omega_j)}\exp(-B_{ij})$$

$$B_{ij} = \frac{1}{8}(\boldsymbol{\mu}_i - \boldsymbol{\mu}_j)^T \left(\frac{\boldsymbol{\Sigma}_i + \boldsymbol{\Sigma}_j}{2}\right)^{-1}(\boldsymbol{\mu}_i - \boldsymbol{\mu}_j) + \frac{1}{2}\ln\frac{\left|\frac{\boldsymbol{\Sigma}_i + \boldsymbol{\Sigma}_j}{2}\right|}{\sqrt{|\boldsymbol{\Sigma}_i||\boldsymbol{\Sigma}_j|}}$$

Building templates for instances of instruction execution, the 30 errors in 30,000 tests correspond to 4 out of 1,028,895 pairs that have the smallest Bhattacharyya distances (from 3.98 to 11.45), showing that the multi-variate Gaussian models are good approximators of the signals. In contrast, for templates of instruction operations, the Bhattacharyya distances of the majority of template pairs, especially logic and arithmetic operations, are near zero, corresponding to recognition rates near to those of random guess.

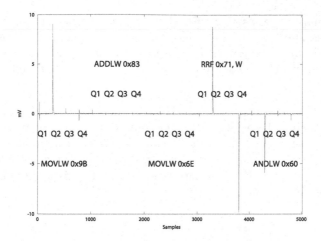

Fig. 3. Difference between two measurements. Although the same program is executing, the register values are different.

4 Data Effects

To discover the effects of runtime status such as bus traffic, we change testing programs by modifying initial values of registers and rerun the measurements. Because register values affect results of conditional branches, code near conditional branches is adjusted, so that only the instruction immediate after each conditional branch test is different while majority of instruction execution stays the same. The difference between the two resulting measurements is shown in Figure 3.

The measurements of "MOVLW 0x9B" have significant difference at the edge of Q2. After executing "MOVLW 0x9B", the measurements of "ADDLW 0x83" and "MOVLW 0x6E" are nearly identical. Executing "RRF 0x71,W" differs at Q2 and Q4, whereas executing "ANDLW 0x60" has significant difference at Q2 and slight difference at Q4. Q1 and Q3 are on the other hand almost the same at all time. This phenomenon coincides with the architecture description in [2]: for instruction execution, instruction is latched in Q1, data memory is read in Q2 (operand read), data is processed in Q3, and in Q4 data memory is written (destination write). After executing "MOVLW 0x9B", the working register and the STATUS register are the same [2], and the traffic on the data bus during operand read and destination write is therefore the same, which leads to the same side-channel measurements. The contents of the file register 0x71 are different, which results in different traffic on the data bus and accordingly different measurements at Q2 and Q4. The result of "RRF 0x71,W" is written to the working register, and thus causes further differences at Q2 and Q4 when executing "ANDLW 0x60". On the other hand, Q1 and Q3 do not show heavy data dependency, even though data is processed in Q3.

---

[2] The STATUS register is affected by previous code not shown.

Further analysis shows that there are strong linear relationships between runtime status and side-channel measurements. Let runtime status at time t be a vector of random variables $\boldsymbol{D}$, the power consumption at t be a random variable Y, the linear dependence between Y and $\boldsymbol{D}$ is formulated as

$$Y = \boldsymbol{a}^T \boldsymbol{D} + b$$

where $\boldsymbol{a}$ is a vector of weights, b encloses remaining components in the power consumption at time t including offsets, time-dependent components, and noise, and is assumed independent from other variables [8]. For two random variables $X = \boldsymbol{a}^T \boldsymbol{D}$ and Y, the Pearson correlation coefficient is a measure of linear dependence between X and Y:

$$r = \frac{cov(X, Y)}{\sigma_X \sigma_Y} = \frac{\sigma_X}{\sqrt{\sigma_X^2 + \sigma_b^2}}$$

r tends to ± 1 as σ_b^2 tends to 0. Spearman's rank correlation is the Pearson correlation between weakly-ordered values. The two correlations are identical for values which are monotonically related. Spearman's correlation is more sensitive to outliers.

Analysis shows that the Hamming distance (HD) of PC and (PC+1) influences the peaks in Q1, regardless of operations. This corresponds to the fact that the pipeline depth of the DUT is two: each instruction execution is overlapped with fetching the next instruction, and the PC is incremented in Q1 for instruction fetch.

The Hamming distance of values of operands influences the peaks in Q2. In Q2, different types of operations will load different types of operands. For bit-oriented file register operations and byte-oriented file register operations such as CLRF, MOVWF, RRF, DECFSZ, and BTFSC, the content of the file register is loaded, even if it will not be used in the computation in Q3 (as in CLRF and MOVWF). For literal operations, the literal is loaded. The power consumption is proportional to the Hamming distance of the value already on the bus (which is the result of previous instruction execution), and the data loaded for current instruction execution. For vector $\boldsymbol{D} = (HD(\text{old data on bus}, \text{new data on bus}))$, the regression coefficient vector $\boldsymbol{a}$ is $(2.87, 44.70)$, in mV. The Pearson correlation coefficient (r) is 0.971, and the Spearman's rank correlation coefficient (ρ) is 0.969.

The plateaus following the peaks in Q2 and Q3, are linear to the Hamming weight (HW) of next opcode, regardless of instruction operations. For vector $\boldsymbol{D} = (HW(\text{next opcode}))$, the coefficient vector is $(0.836, 14.41)$, in mV; $r = 1.000$ and $\rho = 0.991$.

The peaks in Q3 are linear to the Hamming weight of next opcode and the Hamming weight of current opcode: for vector $\boldsymbol{D} = (HW(\text{current opcode}), HW(\text{next opcode}))$, the coefficient vector is $(1.32, 0.828, 28.43)$, in mV; $r = 0.998$ and $\rho = 0.998$.

The peaks in Q4 is linear to the Hamming distance of values on the data bus and the Hamming weight of next opcode: For literal operations, vector is

(HD(literal, new value of working register), HW(next opcode)), coefficient vector is $(3.10, 2.19, 34.36)$, in mV; $r = 0.992$ and $\rho = 0.987$. For operations with the working register as destination, the vector is (HD(value of file register, new value of working register), HW(next opcode)), coefficient vector is $(3.00, 2.17, 35.29)$, $r = 0.998$ and $\rho = 0.997$. For operations with the file register as destination, the vector is (HD(old value of file register, new value of file register), HW(next opcode)), coefficient vector is $(3.60, 2.15, 36.22)$, $r = 0.998$ and $\rho = 0.998$. The Hamming distance of values of the STATUS SFR surprisingly does not significantly affect the power consumption in Q4, which is reflected by the fact that its regression coefficient is one order lower than those of other variables.

The relationships reveal several valuable sources of side-channel leakage that can be utilized for different verification purposes. First, they reveal that side-channel measurements have strong dependencies on data and weak dependencies on instruction operations. This explains why templates of logic and arithmetic operations have small Bhattacharyya distances: they have small differences in the Hamming weights of their opcode spaces and the distributions of operands and results (except for COMF, whose Q4 always has large power consumption since its (HD(old value of file register, new value of working/file register)) is always 8). While not helping in template analysis with respect to instruction operations, data dependencies in peaks of Q2 and Q4 help to match data values with operations. Second, the strong linear relationships also help to validate our semantic models. Third, the dependency in opcodes through Q2 to Q4 leaks information about the control flow. While not directly revealing the neighboring opcodes, this helps in identifying some instructions such as NOP (having the unique 0 opcode) and the NOP executed after each branch. Fourth, coefficient vectors of the order of mV per bit, given the dynamic range of the measurements of $(15, 70)$ mV, are resilient to noise in simple (versus differential) power analysis.

To increase the potential SNR of operation-related signals, we generate testing programs composed of code of the same Hamming weight. Except GOTO and instruction types that cannot have targeted Hamming weight (e.g. NOP and CLRW), all logic and arithmetic operations are included. Repeating the experiment, previous conclusions on data dependencies still hold. Q3 has nearly the same value, which can be shown by the small standard deviations (σ) among waveforms. For execution instances, the maximum σ, occurring at the peak of Q3, is 0.324 mV, in contrast with the maximum σ in previous experiments, which is 4.193. For instruction operations, the maximum σ is 0.121, in contrast with the maximum σ in previous experiments, which is 2.495. This implies that Q3 does not yield sufficient margins for classification. Applying various pattern recognition techniques, the best average recognition rate is 33.16% for instruction operations, obtained by SVM with polynomial kernel, five-fold cross-validation. The recognition rate is still much worse than that obtained by template analysis for instruction execution instances, which is 99.53%.

5   Side-channel Programming

Above experiments show that because of significant data dependency of power consumption, side-channel profiling according to instruction operations is unlikely to have high recognition rates or large margins. It is more suitable to use runtime data status for simple power analysis, especially in noisy environments. On the other hand, although there are very strong linear relationships between waveforms and data read in Q2 and destination write in Q4, it is the Hamming distance rather than the exact data that is involved. For a side-channel-aware attacker, it is easy to compute data pairs that have the same Hamming distance with previous data on the bus in Q2, go through different operations, and again have the same Hamming distance with the operands in Q4, thus evading side-channel-based checking. This is feasible even when considering the Hamming weight relationships through Q2 to Q4, since the opcode is quite compact.

The good news is that a change in data may have cascading effects: in order to tamper with data in one instruction, previous and next instructions must be modified accordingly. The developers of the μC can utilize aforementioned data dependencies to guarantee tamper detection. For a given instruction set, the developers can find a trace of side-channel measurements $\{Q2_i, Q3_i, Q4_i\}, i = 1, \ldots, n$ that for any programs, when given a set of initial register values, lead to a unique set of resulting values. The developers can just choose one program that transforms the input to the output. Any tampering with the program can then either be detected from side-channel measurements, or lead to the same unique set of resulting values.

For a simple example, let us confine the instruction set to include only the literal operations {ADDLW, ANDLW, IORLW, XORLW} that perform add/bit-and/bit-or/bit-XOR operations with the working register and a literal, and then write results to the working register. The runtime status that has strong linear relationships with the side-channel measurements includes (HD(old working register,literal)) in Q2, (HD(new working register,literal)) in Q4, and (HW(current opcode)) and (HW(next opcode)) through Q2 to Q4. It is possible to find that given the initial value of the working register 0x55, execution of any four-instruction programs leads to the same resulting working register 0x1F, given the runtime status constraints (HD(old working register,literal)) = $[3, 6, 3, 7]$ for Q2's of the four instructions respectively; (HW(current opcode)) = $[10, 10, 9, 11]$ for Q3's respectively (also for previous Q2, Q3, Q4); (HD(new working register,literal)) = $[5, 4, 2, 1]$ for Q4's respectively. There are two programs of four instructions that satisfy such side-channel constraints: {ADDLW 0x7C, ANDLW 0x3F, XORLW 0xF1, ADDLW 0x3F} and {ADDLW 0x1F, ANDLW 0x9F, XORLW 0xF4, ADDLW 0x3F}, but all lead to the same resulting working register 0x1F. The developers can randomly pick one of the programs, say, {ADDLW 0x7C, ANDLW 0x3F, XORLW 0xF1, ADDLW 0x3F}. Even if an attacker is able to profile the side-channel characteristics of the μC, she can at best modify the code into {ADDLW 0x1F, ANDLW 0x9F, XORLW 0xF4, ADDLW 0x3F}, which results in exactly the same value and thus renders the attack meaningless, since other modifications will violate the side-channel constraints.

Data: $\forall q2 = [q2(1), \ldots, q2(n)], q3 = [q3(1), \ldots, q3(n)], q4 = [q4(1), \ldots, q4(n)], W_0, F$

Result: $w, num, op, opr, w1p, w1$

```
genPrgm(q2, q3, q4, W₀, F)
begin
    w(1) ← {W₀}
    for i = 1, ..., n do
        for w₀ ∈ w(i) do
            Opr ← {x|HD(x, w₀) = q2(i)}
            for f ∈ F do
                for x ∈ Opr do
                    y ← f(w₀, x)
                    if HW(x) + HW(opcode of f) = q3(i) and HD(x, y) = q4(i)
                    then
                        num(i) ← num(i) + 1
                        op(i, num(i)) ← f
                        opr(i, num(i)) ← x
                        w1p(i, num(i)) ← w₀
                        w1(i, num(i)) ← y
                        w(i + 1) ← w(i + 1) ∪ {y}
```

Algorithm 1. genPrgm: Compute programs that satisfy a given side-channel trace

Data: $\forall Q2 = \{q2_i, i = 1, \ldots, M_2\}, Q3 = \{q3_i, i = 1, \ldots, M_3\}, Q4 = \{q4_i, i = 1, \ldots, M_4\}, W_0, F$

Result: $ops, oprs, q2, q3, q4, W_1$

```
genSCP(Q2, Q3, Q4, W₀, F)
begin
    for q2 ∈ Q2 do
        for q3 ∈ Q3 do
            for q4 ∈ Q4 do
                [w, num, op, opr, w1p, w1] ←genPrgm(q2,q3,q4,W₀,F)
                if w(n + 1) is Singleton then
                    W₁ ← w(n + 1)
                    ops, oprs ← backtrace op and opr through w1 and w1p
                    break to top
```

Algorithm 2. genSCP: Compute combinations of programs and side-channel traces that produce unique output

This leads to the idea of "side-channel programming", in which software engineers utilize side-channel characteristics of existing hardware during development to guarantee tamper detection. General algorithms for finding such combinations of side channel constraints and programs of any length are shown in Algorithms 1 and 2, where W_0 is the initial value of the working register, F is a set of functions that simulate the operations in the instruction set, W_1 is the resulting value of the working register, and $(ops, oprs)$ compose programs that satisfy a n-long side-channel trace $\{q2, q3, q4\}$ and also output a unique W_1. For the above small instruction set, it takes just seconds to find side-channel traces that guarantee unique transformations of input and output on a commercial PC. As the instruction set increases, complexity increases. We leave it as future work to efficiently perform "side-channel programming" for the full instruction set.

6   Conclusion and Future Work

For simple power analysis, we explore whether or not instructions can lead to consistently distinguishable side-channel information, and if so, how the side-channel characteristics differ. By building semantic models of the instruction set and cross-validating with side-channel measurements, we show that data dependencies, rather than instruction operation dependencies, are dominant. We reveal strong linear relationships between runtime status and side-channel measurements, which enable "side-channel programming" that utilizes side-channel characteristics of existing hardware in software development to provide external verification of software integrity. We show how to generate combinations of side-channel constraints and programs of any length for a subset of the instruction set that guarantee a unique transformation of a given input, so that any tampering with the program by a side-channel-aware attacker can either be detected, or lead to the same unique set of input and output. Our future work involves side-channel programming for the full instruction set.

Side-channel characteristics are determined by the IC design of the DUT. The comparatively small instruction set and simple architecture of the μC under test greatly ease side-channel analysis so that the problem is tractable in reasonable period of time. As more complex IC designs are used in embedded systems, instruction sets support more operations executed in a variable number of instruction cycles, pipelines get deeper and more complex, and more components function in parallel. And therefore significantly more factors will need to be incorporated into the semantic models. It may not be possible to find side-channel characteristics for more complex ICs as succinct as discovered in this work for a simple IC. It is, however, fundamentally possible to derive side-channel characteristics as long as the IC operates deterministically. Our future work also involves applying the proposed approach to other microcontrollers/microprocessors.

Acknowledgments. This work was partially funded by NIH grant 1U01EB012470 and NSF grants CNS 1224007, CNS 1239543, and CNS 1253930.

References

1. grsecurity. http://grsecurity.net/
2. PIC16F631/677/685/687/689/690 data sheet. Microchip Technology Inc. (2008). http://ww1.microchip.com/downloads/en/DeviceDoc/41262E.pdf
3. PICmicro mid-range MCU family - reference manual. Microchip Technology Inc. (1997). http://ww1.microchip.com/downloads/en/DeviceDoc/31000a.pdf
4. Trusted computing group (TCG). TPM 2.0 library specification (2014). http://www.trustedcomputinggroup.org/resources/tpm_library_specification
5. Agrawal, D., Archambeault, B., Rao, J.R., Rohatgi, P.: The EM side-channel(s). In: Kaliski Jr., B.S., Koç, Ç.K., Paar, C. (eds.) CHES 2002. LNCS, vol. 2523, pp. 29–45. Springer, Heidelberg (2003)
6. Agrawal, D., Baktir, S., Karakoyunlu, D., Rohatgi, P., Sunar, B.: Trojan detection using IC fingerprinting. In: Proceedings of the IEEE Symposium on Security and Privacy, S&P (2007)
7. Bletsch, T., Jiang, X., Freeh, V.W., Liang, Z.: Jump-oriented programming: a new class of code-reuse attack. In: Proceedings of the ACM Symposium on Information, Computer and Communications Security, ASIACCS (2011)
8. Brier, E., Clavier, C., Olivier, F.: Correlation power analysis with a leakage model. In: Joye, M., Quisquater, J.-J. (eds.) CHES 2004. LNCS, vol. 3156, pp. 16–29. Springer, Heidelberg (2004)
9. Butterworth, J., Kallenberg, C., Kovah, X., Herzog, A.: BIOS chronomancy: fixing the core root of trust for measurement. In: Proceedings of the ACM Conference on Computer and Communications Security, CCS (2013)
10. Chari, S., Rao, J.R., Rohatgi, P.: Template attacks. In: Kaliski Jr., B.S., Koç, Ç.K., Paar, C. (eds.) CHES 2002. LNCS, vol. 2523, pp. 13–28. Springer, Heidelberg (2003)
11. Checkoway, S., Feldman, A.J., Kantor, B., Halderman, J.A., Felten, E.W., Shacham, H.: Can DREs provide long-lasting security? the case of return-oriented programming and the AVC advantage. In: Proceedings of the Conference on Electronic Voting Technology/Workshop on Trustworthy Elections, EVT/WOTE (2009)
12. Clark, S.S., Ransford, B., Rahmati, A., Guineau, S., Sorber, J., Fu, K., Xu, W.: WattsUpDoc: power side channels to nonintrusively discover untargeted malware on embedded medical devices. In: Proceedings of the USENIX Conference on Safety, Security, Privacy and Interoperability of Health Information Technologies, HealthTech, p. 9. USENIX Association, Berkeley (2013)
13. Cui, A., Costello, M., Stolfo, S.: When firmware modifications attack: a case study of embedded exploitation. In: NDSS (2013)
14. Davi, L., Sadeghi, A.-R., Lehmann, D., Monrose, F.: Stitching the gadgets: on the ineffectiveness of coarse-grained control-flow integrity protection. In: Proceedings of the USENIX Security Symposium, SEC (2014)
15. Duflot, L., Perez, Y.-A., Morin, B.: What If you can't trust your network card? In: Sommer, R., Balzarotti, D., Maier, G. (eds.) RAID 2011. LNCS, vol. 6961, pp. 378–397. Springer, Heidelberg (2011)
16. Eisenbarth, T., Paar, C., Weghenkel, B.: Building a side channel based disassembler. In: Gavrilova, M.L., Tan, C.J.K., Moreno, E.D. (eds.) Transactions on Computational Science X. LNCS, vol. 6340, pp. 78–99. Springer, Heidelberg (2010)
17. Falliere, N., Murchu, L.O., Chien, E.: W32. stuxnet dossier version 1.4 (2011)

18. Francillon, A., Castelluccia, C.: Code injection attacks on harvard-architecture devices. In: Proceedings of the ACM Conference on Computer and Communications Security, CCS (2008)
19. Göktas, E., Athanasopoulos, E., Bos, H., Portokalidis, G.: Out of control: overcoming control-flow integrity. In: Proceedings of the IEEE Symposium on Security and Privacy, S&P (2014)
20. Goldack, M.: Side-channel based reverse engineering for microcontrollers. Master's thesis, Ruhr-Universität Bochum, Germany (2008)
21. Gu, L., Ding, X., Deng, R.H., Xie, B., Mei, H.: Remote attestation on program execution. In: Proceedings of the ACM Workshop on Scalable Trusted Computing, STC (2008)
22. Guo, S., Zhao, X., Zhang, F., Wang, T., Shi, Z., Standaert, F.-X., Ma, C.: Exploiting the incomplete diffusion feature: A specialized analytical side-channel attack against the AES and its application to microcontroller implementations. IEEE Transactions on Information Forensics and Security 9(6) (2014)
23. Hanna, S., Rolles, R., Molina-Markham, A., Poosankam, P., Fu, K., Song, D.: Take two software updates and see me in the morning: the case for software security evaluations of medical devices. In: Proceedings of the USENIX Conference on Health Security and Privacy, HealthSec (2011)
24. Jin, Y., Makris, Y.: Hardware trojan detection using path delay fingerprint. In: Proceedings of the IEEE International Workshop on Hardware-Oriented Security and Trust, HST (2008)
25. Nohl, K., Krißler, S., Lell, J.: BadUSB - on accessories that turn evil. https://srlabs.de/blog/wp-content/uploads/2014/07/SRLabs-BadUSB-BlackHat-v1.pdf
26. Kocher, P.C., Jaffe, J., Jun, B.: Differential power analysis. In: Wiener, M. (ed.) CRYPTO 1999. LNCS, vol. 1666, pp. 388–397. Springer, Heidelberg (1999)
27. Li, Y., McCune, J.M., Perrig, A.: VIPER: verifying the integrity of PERipherals' firmware. In: Proceedings of the ACM Conference on Computer and Communications Security, CCS (2011)
28. Mangard, S., Oswald, E., Popp, T.: Power Analysis Attacks: Revealing the Secrets of Smart Cards, 1st edn. Springer Publishing Company, Incorporated (2010)
29. Mason, J., Small, S., Monrose, F., MacManus, G.: English shellcode. In: Proceedings of the ACM Conference on Computer and Communications Security, CCS (2009)
30. McCune, J.M., Li, Y., Qu, N., Zhou, Z., Datta, A., Gligor, V., Perrig, A.: TrustVisor: efficient TCB reduction and attestation. In: Proceedings of the IEEE Symposium on Security and Privacy, S&P (2010)
31. Msgna, M., Markantonakis, K., Naccache, D., Mayes, K.: Verifying software integrity in embedded systems: a side channel approach. In: Prouff, E. (ed.) COSADE 2014. LNCS, vol. 8622, pp. 261–280. Springer, Heidelberg (2014)
32. Nakutis, Z.: Embedded systems power consumption measurement methods overview (2009)
33. Rodríguez, F., Serrano, J.J.: Control flow error checking with ISIS. In: Yang, L.T., Zhou, X., Zhao, W., Wu, Z., Zhu, Y., Lin, M. (eds.) ICESS 2005. LNCS, vol. 3820, pp. 659–670. Springer, Heidelberg (2005)
34. Seshadri, A., Perrig, A., Doorn, L.V., Khosla, P.: SWATT: software-based ATTestation for embedded devices. In: Proceedings of the IEEE Symposium on Security and Privacy, S&P (2004)
35. Skorobogatov, S., Woods, C.: Breakthrough silicon scanning discovers backdoor in military chip. In: Prouff, E., Schaumont, P. (eds.) CHES 2012. LNCS, vol. 7428, pp. 23–40. Springer, Heidelberg (2012)

36. Soll, O., Korak, T., Muehlberghuber, M., Hutter, M.: EM-based detection of hardware trojans on FPGAs. In: IEEE International Symposium on Hardware-Oriented Security and Trust, HOST, May 2014
37. Song, P., Stellari, F., Pfeiffer, D., Culp, J., Weger, A., Bonnoit, A., Wisnieff, B., Taubenblatt, M.: MARVEL: malicious alteration recognition and verification by emission of light. In: IEEE International Symposium on Hardware-Oriented Security and Trust, HOST (2011)
38. Stajano, F., Anderson, R.: The grenade timer: fortifying the watchdog timer against malicious mobile code. In: Proceedings of International Workshop on Mobile Multimedia Communications, MoMuC (2000)
39. Strobel, D., Oswald, D., Richter, B., Schellenberg, F., Paar, C.: Microcontrollers as (in)security devices for pervasive computing applications. Proceedings of the IEEE **102**(8) (2014)
40. Sugawara, T., Suzuki, D., Saeki, M., Shiozaki, M., Fujino, T.: On measurable side-channel leaks inside ASIC design primitives. In: Bertoni, G., Coron, J.-S. (eds.) CHES 2013. LNCS, vol. 8086, pp. 159–178. Springer, Heidelberg (2013)
41. Theodoridis, S., Koutroumbas, K.. Pattern Recognition, 4th edn. Academic Press (2008)
42. Xu, R., Saïdi, H., Anderson, R.: Aurasium: practical policy enforcement for android applications. In: Proceedings of the USENIX Security Symposium, SEC (2012)
43. Yang, Y., Su, L., Khan, M., Lemay, M., Abdelzaher, T., Han, J.: Power-based diagnosis of node silence in remote high-end sensing systems. ACM Trans. Sen. Netw. **11**(2), 33:1–33:33 (2014)
44. Zhang, F., Wang, H., Leach, K., Stavrou, A.: A framework to secure peripherals at runtime. In: Kutyłowski, M., Vaidya, J. (eds.) ESORICS 2014, Part I. LNCS, vol. 8712, pp. 219–238. Springer, Heidelberg (2014)
45. Zhou, Z., Gligor, V.D., Newsome, J., McCune, J.M.: Building verifiable trusted path on commodity x86 computers. In: Proceedings of the IEEE Symposium on Security and Privacy, S&P (2012)

Remote Activation of Hardware Trojans via a Covert Temperature Channel

Priyabrat Dash, Chris Perkins, and Ryan M. Gerdes(✉)

Utah State University, Logan, UT 84322, USA
priyabrat.dash@aggiemail.usu.edu, perkinsck@gmail.com,
ryan.gerdes@usu.edu

Abstract. A hardware trojan (HT) is produced through the malicious tampering of an integrated circuit design. Depending on its placement and purpose, an HT may cause data leakage or corruption, computational errors, reduced system performance, and temporary or permanent denial-of-service through the disabling or destruction of the chip. The varied geographic locales involved in designing, fabricating, and testing a design allow an attacker ample opportunity to insert an HT. In this paper we propose a method to enable the remote activation of HT, via a covert temperature channel, across a network. Through experimentation, our activation method is shown to be feasible on modern computers. In addition, its design is tolerant of process variation to ensure that it can be reliably fabricated. The design was validated using industry standard STMicroelectronics 65 nm technology and shown to be undetectable against present detection techniques. We discuss the major challenges associated with such HT and future research needs to address them.

Keywords: Hardware Trojan · Remote activation · Covert channel · Detection

1 Introduction

Electronic devices are integral to almost every aspect of our lives, but the emergence of hardware specific threats has led some to reconsider the trustworthiness of the hardware used for information processing [2]. Globalization and cut-throat competition in the electronics industry has led to the outsourcing of integrated circuit (IC) manufacturing to untrustworthy foundries [23]. Because chip designers are no longer in control of the production of ICs, affordable, yet unreliable, third-party fabricators make it possible for attackers to make malicious modifications to a circuit before it is fabricated. Additionally, attackers could modify designs through the compromise of the computer aided design (CAD) tools used by designers; malicious circuitry may also already exist in the blackbox intellectual property (IP) modules commonly used in IC design. These malicious and unintended additions to ICs are called hardware Trojans (HT), and they are of particular concern to military, financial and industrial sectors as they can lead to functionality errors, performance reduction, denial-of-service, or information leakage [9].

© Institute for Computer Sciences, Social Informatics and Telecommunications Engineering 2015
B. Thuraisingham et al. (Eds.): SecureComm 2015, LNICST 164, pp. 294–310, 2015.
DOI: 10.1007/978-3-319-28865-9_16

In an attempt to evade detection, HT are often composed of two parts: the payload, and the trigger [22]. The payload is the circuitry designed to effect the goal of the attacker through interaction with the targeted IC. The trigger is intended to keep the trojan stealthy by activating the payload only after some attacker-defined event has taken place.

In this paper, we devise a remotely activated *analog* HT trigger that enables the payload when a certain temperature is reached at the core of the infected circuit. Our target is a chip residing on, or connected to, the logic board in a computer connected to the network. The trigger is influenced via a covert temperature channel, wherein an attacker is able the raise the computer's temperature remotely by sending a large number of requests to the target computer over the network.

A temperature sensitive trigger is ideal from an attacker's point of view for two reasons. Firstly, the possibility of remote activation allows an attacker to achieve their ends without physical access to a target device. Secondly, an analog temperature switch-based trigger is much smaller and quieter—i.e. its area and static and dynamic power draw are lower—than the combinatorial and sequential circuits conventionally used to trigger trojans. As will be shown in Section 6, our trigger, which consists of a temperature switch (tuned to respond to a specific temperature) along with a simple temperature sensor, uses much less power than can be detected using current power-based side channel detection techniques [4]. It should be noted that, rather than introducing an additional temperature sensor, it would be possible to hijack the signal from a temperature sensor that may already be present in an IC (such additions are extremely common for monitoring), making our trojan trigger even stealthier. Because of its analog nature and lack of interaction with the digital circuitry of the IC, our trojan is also able to evade parametric detection techniques such as path delay [14].

Our threat model is detailed and validated in Section 2, while we discuss our trigger design in Section 3. In Section 4, we present a modification to our design that ensures it is tolerant to the process variation inherent in modern fabrication; the design is verified via simulation in Section 5. Section 6 demonstrates that our trigger is able to evade current detection approaches. Related trojans/triggers are discussed in Section 7. Finally, Section 8 concludes the paper.

2   Threat Model

We consider an attacker who has implanted a gate-level trojan into a component of interest that is later installed into a computer with a network interface offering some service (e.g. web or database server; Figure 1). It is assumed that the attacker knows the proximity of the infected component to the CPU in the computer, and that the computer itself is in an environment with a steady, easily predicted ambient temperature, such as a temperature controlled data center. The trojan is composed of an internal trigger and payload; through remote interaction with the computer the attacker is able to induce an internal state that triggers the payload. Specifically, the internal trigger is designed to activate the payload when the temperature of the component exceeds a pre-defined threshold; i.e. we utilize a temperature-based covert channel [29]. Remote activation

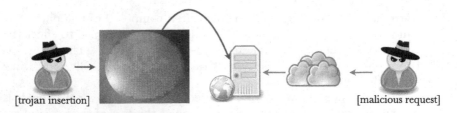

Fig. 1. Threat model: an attacker implants a temperature-triggered hardware trojan into component that is installed in a server. The attacker activates the trojan by sending it spurious requests that cause utilization to increase, causing a rise in temperature that triggers the trojan.

is achieved by sending requests to the service running on the computer at a rate sufficient to increase the CPU utilization, and hence the temperature of the computer [18]. For example, in the case of a webserver an attacker in control of a botnet could initiate new connections or issue page requests to cause excess resource consumption. If the network interface is Internet/externally facing the attacker could initiate the attack remotely, otherwise they would require access to the private network on which the computer resides.

The payload will depend on the goals of the attacker and the component in which the trojan is implanted. For example, data corruption or leakage could be effected if the trojan is located in a southbridge-like component, controller for the data storage device, memory controller, or even peripheral component (e.g. Ethernet card). The attacker could also opt to simply disable the computer by disconnecting the supply voltage of one of these components during the duration of the attack, or even permanently by creating a short inside the component that results in burnout.

Validation of Threat Model

While the existence of temperature-based covert channels is well established, existing work has focused on either coarse-grained case temperature or CPU temperature measurement [18,29]. Our threat model specifies that the attacker knows only the proximity to the CPU. Thus, to establish the temperature threshold at which to trigger the payload, the attacker must know how CPU utilization will affect different regions of the computer.

To this end, we measured the temperature inside a Dell Optiplex 960 at four different locations (Figure 2), using calibrated Texas Instruments LM35A temperature sensors (accuracy ±0.2° [25]), at different CPU utilization levels. The sampling rate was 100 S/s; every second the last 100 samples would be averaged to obtain the temperature for the previous second. The cpulimit program was used to control the utilization of the resource consumption busy program, which spawns a specified number of threads that each execute an infinite loop [1]. Data was collected for several utilization levels (e.g. 0,10,100,400%) and profiles (cycling between different utilization levels) over the course of many days,

Fig. 2. The experimental setup used to validate the threat model. Sensor locations are located at circles. The case was closed during experiments

of which Figure 3 is representative. In this experiment we varied the utilization level periodically: one hour at 400% and one hour at idle (the processor in the computer is dual core with Hyperthreading enabled). We see that sensors closest to the CPU experience the greatest increase in temperature, but that in each case at least 1° increase is observed.

Thus, in this instance, it is feasible for an attacker to design a temperature trigger based on the crossing of a threshold temperature and still have it be effective at differing positions in the computer. Additionally, we note that the maximum temperature achieved through our testing predictably occurred after 25 minutes of 400% utilization (Figure 3), a condition, given the underutilization of most datacenter servers [6,7], that is unlikely to occur during regular or even heavy usage. This helps to minimize the chance that a trojan will be activated by benign workloads. Finally, it is possible that such increased, unscheduled CPU activity could set off CPU workload monitor alarms. The attacker would need to be aware of this possibility and initiate an attack at times when the targeted machine is untended (e.g. during the nighttime) or set a target temperature that can be attained before intervention can be performed.

3   Hardware Trojan Trigger Design

An effective HT trigger needs to be accurate and stealthy in its operation. An accurate trigger will only switch the payload on after a specific event defined by an attacker has taken place. Our trigger consists of an analog temperature sensor circuit along with a multistage inverter designed to switch on at a certain triggering temperature using a voltage signal provided by the sensor (Figure 4). The output of the switching circuitry is connected to the gate of a MOSFET, whose

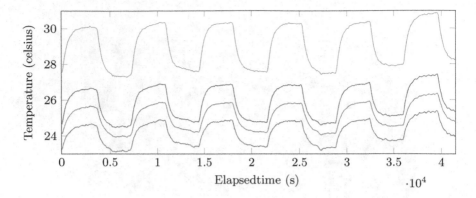

Fig. 3. Temperature at different locations inside the computer with a varying utilization level (0% to 400% periodic). The line color corresponds to the sensor locations given in Figure 2.

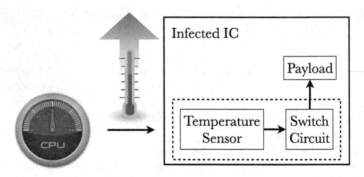

Fig. 4. The proposed method for triggering the payload of a HT: Increased CPU utilization causes a rise in the temperature of an infected IC. The trojan trigger utilizes a low-power temperature sensor to feed switching circuitry designed to activate the payload when the IC temperature exceeds a given threshold.

drain and source are connected to the payload ground line and the IC ground, respectively. When the switching output is logic high the MOSFET switch is closed, allowing power to flow to the payload. The transition temperature at which the switching occurs is predetermined by the attacker before insertion, as per Section 2. We now highlight the design of the sensing and switching components of the trigger.

3.1 Temperature Sensor

The temperature sensor circuit used for our simulations is a BiCMOS design based on the work of [27]. It consists of a cascaded configuration of p-type MOSFETs and pnp BJTs (Figure 9, Appendix). The output of the sensor V_{sen} is the sum of emitter-base voltage V_{eb} of the BJT $Q2$ and source-gate voltage

V_{sg} of the pMOSFET $M2$ ($M1$ is cascaded to the emitter of $Q2$ to obtain the summed output). Under stable biasing both V_{eb} and V_{sg} exhibit negative temperature dependence. As V_{eb} and V_{sg} exhibit complimentary non-linearity against temperature, the linear combination of both voltages results in a high linearity temperature sensor. The pMOSFET portion of the current reference circuit ($M4$ and $M6$) provides stable biasing for $M2$. $Q1$ and $Q2$ are placed in a current mirror configuration ensuring that the collector currents in both $Q1$ and $Q2$ remain the same. This configuration acts as bias for the pnp BJT $Q2$, thereby reducing power consumption and augmenting the decrease in nonlinear deviations in V_{eb}.

The temperature sensor was selected based on the following criteria:

1. *Sensitivity*: This refers to the amount that the output voltage of the sensor changes per degree Celsius. Typical values for solid state temperature sensors range from ± 0.5mV° to ± 9mV° [10]. The higher the sensitivity the fewer the number of stages needed in the switching circuitry, which reduces overall power consumption (discussed in Section 3.2). The nominal sensitivity of our sensor is -3.4mV° with a linearity of 99.96% [27]. We increased the sensitivity of the circuit to -10.12mV° by increasing the width of the $M1$ transistor by 5.3 m.

2. *Power*: The power of the overall design should be minimized. This circuit used 56.31nW at 1.2V, the lowest power circuit we could find.

3. *Positive or negative voltage correlation*: Refers to whether the output voltage of the sensor increases or decreases with an increase/decrease in temperature. Again, this affects our switching circuitry: a positive correlation requires an even number of switching stages (four or six) to ensure that output of the final stage is high to activate our payload power switch. Our sensor has a negative correlation, therefore the switching circuit can use an odd number of stages, which results in fewer inverters and hence less power.

3.2   Switching Circuitry

The overriding concern for our trigger is that the voltage present at the gate of the payload power switch is high at exactly the temperature selected by the attacker but not before. That is, the transition region between switch on and off should be very small. To accomplish this we designed switching circuitry (Figure 10, Appendix) consisting of five common source amplifier stages in sequence [10].

The first stage has its amplifying transistor's gate attached to the output of the temperature sensor. The basic operation is that the final stage T_{out} will remain at a low voltage until the infected IC heats up to the trigger temperature and then it will quickly transition to the logic high value of the payload supply switch. The logic level of the switch circuit should remain low until the trigger temperature is reached to avoid false triggers. The transition point must reside at an input voltage that corresponds to a temperature just below the maximum temperature for swift response.

The transition from low logic to high logic has to be without any delay for smooth payload activation. Therefore the sensitivity of the switch circuit

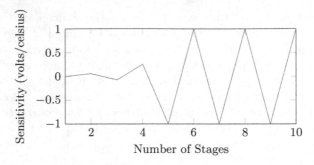

Fig. 5. The effective sensitivity of our temperature sensor at the output of our switching circuitry versus the number of stages in the switch.

is increased by adding additional inverter stages for sharp edge transition. In Figure 5 the sensitivity of individual stages is plotted. The sensitivity values are positive for an even number of stages and negative for odd stages. It can be seen that after the initial increase from stage one to stage five the value remains constant. That is, for a negative correlation sensor, adding additional stages will only increase the power consumption without any improvement in the sensitivity. Thus, the ideal number of stages for our switching circuitry is five, in terms of both minimizing power consumption and providing a fast switching response.

The transition point of the switch circuit—i.e. the temperature at which payload is activated—can be selected by changing the bias voltage of the transistors in a particular stage. For an n-stage circuit, the relationship between the output of a stage can be formulated with respect to the output of the previous stage as:

$$V_i = VDD - \frac{\beta n}{2} \left(V_{i-1} - V_{th} \right)^2 R_{pmos} \tag{1}$$

where V_i is the output of the i-th stage, VDD is the supply voltage, β the transistor's gain, V_{th} the threshold voltage of the transistor, and R_{pmos} the derivative of the drain current I_D with respect to drain-to-source voltage V_{DS} of the pmos transistor. The above equation is for the case of an ideal MOSFET; however, the exact values obtained from simulation are close to the values obtained by the above equation (error range of 11.82mV to -2.72mV).

Unfortunately, this switching architecture is extremely sensitive to changes in threshold voltage. For example, a change in the threshold voltage by 1mV results in a change in the transition point by far more than 1mV. This is quite a significant problem with regards to the accuracy of the attack temperature, as threshold voltage is deeply affected by process variation. That is, a significant change in V_{th} will cause the payload to be powered at a temperature other than that stipulated by the attacker. In varying the parameters that affect V_{th} in a Monte Carlo simulation, we observed a standard deviation of the threshold voltage of 45.62mV. Therefore we have need of a process tolerant switching circuitry to ensure robust and accurate trigger operation.

4   A Process Invariant Design

Continuous advancement in transistor dimensions scaling has led to rampant variations in process parameters affecting the operations of integrated circuits. Variability in channel length (L), oxide thickness (T_{ox}), and transistor threshold voltage (V_{th}) increase drastically in the nanometer technology [8]. Process variation in nanometer technology is categorized into random variations and systematic variations [3]. The systematic variations are caused by device manufacturing process variation such as chemical-mechanical planarization (CMP) [13]. Random variations, mainly caused by geometrical abnormalities, are considered to be the major contributors in 65 nm technology, with L and V_{th} being the most significant contributors to the random component [30]. In the case of our trigger, random parametric variations (threshold voltage and geometrical abnormalities), over which the attacker has no control, lead to unreliable triggering at different temperatures. Therefore the need for process tolerant circuitry, with a small area overhead, is unavoidable.

In this section we present a self-tuning inverter comparator circuit, based on the work of [21], in combination with the parallel gates technique [12], to achieve significant improvement in the circuit level variation tolerance. Our HT trigger of Figure 4 is thus slightly modified to incorporate this new circuitry: the output of the temperature sensor is connected to a self-tuning inverter circuit which in turn is fed to parallel gate inverter chains, replacing our original switching circuitry, to obtain a highly reliable temperature dependent trigger switch. Incorporating a self-tuning inverter comparator circuit gives complete controllability to the attacker to choose the temperature at which the trojan is activated. The process and temperature variation tolerant architecture provides error free targeted trigger temperature operation.

4.1   Self-tuning Inverter Comparator Circuit

The inverter comparator circuit (Figure 11, though designed for PWM application [21], is ideal for use in our trojan circuit due its low voltage operating range, low power consumption, and small area. The basic purpose of the circuit is to set its inherent threshold voltage to a predetermined voltage, independent of process and temperature variation; this is achieved via the principle of negative feedback. The inverter comparator consists of master and slave sub-circuits (Figures 11(a) and 11(b)), with the transistors of both designed to be of the same dimensions. The transistors $MM2$ and $MM3$ act as inverters, generating the desired output voltage to tune the transistors $MM1$ and $MM4$ at the supply rails. The supply rail transistors act as variable resistors to balance the variation in the master input through a negative feedback loop (wire $w1$).

The inherent threshold voltage can be altered according to the attacker's need by changing the voltage at the master circuit's bias node (connection between $MM1$ and $MM4$ in Figure 11(a), Appendix) to the desired threshold value; i.e. the voltage at this node determines the inverter's threshold voltage. In the cases where changing the voltage at the bias node using a voltage source would be undesirable or impossible, bias resistors can also be used to change the inherent threshold voltage value, to a limited extent. For example, the threshold voltage can be set at 0.5 VDD by using equal bias resistors ($R1$ and $R2$ in Figure 11(a)). A threshold voltage of 0.5 VDD equals to 600 mV at $VDD = 1.2$V, which causes the inverter logic in the master-slave circuit to switch at a temperature of 27°. The Miller capacitor C prevents tuning error and undesired oscillations by providing high DC gain and low AC gain, respectively. The output of the master-slave circuit, S_{out}, thus provides our cascaded inverter stages with an appropriately biased, self-tuning input.

4.2   Parallel Gate Inverter Circuit

Even with the inclusion of a self-tuning inverter comparator circuit, our simple cascade of inverter stages circuit is still subject to high output variability due to the sensitivity of the cascaded-inverter circuitry to threshold voltage variations of nMOS and pMOS transistors. This is because small process-induced variability present in early stages can be amplified until they lead to very large fluctuations in the trojan trigger temperature. Therefore, the need for variation tolerant inverter stages arises. The use of programmable threshold voltage inverters [20] would lead to larger inherent voltage deviation, and the power overhead associated with them is proportional to the bit count of digital circuits used to program the inherent voltage. Body biasing techniques [26] have also been proposed, but they are not suitable for our purpose as they are not efficient in tackling random variations and also increase the circuit complexity (area and power consumption).

The standard deviation of the threshold voltage of a transistor is inversely proportional to the square root of the width of the transistor[19]. We therefore increased the width of the transistors in the inverter circuit but failed to observe a drastic reduction in output variation. It wasn't until we also connected the transistors in parallel (effectively increasing the width of the entire inverter) that the random variations were reduced to an acceptable level. The efficacy of the parallel structure can be explained by noting that the variations in each transistor of an inverter is independent of the another transistor, hence using single gates lead to the amplification of the overall random variation in the circuit. Using a parallel gate structure as in Figure 12, Appendix, on the other hand, leads to nullification of independent V_{th} variations in the corresponding parallel transistors [12]. The parallel gate design also leads to a decrease in the input and output capacitance leading to marginally less dynamic power consumption. The higher area overhead is negated when the positive impact it has on suppressing the process variation is considered.

5   Simulation

For the trigger circuit design and Monte-Carlo simulations Cadence Virtuoso IC 6.1.5 with 65 nm, 1.2 V technology library CORE65LPSVT of STMicroelectronics was used. The circuit simulator involved was Spectre. The 65 nm technology was part of an STMicroelectronics kit used for standard, industrial circuit design and simulations.

Initial simulation of the temperature sensor with the five stage inverter stage led to a sharp switch from low to high at the T_{out}. The operation for a single sweep maintains the switch transition at the required temperature levels. But the simulation results above do not take process variation into account. Therefore we ran a Monte-Carlo simulation with the STMicroelectronics kits inherent parameter variations values in the model files. The resultant output was very disappointing, as for only 10 iterations the standard deviation of the transition point was 26.26°. Large fluctuations from the desired trigger temperature can cause uncertainty in executing the attack. It was a challenge to maintain the low area and power consumption of the circuit. Numerous process variations tolerant circuit lead to very high area and power overhead. Therefore a trade-off between area, power and standard deviation was made improve the performance of the trojan trigger.

The simulation result using our process tolerant circuit was improved and displayed accurate functioning of the trojan. The self-tuning inverter circuit along with parallel gate structure when ran for 100 iterations of Monte-Carlo simulations resulted in a standard deviation of 1.48° (Figure 6), which is acceptable in a real attack scenario. We note that should an attacker be in a position to select which chips are shipped to end-users, then they could select for shipment only those chips that trigger most closely to the desired temperature.

The final total power consumption of our process tolerant trigger circuit was 72.34nW, with the temperature sensor occupying 18.36 m with a draw of 46.31nW, the self-tuning inverter 6.52 m and 17.67nW, and the parallel gates 1.52 m and 8.36nW. The pMOS transistors width for the parallel gate circuit

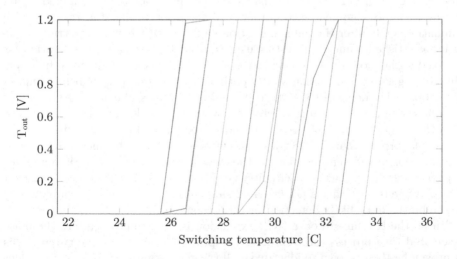

Fig. 6. The switching temperature for the final stage of the process resistant trojan circuitry for 100 Monte Carlo simulations. Target switching temperature was 30°. In 100 simulations a standard deviation of only 1.48° was observed.

were half that of five stage switch circuit. Therefore the area overhead was marginally more and the power consumption was also less considering a bigger circuit. The temperature sensor circuit used in our design can be directly used from one of the many target device motherboard temperature sensors. Utilizing on chip sensor will decrease the area requirement and power consumption of the trojan trigger making it even more difficult to detect.

6   Detectability of Design

Trojan detection is challenging because conventional post manufacturing test and validation processes are often incapable of discovering trojans with effective triggers. Assumption of trigger nodes in a basic benchmark circuit can itself lead to very large trigger sample space, making it almost impractical to test [5]. Therefore, deterministic and exhaustive testing approaches are infeasible. Many detection techniques have been proposed: activation techniques, which attempt to trigger trojans through various possible input combinations; side channel techniques, which monitor circuit side-channel parameters to discover abnormalities [4,17]; design for trust, which modifies the design process to make trojan insertion difficult [24]; and reverse engineering, which thoroughly examines the physical manifestation of the circuit [15]. While these techniques are effective, they are not comprehensive enough to eradicate trojans from modern circuitry. Additionally, these techniques commonly require a genuine, clean reference netlist to find any difference.

An ideal detection technique would be 1) able to detect small trojans, 2) nondestructive, 3) scalable, and 4) authenticate chips in a short time. We consider a few comprehensive detection techniques to evaluate our trigger's detectability. The analog nature of the circuit makes it difficult to analyze the mixed signal circuit as it does not cause any abnormal behavior during the target device simulation. Only after the implementation can it go active when the trigger condition is satisfied. Functional testing using automatic test pattern generation for a mixed signal would not be able to detect it, as it does not alter the functionality of a genuine IC. Similarly, the path delay analysis [14], which examines the propagation delay of the critical paths in a circuit and compares the values obtained with those of a non-infected IC, would be evaded as our trigger is not on a the functional path of the IC. Trojan detection and isolation using current transient current analysis [28] detects switching activity by measuring power consumption at different locations in the chip. Given the published data and our trigger power draw, the trojan circuitry could hide safely in the process variation. We therefore believe that a power-based side channel analysis, as exemplified by [4], to be the most likely detection method to succeed.

In [4] the Karhunen-Loeve (KL) expansion is used to differentiate the noise associated with process variation from the power consumed by the trojan. This approach has been shown to identify small trigger instances with area equivalent to 0.01% of the total size of the circuit, in the presence of random parameter variation as high as ±7.5%. The method works by determining the eigenvalue

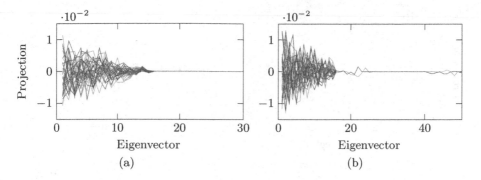

Fig. 7. The eigenvalue spectrum of the trojan (blue) and non-trojan (green) traces. (a) 30 and (b) 50 contiguous points of 16 traces for the non-trojan and trojan devices.

spectrum of the residuals of the signals after measurement noise and nominal power consumption are removed from a power trace for the IC. The spectrum of a trace from a non-trojan device will tend to zero as the number of eigenvectors increases; because of the additional signal (that of the trojan circuitry) the spectrum of a trojan trace will not approach zero at the same rate as the non-trojan.

We used a 256-bit AES circuit as the benchmark circuit to evaluate its detectability. The circuit was re-synthesized, flattened, power optimized, and then analyzed for power consumption, as outlined in [4]. Synopsys Core Synthesis Tools with 65nm, 1.2V technology library CORE65LPSVT of STMicroelectronics was used for the synthesis of the circuit with and without the Trojan. We used Cadence NCSim for the circuit simulation and switching activity analysis. Synopsys PrimeTime PX was used for power analysis and trace file generation. All the power traces were obtained by a time based power simulation with a 50 MHz clock frequency.

The process corner Synopsys library files from the CORE65LPSVT were used to create power traces with differing levels of process noise, as follows: Each sample point of a record would consist of a value picked at random in the range of the best and worst case. The nominal case was deemed to be the average of the best and the worst case. Process noise was recovered by subtracting the nominal case from the generated traces. Following the procedure outlined by [4], we performed the KL analysis on the portions of the trace with the *lowest* process noise, consisting of 30 and 50 contiguous points using 16 traces for each of the non-trojan and trojan traces (Figures 7(a) and 7(b)). We used the same points with 300 and 500 traces, respectively (Figures 8(a) and 8(b)). A worst case analysis, consisting of 600 points from low-noise regions of the trace, along with 6000 traces for the non-trojan and trojan was also undertaken. In all cases the eigenvalue spectrums do not separate at any sample point and are indistinguishable; thus, the trigger is undetectable.

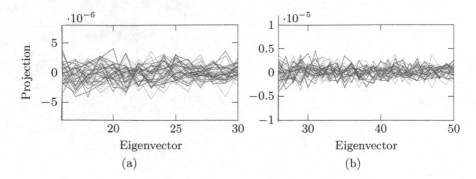

Fig. 8. The eigenvalue spectrum of high-order eigenvectors (where differences should be apparent) for the trojan (blue) and non-trojan (green) traces. (a) 30 and (b) 50 contiguous points of 300/500 traces for the non-trojan and trojan devices.

7   Related Work

There have been numerous active research papers on trojan detection techniques and implementations [9]. Different trojan implementations with effects on circuit parameters such as power, delay, and performance have been proposed [23]. Trojans can also lead to circuit degradation without affecting the overall functionality over a large period of time [9]. Most closely related to our work are trojans that leveraged thermal emissions to leak of data [16], and were triggered via a thermal process [11]. In this latter work, a thermally triggered trojan was implemented on a BASYS FPGA board. An increase in circuit activity increased the temperature causing the Trojan to trigger. Ring oscillators and counters were used to obtain the desired temperature level; i.e. the temperature was artificially increased through high power consuming hardware implanted by the attacker. Though the trigger was thermal based they needed physical access to the board; also, the use of registers needed to activate the trojan would lead to noticeable power consumption. Our low power trigger works in a mixed signal circuit without the need for any physical access to the target device.

8   Conclusion

In this paper, we have presented a fully functional hardware trojan trigger which targets computer logic boards but can also be extended to be maliciously included in any networked device. The trojan can be triggered remotely by increasing the core temperature of the targeted IC through increased network activity, which in turn leads to higher core utilization levels. The low power consumption, high process tolerant operation, and analog implementation mark the trigger as a very potent trojan example. Adversaries with such flexible, accurate and undetectable trojans pose a major threat to IC security. This new attack vector points to the need for improved methods for detecting and preventing mixed signal hardware trojans.

Acknowledgements. The authors are grateful to Dr. Chris Winstead of Utah State University for providing technical guidance on the cascaded switching circuitry and use of his laboratory facilities.

References

1. CPU usage limiter for Linux (2015). https://github.com/opsengine/cpulimit
2. Abramovici, M., Bradley, P.: Integrated circuit security: new threats and solutions. In: Proceedings of the 5th Annual Workshop on Cyber Security and Information Intelligence Research: Cyber Security and Information Intelligence Challenges and Strategies, pp. 55. ACM (2009)
3. Agarwal, K., Nassif, S.: Characterizing process variation in nanometer CMOS. In: 44th ACM/IEEE Design Automation Conference, DAC 2007, pp. 396–399. IEEE (2007)
4. Agrawal, D., Baktir, S., Karakoyunlu, D., Rohatgi, P., Sunar, B.: Trojan detection using IC fingerprinting. In: IEEE Symposium on Security and Privacy, SP 2007, pp. 296–310. IEEE (2007)
5. Banga, M., Chandrasekar, M., Fang, L., Hsiao, M.S.: Guided test generation for isolation and detection of embedded trojans in ICs. In: Proceedings of the 18th ACM Great Lakes symposium on VLSI, pp. 363–366. ACM (2008)
6. Barroso, L.A., Clidaras, J., Hölzle, U.: The datacenter as a computer: An introduction to the design of warehouse-scale machines. Synthesis Lectures on Computer Architecture **8**(3), 1–154 (2013)
7. Benik, A., Ventures, B.: The sorry state of server utilization and the impending post-hypervisor era (2013). https://gigaom.com/2013/11/30/the-sorry-state-of-server-utilization-and-the-impending-post-hypervisor-era/
8. Bernstein, K., Frank, D.J., Gattiker, A.E., Haensch, W., Ji, B.L., Nassif, S.R., Nowak, E.J., Pearson, D.J., Rohrer, N.J.: High-performance CMOS variability in the 65-nm regime and beyond. IBM Journal of Research and Development **50**(4.5), 433–449 (2006)
9. Chakraborty, R.S., Narasimhan, S., Bhunia, S.: Hardware trojan: threats and emerging solutions. In: IEEE International High Level Design Validation and Test Workshop, HLDVT 2009, pp. 166–171. IEEE (2009)
10. Chang, M.H., Liu, C.P., Huang, H.P.: Chip implementation with combined temperature sensor and reference devices based on DZTC principle. Electronics Letters **46**(13), 919–921 (2010)
11. Chen, Z., Guo, X., Nagesh, R., Reddy, A., Gora, M., Maiti, A.: Hardware trojan designs on BASYS FPGA board. Embedded system challenge contest in cyber security awareness week-CSAW (2008)
12. Garg, R., Khatri, S.P.: A variation tolerant circuit design approach using parallel gates
13. He, L., Kahng, A., Tam, K.H., Xiong, J.: Simultaneous buffer insertion and wire sizing considering systematic CMP variation and random leff variation. IEEE Transactions on Computer-Aided Design of Integrated Circuits and Systems **26**(5), 845–857 (2007)

14. Jin, Y., Makris, Y.: Hardware trojan detection using path delay fingerprint. In: IEEE International Workshop on Hardware-Oriented Security and Trust, HOST 2008, pp. 51–57. IEEE (2008)

15. Kash, J.A., Tsang, J.C., Knebel, D.R.: Method and apparatus for reverse engineering integrated circuits by monitoring optical emission (December 17, 2002), US Patent 6,496,022

16. Kiamilev, F., Hoover, R., Delvecchio, R., Waite, N., Janansky, S., McGee, R., Lange, C., Stamat, M.: Demonstration of hardware trojans. DEFCON, 16 (2008)

17. Lin, L., Burleson, W., Paar, C.: Moles: malicious off-chip leakage enabled by side-channels. In: Proceedings of the 2009 International Conference on Computer-Aided Design, pp. 117–122. ACM (2009)

18. Liu, H.: A measurement study of server utilization in public clouds. In: Proceedings of the 2011 IEEE Ninth International Conference on Dependable, Autonomic and Secure Computing, DASC 2011, pp. 435–442. IEEE Computer Society, Washington, DC (2011). http://dx.doi.org/10.1109/DASC.2011.87

19. Orshansky, M., Nassif, S., Boning, D.: Design for manufacturability and statistical design: a constructive approach. Springer Science & Business Media (2007)

20. Segura, J., Rossello, J., Morra, J., Sigg, H.: A variable threshold voltage inverter for CMOS programmable logic circuits. IEEE Journal of Solid-State Circuits 33(8), 1262–1265 (1998)

21. Tan, M.T., Chang, J.S., Tong, Y.C.: A process-and temperature-independent inverter-comparator for pulse width modulation applications. Analog Integrated Circuits and Signal Processing 27(1–2), 95–107 (2001)

22. Tehranipoor, M., Wang, C.: Introduction to Hardware Security and Trust. SpringerLink: Bücher. Springer (2011). https://books.google.com/books?id=bNiw9448FeIC

23. Tehranipoor, M., Koushanfar, F.: A survey of hardware trojan taxonomy and detection (2010)

24. Tehranipoor, M., Salmani, H., Zhang, X., Wang, X., Karri, R., Rajendran, J., Rosenfeld, K.: Trustworthy hardware: Trojan detection and design-for-trust challenges. Computer 7, 66–74 (2010)

25. Instruments, T.: LM35 Precision Centigrade Temperature Sensors. datasheet (2015)

26. Tschanz, J., Bowman, K., De, V.: Variation-tolerant circuits: circuit solutions and techniques. In: Proceedings of the 42nd Annual Design Automation Conference, pp. 762–763. ACM (2005)

27. Wang, R.L., Yu, C.W., Yu, C., Liu, T.H., Yeh, C.M., Lin, C.F., Tsai, H.H., Juang, Y.Z.: Temperature sensor using BJT-MOSFET pair. Electronics Letters 48(9), 503–504 (2012)

28. Wang, X., Salmani, H., Tehranipoor, M., Plusquellic, J.: Hardware trojan detection and isolation using current integration and localized current analysis. In: IEEE International Symposium on Defect and Fault Tolerance of VLSI Systems, DFTVS 2008, pp. 87–95. IEEE (2008)

29. Zander, S., Branch, P., Armitage, G.: Capacity of temperature-based covert channels. Communications Letters, IEEE 15(1), 82–84 (2011)

30. Zhao, W., Liu, F., Agarwal, K., Acharyya, D., Nassif, S.R., Nowka, K.J., Cao, Y.: Rigorous extraction of process variations for 65-nm CMOS design. IEEE Transactions on Semiconductor Manufacturing 22(1), 196–203 (2009)

Appendix: Circuits Used in the Trojan Trigger Design

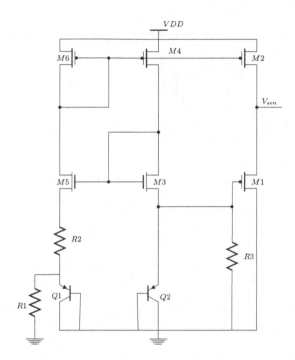

Fig. 9. The low power BiCMOS temperature sensor circuit used in our trojan trigger. Based on [27]. The temperature sensor circuit is the core of the trigger as it must accurately produce the voltage that corresponds to the selected triggering temperature. The output of the temperature sensor V_{sen} is given to the switch circuit.

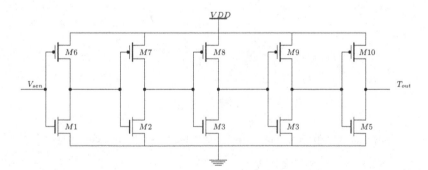

Fig. 10. A cascaded chain of inverters that switch from logic 0 to VDD at a particular temperature. The input to the inverter chain is V_{sen}, the output given from the temperature sensor circuit. When the output $T_{out} = VDD$ the trojan is triggered. Multiple states are added to get a sharp transition and correct inversion of the logic only at the specified temperature. Our switch circuit has an odd number of inverter stages as the temperature sensor has a negative sensitivity.

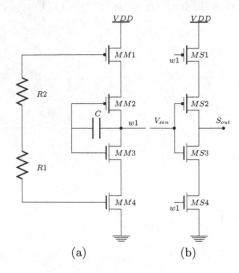

Fig. 11. The (a) master and (b) slave portions of our self-tuning comparator circuit. The purpose of the circuit is to ensure that the first stage of the cascaded inverters has a very low V_{th} variation, as switching variation caused by deviation in V_{th} is amplified through each stage of the inverter chain. The output S_{out} serves as the input to the cascade of parallel gates.

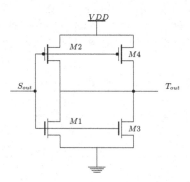

Fig. 12. The process invariant parallel-gate switching circuitry.

Web and Network Security

Route Leaks Identification
by Detecting Routing Loops

Song Li[1], Haixin Duan[2]([✉]), Zhiliang Wang[2], and Xing Li[1]

[1] Department of Electronic Engineering, Tsinghua University,
Beijing 100084, China
lisong10@mails.tsinghua.edu.cn, Xing@cernet.edu.cn
[2] Institute of Network Science and Cyberspace, Tsinghua University,
Beijing 100084, China
duanhx@tsinghua.edu.cn, wzl@csnet1.cs.tsinghua.edu.cn

Abstract. Route leaks have become an important security problem of inter-domain routing. Operators increasingly suffer from large-scale or small-scale route leak incidents in recent years. Route leaks can redirect traffic to unintended networks, which puts the traffic at risk of Man-in-the-Middle attack. Unlike other security threats such as prefix hijacking that advertises bogus BGP route, route leaks announce routes which are true but in violation of routing policies to BGP neighbors. Since the routing policies are usually kept confidential, detecting route leaks in the Internet is a challenging problem. In this paper, we reveal a link between routing loops and route leaks. We find that some route leaks may cause routing loops. Hence detecting routing loops is expected to be able to identify route leaks. We provide theoretical analysis to confirm the expectation, and further propose a detection mechanism which can identify the leaked route as well as the perpetrator AS. Our mechanism does not require information about routing policies. It passively monitors BGP routes to detect route leaks and hence it is lightweight and easy to deploy. The evaluation results show that our mechanism can detect a lot of route leaks that occur in the Internet per day.

Keywords: AS relationship · Routing policies · Route leaks · Routing loops · Identification

1 Introduction

Border Gateway Protocol (BGP) is a path-vector routing protocol which undertakes the exchange of reachability information between Autonomous Systems (ASes). While BGP is crucial to the Internet, it is often under threats of attack and misconfiguration due to lack of built-in security mechanism. Among the threats, prefix hijacking has been considered the main security problem. Prefix hijacking can take over the victim's IP prefix by advertising bogus BGP routes. In order to prevent prefix hijacking, a number of solutions [18,24,26,20] have been proposed to ensure the correctness of BGP routing messages.

© Institute for Computer Sciences, Social Informatics and Telecommunications Engineering 2015
B. Thuraisingham et al. (Eds.): SecureComm 2015, LNICST 164, pp. 313–329, 2015.
DOI: 10.1007/978-3-319-28865-9_17

In this paper, we discuss another important BGP security problem: route leaks, which draw the attention of many researchers recently [28,15]. Different from prefix hijacking, route leaks do not advertise bogus BGP routes, but leak routes in violation of routing policies to BGP neighbors. In other words, in a route leak, the content of the leaked route is true, but the propagation of the route is erroneous.

Routing policies are usually used to control the chosen and propagation of BGP routes. They are created based on the business relationships between ASes. In general, the business relationships are divided into three categories [12]: provider-to-customer (p2c), peer-to-peer (p2p), and sibling-to-sibling (s2s). In a provider-to-customer relationship, the customer AS pays the provider AS for traffic destined for the rest of the Internet. In a peer-to-peer relationship, the peering ASes have a settlement-free agreement which means neither AS pays the other for the traffic destined to each other and their customers. In a sibling-to-sibling relationship, the two ASes are administrated by the same organization and they can freely exchange traffic without any expenses.

Previous research [12,13] shows that an AS commonly adopts the following import and export routing policies according to the business relationships:

- Import policy: A customer-learned route is preferred over peer-learned route over provider-learned route.
- Export policy: A customer-learned route can be exported to all neighbors; a provider-learned route or peer-learned route can only be exported to customers.

The export policy is also known as the *valley-free rule*. When an AS advertises a route that violates the valley-free rule, it can be considered a route leak. According to the neighbor's import policy, the leaked route may be selected as the new best BGP route, which will result in the relevant traffic being redirected to the leaking AS. For instance, on February 23rd, 2012, the Australian route leak incidents [16] misrouted large amount of traffic to AS38285, and led to the interruption of Internet service in the country.

As more and more route leak incidents and their serious impacts are being reported [3,7], it becomes necessary to detect or prevent route leaks in the Internet. There are numerous BGP security proposals [18,21,31] so far. They have focused on detection or prevention of bogus BGP routes. However, because route leaks announce valid routes rather than bogus routes to BGP neighbor, those solutions cannot defend against route leaks [16]. Another common way to prevent route leaks is using route filter to reject the leaked routes. But as mentioned in [16], it is difficult to maintain an accurate and timely route filter in practice, especially for the larger providers.

In this paper, we reveal a link between routing loops and route leaks. According to BGP rules for route selection, when an AS receives a loop route with its own ASN in the AS-Path, the route will be ignored. However, we find that the ignored loop routes received from a peer or customer may imply that there are route leaks which have occurred in the route. We further present a mechanism which identifies route leaks by detecting routing loops. Our mechanism can monitor the route leaks that occur in the Internet without having to know routing policies. Moreover, it can identify the leaking AS (i.e., the perpetrator AS), which is beneficial to mitigate the impact of route leaks in time.

The rest of the paper is organized as follows. Section 2 provides a brief background on route leaks. In Section 3 we discuss the link between routing loops and route leaks, and present the theorems and approaches for route leaks identification. Section 4 provides the detection results of our approach. Some discussions about the detection are given in Section 5. We describe the related work in Section 6. Finally, Section 7 concludes the paper.

2 Route Leaks

Route leaks have often been discussed in the Internet community. However, there has been no exact definition of route leaks until recently [9,28]. A route leak involves three parties: the sending AS, the leaking AS and the receiving AS. It occurs when the leaking AS mistakenly propagates the route learned from the sending AS into the receiving AS in violation of the valley-free rule. In this sense, a route leak can be expressed as an anomalous AS triple (u_{i-1}, u_i, u_{i+1}) which we call *leaking triple*, where u_i is the *leaking AS*.

According to different methods of violating the valley-free rule, route leaks can be grouped into the following four categories:

- **Provider-Provider leaking**: A provider route is mistakenly announced to another provider. The leaking pattern is p2c-c2p.
- **Provider-Peer leaking**: A provider route is mistakenly announced to a peer. The leaking pattern is p2c-p2p.
- **Peer-Peer leaking**: A peer route is mistakenly announced to another peer. The leaking pattern is p2p-p2p.
- **Peer-Provider leaking**: A peer route is mistakenly announced to a provider. The leaking pattern is p2p-c2p.

Figure 1 shows the four types of route leaks. The impact of route leaks on the receiving AS is it can lead to traffic redirection. For instance, in Figure 1(a),

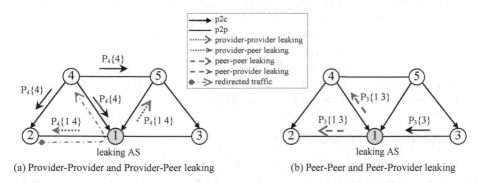

(a) Provider-Provider and Provider-Peer leaking   (b) Peer-Peer and Peer-Provider leaking

Fig. 1. Four types of route leaks

AS1 leaks the route learned from AS4 into AS2. According to the import policies of AS2, the leaked route (peer-learned route) is preferred over the existing BGP route (provider-learned route) in its routing table. Therefore, its traffic destined for AS4 will be redirected to AS1, which gives AS1 a chance to perform a Man-in-the-Middle (MITM) attack [23,17].

3   Routing Loops and Route Leak Detection

Intuitively, we need to know about the AS relationships between ASes in order to identify route leaks. However, the business relationships and routing policies are often kept confidential, which makes the identification of route leaks hard. In this section, we present a novel method to detect route leaks without having to know the relationships.

3.1   Routing Loops Caused by Route Leaks

As a path vector routing protocol, BGP eliminates routing loops by checking if its own AS number (ASN) is contained in the AS-Path of received route. In general, an AS is less likely to receive a route containing its ASN in the AS-Path from its neighbors. This is because its neighbor will usually select the direct link between them as the best path to it. For example, in Figure 2(a), AS1 has three neighbors and it announces prefix P_1 to them. There are two routes for prefix P_1 in the routing table of AS2. One is {1}, and the other is {4 1}. Certainly, AS2 will select {1} as the best path to its neighbor AS1 rather than {4 1}. Therefore, AS2 will not propagate {4 1} into AS1 and AS1 will not receive a route {2 4 1} that contains its own ASN.

However, that could change in a route leak case. For instance, in Figure 2(b), AS3 violates the valley-free rule and leaks the route learned from AS1 into AS2. And hence there are three routes for prefix P_1 in the routing table of AS2. Since AS3 is the customer of AS2, AS2 will select the leaked route {3 1} as the new best path to AS1 according to the common import policy. In the next step, AS2 will announce a new route {2 3 1} to AS1. And as a result, AS1 will receive a route that contains its own ASN from its neighbor AS2, i.e., it receives a route with routing loop from a peer neighbor (AS2). Similarly, in Figure 2(c), the route leak will also make AS4 receive a loop route with its own ASN in the AS-Path from a customer neighbor (AS2).

Since the above examples illustrate route leaks may cause routing loops, it is intuitively expected that detecting routing loops in the Internet may identify route leaks. We confirm this expectation below.

3.2   Route Leak Identification

First, it is important to note that the following conclusions do not consider the complex relationships such as *sibling* and *mutual transit* [12,22]. Because the sibling ASes belong to the same organization, they can exchange routes of

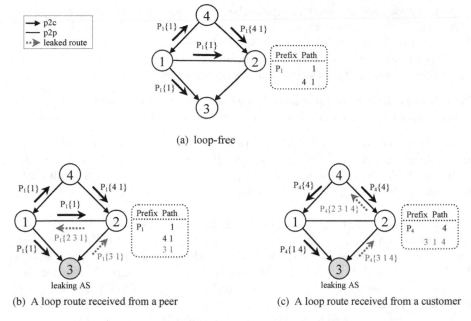

Fig. 2. Routing loops caused by route leaks

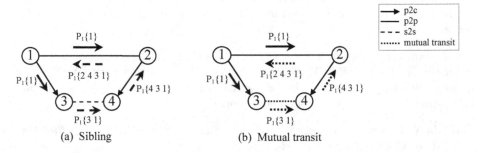

Fig. 3. Routing loops caused by complex relationships of sibling and mutual transit

each other's customers, peers and providers. Therefore, as Figure 3(a) shows, the sibling relationship can result in routing loops like route leaks do. Similarly, as shown in Figure 3(b), the mutual transit AS pair provide transit service mutually, which can also lead to routing loops. We will discuss the method of distinguishing the routing loops caused by route leaks, sibling and mutual transit relationships in the next section.

Second, we introduce the definition of downhill AS-Path [12]. A downhill AS-Path $(u_1, ..., u_n)$ means that for $1 \leq i < n$, the relationship of (u_i, u_{i+1}) is p2c or s2s.

Hypothesis 1. *An AS does not have a p2p or c2p relationship with any AS behind it in a downhill path.*

This hypothesis is based on the valley-free rule and the acyclic type-of-relationship [19]. It means that if $(u_1, ..., u_n)$ is a downhill path, for $1 < i \leq n$, the relationship between u_1 and u_i cannot be p2p or c2p. Here we introduce this hypothesis to assume that the Internet AS topology is a directed acyclic graph [19]. Given the hypothesis, we present the following theorem.

Theorem 1. *Under the hypothesis 1, if an AS receives a route that is originated by itself from its peer or customer, then it can identify the route is a leaked route.*

Proof. We prove by contradiction. Suppose X and Y are BGP neighbors, and the relationship between them is p2p/p2c. If X receives a route originated by itself from Y, let us suppose the route is $\{Y, ..., X\}$. And then we get a full route propagation AS-Path $\{X, Y, ..., X\}$, which includes a routing loop originated from X.

Let us assume that the AS-Path $\{X, Y, ..., X\}$ conforms to the valley-free rule. Because $\{X, Y\}$ is a p2p/p2c link, the path $\{Y, ..., X\}$ can then only be a downhill path according to the valley-free rule. However, given that the relationship between Y and X is p2p/c2p, this means that Y has a p2p/c2p relationship with an AS behind it (i.e., X) in the downhill path $\{Y, ..., X\}$. Clearly it contradicts the hypothesis 1. Therefore, the preceding assumption that the AS-Path $\{X, Y, ..., X\}$ is valley-free is not true, i.e., the route $\{Y, ..., X\}$ is a leaked route.

Corollary 1. *Under the hypothesis 1, if an AS receives a route that contains its own ASN from its peer or customer, then it can identify the route is a leaked route.*

Proof. Similarly, suppose X receives the route $\{Y, ..., X, ...\}$, where Y is its peer or customer. According to Theorem 1, the route propagation path $\{X, Y, ..., X\}$ is not valley-free. Therefore, the propagation path $\{X, Y, ..., X, ...\}$ is also not valley-free, i.e., $\{Y, ..., X, ...\}$ is a leaked route.

Corollary 2. *Under the hypotheses 1, if a tier-1 AS receives a route that contains its own ASN, then we conclude that*
(1) The route is a leaked route.
(2) If there is only one route leak in the route, then the leaking AS is located in the loop and the route leak is a Provider-Provider leaking.

Proof. Since the route received by a tier-1 AS must come from a peer or customer, it is easy to draw the first conclusion based on Corollary 1. For the second conclusion, we suppose that X is the tier-1 AS, and $\{u_1, ..., u_n, X, ...\}$ is the route it receives. Then we have a propagation path $\{X, u_1, ..., u_n, X, ...\}$. According to Theorem 1, the sub-path $\{X, u_1, ..., u_n, X\}$ is not valley-free, i.e., there must be route leaks occur in the loop. Consequently, if there is only one route leak in the path $\{X, u_1, ..., u_n, X, ...\}$, the leaking AS should be located in the loop path $\{X, u_1, ..., u_n, X\}$.

Next, we prove that the only one route leak is Provider-Provider leaking by contradiction. Suppose the route leak is a Provider-Peer leaking, i.e., the leaking pattern is p2c-p2p. Given that X is a tier-1 AS, the sequence of relationships in the loop path $\{X, u_1, ..., u_n, X\}$ will be $\{p2p/p2c, ..., p2c - p2p, ..., c2p/p2p\}$. According to the valley-free rule, there are at least two route leaks in the path. One is p2c-p2p, and the other occurs in $\{p2p, ..., c2p/p2p\}$. Therefore, it contradicts the precondition that there is only one route leak in the route. In the case of Peer-Peer or Peer-Provider leaking, a similar argument applies. Therefore, the route leak can only be a Provider-Provider leaking.

Hypothesis 2. *The relationship between a tier-1 AS and its non-tier-1 neighbor is p2c.*

This hypothesis is based on the fact that the tier-1 ASes are at the top of the hierarchy of the Internet. And hence in the vast majority of cases, it is reasonable that they provide transit services for their non-tier-1 neighbors.

Corollary 3. *Under the hypotheses 1, 2, if a route contains two non-adjacent tier-1 ASes, then we conclude that*
(1) The route is a leaked route.
(2) If there is only one route leak in the route, then the leaking AS is located between the two non-adjacent tier-1 ASes and the route leak is a Provider-Provider leaking.

Proof. We begin with the proof of (1). Suppose the route that contains two non-adjacent tier-1 ASes is $\{..., Y, u_1, ..., u_n, X, ...\}$, where Y and X are tier-1 ASes and u_i is non-tier-1 AS. This implies that there is a best BGP route $\{u_1, ..., u_n, X, ...\}$ in the routing table of Y.

Because tier-1 ASes peer with each other and form a full mesh topology [11], Y and X must be neighbors and their relationship is p2p. Given that u_1 is a non-tier-1 AS (i.e., it should be a customer of Y according to hypothesis 2), Y will advertise the customer route $\{u_1, ..., u_n, X, ...\}$ to X. Therefore, X will receive a route $\{Y, u_1, ..., u_n, X, ...\}$ that contains its own ASN from its peer (Y). Hence, according to Corollary 2, the route $\{Y, u_1, ..., u_n, X, ...\}$ must be a leaked route. And consequently, the route $\{..., Y, u_1, ..., u_n, X, ...\}$ is also a leaked route.

Next, we prove (2). First, let's consider the route propagation path - $\{X, Y, u_1, ..., u_n, X, ...\}$. According to Corollary 2, the leaking AS must be located in the loop $\{X, Y, u_1, ..., u_n, X\}$. Given that $\{Y, u_1\}$ is a p2c link, we can conclude that Y is not a leaking AS. As a result, the leaking AS should be located in $\{Y, u_1, ..., u_n, X\}$, i.e., between X and Y. Second, if there is only one route leak in the route $\{Y, u_1, ..., u_n, X\}$, it can be proved as in Corollary 2 that the route leak must be a Provider-Provider leaking.

3.3 Leaking AS Identification

Once a leaked route is detected, the most important thing is to identify the leaking AS to mitigate and eliminate the impact of route leaks. The Corollary 2 and Corollary 3 give the general location of the route leak. We now discuss a way to further determine the specific position of the leaking AS.

First, in Corollary 2 the route leak has been proved to be a Provider-Provider leaking, i.e., the pattern of the loop path $\{X, u_1, ..., u_n, X\}$ is: $\{p2p/p2c, ..., p2c-c2p, ..., c2p/p2p\}$. This means that the leaking AS is at the bottom of the valley path.

Second, according to [12], it is reasonable that a provider network is typically larger than its customer network and hence it is common that a provider AS has a higher degree than its customer does. To verify this point, we counted the degrees of ASes in the Internet topology derived from BGP data in Routeviews [8], and validated that 98.34% of the p2c links in the largest ground-truth data of AS relationships [22] conform to the assumption that the provider's degree is higher than the customer's degree.

Hence, on the basis of the above analysis, it is extremely likely that in Corollary 2 the leaking AS should be the AS with the lowest degree in the loop path. Similarly, in Corollary 3, the leaking AS is supposed to be the AS with the lowest degree located between the two non-adjacent tier-1 ASes.

3.4   Detection Mechanism

The Theorem 1 and Corollary 1 can be used to detect route leaks in an AS. The Corollary 2 and Corollary 3 can be exploited to build a distributed system to detect route leaks that occur in the Internet. Figure 4 shows the architecture of our route leaks identification system. Our system consists of three modules: routes collection module, sibling and mutual transit inference module and leak identification module.

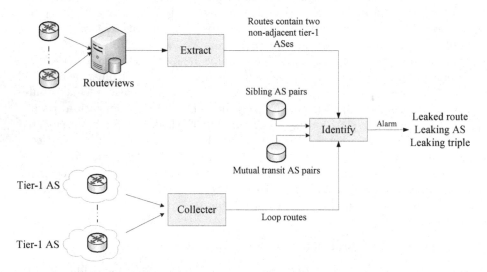

Fig. 4. Architecture of route leaks identification system

Algorithm 1. Route leaks detection algorithm

Input: Routes collected by Routeviews that contain two non-adjacent tier-1 ASes
        Loop Routes received by tier-1 ASes
        P_s: Set of sibling AS pairs
        P_m: Set of mutual transit AS pairs

Output: L_r: The leaked route
          L_{AS}: The leaking AS
          L_{tp}: The leaking triple

1: **if** route contains two non-adjacent tier-1 ASes: $\{..., Y, u_1, ..., u_n, X, ...\}$ **then**
2:     extract sub-path $l : \{Y, u_1, ..., u_n, X\}$
3:     **for** $1 \leq i < n$ **do**
4:        **if** $\{u_i, u_{i+1}\} \in P_s$ or $\{u_i, u_{i+1}\} \in P_m$ **then**
5:           **return**
6:        **end if**
7:     **end for**
8:     $L_r \leftarrow \{..., Y, u_1, ..., u_n, X, ...\}$
9:     find that u_j such that $degree[u_j] = \min\limits_{1 \leq i \leq n} degree[u_i]$
10:    $L_{AS} \leftarrow u_j$
11:    $L_{tp} \leftarrow \{u_{j-1}, u_j, u_{j+1}\}$
12: **end if**

13: **if** route contains routing loop: $\{X, u_1, ..., u_n, X, ...\}$ **then**
14:    extract the loop path $l : \{X, u_1, ..., u_n, X\}$
15:    **for** $1 \leq i < n$ **do**
16:       **if** $\{u_i, u_{i+1}\} \in P_s$ or $\{u_i, u_{i+1}\} \in P_m$ **then**
17:          **return**
18:       **end if**
19:    **end for**
20:    $L_r \leftarrow \{X, u_1, ..., u_n, X, ...\}$
21:    find that u_j such that $degree[u_j] = \min\limits_{1 \leq i \leq n} degree[u_i]$
22:    $L_{AS} \leftarrow u_j$
23:    $L_{tp} \leftarrow \{u_{j-1}, u_j, u_{j+1}\}$
24: **end if**
25: **return**

1. **Routes collection module**: This module collects anomalous routes from Routeviews and tier-1 ASes. According to Corollary 3, we extract those routes that contain two non-adjacent tier-1 ASes from Routeviews. And based on Corollary 2, we also collect loop routes received by tier-1 ASes for detecting route leaks.
2. **Sibling and mutual transit inference module**: This module is an assistant module. It infers the AS relationships of sibling and mutual transit. The inference methods are described in the next section. It should be mentioned that the inferred database will be updated periodically (one month).

3. **Leak identification module**: This module detects route leaks from the collected routes. The detection algorithm is summarized in Algorithm 1. The route will first be checked if it contains sibling or mutual transit AS pairs. If not, then it will be identified as a leaked route and the leaking AS will be further identified using the method presented above. Once the leaking AS is determined, the leaking triple is also figured out, i.e., the route leak incident is identified.

As we can see, the route leaks identification system does not need information about routing policies. It only performs passive monitoring of BGP routes to detect route leaks that occur in the Internet, and hence it is lightweight and easy to deploy.

4   Detection Results

In this section, we present the detection results of route leaks. Our route leaks identification system has been deployed since 01/01/2015. At present, the system only collects BGP routes from Routeviews. Collecting loop routes from tier-1 ASes needs to contact with their operators one by one and is a part of our future work. Nonetheless, it does not affect the evaluation of the effectiveness of our mechanism, because the detection algorithms for the two types of input data (i.e., loop routes and routes containing two non-adjacent tier-1 ASes) are nearly identical, as illustrated in Algorithm 1.

For illustrative purposes, we provide detection results of one month from 01/01/2015 to 01/31/2015. It should be mentioned that we selected the ASes in the clique inferred by [22] as tier-1 ASes. There were 471458 routes that contain two non-adjacent tier-1 ASes (we call them *T1-T1* routes) in the month. As mentioned in the above section, those routes can be caused by route leaks or complex relationships of sibling and mutual transit.

4.1   T1-T1 Routes Caused by Complex Relationships of Sibling and Mutual Transit

Our detection system used the AS-to-organization data [1] derived from WHOIS database to infer the sibling ASes. Those ASes belong to the same organization were inferred to be siblings. There were 631995 sibling AS pairs in total.

Next, the set of mutual transit ASes is inferred as follows. Suppose a route containing a tier-1 AS is $\{..., T1, u_1, ..., u_i, u_{i+1}, ..., u_n\}$, where $T1$ is the tier-1 AS. According to the heuristic algorithm described in [25,22] (i.e., the links seen by a tier-1 AS are p2c), the link (u_i, u_{i+1}) should be p2c. Hence, if the reverse-link (u_{i+1}, u_i) is also seen by a tier-1 AS, i.e., there exists another route $\{..., T1, u_1, ..., u_{i+1}, u_i, ..., u_m\}$ in the global routing table, the relationship of (u_i, u_{i+1}) is probably mutual transit. Note that a route leak can also results in the reverse-link (u_{i+1}, u_i) being seen by a tier-1 AS. To distinguish between them, our system picked out all the AS pairs that both their forward-link and reverse-link were seen by tier-1 ASes every day during the last month. We believe that

Table 1. Results for the detected T1-T1 routes

T1-T1 routes	Number	Percent
Routes containing sibling ASes	31236	6.60%
Routes containing mutual transit ASes	98635	20.90%
Leaked routes	341587	72.50%

those AS pairs are mutual transit because they lasted for one month, whereas a route leak would generally last much shorter.

With the sibling and mutual transit data, our system filtered out the T1-T1 routes that contain sibling ASes and mutual transit ASes. Table 1 shows the results for the detected T1-T1 routes. There are less than one-third of T1-T1 routes that are caused by sibling and mutual transit relationships, and the rest of routes are identified as leaked routes. It should be mentioned that because the inferred siblings and mutual transit ASes may be incomplete, the identified leaked routes are *probable* leaked routes. Below we analyze those probable leaked routes in detail.

4.2   Analysis of Leaked Routes

As illustrated in Section 3.4, our detection system identifies the leaked route as well as the leaking AS and leaking triple. There were 268 leaking ASes and 447 leaking triples that were extracted from the 341587 leaked T1-T1 routes. As mentioned in Section 2, a route leak incident can be represented as a leaking triple. Figure 5 shows the number of leaking triples (i.e., route leak incidents) per day.

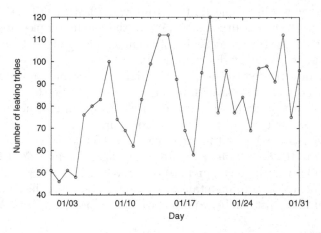

Fig. 5. Number of leaking triples (route leak incidents) per day

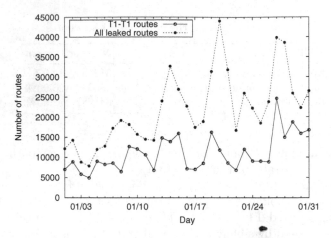

Fig. 6. Number of leaked routes per day

Note that not just the detected T1-T1 routes, any route containing those leaking triples in the routing table were leaked routes. To gain insight into the leaking triples, we also filtered out all routes that contain them in the month. Figure 6 shows the number of leaked routes per day. By comparing Figure 5 with Figure 6, it can be seen that there was no positive correlation between the number of route leak incidents and the number of leaked routes. This is because there are big differences in the impact of route leak incidents (i.e., how many ASes adopted the leaked routes). Some route leaks polluted quite a number of ASes in the Internet, and other route leaks only impact a few ASes.

Since the route leak incident usually results from misconfigurations [30], the leaking triple should be an anomaly and hence it should not appear or seldom appeared in the global routing table before. To verify this, we studied the days of appearance of the leaking triples in the Routeviews last month (i.e., December 2014). As Figure 7 shows, although 61.5% of the leaking triples appeared less than 2 days, it is surprising that 28.4% of them appeared more than 5 days and 9.6% of them appeared every day last month.

We further investigated the long-term leaking triples that appeared for more than 5 days. The prefix list based filtering was found to be the major cause of the route leaks with a long persistency. Figure 8 shows an instance of long-term route leaks caused by the prefix list based configuration.

In Figure 8, AS53309 is multi-homed to AS19109 and AS11232, and it owns two prefixes: 74.116.252.0/23 and 74.116.254.0/23. As a provider of AS53309, AS11232 provides transit to the prefixes of AS53309. Usually AS11232 will use the prefix list of AS53309 to maintain a route filter. That is, the route with the prefix included in the list can be exported to its own providers (i.e., AS3356 and AS2828).

Most of the time, the above prefix list based filtering works properly. However, we found that in a special case of traffic engineering, the prefix list based

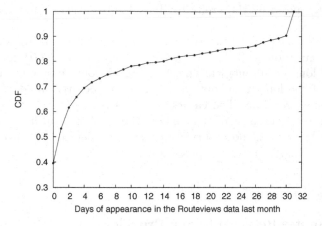

Fig. 7. Distribution of the leaking triples as a function of their days of appearance

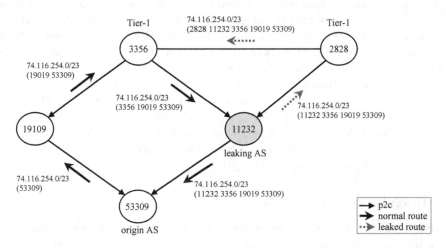

Fig. 8. An instance of long-term route leaks caused by prefix list based filtering

configuration can lead to route leaks. For instance, due to possible traffic engineering policy, AS53309 did not announce the prefix 74.116.254.0/23 to AS11232 and only announced it to AS19019 during December 2014. Consequently, there was only one route destined for 74.116.254.0/23 in the routing table of AS11232, which was {3356 19019 53309}. Since the prefix of the route can pass through the route filter, AS11232 propagated the route to its upstream provider AS2828. As a result, a typical Provider-Provider leaking occurred.

Note that besides the traffic engineering, when the link between AS11232 and AS53309 fails, the prefix list based configuration can also result in the route leak above, as illustrated in [30].

It is reasonable that once the prefix list based filtering was configured, it would not be changed unless the customer updates their prefix list. Therefore, the route leaks caused by the prefix list based configuration would last a long time.

From Figure 8, we can see that the key feature of route leaks caused by prefix list based configuration is the leaking AS and origin AS are BGP neighbors. By checking if the long-term route leaks meet this condition, we found that there are about 62.2% of the long-term route leaks that can be attributed to the prefix based export configuration. The causes behind the rest long-term route leaks were hard to identify because of the confidentiality of the routing policies. And as a future work, we will do a survey of the ISP operators involved in those long-term route leaks to learn the possible causes.

5   Discussion

5.1   Loop Routes Received from a Provider

We have proved that a loop route received from a peer or customer should be a leaked route. However, some operators in the NANOG [6] mailing list provided us with several loop routes received from their providers [5]. We studied those loop routes and found that they were not leaked routes and also caused by the traffic engineering illustrated in Figure 8.

As we can see in Figure 8, there are two ASes that receive loop routes. One is AS3356, and the loop route it receives is from a peer. The other is AS53309, and the loop route is received from a provider. According to the valley-free rule, the former loop route is a leaked route and the latter is not. Hence, it can be seen from this example that when an AS receives a loop route from its provider, it cannot identify the route is a leaked route.

5.2   Complex Routing Policies

The term "route leaks" in our discussion refer to route advertisements that violate valley-free rule. However, routing policies between ASes in the Internet are sometimes complex than the valley-free rule. For example, one of the long-term leaking triples we detected is {2914 17676 209}. Since AS2914 and AS209 are tier-1 ASes and AS17676 is a non-tier-1 AS, this triple is typically in violation of the valley-free rule. But the results queried from IRR database [4] show that AS17676 has complex routing policies which announce routes learned-from AS209 to AS2914 and its other providers. This means that although the triple {2914 17676 209} is not valley-free according to our definition, it is in a special arrangement and not a real route leak.

Therefore, it should be emphasized again that the route leaks identified by our system are advertisements in the sense of valley-free violation.

5.3   Limitations

Our detection system also has a few limitations. First, as mentioned in Section 4.1, the inferred siblings and mutual transit ASes may be incomplete, which might lead to false positives in detection of route leaks. Second, our system identifies the leaking AS by comparing the degrees of ASes. But as described in Section 3.3, it cannot be 100 percent certain that a provider AS has a higher degree than its customer does. Hence the identified leaking AS might be false in a few rare cases.

6   Related Work

While most existing work on BGP security has focused on the *correctness of routing information*, some studies have been concerned with the *correct application of routing policies*. More than a decade ago, Mahajan et al. [30] studied the export misconfiguration (i.e., route leak) which violates the export routing policy. Then in [27,14], the valley-free violation in inter-domain routing has been characterized and investigated. And recently, researchers formally define the advertisement of BGP routes in violation of the valley-free rule as "route leaks" [9,28].

There are a few proposals on prevention or detection of route leaks. Qiu et al. [27] proposed a prevention mechanism that carries pattern information of path in a transitive attribute. The new transitive attribute can be used by the receiver to determine if the advertisement is a leaked route. Although their mechanism can prevent propagating the leaked routes without revealing AS relationships, but it would fail when the attached pattern information is tampered by attackers. Another two similar approaches [29,10] also insert a flag in the BGP route to mark the target (i.e., customer, peer or provider) of the advertisements, and they further protect the integrity of flags by using cryptographic techniques such as S-BGP [18] and BGPSEC [21]. However, they may face challenges because those cryptographic techniques will cause high resource overhead and it is far from the full deployment of them. In [28], three detection approaches are presented to identify route leaks. Although they can address different types of route leaks, but some of them require advertisements of false prefixes, which may be unacceptable for operators.

Compared to the prevention mechanisms [27,29,10], our approach does not require modification of BGP protocol. Moreover, unlike the detection mechanism in [28] that can only be used by an AS to detect the leaked routes for its sake, our approach can monitor the route leaks that occur around the Internet and further identify the leaking AS and leaking triple.

7   Conclusions and Future Works

Route leaks detection is a challenging problem due to the confidential nature of business relationships and routing policies between ASes. In this paper, we studied the routing loops caused by route leaks and presented a novel mechanism that identifies route leaks by monitoring routing loops. We provided a theoretical analysis of the link between routing loops and route leaks. The theoretical analysis shows that when an AS receives a route with loop from its peer or customer, there should be route leaks that occur in the route. We further extended the theorem to the case of tier-1 ASes, and proposed a system to detect the leaked routes in the Internet. In addition to the leaked route, our system can identify the leaking AS and the leaking triple which can be helpful for mitigating and eliminating the impacts of route leak incidents in time. The detection results show that our system can discover a lot of route leak incidents that occur in the Internet per day.

As part of our future work, we will continue building the submodule of gathering loop routes from tier-1 ASes. We plan to start with those tier-1 ASes that peered with our campus network (The China Education and Research Network, CERNET [2]). We believe that once such a submodule is completed, we can detect more route leaks by exploiting those routing loops.

Acknowledgement. The authors would like to thank Randy Bush for his helpful comments. This work was supported by National Natural Science Foundation of China (Grant Nos. 61472215).

References

1. The caida as organizations dataset - 20150101. http://data.caida.org/datasets/as-organizations
2. Cernet homepage. http://www.edu.cn/english_1369/index.shtml
3. Chinese routing errors redirect russian traffic. http://research.dyn.com/2014/11/chinese-routing-errors-redirect-russian-traffic
4. Irr - internet routing registry. http://www.irr.net
5. look for bgp routes containing local as#. http://mailman.nanog.org/pipermail/nanog/2015-January/072922.html
6. Nanog. http://www.nanog.org
7. Routing leak briefly takes down google. http://research.dyn.com/2015/03/routing-leak-briefly-takes-google
8. University of oregon route views project. http://www.routeviews.org
9. Dickson, B.: Route leaks - definitions (2012). http://tools.ietf.org/html/draft-dickson-sidr-route-leak-def-03
10. Dickson, B.: Route leaks - requirements for detection and prevention thereof (2012). http://tools.ietf.org/html/draft-dickson-sidr-route-leak-reqts-02
11. Faratin, P., Clark, D.D., Bauer, S., Lehr, W.: Complexity of internet interconnections: Technology, incentives and implications for policy (2007)
12. Gao, L.: On inferring autonomous system relationships in the internet. IEEE/ACM Trans. Netw. **9**(6), 733–745 (2001)
13. Gill, P., Schapira, M., Goldberg, S.: A survey of interdomain routing policies. Computer Communication Review **44**(1), 28–34 (2014)
14. Giotsas, V., Zhou, S.: Valley-free violation in internet routing–analysis based on bgp community data. In: 2012 IEEE International Conference on Communications (ICC), pp. 1193–1197. IEEE (2012)
15. Goldberg, S.: Why is it taking so long to secure internet routing? Communications of the ACM **57**(10), 56–63 (2014)
16. Huston, G.: Leaking routes (2012). http://labs.apnic.net/?p=139

17. Huston, G.: Mitm and routing security (2013). http://labs.apnic.net/?p=447
18. Kent, S., Lynn, C., Seo, K.: Secure border gateway protocol (s-bgp). IEEE Journal on Selected Areas in Communications **18**(4), 582–592 (2000)
19. Kosub, S., Maaß, M.G., Täubig, H.: Acyclic type-of-relationship problems on the internet. In: Erlebach, T. (ed.) CAAN 2006. LNCS, vol. 4235, pp. 98–111. Springer, Heidelberg (2006)
20. Lepinski, M., Kent, S.: An Infrastructure to Support Secure Internet Routing. RFC 6480, February 2012
21. Lepinski, M., Turner, S.: An overview of bgpsec (2015). http://tools.ietf.org/html/draft-ietf-sidr-bgpsec-overview-07
22. Luckie, M., Huffaker, B., Dhamdhere, A., Giotsas, V., et al.: As relationships, customer cones, and validation. In: Proceedings of the 2013 Conference on Internet Measurement Conference, pp. 243–256. ACM (2013)
23. McPherson, D., Amante, S., Osterweil, E., Mitchell, D.: Route-leaks & mitm attacks against bgpsec, April 2014. http://tools.ietf.org/html/draft-ietf-grow-simple-leak-attack-bgpsec-no-help-04
24. Ng, J.: Extensions to bgp to support secure origin bgp (sobgp), April 2004. http://tools.ietf.org/html/draft-ng-sobgp-bgp-extensions-02
25. Oliveira, R., Willinger, W., Zhang, B., et al.: Quantifying the completeness of the observed internet as-level structure (2008)
26. van Oorschot, P.C., Wan, T., Kranakis, E.: On interdomain routing security and pretty secure bgp (psbgp). ACM Transactions on Information and System Security (TISSEC) **10**(3), 11 (2007)
27. Qiu, S.Y., McDaniel, P.D., Monrose, F.: Toward valley-free inter-domain routing. In: IEEE International Conference on Communications, ICC 2007, pp. 2009–2016. IEEE (2007)
28. Siddiqui, M., Montero, D., Serral-Gracià, R., Yannuzzi, M.: Self-reliant detection of route leaks in inter-domain routing. Computer Networks **82**, 135–155 (2015)
29. Sundaresan, S., Lychev, R., Valancius, V.: Preventing attacks on bgp policies: One bit is enough (2011)
30. Wetherall, D., Mahajan, R., Anderson, T.: Understanding bgp misconfigurations. In: Proc. ACM SIGCOMM (2002)
31. Zhang, Z., Zhang, Y., Hu, Y.C., Mao, Z.M., Bush, R.: Ispy: detecting ip prefix hijacking on my own. ACM SIGCOMM Computer Communication Review **38**(4), 327–338 (2008)

PULSAR: Stateful Black-Box Fuzzing of Proprietary Network Protocols

Hugo Gascon[✉], Christian Wressnegger, Fabian Yamaguchi,
Daniel Arp, and Konrad Rieck

Computer Security Group, University of Göttingen, Göttingen, Germany
{hgascon,christian.wressnegger,fabian.yamaguchi,
darp,konrad.rieck}@uni-goettingen.de

Abstract. The security of network services and their protocols critically depends on minimizing their attack surface. A single flaw in an implementation can suffice to compromise a service and expose sensitive data to an attacker. The discovery of vulnerabilities in protocol implementations, however, is a challenging task: While for standard protocols this process can be conducted with regular techniques for auditing, the situation becomes difficult for proprietary protocols if neither the program code nor the specification of the protocol are easily accessible. As a result, vulnerabilities in closed-source implementations can often remain undiscovered for a longer period of time. In this paper, we present PULSAR, a method for stateful black-box fuzzing of proprietary network protocols. Our method combines concepts from fuzz testing with techniques for automatic protocol reverse engineering and simulation. It proceeds by observing the traffic of a proprietary protocol and inferring a generative model for message formats and protocol states that can not only analyze but also simulate communication. During fuzzing this simulation can effectively explore the protocol state space and thereby enables uncovering vulnerabilities deep inside the protocol implementation. We demonstrate the efficacy of PULSAR in two case studies, where it identifies known as well as unknown vulnerabilities.

Keywords: Model-based fuzzing · Vulnerability discovery · Protocol reverse engineering

1 Introduction

A myriad of network services and protocols is employed in today's computer networks, ranging from classic protocols of the Internet suite to proprietary binary protocols implemented only by particular vendors. While these network services steadily expand their capabilities, securing their functionality still remains a challenging task: A single vulnerability in the implementation of a protocol can suffice to undermine the security of a network service and expose sensitive data to an attacker. For example, a flaw in the implementation of the universal plug-and-play protocol rendered roughly 23 million routers vulnerable to attacks from the Internet [27].

© Institute for Computer Sciences, Social Informatics and Telecommunications Engineering 2015
B. Thuraisingham et al. (Eds.): SecureComm 2015, LNICST 164, pp. 330–347, 2015.
DOI: 10.1007/978-3-319-28865-9_18

Several methods for locating and eliminating vulnerabilities in protocol implementations have been proposed in the last years, each addressing different aspects of the problem. For example, if the implementation of the protocol is easily accessible, different techniques from program analysis can be applied for hunting down security flaws, such as white-box fuzzing [e.g., 13,15], dynamic taint tracking [e.g., 9,34], symbolic execution [e.g., 7,31] and static code analysis [e.g., 18,25,36,37]. The situation, however, changes fundamentally if neither the code nor the specification of the protocol are directly accessible. While in some cases there are means for retrieving the implementation of a protocol, for example by reading out a firmware image or reverse-engineering a binary package, the complexity of this effort may still impede a sufficient security analysis.

Only few approaches exist [14,17] that can help spotting vulnerabilities in settings where code and specifications are hard to obtain. These approaches provide first means for automatically inferring fuzzers for proprietary protocols if a program analysis is not possible or difficult to carry out. Due to the lack of insights in the protocol code; however, these approaches are not capable of guiding the fuzzing process through the implementation. As a consequence, flaws that are linked to deep states in the protocol implementation are hard to reach efficiently.

In this paper, we present PULSAR, a method for stateful black-box fuzzing of proprietary network protocols. Our method combines concepts from fuzz testing with techniques for automatic protocol reverse engineering and simulation. It proceeds by observing the network traffic of an unknown protocol and inferring a generative model for message formats and protocol states that can not only analyze but also simulate communication. In contrast to previous approaches, this model enables effectively exploring the protocol state space during fuzzing and directing the analysis to states which are particularly suitable for fuzz testing. This *guided fuzzing* allows for uncovering vulnerabilities deep inside the protocol implementation. Moreover, by being part of the communication, PULSAR can increase the coverage of the state space, resulting in less but more effective testing iterations.

We empirically evaluate the capabilities of PULSAR in two case studies. First, we analyze the standard text-based protocol FTP as an illustrative example and then proceed to applying PULSAR to the proprietary binary protocol OSCAR, implemented in many instant messengers. To demonstrate the efficacy of simulating network communication, we direct our fuzzer against clients of the respective protocols, as these are harder to test with regular fuzzers due to their active role in the communication. In both case studies, PULSAR is able to spot known flaws in these clients, but also hints us to previously unknown vulnerabilities.

The rest of the paper is organized as follows: we introduce our method for stateful fuzzing of proprietary protocols in Section 2 and evaluate its efficacy in Section 3. Limitations and related work are discussed in Section 4 and 5, respectively. Section 6 concludes the paper.

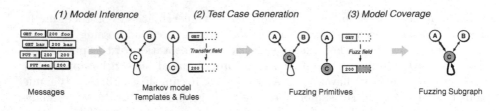

Fig. 1. Overview of PULSAR and the different analysis steps.

2   Methodology

The goal of PULSAR is to be able to effectively fuzz the implementation of proprietary protocols for which no specification exits and the underlying code is hard to analyze. In order to achieve this, our method starts by inferring a model of the protocol including its state machine and the format of the messages. The combination of both elements allow us to actively control the communication in order to guide the fuzzing process and to build faulty inputs that are sent to the network service. As explained in Figure 1, PULSAR proceeds in the following steps:

1. *Model inference.* A sample of network traces from the protocol under test is captured and a model is inferred from its messages. This include a Markov model representing the state machine of the protocol, templates that identify the format of the messages and rules that track the data flow between messages during communication.

2. *Test case generation.* The extracted templates and rules enable defining a set of fuzzing primitives that can be applied to message fields at specific stages of the communication. Using these primitives, test cases for black-box fuzzing are automatically generated.

3. *Model Coverage.* To increase the coverage of the security analysis, protocol states that are particularly suitable for fuzzing are selected. To this end, the fuzzer is guided to subgraphs in the state machine that are rarely visited and contain the largest number of messages with variable input fields.

PULSAR is implemented as an open-source tool[1] that once placed in the network can operate as a service or client and simulate communication with the corresponding party. In the following we describe the three steps conducted by PULSAR in more detail.

2.1   Model Inference

While model-based fuzz testing outperforms brute force fuzzing [30], it also does rely heavily on the quality of the specification used for the generation of the test

---

[1] https://github.com/hgascon/pulsar

cases. In the case of fuzzers whose goal is to identify errors in the implementation of well-known protocols, these models can be built on the basis of existing RFCs or proper documentation. On the contrary, poorly documented or totally closed proprietary protocols represent a tough challenge for such methods.

To address this problem, our method builds on the techniques introduced by Krueger et al. with PRISMA [19], a probabilistic approach to model both the message content and the state machine of an unknown protocol solely relying on standard captures of network traffic. The quality of these models surpasses that of previous works targeting the problem of reverse engineering network protocols without the need to access the binary implementation. As detailed in Section 3, the inferred model allows our method not only to generate relevant security test cases but to simulate the inputs and outputs of a real entity within the environment of the system under test.

Data Acquisition. In a real scenario, a software application usually communicates with different entities in the network, establishing several connections based on different protocols. As a fuzzing session of PULSAR targets an individual service, we start by capturing all traffic transmitted and received by an application between a unique combination of source and destination IPs and PORTs. Then, we re-assemble the captured packages and feed the complete streams into a session extractor. A session identifier is assigned to each one of the streams. If no packet is received for a selected time interval, a session will be marked as terminated, so that a new packet within the same connection will belong to a new session. The interval can be provided as a parameter and tuned to suit the rate of new connections established by the application under test.

We need to note here that a model learned from network traces alone may naturally lack parts of the functionality of the protocol if this functionality has not been observed during the training phase. Therefore, the analyst can generate specific interactions with the test application to model the inputs and outputs of the system that need to be audited.

Message Clustering. After traffic recording and session identification, we model each message as a sequence of bytes. To infer common structures among the series of messages we begin by mapping these sequences of bytes into a finite-dimensional vector space for clustering by the following two strategies.

For text-based protocols, where messages are typically formed by string tokens separated by pre-defined characters, each dimension is associated with an individual token in the feature vector. Thus, each dimension indicates the occurrences of a specific token within a message. In the case of binary protocols, we follow a similar approach where each individual n-gram (i.e., series of bytes of a specific length) within a message is mapped to the correspondent dimension in the feature vector. As the goal of this analysis phase is to model the different types of messages of the protocol, we proceed with a dimensionality reduction phase that allows the clustering algorithm to focus on the most discriminative characteristics from each message. Following the design of PRISMA [19], we use a simple statistical test [16] to remove volatile features, such as cookies and random strings, and constant elements that occur in almost every message.

Once that each message is represented as a vector, we use the Euclidean distance as similarity metric to apply the clustering algorithm. This allow us to extract common message structures which typically occur during a certain stage of the modeled protocol. Since most protocols are assembled from parts, we apply the non-negative matrix factorization algorithm (NMF) for part-based clustering [21]. NMF is an effective and well-known clustering algorithm that represents given data as a factorization of the data matrix (features × traces). After elimination of duplicated entries, the solution to the optimization problem let us identify clusters of messages that share similar structure and therefore belong to the same type.

Protocol State Machine. Network protocols are inherently defined by their state machine. As the exact state machine can only be inferred from the actual implementation of the protocol, PULSAR approximates the state machine from observed network traces. To this end, we annotate each message indicating if it has been generated by the client or the server. For this annotated version, a sliding window of size two links each message to previously observed traces. By computing the probabilities over these linked messages, we finally arrive at a second order Markov model that provides a probabilistic approximation of the real state machine.

Next, we minimize this Markov model into a deterministic finite automaton (DFA). To this end, we keep transitions with probabilities larger than zero and their associated states and at each transition we modify the DFA to accept the event of the second state. The DFA minimization algorithm introduced by Moore [26] let us generate an equivalent DFA that accepts the same language but with a smaller number of states, which allows the security analyst to manually inspect the model if required.

Message Format. In the clustering step we identify common tokens in the recorded messages. The position where these tokens occur in a session during the communication can be linked to a correspondent transition in the state machine. This enables us to correlate tokens with the state of the service. By analyzing the tokens of messages which are observable at the same state, we can improve the initial clustering stage and extract generic format definitions for these messages that we call *templates*.

In particular, after tokenizing each message according to the type of protocol (i.e. text-based or binary) and the embedding used (i.e. token or byte n-gram), we assign each message of a session to the corresponding state of the Markov model. For each one of the states we generate a unique group for all messages with the same number of tokens. If all messages within a group contain the same token at a specific position, this token is fixed as a constant. On the contrary, we consider tokens that differ even if only once as variables and its position is defined as a *field*. As a result, each state of the Markov model is associated with

	State A_S	State B_C	State C_S
Session 1	ftp 3.14	USER anon	331 User anon ok
Session 2	ftp 3.12	USER ren	331 User ren ok
	⋮	⋮	⋮
Session n	ftp 2.0	USER liz	331 User liz ok
Template	ftp □	USER □	331 User □ ok

Fig. 2. Example of template generation for a simplified FTP communication.

a series of templates that represent the generic type of messages that may be observed at such state of the communication.

Figure 2 presents a generic example of the process based on a series of FTP messages from different sessions.

Data Flow. Once the session information, the Markov model and the message templates are defined, we infer a set of *rules* to characterize the flow of information between different messages during a session. More specifically, we establish dependencies so that data found in a preceding message can be used to fill the different fields in a subsequent message.

In particular, we consider each possible combination of template occurrences for the horizon of length $k = 2$, i.e. (t_{-2}, t_{-1}, t_0) and find all messages assigned to these k templates which are sent in a session in this exact order. For each field f in such templates, we look for a rule that let us fill f with data content of a different field from previous messages. If no rule matches, the tokens are recorded and a new data rule is defined, indicating how to fill f with a random choice over previously seen data.

Table 1 describes the different type of rules we have implemented in our system. For instance, in the example from Figure 2 the field associated with the state C can be filled with the field of the previous message in all cases.

Table 1. Rules checked during model building. Parameters like d and s are automatically inferred from the training data.

Rule Description
Copy Exact copy of the content of one field to another.
Seq. Copy of a numerical field incremented by d.
Add Copy the content of a field and add data d to the front or back.
Part Copy the front or back part of a field split by separator s
Data Fill the field by randomly picking data d which we have seen before.

2.2 Test Case Generation

Up to this point, PULSAR is able to simulate both ends of the communication with high accuracy. Furthermore, the templates and fields in our model give us the opportunity to feed the other side of the connection with faulty inputs at a certain point in a session. By applying fuzzing primitives to the data provided by the rules, we can send an ill formatted message when the service expects to parse a variable data field controlled by the remote side.

In particular, the system proceeds as follows: When a message from the other end of the communication is received, it is matched to one of the templates of the states for which a valid transition exist. As the state machine of the protocol is defined as a Markov model of second order, a valid transition is represented by the new matched template and the two previously matched templates in the form of a chain $A{:}B{:}C$. This means that if templates A and B have been observed, our system will try to match a received message to the template C that allow this transition. The set of rules for this transition is used by the system to build the next message in the case that a response is required.

In some cases, the received message at a certain stage of the communication may differ from that observed in the training data. As a result, some tokens or bytes may not allow for an exact template match even if the semantics of the message are expected by the model. Thus, to trigger a transition we use the Levenshtein string distance to measure the similarity between the received message and all reachable templates and select the most similar template as a match. This type of *semi-valid* transition has two effects. In the first place, the probability of reaching a "fuzzable" state is increased and second, if the semantics from the similarity matched template are too far from the semantics of the correct message, the response can be understood as a faulty input in itself. From the fuzzing perspective this is equivalent to a jump to an erroneous state in the real state model of the protocol. This situation may also led to errors in implementations where the network service is not able to handle a wrong sequence of messages during a session or a message from a different session.

After selecting a template D , we use the rules describing the transition $B{:}C{:}D$ in combination with a fuzzing primitive to build the next message. Possible primitives to select during testing include: *invalid UTF-8 byte sequence*, *constant string overflow* or *random string overflow* with or without a percentage of non-alphanumeric characters. A modular architecture allows for new fuzzing primitives to be added by the community to our open-source tool independently of the fuzzer implementation.

2.3 Model Coverage

A classic problem shared by random and more advanced model-based fuzzers is that of achieving a high coverage of the testing space. In the case of PULSAR, the system is able to fuzz the communication but also to be an active part of it as a network service. This allow us to guide the interaction between both ends and can be exploited in order to reach in less time those states where messages can be fuzzed.

After a message has been received and matched to a template, we must select a valid response template. For the purpose of simulating traffic as closed as possible to the real protocol the response template can be chosen according to the probability observed for each transition in the training data. However, when a fuzzing session is active, we define the *fuzzing subgraph* (FS) algorithm to effectively select the next response.

The FS algorithm controls the progress of the fuzzer across consecutive iterations and along the different states of the model, that is, new connections initiated by the application under test when a session is terminated. Its ultimate purpose is not only to increase the exploration of the model but to reach fuzzable states faster.

The algorithm proceeds as follows:

1. When a new fuzzing process is started, a *fuzzing mask* is assigned to each one of the templates. A fuzzing mask is a binary array of size equal to the number of fields in a template and indicates what fields are to be fuzzed the next time this template is selected to build a message. If a template has N fields, there exist 2^N possible fuzzing masks for each one of the templates. Initially, each mask is set to 2^N.

2. A *subgraph* is defined by a root state and all the states that can be reached in D transitions. The fuzzing weight of the subgraph is defined as the sum of the weights of its states. The weight of a state is computed as the sum of the fuzzing masks of its templates at a certain point in time.

3. When a message is received and matched, the state with the highest *subgraph* weight is selected from all states that represent a valid transition. The response template is chosen from this state according to the probability of occurrence in the training data.

4. The communication continues until a fuzzable state is reached. When a template is selected for fuzzing its fuzzing mask is decreased by one.

Modifying the fuzzing mask changes what fields of a template are fuzzed the next time the template is selected. Moreover, it also decreases the fuzzing weight of its state and previous states' subgraphs. As a result, the paths in the model with more fuzzing opportunities at early stages will be walked first. As the fuzzing masks of these templates decrease, the weight of the *subgraph* will also decrease, allowing for the exploration of adjacent paths in the model. If all states reachable from the current state through a valid transition have the same *subgraph* weight, we select the next state randomly.

3   Case Studies

We proceed to demonstrate the capabilities of PULSAR in two case studies with real-world protocols. In particular, we evaluate our method's ability to derive stateful fuzzers for the well-known protocol FTP (Section 3.1) as well as for the proprietary protocol OSCAR as used by different instant messengers (Section 3.2).

3.1   Core FTP Client

At first, we evaluate our method's ability to automatically discover vulnerabilities in implementations of a classic text-based protocol. To this end, we employ PULSAR to identify flaws in the Core FTP Client[2], a commercial, closed-source FTP client. This program has been found to contain several buffer overflow vulnerabilities, providing us with up-to-date ground truth for our analysis.

In June 2014, Gabor Seljan reported several heap-based buffer overflows in the Core FTP Client that can possibly be exploited by attackers to run arbitrary code in the context of the FTP client (CVE-2014-4643). These buffer overflows can be triggered by sending overly long responses to client requests in various stages of the communication. Clearly, to trigger these vulnerabilities the client needs to transition into the vulnerable state. Hence, suitable responses must be returned by the server and thus Seljan manually prepared a sequence of server responses in his proof-of-concept exploit.

In order to automatically identify these vulnerabilities in the FTP client, we record 987 traces from usual interaction between the client and the server running vsftpd[3]. Based on these traces PULSAR automatically generates the state machine depicted in Figure 3 as well as the corresponding message templates and rules. States containing templates with variable fields are shaded for both ends of the communication.

Every state in the state machine is labeled according to the terminology defined by the Markov model: Namely, the observed event that triggers the transition to that state and the event that is generated from this state. For instance, an event labeled X.UAC, Y.UAS indicates that a message from the client UAC has been observed and a response from the server UAS is required at this stage and vice versa. X and Y indicate the cluster identifier of the messages and the templates associated with that state. In case that templates *without* fixed tokens are assigned to that state the identifier is set to *. This also implies that the template is formed only by fields split by separators.

By using the state machine generated by PULSAR we are able to trigger all of the 6 vulnerabilities reported by Seljan in the scope of CVE-2014-4643 and two previously unknown buffer overflows vulnerabilities. Note that our approach does not require any prior knowledge of the FTP protocol or programming to trigger these bugs. Instead, it merely requires an independently learned state machine in order to impersonate a FTP server and have the client connect to it.

Figure 4 shows the two message sequences exchanged between the client and the fake FTP server—mimicked by PULSAR—resulting in the discovery of the two buffer overflows. In both sequences PULSAR first imitates the login procedure,

---

[2] http://www.coreftp.com
[3] http://vsftpd.beasts.org

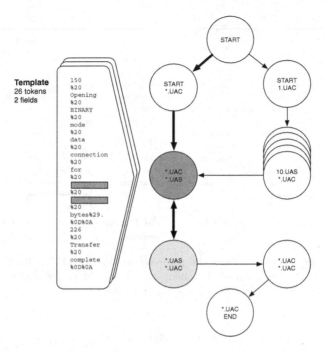

Fig. 3. State machine and example of template generated from FTP traces. The template contain 26 tokens and 2 of them are identified as variable fields.

allowing the client to authenticate itself by issuing a USER followed by a PASS command. The client then issues a PWD command in order to determine the current working directory to which the fake server responds with a seemingly valid directory. Next the client attempts to enter *active mode* by sending the PORT command to the server.

At this point in the communication the message sequences of Figure 4(b) and 4(a) diverge. While in Figure 4(b) PULSAR immediately responds with an overly long string causing the client to crash, in Figure 4(a) a valid response is sent back to the client and the dialog is kept alive. Subsequently the client issues the LIST command and crashes as result of an overly long response. Note that the client only crashes in response to the LIST command after entering active mode while remaining operational in passive mode. This highlights the necessity of stateful fuzzing to identify vulnerabilities located at deeper levels of the state machine.

3.2   Pidgin ICQ/AIM

In our second experiment, PULSAR is employed to learn a state machine for the *Open System for Communication in Realtime* (OSCAR) protocol, a lesser known binary protocol used by the AOL Instant Messenger and ICQ. OSCAR is an exceptionally complex protocol with a login procedure that comprises four stages

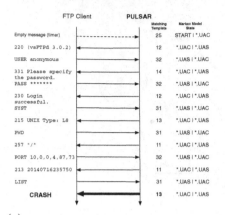
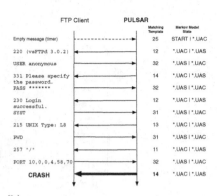

(a) Messages triggering a crash after a LIST command.

(b) Messages triggering a crash after a PORT command.

Fig. 4. Sequences of messages sent and received by the Core FTP client and PULSAR which lead to the termination of the client as a result of buffer overflows when the responses to the LIST and PORT commands are parsed.

and involves two independent servers, the *authorization server* and the *BOS server*. The authorization server has the responsibility to verify user credentials, generate an authorization cookie and redirect to a BOS server for all further processing.

In the past, several vulnerabilities in processing of BOS server messages have been identified in the popular instant messengers Pidgin and Adium. In particularly, several remotely triggerable crashes are known, which result from insufficient validation of UTF-8 strings sent to the client by the BOS server (CVE-2011-4601). We explore whether PULSAR is capable of automatically triggering these bugs, by generating a state machine for the BOS server from 512 network traces. To ensure that our BOS server is contacted, a firewall rule for **netfilter** is used to redirect all traffic sent to the real BOS IP address to our server, thus allowing the client to perform the first login stage with a real authorization server but effectively redirecting to our system all further requests issued from the client to the real BOS server.

Figure 5 shows the state machine learned for the communication between the ICQ/AIM client and the BOS server on port 5190. For clarity, large paths without fuzzable states are shown piled. The path through the model from the beginning of the communication to the state where the fuzzed message triggers the error in the client is highlighted.

Figure 6 shows in more detail the sequence of messages exchanged between Pidgin and the fake BOS server simulated by PULSAR. In combination with the Markov model it can be seen how the system is able to correctly complete the protocol negotiation phase with the client. After this phase, the client considers itself completely authenticated and the user can start interacting with the

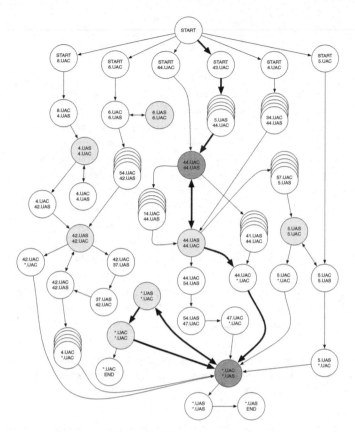

Fig. 5. Markov Model from OSCAR traces.

application. When the user requests to add a buddy to the list, our system fuzzes the response with an invalid UTF-8 sequence that triggers the crash of the client.

In summary, this experiment shows that PULSAR is capable of learning even complex and unusual binary protocols and trigger vulnerabilities deep within the state machine.

4   Limitations

Our experiments show that PULSAR is capable of identifying security flaws inside protocol implementations. Since the discovery of vulnerabilities, however, cannot be fully automated in the generic case due to Rice theorem [29], our method naturally has certain limitations. In this section, we examine these limitations and discuss possible improvements.

Our system strongly relies on the comprehensiveness and completeness of the observed network traffic and is thus unable to model protocol paths which do not occur in this traffic. This is a common problem of automatic inference

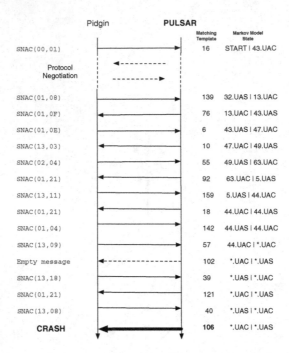

Fig. 6. Sequence of messages sent and received by the ICQ/AIM client and PULSAR to produce a crash as a result of a missed format verification when parsing a negative response to a buddy list request.

approaches and can not be completely solved. Yet, it can at least be alleviated by incorporating knowledge about the protocol under test. For example, the analyst can specifically induce and record protocol functionality that is security sensitive or might be prone to vulnerabilities. Moreover, depending on the particular environment, the analyst may change relevant parameters of the protocol, such as addresses and usernames, to help constructing corresponding templates and rules in the model.

Similarly, our approach does not reconstruct type information of fields which can be help to significantly reduce the range of tested values, thus improving the efficiency of fuzzing. As a remedy, the analyst might manually assign types to certain fields. However, the presented results show that our approach is already capable to identify vulnerabilities without this information—thereby compensating the lack of type information.

As most network monitoring approaches, PULSAR is unable to deal with encrypted network traffic. Although this problem can not be solved in general, it might in some cases be possible to inspect traffic through a proxy that acts as man in the middle. The model can then be learned from the collected traffic prior to forwarding it to the destination. Similarly, the final fuzzing can be conducted by transmitting fuzzed messages directly through the proxy.

5   Related Work

PULSAR unites two research areas from computer security in the scope of network protocols: First, we reverse engineer the protocol by automatic inference and second, based on the learned specification fuzzy testing is applied to the communications parties in order to reveal security vulnerabilities in the implementations. In the following we attempt to provide an overview of work conducted in these two vivid fields of research.

Protocol Re-engineering. Originally, the task of reverse engineering a network protocol has been a time-consuming, demanding and above all, manual task. Over almost a decade of research, however, the community has significantly advanced this field by proposing numerous techniques for automating the task of protocol re-engineering.

Nowadays, state-of-the-art methods can be divided into two orthogonal strains of research: On the one hand, methods that utilize and instrument an existing implementation based on, for instance, dynamic taint-analysis [6,9,11, 24,28,34] and on the other hand, those that attempt to derive the protocol specification from recorded network data only [8,10,19,20,22,23,33]. The task of deriving a protocol model is especially challenging in case the analyst does not have access to a concrete implementation showcasing the protocol interaction, but network recordings only. This exactly is the specific field of operation PULSAR acts in and therefore, we subsequently discuss this line of research in more detail. Another key distinction can be made between stateless [5,10,20] and stateful protocol inference [8,19,23,33]. Common to all approaches on reversing engineering network protocols is the need to differentiate variable from constant segments in the transferred data. In this respect many methods are based on or influenced by early work from Beddoe [4] and the *Protocol Informatics Project* [3] where sequence alignment algorithms from the field of bioinformatics were used to break up the protocol's messages into their individual components.

Roleplayer [10], for instance, extends this by certain heuristics for identifying IP addresses and domain names. In essence the method does not respect temporal states but already addresses the need for inter-field relations. Leita et al. [23] present a system (ScriptGen) that also makes use of sequence alignment algorithms but splits up its application over two phases of different granularity. A later extension of ScriptGen [22] is more relevant in our context. The authors enhance the approach such that it is able to address intra- as well as inter-protocol dependencies of variable fields and contents. This is particularly important for keeping alive recreated dialogs in a meaningful way. PRISMA [19]—the protocol inference framework we chose to build our method on—is able to accomplish this as well. Similarly, the authors of [33] make use of a Markov model and a layered application of the sequence analysis proposed by Beddoe just as ScriptGen does. Unfortunately, this approach is not able to relate variable fields over temporal states.

Protocol Fuzzing. Using fuzz testing it is possible to uncover security flaws in software by strategically generating input in an automated fashion [see 32]. Two levels of abstraction can be discriminated here: (a) *black-box fuzzing* [35] where a tester observes the software from the "outside" only seeing what in- and output is passed in or out respectively, and (b) *white-box fuzzing* [13] that allows the tester to inspect the code (either binary or source code) and for instance, make use of symbolic execution and constraint solving.

This separation obviously applies to protocol fuzzing as well. In this context however, it is crucial to differentiate between stateless and stateful systems. Fuzzing multi-party communication in a completely random fashion is foredoomed to fail. Only with the knowledge of the protocol's states and semantics at hand it is possible to navigate the fuzzer through the communication. This lead to stateful network fuzzers like KiF [1], SNOOZE [2] or Peachfuzzer [9,12], whereby one differentiates special purpose [1], specification-based [e.g., 12] and model-based [e.g., 9,14,17] fuzzers. The latter kind is usually powered by protocol inference as discussed in the previous paragraph and as implemented by PULSAR. Our approach differs from this work in that it operates in absence of the code and the specification for a protocol and thus comes handy in cases where proprietary protocols are used, for example, in embedded systems.

Closest to PULSAR are the approaches AutoFuzz [14] and the system described by Hsu et al. [17], which both also infer the protocol state machine and message formats from network traffic alone. Although these approaches share the same practical setting with PULSAR, they do not make use of the inferred information for fully simulating communication, likely due to the absence of dependence rules that enable us to let data flow between protocol states.

6   Conclusion

Finding vulnerabilities in the implementations of proprietary protocols is a challenging problem of computer security. In this paper, we present a novel method for black-box fuzzing that can help to spot vulnerabilities in protocol implementations, even if neither the code nor the specification of the protocol are available. To this end, our method PULSAR builds on concepts of protocol reverse engineering and simulation that enable us to automatically infer and guide fuzzers for proprietary protocols. Our evaluation demonstrates the utility of such fuzzers, where we identify vulnerabilities in the implementations of a text-based and a binary protocol.

While we have applied PULSAR against rather common network protocols, the method is also suitable for searching bugs in unusual implementations, such as in embedded devices inside cars and industrial control systems. Due to the capability of operating without code and specification, a collection of network traces is sufficient for PULSAR to infer a first fuzzer for an unknown protocol. Moreover, the simple design of the generative model inferred by PULSAR also enables a practitioner to inspect and manually refine the model which provides a bridge to regular fuzzing with manually crafted protocol grammars.

Acknowledgements. The authors gratefully acknowledge funding from the German Federal Ministry of Education and Research (BMBF) under the project INDI (6KIS0154K) and the German Research Foundation (DFG) under the project DEVIL (RI 2469/1-1).

References

1. Abdelnur, H.J., State, R., Festor, O.: KiF: a stateful SIP fuzzer. In: Proc. of International Conference on Principles, Systems and Applications of IP Telecommunications (IPTCOMM), pp. 47–56 (2007)
2. Banks, G., Cova, M., Felmetsger, V., Almeroth, K., Kemmerer, R., Vigna, G.: SNOOZE: toward a stateful NetwOrk prOtocol fuzZEr. In: Katsikas, S.K., López, J., Backes, M., Gritzalis, S., Preneel, B. (eds.) ISC 2006. LNCS, vol. 4176, pp. 343–358. Springer, Heidelberg (2006)
3. Beddoe, M.: The protocol informatics project, July 2015. http://www.4tphi.net/~awalters/PI/PI.html
4. Beddoe, M.A.: Network protocol analysis using bioinformatics algorithms. Technical report, McAfee Inc. (2005)
5. Bossert, G., Guihéry, F., Hiet, G.: Towards automated protocol reverse engineering using semantic information. In: Proc. of ACM Symposium on Information, Computer and Communications Security (ASIACCS) (2014)
6. Caballero, J., Yin, H., Liang, Z., Song, D.: Polyglot: automatic extraction of protocol message format using dynamic binary analysis. In: Proc. of ACM Conference on Computer and Communications Security (CCS) (2007)
7. Cha, S.K., Avgerinos, T., Rebert, A., Brumley, D.: Unleashing mayhem on binary code. In: Proc. of IEEE Symposium on Security and Privacy, pp. 380–394 (2012)
8. Cho, C.Y., Babić, D., Shin, E.C.R., Song, D.: Inference and analysis of formal models of botnet command and control protocols. In: Proc. of ACM Conference on Computer and Communications Security (CCS) (2010)
9. Comparetti, P.M., Wondracek, G., Kruegel, C., Kirda, E.: Prospex: protocol specification extraction. In: Proc. of IEEE Symposium on Security and Privacy (2009)
10. Cui, W., Paxson, V., Weaver, N.C., Katz, R.H.: Protocol-independent adaptive replay of application dialog. In: Proc. of Network and Distributed System Security Symposium (NDSS) (2006)
11. Cui, W., Peinado, M., Chen, K., Wang, H.J., Irun-Briz, L.: Tupni: automatic reverse engineering of input formats. In: Proc. of ACM Conference on Computer and Communications Security (CCS) (2008)
12. Deja vu Security. Peachfuzzer, July 2015
13. Godefroid, P., Levin, M.Y., Molnar, D.: SAGE: whitebox fuzzing for security testing. Communications of the ACM **55**(3), 40–44 (2012)
14. Gorbunov, S., Rosenbloom, A.: AutoFuzz: Automated network protocol fuzzing framework. International Journal of Computer Science and Network Security (IJCSNS) **10**(8), 239–245 (2010)
15. Haller, I., Slowinska, A., Neugschwandtner, M., Bos, H.: Dowsing for overflows: a guided fuzzer to find buffer boundary violations. In: Proc. of USENIX Security Symposium, pp. 49–64 (2013)
16. Hastie, T., Tibshirani, R., Friedman, J.: The Elements of Statistical Learning: data mining, inference and prediction. Springer Series in Statistics. Springer, New York (2001)

17. Hsu, Y., Shu, G., Lee, D.: A model-based approach to security flaw detection of network protocol implementations. In: Proc. of IEEE International Conference on Network Protocols (ICNP), pp. 114–123 (2008)

18. Jang, J., Agrawal, A., Brumley, D.: ReDeBug: finding unpatched code clones in entire os distributions. In: Proc. of IEEE Symposium on Security and Privacy (2012)

19. Krueger, T., Gascon, H., Krämer, N., Rieck, K.: Learning stateful models for network honeypots. In: Proc. of ACM Workshop on Artificial Intelligence and Security (AISEC), pp. 37–48, October 2012

20. Krueger, T., Krämer, N., Rieck, K.: ASAP: automatic semantics-aware analysis of network payloads. In: Dimitrakakis, C., Gkoulalas-Divanis, A., Mitrokotsa, A., Verykios, V.S., Saygin, Y. (eds.) PSDML 2010. LNCS (LNAI), vol. 6549, pp. 50–63. Springer, Heidelberg (2010)

21. Lee, D., Seung, H.: Learning the parts of objects by non-negative matrix factorization. Nature **401**, 788–791 (1999)

22. Leita, C., Dacier, M., Massicotte, F.: Automatic handling of protocol dependencies and reaction to 0-day attacks with ScriptGen based honeypots. In: Zamboni, D., Kruegel, C. (eds.) RAID 2006. LNCS, vol. 4219, pp. 185–205. Springer, Heidelberg (2006)

23. Leita, C., Mermoud, K., Dacier, M.: Scriptgen: an automated script generation tool for honeyd. In: Proc. of Annual Computer Security Applications Conference (ACSAC) (2005)

24. Lin, Z., Jiang, X., Xu, D.: Automatic protocol format reverse engineering through context-aware monitored execution. In: Proc. of Network and Distributed System Security Symposium (NDSS) (2008)

25. Livshits, B., Lam, M.S.: Finding security vulnerabilities in java applications with static analysis. In: Proc. of USENIX Security Symposium (2005)

26. Moore, E.F.: Gedanken-experiments on sequential machines. Automata Studies **34**, 129–153 (1956)

27. Moore, H.: Security flaws in universal plug and play: Unplug. don't play. Technical report, Rapid 7 (2013)

28. Newsome, J., Brumley, D., Franklin, J.: Replayer: automatic protocol replay by binary analysis. In: Proc. of ACM Conference on Computer and Communications Security (CCS) (2006)

29. Rice, H.G.: Classes of recursively enumerable sets and their decision problems. Transactions of the American Mathematical Society **74**, 358–366 (1953)

30. Schieferdecker, I., Grossmann, J., Schneider, M.: Model-based security testing. Electronic Proceedings in Theoretical Computer Science **80**, 1–12 (2012)

31. Schwartz, E., Avgerinos, T., Brumley, D.: All you ever wanted to know about dynamic taint analysis and forward symbolic execution (but might have been afraid to ask). In: Proc. of IEEE Symposium on Security and Privacy, pp. 317–331 (2010)

32. Sutton, M., Greene, A., Amini, P.: Fuzzing: Brute Force Vulnerability Discovery. Addison-Wesley Professional (2007)

33. Whalen, S., Bishop, M., Crutchfield, J.P.: Hidden markov models for automated protocol learning. In: Jajodia, S., Zhou, J. (eds.) SecureComm 2010. LNICST, vol. 50, pp. 415–428. Springer, Heidelberg (2010)

34. Wondracek, G., Comparetti, P., Kruegel, C., Kirda, E.: Automatic network protocol analysis. In: Proc. of Network and Distributed System Security Symposium (NDSS) (2008)

35. Woo, M., Cha, S.K., Gottlieb, S., Brumley, D.: Scheduling blackbox mutational fuzzing. In: Proc. of ACM Conference on Computer and Communications Security (CCS) (2013)
36. Yamaguchi, F., Maier, A., Gascon, H., Rieck, K.: Automatic inference of search patterns for taint-style vulnerabilities. In: Proc. of IEEE Symposium on Security and Privacy (S&P), May 2015
37. Yamaguchi, F., Wressnegger, C., Gascon, H., Rieck, K.: Chucky: exposing missing checks in source code for vulnerability discovery. In: Proc. of ACM Conference on Computer and Communications Security (CCS), pp. 499–510, November 2013

You Are How You Query: Deriving Behavioral Fingerprints from DNS Traffic

Dae Wook Kim[(✉)] and Junjie Zhang

Wright State University, Dayton, USA
{kim.107,junjie.zhang}@wright.edu

Abstract. As the Domain Name System (DNS) plays an indispensable role in a large number of network applications including those used for malicious purposes, collecting and sharing DNS traffic from real networks are highly desired for a variety of purposes such as measurements and system evaluation. However, information leakage through the collected network traffic raises significant privacy concerns and DNS traffic is not an exception. In this paper, we study a new privacy risk introduced by passively collected DNS traffic. We intend to derive *behavioral fingerprints* from DNS traces, where each behavioral fingerprint targets at uniquely identifying its corresponding user and being immune to the change of time. We have proposed a set of new patterns, which collectively form behavioral fingerprints by characterizing a user's DNS activities through three different perspectives including the domain name, the inter-domain relationship, and domains' temporal behavior. We have also built a distributed system, namely *DNSMiner*, to automatically derive DNS-based behavioral fingerprints from a massive amount of DNS traces. We have performed extensive evaluation based on a large volume of DNS queries collected from a large campus network across two weeks. The evaluation results have demonstrated that a significant percentage of network users with persistent DNS activities are likely to have DNS behavioral fingerprints.

Keywords: Domain Name System · Behavioral fingerprints · Privacy

1 Introduction

The Domain Name System (DNS) plays an indispensable role in the Internet by providing fundamental two-way mapping between domains and Internet Protocol (IP) addresses. Its practical usage has gone far beyond the domain-IP mapping service: it supports many critical network services such as traffic balancing [1] and content delivering [2]; it is also leveraged by attackers to build agile and robust malicious cyber infrastructures, where salient examples include fast-flux [3], random domain generator [4], and covert channels [5]. The importance and prevalence of DNS signifies the demand of its traces collected from real networks, which are essential for many DNS-relevant designs by serving as benchmark data or ground truth. For instance, DNS traces have been collected

© Institute for Computer Sciences, Social Informatics and Telecommunications Engineering 2015
B. Thuraisingham et al. (Eds.): SecureComm 2015, LNICST 164, pp. 348–366, 2015.
DOI: 10.1007/978-3-319-28865-9_19

to evaluate DNS cache algorithms [6] and to train statistical models for malicious domain detection [7,8]. Although the specific type and granularity of information extracted from DNS traces may vary for different applications, the demand for DNS traces is generally increasing.

Despite their practical values, DNS traces may introduce significant privacy concerns. For example, DNS queries that are triggered by the prefetching mechanisms of popular browsers can leak users' search engine queries [9]; DNS queries can also reveal the types of operating systems [10]. In this project, we study a new privacy risk introduced by passively collected DNS traffic: to which extent network users can be uniquely identified merely based on the way they issue DNS queries? In other words, we intend to derive *behavioral fingerprints* from DNS traces, where each behavioral fingerprint targets at uniquely identifying its corresponding user and being immune to the change of time. Such DNS-based behavioral fingerprints, once successfully derived, have strong privacy implications. For example, they can be used to de-anonymize the DNS traces with anonymized sources. To be more specific, when DNS traces are shared, the source (e.g., the IP address) that issues the DNS query is usually anonymized (e.g., by obscuring the IP address using hash functions). However, one can learn behavioral fingerprints from un-anonymized DNS traces and use the acquired fingerprints to reveal the presence of specific users in (other) anonymized traces. In addition, if one can get access to DNS traces collected from multiple access networks (e.g., through open DNS services or collecting traces from multiple networks), he/she can track users' locations across different networks by using behavioral fingerprints to reveal users in DNS traces.

This paper aims at investigating the extent to which behavioral fingerprints can be derived and measuring their accuracy on identifying the presence of corresponding network users. As a means towards this end, we have proposed a set of new patterns, which collectively form behavioral fingerprints. We also built a distributed, scalable system, namely *DNSMiner*, to automatically derive DNS-based behavioral fingerprints from a massive amount of DNS traces. Specifically, we make the following contributions in this paper.

- We have designed five new patterns including *domain set, domain sequence, window-aware domain sequence, period behavior,* and *hourly behavior,* which collectively form behavioral fingerprints. These patterns systematically characterize DNS behaviors from three aspects including the domain name, the inter-domain relationship, and the temporal behavior. Although more patterns might be discovered to enhance behavioral fingerprints, our proposed patterns serve as a lower bound of the capabilities to use DNS behaviors to fingerprint network users.
- We have built a system, namely *DNSMiner*, to automatically mine behavioral fingerprints from a massive amount of DNS traces. The design of the system leverages the MapReduce distributed infrastructure to scale up the system performance. After being deployed in a 15-nodes Hadoop platform, *DNSMiner* can process more than 467 million DNS queries using approximately 4 hours.

- We have performed extensive evaluation based on a large volume of DNS queries collected from a large campus network across two weeks.
The experimental results demonstrated that the behavioral fingerprints derived from a historical DNS stream can effectively identify users in a new DNS stream. To be more specific, 69.63% of users, who have behavioral fingerprints in the historical DNS stream and experience persistent DNS activities in the new DNS stream, can be identified using their behavioral fingerprints. Among these identifiable users, our system accomplishes a high accuracy of 98.74% and a low false positive rate of 1.26%.

The rest of this paper proceeds as follows. Section 2 elaborates the related work. Section 3 shows the system design and Section 4 presents the evaluation results. We discuss the possible limitations and potential solutions in Section 5, and Section 6 concludes.

2   Related Work

Information leakage through collected network data has been recognized as a significant privacy concern, thereby attracting a lot of research efforts. A rich body of literature [11–16] have been proposed to infer application-level users' activities from (encrypted) network traffic. Chen et al. [13] have leveraged communication patterns of HTTP connections to infer the activities taken by browser users. In [14,15], Wright et al. have built statistical models to reveal languages and even spoken phases from encrypted VoIP traffic. Zhang et al. [16] designed a hierarchical classification system to identify users' online activities (i.e., a user's running applications) based on network-level traffic patterns. Sun et al. [11] also created traffic signatures to reveal webpages visited by users in encrypted network traffic. Different from these works that focus on inferring users' activities, our work targets at inferring users' identities.

Pang [17] et al. generated user fingerprints based on encrypted wireless traffic patterns. However, compared to deriving user fingerprints from wireless traffic, fingerprinting users based on DNS traffic is faced with unique challenges since DNS traffic has less semantics. Particularly, although encrypted, the wireless traffic can expose the set of SSIDs, packet sizes, and MAC protocol fields used by a user. Comparatively, DNS queries only make visiable the domain name and the timestamp if the source IP is anonymized. Therefore, how to design effective patterns based on semantic-limited DNS queries becomes the key of our solution. The work closest to ours is [18], where Herrmann et al designed a learning-based approach to attribute sessions of DNS queries to their corresponding users. However, our work significantly differs from the method proposed in [18] from two perspectives. First, a single feature, the visiting frequency of popular domains for each host, was adopted in [18] to characterize users' behaviors while we designed multifaceted features (i.e., total 5 features) to systematically characterize users' behaviors from three different perspectives. Second, the method [18] needs to separate a DNS stream into sessions according to the timestamp of DNS queries,

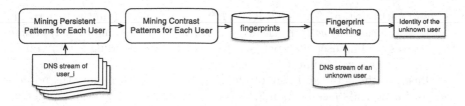

Fig. 1. *DNSMiner* architecture

which implies the necessity for fine-grained timing information for DNS queries. Despite the fact that our current implementation also used timestamp for DNS queries, the first pattern (i.e., the domain set pattern) is time-independent; the second and third patterns (i.e., the domain sequence and window-aware domain sequence patterns) only concern the order in which DNS queries are issued in each day. This implies that our mehtod can be used in DNS streams with coarse-grained timing information. In fact, the domain sequence and window-aware domain sequence patterns collaboratively accomplished a high detection rate of 90.72% in our experiment. A few projects [9,10] investigated information leakage from the same type of network traffic used by our work - the passively collected DNS packets. However, their objectives are different from ours. To be specific, Krishnan et al. [9] aimed at recovering search engine queries by investigating correlated domain names and Matsunaka et al. [10] intended to fingerprint operating systems rather than network users.

Several methods [19–21] have been proposed to de-anonymize network data. Specifically, Coull et al. [19] has proposed techniques to de-anonymize network flows by comparing the objects from the unanonymized and anonymized network data directly. Narayanan et al. [20] and Wondracek et al. [21] have leveraged the topology of an unanonymized social network to effectively identify users in an anonymized social network. Despite the fact that our method leverages different data sources, we do not need auxiliary information (e.g., the context of the anonymized data and additional topologies of unanonymized social networks). Nevertheless, DNS behavioral fingerprints extracted by our method complement existing methods [17,19–21].

3 System

The architectural overview of *DNSMiner* is presented in Fig. 1. *DNSMiner* takes as input a set of DNS-query streams, which is denoted as $\mathcal{S} = \{S_1, S_2, \ldots, S_N\}$. Each stream (e.g., S_i) contains DNS queries issued by a user (e.g., u_i) over a certain time period (e.g., several days). A stream is a series of tuples, where each tuple is denoted as $< u, domain, timestamp >$. u, $domain$, and $timestamp$ refer to the user identity, domain name, and the querying time, respectively. In a network where an IP address can be associated with a user, we can use IP addresses to represent users' identities. *DNSMiner* aims at generating a DNS-based behavioral fingerprint, namely $\mathcal{F}_i$, for a user u_i, where $\mathcal{F}_i$ is defined as a finite set of patterns (i.e., $\mathcal{F}_i = \{F_i^1, F_i^2 \ldots F_i^K\}$). Each pattern in the fingerprint is named as a *fingerprint pattern*. Ideally, fingerprint patterns should be i) *unique* to their corresponding user (i.e., persistent to their corresponding users) and ii) *immune* to the change of time.

To illustrate the detailed design of *DNSMiner*, we first formulate the mining process of fingerprints (see Section 3.1). Next, we will discuss specific patterns used by *DNSMiner* and the motivations behind their design (see Section 3.2). Finally, we briefly describe the implementation of *DNSMiner* that takes advantage of MapReduce [22] to achieve high scalability (see Section 3.3).

3.1   Problem Formulation

Pattern Mining. *DNSMiner* aims at mining fingerprint patterns that exhibit both significant persistence and uniqueness to a user. Towards this end, we start from defining *persistence* and *uniqueness* of a fingerprint pattern. *DNSMiner* aggregates the DNS stream from a user (e.g., u_i) into a set of transactions (denoted as $\mathcal{T}_i = \{T_i^1, T_i^2, \ldots, T_i^M\}$), where each transaction T_i^k is a set of tuples issued by u_i within the same epoch. Since Internet activities usually exhibit strong diurnal patterns [23], we currently use one day to represent an epoch. We denote "T_i^k satisfies F" if the pattern F is observed in T_i^k. The specific meaning of "satisfy" varies for different patterns and we will illustrate it along with the introduction of the patterns. For instance, if F is a set of domains, then T_i^k *satisfies* F when all domains in F are contained in the set of domains that are extracted from all tuples in T_i^k. We introduce a function $mt(F, \mathcal{T}_i)$ that returns all transactions in $\mathcal{T}_i$ that satisfy F. Specifically, $mt(F, \mathcal{T}_i)$ is defined as

$$mt(F, \mathcal{T}_i) = \{T_i^k \in \mathcal{T}_i \mid T_i^k \ satisfies \ F\} \tag{1}$$

We subsequently define a function $supp(F, \mathcal{T}_i)$ to quantify the persistence of a pattern (i.e., F) across the transactions generated by a user u_i. Its formal definition is presented as

$$supp(F, \mathcal{T}_i) = \frac{|mt(F, \mathcal{T}_i)|}{|\mathcal{T}_i|} \tag{2}$$

The $supp(F, \mathcal{T}_i)$ characterizes two trends. If a pattern F is persistent to u_i, $supp(F, \mathcal{T}_i)$ tends to be large. In contrast, a transient pattern is inclined to yield small $supp()$ value. We use a pre-defined threshold, namely α, to discriminate between persistent patterns and transient ones. To be more specific, F is considered to be persistent to u_i if $supp(F, \mathcal{T}_i) \geq \alpha$. We denote the set of persistent patterns for a user u_i as $P(\mathcal{T}_i)$, where $P(\mathcal{T}_i) = \{F | supp(F, \mathcal{T}_i) \geq \alpha\}$.

However, the high persistence of a pattern does not guarantee its uniqueness since a persistent pattern for u_i could also be a persistent pattern for an another user. We therefore define another metric, namely *contrast confidence*, to quantify uniqueness of a persistent pattern (e.g., F) for a user u_i (i.e., how well it F can differentiate u_i from other users).

$$conf(F, \mathcal{T}_i) = \frac{supp(F, \mathcal{T}_i)}{\sum_{F \in P(\mathcal{T}_j)} supp(F, \mathcal{T}_j)}, where \ F \in P(\mathcal{T}_i) \tag{3}$$

$conf(F, \mathcal{T}_i)$ characterizes the following trends: if a pattern is persistent to many users, then its contrast confidence tends to be low; otherwise, its contrast confidence tends to be high. Again, a threshold β is introduced in our current design to differentiate these two trends. A persistent pattern F will be considered as a fingerprint pattern for u_i if $conf(F, \mathcal{T}_i) \geq \beta$.

Pattern Matching. Given an unknown user u_u and his/her associated DNS stream, the pattern matching phase of *DNSMiner* aims at identifying whether this DNS stream can be attributed to any known user. To this end, *DNS-Miner* will first follow the same method discussed in Section 3.1 to obtain persistent patterns for u_u. Specifically, we will derive a set of DNS transactions (denoted as $\mathcal{T}_u$) for the unknown user u_u and subsequently identify persistent patterns $P(\mathcal{T}_u)$. It is worth noting that the same criteria for epoch representation (e.g., 24 hours) and the same value of α will be applied. Next, we will evaluate the similarity between an unknown user u_u and a known user u_i, whose fingerprint is denoted as $\mathcal{F}_i$. A distance function, denoted as $dist(u_u, u_i)$, is consequently defined as

$$dist(u_u, u_i) = 1 - \frac{\sum conf(F_i^k, \mathcal{T}_i)}{\sum conf(F_i^j, \mathcal{T}_i)}, \tag{4}$$
$$where \ F_i^k \in P(\mathcal{T}_u) \cap \mathcal{F}_i \ and \ F_i^j \in \mathcal{F}_i$$

$\sum conf(F_i^k, \mathcal{T}_i)$ is the accumulated confidence for all patterns that belong to the intersection of u_i's fingerprint patterns and u_u's persistent patterns; $\sum conf(F_i^j, \mathcal{T}_i)$ is the accumulated confidence for all patterns in u_i's fingerprint. If $P(\mathcal{T}_u) \cap \mathcal{F}_i$ accounts for a large percentage of patterns in $\mathcal{F}_i$, which implies that two users tend to be similar, the distance tends to be small. If multiple users who have fingerprints have non-zero distance wtih u_u, we assign u_u to the user who has the smallest distance.

It is worth noting that a user with transient DNS behaviors may introduce a large volume of noises when discovering persistent patterns. For example, if a user is only active for one epoch (i.e., there is only one transaction for this user), then all of patterns for this user would be persistent since they are active for that transaction, resulting 100% for the $supp()$ function. A large number of "persistent" patterns generated by transient users may significantly affect the effectiveness for both pattern generation and matching. In the pattern generation phase, these patterns may drastically decrease the contrast confidence of persistent patterns for persistent IPs. In the pattern matching phase, a transient user is likely to have a large overlap with a known user with respect to their patterns, which implies a false positive. Therefore, in our current design, we only consider those users (or IP addresses) that are sufficiently persistent by themselves. Specifically, if a set of users (or IP addresses) subject to analysis have up to M transactions, our implementation only considers those IP addresses that are active for at least $\frac{M}{2}$ transactions. For example, if a set of IP addresses have up to 7 transactions, we will only analyze their users that are active for at least 4 transactions.

3.2 Patterns

The querying behaviors of DNS are closely related to networking activities of individual users. For example, visiting a website or starting a network application (e.g., an instant messenger) usually triggers the resolution of associated domain(s). The routine and personal networking activities of a user may lead to persistent DNS patterns that are unique to him/her. Based on this intuition, we have designed five types of DNS patterns that characterize a user's DNS querying behaviors from three perspectives, including the domain name (i.e., Pattern 1), the inter-domain relationship (i.e., Pattern 2 and 3), and temporal behavior (Pattern 4 and 5). In this section, we will present the definitions of these patterns and the motivation behind their design.

Pattern 1 - Domain Set: A user may have steady interest for certain websites and use some applications routinely. These activities are likely to result in a set of domains that are repeatedly queried by this user across multiple epochs. Since the interest and application usage patterns are highly personal, the repeatedly queried domains may vary drastically across different network users. We therefore introduce the *domain set* pattern (denoted as F_{domain}), which is simply a set of domains that meets the requirements of persistence and uniqueness. Particularly, a transaction T satisfies the domain name pattern F_{domain} if all domains in F_{domain} are observed in transaction T.

In order to identify F_{domain} ideally, we can enumerate all possible domain set based on all domains derived from each transaction of a user, where the smallest domain set contains a single domain from this transaction and the largest domain set contains all domains in this transaction. We can then evaluate the persistence and uniqueness of these domain sets. Unfortunately, when the number of domains involved in a transaction is large, the sheer volume of domain sets will become overwhelming. In order to solve this problem, we generate domain sets that contain up to N unique domains, where $N = 2$ for our current implementation.

Table 1 presents an illustrative example: two users, u_1 and u_2, are active across five consecutive epochs, resulting in five transactions, respectively. All domains queried by u_1 and u_2 for each epoch are listed in the second and third columns in Table 1. If we configure $\alpha = \frac{3}{5}$, the u_1 has persistent F_{domain} patterns including {a}, {b} and {a,b} since $supp(\{a\}, T_1) = \frac{|mt(\{a\}, T_1)|}{|T_1|} = \frac{3}{5} \geq \frac{3}{5}$, $supp(\{b\}, T_1) = \frac{|mt(\{b\}, T_1)|}{|T_1|} = \frac{3}{5} \geq \frac{3}{5}$, and $supp(\{a,b\}, T_1) = \frac{|mt(\{a,b\}, T_1)|}{|T_1|} = \frac{3}{5} \geq \frac{3}{5}$. Similarly, u_2 will have two persistent patterns including {a} and {b}, where $supp(\{a\}, T_2) = \frac{|mt(\{a\}, T_2)|}{|T_2|} = \frac{3}{5} \geq \frac{3}{5}$ and $supp(\{b\}, T_2) = \frac{|mt(\{b\}, T_2)|}{|T_2|} =$

Table 1. Transactions and their associated domains for two users across 5 epochs, where {a,b} becomes the *domain set* fingerprint pattern for u_1.

Transaction	Domains		Epoch
	u_1	u_2	
T_1	a, b, c, d	a, c	1
T_2	a, b	a, e	2
T_3	b, a, f, k	a, b, c	3
T_4	e, f	b, k	4
T_5	c, d	b	5

$\frac{3}{5} \geq \frac{3}{5}$. Considering only these two users, it is easy to reach a conclusion that $conf(\{a\}, T_1) = \frac{1}{2}$, $conf(\{b\}, T_1) = \frac{1}{2}$, $conf(\{a,b\}, T_1) = 1$, $conf(\{a\}, T_2) = \frac{1}{2}$, and $conf(\{b\}, T_2) = \frac{1}{2}$. If we set $\beta = 60\%$, {a,b} becomes the fingerprint pattern for u_1.

Pattern 2 - Domain Sequence: A network user's routine networking activities could involve his/her individualized preferences and the order in which network activities are carried might be able to reflect such preferences. We consequently define a *domain sequence* pattern denoted as F_{seq}, where F_{seq} is a finite sequence of domains. Given two domains in F_{seq} (i.e., $d_i \in F_{seq}$ and $d_j \in F_{seq}$), $d_i \preceq d_j$ means that d_i is issued before d_j.

Similar to the domain set pattern, the ideal implementation to derive domain sequence patterns should consider domain sequences with all possible lengths derived from a transaction. Unfortunately, the ideal solution could result in a prohibitively huge volume of domain sequence patterns when the number of domains contained in a transaction becomes large. Therefore, we only generate domain sequence patterns composed of two domains. To be more specific, $F_{seq} = (d_i, d_j)$ where $d_i \preceq d_j$ in the transaction.

Compared to domain set patterns, domain sequence patterns offer an additional dimension to differentiate two users. For example, if two users visit `facebook` and `twitter` routinely, they will have two identical F_{domain} patterns (i.e., "www.facebook.com" and "www.twitter.com"). However, if the first user always visits `facebook` before `twitter` while the second user follows the reverse order, *DNSMiner* will generate two disparate persistent domain sequence patterns (i.e., $(www.facebook.com, www.twitter.com)$ and $(www.twitter.com, www.facebook.com)$) for these two users, respectively.

Pattern 3 - Window-Aware Domain Sequence: *DNSMiner* further expands the domain sequence patterns by incorporating the first and last time when a domain is visited. Specifically, rather than considering every possible pairwise sequence for d_i and d_j from all tuples within a transaction, *DNSMiner* considers the tuples in which d_i and d_j are first and last observed. To this end, we extract a 3-tuple for each domain (e.g., d_i) in a transaction denoted as $< d_i, s_i, e_i >$, where s_i and e_i refer to the first and last time d_i is observed in the transaction, respectively. In order to illustrate the design of this

Table 2. Window-Aware Patterns

Window-Aware Patterns	p_*'s Value
$< d_i, d_j, ss, p_1 >$	if($s_i < s_j$) $p_1 = 0$; else $p_1 = 1$;
$< d_i, d_j, se, p_2 >$	if($s_i < e_j$) $p_2 = 0$; else $p_2 = 1$;
$< d_i, d_j, es, p_3 >$	if($e_i < s_j$) $p_3 = 0$; else $p_3 = 1$;
$< d_i, d_j, ee, p_4 >$	if($e_i < e_j$) $p_4 = 0$; else $p_4 = 1$;

Table 3. A sequence of DNS queries

Timestamp	t_0	t_1	t_2	t_3	t_4	t_5
Domain	a	b	a	b	b	a

pattern, we consider two domains, d_i and d_j, whose 3-tuples are $< d_i, s_i, e_i >$ and $< d_j, s_j, e_j >$, respectively. Without loss of generality, we assume that d_i alphabetically precedes d_j. The comparison of both starting and ending times of these two domains will result in four 4-tuples as illustrated in Table 2. The third element in a 4-tuple indicates how two domains are compared. For example, "ss" indicates that d_i's starting time is compared to d_j's starting time and "se" indicates the comparison between d_i's starting time and d_j's ending time. The second column in Table 2 shows rules we have used to assign values for the fourth variable. It is worth noting that these four window-aware sequence patterns might not be independent. For example, if p_3 in $< d_i, d_j, es, p_3 >$ is 0, which means that the last time we observe d_i precedes the first time we observe d_j, then all p_* variables in other 4-tuples for d_i and d_j will always be 0. We exploit such dependency in our implementation to reduce the number of patterns yielded for each pair of domains.

Table 3 illustrates a series of domains queried by a user together with their timestamps, where all these domains belong to one transaction and $t_0 < t_1 \ldots t_4 < t_5$. For this user, two 3-tuples in the form of $< d_i, s_i, e_i >$ will be derived, including $< a, t_0, t_5 >$ and $< b, t_1, t_4 >$. For example, $< a, t_0, t_5 >$ indicates that the domain a is first and last queried in this transaction at t_0 and t_5, respectively. We follow the definition of window-aware patterns as indicated in Table 2 to derive four window-aware patterns for this example, which includes $< a, b, ss, 0 >$, $< a, b, se, 0 >$, $< a, b, es, 1 >$, and $< a, b, ee, 1 >$. As indicated in this example, some patterns may imply others, making it possible to simplify the generation of window-aware patterns. For example, if we know $< a, b, ss, 0 >$, we can directly conclude that $< a, b, se, 0 >$ without generating it from data.

Pattern 4 - Period Behavior: Network users' networking activities often exhibit strong temporal patterns. For example, a user could visit a news website every morning while an another user surfs it over every afternoon. Consequently, each domain together with its temporal information may well represent a user. We therefore introduce the *Period Behavior* pattern (denoted as F_{period}), which is defined as a domain-period combination. The "period" refers to a tag indicating "morning", "afternoon", and "evening". In order to derive such

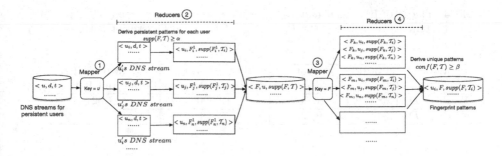

Fig. 2. *DNSMiner* implementation of identifying persistent patterns

pattern, we first map the timestamp of each tuple into one of three period tags, where "morning", "afternoon", and "evening" stand for [5:00AM, 11:00AM), [11:00AM, 5:00PM), and [5:00PM, 5:00AM), respectively. Next, for each tuple, we integrate its domain and its corresponding period tag into a domain-period combination. For example, *(www.facebook.com, 2013-09-17 08:30:23)*, a tuple in a DNS stream, will generate *(www.facebook.com, morning)* as its Period Behavior pattern.

Pattern 5 - Hourly Behavior: We further introduce the *Hourly Behavior* pattern to characterize a user's networking activities at a finer granularity. Rather than mapping a timestamp into a period tag, *DNSMiner* maps a timestamp to its corresponding hour, thereby leading to a domain-hour combination denoted as F_{hourly}. For instance, the tuple *(www.facebook.com, 2013-09-17 08:30:23)* will be mapped into *(www.facebook.com, 08)*.

3.3   System Implementation

A network user may generate a large number of DNS queries. As the number of network users increases, the scalability of *DNSMiner* becomes a concern. To address the challenge, we have implemented *DNSMiner* using the Hadoop MapReduce platform. The two phases of Map and Reduce workflows in the implementation are presented in Fig. 2. *DNSMiner* first identifies persistent patterns for each user. Since the identification of persistent patterns for each user is independent to that for other users, we can easily parallelize the computation by partitioning/mapping tuples (i.e., $< uid, domain, timestamp >$) into reducers based on their *uids* (i.e., the step ① in Fig. 2). Each reducer will then enumerate all patterns for each transaction of u_i; for each derived pattern F_i^j, its *supp*() value in the context of u_i will be subsequently calculated; we consequently apply the predefined threshold α and preserve all persistent patterns (i.e., patterns whose *supp*() values are greater than α). These three actions together are performed in reducers for the step ② in Fig. 2. Next, we partition patterns together with their associated *uids* and *supp*() values into reducers, where the

Table 4. The # of IPs in D_1 and D_2, # of persistent IPs ($|P_1|$ and $|P_2|$), # of IPs with persistent patterns in P_1 and P_2, and # of IPs with fingerprint patterns in D_1 (i.e., $|FP_1|$)

Week	# of IPs	# of Persistent IPs	# of IPs with Persistent Patterns	# of IPs with Fingerprint Patterns
Week 1 (D_1)	55,459	16,003	12,900	11,921
Week 2 (D_2)	54,751	9,120	7,119	-

pattern serves as the key (the step ③ in Fig. 2). Finally, each reducer will calculate the contrast confidence for each pattern with respect to each user and yield those unique ones in the step ④ (e.g., $conf(F, T) \geq \beta$).

4   Experiments

We have evaluated *DNSMiner* using DNS queries collected from a large campus network. Our evaluation aims at answering three questions: "Can DNS-based fingerprints effectively identify their corresponding network users?", "How do parameter values impact *DNSMiner*'s effectiveness?", and "How effective is each category of patterns?".

4.1   Data and Experiment Setup

We obtained DNS queries collected from a large campus network of Xi'an Jiaotong University, China, where the DNS queries are collected below the major recursive DNS servers used by the campus network. Aiming at facilitating the network management, the campus network assigns *static* IP addresses to the vast majority of its users after they register at the network management center. Only a few buildings use dynamic IP addresses and we have excluded DNS queries issued from their corresponding subnets. Sensors were deployed to collect DNS queries that are issued by all hosts in campus network. For each DNS query, three pieces of information were extracted, including the domain name, the timestamp, and the IP address that issues this query. We collected two sets of DNS queries from two consecutive weeks at September 2013, which are denoted as D_1 and D_2, respectively. As illustrated in the second column of Table 4, D_1 and D_2 contain 55,459 and 54,751 unique IP addresses, respectively. Both D_1 and D_2 contain a large number of DNS queries (i.e., 467,388,490 queries in D_1 and 238,993,575 in D_2).

As Internet activities typically show diurnal patterns [23,24], we considers one day as one epoch. Specifically, an epoch starts from 5:00AM and lasts for 24 hours. Both transaction-sets for fingerprint extraction and matching contain 7 epochs (i.e., for 7 consecutive days). We configure $\alpha = \frac{5}{7}$, which means that a fingerprint pattern has to be persistent for at least $\frac{5}{7}$ out of the active days for its corresponding IP address. We also set $\beta = 60\%$.

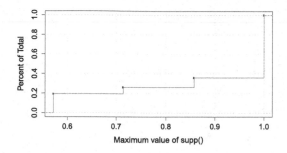

Fig. 3. The CDF distribution of the maximum *supp*() for all persistent IP addresses in D_1 (i.e., all IPs in P_1). A significant percentage (64.18%) of IPs in P_1 have patterns that are persistent across 7 epochs.

We use the queries of the first 7 days (i.e., D_1) to derive DNS fingerprints and those of the remaining week (i.e., D_2) to evaluate the extent to which the fingerprints can effectively de-anonymize users in a new DNS stream. As we have discussed in Section 3, IP addresses with transient DNS behaviors are likely to introduce noises. Therefore, we only consider those IP addresses that experience sufficient persistence by themselves. Specifically, since D_1 and D_2 contain up to 7 transactions, we preserve those IP addresses that are active for at least half of the 7 transactions (i.e., for at least 4 transactions). We use P_1 to represent a set of persistent IPs in D_1 and P_2 in D_2. As illustrated in Table 4, P_1 and P_2 contain 16,003 and 9,120 IP addresses, respectively.

4.2 Fingerprint Extraction

The first step of *DNSMiner* is to assess the persistence of patterns for each IP address in P_1. Specifically, for each IP address in P_1, we extract all of its patterns, investigate their *supp*() values, and preserve those whose *supp*() values are greater than the predefined threshold α. We identify the maximum *supp*() value for each IP address and plot the distribution of maximum *supp*() value for all IPs in P_1 in Fig. 3. As illustrated in the distribution, a significantly large percentage of persistent IPs (i.e., IPs in P_1) indeed have persistent patterns. Particularly, 64.18% of IPs in P_1 have the maximum *supp*() value of 1, indicating that each of these IPs has repeatedly shown at least one pattern across entire 7 epochs. In addition, a large percentage of 80.60% of IPs in P_1 have at least one persistent pattern whose *supp*() value is greater than $\alpha = \frac{5}{7}$. This results in 12,900 IPs with persistent patterns in P_1, which account for totally 313,248,287 persistent patterns.

The second step of *DNSMiner* is to investigate the uniqueness of persistent patterns based on their contrast confidence (i.e., $conf(F_i^j, \mathcal{T}_i)$). Again, $conf(F_i^j, \mathcal{T}_i)$ quantifies the uniqueness of a pattern F_i^j to its corresponding user u_i. In order to visualize the experiment results, for each IP with persistent patterns, we derive the highest contrast confidence for all its persistent patterns; we then present the distribution of the highest contrast confidence values for

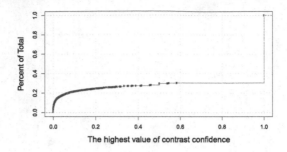

Fig. 4. The CDF distribution of the highest contrast confidence for each IP address that has at least one persistent pattern. Approximately 70% have *unique* persistent patterns (i.e., with contrast confidence of 1).

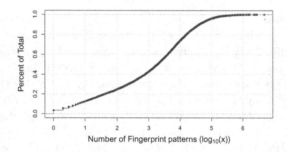

Fig. 5. The CDF distribution of the number of fingerprint patterns for each IP address. IP addresses with fingerprint patterns tend to have a large number of fingerprint patterns.

these IPs in Fig. 4. As illustrated in Fig. 4, about 70% percentage of IPs with persistent patterns have patterns whose contrast confidence is 1, which indicates that these patterns are unique for their corresponding users. In *DNSMiner*, we use the predefined threshold $\beta = 60\%$ to further identify those persistent that also experience significant uniqueness (i.e., fingerprint patterns). Totally, *DNS-Miner* has identified 11,921 IP addresses that have fingerprint patterns, where these IP addresses form a set namely FP_1 and $FP_1 \subseteq P_1$. *DNSMiner* totally generated 222,508,026 fingerprint patterns, among which the domain set pattern, the domain sequence pattern, the window-aware domain sequence pattern, the period pattern, and hourly behavior pattern account for 16.43%, 11%, 72.51%, 0.02%, and 0.04%, respectively. We count the total number of fingerprint patterns for each IP address and plot their distribution in Fig. 5. The distribution indicates that these IPs tend to have a large number of DNS fingerprint patterns, implying strongly discriminative DNS behaviors. Particularly, more than 78% of IP addresses in FP_1 have at least 100 fingerprint patterns.

Table 5. The accuracy of identifying users in a new DNS stream D_2 using fingerprint patterns extracted from a historical DNS stream D_1. Among 69.63% IPs that are identified by fingerprint patterns, 98.74% are correctly revealed.

Week	$|P_2|$	$||FP_1 \cap P_2||$	$|K|$	$||KC||$	$|KI|$	II(%)	DR(%)	FP(%)
Week 2 (D_2)	9,120	4,894	3,408	3,365	43	69.63	98.74	1.26

4.3 Fingerprint Matching

As introduced in Section 4.2, FP_1 represents a set of IPs in D_1 whose DNS behavioral fingerprints have been derived by *DNSMiner*. We also use P_1 and P_2 to represent sets of persistent IPs for D_1 and D_2, respectively. For fingerprint matching, *our objective is to use fingerprint patterns for IPs in FP_1 to reveal their presence in P_2*. Specifically, we perform the pattern matching as discussed in Section 3 to identify all IPs in P_2 whose distance (i.e., $dist(u_u, u_i)$) is smaller than 1 compared to any IP in FP_1, where these IPs together form a set named as K. K can be further divided into two sets, namely KC and KI, which represent the IPs that are correctly and incorrectly identified, respectively (i.e., $K = KC \cup KI$). Subsequently, we define the following three metrics to quantify the effectiveness of fingerprint patterns.

- The percentage of identified IP addresses (**II**): $\frac{|K|}{|FP_1 \cap P_2|}$. We expect *DNS-Miner* to identify all IPs in $FP_1 \cap P_2$ since IPs in $FP_1 \cap P_2$ indeed have fingerprint patterns in the first week and are persistent in the second week. $\frac{|K|}{|FP_1 \cap P_2|}$ represents the overall effectiveness on identifying IPs in a new DNS stream.
- The detection rate: $\frac{|KC|}{|K|}$ (**DR**). This ration shows the ratio of the number of correctly identified IPs over the number of all identified IPs.
- The false positive rate: $\frac{|KI|}{|K|}$ (**FP**). This ration shows the ratio of the number of incorrectly identified IPs over the number of all identified IPs.

We have performed the evaluation of fingerprint matching using the DNS stream of D_2, where the evaluation results are presented in Table 5. Specifically, 4,894 IPs in P_2 (i.e., persistent IPs in the second week) have fingerprint patterns in the first week (i.e., $|FP_1 \cap P_2| = 4,894$). In other words, the ideal objective is to identify all these 4,894 IPs in the DNS stream of the second week (i.e., D_2) using their fingerprint patterns extracted from the first week (i.e., D_1). The matching results show that totally 3,408 IPs have been identified, resulting in the percentage of identified IPs of 69.63%. Among these 3,408 IP addresses, 3,365 IPs are correctly attributed to those IPs in FP_1, resulting a high detection rate of 98.74% and a low false positive rate of 1.26%.

We have deployed *DNSMiner* on a Hadoop platform with 15 nodes. The entire process for both extracting and matching fingerprint patterns consumes approximately 4 hours.

Table 6. The detection performance under different α and β values. "PI" indicates the percentage of IPs in P_1 that have fingerprint patterns; "II" is denoted as the percentage of IPs in $FP_1 \cap P_2$ that are detected by fingerprint patterns; "DR" and "FP" refer to the detection rate and false positive rate, respectively.

Parameter	$\alpha = 4/7$				$\alpha = 5/7$			
	PI(%)	II(%)	DR(%)	FP(%)	PI(%)	II(%)	DR(%)	FP(%)
$\beta = 30\%$	74.04	68.91	92.42	7.58	72.48	68.16	94.17	5.83
40%	73.28	69.45	93.33	6.67	71.29	68.70	95.81	4.19
50%	72.66	70.02	96.09	3.91	70.95	69.26	98.56	1.44
60%	72.35	70.39	96.25	3.75	70.82	69.63	98.74	1.26
70%	71.98	70.43	95.79	4.21	70.65	69.69	97.45	2.55
80%	71.86	70.49	94.78	5.22	70.36	69.77	96.16	3.84
	$\alpha = 6/7$				$\alpha = 7/7$			
	PI(%)	II(%)	DR(%)	FP(%)	PI(%)	II(%)	DR(%)	FP(%)
$\beta = 30\%$	68.98	62.00	90.19	9.81	48.02	43.80	87.80	12.20
40%	67.66	62.50	91.74	8.26	47.53	44.15	88.85	11.15
50%	66.56	63.01	93.93	6.07	47.46	44.51	90.74	9.26
60%	66.29	63.34	94.04	5.96	47.34	44.74	90.82	9.18
70%	65.80	63.42	93.83	6.17	47.27	44.83	89.37	10.63
80%	65.01	63.68	93.07	6.93	47.15	44.99	89.14	10.86

4.4 Evaluating the Impact of Parameter Values

DNSMiner needs two parameters including α and β to be configured. While the evaluation result based on the current configuration ($\alpha = \frac{5}{7}$ and $\beta = 60\%$) yields a high detection rate, we further investigate how parameter values affect the system effectiveness. Specifically, we assign a wide range of values to α (i.e., $\alpha = \frac{4}{7}, \frac{5}{7}, \frac{6}{7}, \frac{7}{7}$) and β (i.e., $\beta = 30\%, 40\%, 50\%, 60\%, 70\%, 80\%$) and then perform the fingerprint extraction and matching for each combination of α' and β' values. The experimental results are summarized in Table 6, where each cell in the table contains i) the percentage of IPs in P_1 that have fingerprint patterns (i.e., $\frac{|FP_1|}{|P_1|}$), ii) the percentage of identified IPs (i.e., $\frac{|K|}{|FP_1 \cap P_2|}$), iii) the detection rate (i.e., $\frac{|KC|}{|K|}$), and iv) the false positive rate (i.e., $\frac{|KI|}{|K|}$). Fig. 6 visualizes the trend of detection rates when α increases from $\frac{4}{7}$ to $\frac{7}{7}$ for a fixed value of β.

As indicated by the experimental results, when both α and β increase, the percentage of IPs in P_1 that have fingerprint patterns drops. For example, 74.04% of IPs in P_1 have fingerprint patterns given $\alpha = \frac{4}{7}$ and $\beta = 30\%$ while the percentage is 47.15% given $\alpha = \frac{7}{7}$ and $\beta = 80\%$. The changes of α and β affect K and FP_1 simultaneously, thereby impacting the percentage of identified IP addresses (i.e., $\frac{|K|}{|FP_1 \cap P_2|}$). This measure stays very stable (i.e., close to 70%) when $\alpha = \frac{4}{7}, \frac{5}{7}$ and all β values under investigation. When $\alpha \geq \frac{6}{7}$, this measure drops significantly (i.e., around 63% for $\alpha = \frac{6}{7}$ and 44% for $\alpha = \frac{7}{7}$). Despite the fluctuation of the percentage of persistent IPs with fingerprint patterns and the percentage of identified IP addresses along with the changes of α and β, *DNSMiner*

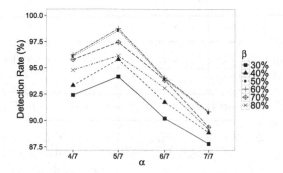

Fig. 6. The trend of detection rates when α increases given a fixed value for β, where *DNSMiner* achieves the best accuracy of 98.74% when $\alpha = 5/7$ and $\beta = 60\%$)

Table 7. The detection performance of *DNSMiner* for each category of patterns: "Domain name" refers to the domain set pattern; "Inter-domain relationship" includes the domain sequence pattern and window-aware domain sequence pattern; "Temporal behavior" contains period and hourly behavior pattern.

Pattern Category	II(%)	DR(%)	FP(%)
Domain name	29.65	85.83	14.17
Inter-domain relationship	43.21	90.72	9.28
Temporal behavior	32.50	87.90	12.10

accomplishes high detection performance. Specifically, for all combinations of α and β values in our experiments, the detection rates are above 87.80%. Particularly, when we configure $\frac{4}{7} \le \alpha \le \frac{6}{7}$, all β values lead to detection rates higher than 90%. Such experiment results imply that our method accomplishes the high detection accuracy over a wide range of parameter values. Nevertheless, considering the percentage of users with fingerprint patterns (i.e., "PI") and the percentage of identified IPs (i.e., "II"), $\alpha \in [\frac{4}{7}, \frac{5}{7}]$ and $\beta \in [40\%, 70\%]$ yield the best detection performance with approximately (i.e., approximately 70% for both "PI" and "II", and detection rates higher than 95%).

We have also investigated the detection performance of *DNSMiner* when only a category of patterns are used and the experiment results are presented in Table 7, where $\alpha = \frac{5}{7}$ and $\beta = 60\%$. As indicated in Table 7, patterns belonging to the category of the inter-domain relationship resulted in the best detection rates (i.e., a detection rate of 90.72% and a false positive rate of 9.28%) compared to patterns in the other two categories. Nevertheless, all these patterns collectively accomplish the best detection performance as indicated in Table 6, indicating that all patterns complement each other in *DNSMiner*.

5   Discussion

DNSMiner currently concentrates on network users whose DNS activities are persistent. For example, network users who were active for at least 4 days out of 7 days were considered in our experiments. Despite the fact that such design mitigates the noises caused by network users with transit DNS activities, it may actually result in limitations for the practical usage of *DNSMiner*. First, *DNSMiner* by design cannot generate fingerprint patterns for those network users with transit DNS activities. Second, *DNSMiner* requires that DNS queries can be attributed to their corresponding users over a relative long period (e.g., across the epochs for fingerprint generation). Specifically, when we use an IP address to represent a user, the IP address should not change across the epochs for pattern generation and matching. For networks using static IP addresses, this limitation can be easily overcome, which is actually the case for our evaluation. However, when the IP address associated with a user changes frequently (e.g., in networks that use dynamic IPs with small lease time), it becomes a challenging problem to directly attribute IP addresses to their corresponding users across a series of epochs.

We acknowledge such limitations in the current design and our future work will focus on systematically addressing them. Specifically, a few potential improvements can be explored. First, we plan to design an algorithm that can adaptively define epochs for each IP address and aggregate them into transaction set according to the DNS activities of this IP address. Particularly, the transaction set will be discovered in a way that it is very unlikely for the host to change its IP address across the epochs belonging to this transaction set. Second, rather than manually defining fingerprint patterns, we intend to propose methods that can automatically generate patterns and perform pattern selection. Particularly, we expect that the patterns will give more weight on characterizing the short-term DNS activities of a user.

6   Conclusion

This paper presents a novel system, *DNSMiner*, to automatically derive behavioral fingerprints from DNS queries, where behavioral fingerprints are expected to reveal the presence of their corresponding users in new DNS streams whose identities are unknown (e.g., anonymized). A behavioral fingerprint is composed of a collection of patterns that systematically characterize each user's DNS activities from three different perspectives including the domain name, the inter-domain relationship, and the temporal behavior. The extensive evaluation based on DNS queries collected from a large campus network has demonstrated that these patterns can accomplish a high detection accuracy of 98.74% and a low false positive rate of 1.26%. Despite its high detection accuracy, more patterns could be discovered and incorporated into *DNSMiner*. Nevertheless, *DNSMiner* demonstrates the lower bound of the effectiveness of using DNS-based patterns to reveal users' presence in network traffic.

References

1. Shaikh, A., Tewari, R., Agrawal, M.: On the effectiveness of dns-based server selection. In: INFOCOM (2001)
2. Vakali, A., Pallis, G.: Content delivery networks: Status and trends. IEEE Internet Computing **7**(6), 68–74 (2003)
3. Holz, T., Gorecki, C., Rieck, K., Freiling, F.C.: Measuring and detecting fast-flux service networks. In: NDSS (2008)
4. Antonakakis, M., Perdisci, R., Nadji, Y., Vasiloglou II, N., Abu-Nimeh, S., Lee, W., Dagon, D.: From throw-away traffic to bots: detecting the rise of dga-based malware. In: USENIX Security Symposium (2012)
5. Paxson, V., Christodorescu, M., Javed, M., Rao, J.R., Sailer, R., Schales, D.L., Stoecklin, M.P., Thomas, K., Venema, W., Weaver, N.: Practical comprehensive bounds on surreptitious communication over dns. In: USENIX Security (2013)
6. Jung, J., Sit, E., Balakrishnan, H., Morris, R.: Dns performance and the effectiveness of caching. IEEE/ACM Transactions on Networking **10**(5), 589–603 (2002)
7. Bilge, L., Kirda, E., Kruegel, C., Balduzzi, M.: Exposure: finding malicious domains using passive dns analysis. In: NDSS (2011)
8. Antonakakis, M., Perdisci, R., Lee, W., Vasiloglou II, N., Dagon, D.: Detecting malware domains at the upper dns hierarchy. In: USENIX Security Symposium (2011)
9. Krishnan, S., Monrose, F.: Dns prefetching and its privacy implications: when good things go bad. In: Proceedings of the 3rd USENIX Conference on Large-scale Exploits and Emergent Threats: Botnets, Spyware, Worms, and More. USENIX Association (2010)
10. Matsunaka, T., Yamada, A., Kubota, A.: Passive os fingerprinting by dns traffic analysis. In: 2013 IEEE 27th International Conference on AINA (2013)
11. Sun, Q., Simon, D.R., Wang, Y.-M., Russell, W., Padmanabhan, V.N., Qiu, L.: Statistical identification of encrypted web browsing traffic. In: Proceedings 2002 IEEE Symposium on Security and Privacy, pp. 19–30. IEEE (2002)
12. Liberatore, M., Levine, B.N.: Inferring the source of encrypted http connections. In: Proceedings of the 13th ACM Conference on Computer and Communications Security (2006)
13. Chen, S., Wang, R., Wang, X., Zhang, K.: Side-channel leaks in web applications: a reality today, a challenge tomorrow. In: 2010 IEEE Symposium on Security and Privacy (SP), pp. 191–206. IEEE (2010)
14. Wright, C.V., Ballard, L., Monrose, F., Masson, G.M.: Language identification of encrypted voip traffic: Alejandra y roberto or alice and bob. In: Proceedings of USENIX Security Symposium (2007)
15. Wright, C.V., Ballard, L., Coull, S.E., Monrose, F., Masson, G.M.: Spot me if you can: uncovering spoken phrases in encrypted voip conversations. In: IEEE Symposium on Security and Privacy, SP 2008. IEEE (2008)
16. Zhang, F., He, W., Liu, X., Bridges, P.G.: Inferring users' online activities through traffic analysis. In: Proceedings of WiSec (2011)
17. Pang, J., Greenstein, B., Gummadi, R., Seshan, S., Wetherall, D.: 802.11 user fingerprinting. In: MobiCom (2007)
18. Herrmann, D., Banse, C., Federrath, H.: Behavior-based tracking: Exploiting characteristic patterns in dns traffic. Computers & Security **39**, 17–33 (2013)

19. Coull, S.E., Wright, C.V., Keromytis, A.D., Monrose, F., Reiter, M.K.: Taming the devil: techniques for evaluating anonymized network data. In: Proceedings Network and Distributed System Security Symposium 2008, February, 10–13, San Diego, California, pp. 125–135. Internet Society 2008 (2008)
20. Wondracek, G., Holz, T., Kirda, E., Kruegel, C.: A practical attack to de-anonymize social network users. In: 2010 IEEE Symposium on Security and Privacy (SP) (2010)
21. Narayanan, A., Shmatikov, V.: De-anonymizing social networks. In: 2009 30th IEEE Symposium on Security and Privacy, pp. 173–187, May 2009
22. Dean, J., Ghemawat, S.: Mapreduce: simplified data processing on large clusters. Communications of the ACM **51**(1), 107–113 (2008)
23. Shafiq, M.Z., Ji, L., Liu, A.X., Wang, J.: Characterizing and modeling internet traffic dynamics of cellular devices. In: ACM SIGMETRICS (2011)
24. Dagon, D., Zou, C., Lee, W.: Modeling botnet propagation using time zones. In: NDSS (2006)

Enhancing Traffic Analysis Resistance for Tor Hidden Services with Multipath Routing

Lei Yang and Fengjun Li[✉]

The University of Kansas, Lawrence, KS 66045, USA
{lei.yang,fli}@ku.edu

Abstract. Hidden service is a very important feature of Tor, which supports server operators to provide a variety of Internet services without revealing their locations. A large number of users rely on Tor hidden services to protect their anonymity. Around 30,000 servers are running hidden services every day [21]. However, hidden services are particularly vulnerable to traffic analysis attacks especially when the entry guard of a hidden server is compromised by an adversary. In this paper, we propose a multipath routing scheme for Tor hidden servers (mTorHS) to defend against traffic analysis attacks. By transferring data through multiple circuits between the hidden server and a special server rendezvous point (SRP), mTorHS is able to exploit flow splitting and flow merging to eliminate inter-cell correlations of the original flow. Experiments on the Shadow simulator [11] show that our scheme can effectively mitigate the risk of traffic analysis even when robust watermarking techniques are used.

Keywords: Tor · Hidden services · Anonymity network · Privacy · Multipath routing · Watermarking attack

1 Introduction

To address people's needs for privacy, many low-latency anonymity systems have been proposed to provide anonymity for Internet communications. Among them Tor [5] is the most popular and widely deployed low-latency anonymous communication system today, providing anonymity to millions of users on a daily basis [20]. One major reason that contributes to the success of Tor is its comprehensive anonymous services, which provide three types of anonymity [17], i.e., *sender anonymity*, *receiver anonymity* and *sender-receiver unlinkability*. In particular, Tor allows general users to access Internet sites without disclosing their actual identities to the destination and prevents adversaries from linking two communicating parties (i.e., sender anonymity and unlinkability for general users). Besides, Tor also allows server operators to hide their locations while providing a variety of Internet services via so-called *Tor hidden services*. This is a very appealing feature that makes Tor stand out. Other popular low-latency anonymity systems such as Anonymizer [10] and Java Anon Proxy (JAP) [3]

© Institute for Computer Sciences, Social Informatics and Telecommunications Engineering 2015
B. Thuraisingham et al. (Eds.): SecureComm 2015, LNICST 164, pp. 367–384, 2015.
DOI: 10.1007/978-3-319-28865-9_20

do not support such hidden service, since it is out of the scope of their initial designs. Anonymous publishing is of great importance especially for people in countries with strict censorship, therefore, a large number of users with strong anonymity needs deploy their services such as SSH, instant messaging and web servers on the Tor network for its practical support to location-hidden services and low latency. According to the statistics of Tor Project [21], around 30,000 hidden servers are active daily in the Tor network.

However, according to recent studies Tor hidden services are still under the risk of de-anonymization due to specialized traffic analysis attacks [16,4]. It is argued that the current Tor design is vulnerable to traffic analysis attacks if the adversary can monitor a user's traffic entering and leaving the anonymous network at both sender and receiver ends. Since the malicious client always resides at one end of the anonymous path, she can successfully perform the traffic analysis attack if she is able to observe the traffic at the hidden server end. Øverlier et al. proposed the first documented attack against Tor hidden services by exploiting traffic analysis techniques. They experimentally verified that a hidden server can be located within a short period of time if the adversary is able to control one Tor (or preferably two) router(s) [16]. Biryukov et al. also confirmed the practicality of traffic analysis attacks by conducting an opportunistic de-anonymization attack to Tor hidden services [4]. The effectiveness of such attacks is mainly caused by the low latency in anonymized paths, which unwillingly preserves the inter-cell timing correlation between the original flow and the anonymized flow. The adversary can exploit traffic analysis techniques to correlate common patterns between the original flow and the anonymized flow to infer identities and relations of the communicating parties. Therefore, the key to mitigating the threats of traffic analysis attacks is to reduce the timing correlation between cells. Dummy traffic is considered as an effective countermeasure to obscure the timing features of the original flow [18]. However, due to the high cost introduced by dummy traffic, it is not a practical solution for the already heavily loaded Tor network.

In this paper, we propose a multipath routing scheme for Tor hidden services (mTorHS) to defend against traffic analysis attacks. Our scheme routes data cells between the rendezvous point and the hidden server through multiple circuits, which exploits flow splitting and flow merging functionalities of multipath routing to remove identifiable patterns of the original flow. Through experiments on the Shadow simulator [11], we show that mTorHS is resistant to traffic analysis, even when robust watermarking-based techniques are employed. In addition, by integrating multi-flow detection scheme [13] into mTorHS, our scheme is able to combine multiple watermarked flows to detect the presence of watermarks, if they have not been completed destroyed by multipath routing.

Because a large number of abbreviations are used in this paper, we summarize the notions in Table 1. The remainder of this paper is organized as follows. After introducing the background of Tor hidden services and two representative traffic analysis attacks against Tor hidden services in Section 2, we present the threat model in Section 3. Then, we elaborate the detailed design of our multipath Tor

Table 1. Definitions of abbreviations used in this paper.

Abbreviation	Term	Abbreviation	Term
HS	Hidden server	SRP	Server's rendezvous point
Alice	Malicious client	RC	Rendezvous cookie
RP	Rendezvous point	DH	Diffie-Hellman
OR	Onion router	IP	Introduction point

hidden services in Section 4. In Section 5, we experimentally evaluate the effectiveness of mTorHS against a very robust watermarking-based attack. Finally, we review the related work in Section 6 and conclude this paper in Section 7.

2 Background

2.1 Tor

The onion-routing-based Tor network is an overlay network contributed by volunteers running Onion Routers (ORs). A client selects three routers by default to establish a circuit to the destination that he wants to access. Then, he packs them into 512-byte cells, encrypts data packets in layers and sends data cells through the circuit. Each router along the circuit peels off one layer of encryption and forwards the cell to the next router until it reaches the last relay (known as "exit"), which further forwards the data to the original destination. Each hop only knows who has sent the data (predecessor) and to whom it is relaying (successor) due to the layered encryption. A router processes the cells that are addressed to itself following the command in the cell, otherwise it simply relays the irrelevant cell to the next hop.

2.2 Tor Hidden Services

The Tor hidden services proposed in [5] use rendezvous points(RPs) to support hidden TCP-based services, such as web servers and instant messaging servers, without revealing real IP addresses of hidden servers. Figure 1 illustrates basic components of Tor hidden services: (1) To make a service reachable, the hidden server (HS) selects several routers at random as introduction points (IPs) and builds circuits to them. IPs wait for connections on behalf of the hidden server. (2) HS then uploads its service descriptor to the hidden service directory (HSDir). The descriptor containing its public key and a set of introduction points signed by the private key. After this step, HS is ready to accept connections from clients. (3) To connect to the hidden service, we assume a client (Alice) learns about HS's onion address out of band. Then, Alice contacts HSDir and retrieves the service descriptor of HS using this onion address. (4) After getting the set of introduction points and HS's public key from the service descriptor, Alice randomly selects a router as the rendezvous point (RP) by assigning it a rendezvous cookie (RC) which is a one-time secret, and builds a circuit to it (i.e.,

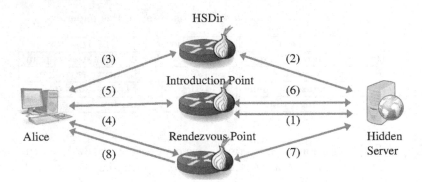

Fig. 1. Tor hidden services architecture

client circuit). (5) After that, Alice sends an introduce message to one of the introduction points and (6) asks the IP to forward it to HS. The message containing the rendezvous cookie, RP address and the first part of a Diffie-Hellman (DH) handshake is encrypted by HS's public key. (7) After decrypting the introduce message, HS establishes a new circuit to Alice's RP (i.e., hidden server circuit), and sends a rendezvous cell with RC and the second part of DH handshake. (8) RP then relays the rendezvous cell to Alice. After verifying RC and generating the end-to-end session key, Alice and HS start communicating with each other through RP.

Because every connection (depicted by solid blue line in Figure 1) is a multihop Tor circuit, no one can learn the actual IP address of either end of the connection. It is worth noting that the complete path between Alice and HS generally consists of six routers in two circuits as shown in Figure 2: among them, three routers including the rendezvous point are selected by Alice, and the other three are chosen by HS. It was intuitively expected that network delay jitter and flow mixing introduced by the six-hop path will make the original flow indistinguishable from other flows, so that the adversary can neither correlate the communication between Alice and HS nor identify the real IP address of HS.

2.3   Traffic Analysis Attack against Hidden Services

It is recognized that Tor hidden service is vulnerable to traffic analysis attacks. In general, traffic analysis attacks can be classified into two categories: *passive* traffic analysis and *active* traffic analysis. Passive traffic analysis correlates the sender's outgoing traffic with the receiver's incoming traffic by comparing the traffic features, such as packet timings and counts. To launch a successful passive traffic analysis, the adversary needs to monitor the traffic for a long time to obtain a reliable traffic pattern. The biggest advantage of passive traffic analysis is its stealth, but it is time-consuming and less accurate compared with the active attacks. To improve the accuracy and reduce the cost, many active traffic analysis techniques have been proposed to generate traffic with a special pattern at one end of the communication path and identify it at the other end.

The security of Tor hidden services was first challenged by Øverlier et al. [16]. They experimentally attacked an early version of hidden services in which the entry guard protection mechanism has not yet been implemented in Tor. In response to a client request, HS will randomly select three routers to build a circuit to RP. Assume a malicious client controls a set of routers in the Tor network. By establishing a large number of connections to HS, she can eventually force HS to choose an entry router (i.e., the fist hop of a circuit) that she controls. Then by requesting files of different sizes at different time from HS, the attacker can generate a special traffic signature and exploit simple traffic analysis techniques (e.g., packet counting combined with timing information) at the malicious entry node and the RP to correlate flows with the same traffic pattern.

Another attack is proposed by Biryukov et al. [4]. They generated traffic with a special pattern and applied packet counting traffic analysis to identify flows with the injected pattern. For example, a malicious RP can send 50 *padding* cells and a *destroy* cell to HS after receiving the rendezvous cell in Step (7) (as shown in Figure 1). If the corresponding malicious entry guard observes 53 cells (including the destroy cell, 50 padding cells and 2 additional *extended* cells in circuit construction) going towards HS and 3 cells (including the rendezvous cell and 2 *extend* cells) leaving HS, the adversary can decide that this malicious guard node is chosen as the entry node by HS.

However, these two attacks also suffer drawbacks. Since Øverlier's attack was conducted in the early stage of Tor with much fewer routers, clients and hidden servers, at that time their generated traffic pattern was unique enough and hence can be preserved after going through the Tor network. Nevertheless, the current Tor with much more traffic will make this simple packet counting based analysis less effective. For Biryukov's attack, because special cells (i.e., *padding* cells) are used to generate a unique traffic signature, it may not be invisible to hidden server. Therefore, more advanced active watermarking-based traffic analysis techniques [23,14,9,8] are proposed, which can make the traffic analysis attacks targeting Tor hidden services more efficient and stealthy. They embed a specific traffic pattern to the victim's flow on the sender side by manipulating the timings of selected cells. The adversary breaks the anonymity guarantee if the watermark is uniquely identified on the receiver side. Compared to passive traffic analysis and other active traffic analysis techniques, watermarking is more robust to flow transformations such as dummy traffic, flow mixing, traffic padding and network jitter, so it is considered a more efficient and severe threat to Tor hidden services.

3   Overview of the Problem and the Threats

The attacks described in Section 2.3 show that the adversary can successfully correlate two communicating parties if she is able to observe the traffic at two ends of a Tor circuit. As shown in Figure 2, the anonymous path between a client and the hidden service server consists of 6 hops. Since a malicious client is always at one end of the path, she only needs to trick HS to choose a compromised

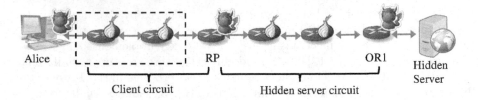

Fig. 2. Threat model in this paper where RP and OR1 are controlled by the adversary

router controlled by herself, i.e., OR1. Her success rate relies on the proportion of compromised routers in the Tor network. Therefore, this attack particularly threatens the hidden services. Moreover, the adversary can further select a node that she controls to be the rendezvous point and build a one-hop circuit to this RP. In this way, she can shorten the path to four and thus reduce the latency between herself and HS to help correlate the traffic pattern. To mitigate this threat, efforts can be made from two perspectives: (1) preventing an adversary from controlling both ends of a circuit to impede the occurrence of traffic analysis (2) reducing the success rate of traffic analysis even when both ends of a circuit are compromised.

The concept of "entry guards" [16] is introduced into the current Tor design to solve this problem following the first direction. Entry guards are a set of routers that are considered reliable by a Tor node to be the first relay of an anonymous path. By default, each user constructs its guard set of three routers, which will expire in 30 to 60 days. After that, the entry guards will be reselected. With entry guards, whenever the hidden server builds a circuit to the rendezvous point in response to a client's request, it will pick an entry guard from the set for its first hop instead of choosing a random router in the network. Since the entry guards are evaluated by several measures and considered reliable, they are less likely to be controlled by the adversary. As a result, the chance that an adversary controls both ends of a circuit is significantly reduced. However, it is unreliable that the security of hidden servers merely relies on the goodness of the entry guard set. Given enough time, a user will eventually select a malicious entry node into his guard set. Johnson et al. showed that for an adversary with moderate bandwidth capacity, it only takes 50 to 60 days to include a malicious router to a user's guard set [12]. As noted by Elahi et al., the design of entry guard is still an unclear research problem [6] and subtle parameter selection is required to achieve expected protection. Therefore, it is critical to develop protection mechanisms which are parallel to the entry-guard-based solution to enhance the resistance of Tor hidden services to traffic analysis attacks in case the guard set is compromised.

In this paper, we make efforts following the second direction to reduce the success rate of traffic analysis when the attacker has successfully controlled both ends of a Tor circuit. Our work can be applied in concert with entry guard protection mechanism. Figure 2 illustrates our threat model. We assume an adversary Alice pretends to be a client of the hidden server and tricks the hidden server to select a node controlled by her (OR1) to be the entry node in the return anonymous path. Alice then selects another controlled router as the rendezvous point. We assume Alice can exploit any traffic analysis technique to passively observe or actively manipulate the traffic passing through OR1 and RP. The primary goal of the traffic analysis is to identify flows with the same traffic pattern at OR1 and RP to confirm that both malicious nodes are recruited in HS's circuit, from which she can learn the location of the hidden server.

4   Multipath Tor Hidden Services (mTorHS)

To prevent the adversary's RP and entry node from correctly identifying the traffic pattern, we present a multipath routing scheme for Tor hidden services. This scheme is based on the key insight that the traffic pattern observed or intentionally generated at the malicious entry guard (e.g., OR1) will be somewhat distorted by flow splitting and flow merging operations in multipath routing and by the multiple routes with different network dynamics. The architecture of mTorHS is illustrated in Figure 3. Different from the selection of rendezvous point in the current Tor implementation, the hidden server also selects its own "rendezvous point". To distinguish two rendezvous points, the one selected by the client is denoted as "CRP" and the one selected by hidden server is denoted as "SRP". In respond to a client's request, HS builds an anonymous tunnel consisting of m circuits, where m is a server specific parameter. HS then splits the original flow onto m subflows and attaches each subflow to a circuit in the tunnel. All m circuits will go through the same entry guard OR1 and merge at SRP, which further relays the merged flow towards the client. Next we will present the detailed process of connection initiation and data transmission.

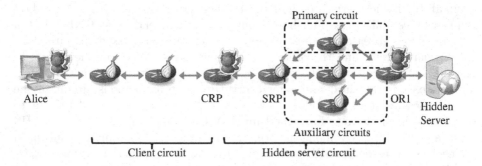

Fig. 3. mTorHS architecture

4.1   Connection Initialization at Client Side

For the client, the connection initialization remains the same as the current Tor hidden services (i.e., *step 3-6* in Section 2.2). More specifically, Alice first selects a client rendezvous point (CRP) and constructs a rendezvous circuit to it by sending an establish_rendezvous request. Then, she builds an introduce circuit to one of HS's introduction points and sends an introduce request, which requests for the hidden service at HS and informs HS with CRP's address (i.e., fingerprint).

4.2   Multipath Tunnel Construction on Hidden Server Side

After receiving the introduce request, HS decrypts it with its private key and extracts the fingerprint of CRP, rendezvous cookie (RC) and the DH handshake message. Then, HS selects its own rendezvous point (SRP) and constructs a multipath tunnel to SRP, following the same approach described in [24].

SRP Selection. The selection of SRP is very critical. From Figure 3, we see that subflow merging occurs at SRP. Hence, even when multipath routing is adopted between SRP and HS, if the adversary controls SRP and OR1, she can observe traffic patterns before merging from both ends of each subflow and thus perform traffic analysis successfully. The adversary may follow the same strategy as described in [16] to trick HS into selecting a controlled node as SRP by continuously sending a large number of requests. If HS selects a new SRP for each received access request, it may eventually select one of the compromised router. Inspired by the entry guard idea, we propose "rendezvous guard" for SRP selection, which is a set of reliable routers selected by the hidden server. A hidden server initially selects three routers to compose its rendezvous guard set, each of which stays in the set for a random period between 30 and 60 days. Whenever HS builds a rendezvous circuit in response to the client request, it sticks to the same rendezvous guard set and randomly picks one router from it.

Tunnel Initialization. As discussed previously, mTorHS constructs a tunnel with multiple circuits to SRP instead of one anonymous circuit to CRP. In the original Tor hidden service design, the hidden server responds to an introduce request by establishing a four-hop anonymous circuit ending at CRP selected by the client. To ease the presentation, we denote this anonymous circuit as the primary circuit and the other $m - 1$ anonymous circuits in the tunnel as the auxiliary circuits. As shown in Figure 3, all circuits merge at the SRP. Therefore, it is the third router for every three-hop anonymous circuit in the tunnel. Besides that, HS follows the default Tor path selection algorithm to select all other routers to form the tunnel. When the circuit is established, HS sends a multipath_m cell[1] along the primary circuit to SRP to request a multipath connection. In response, SRP generates a unique 32-bit tunnel identifier (TID) and incorporates it into the replied multipath_ack_m cell to indicate a successful multipath tunnel construction. With TID, HS adds each auxiliary circuit to the tunnel by sending a join_m request to SRP along the circuit. SRP acknowledges each successful joining with a joined_m message. Finally, when HS receives $m - 1$ acknowledgments, a multipath tunnel is successfully constructed. Note that all

---

[1] To distinguish from the commands in current Tor, all the newly added commands in mTorHS will end with an m.

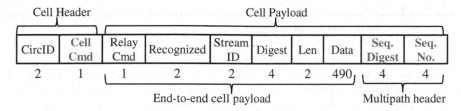

Fig. 4. mTorHS cell format

the cells are layered encrypted so only HS and SRP at two ends see *TID* and the newly added tunnel construction command. This prevents the entry and middle nodes of HS's circuit from linking *TID* with HS. In fact, they even do not know if they are involved in any tunnel construction.

Once the tunnel is established, HS follows the same process of the current hidden service protocol to extend path construction to CRP and the client. In particular, HS sends a rendezvous1 cell containing DH handshake message and rendezvous cookie (RC) to CRP along the primary circuit, which verifies RC and joins the client's circuit with the server's primary circuit. Then, CRP sends a rendezvous2 cell containing the DH handshake message to the client to finish the construction. Note that from CRP's view, it sees only the primary circuit connecting itself to SRP, and hence it has no idea about how many circuits are involved in the multipath tunnel between SRP and HS.

Tunnel Management. The hidden server can add new auxiliary circuits or tear down any existing circuit in the tunnel after it is established. In particular, a new auxiliary circuit can join the tunnel by sending a join_m command with the corresponding *TID*. To tear down a circuit, HS immediately stops sending on this circuit and informs SRP to drop it using a drop_m message. Note that the number of cells that have already been sent on this circuit (denoted as n_s) should also be passed to SRP to avoid packet loss. After receiving drop_m cell, SRP extracts n_s and replies with a dropped_m cell after it receives the remaining n_s cells. Finally, HS tears down the circuit when it receives the dropped_m message. Since each tunnel is constructed in response to a client's request, it will be closed after the request is completed. However, this will not result in the closure of all circuits in the tunnel, since the circuits may be reused for other purposes until it gets "dirty" - after its lifetime exceeding 10 minutes and no streams on it, similar as in Tor circuit management.

4.3   Data Transmission between Client and HS

Once the connection is set up, the client and HS can communicate through the anonymous path consisting of the server's and the client's anonymous circuits joined at CRP. Data cells between SRP and HS can be routed through any circuit in the tunnel. To indicate a cell is a multipath cell used in mTorHS, we add a new cell command (i.e., MULTIPATH_CELL). HS is responsible for assigning data cells to circuits. Obviously, if HS schedules consecutive cells onto a same subflow, it is highly likely that the traffic pattern inserted by the malicious guard on this subflow will be preserved in the merged flow and detected by the malicious CRP. To reduce the likelihood of inter-cell correlations, HS randomly assigns data cells to subflows with different capacities. As a result, a data cell from a fast circuit needs to wait at SRP for earlier cells arriving from slow subflows to be merged in an orderly manner. In this way, we utilize the network properties of different circuits to distort or destroy potential traffic patterns inserted by the malicious guard. This greatly reduces the likelihood of inter-cell correlation (we will explain this in Section 4.4).

Data Cell Format. Since the capacity of each circuit in the tunnel varies, different delays will be introduced to these subflows. Therefore, the data cells in different subflows may arrive at SRP out of order. To solve this issue, we modify the format of Tor data cell to incorporate a 4-byte *sequence digest* and a 4-byte *sequence number* for multipath data packets, as shown in Figure 4. Originally the 512-byte cell consists of a 3-byte cell header including a circuit identifier and a cell command for cell type, and 509-byte cell payload with a payload header and the payload data. We use 8 bytes of the cell payload as *multipath header* for cell reordering, where 4 bytes are used as sequence digest for integrity check and 4 bytes are used for sequence number. The multipath header is only used by SRP and HS to reorder data cells, and the remaining 501-byte end-to-end cell payload is used to carry the real payload data between client and HS.

Data Cell Encryption. In Tor anonymous routing, data cells are encrypted in layers with the shared session keys of the intermediate relays in the order of their relative positions in the anonymous path. Since the end-to-end cell payload and the multipath header are designed for the client and SRP respectively, HS needs to encrypt the two parts separately. The end-to-end cell payload should be encrypted in *five* layers with the inner-most layer encrypted by the end-to-end session key and the outer-most layer encrypted by the key of OR1, while the multipath header is only encrypted in *three* layers with the keys of SRP, the middle router OR2 and the entry router OR1, respectively. When an intermediate router receives a multipath cell, it applies its secret session key onto both end-to-end cell payload and the multipath header to unwrap one encryption layer. Consequently, at SRP the multipath header will be completely unwrapped and recognized by SRP for further processing, while the end-to-end cell payload is still encrypted and remains secure.

Data Cell Reordering. To merge multiple circuits in a tunnel, SRP orders the received cells from all circuits according to their sequence number and temporarily stores the out-of-order cells in a buffer. When SRP receives a multipath data cell from a subflow, it first decrypts the multipath header and generates a digest for the last four bytes of the multipath header using the symmetric key shared with HS. If it is the same as the received sequence digest, SRP verifies the sequence number is not tampered. If the sequence number of this cell is what SRP expects, it will be immediately forwarded to CRP, otherwise it will be stored and ordered according to the sequence number. The multipath header

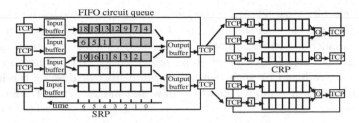

Fig. 5. Tor router queuing architecture [2]

field is only used for data cell reordering. Hence, after SRP reorders the cells and merges them into one output stream, this field becomes useless. To avoid unnecessary information leak, SRP will replace it with random bits. Similarly, when the client sends data to HS, the client reserves these eight bytes for SRP by padding them with random numbers.

4.4   Discussions

In Tor network, two Tor routers are connected over a TCP connection, which is multiplexed by several circuits. Due to the multiplexing of a TCP connection, flow mixing actually occurs at every router. However, we argue that the cell distribution is well preserved after flow mixing so that a maliciously inserted traffic pattern can still be observed by the attacker. First, let us explain the data cell processing at a Tor router. When a cell arrives from a TCP connection, it triggers the *connection read event* of libevent to first put it into the application-layer input buffer and then send to the corresponding circuit queue according to its circuit identifier. As shown in Figure 5, five different circuits arrive SRP from four TCP connections. Then, a *connection write event* will select a circuit based on pre-determined scheduling algorithms such as priority-scheduling [19] to pull cells from the circuit queue and send them to the output buffer. As a low-latency system, a router will send out cells in the circuit queue as fast as possible until the output buffer is full. Therefore, it is not surprising that cells from a same subflow will be outputted in a batch with inter-cell features well preserved.

In this paper, we propose a multipath routing approach that introduces an interdependent subflow mixing to SRP data cell processing. For example, in Figure 5 suppose the circuits in gray belong to the same tunnel. Each of them is associated to a subflow, which transfers a portion of data cells. Since the malicious guard has no clue about the flow membership of the subflows passing through it, it has to treat each subflow independently when inserting detectable traffic patterns. Oppositely, SRP will treat subflows of a same flow in a way that considers flow interdependency. In particular, when subflows are merged at SRP, cells from one subflow may be inserted into two cells that are adjacent in another subflow. This interpolation causes difficulty in pattern detection on the merged flow. Passive traffic analysis such as packet counting will fail. More-over, due to differences in router bandwidth and other network dynamics, the capacity of circuits vary [22,24]. Some cells with larger sequence numbers from a fast circuit (e.g., cell 4 on the first circuit in Figure 5) may arrive earlier than those with smaller sequence numbers but assigned to a slow circuit (e.g., cell 1 on the second circuit). The cells must be reordered at SRP. Consequently, the waiting time introduced by such reordering will distort or destroy the inter-cell timing correlations of a manipulated subflow and makes active traffic analysis less effective.

5   Experiment Evaluation

In this section we test the performance of mTorHS against a well-known active traffic analysis scheme, i.e., interval centroid-based watermarking (ICBW) [23], and evaluate the enhanced anonymity in our multipath hidden services. In particular, we conducted experiments with the Shadow simulator [11], which is an accurate, discrete event simulator running real Tor protocol over a simulated Internet topology. We implemented the multipath Tor router (please read [24] for details) and plugged it into the Shadow simulator to support multipath hidden services in a private Tor network. We also implemented an adversary node following the threat model described in Section 3, which first inserted watermarks to flows at the malicious entry guard OR1 using ICBW protocol, and then examined packets at the malicious client rendezvous point for expected traffic signatures.

5.1   Implementing ICBW Watermarking Scheme

To assess the resistance of the proposed scheme against traffic analysis, we implemented a state-of-the-art traffic watermarking scheme, the interval centroid-based watermarking (ICBW) protocol to attack low-latency anonymity systems [23]. The ICBW was verified on a leading commercial anonymizing service platform www.anonymizer.com as an effective attack. Here we briefly explain its working mechanism. As illustrated in Figure 6, ICBW embeds a watermark into a sufficiently long flow by intentionally changing the centroid of several randomly selected intervals. This scheme divides the duration of flow starting from an offset O into $2n$ intervals of equal length T. The centroid is then calculated by averaging each packet's relative arrival time to the start of its interval. The intervals are randomly grouped into two subsets ($\{I_{A_1}, ..., I_{A_l}\}$ and $\{I_{B_1}, ..., I_{B_l}\}$), each with l elements. Each element in set A and B contains r intervals for redundancy such that $n = rl$. The random grouping is illustrated in Figure 6a. To encode a watermarking bit 1 (or 0), two elements (I_{A_i} and I_{B_j}) of the set A and B are selected, respectively. The packets in all intervals of I_{A_i} (or I_{B_i}) will be delayed by a maximum value of a. Figure 6b illustrates the delaying, which actually changes the distribution of relative arrival time from $U(0, T)$ to $U(a, T)$ where $U(,)$ stands for uniform distribution. After encoding, the difference between the average centroids of I_A and I_B will be $\frac{a}{2}$ for watermark bit 1 and $-\frac{a}{2}$ for watermark bit 0. To decode, the decoder starts from the same offset O and checks the

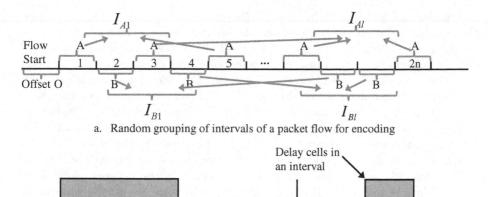

a. Random grouping of intervals of a packet flow for encoding

b. Distribution of cell timing before and after delaying

Fig. 6. Random grouping intervals for a packet flow in ICBW [13,23]

existence of the watermark. Because each watermark bit is encoded by averaging the delays of packets that are randomly selected from many intervals, ICBW is very robust to network delay jitter and flow mixing along a circuit. We refer the readers to [23] for details.

For ICBW, we follow the suggested parameter setting: 32-bit watermarks are randomly generated and the redundancy r is set to 20. The interval length T and the maximum delay a are set to 500ms and 350ms, respectively. We use an offset $O = 10s$ to delay cells in the selected intervals according to the watermark bits at the malicious guard and meanwhile log the arrival time of each cell using the same offset at CRP. From the logged arrival time we compute the difference between the average centroid of I_A and I_B to derive a watermark bit 1 if it is closer to $\frac{a}{2}$ or 0 if it is closer to $-\frac{a}{2}$. Hamming distance, which is the number of mismatched bits, is computed between the derived watermark and the original watermark to evaluate how successful the watermarking attack is. Since the network delay is unknown, a set of different offsets are tested. The one that matches most to the inserted watermarks is chosen as the correct decoding offset to decode the watermark.

5.2 Implementing mTorHS

We implemented mTorHS on Tor v0.2.5.6-alpha. The construction of the client's circuit remains the same as in the current Tor hidden service design, but we change the implementation for the server circuit construction. As explained previously, the server's circuit consists of an entry guard, a middle relay, SRP and CRP. Since we assume the malicious client controls the guard node and CRP, we fix the selection of the two nodes in the implementation. The middle relay is randomly selected from the Tor router set and SRP is randomly selected from the "rendezvous guard set". For simplicity, in our current implementation we form the rendezvous guard set with routers flagged as entry guard. This is because the concept of "rendezvous guard set" is derived from the idea of entry guard set to denote a set of routers trusted by the hidden server. In the future, we will develop selection criteria to assist the selection of reliable rendezvous guards.

Finally, we build a small private Tor network in the Shadow simulator with 50 Tor routers, 1 hidden server, 20 general HTTP servers, 1 malicious client and 100 general web clients to run our experiments. Among the 50 routers, two are configured as malicious CRP and OR1. This is a general case for evaluation. Obviously, the fewer the general clients in the network, the more likely the adversary identifies the hidden server. So, we choose an extreme setting for comparison, where the adversary is the only client in the network. As pointed out by Wang et al. in [23], the longer the flow, the more robust the watermark. To ensure a sufficiently long flow for successful watermarking, we let the client to request a 100MiB file at the hidden server under both settings.

5.3   Results

We perform the ICBW attack on the original Tor and the proposed mTorHS, where m is set to 2, 4, 6 and 8. To rule out random noise, we repeat the watermarking attack for ten times for each setting. The results shown below are the average results of ten experiments. Table 2 shows the comparison in terms of Hamming distance between Tor and mTorHS under different settings. A larger Hamming distance indicates that the anonymity system can better transform the original flow and prevent the traffic analysis. No matter in general cases or extreme cases, mTorHS can better obscure the embedded watermark in the victim's flow. The Hamming distance achieved on mTorHS is always larger than the maximum Hamming distance threshold (i.e., 8) [23]. When the Hamming distance exceeds the threshold, the adversary has less confidence to correlate the watermarked flow to the suspected flow. We note that with m increasing, the Hamming distance does not increase obviously. One reason might be that when we decode the watermark, we tried a set of different offsets and picked the minimum value.

Table 2. Comparison of Hamming distance between Tor and mTorHS with different m where each flow is encoded using different watermarks.

	Tor	mTorHS			
		m=2	4	6	8
General case	6	9	9	10	12
Extreme case	3	8	9	9	11

From the adversary's perspective, if she wants to circumvent the multipath routing scheme, she should use the same watermark for different flows. Since two circuits between OR1 and HS multiplex the common TCP connection, the cells that HS sends out through two different subflows arrive at OR1 within the same coding interval of 500ms. If the adversary uses different watermarks to encode them, it is possible that one subflow is delayed while the other one not, which causes the distribution of the delayed subflow is squeezed to $U(a, T)$ while the other one is still $U(0, T)$. When SRP receives these cells from two subflows, SRP will merge them so that the distribution of the merged flow will be a uniform distribution $U(x, T)$ where $0 < x < a$ depending on which subflow the majority of the cells belong to. Therefore, when the malicious CRP receives the merged subflow, she cannot recover the correct centroid of this interval. To avoid this, the adversary ought to use the same watermark to encode all flows going through OR1 so that they will have a same distribution. When they are merged at SRP, the merged flow still preserves the distribution. Table 3 shows the results when the adversary embeds the same watermark to all flows. In order to verify this assumption without being influenced by general traffic, we perform this experiment in the extreme cases. As shown in Table 3, when the same number of subflows are used, the Hamming distance of the merged flow in cases where a same watermark is embedded is always smaller than the one when different watermarks are used.

Table 3. Comparison of Hamming distance between Tor and mTorHS with different m where all flows are encoded using the same watermark.

	Tor	mTorHS			
		m=2	4	6	8
Extreme case	3	4	7	6	7

However, once the adversary encodes multiple flows with the same watermark, her watermarking is vulnerable to the multi-flow attacks [13] (from the defending perspective, we call it multi-flow detection (MFD) in this paper.) The idea of MFD is that the MFD detector will aggregate all flows into a single flow after it collects a number of watermarked flows. This aggregation scheme in MFD is different from our subflow mixing, which overlaps the relative arrival time of each flow to the same start. If several abnormally long periods of silence (i.e., no packets for hundreds of milliseconds) are observed in the aggregated flow, the detector considers the presence of watermarking attack, extracts the watermarking keys and removes the watermarks from the observed flows. Since SRP merges multiple subflows, which is naturally compatible to MFD, we deploy the MFD detector at SRP. Figure 7 shows the aggregated arrival time of six flows with and without the presence of watermark. Compared to the aggregated unwatermarked flows, the silence of the victim's aggregated flow is more obvious and periodic. Once SRP recognizes the existence of a watermark with higher confidence, it can remove it by randomly delaying some cells on the suspicious flow.

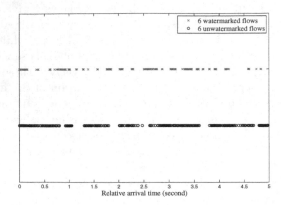

Fig. 7. Comparison of time pattern of the aggregated flow between watermarked flows and unwatermarked flows.

6   Related Work

Attacks to Hidden Services. In addition to the two traffic analysis attacks against Tor hidden services discussed in Section 2.3, clock skew based attacks are also proposed to break the anonymity of hidden servers. [15,25] found that the load changes on the victim's computer will result in temperature changes, which further cause the victim's clock to deviate from the real clock time and results in *clock skew*. Therefore, the adversary can periodically build many connections to the victim to generate a specific clock skew pattern. Meanwhile, she can measure the clock skew of a set of candidates and tries to detect a matched pattern.

Multipath Routing for Performance. The solution proposed in this work is based on multipath routing in the current Tor network. Other multipath routing schemes [1,24] have been proposed to improve the performance for general clients on Tor. Alsabah et al. [1] exploited multipath routing solutions to improve the performance for bridge and video streaming users, while Yang et al. [24] proposed a scheme to better utilize low-capacity routers to support bandwidth-intensive applications. We adopted the design of [24] in this work, but any multipath routing based approach can be applied in the proposed scheme.

Defense for Hidden Services. Entry guard proposed in [16] is an effective solution to protect hidden servers. Elahi et al. implement a framework to study Tor's entry guard design and empirically explores how the parameters affect the anonymity [6]. Besides, Hopper proposed a protection mechanism for Tor hidden services from another perspective – he explored the challenges in protecting Tor hidden services against botnet abuse [7].

7   Conclusion and Future Work

Tor hidden service is a very important tool to provide receiver anonymity to server operators, but it is vulnerable to traffic analysis attacks especially when the entry guard protection is broken. In this paper, we propose a multipath routing based scheme that exploits flow mixing and flow merging to distort or destroy inserted traffic patterns in a victim's flow. We believe this is an effective complement to the existing protection mechanism. Besides, since the multipath architecture is naturally compatible to detection mechanisms based on multiflows, it can be further integrated with multiflow detection protocols to detect the presence of watermarks. We experimentally verify the effectiveness of our scheme in defending one of the most robust watermarking schemes on the Shadow simulator.

The performance issues of Tor have been recognized as a big obstacle impeding Tor's further expansion, so it is important to evaluate the cost introduced by our proposed multipath routing architecture. Based on the findings of other multipath routing work on general Tor services [1,24], we believe that the multipath routing schemes usually improve the performance when a larger aggregated auxiliary circuits bandwidth contributes to the tunnel. However, the proposed multipath hidden services introduce more complexity to onion routers (e.g., separate encryption for end-to-end data and multipath header). In our future work, in addition to the evaluation on the Shadow simulator, we will also deploy multiple onion routers in the live Tor network to explore its impact on the performance of Tor hidden services. Besides, we will also test different scheduling schemes when HS splits traffic to multiple subflows, e.g., round-robin and proportional scheduling.

Acknowledgments. This work was partially supported by the National Science Foundation under Award EPS0903806, KU General Research Fund under Award GRF2301075, and KU Research Investment Council Strategic Initiative Grant under Award INS0073037.

References

1. AlSabah, M., Bauer, K., Elahi, T., Goldberg, I.: The path less travelled: overcoming Tor's bottlenecks with traffic splitting. In: De Cristofaro, E., Wright, M. (eds.) PETS 2013. LNCS, vol. 7981, pp. 143–163. Springer, Heidelberg (2013)
2. AlSabah, M., Bauer, K., Goldberg, I., Grunwald, D., McCoy, D., Savage, S., Voelker, G.M.: DefenestraTor: throwing out windows in Tor. In: Fischer-Hübner, S., Hopper, N. (eds.) PETS 2011. LNCS, vol. 6794, pp. 134–154. Springer, Heidelberg (2011)
3. Berthold, O., Federrath, H., Köpsell, S.: Web MIXes: a system for anonymous and unobservable internet access. In: Federrath, H. (ed.) Anonymity 2000. LNCS, vol. 2009, pp. 115–129. Springer, Heidelberg (2001)
4. Biryukov, A., Pustogarov, I., Weinmann, R.: Trawling for Tor hidden services: detection, measurement, deanonymization. In: 2013 IEEE Symposium on Security and Privacy (SP), pp. 80–94. IEEE (2013)
5. Dingledine, R., Mathewson, N., Syverson, P.: Tor: the second-generation onion router. In: Proc. of the 13th USENIX Security Symposium (2004)

6. Elahi, T., Bauer, K., AlSabah, M., Dingledine, R., Goldberg, I.: Changing of the guards: a framework for understanding and improving entry guard selection in Tor. In: Proceedings of the 2012 ACM Workshop on Privacy in the Electronic Society, pp. 43–54. ACM (2012)
7. Hopper, N.: Challenges in protecting tor hidden services from botnet abuse. In: Christin, N., Safavi-Naini, R. (eds.) FC 2014. LNCS, vol. 8437, pp. 316–325. Springer, Heidelberg (2014)
8. Houmansadr, A., Borisov, N.: Swirl: a scalable watermark to detect correlated network flows. In: Proceedings of the Network and Distributed Security Symposium - NDSS 2011. Internet Society, February 2011
9. Houmansadr, A., Kiyavash, N., Borisov, N.: Rainbow: a robust and invisible non-blind watermark for network flows. In: Proceedings of the Network and Distributed Security Symposium - NDSS 2009. Internet Society, February 2009
10. Anonymizer Inc. Anonymizer. https://www.anonymizer.com/
11. Jansen, R., Hopper, N.: Shadow: running Tor in a box for accurate and efficient experimentation. In: Proceedings of the Network and Distributed System Security Symposium - NDSS 2012, February 2012
12. Johnson, A., Wacek, C., Jansen, R., Sherr, M., Syverson, P.: Users get routed: traffic correlation on Tor by realistic adversaries. In: Proceedings of the 20th ACM Conference on Computer and Communications Security (2013)
13. Kiyavash, N., Houmansadr, A., Borisov, N.: Multi-flow attacks against network flow watermarking schemes. In: USENIX Security Symposium (2008)
14. Ling, Z., Luo, J., Yu, W., Fu, X., Xuan, D., Jia, W.: A new cell counter based attack against Tor. In: Proceedings of the 16th ACM Conference on Computer and Communications Security, pp. 578–589. ACM (2009)
15. Murdoch, S.J.: Hot or not: revealing hidden services by their clock skew. In: Proc. of the 13th ACM Conf. on Computer and Communications Security (2006)
16. Øverlier, L., Syverson, P.: Locating hidden servers. In: Proceedings of the 2006 IEEE Symposium on Security and Privacy, May 2006
17. Pfitzmann, A., Waidner, M.: Networks without user observability. Computers & Security 6(2), 158–166 (1987)
18. Shmatikov, V., Wang, M.-H.: Timing analysis in low-latency mix networks: attacks and defenses. In: Gollmann, D., Meier, J., Sabelfeld, A. (eds.) ESORICS 2006. LNCS, vol. 4189, pp. 18–33. Springer, Heidelberg (2006)
19. Tang, C., Goldberg, I.: An improved algorithm for Tor circuit scheduling. In: Proc. of the 2010 ACM Conf. on Computer and Communications Security (2010)
20. TorProject. Estimated Number of Clients in the Tor Network. https://metrics.torproject.org/clients-data.html
21. TorProject. Unique .onion Address. https://metrics.torproject.org/hidserv-dir-onions-seen.html
22. Wang, T., Bauer, K., Forero, C., Goldberg, I.: Congestion-aware path selection for Tor. In: Keromytis, A.D. (ed.) FC 2012. LNCS, vol. 7397, pp. 98–113. Springer, Heidelberg (2012)
23. Wang, X., Chen, S., Jajodia, S.: Network flow watermarking attack on low-latency anonymous communication systems. In: IEEE Symposium on Security and Privacy, SP 2007, pp. 116–130. IEEE (2007)
24. Yang, L., Li, F.: mTor: a multipath Tor routing beyond bandwidth throttling. In: 2015 IEEE Conference on Communications and Network Security (CNS). IEEE (2015)
25. Zander, S., Murdoch, S.J.: An improved clock-skew measurement technique for revealing hidden services. In: USENIX Security Symposium (2008)

An Improved Method for Anomaly-Based Network Scan Detection

Ashton Webster$^{(\boxtimes)}$, Margaret Gratian, Ryan Eckenrod, Daven Patel,
and Michel Cukier

University of Maryland, College Park, USA
{awebste2,mgratian,eckenrod,dpatel19,mcukier}@umd.edu

Abstract. Network scans, a form of network attacker reconnaissance, often preface dangerous attacks. While many anomaly-based network scan detection methods are available, they are rarely implemented in real networks due to high false positive rates and a lack of justification for the chosen attribute sets and machine learning algorithms. In this paper, we propose a new method of scan detection by selecting and testing combinations of attribute sets, machine learning algorithms, and lower bounded data to find a Local Optimal Model.

Keywords: Machine learning · Network intrusion detection · Anomaly-based detection · Network security · Scanning

1 Introduction

Each year, new and devastating cyber attacks amplify the need for robust cybersecurity practices. Preventing novel cyber attacks requires the invention of intrusion detection systems (IDSs) that can identify previously unseen attacks. To this end, many researchers have attempted to produce anomaly-based IDSs using machine learning techniques [1, 2, 3, 4]. However, anomaly-based IDSs are not yet able to detect malicious network traffic consistently enough to warrant implementation in real networks [2, 5]. It remains a challenge for the security community to produce anomaly-based IDSs that are suitable for adoption in the real world [5, 6].

One promising field of study has been anomaly-based network scan detection. This line of research aims to detect network scans that often precede cyber attacks so that potential attackers can be identified and blocked. Specifically, many researchers have focused on using network flow data as an anomaly-based scan detection medium [7, 8, 9]. To improve upon previous research in this field, we present a method for identifying an effective network flow-based machine learning model for scan detection on a given network. Network administrators utilizing this method on their own networks can use the scan detection models produced to create personalized anomaly-based scan detection systems. In addition, we present an application of this method on the University of Maryland network.

The remainder of this paper is organized as follows. Section 2 details the background of this paper and related work. Section 3 lists our contributions and defines terms specific to this paper. Section 4 details our method and an application of this

© Institute for Computer Sciences, Social Informatics and Telecommunications Engineering 2015
B. Thuraisingham et al. (Eds.): SecureComm 2015, LNICST 164, pp. 385–400, 2015.
DOI: 10.1007/978-3-319-28865-9_21

method on the University of Maryland network. Section 5 presents and discusses the results obtained and the possible limitations for our method. Finally, Section 6 presents the conclusion.

2   Background

2.1   Scanning

Network scanning, a form of network reconnaissance, often prefaces a cyber attack [7, 10]. Through various scanning techniques, an attacker will attempt to gain information about network configurations, server implementations, and potential vulnerabilities before launching more invasive exploits. Thus, scan detection is vital to the security of a network [1].

Scans can be classified into two broad categories: vertical and horizontal [10]. Vertical scans are directed at a specific host and include an in-depth examination of ports and protocols being used by the host. Horizontal scans sweep over several hosts within the targeted network and seek general information about configurations, operating system versions, and more. Vertical and horizontal scans can also be made "stealthy" by increasing the time between each successive port contact to avoid detection [11].

Rule-based thresholding is the most common method of scan detection [1, 7]. IP addresses are declared as scanners after their connection attempt count exceeds a predetermined limit. This method has a low detection rate and an "unacceptable" false alarm rate [1, 6]. Other rule-based processes are burdensome, time consuming, and prone to human error; scan detection is often skipped or overlooked for this reason [9, 12].

2.2   Anomaly Detection Systems in Scan Detection and Machine Learning

At the most fundamental level, anomaly detection involves examining data for unusual patterns [3]. This method of detection aims to classify data as either normal or abnormal based on a given definition of normalcy. In the context of anomaly-based scan detection, we use the terms 'benign' to describe normal network users and 'malicious' to describe network scanners. For the purpose of this paper, we define a user as a unique source IP address producing traffic on a network.

In an anomaly-based scan detection system, a normal network user profile is created and anomalies are treated as network scans. The system's classification success is dependent upon the number of true positives, true negatives, false positives, and false negatives it produces [13]. Based on this convention, these terms are defined as follows:

True positives: The number of correctly labeled malicious users.
False positives: The number of benign users incorrectly labeled as malicious.
False negatives: The number of malicious users incorrectly labeled as benign.
True negatives: The number of correctly labeled benign users.

In applying anomaly-based scan detection, an important goal to strive for is the reduction of false negatives and false positives [14]. This is because false positives result in a waste of resources, while false negatives result in undetected malicious activity [2, 5, 7].

Machine learning classifies data instances using a set of predictive heuristics [12]. This technique uses learning algorithms and input data to create a predictive mathematical model for classifying further data. Machine learning has been proven to be a useful tool for anomaly detection, with successful applications in fields such as keystroke dynamics, malicious system trace detection, and user behavior at the command line [4, 15, 16]. We will refer to machine learning models created for scan detection as 'scan detection models.'

2.3   Previous Work

Previous studies have analyzed the effectiveness of network flow-based scan detection models [7, 8, 17]. Network flow is a protocol for recording network traffic between two IP addresses and has proven to be a useful source of data for machine learning [8, 17, 18, 19]. When using network flow records, a minimum is often set on the number of network flow records a user must produce in order to be classified as a normal user or network scanner. This practice of setting a minimum number of records will be referred to as setting a 'lower bound.' This lower bound is similar to one used by the Threshold Random Walk scan detection method [17], which determines a minimal number of connection attempts a source IP address must make to distinct destination IP addresses to be accurately classified. However, network flow-based scan detection studies often choose a lower bound without giving a strong justification for the choice [7]. Moreover, other studies attempt to classify IP addresses that have only produced one record, without verifying in detail whether one record provides enough data to make an accurate classification [19].

Another important aspect of creating scan detection models is the calculation of network flow attributes. Among the attributes calculated, researchers often attempt to identify a subset of the attributes that enables high classification performance when used to create scan detection models [8, 9]. This process (called attribute set selection) reduces storage costs and computing complexity, and it eliminates extraneous attributes that reduce the accuracy of machine learning classification [14, 20, 21]. Although other researchers often identify and utilize a reduced attribute set using an attribute selection algorithm [8, 9], there may exist other attribute sets which will better classify the users. Since the "quality of the... [attribute set] is crucial to the performance of a [machine learning] algorithm," it is essential to test and evaluate multiple attribute sets [14]. Similarly, many studies classify users using only one or very few machine learning algorithms, and thus can only make claims about a specific group of algorithms and their classification success [7, 19].

Despite extensive research, the strategy of using anomaly-based scan detection in concert with machine learning has been "rarely employed in operational 'real world' settings" [2]. One of the primary challenges with machine learning applications is developing a realistic and accurately labeled network dataset for training; this issue stems from the loose definition of the term 'scan' and the high variability of networks [2]. Other studies use publicly available datasets that are over fifteen years old or are known to inaccurately model real networks [7, 12], such as the DARPA - 98/99, the KDD-99, and the Kyoto 2006 datasets [22, 23, 24]. Furthermore, some papers seek to make claims about scan detection on datasets that have a disproportionately high number of malicious sources [5, 8]. This leads to training machine learning models on datasets that are not large enough or representative enough of the desired network to make successful classifications and prevents the work from being generalized to most other networks [2, 12, 22, 23].

3   Contributions

Motivated by previous work and the challenges associated with anomaly-based scan detection using network flow records, we present a general method for creating improved machine learning scan detection models. In order to precisely define our task, we introduce the following terms:

Aggregate Metric Value (AMV): A value calculated based on multiple classification metrics for a given scan detection model. For the purpose of this paper, we use the average of accuracy, precision, and sensitivity.

Local Optimal Model (LOM): The scan detection model with the highest performance based upon a given AMV among all of the models generated.

We frame scan detection model creation as an optimization problem with three variables: (1) a network flow attribute set, (2) a machine learning classifier, and (3) a lower bound. Our method creates multiple scan detection models based upon combinations of these variables. The AMV of each model is then calculated to find a specific network's LOM. This framework for scan detection model creation seeks to resolve challenges inherent in using machine learning for scan detection, including network-specific models and arbitrary selection of attribute sets, machine learning algorithms, and lower bounds.

By proposing a solution to this problem, we contribute the following:

- We provide a customizable method of identifying the combination of attribute set, machine learning classifier, and lower bound that creates a Local Optimal Model for a specific network.
- We compare and evaluate the implications of applying lower bounds on the number of records necessary for classification.
- We demonstrate an application of this method on the University of Maryland network.

Our method utilizes supervised machine learning and is outlined by the work flow diagram in Figure 1. To implement machine learning for our experiment, we selected the Weka machine learning library [25].

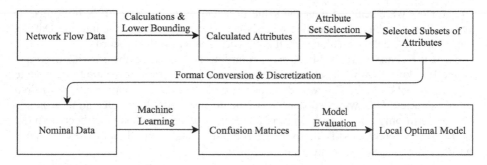

Fig. 1. This work flow diagram of our method provides an overview of the process of collecting network flow data, deriving attributes for each network user for several lower bounds, selecting attribute sets, creating scan detection models using machine learning, and finally evaluating the resulting models to find the LOM.

4   Method

4.1   Network Flow Data Collection

Network flow data must first be collected over a network. Two sets of network flow data should be collected so that scan detection models can be trained on one set and tested on the other. Having independent training and testing datasets avoids the potential issue of overfitting the training data [26]. An additional step that can be taken is to inject network scans into the data. Injecting scans will ensure that the data contains some scans, but can also corrupt the dataset as discussed in Section 5.5.

For our experiment, we chose to create a scan detection model for the University of Maryland network. We collected the network's Cisco NetFlow [18] data over the month of November and nine days of December, 2013. We trained scan detection models using the month of November data, which we will call Dataset 1, and tested the models on the nine days of December data, which we will call Dataset 2. As the datasets were collected, they were inserted into two separate databases.

To challenge our models to detect stealthy network scans that might occur on a network, we chose to inject a sample of stealthy scans into each dataset. We set up a network of 32 virtual machines (VMs) to develop stealth scanning profiles. On the network, the open source scanning tool Nmap [27] was used to test different scans against the Snort IDS [28]. In order for the scans to be representative of stealth scans, Snort was configured with the strictest port scanning thresholds available. Stealth scanning profiles for horizontal and vertical scanning were derived from extensive testing against Snort and research into stealth scanning behavior. It was found that the slightest modifications from the default Nmap settings proved sufficient to evade Snort. The scans were developed with the additional goal of discovering enough host information to launch an exploit or attack while sending a small number of port probes over a one month period.

Once we were confident that our scan profiles were representative of stealth scanning, we configured a network to perform these scans. Five VMs were set up to scan two Class C subnets of the University of Maryland network multiple times.

The subnets were scanned over the same time period as the network's flow records were collected. Thus, the scanning records were inserted in real time into the Dataset 1 and Dataset 2 databases alongside the network's inherent flow records.

Once the scans were finished, each complete scan was relabeled with a unique source IP address within its network flow data so that every scan seemed to originate from a new IP address. This was done because more than five scanners were desired for the dataset. This was also done to replicate the difficulty of detecting scanners who perform only a few scans. In turn, the scan detection models must become more robust to accurately classify these users. The list of malicious IP addresses produced in this step was stored separately for labeling.

4.2   Network Flow Data Labeling

Once the network flow data has been collected, every user must be labeled as malicious or benign in order to perform supervised machine learning. For simplicity, our method identifies a network user as any unique source IP address that accesses a network. The advantage of injecting scans into the dataset is that the injected IP addresses can be labeled as malicious because they are the output of the Nmap scans. Labeling the remainder of the network users confidently is much more difficult. It is a time consuming and imperfect process as described in Section 5.5. To label any inherent malicious users within the data, a set of heuristics that identifies a user as a network scanner based upon the user's network flow data must be defined and applied. These heuristics can be based upon accepted definitions of scans or based on the specific network's configuration. For example, if access to port 22 is closed on the network and analyzing network flow records reveals a user attempted to access the port on several hosts, the user could potentially be labeled a scanner. Users that do not fit these heuristics should be labeled as benign users.

In our dataset, the labeling process occurred as part of the network flow attribute calculations. Users were automatically labeled as malicious if they were among the injected scans. For non-injected users, we defined a strict set of heuristics to identify any network scanners on the university network. A user was labeled as malicious if the IP address displayed horizontal or vertical scan detection behavior on the network. Additionally, any user who attempted to access a single closed port on the network was labeled as a scanner. All other users were labeled as benign.

4.3   Attribute Calculation

Statistics about a user's network flow data must be calculated to classify the user as malicious or benign using machine learning. Choosing which network flow attributes to calculate is the first step in this process. Any attribute that is believed to differ between benign network users and malicious users can be chosen. Other researchers have identified potentially useful attributes [7, 8, 19]. Once the attributes have been selected, they need to be calculated for each user that accessed the network. The user's label must be added to calculated attributes for use by the machine learning algorithms. An additional attribute that can be calculated in this step is the number of network flow records that the user produced. This attribute can be used to quickly implement lower bounding in the next step.

To perform these operations with our data, we first compiled a list of 34 network flow attributes to calculate based on the attributes used by Gates et al. [8] and Williams et al. [19]. A full listing can be can be found in Appendix A. We then created a script that individually queried the Dataset 1 and Dataset 2 databases for each user's network flow records. The 34 attributes, the user's label, and the number of records produced by the user were then calculated for each IP address in each set. This process generated two CSV files: a training dataset of Dataset 1's users and corresponding calculations, and a testing dataset that contained Dataset 2's users and calculations.

4.4 Lower Bounding

A lower bound refers to the minimum number of network flow records a user must produce to be classified. Our study introduces the concept of varying lower bounds during model creation to discover how lower bounds affect a model's AMV. Different lower bounds should be chosen in search of the LOM as they may impact the AMV, as demonstrated by our findings. To test the application of lower bounds, network users that did not produce certain numbers of network flow records should be removed from the calculations dataset. Each lower bounded set of calculations should be saved separately for evaluation.

For our experiment, we chose to test the lower bounds of 2, 4, 6, 8, 10, 30, and 50 network flows, as well as no lower bound (a bound of 1 record). To perform the lower bounding, each calculation file was copied and all IP addresses that did not produce the minimum number of records removed from the file. The resulting files and the number of benign and malicious IP addresses left in each is detailed in Table 1.

Table 1. Number of Malicious and Benign Users

Lower Bound	Dataset 1		Dataset 2	
	Benign	Malicious	Benign	Malicious
1	149,600	91	103,663	57
2	115,475	86	88,042	57
4	85,874	85	73,328	57
6	71,836	83	65,446	56
8	63,384	83	59,821	56
10	57,500	78	55,918	56
30	33,913	59	39,396	50
50	25,536	56	32,943	40

4.5 Attribute Discretization

Before attribute selection or model creation can occur, the attribute calculations must be converted into a machine learning format and discretized. The conversion is a simple formatting change into a syntax on which machine learning algorithms can operate. Then the calculations must be discretized so that each attribute's range of calculated values for the users is no longer continuous but in nominal, categorized sets of values useful for machine learning.

In order for our data to be utilized by the Weka library, our calculations in CSV format were converted to ARFF (Attribute-Relation File Format) by means of a simple translation script. The ARFF files were then discretized using a modified version of Fayyad and Irani's Minimum Description Length (MDL) discretize function implemented in the Weka library that split an attribute's range of values at least once ("binary discretization") [30]. Without this modification, some attribute ranges would not have been split at all, resulting in only one discretized category for those attributes. Having a singular category for an attribute renders the attribute useless for classification since all users will have the same value for the attribute.

4.6   Attribute Set Selection

Following discretization, network flow attribute sets must be identified in order to build scan detection models. An attribute set refers to a subset of all the network flow attributes that were calculated for each IP address. Prior research has shown that choosing to classify instances based upon a strongly predictive subset of attributes instead of using all attributes can increase classification performance [30, 31]. Attribute sets are thus the second variable component of scan detection model creation that must be explored in search of the LOM.

Attribute sets can be selected in a number of ways. Every combination of the network flow attributes could be selected as an attribute set. However, testing all of the sets may prove infeasible if many attributes were calculated because the number of tests necessary grows exponentially with the number of attributes. Attribute sets can alternatively be selected manually or through the use of attribute selection algorithms. These algorithms are designed to identify which attributes are the most useful for distinguishing items of one labeled class from items of another class for a given dataset.

Given the 34 network flow attributes we identified and calculated for each user, selecting every possible attribute set combination for testing was deemed infeasible because there are 17 billion ways of combining the attributes into subsets. We therefore turned to the Weka machine learning library for attribute selection algorithms. Making no assumptions about which network flow attributes would best differentiate normal network users from network scanners, we solely relied upon these algorithms to identify useful attribute sets to test.

There are two types of attribute selection algorithms in the Weka library: subset evaluators and attribute evaluators. Subset evaluators attempt to identify the subset of all attributes that best differentiates between classes, while attribute evaluators simply rank all attributes by their perceived usefulness for differentiating between classes [32]. For our experiment, we selected every subset evaluator algorithm Weka provided that returned non-empty attribute sets, and we selected every attribute evaluator algorithm that ranked at least five attributes with nonzero scores. Thus, the CFS and Consistency subset evaluators were chosen along with the Chi-Squared, Gain Ratio, Info Gain, and Symmetrical Uncertainty attribute evaluators.

These algorithms were run on each of Dataset 1's lower bounded files. Since each attribute evaluator returned only rankings of attributes instead of a subset of them, constructing subsets from these rankings required choosing some number of the highest ranked attributes from the ranking list. For each of the attribute evaluator algorithms we chose, we decided to create six subsets based upon the rankings re-turned. The first subset contained the best 5 attributes, the second contained the best 10 attributes, the third contained the best 15 attributes, and so on up to the sixth sub-set, which contained the best 30 attributes. We also selected a control attribute set where all 34 attributes were selected. Along with the two subsets created by the subset evaluators, this amounted to 27 selected attribute sets per lower bounded file. In some cases, duplicate subsets were produced across algorithms and files with different low-er bounds, so the final number of unique subsets created for testing was 122.

4.7   Machine Learning Model Creation

After attribute selection, machine learning algorithms must be selected so that scan detection models can be created and tested. Different machine learning algorithms may classify a dataset differently and are thus the third variable that should be tested in search of the LOM. Machine learning algorithm selection can be based upon the unique benefits of certain algorithms, an algorithm's classification performance in other settings, the distribution of malicious and benign users within the data, or some other prior knowledge. Since justifying the selection of a machine learning algorithm can still be challenging, we propose selecting many algorithms to test in order to compare their classification results.

Once the machine learning algorithms are selected, scan detection models are created by training each algorithm on the training datasets according to attribute sets. Each algorithm should train on each training dataset generated by applying a lower bound, using every attribute set selected for testing. This results in one unique scan detection model for every combination of the three variables. Afterwards, the models are tested on the corresponding lower bound testing dataset. The output of this stage is a classification confusion matrix for each of the scan detection models.

For our experiment, we selected the following five machine learning algorithms implemented in the Weka Machine Learning Library: Random Forest, AODE, PRISM, SMO, and Decision Table. We sampled algorithms from different categories of machine learning algorithms, including Tree Based (Random Forest), Rule Based (Decision Table), and Bayes (AODE), among others. We trained each of these ma-chine learning algorithms on each of the 8 lower bounds files with each of the 122 attribute sets, resulting in 4,880 unique scan detection models. We then tested every scan detection data model on the corresponding lower bounded data from Dataset 2 with the same attribute sets to generate a set of confusion matrices for comparison of the models.

4.8   Model Evaluation

Once scan detection models are created and confusion matrices are generated from testing, classification metrics can be derived from the matrices to determine which model best classified the data. Models can be evaluated according to a single metric such as accuracy. However, the base rate fallacy is a serious problem for scan detec-tion, as the vast majority of the network users are usually benign [5]. This means that if a model classified every user as benign, it will still have a high classification accuracy. Therefore, it is advisable to combine and weigh multiple classification metrics into a single score: what we call an Aggregate Metric Value (AMV). We term the model with the highest AMV to be the Local Optimal Model (LOM). The general method to produce a simple weighted AMV is as follows:

$$\sum_{i=0}^{n} w_i * m_i \tag{1}$$

where w_i is the assigned weight for the metric m_i and n is the total number of metrics.

Once an AMV is selected, it should be calculated for every scan detection model generated from the previous step based upon its testing confusion matrix. Models can then be sorted by descending AMV to find the LOM. If the AMV of this model is deemed sufficient, it can be deployed as an anomaly-based scan detection system on the live network. For our data, we used the following AMV, based on conventional definitions of precision (p), sensitivity (s), and accuracy (a):

$$AMV = \frac{1}{3} * p + \frac{1}{3} * s + \frac{1}{3} * a \tag{2}$$

where

$$p = \frac{TP}{TP+FP} \tag{3}$$

$$s = \frac{TP}{TP+FN} \tag{4}$$

$$a = \frac{TP+TN}{TP+FP+TN+FN} \tag{5}$$

We calculated this AMV for each of the 4,880 scan detection models generated in the previous step and sorted by descending AMV to find the LOM for our data.

5 Results and Discussion

The following section presents the results of implementing our method on the University of Maryland network. With these results, we will illustrate how each variable of lower bound, attribute set, and machine learning classifier impacts the AMV performance of a scan detection model. While we analyze which values of the variables performed well on our network dataset, we recognize that these specific values may not extend to other networks.

Table 2 displays the classification results of the LOMs created based on different AMVs. From this table, we see that the selection of our AMV for model evaluation returns nearly three times as many correctly identified scans than evaluating solely by accuracy. While evaluating models by our AMV identified the same LOM as evaluating by precision, this is simply a coincidence based on our particular selection of AMV as the average of sensitivity, precision, and accuracy.

Table 2. Comparison of AMVs

Metric	Lower Bound	True Positives	False Positives	False Negatives	True Negatives
Accuracy	1	6	4	51	103659
Precision	4	17	4	40	73324
Sensitivity	1	57	103612	0	51
Our AMV	4	17	4	40	73324

5.1   The Role of Lower Bound on Metric Performance

One of the unique aspects of our method is treating lower bound as another scan detection model input variable. Table 3 compares the models with the same machine learning classifier and attribute set as our LOM, but with different lower bounds. The table illustrates a noticeable drop in performance if a lower bound other than 4 is chosen. If no lower bound is used, (designated by the lower bound row 1) only two instances are correctly classified as malicious. These results suggest that evaluating multiple lower bounds can produce models with higher AMV performance.

The tradeoff of using lower bounds is that the model ignores users who only produce a few network flow records. Essentially, this is equivalent to requiring network scans to consist of at least a minimum number of flows. It is possible that the unlabeled users for one model could be labeled as malicious in another model with a different lower bound. However, neither model is "mislabeling" the data, as they are attempting to detect scans based on fundamentally different definitions. Based on these facts, it is important to note that the LOM returned by our method will use the definition of a scan based on the lower bound with the best performance for the given AMV.

Table 3. Comparison of Lower Bounds by Descending AMV

Lower Bound	True Positives	False Positives	False Negatives	True Negatives	Our AMV
4*	17	4	40	73324	0.7024
6	15	9	41	65437	0.6307
10	10	8	46	55910	0.5777
8	12	13	44	59808	0.5644
2	4	4	53	88038	0.5232
30	5	10	45	39386	0.4773
1	2	4	55	10365	0.4560
50	4	11	36	32932	0.4551

*Lower bound selected by method

5.2   The Role of Attribute Sets on Metric Performance

Table 4 shows the impact of the attribute set on performance, controlling for the lower bound and classifier. The impact of attribute set is more subtle than machine learning algorithm or lower bound selection, resulting in only minor variations in the false positive rate and the number of correctly classified instances. This reflects the tendency of the method to generate multiple viable attribute sets.

Table 4. Comparison of Top 5 Attribute Sets by Descending AMV

Rank	True Positives	False Positives	False Negatives	True Negatives	Our AMV
1*	17	4	40	73324	0.7024
2	18	6	39	73322	0.6884
3	18	6	39	73322	0.6884
4	14	4	43	73324	0.6743
5	16	6	41	73322	0.6701

*Attribute set selected by method

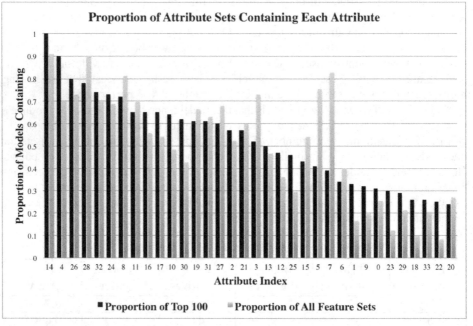

Fig. 2. Proportion of top 100 models and all models containing each attribute

Figure 2 displays two calculations: (a) the proportion of the attribute sets from the top 100 models containing a given attribute and (b) the proportion of all attribute sets containing a given attribute. Every one of the top 100 models' attribute sets contained attribute 14, "rt_std_pttrn" (see Appendix A for details). One interesting finding is that although more than 70% of all the attribute sets generated by the attribute selection algorithms contained attributes 5 and 7, the attributes were only present in the top 100 models about 40% of the time. This suggests that attribute set selection algorithms may choose attributes that appear less frequently in the attribute sets of models with the highest AMVs. This reinforces the importance of trying various combinations of attribute sets for comparison based on results.

5.3   The Role of Machine Learning Classifiers on Metric Performance

By controlling for lower bound and attribute set, Table 5 shows that machine learning algorithm selection has a significant impact on AMV performance. Random Forest outperforms the other algorithms by a considerable margin in terms of false positive rate, with only 4 false positives for the 17 correctly identified scans.

Table 5. Comparison of Machine Learning Algorithm by Descending AMV

Classifier	True Positives	False Negatives	False Positives	True Positives	Our AMV
Random Forest*	17	40	4	73324	0.7024
AODE	14	43	38	73290	0.5046
Prism	24	30	425	72883	0.4972
SMO	1	56	18	73310	0.3564
Decision Table	0	57	67	73261	0.3328

*Machine learning algorithm selected by method

For classifiers, Random Forest was the most successful at achieving high AMV values. In fact, the top 26 models by AMV were all achieved using Random Forest, with AODE first appearing at position 27. The Prism machine learning algorithm was not used to generate any of the top 100 results, largely due to its propensity to label large portions of the data as malicious.

6   Conclusions

By treating the creation of scan detection models as an optimization of an AMV using the best combination of lower bound, attribute set, and machine learning algorithm, a flexible framework for identifying LOMs is created. We were able to evaluate our model on the University of Maryland network and successfully identify the LOM. Our results demonstrate that different lower bounds, attribute sets, and machine learning algorithms are necessary to evaluate because they impact the AMV of a scan detection model. We improve upon an arbitrary selection of these variables when creating models by using a model's performance to justify the variables' values. This will provide a more practical method of creating network specific scan detection models in operational settings.

While our method successfully identified the LOM for the University of Maryland network, the method should be easily extendable to other networks. Network administrators should start by selecting their own network flow attributes to calculate. Then, they can create models using their own selection of lower bounds, attribute sets, and machine learning algorithms. Finally, the models should be compared using a customized AMV to produce a network specific LOM.

Despite our method's benefits, it is limited by its reliance upon supervised machine learning. Performing supervised learning requires every source IP address in the network flow data to be labeled as malicious or benign prior to testing. This labeling is time consuming, and it requires a network administrator to have thorough knowledge of a network's configuration and network scans to label every IP address in the network flow data confidently. Even if a network administrator labels every IP address according to some strict set of heuristics, there is no ground truth regarding which users are truly scanners. We attempted to counteract this problem by injecting scans into the network flow data that could be labeled with ground truth. However, injecting anomalous data into a network dataset can make the dataset no longer representative of a real world network [25, 34].

The alternative approach of semi-supervised machine learning would require administrators to only label a few IP addresses in the network that are known to be malicious or benign such as injected network scans or websites commonly visited over the network. An avenue for future research is evaluating if applying semi-supervised learning to such a method can produce scan detection models with classification success similar to that of models produced using supervised learning.

Appendix A: Calculated Network Flow Attributes

Network Flow Attributes Calculated for Each Source IP Address		
Index	Attribute	Description
0	rt_w/o_ACK	Ratio of flows that do not have the ACK bit set to all flows
1	rt_under_3	Ratio of flows with fewer than 3 flows to all flows
2	max_ips_1sub	Maximum number of IP addresses contacted in any one /24 subnet
3	max_high	Maximum number of high destination ports contacted on any one host
4	max_low	Maximum number of low destination ports contacted on any one host
5	max_cnsc_high	Maximum number of consecutive high destination ports contacted on any one host
6	max_cnsc_low	Maximum number of consecutive low destination ports contacted on any one host
7	num_uniq_dsts	Number of unique destination IP addresses contacted
8	num_uniq_srcp	Number of unique source ports
9	avg_srcp/dest	Average number of source ports per destination IP address
10	rt_std_flags	Ratio of flows with "standard" flag combinations (SYN and ACK set, along with either the FIN or RST bit set) to all flows
11	rt_over_60	Ratio of the number of flows with the average bytes/packet > 60 to all flows
12	med_pack/dst	Median value of packets per destination IP address
13	rt_std_pttrn	Ratio of flows with "standard" combination (standard flag combination and at least three packets and at least 60 bytes/packet on average) to all flows
14	rt_bksctr_pttrn	Ratio of flows with backscatter combination (RST, RST-ACK, or SYN-ACK for the flag combination and the average number of bytes/packet is <= 60 and the number of packets per flow is <= 2) to all flows
15	rt_dst	Ratio of unique destination IP addresses to the number of flows
16	rt_srcp	Ratio of unique source ports to the number of flows
17	rt_bksctr_flags	Ratio of flows with backscatter flag combinations (R/RA/SA) to all flows
18	min_pack	Minimum number of packets of any one flow

19	max_pack	Maximum number of packets of any one flow
20	mean_pack	Mean packets per flow
21	std_dev_pack	Standard deviation of packets per flow
22	min_dur	Minimum duration of any one flow
23	max_dur	Maximum duration of any one flow
24	mean_dur	Mean duration per flow
25	std_dev_dur	Standard deviation of duration per flow
26	min_bytes	Minimum number of bytes of any one flow
27	max_bytes	Maximum number of bytes of any one flow
28	mean_bytes	Mean bytes per flow
29	std_dev_bytes	Standard deviation of bytes per flow
30	min_bpp	Minimum number of bytes per packet of any one flow
31	max_bpp	Maximum number of bytes per packet of any one flow
32	mean_bpp	Mean bytes per packet per flow
33	std_dev_bpp	Standard deviation of bytes per packet per flow

Acknowledgements. We would like to thank Benjamin Klimkowski and Bertrand Sobesto for their assistance on this project. This material is based upon work supported by the National Science Foundation under Grant No. 1223634.

References

1. Dua, S., Xian, D.: Data Mining and Machine Learning in Cybersecurity. Auerbach, Boca Raton (2011)
2. Sommer, R., Paxson, V.: Outside the closed world: on using machine learning for network intrusion detection. In: IEEE Symposium on Security and Privacy, Oakland (2010)
3. Denning, D.E.: An Intrusion-Detection model. IEEE Transactions on Software Engineering (1987)
4. Lane, T.D.: Machine Learning Techniques for Computer Security Domain of Anomaly Detection. Purdue University, Department of Electrical and Computer Engineering and the COAST Laboratory (1998)
5. Axelsson, S.: The Base-Rate Fallacy and the Difficulty of Intrusion Detection. ACM Transactions on Information and System Security (TISSEC), 2008
6. Lippmann, R.P., et al.: Evaluating intrusion detection systems: the 1998 DARPA off-line intrusion detection evaluation. In: DARPA Information Survivability Conference and Exposition (2000)
7. Simon, G.J., et al.: Scan detection: a data mining approach. In: Proceedings of the Sixth SIAM International Conference on Data Mining, SIAM (2006)
8. Gates, C., et al.: Scan detection on very large networks using logistic regression modeling. In: Proceedings of the IEEE Symposium on Computers and Communications (2006)
9. Ertöz, L., et al.: Scan Detection - Revisited. Technical Report AHPCRC 127, University of Minnesota – Twin Cities (2004)
10. Bhuyan, M.H., Bhattacharyya, D.K., Kalita, J.K.: Surveying Port Scans and Their Detection Methodologies. The Computer Journal (2011)

11. Yegneswaran, V., Barford, P., Ullrich, J.: Internet intrusions: global characteristics and prevalence. In: SIGMETRICS Performance Evaluation. ACM, New York (2003)
12. Symons, C.T., Beaver, J.M.: Nonparametric semi-supervised learning for network intrusion detection: combining performance improvements with realistic in-situ training. In: Proceedings of the 5th ACM Workshop on Artificial Intelligence and Security (2012)
13. Davis, J., Goadrich, M.: The relationship between precision-recall and ROC curves. In: Proceedings of the 23rd ACM International Conference on Machine Learning (2006)
14. Nguyen, T.T.T., Armitage, G.: A Survey of Techniques for Internet Traffic Classification using Machine Learning. Communications Surveys & Tutorials (2008). IEEE
15. Killourhy, K.S., Maxion, R.: Comparing anomaly-detection algorithms for keystroke dynamics. In: International Conference on Dependable Systems & Networks (2009)
16. Lee, W., Stolfo, S.J., Chan, P.K.: Learning patterns from unix process execution traces for intrusion detection. In: AAAI Workshop on AI Approaches to Fraud Detection and Risk Management (1997)
17. Jung, J., et al.: Fast portscan detection using sequential hypothesis testing. In: IEEE Symposium on Security and Privacy (2004)
18. Cisco: Introduction to Cisco IOS Network Flow, March 2015. www.cisco.com
19. Williams, N., Zander, S., Armitage, G.: A Preliminary Performance Comparison of Five Machine Learning Algorithms for Practical IP Traffic Flow Classification. SIGCOMM Computer Communication Review 36(5), 5–16 (2006)
20. Dash, M., Liu, H., Motoda, H.: Consistency based feature selection. In: PADKK 2000 Proceedings of the 4th Pacific-Asia Conference on Knowledge Discovery and Data Mining, Current Issues and New Applications (2000)
21. Witten, I.H., Frank, E., Hall, M.A.: Data Mining: Practical Machine Learning Tools and Techniques, 2nd edn. Morgan Kaufman, Burlington (2005)
22. Tavallaee, M., et al.: A detailed analysis for the KDD CUP 99 data set. In: IEEE Symposium on Computational Intelligence for Security and Defense Applications (2009)
23. Song, J., et al.: Statistical analysis of honeypot data and building of kyoto 2006+ dataset for NIDS evaluation. In: Proceeding of the First Workshop on Building Analysis Datasets and Gathering Experience Returns for Security (2011)
24. McHugh, J.: Testing Intrusion Detection Systems: A Critique of the 1998 and 1999 DARPA Intrusion Detection System Evaluations as Performed by Lincoln Laboratories. ACM Transactions on Information and System Security, November 2000
25. The University at Waikato: Weka 3: Data Mining Software in Java, March 2015. http://www.cs.waikato.ac.nz/ml/
26. Dietterich, T.: On Overfitting and Undercomputing in Machine Learning. ACM Computing Surveys (1995)
27. Nmap, March 2015. http://nmap.org/
28. Cisco. Snort, March 2015. https://www.snort.org/
29. Fayyad, U.M., Irani, K.B.: Multi-interval discretization of continuous-valued attributes for classification learning. In: International Joint Conferences on Artificial Intelligence (1993)
30. Jain, A., Zongker, D.: Feature Selection: Evaluation, Application, and Small Sample Performance. IEEE Transactions on Pattern Analysis and Machine Intelligence (1997)
31. Jain, A.K., Chandrasekaran, B.: Dimensionality and sample size considerations in pattern recognition practice. In: Handbook of Statistics (1982)
32. University of Waikato: Performing Attribute Selection. https://weka.wikispaces.com/Performing+attribute+selection
33. Mahoney, M.V., Chan, P.K.: An analysis of the 1999 DARPA/lincoln laboratory evaluation data for network anomaly detection. In: Proceedings of the 6th Intl. Symposium on Recent Advances in Intrusion Detection (2003)

Why Web Servers Should Fear Their Clients
Abusing Websockets in Browsers for DoS

Juan D. Parra Rodriguez[✉] and Joachim Posegga

Institute of IT-Security and Security Law, University of Passau,
Innstraße 43, Passau, Germany
{dp,jp}@sec.uni-passau.de

Abstract. This paper considers exploiting browsers for attacking Web servers. We demonstrate the generation of HTTP traffic to third-party domains without the user's knowledge, that can be used e.g. for Denial of Service attacks.

Our attack is primarily possible since Cross Origin Resource Sharing does not restrict WebSocket communications. We show an HTTP-based DoS attack with a proof of concept implementation, analyse its impact against Apache and Nginx, and compare the effectiveness of our attack to two common attack tools.

In the course of our work we identified two new vulnerabilities in Chrome and Safari, i.e. two thirds of all browsers in use, that turn these browsers into attack tools comparable to known DoS applications like LOIC.

Keywords: Denial of Service · Browser security · Web security · HTML5 security

1 Introduction

The last two decades of Web technology were governed by making Web browsers more powerful, thus increasing the computational power at the "edges" of the Internet. In particular, the power of JavaScript within the browser has grown immensely since its inception. Although this is indeed very profitable for Web developers, the potential for abuse of clients has also grown: at the moment, there are browser compatible JavaScript libraries for controversial purposes, such as bitcoin mining [7,19], cracking of cryptographic hashes [2,20], port-scanning [16], TOR network bridging [9], and even an attack that can use the users' disk space beyond reasonable limits [1,6]. These are some examples where functionality is pushed beyond its "intended" behaviour.

In spite of how worrisome the aforementioned examples may be, this paper has a narrower scope and is limited to analysing a particular attack misusing browsers, namely, using WebSockets for Denial of Service (DoS) against regular Web servers. This attack has an increased surface in comparison to existent WebSocket-based DoS attacks, which targeted only servers implementing the WebSocket protocol[15,26]. The main contributions of this paper can be summarized as follows:

© Institute for Computer Sciences, Social Informatics and Telecommunications Engineering 2015
B. Thuraisingham et al. (Eds.): SecureComm 2015, LNICST 164, pp. 401–417, 2015.
DOI: 10.1007/978-3-319-28865-9_22

- Assess protection mechanisms from browsers against malicious code using WebSockets to perform DoS attacks against third parties. Our analysis led us to discover two previously unknown vulnerabilities affecting two famous browsers.
- Evaluate and compare the impact of our attack executed in different browsers by measuring network traffic and connections on the server side. The results are further compared with two native tools doing HTTP and SYN flood DoS attacks: LOIC [18], and Syn-GUI [10].

At the time of writing, browser statistics [28] indicate that 64.9% of users utilize Chrome (or Chromium), while Safari is used by 3,8% of the market. These are the browsers most affected by our findings, so roughly two thirds of the browsers' population can be employed to execute the DoS attack as presented in this paper. Furthermore, every browser supporting WebSockets can already contribute to the DoS attack although to a lesser extent.

The rest of the paper is organized as follows. First, we explain the details of our attack in Section 2. Next, we describe our attack in Section 3. Section 4 shows the physical set up, measurements acquired and the discussion of the results. Then, related work is covered in Section 5. Finally, we draw conclusions from our research in Section 6.

2   Attack Details

DoS attacks from browsers scale very well since malicious content delivered to the client can be rather small, and it is delivered only once. As shown in Figure 1, as soon as the content is conveyed, the Web browser will open as many connections as possible to the third-party domain (i.e. victim) without the end-user noticing any of it.

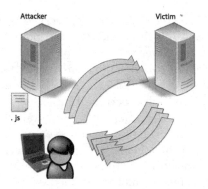

Fig. 1. Attack

Browsers can spawn threads to execute heavy computation in the background called WebWorkers [12]. We spawn 4 WebWorkers in the attack. Inside each Web-Worker, a function opening the socket is called 500 times, although it could also be called endlessly if desired. In our particular case, the number of threads and the number of sockets were selected after testing which configuration performed best across different browsers. The code for each WebWorker should resemble the following snippet:

```
var j = 0;
for(j=0; j<500; j++)
{
   socket();
}
```

Due to the asynchronous nature of JavaScript, an infinite recursion is required to keep a connection open at all times. To implement this, a callback is provided to the socket's close event handler so the socket creation function is called again recursively. This is an example attacking victim.domain.

```
function socket(){
        var wsUri = "ws://victim.domain";
        var websocket = new WebSocket(wsUri);
        websocket.onclose = function(evt) {
                socket();
        };
}
```

Although the WebSocket connection request is not really a "typical" GET request, it is enough to make the server reply back with the content of the Web site; therefore, using this code allows to successfully open HTTP connections with third-parties, i.e victim servers.

Aside from Chrome (also Chromium), and Safari, this attack also affects a more modest browser called Rekonq; nonetheless, measurements for this browser were omitted due to its low current participation on the browser's market.

3 Attack Prerequisites and Synergies

Analysing the aspects leading to the attack, and the facets intensifying its impact is of paramount importance. This allows us to extract lessons learnt which can be capitalized in the future. In this section we discuss the two triggering factors for the attack, i.e. CORS and the lack of backward protocol compatibility. Afterwards, a synergy increasing the power of the attack is presented.

3.1 Cross Origin Resource Sharing

Cross Origin Resource Sharing (CORS) provides a mechanism to enable client-side sharing of cross-origin requests [14]. It is an opt-in mechanism empowering hosts to allow other domains to request their content through the browser. In general, when the browser loads a Web site (Origin1.com) as depicted in step (1) of Figure 2, and the loaded site (Origin1.com) contains JavaScript code

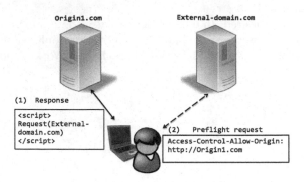

Fig. 2. Pre-flight request CORS

attempting to acquire content from an external domain (External-domain.com), the browser must determine, by means of a preflight request, whether the third-party domain wants to serve HTTP requests commenced by Origin1.com.

As shown in step (2) of Figure 2, the preflight request to the third-party domain (External-domain.com) gives information to the browser regarding the HTTP methods and origins allowed by the third-party server (External-domain.com). Subsequently, this information is used by the Web browser to decide whether HTTP requests should be sent to the third-party domain or not.

In theory, CORS would block DoS attacks against third-party domains, since it would require the victim to include the attacker's domain in their preflight request: a highly unlikely scenario. However, in practice, certain requests such as image requests, iframe content requests, or creation of WebSockets are not forbidden to avoid hindering functionality in Web sites. This yields the possibility to generate certain requests to third-party domains making not only DoS, but also other attacks such as port scanning possible.

3.2 Lack of Backward Protocol Compatibility

Huang et al. [13] have shown how the WebSocket handshake definition, as a sequence of HTTP messages, brings security problems. Although not related to DoS attacks, Huang et al. discovered that an HTTP header misinterpretation allowed to poison the cache of transparent proxies in the network. This attack forced every proxy client to load malicious content delivered by the attacker. We exploited a different aspect of the WebSocket handshake, yet related to their work since it benefits from an HTTP header omission. The issue pertains to the first message of the WebSocket handshake, which is an HTTP GET request with additional headers (e.g. Upgrade, Connection, Sec-WebSocket-Key) [21].

Whereas the WebSocket specification contemplates how a WebSocket server deals with additional headers in the handshake, it disregards how a regular Web server would reply to such request. Currently, when a WebSocket handshake is sent to a plain Web server, the server will interpret the request as a regular GET request, ignoring additional headers, and sending the content of the main page back. In this way, an attacker can generate requests for content to third-party Web servers just by attempting to open a WebSocket with the host, even though they are not WebSocket servers.

3.3 Browser Vulnerabilities

Antonatos et al. [4] have used several data sources, ranging from Alexa ranking [3] to an instrumentation of their institution's Web site to study users' behaviour, in order to estimate from a theoretical perspective the impact of a DoS attack abusing Web browsers. Their work revealed that the mean time that users keep pages on their browsers open is around 74 minutes. They also conclude that abusing browsers is a real threat; especially, because according to their results, more than 20 percent of typical commercial sites could abuse 10.000 clients, and 4 to 10 percent of randomly selected sites can use more than 1.000 browsers.

We have discovered two new vulnerabilities, increasing the aggressiveness of a DoS attack, after testing the most known browsers supporting WebSockets: Chrome, Chromium, Firefox, Safari, and Opera. One vulnerability affects Chromium and Chrome, and another one affects Safari. In this context, even though browser vulnerabilities are not a prerequisite, they create a powerful synergy with the DoS attack. In the presence of a browser vulnerability, less popular sites would still constitute a powerful ally for an attacker because clients would generate more traffic than intended.

The Chrome (and Chromium) networking stack follows an asynchronous design philosophy for performance reasons. Chrome was designed to restrict the amount of connections generated by WebSocket handshakes. However, this verification was implemented synchronously. As a result, when the user left the malicious (or compromised) Web site, all the queued connections to third-party domains were opened. We reported this behaviour through the Chromium bug tracking site, i.e. the Open Source project in which Google Chromium is based upon. This issue has been fixed by Chromium developers in the Chromium master branch [22]. Also, we found, and reported through the apple's developers bug reporting site, that Safari does not cap the amount of connections generated by WebSocket handshakes per tab. For both vulnerabilities, using WebWorkers exacerbated the effect of the attack by opening several WebSocket connections concurrently.

4   Testing and Analysis

In order to assess whether our attack is feasible in the real world, its impact must be measured and compared to applications designed for DoS. In this section we describe the physical and virtual set-up used to confirm the feasibility of our attack, as well as the measurements obtained and the discussion around them.

4.1 Set up

As illustrated on Figure 3, one router (MikroTik RouterBoard RB750 Series)
and four physical machines were used: three Dell Inspiron 15 with 6 GB RAM
memory and with an Intel(R) Core(TM) i5-4200U CPU @ 1.60GHz processor (in
gray), and one Lenovo T430S with 16 GB RAM memory and with an Intel(R)
Core(TM) i7-3520M CPU @ 2.90GHz processor (in white). All the network connections used Ethernet cables to ensure a fast, and reliable physical connection
between the physical machines. On every one of the Dell machines, a fresh installation of Kubuntu 13.10 saucy was performed; also, an Ubuntu 12.04 TLS was
installed in the Lenovo T430S hosting the attacker's Web site.

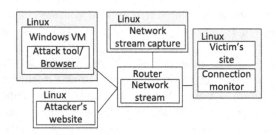

Fig. 3. Testing environment

One of the Dell machines running Kubuntu had a VirtualBox Version 4.3.18
r96516 with a virtual machine running Windows 7 Enterprise Service Pack1,
where all the attacks were executed from. This machine was configured with
a Bridged VirtualBox network adapter, 4 GB of RAM memory, and 1 CPU
core without capping the execution. Inside this Virtual machine the following
programs were used for benchmarking the DoS attack: LOIC version 1.0.7.42,
and Syn-GUI version 2.0. The browsers compared to the DoS tools were executed
on the same virtual machine using Chrome version 39.0.2171.95 Official Build,
and Safari Windows version 5.1.7. The choice for the SYN-flood tool and Safari's
version was stirred by our need to execute every attack on the same platform,
i.e. the Windows virtual machine. Nevertheless, the same behaviour observed in
Safari version 5.1.7, was also observed in newer versions running in Mac OSX
systems.

Due to the popularity of Apache and Nginx [25] they were used to run the
victim's Web site on one of Dell machines natively in Kubuntu. The Apache
version was 2.4.6, and the Nginx version was 1.4.1. Both servers were used in
their default configuration, delivering only static (HTML) content.

On the network side, to hinder the interference of network capturing with the
measurements as much as possible, the router forwarded the traffic between the
victim site and the host running the attack to an external host (above, connected
with dashed line) for further offline analysis. The external host received the
traffic encapsulated with TaZmen Sniffer Protocol (TZSP), a protocol designed

to encapsulate network traffic over the wire. Afterwards, the external host stored the traffic at the end of the experiment. This configuration delivered better results than capturing and storing traffic inside the router.

On the victim's server, the total amount of TCP connections to port 80 (used by the Web servers) listed by the Operating System was stored every 100 milliseconds (ms) approximately. This connection count included not only the fully established connections (i.e. ESTABLISHED state), but also those which were in an intermediate step or momentarily unused, such as those with state SYN_RECV, TIME_WAIT, or FIN_WAIT. This approach was preferred because it was observed that depending on server implementation aspects, connections may be left inactive for longer or shorter periods depending on how the socket and thread pools are handled. Also, the efficiency of the server can affect the time required to fully establish or close the socket from the moment when a SYN, or FIN packet is received respectively.

4.2 Measurements

For each server, a series of measurements were conducted while they were attacked by two DoS tools and the two most affected browsers. Before each measurement, the server was restarted in order to avoid affecting server performance due to previous execution of attacks.

For Safari, Chrome, as well as for every DoS tool (i.e. LOIC and Syn-GUI), a 20 second attack was performed. In the case of Chrome, a massive number of connection requests was generated when the user left the Web site. As a result, the measurements for Chrome were performed by opening the malicious Web site, waiting for 20 seconds in the Web site, and then closing the tab. Naturally, in the case of Chrome, the aggressiveness of the attack is proportional to the amount of time spent on the malicious page.

From Figure 4 to Figure 9, the left Y axis represents the network statistics obtained by counting the number of packets in a 100 milliseconds timespan that matched certain criteria. The values plotted therein contain the following measurements: the amount of SYN packets sent by the client (black continuous line), the number of acknowledged connections from the server (red dots), and the amount of HTTP requests answered by the server successfully (gray impulses filling the curve). On the right hand Y axis, the number of connections on the server side is shown with a dashed blue line. Unfortunately, unlike the left Y axis, due to the divergence of the number of connections, the right Y axis scale has to be adapted accordingly from graph to graph.

From now on, each subsection will show the results for a given attack tool, such as Chrome, Safari or LOIC, for both target servers, i.e. Apache and Nginx. At the end, we dedicate a subsection to the results obtained when attempting the attack after a security patch has been applied on Chromium.

Chrome. In Figure 4 and 5, when the user leaves the tab roughly at the 20th second of the measurement, there is a peak of SYN packets sent by the browser,

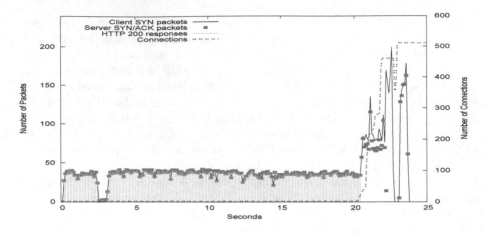

Fig. 4. Chrome-Apache

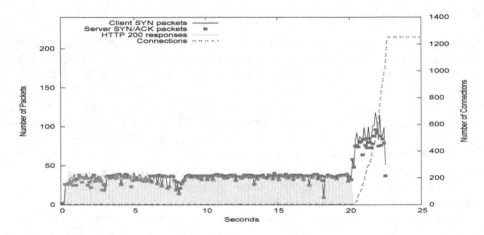

Fig. 5. Chrome-Nginx

i.e 100-200 packets/100 ms for Apache, and 100-150 packets/100 ms for Nginx. At this point, the Web server stops replying with content.

The fact that the Web server does not reply is evidenced by the lack of gray filling under the curve. Additionally, the server fails to acknowledge all the connections requested, which is visible because the values for the number of acknowledgements, represented as red dots, appear below the continuous black line depicting the number of connection requests, i.e. SYN packets.

Also, whereas the network traffic is similar in both captures for Chrome, i.e. Apache and Nginx, the amount of server side connections for Nginx is more than twice of the values observed for Apache, reflecting that Nginx opens more connections on the operating system level than Apache.

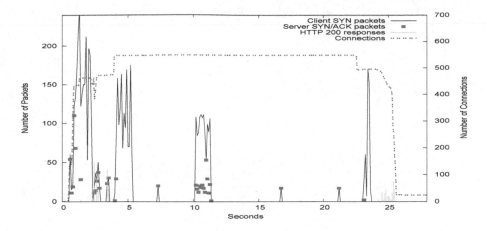

Fig. 6. Safari-Apache

Safari. Safari can inhibit Apache from replying content from the beginning of the attack. It can be seen in Figure 6 that, due to the peak of SYN packets sent by Safari, the connections are not even acknowledged by the server, and the HTTP responses are scarce and severely delayed. Further, when comparing the two browsers for the Apache measurements, The number of SYN packets is slightly higher in the case of Safari, i.e. 150-250 instead of 100-200 packets/100 ms in the case of Chrome.

In the case of Safari attacking Nginx in Figure 7, peaks of SYN packets having 50-120 packets/100 ms force the server to stop replying to the HTTP requests temporarily, however, Nginx starts to provide HTTP responses afterwards. Eventually, it almost replies for every connection request. As expected, Nginx opens a higher amount of connections than Apache on the Operating System level, just like in the previous case.

LOIC. LOIC is a Windows application commonly used to perform DoS attacks. This tool can be compared to the browser attack because it attempts to flood the Web server with HTTP messages using a parametrizable amount of threads.

At first, we tested LOIC with 4 threads to have equivalent conditions to our attack from the browsers; however, the impact was significantly lower than using Safari or Chrome. As a result, this was modified to use the default configurations, i.e. 10 threads and wait for server response, while our attack had 4 WebWorkers, i.e. browser threads.

There are several differences in the network traffic when Chrome and Safari are compared to LOIC's attack against Apache and Nginx, see Figure 8 and Figure 9. For example, when the user leaves the tab in Chrome or when the attack is performed in Safari, the amount of SYN packets, and network traffic produced in general, is considerably higher than the traffic produced by LOIC.

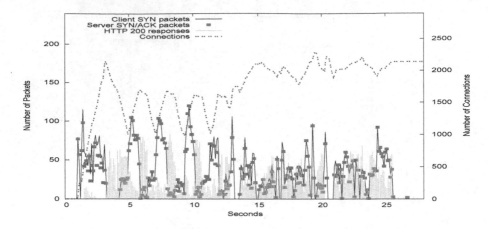

Fig. 7. Safari-Nginx

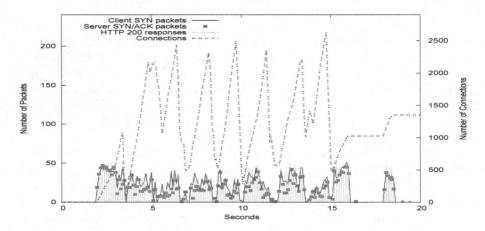

Fig. 8. LOIC-Apache

This situation allows Chrome and Safari to coerce Apache and Nginx to stop replying, which is not achieved by LOIC.

However, LOIC has higher impact than the browsers on the amount of connections opened on the server side by Nginx and Apache. Moreover, in the particular case of LOIC's attack against Nginx, a special behaviour was observed. LOIC induces a concurrency problem for Nginx due to the amount of opened connections on the server side.

For Linux systems each socket is treated as a file descriptor [17], and in the particular case of LOIC against Nginx, the number of connections is consistently around 2500 connections for periods of up to 5 seconds. As a result, Nginx replies with an HTTP 500 error code, see black triangles in Figure 9, due to too many open file descriptors, which is evidenced in the log files.

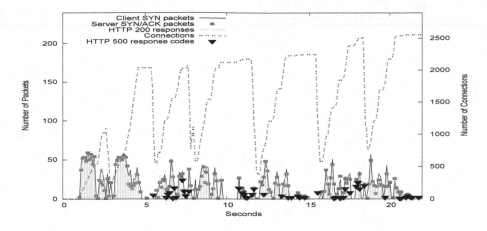

Fig. 9. LOIC-Nginx

Syn-GUI. Syn-GUI implements a SYN flood attack by sending SYN packets massively to the server without implementing the HTTP protocol in the application layer, as previously mentioned attacks do. Comparing the browser attack to a SYN flood attack is relevant, since the strongest property observed for browsers was the power to generate a high amount of SYN packets during the initial hand shake of the TCP connection. As a result, the analysis presented hereafter focuses only on this aspect; also, because other measurements, such as the number of HTTP responses cannot apply to a SYN flood attack.

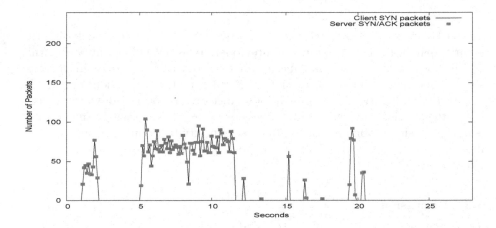

Fig. 10. SynGUI-Apache

As it can be seen in Figure 10 and Figure 11, the peaks of SYN packets sent by Syn-GUI are still smaller compared to the peaks observed for Chrome and

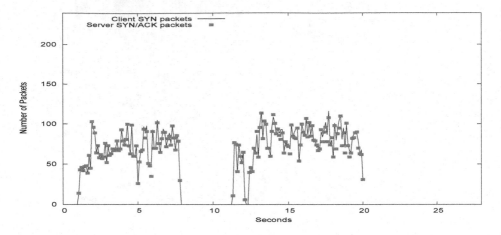

Fig. 11. SynGUI-Nginx

Safari. However, the amount of SYN packets is higher that the packets sent by LOIC.

Withal, it must be mentioned that certain countermeasures are effective against SYN flood attacks, but they fail to thwart LOIC or the browser attack. For example, SYN cookies avoid the allocation of resources on the server side until the TCP connection is actually opened. Although this would be effective against a SYN flood, it will not work neither against LOIC, nor against the browsers because they actually open the TCP connections and send HTTP request to the server subsequently.

Fixed Browser. We executed the trunk raw build of Chromium, including the security patch, to test the fix of the previously reported vulnerability. For this graph, both of the Y axes have been adjusted to a narrower scale in order to show the behaviour of the packets in the network and the connections opened. In Figure 12 and Figure 13, the amount of connections is controlled when the user leaves the tab. Further, the number of requests, and SYN packets in the network is not increasing beyond 8 packets/100 ms: A pretty low value, considering that it was around 40 packets/100 ms in the unpatched version, even before the user left the tab.

4.3   Discussion

The comparison between browsers and the SYN flood tool demonstrated that the amount of connection requests generated from the browser is comparable to the number of requests generated by the SYN flood application. Nevertheless, abusing browsers has an additional advantage in respect to SYN flood: the browser implements the whole TCP, and HTTP network stack. As a result, countermeasures against browsers need to be more complex; for example, SYN

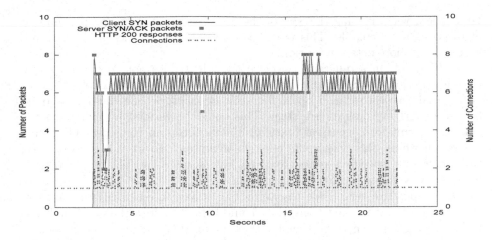

Fig. 12. Chromium Fixed-Apache

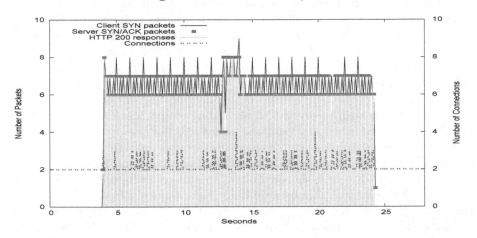

Fig. 13. Chromium Fixed-Nginx

cookies would thwart the SYN flood attack, yet they will fail against a Web browser attack.

Moreover, Safari and Chrome hinder the server from replying requests right after the attack is performed due to the sudden increase of TCP connection requests. To mitigate the impact from an attack exploiting browsers on the server side, configuring firewall rules to drop SYN packets after a certain amount of connections has been reached with given IP seems reasonable. However, these rules would have to be generated dynamically; especially, because different browsers execute the malicious JavaScript code while they visit the malicious Web site. This makes the set of browsers to be banned a constantly moving target, due to the high churn of visitors that a Web site has. Furthermore, if the browser attack is programmed in a less aggressive manner, recognition on the server side could be avoided, yet achieving the goal of the attack as long as the proper amount of browsers are available. This is the case of existent attacks [4,5] which are described in more detail in Section 5.

LOIC excels in a different aspect. Although it does not coerce the server to stop replying like Safari or Chrome, is capable to force Nginx to reply with an internal server error as it opens more file descriptors than the limit allowed by the underlying operating system. This could be tackled by increasing the maximum limit for concurrent opened file descriptors in the server Operating System; however, this only would cure the symptom. To solve this problem on the server side, specific business logic on how sockets and file descriptors are handled by Nginx would have to be modified.

So far, possible server-side countermeasures have been discussed. Now, we focus on client-side modifications which could help to address the problem. It has been previously shown, in Section 4.2, that the fixed Chromium version behaves mercifully with the server. Withal, It must be noted that although this diminishes the power of one single browser against a server, the problem of detecting when several browsers are colluding against a domain remains unsolved. We consider that employing machine learning techniques for malicious JavaScript code detection can help to detect properties of the DoS attacks [8,23]. Further, a technique favouring early detection malicious code, such as the work presented Schütt et al. [24], may be the best match in order to stop the attack as early as possible. However, the main challenge is the identification of the proper features to process in the algorithms, as well as finding proper data sets, so learning algorithms can be trained and validated afterwards.

Last but not least, from the measuring perspective, collecting network traffic during a DoS attack characterizes it better than only counting TCP connections on the server side; however, this method still yields results specific to the server platform. This is unavoidable because there are a number of possible resources that could be exhausted, such as open ports, files opened by the server, CPU time, etc. However, common patterns observed allowed us to conclude which are the strong and weak points of each attack and how they perform.

5   Related Work

Puppetnets was a term coined by Antonatos et al. for a botnet of browsers executing port-scanning, DoS, and worm propagation [4]. The authors described a simple DoS attack which did not exploit any implementation aspects of the browser. Still, they spent significant efforts on estimating the impact of an eventual attack. Their findings indicate that around 20 percent of commercial sites could be used to steer around 10.000 browsers, while the top-500 popular sites could leverage up to 100.000 browsers. They enumerate several possible countermeasures against the three aforementioned attacks, but they concluded that none of the presented options was completely satisfying. Athanasopoulos et al. performed measurements on the network level focused on the impact of RTT times in the generation of HTTP traffic from browsers, yet leaving any practical

DoS evaluation of the scope of the paper. Instead, we focus on the validation of the attack by demonstrating its impact on real world server implementations, and the generation of traffic from one browser.

Grossman et al. [11] presented that it is possible to use browsers to conduct a DoS attack using Ad Networks to deliver the malicious JavaScript code, yet spending a small amount of money. Furthermore, although the DoS attack is already feasible due to the wide reach of an Add Network, its power can be further increased when there is a vulnerability on the browser's side. Grossman et al. discovered a vulnerability in Firefox. The exploitation consisted of using the browser's JavaScript API to attempt to load an image, but changing the HTTP scheme to FTP in the url. This allowed an attacker to create a higher amount of requests. Instead, we use the WebSocket API combined with the spawning of WebWorkers to generate requests from the browser, and we found a vulnerability affecting the handling of WebSocket handshakes for Chrome, and Chromium, and another one for Safari. Grossman et al. show the effectiveness of the attack by measuring the amount of HTTP connections on the server side for one server implementation, i.e. Apache. Instead, we monitored not only the established connections on the server side, but also the network traffic on the router level for two different server implementations, i.e. Apache and Nginx. This allows us to analyse more deeply the impact of each attack. Moreover, the comparison between common DoS tools and the proposed browser attack is also missing in the work presented by Grossman et al.

According to a recent technical report [5,27], an anti-censorship project in China called GreatFire.org suffered a large scale DoS attack. The attack was executed from browsers of innocent Web site visitors located all around the world. The report includes the JavaScript code suspected of launching the attack. The presented code lacks of the mixture of WebWorkers and WebSockets presented in our work. In contrast to our approach, the discovered attack sends GET requests using the AJAX get function provided by jQuery. This shows that it neither employs WebWorkers, nor exploits cross-protocol or browser implementation problems to increase its power, as we do.

There is also existing work on executing DoS attacks using WebSockets from browsers [15,26]; however, this kind of attack only targets WebSocket-enabled servers, and the existent work does not include detailed measurements. More to the point, our attack has an increased surface in comparison to the existent WebSocket-based DoS attacks, since it can be directed against any Web server, even if it does not implement the WebSocket protocol.

6   Conclusion and Future Work

We showed in our paper how to turn modern Web browsers into attack tools by exploiting certain features of WebSockets. We measured the effectiveness of our attack, against two different Web server implementations, by combining server side measurements of the number of TCP connections with a network layer capture analysis. This allows us to confirm that the impact of the DoS attack from browsers is comparable, or in some cases more effective than using DoS tools.

The massive DoS attack discovered recently [5,27] shows the significance of studying and understanding DoS attacks steering innocent browsers against victim servers, such as the attack discovered in our research. Also, Google Chromium's team decision to implement a security patch based on our vulnerability report reassures the relevance of the proposed attack, and it also enables our research to achieve real world impact. However, from a wider perspective, we consider that the criteria for moving functionality to the client side should be further researched, so future attacks can be prevented. For instance, if infinite trivial recursions including network operations such as the one presented would be forbidden, the attack would have been less powerful. Besides, preventing WebWorkers to open WebSockets, like Firefox does, would have also been a good countermeasure to limit the power of the attack. This proves, once again, that taking the least-privilege path when enabling functionality will always be the most secure approach.

Also, since the first study of browser-based DoS attacks [4], its detection has proven to be a difficult due to the number of possibilities to obfuscate, and dynamically modify and execute JavaScript code. We consider that future research efforts should study the feasibility of applying advanced algorithms, e.g. machine learning detection methods [8,23,24], for code property detection to assess their usefulness in this realm.

Finally, the risk of malicious code being executed transparently to the user could be mitigated by developing specific mechanisms within the browser. For instance, users could be empowered to control or monitor browser resource usage such as number of connections, number of spawned threads, etc.

Acknowledgements. The research leading to these results has received funding from the European Union's FP7 project COMPOSE, under grant agreement 317862. Further, the authors would like to thank Oussama Mahjoub for providing valuable insights during the collection of network captures.

References

1. Introducing the new HTML5 Hard Disk Filler API (2013). http://feross.org/fill-disk/
2. MD5-Password-Cracker (2013). https://github.com/feross/md5-password-cracker.js/
3. The top 500 sites on the web (2015). http://www.alexa.com/topsites
4. Antonatos, S., Akritidis, P., Lam, V.T., Anagnostakis, K.G.: Puppetnets: Misusing Web Browsers As a Distributed Attack Infrastructure. ACM Trans. Inf. Syst. Secur. **12**(2) (2008)
5. Using Baidu to steer millions of computers to launch denial of serviceattacks (2015). https://drive.google.com/file/d/0ByrxblDXR_yqeUNZYU5WcjFCbXM/view
6. Web code weakness allows data dump on PCs (2008). http://www.bbc.co.uk/news/technology-21628622
7. Bitcoin Miner for Websites (2011). http://www.bitcoinplus.com/miner/embeddable

8. Cova, M., Kruegel, C., Vigna, G.: Detection and analysis of drive-by-download attacks and malicious javascript code. In: Proceedings of the 19th International Conference on World Wide Web, WWW 2010, pp. 281–290. ACM, New York (2010)
9. Fifield, D., Hardison, N., Ellithorpe, J., Stark, E., Boneh, D., Dingledine, R., Porras, P.: Evading censorship with browser-based proxies. In: Fischer-Hübner, Simone, Wright, Matthew (eds.) PETS 2012. LNCS, vol. 7384, pp. 239–258. Springer, Heidelberg (2012)
10. SynGUI (2014). http://download.cnet.com/SynGUI/3000-18510_4-10915777.html
11. Grossman, J., Johansen, M.: Million Browser Botnet (2013). https://www.blackhat.com/us-13/briefings.html
12. Hickson, I.: Web workers. Candidate recommendation, W3C, May 2012. http://www.w3.org/TR/2012/CR-workers-20120501/
13. Huang, L.S., Chen, E.Y., Barth, A., Rescorla, E., Jackson, C.: Talking to yourself for fun and profit. In: Proceedings of W2SP, pp. 1–11 (2011)
14. Kesteren, A.V.: Cross-Origin Resource Sharing. W3C recommendation, W3C, January 2014. http://www.w3.org/TR/2014/REC-cors-20140116/
15. Kulshrestha, A.: An Empirical study of HTML5 Websockets and their Cross Browser behavior for Mixed Content and Untrusted Certificates. International Journal of Computer Applications 82(6), 13–18 (2013)
16. Kuppan, L., Saindane, M.: JS Recon (2010). http://www.andlabs.org/tools/jsrecon/jsrecon.html
17. Linux Programmer's Manual (2015). http://man7.org/linux/man-pages/man2/select.2.html
18. A Network Stress Testing Application (2014). https://sourceforge.net/projects/loic/
19. Matthews, N.: jsMiner (2011). https://github.com/jwhitehorn/jsMiner
20. Matthews, N.: Ravan: JavaScript Distributed Computing System (BETA) (2012). http://www.andlabs.org/tools/ravan.html
21. Melnikov, A.: The websocket protocol. RFC 6455, RFC Editor, December 2011. http://tools.ietf.org/html/rfc6455
22. Rice, A.: Chromium Code Reviews Issue 835623003: Add a delay when unlockingWebSocket endpoints. (Closed) (2015). https://codereview.chromium.org/835623003
23. Rieck, K., Krueger, T., Dewald, A.: Cujo: efficient detection and prevention of drive-by-download attacks. In: Proceedings of the 26th Annual Computer Security Applications Conference, ACSAC 2010, pp. 31–39. ACM, Austin (2010)
24. Schütt, K., Kloft, M., Bikadorov, A., Rieck, K.: Early detection of malicious behavior in JavaScript code. In: Proceedings of the 5th ACM Workshop on Security and Artificial Intelligence, AISec 2012, pp. 15–24. ACM, Raileigh (2012)
25. Web Server Usage Statistics (2015). http://trends.builtwith.com/web-server
26. Shema, M., Shekyan, S., Toukharia, V.: Hacking with WebSockets (2012). http://media.blackhat.com/bh-us-12/Briefings/Shekyan/BH_US_12_Shekyan_Toukharian_Hacking_Websocket_Slides.pdf
27. Internet activists blame China for cyber-attack that brought down GitHub (2015). http://www.theguardian.com/technology/2015/mar/30/china-github-internet-activists-cyber-attack
28. Browser Statistics (2014). http://www.w3schools.com/browsers/browsers_stats.asp

An Attribute-Based Signcryption Scheme to Secure Attribute-Defined Multicast Communications

Chunqiang Hu[1], Xiuzhen Cheng[1], Zhi Tian[2], Jiguo Yu[3]($\boxtimes$),
Kemal Akkaya[4], and Limin Sun[5]

[1] Department of Computer Science, George Washington University,
Washington, DC, USA
{chu,cheng}@gwu.edu
[2] Electrical and Computer Engineering Department,
George Mason University, Fairfax, USA
ztian1@gmu.edu
[3] School of Information Science and Engineering,
Qufu Normal University, Qufu, China
jiguoyu@sina.com
[4] Electrical and Computer Engineering Department,
Florida International University, Miami, USA
kakkaya@fiu.edu
[5] Beijing Key Laboratory of IOT Information Security Technology,
Institute of Information Engineering, CAS, Beijing, China
sunlimin@iie.ac.cn

Abstract. We consider a special type of multicast communications existing in many emerging applications such as smart grids, social networks, and body area networks, in which the multicast destinations are specified by an access structure defined by the data source based on a set of attributes and carried by the multicast message. A challenging issue is to secure these multicast communications to address the prevalent security and privacy concerns, i.e., to provide access control, data encryption, and authentication to ensure message integrity and confidentiality. To achieve this objective, we present a signcryption scheme called CP_ABSC based on Ciphertext-Policy Attribute Based Encryption (CP_ABE) [2] in this paper. CP_ABSC provides algorithms for key management, signcryption, and designcryption. It can be used to signcrypt a message/data based on the access rights specified by the message/data itself. A multicast destination can designcrypt a ciphertext if and only if it possesses the attributes required by the access structure of the data. Thus CP_ABSC effectively defines a multicast group based on the access rights of the data. CP_ABSC provides collusion attack resistance, message authentication, forgery prevention, and confidentiality. It can be easily applied to secure push-based multicasts where the data is pushed from the source to multiple destinations and pull-based multicasts where the data is downloaded from a repository by multiple destinations. Compared to CP_ABE, CP_ABSC combines encryption with signature at a lower computational cost for signcryption and a slightly higher cost in designcryption for signature verification.

© Institute for Computer Sciences, Social Informatics and Telecommunications Engineering 2015
B. Thuraisingham et al. (Eds.): SecureComm 2015, LNICST 164, pp. 418–437, 2015.
DOI: 10.1007/978-3-319-28865-9_23

Keywords: Ciphertext-Policy Attribute Based Signcryption · Secure multicast communications · Push-based multicast · Pull-based multicast

1 Introduction

We consider a special type of multicast communications existing in emerging applications such as smart grids, social networks, and body area networks: a multicast message carries an access structure specified by the data source based on a set of attributes to define the right set of destinations - a recipient of the message can read the data only if it possesses the set of attributes required by the data source. Such multicasts can be either *push-based* or *pull-based*. For examples, a service provider in smart metering can employ push-based multicast to deliver a software update command to the smart meters of model A or B located at a certain area manufactured by company X after the year Y and the message carries an access structure defined by attributes {*location, time, company, model*} based on the AND and OR relations; a smart meter reading together with its access policy (e.g., only the service providers in Washington DC or Bethesda MD can access this data), again defined by AND and OR relations, can be stored in a data repository for future downloads (being pulled) by the service providers designated by the attributes (e.g., service providers in Washington DC or Bethesda MD).

Push-based multicasts under our consideration are very similar to the traditional ones except that no identities of the destinations are carried by the message; pull-based multicasts require the data to be stored in a repository and then downloaded by multiple users on-demand. Both multicast scenarios require the data to be protected for confidentiality, integrity, authentication, and access control. Specifically,

- All the multicast messages must be protected from adversaries as the data may disclose private information of the data source. For example, the electricity usage data could reveal the activities of the residents in a household [6], which places a significant privacy concern.
- The data source should provide access control and intelligently determine who should or should not have access to its data. An access structure should be defined based on the attributes required by the data source. The data should be accessible only by the destinations specified by the data source; no third party including the data repository should be able to read the data.
- The authenticity of the data source and the integrity of the data should be verifiable.

To achieve these objectives, we propose a signcryption scheme termed CP_ABSC based on Ciphertext-Policy Attribute-based Encryption (CP_ABE) [2] to address the secure multicast problem and provide the required security services mentioned above. CP_ABSC combines signature and encryption, and provides a new mechanism for data encryption, access control, and authentication to ensure security and privacy. The basic idea of CP_ABSC is to signcrypt a data item based on its access policy (represented by an access tree and specified by the data (data source) itself) and designcrypt the corresponding ciphertext with a secret key computed from a set of attributes. The access tree defines the access rights of the data based on the attributes and is carried by the ciphertext. This implies that any user possessing the set of attributes that satisfy the access policy defined by the data itself can access the data. Because a multicast group is uniquely defined by the data itself via the access policy, secure multicasts are effectively achieved. Moreover, other than supporting the traditional push-based multicast that "pushes" the data to all destinations, CP_ABSC can also support pull-based multicast, in which the data is stored in a repository and delivered to a multicast destination only when the destination needs the data and actively "pulls" the data.

The contributions of this paper can be summarized as follows:

- We develop a novel scheme called Ciphertext-Policy Attribute Based Signcryption (CP_ABSC) based on CP_ABE, which ensures security and privacy of the data by combining signature and encryption without requiring a certificate for verification.
- We prove the correctness of the proposed scheme and analyze its efficiency and feasibility. In particular, we discuss the security of the proposed scheme under four major attack scenarios: collusion, message authentication, forgery, and confidentiality. We also conduct a quantitative performance analysis, and our results indicate that the proposed CP_ABSC is efficient and feasible.
- We demonstrate how to apply the proposed signcryption scheme to secure different multicast communications in smart grids. Particularly, we develop a protocol to secure the instructions sent from utility companies to smart meters (push-based multicast); we also develop a procedure for the smart meter data to be securely stored and accessed by different service providers based on CP_ABSC (pull-based multicast).

The remainder of this paper is structured as follows: In Section 2, we present the motivations, our system model, and the most related work. Section 3 proposes our signcryption scheme CP_ABSC and illustrates how to use it to secure multicast communications. Section 4 proves the correctness of CP_ABSC and analyzes its security strength and computational cost. Conclusions and future research are presented in Section 5.

2   Motivations, System Model, and Related Work

In this section, we describe a few real world applications to motivate our problem formulation, present our system model, and then summarize the most related research.

2.1   Push-Based Multicast Communications

Traditional multicast communications are usually *push-based*, in which the data source pushes the data to all recipients (the multicast destinations) whose

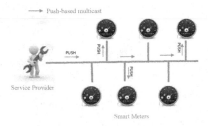

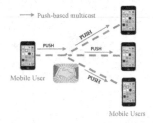

Fig. 1. Commands broadcast in smart metering

Fig. 2. Friend discovery in Social networks

identities are unique and known to the source ahead of time via one or more simultaneous transmissions. In this study, we consider a variation of the traditional multicast, in which the destinations are defined based on a set of attributes, i.e., the destinations must possess certain attributes in order to receive a multicast message. Such multicasts are popular in emerging applications such as smart grids and social networks.

Fig.1 illustrates a push-based multicast in smart metering, in which a service provider sends instructions or commands to a group of smart meters specified by their locations, models, the connected smart devices, and other attributes. For example, a service provider may broadcast a critical software update message to all smart meters at the Inverness Village whose connected devices include the smart fridges with model number 00000 or 11111 manufactured by XYZ company. This multicast message does not need to specify the identities of the smart meters (and smart devices); instead, it carries the following access structure defined by AND and OR relations: *Inverness Village AND smart fridges AND manufactured by XYZ company AND (model 00000 OR model 11111)*. Such an access structure clearly specifies the set of destinations that should receive the multicast message - it may not be practical to include a unique identity for each device in the multicast message. A similar scenario is observed in friend discovery in mobile social networks (see Fig. 2), in which a user who wants to make friends who share similar interests (reading certain types of novels, traveling to the east coast, enjoying sea food, etc.) broadcasts a query message carrying an access structure that specifies the type of friends the user is looking for.

These applications require a secure push-based multicast that can provide *access control* (not every recipient should be able to access the content of the message), *data encryption* (the query or the instruction should be kept confidential), and *authentication* (the data source should be verifiable and the data integrity should be protected) to ensure message integrity and confidentiality. But unfortunatley push-based multicast authentication schemes such as TELSA, Biba, HORS, and OTS [8,10,13–16,20] focus on authentication while ignoring access control and confidentiality. Moreover, the multicast destinations in our problem are defined by an access structure specified by the data source, which renders many popular secure multicast protocols inapplicable.

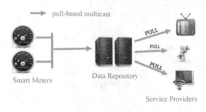
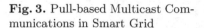
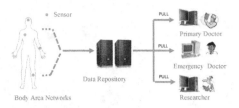

Fig. 3. Pull-based Multicast Communications in Smart Grid

Fig. 4. Pull-based Multicast Communications in BANs

2.2 Pull-Based Multicast Communication

A *pull-based* secure multicast in which the data is stored after being generated and later is pulled by multiple authorized users may be as desirable for some cases in applications such as smart grids and body area networks. For example, multiple service providers may need to retrieve the electricity usage data of a smart meter for different purposes at different times; thus the smart meter should store its data at a data repository for future downloads. This poses significant security and privacy concerns because the access of the data in a data repository is completely out of the control of the smart meter who generated the data but it should be the smart meter's decision whether or not to disclose its electricity usage of certain smart devices to certain service providers – a service provider in California may not need the utility usage data of a microwave in a house at Washington DC. Moreover, not all service providers need the same data. Thus smart meters should have the right to decide who should have the access right to their data. Fig. 3 illustrates such a pull-based multicast scenario in smart metering. Fig. 4 demonstrates a similar example in body area networks (BANs), in which the data collected by the body sensors is stored in a data repository and later accessed by different people for different purposes: the primary doctor has the full access rights to pull the patient's medical information while a nurse is able to read only the meta data.

These applications require the data source to specify the set of users that can access the data: different users should have different access right to different data stored in the repository. Similar to the push-based multicast mentioned in Section 2.1, we resort to an access structure defined by the data source: only the user who possesses certain attributes can access the data stored in the data repository. This implies that the data source should store the access structure defining the access right in the repository as well. Note that pull-based multicast allows the destinations to actively and asynchronously pull the data from the repository while push-based multicast feeds the data to all destinations at one time.

2.3 System Model

We make the following observations from the application scenarios described in Sections 2.1 and 2.2: The multicast destinations are defined by a set of attributes forming an access structure specified by AND and OR relations. The message caring the data does not carry the identity of the destinations but carry an access structure: any user receiving the data is able to access the data only if it possesses the attributes specified in the access structure. Such multicast should provide access control, data encryption, confidentiality, and authentication to protect the data and the data source. These observations motivate us to consider a communication system depicted in Figure 5.

There are four entities in our system model: Key Generation Center (KGC), Data Source, Destinations, and Data Repository. The KGC generates and distributes keys for all entities. A data source produces the data to be broadcasted and defines the access structure of the data; it is assumed to have sufficient computational capacity to signcrypt the data. Destinations are defined by an access structure carried by the data; they are able to designcrypt a message and verify the authenticity of the source and the integrity of the data. A data repository stores signcrypted data generated by a data source.

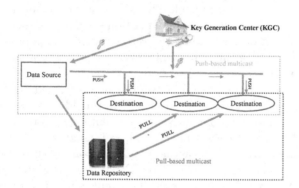

Fig. 5. A generical communication architecture.

This system model involves two types of multicasts: the multicast from a data source to all the destinations defined by an access structure (push-based multicast), and the retrieval of the data from a repository by multiple destinations (pull-based multicast).

2.4   Related Work

The most related works are IBE and ABE, which have received a significant amount of attention in recent years. There exists two different and complementary notions of ABE: Key-Policy ABE (KP-ABE) [5] and Ciphertext-Policy ABE (CP-ABE) [2]. In KP-ABE, encryption is completely determined by the full set of descriptive attributes possessed by the data source while the decryption key is computed by a Key Generation Center (KGC) from an access policy defined by the KGC. In order to decrypt a ciphertext, a user must go to KGC to get a decryption key. In CP-ABE, encryption is completely determined by an access tree defined from the set of attributes possessed by the data source, and the ciphertext carries the access policy; the decryption key is computed by KGC and is associated with a user possessing a certain set of descriptive attributes. In other words, KGC helps a user compute a deception key based on the user's attributes. A user can decrypt a ciphertext if and only if its attributes satisfy the access tree carried by the ciphertext. Therefore in CP_ABE, a data source is able to intelligently decide who should or should not have access to its data. A new construction of CP_ABE, named Constant-sized CP_ABE (denoted as CCP_ABE), was presented in [21], which reduces the ciphertext length to a constant size for an AND gate access policy with any given number of attributes at the cost of long secret keys and complicated access structures.

A scheme that employs IBE to provide a zero-configuration encryption and authentication solution for end-to-end secure communications was proposed in [19]. The concept of IBE was utilized by [11] to construct a signature and later verify the signature. KP_ABE was adopted by [3] to broadcast a single encrypted message to a specific group of users. The Lewko-Waters ABE scheme [9], was used by [17] to ensure access control. The above schemes can not ensure message integrity and confidentiality. A signcryption scheme based on KP_ABE was proposed in [4], which does not meet the requirements of many practical applications as the data source can not intelligently decide who should or should not have access to its data.

In this paper, we present a signcryption scheme termed Ciphertext-Policy Attribute-Based SignCryption (CP_ABSC) to provide the security services required by the multicast communications mentioned above. Compared to CP_ABE, CP_ABSC provides both encryption and signature without significantly increasing the computational cost (actually only the computational cost of designcryption is slightly increased compared to CP_ABE due to signature verification in CP_ABSC). CP_ABSC has strong security strength in terms of collusion resistance, message authentication, forgery prevention, and confidentiality.

3   CP_ABSC: A Ciphertext-Policy Attribute Based Signcryption Scheme

3.1   Preliminary Knowledge for CP_ABSC

Bilinear Mapping and the Bilinear Diffie-Hellman Problem. Let $\mathbb{G}_1$, $\mathbb{G}_2$, and $\mathbb{G}_3$ be three bilinear groups of prime order p, and let g_1 be a generator of $\mathbb{G}_1$ and g_2 be a generator of $\mathbb{G}_2$. Our proposed scheme makes use of a bilinear mapping: $e : \mathbb{G}_1 \times \mathbb{G}_2 \to \mathbb{G}_3$ with the following properties:

1. *Bilinear:* A mapping $e : \mathbb{G}_1 \times \mathbb{G}_2 \to \mathbb{G}_3$ is bilinear if and only if for $\forall P \in \mathbb{G}_1, \forall Q \in \mathbb{G}_2$, and $\forall a, b \in \mathbb{Z}_p$, $e(P^a, Q^b) = e(P, Q)^{ab}$ holds. Here $\mathbb{Z}_p = \{0, 1, \ldots, p-1\}$ is a Galois field of order p.
2. *Non-degeneracy:* The generators g_1 and g_2 satisfy $e(g_1, g_2) \neq 1$.
3. *Computability:* There is an efficient algorithm to compute $e(P, Q)$ for $\forall Q \in \mathbb{G}_2$.

With a bilinear mapping, one can get the following **Bilinear Diffie-Hellman problem (BDH)**: Given three groups $\mathbb{G}_1$, $\mathbb{G}_2$, and $\mathbb{G}_3$ of the same prime order p. Let $e : \mathbb{G}_1 \times \mathbb{G}_2 \rightarrow \mathbb{G}_3$ be a bilinear mapping and g_1, g_2 be respectively the generators of $\mathbb{G}_1$ and $\mathbb{G}_2$. The objective of BDH is to compute $e(g_1, g_2)^{abc}$, where $a, b, c \in \mathbb{Z}_p$, from the given $(g_1, g_1^a, g_1^c, g_2, g_2^a, g_2^b)$.

Note that the hardness of the CBDH - i.e., the Computational Bilinear Diffie-Hellman problem (CBDH) - forms the basis for the security of our scheme.

Secret Sharing. Another important cryptographic primitive used by our CP_ABSC is secret sharing [7,18]. In the context of a *dealer* sharing a secret with n *participants* $u_1, \ldots, u_n$, a participant learns the secret if and only if it can cooperate with at least $t - 1$ other participants (on sharing what they learn from the dealer), where $t \leq n$ is a pre-determined parameter. The secret to be shared by the dealer is $s \in \mathbb{Z}_p$, where $p > n$. Before secret sharing, each participant u_i holds a pairwise secret key $k_i \in \mathbb{Z}_p$, which is only known by u_i and the dealer.

The dealer follows a two-step process. First, it constructs a polynomial function $f(z)$ of degree $t - 1$, i.e., $f(z) = s + \sum_{j=1}^{t-1} a_j z^j$, by randomly choosing $t - 1$ i.i.d. coefficients (the a_j's) from $\mathbb{Z}_p$. Note that all (additive and multiplicative) operations used in (3.1) and throughout the rest of the paper are modular arithmetic (defined over $\mathbb{Z}_p$) as opposed to real arithmetic. Also note that s forms the constant component of $f(z)$ - i.e., $s = f(0)$. Then, in the second step, the dealer transmits to each u_i a secret share $s_i = f(k_i)$ computed from k_i, the secret key known only by u_i and the dealer.

We now show how t or more users can cooperate to recover s by sharing the secret shares received from the dealer. Without loss of generality, let $u_1, \ldots, u_t$ be the cooperating users. These t users can reconstruct the secret $s = f(0)$ from $s_1 = f(k_1), \ldots, s_t = f(k_t)$ by computing

$$s = f(0) = \sum_{j=1}^{t} \left(s_j \prod_{i \in [1,t], i \neq j} \frac{0 - k_i}{k_i - k_j} \right). \tag{1}$$

Note that the cumulative product in (1) is essentially a Lagrange coefficient. The correctness of (1) can be easily verified based on the definition of $f(z)$.

3.2   Access Control Policy – The Access Tree

Our main idea is to design an attribute-based signcryption scheme that views an identity as a set of attributes, and enforces a lower bound on the number of common attributes between a user's identity and its access rights specified by the sensitive data. We use an access tree structure proposed by [2], which is illustrated in Figure 6, to control the user's access to the encrypted data. In Figure 6, each non-leaf node x is associated with two parameters, num_x and k_x, where num_x is the number of child nodes of node x, and $k_x \in [1, num_x]$ is its threshold value indicating that node x performs the OR operation over all

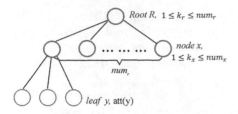

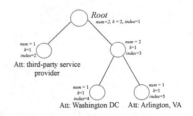

Fig. 6. An access control tree structure

Fig. 7. An example access control structure

subsets of k_x child nodes of x, with each subset supporting an AND operation; each leaf node x is described by an attribute and a threshold value $k_x = 1$. We also associate an index with each node x in T, denoted by $index(x)$. Since a tree with $|S|$ number of attributes can have at most $2|S| - 1$ nodes, we can assign a unique number in $\{1, 2, \cdots, 2|S| - 1\}$ to each node in the tree based on pre-order tree traversal. Other tree traversal techniques such as in-order or post-order can also be applied. Let $parent(x)$ be the parent node of x in T.

Note that any attribute-based access structure can be represented by a tree T shown in Figure 6. For example, the following access structure may be specified for a data item: *Third-Party Service Provider* AND *Arlington, VA* OR *Washington, DC*, which indicates that only the third-party service providers in Arlington, VA or Washington, DC have the access to this data. Thus a user located in Washington DC with a set of attributes {*Third-Party Service Provider, Washington DC, Air-Conditioner*} has an access right to the data mentioned above. The corresponding access control tree for this example is illustrated in Figure 7. The indices of the root node and its two children are respectively 1, 2, and 3 based on pre-order tree traversal.

3.3   CP_ABSC: Ciphertext-Policy Attribute Based Signcryption

In this subsection, we propose our CP_ABSC, a Ciphertext-Policy Attribute-Based SignCryption scheme. CP_ABSC consists of four primary algorithms. Algorithm 1 is executed by KGC to provide system initialization. It generates and distributes to all the involved entities the public parameters of the system.

Algorithm 2 is also executed by *KGC* to generate three keys for an attribute set S: the key SK for ciphertext designcryption, the signing key K_{sign} for signing the ciphertext message, and the verification key K_{ver} for signature verification. For example, a utility company possessing the attribute set S can use its signing key K_{sign} to sign its commands or instructions sent to the smart meters, and use its designcryption key SK to designcrypt the smart meter data stored in ciphertext format (signcrypted data) at the data repositories; its verification key k_{ver} is published for others to verify the signature of its ciphertext.

Algorithm 3 details the signcryption procedure, which is the core of the proposed CP_ABSC. This algorithm is mainly performed by data sources to signcrypt its data before transmitting to the data repositories or to other receivers.

Algorithm 1 System Initialization

1: Select a prime p, the generators g_1 and g_2 for $\mathbb{G}_1$ and $\mathbb{G}_2$, respectively, and a bilinear mapping $e : \mathbb{G}_1 \times \mathbb{G}_2 \to \mathbb{G}_3$.
2: Choose two random exponents $\alpha, \beta \in \mathbb{Z}_p$.
3: Select a hash function $H_1 : \{0,1\}^* \to \mathbb{Z}_p$. This function H_1 is viewed as a random oracle.
4: Publish the public parameters given by

$$PK = (p, \mathbb{G}_1, \mathbb{G}_2, H_1, g_1, g_2, h = g_1^\beta, t = e(g_1, g_2)^\alpha) \qquad (2)$$

5: Compute the master key $MSK = (\beta, g_2^\alpha)$.

Algorithm 2 Key Generation (MSK, S)

Inputs: The master key MSK and a set of attributes S belonging to an entity.

1: Select random numbers $r_{en}, r_{sn} \in \mathbb{Z}_p$
2: Compute the secret key component $D_{en} = g_2^{\frac{(\alpha + r_{en})}{\beta}}$ and signing key $K_{sign} = g_2^{\frac{(\alpha + r_{sn})}{\beta}}$.
3: **for** each attribute $j \in S$ **do**
4:     Select a random number $r_j \in \mathbb{Z}_p$
5:     Compute the secret key components $D_j = g_2^{r_{en}} \cdot g_2^{(H_1(j) \cdot r_j)}$ and $D'_j = g_2^{r_j}$
6: **end for**
7: The secret key SK for designcryption is:

$$SK = (D_{en}, \forall j \in S : D_j, D'_j). \qquad (3)$$

8: Compute the verification key: $K_{ver} = g_2^{r_{sn}}$
9: Send SK and K_{sign} to the owner of the attribute set S, and publish K_{ver} for others to verify the owner of S.

In a typical application, a data source encrypts a message/data whose access control is specified by an access tree T, and signs the message with its signing key. Note that Lines 1 to 7 is executed only once for all the data with the same access structure. Algorithm 3 is designed to provide confidentiality, access control, integrity, authentication, and non-repudiation to ensure the security and privacy of the data sources. Note that encryption is completely determined by the access policy of the data itself.

Algorithm 4 implements verification and decryption. The ciphertext receivers execute it to decrypt the ciphertext according to their attributes. Note that Algorithm 4 calls a function *DecryptNode* described in Algorithm 5, which was originally proposed by [2]. Here we include *DecryptNode* for completeness and to help the readers without the knowledge of CP_ABE to understand CP_ABSC.

Algorithm 3 SignCryption(M, T, K_{sign})

Inputs: The public parameter PK; plaintext message M; the tree T rooted at node R specifying the access control policy of message M; and the signing key K_{sign}.

1: Choose a polynomial q_x and sets its degree $d_x = k_x - 1$ for each node x in the tree T.
2: Choose a random number $s \in \mathbb{Z}_p$ and sets $q_R(0) = s$;
3: Choose d_R random numbers from $\mathbb{Z}_p$ to completely define the polynomial q_R.
4: **for** any other node x in T **do**
5:     Set $q_x(0) = q_{parent(x)}(index(x))$.
6:     Select d_x random numbers from $\mathbb{Z}_p$ to completely define q_x.
7: **end for**
8: Let Y be the set of leaf nodes in T. The ciphertext CT is constructed based on the access tree T as follows:

$$CT = (T, \tilde{C} = M \oplus t^s, C = h^s, \forall y \in Y : C_y = g_1^{q_y(0)}, C'_y = g_1^{(H_1(att(y)) \cdot q_y(0))}) \quad (4)$$

9: Choose a random $\zeta \in \mathbb{Z}_p$; compute $\delta = e(C, g_2)^\zeta$, $\pi = H_1(\delta|M)$, and $\psi = g_2^\zeta \cdot (K_{sign})^\pi$.
10: Output the message:

$$CT_{sign} = (T, \tilde{C}, C, \forall y \in Y : C_y, C'_y; W = g_1^s, \pi, \psi)$$

Algorithm 4 DeSignCryption (CT_{sign}, SK, S)

Inputs: The $CT_{sign} = (CT, W, \pi, \psi)$; the private key SK for designcryption; and the set of possessed attributes S.

1: $A = DecryptNode(CT, SK, R)$
2: **if** $A \neq \perp$ **then**
3:     $\tilde{A} = e(C, D_{en})/A$
4: **end if**
5: Compute

$$\delta' = \frac{e(C, \psi)}{(e(W, K_{ver}) \cdot \tilde{A})^\pi} \quad (5)$$

6: **if** $H_1(\delta'|M') = \pi$ **then**
7:     return $M = M'$
8: **end if**
9: Return $\perp$

3.4 CP_ABSC v.s. CP_ABE

In this section, we compare CP_ABSC and CP_ABE[2] to illustrate their differences. The characteristics of CP_ABSC and CP_ABE are summarized in Table 1.

Algorithm 5 Function $DecryptNode\ (CT, SK, x)$

Inputs: A ciphertext $CT = (T, \tilde{C}, C, \forall y \in Y : C_y, C'_y)$; the secret key SK, which is associated with a set S of attributes, the node x from T.

1: **if** x is a leaf node of T **then**
2:     Let $i = att(x)$
3:     **if** $i \in S$ **then**

$$\text{Return } F_x = \frac{e(C_i, D_i)}{e(C'_i, D'_i)} = e(g_1, g_2)^{r_{en} q_x(0)} \tag{6}$$

4:     **else** Return $\perp$
5:     **end if**
6: **else**
7:     **for** Each child node z of x **do**
8:         $F_z = DecryptNode(CT, SK, z)$
9:     **end for**
10: **end if**
11: Let S_x be an arbitrary k_x-sized set of child nodes of x such that $F_z \neq \perp$ for $\forall z \in S_x$.
12: **if** S_x exists **then**
13:     **for** Each node $z \in S_x$ **do**
14:         $i_z = index(z)$
15:         $S'_z = \{index(z) \ || \ z \in S_x\}$
16:         $\triangle_{i_z, S'_z}(y) = \prod_{j \in S'_z, j \neq i_z} \frac{y-j}{i_z - j}$
17:     **end for**
18:     Return

$$F_x = \prod_{z \in S_x} F_z^{\triangle_{i_z, S'_z}(0)} = \prod_{z \in S_x} (e(g_1, g_2)^{r_{en} \cdot q_z(0)})^{\triangle_{i_z, S'_z}(0)}$$
$$= \prod_{z \in S_x} e(g_1, g_2)^{r_{en} \cdot q_x(i_z) \cdot \triangle_{i_z, S'_z}(0)} = e(g_1, g_2)^{r_{en} \cdot q_x(0)}$$

19: **else**
20:     Return $F_x = \perp$
21: **end if**

System Initialization. This procedure creates the groups, the group generators, and the bilinear mapping. The difference between CP_ABSC and CP_ABE is that the former uses asymmetric groups while the latter uses symmetric groups.

Key Generation. The Key Generation algorithm in our scheme CP_ABSC is different from the key generation in CP_ABE [2] in two aspects: i) since we are designing a signcryption scheme, we need to compute a signing key (which will be sent to the signcryptor) and a verification key (which will be public) while CP_ABE only needs one key for decryption; and ii) due to the fact that CP_ABSC utilizes asymmetric groups, its key generation is more computationally efficient than the one proposed in [2] according to our comparison study in Section 4.3.

Table 1. Comparison between CP_ABE and CP_ABSC

The scheme	System Initialization	Key Generation	Encryption	Decryption
CP_ABE [2]	symmetric groups	private(encrypt) key	encryption	decryption
CP_ABSC	asymmetric groups	private(encrypt+sign) key	signcryption	decryption& verification

Encryption (SignCryption). The SignCryption in CP_ABSC combines signature and encryption, while the one in [2] performs only encryption. The computational cost of our SignCryption algorithm is less than the sum of the two computations (encryption and signature), and is also less than that of the encryption algorithm in [2], according to our analysis in Section 4.3, which is attributed to the adopted asymmetric groups.

Decryption (DeSignCryption). The DeSignCryption in CP_ABSC includes decryption and verification, while the decrypt algorithm in [2] performs only decryption. The computational cost of DeSignCryption is only slightly higher than that of the decyption algorithm in [2], according to our analysis in Section 4.3.

3.5   Application of CP_ABSC in Smart Grids

In this section, we illustrate how to use CP_ABSC to secure the two typical multicast communications in a smart grid. Initially, KGC computes the public parameters PK according to Algorithm 1, and posts PK to all active entities (smart meters and service providers) in the system. Each entity also needs to register with KGC to get the corresponding keys computed from Algorithm 2. For example, a utility company needs a private key SK for designcryption based on its access attributes, a signing key K_{sign} to sign its commands, and a verification key K_{ver} for others to verify its signature.

Push-Based Multicast Communication in Smart Grid. When a service provider wants to send instructions or commands to one or more smart meters, the service provider constructs an access structure T that describes the set of smart meters satisfying the access policy. It then signcrypts an instruction I with a timestamp ts. The timestamp can be the current time or the current time with an expiration time. Generally speaking, the timestamp can help the receivers decide whether or not instruction I is valid and resist replay attacks. The following procedure implements a push-based multicast for a service provider to broadcast I to certain smart meters.

1. The service provider broadcasts the following signcrypted instruction to the smart meters according to Algorithm 3:

$$Service\ provider \rightarrow Smart\ meters : SignCryption(I\|ts, T, K_{sign}).$$

2. When a smart meter receives the signcrypted instruction, it designcrypts and verifies the message according to Algorithm 4. If the verification is passed,

the smart meter executes the instruction and sends a response to the service provider to notify that it has received the instruction (proving that it has the required privilege).
3. When the service provider receives the feedback response, the communication is completed; otherwise, the service provider sends the instruction again.

Pull-Based Multicast Communication in Smart Grid. In order to protect the power usage data, a smart meter signcrypts the data of its household devices using Algorithm 3 based on the access policy specified by the data, and then sends the signcrypted data CT_{sign} to a data repository. When a service provider possessing an attribute set S wants to get the data for a particular household device, it contacts the data repository and gets the signcrypted data CT_{sign}. The following procedure details the process implementing a pull-based multicast.

1. A smart meter signcrypts its reading M with a timestamp ts, $M\|ts$, based on Algorithm 3 and then sends CT_{sign} to the data repository. This step can be performed whenever a new data item is generated.

$$Smart\ meter \rightarrow Data\ repository : CT_{sign}.$$

2. When a service provider holding an attribute set S needs to access the smart meter data, it contacts the data repository to obtain the signcrypted data CT_{sign}:

$$Data\ repository \rightarrow Service\ provider : CT_{sign}.$$

3. Upon receiving the signcrypted data CT_{sign}, the service provider designcrypts CT_{sign} and verifies the message according to Algorithm 4: it first recovers the plaintext M' based on its private key SK and then computes δ'; if $H_1(\delta'|M') = \pi$, which demonstrates the successful designcryption of the data, the service provider accepts M'; otherwise, the message is dropped.

4   Correctness and Performance Analysis

In this section, we prove the correctness of CP_ABSC and analyze its security strength. We also carry out a simulation based performance analysis to quantitatively study the efficiency and computational cost of CP_ABSC.

4.1   The Correctness of CP_ABSC

In this subsection, we show that CP_ABSC is indeed feasible and correct. First, from the decryption procedure we have

$$M' = \tilde{C} \oplus \tilde{A} = \tilde{C} \oplus (\frac{e(C, D)}{A}) = \tilde{C} \oplus (\frac{e(C, D)}{A})$$

$$= \tilde{C} \oplus (\frac{e(h^s, g_2^{(\alpha+r_{en})/\beta})}{e(g_1, g_2)^{r_{en}s}}) = M \oplus e(g_1, g_2)^{\alpha s} \oplus (\frac{e(g_1^{\beta s}, g_2^{\alpha+r_{en}/\beta})}{e(g_1, g_2)^{r_{en}s}})$$

$$= M \oplus e(g_1, g_2)^{\alpha s} \oplus \left(\frac{e(g_1, g_2)^{\beta s \cdot (\alpha + r_{en})/\beta}}{e(g_1, g_2)^{r_{en} s}} \right)$$

$$= M \oplus e(g_1, g_2)^{\alpha s} \oplus \left(\frac{e(g_1, g_2)^{(\alpha s + r_{en} s)}}{e(g_1, g_2)^{r_{en} s}} \right)$$

$$= M \oplus e(g_1, g_2)^{\alpha s} \oplus e(g_1, g_2)^{\alpha s} = M.$$

which indicates that Algorithm 4 can correctly decrypt the ciphertext if the designcryptor satisfies the access policy (posessing the designcryption key SK).

Second, the receiver verifies whether the message M' has been forged or falsified, and whether the received message is indeed sent by the generator of the message. The designcryptor (the receiver) computes δ' by:

$$\delta' = \frac{e(C, \psi)}{(e(W, K_{ver}) \cdot \tilde{A})^\pi} = \frac{e(g_1^{\beta s}, g_2^{\zeta} \times g_2^{\frac{(\alpha + r_{sn})}{\beta} \pi})}{(e(g_1^s, g_2^{r_{sn}}) \cdot e(g_1, g_2)^{\alpha s})^\pi}$$

$$= e(g_1, g_2)^{\beta s(\zeta + \frac{(\alpha + r_{sn})}{\beta} \pi) - s r_{sn} \pi - \alpha s \pi} = e(g_1, g_2)^{\beta s \zeta + s(\alpha + r_{sn})\pi - s r_{sn}\pi - \alpha s \pi}$$

$$= e(g_1, g_2)^{\beta s \zeta} = e(C, g_2)^{\zeta} = \delta.$$

If $H_1(\delta'|M') = \pi$, M' is valid, i.e., $M = M'$, and the message is not modified and is indeed sent by the generator; otherwise, M' is invalid.

4.2   Security Strength

In this subsection, we analyze the security strength of the proposed scheme CP_ABSC by examining how it can counter four major attacks.

Collusion. In CP_ABSC, the set of attributes composes of the user's identity. In order to provide different types of users with different access rights, the scheme provides an access tree structure for each signcrypted data item, and requires only a subset of the attributes for designcryption. Since the secret key computation involves a unique random number for each attribute in the access policy, our scheme can defend against collusion attacks. For example, assume that neither user U_1 nor user U_2 possesses a sufficient number of attributes to successfully designcrypt the ciphertext CT_{sign} alone but the combined attribute set has sufficient number of attributes for the designcryption. Then U_1 and U_2 may collude by combining their attributes. However, they are not able to combine their secret keys (the SKs) to get a secret key for the combined set of attributes according to Algorithm 2 because the KGC generates different random numbers r_{en} for U_1 and U_2. Thus they could not designcrypt the message, and the proposed scheme is secure against collusion attacks.

Message Authentication. Assume that a user U wants to get a message M from the data repository. Before the data is stored in the data repository, the data generator has signcrypted it with Algorithm 3. When U plans to obtain the

Table 2. The details of Functions and Operations between CP_ABE and our scheme

	CP_ABE [2]	CP_ABSC
Key Generation	$n\mathbb{G}_1 + (n+2)\mathbb{G}_2 + nH_{\mathbb{G}_2}$	$(2n+5)\mathbb{G}_2$
Encryption	$(k+1)\mathbb{G}_1 + k\mathbb{G}_2 + 1\mathbb{G}_3 + kH_{\mathbb{G}_2}$	$(2k+2)\mathbb{G}_1 + 2\mathbb{G}_2 + 2\mathbb{G}_3 + 2$ (pairings)
Decryption	$(2k'+1)$ (pairings)	$(2k'+3)$ (pairings)

Notes: $\mathbb{G}_1$ in the table means an exponentiation operation in $\mathbb{G}_1$ group; $\mathbb{G}_2$ and $\mathbb{G}_3$ are defined similarly. $H_{\mathbb{G}_1}$ means hashing an attribute string or a message into an element in $\mathbb{G}_1$; $H_{\mathbb{G}_2}$ is defined similarly.

Table 3. The Computational Cost (Run Time) of Different Operations in Charm Library

Group	$\mathbb{G}_1$	$\mathbb{G}_2$	$\mathbb{G}_3$	(pairings)	$H_{\mathbb{G}_1}$	$H_{\mathbb{G}_2}$
SS512	3.73	3.70	0.48	3.92	8.34	8.39
MNT159	1.12	9.84	2.62	8.42	0.10	34.82

Notes: Time is in ms. The result in this table is the average of 1000 runs.

data from the data repository, it needs its private key $SK = (D = g_2^{\frac{(\alpha + r_{en})}{\beta}}, \forall j \in S : D_j = g_2^{r_{en}} \cdot g_2^{(H_1(j) \cdot r_j)}, D_j' = g_2^{r_j})$, which is computed by Algorithm 2. Meanwhile, U obtains the data source's verification key from KGC. It designcrypts the ciphertext to get the message M' by Algorithm 4: if $H_1(\delta'|M') = \pi$, the decrypted message M is valid; otherwise, it is discarded.

Forgery. An adversary who wishes to forge the signcryption of a legal user must possess the user's signing key. An adversary cannot infer the signing key K_{sign} or the root node of the access tree T because the random number r for each attribute in S (In Algorithm 2) and the s for the root of T (in Algorithm 3) are chosen randomly and secretly. An adversary cannot create a new, valid ciphertext from other user's ciphertexts. If the adversary changes the ciphertext of a message, the receiver can verify that the ciphertext is illegal by Algorithm 4. Moreover, colluding users can not forge a ciphertext, as analyzed before. Thus we claim that our proposed scheme is unforgeable.

Confidentiality. Decryption requires the knowledge of $e(g_1, g_2)^{\alpha s}$. The decryption procedure takes the same idea as that of CP_ABE [2], and thus CP_ABSC has the same security strength as that of the CP_ABE. The designcryption requires the knowledge of $\delta = e(C, g_2)^\varsigma$. For a passive adversary, the available information is CT_{sign}. It is difficult to get s from the W in CT_{sign} since it is difficult to compute the discrete logarithm problem. Even if the adversary constructs the bilinear mapping e via C and the public parameter g_2 to obtain $e(C, g_2)$, it can not get ς, which is randomly chosen by the signcryptor. The adversary may try to get ς from ψ, but it has to get the K_{sign} first. Even if the K_{sign} is compromised, the adversary still can't get ς from ψ due to the difficulty of computing the discrete logarithm problem. Given the discussion above and the

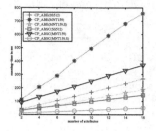 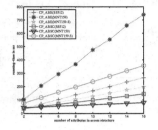 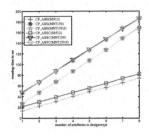

Fig. 8. Key generation time

Fig. 9. Encryption time

Fig. 10. Decryption time

fact that CP_ABE is proven secure under chosen-ciphertext attacks, our scheme is secure under chosen-ciphertext attacks too.

4.3 Efficiency and Cost Analysis

In this subsection, we present a quantitative performance study on CP_ABSC.

Our scheme CP_ABSC does not incur a high computational cost in Key Generation, SignCryption, and DeSignCryption compared to CP_ABE. Table 2 reports the amount of operations performed by CP_ABE and CP_ABSC. The notations are explained as follows: n is the number of attributes a user holds, k is the number of leaf nodes in the access tree T, and k' is the number of attributes a user possesses. $\mathbb{G}_1$ denotes an exponent operation in $\mathbb{G}_1$ group, and the same definitions hold for $\mathbb{G}_2$ and $\mathbb{G}_3$. $H_{\mathbb{G}_1}$ means hashing an attribute or message into an element in $\mathbb{G}_1$, and $H_{\mathbb{G}_2}$ is defined similarly.

Starting with Key Generation, as described in Algorithm 2, there is $2n + 5$ exponent operations in $\mathbb{G}_2$, which includes 5 exponent operations $\{g_2^{r_{en}}, g_2^{\beta}, g_2^{r_{sn}}, D_{en}, K_{sign}\}$, and $2n$ exponent operations $\{D_j, D_j'\}$. In CP_ABE[2], the total operations is $n\mathbb{G}_1 + (n + 2)\mathbb{G}_2 + nH_{\mathbb{G}_2}$.

Moving next to the Signcryption in Algorithm 3, there are $2k + 2$ exponent operations in group $\mathbb{G}_1$ and 2 exponent operations in group $\mathbb{G}_2$. Additionally, there are 2 map operations and 2 pairing. The combined overhead is thus $(2k + 2)\mathbb{G}_1 + 2\mathbb{G}_2 + 2\mathbb{G}_3 + 2$ (pairings). Similarly, in CP_ABE, the total operation is $(k + 1)\mathbb{G}_1 + k\mathbb{G}_2 + 1\mathbb{G}_3 + kH_{\mathbb{G}_2}$.

For Designcryption (in Algorithm 4), there are $(2k'+3)$ (pairings) operations. In CP_ABE, there are $(2k' + 1)$ (pairings) operations.

We run the experiment with Ubuntu 12.04 running as a VM on a MAC-Book Air with one 1.8GHz core and 1GB memory. The implementation uses a Python library called Charm-crypto [1], which is a framework used to prototype advanced cryptosystems such as IBE and IBS (Identity-Based Signature). The core mathematical functions behind Charm are from the Stanford Pairing-Based Cryptography (PBC) library [12], which is an open source C library that performs mathematical operations underlying pairing-based cryptosystems.

We execute the implementation under both symmetric (SS512) and asymmetric groups (MNT159 and MNT159.S), both with 80 bits of security, to compare CP_ABE and CP_ABSC. In SS512, the map is $\mathbb{G}_1 \times \mathbb{G}_2 \to \mathbb{G}_3$, where $\mathbb{G}_1$ and $\mathbb{G}_2$ are the same group. In MNT159, the map is $\mathbb{G}_1 \times \mathbb{G}_2 \to \mathbb{G}_3$, where $\mathbb{G}_1$ and $\mathbb{G}_2$ are different groups, and $\mathbb{G}_2$ and $\mathbb{G}_3$ are extension groups of $\mathbb{G}_1$. The elements in $\mathbb{G}_2$ and $\mathbb{G}_3$ are longer than those in $\mathbb{G}_1$. The longer the element, the larger the computational cost in exponential operations. In MNT159.S, we swapped the $\mathbb{G}_1$ and $\mathbb{G}_2$ group so that most of the key generation operations are in $\mathbb{G}_1$ instead of $\mathbb{G}_2$.

Table 3 lists the run time of each operation and function in SS512 and MNT159. One can see that some operations are more efficient in SS512 than in MNT159 while others are the opposite. For example, the operations $H_{\mathbb{G}_1}$ and $\mathbb{G}_1$ have less run time in MNT159 than in SS512 but the operations of $\mathbb{G}_2$ and $H_{\mathbb{G}_2}$ have less runtime in SS512 than in MNT159.

The performance analysis compares the efficiency and computational cost between CP_ABSC and CP_ABE for Key Generation, Signcryption/Encryption, and Designcryption/Decryption. The results are reported in Figures 8-10. Figure 8 shows the run times of Key Generation. MNT159.S has the best performance since we swapped $\mathbb{G}_1$ and $\mathbb{G}_2$ and most of the operations are in $\mathbb{G}_1$ after the swap. Figure 9 reports the encryption run times. The run time in CP_ABE and that in our scheme CP_ABSC is almost linear with respect to the number of leaf nodes in the access policy. The polynomial operation at leaf nodes does not significantly contribute to the run time. Comparing the run time between CP_ABE encryption and CP_ABSC signcryption, one can see that our scheme costs less time than CP_ABE because we don't need to compute $H_{\mathbb{G}_2}$. Figure 10 illustrates the run times of decryption. Our scheme is slightly higher than that of CP_ABE due to the fact that we add the signature verification process. However, because the computational cost of ABE is more expensive as the number of attributes increases, the cost of signature verification is relatively trivial in practice.

Considering all three processes of KeyGeneration, SignCryption, and DeSignCryption, MNT159.S has considerably better performance than MNT159. We recommend executing the schemes in asymmetric groups and swapping $\mathbb{G}_1$ and $\mathbb{G}_2$ to gain a better performance.

Due to space limitation, we omit the part of comparison between the proposed scheme and Attribute based signature, which will be included in the extended version.

In summary, the run time is predictable for key generation and encryption in our scheme and is correlated with the number of attributes. Comparing the run times of key generation, encryption, and decryption between CP_ABE and our scheme CP_ABSC, the run times of our scheme is a little higher than CP_ABE for some cases. However, considering that our scheme combines encryption and signature, CP_ABSC is feasible and more desirable than the encryption-only CP_ABE.

5 Conclusion and Future Work

In this paper, we present a signcryption scheme called CP_ABSC that can provide access control, data confidentiality, and authentication based on an access structure specified by the to-be-protected data itself. We analyze the computational cost and security strength of CP_ABSC, and illustrate how to apply CP_ABSC to protect the multicast communications in smart grids. Particularly, we employ CP_ABSC to secure two types of multicasts: the push-based multicast of instructions/commands from service providers to smart meters and the pull-based data retrieval from data repositories to service providers.

Our future research lies in the following directions: design more efficient signcryption approaches with less computational and storage requirements; and develop a dynamic scheme that could dynamically add attributes to adapt to the changing requirements of applications.

Acknowledgement. This research is supported by National Natural Science Foundation of China under grant 61373027, and the US National Science Foundation under grants CCF-1442642, IIS-1343976, CNS-1318872, and CNS-1550313.

References

1. Akinyele, J.A., Garman, C., Miers, I., Pagano, M.W., Rushanan, M., Green, M., Rubin, A.D.: Charm: A framework for rapidly prototyping cryptosystems. Journal of Cryptographic Engineering **3**(2), 111–128 (2013)
2. Bethencourt, J., Sahai, A., Waters, B.: Ciphertext-policy attribute-based encryption. In: IEEE Symposium on Security and Privacy, SP 2007, pp. 321–334. IEEE (2007)
3. Fadlullah, Z.M., Kato, N., Lu, R., Shen, X., Nozaki, Y.: Toward secure targeted broadcast in smart grid. IEEE Communications Magazine **50**(5), 150–156 (2012)
4. Gagné, M., Narayan, S., Safavi-Naini, R.: Threshold attribute-based signcryption. In: Garay, J.A., De Prisco, R. (eds.) SCN 2010. LNCS, vol. 6280, pp. 154–171. Springer, Heidelberg (2010)
5. Goyal, V., Pandey, O., Sahai, A., Waters, B.: Attribute-based encryption for fine-grained access control of encrypted data. In: Proceedings of the 13th ACM Conference on Computer and Communications Security, pp. 89–98. ACM (2006)
6. Hart, G.: Nonintrusive appliance load monitoring. Proc. IEEE **80**(12), 1870–1891 (1992)
7. Chunqiang, H., Liao, X., Cheng, X.: Verifiable multi-secret sharing based on lrsr sequences. Theoret. Comput. Sci. **445**, 52–62 (2012)
8. Kgwadi, M., Kunz, T.: Securing rds broadcast messages for smart grid applications. International Journal of Autonomous and Adaptive Communications Systems **4**(4), 412–426 (2011)
9. Lewko, A., Waters, B.: Decentralizing attribute-based encryption. In: Paterson, K.G. (ed.) EUROCRYPT 2011. LNCS, vol. 6632, pp. 568–588. Springer, Heidelberg (2011)
10. Li, Q., Cao, G.: Multicast authentication in the smart grid with one-time signature. IEEE Transactions on Smart Grid **2**(4), 686–696 (2011)

11. Lu, R., Liang, X., Li, X., Lin, X., Shen, X., et al.: Eppa: An efficient and privacy-preserving aggregation scheme for secure smart grid communications. IEEE Trans. on Parallel and Distributed Systems (2012)
12. Lynn, B.: On the implementation of pairing-based cryptosystems. PhD thesis, Stanford University (2007)
13. Neumann, W.D.: Horse: an extension of an r-time signature scheme with fast signing and verification. In: International Conference on Information Technology: Coding and Computing, Proceedings. ITCC 2004, vol. 1, pp. 129–134. IEEE (2004)
14. Perrig, A.: The biba one-time signature and broadcast authentication protocol. In: Proceedings of the 8th ACM conference on Computer and Communications Security, pp. 28–37. ACM (2001)
15. Perrig, A., Canetti, R., Tygar, J.D., Song, D.: The tesla broadcast authentication protocol. CryptoBytes **5**(2), 2–13 (2002)
16. Reyzin, L., Reyzin, N.: Better than BiBa: short one-time signatures with fast signing and verifying. In: Batten, L.M., Seberry, J. (eds.) ACISP 2002. LNCS, vol. 2384, pp. 144–153. Springer, Heidelberg (2002)
17. Ruj, S., Nayak, A., Stojmenovic, I.: A security architecture for data aggregation, access control in smart grids. Arxiv preprint arXiv: 1111.2619 (2011)
18. Shamir, A.: How to share a secret. Commun. ACM **22**(11), 612–613 (1979)
19. So, H.K.H., Kwok, S.H.M., Lam, E.Y., Lui, K.S.: Zero-configuration identity-based signcryption scheme for smart grid. In: IEEE International Conference on Smart Grid Communications, pp. 321–326. IEEE (2010)
20. Wang, Q., Khurana, H., Huang, Y., Nahrstedt, K.: Time valid one-time signature for time-critical multicast data authentication. In: IEEE INFOCOM 2009, pp. 1233–1241. IEEE (2009)
21. Zhou, Z., Huang, D.: On efficient ciphertext-policy attribute based encryption and broadcast encryption. In: Proceedings of the 17th ACM Conference on Computer and Communications Security, pp. 753–755. ACM (2010)

Generation of Transmission Control Rules Compliant with Existing Access Control Policies

Yoann Bertrand$^{(\boxtimes)}$, Mireille Blay-Fornarino, Karima Boudaoud, and Michel Riveill

University of Nice Sophia Antipolis, CNRS, I3S, UMR 7271, 06900 Sophia Antipolis, France {bertrand,blay,boudaoud,riveill}@i3s.unice.fr

Abstract. Access Control (AC) is a well known mechanism that allows access restriction to resources. Nevertheless, it does not provide notification when a resource is retransmitted to an unauthorized third party. To overcome this issue, one can use mechanisms such as Data Loss/Leak Prevention (DLP) or Transmission Control (TC). These mechanisms are based on policies that are defined by security experts. Unfortunately, these policies can contradict existing AC rules, leading to security leakage (i.e. a legitimate user is allowed to send a resource to someone who has no access rights in the AC).

In this article, we aim at creating TC policies that are compliant with existing AC policies. To do so, we use a mapping mechanism that generates TC rules directly from existing AC policies. Thanks to the generated rules, our solution can make inferences to improve existing AC and enhance security knowledge between infrastructures.

Keywords: Security · Access Control · Security policies · Transmission Control · Transmission security · Data Loss Prevention · Data Leak Prevention · Data leakage

1 Introduction

To add security to an infrastructure, one can start by controlling access to certain resources by using Access Control (AC) mechanisms. Unfortunately, traditional AC mechanisms are not useful to notify and manage what can happen to the resource once it is accessed. Indeed, a legitimate user can access then retransmit (legitimately or not) the resource to an unauthorized third party. If the third party does not have access to the resource in the AC, this retransmission can be seen as a violation of AC, and thus, as a data leakage. To tackle this problem, one can use Data Loss/Leak Prevention (DLP) or other Transmission Control mechanisms (TC). Such mechanisms are based on policies that aim at monitoring and notifying unauthorized resource transmission. DLP / TC are often used on top of AC, leading security experts to manage both paradigms. This double management can lead to data leakage.

© Institute for Computer Sciences, Social Informatics and Telecommunications Engineering 2015
B. Thuraisingham et al. (Eds.): SecureComm 2015, LNICST 164, pp. 438–455, 2015.
DOI: 10.1007/978-3-319-28865-9_24

Let us take an example. Imagine an AC policy containing a rule mentioning that *"user Chris can access the resource docA.pdf"* and a TC rule saying that *"Chris can send all pdf files"*. If Chris accesses docA.pdf and wants to send it to Ana (who does not have access to docA.pdf in the AC), several remarks can be made. First of all, the fact that Chris can access docA.pdf does not violate the AC policy. Secondly, the fact that Chris sends docA.pdf to Ana does not violate the TC policy. Nevertheless, the transmission will cause a violation of the AC policy because Ana does not have access to docA.pdf.

This simple, but yet explicit example, shows that even if both AC and TC policies are correct, TC rules can violate existing AC policies and consequently lead to data leakage.

Our objective is to work with Transmission Control (TC) policies that do not contradict the existing Access Control (AC) policies.

To do so, we propose a mechanism that generates TC policies based on existing AC policies. Thanks to the generated TC policies, our solution offers mechanisms that :

- help improving existing AC policies (M1);
- help integration and enhancement of security knowledge between infrastructures or companies (M2).

The rest of the paper is organized as follows. Section 2 presents the main works related to access and transmission control. Section 3 describes the vocabulary we are using. Section 4 details our solution. Section 5 presents the results of our evaluation while section 6 concludes the paper and outlines future works.

2   Related Works

This section presents the main Access Control models and Data Loss/Leak Prevention (DLP) notions. The last part of the section presents existing solutions that aim at linking both AC and TC paradigms in common models or frameworks.

2.1   Access Control Models (AC)

Access Control (AC) encompasses sets of controls to restrict access to certain resources. Several contributions have been made to create efficient and fine-grained AC mechanisms. The following subsections present the main AC models.

Mandatory Access Control (MAC). MAC is a type of access control that secures resources by assigning sensitivity labels on resources and comparing these labels to the accreditation level a user is operating at. These levels are defined and controlled by the system, independently of user operations and choices. MAC is often used in confidential and military infrastructures. Famous models, such as Bell-LaPadula [1] or Biba [2] are based on MAC principles.

Discretionary Access Control (DAC). DAC allows users to determine and set the permissions over all the resources they own. The main DAC models are Access Control Lists (ACL) and Capability-based access control. Access Control Lists [3] represent resource rights as a table of subjects mapped to their individual rights over the resource. ACLs are data-oriented and provide a straightforward and rather simple way of granting or denying access.

Capability-based [4] access is more subject-oriented. A capability is an unforgeable token used to access a resource. It can be represented as a pair (x, r) where x is the name of a resource and r is a set of access rights. Thus, subject's capabilities are stored with the subject. Systems such as Plessey System 250 [5] are based on capabilities.

Role Based Access Control (RBAC). The paradigm behind RBAC [6] is based on the notion of role. A role is a set of users that share common attributes (for instance, a role "Network-Staff" containing all the network engineers of a company). In this model, users are members of one or several groups and this membership gives them access to certain resources.

Attributes Based Access Control (ABAC). NIST defines ABAC as *"An access control method where subjects requests to perform operations on objects are granted or denied based on assigned attributes of the subject, assigned attributes of the object, environment conditions, and a set of policies that are specified in terms of those attributes and conditions"* [7]. Attributes can represent various things about a subject (age, sex, etc.) or an object (resource security level, type, etc.). Thus, ABAC can be seen as an extension of RBAC.

Policy Based Access Control (PBAC). Policy Based Access Control [8] allows access rules to be defined and updated in a policy-oriented fashion. Policies are sets of rules that can be combined to determine if an access is authorized or not, depending on various attributes regarding the subject, object or environment. For these reasons, PBAC can be viewed as a standardization of ABAC for companies or other governance oriented structures.

Traditional AC models offer an easy way to restrict access to resources. Nevertheless, they do not tackle retransmission problems. To overcome this issue, solutions have been proposed. These solutions include Data Loss/Leak Prevention.

2.2 Data Loss/Leak Prevention (DLP)

This subsection presents the main notions of Data Loss/Leak Prevention[1].

---

[1] DLPs have been described in various terms, including Information Leak Detection and Prevention (ILDP), Information Leak Prevention (ILP) or Content Monitoring and Filtering (CMF). Nevertheless, DLP is the most commonly used name.

Definition and Classification. DLPs have been described as *"systems that monitors and enforce policies on fingerprinted data that are at rest (i.e. in storage), in-motion (i.e. across a network) or in-use (i.e. during an operation) on public or private computer/network."* [9].

Policy Definition. DLPs are based on policies. These policies can help security experts defining fine-grained rules that help the DLP to detect and prevent leakage (for instance: *"deny the transmission if data x is sent to user U1"*). Industrial DLPs, such as the one provided by Symantec[2] or RSA[3], offer graphical user interfaces to generate these rules.

DLP can provide efficient TC mechanisms thanks to policies. As stated in the introduction, such policies can be in contradiction with an existing AC, leading to AC policy violations. To overcome this issue, one solution can be to combine both Access Control and Transmission Control in an unified paradigm and define both aspects at the same time. Such solutions are presented in the next subsections.

2.3   Unifying AC and TC

Several works have been proposed to unify AC and TC in common formalisms or frameworks. By doing so, a security expert can define at the same time both AC and TC policies, reducing the risk of contradiction. This subsection presents the main works in the domain.

Usage Control (UCON). UCON [10] has proposed to add the notion of ongoing usage to AC. Based on the notions of Authorizations, Obligations and Conditions, UCON offers a unified framework that covers traditional AC models and enhance them to tackle prerequisites within network-connected environment. UCON has been followed by many works, tackling policy definition [11], decentralized systems [12] or existing company mechanisms enforcement [13].

Organization Based Access Control (OrBAC). OrBAC defines a conceptual and industrial framework to meet the needs of information security. It covers a lot of issues such as conflict detection [14] or interoperability and deployment in companies Workflows [15]. In [16], OrBAC has been enhance to tackle information flow control problematic.

eXtensible Access Control Markup Language - Data Loss Prevention (XACML-DLP). XACML is a XML standard that defines a declarative AC. In October 2014, a new version of XACML has been implemented. This version,

---

[2] https://www.symantec.com/data-leak-prevention/
[3] http://www.emc.com/security/rsa-data-loss-prevention.htm?fromGlobalSelector

named XACML-DLP[4], embeds both Access Control and Transmission Control in a same formalism.

Linking AC and TC in a common formalism allows security experts to define at the same time both paradigms, reducing the risk of contradiction between them. Nevertheless, these solutions do not use the existing AC. Moreover, they cannot help enhancing the existing AC policies (M1) and ease the integration between companies thanks to inferences (M2). Following sections present a solution providing such mechanisms.

3   Context and Vocabulary

This section gives information about the concepts and vocabulary we are using. It first describes the scope of our study. Then, it presents a generic AC formalism and sets some working hypothesis regarding the existing AC policies.

3.1   Scope of the Study

In this paper, we have considered only 3 actions: Read, Read-Write, and no access. Also, we have decided to represent subjects as individuals instead of roles or groups. In term, we intend to broaden our solution to encompass more sophisticated actions and subjects representation.

Concerning the validation of the generated TC policies, a checking mechanism has been implemented to verify that generated TC rules are coherent with the existing AC policies. In this article, we focus on the generation process itself, for that reason, details about this validation mechanism are intentionally omitted.

3.2   Generic Access Control Model

To take into account the main AC models of the literature, we have been inspired by [17] and more specifically [18] and [19] to represent a generic AC as a set of rules (1). A rule is always composed of three fundamental things; Subject, Action and Resource (2).

$$GenericAC =< \sigma_1, \sigma_2, ..., \sigma_n >, \forall \sigma \in Rules \qquad (1)$$

$$\sigma =< s, a, r >, s \in Subject, a \in Action, r \in Resource \qquad (2)$$

Subjects, Actions and Resources are subsets of Entity (3). An entity can be formalized has a unique identifier (for instance a name) and a set of parameters (i.e. attributes) (4). A parameter can represent for instance a role (ex: role="manager") or an accreditation level (ex: "accreditationLevel = "3"). The main properties of the identifier is that it cannot be empty (5) and it must be unique (6).

---

[4] http://docs.oasis-open.org/xacml/xacml-3.0-dlp-nac/v1.0/csprd01/xacml-3.0-dlp-nac-v1.0-csprd01.html

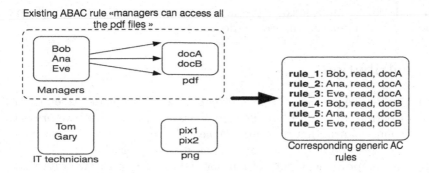

Fig. 1. Correspondences between the ABAC rule "Managers can read all pdf files" and the generic AC rules.

$$\{Subject, Action, Resource\} \subset Entity \tag{3}$$

$$entity = \{identifier, < p_1, p_2, ..., p_n >\} \tag{4}$$

$$\forall e \in Entity, e(identifier) \neq \emptyset \tag{5}$$

$$\forall e_i, e_j \in Entity, e_i(identifier) \neq e_j(identifier) \tag{6}$$

A parameter is a pair of key/value (7). Both key and value cannot be empty (8). For a particular entity (ex: subject "Bob"), two parameters cannot have the same key (9).

$$parameter =< key, value > \tag{7}$$

$$\forall p \in Parameter, p(key) \neq p(value) \neq \emptyset \tag{8}$$

$$\forall (p_i, p_j) \in P^2, p_i(key) \neq p_j(key) \tag{9}$$

Thanks to this formalism, we consider that traditional AC models can be represented. For instance, in the case of ABAC, a rule such as *"every Manager can access all the pdf files in read mode"* is equivalent to an enumeration of the rules (i.e. Cartesian product) among set "Manager" and set "pdf" (see Fig. 1.). We underline that such transformation can generate a huge amount of rules. Nevertheless, conducting tests in Section 5 show that our model is efficient for quite large sets of rules.

We make some hypothesis concerning the original AC. First of all, we consider that the original AC does not contain contradictory rules (for instance, a subject has both access and no access to a particular resource). Secondly, we consider that the correspondence between the original AC and the generic AC rules is not destructive, meaning that the semantic is conserved (no information is added, modified or removed). Finally, we consider that the corresponding generic AC can contain duplicate rules.

In this section, we have presented the generic model used by our solution. This generic model has been defined in order to take into account several AC models such as traditional ACL, RBAC or ABAC. Working hypothesis have been made concerning the correspondence with generic AC rules. The following section describes our contribution in detail.

4   Contribution

In this section, we present our model. The first subsections describe our Transmission Control paradigm (4.1) and representation (4.2). Then, we present the generation mechanism that transforms Access Control policies into Transmission Control policies (4.3). The last subsections present a mechanism that notifies possible AC improvement (4.4) and propose an example to illustrate that our solution can ease integration and improve security knowledge between infrastructures (4.5).

4.1   Transmission Control List

Transmission Control model aims at answering the question: *"who can send what to whom?"*. To do so, we have defined a Transmission Control List (TCL), formalized as a set of transmissions regarding a specific resource (10). Thus, a specific TCL cannot describe transmission rights of more than one resource (11). A transmission embeds the following elements: a source subject (i.e. the sender), a destination subject (i.e. the receiver), the actions of the sender and the receiver and a transmission type (12). A transmission type represents if a transmission is authorized (TRANSMISSION_AUTH) or if the transmission is denied (TRANSMISSION_DEN).

$$\forall tcl \in TCL, tcl = \{resource, < \tau_1, ..., \tau_n >\} \tag{10}$$

$$\forall tcl_1, tcl_2 \in TCL, tcl_1(resource) \neq tcl_2(resource) \tag{11}$$

$$\tau = < sender, receiver, senderAction, receiverAction, type >,$$
$$sender, receiver \in Subject, \tag{12}$$
$$senderAction, receiverAction \in Action, type \in TransmissionType$$

4.2   Representation

For the sake of understanding, we represent ACL and TCL as matrices. ACL can be represented as a two-dimensional matrix, where columns represent resources, rows represent subjects, and intersections represent the action that the corresponding subject can perform on the corresponding resource (Fig. 2.a).

For a specific resource, the corresponding TCL can be represented as a two-dimensional matrix, where rows represent senders, columns represent receivers, and intersections represent the transmission type (ex: TRANSMISSION_AUTH) between the sender and the receiver (Fig. 2.b). We underline that actions of senders and receivers are also conserved in the TCL, due to the TCL formalism defined in 4.1. We also underline that the only subjects that are present in the

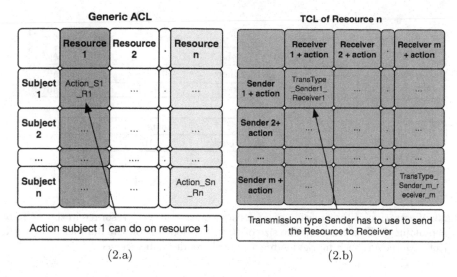

Fig. 2. Graphical representation of a generic ACL (2.a) and a corresponding TCL (2.b)

corresponding TCL are the subjects with an explicit access right to this resource (we call such subjects **"marked subjects"**). Thus, the size of the TCL depends on the number of marked subjects. Indeed, a resource with many access rights in the ACL will generate a bigger TCL than a resource that can be accessed by fewer subjects.

4.3   Generation Mechanisms

After having described both ACL and TCL, we now discuss the generation mechanisms that aim at transforming existing ACL into TCLs. This subsection presents the main parts of the generation mechanism.

Creation of the TCL Structure. To create the general structure of the TCLs, the mechanism starts by retrieving all resources of the ACL. For each resource, the mechanism retrieves every marked subjects. Then, the mechanism creates the general structure of the matrices (one matrix per resource) by adding for each row and column the marked subjects as senders and receivers.

Mapping Rules Concept. Once the TCLs have been generated, they must be filled. A naive approach could be to fill every intersection with TRANSMIS-SION_AUTH, because every subject in a specific TCL is a marked subject and thus, has access to the resource in the original AC (see Fig. 3). Nevertheless, allowing every single transmission between marked subjects can be too permissive. In order to restrict transmissions in certain cases, we have defined Mapping

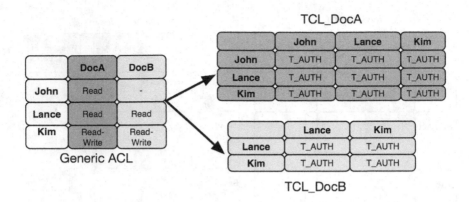

Fig. 3. Illustration of the creation of TCLs structure. For every resource in the ACL, a corresponding TCL is created. The size of the TCL depends on the number of marked subjects. Moreover, each marked subject is both sender and receiver.

Rules (MR). A MR can be represented as a function that takes parameters of a sender, actions, receiver and resource and returns a transmission type (13).

$$f(sender, senderAction, receiver, receiverAction, resource) \rightarrow type$$
$$type \in TransmissionType$$
(13)

For each element of the matrix (i.e. each row/column intersection), the mechanism retrieves all the parameters concerning the sender, the receiver, the action of the sender, the action of the receiver and the resource, then output a transmission type.

To define how the transmission type is chosen depending on the entry parameters, we have defined a syntax. Details about this syntax are given below.

Mapping Rules Syntax. We have defined a syntax called Mapping Rules Syntax (MRS). MRS is based of three different things: targets, operators and inputs. A target can be formalized as an entity and an element (14). An entity can be a sender, a receiver, an action of the sender, an action of the receiver or a resource (15). An element can be an entity identifier (ex: "John"), a parameter key (ex: "role"), or a parameter value (ex: "manager")(16).

$$target = (entity, element) \quad (14)$$
$$entity = \{sender, receiver, senderAction, receiverAction, resource\} \quad (15)$$
$$element = \{identifier, parameter(key), parameter(value)\} \quad (16)$$

MRS uses two types of operators: arithmetic operators and logical operators (17):

$$arithmeticOperator : \{=, \neq, <, >, \geq, \leq\}$$
$$logicalOperator : \{\vee, \wedge\}$$
(17)

Finally, the last component of MRS is the input, which is just a String (i.e. any word in the alphabet $\mathcal{A}$) (18).

$$input \in \mathcal{A}^* \qquad (18)$$

Generic Rules. Thanks to previous definitions, generic rules can be defined and applied. A generic rule is defined by a target, an arithmetic operator, another target and a transmission type (19):

$$genericRule = targetA, arithmeticOperator, targetB \rightarrow type$$
$$targetA, targetB \in Target \qquad (19)$$
$$type \in TransmissionType$$

Generic rules can provide predefined and generic patterns to security experts. For instance, a generic rule such as *"you cannot send any resource to someone with an accreditation level lower than yours"* can be defined. Considering that subjects have a parameter "level" describing such accreditations, the previous generic rule will be:

rule1: (sender, level) > (receiver, level) → TRANSMISSION_DEN

With this formalism, we aim at providing general patterns that can be automatically applied to every row/column intersection. Such mechanism can then easily transform ACLs into TCLs.

Nevertheless, a security expert might want to define particular rules, adapted to her/his business or infrastructure. To do so, we have defined specific rules.

Specific Rules. Our model defines a specific rule as a target, an arithmetic operator and an input (20):

$$specificRule = target, arithmeticOperator, input \rightarrow type \qquad (20)$$

Specific rules are used to define specific conditions on parameter values. A specific rule such as *"if the receiver does not have read and write permission, the transmission is denied"* will be defined by:

rule2:
(receiverAction,identifier) ≠ "Read-write" → TRANSMISSION_DEN

To express even more complex rules, conditions and rules can be combined with logical operators. For instance, a set of conditions can be used to define the rule *"if John sends docA.pdf to a manager, the transmission is authorized"*. This rule will be formalized as follows:

> rule3:
> (sender, identifier) = "John" $\wedge$ (resource, identifier) = "docA.pdf" $\wedge$
> (receiver, identifier) = "manager" $\rightarrow$ TRANSMISSION_AUTH

Thanks to generic and specific rules, conditions on entities and parameters can be defined and applied. Generic rules provide a toolkit that can automatically be applied while specific rules formalism can be used by a security expert to express specific conditions, depending on her/his infrastructure and security concerns.

Confidential Transmission. Because TRANSMISSION_AUTH does not modify the medium, we empathize that sending a resource in cleartext is not secured and can be viewed as sending a resource to everyone. Thus, we have added another type of transmission, called TRANSMISSION_CONF, which allows a security expert to express confidentiality. This transmission type can be used with generic or specific rules. For instance, the rule *"resource 'docX.pdf' needs to be sent with confidentiality"* will be expressed as follows:

> rule4: (resource, identifier) = "docX.pdf" $\rightarrow$ TRANSMISSION_CONF

Conflict Detection. Our model is able to express generic and specific rules. Nevertheless, definition and combinaison of these rules can lead to conflicts. Indeed, imagine for instance that a security expert defines and combines two different rules **r1** and **r2**, where **r1** defines *"When managers are sending a resource, the transmission must have confidentiality property"* and **r2** defines *"John cannot send docA.pdf"* (even if he has access to it in the ACL). Imagine now that John is a manager. The mapping mechanism will have issues deciding which transmission type to apply for every element in the row "John" for the TCL of docA.pdf.

Indeed, for this resource, the system will not be able to determine if the resource can be sent (**r1**) or not (**r2**). To overcome this issue, we have defined several mechanisms.

The first one is to notify the security expert of the inconsistency and ask her/him for an answer. She/he can chose the transmission type of her/his choice, or implement an ad hoc rule.

To avoid multiple notifications, another mechanism that we have defined is the decision strategies (DS). To use decision strategies, a security expert first needs to set levels for transmission type. For our example, we have considered that a denied transmission is more secure than the other types of transmission. Thus, we have chosen the following order:

Level_1: TRANSMISSION_AUTH < Level_2 : TRANSMISSION_CONF <
Level_3: TRANSMISSION_DEN

Once the levels have been defined, the security expert can use one of the following decision strategies:

- HIGHEST: apply the transmission type with the highest level
- LOWEST: apply the transmission type with the lowest level
- MOST PRESENT: apply the transmission type which is the most present in the sequence of rules
- DEFAULT: apply the default transmission type

In our example, the following rule will be applied automatically, depending on the strategy:

Strategy	Applied rule
HIGHEST	r2
LOWEST	r1
MOST PRESENT	cannot answer, DEFAULT is applied
DEFAULT	TRANSMISSION_DEN

To transform AC policies into TC policies, we have defined a specific syntax, called Mapping Rules Syntax (MRS). MRS can express generic and specific rules. Generic rules provide a toolkit that applies generic security policies while Specific rules can be use to define ad hoc rules. Thanks to this syntax, an ACL (which can be represented as a two-dimensional matrix) can be transformed into many TCLs matrices. Each TCL represents all the transmissions marked subjects can/cannot do for a specific resource.

4.4   Inference Mechanisms to Enhance Existing AC Policies (M1)

One of our objective is to provide a solution that is capable of improving an existing AC model. To do so, we use inference mechanisms. This subsection presents the main inferences that our solution is able to make.

Similarities Between Subjects. In the same TCL, if two couples of row/column are identical, it means that for a particular resource, two subjects have the same transmission behavior (i.e. they can send and receive the resource in the same way). If this reasoning is generalized for all TCLs, it means that these two subjects have exactly the same transmission rights for all the resources they have been marked for. Such inference mechanism is able to notify security experts that two or more subjects are similar in terms of transmission rights.

The model is also able to determine if these similar subjects have common parameters (such as "role" or "group"). If the existing ACL is based on RBAC or ABAC, the exact original classification is detected. However, if the original AC was a model without roles or attributes, notifications can help a security expert to have a better understanding of her/his ACL. With this knowledge, the security expert can decide to migrate her/his original ACL to a RBAC or ABAC model, using the notification to create roles or categories. Fig. 4. gives an example of the similarities between subjects.

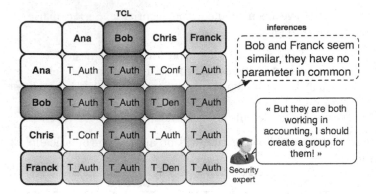

Fig. 4. Representation of the subject similarities mechanism for a single resource. In this case, security expert will be notified that Bob and Franck have the same behavior.

Similarities Between Resources. The same inferences can be applied to resources. In this case, if two TCLs are strictly equivalent, it means that for two different resources, the same subjects have strictly the same transmission behavior. The same assumption can be made for more than two resources. Thus, the same reasoning as subject similarities can be applied, meaning that the model is able to determine if similar resources (in term of transmission behavior) have properties in common (for instance, type="pdf"). Once again, these notifications can help security experts to have a better understanding of the original AC.

4.5   Inference Mechanisms to Help Integration and Enhance Security Knowledge (M2)

Inference mechanisms can also be used to detect security indulgences between two infrastructures regarding the same resources. Indeed, imagine that a company A wants to buy another company B. Both companies can be very different in terms of hierarchy, policies and sensibilities toward security. After the buyout, security experts from company A might have some issues equalizing the two environments. Our solution can be interesting in such case.

Indeed, imagine that documentX.pdf is both used by company A and B. By applying our model in both companies, two different TCLs, TCL_A and TCL_B, will be generated. TCL_A (resp. TCL_B) will represent the transmission behavior of documentX.pdf inside company A (resp. company B). Inferences mechanisms presented previously cannot be applied, mainly because the two companies do not share the same subjects. Nevertheless, it is possible to compare the "tendencies" of the two TCLs. By tendencies, we mean general statistics such as the total number of subjects who have access to the resource (i.e. the size of the TCL) or the transmission types distribution (i.e. the percentage of each transmission type). To give an example, Fig. 5. represents TCL_A as a small matrix filled with confidential transmissions, while TCL_B is represented as a very big TCL with a lot of non-confidential transmissions. Tendencies underline that there is a difference of security level regarding documentX.pdf. With such comparison, our model is able to notify security experts that company B has an indulgent security policy concerning documentX.pdf. Security experts can then modify mapping rules to generate a less permissive TCL_B, or tackle the problem at its root and modify the AC of company B in order to reduce the size of TCL_B.

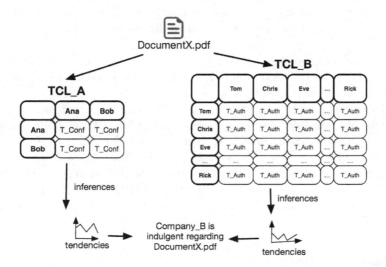

Fig. 5. Illustration of the tendency inferences, applied to a buyout example. Based on tendencies, notification can underline that company B is more indulgent regarding documentX.pdf security.

5   Evaluations

This section presents the results of several tests conducted in order to show that the proposed solution can be applied in real-life scenarios. For these tests, we aim to answer the following three questions:

- **Q1**: Are generation and inference mechanisms time-consuming?
- **Q2**: Is our solution suitable for small and medium-sized companies?
- **Q3**: Do specific ACL characteristics have any effects on the computational time?

5.1   Implementation

To generate ACLs, we have implemented an automatic rules generator. For the tests, several ACLs have been generated in order to simulate small and medium-sized company in term of subjects and resources. Information about these ACLs are given in Table 1. The last column of this table (Ratio) is the proportion between the number of subjects and the number of resources (Ratio = NbResources/NbSubjects). A ratio greater than 1 is more likely to be found in a company. Indeed, the total amount of resources is often bigger than the total amount of subjects. We have based our sets on this assumption and have generated ACLs with different size and ratio. These ACLs try to simulate the amount of subjects and resources that can be found in small and middle-sized companies. We empathize, however, that these ACLs are purely speculative. Future works will focus on asking companies for insight about realistic volumetry and ratios (to that end, an online survey can be found here: http://goo.gl/forms/l0VIKDYBGt).

From a technical point of view, we have used a MacBook Pro Retina (Intel Core i7, 2,4 GHz, 16GB RAM, 256 GB SSD hard drive) and Java 7. Java Virtual Machine has been tweaked with a heap size of 4096 bytes.

We have used two mapping rules. The first one was *"you cannot send a resource to someone with a lower accreditation level than you"* while the second was: *"confidential resources need to be sent with confidentiality property"*. Thus, we have created subjects with a parameter "accreditationLevel" and resources with a parameter "securityLevel". In order not to distort results with human interactions, we have used Decision Strategy "STRONGEST" with the security level described in 4.3. Thus, in case of conflict, the first rule was applied automatically.

5.2   Generation Tests

In these tests, we have measured the time-consumption of the process that allows our model to generate TCLs based on ACL. To do so, we have measured the time between the loading operation of an ACL and the end of the process (i.e. when all TCLs have been generated and saved as serializable objects in the hard drive). Results in Fig. 6.A show the generation process results. For very little set such as ACL1, it takes less than 1 second to compute. For sets ACL2 / ACL3 and ACL4 / ACL5, we can notice that the ratio slightly influences the computation. It can be explained by the fact that for ACL4, the maximum size of a TCL would be 1000 rows and columns (if everyone has access to the corresponding resource), whereas the maximum size of a TCL generated with ACL5 would

Table 1. Access Control Lists used for the tests.

ID	Rules	Subjects	Actions	Resources	Ratio
ACL1	50	10	3	40	4
ACL2	1500	250	3	1000	4
ACL3	1500	50	3	1250	25
ACL4	5000	1000	3	4000	4
ACL5	5000	200	3	4000	20
ACL6	10000	200	3	7000	35

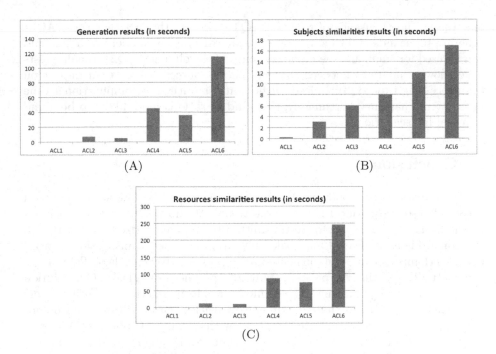

Fig. 6. Results for the generation process tests (A), subjects similarities tests (B) and resources similarities tests (C).

be "only" 200. Thus, these results show that it is algorithmically easier to do operations on a lot of smaller TCLs, rather than manipulating fewer, but bigger ones. Moreover, the saving process that consists of storing the generated TCLs is quite time-consuming, especially for big serialized objects.

Finally, ACL6 results show that our model can compute medium-size companies sets in less than 2 minutes. We consider these results has acceptable, especially for a process that needs to be done several times a day to be up-to-date.

5.3   Inferences Tests

We have tested the subjects and resources inferences mechanisms. Results in figure 6.B show that the subjects similarities computational time depends on the size of the ACL, with no significant impact regarding the ratio. Results in figure 6.C, however, show that ratio has a little impact for resource similarities. Indeed, even if ACL4 has 400 more resources, results shows that resources similarities process in ACL4 is faster than in ACL3. This results can be explained by the fact that once again, it is easier to compare many smaller Java objects.

Thanks to the conducted tests, questions **Q1**, **Q2** and **Q3** have been answered. Results show that the mechanisms involved in our model (i.e. generation and inferences) are quite fast, even with ACLs that embeds hundred of subjects and thousands of resources (**Q1**). Despite the fact that these ACLs generate thousands of TCLs, results have shown that our model is scalable and can be used for small and medium-size companies volumetry (**Q2**). Finally, tests have shown that ratio between subjects and resources can have an impact on the processing time (**Q3**). Indeed, bigger ratio reduces the computational time for some mechanisms. Fortunately, this kind of ratio is more likely to be found in a real life scenario.

6   Conclusion

Over the years, Access Control (AC) mechanisms have been proposed to control access of resources. Unfortunately, traditional AC do not provide notification mechanisms when a resource is retransmitted to an unauthorized third party. To overcome this issue, Data Loss/Leak Prevention or other Transmission Control (TC) mechanisms can be implemented on top of AC. Nevertheless, TC policies can contradict existing AC policies, leading to potential data leaks. One solution can be to link both paradigms in a common formalism, allowing a security expert to define both policies at the same time. Nevertheless, proposed solutions do not always provide TC rules that are compliant with existing AC policies. Moreover, they do not offer notification mechanisms that can help enhancing the existing AC policies and facilitate the integration between companies and infrastructures. To cover these drawbacks, we have defined a new transformation mechanism that takes existing AC policies and generates TC policies. Thanks to the generated TC policies, two notification mechanisms have been implemented.

The first mechanism can help enhancing the existing AC (M1). This mechanism has been implemented thanks to resources and subjects similarities features. Such features can help a security expert to have a better understanding of her/his existing AC, by detecting resources and subjects with the same transmission behavior (Section 4.4). The second mechanism can be used to ease the integration between infrastructure and increase security knowledge (M2). Once again, we have used generated TCLs to infer tendencies that fulfill such purpose. To give an example, we have proposed a simple case study of a company buyout (Section 4.5). Finally, we have tested our solution with various ACLs. Results show that the model is interesting in terms of computational time for small and medium-sized companies.

In the future, we intend to modify our model to take into account more sophisticated entities by using capability-based security. Moreover, we will aim at reasoning with clusters of entities rather than single entities to simplify policy management and reduce the number of generated files. Secondly, we aim at creating realistic ACLs (in term of subjects and resources ratio) by asking companies about the volumetry of their ACLs. Finally, we would like to offer a formalized approach of the complexity of our mechanisms.

References

1. Bell, D.E., La Padula, L.J.: Secure computer systems: Mathematical foundations (No. MTR-2547-VOL-1). MITRE Corp., Bedford (1973)
2. Biba, K.J.: Integrity considerations for secure computer systems. No. MTR-3153-REV-1. MITRE Corp., Bedford (1977)
3. Saltzer, J.H., Schroeder, M.D.: The protection of information in computer systems. Proceedings of the IEEE **63**(9), 1278–1308 (1975). doi:10.1109/PROC.1975.9939
4. Levy, H.M.: Capability-Based Computer System. Butterworth-Heinemann, Newton (1984)
5. Fabry, R.S.: Capability-based addressing. Communications of the ACM **17**(7), 403–412 (1974)
6. Sandhu, R.S., Coyne, E.J., Feinstein, H.L., Youman, C.E.: Role-based access control models. Computer **2**, 38–47 (1996)
7. Hu, V.C., Ferraiolo, D., Kuhn, R., Schnitzer, A., Sandlin, K., Miller, R., Scarfone, K.: Guide to attribute based access control (ABAC) definition and considerations. NIST Special Publication **800**, 162 (2014)
8. Han, W., Lei, C.: A survey on policy languages in network and security management. Computer Networks **56**(1), 477–489 (2012)
9. Shabtai, A., Elovici, Y., Rokach, L.: A survey of data leakage detection and prevention solutions. Springer Science & Business Media (2012)
10. Park, J., Sandhu, R.S.: The UCON ABC usage control model. ACM Transactions on Information and System Security (TISSEC) **7**(1), 128–174 (2004)
11. Hilty, M., Pretschner, A., Basin, D., Schaefer, C., Walter, T.: A policy language for distributed usage control. In: Biskup, J., López, J. (eds.) ESORICS 2007. LNCS, vol. 4734, pp. 531–546. Springer, Heidelberg (2007)
12. Kelbert, F., Pretschner, A.: Decentralized distributed data usage control. In: Kiayias, A., Askoxylakis, I., Gritzalis, D. (eds.) CANS 2014. LNCS, vol. 8813, pp. 353–369. Springer, Heidelberg (2014)
13. Gheorghe, G., Mori, P., Crispo, B., Martinelli, F.: Enforcing UCON policies on the enterprise service bus. In: Meersman, R., Dillon, T., Herrero, P. (eds.) OTM 2010. LNCS, vol. 6427, pp. 876–893. Springer, Heidelberg (2010)
14. Cuppens, F., Cuppens-Boulahia, N., Ghorbel, M.B.: High level conflict management strategies in advanced access control models. Electronic Notes in Theoretical Computer Science **186**, 3–26 (2007)
15. Ayed, S., Cuppens-Boulahia, N., Cuppens, F.: Deploying security policy in intra and inter workflow management systems. In: International Conference on Availability, Reliability and Security, ARES 2009, pp. 58–65. IEEE (2009)
16. Ayed, S., Cuppens-Boulahia, N., Cuppens, F.: An integrated model for access control and information flow requirements. In: Cervesato, I. (ed.) ASIAN 2007. LNCS, vol. 4846, pp. 111–125. Springer, Heidelberg (2007)
17. Barker, S.: Logical approaches to authorization policies. In: Artikis, A., Craven, R., Kesim Çiçekli, N., Sadighi, B., Stathis, K. (eds.) Sergot Festschrift 2012. LNCS, vol. 7360, pp. 349–373. Springer, Heidelberg (2012)
18. Slimani, N., Khambhammettu, H., Adi, K., Logrippo, L.: UACML: unified access control modeling language. In: 2011 4th IFIP International Conference on New Technologies, Mobility and Security (NTMS), pp. 1–8. IEEE (2011)
19. Khamadja, S., Adi, K., Logrippo, L.: An access control framework for hybrid policies. In: Proceedings of the 6th International Conference on Security of Information and Networks, pp. 282–286. ACM (2013)

Crypto, Protocol and Model

A Markov Random Field Approach
to Automated Protocol Signature Inference

Yongzheng Zhang[1], Tao Xu[1,2], Yipeng Wang[1(✉)],
Jianliang Sun[1,2], and Xiaoyu Zhang[1]

[1] Institute of Information Engineering, Chinese Academy of Sciences, Beijing, China
{zhangyongzheng,wangyipeng,zhangxiaoyu,xutao9083,sunjianliang}@iie.ac.cn,
yipeng.wang1@gmail.com
[2] University of Chinese Academy of Sciences, Beijing, China

Abstract. Protocol signature specifications play an important role in networking and security services, such as Quality of Service(QoS), vulnerability discovery, malware detection, and so on. In this paper, we propose ProParser, a network trace based protocol signature inference system that exploits the embedded contextual correlations of n-grams in protocol messages. In ProParser, we first apply markov field aspect model to discover the contextual relations and spatial structure among n-grams extracted from protocol traces. Next, we perform keyword-based clustering algorithm to cluster messages into extremely cohesive groups, and finally use heuristic ranking rules to generate the signature specifications for the corresponding protocol. We evaluate ProParser on real-world network traces including both textual and binary protocols. We also compare ProParser with the state-of-the-art tool, ProWord, and find that our approach performs more accurately and effectively in practice.

Keywords: Protocol signatures · Markov random field · Network security

1 Introduction

Protocol signatures are a set of unique byte subsequences that can be used to distinguish the network traces of individual protocols. Protocol signature specifications play an important role in networking and security services, such as Quality of Service(QoS), Intrusion Detection and Prevention Systems(IDSes/IPSes), malware detection, vulnerability discovery, and so on [5, 15, 16, 25, 27]. To be specific, Internet Service Providers(ISPs) uses protocol signature specifications to understand the components of protocol traffic passing through their networks. With an in-depth analysis of the composition of protocols, ISPs can

This research was supported by the National Natural Science Foundation of China under grant numbers 61402472, 61572496, 61202067 and 61303261, and the National High Technology Research and Development Program of China under grant numbers 2013AA014703 and 2012AA012803.

© Institute for Computer Sciences, Social Informatics and Telecommunications Engineering 2015
B. Thuraisingham et al. (Eds.): SecureComm 2015, LNICST 164, pp. 459–476, 2015.
DOI: 10.1007/978-3-319-28865-9_25

impose meaningful and appropriate policies on protocol traces to provide a better service experience in practice. Furthermore, protocol signature specifications are also crucial for IDSes/IPSes. IDSes/IPSes match the packet payload against the protocol signatures to discover abnormal behaviors or activities in protocol traffic. Besides traffic monitoring and IDSes/IPSes, protocol signature specifications are also helpful for vulnerability discovery. For example, existing penetration testing tools often need protocol signatures to generate the protocol traces for vulnerability detection.

Prior arts for protocol signature inference are generally divided into two categories: reverse engineering-based approaches and network trace-based approaches. In this paper, we concern the problem of automated protocol signature inference based on the packet payload of protocol traces. Notice that many network trace-based approaches have been proposed in prior arts, such as Discoverer [1], ACAS [2], Veritas [20], ProDecoder [3], ProWord [21, 26] and so on. The most recent and relevant work is ProWord [21, 26] proposed by Zhang et al. ProWord is an elegant solution for network trace-based protocol signature specification inference. ProWord has two key modules, and it works as follows: ProWord first breaks packet payload into candidate words based on a modified Voting Experts algorithm. Then, ProWord infers protocol signature specifications by a ranking algorithm that selects the highest ranked words as protocol feature words. However, ProWord has two major limitations. 1). to infer protocol signatures, ProWord breaks the packet payload into a set of candidate words. However, this naive solution ignores the spatial coherence of candidate words in protocol messages, and thus leads to a reduced performance on accuracy in practice. For example, message "MAIL FROM" is a protocol signature of SMTP (Simple Mail Transfer Protocol). However, ProWord often breaks the above signature "MAIL FROM" into two parts, "MAIL" and "FROM". Note that the divided messages "MAIL" and "FROM" are not true protocol signatures for SMTP. 2). The computational efficiency of ProWord presents one of its main limitations. For examples, the memory space requirement in ProWord is very high due to the construction of a prefix tree in the VE algorithm.

In this paper, we propose ProParser, which performs automated protocol signature inference based on the network traces of application protocols. The input of ProParser is the network traces of a given protocol, and the output is the protocol signatures, where each protocol signature is represented by a set of n-grams. ProParser has four functional modules in practice: n-Gram Extraction, Keyword Inference, Message Clustering, and Signature Generation. Specifically, we first extract n-grams from the packet payload of protocol traces. Next, we use a Markov field aspect model to infer protocol keywords, which are used to define protocol signature specifications. Then, we utilize a hierarchical clustering algorithm called sequential Information Bottleneck(sIB) algorithm [6] to group similar protocol messages into clusters of the same type according to their protocol keywords. Finally, we generate the final protocol signatures using heuristic ranking rules that find the invariant field among messages in each cluster. The key novelty of ProPaser lies in its exploitation of the spatial coherence of keywords in protocol messages that is usually missed under the previous conditional independence assumptions. Therefore, ProPaser is a more robust network trace-based system for automated protocol signature inference.

In order to test and verify the effectiveness of ProParser, we apply ProParser on a set of real-world application traces, including a text protocol SMTP and a binary protocol DNS, and then we utilize precision and recall as the metrics to evaluate our experimental results. The experimental results show that ProParser has precisely parsed the protocol signatures with an average recall of 98% and an average precision of 98.5%. In summary, our contributions are highlighted as follows.

- We introduce and present a Markov random field approach to extract the protocol keywords from the packet payload of protocol traces. The proposed approach considers the spatial coherence of keywords in protocol messages that would be missed under the previous conditional independence assumptions.
- We design a system called ProParser, which can automatically infer the protocol signatures of a specific protocol from its real-world traces with no prior knowledge about the protocol specification. We propose a new technique to extract protocol keywords that is independent of the type of the target protocol.
- ProParser is able to handle both textual and binary protocols. Compared to the state-of-the-art method ProWord, our approach performs better experimental results on effectiveness and efficiency.

The rest of the paper is organized as follows. We state our problem scope and review related work in Section 2. We describe the design and technical details of ProParser in Section 3. We present datasets, evaluation methods, experimental results in Section 4. Finally, we conclude the paper in Section 5.

2 Related Work

Prior arts for protocol signature inference can be generally divided into two categories: reverse engineering-based approaches [10, 11, 12, 19] and network trace-based approaches [1, 2, 8, 9, 17-22]. In the remainder of this section, we introduce some typical prior arts of the two categories.

2.1 Reverse Engineering-Based Methods

The reverse engineering based methods implement the executable code and analyze the received application messages to infer protocol signature. Caballero et al. proposed Polyglot, an automatic protocol reverse engineering approach by using dynamic binary analysis [10], they implemented executable codes and monitored the data to extract the protocol signature. Lim et al. implemented an analysis tool which extracts network packet formats by means of working on executable binary code [11]. Cui et al. presented Tupni in [12], a reverse engineering method by analyzing a set of input, including record sequence, record types and input constraints. These researches have some limitations. First, unknown protocols' executable code is often difficult to obtain, even if it is available, it still suffers from tedious manual effort and harsh operating condition. Additionally, reversing process is significantly difficult once the executable code uses code obfuscation or code compression. As a consequence, we assume the executable code of protocols is not available and focus on network trace based methods.

2.2   Network Trace-Based Methods

Cui et al built Discoverer, which automatically extracted protocol signatures from network traces [1]. Discoverer first separated messages into tokens and classified them into clusters based on the token pattern of the messages. Then, Discoverer implemented recursive clustering to divide the clusters into similar clusters with same message formats. Finally, it merged the clusters using sequence alignment to avoid over-classification. However, the predefined delimiters using in tokenization phase are obviously invalid for binary protocols. In the meanwhile, the sequence alignment algorithm is time-consuming and not that necessary to be a part of signature inference. We notice that the protocol signatures represented by n-gram sets are more efficient. By contrast, ProParser does not depend on delimiters and it uses some heretics ranking rules to extract protocol signatures.

Ma et al. built a statistical and structural content model to identify protocol from network traces automatically [14], they believed that the first 64-bytes can approximately draw a complete distribution of the entire session. However, this assumption often does not hold in reality especially for binary protocols. Haffer et al. proposed ACAS, which explored automatically extracting application signatures from IP traffic payload contents [2]. They also regarded first 64 bytes of each TCP Flow as feature vectors leading to the information loss. ProParser use whole bytes of flows to infer protocol signature.

Zhang et al. proposed ProWord [21], an unsupervised approach to extract protocol signature. They built a word segmentation algorithm to generate candidate feature words and then used a ranking algorithm to select the top-k words. Their work achieves decent accuracy and conciseness while suffers from some obvious drawbacks. ProWord broke payloads into candidate words to discover semantics information while its precision and recall are barely satisfactory, especially for binary protocols. By contrast, ProParser can handle these problems because it does not rely on word boundaries. In addition, the signature pruning phase of ProWord needs manual efforts while ProParser is fully-automated.

Finamore et al proposed KISS in [8], which first extract statistical features from network traces, and then build a support vector machines(SVM) based classifier. Zhang et al. vectored captured protocol traces and employed K-means algorithm to cluster them in [17]. Xie et al. proposed a multi-classifier SubFlow using statistical features from network traces in [18]. However, these methods

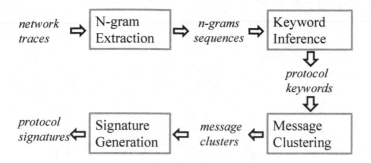

Fig. 1. Architecture of ProParser

suffer from relatively low accuracy caused by protocol behavior confusion or payload byte stuffing. ProParser can address these problems because it has redundant information of protocol messages by using both sematic correlation and statistical distribution.

3   ProParser

The input of ProParser is the network traces of a given protocol, and the output is the protocol signatures, where each protocol signature is represented by a set of n-grams. As shown in Fig. 1, ProParser has four functional modules in practice: n-gram extraction, keyword inference, message clustering and signature generation. Next, we provide the technical details for each module.

3.1 n-Gram Extraction

The input to this n-Gram Extraction module is a set of packet traces of the same protocol, and the output to this module is protocol messages, where each protocol messages is denoted by a sequence of n-grams. An n-gram is defined as a subsequence of n elements contained in a given sequence of at least n elements. For example, considering messsage "\x48\x7e\x0a\x3c\x0d" in BitTorrent protocol, we can decompose it into 3-grams as follows: "\x48\x7e\x0a", "\x7e\x0a\x3c", "\x0a\x3c\x0d". More generally, given a byte sequence "$c_1 c_2 \cdots c_m$", we break it into n-grams as follows, "$c_1 c_2 \cdots c_n$", "$c_2 c_3 \cdots c_{n+1}$", $\cdots$, "$c_{m-n+1} c_{m-n+2} \cdots c_m$". In practice, we note that a larger value of n will generate a tremendous set of n-grams and the execution time is also high, while a smaller value of n will introduce noise data and further identify inaccurate protocol keywords. Therefore, we give a tentative value in this paper, and we set the value of n to be 3.

In addition, we should also consider the total number of n-grams considered in the n-gram vocabulary. Theoretically, a given n-gram collection may involve approximately 256^n items. In reality, more items can provide more semantics information for the protocol under analysis. However, this enormous amount of items causes prohibitively expensive time consumption. In this paper, we select

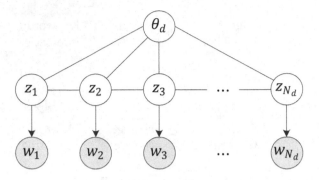

Fig. 2. Markov Random Field Dirichlet Allocation

a P-percent subset from the origin n-gram collection with high frequency of n-gram occurrence to make a trade-off. We vary the range of $P = \{40\%, 60\%, 80\%\}$ to find the most appropriate value for protocol signature inference.

3.2   Keyword Inference

In the module keyword inference, we aim to identify the protocol keywords that are in the given network traces of an application protocol. The input to this module is a sequence of n-grams extracted by the previous module, and the output to this module is a distribution of protocol keywords inferred by ProParser. In prior work, ProDecoder [3] uses a model called Latent Dirichlet Allocation (LDA) to infer protocol keywords from the network traces of individual protocols. However, the basic LDA model is based on a bag-of-words assumption. In other words, LDA model assumes that its n-grams are drawn independently from the keyword mixture $\boldsymbol{\theta}_m$, and thus it ignores the spatial structure of the packet. In practice, we notice that the Markov Random Field model (MRF) can reflect such local interactions for spatial contiguity.

Basic of Markov Field Aspect Model. Given a protocol packet corpus $D \equiv \{\{w_{m,i}\}_{i=1}^{N_m}\}_{m=1}^{M}$ of M packets, where $w_{m,i}$ represents the i-th n-gram in packet m, and N_m is the number of n-grams considered in packet m. Remember that in the basic LDA model, each n-gram $w_{m,i}$ corresponds to a specific keyword indicator $z_{m,i}$. More specifically, each packet m is modeled as a probability distribution of protocol keywords, denoted by $\boldsymbol{\theta}_m = p(\boldsymbol{z}|m)$, where each keyword $z = k \in \{1, \cdots, K\}$ is in turn a probability distribution over the n-gram terms $\boldsymbol{t} = \{u\}_{u=1}^{W}$, denoted by $\boldsymbol{\varphi}_k = p(\boldsymbol{t}|k)$. To improve the spatial coherence for keyword inference, we consider to move from a multinomial distribution over hidden variables $\boldsymbol{z}$ to a representation of Markov random field as shown in Fig. 2. Our Markov random field based inference model can be formulated as a product of MRF and LDA over protocol keyword $\boldsymbol{z}$, and thus the proposed model can be called Latent Dirichlet Markov Random Field model (abbr. LDMRF).

The detailed mathematical derivation of our target posterior distribution $p(\boldsymbol{z}|\mathcal{M}, \boldsymbol{w})$ can be found as follows,

$$
\begin{aligned}
\underbrace{p(\boldsymbol{z}|\mathcal{M}, \boldsymbol{w})}_{\text{Posterior Distribution}} &= \underbrace{p(\boldsymbol{z}|\mathcal{M})}_{\text{MRF}} \cdot \underbrace{p(\boldsymbol{z}|\boldsymbol{w})}_{\text{LDA}} \\
&= \underbrace{\prod_{m=1}^{M} \frac{1}{Z} \psi_c(\boldsymbol{z}_m|\mathcal{M})}_{\text{MRF}} \cdot \underbrace{\prod_{m=1}^{M} \boldsymbol{\theta}_m}_{\text{LDA}} \\
&= \underbrace{\prod_{m=1}^{M} \frac{1}{Z} \prod_{i=1}^{N_m} \psi_c(z_{m,i})}_{\text{MRF}} \cdot \underbrace{\prod_{m=1}^{M} \prod_{i=1}^{N_m} \theta_{m,i}}_{\text{LDA}} \quad (1) \\
&= \frac{1}{Z} \prod_{m=1}^{M} \prod_{i=1}^{N_m} \left(\psi_c(z_{m,i}) \cdot \theta_{m,i} \right) \\
&= \frac{1}{Z} \prod_{m=1}^{M} \prod_{i=1}^{N_m} \left(\exp\{-E_c(z_{m,i})\} \cdot \theta_{m,i} \right)
\end{aligned}
$$

where $\mathcal{M}$ corresponds to the states of Markov random field, and Z is a normalization constant. In addition, ψ_c is a potential function, and E_c denotes clique potential in the Potts model. From Equation 1, we clearly find that the transition of raw LDA to LDMRF is equivalent to placing a Markov random field prior on the probability of keyword $\theta_{m,i}$. Note that determining keyword indicator $\boldsymbol{z}$ of LDMRF model is the core problem of learning the proposed protocol keyword model. By using $\boldsymbol{z}$, we can easily calculate the two types of distributions: (1) the n-gram distribution for each keyword k, denoted φ_k, and (2) the keyword distribution for each packet m, denoted $\boldsymbol{\vartheta}_m$. In the rest of this paper, we use parameter sets $\Phi = \{\varphi_k\}_{k=1}^{K}$ and $\Theta = \{\boldsymbol{\vartheta}_m\}_{m=1}^{M}$ to denote the above two types of distributions, respectively.

Approximate Inference. Next, we would like to discuss about estimating the parameter $\boldsymbol{z}$ in LDMRF. Remember that our target posterior distribution is $p(\boldsymbol{z}|\mathcal{M}, \boldsymbol{w})$, and it can be formulated as follows,

$$
p(\boldsymbol{z}|\mathcal{M}, \boldsymbol{w}) = \frac{p(\boldsymbol{z}, \boldsymbol{w}) \cdot p(\boldsymbol{z}|\mathcal{M})}{p(\boldsymbol{w})} \quad (2)
$$

Note that exact inference of the target distribution $p(\boldsymbol{z}|\mathcal{M}, \boldsymbol{w})$ in the LDMRF model is particularly difficult. Thus, in this paper, we obtain an approximate inference result through Gibbs sampling, an example of Markov Chain Monte Carlo (MCMC) algorithm [7]. Gibbs sampling is an iterative algorithm, where in each iteration the value of each variable is updated by a value drawn from the target distribution of that variable conditioned on the rest of variables. To estimate the parameter z in the LDMRF model, the updating rule for Gibbs sampling algorithm is as follows,

$$p(z_{(m,i)} = k \mid \boldsymbol{z}_{\neg(m,i)}, \boldsymbol{w}, \mathcal{M}) \propto \frac{n_k^{(t)} - 1 + \beta}{\sum_{i=1}^{W} n_k^{(t)} - 1 + W\beta} \cdot \frac{n_m^{(k)} - 1 + \alpha}{\sum_{k=1}^{K} n_m^{(k)} - 1 + K\alpha} \cdot \exp\left(\sum_{i \sim j} \Delta \Lambda(z_{m,i}, z_{m,j})\right),$$ (3)

where $n_k^{(t)}$ is the number of times that n-gram term t is assigned to keyword k, and $n_m^{(k)}$ denotes the number of times that an n-gram from the packet m has been assigned to keyword k. Λ is an indicator function, which decides if the keyword indexes for neighbors $z_{m,i}$ and $z_{m,j}$ are the same. Δ is a strength parameter, and a positive value of Δ awards configurations where neighboring nodes have the same label. After a sufficient number of iterations, the Gibbs sampling algorithm converges, and we can obtain keyword assignments for z, which are then used to estimate the two parameter sets Θ and Φ according to the following equations:

$$\varphi_{k,t} = \frac{n_k^{(t)} + \beta}{\sum_{t=1}^{W} n_k^{(t)} + W\beta}$$ (4)

$$\vartheta_{m,k} = \frac{n_m^{(k)} + \alpha}{\sum_{k=1}^{K} n_m^{(k)} + K\alpha}$$ (5)

Perplexity. In order to ensure that the Gibbs sampling algorithm in LDMRF has converged and that the LDMRF model with the estimated parameter sets θ and ϕ is generalizable, we employ *perplexity* as the metrics to quantify the quality of our estimation. Perplexity, which is defined as follows, is a well-known measure of the ability of a model to generalize to unseen data [24].

$$perplexity(D) = \exp\left\{ -\frac{\sum_{m=1}^{M} \log p(\boldsymbol{w}_m)}{\sum_{m=1}^{M} N_m} \right\}$$ (6)

where N_m is the total number of n-grams in message m. In ProParser, we prefer a lower perplexity score as a lower perplexity score denotes better generalization performance in practice. Perplexity also allows us to determine the right number of keywords for the given corpus of messages.

3.3 Message Clustering

The Message Clustering module aims to partition the messages which contain identified keywords into multiple clusters. The fact that an application protocol always has many types of signatures representing different protocol grammar, so it is critical to guarantee the purity of each cluster, that is, one cluster can contain messages from only one protocol while messages from one protocol can be partitioned into multiple clusters. Take a message set of HTTP as an example. For the following cluster of three messages, the first two messages should be partitioned into one cluster and the third one should be set alone.

1) GET /activity.ini HTTP/1.1
2) GET /stat.xml HTTP/1.1
3) POST / HTTP/1.1

Algorithm 1. Sequential Information Bottleneck

Input: Clustering threshold K; Feature vector X; Maximum iteration M; Convergence multiplier θ.
Output: A partition C of X into K clusters.
  1: **function** sIB(K, X, M, θ)
  2:      Partition $C \leftarrow \phi$
  3:      **for** i^{th} period of partition C_i **do**
  4:          $C_i \leftarrow$ random partition $c_1, c_2, \cdots, c_k$ from X
  5:          $changeFlag \leftarrow 0$, $itFlag \leftarrow 0$
  6:          **while** $itFlag < M$ **and** $changeFlag > \theta|X|$ **do**
  7:              $ifFlag \leftarrow itFlag + 1$
  8:              **for** j **from** 1 **to** $|X|$ **do**
  9:                  pop x from c_j
 10:                  $d(x, c_{new}) \leftarrow argmin_{c \in C} d(x, c_{new})$
 11:                  **if** $d(x, c_{new}) < d(x, c_j)$ **then**
 12:                      insert x into c_{new}
 13:                      $changeFlag \leftarrow changeFlag + 1$
 14:                  **else**
 15:                      insert x into c_j
 16:                  **end if**
 17:              **end for**
 18:          **end while**
 19:          $C \leftarrow argmax_{c \in C} Score(c)$
 20:      **end for**
 21: **end function**

Taking probability correlated keywords as message features, we adopt the sIB clustering algorithm to accomplish this task. This method aims to obtain the relevant information of the messages sharing the same message format, denoted by a cluster. sIB has two objective progresses comparing with aIB, a hierarchical clustering algorithm been used by ProDecoder. First, as an agglomerative clustering method, aIB is irreversible and cannot guarantee the global optimum, sIB performs multiple reruns and multiple iterations in each run to avoid losing the optimal solution. Second, it is observed that sIB has more rapid convergence to global optimum so that decrease the execution time.

The input of sIB is cluster threshold K and the joint probability distribution $p(x, y)$ where the random variable X denotes the message feature vector and random variable Y denotes the relevant features of X. The output of sIB is a partition C with K clusters. Initially, we randomly divide the feature vectors in X into a partition C with K clusters, i.e. $C = \{c_1, c_2, \cdots, c_k\}$. Then we step into a loop. Iteratively, we choose every object $x \in X$ out of its current cluster $c(x)$ and reallocate it to a new cluster C_{new} which satisfies $C_{new} = argmin_{c \in C} cost(x, c)$. The cost function is defined as follows:

$$d(x, c) = (p(x) + p(c)) * JS[p(y|x), p(y|c)], \tag{7}$$

where $p(x)$, $p(y)$ represent cluster prior probabilities, and JS is Jensen-Shannon divergence that represents the possibility of $p(x)$ and $p(y)$ derived from the same distribution and can be calculated by the following equations:

$$D_{kl}(p\|q) = \sum_{x \in X} p(x) \log \frac{p(x)}{p(y)}. \tag{8}$$

$$JS_{\pi_1, \pi_2}(p\|q) = \pi_1 D_{kl}(p\|r) + \pi_2 D_{kl}(q\|r). \tag{9}$$

More details about the above equations can be seen in [6]. There are two stop conditions of the above loop: maximum iterations $maxL$ and convergence multiplier θ, that is, when the time of iteration is greater than $maxL$ or the changed elements in the current loop are less than $\theta * |X|$, the loop is terminated. Now, we obtain a converged partition C^*. We calculate its score $F(C^*) = I(Y; C)$, where $I(Y; C)$ denotes the mutual information between C and Y. The $I(Y; C)$ can be calculated by the following equation:

$$I(Y; C) = \sum_{y, c} p(y, c) \log \frac{p(y, c)}{p(y) p(c)}. \tag{10}$$

In order to find out an optimal partition of X, we run sIB n times with random initialization. As a consequence, we will get a partition set $S = \{C_1, C_2, \cdots C_n\}$, and their corresponding scores $F = \{F(C_1), F(C_2), \cdots, F(C_n)\}$. Finally, we select the partition C^*, which satisfies the equation $C^* = argmax_{C \in S} F(C)$. In ProParser, we heuristically set the cluster threshold K to 1.5 times the number of keywords in keyword inference module. Up to this point, we acquire message clusters with extremely cohesive set of messages.

3.4   Signature Generation

Given the clusters of highly related messages, the main goal of this module is to discover protocol signature represented by the 3-grams, i.e., the invariant part among messages. As shown in Fig. 2, the input of this module is the messages in each cluster and the output is the common subsequence represented by 3-grams. To this end, we exploit a ranking method to identify 3-grams that are most

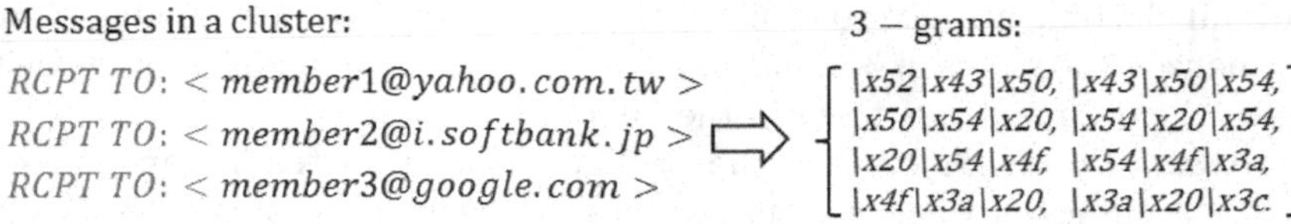

Messages in a cluster:

RCPT TO: < *member1@yahoo.com.tw* >
RCPT TO: < *member2@i.softbank.jp* > $\implies$
RCPT TO: < *member3@google.com* >

3 − grams:

$$\begin{bmatrix} |x52|x43|x50, & |x43|x50|x54, \\ |x50|x54|x20, & |x54|x20|x54, \\ |x20|x54|x4f, & |x54|x4f|x3a, \\ |x4f|x3a|x20, & |x3a|x20|x3c. \end{bmatrix}$$

Fig. 3. An Example of Signature Generation

likely to be the protocol signature. We first grade the possible keywords of each cluster and choose the higher ones as candidates relatively. Then we combine the candidates together and prune the redundancy.

1) 3-*grams Ranking:* Considering messages in a specific cluster, protocol signature can be a set of 3-grams with any length and location, it is important to develop a strategy to identify the proper ones. Inspired by the information retrieval heuristics proposed in [23] and aggregation methods proposed in [21], we build several ranking rules and adapt the heuristics to protocol reverse engineering to choose the accurate 3-grams from aforementioned clusters. The ranking rules consist of frequency rule, location rule and position rule.

Frequency Rule. Given a candidate set S of a cluster, we define the number of occurrence of $s \in S$ as **gram frequency**, the number of message which contains $s \in S$ as **message coverage**. We would like to give a higher score to s with higher gram frequency. If the gram frequency is the same, we appreciate the s with higher message coverage. The intuition of this rule is that we believe the 3-grams with substantial amount of appearance is more likely to be the protocol signature.

Location Rule. We define the specific location with maximum number of occurrence of $s \in S$ as **max location**, the number of message which contains $s \in S$ in the max location as **location coverage**. We are willing to give a higher score to s with higher location coverage. For max location calculation, we count all candidates in every possible location in the message and choose the maximum. The intuition of this rule is we believe that s occurs in several locations in a message while the location with maximum occurrence is more valuable. Also, considering the situation where $s1, s2 \in S$ have the same value of message coverage, $s1$ appears at a fixed location while $s2$ scatters at several locations, we prefer $s1$ apparently.

Position Rule. We define the message byte offset of $s \in S$ as **gram position**. The gram position at the beginning or the end of a message deserves a higher score. The intuition of this rule is that we find the bytes that occur at such position is more likely to be used as a protocol signature.

We compute the scores of candidates using the rules of frequency, location and position separately and combine them by multiplication. This aggregation method is proved to obtain proportional fairness of multipliers in [23].

2) 3-*grams Combination:* Based on the ranking method, we get many 3-grams corresponding to the clusters. Note that the 3-grams may be separated

into several clusters, we need to combine them according to their ranking scores. We normalized the scores of 3-grams in each cluster due to its different capacity, then sum them up and sort them in the decreasing order.

3) *3-grams Pruning:* Note that the quality of the extracted 3-grams directly affects the accuracy of whole system, we establish several pruning rules to eliminate the unreasonable 3-grams.

Length Scale. Message format is designed to exchange data among network hosts, a long signature will burden the data transmission while a short signature lacks the ability to distinguish protocols. In this paper, we control the protocol signature in a reasonable range of [3, 10] for eliminating.

Score Threshold. Based on our ranking method, even candidates with low frequency or coverage can get a score. To increase the compactness of extracted 3-grams, we define a score threshold K and select the top-K 3-grams with higher score, the remaining 3-grams are discarded.

Gram Redundancy. Considering two 3-grams in the gram set, if one with lower score is a substring of another, we will remove it. If one with higher score is a substring of another, we will retain both.

Gram Irrelevance. Irrelevant payload data in protocol traces may generate irrelevant 3-grams, such as date field like "2015/04/15", message ending field like "\x0d\x0a" and message padding field like "\x00\x00\x00". These strings often occur in protocol messages but have no relevance to the protocol, and hence they should be removed.

4 Experimental Results

We evaluate our approach on two kinds of protocols, including textual and binary protocols. ProParser takes network traces of specific protocol as the system input and automatically outputs protocol signatures. In the remainder of this section, we first describe our data sets, then show our evaluation methodology and metrics. Finally, we present the experimental results including parameter tuning, method performance and efficiency. Comparative experimental results are also presented in this section.

4.1 Datasets

Our dataset consists of two well-known protocols, namely SMTP and DNS. We collect the traces from a backbone router of a major ISP on the Internet. The details of the network traces are shown in Table 1. The ground truth of a network trace means its generating application. In order to build the ground truth, we use both the port number and the DPI information to filter network traces. The traces are all raw packets with complete payload semantics. We separate the above mentioned datasets into two parts, one for training and the other for testing. The testing dataset consists of both positive and negative samples. For example, the SMTP set consists of abundant SMTP traces and the same amount of non-SMTP traces, including DNS, HTTP, IMAP and other protocols.

Table 1. Summary of The Traces

Protocol	Size(B)	Packets	Flows	Collection Time
SMTP	673M	1.54M	179K	Aug 2014
DNS	438M	1.33M	145K	Sep 2014

4.2   Evaluation Methodology and Metrics

In this section, we present our evaluation methodology first. We split datasets into two parts, one for training and the other for testing, the training set contains 90% of the dataset traces and the remaining 10% traces contribute to testing set. The amount of each protocol in the dataset is limited because of the high computation complexity of keyword inference and message clustering, while we believe that the number is large enough for extracting good protocol specification. In the training process, we rerun keyword inference several times to adjust the appropriate parameters and perform the message clustering in multiple servers simultaneously to reduce the time consumption. In testing process, we repeat the experiment several times and calculate the average values of metrics to eliminate the variation of different runs.

Table 2. The Confusion Metrics of Trace Prediction

	Actual DNS	Actual not DNS	Total
Predicted DNS	True Positive(TP)	False Positive(FP)	Predicted Positive
Predicted Not	False Negative(FN)	True Negative(TN)	Predicted Negative
Total	Actual Positive	Actual Negative	

To measure the correctness and effectiveness of ProParser, we put forward our evaluation metrics. Given a prediction of packet of targeted protocol, all possible situations are listed in the above confusion table. Table 2 reports the confusion metrics of DNS prediction. There are four possible outcomes of a prediction for a two-class case shown in the table. TP means when the packet is actually positive and is predicted as positive sample correctly. TN means when the packet is actually negative and is predicted as negative sample correctly. FP means when the packet is actually negative but is predicted as positive sample incorrectly. FN means when the packet is actually positive but is predicted as negative sample incorrectly. Based on the above four fundamental measurements, we introduce three evaluation metrics as follows.

$$recall = \frac{TP}{TP + FN}. \tag{11}$$

$$precision = \frac{TP}{TP + FP}. \tag{12}$$

We combine recall and precession into F-Measure to take advantage of their own strengths.

Table 3. Values of Tunable Parameters

Parameter Name	Parameter Value
Iteration in sIB	2000
Rerun Times in sIB	5
Cluster number in sIB	$1.5 * K$
top-k for pruning in Ranking	100
length range$[a, b]$ of 3-grams	$[3, 10]$

$$F - Measure = 2 * \frac{precision * recall}{precision + recall}. \tag{13}$$

4.3 Experimental Results

In this section, we first present the procedure of parameter tuning, and then show the performance and efficiency of our approach. We also exhibit comparative experiments.

1) *Parameter Tuning:* There are several parameters in each module of ProParser. Next, we would like to talk about how to select the optimal parameters in each module. Notice that the parameter tuning is performed only on the training data set, and it is unnecessary for the test data set. We discuss some parameters in details and list others in Table 3 due to space limitation.

Iteration Count L. Gibbs sampling algorithm, used in keyword inference, is an iterative algorithm which is directly relative to the correlation of the n-grams. Thus it is vital to select a proper iteration count L to ensure that the algorithm is convergent. By varying L from 1000 to 10000 and changing P of 40%, 60%, and 80% for DNS and SMTP protocols, respectively, the corresponding perplexity are drawn in Fig. 3. We observe that the complexity values converge at 4000 iterations for DNS and 6000 iterations for SMTP.

Keywords Number K. Keyword number K is another predefined parameter in keyword inference. In this module, markov random field model outputs K keywords with their corresponding probabilities. The K keywords in each message is regarded as K attributes of message clustering. To choose the proper K, we range K from 10 to 180 with a step length of 10 and change P as 40%, 60%, and 80%, respectively. Fig. 4 reports that the perplexity value drops substantially at first and increases gradually later under each P of DNS and SMTP. Thus we record the functional minimum value as the appropriate K for each P of DNS and SMTP.

Strength Parameter Δ. In this part we display the tuning of hyper parameters α, β as well as the strength factor Δ in markov random field model. We fix the proper L and K for each P of each protocol, and then we vary $\alpha = \{0.1, 0.5, 0.9\}$, $\beta = \{0.001, 0.005, 0.01, 0.05, 0.1\}$, $\Delta = \{0.01, 0.05, 0.1, 0.5, 0.9\}$ and $P = \{40\%, 60\%, 80\%\}$ to compute the precision and recall for ProParser. Due to space limitations we will omit the selection of α and β. Next we emphasize the tuning of Δ and the corresponding recall and precision results. Fig. 5

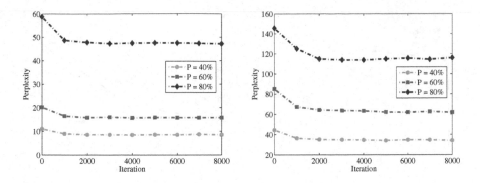

Fig. 4. Selection of Iteration for DNS and SMTP Protocols.

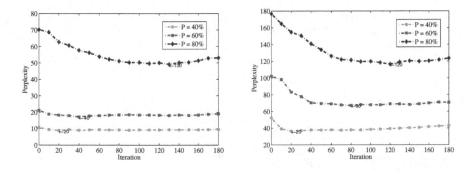

Fig. 5. Selection of the optimal number of keywords for DNS and SMTP.

shows the precision and recall for DNS by varying Δ and P values. The optimal parameter values for SMTP are $\alpha = 0.1$, $\beta = 0.005$, $\Delta = 1.0$ and $P = 0.8$, and the corresponding precision and recall are 98% and 99%. Fig. 6 shows the precision and recall for SMTP by varying Δ and P values. The optimal parameter values for SMTP are $\alpha = 0.1$, $\beta = 0.01$, $\Delta = 1.0$ and $P = 0.8$, and the corresponding precision and recall are 99% and 97%.

2) *Performance Results:* As shown in the parameter tuning, ProParser achieves a decent recall and precision for both textual and binary protocols. We also implement ProWord which is an unsupervised protocol signature extraction approach. Fig. 7 presents the precision and recall for ProParser, with comparison to the results of ProWord. It is obvious that ProParser can significantly enhance the recall without decreasing the precision of ProWord. Additionally, ProWord uses manual inspection for keywords pruning while ProParser is totally automated. Furthermore, ProWord claims that it is more concise and compact with top-K signatures. In oder to hold the decent accuracy, the K of ProWord is 100 while the volume of ProParser is approximately 250. Note that the two

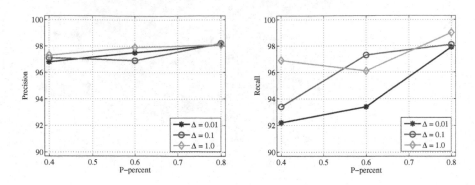

Fig. 6. Precision and Recall of ProParser for DNS.

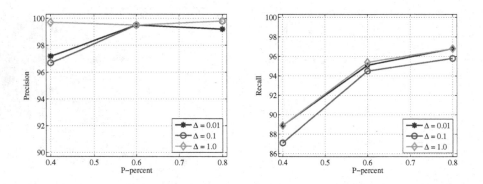

Fig. 7. Precision and Recall of ProParser for SMTP.

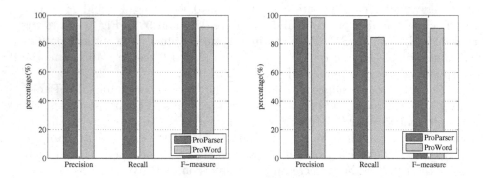

Fig. 8. Comparison of ProParser with ProWord for DNS and SMTP Protocols.

tools both run offline for signature generation, and thus it is not necessary to consider the training latency. The feature matching latencies of the two tools are approximately the same.

5   Conclusion

In this paper, we propose ProParser, a network trace-based approach for auto-mated protocol signature inference. Our method builds on markov random field model to discover sematic relationship and spatial structure of protocol messages, which promotes the effect of message clustering. It also relies on heuristic ranking rules to find the invariant field among protocol messages. We evaluate our protocol signature inference system on real-world network traces including both textual and binary protocols. We also compare ProParser with the state-of-the-art tool, ProWord, and find that our approach performs more accurately and effectively in practice.

References

1. Cui, W., Kannan, J., Wang, H.J.: Discoverer: automatic protocol reverse engineering from network traces. In: Proceedings of the 16th USENIX Security Symposium, pp. 1–14 (2007)
2. Haffner, P., Sen, S., Spatscheck, O., Wang, D.: ACAS: automated construction of application signatures. In: Proceedings of the 2005 ACM SIGCOMM Workshop on Mining Network Data, pp. 197–202 (2005)
3. Wang, Y., et al.: A semantics aware approach to automated reverse engineering unknown protocols. In: Proceedings of the 20th IEEE International Conference on Network Protocol (ICNP), pp. 1–10 (2012)
4. Slonim, N., Tishby, N.: Agglomerative information bottleneck. In: Proceedings of the 12th Neural Information Processing Systems (NIPS), pp. 617–623 (1999)
5. Perdisci, R., Lee, W., Feamster, N.: Behavioral clustering of HTTP-based malware and signature generation using malicious network traces. In: Proceedings of the 7th USENIX Conference on Networked Systems Design and Implementation, pp. 391–404 (2010)
6. Slonim, N., Friedman, N., Tishby, N.: Unsupervised document classification using sequential information maximization. In: Proceedings of the 24th International ACM SIGIR Conference on Research and Development in Information Retrieval, pp. 129–136 (2002)
7. Griffiths, T.L., Steyvers, M.: Finding scientific topics. Proceedings of the National Academy of Sciences of the United States of America **101**, 5228–5235 (2004)
8. Finamore, A., Mellia, M., Meo, M., Rossi, D.: Kiss: Stochastic packet inspection classifier for udp traffic. IEEE/ACM Transactions on Networking, 1505–1515 (2010)
9. Wang, Y., et al.: Biprominer: automatic mining of binary protocol features (PDCAT). In: Proceedings of the 12th IEEE International Conference on Parallel and Distributed Computing, Applications and Technologies, pp. 179–184 (2011)
10. Caballero, J., Yin, H., Liang, Z., Song, D.: Polyglot: automatic extraction of protocol message format using dynamic binary analysis. In: Proceedings of the 14th ACM Conference on Computer and Communications Security, pp. 317–329 (2007)
11. Lim, J., Reps, T., Liblit, B.: Extracting output formats from executables. In: Proceedings of the 13th Working Conference on Reverse Engineering, pp. 167–178 (2006)

12. Cui, W., Peinado, M., Chen, K., Wang, H.J., Irun-Briz, L.: Tupni: automatic reverse engineering of input formats. In: Proceedings of the 14th ACM Conference on Computer and Communications Security, pp. 391–402 (2008)
13. Kannan, J., Jung, J., Paxson, V., Koksal, C.E.: Semi-automated discovery of application session signatures. In: Proceedings of the 6th ACM SIGCOMM Conference on Internet Measurement (IMC), pp. 119–132 (2006)
14. Ma, J., Levchenko, K., Kreibich, C., Savage, S., Voelker, G.M.: Unexpected means of protocol inference. In: Proceedings of the 6th ACM SIGCOMM Internet Measurement Conference, pp. 313–326 (2006)
15. Holger, D., Anja, F., Michael, M., Vern, P., Robin, S.: Dynamic application-layer protocol analysis for network intrusion detection. In: Proceedings of the 15th Conference on USENIX Security Symposium, pp. 257–272 (2006)
16. Yun, X., Wang, Y., Zhang, Y., Zhou, Y.: A Semantics-Aware Approach to the Automated Network Protocol Identification. IEEE/ACM Transactions on Networking **24**(1), 1–13 (2015)
17. Zhang, J., Xiang, Y., Zhou, W., Wang, Y.: Unsupervised traffic classification using flow statistical properties and IP packet payload. Journal of Computer and System Sciences **79**(5), 573–585 (2013)
18. Xie, G., Iliofotou, M., Keralapura, R., Faloutsos, M., Nucci, A.: Subflow: towards practical flow-level traffic classification. In: Proceedings of the 31th Annual International Conference on Computer Communications, pp. 2541–2545 (2012)
19. Cho, C.Y., Babic, D., Shin, R., Song, D.: Inference and analysis of formal models of botnet command and control protocols. In: Proceedings of the 17th ACM Conference on Computer and Communication Security, pp. 426–439 (2010)
20. Wang, Y., Zhang, Z., Yao, D.D., Qu, B., Guo, L.: Inferring protocol state machine from network traces: a probabilistic approach. In: Lopez, J., Tsudik, G. (eds.) ACNS 2011. LNCS, vol. 6715, pp. 1–18. Springer, Heidelberg (2011)
21. Zhang, Z., Zhang, Z., Lee, P.P.C., Liu, Y., Xie, G.: ProWord: an unsupervised approach to protocol feature word extraction. In: Proceedings of the 33th Annual International Conference on Computer Communications, pp. 1393–1401 (2014)
22. Krueger, T., Krämer, N., Rieck, K.: ASAP: automatic semantics-aware analysis of network payloads. In: Dimitrakakis, C., Gkoulalas-Divanis, A., Mitrokotsa, A., Verykios, V.S., Saygin, Y. (eds.) PSDML 2010. LNCS, vol. 6549, pp. 50–63. Springer, Heidelberg (2010)
23. Fang, H., Tao, T., Zhai, C.: A formal study of information retrieval heuristics. In: Proceedings of ACM SIGIR, pp. 49–56 (2004)
24. Azzopardi, L., Girolami, M., van Risjbergen, K.: Investigating the relationship between language model perplexity and ir precision-recall measures. In: Proceedings of the 26th Annual International ACM SIGIR Conference on Research and Development in Informaion Retrieval, pp. 369–370 (2003)
25. Wang, Y., et al.: Using entropy to classify traffic more deeply. In: Proceedings of the 6th International Conference on Networking, Architecture and Storage (NAS), pp. 45–52 (2011)
26. Zhang, Z., Zhang, Z., Lee, P.P.C., Liu, Y., Xie, G.: Toward Unsupervised Protocol Feature Word Extraction. IEEE Journal on Selected Areas in Communications **32**(10), 1894–1906 (2014)
27. Wang, Y., Yun, X., Zhang, Y.: Rethinking robust and accurate application protocol identification: a nonparametric approach. In: Proceedings of the 23rd IEEE International Conference on Network Protocol (ICNP), pp. 1–11 (2015)

How *to Prevent* to Delegate Authentication

Mohsen Alimomeni[(✉)] and Reihaneh Safavi-Naini

University of Calgary, Calgary, AB, Canada
{malimome,rei}@ucalgary.ca

Abstract. We consider *delegation attack* in authentication systems in which a credential holder shares their credentials with a third party that we call *helper*, to allow them to use their account. We motivate this problem and propose a model for non-delegatable authentication and a novel authentication system, based on behavioural biometrics, that achieves non-delegatability. Our main observation is that a user's behaviour in complex activities such as playing a computer game, provides an imprint of many of their personal traits in the form of measurable features, that can be used to identify them. Carefully selected features will be "hard" to pass on to others, hence providing non-delegatability. As a proof of concept we designed and implemented a computer game (a complex activity), and used the feature points in the game play to construct a user model for authentication. We describe our implementation and experiments to evaluate correctness, security and non-delegatability. Compared to using traditional biometrics, the system enhances user privacy because the user model is with respect to an activity and do not have direct relation to the user's identifying information. We discuss our results and deployment of the system in practice, and propose directions for future research.

1 Introduction

We consider the problem of credential sharing, where a user wants to share their credential with a third party with the goal of bypassing the system security. We refer to this as *delegation attack*. The problem naturally arises in authentication systems (e.g. online subscription systems) where users have incentives to share their credentials and let a third party use their privileges, or assume their roles. Traditional authentication systems do not provide protection against this attack. Authentication systems use credentials such as, what a user knows (e.g. passwords, secret keys), what a user has (e.g. tokens, cards), and what a user is (biometric) to ensure correct identity claims. They may also use user *attributes* such as their expected location or distance from the verifier, to provide stronger security guarantees. In all cases security of an authentication system is primarily against an *outside attacker* who, without having access to the user credentials, tries to impersonate them.

We consider a scenario that a user actively shares their credential. In this case security of all known traditional authentication systems will be severely compromised. Systems that rely on secret keys (or passwords) and tokens cannot

© Institute for Computer Sciences, Social Informatics and Telecommunications Engineering 2015
B. Thuraisingham et al. (Eds.): SecureComm 2015, LNICST 164, pp. 477–499, 2016.
DOI: 10.1007/978-3-319-28865-9_26

provide any security guarantee. Biometric systems that rely on the user's unique characteristics (e.g. fingerprint, voiceprint) may also become insecure if the user is willing to share their biometric templates [Fid13]. Systems that use attributes such as distance of a user to the verifier usually rely on a secret key (symmetric or public key) and cannot guarantee security if the secret key is passed on.

Credential sharing is a well known problem in subscription services such as Netflix [Wor13] and online games [TBB12] and can effectively bypass the security of the subscription system. The problem is widely studied and a range of solutions including trusted hardware and tamper-proof software have been proposed. However solutions that provide sufficient usability for the system (e.g. allowing multiple devices), quickly become ineffective. In corporate world credential sharing is a known problem, commonly used for reasons such as ease of access to documents (e.g. an executive shares their password with their assistants to allow them access). A less studied problem however, is credential sharing by dishonest employees with motivations such as employing "cheap labour" from outside the company to perform one's allocated tasks, or organizing more systematic collusion (e.g. espionage) attacks to provide access to outsiders. The former case has been a real concern of software companies where employees delegate software development tasks to developer sites that offer this service [TH13]. Correct authentication of remote users is also increasingly important due to the wider adoption of work-from-home model, and the need for companies to cater for mobile workforce.

An immediate solution for providing security against credential sharing is to use additional factors such as a hardware token, in the authentication process. Tokens however, although make it harder for users to pass on their credentials, cannot protect against credential sharing: a software developer [TH13] in the US outsourced their work to a Chinese firm by sending the RSA token that was required for authentication. A second solution is to use biometric based authentication systems. Biometric templates although in general are unique to individuals, in some cases may be recorded and replayed for authentication [Fid13]. However in the above application scenarios, it is perceivable that one will not be willing to share their biometric data because of the permanency and sensitivity of this data. Biometric systems have disadvantages such as the need for extra hardware and deployment cost, in addition to careful management of the collected biometric data throughout the lifetime of the system. Using biometric authentication in corporate environment also introduces privacy concerns for employees who may move from one employer to another, and do not want to leave a biometric trace behind. A third solution is to strengthen password systems using extra behavioural features of users. Existing behavioural authentication systems capture simple users' behaviours such as keyboard typing pattern or mouse dynamics [MR00] and have no real guarantee that these behaviours cannot be taught or transferred to others. Our method can be seen as developing this approach by designing activities that capture complex non-transferable characteristics of users.

1.1   Our Work

Intuitively, to prevent delegation of authentication credential, one must use intrinsic properties of users that are "hard" to pass on to others. Such properties can be grouped into *personality traits*, and *behavioural* and *cognitive* factors. Identifying individuals using their intrinsic properties have been subject of extensive studies in psychology. Trait theory approach to personality promotes the idea that individuals can be identified through their personality traits such as abstractedness, perfectionism and reasoning. Cattell suggests 16 personality factors [Cat57] are sufficient to identify individuals. Human behaviour refers to one's actions and manners in response to stimuli (inputs) that could be internal or external, and conscious or subconscious. Human behaviour has been shown to be effective in distinguishing individuals [BSR+12,MR00]. Cognitive abilities in domains such as language, reasoning, memory, learning and visual perception, as well as higher order abilities such as intelligence, have been measured through well designed experiments and shown to be able to identify individuals [Car93]. We use *personal traits* to refer to both these types of human intrinsic properties when they are, (i) *measurable* in the interactions of users with the environment, and (ii) are relatively *stable*. Stability of a trait intuitively refers to the property that the measurements of the trait correspond to a narrow probability distribution that could be used to differentiate users in a population. Stable traits may change over time. We assume this change can be represented by a (slow) shift over time. Traits may have different levels of transferability. Some traits may be learnt or imitated by training and practice (with different degrees of success). For example, traits related to the user behaviour (personal preferences) can be learnt more easily than skill based traits such as speed of performing an action.

Our work aims to capture *trait related information* of an individual in a complex activity. A measurement in an activity is modelled by a random variable, representing in general, multiple personal traits. The *user profile* consists of these variable, also called *features*. Features are chosen to be non-delegatable in the sense that they are "hard" to be learnt by a helper that is assisted by the user. We call authentication systems built on these profiles, a *Hard to Delegate (HtD)* authentication system. As a proof of concept we designed and implemented a target shooting game to model a complex activity. In an authentication attempt a *challenge* is presented to the user and their response is received. The challenge is a game (in our case a target), and the response is a set of measurements during their game play (in our case, an arrow shot at the target). The response measurements is matched against the stored user profile. To analyze the system, we first give a formal definition of non-delegatability in authentication systems. This is a new security property that captures protection against a user credential sharing. We then use user experiments in small groups to select non-delegatable features, followed by large group experiments for evaluating correct user authentication. We also design and implement special experiments to show that the system provides protection against non-delegatability.

We note that non-delegatability is a strictly stronger security requirement than user impersonation, because the credential holder assists the attacker to succeed in impersonating them and the proposed system is also a new secure authentication system using user game play.

Selecting Features in Activities. A feature in an activity is a measurement that corresponds to a random variable X. This variable is sampled in each run of the activity, producing a *feature point x*. The randomness of the variable is due to the user's *intrinsic randomness* that results from the complex combination of their personal traits. Suitable features to support non-delegatability must be, (i) strongly correlated with stable user traits and stay stable over time and, (ii) be hard to transfer. Selecting such features in our system has been through small group experiments. The experiments (described in Section 5.3) suggests that selecting effective features is a rich direction for future research. An interesting case is *tightly coupled features* that provide strong non-delegatability. These are pairs of features that are negatively correlated, but successful impersonation requires both to be modified in the same direction. For example in our target shooting game, the speed at which a user aims at the target and the error in hitting the target are negatively correlated (i.e. reducing aim time increases error). However to imitate a (skilled) user one needs to reduce aim time and error at the same time.

Applications. Non-delegatable authentication systems can be used in conjunction with traditional password based (or key-based) authentication to provide non-delegatability. Our motivating example was providing security for work from home environment that could pose major threat to the enterprise network. Another important application is providing protection against credential sharing in massively multiplayer online (MMO) games with incentives such as bypassing subscription fees, allowing a more experienced player to play on one's behalf, or hijacking an account [CH07] to take advantage of the user's progress in the game. An important advantage of behavioural authentication system such as the one proposed in this paper is privacy enhancement because of using the behavioural attributes instead of personally identifiable information.

Ethics Approval. The experiments described in this paper involved human subjects. We obtained ethics approval from the Conjoint Faculties Research Ethics Board at the University of Calgary, under the file number 7630. The first author completed a course on ethics, entiled Ethical Conduct for Research Involving Humans Course on Research Ethics (TCPS 2: CORE). All experiments were performed in accordance with these ethics guidelines.

1.2   Related Works

Behavioural biometrics [Rev08] is a relatively new research area. Human computer interaction based biometrics such as those based on keystroke dynamics[MR00] and mouse movement [PB04], have been shown to be effective way of identifying users. In [YG09], authors showed that measuring the player's strategy in a poker game is effective for user verification. Our approach of using feature points that are behaviour based is distinctly different from collecting feature points related to the user strategy as used in [YG09] for the game of poker. This latter type of points are not chosen for non-delegatability and in fact may be delegatable. Alayed et al. [AFN13] used a first person shooter game to distinguish between normal behaviour of the players, and cheating behaviour. The output of their classifier is a binary value, indicating cheating or no cheating.

Implicit memory for authentication was proposed by Denning et al. [DBvDJ11]. Bojinov et al. [BSR+12] used implicit learning to defend against "rubber hose attacks" in authentication. Implicit learning cannot directly prevent delegation attack because a dishonest user may memorize the password during the training phases and later pass it on to the helper. HtD authentication however can achieve the goals of [DBvDJ11] and [BSR+12] without requiring password.

Paper Organization. Section 2, gives a model for HtD property. Section 3 is on behavioural biometric using complex non-debatable features. Section 4, is our proof of concept game, the collected features of users and describe the experimental setup and the results. Section 3.2 is on deployment issues and attacks on HtE games, and cheat-proofing techniques for preventing these attacks.

2 Non-delegatable Authentication

A HtD system has three computational entities, a Server S, a Client C, and a device D with three interfaces DI_1, DI_2 and DI_3, that are used to present a challenge to the user, collect the response from the user, and communicate with the network, respectively. S sends the challenge to C on the device D using DI_1. The user responds using DI_2 that is passed to C, which is finally forwarded to S via DI_3.

2.1 HtD Authentication Systems

We consider a multiparty setting where participants receive inputs and produce outputs. An honest participant follows the protocol and a dishonest one deviates arbitrarily, in all cases using probabilistic polynomial-time (PPT) algorithms. A participant can be a *prover* denoted by $\mathcal{P}$ (also referred to as a *user* U), a *verifier* denoted by $\mathcal{V}$, or an *adversary* denoted by $\mathcal{A}$. The adversary corrupts participants and uses them to defeat security of the system. The verifier V always behaves honestly. A prover however may be corrupted, in which case it is denoted by $\mathcal{P}^*$. A prover $\mathcal{P}$ has a set of attributes some measurable directly (e.g. location, IP), and some indirectly through *imprints* that are obtained during a user activity. These can be *estimated* through random variables that are measured during user activities. The random variables in general take different values in different measurement rounds, following a (slow changing) distribution. For example, the error in hitting the target in a target shooting game, carries user intrinsic attributes such as their skill level in the game play. A prover $\mathcal{P}$ thus is intrinsically probabilistic and its attributes in general can be represented as a vector of random variables[1].

Authentication Protocol. An HtD authentication protocol is a two party protocol between two interactive PPT algorithms, a trusted verifier V and a prover P. We also use V and P to refer to the verifier and the prover, respectively. A *protocol run (instance)* between P and V is denoted by $exp = V(x; r_V) \rightleftarrows P(y; r_P)$ where x and y are the private values of V and P, respectively, and r_P and r_V are the *explicit* randomness that of the verifier and prover algorithm, respectively. In some protocols (e.g. password authentication) only explicit randomness is used. However protocols can also include the intrinsic randomness of P through user activities. The experiment can be extended to include an adversary A who interacts with the parties in the system. The expanded experiment is shown by $exp = (P(x; r_P) \rightleftarrows A(r_A) \rightleftarrows V(y; r_V))$. A participant in a protocol instance has a *view* consisting of all its inputs, coins, and messages that it can see. The view of A includes all its communications with P and V. At the end of a protocol instance the verifier V outputs $out \in \{0, 1\}$ which is 1 if the authentication claim of the claiming prover is accepted, and 0 otherwise. The prover does not have an output. We use $\Pr_r[E : exp]$ to denote the probability of the event E in the protocol instance, and r to denote that random coins used in the protocol.

Definition 1. *A* Hard to Delegate (HtD) Authentication *system is a tuple* (Reg, P, V) *defined as follows. Reg is a registration protocol, run between P and V that takes a security parameter s, explicit randomness r and implicit randomness of P, and outputs (s_P, s_{V_p}) (denoted by $(s_P, s_{V_p}) \leftarrow Reg(1^s, r, V_{reg}, P_{reg}))$, where s_P and s_{V_p} are the values given to the prover P and the verifier V, respectively. We assume the protocol is always played honestly by the participants (secure registration) and treat it as a single function outputting the pair (s_P, s_{V_p}). The protocols satisfy the following properties.*

1. *Termination:*
   $(\forall s)(\forall r; r_V)$ *if* $(s_P, s_{V_p}) \leftarrow Reg(1^s; r, P_{reg}, V_{reg})$, *and for any run of the protocol* $(R \rightleftarrows V(s_P; r_V))$, *between the verifier and an (unbounded) prover algorithm R, V halts in $Poly(s)$ computational steps;*
2. δ-**correctness***: $(\forall s)$ we have*

$$Pr\left[out = 0 : \frac{(s_P, s_{V_p}) \leftarrow Reg(1^s; r, P_{reg}, V_{reg}))}{P(s_P; r_P) \rightleftarrows V(s_{V_p}; r_V)}\right] \leq \delta$$

   where $s_P \leftarrow Reg(1^s, r, V_{reg}, P_{reg})$, $\Pr[out = 1 : exp]$ is the probability that verifier outputs 1 after the experiment is completed and the probability is over the randomness $\{r; r_P; r_V\}$.
3. ϵ_d-**Delegation resistance** *(ϵ_d-HtD)]*
   The probability that an adversary A (helper colluding with the user) successfully emulates P, given access to registration information (s_P, s'_V), and after

---

[1] A vector of biometric feature points such as fingerprint minutiae that is collected from a user during an authentication session fits this definition also.

observing a number of instances of the authentication protocol $P \rightleftarrows V$, is bounded by ϵ_d:

$$
Pr \left[out = 1 : \begin{array}{c} (s_P, s_{V_p}) \leftarrow Reg(r, P_{reg}, V_{reg}) \\ P(s_P) \rightleftarrows A_1 \rightleftarrows V(s_{V_p}) \\ A_2(s_P, s'_V, View(A_1), aux) \rightleftarrows V(s_{V_p}) \end{array} \right] \leq \epsilon_d
$$

Here $(s'_P, s'_{V_p}) \leftarrow Reg(r, V_{reg}, P_{reg})$, is obtained by the interaction between P and a simulated verifier, and then given to A by P^*. The adversary is shown by a pair of algorithms, (A_1, A_2). A_1 observes authentication sessions between P and V, and provides its view to A_2. We use aux to denote other side information that P^* gives to A.

Remark: Non-delegatability is an insider collusion attack. A corrupted registered participant P^* colludes with the helper A, and gives them their registration information s_P as well as s'_{V_p} that is obtained by simulating the Reg protocol. Note that s'_P and s'_{V_p} will have the same distribution as the same intrinsic randomness of P is used. Security against delegation attack implies security against impersonation attack which is an outsider attack. This can be seen by using $A()$ with no privileged inputs instead of $A(s_P, s'_{V_p}, aux)$.

3   Authentication Games

To construct an HtD authentication system we use a challenge-response protocol where the verifier sends a challenge to the prover and receives a response. We use the following terminology and definitions. A *feature with respect to a game*, or a feature for simplicity, is a random variable that is associated with a game play and can be measured in each instance of the game play. An *identifying feature* is a complex function of one or more identifying personal traits. The measured value of a feature in a game instance is called a *feature point*. A *feature vector* is a vector of feature points that are collected in a game play.

3.1   An Authentication System Using Games

We consider the same setting of Section 2.1, and a two phase authentication system. A prover registers by participating in the registration protocol that is run by the verifier (or a trusted third party) and generates a *profile* of the user. In each instance of the game (a round of challenge-response), a vector of b feature points $F = (f_1, f_2, \ldots, f_b)$ is sampled, and sent to S as the response to the challenge. Let $R_P(n)$ denote a sequence of n feature vectors $F_1, F_2, \ldots, F_n$, that are collected in n consecutive runs of the game. $R_P(n)$ is the user *profile* held by V. That is, Reg algorithm, here the n times game play, is used to produce the profile $R_P(n)$. (For example in our target shooting game, the user will have n runs to throw the arrow at the target.) Note that a user P can always simulate V algorithm and construct $R'_P(n)$. Assuming P game play is stationary, $R'_P(n)$ will have the same distribution as $R_P(n)$. The set of users' profiles forms the profile database DB, that will be used to verify users. During the authentication phase a user will be presented with n' consecutive challenges (game instance) one by one, and the collected set of n' responses (feature vectors) form $R_P(n')$ that will be used by the verification algorithm, to decide whether $R_P(n)$ and $R_P(n')$ are generated by the same $\mathcal{P}$ (same intrinsic distribution). Let $\mathsf{mtc}(R_{P'}(n'), \mathcal{P})$ be a matching algorithm that matches a given set of feature vector $R_{P'}(n')$, against the stored profile $R_P(n)$ of the user $\mathcal{P}$. The matching algorithm uses a distance function (Section 4.2) to compute the distance between $R_{P'}(n')$ and $R_P(n)$, for all $\mathcal{P} \in DB$ and outputs Accept (1) or Reject (0) if the distance was lower than a threshold.

Correctness and Security. For correctness, the distance between $R_P(n)$ and $R_P(n')$ must be small for the same user, and the distance between $R_P(n)$ and $R_{P'}(n)$ must be large for any two distinct users in DB. For security, $\mathcal{P}$'s response must not result in the matching algorithm to output 1, assuming $\mathcal{P}'$ is given the simulated profile of $\mathcal{P}$ (i.e., $R'_P(n)$). We formalize these requirements as follows.

Definition 2. *A $(b, m, n, (\alpha, \beta), \gamma, \mathsf{mtc})$-Authentication Game is a game played between a user $\mathcal{P}$ who is a user in a set of m users, and the server S. In each instance of the game play a vector of b feature points, $(f_1, \ldots, f_b)$, is sampled. The user profile $R_P(n)$ consists of n feature vectors that are sampled in n consecutive rounds of the game. The matching algorithm mtc measures the distance of $R_P(n')$ to user profiles in DB, and outputs 1 if the distance is less than a threshold.*

1. *(α, β)- correctness:*
   - *α-FRR: For $n' < n$, the algorithm mtc outputs 1 with high probability given $R_P(n')$ and P:*

$$\Pr_P \left[\mathsf{mtc}(R_P(n'), P) \neq 1 \right] \leq \alpha.$$

   - *β-FAR: For a user $\mathcal{P}$, the probability that $R_{P'}(n')$ of user $\mathcal{P}' \neq \mathcal{P}$ is matched as $\mathcal{P}$ is bounded:*

$$\forall P, \Pr_{P' \neq P} \left[\mathsf{mtc}(R_{P'}(n'), P) = 1 \right] \leq \beta.$$

2. *γ-Hard to Emulate (HtE): A game satisfies HtE if it is "hard" (measured empirically by the required time and training) for $\mathcal{A}$ to play in lieu of $\mathcal{P}$ and result in mtc to output $\mathcal{P}$ as the matched user. We assume $\mathcal{A}$ has $R_P(n)$, and additional information including possibility of observing game play of $\mathcal{P}$, denoted by Obs. Let $R_A(n')$ denote a set of n' feature vectors collected from $\mathcal{A}$'s game play when it is playing in lieu of $\mathcal{P}$. We require*

$$\Pr_{A \neq P} \left[\mathsf{mtc}(R_A(n'), P) = 1 \mid \mathcal{I} = \{R_P(n), Obs\} \right] \leq \gamma,$$

holds for all P where $\mathcal{I}$ denotes the additional information available to $\mathcal{A}$.

Proposition 1. *An $(b, m, n, (\alpha, \beta), \gamma, \mathsf{mtc})$-authentication game is an authentication system satisfying definition 3, providing δ-correctness, and ϵ_d-resistance against delegation attack. We have $\delta = \alpha + \beta$, $\epsilon_d = \gamma$ and $s = f(b, m, n)$.*

The proposition follows by comparing definitions 1 and 2 and noting that in an authentication game, errors in honest game play of users will be in the form of FRR and FAR. A more detailed argument will be provided in the final version of the paper.

Feature Selection. Features are in general complex functions of multiple personal traits and can range from those that are mostly skill based and so learnable, to those that have deeper cognitive and behavioural base and so harder to learn by others.

Orthogonal Features. Our experiments show that one can use more features to increase accuracy of user authentication. In some cases a similar level of distinguishability can be obtained by reducing the number of features that are less correlated.

Tightly Coupled Features. For security against delegation attack features must be "hard" to transfer to others. For example, choosing objects in categories (e.g. clothing, pets) can be considered a personal trait that can form a feature in a game play. However such preferences cannot be used for HtE authentication as one can effectively pass on their preferences to others. To reduce the success chance of delegation, tightly coupled features can be chosen. These are dependent pairs and an attempt to change one will affect the other. For example, precision and speed of doing a task are tightly coupled features and increasing precision needs higher concentration and so more time, which will decrease the speed of performing the task. Tightly coupled features must be transferred together and this increases the difficulty of training the helper. In the above example training the helper to mimic higher precision of a skilled player should be together with mimicking their higher speed of playing the game.

3.2   Deploying Authentication Games

We analyzed the proposed authentication mechanism assuming a system design that enforces authentication by playing the game. *1- Overtaking network communication:* where the helper injects data packets directly into the network without playing the game. This attack would be successful if a fixed game is used and the user's response can be recorded. *2- Modifying the game client:* where the client software is modified to change the data input by the user to match the stored profile. *3- Automated game play (bot)* where a software is trained to emulate the behaviour of the legitimate prover in the game play. In our game, each challenge is freshly generated and developing a software agent that can learn the user behaviour in a complex game play requires major effort in learning theory and implementation to produce correct response in real time. In Appendix 6 we outline the prevention mechanisms against these attacks.

4   A Proof of Concept HtE Game

Our proposed HtE authentication game is an archery target shooting game. The game has a number of levels. In each level eight features, three primarily skill based, and five mostly behaviour based, are measured. More details on these features are given in Section 4.1. The game provides a clear goal for users to focus on. This is important for providing consistent game play statistics.

4.1   The Game Design

The implementation uses a 2D Physics engine to simulate the shooting of an arrow towards a target. The player drags and tilts the arrow (for example by using mouse) to choose the initial speed and the angle of throw, and release it to the target. The user wins if the arrow hits the centre of the target

Features Selection. In each shot of the arrow the following features are sampled. t_1-*Hit Error*. The distance between the arrow and center of the target after hitting. This is a floating point number in the interval $[-120, 120]$ as shown in Fig. 2.

Fig. 1. Screen-shot of the game

Fig. 2. Hit error

t_2-*Aiming time*. The time in milliseconds that it takes for the player to aim and shoot at the target. This is the time difference between the start of dragging and when the arrow is released which is a positive floating point number in $(0, 10]$. t_3-*Wait time*. The time in milliseconds that it takes for the player to begin dragging a new arrow, after the game is reset . This is a positive floating point number in the $(0, 5]$. t_4, t_5-*Relative initial Mouse click coordinates*. The x, y coordinates of the mouse initial clicking on the screen to drag the arrow, relative to the coordinate of the arrow's tail as the center. These are two floating point numbers greater than 0 and independent of the screen resolution. t_6, t_7-*Initial velocity and angle*. The velocity and relative angle of the arrow when it is released toward the target. t_8-*Miss count*. The number of misses between each two successful shots.

We note that the only varying parameter in the game that affects the measurements of features (e.g. t_1 and t_7) is the target location (in level 4). For both features, we measure them relative to the location of the target center. This makes the user feature points independent of the game parameters and our experiments shows stability of the values of these features over time. Features t_1, t_2, t_6, t_7 and t_8 are mostly based on personal traits such as concentration and cognition, reaction time and coordination: they measure precision and speed of a player in aiming at the target (selecting the angle and velocity of the arrow) considering the variable parameters of the game. Features t_3, t_4 and t_5, measure traits that are mostly subconscious including personal preference in where the arrow is grabbed. Our experiments show that decreasing the hit error and aiming time at the same time, is hard. Thus the pairs (t_1, t_2) and (t_2, t_8) are tightly coupled features: a player trying to decrease the hit error, needs to increase the time of aiming at the target. Our experiments suggest that the features $t_1, \ldots, t_8$ are stable and using consecutive measurements can identify users in a group (Section 5). Removing each of the features from the user game-play will reduce FAR and FRR.

Game Levels. The game design has evolved over a period of 2 months as we performed continued tests with 4 local participants. For our final evaluation using Amazon Mechanical Turks, we used 4 levels. Our observations on the affect of the design on the correctness and security are summarized in Section 5. In the first three levels of the 4 level game, the location of the target is fixed. The first level is the easiest: the target is fixed in the center of the screen and the player has to choose the speed and the angle of throw, and hit the center of the target. In the second level, there is a blocking wall that prevents the player to shoot at the target in straight line (Fig. 1. The player must adjust the angle and speed to prevent hitting the wall. The third level is the same as the first, but the target has a vertical periodic (sinusoidal) movement, and the player must predict the location of the target before releasing the arrow. The forth level is different from the previous 3 levels: the target will jump around and changes its location. It also fades away, and so forces the player to release the arrow within the time period that the target is visible. Otherwise the chance of hitting the target reduces.

4.2   Verification Function

The verification function is a matching algorithm that matches the user response in an authentication attempt against a stored profile. The stored profile $R_P(n)$ is a set of $n = 120$ feature vectors that are collected during the registration phase when the correct user is playing n rounds of the game challenge and response. Each authentication attempt consists of $n' = 30$ rounds of the game challenge and responses, where a user claims identity $\mathcal{P}$. The user profile is stored in the database DB indexed by the user identity and is used to match $R_P(n')$. We experimented with a number of candidate matching algorithms including SVM and random forest method, and chose the following algorithm because it provided the best accuracy (lowest FAR and FRR). The verification function takes as input two sets of feature vectors $R_P(n)$ and $R_{P'}(n')$ and outputs a bit, 1 or 0. The verification function estimates the probability distributions of features using the two sets of feature vectors, and compares the two distributions using statistical distance.

Converting Samples to Distribution. To construct a probability distribution for a feature from the profile (or an authentication attempt), one can construct the corresponding histograms (by defining bins and counting the number of samples in each bin), and then find a suitable parametrized density function that fits the data. Parameters of the density function will be determined using a goodness of fit algorithm, resulting in the probability distribution.

Our empirical results showed that *cumulative distribution function* (cdf) is more effective in distinguishing users. Our goal was thus to construct the cdf associated with a set of feature vectors, $R_P(n) = (F_1, F_2, \ldots, F_n)$, where $F_i = \{f_{1i}, f_{2i}, \ldots, f_{bi}\}, i \in [n]$. Here f_{ji} is the ith measurement of the feature f_j. Constructing the cdf of a multi-dimensional variable depends on the order that the variables are considered (corresponding to feature) and so the final distribution will depend on this order. To overcome this problem, we construct the cdf of each variable independently, use each to calculate a score for the corresponding feature in the authentication data, and then combine the results using the weighted average of these scores. To estimate the cdf of a feature f_j, we first extract the values of f_j from the set of feature vectors $C_j = \{f_{j1}, f_{j2}, \ldots, f_{jn}\}$. Assuming that the elements of C_j are samples of a distribution X, we want to estimate $\mathsf{cdf}(X)$ given by $\mathsf{cdf}(x) = \Pr[X \leq x]$, for a probability distribution $\Pr(X)$. Since we do not have the probability distribution X, we estimate the cdf which we call *empirical distribution function* (edf) by,

$$\mathsf{edf}_{C_j}(x) = \Pr_n[X \leq x] = \frac{1}{n} \sum_{i=1}^{n} I(C_{ji} \leq x),$$ where C_{ji} is the ith element in C_j,

and the function I returns 1 if the input condition is true and 0 otherwise. Thus $\mathsf{edf}_{C_j}(x)$ outputs the fraction of the sample points below value x.

The Distance Function. Given two sets of samples C_j, C'_j of size n and m respectively, we calculate the score as,

$$\mathsf{score}_j = \left(\frac{mn}{m+n}\right)^{1/2} \max_x \left| \mathsf{edf}_{C_j}(x) - \mathsf{edf}_{C'_j}(x) \right|.$$

score_j measures the distance between the two empirical distributions associated with the two sets of sample data. This function had been used in the *Kolmogorov-Smirnov (KS)* test as a measure of similarity between two datasets. The KS test measures the probability that two datasets are generated by the same distribution. The score is illustrated in Fig. 3 for 4 features measured in the game.

Finally, for the two sets of feature vectors $R_P(n)$ and $R_P(n')$, we define the score as a weighted sum of score_j for $j \in [b]$, $\mathsf{score} = \sum_{j=1}^{b} w_j \mathsf{score}_j$, where w_j is the weight of the feature j. The *score* can be considered as a measure of the likelihood that two sets of feature vectors are drawn from the same multivariate distribution. For a given profile $R_P(n)$ of user P and a response set $R_P(n')$, the verification function outputs 1 if the score is less than a threshold τ.

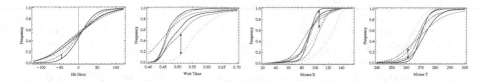

Fig. 3. The smooth edf of the features for 7 random users

5   Experiments

These experiments can be broadly divided into two groups and were performed over a six months period with a total of 186 users. There were 4 local users who participated in our experiments from the design stage, and allowed us to refine the design and parameter selection of the game. For the evaluation of our final design we used Amazon Mechanical Turks. The collected data from this latter group were filtered appropriately to exclude outliers as will be explained below. Our evaluation consists of two types of experiments, first for evaluating correctness and security as given in section 5.2, and second HtE property of the authentication game given in section 5.3.

Graphs in this Section. The figures used in this section illustrate the values of features measured through game play of users. The x-axis represent the feature value and the y-axis is frequency, or probability in the case of PDF or CDF. The graphs describe user behaviour as follows. Graphs for the timing of action such as targeting and wait time, shows the time spent for each feature. The user has spent less time for a feature, if the graph is towards the y-axis with higher peaks closer to value $x = 0$. For the feature "hit error", the user is more skilled in hitting the center of the target if the graph peak is around $x = 0$.

5.1   Considerations in Using Amazon Mechanical Turk

We had to ensure that users play the game consistently and to the best of their ability, and not at random and inconsistent way. To achieve this goal, users were instructed to play the game to achieve a minimum score at each level of the game. The minimum was set to be achievable by the weakest users. In each phase, the users were required to play the game for a required number of rounds without delay in between rounds. We measured timing parameters from the game to verify the users followed the requirements.

We note that feature measurements in general will be affected by the device and software platform including screen resolution or CPU speed. This is a known problem in behavioural authentication system that can be handled by considering multiple profiles for each user and introducing appropriate restrictions during deployment of the system.

5.2   Experiment 1: Correctness and Security

For correctness and security evaluation, we recruited approximately 150 Mechanical Turks, with only 97 of them passing our minimum requirements. Thus 101 users were used in the experiment, including our colleagues.

In the registration phase we collected 120 feature vectors (120 shots to the target) from each user, and in the authentication phase collected 30 feature vectors (on average taking around two minutes to complete) . The data for both phases were collected during a 6 hour period with roughly an hour in between registration and verification. This is to remove effect of learning, change of user experience and the like in measuring correctness. We will deal with these issues separately in Section 5.2.

Correctness (Single User). Our experiments showed that the measured features are fairly stable for user's recorded profiles. This means that the change in the values are so small that does not affect the matching algorithm. We examined users' data in two consecutive time slots and then constructed a histogram of the measurements. Fig. 4 is the histogram (cdf) for the two consecutive measurements for the two features, hit error and aim time, for one user.

In this experiment, we measured the stability of feature values during registration and authentication phases. We measured the distance (as described in Section 4.2) between the profile of the users constructed in the registration phase, and the measured feature vectors during authentication phase. The graphs in Fig. 4 are the histograms of the measured feature points of two features, hit error and aiming time. In each graph, the feature points during the registration and authentication are plotted separately. For 91 users (out of 101), the distance function outputs a very small difference between the registration and authentication data. This shows the stability of features during the two measurements indicating correctness of authentication game. Fig. 4 shows stability of measurements when performed in two consecutive time slots.

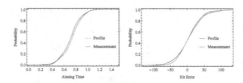

Fig. 4. User verification accuracy; measurements matching the profile

User Learnability and Profile Update. An important issue is the usage of the system over time. When a user profile is constructed at time t_1, one expects all (most) authentication attempts at times $t > t_1$ be successful. However, the change in the user's behaviour and skill over time could result in failed authentication attempt. We asked users to make login attempts over a period of 5 days. Each user on average made 20 login attempts at each level of the game. Fig. 5 shows the change in user behaviour over this period.

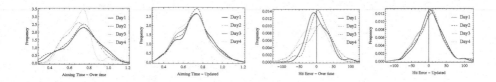

Fig. 5. The smooth histogram of the feature points for 1 user, illustrating how the features change over time.

There are 4 sub-figures in Fig. 5 illustrating the changes of two features, namely aiming time and hit error, over time. All sub-figures are extracted from one user data but the trends were the same for all users. The two sub-figures on the left show the behaviour of the user over time for 5 distinct measurements in the order numbered in the sub-figure legend. As shown in the sub-figures on the left, the behaviour and skill of users change over time and this can result in higher false negative in the matching algorithm. For example for the sub-figure related to aiming time feature, as the user becomes more experienced, less time is spent on aiming the arrow. For example, comparing the graphs on days 1 and 3, the peak of the graph 1 is on feature point 0.75 (seconds) compared to the peak 0.7 (seconds) in graph 3. The average value of aim time decreases as the user becomes more experienced in the game. For the sub-figure related to the hit error, the user's behaviour changes over time, but not necessarily towards lower error.

To compensate the affect of behaviour and skill change, the profiles of users were updated upon each successful login. The sub-figures on the right of Fig. 5 illustrates how updating the profile alleviates this problem. In the sub-figures on the right, the measurements are performed in the same order. For the measurements on days 1 and 3 the profile is updated, and authentication measurements on day 2 and 4 are compared against profile 1 and 3 respectively for verification. The results show that profile update is an important factor in accurate authentication over time. Without profile update around 70% of the authentication attempts (average over all users) failed, and this was mainly after a number of successful verification attempts. With profile update the same collected data showed 93% success rate in verification.

Security Against Impersonation: Multiple Users. Here the goal is to evaluate performance of the system in detecting a false claim: that is a user P' claiming to be P. In this experiment, we used the matching algorithm of Section 4.2 to evaluate how the feature points can distinguish users. The threshold was set to have a low FAR (level 4). Fig. 6 and 3 illustrate the histogram (pdf and cdf resp.) of feature points of 7 users' profiles. The user's histograms were distinguishable and the matching algorithm could correctly verify 91 out of 101 users. From the 9 users who were not verified, 4 were very close to the verification threshold. The other 5 users (all from Mechanical Turk) were far from their

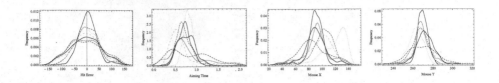

Fig. 6. The smooth histogram of the feature points for 7 users, illustrating how the features can distinguish among a group of people.

profile. However because of using Turks, it was not possible to ensure that the game plays were generated by the same user.

Entropy of the Authentication Information. The simplest attack on an authentication system is guessing attack where the attacker guesses the responses to the challenges. We used min-entropy which is the best success chance of guessing a variable, to measure guessability of a user profile. The measurements used NIST tests for estimating min-entropy explained in [BK12]. The measurements shows that the feature vector for each shot in the game has on average (over all users) at least 32 bits of entropy and so for 30 shots guessing entropy is $960 = 30 \times 32$ bits, making guessing attack impossible.

5.3   Experiment 2: HtE Property

We considered HtE property in the following scenario. A user registers to the system by playing the required number of game instances. The authentication information are passed on to a helper who will try to authenticate as the user. To evaluate HtE property, we considered an experiment where a group of users (helpers) all (independently) aim to emulate a target user. This would give us an estimate of the fraction of population who could successfully emulate the target user. Intuitively, this fraction would depend on the skillfulness of the target player. We chose two skill levels: a higher skill level and a lower skill level. There were a number of challenges in performing the experiment. Firstly, we had to ensure that the users (helpers) are incentivized to do their best to emulate the target users. We provided this incentive to Mechanical Turks who played the role of the helper, by offering a bonus of $20 for the task of successful emulation of the target, in addition to the standard payment. We also provided information that were "helpful" to the Turks so that they can modify their game play towards the target user. Providing plain user profile was soon proved to be not useful. Therefore, we initially provided a set of information about the target user to the Turks, and then provided feedback after each authentication attempt. The set of information included i) a video recording of the target user playing the game, and ii) the statistics of the feature points in the target user's profile such as maximum, minimum and average values of each of the features. The feedback information included i) the statistics of the feature points in the Turk's data from each verification attempt (Table 2), ii) direct instructions on how the user should change behaviour to match the target user as in Table 1, and iii) the graphs comparing the distribution of the target user's profile and the Turk's verification attempt as in Figures 7 (c,d).

In our experiments we hired 2 local users, one a more skilled user and a less skilled one, as delegation targets. We hired 15 Mechanical Turks and 2 local users to emulate each of the target users. The 2 target users also tried to emulate each other, so the total number of participants (who satisfied our requirements) was 36. The Mechanical Turks were selected with varying skill levels, based on their previous scores, and new users who had not played the game before. These choices were to make the experiments unbiased. The user tried to emulate the behaviour of the target users at least 20 times over a period of 5 hours. The task was allowed to be continued if the users were interested in making more attempts to win the bonus payment. In total we had, 904 and 1606 login attempts to emulate the behaviours of the user 1 and 2 respectively.

Our first observation in evaluating HtE property is that any false positives in authentication phase implies that HtE property will not be satisfied. In other words, if the authentication algorithm matches authentication attempts of user A to the profile of user B, this implies that user A can emulate the behaviour of user B. So in experiment 5.2, we counted the number of users who could authenticate as another user. Note that in experiment 5.2, the users were not asked to emulate the behaviour of another user. But their data was close enough to another user that resulted in a false positive.

HtE Property of the Game. A player X from Mechanical Turk was given the following information about the target player Y (local): the record of feature measurements, feature statistics (average, min, max), graphs of feature points (as used by the verification algorithm), the information from visually observing the game play of Y and instructions on how to change behaviour to get closer to user Y. With this, player X had to emulate user Y in several authentication rounds, each consisting of 30 game plays. After each round, we provided feedback (increase or decrease the feature values) to X on how to change their game play to get closer to the target. The player X was also told about how the matching algorithm rated the feature points compared to Y's profile. We had asked player X to play as themselves in their first attempt so that we could compare and measure the progress in the behaviour emulation. We repeated this experiment with direct supervision of the 4 local users, trying to emulate the behaviour of the two target users.

Table 1. Instructions provided after each attempt

Increase aiming time by 0.5 seconds.
Decrease wait time by 0.3 seconds.
Decrease hit error by 10 pixels.
Increase Mouse X by 20 pixels.

Table 2. Statistical information of behaviour

Feature	Min	Max	Average
Aiming time	0.5	2.3	1.2
Wait time	0.2	1.3	0.7
Hit error	-89.45	56.31	5.3

The Affect of Tightly Coupled Features. From the 36 users attempting to emulate the behaviour of our players, three Turks could emulate the behaviour of the local users. However, only one Turk could repeat their success in emulating the behaviour of the weaker user such that the matching algorithm outputs 1 in around 26% of the attempts. We note that the behaviour of this participant was relatively close to the weaker user in their first attempt. The other two participants could only emulate the behaviour of the local users once or twice in all their attempts. In total, for 1606 attempts to emulate the behaviour of the stronger user, only 2 attempts were successful and matching algorithm output 1 with 95% success. For the weaker local user however, out of 904 emulation attempts, 13 attempts were successful.

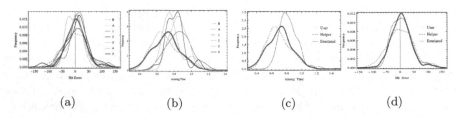

(a)   (b)   (c)   (d)

Fig. 7. (a,b) HtE property; measurements for two single features (c,d) Increase in hit error results in increase in aiming time.

Fig. 7 (a,b) illustrates the attempts made by a user to emulate a second user. The histogram of feature measurements of user X is shown in dashed line before passing on Y's information. The histogram of feature measurements of user Y (from Y's profile) are shown in a blue thick lines. The remaining graphs correspond to attempts made by user X to emulate the behaviour of user Y for two sample features, hit error and aiming time. As shown in the figures, user X has lower hit error initially, while aiming time is roughly similar to Y. But an attempt to increase the hit error results in longer aiming time, even when X is trained to emulate the behaviour of user Y. Therefore user X could not emulate both features at the same time. This is illustrated in Fig. 7 (c,d) for one attempt to simulate the behaviour of another user. In general, time and coordinate related features were harder to emulate. For example the difference in wait time of two users, although it could distinguish the users, but was not significant so that a user can emulate the exact delay of the second user[2].

Stronger Versus Weaker Users: Our experiments showed that it is easier to emulate the behaviour of weaker users compared to the more skilled users and for the former group, a helper could improve its emulation of the target user. For strong users however, some of the users could not have any progress in their emulation attempt and the rest could not get close enough to the behaviour of the target user.

---

[2] The user trying to emulate a second user had this comment: "How can I delay for 0.3 seconds more in each game play?!"

Game Design and Parameters. The game was developed over a period of few months taking into account the effect of varying parts of the game on accuracy of authentication and the HtE property. Using the feedback of the 4 local users, the game variables including the gravitational force, the speed of target movement, appearance of obstacle in the arrow path, and making the target hidden, were modified to examine their effect on correctness, security and HtE properties. We finally selected 4 levels (described in Section 4.1) for the main experiments. Variations such as target movement in the game can significantly reduce convergence of user profiles. This observation was supported by our experiments as shown below. The value of FRR for the 4 levels of the game is 28%, 18%, 24%, 9% and value of FAR is 12%, 6%, 13%, 6% respectively. As can be seen, level 4 results in the lowest FRR and FAR and thus is more suitable for providing non-delegatability. The target in level 4 fades in and out in different locations and this makes it harder to achieve higher scores. The issue that may rise here is that the variations may cause instable feature measurements over time. However, relative measurements (to the variations in the game) can mitigate this issue.

6   Deploying Authentication Games

In the following, we discuss possible attacks and prevention mechanisms on authentication games. There is an ongoing research on the topic of cheat prevention in online games that enables hackers to modify the client, or change the network communication so that they win without playing. A survey and classification of these attacks can be found in [WK12]. The success of an online multi-player game is very much dependent on its fairness among players and thus gaming industry invests on developing anti-cheating mechanisms due to its financial significance.

In the following sections, we will summarize the methods in this line of work that can be used to protect a HtE game against the three mentioned attacks.

Tampering with Network Communication. In this attack the delegatee uses a trained software that can emulate the behaviour of a legitimate prover, to bypass the game client and sends the information to the verifier over network. To prevent this attack we assume a secure communication between the verifier and game client. This can be achieved by obfuscating a shared key K inside the game client. We assume this key is not retrievable/modifiable by the users of the system, neither the prover, not the delegatee. Note that *we do not restrict access to the same game client software by any party*, so the delegatee may acquire a copy of the game client with the same shared key. Assuming the shared key, a secure authentication mechanism can be implemented in the game client to prevent any tampering with the network, including replay attack where the delegatee only replays the responses from the prover. We note that this is not a full proof solution, but it is assumed in many cheat-proofing mechanisms for games [HARD10] as it effectively prevents cheating.

Game Client Modifications. The delegatee might modify the client to bypass the authentication system in two ways. First by installing a cheat along with the game client as a patch or loadable module to help in emulating the behaviour of the prover, and in second method by retrieving/modifying the shared key with the verifier to be able to tamper with the network communication. To mitigate these attacks, authors in [TBB12] propose to symbolically execute the client to find the constraints on the state of the client implied by the responses received from it, and then using constraint solvers to find if such constraints could be generated by user input. An extension of this approach was proposed in [HARD10] which uses Accountable virtual machines (AVM). In this approach, the game is run in a virtual machine that monitors the state of the game during user game play and outputs a log of the game events (e.g. mouse click, key stroke, etc) which will be sent to the verifier. Having all the logs, the verifier can simulate running the game with the events in the log to find inconsistencies. There are also solutions based on tamper-resistant hardware [BM07] that use a dedicated hardware to check the state of the client.

Automated Game Play (bot). A game bot is a software/hardware agent that can emulate game play. In this attack, a game bot can be trained to be able to emulate the behaviour of the prover, without client modification or tampering with the network. For example one type of game bots can generate the sequence of mouse clicks and key strokes to play the game, by image processing the game environment. Depending on the graphics of the game, such tools can get very complex and harder to implement. There are general protection mechanisms to mitigate these attack such as Intel hardware protection mechanism [SGJ07], and software techniques such as human interactive proofs (e.g. Captcha) [MY12]. In [GWXW09], human observational proofs (HOP) are used to distinguish between human and bots. HOPs differentiate bots from human players by monitoring actions taken by the player that are difficult for a bot to perform. [CPC08] tries to distinguish human behaviour from bots by arguing that certain human behaviours are difficult to perform by a bot because they are AI-hard. Note that the methods in [GWXW09, CPC08] collect feature from game play and can be simply incorporated into our proposal by unifying the collected features and doing further analysis on the feature vector to detect bots, and then verify the identity of prover.

D-MiM Attacks. In a delegation Man-in-the-Middle attack (D-MiM) the helper forwards the challenge to the colluder, receive its response and passes it on to the verifier. This attack is only possible if the colluding prover is on-line at the time of the challenge. Although this is a valid attack if the time is coordinated before hand, it becomes increasingly hard if the verifier use the system in *continuous authentication* mode (e.g. in scenario of work-at-home) and send challenge blocks at random times to the user. Similar to other MiM attack, providing protection against D-MiM can be achieved by using extra mechanisms such as distance bounding protocols to verify the distance of the user from the verifier. Note that although distance bounding protocols are primarily for wireless environments, there are distance bounding protocols that work over the Internet. Distance bounding over wired networks has been considered in a number of works. Drimer et al. [DM07] proposed to use DB over wired networks to prevent relay attacks between bank terminals and smart cards. Watson et al. [WSNA+12] also proposed DB to estimate the location of a server over a wired network which describes a method to achieve an estimation error of 67 km for distance.

7   Concluding Remarks

We proposed a novel approach to challenge response authentication using behavioural biometrics in a complex activity. Exploring possible activities that can be used for user authentication, and feature selection for these activities is an interesting direction for future work. Another important direction for future work is privacy of user data. A user profile is a set of feature vectors that is only meaningful with respect to the activity. Developing a privacy model and evaluating it experimentally is also an interesting direction for future research.

Acknowledgement. This research is in part supported by Natural Sciences and Engineering Research Council of Canada.

References

[AFN13]   Alayed, H., Frangoudes, F., Neuman, C.: Behavioral-based cheating detection in online first person shooters using machine learning techniques. In: 2013 IEEE Conference on Computational Intelligence in Games (CIG), pp. 1–8, August 2013

[BK12]   Barker, E., Kelsey, J.: Recommendation for the entropy sources used for random bit generation, August 2012. http://csrc.nist.gov/publications/drafts/800-90/draft-sp800-90b.pdf

[BM07]   Balfe, S., Mohammed, A.: Final fantasy – securing on-line gaming with trusted computing. In: Xiao, B., Yang, L.T., Ma, J., Muller-Schloer, C., Hua, Y. (eds.) ATC 2007. LNCS, vol. 4610, pp. 123–134. Springer, Heidelberg (2007)

[BSR+12]   Bojinov, H., Sanchez, D., Reber, P., Boneh, D., Lincoln, P.: Neuroscience meets cryptography: designing crypto primitives secure against rubber hose attacks. In: Proceedings of the 21st USENIX Conference on Security Symposium, Security 2012, pp. 33–33. USENIX Association, Berkeley (2012)

[Car93]   Carroll, J.B.: Human Cognitive Abilities. Cambridge University Press (1993)

[Cat57]   Cattell, R.: Personality and motivation structure and measurement (1957). http://psychology.about.com/od/trait-theories-personality/a/16-personality-factors.htm

[CH07]   Chen, K.-T., Hong, L.-W.: User identification based on game-play activity patterns. In: Proceedings of the 6th ACM SIGCOMM Workshop on Network and System Support for Games, NetGames 2007, pp. 7–12. ACM, New York (2007)

[CPC08] Chen, K.-T., Kenneth Pao, H.-K., Chang, H.-C.: Game bot identification based on manifold learning. In: Proceedings of the 7th ACM SIGCOMM Workshop on Network and System Support for Games, NetGames 2008, pp. 21–26. ACM, New York (2008)

[DBvDJ11] Denning, T., Bowers, K., van Dijk, M., Juels, A.: Exploring implicit memory for painless password recovery. In: Proceedings of the SIGCHI Conference on Human Factors in Computing Systems, CHI 2011, pp. 2615–2618. ACM, New York (2011)

[DM07] Drimer, S., Murdoch, S.J.: Keep your enemies close: distance bounding against smartcard relay attacks. In: Proceedings of 16th USENIX Security Symposium on USENIX Security Symposium, SS 2007, pp. 7: 1–7: 16. USENIX Association, Berkeley (2007)

[Fid13] Fiddy, H.O.: Method and system for defeat of replay attacks against biometric authentication systems, US Patent 8,508,338 (2013)

[GWXW09] Gianvecchio, S., Zhenyu, W., Xie, M., Wang, H.: Battle of botcraft: fighting bots in online games with human observational proofs. In: Proceedings of the 16th ACM Conference on Computer and Communications Security, CCS 2009, pp. 256–268. ACM, New York (2009)

[HARD10] Haeberlen, A., Aditya, P., Rodrigues, R., Druschel, P.: Accountable virtual machines. In: Proceedings of the 9th USENIX Conference on Operating Systems Design and Implementation, OSDI 2010, pp. 1–16. USENIX Association, Berkeley (2010)

[MR00] Monrose, F., Rubin, A.D.: Keystroke dynamics as a biometric for authentication. Future Generation Computer Systems 16(4), 351–359 (2000)

[MY12] McDaniel, R., Yampolskiy, R.V.: Development of embedded captcha elements for bot prevention in fischer random chess. Int. J. Comput. Games Technol., p. 2:2 (2012)

[PB04] Pusara, M., Brodley, C.E.: User re-authentication via mouse movements. In: Proceedings of the 2004 ACM Workshop on Visualization and Data Mining for Computer Security, pp. 1–8. ACM (2004)

[Rev08] Revett, K., Biometrics, B.: A Remote Access Approach. John Wiley & Sons Ltd. (2008)

[SGJ07] Schluessler, T., Goglin, S., Johnson, E.: Is a bot at the controls?: detecting input data attacks. In: Proceedings of the 6th ACM SIGCOMM Workshop on Network and System Support for Games, NetGames 2007, pp. 1–6. ACM, New York (2007)

[TBB12] Tian, H.Y., Brooke, P.J., Bosser, A.-G.: Behaviour-based cheat detection in multiplayer games with event-B. In: Derrick, J., Gnesi, S., Latella, D., Treharne, H. (eds.) IFM 2012. LNCS, vol. 7321, pp. 206–220. Springer, Heidelberg (2012)

[TH13] Thanh Ha, T.: Us developer outsourced his job to china (2013). http://www.theglobeandmail.com/technology/how-a-model-employee-got-away-with-outsourcing-his-software-job-to-china/article7409256/3/

[WK12] Woo, J., Kim, H.K.: Survey and research direction on online game security. In: Proceedings of the Workshop at SIGGRAPH Asia, WASA 2012, pp. 19–25. ACM, New York (2012)

[Wor13] Wortham, J.: No tv? no subscription? no problem (2013). http://www.nytimes.com/2013/04/07/business/streaming-sites-and-the-rise-of-shared-accounts.html

[WSNA+12] Watson, G.J., Safavi-Naini, R., Alimomeni, M., Locasto, M.E., Narayan, S.: Lost: location based storage. In: Proceedings of the 2012 ACM Workshop on Cloud Computing Security Workshop, CCSW 2012, pp. 59–70. ACM, New York (2012)

[YG09] Yampolskiy, R.V., Govindaraju, V.: Strategy based behavioural biometrics: a novel approach to automated identification. Int. J. Comput. Appl. Technol. **35**(1), 29–41 (2009)

Ciphertext-Policy Attribute-Based Encryption with User and Authority Accountability

Xing Zhang[1(✉)], Cancan Jin[2], Cong Li[2], Zilong Wen[2], Qingni Shen[2], Yuejian Fang[2], and Zhonghai Wu[2]

[1] School of Electronics Engineering and Computer Science, Peking University, Beijing, China
novostary@163.com
[2] School of Software and Microelectronics, Peking University, Beijing, China
jincancan1992@126.com, li.cong@pku.edu.cn, 450275803@qq.com,
{qingnishen,fangyj,zhwu}@ss.pku.edu.cn

Abstract. To ensure the security of sensitive data, people need to encrypt them before uploading them to the public storage. Attribute-based encryption (ABE) is a promising cryptographic primitive for fine-grained sharing of encrypted data. However, ABE lacks user and authority accountability. The user can share his/her secret key without being identified, while key generation center (KGC) can generate any user's secret key. In this paper, we propose a practical large universe ciphertext-policy ABE (CP-ABE) with user and authority accountability in the white-box model. As embedding the user's identity information into this user's secret key directly, the trace stage has only $O(1)$ time overhead. The property of accountability is proved against the dishonest user and KGC in the standard model. We implement our scheme in Charm. Experiments show that CP-ABE of Rouselakis and Waters in CCS 2013 is enhanced in user and authority accountability by our method with small computational cost.

Keywords: Attribute-Based Encryption · User accountability · Authority accountability · White-box model

1   Introduction

Cloud computing is changing the way we deliver large-scale web applications. Various computing resources are delivered as services over the Internet. The openness and sharing of cloud has caused important issues of information security. More and more enterprises and individuals choose to put their data into the cloud. However, cloud service providers are generally assumed to be untrusted parties, that is, they may be curious about the content of their users' data for advertising or even sell the data to data owner's competitors. A natural solution is that data owners should encrypt sensitive data before outsourcing them. Attribute-based encryption (ABE), as an excellent cryptographic access control mechanism, is quite preferable for sharing of encrypted outsourced data.

The concept of ABE was first proposed by Sahai and Waters in 2005 [21]. Then ABE comes into two flavors, key-policy ABE (KP-ABE) [10,19,2] and ciphertext-policy ABE (CP-ABE) [4,8,25]. In KP-ABE, ciphertexts are associated with sets of attributes and user's secret keys are associated with access structures. When ciphertexts are created, data owners do not know who will have access to them later.

B. Thuraisingham et al. (Eds.): SecureComm 2015, LNICST 164, pp. 500–518, 2015.
DOI: 10.1007/978-3-319-28865-9_27

KP-ABE focuses on the specific need of user. Whatever user needs, key generation center (KGC) will generate secret keys corresponding to the proper access structures. In CP-ABE, the situation is the opposite. Users' secret keys are labeled by attributes and ciphertexts are associated with access structures. Before encrypting, the data owner clearly knows what kind of people is allowed to access.

Nevertheless, ABE has a major drawback which is known as the lack of user accountability. As secret keys do not include identity information, a dishonest user need not worry about being caught if this user shares his/her secret key with others or produces a pirate decryption device and sells it on the Internet. Almost all ABE systems suffer from this problem which does not exist in traditional public key encryption (PKE) as users' public keys are certificated with their identities by public key infrastructure (PKI). Thus the general method for user accountability is to embed the identity-related information to the user's secret key. Notice that ABE is a one-to-many communication and its public key in the conventional sense consists of public parameters and attribute sets.

In addition, there is also another problem named the lack of authority accountability. As KGC in ABE has the power to generate secret key for any user with any attribute set, it is hard to distinguish whether the traitor founded by using the technique of user accountability is innocent or not. The general method is to embed secret information which is hidden from the KGC's view into the user's secret key. That secret information can be called key family number [9], which means there are a cluster of secret keys related with each user. We can tell that KGC is to blame if the key family number of the suspected key does not match with that of the accessible users.

There are two models about accountability, white-box model and black-box model. In white-box model, we can get the content of secret key of suspected user. While in black-box model, the secret key is encapsulated in a decryption box. A judge should be able to decide if this box was created by a dishonest user or KGC only by constructing the input and observing the output of the box. Notice that Liu et al. [16] use the word "traceability" other than "accountability". In this paper, they are used interchangeably.

1.1   Related Work

In ABE, most of the concern is user accountability [11] which assuming that the KGC can be trusted. Hinek et al. [11] proposed a token-based ABE. When decrypting, users must request a decryption token from a third party token server. Therefore, the token server is required to be online. Yu et al. [26] proposed a KP-ABE scheme by combining anonymous ABE with traitor tracing in broadcast environments. The content provider would choose particular types of ciphertexts and trick pirate devices into decrypting them. Li et al. [13] proposed an accountable, anonymous CP-ABE. User accountability can be achieved in black-box model by embedding additional user-specific information into the attribute secret key. Liu et al. proposed white-box [16] and black-box [15] traceable CP-ABE respectively. Both can support any monotone access structures while the schemes prior to Liu et al.'s work only support AND gate with wildcards. However, both schemes use bilinear groups of large composite order and are inefficient. Ning et al. [18] proposed a large universe CP-ABE with user accountability in white-box model on bilinear groups of prime order. "Large universe" means that a scheme can support flexible number of attributes. Liu and Wong [17] proposed both large universe KP-ABE and

CP-ABE with user accountability in black-box model on bilinear groups of prime order. The scheme supports revocation for the dishonest user.

Wang et al. [24] achieved authority accountability in white-box model by combining accountable authority identity-based encryption (IBE) [14] and KP-ABE [10]. As the user's secret key contains the secret information unknown to KGC, if KGC forges secret key in accordance with the user's identity, we can find whether KGC or the user is dishonest according the key family number. But yet it does not support large universe.

In multi-authority ABE [6,7], different authorities operate simultaneously and each hands out a user's partial secret key for a different set of attributes. Li et al. [12] proposed a multi-authority CP-ABE scheme with user accountability. However, it only supports access structure with AND gate with wildcards.

1.2   Our Contributions

The main contributions of our work can be summarized as follows.

1) We propose a ciphertext-policy attribute-based encryption scheme with user and authority accountability (UaAA-CP-ABE) in white-box model.

2) Our scheme has the property of large universe and is proved selectively secure in the standard model. The accountability property is also proved against dishonest user and KGC in the standard model.

3) By embedding a user's identity into this user's secret key directly, the only thing needed to do is to check whether the suspected secret key is well-formed at trace stage. If that key is well-formed, we can easily find out the dishonest user or KGC. It is more practical than existing ones [16,18]. More analysis can be seen at Section 1.3.

4) Our scheme is very efficient. We enhance CP-ABE of Rouselakis and Waters [20] in user and authority accountability with small computational cost.

We compare our work with other related works in Table 1.

1.3   Our Main Ideas

In this section we will briefly describe the main ideas in our scheme.

We extend large universe CP-ABE of Rouselakis and Waters [20] to support accountability for user and authority. To find out the identity of the dishonest user, Liu et al. [16] use an identity table to connect the user's identity with secret key. Therefore, the table grows linearly with the number of users in the system. To address this issue, Ning et al. [18] remove the identity table and use Shamir's threshold scheme [23] to trace the dishonest user. As every user has a unique identity ID in the system, can we embed ID into the user's secret key directly? If succeeded, the trace stage would become very simple, the only thing is to check whether the suspected secret key is well-formed or not. Liu et al. [16] in their extensions give some suggestions by using another signature scheme in [5]. However, they do not give a complete construction and proof. And their scheme uses bilinear groups of composite order and merely supports user accountability in white-box model. In our scheme, we successfully embed the signature scheme in [5] into our prime order construction and give complete proof.

Table 1. Comparisons with other related works

Schemes	Category	Large Universe	Supporting Monotonic Access Structure	Order of Bilinear Groups	User Accountability	Authority Accountability	Security Model[1]
LRZ+[13]	CP-ABE	✗	✗	prime	black-box[2]	✗	selectively secure
WCL+[24]	KP-ABE	✗	✓	prime	white-box	white-box	selectively secure
LCW[16]	CP-ABE	✗	✓	composite	white-box	✗	Fully secure
LCW[15]	CP-ABE	✗	✓	composite	black-box	✗	fully secure
NCD+[18]	CP-ABE	✓	✓	prime	white-box	✗	selectively secure
LW[17]	KP-ABE CP-ABE	✓	✓	prime	black-box	✗	selectively secure
RW[20]	CP-ABE	✓	✓	prime	✗	✗	selectively secure
Ours	CP-ABE	✓	✓	prime	white-box	white-box	selectively secure

[1]All schemes are secure in the standard model.

[2][16] gives a "compare-before-output" technique to avoid the tracing algorithm from identifying the dishonest user in Appendix A.

In order to achieve authority accountability, we borrow some ideas from accountable authority IBE [9]. Nevertheless, in IBE, both secret key and ciphertext contain the user's specific identity information. In ABE, the ciphertext is used for sharing and cannot contain the user's specific identity information. However, we finally succeed in embedding secret information hidden from the KGC's view into the user's secret key. We owe it to the secret key and ciphertext structure of Rouselakis and Waters [20] which employ "attribute" layer and "secret sharing" layer and use a "binder term" to connect them. We can embed secret information into the "secret sharing" layer in the user's secret key and need not change the ciphertext. This trick does not affect the normal computation in the decryption phase other than a change in exponential factor.

1.4   Organization

The remainder of the paper is organized as follows. Section 2 introduces the background. In Section 3, we give the formal definition of UaAA-CP-ABE and its security model. Section 4 proposes the construction of our UaAA-CP-ABE scheme. In Section 5, we analyze our proposed scheme in terms of security and performance. Finally, we give a brief conclusion in Section 6.

2   Background

2.1   Access Structures and Linear Secret Sharing Schemes

Definition 1. *(Access Structures [3])* Let $\{P_1, P_2, \ldots, P_n\}$ be a set of parties. A collection $\mathbb{A} \subseteq 2^{\{P_1, P_2, \ldots, P_n\}}$ is monotone if $\forall B, C$: if $B \in \mathbb{A}$ and $B \subseteq C$ then $C \in \mathbb{A}$. An access structure (respectively, monotone access structure) is a collection (respectively, monotone collection) $\mathbb{A}$ of non-empty subsets of $\{P_1, P_2, \ldots, P_n\}$, i.e., $\mathbb{A} \subseteq 2^{\{P_1, P_2, \ldots, P_n\}} \backslash \{\emptyset\}$. The sets in $\mathbb{A}$ are called the authorized sets, and the sets not in $\mathbb{A}$ are called the unauthorized sets.

In our context, the role of the parties is taken by the attributes. In this paper, we mainly focus on monotone access structure.

Definition 2. *(Linear Secret Sharing Schemes (LSSS) [3])* A secret sharing scheme Π over a set of parties $\mathcal{P}$ is called linear (over $\mathbb{Z}_p$) if

1) The shares for each party form a vector over $\mathbb{Z}_p$.

2) There exists a matrix an M with l rows and n columns called the share-generating matrix for Π. For all $i = 1, \ldots l$, the ith row of M we let the function ρ defined the party labeling row i as $\rho(i)$. When we consider the column vector $\vec{z} = (s, z_2, \ldots, z_n)^T$, where $s \in \mathbb{Z}_p$ is the secret to be shared, and $z_2, \ldots, z_n \in \mathbb{Z}_p$ are randomly chosen, the $M\vec{z}$ is the vector of l shares of the secret s according to Π. The share $(M\vec{z})_i$ belongs to party $\rho(i)$.

According to [3], every LSSS according to the above definition also enjoys the linear reconstruction property. Suppose that Π is an LSSS for the access structure $\mathbb{A}$. Let S be any authorized set if $\mathbb{A}(S) = 1$, and let $I \subset \{1, 2, \ldots, l\}$ be defined as $I = \{i : \rho(i) \in S\}$. Then, there exist constants $\{\omega_i \in Z_p\}_{i \in I}$ such that, if $\{\lambda_i\}$ are valid shares of any secret s according to Π, then $\sum_{i \in I} \omega_i \cdot \lambda_i = s$.

2.2   Bilinear Maps

Definition 3. *(Bilinear Maps)* Let $\mathbb{G}_0$ and $\mathbb{G}_1$ be two multiplicative cyclic groups of prime order p. Let g be a generator of $\mathbb{G}_0$ and e be a bilinear map $e : \mathbb{G}_0 \times \mathbb{G}_0 \to \mathbb{G}_1$. The bilinear map e has the following properties:

1) Bilinearity: for all $u, v \in \mathbb{G}_0$ and $a, b \in \mathbb{Z}_p$, we have $e(u^a, v^b) = e(u, v)^{ab}$.

2) Non-degeneracy: $e(g, g) \neq 1$.

3) Computable: there exists an efficient algorithm for $e : \mathbb{G}_0 \times \mathbb{G}_0 \to \mathbb{G}_1$.

Notice that the map e is symmetric since $e(g^a, g^b) = e(g, g)^{ab} = e(g^b, g^a)$.

2.3   Assumptions

In our paper, we adopt the q-type assumption of Rouselakis and Waters' scheme [20].

Assumption 1. q-type assumption

Initially the challenger calls the group generation algorithm with input the security parameter, picks a random group element $g \in \mathbb{G}_0$, and $q + 2$ random exponents $a, s, b_1, b_2, \dots, b_q \in \mathbb{Z}_p$. Then he sends to the adversary the group description $(p, \mathbb{G}_0, \mathbb{G}_1, e)$ and all of the following terms:

$$g, g^s$$
$$g^{a^i}, g^{b_j}, g^{sb_j}, g^{a^i b_j}, g^{a^i b_j^2} \qquad \forall (i, j) \in [q, q]$$
$$g^{a^i b_j / b_{j'}^2} \qquad \forall (i, j, j') \in [2q, q, q] \ with \ j \neq j'$$
$$g^{a^i / b_j} \qquad \forall (i, j) \in [2q, q] \ with \ i \neq q + 1$$
$$g^{sa^i b_j / b_{j'}}, g^{sa^i b_j / b_{j'}^2} \qquad \forall (i, j, j') \in [q, q, q] \ with \ j \neq j'$$

It is hard for the adversary to distinguish $e(g, g)^{sa^{q+1}} \in \mathbb{G}_1$ from an element which is randomly chosen from $\mathbb{G}_1$.

Definition 4. We say that the q-type assumption holds if no probabilistic polynomial time (PPT) adversary has a non-negligible advantage in solving the q-type problem.

Assumption 2. l-Strong Diffie-Hellman assumption [5]

Given a $(l + 1)$-tuple $g, g^x, g^{x^2}, \dots, g^{x^l}$ as input, it is hard for the adversary to output a pair $(d, g^{1/(x+d)})$ where $d \in \mathbb{Z}_p^*$.

Definition 5. We say that the l-SDH assumption holds if no PPT adversary has a non-negligible advantage in solving the l-SDH problem.

2.4   Miscellaneous Primitives

Zero-knowledge Proof of Knowledge of Discrete Log. A zero-knowledge proof[1] is a method by which one party (the prover) can prove to another party (the verifier) that a given statement is true, without conveying any information apart from the fact that the statement is indeed true. As a realistic cryptography application, a zero-knowledge proof of knowledge (ZK-POK) of discrete log protocol [9,22] enables a prover to prove to a verifier that it possesses the discrete log r of a given group element R in question.

3   CP-ABE with User and Authority Accountability

In this section we give the definition and security model of a large universe CP-ABE scheme with user and authority accountability (UaAA-CP-ABE).

---

[1] http://en.wikipedia.org/wiki/Zero-knowledge_proof

3.1   Definition

A UaAA-CP-ABE scheme consists of the following five algorithms:

Setup $(1^\lambda) \to (PK, MK)$: This is a randomized algorithm that takes a security parameter $\lambda \in \mathbb{N}$ encoded in unary. It outputs the public parameters PK and master key MK.

KeyGen $(PK, MK, ID, S) \to SK$: This is a randomized algorithm that takes as input the public parameters PK, the master key MK, a user's identity ID and a set of attributes S. It outputs this user's secret key SK.

Encrypt $(PK, M, \mathbb{A}) \to CT$: This is a randomized algorithm that takes as input the public parameters PK, a plaintext message M, and an access structure $\mathbb{A}$. It outputs the ciphertext CT.

Decrypt $(PK, SK, CT) \to M$: This algorithm takes as input the public parameters PK, a secret key SK for a user ID with a set of attributes S, and a ciphertext CT encrypted under access structure $\mathbb{A}$. It outputs the message M if $\mathbb{A}(S) = 1$.

Trace $(SK_{suspected}) \to$ (A user's ID or "KGC" or $\perp$): This algorithm has two stages. In the first stage, it takes as input a decryption key $SK_{suspected}$ and outputs a user's identity ID with a key family number o or the special symbol $\perp$ if $SK_{suspected}$ is ill-formed. In the second stage, it compares the key family number o' of the secret key of the user ID with o. If $o' = o$, it outputs ID assuming the user ID is dishonest. Otherwise, it outputs "KGC". This definition of Trace is for the white-box setting.

3.2   Selective Security Model for UaAA-CP-ABE

In this part, we will define selective security for our UaAA-CP-ABE scheme. This is described by a game between an adversary $\mathcal{A}$ and a challenger $\mathcal{B}$ and is parameterized by the security parameter $\lambda \in \mathbb{N}$. The phases of the game are as follows.

Init: The adversary $\mathcal{A}$ declares the challenge access structure $\mathbb{A}^*$ which he wants to attack, and then sends it to the challenger $\mathcal{B}$.

Setup: The challenger $\mathcal{B}$ runs the Setup (1^λ) algorithm and gives the public parameters PK to the adversary $\mathcal{A}$.

Phase 1: The adversary $\mathcal{A}$ is allowed to issue queries for secret keys for users with sets of attributes $(ID_1, S_1), (ID_2, S_2), \ldots, (ID_{Q_1}, S_{Q_1})$. For each (ID_i, S_i), the challenger $\mathcal{B}$ calls KeyGen $(PK, MK, ID_i, S_i) \to SK_i$ and sends SK_i to $\mathcal{A}$. The only restriction is that S_i does not satisfy $\mathbb{A}^*$.

Challenge: The adversary $\mathcal{A}$ submits two equal length message M_0 and M_1. The challenger $\mathcal{B}$ flips a random coin $b \in \{0,1\}$, and encrypts M_b with $\mathbb{A}^*$. The ciphertext is passed to $\mathcal{A}$.

Phase 2: Phase 1 is repeated.

Guess: The adversary $\mathcal{A}$ outputs a guess b' of b.

The advantage of an adversary $\mathcal{A}$ in this game is defined as $|\Pr[b' = b] - 1/2|$.

Definition 6. A ciphertext-policy attribute-based encryption scheme with user and authority accountability is selectively secure if all PPT adversaries have at most negligible advantage in λ in the above security game.

3.3   Accountability Model for UaAA-CP-ABE

In this part, we will define three games for accountability, one for the dishonest KGC and two for the dishonest user.

a) The DishonestKGC Game

The intuition behind this game is that an adversarial KGC attempts to calculate user's key family number o in the user's secret key. The DishonestKGC Game for our scheme is defined as follows.

Setup: The adversary (acting as an adversarial KGC) runs the Setup (1^λ) algorithm and gives the public parameters PK and a user's identity ID to the challenger. The challenger checks that PK and ID are well-formed and aborts if the check fails.

Key Generation: The challenger chooses $o \in \mathbb{Z}_p$ randomly and sends w^o to the adversary. The challenger also need to give to the adversary a zero-knowledge proof of knowledge of the discrete log of w^o with respect to w. Then the adversary calls KeyGen $(PK, MK, ID, S) \rightarrow SK$ and sends SK to the challenger. The challenger also check that SK is well-formed and aborts if the check fails.

Key Forgery: The adversary will output a decryption key SK' related with ID. The challenger checks that SK' is well-formed and aborts if the check fails.

Let KW denote the event that the adversary wins this game which happens the key family number of SK' equivalent to SK's. The advantage of an adversary in this game is defined as $Pr[KW]$.

b) The DishonestUser-1 Game

The intuition behind this game is that the adversary cannot create a new ID's secret key or even generate a new key SK'_{ID} with an existed ID appeared at Key Query stage. At Key Query stage, the adversary has already got SK_{ID}. In this game, a new key with an existed ID means that the identity-related information in SK_{ID} is successfully changed by the adversary. A tuple (ID, c) represents identity ID with the identity-related information. The DishonestUser-1 Game for our scheme is defined as follows.

Setup: The challenger runs the Setup (1^λ) algorithm and gives the public parameters PK to the adversary.

Key Query: The adversary issues queries for secret keys for users with sets of attributes $(ID_1, S_1), (ID_2, S_2), \ldots, (ID_q, S_q)$. The challenger responds to each query by calling KeyGen $(PK, MK, ID_i, S_i) \rightarrow SK_i$.

Key Forgery: Eventually, the adversary outputs a decryption key SK related with (ID, c) and wins the game if

(1) (ID, c) is not any of $(ID_1, c_1), \ldots, (ID_q, c_q)$, and

(2) SK is well-formed.

Let $UW1$ denote the event that the adversary wins this game. The advantage of an adversary in this game is defined as $Pr\,[UW1]$.

c) The DishonestUser-2 Game

As the same with DishonestKGC Game, we must assure a dishonest user cannot create another key family number (denoted by o) in that user's secret key. The DishonestUser-2 Game for our scheme is defined as follows.

Setup: The challenger runs the Setup (1^{λ}) algorithm and gives the public parameters PK to the adversary (acting as an adversarial user). The adversary checks that PK are well-formed and aborts if the check fails.

Key Query: The adversary issues queries for secret keys for users with sets of attributes $(ID_1, S_1), (ID_2, S_2), \ldots, (ID_q, S_q)$. The challenger responds to each query by calling KeyGen $(PK, MK, ID_i, S_i) \to SK_i$.

Key Forgery: The adversary will output a decryption key SK related with (ID, c, o) and wins the game if

(1) (ID, c) is one of $(ID_1, c_1), \ldots, (ID_q, c_q)$, we assume (ID, c) is equivalent to (ID_i, c_i), and

(2) o does not equal to o_i, and

(3) SK is well-formed.

Let $UW2$ denote the event that the adversary wins this game. The advantage of an adversary in this game is defined as $Pr\,[UW2]$.

Definition 7. A ciphertext-policy attribute-based encryption scheme with user and authority accountability is fully accountable if all PPT adversaries have negligible advantage in the above three security games.

4   Our Construction

Let $\mathbb{G}_0$ be a bilinear group of prime order p, and let g be a generator of $\mathbb{G}_0$. In addition, let $e: \mathbb{G}_0 \times \mathbb{G}_0 \to \mathbb{G}_1$ denote the bilinear map. A security parameter λ will determine the size of the groups. For the moment we assume that users' identity IDs and attributes are elements in $\mathbb{Z}_p^*$, however, IDs and attributes can be any meaningful unique strings using a collision resistant hash function $H: \{0,1\}^* \to \mathbb{Z}_p^*$.

Our construction follows.

Setup $(1^{\lambda}) \to (PK, MK)$: The algorithm calls the group generator algorithm $\mathcal{G}(1^{\lambda})$ and gets the descriptions of the groups and the bilinear mapping $D = (p, \mathbb{G}_0, \mathbb{G}_1, e)$. Then it picks the random terms $g, u, h, w, v \in \mathbb{G}_0$ and $\alpha, x, y \in \mathbb{Z}_p$. The published public parameters PK are

$$(D, g, u, h, w, v, X = g^x, Y = g^y, e(g, g)^{\alpha}).$$

The master key MK are (α, x, y).

KeyGen $(PK, MK, ID, S = \{A_1, A_2, \ldots, A_k\} \subseteq \mathbb{Z}_p) \to SK$: After the user ID is authenticated, the KGC gets w^o from ID where ID chooses $o \in \mathbb{Z}_p$ randomly. ID also needs to give to KGC a zero-knowledge proof of knowledge of the discrete log (as in Section 2.5) of w^o with respect to w. Then it picks $k + 2$ random nents $c, r, r_1, r_2, \ldots, r_k \in \mathbb{Z}_p$. It outputs this user's secret key SK (Notice that $N_3 = o$ is owned by the user secretly, and is part of SK):

$$S, K_1 = g^{\alpha/(x+ID+yc)}w^{o \cdot r}, N_1 = ID, N_2 = c, N_3 = o, L_1 = g^r, L_2 = g^{xr}, L_3 = g^{yr},$$
$$\{K_{i,2} = g^{r_i}, K_{i,3} = (u^{A_i}h)^{r_i}v^{-(x+ID+yc)r}\}_{i \in [k]}.$$

Here $1/(x + ID + yc)$ is computed modulo p. In the unlikely event that $x + ID + yc = 0$ we will pick another random c.

Encrypt $(PK, m, (M, \rho)) \rightarrow CT$: To encrypt a message $m \in \mathbb{G}_1$ under an access structure encoded in an LSSS policy (M, ρ). Let the dimensions of M be $l \times n$. Each row of M will be labeled by an attribute and $\rho(i)$ denotes the label of ith row $\vec{M}_i$. Choose a random vector $\vec{z} = (s, z_2, \ldots, z_n)^T$ from $\mathbb{Z}_p^n$ where s is the random secret to be shared among the shares. The vector of the shares is $\vec{\lambda} = (\lambda_1, \lambda_2, \ldots, \lambda_l)^T = M\vec{z}$. It then chooses l random value $t_1, t_2, \ldots, t_l \in Z_p$ and publishes the ciphertext as:

$$CT = ((M, \rho), C = me(g, g)^{\alpha s}, D_1 = g^s, D_2 = g^{xs}, D_3 = g^{ys},$$
$$\{C_{i,1} = w^{\lambda_i}v^{t_i}, C_{i,2} = (u^{\rho(i)}h)^{-t_i}, C_{i,3} = g^{t_i}\}_{i \in [l]}).$$

Decrypt $(PK, SK, CT) \rightarrow m$: To decrypt the ciphertext CT with the decryption key SK, proceed as follows. Suppose that S satisfies the access structure and let $I = \{i: \rho(i) \in S\}$. Since the set of attributes satisfy the access structure, there exist coefficients $\omega_i \in \mathbb{Z}_p$ such that $\sum_{\rho(i) \in I} \omega_i \cdot \vec{M}_i = (1, 0, \ldots, 0)$. Then we have that $\sum_{\rho(i) \in I} \omega_i \lambda_i = s$. Now it calculates

$$E = e(K_1, D_1^{ID}D_2 D_3^c) = e(g, g)^{\alpha s}e(g, w)^{(x+ID+yc)rso}.$$
$$F = \prod_{i \in I}(e(L_1^{ID}L_2 L_3^c, C_{i,1})e(K_{i,2}, C_{i,2})e(K_{i,3}, C_{i,3}))^{\omega_i} = e(g, w)^{(x+ID+yc)rs}.$$
$$m = CF^o/E.$$

Trace $(SK_{suspected}) \rightarrow$ (A user's ID or "KGC" or $\perp$) : If $SK_{suspected}$ is ill-formed, the algorithm will output the special symbol $\perp$. Otherwise, it outputs $N_1 = ID$ and key family number $N_3 = o$ in $SK_{suspected}$. If ID does not exist, the algorithm outputs "KGC" which means the dishonest KGC create a fake user's identity. Otherwise, it compares o with the key family number o_{ID} of the secret key of a real user ID. If $o = o_{ID}$, it outputs ID assuming the user ID is dishonest. Otherwise, it outputs "KGC". Notice that we do not need to compare the signature part $N_2 = c$ in these two keys, because key family number N_3 is enough to distinguish dishonest user or KGC.

5   Analysis of Our Proposed Scheme

5.1   Selective Security Proof

In our original scheme, the KGC does not have complete control over SK because it does not know o in w^o. For this reason, the scheme is difficult to be proved selectively secure. A similar situation occurs in accountable authority identity-based encryption (A-IBE) scheme [9]. In the part of security proof of A-IBE, the simulator uses a knowledge extractor to extract the discrete log. In our proof, we will use the same technology and assume that the simulator knows o.

In the selective security proof, we will reduce the selective security of our CP-ABE scheme to that of Rouselakis and Waters' [20] which is proved selectively secure under Assumption 1.

Theorem 1. If Rouselakis and Waters' scheme [20] is selectively secure, then all PPT adversaries with a challenge matrix of size $l \times n$, where $l, n \leq q$, have a negligible advantage in selectively breaking our scheme.

Proof. To prove the theorem we will suppose that there exists a PPT adversary $\mathcal{A}$ with a challenge matrix that satisfies the restriction, which has a non-negligible advantage $Adv_{\mathcal{A}}$ in selectively breaking our scheme. Using this adversary we will build a PPT simulator $\mathcal{B}$ that attacks Rouselakis and Waters' scheme (Sim_{RW}) [20] with a non-negligible advantage.

Init: The adversary $\mathcal{A}$ declares a challenge access policy $\mathbb{A}^* = (M^*, \rho^*)$ which he wants to attack, and then sends it to the challenger $\mathcal{B}$. $\mathcal{B}$ sends this received challenge access policy to Sim_{RW}. Notice that M^* is a $l \times n$ matrix, where $l, n \leq q$. Each row of M^* will be labeled by an attribute and $\rho^*(i)$ denotes the label of ith row of M^*.

Setup: $\mathcal{B}$ gets the public parameters $PK_{RW} = (D, g, u, h, w, v, e(g,g)^\alpha)$ from Sim_{RW}. Then $\mathcal{B}$ chooses $x, y \in \mathbb{Z}_p$ randomly, and gives the public parameters PK= $(D, g, u, h, w, v, g^x, g^y, e(g,g)^\alpha)$ to $\mathcal{A}$. Notice that this way α is information-theoretically hidden from $\mathcal{B}$.

Phase 1: Now $\mathcal{B}$ has to produce secret keys for tuples which consists of non-authorized sets of attributes $S = \{A_1, A_2, \dots, A_k\}$, a user's identity ID, and an element w^o computed with a zero-knowledge proof. The only restriction is that S does not satisfy $\mathbb{A}^*$. As analysis in the beginning part of this section, we assume $\mathcal{B}$ knows o. At first, $\mathcal{B}$ will issue S to Sim_{RW} and get the corresponding decryption key as follows:

$$S, \widetilde{K_1} = g^\alpha w^{\tilde{r}}, \widetilde{L_1} = g^{\tilde{r}}, \{\widetilde{K}_{i,2} = g^{\tilde{r}_i}, \widetilde{K}_{i,3} = (u^{A_i}h)^{\tilde{r}_i}v^{-\tilde{r}}\}_{i \in [k]}.$$

Then $\mathcal{B}$ picks random exponents $c \in \mathbb{Z}_p$, and sets $r = \tilde{r}/((x + ID + yc) \cdot o)$ and $\{r_i = \tilde{r}_i/o\}_{i \in [k]}$ implicitly. Here $1/(x + ID + yc)$ is computed modulo p. In the unlikely event that $x + ID + yc = 0$, $\mathcal{B}$ will pick another random c. Then $\mathcal{B}$ computes

$$K_1 = \widetilde{K_1}^{1/(x+ID+yc)} = g^{\alpha/(x+ID+yc)}w^{\tilde{r}/(x+ID+yc)} = g^{\alpha/(x+ID+yc)}w^{o \cdot r}.$$
$$L_1 = \widetilde{L_1}^{1/((x+ID+yc) \cdot o)} = g^{\tilde{r}/((x+ID+yc) \cdot o)} = g^r, L_2 = L_1^x = g^{xr}, L_3 = L_1^y = g^{yr}.$$
$$\{K_{i,2} = (\widetilde{K}_{i,2})^{1/o} = g^{\tilde{r}_i/o} = g^{r_i}\}_{i \in [k]}.$$
$$\{K_{i,3} = (\widetilde{K}_{i,3})^{1/o} = (u^{A_i}h)^{\tilde{r}_i/o}v^{-\tilde{r}/o} = (u^{A_i}h)^{r_i}v^{-(x+ID+yc)r}\}_{i \in [k]}.$$

Finally, $\mathcal{B}$ sends the decryption key $SK = (S, K_1, N_1 = ID, N_2 = c, L_1, L_2, L_3, \{K_{i,2}, K_{i,3}\}_{i \in [k]})$ to $\mathcal{A}$. Notice that $N_3 = o$ is owned by $\mathcal{A}$.

Challenge: The adversary $\mathcal{A}$ submits two equal length message m_0 and m_1. Then $\mathcal{B}$ submits m_0 and m_1 to Sim_{RW}, and gets the challenge ciphertext as follows:

$$((M^*, \rho^*), C, D_1 = g^s, \{C_{i,1} = w^{\lambda_i}v^{t_i}, C_{i,2} = (u^{\rho(i)}h)^{-t_i}, C_{i,3} = g^{t_i}\}_{i \in [l]}).$$

Notice that C has two forms indeed according to the proof part of Rouselakis and Waters' scheme [20], one is well-formed ($m_b e(g,g)^{\alpha s}$), and the other is random.

Then $\mathcal{B}$ computes $D_2 = D_1^x = g^{xs}, D_3 = D_1^y = g^{ys}$. Finally, $\mathcal{B}$ sends the challenge ciphertext $CT = ((M^*, \rho^*), C, D_1, D_2, D_3, \{C_{i,1}, C_{i,2}, C_{i,3}\}_{i \in [l]})$ to $\mathcal{A}$.

Phase 2: Phase 1 is repeated.

Guess: The adversary $\mathcal{A}$ outputs a guess b' of b to $\mathcal{B}$. Then $\mathcal{B}$ sends b' to Sim_{RW}.

Since the distributions of the public parameters, secret keys and ciphertexts of our scheme and Rouselakis and Waters' in the above game are the same, the adversary in selectively breaking Rouselakis and Waters' scheme has the same advantage as adversary $\mathcal{A}$ in selectively breaking our scheme. As Rouselakis and Waters' scheme is selectively secure, so do ours. □

5.2 Accountability Proof

a) Analysis of the DishonestKGC Game

Theorem 2. Assuming that computing discrete logarithm is hard in $\mathbb{G}_0$, the advantage of an adversary in the DishonestKGC Game is negligible for our scheme.

Proof. To prove the theorem we will suppose that there exists a PPT adversary $\mathcal{A}$ which has a non-negligible advantage $Adv_{\mathcal{A}}$ in the DishonestKGC Game in our scheme. Using this adversary we will build a PPT simulator $\mathcal{B}$ that attacks the discrete logarithm problem with a non-negligible advantage. $\mathcal{B}$ proceeds as follows.

Setup: The adversary $\mathcal{A}$ (acting as an adversarial KGC) runs the Setup (1^λ) algorithm and gives the public parameters PK= $(D, g, u, h, w, v, g^x, g^y, e(g,g)^\alpha)$ and a user's identity ID to the simulator $\mathcal{B}$. $\mathcal{B}$ checks that PK and ID are well-formed and aborts if the check fails.

Key Generation: $\mathcal{B}$ invokes the challenger $\mathcal{C}$, passes on w to it and gets a challenge $W = w^o \in \mathbb{G}_0$. Then $\mathcal{B}$ engages in the key generation protocol with $\mathcal{A}$ to get a decryption key for ID as follows. Notice that $\mathcal{B}$ should give to $\mathcal{A}$ a zero-knowledge proof of knowledge of the discrete log of w^o with respect to w, however, $\mathcal{B}$ does not know o. A similar situation occurs in A-IBE [9]. In the part of security proof of the FindKey game in A-IBE, $\mathcal{B}$ simulates the required proof without knowledge of o. In our proof, we will use the same technology and assume that $\mathcal{B}$ successfully gives to $\mathcal{A}$ a zero-knowledge proof of knowledge. Then $\mathcal{A}$ calls KeyGen ($PK, MK, ID, \mathcal{S}) \rightarrow SK$ and sends SK to $\mathcal{B}$.

Key Forgery: $\mathcal{A}$ will output a decryption key $SK' = (\mathcal{S}, K_1, N_1 = ID, N_2 = c, N_3 = o', L_1, L_2, L_3, \{K_{i,2}, K_{i,3}\}_{i \in [k]})$ related with ID. $\mathcal{B}$ checks that SK' is well-formed and aborts if the check fails. If SK' is well-formed, $\mathcal{B}$ sends o' to $\mathcal{C}$.

If $Adv_{\mathcal{A}}$ in the DishonestKGC Game is non-negligible, we have built a PPT simulator $\mathcal{B}$ that attacks the discrete logarithm problem with a non-negligible advantage. Since computing discrete logarithm is believed to be difficult, there does not exist a PPT adversary $\mathcal{A}$ which has a non-negligible advantage $Adv_{\mathcal{A}}$ in the DishonestKGC Game in our scheme. □

b) Analysis of the DishonestUser-1 Game

Theorem 3. The advantage of an adversary in the DishonestUser-1 Game is negligible for our CP-ABE scheme under the l-SDH assumption.

Proof. To prove the theorem we will suppose that there exists a PPT adversary $\mathcal{A}$ which has a non-negligible advantage $Adv_{\mathcal{A}}$ in the DishonestUser-1 Game in our scheme (the probability that $\mathcal{A}$ wins the game is at least ϵ). Using this adversary we will show how to build a PPT simulator $\mathcal{B}$ that is able to solve the l-SDH assumption with a non-negligible advantage.

We first give some intuition for the proof. Assuming $\mathcal{A}$ issues q queries, For each secret key, we record a tuple $(ID_i, c_i, d_i = ID_i + yc_i)$. At Key Forgery stage, the adversary outputs a decryption key SK related with $(ID^*, c^*, d^* = ID^* + yc^*)$. There are two possibilities when the adversary wins the game, $d^* \in \{d_i\}_{i \in [q]}$ or $d^* \notin \{d_i\}_{i \in [q]}$. We distinguish between two types of adversaries.

Type-1 adversary: an adversary that either
1) makes a secret key query for user's identity $ID = -x$ at Key Query stage, or
2) outputs a decryption key SK related with $d^* \notin \{d_i\}_{i \in [q]}$ at Key Forgery stage.

Type-2 adversary: an adversary that both
1) never makes a secret key query for user's identity $ID = -x$ at Key Query stage, and
2) outputs a decryption key SK related with $d^* \in \{d_i\}_{i \in [q]}$ at Key Forgery stage.

We will show that either adversary can be used to solve the l-SDH assumption. However, the simulator $\mathcal{B}$ works differently for each adversary type. Thus, $\mathcal{B}$ will choose a random bit $b_{mode} \in \{1, 2\}$ that indicates its guess for the type of adversary that $\mathcal{A}$ will emulate.

$\mathcal{B}$ is given a bilinear mapping $D = (p, \mathbb{G}_0, \mathbb{G}_1, e)$ and a random instance $(A_0 = g', A_1 = (g')^x, A_2 = (g')^{x^2}, ..., A_l = (g')^{x^l}) \in \mathbb{G}_0^{l+1}$ of the l-SDH problem for some unknown $x \in \mathbb{Z}_p^*$. Then $\mathcal{B}$ proceeds as follows.

Setup: $\mathcal{B}$ chooses $q = l - 1$ random elements $d_1, d_2, ..., d_q \in \mathbb{Z}_p^*$. Let $f(z)$ be the polynomial $f(z) = \prod_{i=1}^{l-1}(z + d_i)$. Expand $f(z)$ and write $f(z) = \sum_{i=0}^{l-1} \eta_i z^i$ where $\eta_0, \eta_1, ..., \eta_{l-1} \in \mathbb{Z}_p$ are the coefficients of the polynomial $f(z)$. Compute:

$$g \leftarrow \prod^{l-1} A_i^{\eta_i} = (g')^{f(x)} \text{ and } Z \leftarrow \prod_{i=1}^{l} A_i^{\eta_{i-1}} = (g')^{xf(x)} = g^x.$$

Notice that we may assume that $f(x) \neq 0$, otherwise, $x = -d_i$ for some i which means that $\mathcal{B}$ just obtains the secret key x of the l-SDH problem.

Then $\mathcal{B}$ picks the random terms $u, h \in \mathbb{G}_0$, $\alpha, \mu, \pi \in \mathbb{Z}_p$ and

If $b_{mode} = 1$, $\mathcal{B}$ picks a random $y \in \mathbb{Z}_p^*$ and gives $\mathcal{A}$ the public parameters $PK_1 = (D, g, u, h, w = g^\mu, v = g^\pi, X = Z = g^x, Y = g^y, e(g, g)^\alpha)$.

If $b_{mode} = 2$, $\mathcal{B}$ picks a random $x' \in \mathbb{Z}_p^*$ and gives $\mathcal{A}$ the public parameters $PK_2 = (D, g, u, h, w = g^\mu, v = g^\pi, X = g^{x'}, Y = Z = g^x, e(g, g)^\alpha)$.

Notice that in either case, $\mathcal{B}$ provides the adversary $\mathcal{A}$ with a valid public parameters.

Key Query: The adversary $\mathcal{A}$ can issue up to q queries for secret keys adaptively. In order to respond, $\mathcal{B}$ maintains a list H-list of tuples (ID_i, c_i, W_i). Then for the ith query (ID_i, S_i):

Let $f_i(z)$ be the polynomial $f_i(z) = f(z)/(z + d_i) = \prod_{j=1, j \neq i}^{l-1}(z + d_i)$. Expand $f_i(z)$ and write $f_i(z) = \sum_{j=0}^{l-2} \beta_j z^j$ where $\beta_0, \beta_1, \dots, \beta_{l-2} \in \mathbb{Z}_p$ are the coefficients of the polynomial $f_i(z)$. Compute

$$\sigma_i \leftarrow \prod_{j=0}^{l-2} A_j^{\beta_j} = (g')^{f_i(x)} = g^{1/(x+d_i)}.$$

If $b_{mode} = 1$, check if $g^{-ID} = X$. If so, $\mathcal{B}$ just obtains the secret key x of the l-SDH problem which allows it to compute $(d, g^{1/(x+d)})$ for any d easily. At this point $\mathcal{B}$ successfully solves the l-SDH assumption.

Otherwise, $\mathcal{B}$ sets $c_i = (d_i - ID_i)/y \in \mathbb{Z}_p^*$. If $c_i = 0$, $\mathcal{B}$ reports failure and aborts. Otherwise, it picks $k + 1$ random exponents $r, r_1, r_2, \dots, r_k \in \mathbb{Z}_p$ and outputs ID_i's secret key SK_i (o is owned by the adversary secretly, and is part of SK_i)

$$S, K_1 = \sigma_i^{\alpha} w^{o \cdot r} = g^{\alpha/(x+ID_i+yc_i)} w^{o \cdot r}, N_1 = ID_i, N_2 = c_i, N_3 = o,$$
$$L_1 = g^r, L_2 = X^r = g^{xr}, L_3 = Y^r = g^{yr},$$
$$\{K_{i,2} = g^{r_i}, K_{i,3} = (u^{A_i} h)^{r_i} X^{-\pi r} v^{-(ID+yc)r} = (u^{A_i} h)^{r_i} v^{-(x+ID_i+yc_i)r}\}_{i \in [k]}.$$

Apparently, this is a valid user's secret key.

If $b_{mode} = 2$, $\mathcal{B}$ sets $c_i = (x' + ID_i)/d_i \in \mathbb{Z}_p^*$. If $c_i = 0$, $\mathcal{B}$ reports failure and aborts. Otherwise, it picks $k + 1$ random exponents $r, r_1, r_2, \dots, r_k \in \mathbb{Z}_p$ and outputs ID_i's secret key SK_i (o is owned by the adversary secretly, and is part of SK_i)

$$S, K_1 = \sigma_i^{\alpha/c_i} w^{o \cdot r} = g^{\alpha/(x'+ID_i+xc_i)} w^{o \cdot r}, N_1 = ID_i, N_2 = c_i, N_3 = o,$$
$$L_1 = g^r, L_2 = X^r = g^{x'r}, L_3 = Y^r = g^{xr},$$
$$\{K_{i,2} = g^{r_i}, K_{i,3} = (u^{A_i} h)^{r_i} v^{-(x'+ID_i)r} Y^{-\pi c_i r} = (u^{A_i} h)^{r_i} v^{-(x'+ID_i+xc_i)r}\}_{i \in [k]}.$$

Apparently, this is a valid user's secret key, too.

In either case $\mathcal{B}$ adds the tuple $(ID_i, c_i, W_i = g^{ID_i} Y^{c_i})$ to the H-list.

Key Forgery: Eventually, the adversary outputs a decryption key SK related with (ID^*, c^*) where SK is well-formed and (ID^*, c^*) is not any of $(ID_1, r_1), \dots, (ID_q, r_q)$. Notice that by adding dummy queries as necessary, we may assume that the adversary made exactly $l - 1$ queries. Let $W^* = g^{ID^*} Y^{c^*}$. Then $\mathcal{B}$ searches W^* from the H-list. There are two possibilities:

Type-1 adversary: No tuple of the form $(\cdot, \cdot, W^*)$ appears on the H-list.

Type-2 adversary: The H-list contains at least one tuple (ID_j, c_j, W_j) such that $W_j = W^*$.

Let $B_{type} = 1$ if $\mathcal{A}$ produced a type-1 adversary. Otherwise, set $B_{type} = 2$. If $b_{mode} \neq B_{type}$, $\mathcal{B}$ reports failure and aborts.

If $b_{mode} = B_{type} = 1$, check if $g^{-ID} = X$. If so, $\mathcal{B}$ can solve the l-SDH assumption successfully. Otherwise, compute

$$\sigma^* = (K_1 L_1^{-\mu N_3})^{1/\alpha} = g^{1/(x+ID^*+yc^*)} = (g')^{f(x)/(x+ID^*+yc^*)}.$$

Let $d^* = ID^* + yc^*$. Notice that $d^* \notin \{d_i\}_{i \in [l-1]}$ when adversary is type-1.

Using long division we write the polynomial f as $f(z) = \gamma(z)(z + d^*) + \gamma_{-1}$ for some polynomial $\gamma(z) = \sum_{i=0}^{l-2} \gamma_i z^i$ and $\gamma_{-1} \in \mathbb{Z}_p$. Then $f(z)/(z + d^*) = \gamma_{-1}/(z + d^*) + \sum_{i=0}^{l-2} \gamma_i z^i$ and hence

$$\sigma^* = (g')^{\gamma_{-1}/(x+d^*) + \sum_{i=0}^{l-2} \gamma_i x^i}.$$

Notice that $\gamma_{-1} \neq 0$, since $f(z) = \prod_{i=1}^{l-1}(z + d_i)$ and $d^* \notin \{d_i\}_{i \in [l-1]}$. Then $\mathcal{B}$ computes

$$(\sigma^* \cdot \prod_{i=0}^{l-2} A_i^{-\gamma_i})^{1/\gamma_{-1}} = ((g')^{\gamma_{-1}/(x+d^*)} \cdot (g')^{\sum_{i=0}^{l-2} \gamma_i x^i} \cdot \prod_{i=0}^{l-2} (g')^{-\gamma_i x^i})^{1/\gamma_{-1}}$$

$$= (g')^{1/x+d^*}.$$

and returns $(d^*, (g')^{1/(x+d^*)})$ as the solution to the l-SDH problem.

If $b_{mode} = B_{type} = 2$, let (ID_j, c_j, W_j) be a tuple on the H-list where $W_j = W^*$. Since $Y = g^x$, we know that $g^{ID_j} g^{xc_j} = g^{ID^*} g^{xc^*} \Rightarrow ID_j + xc_j = ID^* + xc^*$. We know that $(ID_j, c_j) \neq (ID^*, c^*)$, otherwise, the adversary failed to forge a secret key SK and would lose the game. Therefore, $x = (ID^* - ID_j)/(c_j - c^*) \in \mathbb{Z}_p^*$. As $\mathcal{B}$ knows x, $\mathcal{B}$ can solve the l-SDH assumption successfully.

Now we complete the description of simulator $\mathcal{B}$. Notice that,

1) the view from $\mathcal{A}$ is independent of the choice of b_{mode},
2) the public parameters are uniformly distributed, and
3) the secret keys that $\mathcal{A}$ queries are well-formed.

Therefore, $\mathcal{A}$ produces a valid secret key with probability at least ϵ.

It remains to bound the probability that $\mathcal{B}$ does not abort. We argue as follows:

If $b_{mode} = B_{type} = 1$, $\mathcal{B}$ aborts when $\mathcal{A}$ forged a secret key with $d^* \in \{d_i\}_{i \in [l-1]}$. This happens with probability at most $(l-1)/p$.

If $b_{mode} = B_{type} = 2$, $\mathcal{B}$ does not abort.

Since b_{mode} is independent of B_{type} we have that $\Pr[b_{mode} = B_{type}] = 1/2$. It now follows that $\mathcal{B}$ produces a valid tuple $(d, (g')^{1/(x+d)})$ with probability

$$\Pr[\mathcal{B} \text{ not abort \&\& win}|b_{mode} = B_{type} = 1] \cdot \Pr[b_{mode} = B_{type} = 1] +$$
$$\Pr[\mathcal{B} \text{ not abort \&\& win}|b_{mode} = B_{type} = 2] \cdot \Pr[b_{mode} = B_{type} = 2]$$
$$= \epsilon \cdot (1 - (l-1)/p) \cdot 1/4 + \epsilon \cdot 1/4 = \epsilon/2 - (l-1) \cdot \epsilon/(4p) \approx \epsilon/2. \quad \square$$

c) Analysis of the DishonestUser-2 Game

Theorem 4. Assuming that computing discrete logarithm is hard in $\mathbb{G}_0$, the advantage of an adversary in the DishonestUser-2 Game is negligible for our scheme.

Proof. To prove the theorem we will suppose that there exists a PPT adversary $\mathcal{A}$ which has a non-negligible advantage $Adv_{\mathcal{A}}$ in the DishonestUser-2 Game in our scheme. Using this adversary we will build a PPT simulator $\mathcal{B}$ that attacks the discrete logarithm problem (g, g^z) with a non-negligible advantage. $\mathcal{B}$ proceeds as follows.

Setup: $\mathcal{B}$ runs the Setup (1^λ) algorithm and gives the public parameters PK to the adversary $\mathcal{A}$. Notice that the generation of w, v is different from the original Setup. $\mathcal{B}$ picks the random terms $\omega, \mu \in \mathbb{Z}_p$ and calculates $w = g^\omega, v = g^\mu$. However, in $\mathcal{A}$'s view, they are identical.

Key Query: The adversary $\mathcal{A}$ issues queries for secret keys for users with sets of attributes $(ID_1, S_1), (ID_2, S_2), \dots, (ID_q, S_q)$. As space limited, we only give the different parts from the original KeyGen here. For query i, when $\mathcal{A}$ gives $\mathcal{B}$ a zero-knowledge proof of knowledge of the discrete log of w^{o_i} with respect to w, $\mathcal{B}$ will use a knowledge extractor [9] to extract the discrete log o_i. Then $\mathcal{B}$ chooses $\gamma_i \in \mathbb{Z}_p$ and implicitly sets $r^{(i)} = \gamma_i \cdot z$. $\mathcal{B}$ can calculate $w^{o_i \cdot r^{(i)}}$ by $(g^z)^{\omega \cdot o_i \cdot \gamma_i}$. $\mathcal{B}$ can use the same method to calculate $g^{r^{(i)}}, g^{xr^{(i)}}, g^{yr^{(i)}}, v^{-(x+ID+yc)r^{(i)}}$ even if $\mathcal{B}$ does not know z. Other parts in the secret key will follow the same method in KeyGen. Finally, $\mathcal{B}$ sends SK_i to $\mathcal{A}$.

Key Forgery: The adversary $\mathcal{A}$ outputs a decryption key SK related with (ID, c, o). We assume (ID, c) is equivalent to (ID_i, c_i) and o does not equal to o_i. In this case, $\mathcal{A}$ generates a new secret key successfully.

Now we will analyze the security of the discrete logarithm problem. Let's review the user's secret key firstly. For simplicity, we omit i and (i) in o_i and $r^{(i)}$:

$$S, K_1 = g^{\alpha/(x+ID+yc)} w^{o \cdot r}, N_1 = ID, N_2 = c, N_3 = o,$$
$$L_1 = g^r, L_2 = g^{xr}, L_3 = g^{yr}, \{K_{i,2} = g^{r_i}, K_{i,3} = (u^{A_i} h)^{r_i} v^{-(x+ID+yc)r}\}_{i \in [k]}.$$

And the adversary $\mathcal{A}$ outputs a forged secret key SK' where $o' \neq o$:

$$S', K_1' = g^{\alpha/(x+ID+yc)} w^{o' \cdot r'}, N_1' = ID, N_2' = c, N_3' = o',$$
$$L_1' = g^{r'}, L_2' = g^{xr'}, L_3' = g^{yr'}, \{K_{i,2}' = g^{r_i'}, K_{i,3}' = (u^{A_i} h)^{r_i'} v^{-(x+ID+yc)r'}\}_{i \in [k']}.$$

Firstly, we will analyze K_1 and K_1'. As $\alpha/(x + ID + yc)$ and r in K_1 is information-theoretically hidden from $\mathcal{A}$. If $\mathcal{A}$ can forge K_1' successfully, then we can assume that $K_1' = K_1 \cdot w^{f_1} \Rightarrow o \cdot r + f_1 = o' \cdot r'$. Similarly, since $x + ID + yc$ in $K_{i,3}$ is information-theoretically hidden from $\mathcal{A}$, if $\mathcal{A}$ can forge $K_{i,3}'$ successfully, we can assume that $K_{i,3}' = (K_{i,3})^{f_2} \Rightarrow r \cdot f_2 = r'$. Then we get two equations:

$$\begin{cases} o \cdot r + f_1 = o' \cdot r' \\ r \cdot f_2 = r' \end{cases}.$$

From $\mathcal{A}$'s view, $\mathcal{A}$ knows o, o', f_1, f_2. If $o' \cdot f_2 \neq o$, then $r = f_1/(o' \cdot f_2 - o)$. Apparently, the probability of $o' \cdot f_2 = o$ is negligible. Then $\mathcal{A}$ can compute r. As r equals to $\gamma_i \cdot z$, then $z = r/\gamma_i$. Therefore, if $\mathcal{A}$ forges a secret key SK' where $o' \neq o$, we can conclude that $\mathcal{A}$ have solved the discrete logarithm problem. However, as we assumed that computing discrete logarithm is hard in $\mathbb{G}_0$, then $\mathcal{A}$ cannot forge a secret key SK' where $o' \neq o$. Therefore, the advantage of an adversary in the DishonestUser-2 Game is negligible for our scheme. $\square$

5.3   Performance Analysis

There are two aspects to consider for performance analysis, the performance of normal functions and the capability of the accountability. As for accountability, the advantage of our scheme is obvious and we have explained it in Section 1.3. Therefore, we mainly focus on the performance of normal functions in this section. We compared our scheme with Rouselakis and Waters (RW'13) [20] as ours is based on RW'13. We wanted to know how much computational efficiency to lose for security enhancements of RW'13. We implemented both schemes in Charm[2] [1]. We use

---

[2] You can download our codes from https://github.com/zlwen/charm-example.

"SS512" elliptic curve group. All our tests were executed on a Intel(R) Core(TM) i7-3770 CPU (3.40GHz) with 8.0GB RAM running Windows 8.1 Pro and Python 3.4.3 and sampled 20 times.

As the Setup stage is stable, we do not show the time in the figure. Ours spend 71.5 milliseconds and 56 milliseconds for RW'13. These are very small values. Fig. 1 shows the computation cost in KeyGen, Encrypt, and Decrypt under various conditions. In the Setup stage, attribute number of users starts from 5 to 60 and increases 5 every time. In the Encrypt stage, attribute number of ciphertext policies starts from 5 to 60 and increases 5 every time. They are connected by the AND gate. As can be seen from the figure, the time is very close to each experiment. We find that the differences of Encrypt and Decrypt time are nearly constant in these test cases. The Encrypt time of our scheme is 0.015s bigger than RW'13 [20] and the Decryption time is 0.032s. The difference of KeyGen time between our scheme and RW'13 [20] grows slowly from 0.016s to 0.021s. Therefore, our scheme is very efficient. Notice that the encryption time of our scheme in the figure is only for KGC. Users also need to give to KGC a zero-knowledge proof of knowledge of the discrete log of w^o with respect to w.

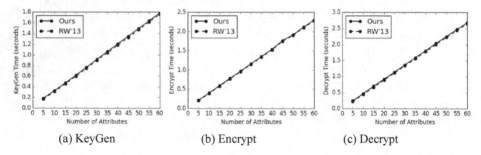

(a) KeyGen   (b) Encrypt   (c) Decrypt

Fig. 1. Comparison of KeyGen, Encrypt and Decrypt

6   Conclusion

The lack of user and authority accountability is an important challenging issue in ABE. The user is able to share his/her secret key and abuse his/her access privilege without being identified, and KGC can generate any user's secret key. In this paper, we propose a practical large universe CP-ABE with user and authority accountability. We can trace the dishonest user or KGC in white-box model. We prove our scheme selectively secure in the standard model under q-type assumption. We also prove the accountability property against dishonest user and KGC in the standard model. In the future work, we intend to construct a scheme which can support user and authority accountability in black-box model. And another future research direction is how to revoke the dishonest user after the user is found.

Acknowledgments. This work is supported by the National High Technology Research and Development Program ("863" Program) of China under Grant No. 2015AA016009, the National Natural Science Foundation of China under Grant No. 61232005, and the Science and Technology Program of Shen Zhen, China under Grant No. JSGG2014051 6162852628.

References

1. Akinyele, J.A., Garman, C., Miers, I., Pagano, M.W., Rushanan, M., Green, M., Rubin, A.D.: Charm: a framework for rapidly prototyping cryptosystems. Journal of Cryptographic Engineering **3**(2), 111–128 (2013)
2. Attrapadung, N., Libert, B., de Panafieu, E.: Expressive key-policy attribute-based encryption with constant-size ciphertexts. In: Catalano, D., Fazio, N., Gennaro, R., Nicolosi, A. (eds.) PKC 2011. LNCS, vol. 6571, pp. 90–108. Springer, Heidelberg (2011)
3. Beimel, A.: Secure schemes for secret sharing and key distribution. Ph.D. thesis, Israel Institute of Technology, Technion, Haifa, Israel (1996)
4. Bethencourt, J., Sahai, A., Waters, B.: Ciphertext-policy attribute-based encryption. In: IEEE Symposium on Security and Privacy, pp. 321–334 (2007)
5. Boneh, D., Boyen, X.: Short signatures without random oracles. In: Cachin, C., Camenisch, J.L. (eds.) EUROCRYPT 2004. LNCS, vol. 3027, pp. 56–73. Springer, Heidelberg (2004)
6. Chase, M.: Multi-authority Attribute Based Encryption. In: Vadhan, S.P. (ed.) TCC 2007. LNCS, vol. 4392, pp. 515–534. Springer, Heidelberg (2007)
7. Chase, M., Chow, S.S.: Improving privacy and security in multi-authority attribute-based encryption. In: ACM Conference on Computer and Communications Security, pp. 121–130 (2009)
8. Cheung, L., Newport, C.: Provably secure ciphertext policy ABE. In: ACM Conference on Computer and Communications Security, pp. 456–465 (2007)
9. Goyal, V.: Reducing trust in the PKG in identity based cryptosystems. In: Menezes, A. (ed.) CRYPTO 2007. LNCS, vol. 4622, pp. 430–447. Springer, Heidelberg (2007)
10. Goyal, V., Pandey, O., Sahai, A., Waters, B.: Attribute-based encryption for fine-grained access control of encrypted data. In: ACM Conference on Computer and Communications Security, pp. 89–98 (2006)
11. Hinek, M.J., Jiang S., Safavi-Naini, R., Shahandashti, S.F.: Attribute-based encryption with key cloning protection. Cryptology ePrint Archive, Report 2008/478 (2008). http://eprint.iacr.org/
12. Li, J., Huang, Q., Chen, X., Chow, S.S., Wong, D.S., Xie, D.: Multi-authority ciphertext-policy attribute-based encryption with accountability. In: ACM Conference on Computer and Communications Security, pp. 386–390 (2011)
13. Li, J., Ren, K., Zhu, B., Wan, Z.: Privacy-aware attribute-based encryption with user accountability. In: Samarati, P., Yung, M., Martinelli, F., Ardagna, C.A. (eds.) ISC 2009. LNCS, vol. 5735, pp. 347–362. Springer, Heidelberg (2009)
14. Libert, B., Vergnaud, D.: Towards black-box accountable authority ibe with short ciphertexts and private keys. In: Jarecki, S., Tsudik, G. (eds.) PKC 2009. LNCS, vol. 5443, pp. 235–255. Springer, Heidelberg (2009)
15. Liu, Z., Cao, Z., Wong, D.S.: Blackbox traceable CP-ABE: how to catch people leaking their keys by selling decryption devices on eBay. In: ACM Conference on Computer and Communications Security, pp. 475–486 (2013)
16. Liu, Z., Cao, Z., Wong, D.S.: White-box traceable ciphertext-policy attribute-based encryption supporting any monotone access structures. IEEE Transactions on Information Forensics and Security **8**(1), 76–88 (2013)
17. Liu, Z., Wong, D.S.: Practical attribute based encryption: traitor tracing, revocation, and large universe. Cryptology ePrint Archive, Report 2014/616 (2014). http://eprint.iacr.org/

18. Ning, J., Cao, Z., Dong, X., Wei, L., Lin, X.: Large universe ciphertext-policy attribute-based encryption with white-box traceability. In: Kutyłowski, M., Vaidya, J. (eds.) ICAIS 2014, Part II. LNCS, vol. 8713, pp. 55–72. Springer, Heidelberg (2014)
19. Ostrovsky, R., Sahai, A., Waters, B.: Attribute-based encryption with non-monotonic access structures. In: ACM Conference on Computer and Communications Security, pp. 195–203 (2007)
20. Rouselakis, Y., Waters, B.: Practical constructions and new proof methods for large universe attribute-based encryption. In: ACM Conference on Computer and Communications Security, pp. 463–474 (2013)
21. Sahai, A., Waters, B.: Fuzzy identity-based encryption. In: Cramer, R. (ed.) EUROCRYPT 2005. LNCS, vol. 3494, pp. 457–473. Springer, Heidelberg (2005)
22. Schnorr, C.-P.: Efficient identification and signatures for smart cards. In: Brassard, G. (ed.) CRYPTO 1989. LNCS, vol. 435, pp. 239–252. Springer, Heidelberg (1990)
23. Shamir, A.: How to share a secret. Communications of the ACM **22**(11), 612–613 (1979)
24. Wang, Y., Chen, K., Long, Y., Liu, Z.: Accountable authority key policy attribute-based encryption. Science China Information Sciences **55**(7), 1631–1638 (2012)
25. Waters, B.: Ciphertext-policy attribute-based encryption: an expressive, efficient, and provably secure realization. In: Catalano, D., Fazio, N., Gennaro, R., Nicolosi, A. (eds.) PKC 2011. LNCS, vol. 6571, pp. 53–70. Springer, Heidelberg (2011)
26. Yu, S., Ren, K., Lou, W., Li, J.: Defending against key abuse attacks in KP-ABE enabled broadcast systems. In: Chen, Y., Dimitriou, T.D., Zhou, J. (eds.) SecureComm 2009. LNICST, vol. 19, pp. 311–329. Springer, Heidelberg (2009)

A Decentralized Access Control Model
for Dynamic Collaboration of Autonomous Peers

Stefan Craß[(⊠)], Gerson Joskowicz, and Eva Kühn

Institute of Computer Languages, TU Wien, Argentinierstr. 8, Vienna, Austria
{sc,gj,ek}@complang.tuwien.ac.at

Abstract. Distributed applications are often composed of autonomous components that are controlled by different stakeholders. Authorization in such a scenario has to be enforced in a decentralized way so that administrators retain control over their respective resources. In this paper, we define a flexible access control model for a data-driven coordination middleware that abstracts the collaboration of autonomous peers. It supports the definition of fine-grained policies that depend on authenticated subject attributes, content properties and context data. To enable peers to act on behalf of others, chained delegation is supported and permissions depend on trust assumptions about nodes along this chain. Besides access to data, also service invocations, dynamic behavior changes and policy updates can be authorized in a unified way. We show how this access control model can be integrated into a secure middleware architecture and provide example policies for simple coordination patterns.

Keywords: ABAC · Delegation · P2P · Coordination middleware

1 Introduction

Modern distributed systems are often not managed by a single organization, but require collaboration of multiple stakeholders that provide data and offer services. Due to evolving application requirements and availability of different providers for specific tasks, distributed workflows should be dynamically configurable and enable ad-hoc coordination. Examples for such complex interactions include cloud-based business-to-business transactions, peer-to-peer (P2P) networks that enable efficient data replication, and connected smart devices.

As mutual trust cannot be assumed in such dynamic communication networks, a suitable access control model is necessary that enables participants to specify who can access their data and services. To address the flexibility of distributed systems with dynamically changing security requirements, each member shall be able to manage its own access control policy independently of others [1]. This requires an authentication concept that supports identity providers from different security domains, which may be linked to different trust levels. In order to cope with indirect access on behalf of other users, support for delegated identities is needed. For instance, a customer may want to access a company's data

© Institute for Computer Sciences, Social Informatics and Telecommunications Engineering 2015
B. Thuraisingham et al. (Eds.): SecureComm 2015, LNICST 164, pp. 519–537, 2015.
DOI: 10.1007/978-3-319-28865-9_28

storage via a cloud service. The company may allow a trusted cloud service to read data associated with the delegating customer, while denying direct customer access in order to make security administration simpler and more reliable.

In order to adhere to the principle of least privilege, permissions shall be specifiable in a fine-grained way. Access decisions may depend on the environmental context (e.g. previous interactions), while the administration of policies itself shall be governed with meta-level policies [2]. For instance, resource owners may delegate their administrator privileges to other trusted users, or a cloud provider may allow users to control access to their deployed services themselves.

Current security mechanisms for distributed systems usually rely on centralized servers, which limits their use to networks controlled by a unified administration. There still is a lack of powerful security models for the collaboration of autonomous peers in dynamic scenarios. Although some research has been done on decentralized authentication and authorization [3,4,5], most approaches do not model fine-grained access control policies that support content- and context-based rules as well as arbitrary forms of delegation.

In this paper, we present a flexible and expressive security concept that targets the dynamic coordination of autonomous components in a fully decentralized environment. We assume that applications are designed using a data-driven coordination model [6], which hides the complexity of remote communication and provides intelligible abstractions for service invocation and data access. Application logic is encapsulated in decoupled software components termed *peers*, whose interactions are specified declaratively. Although the security mechanisms are shown in the context of this specific architecture, the concept is applicable to any business process that is implemented using interconnected components.

We propose an extended middleware architecture for this coordination model called *Secure Peer Space* that enables decentralized authorization with support for complex delegation chains and fine-grained access control rules. Rules depend on the accessed content, the environmental context and the subject. We combine elements of attribute-based and discretionary access control, as decisions are based on authenticated attributes, while each owner of a peer may govern access to its own services and data. In contrast to usual access control concepts that place controls on few entry points, we support access control at any involved component of a workflow. The access control model is suitable for cross-organizational collaboration, as it provides a way to specify trust in attributes from distributed sources. It is also possible to depict multitenant scenarios, as users may dynamically inject sub-peers into another peer if permitted by its owner. The security mechanisms, including policy administration, are largely bootstrapped using existing coordination features of the middleware.

The paper is structured as follows: Section 2 describes the addressed coordination middleware. On top of that, Section 3 presents a security concept and a middleware architecture for the Secure Peer Space. Section 4 provides examples for the usage of this secure middleware in the form of reusable coordination patterns. Section 5 discusses the benefits of the presented approach and compares it to related work. Finally, Section 6 concludes the paper and outlines future work.

2   Modeling Coordination with the Peer Model

When designing distributed applications, middleware can help to hide the complexity of remote communication and offer proven coordination primitives for common tasks like synchronization, data access and service invocations. A coordination model provides a high-level abstraction on how to program the coordination logic of a distributed system, i.e. the interactions of individual software components. The *Peer Model*, originally described in [6], allows for modeling of data-driven workflows among highly decoupled components (i.e. peers) in a distributed environment. In the following, we describe the basic concepts of the Peer Model and its associated middleware runtime, the *Peer Space*.

A peer is an addressable component consisting of *space containers* [7], which hold its internal state, and *wirings*, which connect containers within and between peers. Thus, wirings describe the component behavior and its coordination logic. Space containers, which are inspired by Linda tuple spaces [8], store typed data items termed *entries* and provide methods to write and query them. Different kinds of data and messages that are required in a distributed system can be modeled by entries, including events, user data, service requests and responses. Besides its payload, each entry contains a set of (possibly nested) key/value pairs termed *coordination properties*, which determine how an entry is affected by wirings. Each peer provides a *Peer-In-Container* (**PIC**) and a *Peer-Out-Container* (**POC**), forming its input and output stages, respectively. Peers may also be nested so that parts of their functionality are encapsulated into sub-peers.

Wirings are triggered by a specific combination of entries, execute application-specific logic and output their results as entries. A wiring consists of one or more *guards*, zero or more *services* and zero or more *actions*. Guards impose certain conditions on the content of containers. When all guards of a wiring are fulfilled, they provide the services with a set of input entries from these containers. The services may modify the entries or create new ones based on the input. The resulting output entries are then distributed to their target containers by the actions. A wiring may only access containers of the enclosing peer and those of its direct sub-peers. Each guard is specified via a source container, an operation type, and a query that selects a certain subset of entries in the given container. By default matching entries are deleted from the source container when a wiring is triggered (operation type "**move**"), but they may also be only read (operation type "**copy**"). The query consists of the required entry type, optional selectors on further coordination properties (e.g. "$[size < 10 \, kB]$"), and a count parameter, which defines the minimum and maximum number of entries to be selected (default: $min = max = 1$). A query is only fulfilled when at least the minimum number of entries matching the type and selector criteria are available in the source container. After the services have been executed, the actions operate on the resulting entries. Each action has a query that selects from these entries and a target container where matching entries are written to. Unlike guards, an action does never block as the output entries are fixed after service execution.

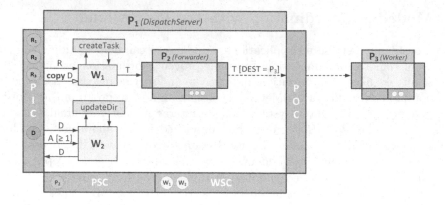

Fig. 1. Peer Model example with dynamic state.

The Peer Space middleware runtime executes the modeled wirings and realizes remote communication between peers. We denote a specific instance of a collaborative interaction as a *flow*, which is usually started by a single user request and may involve the (possibly concurrent) execution of several wirings located at multiple (possibly distributed) peers. To provide the glue that creates a distributed process out of the modeled behaviors of involved peers, there are several predefined coordination properties that determine how entries are treated: A unique **FlowID** helps the framework to correlate entries that belong to the same flow. Timing constraints may be addressed by time-to-live (**TTL**) and time-to-start (**TTS**) properties, which limit the lifecycle of an entry and delay its activation, respectively. The destination (**DEST**) property of an entry provides the mechanism to model directed remote communication. It specifies the target container using the address of its peer and a container name (default: *PIC*). The entry is then injected into this container by the Peer Space.

We also introduce a meta-model approach for the dynamic adaptation of behavior by adding and replacing wirings and peers. Besides PIC and POC, each peer also has a *Wiring Specification Container* (**WSC**) and a *Peer Specification Container* (**PSC**). Each wiring corresponds to a meta entry in the WSC that includes the wiring specification as payload. Similarly, the PSC contains the specification entries for each direct sub-peer. The behavior of the sub-peers is then specified recursively. These meta entries may be accessed like regular entries in a PIC or POC. Thus, they can be injected via remote communication, may be written or deleted by local wirings and are garbage-collected based on their TTL. This mechanism is also required to allow queries with parameters that dynamically depend on the application logic. For that, a wiring must create a suitable wiring specification entry in its service and write it to the WSC of the corresponding peer. Depending on its specification, such a dynamic wiring may run as continuous subscription until explicitly deleted or only as a one-off query.

Fig. 1 outlines an example model that dispatches tasks to remote worker peers based on client requests and a configurable lookup directory. Wiring W_1

takes one request (of type R) and a copy of its internal lookup directory D from the PIC of peer P_1 and passes them to its service, which creates a task of type T for a specific worker peer. The wiring's action writes this entry to the PIC of sub-peer P_2, which is responsible for reliably forwarding the task to the target peer. Its sending action is indicated by the dashed arrows, which can be viewed as wirings that are dynamically set by the runtime when it encounters an entry with a specified destination, like P_3 in our example. To keep the model simple, the internal behavior of P_2 and P_3 is not detailed here. The second wiring W_2 updates the lookup directory by taking the corresponding entry together with any new advertisements of type A that have been sent to the peer to indicate changes in the list of available peers. The example also shows the dynamic state of the model during execution. We assume that there are currently three requests and one directory entry in the PIC of P_1. This means that W_1 can be triggered three times, while W_2 is currently waiting for at least one entry of type A. Finally, the figure also depicts the meta model, as sub-peers and wirings are represented by corresponding entries in the PSC and WSC, respectively.

3 Security for the Peer Model

The Peer Model supports a flexible and comprehensible way of modeling coordination within distributed applications, but it lacks a suitable security model. In the following, we describe Peer Model extensions that provide the required security concepts and a corresponding middleware architecture for the Secure Peer Space. The main elements are an attribute-based representation of identities with support for chained delegation, a fine-grained rule-based authorization mechanism for access to entries in regular containers and the meta model, and a secure runtime architecture that authenticates incoming entries and enforces access control on them. The proposed security concept is based on previous work on an access control model for space containers [9], which is adapted to the needs of the Peer Model. Major additions are a trust model based on delegation chains, support for dynamic behavior changes via meta containers, and the introduction of hierarchic policies based on nested peers.

3.1 Identity Representation with Delegation Support

A unified representation of identities forms the foundation of the decentralized security model. We use the notion of a *principal*, which represents a specific user (i.e. a system or a person) within the distributed system. The identity of a principal is represented by a data set managed by an *identity provider*. For each runtime, there is an explicit principal termed *runtime user* that represents the Peer Space when communicating with remote runtimes.

Management of permissions must be scalable. Instead of assigning permissions to each user separately, access control should rely on roles and other attributes of authenticated principals. Therefore, the Secure Peer Space supports attribute-based access control (ABAC) [10], where rules depend on one or more validated attributes. Role-based access control (RBAC) [11], where rules grant access for principals with specific roles, can be seen as a special case of ABAC, as role information can be included via attributes. Additional attributes may vary, but at least a user ID and an associated domain (e.g. the user's organization) must be included to be able to uniquely identify the principal.

Access control in the Secure Peer Space targets any operation on containers, which includes (possibly consuming) queries by wiring guards, write operations by wiring actions and entry injection via remote communication. The responsible entity for a specific operation with regard to access control is called the *subject*. A subject may correspond to a single principal, but it may also represent a composition of several principals in case of delegation. The subject that writes an entry to a container is assigned as the *entry owner*. Its identity is represented via nested *subject properties*, which are a special form of coordination properties that are attached to each entry and represent the authenticated attributes.

As peers and wirings are specified by writing entries into meta containers, they also have dedicated owners, which are called *peer owners* and *wiring owners*, respectively. Peer owners are able to administrate the access control policies of their peers, which is detailed in Section 3.2. Wirings and sub-peers are usually created by the owner of their parent peer, but they may also be inserted dynamically by different subjects that were authorized by the peer owner. Whenever a wiring tries to select entries from a container via its guards, the wiring owner is the relevant subject for checking if the wiring is allowed to do so. Similarly, when entries need to be written by a wiring action, the corresponding wiring owner determines the subject relevant for access control and thus also the owner of the emitted entries. The entry owner is not necessarily the original creator of an entry. Even if a wiring modifies only some properties of an entry or simply forwards it to another container, the entry owner is changed. A wiring may choose to use *direct access* and set the entry owner to the wiring owner, or it may apply *indirect access* on behalf of another subject to support delegation.

The simplest way to model delegation would be for a server to use the provided credentials from a user to authenticate at another site and perform some action on the user's behalf. However, this would allow servers to impersonate other principals, which is not feasible as we do not assume inherent trust in any principal. The path to the ultimate target of a request from the initial request issuer may involve several machines that are not equally trusted [12]. A suitable delegation concept for the Secure Peer Space must therefore support chained delegations (e.g. $User1$ delegates to $User2$, who delegates to $User3$ etc.) and allow access control decisions that depend on a combination of the involved principals. The first element of the delegation chain is the initial issuer of a request, while the last element corresponds to the principal that has actually written the entry to its current container. For better readability, we depict a subject by listing the principals in reverse order ($User3$ **for** $User2$ **for** $User1$). For most examples in this paper, we just specify the principals' user IDs, even though their identities actually consist of multiple attributes that are stored in the subject properties.

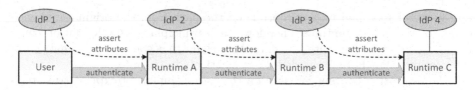

Fig. 2. Chained authentication with different identity providers.

Delegation is triggered when a service within a wiring emits an entry using indirect access mode. Subject properties of an entry cannot be directly manipulated by the service, which prevents malicious wirings from issuing requests or writing data on behalf of arbitrary principals. Instead, they may select any of the owners of their input entries as delegating subject. Thus, a wiring with owner A that fetches two entries with owners B and C, respectively, may use the subjects "A **for** B", "A **for** C", or simply "A" (when using direct access). When another wiring (with owner D) subsequently copies or moves this new entry, it may itself use indirect access and add its own identity to the delegation chain (e.g. "D **for** A **for** B"). This approach prevents impersonation, as the wiring owner is always included as the responsible actor for any action performed by the wiring. Thus, delegation may be used to restrict access based on the identity of the delegating subject, but not to escalate the privileges of the wiring owner, which still has to be authorized to induce the subsequent steps in the flow.

As authentication is performed in a decentralized way, additional challenges arise. Principals that are part of a subject need not necessarily be directly authenticated at the local Peer Space. For instance, when a delegation chain spans several runtimes with runtime users U_1 to U_n, the last Peer Space only directly authenticates U_{n-1} and it has to trust this runtime that U_{n-2} has indeed been correctly authenticated and so forth. A similar problem occurs when a wiring with an owner different from the local runtime user wants to send an entry to a remote Peer Space (using the DEST property). As the runtime must not impersonate the wiring owner directly, it authenticates at the remote site using the identity of its own runtime user, while claiming that the wiring owner has been authenticated at its site (or at another runtime that it trusts).

Each principal in a delegation chain may be authenticated by a different Peer Space runtime, which is illustrated in Fig. 2. In this example, a separate entity (IdP 1-4) is responsible for asserting attributes for each principal, but multiple runtimes may also share the same identity provider. The identity providers act as anchors of trust, which prove the validity of the authenticating principal's identity using some form of authentication mechanism (e.g. certificates) not detailed in this paper. However, they are not responsible for the identity of any previously authenticated principal in the chain. Instead, the runtime that has authenticated a principal has to guarantee the validity of the claimed subject properties when it forwards this information. It is not only necessary to trust that the principals in the delegation chain are in fact acting legitimately on behalf of previous principals, but also that the claimed identities of these principals are in fact valid and were not modified by any runtime on the path from the original authenticator to the current runtime. Therefore, each principal in the delegation chain is associated with a separate authentication chain that specifies the identities of the runtimes that have forwarded its authenticated attributes.

The delegation concept is based on the establishment of explicit trust relationships among collaborating principals by means of access control rules. Each peer owner can independently select which forms of delegations are trusted by including constraints on the delegation and authentication chains of an incoming entry. For instance, it may be specified that only peers with a certain role may act on behalf of other principals and that owners of the delegating peers must be authenticated by a runtime owned by a specific organization. If such rules are defined for every peer, an explicit chain of trust can be established that states which peers and runtimes are trusted to act on behalf of prior peers.

As the entries that constitute a delegated access and their authentication data are relayed on the same path (via the participating Peer Spaces), the delegation chain and the individual authentication chains can be combined in a single data structure called *subject tree*. The root of this tree represents the local runtime user. Its direct children are the principals within the subject that were directly authenticated by the runtime. Each inner node depicts a runtime user that has been authenticated by its parent and has authenticated its children. The leaves correspond to principals that are part of the delegation chain, while the path from each leaf to the root forms the respective authentication chain. The order of principals in the delegation chain is defined via a left-to-right tree traversal.

This subject tree is iteratively extended as entries are processed and forwarded along a flow. When an entry is received from a remote runtime, the authenticated security attributes of the sender are written to the root node of the entry's subject tree. Then, the local runtime user is added as the new root. When a service triggers delegation using indirect access, the subject trees of the delegating input entry owner and the wiring owner are merged to form the subject tree for the output entries. As both root nodes represent the local runtime user, they are replaced by a common root, whereas the child nodes associated with the wiring owner are placed after those of the input entry owner to ensure the correct order of the delegation chain.

An example for such a subject tree is shown in Fig. 3, which can be mapped to the Peer Model example from Fig. 1. The subject tree depicts the owner of the task entry that arrives at peer P_3, assuming that the original request came from another remote peer P_0 owned by user "evakuehn" from TU Wien and that P_1 together with its sub-peer and wirings are owned by a system user from organization "OrgA". Each of the three peers P_0, P_1 and P_3 are hosted by different Peer Space runtimes with separate runtime users. The delegation chain can be represented as "*SystemUser* **for** *evakuehn*", whereas the other principals are part of the authentication chains. User "evakuehn" has been authenticated by runtime user "SBCServer" when she has registered P_0. When sending the request from P_0, this runtime then authenticates at the runtime of P_1 (with runtime user "Server123"), which happens to be a cloud node that may host

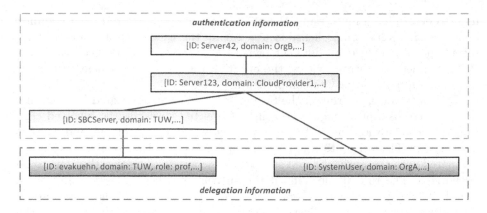

Fig. 3. Subject tree example for delegation.

peers of different companies and has also earlier authenticated the owner of P_1 as "SystemUser". This runtime then provides its authentication data together with the forwarded claims of the other principals to the final target runtime, which is owned by the runtime user "Server42" from organization "OrgB". The target peer has to specify if it trusts such a subject tree via its access control rules. For the textual representation of a subject tree, we depict authentication chain edges with the "@" symbol. The example subject tree can thus be abbreviated as "$(SystemUser$ **for** $(evakuehn@SBCServer))@Server123@Server42$".

3.2 Rule-Based Authorization

Based on the proposed delegation concept, a decentralized authorization mechanism can be defined, where for every peer an access control policy is specified by its owner. Each policy consists of a set of access control rules that need to be evaluated to form an access decision. It determines which entries can be written to as well as read or removed from a container. As all interactions in the Peer Model are based on entries, this protects access to a peer's internal state and its services. Due to the data-centric modeling of service invocations, requests as well as their responses can be authorized. Rules may not only apply to regular peer containers, but also to the meta containers that specify sub-peers and wirings. Thus, a peer owner may allow trusted subjects to inject their own logic into the peer, which supports the management of multitenant environments.

Fine-grained access control policies should exceed the expressiveness of simple access control lists on peers or containers. Therefore, we adapt a policy language from our previous work on secure space containers [9] to domain-specific assumptions introduced by the Peer Model. This approach is inspired by the XACML standard [13], which provides a declarative, XML-based language for expressing access control policies based on authenticated subject attributes, used operations, accessed content, and context-dependent conditions. Rules may either permit or deny a specific access request, whereas combination algorithms are used to determine a final result. However, XACML policies are rather complex and often not very comprehensible. As during the execution of a flow usually several peers managed by different owners are involved, which need to define their own access control policies, the effect of the individual policies and their combination must be easy to comprehend.

Each access control rule in the Secure Peer Space is associated to a specific peer and consists of a unique ID, a list of affected subjects, the involved containers and operations as well as restrictions on the entry content and context information. The **subjects** field contains one or more *subject templates* that are compared with the authenticated subject of the access operation that has to be authorized. The rule applies only if the subject matches at least one of these templates. Such a template is represented by a tree where each node consists of a set of predicates on the subject properties of the corresponding principal in the subject tree. These predicates resemble the selectors used in guard and action queries and may check for equality or inequality with a specific value or use comparison operators (e.g. "$age \geq 18$"). Additionally, wildcards for single nodes ("*") and chains ("**") are supported. A subject tree node matches its corresponding node in the template if each of its predicates is fulfilled. The root node can be omitted, as it always corresponds to the local runtime user. An example template that matches the subject tree from Fig. 3 would be "($[domain = OrgA]$ **for** ($[domain = TUW, role = prof]$ @ **)) @ $[domain = CloudProvider1]$". This means that the rule targets delegated access by any peer from organization "OrgA" on behalf of a professor from TU Wien, which was transmitted via a runtime managed by the organization of "CloudProvider1". The wildcard states that the creator of the rule does not care whether the professor was directly authenticated at the cloud provider or indirectly via a chain of one or more other runtimes. Thus, it is not guaranteed that this authentication data was relayed only along trusted nodes. However, it could be assumed that the cloud provider is already responsible for doing these kind of checks. If every runtime trusts its direct predecessors in a flow to only accept input from other trusted nodes, a chain of trust can be established that allows for very simple subject templates.

The **resources** field specifies the container(s) for which the rule applies, while the **operations** field distinguishes between three access types: **read**, **take**, and **write**. Read access is relevant for copy guards, while take privileges are required by move guards. Write permissions are necessary for actions, including those that inject entries into remote containers via the DEST property.

The optional **scope** field states for which kind of entries the rule is valid. This is expressed via the same query mechanism as used by guards and actions, however without the count parameter. Thus, the rule's scope may be restricted to a certain entry type or to entries with specific coordination properties. A combination of queries using disjunction, conjunction and negation is possible, thus enabling complex rules. The optional **condition** field allows restrictions based on the current state of the peer, which depicts context information that may depend on previous interactions. It consists of one or more *condition predicates* that can be combined using disjunction, conjunction and negation. Each predicate consists of a container name and a query as used by the scope mechanism. If at least one entry in the specified container matches the query, the predicate is fulfilled. The rule only applies if the combination of predicates is satisfied. A condition may, e.g., be used in rules that allow access to a container only if an internal state entry in the PIC has a specific value or if a specific sub-peer is registered in the PSC. For our example, a rule that allows users to write requests to the PIC of P_1 may be defined as follows:

SUBJECTS: $[role = prof]$ @ $[ID = SBCServer,\ domain = TUW]$
RESOURCES: PIC
OPERATIONS: $write$
SCOPE: R
CONDITION: $PIC \triangleright D\ [peerCount > 0]$

The subject template matches any professor that was authenticated via a specific runtime user from TU Wien. The scope limits permissions to entries of type R, while the condition checks that the coordination property *"peerCount"* of the directory entry D in the PIC has a value greater than zero, which prevents access when no peers are available that are able to process tasks.

In contrast to XACML, we support only "permit" rules, which simplifies the combination of rules for finding an access decision. If access to a specific entry for a given subject is not permitted by at least one active rule, it is automatically denied. Due to the fine-grained rules and the possibility to specify hierarchic security policies (one for each sub-peer), most access restrictions can still be expressed easily. A rule permits access if the subject tree of an operation matches any given subject template, the operation type and the accessed container are included in the rule, the condition (if available) evaluates to true and the written or selected entries fulfill the scope query. If no scope query is specified, access to the whole container is granted. Access control is transparent for wirings: Guards only select entries from the subset of entries the wiring owner is permitted to access, while other entries are not visible by the query mechanism. Thus, a wiring cannot distinguish if an entry does not exist or if the subject does not have the necessary permissions. When actions try to write entries to a container, the set subject must be allowed to write each of them, otherwise the action is skipped.

In order to let permissions not only depend on the context of the peer, but also on the context of the accessing subject, we introduce *context variables* that can be used instead of any coordination property value in scope and condition queries as well as subject templates. These variables are prefixed with a "$" symbol followed by a name that represents a specific subject property for the current access. To simplify the specification of such constraints, the original issuer of a flow (i.e. the leftmost leaf in the subject tree) is aliased as "originator". This allows, e.g., to specify that the domain of a runtime user in the authentication chain must be the same as the domain of the original issuer of a request (*"domain = $originator.domain"* in the subject template), or that entries may only be accessed on behalf of the principal that was responsible for writing them (*"originator = $originator"* in a scope query).

To reduce the number of rules and prevent users from being locked out of their own peers, peer owners may implicitly access their own containers without any restrictions. However, if delegation is used (peer owner on behalf of another subject), explicit access control rules are required, which supports restrictions based on the identity of the delegating subject.

3.3   Secure Runtime Architecture

The security concept can be integrated into the Peer Space runtime architecture, resulting in the Secure Peer Space. The runtime hosts peers and is responsible for storing entries, executing wirings, handling remote communication as well as enforcing authentication and authorization. Fig. 4 shows the architecture of this middleware framework. As the runtime has input and output stages in the form of a remote communication interface, it can be represented in the meta model by a *runtime peer* that is owned by the runtime user. Incoming entries are written to the PIC and dispatched to the corresponding peer, either according to the address in the given DEST property or using explicit wirings. Similarly, entries that need to be sent to a remote runtime are written to the POC. Top-level peers and wirings can be added by writing to the PSC and WSC of the runtime peer.

Authentication is done by an *authentication manager* that intercepts received entries before writing them to the PIC of the runtime peer (or to a meta container, e.g. when adding peers). It is responsible for verifying the credentials that were sent with each entry. If authentication is successful, the authenticated attributes are attached to the entry's subject tree, otherwise the entry is discarded. The authentication manager may be configured to accept attributes from one or more identity providers, which may be restricted to specific domains to prevent that an identity provider for one organization issues identities associated with a competitor. The security mechanism is independent of the used authentication method, whose details are therefore out of scope of this paper. Identity providers may either directly communicate with the authentication manager or indirectly via information already included in the received entry. As the level of trust in a subject may depend on the used authentication method and the responsible identity provider, information about the authentication context is also included in the subject properties by the authentication manager.

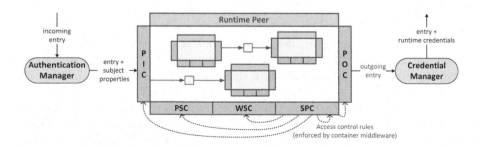

Fig. 4. Secure Peer Space runtime overview.

Before an entry is sent to a remote runtime, the *credential manager* attaches the credentials of the runtime user to the outgoing entry (e.g. by using a digital signature), so that the remote runtime's authentication manager may correctly authenticate the entry. We assume that the used communication channels are cryptographically secured to ensure confidentiality and integrity for entries.

The access control policy for each peer is managed via an additional meta container named *Security Policy Container* (**SPC**) that holds the access control rules as individual entries. The policy can be managed by writing and removing rules via (dynamic) wirings, which allows for flexible permission changes. Rules may target any container of the corresponding peer, including the SPC itself. Thus, a peer owner may grant administrator privileges to another subject by specifying a rule that permits (possibly restricted) access to the SPC.

The policy for the entire Peer Space is defined in a hierarchic way via the SPCs of the runtime peer and all hosted (sub-)peers. An administrator may define general rules that specify who is trusted to communicate with the Peer Space, while the owners of the hosted peers may restrict access to their services to specific subjects. If necessary, more fine-grained permissions may be set in sub-peers. As entries are always passed up or down along this hierarchy, each involved stakeholder can control what kind of interactions are allowed. This also applies when using the remote communication mechanism, as the runtime moves an entry with set DEST property recursively through the POC of each parent peer until the POC of the runtime peer is reached. On the receiving side, the entry recursively passes the PICs of child peers until the destination is reached. The entry owner must be permitted to write to each of these containers.

The enforcement of the access control policy can be embedded into the container implementation using a mechanism described in [14]. Each container access is intercepted and evaluated with regard to the active policy stored in the responsible SPC. The runtime determines rules with matching subject, operation and container. Then, conditions are evaluated by querying the specified containers. Finally, for all remaining (i.e. applicable) rules the scope is evaluated, either on the set of written entries or on the entire container (for read/take access). The container operation is only performed if it is allowed according to the specified rules, whereas denied entries are treated as invisible for query operations.

4   Secure Coordination Patterns

Coordination patterns provide reusable design solutions to recurring problems for the interaction of autonomous components. Due to the high decoupling provided by the Peer Model, complex applications may be designed by configuring and composing such "building blocks" consisting of several peers and their coordination logic [15]. In the following, we outline two coordination patterns with respective access control rules as examples for the usage of the Secure Peer Space.

4.1   Request-Response with Cloud Service

For the first example, we address a request-response scenario, where a client peer sends a request entry (*Req*) to a server peer, which generates a response entry (*Resp*) that is returned to the client. The server is hosted at a generic cloud platform that may act as runtime peer for several server peers managed by different principals. The Peer Model representation of this pattern is depicted in Fig. 5, which also shows the relevant security attributes of the peer owners and the subjects for the individual operations. For the sake of simplicity, we assume that all principals share a domain. To prevent misuse, several access control rules need to be defined by the respective peer owners. For the server peer *AppPeer*1 (owned by *App*1), the following rules may be defined in its SPC:

SUBJECTS: [*role = Client*]   **SUBJECTS:** [*ID = App*1] **for ****
RESOURCES: *PIC*   **RESOURCES:** *POC*
OPERATIONS: *write*   **OPERATIONS:** *write*
SCOPE: *Req*   **SCOPE:** *Resp*

The first rule allows clients to invoke the server using a request entry, while the second rule indicates that there are no restrictions on whose behalf a response entry may be sent. Taking a request from its PIC is implicitly allowed for the peer owner *App*1. The same (or more general) rules must also be set by the owner of the runtime peer *CloudRTP*. To enable the dynamic adaptation of server peers via meta containers, additional rules have to be specified by the runtime user, which are not detailed here. Finally, the client, which owns runtime peer *ClientRTP*, may want to ensure that a server only sends a response entry when it acts on the client's behalf. That is achieved using the following rule:

SUBJECTS: ([*role = Server*] **for** [*ID = User*1]) @ [*ID = Cloud*1]
RESOURCES: *PIC*
OPERATIONS: *write*
SCOPE: *Resp*

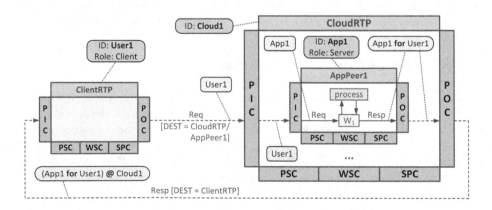

Fig. 5. Cloud-based request-response pattern with responsible subjects.

4.2   Data Exchange via Shared Memory

The second example outlines a shared memory on a server peer that can be accessed by several nodes that want to exchange data. A possible use case would be home automation, where several devices may want to exchange sensor data to collaboratively achieve a task. Fig. 6 depicts such a scenario, where two robot peers that are part of an alarm system application share their sensor data via a central home server. The following rule regulates access to this storage peer:

SUBJECTS: $[role = Node]$
RESOURCES: PIC
OPERATIONS: $write, read, take$
SCOPE: $Data\ [originator.app = \$originator.app]$

It ensures that any peer with role $Node$ may write and retrieve data entries. However, data may only be accessed within the same application, which prevents, e.g., that the entertainment system reads sensitive data from the alarm system. This is achieved via a context-aware selector in the scope, which ensures that only entries sharing the subject property app with the entry owner are considered. Optionally, the rule may be extended with additional conditions, e.g. to ensure that the application is currently active based on a status entry. Read and take access are realized via dynamic wirings. In the example, $RobotPeer2$ retrieves the data of $RobotPeer1$ by writing the wiring specification for W_1 to the WSC of $StoragePeer$. This requires additional rules that allow write access for nodes to the WSC and the POC, as well as a rule on $RobotPeer2$ that permits the dynamic wiring to respond via the PIC of the robot peer, using "$[ID = Robot2]\ @\ [role = Server]$" as subject template to express trust in the server.

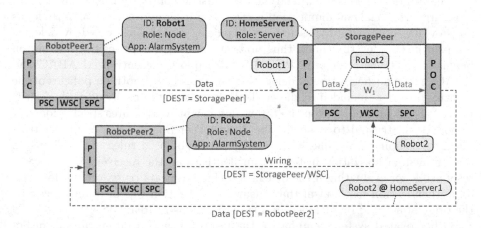

Fig. 6. Shared memory pattern in home automation scenario with responsible subjects.

5   Discussion and Related Work

The proposed Secure Peer Space architecture offers an abstraction for modeling secure collaboration of autonomous peers in distributed systems with fine-grained, context-aware permissions for stored data as well as service invocations. Due to its explicit trust model, it supports multiple identity providers and heterogeneous authentication mechanisms. Authorization is decentralized, as each user regulates access to its own peers based on the trustworthiness of the request issuer, the delegated principals, and the involved runtimes. Also for multitenant environments, security constraints can be expressed in a natural way due to the support for access control on meta-model operations and the hierarchical layers of protection provided by the nested peer structure. As policy administration is bootstrapped using meta containers, a holistic security model for collaborative scenarios is provided that allows for specifying flexible access control rules targeting all kind of peer interactions and administrator tasks.

The underlying Peer Model separates coordination and computation in a business process, while the proposed concept adds access control in a decoupled way. Consequently, each component can be administered independently allowing reuse of secured peers in different workflows. As a tradeoff, administrators have to know the basic functionality of involved peers. While simpler ways of handling authorization are possible, the expressiveness of our model enables the definition of complex constraints that would otherwise have to be included directly in the application code. If such complexity is not desirable, an actual implementation could simplify rules, e.g. by defining the scope only by means of entry types and omitting conditions. It is also possible to model a peer that dynamically changes rules based on a high-level security policy, which may be easier to comprehend than the combination of individual rules in different policy containers.

Chained delegations are already an established concept for access control in cross-organizational communication networks. Earlier approaches [3,12,16] focus on providing cryptographic assurance that delegation is authorized by delegating principals along the chain, thus preventing malicious nodes from acting on behalf of arbitrary principals. PERMIS [4] supports decentralized ABAC and RBAC, where authorization of delegation chains is based both on policies of the identity provider (included in the credentials) and of the receiving node. Trust-related access control rules on the target define which attributes specific identity providers are trusted to issue. In the Secure Peer Space, we use subject templates to combine such rules with regular privilege-based rules. As we focus on fine-grained authorization instead of authentication, the receiver of an entry is responsible for evaluating if the delegation chain appears trustworthy. However, an authentication mechanism that ensures a delegation was also authorized by the originator could be included in a similar way as in PERMIS.

Other related systems emphasize the importance of a decentralized authorization approach, but do not support delegation chains. P-Hera [5] provides secure content hosting for P2P infrastructures, where resource and data owners can dynamically establish trust via fine-grained XACML rules. Similar to the Secure Peer Space, each subject may express its own constraints based on its role in the network. Opyrchal et al. [17] suggest an access control model for a publish-subscribe middleware in pervasive environments, where owners can authorize other users to subscribe to their events. Fine-grained rules can be specified using conditions on attributes of the request, the addressed event, and context information. As in our approach, secure policy administration is bootstrapped via rules that allow users to modify a policy. LGI [1] provides a secure message exchange mechanism for open groups of distributed agents. Members may independently define their own access control policy, as long as it conforms to a common coalition policy. Expressive Prolog-based rules can be specified that may depend on the current state of the interaction. The Secure Peer Space also supports a hierarchy of policies via nested peers. A shared policy may be enforced by an administrator that manages distributed coalition peers, which contain sub-peers owned by the respective members. TuCSoN [18] supports coordination via distributed tuple spaces connected in a tree topology, where gateway nodes control visibility and authorization of their children. Such an architecture may also be enforced with the Secure Peer Space by only allowing access if an entry was forwarded by a gateway peer. Like in our runtime architecture, access control is realized using features of the space-based middleware itself. Similar to our approach, SMEPP [19] is a service framework on top of a tuple space abstraction, where service requests and replies are modeled as data entries in shared spaces. However, access control is based on groups and thus rather coarse-grained.

6   Conclusion

We have presented a decentralized access control model that addresses interactions of autonomous peers which do not fully trust each other. Each principal may specify its own security policy that governs access to its data and services. By using the Peer Model as a data-driven abstraction for collaborative workflows and meta-level operations, we are able to specify a wide range of security constraints via fine-grained rules on (meta) containers that depend on properties of the authenticated subject, the accessed entries and context data. Due to an expressive delegation mechanism, trust-based rules can be specified that depend not only on the request originator, but also on the trustworthiness of users that have forwarded the request and security attributes of other principals.

For the proposed middleware architecture, we are currently developing a prototype that should be applicable for different domains, including cloud architectures and P2P networks. Even in situations where the runtime itself is not feasible, e.g. due to limited resources of embedded systems, the secured Peer Model version can still be helpful in the design phase to model all kind of security constraints in a unified way. Future work will also involve additional research on secure coordination patterns in order to provide an extensive pattern catalogue that covers the most relevant forms of interaction in collaborative scenarios.

Acknowledgments. We would like to thank Lukas Bitter, Stephan Cejka, Thomas Hamböck, and the anonymous reviewers for their helpful comments.

References

1. Ao, X., Minsky, N.H.: Flexible regulation of distributed coalitions. In: Snekkenes, E., Gollmann, D. (eds.) ESORICS 2003. LNCS, vol. 2808, pp. 39–60. Springer, Heidelberg (2003)
2. Ahmed, T., Tripathi, A.R.: Security Policies in Distributed CSCW and Workflow Systems. IEEE Transactions on Systems, Man, and Cybernetics - Part A: Systems and Humans 40(6), 1220–1231 (2010)
3. Gomi, H., Hatakeyama, M., Hosono, S., Fujita, S.: A delegation framework for federated identity management. In: 2005 Workshop on Digital Identity Management, pp. 94–103. ACM (2005)
4. Chadwick, D., Zhao, G., Otenko, S., Laborde, R., Su, L., Nguyen, T.A.: PERMIS: A modular authorization infrastructure. Concurrency Computation Practice and Experience 20(11), 1341–1357 (2008)
5. Crispo, B., Sivasubramanian, S., Mazzoleni, P., Bertino, E.: P-Hera: scalable fine-grained access control for P2P infrastructures. In: 11th International Conference on Parallel and Distributed Systems, vol. 1, pp. 585–591. IEEE (2005)
6. Kühn, E., Craß, S., Joskowicz, G., Marek, A., Scheller, T.: Peer-based programming model for coordination patterns. In: De Nicola, R., Julien, C. (eds.) COORDINATION 2013. LNCS, vol. 7890, pp. 121–135. Springer, Heidelberg (2013)
7. Kühn, E., Mordinyi, R., Keszthelyi, L., Schreiber, C.: Introducing the concept of customizable structured spaces for agent coordination in the production automation domain. In: 8th International Conference on Autonomous Agents and Multi-agent Systems, vol. 1, pp. 625–632. IFAAMAS (2009)
8. Carriero, N., Gelernter, D.: Linda in context. Communications of the ACM 32(4), 444–458 (1989)
9. Craß, S., Dönz, T., Joskowicz, G., Kühn, E., Marek, A.: Securing a Space-Based Service Architecture with Coordination-Driven Access Control. Journal of Wireless Mobile Networks, Ubiquitous Computing, and Dependable Applications 4(1), 76–97 (2013)
10. Yuan, E., Tong, J.: Attributed based access control (ABAC) for web services. In: 2005 IEEE International Conference on Web Services, pp. 561–569. IEEE (2005)
11. Sandhu, R.S., Coyne, E.J., Feinstein, H.L., Youman, C.E.: Role-based access control models. Computer 29(2), 38–47 (1996)
12. Lampson, B., Abadi, M., Burrows, M., Wobber, E.: Authentication in distributed systems: theory and practice. ACM Transactions on Computer Systems 10(4), 265–310 (1992)
13. Moses, T.: eXtensible Access Control Markup Language (XACML) Version 2.0. Standard, OASIS (2005)
14. Craß, S., Dönz, T., Joskowicz, G., Kühn, E.: A coordination-driven authorization framework for space containers. In: 7th International Conference on Availability, Reliability and Security, pp. 133–142. IEEE (2012)
15. Kühn, E., Craß, S., Schermann, G.: Extending a peer-based coordination model with composable design patterns. In: 23rd Euromicro International Conference on Parallel, Distributed and Network-Based Processing, pp. 53–61. IEEE (2015)
16. Gasser, M., McDermott, E.: An architecture for practical delegation in a distributed system. In: IEEE Computer Society Symposium on Research in Security and Privacy, pp. 20–30. IEEE (1990)

17. Opyrchal, L., Prakash, A., Agrawal, A.: Designing a publish-subscribe substrate for privacy/security in pervasive environments. In: 2006 ACS/IEEE International Conference on Pervasive Services, pp. 313–316. IEEE (2006)
18. Cremonini, M., Omicini, A., Zambonelli, F.: Coordination and access control in open distributed agent systems: the TuCSoN approach. In: Porto, A., Roman, G.-C. (eds.) COORDINATION 2000. LNCS, vol. 1906, pp. 99–114. Springer, Heidelberg (2000)
19. Benigni, F., Brogi, A., Buchholz, J.L., Jacquet, J.M., Lange, J., Popescu, R.: Secure P2P programming on top of tuple spaces. In: 17th Workshop on Enabling Technologies: Infrastructure for Collaborative Enterprises, pp. 54–59. IEEE (2008)

Using a 3D Geometrical Model to Improve Accuracy in the Evaluation and Selection of Countermeasures Against Complex Cyber Attacks

Gustavo Gonzalez Granadillo$^{(\boxtimes)}$, Joaquin Garcia-Alfaro, and Hervé Debar

Institut Mines-Telecom, Telecom Sudparis, SAMOVAR UMR 5157,
9 Rue Charles Fourier, 91011 Evry, France
{gustavo.gonzalez_granadillo,joaquin.garcia_alfaro,
herve.debar}@telecom-sudparis.eu

Abstract. The selection of security countermeasures against current cyber attacks does not generally perform appropriate assessments of the attack and countermeasure impact over the system. In addition, the methodologies used to evaluate and select countermeasures are generally based on assumptions, estimations, and expert knowledge. A great level of subjectivity is considered while estimating parameters such as benefits and importance of the investment in cost sensitive models. We propose in this paper a decision support tool that uses a Return On Response Investment (RORI) metric, and a 3D geometrical model to simulate the impact of attacks and countermeasures on the system. The former is a cost sensitive model used to evaluate, rank and select security countermeasures against complex cyber attacks. The latter, is a tool that represents the impact of attacks and countermeasures in a three dimensional coordinate system. As a result, we are able to automatically select mitigation strategies addressing multiple and complex cyber attacks, that are efficient in stopping the attack and preserve, at the same time, the best service to legitimate users. The implementation of the tool and main results are detailed at the end of the paper to show the applicability of our model.

Keywords: Countermeasure selection · Geometrical volume · Security impact · CARVER · Response actions

1 Introduction

Innovation in Information Technology has brought numerous advancements but also some consequences. Cyber attacks have evolved along with technology, reaching a state of high efficiency and performance that makes the detection and reaction process a challenging task for security administrators.

Current research focuses on approaches to detect such sophisticated attacks and to demonstrate their robustness and the difficulty in their mitigation [1,3].

© Institute for Computer Sciences, Social Informatics and Telecommunications Engineering 2015
B. Thuraisingham et al. (Eds.): SecureComm 2015, LNICST 164, pp. 538–555, 2015.
DOI: 10.1007/978-3-319-28865-9_29

On the contrary, research on mitigation strategies receives considerably less attention, owing to the inherent complexity in developing and deploying responses in an automated fashion. Mitigation strategies are part of a reaction process that requires security administrators to remediate to threats and/or intrusions by selecting appropriate security countermeasures.

The definition of countermeasures to protect these systems is a process that requires a great expertise and knowledge. Inappropriate countermeasures may result in disastrous consequences for the organization [5]. Typically, the selection of a given countermeasure requires a manual intervention of security operators. No appropriate assessment of the countermeasure impact over the system is currently performed, and service dependencies among the numerous components of large systems in complex environments are not considered.

There is a need for automated mitigation strategies addressing multiple and complex cyber attacks that enable to select optimal countermeasures that are efficient in stopping the attack and preserve, at the same time, the best service to legitimate users.

An attack surface with regard to an information system being attacked is defined as a model that measures quantitatively the level of exposure of a given system, i.e., the reachable and exploitable vulnerabilities existing on the system [11].

Howard et al., [6] consider three dimensions to determine the attack surface of an operating system (e.g. Linux, Windows): Target and enablers, Channels and protocols, and Access rights. However, the approach does not provide a systematic method to assign weights to the attack vectors; it focuses on measuring the attack surfaces of operating systems; and it is not possible to determine if all attack vectors have been identified.

Manadhata et al. [10] measure the attack surface of a software system (e.g., IMAP server, FTP daemons, Operating Systems) based on the analysis of its source code, through three dimensions: methods, channels, and data. However, in the absence of source code, the proposed methodology is useless. The damage potential estimation includes only technical impact (e.g., privilege elevation) and not monetary impact (e.g., monetary loss). The model only compares the level of attackability between two similar systems; no attempt has been made to compare the attack surface of different system environments. The method does not make assumptions about the capabilities of attackers or resources in estimating the damage potential-effort ratio. The methodology does not allow the security administrator to evaluate multiple attacks occurring simultaneously in a given system.

Petajasoja et al. [13] propose an approach to analyze a system's attack surface using CVSS. As a result, it is possible to identify most critical interfaces in order to prioritize the test effort. However, this approach limits the attack surface to known vulnerabilities, it is not meant to be used as a reaction strategy and only compares relative security of similar infrastructures.

Microsoft has recently developed an attack surface analyzer tool [4], that identifies changes made to an operating system attack surface by the installation of new software. However the tool can be used only for Windows operating systems and is useless to measure a network attack surface.

Taking into account the aforementioned limitations, we propose in this paper a method of selecting countermeasures for a service of an information system, against complex cyber attacks. The method comprises:

- identifying elements of the service exposed to the cyber attack(s),
- calculating the return on response investment (RORI) of each countermeasure with respect to the cyber attack(s),
- ranking the countermeasure(s) on the basis of the RORI metric
- simulating the impact of the attack(s) and countermeasure(s) on the system, the countermeasure to be implemented being selected as a function of the result of the simulation.

The rest of the paper is structured as follows: Section 2 introduces the Return On response Investment (RORI) index. Section 3 describes our proposed geometric volume model and details the different types of volumes considered in the approach, as well as the system dimensions. Section 4 discusses the methodologies to select optimal countermeasures. Section 5 presents our approaches to calculate the financial impact of attacks and countermeasures. Section 6 presents our model implementation and main results. Finally, conclusions and perspective for future work are presented in Section 7.

2   Return on Response Investment

The Return On Response Investment (RORI) was first introduced by Kheir et al. [8] as an extension of the Return On Security Investment ROSI [14]. RORI identifies three cost dimensions for intrusion response i.e. the response collateral damages (CD), the response operational costs (OC), and the response goodness (RG). This latter is computed as the difference between the expected intrusion impact before response (ICb) and the combined impact of intrusion and response (RC).

The deployment of the RORI index into real world scenarios has presented the following shortcomings:

- The absolute value of parameters such as ICb and RC is difficult to estimate, whereas a ratio of these parameters is easier to determine, which in turn reduces errors of magnitude.
- The RORI index is not defined when no countermeasure is selected. Since the operational cost (OC) is associated to the security measure, the RORI index will lead to an indetermination when no solution is enacted (hereinafter denoted as NOOP).
- The RORI index is not normalized with the size and complexity of the infrastructure.

Gonzalez Granadillo et al. [5] propose an improvement of the RORI index by taking into account not only the countermeasure cost and its associated risk mitigation, but also the infrastructure value and the expected losses that may occur as a consequence of an intrusion or attack. The improved RORI handles the choice of applying no countermeasure and provides a response that is relative to the size of the infrastructure. RORI is used as a quantitative approach to evaluate, rank, and select a set of countermeasures. The proposed RORI index is calculated according to Equation 1.

$$RORI = \frac{(ALE \times RM) - ARC}{ARC + AIV} \tag{1}$$

Where:

- The Annualized Loss expectancy (ALE) refers to the impact cost that is produced in the absence of countermeasures. It is expressed in currency per year and includes loss of assets (L_a), loss of data (L_d), loss of reputation (L_r), legal procedures (LP), loss of revenues from clients or customers (L_{rc}), as well as other losses (L_o), contracted insurances (Ins), and the annual rate of occurrence (ARO) of the attack.
  $ALE = (L_a + L_d + L_r + LP + L_{rc} + L_o - Ins) \times ARO$
- The Annual Infrastructure Value (AIV) corresponds to the fixed costs that are expected on the system regardless of the implemented countermeasure. AIV is strictly positive and is expressed in currency per year. AIV includes the following costs: equipment costs (C_e), personnel costs (C_p), service costs (C_s) and other costs (C_o), as well as the resell value (V_r).
  $AIV = C_e + C_p + C_s + C_o - V_r$
- The Risk Mitigation (RM) refers to the risk reduction associated with a given countermeasure. RM is computed as the product of the Countermeasure Coverage (Cov, which corresponds to the percentage of the attack covered by the countermeasure) and the Effectiveness Factor (EF, which refers to the degree at which a countermeasure protects a target against an attack).
  $RM = Cov + EF$
- The Annual Response Cost (ARC) refers to the costs associated to a given countermeasure. ARC is always positive and expressed in currency per year. It includes direct costs such as the cost of implementation (C_{impl}), the cost of maintenance (C_{maint}), as well as other direct costs (C_{od}) and indirect costs (C_i) that may originate from the adoption of a particular countermeasure.
  $ARC = C_{impl} + C_{maint} + C_{od} + C_i$

3   3D Geometrical Model

In analogy with access control models [7,9], we identified three main dimensions that contribute directly to the execution of a given attack: User account (subject), Resource (object), and Channel (the way to execute actions, e.g., connect, read, write, etc). This latter is represented as the transitions between subjects and objects. For instance, in order to access a web-server (object) of a given organization, a user (subject) connects to the system by providing his/her login and password (action).

3.1 Coordinate System

Our geometric model is proposed to represent services, attacks and countermeasures in a three dimensional coordinate system (i.e., user account, channel, and resource).

User Account: A user account is a unique identifier for a user in a given system that allows him/her to connect and interact with the system's environment. A user account is associated to a given status in the system, from which his/her privileges and rights are derived (i.e., system administrator, standard user, guest, internal user, or nobody).

Channel: In order to have access to a particular resource, a user must use a given channel. We consider the IP address and the port number to represent channels in TCP/IP connections. However, each organization must define the way its users connect to the system and have access to the organization's resources.

Resource: A resource is either a physical component (e.g., host, server, printer) or a logical component (e.g., files, records, database) of limited availability within a computer system. We defined two levels of privileges (i.e., kernel, user), and seven levels of transitions (i.e., read, write, execute, and their combinations),

Table 1. Weighting Factor (WF) Results

	Dimension	C	A	R	V	E	R	Total	WF
User Account	Super Admin	10	9	8	10	10	9	56	5
	System Admin	8	8	7	9	8	7	47	4
	Standard User	6	7	6	7	7	5	38	3
	Internal User	4	5	4	6	5	5	29	2
	Guest	3	3	2	5	4	2	19	1
	Nobody	1	1	1	1	1	1	6	0
IP-Port	Class 1	10	9	8	8	7	8	50	4
	Class 2	8	7	6	5	5	6	39	3
	Class 3	7	8	5	7	5	6	38	3
	Class 4	3	2	3	4	3	5	20	1
	Class 5	2	1	1	3	1	1	9	0
	Public	8	7	5	7	6	5	37	3
	Private	5	1	4	3	4	3	20	1
	Reserved/ Special purpose	2	1	3	1	1	1	9	0
Resource	Kernel & R-W-X	10	10	9	9	9	9	56	5
	Kernel & W-X/R-X/R-W	8	9	9	9	7	8	50	4
	Kernel & W/X	6	7	7	8	7	5	40	3
	Kernel & R / User & R-W-X	5	5	7	7	6	6	36	3
	User & W-X/R-X/R-W	5	5	6	5	4	5	30	2
	User & W/X	3	3	5	3	2	3	19	1
	User & R	1	2	2	1	1	3	10	0

and we assigned numerical values to each privilege and transitions based on their characteristics.

Each dimension contributes differently in the volume calculation. This contribution represents the criticality of a given element in the execution of an attack. Following the CARVER methodology [12], which considers multiple criteria (i.e., criticality, accessibility, recuperability, vulnerability, effect, recognizability), we assign numerical values on a scale of 1 to 10 to each entity within the dimension. Table 1 summarizes this information.

As a result, we are able to represent graphically services, attacks and countermeasures in the same coordinate system. It is therefore possible to determine through geometrical operations the impact of attacks and countermeasures within a particular system, the residual risk (i.e., the volume of the system that is being attacked but is not covered by any countermeasure), as well as, the potential collateral damage (i.e., the volume of the system that is not being attacked but is covered by a countermeasure, and whose implementation could cause a damage over the target element).

3.2   Volume Calculation

The projection of the three axis in our coordinate system generates a parallelepiped in three dimensions. For a system S, having three vectors $\mathbf{Co_{Acc}(S)}$, $\mathbf{Co_{Cha}(S)}$ and $\mathbf{Co_{Res}(S)}$ in a three dimensional space $\mathbb{R}^3$, these vectors form three edges of a parallelepiped. The volume of this parallelepiped is equal to the absolute value of the scalar triple product of all three vectors, as shown in Equation 2.

$$V(S) = |Co_{Acc}(X) \cdot (Co_{Cha}(X) \times Co_{Res}(X))| \tag{2}$$

The volume calculation requires the computation of the contribution of each axis represented in the coordinate system. This contribution is determined as the sum of each set of axis entities (e.g., user account type, port class, resource type) times its associated weighting factor, as shown in Equation 3.

$$Co_{Axis}(S) = \sum_{i=0}^{n} Count(E \in Type_{Axis}(S)) \times WF(Type_{Axis}(S)) \tag{3}$$

3.2.1   System Volume

It represents the maximal space a given system (e.g., S1) is exposed to users and attackers. This volume includes tangible assets (e.g., PCs, mobile phones, network components, etc.), as well as intangible assets (e.g., confidential information, business reputation, etc) that are vulnerable to known and unknown threats. Each of these assets are represented in the system volume as user accounts, channels, and/or resources. The system volume is calculated as the product of its dimension's contribution, as shown in Equation 4.

$$SV(S) = Co_{Acc}(S) \times Co_{Cha}(S) \times Co_{Res}(S) \tag{4}$$

3.2.2 Attack Volume

Within the complete system volume exposed to attackers (including all possible vulnerable resources of the given system), we concentrate on a given attack to identify the portion of the volume being targeted based on the vulnerabilities it can exploit. These vulnerabilities are related to all the dimensions that comprise the system volume (i.e., user accounts, channels, and resources). The attack volume is calculated as the product of its dimension's contribution, as shown in Equation 5.

$$AV(A) = Co_{Acc}(A) \times Co_{Cha}(A) \times Co_{Res}(A) \qquad (5)$$

The coverage (Cov) of a given attack (A) respect to a given system (S) is a value that ranges between zero and one. Such coverage is computed as the ratio between the attack volume overlapping with the system volume $(AV(A \cap S))$ and the system volume $(SV(S))$, as shown in Equation 6:

$$Cov(A/S) = \frac{AV(A \cap S)}{SV(S)} \qquad (6)$$

Where $AV(A \cap S)$ represents the volume that results from the elements of system (S) that are compromised by attack (A).

3.2.3 Countermeasure Volume

The countermeasure volume represents the level of action that a security solution has on a given system. In other words, the countermeasure volume is the percentage of the system volume that is covered and controlled by a given countermeasure. An attack is covered by a countermeasure if their volumes overlap. The countermeasure can exceed the attack volume and cover part of the system that is not covered by the attack. The countermeasure volume is calculated as the product of its dimension's contribution, as shown in Equation 7.

$$CV(C) = Co_{Acc}(C) \times Co_{Cha}(C) \times Co_{Res}(C) \qquad (7)$$

The coverage (Cov) of a given countermeasure (C) respect to a given attack (A) is a value that ranges from zero to one. Such coverage is calculated as the ratio between the countermeasure volume overlapping with the attack volume $(CV(C \cap A))$ and the attack volume $(AV(A))$, as shown in Equation 8:

$$Cov(C/A) = \frac{CV(C \cap A)}{AV(A)} \qquad (8)$$

Where $AV(C \cap A)$ represents the volume that results from the elements of attack (A) that are mitigated by countermeasure (C). From Equation 8, the higher the ratio, the greater the mitigation level.

4 Countermeasure Evaluation

The process of evaluating and selecting security countermeasures is depicted in Figure 1. The process starts by receiving an alert indicating the presence of a malicious entity in the system (1). A determination is made as whether the system detected multiple attacks (2). In such a case, the system calculates the impact of multiple simultaneous attacks (2a). For this, the system represents graphically each attack in our 3D coordinate system, and calculates their coverage with respect to the system (using Equation 6). Such coverage is then transformed into the annual loss expectancy as detailed in Section 5.

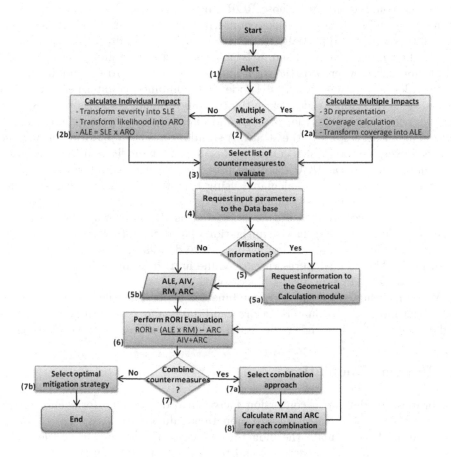

Fig. 1. Countermeasure Selection Process

In case the system detects only one attack (2b), the system calculates the monetary impact of such attack (i.e., ALE) using a methodology as the one described in Section 2. Then, the system selects the countermeasure candidates to be evaluated (3). In order to perform the countermeasure evaluation, the system requests the input parameters (ALE, AIV, RM, and ARC) to the internal database (4). If parameters such as the ALE or the RM are missing for that particular attack (5), the system will request them to the graphical representation module (5a). Upon reception of all the parameters (5b), the system performs the individual evaluation of all the countermeasures (6).

The resulting RORI indicates the expected return that can be obtained if a given countermeasure is implemented in the system to mitigate the effects of a given attack. A determination is made as whether countermeasures could be combined (7). In such a case, it is necessary to select the desired approach to combine countermeasures (e.g., perform all possible combinations, combine only those countermeasures whose RORI index is above the average or a pre-defined threshold), and to consider countermeasures that are totally restrictive, mutually exclusive and partially restrictive in order to obtain the list of combinable countermeasures (7a). Then, it is possible to generate groups of 2, 3, ..., n countermeasures, where n is the total number of elements to be combined.

In order to calculate the RORI index for combined countermeasures, it is necessary to determine their risk mitigation and annual response cost (8). For that we need to calculate the coverage and effectiveness of each group of countermeasures with respect to the attack. A simulation is then performed using our geometric volume tool, which considers Resources, Channels, and User accounts (hereinafter denoted as RCU) that are protected by each countermeasure. The countermeasure coverage is calculated using Equation 8. Then we can compute the RORI for each group of countermeasures (6), taking into account that the cost of multiple countermeasures is estimated as the sum of all the individual countermeasure costs and the risk mitigation of a combined solution is calculated as the probability of the union of events. More details of these calculations are given in [5]. The Annual Infrastructure Value and the Annual Loss Expectancy remains unchangeable for all combined solutions.

When no other countermeasure combination is possible, the system compares the RORI index of all countermeasure candidates and selects the one with the highest value (7b). The higher the RORI index, the better for the organization.

5   Impact Calculation

We propose to develop a conversion factor in order to transform cubic units (hereinafter denoted as $units^3$) into monetary values (e.g., , €). For this purpose, we need to estimate the monetary value of the system (e.g., the dollar value of the whole infrastructure), and to calculate its volume (as proposed in Equation 4). The conversion factor will be, therefore, the resulting value between these two parameters (e.g., $/units^3$).

By calculating the volume of attacks and countermeasures on the system, we are able to determine the monetary impact value for single and/or multiple entities.

5.1   Attack Impact

The Annual Loss Expectancy measures the monetary impact of a given attack over a target system. Several methodologies have been developed to compute this metric. The simplest way to compute it is by the product of the single loss expectancy (SLE) and the annual rate of occurrence (ARO) [2].

For single attacks, we compute its volume on the system (in $units^3$) and we calculate the corresponding monetary value using the previous conversion factor (CF). The resulting value represents the SLE of such attack on the system, and the ARO (i.e., Likelihood) is estimated as the number of times per year an attack is expected to occur in the system [2]. For instance, let us assume that the volume of attack A_1 is calculated as $AV(A_1) = 100,000$ $units^3$, and the conversion factor $CF = 0.1$ €/$unit^3$. The single loss expectancy for A_1 is therefore, $SLE(A_1) = 10,000.00$ €. Considering that A_1 has a likelihood estimated as 12 times per year, we calculate the annual loss expectancy as: $ALE(A_1) = 120,000.00$ €/year.

For multiple attacks occurring simultaneously in the system, we determine the union and/or intersection of the different volumes, and we estimate the total volume of the group of attacks (in $units^3$). The resulting volume is then transformed into its corresponding monetary value in order to calculate their single loss expectancy. The ALE is then computed as the product of the SLE and the ARO. This value is further used in the countermeasure evaluation process.

5.2 Countermeasure Impact

Each countermeasure is represented as a geometrical figure that covers a set of resources, channels, and users (RCU) from a given system. Such coverage is calculated using Equation 8. For this, it is necessary to determine the RCU elements that belong to both: the attack and the selected countermeasure.

For instance, considering that A_1 affects resources R1:R3 (WF=5), channels Ch1:Ch3 (WF=3), and users U1:U3 (WF=2), the attack volume is equivalent to ($AV(A_1) = (3 \times 5) \times (3 \times 3) \times (3 \times 2) = 810$ $units^3$); and countermeasure C_1 protects resources R2:R5, channels Ch2:Ch5, and users U2:U5, ($CV(C_1)=$ 1,920 $units^3$), the RCU elements that are covered by C_1 respect to A_1 are the following: R2:R3, Ch2:Ch3, U2:U3. The coverage volume of C_1 with respect to A_1 is therefore equivalent to:

$$CV(C_1 \cap A_1) = [(2 \times 5) \times (2 \times 3) \times (2 \times 2)] = 240 \ units^3.$$

The coverage of C_1 with respect to A_1 is calculated as:

$$Cov(C_1/A_1) = \frac{240 units^3}{810 units^3} = 0,2962\%$$

As a result, only 29,62% of the total volume of A_1 is covered by C_1. This value helps improving the accuracy in the evaluation and selection of security counter-measures. The remaining 70,38% of the attack is considered as a residual risk.

6 Implementation and Results

We developed a Python software application to generate the graphical representation of multiple attacks and countermeasures within a particular system, and to evaluate, rank, and select optimal countermeasures against complex attacks. This section describes the tool and the resulting geometrical figures, as well as, the approach to calculate the monetary impact of attacks and countermeasures and the process of countermeasure selection.

A software prototype of our approach is available at http://j.mp/3d-rori. It implements all the modules introduced in this section, i.e., input data, RORI and geometrical calculation, and graphical representation. The prototype has been implemented using the Python language. It has been tested using real-world scenarios.

6.1 Tool Description

Our proposed tool is composed of three modules: Input data processor, RORI & Geometrical Calculation, and Graphical Representation, as depicted in Figure 2. For more information about the tool, please see http://j.mp/3d-rori.

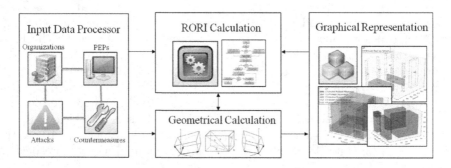

Fig. 2. Decision Support Tool

6.1.1 Input Data Processor : This module stores information about the Organization, Policy Enforcement Points (PEPs), Attacks, and Countermeasures.

Organization: provides information of a given organization regarding its security infrastructure (e.g., name, description, annual infrastructure value). An organization has one or more Policy Enforcement Point -PEP (RFC2904) , and it is exposed to one or many attacks.

PEPs: refer to the list of security equipments i.e., Policy Enforcement Points that are associated to a given organization to protect the confidentiality, integrity and availability of its resources against attacks. Examples of PEPs are: firewall, IDS, Access Control, SIEMs, etc. The tool allows assigning a name, a category and the countermeasures that the PEP can implement on the system, as well as the annual cost of each PEP. The sum of all PEP's annual costs represents the annual infrastructure value.

Attacks: correspond to any kind of detrimental event (e.g., intrusions, attacks, errors) to which the organization is exposed and that could cause damage to the system's organization. Each attack is assigned a name, a description, a risk level (e.g., low, medium, high), and one or more countermeasures. In addition, it is possible to assign one or more attacks to a given organization, with a given likelihood and severity, the product of these two parameters represents the annual loss expectancy.

Countermeasures: are mitigation actions used to stop or minimize the impact of a given attack. Countermeasures are assigned a name, a description, a percentage of the risk that is mitigated, the annual response cost, and restrictions if they exist. A countermeasure is associated to one or more attacks.

6.1.2   RORI & Geometrical Calculation: This module allows to perform the evaluation, rank and selection of individual and combined countermeasures against a cyber attack in a given organization. it uses the Return On Response Investment (RORI) metric to compare multiple alternatives. It communicates with the geometrical calculation sub-module to obtain more accurate information about input parameters, in particular the financial impact of individual and multiple attacks (i.e. ALE), as well as the impact coverage of single and multiple countermeasures (i.e., Cov(CM)).

6.1.3   Graphical Representation: This module provides a graphical representation of attacks and countermeasures in a three-dimensional coordinate system (i.e., Resource, Channel, and User account - RCU), making it possible to identify the size of each attack and countermeasure in a given system, as well as priority areas (e.g., areas affected by most attacks, or those with insufficient protection).

6.2   Use Case: Olympic Games

For testing purposes, we stored the RCU information of a target system from an Olympic Games scenario. The case study responds to the needs of improving the security of a system whose mission is to provide services and real time information for games of around 20 disciplines that spans more than 60 competition and non-competition venues, involving more than 10,000 athletes, 20,000 members of the media, and 70,000 volunteers.

The target system has 100 network resources (e.g, workstations, databases, servers, etc.); 171 channels (e.g., public IP address, credential connections); and 71 user accounts (e.g, IT professionals, partner staff, volunteers). Table 2 summarizes this information.

Table 2. RCU Information of the target system

Dimension	Range	Description	Q	WF	Range
Resource	R1:R16	Server	16	5	0:80
	R17:R17	Access Control Tool	1	4	80:84
	R18:R19	Database	2	4	84:92
	R20:R22	IDS	3	4	92:104
	R23:R25	Firewall	3	4	104:116
	R26:R35	Network device	10	4	116:156
	R36:R100	Workstation	65	3	156:351
Channel	Ch1:Ch91	Public IP address	100	3	0:300
	Ch92:Ch103	Credentials	71	3	300:513
User Account	U1:U40	IT professional	40	4	0:160
	U41:U47	Partner staff	7	3	160:181
	U48:U71	Volunteer	24	1	181:205

The annual infrastructure value (AIV) has been calculated as 12.800 €/year. This latter corresponds to the annualized cost of operation and maintenance of the security infrastructure. Applying Equation 4, we calculate the volume of system S1 as: $SV(S1) = (351) \times (513) \times (205) = 36{,}912{,}915$ $units^3$. Considering that the complete infrastructure value is estimated as 450,000 euros, the conversion factor (currency/$units^3$) is therefore computed as: $CF = 450{,}000/36{,}912{,}915 = 0.01219086$ €/$unit^3$.

6.3   Attack Scenario

A first attack (i.e., A1) is detected in the Olympic Games scenario. The general process starts when the attack accesses the URL of an external web application and studies its behavior (the attacked web application could also be internal). Then, he/she rewrites the URL of the web application to bypass any implemented security check (login, cookies, session). As a result, the attacker bypasses security checks and accesses restricted information.

Attack A1 affects resources R1:R12 (range 0:60), channels Ch1:Ch12 (range 0:36), and users U1:U71 (range 0:205). The volume of A1 is calculated using Equation 5 as: $AV(A1) = (12 \times 5) \times (12 \times 3) \times [(40 \times 4) + (7 \times 3) + (24 \times 1)] = 442{,}800$ $units^3$.

A second attack (i.e., A2) is executed simultaneously on the system. A2 is based on modification of data sent between client and web applications in HTTP headers, requests for URLs, form fields, and cookies. This kind of attack allows unauthorized access to restricted information and operations. It affects resources R9:R16 (range 40:80), channels Ch1:Ch16 (range 0:48), and users U1:U71 (range 0:205). The attack volume is calculated as: $AV(A2) = (8 \times 5) \times (8 \times 3) \times [(40 \times 4) + (7 \times 3) + (24 \times 1)] = 393{,}600$ $units^3$.

Attacks A1 and A2 are partially joint, each attack has an estimated "Significant" severity Level and a "High" likelihood (one attempt per month, starting four months prior to the Games event). The union of both attacks is treated as a new attack (i.e., $A3 = A1 \cup A2$) that affects resources R1:R16 (range 0:80), channels Ch1:Ch16 (range 0:48), and users U1:U71 (range 0:205), and whose volume is calculated as: $AV(A3) = (16 \times 5) \times (16 \times 3) \times [(40 \times 4) + (7 \times 3) + (24 \times 1)] = 787{,}200$ $units^3$.

Applying the previously calculated conversion factor, we obtain the monetary impact loss expected from the combined attack as: $SLE(A3) = 787{,}200$ $units^3 \times 0.0121986$ €$/unit^3 = 9{,}596.65$ €. Using the Lockstep methodology [2], we transform the likelihood value into the annual rate of occurrence (i.e., high likelihood $= 12$), then the ALE for attack A3 is expected to be equivalent to: $ALE(A3) = 115{,}159.69$ €/year. This latter is the monetary impact expected on the system in yearly basis, if both attacks are realized.

6.4 Countermeasure Analysis

The following are sample countermeasures associated to attack A3, (i.e., the combination of URL-rewriting attack 'A1', and data modification attack 'A2'). We assume security experts providing the list of countermeasures.

- **C0. No Operation (NOOP):** This solution considers to accept the risk and does not require any modifications. The cost and risk mitigation level are equal to zero.
- **C2. Activate abnormal behavior rules:** this countermeasure requires to update the existing rules (i.e., default security policies) to be more restrictive and/or to activate new rules that disable other less restrictive ones.
- **C6. Deny or redirect requests:** URL requests coming from origins that are generating an unusual amount of requests are denied or redirected. This is similar to blocking requests from the offending IPs. The downside is that false positives may be denied access to the URL resources.
- **C7. Disable URL-rewriting mode:** either at the server side or at the application level. An attractive option is a Servlet filter which wraps the response object with an alternate version and changes the encoded URL and related methods into no-operations. However, disabling also defensive URL rewriting increases the risk of other attacks.
- **C8. Activate automatic expiring URLs:** a URL that expires a short period of time after it is requested (e.g., 10 minutes) would greatly reduce the window of opportunity for an attacker to perform a URL rewriting attack but still allow legitimate users enough time to work with the resource.
- **C9. Enable HTTPS:** when enabling HTTPS security, some systems allow applications to obtain the SSL/TLS session identifier. The use of SSL/TLS

session identifier is suitable only for critical applications, such as those on large financial sites, due to the size of the systems.

- **C13. Generate new SID:** even though an attacker may trick a user into accepting a known SID, the SID will be invalid when the attacker attempts to reuse the SID. However, session regeneration is not always possible. Problems (e.g., logouts, session separation, etc.) are known to occur when third-party software such as ActiveX or Java Applets is used, and when browser plug-ins communicate with the server. For this reason, session regeneration is only advised when performing sensitive operations or accessing sensitive links.

Table 3 summarizes the RCU information of each security solution except for C0 (NOOP), since this latter implies no changes in the system. In addition, we provide information about the coverage of each countermeasure based on the detected attack. Such coverage is calculated using geometrical operations from the geometrical calculation module. For instance, having the RCU of attack A3 (0:80, 0:48, 0:205), and the RCU of countermeasure C2 (0:156, 0:105& 300:513, 0:205) we compare both entities and we obtain the RCU intersection (i.e., 0:80, 0:48, 0:205), then we compute the volume (using Equation 7) and we determine the percentage of the attack volume that is covered by the countermeasure volume (using Equation 8). As a result, C2 covers 100% of attack A3.

Table 3. RCU Information of the security countermeasures

CM	Resource	Range	Channel	Range	User	Range	Coverage
C2	R1:R35	[0,156]	Ch1:Ch35& Ch101:Ch171	[0,105]& [300,513]	U1:U71	[0,205]	1.00
C6	R1:R17& R20:R25	[0,84]& [92,116]	Ch1:Ch17& Ch20:Ch25	[0,51]& [57,75]	U1:U71	[0,205]	1.00
C7	R1:R13	[0,80]	Ch1:Ch13	[0,39]	U1:U71	[0,205]	0.81
C8	R1:R13& R36:R100	[0,80]& [156,351]	Ch1:Ch13& Ch36:Ch100	[0,39]& [105,300]	U1:U71	[0,205]	0.81
C9	R1:R16	[0,80]	Ch1:Ch16	[0,48]	U1:U71	[0,205]	1.00
C13	R1:R17	[0,84]	Ch1:Ch17	[0,51]	U1:U71	[0,205]	1.00

We determine the annual response cost and effectiveness of each security countermeasure. The risk mitigation value (RM) is calculated as the product of the Effectiveness (EF) and the Coverage (COV). This latter is obtained via the geometrical calculation module. The RORI index is calculated using Equation 1. Table 4 summarizes this information.

From the list of proposed countermeasures, C7 (Disable URL-rewriting mode) provides the highest RORI index. By taking this action, the risk is expected to be reduced 72%, resulting in a RORI index of 0.609. The graphical representation of each countermeasure vs. the detected attacks is depicted in Figure 3, where the blue parallelepiped represents attack A3 and the green parallelepiped represents the countermeasures.

Table 4. Countermeasure Evaluation Information

CM	EF	COV	RM	ARC	RORI	Restriction
C0	0.00	0.00	0.00	0.00	0.00	all
C2	0.68	1.00	0.68	400.00	0.590	C0
C6	0.55	1.00	0.55	500.00	0.472	C0
C7	0.89	0.81	0.72	700.00	0.609	C0
C8	0.79	0.81	0.64	450.00	0.552	C0
C9	0.49	1.00	0.49	550.00	0.418	C0
C13	0.39	1.00	0.39	250.00	0.342	C0

Attack A3 remains the same (in size and affected elements) for all the different cases, whereas countermeasures change their size according to the elements they cover. Therefore, the bigger the countermeasure, the smaller the graphical representation of the attack. That explains why in Figure 3(a) the attack looks smaller than the one represented in Figure 3(c).

We evaluated all possible combinations of security countermeasures (considering mutually exclusive, partially restricted and totally restrictive countermeasures) and taking into account that for a combined solution, the cost is computed as the sum of all the individual countermeasure costs (Pessimistic Approach) and the risk mitigation is calculated as the probability of the union of events (using the effectiveness and coverage parameters as detailed in [5]). The Annual Infrastructure Value and the Annual Loss Expectancy remains the same for all combined solutions. Table 5 presents the results of the five best combinations of security countermeasures.

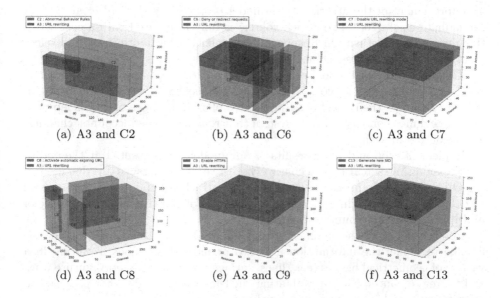

(a) A3 and C2   (b) A3 and C6   (c) A3 and C7

(d) A3 and C8   (e) A3 and C9   (f) A3 and C13

Fig. 3. Graphical representation of attack A3 and all individual countermeasures

Table 5. Countermeasure Combination Results

N	CM_c	EF_c	COV_c	RM_c	ARC_c	RORI_c
1	C2+C7	0.68	0.81	0.85	1,100.00	0.695
2	C2+C7+C13	0.39	0.81	0.85	1,350.00	0.681
3	C2+C7+C8	0.68	0.71	0.86	1,550.00	0.679
4	C6+C7	0.55	0.81	0.82	1,200.00	0.669
5	C2+C6+C7	0.55	0.81	0.85	1,600.00	0.668

From Table 5, the value of EF_c corresponds to the minimum effectiveness value of the combined solution, whereas COV_c corresponds to the value of the intersection coverage of the combined countermeasures. RM_c and ARC_c represent the risk mitigation and the annual response cost respectively for each combination. RORI_c is the resulting RORI index for the combination.

After comparing the RORI index on all the different options, we determined that the best solution is to combine C2 and C7, which proposes to activate abnormal behavior rules and to disable URL-rewriting mode. As a result, the risk is expected to be reduced 85%, and the RORI index is expected to be 0.695. This combined solution becomes the selected countermeasure for a combined attack based on URL-rewriting and data modification in the attack scenario described in Section 6.3.

7   Conclusion and Future Work

In this paper we introduced a 3D geometrical model (i.e., Attack volume), as an improvement of the attack surface model proposed by Howard et al. [6] and Manadhata et al. [10] . The attack volume is fully integrated with a cost sensitive metric (i.e., Return On Response Investment) to evaluate, rank and select security countermeasures against complex attack scenarios.

The 3D geometrical model proposes to measure the volume of multiple entities (e.g., system, attack, countermeasures) by using geometrical operations in order to calculate their coverage. Entities are plotted as cubes or parallelepipeds in a three dimensional coordinate system that represents user accounts, channels and resources in each axis.

Implementation and main results of our model are presented at the end of the paper, using a real case scenario where two cyber attacks are detected in the Olympic Games Infrastructure. Using the attack volume model, we improve RORI results by providing more accurate values of the the financial impact of multiple attacks and countermeasures.

Considering that the number of axis could change, the system should be flexible to model the information into two or more dimensions, resulting in a variety of geometrical figures (e.g., lines, surfaces, hyper-cubes, etc). Future work will therefore concentrate in evaluating such figures through other geometrical operations (e.g., length, area, hyper-volume).

Acknowledgements. The research in this paper has received funding from the Information Technology for European Advancements (ITEA2) within the context of the ADAX Project (Attack Detection and Countermeasure Simulation), and the PANOPTESEC project, as part of the Seventh Framework Programme (FP7) of the European Commission (GA 610416). Authors would like to thank the MAnagement of Security information and events in Service InFrastructures (MASSIF) projet and the use case providers for their contribution of a real case study.

References

1. Agarwal, P., Efrat, A., Ganjugunte, S., Hay, D., Sankararaman, S., Zussman, G.: Network vulnerability to single, multiple and probabilistic physical attacks. In: Military Communications Conference (2010)
2. Consulting, L.: A Guide for Government Agencies Calculating ROSI. Technical report (2004). http://lockstep.com.au/library/return_on_investment
3. Fan, J., Gierlichs, B., Vercauteren, F.: To infinity and beyond: combined attack on ECC using points of low order. In: Preneel, B., Takagi, T. (eds.) CHES 2011. LNCS, vol. 6917, pp. 143–159. Springer, Heidelberg (2011)
4. Fisher, D.: Microsoft releases attack surface analizer tool (2012). http://threatpost.com/en_us/blogs/microsoft-releases-attack-surface-analyzer-tool-080612
5. Granadillo, G.G., Belhaouane, M., Debar, H., Jacob, G.: RORI-based countermeasure selection using the orbac formalism. International Journal of Information Security **13**(1), 63–79 (2014)
6. Howard, M., Wing, J.: Measuring relative attack surfaces. In: Computer Security in the 21st Century, pp. 109–137 (2005)
7. Kalam, A.A.E., Baida, R.E., Balbiani, P., Benferhat, S., Cuppens, F., Deswarte, Y., Miege, A., Saurel, C., Trouessin, G.: Organization based access control. In: 8th International Workshop on Policies for Distributed Systems and Networks (2003)
8. Kheir, N., Cuppens-Boulahia, N., Cuppens, F., Debar, H.: A service dependency model for cost-sensitive intrusion response. In: Gritzalis, D., Preneel, B., Theohari-dou, M. (eds.) ESORICS 2010. LNCS, vol. 6345, pp. 626–642. Springer, Heidelberg (2010)
9. Li, N., Tripunitara, M.: Security analysis in role-based access control. ACM Transactions on Information and System Security **9**(4), 391–420 (2006)
10. Manadhata, P., Wing, J.: An attack surface metric. In: IEEE Transactions on Software Engineering (2010)
11. Northcutt, S.: The attack surface problem. In: SANS technology Institute Document (2011). http://www.sans.edu/research/security-laboratory/article/did-attack-surface
12. F. of American Scientists: Special operations forces intelligence and electronic warfare operations. Appendix D: Target Analysis Process (1991). http://www.fas.org/irp/doddir/army/fm34-36/appd.htm
13. Petajasoja, S., Kortti, H., Takanen, A., Tirila, J.: Ims threat and attack surface analysis using common vulnerability scoring system. In: 35th IEEE Annual Computer Software and Applications Conference Workshops (2011)
14. Sonnenreich, W., Albanese, J., Stout, B.: Return On Security Investment (rosi) - A Practical Quantitative Model. Journal of Research and Practice in Information Technology **38**(1) (2006)

Poster Session

POSTER: API-Level Multi-policy Access Control Enforcement for Android Middleware

Dongdong Tian[1,2], Xiaohong Li[1,2(✉)], Jing Hu[1,2],
Guangquan Xu[1,2], and Zhiyong Feng[1,2]

[1] School of Computer Science and Technology, Tianjin University, Tianjin, China
{tianddong,xiaohongli,mavis_huhu,losin,zyfeng}@tju.edu.cn
[2] Tianjin Key Laboratory of Cognitive Computing and Application,
Tianjin University, Tianjin, China

Abstract. This paper proposes *MpDroid*, an API-level multi-policy access control enforcement based on the 'Rule Set Based Access Control' (RSBAC) framework. In the *MpDroid*, we monitor and manage resources, services and Android inter-component communication (ICC) based on multiple policies mechanism, so as to restrict the applications access to the sensitive APIs and prevent privilege escalation attacks. When installing an application, we build the mapping relationships between sensitive APIs and the application capability. Each rule in the user-defined and context policies is regarded as a limitation of the application capability. Moreover, system policy is used for matching the illegal ICC communications. Experimental results showed that we can realize the API-level access control for Android middleware, and prevent the illegal ICC communication on the Android 4.1.4.

Keywords: Android middleware · Multi-policy · Permission re-delegation · Inter-component communication · Privilege escalation attacks

1 Introduction

Apex [1] allows to selectively grant permissions at install time, and defines constrains at runtime. MockDroid [2] allows to provide fake or 'mock' data to applications by the user-defined policies. CRePE[3] designs a fine-grained framework by introducing the context policy. Saint [4] proposals a novelty framework that developers design policies based on application requirement. Xmandroid [5] deals with privilege escalation attacks based on the system policy that calling and callee permissions are matched. However, None of them can design a flexible and security framework that comprehensively solves the problem of Android framework.

In this paper, we expand the android framework layer based on the RSBAC. We monitor and manage resources, services and Android inter-component communication (ICC) based on multiple policies mechanism, so as to restrict the applications access to the sensitive APIs and prevent privilege escalation attacks. Our *MpDroid* is integrated into the Android system, which can be used to realize the permission management. It is applied to manage android market applications in this paper.

© Institute for Computer Sciences, Social Informatics and Telecommunications Engineering 2015
B. Thuraisingham et al. (Eds.): SecureComm 2015, LNICST 164, pp. 559–562, 2015.
DOI: 10.1007/978-3-319-28865-9_30

2   MpDroid Architecture

The *MpDroid* Architecture was inspired by RSBAC [6]. In RABAC framework, users should define some policies for constraining capabilities of subject and object. In our framework, AEC is responsible for obtaining the request of the subject and analysis the object type. As the subject always is the application and the object type belongs to resource, service, component or application. Then AEC transfers the request and the object property to the ADM, in which the states of subject and object are loaded. In this paper, we name these states as Application State (AS). AS are three-tuple $S(type, S_{cap}, S_{compo})$, where type is the application type, S_{cap} is the set of application capabilities and S_{compo} is the set of application components.

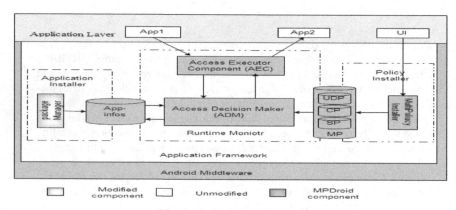

Fig. 1. MpDroid Architecture

3   Experiment

The malicious samples are from VirusTotal Malware Intelligence Service [7], Android Malware Genome Project [8] (Totally 118 applications). The benign samples are from the Google Play application market of top 50 popular software. The experiments can be classified as following:

Table 1. The experiment of access API

Experiment samples	The number of access sensitive API	Access entities of system component	The number of rules for access control
Known Attacks[32,33]	623	Location/Bluetooth Manager, Telephony/SMS Manager, Calendar/ Contact Content Provider, Internet	623 rules in UDP, 977 rules in CP
Walk and Text	5	Contact Content Provider, SMS/Telephony Manager	5 rules in UDP, 10 rules in CP
What's App	9	Contact Content Provider, SMS/Telephony Manager, Internet	9 rules in UDP, 15 rules in CP
Twitter	7	Contact Content Provider, SMS/Telephony Manager	7 rules in UDP, 12 rules in CP

Table 2. The experiment of ICC communication

Experimental Samples	Escalation type	($S_{callingUid}$, $S_{calleeUid}$,Policies)
Malicious contacts manager (READ_CONTACTS) and malicious wallpaper (INTERNET)	Colluding applications	$S_{calleeUid}.type$=untrust_app, $S_{callingUid}.S_{cap}$ =read_contacts $S_{calleeUid}.type$ = untrust_app $S_{callingUid}.S_{cap}$ = Internet Policy = SP
Malicious location manager (ACCESS_FINE_LOCATION) and malicious wallpaper (INTERNET).	Colluding applications	$S_{callingUid}.type$ $S_{calleeUid}.type$ =untrust_app, $S_{callingUid}.S_{cap}$ =access_fine_location = untrust_app $S_{callingUid}.S_{cap}$ =Internet Policy = SP
Malicious app (No CALL_PHONE) and vulnerable dialer [17]	Confused deputy attacks	$S_{calleeUid}.type$ =untrust_app, $S_{callingUid}.S_{cap}$ =NULL $S_{calleeUid}.type$ = system_app $S_{callingUid}.S_{cap}$ = send_sms Policy = SP
Malicious contact manager (READ_CONTACT) and vulnerable SMS sender (SEND_SMS).	Confused deputy attacks	$S_{calleeUid}.type$ =untrust_app, $S_{callingUid}.S_{cap}$ =read_contacts $S_{calleeUid}.type$ = system_app $S_{callingUid}.S_{cap}$ = send_sms Policy = SP

The subject which sends request to the Service/Providers are tagged by AEC. Our policy serves as a kind of firewall, making it much more difficult for applications to use the default permission to access the sensitive data. We test experiment samples by applying UDP and CP to the system to prevent the application access to the sensitive API. For example, the application, Walk and Text, gains the telephone number and device id, and uploads that to the remote server. The application accesses 5 sensitive API. In the experiment, we success in managing every behavior using policies. The ICC communication can be defined as the tuple $(S_{callingUid}, S_{calleeUid}, Policies)$ .The *MPDroid* runtime control is achieved by mapping the AS and policy to the parameters. We use the tuple $(S_{callingUid}, S_{calleeUid}, Policies)$ to realize access control (Table 2). Attacks targeting confused deputies in system component are tackled by the system policy. By assigned application types, we can address the ICC between colluding applications.

Table 3. The time consuming comparison of access API

	Sample Numbers	Number of access the sensitive API	Average time consumes(ms)
The original API access	50	269	0.149
MpDroid API access	50	281	0.399

Table 4. The time consuming comparison of ICC

	ICC call times	Average time	Std. Dev(ms)
The Original Reference Monitor	80721	0.168	18.932
MpDroid ICC	87453	6.334	45.128

As Table 3 shows, When running the applications in the original system, the results is nearly 0.153ms. When running the applications in the *MpDroid*-based Android system, the average time is 0.399ms. Table 4 lists our performance results. In total 80721 ICC calls occurred during the testing. The average runtime for original Reference Monitor time is 0.168ms, and the MpDroid ICC time is 6.334ms.

4   Conclusions

In this paper, we propose a multi-policy access control enforcement *MpDroid* based on RSBAC framework. Multiple policies makes our framework more efficient to resist the diverse attacks. The experiment results shows that we can realize the API-level access control for Android middleware, and prevent the illegal ICC communication on the Android 4.1.4. The system policy time consuming is 6.334ms. However, from the experiment, we learn some collusion attacks that can not be fully tackled by system policy. Besides, we hope we can make more efficiency policy to deal with more attacks.

Acknowledgments. This work has partially been sponsored by the National Science Foundation of China (No. 91118003, 61272106, 61003080) and 985 funds of Tianjin University, Tianjin Research Program of Application Foundation and Advanced Technology under grant No. 15JCYBJC15700.

References

1. Nauman, M., Khan, S., Zhang, X.: Apex: extending Android permission model and enforcement with user-defined runtime constraints. In: Proceedings of the 5th ACM Symposium on Information, Computer and Communications Security, ASIACCS 2010 (2010)
2. Mueller, K., Butler, K.: Flex-P: flexible Android permissions. In: IEEE Symposium on Security and Privacy, Poster Session (2011)
3. Conti, M., Nguyen, V.T.N., Crispo, B.: CRePE: context-related policy enforcement for Android. In: Tsudik, G., Magliveras, S., Ilić, I., Burmester, M. (eds.) ISC 2010. LNCS, vol. 6531, pp. 331–345. Springer, Heidelberg (2011)
4. Ongtang, M., McLaughlin, S., Enck, W., McDaniel, P.: Semantically rich application-centric security in Android. In: IEEE Computer Society, ACSAC 2009 (2009)
5. Bugiel, S., Davi, L., Dmitrienko, A., Fischer, T., Sadeghi, A.: XManDroid: a new Android evolution to mitigate privilege escalation attacks. Technische Universität Darmstadt; 2011a [Technical Report; Technical Report TR-2011-04]
6. Ott, A., Fischer-Hübner, S.: The 'rule set based access control'(RSBAC) framework for linux. In: Proceedings of the 8th International Linux Kongress (2001)
7. VirusTotal Malware Intelligence Services. https://secure.vtmis.com/vtmis/
8. Zhou, Y., Jiang, X.: Dissecting android malware: characterization and evolution. In: S&P. IEEE Computer Society (2012)

POSTER: Reliable and Efficient Protection of Consumer Privacy in Advanced Metering Infrastructure

Vitaly Ford[✉] and Ambareen Siraj

Computer Science Department, Tennessee Technological University,
Cookeville, TN 38505, USA
vford42@students.tntech.edu, asiraj@tntech.edu

Abstract. We are investigating a novel approach towards reliable and efficient protection of consumer privacy in the Advanced Metering Infrastructure (AMI). In the smart grid, one of the main concerns of consumers is associated with the usage of the smart meters and how utility companies handle energy consumption data, which can potentially reveal sensitive and private information about consumers. Current solutions provide privacy-preserving protocols using zero-knowledge proofs and homomorphic encryption, which work on aggregated smart meter data. There is still lack of an integrated solution that enables privacy preservation with access to fine-grained data such that opportunities of making energy consumption more efficient are not sacrificed. Such access will also enable other forms of advanced intelligent analysis like energy fraud detection. In this regard, we propose a three-tier privacy preservation model that includes secure communication among smart meters, utility company, and a Trusted Third Party (TTP) using Certificateless Public Key Encryption and AES 128. It is a flexible framework allowing protection of consumer privacy such that only consumers can securely retrieve their fine-grained readings through the TTP's web-portal. This protocol supports dynamic rate utilization as well as data mining for advanced analysis. In addition, the proposed secure framework satisfies computational resource limitations in the Advanced Metering Infrastructure and provides a scalable solution for efficient consumer privacy-preserving billing.

Keywords: Security · AMI · Privacy-preserving protocol

1   Introduction

We introduce a three-tier model for secure smart meter communication that enables consumer's privacy preservation as well as retention of fine grained data analysis capability. The model comprises of Smart Meters (SMs), Utility Companies (UCs), and a Trusted Third Party (TTP). TTP has direct access to fine-grained consumer data and has the capability to include additional advanced analysis features, such as fraud detection. The data are secured in such a way that TTP cannot link energy consumption readings with any particular consumer. In the proposed model, SMs encrypt all the energy consumption data and send the encrypted traffic to TTP through a separate collector entity in the UC's

© Institute for Computer Sciences, Social Informatics and Telecommunications Engineering 2015
B. Thuraisingham et al. (Eds.): SecureComm 2015, LNICST 164, pp. 563–566, 2015.
DOI: 10.1007/978-3-319-28865-9_31

smart metering network. However, UC can only relay the energy measurements to TTP without having the ability to decrypt them.

Many existing solutions [2, 3, 4] propose different protocols that have to be used in the smart grid at the same time for load monitoring, aggregation, billing and fraud detection. Instead of using varied protocols for the above-mentioned operations, the proposed architecture utilizes one protocol with minimal overhead to SMs.

2   Approach

The following describes the proposed model for the AMI infrastructure. The three-tier system consists of SMs, UCs, and TTP storage system. TTP is an independent private organization, whose service is purchased by UCs. TTP can manage meter data from several different electricity providers and thus release the AMI infrastructure from unnecessary computations, such as aggregation, fraud detection, and energy consumption analysis. There is also a collector(s) installed by UC, which facilitates collection of energy consumption data from various SMs. Fig. 1 shows the high-level architecture (solid lines correspond to an internal UC network and dashed lines correspond to the Internet connectivity).

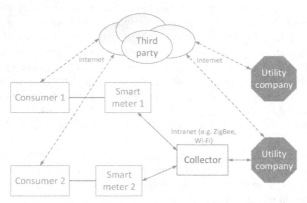

Fig. 1. Proposed architecture

In the proposed model (Fig. 1), TTP is connected to UC via the IP-based communication line in the Internet. SMs are not directly connected with the TTP and instead connected through UC. This is because SMs connect with their UCs via an internal network to decrease the possibility of attacks that are common in the Internet.

In this model, UC deploys SMs and has limited control over them. The control is restricted for preserving consumer privacy and UCs are only allowed to provide administrative support for AMI, such as verifying SMs availability.

When UC deploys SM, it generates a random identification number (ID) for SM in the household. SM and TTP initiate a Certificateless Public Key Exchange Protocol (CLPKE) [1], where UC serves as the Key Generation Center. Once public/private keys are distributed to both parties, TTP generates a session key for securely communicating energy consumption data from SM to TTP and sends it via an encrypted connection (using public/private keys) to SM. SM stores the session key in its TPM and uses it for sending energy readings to TTP via UC.

SM encrypts energy consumption (*EC*) measurements and sends them to the collector. The main responsibility of the collector is to temporarily store the encrypted *EC* data and send them to UC in a predefined time interval. UC forwards the encrypted *EC* data to TTP. Without knowledge of the key, UC cannot decrypt the data and thus, privacy is preserved for their clients. TTP decrypts all received data and stores them in its database.

At the time of billing, UC sends TTP a request for *EC* readings to be billed, including the anonymized meter's ID and price ranges for different periods of time. TTP authenticates UC, queries the requested data from its database, and aggregates energy on a daily/monthly basis depending on the policy and bill calculation requirements.

When a consumer receives the bill, he/she can check the correctness of the billing computations. Consumers can connect to the TTP web-service, authenticate without revealing their real identity, and gain access to their fine-grained data.

The features of the proposed protocol are as follows:

- Energy data are encrypted by SMs and anonymized by UC prior to being sent to TTP.
- Lightweight efficient encryption is used for the main parts of communication. We use Advanced Encryption Standard (AES) 128-bit keys for securing communication between SM and UC as well as SM and TTP.
- UC forwards the anonymized and encrypted data to TTP via a wide area network. UC cannot decrypt the data, preserving consumer privacy.
- UC can acquire aggregated decrypted data from TTP on request for billing purposes.
- TTP cannot identify real consumers because of anonymization of SM's ID.
- Additional consumer energy consumption analysis can be done at TTP without disclosure of any sensitive information about consumers.
- UC cannot ask a consumer to pay a fee different from the one that was produced by TTP for billing.

3   Protocol Phases

There are three main phases in the proposed protocol: *registration phase* (Fig. 3), *session key exchange phase* (Fig. 4), and *data transmission phase* (Fig. 5). The *registration phase* describes the steps that SMs and TTP have to follow for receiving their public/private key pairs from UC based on the CLPKE [1]. Those keys will allow SM and TTP to establish a secure and private connection for exchanging a session key used for further communication between SM and TTP at the *data transmission phase*.

1) *Registration phase.*

UC serves as a Key Generation Center. SMs and TTP communicate with UC in order to obtain public/private keys. Any communication between SM and UC is encrypted with the pre-shared key S_{SM-UC}. When SM sends UC an encrypted (with S_{SM-UC}) message, it concatenates its ID_{SM} so that UC can identify the meter upon receiving the message and decrypt it accordingly. The message consists of a request to generate keys and a timestamp against replay attacks. UC generates the keys and sends them to SM. UC and TTP have to establish a *TLS* connection before UC sends the keys for TTP.

2) *Session key exchange phase.*

When SM and TTP complete the registration phase, they initiate a session key exchange phase in order to share a secret key used for encrypting/decrypting fine-grained meter readings. SM uses TTP's public key for encrypting the message containing a request to share a key and a random number used as an extra security measure against man-in-the-middle attacks. In addition, SM sends an HMAC to preserve integrity. Upon receiving the message, TTP generates the session key $S_{SM\text{-}TTP}$, concatenates the random number, encrypts the packet with SM's public key, and forwards it to SM via UC.

3) *Data transmission phase.*

The session key established at the *session key exchange* phase is used for sending meter readings from SM to TTP. Thus, only SM and TTP can decrypt the fine-grained measurements. SM sends energy consumption (EC) along with a timestamp t to UC by encrypting the data with $S_{SM\text{-}TTP}$. It also concatenates an HMAC to the message by hashing $EC \mid\mid t$ and its real ID_{SM}. UC verifies HMAC and forwards the received data to TTP, replacing ID_{SM} with an-ID_{SM} found in its table mapping real ID_{SM} with the anonymized an-ID_{SM}. TTP decrypts $EC \mid\mid t$ by using $S_{SM\text{-}TTP}$ and retrieves the data.

4   Conclusion and Future Work

Proposed secure AMI preserves consumer privacy in terms of billing and advanced fine-grained data analysis, such as fraud detection. It takes into account the limited capabilities of Smart Meters and can be implemented with minimum changes to the current grid. Also, consumers can access their own fine-grained data stored at TTP. We are currently working on formal and empirical evaluation of the proposed privacy preserving protocol for AMI infrastructure.

Acknowledgements. This work is supported by the Center for Energy Systems Research of Tennessee Tech University. We are thankful to Michael Pyle, Chief Security Officer and VP of Cyber Security at Schneider Electric, Nashville TN, for his invaluable comments and feedback.

References

1. Sun, Y., Zhang, F.T., Baek, J.: Strongly secure certificateless public key encryption without pairing. In: Bao, F., Ling, S., Okamoto, T., Wang, H., Xing, C. (eds.) CANS 2007. LNCS, vol. 4856, pp. 194–208. Springer, Heidelberg (2007)
2. Joye, M., Libert, B.: A scalable scheme for privacy-preserving aggregation of time-series data. In: Sadeghi, A.-R. (ed.) FC 2013. LNCS, vol. 7859, pp. 111–125. Springer, Heidelberg (2013)
3. Lin, H.-Y., Tzeng, W.-G., Shen, S.-T., Lin, B.-S.P.: A practical smart metering system supporting privacy preserving billing and load monitoring. In: Bao, F., Samarati, P., Zhou, J. (eds.) ACNS 2012. LNCS, vol. 7341, pp. 544–560. Springer, Heidelberg (2012)
4. Ruj, S., Nayak, A., Stojmenovic, I.: A security architecture for data aggregation and access control in smart grids. arxiv.org/pdf/1111.2619.pdf

POSTER: A Security Adaptive Steganography System Applied on Digital Audio

Xuejie Ding, Weiqing Huang, Meng Zhang[✉], and Jianlin Zhao

Institute of Information Engineering, Chinese Academy of Sciences, Beijing 100093, China
{dingxuejie,huangweiqing,zhangmeng,zhaojianlin}@iie.ac.cn

Abstract. As a kind of covert communication technology, stegangoraphy can transmit cryptography using public cover on the internet. However, the behavior is easy to be found because of the cover distortion. To solve this problem, we define two distortion functions to measure the impact of embedding secret. They are called cover perception distortion (CPD) and statistical property distortion (SPD). Then a security stegangoraphy strategy can be generated adaptively by minimizing the two distortion functions. The experiment results demonstrate the effectiveness of our work.

Keywords: Steganography · Steganalysis · Distortion function · Modify path · Modify style

1   Introduction

Steganography can embed secret to the open cover such as images, audio and video in public communication mode without arousing suspicion. Compared with other kinds of multimedia, hiding data in audio is more challenging because of the sensitivity of human auditory system (HAS).

In the past years, several methods have been proposed based on the characteristics of digital audio signals and the human auditory system (HAS). Among the embedding algorithms, the least significant bits (LSB) substitution is one of the earliest techniques and used widely in audio and other media types. Hiding data in LSBs of audio samples can obtain the high data rate of embedding information, but it also faces challenges of various steganalysis system. So many kinds of algorithm based on LSBs have been proposed to improve the security with different transform domain or different embedding rules.

The goal of this paper is to design an audio steganography method which is more undetectable and imperceptibility. The novelty of this work is derived from distortion minimizing framework in image field [2]. We construct an embedding strategy includes security modify path and riskless modify style. They are established adaptively depends on minimizing two distortion functions. In details, first, every element in cover is assigned by the value of CPD, and then STCs is employed to find an optimal path. The elements belong to the modify path can be seen the less important parts according to CPD. Different from exiting distortion functions, the CPD is attained by an unsupervised algorithm. At last, SPD is used to determine the modify style for the elements on the path.

B. Thuraisingham et al. (Eds.): SecureComm 2015, LNICST 164, pp. 567–571, 2015.
DOI: 10.1007/978-3-319-28865-9_32

2   Proposed Method

The principle of novel steganography system is shown as follow, which can generate the embedding strategy adaptively for different covers.

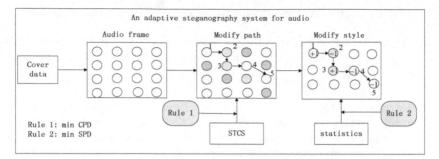

Fig. 1. The principle of novel steganography system

From Fig.1, we can see there are three key steps in the novel steganography system, they are depicted as follows.

Step 1(framing and DCT): We divide the audio cover $x(t)$ into D non-overlapping frames x_i, each frame is L samples. These DCT coefficients of each frame collectively form the new data matrix $X = [X(1), \cdots X(D)]$.

Step 2 (Finding security modify path): A perception value is assigned for each element in cover, which represents the influence strength when the corresponding element is modified. The distortion function is defined as,

Rule 1: $$MP(X, Y) = \arg\min D_{CPD}(X, Y) \tag{1}$$

Then STCs [2] is employed to find a modify path which is subject to make the $D_{CPD}(X, Y)$ is minimal as Rule 1 describes.   The theory of independent component analysis (ICA) is applied to construct CPD, and the procedure is shown in Fig. 2.

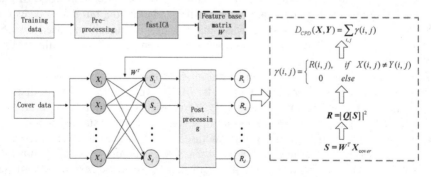

Fig. 2. The procedure of constructing CPD

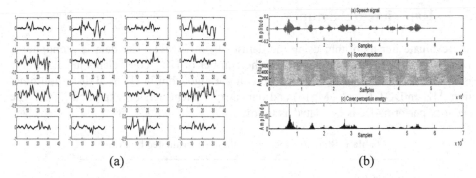

(a)   (b)

Fig. 3. Related results of CPD (a) Feature base matrix W (b) An example for distribution of cover perception energy.

Step 3 (Generating optimal modify strategy): The sender has to introduce modifications from cover X to stego Y at LSB. We design a distortion function to decide the modify style (-1 or $+1$) which is based on the statistical property of cover.

Rule 2:
$$MS(X,Y) = \arg\min D_{SPD}(X,Y) \tag{2}$$

The modify style is chosen when the $D_{SPD}(X,Y)$ is minimal as shown in rule2. Specially, generalized Gaussian distribution (GGD) is introduced to estimate the distribution of the DCT coefficients of each frame. The shape parameter is used to construct SPD as follows.

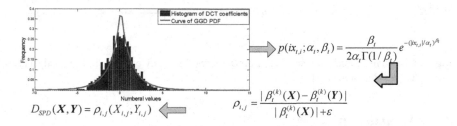

Fig. 4. The procedure of constructing SPD

The stego audio is attained after the inverse DCT of Y. The secret can be extracted as (3) after the LSB of coefficients $\tilde{Y}$ are extracted.

$$\tilde{Y}H^T = m \tag{3}$$

Where $H \in \{0,1\}$ is the parity check matrix of the used STCs shared between sender and receiver.

3   Experimental Setup

We evaluate our algorithm using the dataset from TIMIT. The data is monophonic waveform with 16-kHz sampling. And the number of DCT coefficients in each frame is 1024. Our method is in comparisons with the algorithm in [1] used distortion function AIH-IntDCT (blocks M=16) and our improvement version exploited STCs. The security performance is evaluated as follows.

Table 1. Ratio of Score lower than 3.8 evaluated by PESQ

Payload (bpf)	Algorithms		
	AIH-IntDCT	AIH-IntDCT-STC	Our method
0.1	2.2%	0	0
0.2	3%	0.8 %	0
0.3	4.5%	0.9%	0.52%
0.4	12.5%	8.2%	7.2%
0.5	13.5%	9.6%	7.4%

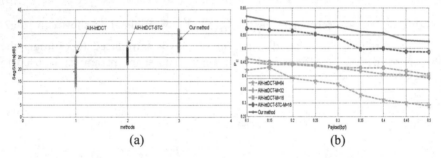

(a)   (b)

Fig. 5. Objective evaluation results: (a) SegSNRs results at payload 0.5 (b) Steganalysis results using CC-PEV features in [3].

4   Conclusion

With the motivation to improve security, two distortion functions have been constructed to measure the impact of embedding secret. They guide the embedding positions and strategy respectively. Experiment results have shown that our method has good performance with lower distortion and larger error detection.

Acknowledgement. This work is supported by the "Strategic Priority Research Program" of the Chinese Academy of Sciences, Grant No. Y2W0012306.

References

1. Huang, X., Ono, N., Echizen, I., Nishimura, A.: Reversible audio information hiding based on integer DCT coefficients with adaptive hiding locations. In: Shi, Y.Q., Kim, H.-J., Pérez-González, F. (eds.) IWDW 2013. LNCS, vol. 8389, pp. 376–389. Springer, Heidelberg (2014)
2. Filler, T., Judas, J., Fridrich, J.: Minimizing Additive Distortion in Steganography Using Syndrome-Trellis Codes. IEEE Trans. Inf. Forensics Security 6(3), 920–934 (2011)
3. Kondovsky, J., Fridrih, J.: Calibration revisited. In: Proceedings of the 11th ACM Multimedia and Security Workshop, Princeton, NJ, September 7–8, 2009

POSTER: Semantics-Aware Rule Recommendation and Enforcement for Event Paths

Yongbo Li$^{(\boxtimes)}$, Fan Yao, Tian Lan, and Guru Venkataramani

George Washington University, Washington D.C. 20052, USA
{lib,albertyao,tlan,guruv}@gwu.edu

Abstract. With users' increasing awareness of security and privacy issues, Android's permission mechanism and other existing methods fall short to provide effective protection over user data. This paper presents SARRE, a Semantics-Aware Rule Recommendation and Enforcement system to detect critical information outflows and prevent information leakage. SARRE leverages runtime monitoring and statistical analysis to identify system event paths. Then, an online recommendation algorithm is developed to automatically assign and enforce a semantics-aware security rule to each event path. Our preliminary results on real-world malware samples and popular apps from Google Play show that the recommended rules by our system are effective in preventing information leakage and enabling protection policies for users' private data.

1 Motivation

With its increasing popularity among all smartphone platforms, Android continues to claim the largest share of malware [1], a lot of which collects and leaks users' private data. In addition, users' information can even leak out through apps downloaded from Google Play [7]. Information leakage and user privacy remain to be challenging problems for hardening smartphone security.

The limitations of Android's current permission-based security mechanism have been well recognized in prior work [6]. A number of proposals are made to tackle this challenging problem using techniques such as enhanced Access Control [6] and data obfuscation [8]. However, the burden of manually constructing extensive security rules for various apps still lies with smartphone users or app developers, who may find it overly convoluted and difficult to adjust on the fly. The problem is further complicated when different information flows accessing the same data require differentiated security rules. For instance, while GPS coordinates are routinely queried by information flows in map/tracking apps, it could raise serious privacy concerns if they are accessed by an alarm clock app, whether it contains repackaged malware or advertisement libraries collecting users' location. Recent studies have begun to investigate automated rule assignment in smartphone systems [5], but only consider a one-size-fits-all solution for each data source and fall short on providing fine-grained security rules for different information flows and app semantics.

© Institute for Computer Sciences, Social Informatics and Telecommunications Engineering 2015
B. Thuraisingham et al. (Eds.): SecureComm 2015, LNICST 164, pp. 572–576, 2015.
DOI: 10.1007/978-3-319-28865-9_33

2   Our Approach

We propose SARRE, a Semantics-Aware Rule Recommendation and Enforcement system that automatically assigns and enforces security rules for event paths to prevent information leakage. SARRE consists of four main parts: (i) *Event Monitor*, (ii) *Path Identifier*, (iii) *Rule Recommender*, and (iv) *Camouflage Engine*. The interconnections between different parts are depicted in Figure 1.

Event Monitor intercepts and logs timestamped events (within a configurable list) at Android's framework level. Monitored events include: (i) apps' calls to APIs that can be leveraged for data collection, processing, and transmission, such as API calls to access location and network services; and (ii) other system events or phone state changes that are not directly related to information flows, but facilitate characterization of them, for example, incoming phone calls and new SMS notifications frequently serve as different triggers for information flows. The log files generated by *Event Monitor* are encrypted and transmitted periodically to *Path Identifier* by *Secure Sender*.

Path Identifier quantifies the correlations between events within the log file through statistical analysis to construct an Event Graph for each app. Each vertex on the graph is a monitored event, and an arc between two events exists if and only if their correlation is statistically significant. A weight is assigned to each arc measuring the correlation significance. *Path Identifier* then leverages our path cover algorithm to extract the event paths with largest accumulated weights, covering all the events' occurrences in the log file. The Event Graph constructed for a malware sample *com.nicky.lyyws.xmall* [2], is depicted in Figure 2. Because of space limitation, the event names are shown in an abbreviated manner. The numbers at the end of vertices denote counts of event occurrences in the log file. Paths identified for this sample are also shown in the figure.

Next, *Rule Recommender* assigns fine-grained security rules to newly-identified event paths. A rule R_r is numerically denoted and $R_r \in [0,1]$, indicating level of protection needed for the sensitive data associated with the event path. In specific, the recommender leverages two types of knowledge: (i) known security rules of similar paths and (ii) the corresponding apps' semantic information. A recommendation is made for an event path by calculating the weighted

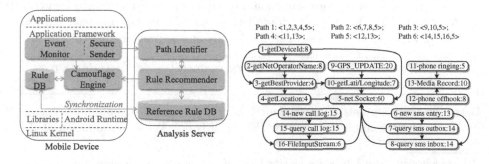

Fig. 1. Overview of System Design   **Fig. 2.** Event Graph and paths of *nickispy*

average of the rules for K nearest event paths with matched semantic information. This approach allows SARRE to construct security rules that are both effective and in-context in an unsupervised manner.

Finally, recommended security rules are enforced by *Camouflage Engine* for the sensitive information flows on event paths at run time. The camouflage action is selected based on the underlying data property. For example, numerical GPS coordinates can be obfuscated by adding random noise to reduce their resolutions, while fields in structured data like contacts data can be selectively hidden depending on the recommended security rule.

3   Evaluation of Effectiveness

We prototyped SARRE on Android Open Source Project v4.1.2. We collected malware samples from an online sharing site [4], and top ranking apps on Google Play. Then, we manually select one from some pre-defined labels[1] such as *Games* and *Social* to each sample based on the app description. The label denotes the app's declared functionality, and serves as the semantic information in current evaluation. We present the effects of the recommended rules for two examples.

– *My Tracks:* Since malware normally doesn't present harvested data when stealthily eavesdropping on users' location, we use a tracking app *My Tracks* to emulate malware by intentionally replacing its actual label 'Tracking/Maps' with 'Games'. We choose a tracking app because it has a UI showing GPS coordinates update, which makes it convenient to compare the data when different rules are enforced. An event path identified for *My Tracks* involving location data is written in an abbreviated manner, as follows:

GPS updated $\rightarrow$ *getLocation* $\rightarrow$ *Socket.getOutputStream* $\rightarrow$ *Socket.connect*

The recommended rule for this path is 0.4, which means a security action corresponding to 0.4 needs to be applied when it shows up in a game app. When we replace the actual label 'Tracking/Maps' back, the rule recommended is 1, meaning such an event path in a 'Tracking/Maps' app should be left intact. The tracks with rules 1 and 0.4 enforced are shown in Figure 3. Malware like *nickispy* [2] eavesdropping users' location exhibit similar event paths, and after rule enforcement the location data sent should be similar to the right one in Figure 3.

– *Love Chat [3]:* This malware doesn't show an UI, but has an event path as follows, in which data is accessed, stored locally and sent out by network socket.

getLine1Number $\rightarrow$ *getDeviceId* $\rightarrow$ *query(contacts)* $\rightarrow$ *io.FileOutputStream* $\rightarrow$ *Socket.getOutputStream*

Based on this sample's declared functionality, we attach 'Communication' as its label. The recommended rule for this path is 0.2. With examination of the

---

[1] In our design, such labels are assigned by our system based on apps' functionality descriptions, and they cannot be manipulated by the apps.

Fig. 3. Intact track (left) when rule **Fig. 4.** Contacts on the phone (left) and data '1' is enforced, and track with noise sent by *Love Chat* when rule '1' (upper right) (right) when rule '0.4' is enforced   or '0.2' (lower right) is enforced

Reference Rule DB, we see that although this malware disguises as a 'Communication' app, it doesn't get a rule with large number, because paths similar to the above path are popular among privacy-stealing malware, but not 'Communication' apps. This makes sense and shows the necessity to use event path as reference for rule recommendation. To see the enforcement effect, we redirect packets sent by this sample to an external server. We input some made-up contacts data on the phone as shown in Figure. 4 (left). The contents in the files that are sent to the external server before and after rule enforcement are also shown in the figure (right). We can see the effectiveness of the rule enforcement by hiding contacts' first names and scrabbling some digits in the phone numbers.

Acknowledgments. This work is supported, in part, by the Office of Naval Research under grant No. N00014-15-1-2210. Any opinions, findings, and conclusions expressed in this material are those of the authors and do not necessarily reflect the views of the Office of Naval Research.

References

1. Android still triggers the most mobile malware. http://goo.gl/FXTGsi
2. Malware with package name *com.nicky.lyyws.xmall*. http://goo.gl/U7D2FW
3. Malware with package name *com.yxx.jiejie*. http://goo.gl/CpkioI
4. Mobile malware sharing website. http://goo.gl/YNIOLg
5. Chakraborty, S., Shen, C., Raghavan, K.R., Shoukry, Y., Millar, M., Srivastava, M.: ipShield: a framework for enforcing context-aware privacy. In: NSDI (2014). USENIX
6. Demetriou, S., Zhou, X., Naveed, M., Lee, Y., Yuan, K., Wang, X., Gunter, C.A.: What's in your dongle and bank account? mandatory and discretionary protection of android external resources. In: NDSS (2015)

7. Enck, W., Gilbert, P., Han, S., Tendulkar, V., Chun, B.-G., Cox, L.P., Jung, J., McDaniel, P., Sheth, A.N.: Taintdroid: an information-flow tracking system for real-time privacy monitoring on smartphones. In: ACM TOCS (2014)

8. Zhou, Y., Zhang, X., Jiang, X., Freeh, V.W.: Taming information-stealing smartphone applications (on android). In: McCune, J.M., Balacheff, B., Perrig, A., Sadeghi, A.-R., Sasse, A., Beres, Y. (eds.) Trust 2011. LNCS, vol. 6740, pp. 93–107. Springer, Heidelberg (2011)

POSTER: An Approach to Assess Security, Capacity and Reachability for Heterogeneous Industrial Networks

Apala Ray[1,3]([✉]), Johan Åkerberg[2,3], Mats Björkman[3], and Mikael Gidlund[4]

[1] ABB Corporate Research, Bangalore, India
apala.ray@in.abb.com
[2] ABB AB; Corporate Research, Vasteras, Sweden
[3] School of Innovation, Design, and Technology, Mälardalen University,
Vasteras, Sweden
[4] Mid Sweden University, Sundsvall, Sweden

Abstract. Industrial plants are heterogeneous networks with different computation and communication capabilities along with different security properties. The optimal operation of a plant requires a balance between communication capabilities and security features. A secure communication data flow with high latency and low bandwidth does not provide the required efficiency in a plant. Therefore, we focus on assessing the relation of security, capacity and timeliness properties of an industrial network for overall network performance.

Keywords: Security modeling · Network assessment · Routing · Path planning

1 Introduction

The goal of industrial automation is to automate the operations involved in industrial processes with minimal or reduced human intervention. Technological advances in terms of computing power and communication capabilities bring operational benefits inside plants, but also increase the exposure of cyber security attacks. Therefore, industrial automation security has constantly gained attention over the last years both in academia and in industry. Along with cyber security requirements on industrial plants, it is also necessary to consider other important requirements of plants in terms of availability and timeliness. Therefore, it is important to understand the network capabilities during network design to avail the required network performance in a heterogeneous network system. The network planning phase should capture the properties of the system and identify constraints on the network to achieve an overall secure solution. In this work, we explore how a network path can be chosen inside a plant between two devices, where the network will consider the required levels of communication security, capacity and timeliness. In a multi-hop heterogeneous network, data communication between source and destination can be possible through multiple paths involving devices with varying capabilities. The problem is that, some

© Institute for Computer Sciences, Social Informatics and Telecommunications Engineering 2015
B. Thuraisingham et al. (Eds.): SecureComm 2015, LNICST 164, pp. 577–580, 2015.
DOI: 10.1007/978-3-319-28865-9_34

devices can score high on one particular performance parameter, whereas, score very low on other performance parameters. If the decision of choosing a flow path between a source and destination is done based on one performance criteria only, such as, security or path reachability or link capacity, then one segment of a network may be overloaded.

There is a set of work where different models are used to assess network security. Security monitoring and incident modeling by combing automated analysis of data from security monitors and system logs with human expertise is shown in [1]. There are some research on attack graph construction and performance evaluation [2]. in [3], two layers attack graph is proposed. Attack models also can be used to assess network security. A hierarchical attack representation model is proposed in [4], where a two-layer hierarchy is proposed to separate the network topology information from the vulnerability information of each host. A ranking scheme to identify a relevant portion of the attack graph is proposed in [5]. In [6], a framework for an experimentation environment for network industrial control system is proposed which can reproduce concurrently physical and cyber systems. Most of these work focus on run-time analysis of network traffic or generate attack graphs. In this paper, we provide a model which can be used during network design to identify optimized network paths.

2   Proposed Idea

To assess security, capacity and reachability for heterogeneous industrial networks, we propose to analyze the systems globally, identifying flow paths based on application requirements and directing resources efficiently to increase the confidence in the system. For an efficient flow path estimation, our model requires the topology of the system along with the performance related attributes as input. The key performance indicators required for successful operations of a network are also identified. Once we have a mathematical model, then we can

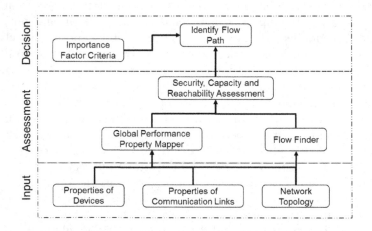

Fig. 1. Architecture for Secure and Robust Path Identification

individually analyze the effect of each key performance indicator on a network flow. Based on this analysis, we can study the effects of a local performance indicator of each node on the global performance indicator of a flow path keeping overall security, capacity and timeliness in the system. This helps us to rank the each communication flow path based on the key performance indicators of the network. This information is useful when designing a plant with a service level agreement. Figure 1, presents the architecture of the component required for path identification.

3   Results

Figure 2 shows the result from our proposed model. We apply the proposed idea on an example network to analyze the network flow value. We consider a small network and estimate the flow value of each flow path. Then we present how the flow value between two devices changes based on the change in local performance metrics *node assurance value*, *link capacity* and *hop count.*

We can see from the graph that with an increase of *node assurance value* the *flow value* gradually increases until the *node assurance value* reaches maximum allowed limit. With the increase of *link capacity*, the *flow value* increases until it reaches the minimum of the rest of *link capacity* set in the flow path. Once the *link capacity* reaches the minimum of the set, there is no change in the flow value. The increase of *hop count* decreases the *flow reachability* and in turn decreases the *flow value.*

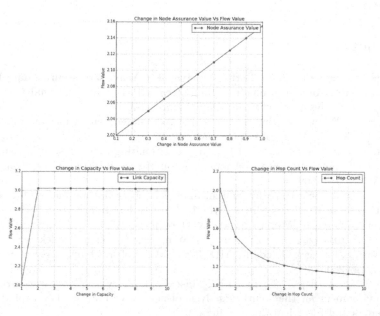

Fig. 2. Change in Flow Value with change in Node Assurance Value, Link Capacity Value and Hop Count

4   Conclusions

We introduce a concept to balance secure, high capacity and reachable flow path in a heterogeneous industrial network during planning phase. We use the concept of *flow awareness value* to determine the trustworthiness of a network. This value is a probabilistic measure of confidence in the security properties of devices and communication flows. The *flow awareness value* captures the risk of a flow path getting affected from the nodes in the flow path. We also introduce the concept of link bandwidth and hop count to model the *flow capacity* and *flow reachability*. This model can assist plant operators to rank each communication flow path based on security, capacity and reachability. We have observed that, if there is a bottleneck with a low capacity link in the network, the increase of trustworthiness of nodes will not improve the flow path value. Similarly, if we have a high number of intermediate nodes with low capacity and high security between the source node and destination node, we might not get a high rank flow path. This type of information is useful when designing a plant with a service level agreement.

In this network model, we do not consider the throughput of the system which can be an average rate of successful message delivery over a communication link. This throughput can only be available to the network operator during run-time when the message sending rate is also available along with the fixed topology. Therefore, we need to analyze the working flow paths rather than all possible flow paths. Then we can validate the performance of a network after choosing the identified flow path as described in our model. We plan to explore this option in our next work.

References

1. Sharma, A., Kalbarczyk, Z., Barlow, J., Iyer, R.: Analysis of security data from a large computing organization. In: 2011 IEEE/IFIP 41st International Conference on Dependable Systems Networks (DSN), June 2011
2. Sheyner, O., Haines, J., Jha, S., Wing, R.: Automated generation and analysis of attack graphs. In: Technical Report CMU (2002)
3. Xie, A., Cai, Z., Tang, C., Hu, J., Chen, Z.: Evaluating network security with two-layer attack graphs. In: Proc. of Annual Computer Security Applications Conference (ACSAC 2009) (2009)
4. Hong, J., Kim, D.-S.: Harms: hierarchical attack representation models for network security analysis. In: Proceedings of the 10th Australian Information Security Management Conference, Western Australia, December 2012
5. Mehta, V., Bartzis, C., Zhu, H., Clarke, E.: Ranking attack graphs. In: Zamboni, D., Kruegel, C. (eds.) RAID 2006. LNCS, vol. 4219, pp. 127–144. Springer, Heidelberg (2006)
6. Genge, B., Siaterlis, C., Fovino, I.N., Masera, M.: A cyber-physical experimentation environment for the security analysis of networked industrial control systems. Computers and Electrical Engineering (2012)

POSTER: An Online Prefix-Preserving IP Address Anonymization Algorithm for Passive Measurement Systems

Kai Cao[1], Yunchun Li[1(✉)], Hailong Yang[1], Jiqiang Tang[2], and Xiaoxiang Zou[2]

[1] Sino-German Joint Software Institute, School of Computer Science and Engineering,
Beihang University, Beijing, China
lych@buaa.edu.cn

[2] National Computer Network Emergency
Response Technical Team/Coordination Center (CNCERT/CC), Beijing, China

Abstract. To strike a balance between usefulness of network traces and privacy protection, offline prefix-preserving anonymization has been studied extensively to anoymize IP addresses while preserving their prefix nature. In this paper, a novel Dynamic Subtree-scheduling Packet Anonymization scheme called DS-PAn is developed for measurement systems based on the prefix-preserving algorithm Crypto-PAn. DS-PAn makes online anoymization practical to be operated at a high rate, while using less memory compared to precomputed Crypto-PAn. Performance evaluations validate that the proposed algorithm outperforms the conventional anonymization mechanism in terms of computation speed as well as memory requirement.

Keywords: IP address anonymization · Dynamic subtree-scheduling · Crypto-PAn

1 Introduction

Network traces are valuable data for network researchers. Sensitive header fields need to be sanitized before the trace is made public. Prefix-preserving IP address anonymization is implemented in TCPDpriv[1] and Crypto-PAn[2], and seems to be suit for offline way. However, when online anonymization is required with a case that traffic traces are anonymized as soon as they are collected in a measurement node, the performance of offline anonymization algorithm should be improved. In this paper, we present a novel IP address anonymization algorithm based on Crypto-PAn and it is able to anonymize IP address at line speed with moderate memory requirement.

2 Crypto-PAn

The anonymization is a one to one mapping from original IP addresses to anonymized ones. Let f_i be a function from $\{0,1\}^i$ to $\{0,1\}$, for $i = 1,2,\cdots,31$ and f_0 is a constant function, and f_i is defined as

$$f_i(a_1 a_2 \cdots a_i) := L\big(R(P(a_1 a_2 \cdots a_i), k)\big)$$

© Institute for Computer Sciences, Social Informatics and Telecommunications Engineering 2015
B. Thuraisingham et al. (Eds.): SecureComm 2015, LNICST 164, pp. 581–584, 2015.
DOI: 10.1007/978-3-319-28865-9_35

where L returns the "least significant bit" and R represents Rijndael cryptographic computation and P is a padding function. Then given the original address $a = a^1 a^2 \cdots a^n$, the anonymization function could be defined as:

$$F(a) := a'_1 a'_2 \cdots a'_n$$

where $a'_i = a_i \oplus f_{i-1}(a_1 a_2 \cdots a_{i-1})$, $i = 1,2 \cdots n$.

Since the input of f_i is a bit sequence whose length varies from 0 to 31, and the output is a 0 or 1, the results of f_i can be organized as a perfect binary tree, as shown by Figure 1, where a black node represents 1 and a white node represents 0.

3   The Proposed Algorithm

3.1   DS-PAn Algorithm

For the proposed anonymization scheme DS-PAn, the anonymization tree is divided into two parts: the first k levels of the anonymization tree (level 0 to level k-1) stay unchanged, and the remaining part of anonymization tree is comprised of 2^k subtrees, as shown in Figure 1.

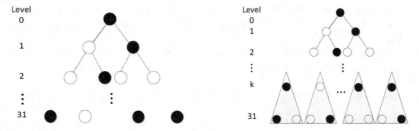

Fig. 1. Anonymization trees of Crypto-PAn and DS-PAn

When k is 24, for example, the the first 24 bits of the original IP address is anonymized as precomputed Crypto-PAn, and the remaining 8 bits are anonymized according to one of the 2^{24} subtrees. If the desired subtree has been computed and stored in memory, it is accessed directly, otherwise the corresponding subtree has to be calculated and stored to memory for later use.

As more IP addresses are anonymized, the subtrees stored in memory will increase gradually. Subtree removal is necessay when memory limitation is reached. We refer to this strategy that subtrees are dynamically constructed and destructed during the anonymization process as subtree scheduling.

When k is larger than 24, the size of subtree is smaller, thus constructing a subtree is quicker. However, the number of subtrees grows, so managing these subtrees is more time-consuming. When k is set to a smaller number, constructing a subtree may take more time, but it is less likely that an inserting or removing action is needed.

3.2   Detail of Anonymization Tree

The detailed design of DS-PAn is demonstrated in Figure2. For simplicity, it shows a scenario in which only 3 subtrees exist in memory. If the maximum size of pointers array is 32, for example, then 5 bits is long enough for each pointer index. A pointer index either denotes the position of a pointer in pointer array or is null, which means the corresponding subtree is not in memory.

When accessing a subtree, DS-PAn first look up the pointer index using the k-bit prefix of the original IP address, if the corresponding index is not null, then the position of the pointer to the desired subtree can be reached directly in pointer array by index. Otherwise, the subtree is not in memory, it need to be computed immediately and the corresponding pointer need to be inserted into a proper position in pointer array.

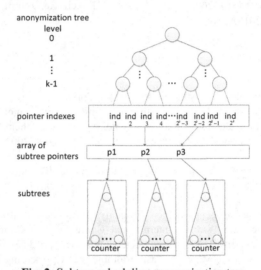

Fig. 2. Subtree-scheduling anonymization tree

Note that every subtree has a counter with it. The counter counts the time of accesses, and is used to determine which subtree should be removed when necessary.

4   Performance Evaluation

The performance of different algorithms is compared and listed in Table 1.

Table 1. Performance of Crypto-PAn and DS-PAn

	Initialization time (s)	Speed (IP addresses /s)	Memory (MB)
Crypto-PAn	0	344687	0
Crypto-PAn (precomputed)	113	3396960	512
DS-PAn (k=21)	0.056	1448964	71

5   Conclusion

In this paper, we presented a novel prefix-preserving IP address anonymization algorithm called DS-PAn which is capable of online IP address anonymization on commodity hardware. When adequately configured, DS-PAn is able to provide link-rate anonymization speed while eliminating the initialization delay and requiring small memory. The performance improvement is achieved by precomputation and the utilization of localized distribution of IP addresses in network traces, thus the security level of DS-PAn is completely the same as Crypto-PAn.

Acknowledgments. This work was supported by the National Natural Science Foundation of China (Grant No. 61361126011) and National Hi-tech R&D program of China (863 program) (Grant No. 2015AA01A301).

References

1. Minshall, G.: Pdpfiv. http://fly.isti.cnr.it/software/tcpdpriv/
2. Xu, J., Fan, J., Ammar, M.H., et al.: Prefix-preserving ip address anonymization: measurement-based security evaluation and a new cryptography-based scheme. In: Proceedings of the 10th IEEE International Conference on Network Protocols, 2002, pp. 280–289. IEEE (2002)
3. Ramaswamy, R., Wolf, T.: High-speed prefix-preserving IP address anonymization for passive measurement systems. IEEE/ACM Transactions on Networking **15**(1), 26–39 (2007)
4. Seppänen, K.: A fast and secure method for anonymizing packet traffic and call traces. In: Proceedings of the 12th WSEAS International Conference on Communications. World Scientific and Engineering Academy and Society (WSEAS), pp. 340–346 (2008)
5. Zhang, P., Huang, X., Luo, M., et al.: Fast restorable prefix-preserving IP address anonymization for IPv4/IPv6. The Journal of China Universities of Posts and Telecommunications **17**, 93–98 (2010)

POSTER: Ciphertext-Policy Attribute-Based Encryption Method with Secure Decryption Key Generation and Outsourcing Decryption of ABE Ciphertexts

Yuejian Fang[✉], Zilong Wen, Qingni Shen, Yahui Yang, and Zhonghai Wu

School of Software & Microelectronics, Peking University, Beijing, China
{fangyj,qingnishen,yhyang}@ss.pku.edu.cn,
{zlwen,wuzh}@pku.edu.cn

Abstract. Attribute-based encryption (ABE) allows user to encrypt and decrypt data based on user attributes, and can be applied in some promising area such as mobile cloud storage. Since these are massive users in these applications, secure online transmission of decryption key is necessary. In this paper, a cipher-text-policy attribute-based encryption (CP-ABE) method with secure decryption key generation and outsourcing decryption of ABE ciphertexts is proposed. In the method, a user's public key information is embedded into his decryption key in the key generation algorithm. Both the user's decryption key and private key are needed to decrypt a ciphertext. With only the decryption key, a ciphertext cannot be decrypted, so the decryption key is secure and can be directly transmitted online. This saves some costs comparing to other transmission approaches, such as Secure Sockets Layer (SSL). Furthermore, the method supports outsourcing the decryption of ABE ciphertexts. Our analysis and experiment results prove that our method is more efficient than the existing outsourcing methods which generally use key transformation technique.

Keywords: CP-ABE · Secure decryption key generation · Outsourcing · Mobile cloud storage

1 Introduction

Attribute-based encryption provides a solution for a user to specify access control policy without prior knowledge of who will receive the use's messages. ABE can be applied in some new promising areas, such as mobile cloud storage [1]. Since these are massive users in these applications, secure online transmission of decryption key is necessary. An existing solution is to use SSL. There are much costs of SSL including setup, identification and key exchange, data encryption/decryption, etc.

In mobile cloud storage, since the size of ciphertext and the decryption time grow with the complexity of the access formula in ABE, the decryption process becomes a burden for mobile devices with limited computation ability. Some research works provide methods for outsourcing the decryption of ABE ciphertext [2-4]. The disadvantage of the existing outsourcing method is that the key transformation time grows linearly with the number of attributes, and this cost is not negligible for mobile devices in mobile cloud storage applications.

© Institute for Computer Sciences, Social Informatics and Telecommunications Engineering 2015
B. Thuraisingham et al. (Eds.): SecureComm 2015, LNICST 164, pp. 585–589, 2015.
DOI: 10.1007/978-3-319-28865-9_36

Our Contribution. In this paper, we propose a simple and efficient ciphertext-policy attribute-based encryption method with secure decryption key generation and outsourcing decryption of ABE ciphertexts.

In the set up algorithm of the method, each user establishes his public/private key. A user's public key information is embedded into his decryption key in the decryption key generation algorithm. In the decryption algorithm, both a user's decryption key and private key are needed to decrypt a ciphertext. With only the decryption key, ciphertext cannot be decrypted, so the decryption key can be directly transmitted online. It is secure from online attack, such as stealing by attackers. In existing secure transmission approaches, such as SSL, the user's key is regarded as structureless data bytes. Comparing to our method, SSL incurs extra costs, including extra costs data encryption/decryption.

The decryption algorithm of the method is divided into two stages. In the first stage, only the user's decryption key is used and a middle result is obtained. If the user decides to outsource the first stage computation to a third party, such as a cloud proxy, he sends his decryption key to the cloud. The cloud proxy gets the ciphertext and computes a middle result with the decryption key. The middle result is an ElGamal type ciphertext, and the cloud proxy can't further decrypt it. In the second stage, a user uses his private key, and uses part of his decryption key if needed, to get the final decrypted message. The advantage of our method is that the decryption key can be directly sent to the third party, while in the existing outsourcing methods, the user needs to use a secret key to turn his decryption key into a single transformation key, then he sends the transformation key to the third party. So our method is more efficient than the existing methods with outsourcing of ABE ciphertexts.

2   Our Construction

In this chapter, we give our new construction of CP-ABE algorithms that apply our method in research work [5]. The detailed description is given below.

Set up $(\lambda) \rightarrow GP$. The setup algorithm takes as input a security parameter λ, it first generates $(q, \mathbb{G}, \mathbb{G}_T, e)$, where q is a λ-bit prime, $\mathbb{G}_0$ and $\mathbb{G}_1$ are two multiplicative cyclic groups with prime order q, Let g be a generator of $\mathbb{G}$ and e is the bilinear pairing $e: \mathbb{G}_0 \times \mathbb{G}_0 \rightarrow \mathbb{G}_1$. Next it chooses $H: \{0,1\}^* \rightarrow \mathbb{G}$.

The authority chooses random exponent $\alpha, \beta \in \mathbb{Z}_p$ as its master key($MK_A = \{\alpha, \beta\}$, his public parameters are: $PK_A = \{e(g,g)^\alpha, h = g^\beta, f = g^{1/\beta}\}$.

Each user j chooses a random exponent $\alpha_j \in \mathbb{Z}_p$ as his private key, and computes the corresponding public key $PubK_j$ as g^{α_j}.

Message Encryption(PK_A, M, $\mathbb{A}$). A user encrypts a message M under tree access structure $\mathcal{T}$ as follows:

The algorithm first chooses a tree access structure $\mathcal{T}$ the same as in [5], and then the cipher-text is then constructed by giving the tree access structure $\mathcal{T}$ as follows:

$$CT = (\mathcal{T}, \tilde{C} = Me(g,g)^{\alpha s}, C = h^s, \forall y \in Y: C_y = g^{q_y(0)},$$

$$C_y' = H(att(y))^{q_y(0)})$$

KeyGen($MK_A, S, PubK_j$). Suppose user j with public key g^{α_j} holds a set of attribute S. The authority generates user j's decryption key. The algorithm chooses random $r \in \mathbb{Z}_p$, and then chooses random $r_k \in \mathbb{Z}_p$ for each attribute $k \in S$. Then it computes the decryption key as

$$SK_j = (D = g^{\frac{\alpha_j(\alpha+r)}{\beta}}, \forall k \in S: D_k = g^{\alpha_j r} \cdot H(k)^{r_k}, D_j' = g^{r_k})$$

FirstStageDecrypt (CT, SK_j). If the user decides to outsource the first stage computation to a third party, such as a cloud proxy, then the cloud proxy performs all the computation of this stage. The detailed process is described is as follows.

If the node x is a leaf node then we let $k = att(x)$, and define as follows: If $k \in S$, then

$$DecryptNode(CT, SK_j, x) = \frac{e(D_k, C_x)}{e(D_k', C_x')} = \frac{e(g^{\alpha_j r} \cdot H(k)^{r_k}, g^{q_x(0)})}{e(g^{r_k}, H(k)^{q_x(0)})}$$

$$= \frac{e(g^{\alpha_j r}, g^{q_x(0)})e(H(k)^{r_k}, g^{q_x(0)})}{e(g^{r_k}, H(k)^{q_x(0)})} = e(g, g)^{\alpha_j r q_x(0)}$$

If $i \notin S$, then we define $DecryptNode(CT, DK_j, x) = \bot$. We now consider the recursive case when x is a non-leaf node. Then let S_x be an arbitrary k_x-sized set of child nodes z such that $F_z \neq \bot$. If no such set exists then the node was not satisfied and the function returns $\bot$. Otherwise, we compute

$$F_x = \prod_{z \in S_x} F_z^{\Delta_{i,S_x'}(0)}, i = index(x), S_x' = \{index(z): z \in S_x\}$$

$$= \prod_{z \in S_x} (e(g, g)^{\alpha_j r \cdot q_x(i)})^{\Delta_{i,S_x'}(0)} = e(g, g)^{\alpha_j r \cdot q_x(0)}$$

If the tree is satisfied by S, we set $CT_P = DecryptNode(CT, SK_j) = e(g, g)^{\alpha_j r \cdot q_R(0)} = e(g, g)^{\alpha_j r \cdot s}$.

SecondStageDecrypt ($\tilde{C}, CT_P, SK_j, PriK_j$). User j now decrypts $\tilde{C}$ with part of his decryption key SK_j and his private key $PriK_j$ by computing:

$$\frac{\tilde{C}}{(e(C, D)/CT_P^{\frac{1}{\alpha_j}}} = \frac{Me(g, g)^{\alpha s}}{(e(h^s, g^{\frac{\alpha_j(\alpha+r)}{\beta}})/(e(g, g)^{\alpha_j r \cdot s}))^{\frac{1}{\alpha_j}}} = M$$

The security proof of the construction is omitted for sake of space.

3   Performance

We implemented our new scheme of CP-ABE with access tree structure, and evaluated the performance. We made comparison with the existing method with key transformation technique [2] (shown with "-T" in the figure). We ran the tests on two hardware platforms: a 3.3 GHz Intel Core Duo platform with 4 GB RAM running Linux Kernel version 3.2.0, and a Google Nexus one mobile phone with 1 GHz Qualcomm Snapdragon (QSD) single core processor, 512 MB ARM running Android 2.3. We generated a collection of 100 distinct ciphertext policies of the form (A_1 AND A_2 AND ... AND A_N), where A_i is an attribute. Each experiment was repeated vast times and averaged to obtain our decryption timings. The results are shown in Fig. 1.

Comparing the existing transmission approach such as SSL using HTTPS protocol, the decryption key generated in our method can be directly transmitted online using HTTP protocol. The key generation time of the method (SDKeyGen) with key transformation technique (KeyGen-T) need much more time. The main advantage of our method is that our method needs no key transformation, so the key generation time of our method is much smaller than the corresponding time of the method with key transformation technique.

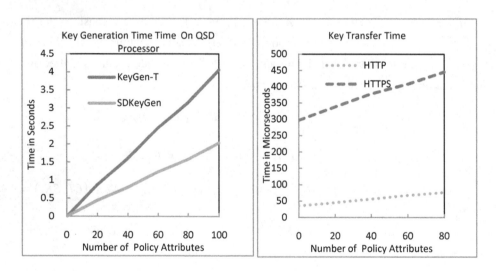

Fig. 1. Results with our CP-ABE scheme

4   Conclusion

In this paper, we propose a simple and efficient ciphertext-policy attribute-based encryption method with secure decryption key generation and outsourcing decryption of ABE ciphertexts. The analysis and experiments show that our method is more efficient than SSL and existing methods with outsourcing of ABE ciphertexts.

Acknowledgments. This work is supported by the National High Technology Research and Development Program ("863" Program) of China under Grant No. 2015AA016009, the National Natural Science Foundation of China under Grant No. 61232005, and the Science and Technology Program of Shen Zhen, China under Grant No. JSGG20140516162852628.

References

1. Zhou, Z., Huang, D.: Efficient and secure data storage operations for mobile cloud computing. In: Proceedings of the 8th International Conference on Network and Service Management, pp. 37–45 (2012)
2. Green, M., Hohenberger, S., Waters, B.: Outsourcing the decryption of ABE ciphertexts. In: Proceedings of the 20th USENIX Conference on Security, pp. 34–34 (2011)
3. Li, J., Huang, X., Li, J., Chen, X.: Securely Outsourcing Attribute-based Encryption with Checkability. IEEE Transactions on Parallel and Distributed Systems **25**(8), 2201–2220 (2014)
4. Lai, J., Deng, R.H., Guan, C., Weng, J.: Attribute-Based Encryption With Veriable Outsourced Decryption. IEEE Transactions on Information Forensics and Security **8**, 1343–1354 (2013)
5. Bethencourt, J., Sahai, A., Waters, B.: Cipheretxt-policy attribute-based encryption. In: IEEE Symposium on Security and Privacy, pp. 321–334 (2007)

POSTER: Context-Adaptive User-Centric Privacy Scheme for VANET

Karim Emara[1,2]([✉]), Wolfgang Woerndl[1], and Johann Schlichter[1]

[1] Department of Informatics, Technical University of Munich (TUM),
Boltzmannstr. 3, 85748 Garching, Germany
{emara,woerndl,schlichter}@in.tum.de
[2] Faculty of Computer and Information Sciences, Ain Shams University,
Khalifa El-Maamon St., Abbasiya, Cairo 11566, Egypt
karim.emara@cis.asu.edu.eg

Abstract. Vehicular adhoc network allows vehicles to exchange their information for safety and traffic efficiency. However, exchanging information may threaten the driver privacy because it includes spatiotemporal information and is broadcast publicly on a periodical basis. In this paper, we propose a context-adaptive privacy scheme which lets a vehicle decide autonomously when to change its pseudonym and how long it should remain silent to ensure unlinkability. This scheme adapts dynamically based on the density of the surrounding traffic and the user privacy preferences. According to the experimental results, the proposed scheme demonstrates a significant reduction in traceability with a better quality of forward collision warning application compared with the random silent period scheme.

Keywords: Context-adaptive privacy · Safety application · Forward collision warning · Random silent period

1 Introduction

Vehicular adhoc networks (VANET) are those networks formed among vehicles and roadside units (RSUs) to provide diverse traffic-related and infotainment applications. VANET is envisioned to enhance traffic safety and efficiency by increasing the awareness of vehicles about their surrounding traffic. To attain this awareness in real-time, vehicles are required to broadcast periodically their current state (i.e., position, speed, heading, etc.) in authenticated *beacon* messages. These messages may threaten the driver location privacy when they are collected by an external eavesdropper because the driver trajectories can be re-identified [1]. There are many privacy schemes that suggest to preload vehicles with a pool of pseudonyms where a single pseudonym is used at a time and changed periodically [7]. However, it is required to change pseudonyms in an unobserved zone in which the adversary cannot monitor the vehicle movements. This zone is often realized by a silent period [8] or in predetermined locations

© Institute for Computer Sciences, Social Informatics and Telecommunications Engineering 2015
B. Thuraisingham et al. (Eds.): SecureComm 2015, LNICST 164, pp. 590–593, 2015.
DOI: 10.1007/978-3-319-28865-9_37

(i.e., mix-zone) [6]. The silent period scheme lets a vehicle stop sending messages for a random period before changing its pseudonym. After this period, the vehicle resumes broadcasting beacon messages with a new pseudonym. When it is sufficiently long, a silent period prevents an adversary from tracking vehicle movements and linking old and new pseudonyms but at the cost of safety. Therefore, it is important to consider the impact of a privacy scheme on safety applications to better understand this trade-off between privacy and safety.

In this paper, we propose a context-adaptive privacy scheme (CADS) that utilizes silent period to deliver unlinkability among subsequent pseudonyms. This scheme is a significant improvement of our recent work, context-aware privacy scheme (CAPS) [4]. The CADS minimizes the required parameters by adapting the internal logic according to the density of the surrounding traffic. We integrate also the driver privacy preferences into the scheme to offer privacy constraints only when it is needed by the driver which minimizes the costs on the safety applications.

2 Methodology

The system and adversary models are assumed to be similar to those proposed in [4]. We used realistic vehicle traces [9] for Cologne city and selected half an hour for the middle 64 km^2 region. The resultant traces are 19,704 where each vehicle appears once with an increasing density ranging from 1,929 to 4,572 simultaneous vehicles in the first and last time steps, respectively. Finally, we add a random noise of 0.5 m to positions.

For privacy evaluation, the vehicle tracker proposed in [2,3] is employed to measure the *traceability* Π of vehicles as explained in [4]. Some vehicles never change their pseudonyms during their lifetime. Thus, the *normalized traceability* Π_n is additionally calculated by excluding these vehicles. For the QoS evaluation of safety applications, we employ our methodology proposed in [5] to evaluate the impact of a privacy scheme on a forward collision warning (FCW) application. In this method, the probability of correctly calculating the main application factors is estimated using Monte Carlo analysis.

3 Context-Adaptive Privacy Scheme (CADS)

The CADS improves the CAPS by allowing a driver to choose low, normal or high privacy preferences. The CADS also minimizes the required parameters by dynamically adapting its context-awareness module according to the density of the surrounding traffic. To optimize the scheme parameters with respect to the surrounding traffic, we investigate the performance of the CAPS in different densities. First, we select two relatively short sub-datasets from the realistic vehicle traces with low and high traffic densities, respectively. Second, the CAPS is evaluated using each sub-dataset with several parameter combinations and obtain the resulting privacy and safety metrics. Third, the results of the sub-dataset experiments are divided into three categories according to the achievable

privacy. Fourth, we identify the parameters that result in the best compromise
between privacy and safety in each category. Last but not least, these categorized
parameters of each density are integrated into CADS and bound according to
the real-time vehicle density and the input privacy preference.

The CADS was evaluated in two different scenarios. In the first scenario,
all drivers select the same privacy preference whether low, normal or high level.
Figure 1(a) displays the Π, Π_n and the QoS of each privacy preference. As a kind
of comparison, the measurements for the CAPS scheme of 11 s maximum silent
time are shown as dashed lines. The Π and Π_n of CADS decreases when vehicles
use a higher privacy level with a concurrent slight decrease in the QoS application. Compared to the CAPS, CADS achieves a better compromise between
traceability and QoS.

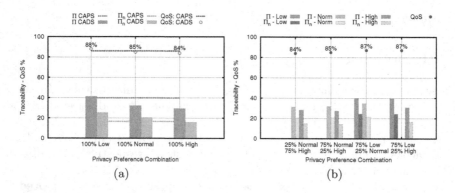

Fig. 1. The CADS evaluation when (a) all vehicles use the same privacy preference
compared to the CAPS of 11 s max silent time and (b) vehicles use a random privacy
preference based on the specified percentages

In the second scenario, vehicles randomly select the preferred privacy level
based on given percentages. The purpose of this scenario is to confirm the
enhancement of privacy when some vehicles use a higher privacy level than
others. Each experiment is repeated five times using a different random assignment of privacy preferences to vehicles. The mix of low, normal and high privacy preferences for each of the four experiments is specified along the x-axis of
Figure 1(b). Although the groups tested in the first two experiments had different
percentages of normal and high privacy preferences, we found similar (normalized) traceability achievable by each group in both experiments. Furthermore,
the high privacy preference group in the fourth experiment achieves a lower traceability than that achieved by the normal group in the third experiment. Also,
the high privacy group in the fourth experiment achieves a higher traceability
than that achieved by the same group in the second experiment. This result may
attributed to the major privacy preference group being low in the fourth experiment but normal in the second. Regarding the QoS, we notice that it follows

the QoS of the major group with a slight effect from the minor. For example, the QoS in the first experiment is the same as that in the 100% high-privacy experiment, and the QoS in the fourth experiment is similar to that in the 100% low-privacy experiment. From all these observations, we can conclude that the traceability is mainly affected by the configured privacy preference with a slight effect from the surrounding traffic. However, this slight change in traceability is compensated positively in the QoS.

4 Conclusion

In this paper, the context-adaptive privacy scheme (CADS) is proposed and evaluated. In CADS, a driver can choose the desired privacy level and the scheme can automatically identify the appropriate parameters that fit this desired level based on the real-time traffic density. Based on the experimental results, CADS reduces traceability than the CAPS does when normal or high privacy levels are selected with a slight reduction in the QoS. In future work, we will compare CADS with advanced privacy schemes such as mix-zones.

References

1. Emara, K.: Location privacy in vehicular networks. In: 2013 IEEE 14th International Symposium on World of Wireless, Mobile and Multimedia Networks (WoWMoM), pp. 1–2, June 2013
2. Emara, K., Woerndl, W., Schlichter, J.: Beacon-based Vehicle Tracking in Vehicular Ad-hoc Networks. Tech. rep., TECHNISCHE UNIVERSITÄT MÜNCHEN, April 2013. http://mediatum.ub.tum.de/attfile/1144541/hd2/incoming/2013-Apr/691293.pdf
3. Emara, K., Woerndl, W., Schlichter, J.: Vehicle tracking using vehicular network beacons. In: Fourth International Workshop on Data Security and PrivAcy in wireless Networks 2013 (D-SPAN 2013), Madrid, Spain, June 2013
4. Emara, K., Woerndl, W., Schlichter, J.: Caps: context-aware privacy scheme for vanet safety applications. In: Proceedings of the 8th ACM Conference on Security & Privacy in Wireless and Mobile Networks, WiSec 2015, pp. 21: 1–21: 12. ACM, New York (2015). http://doi.acm.org/10.1145/2766498.2766500
5. Emara, K., Woerndl, W., Schlichter, J.: On evaluation of location privacy preserving schemes for VANET safety applications. Computer Communications **63**, 11–23 (2015)
6. Freudiger, J., Raya, M., Flegyhzi, M., Papadimitratos, P., Hubaux, J.P.: Mix-zones for location privacy in vehicular networks. In: ACM Workshop on Wireless Networking for Intelligent Transportation Systems (WiN-ITS), Vancouver, August 2007
7. Petit, J., Schaub, F., Feiri, M., Kargl, F.: Pseudonym Schemes in Vehicular Networks : A Survey. IEEE Communications Surveys & Tutorials (c), 1–31 (2014)
8. Sampigethaya, K., Huang, L., Li, M., Poovendran, R., Matsuura, K., Sezaki, K.: Caravan: providing location privacy for vanet. In: Embedded Security in Cars (ESCAR) (2005)
9. Uppoor, S., Fiore, M.: Vehicular mobility trace of the city of cologne, germany (2011). (accessed January 20, 2015) http://kolntrace.project.citi-lab.fr/

POSTER: A Collaborative Approach on Behavior-Based Android Malware Detection

Chanwoo Bae[✉], Jesung Jung, Jaehyun Nam, and Seungwon Shin

Korea Advanced Institute of Science and Technology (KAIST),
Daejoen, Republic of Korea
{cwbae,taegm01,namjh,claude}@kaist.ac.kr

1 Introduction

The popularity of smart devices has grown rapidly in recent years, and now they are necessary elements connecting us to the Internet everywhere. As the number of smartphone users has explosively increased, malware authors are moving their targets from legacy computers to the smart devices. Therefore, we are facing new types of threats.

Many research proposals have been suggested so far to detect and prevent those threats, and these can be classified into two main categories: (i) static analysis, which investigates the source code of malware to detect malicious behavior [1–3]. and (ii) dynamic analysis, which monitors the runtime behavior of malware to detect its forbidden operations [4,5]. Each method has clear advantages and disadvantages. While the static method does not add much overhead to the device, it can be evaded by some advanced attack methods (e.g., obfuscation). The dynamic analysis method provides better chances of detection even if the malware employs some advanced evasion ways, however, it commonly adds more overhead to the device.

Observing that dynamic analysis method can increase the chance of malware detection, we have investigated if it is possible to employ a dynamic analysis method, but with less cost to the smartphone. And, we have found that correlating several different features that do not add much overhead can present similar detection results compared to existing detection systems based on dynamic analysis.

In our approach, we minimize the use of high overhead functions (e.g., control-flow tracking) and replace them to lightweigt features (e.g., function call monitoring). Here is the approach how we have leveraged those features instead of using high overhead operations. First, we monitor the network connections. It is likely that malicious apps are trying to connect to some suspicious hosts with relatively poor reputations. By watching whom, an app connects to, we can infer its malicious behavior (a good heuristic for malware detection). Second, all Android apps run on application program interface (API) provided by Android platform. Hence, malicious behavior of an Android app can be monitored by capturing the invocation of some sensitive Android APIs. Third, we monitor pattern of permission usage of an app. By monitoring the permission usage, we can verify malicious behaviors which are related to those permissions.

© Institute for Computer Sciences, Social Informatics and Telecommunications Engineering 2015
B. Thuraisingham et al. (Eds.): SecureComm 2015, LNICST 164, pp. 594–597, 2015.
DOI: 10.1007/978-3-319-28865-9_38

2   System Architecture

Our system consists of three engines: (i) host domain reputation analysis engine, (ii) critical API call pattern analysis engine and (iii) Android permission use analysis engine. Each of them makes own decision whether a monitored app is malicious, then, the correlator takes all decisions and combines them into a final decision. To employ multiple engines is a good way in reducing the chance of missing malicious apps by compensating errors with ohters' decisions.

Host Domain Reputation Analysis Engine. It is likely that malicious apps are connecting to the host with bad domain (or low reputation). By leveraging this fact, we have designed the host domain reputation analysis engine which monitors to whom the monitored app connects to. In this design, we try to leverage existing knowledge, and we select features employed by the work of EXPOSURE [6], which is known as a decent malicious domain detection system.

To build this engine, we use the Support Vector Machine (SVM), one of the most popular machine-learning classifiers. To train the model, we have collected sample malicious/benign domains (we have collected them from the local DNS server on campus from July to August in 2013) and built a SVM model.

Critical API Call Pattern Analysis Engine. We have observed that there is a special set of APIs frequently or hardly invoked by malwares (let us call those critical APIs). Based on this, we have designed the second engine that monitors the invocation of critical APIs. We have followed three steps to build our engine;

(i) Critical APIs Extraction: By running malicious/benign apps, we have extracted APIs that are frequently used by malicious apps but seldom by benign apps and vice versa. We further use this list of APIs as critical APIs.

(ii) Training a Model: We group apps into clusters by the pattern of using critical APIs. We extract call ratios of every single app from sample (by running them), make groups (or clusters) by K-means which is a well-known clustering algorithm. Apps whose call ratios of critical APIs are in the same cluster must have the similar pattern of usage of those APIs.

(iii) App Prediction: In this phase, we finally predict whether a unknown app is malicious or benign. From apps, extracting call ratio of critical APIs, we match this to the most close cluster. By figuring out the portion of malicious apps in that cluster, this engine could determine its decision.

Android Permission Use Analysis Engine. Like critical APIs, there also is a set of permissions that well-used by malicious apps (let this be critical permissions). We have extracted critical permissions as same as we did for the critical APIs. By training a SVM model based on usage of critical permissions, the third engine has been finally built.

Correlation Engine. To build a correlation engine, we again use SVM-classifier. We have let the sample apps be tested by three engines, and collected their responses, then finally trained our model for the correlation engine. When predicting an unknown app, the correlation engine makes a final decision with decisions from three engines and pre-trained model.

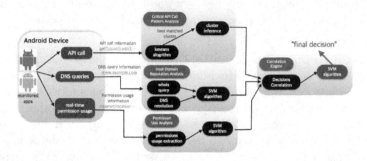

Fig. 1. System design of a malware detection system

3   Evaluation

Collection of Malware/Benign Apps. To train models and test our system, we have downloaded malware sample (795 apps) from the drebin[1]. Also we have collected benign apps (826 apps) by crawling and downloading from Google Playstore which is the official app market of Google. We have divided them into training sample and test sample (half for the training, half for the test).

The Precision of Single Engine. To show the precision of our system, we first measured the efficiency of each engine. The results are shown in table 1.

Table 1. The Precision of Each Engine

engine	result
Host Domain Reputation Analysis Engine	87 apps out of 415 benign apps which have connected to at least one remote host, were alarmed, 173 apps out of 340 malicious apps (with at least one connection) were alarmed.
Critical API Call Pattern Analysis Engine	358 apps out of 413 benign apps have been rightly not flagged (86.80%) and, 363 apps out of 398 malicious apps have been rightly flagged (91.39%).
Android Permission Use Analysis Engine	394 apps out of 413 benign apps have been rightly not flagged (95.40%) and, 283 apps out of 398 malicious apps have been rightly flagged (71.11%).

[1] The link for download is http://user.informatik.uni-goettingen.de/~darp/drebin/

Final Decision. As we mentioned previous section, each engine makes its own decision and then these are correlated into a final decision. Table 2 presents how precise the final decision is. Through the result, we found that, by combining decisions from multiple engines, the precision gets better.

Table 2. The Precision of Final Decision

by SVM	predicted as benign	predicted as malware	precision rate	by Naive Bayes	predicted as benign	predicted as malware	precision rate
benign	350	63	84.75%	benign	358	55	86.68%
malware	8	390	97.99%	malware	26	372	93.47%
TN& TP	97.77%	86.09%	91.25%	TN& TP	93.23%	87.12%	90.01%
Decision Tree	predicted as benign	predicted as malware	precision rate	majority rule	predicted as benign	predicted as malware	precision rate
benign	395	18	95.64%	benign	320	93	77.48%
malware	78	320	80.40%	malware	26	372	93.47%
TN& TP	83.35%	94.67%	88.16%	TN& TP	92.49%	80.00%	85.33%

The tables show results each by SVM (upper left), by Naive Bayes (upper right), by Decision Tree (bottom left) and with the decision by majority (bottom right).

Performance. For the last, we have measured performance of our system (i.e., performance overhead). We have run two widely-used Android benchmark tools: Vellamo Benchmark and GFX Bench.[2] The results show that our system has caused 7.27% and 0.16% (by average of three tasks) performance overhead from each benchmark tool.

References

1. Mu, Z., Heng, Y., Zhiruo, X.: Semantics-aware android malware classification using weighted contextual api dependency graphs. In: ACM CCS, Arizona (2014)
2. Yajin, Z., Zhi, W., et al.: Hey, you, get off of my market: detecting malicious apps in official and alternative android markets. In: NDSS, San Diego (2012)
3. Kevin, Z.C., Noah, J., et al.: Contextual policy enforcement in android applications with permission event graphs. In: NDSS, San Diego (2013)
4. William, E., Peter, G., et al.: TaintDroid: an information-flow tracking system for realtime privacy monitoring on smartphones. In: USENIX OSDI, Vancouver (2010)
5. Iker, B., Urko, Z., Simin, N.: Crowdroid: behavior-based malware detection system for android. In: ACM Workshop on Security and Privacy in Smartphones and Mobile Devices, Chicago (2011)
6. Leyla, B., Engine, K., et al.: EXPOSURE: finding malicious domains using passive DNS analysis. In: NDSS, San Diego (2011)

---

[2] The unique app ID of Vellamo is com.quicinc.vellamo, that of GFX Bench is net.kishonti.gfxbench.gl. Both two apps are available in Goolgle Playstore for free.

POSTER: Using Improved Singular Value Decomposition to Enhance Correlation Power Analysis

Degang Sun[1], Xinping Zhou[1,2], Zhu Wang[1(✉)], Changhai Ou[1,2],
Weiqing Huang[1], and Juan Ai[1,2]

[1] Institute of Information Engineering, Chinese Academy of Sciences,
Beijing, People's Republic of China
{sundegang,zhouxinping,wangzhu,ouchanghai,huangweiqing,aijuan}@iie.ac.cn
[2] University of Chinese Academy of Sciences, Beijing, People's Republic of China

Abstract. Correlation Power Analysis (CPA) is one of effective means of power analysis in side channel analysis. The noisy power traces can affect the power of CPA. It is significant to select the helpful power traces to improve the efficiency of analysis. In this paper, we present a new preprocessing method that is based on Improved Singular Value Decomposition (ISVD) for selecting the traces when using CPA to attack. The ISVD is a combination of SVD and Z-score. Experimental results show that our method is effective to improve the efficiency when analyzing both the unprotected implementation and the masked implementation.

Keywords: Improved Singular Value Decomposition · Side Channel Attack · Correlation Power Analysis · Selecting traces

1 Introduction

When performing a real power analysis attack on cryptographic device, the number and dimension of power traces are always very large. For the goal of high efficiency of attack, many researches pay attention on how to decrease the dimension. We think it is necessary to select a helpful subset of power traces to improve the efficiency when performing CPA. However, of the today,there are rare literature on selecting power traces for CPA. In paper [4],the authors present a method by using the mean and variance of the power consumption on the most relevant time to the processed data. This method require the exact time when processing data. We think this assumption is stringent, our method just need the near range that contains the point of data processing. Paper [3] proposed a method that is based on Principal Component Analysis (PCA). They sort the power traces by the first principle component of the noise matrix. The efficiency is desirable. Nevertheless, the methods proposed in these papers only focus on the unprotected implementation and did not demonstrate whether it is effective on protected implementation.

© Institute for Computer Sciences, Social Informatics and Telecommunications Engineering 2015
B. Thuraisingham et al. (Eds.): SecureComm 2015, LNICST 164, pp. 598–601, 2015.
DOI: 10.1007/978-3-319-28865-9_39

In this paper, we propose a new method that combine the SVD and Z-score to develop improved singular value decomposition to select power traces when performing CPA. The selected traces by this method can easily recover the key. We utilize this method both on unprotected implementation and masked implementation. The efficiency is outstanding and it can practically improve the effiency of CPA.

2   Background Knowledge

2.1   SVD

In the fields such as picture processing and machine learning, the data is always very large. In this scenario, the feature should be extracted to present the original data. Eigenvector is one of the methods that can achieve the purpose. We denote the original data is $A \in \mathbf{R}^{n \times n}$. The eigenvector $\nu \in \mathbf{R}^{n \times 1}$ can be computed by $A\nu = \lambda\nu$. The eigenvalue decomposition is a good method to extract the characteristic but the precondition is that the array of data must be square matrix. In the condition where data is not square matrix, the SVD is an alternate method. SVD is a method that can decompose any kind of array into lower dimension matrix and extract the characteristic of the original data. Further details on SVD may be found in [2].

2.2   ISVD

Before calculating the singular value, we introduce the Z-$score$ to eliminate the huge difference of row vectors of $A^T A$. The calculation of Z-$score$ as follow,

$$z = \frac{x - u}{\sigma} \tag{1}$$

where x is row vectors of matrix, u is the mean vector of all row vectors of matrix, σ is the standard deviation of x, z is the row vectors after processing.

3   Using ISVD in CPA

Let m power traces also known as samples and each of them contain n variables also known as sample points be $L \in \mathbf{R}^{m \times n}$. This is not a square matrix. However, we can calculate its singular values and corresponding singular vectors. We first let L be the A^T of Equation (3), so it is converted into

$$(LL^T)\nu = \lambda\nu \tag{2}$$

Before calculating Equation (2). We normalize the matrix LL^T by Z-score described in subsection 2.2 to ensure the amount of positive eigenvalue is equal to m. We denote $B = Z\text{-}score(LL^T)(B \in \mathbf{R}^{m \times m})$, the problem changes to calculate

$$B\nu = \lambda\nu \tag{3}$$

From Equation (3), we can acquire all the singular values λ_i and corresponding singular vectors $\nu_i \in \mathbf{R}^{m \times 1}(i \in [1, m])$. The eigenvectors can be used to represent the original data, so we suppose the singular vector corresponding to the biggest singular value should contain most of information about the original data. Note that the dimension of singular vector is equal to the number of samples. So we can sort the first singular vector ν' from large to small and get the corresponding index. The algorithm of this method is presented in Algorithm 1.

Algorithm 1. ISVD for Selecting Power Traces

Input: $L \in \mathbf{R}^{m \times n}$ (represents m power traces and n sample points),
        k(represents the needed number of power traces ,and $k \leq m$)
Output: Select(1:k)(represents the indexes of selected traces)
1: **function** ISVD(L,k)
2:     $A = LL^T$
3:     $B = Z\text{-}score(A)$
4:     Calculate λ_i, ν_i,such that $B\nu_i = \lambda_i \nu_i (i = 1, 2, \ldots, m)$
5:     Choose the ν' corresponding to the largest λ
6:     Sort ν' by descend, and get the corresponding subscript Order(1 : m)
7:     Select(1:k)= Order(1:k)
8:     Return Select(1:k)
9: **End function**

---

4 Experiments

In this section, we will perform a series of experiments on both unprotected implementation and protected implementation, the real power traces come from the DPA contest [1](the data of DPA contest are public data and they are widely used in testing methods in side channel attack). We use CPA based on our selecting method and randomly choosing method to analysis. Besides, for comparison, the PCA method that proposed in [3] is also used in the experiments. Success Rate (SR) proposed in [5] will be used as the evaluation metric. SR is defined as the probability that one can successfully recover the correct key, and it is widely used in side channel attacks to evaluate the key-recovery efficiency of an attacking method.

4.1 Unprotected Implementation

The power traces of unprotected implementation comes from DPA Contest v2. This attack is performed by first-order CPA by the selecting methods. The result is shown in Fig. 1 (a).

4.2 Protected Implementation

The power traces are acquired from DPA Contest v4. This attacks is performed by second-order CPA by the selecting methods.The result is showed in Fig. 1

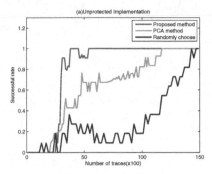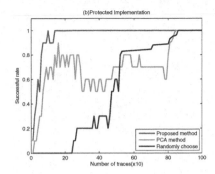

Fig. 1. (a)Success rates by using first-order CPA based different methods of selecting traces on DPA Contest v2.(b)Success rates by using second-order CPA based different methods of selecting traces on DPA Contest v4.

(b). The real experiments on both unprotected and protected implementation verify that the practical advantage of our method is remarkable.

5   Conclusions

In this paper, we proposed a method that using the improved singular value decomposition of the original power traces to select traces in order to enhance the efficiency of CPA. This method can select the power traces of high signal to noise ratio for analysis. This method is useful when performing the first-order CPA on the unprotected implementation and when performing the second-order CPA on the masked implementation. The results of experiments indeed verify the conclusion.

Acknowledgment. This research is supported by the Nation Natural Science Foundation of China (No.61372062).

References

1. DPA Contest. http://www.dpacontest.org/home/
2. Golub, G.H., Reinsch, C.: Singular value decomposition and least squares solutions. Numerische Mathematik **14**(5), 403–420 (1970)
3. Kim, Y., Ko, H.: Using principal component analysis for practical biasing of power traces to improve power analysis attacks. In: Lee, H.-S., Han, D.-G. (eds.) ICISC 2013. LNCS, vol. 8565, pp. 109–120. Springer, Heidelberg (2014)
4. Kim, Y., Sugawara, T., Homma, N., Aoki, T., Satoh, A.: Biasing power traces to improve correlation power analysis attacks. In: First International Workshop on Constructive Side-Channel Analysis and Secure Design (COSADE 2010), pp. 77–80 (2010)
5. Standaert, F.-X., Malkin, T.G., Yung, M.: A unified framework for the analysis of side-channel key recovery attacks. In: Joux, A. (ed.) EUROCRYPT 2009. LNCS, vol. 5479, pp. 443–461. Springer, Heidelberg (2009)

ATIS 2015: 6th International Workshop on Applications and Techniques in Information Security

Securing Application with Software Partitioning: A Case Study Using SGX

Ahmad Atamli-Reineh[(✉)] and Andrew Martin

Department of Computer Science, University of Oxford, Oxford, UK
{ahmad.atamli,andrew.martin}@cs.ox.ac.uk

Abstract. Application size and complexity are the underlying cause of numerous security vulnerabilities in code. In order to mitigate the risks arising from such vulnerabilities, various techniques have been proposed to isolate the execution of sensitive code from the rest of the application and from other software on the platform (e.g. the operating system). However, even with these partitioning techniques, it is not immediately clear exactly *how* they can and should be used to partition applications. What overall partitioning scheme should be followed; what granularity of the partitions should be. To some extent, this is dependent on the capabilities and performance of the partitioning technology in use. For this work, we focus on the upcoming Intel Software Guard Extensions (SGX) technology as the state-of-the-art in this field. SGX provides a trusted execution environment, called an *enclave*, that protects the integrity of the code and the confidentiality of the data inside it from other software, including the operating system. We present a novel framework consisting of four possible schemes under which an application can be partitioned. These schemes range from coarse-grained partitioning, in which the full application is included in a single enclave, through ultra-fine partitioning, in which each application secret is protected in an individual enclave. We explain the specific security benefits provided by each of the partitioning schemes and discuss how the performance of the application would be affected. To compare the different partitioning schemes, we have partitioned OpenSSL using four different schemes. We discuss SGX properties together with the implications of our design choices in this paper.

1 Introduction

Applications have grown tremendously in functionality and size. This growth in sensitive applications and libraries such as Apache and OpenSSL has long ago surpassed the feasible limit for assurance techniques such as formal verification to verify the correctness of the code, and numerous factors have rendered manual review equally insufficient for that task. Accompanying the growth of the code in these applications, more classes of vulnerabilities have been identified, such as stealing secrets and modifying sensitive code [1] [2]. An example that demonstrates this was the HeartBleed bug in the OpenSSL library where an attacker was able to obtain sensitive information including user names and passwords, credentials, and sensitive keys from remote servers [3].

© Institute for Computer Sciences, Social Informatics and Telecommunications Engineering 2015
B. Thuraisingham et al. (Eds.): SecureComm 2015, LNICST 164, pp. 605–621, 2015.
DOI: 10.1007/978-3-319-28865-9_40

Much research has considered the design of systems based on well-known operating systems and hardware components to protect sensitive code. Many of these systems leverage virtualisation and trusted computing to isolate the execution of the entire application [4–12]. However, many applications have thousands lines of code which makes it hard to gain assurance that no vulnerability exists in the code. Moreover, when virtualisation is used to provide isolation between different executions, there are many trust assumptions that make these systems limited in their security properties. For example, the Virtual Machine Monitor (VMM) or the code providing isolation needs to be trusted, loading the Trusted Computing Base (TCB) with thousands lines of code. The TCB is defined by the size of code that runs inside the same environment such as an isolated environment. The isolation of a software partition protects the data and the execution from external code, e.g. the OS and applications running in the same system. It follows that software partitioning of the application into several trusted partitions and untrusted partition, is expected to produce smaller partitions of code when considering the whole application as one partition. The latter, when partitioning to smaller chunks is feasible, may allow to formally verify the partition, which is protected by an isolated environment from external code and vulnerabilities such as vulnerabilities in other partitions of the same application.

Other systems [13–20] provide isolation for the execution of a sensitive code without defining the portion of the application running on the trusted space, the granularity of these approaches to port sensitive code, or the feasibility to port small code such as merely few methods of an existing library. For instance, the TrustVisor [14] authors appreciate the complexity of porting security sensitive code in trusted environment. Porting security sensitive code is straightforward if the program is privilege-separated and modular. However, it is a greatest challenge in complex applications such as Apache + OpenSSL [14].

To overcome the above mentioned shortcomings, processor extensions have been proposed in several pieces of research [21,22] to protect software execution and reduce the TCB. Protecting the code execution of the TCB is achieved with *Trusted Execution Environment* (TEE) in hardware, which prevents external software from tampering with the execution, or modifying an existing code/data. Intel has also proposed security extensions to Intel? Architecture called Intel? Software Guard Extensions (Intel? SGX) [23],extensions that enable provisioning of sensitive data within applications. These extensions allow an application to instantiate a protected container to ensure the confidentiality and integrity of the data even in the presence of malware, while also relying on hardware to prevent external access to the container's memory area. The protected container protects the inner code/data from external software, even privileged one, and is referred to as an *enclave*.

Generally, the code and data are freely available for inspection and analysis prior to loading them into the enclave. Once loaded into the enclave and measured, they become protected against external software access. In order to store data outside the enclave's boundary, e.g. on the disk, the application can request from the enclave to seal the data beforehand. Furthermore, the platform key, which is used to encrypt the data, ties the data to the platform and can be used to report platform identity to remote parties. Overall, these capabilities extend the ability of enterprises and personnel to design secure applications by relying strongly on hardware instead of traditional software techniques. The aforementioned hardware provides another layer of protection against exploits of vulnerabilities missed by the tools verifying the correctness of the code or in manual reviews.

However, even though many technologies are available, it is not necessarily obvious exactly *how* they can and should be used to partition applications. For some simple cases, the choice of partitioning scheme might indeed be obvious, but as applications increase in size and complexity, the number of possible partitioning schemes increases and the choice of the optimal approach becomes a very important non-trivial consideration. From a technical perspective, partitioning schemes vary in terms of the security guarantees they provide and their impact on the performance of the application. The choice of partitioning scheme has also other indirect implications, such as the effort for the application developers or software maintainers, but these are beyond the scope of this paper.

In this paper we investigate different software partitioning schemes using protected container, a TEE, to protect secrets from vulnerabilities in applications. Each scheme defines a different TCB size in each partition, which has immediate consequences on the economics of the TCB assurance process, in particular, its relation to the number of undetected vulnerabilities.

As a rule, we isolate software partitions as defined in each scheme, and use an enclave to protect its execution and data from access by untrusted code. Previous research [23]addressed the threat model and components of SGX; our paper explores the use of hardware primitives, such as those offered by SGX, to provide secure design of applications through partitioning to keep the confidentiality and integrity of application's data. We implement two of the four partitioning schemes using SGX and test their ability to protect the system against an exploit of the *HeartBleed* bug.

Our main contributions are:

- Proposing framework for different software partitioning schemes of an application.
- Investigation of different software-partitioning schemes using SGX, with an empirical focus.
- Proposing and investigating an evaluation matrix for partitioning schemes.

The paper is divided into seven sections. Section 2 provides a brief background on SGX and some of its instructions and features. Section 3 discusses the rationale of this paper, objectives, and adversary model. In section 4 we demonstrate the rationale behind software partitioning and several partitioning schemes. Section 5 presents a real-world case study partitioned based on our proposed schemes, with security and efficiency evaluation of each scheme. Section 6 discusses related work, and finally section 7 concludes the paper.

2   Background

2.1   Isolation Mechanisms

In this section we list different mechanisms used for isolation, and briefly list examples of systems that make use of such mechanisms.

2.1.1   Software-Enforced Isolation

There are several ways to create separation between partitions. The most common approach used in software is using privileged code such as an OS or Virtual Machine Monitor(VMM) that enforces access control semantics [14]. A VMM will typically use hardware assistance for virtualisation, however the access control is enforced by software using meta-data of a memory address table. In contemporary operating systems the OS enforces access control between processes. Each process has its own code and data in memory, and the OS prevents one process from accessing another process space, that includes memory addresses and code.

2.1.2   Hardware-Enforced Isolation

In order to isolate a partition from the rest of the system, hardware primitives have been proposed to provide TEE [13,21]. The TEE isolates the code execution from the rest of the system in hardware and enforces memory access semantics between the code running in the TEE. We refer to the code in the TEE as trusted code, and the code of the rest of the system as untrusted code. Arm TZ allows switching to a TEE from the untrusted space on TEE instruction invocation: the hardware moves the processor to TEE mode where data and code are separated from the rest of the system.

2.2   Software Guard Extensions (SGX)

An overview of the SGX protection model [24] was given by Mckeen et al. In their paper they present the core of this technology, the extensions that enable instantiating a protected container, describe the SGX instruction set, security model, threat model, and the hardware component on which this technology is based. In this section we give the background on SGX and its protection capabilities that is relevant to this work.

- **Enclave** - Intel SGX provides hardware features that creates a form of user-level TEE. The enclave is an isolated region of code and data within an application's address space. Data within an enclave can be accessed only with code within the same enclave. The enclave is able to protect its data using Enclave Page Cache (EPC); a secure storage used by the processor to store pages when they are part of an executing enclave. The EPC is built from chunks of 4KB pages; aligned on a 4KB boundary and each page has security attributes in the Enclave Page Cache Map (EPCM), an internal micro-architecture structure that is not accessible by software. It tracks the content of each EPC page, and enforces access control for accessing the pages.

- **Measurement** - a cryptographic hash of the code and data residing in an enclave at the time of initialisation. The measurement is used to verify that the loaded enclave is what the enclave claims it is.

2.2.1 SGX Enclave Instructions and Protection Rings

The enclave instructions available with SGX are divided under two protection rings; ring 0 and ring 3 [25]. The allowed set of instructions is determined according to the privilege level of the executing software. For the most part, ring 0 instructions; ECREATE, EADD, and EINIT are used for EPC management thus executed by privileged software such as OS and VMM. While ring 3 instructions e.g. EENTER, EEXIT, EGETKEY, EREPORT, and ERESUME are used by the user-space software to execute functionality within or between enclaves.

2.2.2 Enclave Life Cycle

In order to provide strong security features, managing an enclave is done in hardware through enclave build instructions. To create an enclave, ECREATE instruction is used. It builds the enclave and sets base and range addresses. Once an enclave is created, EADD is used to add 4KB protected pages of data and code. This is followed by measuring the enclave's content using EEXTEND to protect the integrity of the data within the enclave. To elaborate on the latter, adding and measuring the enclave's pages are done by software prior to EINIT instruction. Once called, it finalises the measurement of the enclave and establishes an enclave identity. Executing within an enclave prior to this instruction is not allowed. On success of EINIT, entry to the enclave is enabled and permitted to run on the processor in privileged mode called *enclave mode*.

In order to enter and exit the enclave under program control, EENTER and EEXIT are used respectively. On enclave entry, the cached addresses are flushed, including addresses that overlap with the addresses used by the enclave to ensure the protection of the memory accesses within the enclave. Similarly, on enclave exit any cached addresses referring to the protected space in an enclave are cleared. The purpose of this is to prevent external software from using the cached addresses to access the enclave's protected memory.

2.2.3 Asynchronous Exit and Resuming Execution

Exiting the enclave asynchronously occurs due to events such as exceptions and interrupts in which the processor handles such events by invoking the internal routine Asynchronous Exit (AEX). The AEX saves the registers used by the enclave which are consequently cleared to prevent leaking secrets. In particular, one saved address to be stored is the location of the returning address, also called the faulting address, where the execution resumes on the resuming enclave's execution. While saving the enclave's state is essential for resuming the enclave's execution, equally important is clearing the data used by the enclave to prevent secret exposure. Once AEX finishes execution, the processor exits enclave mode and goes back to normal mode where every instruction is treated as an external instruction.

On the other hand, the ERESUME instruction restores the enclave's state and gives back control to the enclave from the point it was interrupted. It is important to mention that the event whom the AEX was called upon may be triggered again in case of failure when the event is an exception or faults within the enclave.

3   Objectives and Adversary Model

3.1   Security Objectives

Applications consist of data, e.g. keys, passwords, and code of third-party libraries such as OpenSSL. Protecting secrets is a major priority; an application would like to keep the confidentiality and integrity of these secrets, and the integrity of the code executing using these secrets. The exposure of one element is enough to compromise the entire system. Furthermore, sensitive parts of an application constitute a small fragment of the code as a whole in most applications. Thus, isolating the data storage and execution of sensitive parts from the rest can decrease the impact of vulnerabilities.

Our security objective is to keep the *Confidentiality* even in the presence of malware (including malware running within the privileged operating system), and reduce the impact of vulnerabilities in code. It has been shown that hardware-assisted partitioning technology, such as Intel SGX, can be used to achieve this [23,26].

The enclave keeps the confidentiality of the data by encrypting its content when leaving the processor in enclave mode e.g. in memory. Our objective is to protect secrets such as passwords, keys, and sensitive code from vulnerabilities in applications. One approach to achieving this when considering a trusted OS is to use a different process for each partition,relying on the OS to enforce memory access control semantics between processes. However, we assume untrustworthy OS, an OS that might have vulnerability or malware, thus, using the processes is not an option. To elaborate on the latter, we do not consider an OS that is untrustworthy as a result of an adversary booting malicious OS. We assume that the OS is coming from trusted source but may have vulnerabilities or malware which may risk the exposure of secrets in applications.

It is important to note that using systems with one TEE such as ARM Trust-Zone [21], and Flicker [13] does not scale in flexibility for partitioning applications. These systems address how to isolate trusted code from untrusted code using one TEE, and managing the TEE for different partitions requires intervention of software and not hardware. On the other hand, SGX does allow instantiating of many containers using hardware operations, thus, it is well suited for our partitioning schemes and in evaluating the security of each scheme.

3.2   Adversary Model

In this paper, we consider an adversary with the capabilities to insert malware into the system, read the memory, and manipulate the OS including booting another OS. An adversary aims to exploit vulnerabilities in application code who may be able to obtain secrets or cause malfunction, which eventually may lead to exposure or modification of sensitive data. The adversary may have knowledge of the software running, but does not have physical access to the system's CPU and physical parts of the platform including memory controller or the buses interconnecting between platform components [27,28]. The adversary may be an insider with a limited physical access to the system, or a remote adversary. We do not aim to protect against attacks such as denial of service or side channel attacks.

4   Application Software Partitioning

We are proposing a partitioning scheme framework and that will be illustrated and explained with a concrete example of OpenSSL. However, the approach taken here is applicable to all types of applications that protect secret data. In the trusted part we would like to port sensitive functions and data such as hashing functions, random number generator, certificates, keys and passwords. The untrusted code will be located out of the TEE with the ability to call protected functions to be executed in TEE. While the untrusted code may be able to request for encryption and decryption services from the trusted code, it is unable to read/write the keys and the cryptographic functions that reside within a TEE to provide these services. The untrusted code may merely call the interface TEE functions for execution. The trusted part is considered as a *Black Box* to the untrusted part, thus, protecting the confidentiality and integrity of the code and data.

The application must be partitioned into several parts by identifying the sensitive partitions that require isolation from other parts of the application. The design guideline is to keep a sensitive partition minimal and within feasibility borders to allow formal verification of the code. While the TEE can protect its execution and secrets from external vulnerabilities, it does not protect against badly written code with flaws. Thus, a partition with small code is a corner stone for designing a secure application and has been long advocated by Saltzer and Schroeder [29]. However, it is important to bear in mind the efficiency of the execution when partitioning the code. A partition scheme that substantially impairs system efficiency will often be unfeasible regardless of its security characteristics.

4.1   Partitioning Schemes

In this section, we describe several possible partitions schemes. We start with basic partitioning configuration and develop it further as a function of the TCB and number of enclaves that yield different partitioning schemes. These schemes may differ in their ability to protect the confidentiality of the data, which we will be investigating in more details in section 5.

Initially, we started by defining a partitioning scheme that considers two guidelines: 1) the number of available enclaves 2) the TCB size inside each enclave. In scheme 1, we started with the most basic configuration, one enclave and without any limitation on the size of the TCB inside that enclave. Our aim is clear and simple; to protect the secrets as described in detail in section 3 from the rest of the code. In scheme 2, we chose to increase the number of enclaves by one, two enclaves with a reduction in the TCB as explained in 4.1.2, which led us to scheme 3. In Scheme 2, the size of the TCB inside each enclave is reduced to an optimal level. However, accounts/connections/users have to use the only available two enclaves, thus, no separation between the different accounts/connections/users. In scheme 3, we built on scheme 2 and adopted a similar TCB inside an enclave but with open approach toward the number of enclaves that isolate between different accounts/connections/users. Scheme 3 proved to be very complex both for security and implementation. For instance, a trusted channel is needed between every two enclaves that wished to talk to each other, thus, with the adopted open approach in scheme 3 many trusted channels are needed. Also, with this approach every piece of code inside an enclave needed to be duplicated for full separation between the accounts/connections/users. Hence, we identified a potential implementation and performance issues prior to evaluating the approach. It follows, in scheme 4 we took scheme 3 and optimised it by considering reducing the number of enclaves, TCB, and duplication of code.

4.1.1   Scheme 1 - Whole Application

In this scheme we choose to put part of an application such as a library inside one enclave. The residents of the enclave which may be code and data, include all secrets such as keys (e.g. private key, storage key, session key), passwords, credentials, and the code.

4.1.2   Scheme 2 - All Secrets

In this scheme we apply smaller granularity compared to scheme 1. We use two enclaves, we divide the code in two partitions, based on the frequency of accessing the code and port the code that generates secrets and has high frequency for accessing the secrets. The rationale is to opt-out the code that does not have high frequency of accessing the secrets which will result in reduction of code's lines number, hence, reduction of the TCB. However, it is important to mention that an application with different users has all its users' secrets within the same enclave. Thus, it is the responsibility of the software running inside the same enclave to enforce isolation between users' data.

4.1.3   Scheme 3 - Separate Secret

Scheme 3 is smaller in granularity compared to the previous two schemes. We use multiple enclaves to secure the secretes. Each enclave contains one secret such that each key resides in a separate enclave. For example code using the session key lies in one enclave and code using the private key lies in another enclave. We use multiple enclaves per account/user/connection, where each enclave contains the secrets generation relevant code and its relevant key, and one enclave for the code that has high frequency of accessing the code after generation.

4.1.4   Scheme 4 - Hybrid

In this scheme we apply smaller granularity than Scheme 1 and Scheme 2 but less than Scheme 3. We use multiple enclaves to protect Application's secretes. Each account/user/connection has a separate enclave. One enclave per account/user/connection, that includes keys (e.g. private key, session key), generation code, and functions with high frequency for accessing the secrets. For example, an application with multiple users, each user's secrets reside within the same enclave. However, in order to reduce the number of enclaves used, we use an enclave that contains code but not secrets to give services to all accounts. When a secret is needed, it's sent to another enclave which is assumed not to store any data. This scheme is similar to scheme 2 in the definition of the TCB residing inside an enclave, however, while scheme 2 has all secrets of all users/connections/account in an enclave, scheme 4 isolates between users/connections/account by having enclave for each. On the other hand, scheme 4 is similar to scheme 3 in the way it isolates the secrets of each users/connections/account.

4.2   Partitioning Using SGX

The application uses SGX to protect the execution of sensitive partitions by porting different sensitive partition into different enclaves. The number of TCBs is the influential factor for the number of partitions constructed prior to running the application, and during the run time, SGX enforces access between these partitions. It is important to mention that porting the code to run in trusted space is not the only action required when partitioning the code, the same ported code should be able to handle I/O operations and external operations and exit enclave mode when necessary. The interface to the enclave is limited and the creation process requires the intervention of privileged software that runs in ring 0, e.g. SGX driver. As a rule, the privileged software creates an enclave using ECREATE, adds, and measures the code of the desired partition. It uses EADD and EEXTEND respectively to perform the latter, which is then followed by EINIT to finalise the creation process, and entering the enclave by the same application that created it. In order to enter an enclave, the application uses synchronous entry instruction EENTER to switch the processor to enclave mode and to execute the relevant call.

As an essential part of the design, I/O operations are excluded from the enclave since they require the intervention of the OS, thus, when I/O operation is required, synchronous exit (EEXIT) is called to switch the processor to normal mode to handle the requested external operation. In a similar way the OS interrupts are handled through *Asynchronous Exit and Resuming Execution instructions*. Once done, the trusted part resumes by re-entering the enclave with ERESUME.

Once the enclave finishes execution it exits the enclave mode using EEXIT and the processor returns to normal mode of execution. The life cycle of the enclave and its content can be terminated by the application using privileged software; the privileged software tears down the pages inside the enclave (EREMOVE) and removes all the meta-data associated with it.

5   Security and Efficiency Evaluation

We use a *MiniServer + OpenSSL* library to examine several software partitioning schemes. The MiniServer is a web server that serves multiple clients and provides authentication, and secure communication channel. The MiniServer runs on Linux and uses merely minimal code to establish secure connections with clients. Furthermore, it uses the OpenSSL library for establishing secure connection between the server and the client [30].

To meet our objectives we choose to consider two main components in the SSL protocol: the handshake protocol and the data exchange. During the handshake, the client and the server generate keys which are unique for each connection session. The session defines a set of cryptographic security parameters which can be shared among multiple connections. For the most part, the handshake protocol allows the server and the client to authenticate each other and to negotiate a cryptographic suit. The handshake protocol consists of several messages exchanged between a client and a server prior to establishing a secure channel. It is followed by the second part of the protocol execution in which data is exchanged between client and server.

In order to evaluate the security and efficiency of the proposed schemes we consider partitioning the OpenSSL library 1.0.2-beta1. On the security side we investigate: 1) the ability of a scheme to protect against vulnerabilities in code such as the HeartBleed vulnerability; 2) the number of trusted channels required between partitions; and 3) the size of the TCB. Our primary reason for considering these evaluation items is their impact on the attack surface. For example, the size of the TCB has a direct impact on the number of vulnerabilities in code. Also, an application with various enclaves requires trusted channels for communicating between these enclaves, thus increasing the complexity of the system and expanding the attacks surface since there are more components to protect. On the efficiency side, we consider the number of enclaves, the number of entries to these enclaves, and the size of each enclave. Moreover, context switching is required when moving in to and out of the enclave, introducing an overhead that increases with the number of enclaves and entries to these enclaves. We evaluate the security and efficiency of the proposed partitioning schemes from section 4 and present the calculated results in table 1.

5.1   Case Study

In this section we use the OpenSSL library to examine the proposed software partitioning schemes. In particular, we choose a vulnerability from the buffer over-read class of attacks, the *HeartBleed* vulnerability [31], to evaluate each scheme. The aforementioned vulnerability will demonstrate the ability of each scheme to meet our objective of protecting the private and session keys. While, a straightforward solution is to fix the vulnerability when found, our proposed method of isolating software partitions from each other aims to counter the over-read class of attacks when a vulnerability is missed during the verification process.

The vulnerability known as HeartBleed results from missing bounds check in the heart beat extension which is a 'keep-alive' mechanism between two end-points to keep the connection alive. The latter was classified as a buffer over-read vulnerability and it allows more data to be read than was initially negotiated between the client and server, thus revealing secrets and sensitive data. The sensitive data is not limited to secret keys used within the OpenSSL library, but also includes user names and passwords of the application that happen to be in the requested memory space. For the most part, applications rely on privileged software such as the OS to prevent external access to an application space. However, in the presence of vulnerability in an application such as in a third-party library, the OS does not play any part in protecting the data of the entire application, specifically, data that is generated by the application but not used by the imported third-party library.

5.2   First Scheme - Whole Application as One Partition

In the first scheme the entire SSL library resides in a single enclave and includes the heart beat code. The code within an enclave has memory access to every memory address inside the same enclave, thus when a client requests more data than it has sent, the heart beat code is still able to extract the requested length, notwithstanding its content e.g. session and private keys, and send it back to the client. Moreover, data from the application using OpenSSL, such as user-names and passwords, can be extracted when residing in adjacent memory addresses to the requested data. Hence, the rest of the application is vulnerable to secrets exposure.

Using TEE does not protect against vulnerabilities in the code. While the data is protected with encryption from external software when it resides in the memory, it is not protected from vulnerabilities that reside in the enclave. To illustrate this using the HeartBleed example, the heart beat code resides within an enclave, thus it is part of the same TCB that contains the secret keys and functions used during the SSL session. As a result, the security properties provided by the enclave are transparent to the contained software, and accessing secrets from an inner function, such as the heart beat code, can be achieved without the enclave's interference.

Scheme 1 uses one enclave and thus doesn't require any trusted channels. However, the big drawback is the large size of TCB that includes the buffer over-read vulnerability, which in return it doesn't protect the confidentiality of secrets upon implementation.

5.3   Second Scheme - All Secrets

In the second scheme we used two enclaves to isolate part of the OpenSSL library including the handshake protocol, private key, session key, and data exchange. We partition the code such that only key handling the code (both session and private) are inside the enclave, but heartbleed code is outside that enclave.

Scheme 2 protects against exploitation of the HeartBleed vulnerability since the heart-beat code can not access the session key which is encrypted in memory as part of an enclave. The TCB is smaller than that of scheme 1. However, other secrets of the application, such as the user-names and passwords of the server which are not part of the enclave, are not protected. Also, one might question the security of having all the session keys within the same enclave used by the same code. To state the obvious, mutual exclusion between the different sessions is not achieved with this scheme.

5.4 Third Scheme - Separate Secrets

In scheme 3 each connection has two enclaves, one for the handshake protocol and session key, and one for the data exchange. To elaborate on the latter, since each connection has two enclaves, it's obvious that some duplication of code is inevitable. Nonetheless, the private key resides in a different enclave and can be used by other enclaves that require access to it.

In scheme 3 isolating each secret in a different enclave protects against code vulnerabilities, such as HeartBleed, compromising the confidentiality or integrity of the session key or private key. The TCB in each of the enclaves is significantly smaller than in scheme 1 . However, this approach brings with it other challenges: In order to prevent malicious software from exploiting the different enclaves, a trusted channel must be established between the different enclaves to assure secure communication and execution of the partitions combined. The latter may impair the execution efficiency in favour of isolating connections. However, more detailed empirical work is needed to examine this, which is beyond the scope of this paper.

5.5 Fourth Scheme - Hybrid Software Partitioning

In this approach we considered a hybrid partitioning of the code, which is a combination of the aforementioned schemes. The main code resides in the untrusted space and only a part of the code and data resides in the enclave. The heart beat code resides in the untrusted space of the application and is thus unable to access the secrets within the enclave. The heart beat code could reside in a separate enclave if need be. The main focus of our design is on partitioning the application in such a way that sensitive partitions with secrets are isolated from other unrelated partitions. In scheme 4, the TCB is smaller than in schemes 1 and isolation between the sessions is achieved. However, TCB is not as small as in scheme 3. The advantage of scheme 4 over scheme 3 is a reduction in the number of enclaves. The number of trusted channels required between different enclaves is smaller, which results in less overhead in the system and the trusted channel being a target for adversaries. To test this framework, we implemented the hybrid approach using SGX - a combination that proved to be resilient to read-overflow vulnerabilities such as HeartBleed. In addition, with this scheme the size of the TCB inside the enclave proved to be much smaller than scheme 1. In table 1 we summarise the analysis of the 4 different partition schemes discussed.

Table 1. Comparison between the 4 schemes

	Whole Application	All Secrets	Separate Secret	Hybrid
Number of Enclaves (10 Connections)	1	2	21	11
Trusted Channels between Enclaves (One connection)	0	0	3	2
TCB in enclave	L	S	S	S
Duplication of Code	No	No	Yes	Yes
Capacity Used	M	S	L	M - L

Size Scale : L - Large, M - Medium , S - Small

6   Related Work

In the last decade the topic of executing sensitive code in isolated and trusted environment has caught the attention of many researchers. McCune et al. presented Flicker [13]- an infrastructure for code execution in isolated and trusted environment. In their work they rely merely on 250 lines of code in the TCB to provide strong isolation. For the most part, they appreciate that 250 lines of code is a tiny code, therefore formal assurance of its execution is more trusted as a result of the feasibility to verify the code. Nonetheless, an application running in an isolated execution environment can be thousands of line of code and isolation between several parts in the application space is essential to prevent exploits by unfortunate vulnerabilities. The same group presented TrustVisor [14] a pointed purpose hypervisor that provides code and data integrity and secrecy for sensitive portions of an application. TrustVisor provides application developers with a strong secure environment for code execution and data storage on untrusted platforms. Moreover, they argue that small TCB code is easier to be formally verified, thus, it is more trusted when executing in TEE. Another research effort that takes a similar approach is that of Singaravelu et al. [32] where they showed that reducing TCB complexity can result in enhancing the security of the sensitive part of the application. The sensitive part is executed in a process called AppCore while the rest of the application is executed on a virtualised untrusted operating system. This approach is supported by three real world case-study applications.

In [33] Strackx proposed Fides: a security architecture that consists of two parts: a run-time security architecture and a compiler. The run-time security architecture is based on memory access control to protect applications. The modules are divided into a private section, where sensitive data is protected and accessed by the relevant module through limited interface, and a public section that contains the module's code. The second part is the compiler which is responsible for compiling standard C code into protected modules. In another work [34], Cheng et al. presented DriverGuard, a hypervisor protection mechanism to shield I/O flow from a malicious kernel. DriverGuard protects a tiny fraction of the code that is sensitive, such as biometric authentication. However, they assume secure boot-up and load-time attestation to ensure the hypervisor's security in the bootstrapping phase.

In [10] Li et al. introduce MiniBox, a two way sandbox that isolates the memory space between OS protection modules and applications. Unlike most approaches it aims to protect the OS from untrusted applications, but also protects the applications from a malicious OS. In Minibox, the authors focus on the two-way Sandboxing and don't address the porting efforts for legacy code, and suffice by mentioning that the porting efforts are similar to the porting effort on NaCl [17].

In [35] Vasiliadis et al. introduce PixelVault, a system that uses GPUs to secure cryptographic keys. In PixelVault the private key is created inside the GPU and never leaves or leaks it even in the presence of malicious OS. However, this is limited to the private key since PixelVault can not use the GPU to secure keys negotiated at run-time such as the session key or key pairs. Thus, malicious software can act as a man in the middle.

Partitioning privileges between hardware and software is not a new paradigm [36]. Hardware/Software partitioning has shown improvement in performance, energy consumption, and optimised run-time. However, there hasn't been much work that addresses hardware and software partitioning from security point of view.

Our approach differs in the granularity and feasibility of isolating sensitive code. Most approaches rely on software to isolate the execution of sensitive code from the rest of the system. These approaches face significant difficulties when partitioning the code into trusted and untrusted sections. While it is straightforward to isolate an entire application using SGX, it is still feasible for programmers to partition the code into trusted and untrusted sections even when the application is not modular or privilege-separated. Unlike some hardware-based isolation techniques, SGX enables concurrent execution of more than one secure enclave. This allows applications to use various different partitioning schemes to achive the required balance between security and performance.

7   Conclusions and Future Work

In order to protect the execution of sensitive code and data, it is desirable to use a trusted execution environment that does not include untrusted entities such as the OS. This can be achieved by keeping the TCB as small as possible and excluding irrelevant parts of the code. Fine-grained software partitioning of the code provides a good means of isolating different parts of the application and defining trust relationships between the partitions. Such an approach can protect the execution of a sensitive code from untrusted partitions when access is enforced properly. SGX proves to be a good candidate that keeps the OS out of the TCB and protects the execution of a partition from untrusted code using hardware. It is widely expected that the adoption of technologies like SGX will facilitate the design of secure applications and add another level of protection against various vulnerabilities in the code. In this paper we have proposed a framework that describes exactly *how* these technologies could be used to achieve this. We have explored four possible partitioning schemes that differ in terms of security guarantees and performance. We have demonstrated how our schemes could be realized using SGX to secure the execution of low level sensitive code in the SSL library as a proof of concept to our claims.

Another key point is that although the TEE is an important and desirable security feature, it is not a silver bullet against vulnerabilities in code. We demonstrate a logical use of TEE and the feasibility of different software partitioning schemes with SGX in merely one example: the OpenSSL library. In future work we plan to perform broader research on fine-grained software partitioning using SGX with different applications that includes bench-marking each of the schemes described above. Eventually, we intend to develop a methodology to help developers partition applications effectively using these new technologies in order to balance security with performance.

Acknowledgement. We appreciate the assistance and collaboration of Intel Labs, especially Mona Vij, and Somnath Chakrabarti. The authors would also like to thank Xiaowei Jiang, Andrew Paverd for the discussions and fruitful comments on this manuscript.

References

1. Misra, S.C., Bhavsar, V.C.: Relationships between selected software measures and latent bug-density: guidelines for improving quality. In: Kumar, V., Gavrilova, M.L., Tan, C.J.K., L'Ecuyer, P. (eds.) ICCSA 2003. LNCS, vol. 2667, pp. 724–732. Springer, Heidelberg (2003)
2. One, A.: Smashing the stack for fun and profit. Phrack Magazine **7**(49), 14–16 (1996)
3. Sullivan, N.: Staying ahead of OpenSSL vulnerabilities – CloudFlare Blog (2014)
4. England, P., Lampson, B., Manferdelli, J., Peinado, M., Willman, B.: A trusted open platform. Computer **36**(7), 55–62 (2003)
5. Chen, X., Garfinkel, T., Lewis, E.C., Subrahmanyam, P., Waldspurger, C.A., Boneh, D., Dwoskin, J., Ports, D.R.: Overshadow: a virtualization-based approach to retrofitting protection in commodity operating systems. ACM SIGOPS Operating Systems Review **42**, 2–13 (2008)
6. Martignoni, L., Poosankam, P., Zaharia, M., Han, J., McCamant, S., Song, D., Paxson, V., Perrig, A., Shenker, S., Stoica, I.: Cloud terminal: secure access to sensitive applications from untrusted systems. In: USENIX Annual Technical Conference, pp. 165–182 (2012)

7. Garfinkel, T., Pfaff, B., Chow, J., Rosenblum, M., Boneh, D.: Terra: A virtual machine-based platform for trusted computing. ACM SIGOPS Operating Systems Review **37**, 193–206 (2003)
8. Ta-Min, R., Litty, L., Lie, D.: Splitting interfaces: making trust between applications and operating systems configurable. In: Proceedings of the 7th Symposium on Operating Systems Design and Implementation, pp. 279–292. USENIX Association (2006)
9. Paverd, A.J., Martin, A.P.: Hardware security for device authentication in the smart grid. In: Cuellar, J. (ed.) SmartGridSec 2012. LNCS, vol. 7823, pp. 72–84. Springer, Heidelberg (2013)
10. Li, Y., McCune, J., Newsome, J., Perrig, A., Baker, B., Drewry, W.: Minibox: a two-way sandbox for x86 native code. In: 2014 USENIX Annual Technical Conference (USENIX ATC 2014). USENIX Association (2014)
11. Hofmann, O.S., Kim, S., Dunn, A.M., Lee, M.Z., Witchel, E.: Inktag: secure applications on an untrusted operating system. ACM SIGPLAN Notices **48**(4), 265–278 (2013)
12. Atamli, A.W., Martin, A.: Threat-based security analysis for the internet of things. In: 2014 International Workshop on Secure Internet of Things (SIoT), pp. 35–43. IEEE (2014)
13. McCune, J.M., Parno, B.J., Perrig, A., Reiter, M.K., Isozaki, H.: Flicker: An execution infrastructure for tcb minimization. SIGOPS Oper. Syst. Rev. **42**(4), 315–328 (2008)
14. McCune, J., Li, Y., Qu, N., Zhou, Z., Datta, A., Gligor, V., Perrig, A.: Trustvisor: efficient tcb reduction and attestation. In: 2010 IEEE Symposium on Security and Privacy (SP), pp. 143–158, May 2010
15. Azab, A.M., Ning, P., Zhang, X.: Sice: a hardware-level strongly isolated computing environment for x86 multi-core platforms. In: Proceedings of the 18th ACM Conference on Computer and Communications Security, pp. 375–388. ACM (2011)
16. Sahita, R., Warrier, U., Dewan, P.: Protecting critical applications on mobile platforms. Intel Technology Journal **13**(2) (2009)
17. Yee, B., Sehr, D., Dardyk, G., Chen, J.B., Muth, R., Ormandy, T., Okasaka, S., Narula, N., Fullagar, N.: Native client: a sandbox for portable, untrusted x86 native code. In: 2009 30th IEEE Symposium on Security and Privacy, pp. 79–93. IEEE (2009)
18. Dewan, P., Durham, D., Khosravi, H., Long, M., Nagabhushan, G.: A hypervisor-based system for protecting software runtime memory and persistent storage. In: Proceedings of the 2008 Spring Simulation Multiconference, pp. 828–835. Society for Computer Simulation International (2008)
19. Singaravelu, L., Pu, C., Härtig, H., Helmuth, C.: Reducing tcb complexity for security-sensitive applications: Three case studies. ACM SIGOPS Operating Systems Review **40**, 161–174 (2006)
20. Cheng, Y., Ding, X., Deng, R.: Appshield: Protecting applications against untrusted operating system. Singaport Management University Technical Report, SMU-SIS-13 **101** (2013)
21. ARM: ARM TrustZone
22. McCune, J.M., Parno, B., Perrig, A., Reiter, M.K., Seshadri, A.: How low can you go?: Recommendations for hardware-supported minimal tcb code execution. SIGARCH Comput. Archit. News **36**(1), 14–25 (2008)
23. Hoekstra, M., Lal, R.: Using innovative instructions to create trustworthy software solutions. In: Proceedings of the 2nd International Workshop on Hardware and Architectural Support for Security and Privacy (2013)

24. McKeen, F., Alexandrovich, I., Berenzon, A.: Innovative instructions and software model for isolated execution. In: HASP (2013)
25. Schroeder, M.D., Saltzer, J.H.: A hardware architecture for implementing protection rings. Communications of the ACM 15(3), 157–170 (1972)
26. Baumann, A., Peinado, M., Hunt, G.: Shielding applications from an untrusted cloud with haven. In: USENIX Symposium on Operating Systems Design and Implementation (OSDI) (2014)
27. Zhang, Y., Juels, A., Reiter, M.K., Ristenpart, T.: Cross-vm side channels and their use to extract private keys. In: Proceedings of the 2012 ACM Conference on Computer and Communications Security, CCS 2012, pp. 305–316. ACM, New York (2012)
28. Fan, J., Guo, X., De Mulder, E., Schaumont, P., Preneel, B., Verbauwhede, I.: State-of-the-art of secure ecc implementations: a survey on known side-channel attacks and countermeasures. In: 2010 IEEE International Symposium on Hardware-Oriented Security and Trust (HOST), pp. 76–87. IEEE (2010)
29. Saltzer, J.H., Schroeder, M.D.: The protection of information in computer systems. Proceedings of the IEEE 63(9), 1278–1308 (1975)
30. OpenSSL Software Foundation: OpenSSL Library Version 1.0.2a
31. Mehta, N.: Codenomicon: The Heartbleed Bug
32. Singaravelu, L., Pu, C., Härtig, H., Helmuth, C.: Reducing tcb complexity for security-sensitive applications: Three case studies. SIGOPS Oper. Syst. Rev. 40(4), 161–174 (2006)
33. Strackx, R., Piessens, F.: Fides: selectively hardening software application components against kernel-level or process-level malware. In: Proceedings of the 2012 ACM Conference on Computer and Communications Security, CCS 2012, pp. 2–13. ACM, New York (2012)
34. Cheng, Y., Ding, X., Deng, R.H.: DriverGuard: a fine-grained protection on I/O flows. In: Atluri, V., Diaz, C. (eds.) ESORICS 2011. LNCS, vol. 6879, pp. 227–244. Springer, Heidelberg (2011)
35. Vasiliadis, G., Athanasopoulos, E., Polychronakis, M., Ioannidis, S.: Pixelvault: using gpus for securing cryptographic operations. In: Proceedings of the 2014 ACM SIGSAC Conference on Computer and Communications Security, CCS 2014, pp. 1131–1142. ACM, New York (2014)
36. Stitt, G., Lysecky, R., Vahid, F.: Dynamic hardware/software partitioning: a first approach. In: Proceedings of the 40th Annual Design Automation Conference, DAC 2003, pp. 250–255. ACM, New York (2003)

Image Spam Classification Using Neural Network

Mozammel Chowdhury[1(✉)], Junbin Gao[1], and Morshed Chowdhury[2]

[1] School of Computing and Mathematics, Charles Sturt University, Bathurst, Australia
{mochowdhury,jbgao}@csu.edu.au
[2] School of Information Technology, Deakin University, Geelong, Australia
muc@deakin.edu.au

Abstract. Spam, an unsolicited or unwanted email, has traditionally been and continues to be one of the most challenging problems for cyber security. Image-based spam or image spam is a recent trick developed by the spammers which embeds malicious image with the text message in a binary format. Spammers use image based spamming with the intention of escaping the text based spam filters. On the way to detect image spam, several techniques have been developed. However, these techniques are vulnerable to most recent image spam and exhibit lack of competence. With a view to diminish the limitations of the existing solutions, this paper proposes a robust and efficient approach for image spam detection using machine learning algorithm. Our proposed system analyzes the file features together with the visual features of the embedded image. These features are used to train a classifier based on back propagation neural networks to detect the email as spam or legitimate one. Experimental evaluation demonstrates the effectiveness of the proposed system comparable to the existing models for image spam classification.

Keywords: Image spam · Spam filtering · Machine learning · BPNN

1   Introduction

Nowadays, e-mails have become a very common and convenient medium to millions of people worldwide for daily communications due to the rapid advances of Internet. However, along with the emergent significance of the emails, there has been a striking growth of spam in recent years which has become a key problem to the internet users and vendors. Spam is commonly defined as an unsolicited or unwanted bulk e-mail sent indiscriminately, directly or indirectly, by a sender having no current relationship with the recipients [1]. The current trend of spam messages alarms that it will climb to 95% of the total email traffic very shortly, which was accounted about 70% in 2012 [2]. Due to the recent upsurge in spam emails, it has been a significant concern for the researcher to develop unbeaten techniques for fighting against spam.

Until last decade, the spam messages were based on textual content only. That's why, the spam filters [3-6] were designed to analyze only the text content of the messages to classify them as spam or legitimate email. However, in recent years, spammers has introduced a new trick by developing multimedia enriched spam, where the

B. Thuraisingham et al. (Eds.): SecureComm 2015, LNICST 164, pp. 622–632, 2015.
DOI: 10.1007/978-3-319-28865-9_41

text message is embedded into the attached image with an intention to defeat the text-based anti-spam filters. Fig. 1 shows the examples of spam images. Approaching to detect and filter image spam, several techniques have been recently proposed [7-12]. However, these proposed solutions exhibit several weaknesses and their effectiveness has not been thoroughly investigated so far.

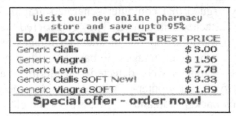 

Fig. 1. Examples of spam images: (a) image with embedded text (b) image with text and picture.

Many researchers have contributed to fight against the arms racing of spam by developing new techniques. In recent years, machine learning based text categorization techniques have been widely investigated for textual content analysis [13-17]. The success of machine learning techniques for text categorization has inspired researchers to explore learning algorithms in developing spam filtering. In particular, Bayesian techniques and Support Vector Machines (SVM) are most effective methods for text categorization, which are widely used by the researchers for spam classification [3].

It is a matter of fact that the unbeaten response of the content-based filters has forced spammers to originate increasingly complex attacks to escape these filters. On the way to struggle against the spammers' tricks, researchers have employed learning capability with these filters to train those using machine learning algorithms. Learning-based filters have the potential to learn and enhance the self-performance at real-time, so that they can adapt themselves to the wide genre of spam.

In this paper, a new architecture of spam classification has been proposed based on back propagation neural network (BPNN). The system will analyze the file features of the embedded image and extract the low level visual features as well. These features are then fed into the BPNN classifier to train the network. To test the effectiveness of the proposed network and verify the accuracy, we use a large data set consisted of both spam and non-spam images. Experimental evaluation confirms that the proposed system is robust and efficient to detect the embedded message as spam or legitimate email.

The remainder of the paper is organized as follows. Section 2 provides an overview of relevant work in this research area. Section 3 describes our proposed approach for image spam classification. Section 4 demonstrates the experimental results and performance of the proposed system with a critical discussion. Finally, Section 5 concludes the paper with future research directions.

2   Related Works

Many techniques have been proposed by the researchers in last recent years for detecting image spam. In this section we provide a brief discussion on relevant work in image spam classification.

Wu *et al.* [18] proposed an image spam classification technique based on text area and low-level features of the image. They argued that computer-generated graphics like banner, advertisement are spam images attached with emails. They considered the ratio of the banners and graphic images to the total number of attached images as features based on the assumption that most of the spam images are banners and computer-generated graphics as advertisements. Banners were detected considering the aspect ratio, height, and width. To identify the computer-generated graphics they assumed that graphics contain homogeneous background and less texture. A one class classifier based on SVM was used in their work.

Aradhye *et al.* [19] proposed a technique for image spam detection based on extracted overlay text and color features. It can monitor outbound e-mails by corporations to detect communications including proprietary or confidential material of the corporation. The method consists of three stages: (i) extraction of the text containing in the spam image, (ii) identification of spam-indicative features from the image, and (iii) learning the features with a SVM for image spam categorization.

A fast classifier using Maximum entropy, Naïve Bayes and Decision tree was proposed by Dredze *et al.* [20] based on image metadata and low-level features. The technique exploits information like image height, width, aspect ratio, file format (e.g., gif, jpg), and file size. Visual features like average red, green and blue values, features based on edge detection were also considered.

Wang *et al.* [21] proposed an image spam classification technique based on low-level features and similarity of images. The similarity measure is estimated for each set of features. The distance measure is then compared to a threshold. The threshold is set different for each feature space. Based on the threshold value, the image is detected as spam or legitimate one. The image features are extracted from color histograms, Haar wavelet transform, and edge orientation histograms. They used Nearest neighbour detection in their technique.

Another image spam classification algorithm based on low level image processing technique was proposed by Biggio *et al.* [22]. This method can recognize the noisy texts in the malicious image. This technique can identify the presence or absence of noisy text, or measure the amount of noise in a proper scale.

Mehta *et al.* [8] proposed a two-class SVM classifier based on the low level color features and similarity of images. Their proposal assumed that spam images are artificially generated and are related to color, shape and texture of the images. Their distribution was approximated with Gaussian mixture models. They stated that the low-level features could help the email recipients to achieve the highest capability for discriminating the spam and non-spam images.

Zhang *et al.* [23] proposed a technique based on image similarity where similarity is computed on the basis of color, texture, and shape features of the image. They used a two-class SVM classifier trained on spam and legitimate images. This technique consists of three steps: (i) image segmentation, (ii) feature extraction and similarity calculation and (iii) spam image clustering.

Bowling *et al.* in [24] suggested an approach for image spam classification using artificial neural networks. Their method identifies image spam by training an artificial neural network. The process consists of three steps. The initial step is the image preparation. In the next step the neural network is trained with training data. In the final stage, the neural network is tested to identify whether the embedded image is spam or non-spam. The neural network was implemented with 22,500 inputs, two hidden layers of 50 or 75 nodes each, and one output node. The input nodes are the pixels of an image. The output layer is the +1 or -1 indicating spam or non-spam.

3   Proposed Architecture of Image Spam Detection Technique

The overall framework of our proposed method for image spam detection is shown in Fig. 2. The aim of this paper is to develop a classifier that can detect the image spam and legitimate emails. The proposed system consists of three main components: (i) Features extraction, (ii) Features selection and (iii) BPNN Classification. This section presents the proposed methodology for extracting the feature points from the embedded image and a feed forward back propagation neural network, which pretends as a classifier for detecting the image as spam or legitimate one.

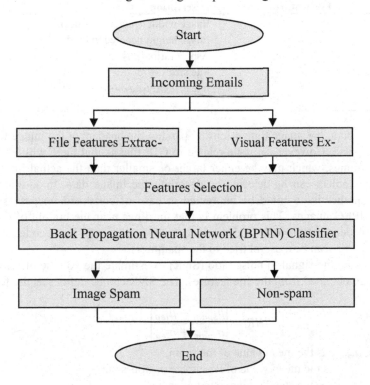

Fig. 2. Proposed approach for image spam classification.

3.1   Features Extraction and Selection

One of the key tasks underlying image spam classification is feature extraction. This paper extracts two types of features for image spam classification: one is file features and another is visual or color features of the image. Selected features are then feed forward to BPNN classifier.

3.1.1   File Features Extraction

Image spam can be detected based on their file type. The authors [11] derive some features of the image file for detecting image spam using decision trees and support vector machine. In this work, we only extract the basic file features of an image with an intension of requiring low computation cost. The basic useful features of an image file include: image file type, file size and the dimension (width and height) denoted in the header of the image file. Empirically we find that image spam mostly contains images of GIF (graphics interchange format), PNG (portable network graphics) or JPEG (joint photographic experts group) file types. Therefore, we consider these three image file formats in our work. The file features of an image are reported in Table 1.

Table 1. File features of an image

File features	Description
f_1	Image width denoted in header
f_2	Image height denoted in header
f_3	Aspect ratio: f_1/f_2
f_4	File size
f_5	Image area: $f_1 \times f_2$
f_6	Compression: f_5/f_4

We can obtain the image dimensions by parsing the headers of the image files with a minimal parse. However, an issue related to GIF files is that there will be presence of virtual frames, which may be either larger or smaller than the actual image width [11]. This problem can be detected by decoding the image data. In addition to this problem, another issue could be impressed in case of corrupted images as well as PNG and JPEG images. This problem is that the lines near the bottom of the image will not be decoded properly and no further image data can be decoded after that point. This issue can be a useful trick to the spammers.

We measure the signal to noise ratio (SNR) to estimate the volume of information in the image obtained from the file features. The SNR can be defines as the following equation:

$$SNR = \left| \frac{\mu_{spam} - \mu_{leg}}{\sigma_{spam} + \sigma_{leg}} \right| \tag{1}$$

where, μ_{spam} is the mean value of the spam,

μ_{leg} is the mean value of legitimate or non-spam,

σ_{spam} is the standard deviation of spam,

σ_{leg} is the standard deviation of legitimate or non-spam.

The mean value of the binary features reflect the percentages of images in the respective formats. The feature f6 is the most informative feature beyond the binary image file that retains the amount of compression. The compression is better if more number of pixels is stored per byte.

3.1.2 Visual Features Extraction

The spammers usually design the spam messages using highly contrasting colors with an intention that the spam emails should be easily noticeable by the users [10, 18]. Based on this constraint, we use HSI (Hue, Saturation, and Intensity) color histogram to extract the visual features from the image. HSI color space is different from the RGB color space and it separates out the intensity from the color information. Intensity represents the value or brightness of a color, which is decoupled from the color information in the represented image. Fig. 3 shows a three dimensional representation of the HSI color space. The central vertical axis represents the intensity. Hue defines the angle relative to the red axis, and Saturation is the depth or purity of the color measured from the radical distance from the central axis with value between 0 at the center to 1 at the outer surface. This histogram is converted into three bins and passed into neural networks.

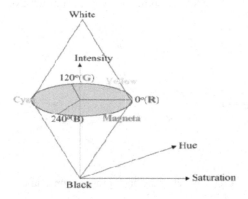

Fig. 3. Representation of HSI color space.

We can convert the RGB color space into HIS color space as follows:

$$I = \frac{1}{3}(R + G + B)$$ (2)

$$S = 1 - \frac{3}{R + G + B}[min\ (R, G, B)]$$

$$H = cos^{-1}\left[\frac{\frac{1}{2}[(R - G) + (R - B)]}{\sqrt{(R - G)^2 + (R - B)(G - B)}}\right]$$

3.2   The BPNN Classifier Model

A back-propagation neural network (BPNN) is a multi-layer artificial neural network consists of neurons [2, 24]. The layers are fully connected, that is, every neuron in each layer is connected to every other neuron in the adjacent forward layer and each connection has a weight associated with it. Back propagation algorithm presents a training sample to the neural network and compares the obtained output to the desired output of that sample. It calculates the error in each output neuron. BPNN adjusts the weights of each neuron to minimize the error. BPNN is used as a supervised training model for classification of image spam using the optimum feature vectors extorted from an image. It recognizes the data and test how well it has learned from the previous set of data.

Fig. 4 shows the architecture of the back-propagation neural network. The network consists of one input layer with 20 neurons and two hidden layers with 80 neurons and one output layer with a single neuron. The input nodes take the pixel values of an image. The output layer results -1 or 1 indicating non-spam or spam image respectively. The indices, i, j, k, refer to the neurons in the input, hidden and output layers, respectively. Input signals are propagated through the network from left to right, and error signals from right to left. The symbol w_{ij} denotes the weight for the connection between neuron i in the input layer and neuron j in the hidden layer, and the symbol w_{jk} the weight between neuron j in the hidden layer and neuron k in the output layer.

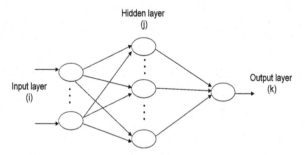

Fig. 4. The model of the back-propagation neural network

To propagate error signals, we start at the output layer and work backward to the hidden layer. The error signal at the output of neuron k at the pth training cycle (iteration) is given as:

$$e_k(p) = d_k(p) - y_k(p) \tag{3}$$

The instantaneous value of error energy for neuron k is,

$$E(i) = \frac{1}{2}e_k^2(p) \tag{4}$$

The total error energy $E(p)$ can be computed by summing up the instantaneous energy over all the neurons in the output layer:

$$E(p) = \sum_{k \in C}\frac{1}{2}e_k^2(p) \; ; \text{C is a set of all output neurons} \tag{5}$$

The sigmoid function transforms the input, which can have any value between plus and minus infinity, into a reasonable value in the range between 0 and 1. The input value is passed through the sigmoid activation function. The sigmoid function can be expressed as,

$$R = \frac{1}{1-e^{-x}} \tag{6}$$

Fig. 5 show the flow diagram of the BPNN classifier model.

Start

Initialization

Initialize the threshold values θ_j, a positive constant learning rate α, with random number within the range $[-2.4/F_i, 2.4/F_i]$, where F_i is the maximum number of inputs connected to the single neuron.

Activation

Activate the input layer by presenting all samples repeatedly to the classifier. Set the desired output layer and then calculate the actual output of the output layer.

    a)   Calculate the actual output of the neuron in the hidden layer(s) at p^{th} training cycle:

$$y_j(p) = R\left(\sum_{i=1}^{n} x_i(p)w_{ij}(p) \right) \quad ; \text{R is the sigmoid function}$$

    b)   Calculate the output of the neuron of the output layer:

$$y_k(p) = R\left(\sum_{j=1}^{m} y_j(p)w_{jk}(p) \right)$$

Training

a) Compute error signals at the output and the hidden layers (back propagation step):

$$e_k(p) = y_k(p) - d_k$$
$$\delta_k(p) = y_k(p)[1 - y_k(p)]e_k(p)$$
$$\delta_j(p) = y_j(p)[1 - y_j(p)]\sum_{k=1}^{l} \delta_k(p)w_{jk}(p)$$

b) Update the weights related to hidden and output layers:

$$w_{jk}(p+1) = w_{jk}(p) - \alpha\delta_k(p)y_j(p)$$
$$w_{ij}(p+1) = w_{ij}(p) - \alpha\delta_j(p)x_i(p)$$

Iteration

Increase iteration p: $p = p + 1$ process until convergence.

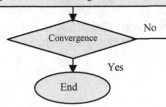

Convergence — No

Yes

End

Fig. 5. Flowchart of Back Propagation Algorithm.

4   Experimental Evaluation

We develop an efficient image spam classification system based on image features using back propagation neural network. A histogram based method is used for visual features extraction. The file features of the image are selected based on the file type, file size and dimension of the image file. Experimental evaluations demonstrates the effectiveness of the propose system. To test our algorithm, we use a benchmark data set developed by G. Fumera *et al.* [17]. The corpora contains 5087 images combined of 3209 spam and 1878 non-spam images.

We evaluate our system by estimating three performance measures: Accuracy (A), Precision (P), and Recall (R). The measures can be defined as follows:

$$Accuracy \quad = \frac{TP + TN}{TP + FP + TN + FN} \tag{7}$$

$$Pr\ ecision \quad = \frac{TP}{TP + FP} \tag{8}$$

$$Re\ call \quad = \frac{TP}{TP + FN} \tag{9}$$

where,

   TP (true positive) = No of spam emails and identified as spam,
   FP (false positive) = No of non-spam emails but identified as spam,
   TN (true negative) = No of non-spam emails and identified as non-spam,
   FN (false negative) = No of spam emails but identified as non-spam.

False positives are generally considered to be more harmful than false negatives. Therefore, our target is to ensure the low false alarm rate. If the value of precision is high, it obviously indicates that the false negative is high. In other words, the detector has misclassified many spam messages as legitimate (non-spam) message. On the other hand, a high recall indicates that the false positive is high, i.e. many legitimate messages are misevaluated as spam. We concern about the trade-off that exists between the spam and non-spam when we consider precision and recall values.

Table 2 illustrates the Signal to Noise ratio (SNR) for spam and non-spam image of GIF, JPEG and PNG format. Based on the SNR obtained for different features of an image it is possible to isolate spam message from the legitimate message. By analyzing our test dataset we find that most of the spam images in e-mails are GIF and non-spam images are JPEG type. A comparison of the performance between our proposed technique and other methods is reported in Table 3. Experimental results confirm that our proposed spam detection technique gives better performance comparable to existing methods.

Table 2. File features of an image

File features	JPEG	GIF	PNG
f_1	0.268	0.192	0.498
f_2	0.298	0.144	0.273
f_3	0.010	0.032	0.312
f_4	0.283	0.131	0.625
f_5	0.312	0.803	0.451
f_6	0.271	0.545	1.489

Table 3. Performance comparison of the proposed system with other techniques.

Measures	Accuracy (%)	Precision (%)	Recall (%)
Naïve Bayes	94.53	83.15	96.65
SVM	95.09	96.38	97.04
BPNN (proposed)	97.89	93.75	98.02

5   Conclusion

In this paper, we present an efficient and robust method for image spam classification using back propagation neural network. The system analyzes the file features of the embedded image and extract the low level visual features as well. A gradient histogram based algorithm is utilized to extract the color feature points from the image. The extracted file features as well as the visual features are feed forwarded to the BPNN classifier to train the network. Experimental results confirms the effective performance of our proposed system comparable to the state-of-the-art methods. The results show the performance near to 98% accuracy and 0.03 false positive rate. Our future plan is to improve the algorithm to develop a complete classification system that is also capable of detecting textual spam image.

References

1. Das, M., Prasad, V.: Analysis of an Image Spam in Email Based on Content Analysis. International Journal on Natural Language Computing (IJNLC) **3**(3), 129–140 (2014)
2. Patil, D., Turukmane, A.: Design and Development of Decision Making Model for Spam email Classification Using Neural Network. International Journal on Recent and Innovation Trends in Computing and Communication **3**(2), 327–330 (2015)
3. Islam, M.R., Zhou, W., Choudhury, M.U.: Dynamic feature selection for spam filtering using support vector machine. In: IEEE/ ACIS (ICIS) (2007)
4. Islam, R., Zhou, W.: An adaptive model for spam filtering using machine learning algorithms. In: 7th Int. Conference on Algorithms and Architecture for Parallel Processing (ICAAPP), Hangzhou, China (2007)
5. Sasaki, M., Shinnou, H.: Spam detection using text clustering. In: IEEE Proceedings of the International Conference on Cyber Worlds (2005)

6. Deshpande, V.P., Erbacher, R.F., Harris, C.: An evaluation of naïve bayesian anti-spam filtering techniques. In: Proceedings of the IEEE Workshop on Information Assurance, pp. 333–340 (2007)
7. Liu, Q., Qin, Z., Cheng, H., Wan, M.: Efficient modeling of spam images. In: 2010 Third International Symposium on Intelligent Information Technology and Security Informatics (IITSI), pp. 663–666 (2010)
8. Mehta, B., Nangia, S., Gupta, M., Nejdl, W.: Detecting image spam using visual features and near duplicate detection. In: Proceedings of the 17th International Conference on World Wide Web, pp. 497–506. ACM (2008)
9. Li, P., Yan, H., Cui, G., Du, Y.: Integration of Local and Global Features for Image Spam Filtering. Journal of Computational Information Systems 8(2), 779–789 (2012)
10. Wang, C., Zhang, F., Li, F., Liu, Q.: Image spam classification based on low-level image features. In: Proceedings of the ICCCAS, pp. 290–293 (2010)
11. Krasser, S., Tang, Y., Gould, J., Alperovitch, D., Judge, P.: Identifying image spam based on header and file properties using C4.5 decision trees and support vector machine. In: IEEE Workshop on Information Assurance (2007)
12. Liu, T., Tsao, W., Lee, C.: A high performance image-spam filtering system. In: Ninth International Symposium on Distributed Computing and Applications to Business, Engineering and Science 2010, pp. 445–449 (2010)
13. Lai, C.-C., Wu, C.-H., Tsai, M.-C.: Feature selection using particle swarm optimization with application in spam filtering. Int. Journal of Innovative Computing 5(2), 423–432 (2009)
14. Koprinska, I., Poon, J., Clark, J., Chan, J.: Learning to classify e-mail. Information Sciences 177(10), 2167–2187 (2007)
15. Meyer, T.A., Whateley, B.: Spam bayes: effective open-source, Bayesian based, email classification system. In: First Conf. on Email and Anti-Spam (CEAS) (2004)
16. Drucker, H., Wu, D., Vapnik, V.N.: Support vector machines for spam categorization. IEEE Trans. on Neural Networks 10(5), 1048–1054 (1999)
17. Fumera, G., Pillai, I., Roli, F.: Spam Filtering based on the Analysis of Text Information Embedded into Images. Journal of Machine Learning Research (Special Issue on Machine Learning in Computer Security) 7, 2699–2720 (2006)
18. Wu, C.-T., Cheng, K.-T., Zhu, Q., Wu, Y.-L.: Using visual features for anti-spam filtering. In: Proceedings of the IEEE International Conference Image Processing, vol. 3, pp. 501–504 (2005)
19. Aradhye, H.B., Myers, G.K., Herson, J.A.: Image analysis for efficient categorization of image-based spam e-mail. In: 8th International Conference on Document Analysis and Recognition (ICDAR 2005), vol. 2, pp. 914–918 (2005)
20. Dredze, M., Gevaryahu, R., Elias-Bachrach, A.: Learning fast classifiers for image spam. In: Proceedings of the 4th Conf. Email Anti-spam (CEAS) (2007)
21. Wang, Z., Josephson, W., Lv, Q., Charikar, M., Li, K.: Filtering image spam with near-duplicate detection. In: Proceedings of the 4th Conf. Email Anti Spam (CEAS) (2007)
22. Biggio, B., Fumera, G., Pillai, I., Roli, F.: Image spam filtering by content obscuring detection. In: 4th Conference on Email and Anti-Spam (CEAS) (2007)
23. Zhang, C., Chen, W.-B., Chen, X., Tiwari, R., Yang, L., Warner, G.: A Multimodal Data Mining Framework for Revealing Common Sources of Spam Images. Journal of Multimedia 4(5), 313–320 (2009)
24. Bowling, J.R., Hope, P., Liszka, K.J.: Spam image identification using an artificial neural network. In: MIT Spam Conference (2008)

An Effective t-way Test Data Generation Strategy

Khandakar Rabbi[(⊠)] and Quazi Mamun

School of Computing and Mathematics, Charles Sturt University, Bathurst, Australia
{krabbi,qmamun}@csu.edu.au

Abstract. Software testing is an integral part of software development life cycle which ensures the quality of the software. An exhaustive testing is not always possible because of combinatorial optimisation problem. Thus, in the software testing phase, generation of optimal number of test data accelerate the overall software testing process. We identified that the reduction of interactions among the input parameters significantly reduces the number of test data and generate an optimal test data set. This interaction is known as 't'-way interaction. Over the last decade, a large number of 't'-way test data generation strategies have been developed. However, generating optimum number of test data appears to be a NP-hard problem where the test data generation time becomes significantly higher. This paper proposes an effective test data generation strategy based on 'Kids Card' game known as MTTG. The proposed strategy significantly reduces the test data generation time. The result and discussion section shows that, MTTG outperforms all other strategies.

Keywords: t-way testing · Test data generation strategy · Test optimization · NP-Hard problem

1   Introduction

On 4th June 1996, the European Space Agency launched the maiden flight of the Ariane 5. But it exploded 40 seconds after lift-off at an altitude of 3700 m. This accident was investigated by the Massachusetts Institute of Technology research team. Their report indicated that, a component was erroneously putting a 64-bit floating number into a 16-bit floating number. This eventually causes overflow error which affects rocket alignment [1]. This error was caused by lack of software testing which can be disastrous and life threatening.

About 50% of the total cost and resources are allocated to software testing which is considered an important and integral part of the software develop life cycle. Paying attention to the software testing can lead to an overall reduction in costs. The cost reduction can be achieved through process automation. However, an optimum and effective test data set by reducing the amount of test data required can also reduce the overall software testing costs [4-21]. To understand what the test data is and its magnitude, let's consider a very simple system having 5 parameters with 10 values each. It produces 10^5 number of test data. To a further extend, if we consider Figure 1, which is a single *'Indents and Spacing'* under the *'Paragraph'* dialog in *'Microsoft Word'*. It consists of non-uniform parameterized values i.e. one parameter 'Alignment' which has four values, *'Outline level'* has 10 values, *'Indentation Special'* has

© Institute for Computer Sciences, Social Informatics and Telecommunications Engineering 2015
B. Thuraisingham et al. (Eds.): SecureComm 2015, LNICST 164, pp. 633–648, 2015.
DOI: 10.1007/978-3-319-28865-9_42

two values and '*Line Spacing*' has six values. Therefore, this single tab will have about 1^4 x 1^{10} x 1^2 x 1^6 = 480 numbers of test data. A manual testing will take about 24 hours to complete the testing of this tab [22]. When the system becomes more complex, number of test data increase exponentially.

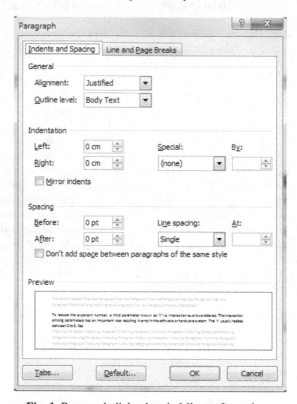

Fig. 1. Paragraph dialog box in Microsoft word.

To reduce the exponent number, a third parameter known as 't' i.e. interaction level is considered. This interaction among parameters has an important role resulting in error in the software or hardware system. The 't' usually resides between 2 to 6. Research indicates that the appropriate reduction of the 't' significantly reduces the number of test data by maintaining the standard quality. When the value of the 't' is 2, it is known as 2-way testing or pairwise testing. On the other hand, when 't' is greater than 2 (t > 2), it is known as t-way testing. The value of 't' ranges from 2 up to a maximum number which is equal to the number of input variables. In the field of software testing, it is referred to as t-way testing.

Researchers have developed many t-way test data generation strategies to optimize the number of test data including OA [22], CA [23], MCA [24], TConfig [25], CTS [26], AllPairs [27], AETG [28], mAETG [29], TCG [30], mTCG [31], GA [14], ACA [14], IPO [32], IPOG [3], Jenny [20], TVG [19], ITCH [33], GTway [34], PSTG [35]. A brief description and scrutinizing analysis has been conducted throughout the appropriate section of this paper. Our empirical analysis identifies a basic problem in current test data generation strategies. Exhaustive analysis of test data produces combinatorial explosion problem (CEP) [3-21] which is also a NP-hard problem in common scientific and mathematical practice [5-21]. Thus, no abovementioned strategy can produce optimum number of test data in every input configuration. In addition to that, we also identifies that the complexity of the algorithm is very high and take non-polynomial time to generate the optimum test data set. Much effort has been expended to optimize the principal problem (CEP) through traditional computing analysis over the past decade [29-32]. However, through parallelization, CEP may be alleviated, but the development of complex software and hardware still poses the same question to the researchers. In addition, the parallel computing for test data generation is an expensive solution. Apart from this, the problem is also known as the NP-hard problem, where it is impossible to produce the optimum solution in every case (because of the nature of the problem itself). However, our study shows that most of the strategies take substantial time to produce the optimal test data. We have also identified the following research question [22, 29-37]:

1. What is the optimal and smaller set of test data to choose over the large dataset i.e. what strategy to choose that can produce optimal test data set?
2. Which test data generation strategy to choose in terms of complexity i.e. which strategy to choose that can produce faster test data?
3. What strategy to choose that supports maximum interaction level?

In the next section, we examined the available t-way test data generation strategies and explored the significance of generating a faster test data generation strategy.

2   Literature Review

Many attempts are taken to classify the existing t-way and pairwise test data generation strategies. *Cohen et. al.* has classified the number of test date generation strategies mainly into two groups (Cohen et. al. 2004). i) algebraic strategies ii) computational strategies. Grindal et. al. extends and expands the abovementioned strategies and identified three main sub-categories based on the randomness of the solution of the strategy: i) Non-deterministic ii) Deterministic iii) Compound. Non-deterministic strategies always produce random number of test data in each execution. It employs a random selection of test data over the search space. Artificial intelligence strategies are found to be non-deterministic. Thus, each solution produces different number of test data. On the other hand deterministic strategies appear to be producing same test data set in each execution. Usually, algebraic strategies found to be deterministic. Compound strategies are the combination of both deterministic strategy and non-deterministic strategy. The following sub-section analysied available 't' way test data generation strategies.

2.1   Analysis of Test Data Generation Strategies

There are few strategies which uses arithmetic operation to generate test. These strategies are usually arithmetic strategies. All most all of these strategies are limited to 2-way interaction level. To generate test data, these strategies are based on OA (Orthogonal Array), CA (Covering Array) and Mixed Level Covering Array (MCA). Orthogonal Arrays (OA) uses few different algebraic and the mathematical concepts [22]. This strategy uses 'Latin squares' to generate test data which significantly used in compiler design [22]. Analysis shows that OA strategy is deterministic. But the biggest impediment of orthogonal array is it's limitation to pairwise test data generation. It only uses symbolic data and no real data is uses as a part of data generation. Thus the practitioner's require mapping the real data with the symbolic data before operating the strategy. In addition, OA cannot support non-uniform input configuration which means each parameters require same number of values. Having the similarity with orthogonal array, CA is another form of array which can generate test data set. The major different of CA is it reduced the restriction of $\lambda=1$ which has been mentioned in other section. CA is also a deterministic approach. The major difference between CA and OA is CA supports 3-way test data generation where OA only supports pairwise or 2-way test data generation. Similar to OA, CA also cannot support non-uniform values. In addition, the strategy doesn't consider real input data as part of test data generation.

William et al. in 2000 proposed a computational tool using both OA and CA. He proposed an algorithm that can generate OA which in terms can be used as an initial block of larger CA. Thus his proposed algorithm uses both algebraic and combinatorial approach to generate test data set. TConfig is a deterministic approach. Although it uses the basics of OA and CA, it can support non-uniform values. It overcomes the limitation of CA and OA, however it is still limited to 6-way test data generation. Input configuration can be both symbolic and real data. Combinatorial Test Services (CTS) uses algebraic recursion as part of the generation of test data set. The algorithm uses C++ programming language. It is also referred as combinatorial recursive construction. It analyse all the possible input configurations. Based on the configurations, it selects the best covering array. The covering array can generate best test data set. CTS is a deterministic approach with the support of both uniform and non-uniform input configurations. However, input configurations can only be index values, thus no actual data can be used as a part of test data generation. Considering interaction level, CTS only supports only 2-way and 3-way. There are no published works found on AllPairs. It is mostly a tool developed in Perl (programming language) by Bach et al. in 2004. Later on, Cunningham developed a Java version of the tool. The tool only supports pairwise test data generation. The complexity of the tool is low. The tool generates test data in a deterministic approach. The tool supports both index values and real values as part of test data generation. In addition, the tool also supports non-uniform parameterized values. AETG starts with empty test data set and then add as many test data in the empty set. Finally choose the best test data which covers the most interaction levels. Our observation states that, AETG is the first computational strategy proposed by Cohen et al. in 1994. Later on few modifications alone with comparative results were shown in different publications. Analysis shows that AETG is a random approach which means it generates different number of test data set in different execution. Though the authors claim that AETG supports general t-way strategies but the publish results was limited to pairwise and 3-way. Input configuration was limited to index values, thus there were no supports for real data. However, AETG supports non-uniform values. A modified version of AETG was proposed by

Myra in her PhD thesis (2004). She has shown two basic difference of mAETG as compared to AETG. First difference was the randomness. Although AETG was non-deterministic, the number of test data was same for same configuration (the test data set was different). mAETG has a variable number of test data, which means it generate different number of test data for same input configuration in different execution. Second difference was the way to choose uncovered pairs. AETG was selecting the covered pairs first then later on it chooses the uncovered pairs randomly where mAETG chooses highly covered pairs first then it fix some variable to choose the uncovered pairs. Like AETG, mAETG is non-deterministic. mAETG can only support pairwise and 3-way test data generation. Input configurations are index values and no support for actual data. mAETG also supports non-uniform values.

TCG is a deterministic strategy. Yu-Wen et al. used TCG in 2000 used as a test data generator in 'Jet Propulsion Laboratory'. The algorithm used in TCG is similar to AETG which first generates empty test set and then add single test data until all t-way interaction is covered. Despite of that similarity, the test data generation is TCG always generates same test data in the same input configuration each time. TCG only supports pairwise test data generation. For the input configuration, it can only be symbolic. There is no support for actual data to be used. However, the strategy appears to be supporting non-uniform values. Similar to mAETG, Myra modified the original TCG and proposed mTCG. She modified the original rule based test data selection process to random based test data selection process. In the test data generation process, when mTCG finds the same test data covering similar number of pairs, mTCG choose any one randomly. Since mTCG uses random selection of test data, it is a non-deterministic approach. The strategy is limited to pairwise thus there is no support for 3-way. Input configuration can only be index values and there are no supports for actually data. However, mTCG can support non-uniform parameterized values.

For the first time, Shiba et al. in 2004 modified the original AETG and proposed an artificial intelligent based strategy known in test data generation. Each test data in GA is defined as chromosome. A number 'm' will generate randomly which is known as candidate test data. These test data will loop through an evaluation process. After that there will be crossover and mutation candidates based on few criteria and finally a set of test data will be chosen from that candidate set. Our analysis shows that GA is non-deterministic. Regarding t-way interaction, GA can only support t up to 3 levels. About the input configuration there is no support for actual data to be used as a part of test data generation. However, test data generation from non-uniform values are also supported by GA. Apart from GA, Shiba et al. worked on other artificial intelligent based strategy and implemented artificial ant colony algorithm in test data generation. ACA also used AETG as a base algorithm to generate test data. Implementation of ACA is a motivation of nature and an understanding how ants select their best path in orders to find out foods from various locations. ACA is a random search process thus appears to be non-deterministic. It can only supports pairwise and t = 3. There is no supports for real data to be used as a part of test data generation. However, ACA also supports non-uniform parameterized values.

IPO is a deterministic approach and the test data generation of IPO is very fast comparing to other test data generation strategies. It was first implemented in a tool called PairRest. IPO first generate an exhaustive number of test data from the first two pairs. After than other parameters are added by checking that if that parameter's value is paying the highest number of coverage or not. In the way it adds new values at the end of the each test data set and completes a test data set. IPO generates same number of test data in same input configuration which is a deterministic approach. IPO only support pairwise test data generation thus no supports for t=3. In input configuration IPO cannot support real input values and only supports index values. Our analysis also shows that IPO supports non-uniform values. IPOG is a basic strategy which is implemented in a popular tool known as FireEye. Development of FireEye tool was a collaboration work among ITL (Information Technology Laboratory) and NIST (National Institute of Standard and Technology) and the University of Texas, Arlington. The basic of IPOG is similar to IPO. It is developed to support higher t which was not supported in IPO. IPOG is a deterministic strategy and the supporting interaction level is up to 6. Input configuration can only be symbolic and no original data can be used as a part of test data generation. However, IPOG supports non-uniform parameterized values.

Jenkins in 2003 proposed a tool to generate test data which is known as Jenny. Jenkins stated that, Jenny starts generating test data by covering 1-way first, then 2-way, after that 3-way and until the proposed t-way. After generating 1-way, it checks if all 2-way has been covered or not. And when it covers 2-way, it checks that all 3-way has been covered or not. This is the way when the defined t-way covered, it release the test data set. Jenny produces same number of test data every time, shows that it is deterministic. Regarding interaction level, Jenny supports 't' up to 8. About input configuration, Jenny doesn't support original input as a part of test data generation. Jenny also supports non-uniform values. Test Vector Generation (TVG) is a tool proposed and developed by Schroeder et al. in 2003. The tool consists of three techniques. In the first technique, it produces test data randomly which supports only pairwise interactions. On the secondly technique, it was extended to support higher t-way interaction. And in the third technique, TVG uses an input and output relationships to reduce the number of exhaustive test data, hence generate the complete test data set. TVG is a deterministic strategy. As mentioned previously, TVG's second technique supports higher 't', however it is limited to '5' level only. In the input configuration, both real input and symbolic input can be uses in the part of test data generation. In addition, TVG can also support non-uniform parameter values.

IBM developed test data generation strategy which is known as ITCH. And the windows version of the tool is known as WITCH. In ITCH, user can specify the number of test data. Based on that number ITCH, choose the proper interaction levels. Users can also specify the 't' levels, which in terms can generate the number of test data set. It appears that ITCH is a deterministic strategy. Our observation also stated that, ITCH can support only 4 levels of interaction. Input configurations can be both symbolic and real data. In addition, ITCH can support non-uniform parameterized values. Klaib et al. in 2009 proposed a backtracking based test data generation strategy. It uses the basic IPO to choose the best coverable test data set. Once all the interactions are covered, it uses a backtracking algorithm to choose other test data set. He has also provided automation support in test data execution. Our analysis found that, GTway can support as much as 12 interaction levels. Input configuration can be both symbolic and real data. In addition, GTway also supports non-uniform parameterized values.

3   Design of MTTG

The proposed strategy has been created inspiring kids "Set" game, where the deck has total of 81 cards varying in four features: number (one, two, or three); symbol (diamond, squiggle, oval); shading (solid, striped, or open); and color (red, green, or purple) There are various versions of the game is available. However, in the most playing game, a player randomly take cards from the deck and try to make a complete 'Set' of a particular card by transferring to other members. The proposed strategy utilises the same strategy used in the 'Set' game. The cards are illustrated as the individual test data. Each test data is categorised by the combination of different parameters. A unique strategy runs over all the parameters, identifies the missing parameter and replaces it with a most effective parameter. The overall design can be divided into 3 major steps.

3.1   Step 1: Development of N-Tuples:

In first steps, the strategy reads the number of parameters and values and creates the N-Tuples. The number of N-Tuples depends on the 't' i.e. interaction level. Figure 2 shows an N-Tuples generated from 3 parameters and 2 values in a 2-way/pairwise interaction.

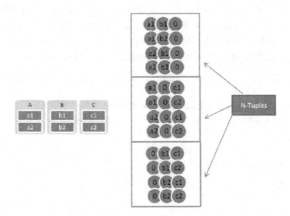

Fig. 2. Illustration of N-Tuples

The following equation has been used when creating N-Tuples:

$$N = p! \frac{t!}{(P - t)!}$$

Where, N denotes N-Tuples, t denotes the interaction level and P is the number of parameters.

3.2   Step 2: Identification of 'Missing Parameter'

In the second step, MTTG reads all the N-Tuple values. It identifies the missing parameter and adds 0 to the missing parameter of that Tuple. Thus MTTG an iteratively search the missing parameter and can replace it with the best possible value to produce the 'Set'. Figure 3 illustrates the missing parameter.

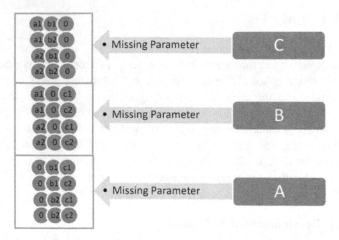

Fig. 3. Identification of Missing parameter

3.3   Step 3: Updating the Missing Parameter

This step involves searching for the 0th parameter and replacing it with an appropriate value so that a best coverage is possible. Replacing is possible based on two selection criteria i) Appropriate parameter ii) Appropriate value of the parameter. The algorithm 'Test data construction' has been shown as a pseudocode in the Figure 4.

```
Begin
  Let N_T = {} as a dataset represents the N-Tuples
  Let N_ST = {} as empty dataset represents the subset of N_T
based on specific single Tuple.
  Let N_TS = {} as final test data set
For each value 'N' in N_T
      N_ST = N
      For each value V in N_ST
      If V == 0
            Read position of 'V' as P
            Find position of Parameter from P
      End If
      End For
      For each values in P
            Replace 0 with the values
            Create test data C
            Calculate coverage of C = P_C
      If P_C == 'Acceptable Number'
            Add C to N_ST
      End if
      End For
  End For
  End
```

Fig. 4. Test data generation pseudo code.

4   MTTG Flowchart

The flowchart of MTTG has been shown in the Figure 5. It starts with 'Generate Pair' section when the pairs are generated based on the interaction level. N-tuples are generated based on a formula from the generated pair. The N-Tuples are iterated bases on the coverage. It reads 0th parameter, replace with a possible value and calculate the coverage. If the coverage is acceptable, the test data is added to the final test data set.

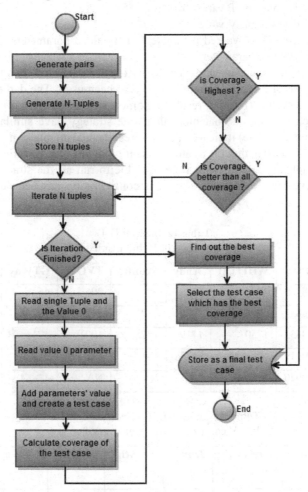

Fig. 5. Complete workflow of MTTG

5   Results and Discussions

To evaluate the MTTG, we carried out a number of experiments both in terms of 'Number' of test data and the test data generation 'Time' i.e. complexity. The overall experiments are divided into four different groups:

G-1: 'P' and 'V' is constant, 't' varies from 2 to 6.
G-2: 't' and 'V' is constant, P varies from 5 to 15.
G-3: 'P' and 't' is constant, V varies from 2 to 10.
G-4: TCAS dataset. 12 10-valued parameters, 1 4-valued parameters, 2 3-valued parameters and 7 2-valued parameters.

The results for test data size and complexity are separated into two tables for each group. Hence there are eight different tables have been used. The darken cell in each row represents the outperforming result. In some cases, there are more than one darken cell in each row means that more than one strategy have similar results. Cell marking NA (not available) indicates there are results unavailable or no published. NS (not supported) indicates that the strategy doesn't support that specific configuration. Regarding complexity analysis, we were not able to run all the strategies into same platform however, a near proximity system configuration has been utilised for the evaluation.

Table 1a. Size for G-1
P & V constants (10, 5), but t varied up to 6

T-Way	IPOG	WHITCH	Jenny	Tconfig	TVG II	GTWay	MTTG
2	48	45	45	48	50	46	58
3	308	225	290	312	342	293	372
4	1843	1750	1719	1878	1971	1714	2194
5	10119	NS	9437	NA	NA	9487	11384
6	50920	NS	NS	NA	NA	44884	54166

Table 1b. Complexity (in Seconds) for G-1
P & V constants (10, 5), but t varied up to 6

T-Way	IPOG	WHITCH	Jenny	Tconfig	TVG II	GTWay	MTTG
2	0.11	1	0.43	1	0.141	0.265	0.019
3	0.56	23	0.78	88.62	5.797	6.312	0.193
4	6.38	350	17.53	>8hr	276.328	201.235	1.533
5	63.8	NS	500.93	>24hr	>24hr	3636.110	8.277
6	791.35	NS	NS	>24hr	>24hr	21525.063	24.719

Table 1a and 1b shows the result of G-1 in terms of Size and Time respectively. In terms of test data size WITCH, Jenny and GTway has outperform all other strategies. However, In terms of test data generation time, MTTG outperforms all others. The last row where 't' = 6 shows a significant improvement of complexity comparing other strategies.

Table 2a. Size for G-2
t & V constants (4, 5), but P varied (from 5 up to 15)

P	IPOG	WHITCH	Jenny	Tconfig	TVG II	GTWay	MTTG
5	784	625	837	773	849	731	730
6	1064	625	1074	1092	1128	1027	1032
7	1290	1750	1248	1320	1384	1216	1321
8	1491	1750	1424	1532	1595	1443	1614
9	1677	1750	1578	1724	1795	1579	1890
10	1843	1750	1719	1878	1971	1714	2194
11	1990	1750	1839	2038	2122	1852	2485
12	2132	1750	1964	NA	2268	2022	2807
13	2254	NA	2072	NA	2398	2116	3165
14	2378	NA	2169	NA	NA	2222	3564
15	2497	NA	2277	NA	NA	2332	3884

Table 2b. Complexity (in Seconds) for G-2 t & V constants (4, 5), but P varied (from 5 up to 15)

P	IPOG	WHITCH	Jenny	Tconfig	TVG II	GTWay	MTTG
5	0.19	5.26	0.44	31.46	1.468	0.047	0.32
6	0.45	14.23	0.71	231.56	5.922	0.563	0.45
7	0.92	59.56	1.93	1,120	18.766	3.046	0.63
8	1.88	115.77	4.37	>1hr	55.172	15.344	0.88

Table 2b. *(continued)*

9	3.58	210.87	9.41	>3hr	132.766	63.516	1.28
10	6.38	350	17.53	>8hr	276.328	201.235	1.53
11	10.83	417	30.61	>23hr	548.703	599.203	2.94
12	17.52	628.94	50.22	>24hr	921.781	1682.844	4.71
13	27.3	>24hr	76.41	>24hr	1565.5	4573.687	7.40
14	41.71	>24hr	115.71	>24hr	>24hr	11818.281	11.96
15	61.26	>24hr	165.06	>24hr	>24hr	28793.360	18.74

Table 2a and 2b shows the result of G-2 in terms of Size and Time respectively. In terms of test data size, there is a uniformed distribution was found. Almost all strategies have achieved good results into a particular configuration. However, In terms of test data generation time, MTTG outperforms all others.

Table 3a. Size for G-3
P & t constants (10, 4), but V varied (from 2 up to 10)

V	IPOG	WHITCH	Jenny	Tconfig	TVG II	GTWay	MTTG
2	46	58	39	45	40	46	50
3	229	336	221	235	228	224	277
4	649	704	703	718	782	621	1950
5	1843	1750	1719	1878	1971	1714	2194
6	3808	NA	3519	NA	4159	3514	4531
7	7061	NA	6482	NA	7854	6459	8245
8	11993	NA	11021	NA	NA	10850	13928
9	19098	NA	17527	NA	NA	17272	21944
10	28985	NA	26624	NA	NA	26121	32966

Table 3b. Complexity (in Seconds) for G-3 (Time)
P & t constants (10, 4), but V varied (from 2 up to 10)

V	IPOG	WHITCH	Jenny	Tconfig	TVG II	GTWay	MTTG
2	0.16	1	0.47	14.43	0.297	1.282	0.04
3	0.547	120.22	0.51	379.38	3.937	7.078	0.18
4	1.8	180	4.41	>1hr	46.094	25.250	1.34
5	6.33	350	17.53	>8hr	276.328	201.235	1.69
6	16.44	>24hr	134.67	>24hr	1,273.469	765.453	3.81
7	38.61	>24hr	485.91	>24hr	4,724	2389.812	6.78
8	83.96	>24hr	1410.27	>24hr	>24hr	6270.735	10.66
9	168.37	>24hr	2125.8	>24hr	>24hr	15672.531	16.18
10	329.36	>24hr	5458	>24hr	>24hr	35071.672	24.28

Table 3a and 3b shows the result of G-3 in terms of Size and Time respectively. In terms of test data size GTway has outperform almost all other strategies. However, In terms of test data generation time, MTTG outperforms all others.

Table 4a. Size for G-4
TCAS Module (12 multi-valued parameters, t varied from 2 to12)

T-Way	IPOG	WHITCH	Jenny	Tconfig	TVG II	GTWay	MTTG
2	100	120	108	108	101	100	100
3	400	2388	413	472	434	402	406
4	1361	1484	1536	1476	1599	1429	1404
5	4219	NS	4580	NA	4773	4286	4355
6	10919	NS	11625	NA	NS	11727	13667
7	NS	NS	27630	NS	NS	27119	35313
8	NS	NS	58865	NS	NS	58584	70600
9	NS	NS	NA	NS	NS	114411	127811
10	NS	NS	NA	NS	NS	201728	212400
11	NS	NS	NA	NS	NS	230400	230400
12	NS	NS	NA	NS	NS	460800	460800

Table 4b. Complexity (in Seconds) for G-4
TCAS Module (12 multi-valued parameters, t varied from 2 to 12)

T-Way	IPOG	WHITCH	Jenny	Tconfig	TVG II	GTWay	MTTG
2	0.8	0.73	0.001	>1hr	0.078	0.297	0.07
3	0.36	1,020	0.71	>12hr	2.625	1.828	0.13
4	3.05	5,400	3.54	>21hr	104.093	58.219	1.00
5	18.41	NS	43.54	>24hr	1,975.172	270.531	5.47
6	65.03	NS	470	>24hr	NS	1476.672	19.36
7	NS	NS	2461.1	NS	NS	4571.797	41.90
8	NS	NS	11879.2	NS	NS	10713.469	53.59
9	NS	NS	>1day	NS	NS	14856.109	45.29
10	NS	NS	>1day	NS	NS	10620.953	27.43
11	NS	NS	>1day	NS	NS	363.078	12.92
12	NS	NS	>1day	NS	NS	12.703	8.06

Table 4a and 4b shows the result of G-4 in terms of Size and Time respectively. In terms of test data size GTway and IPOG has better results than others. However, In terms of test data generation time, MTTG outperforms all others. Based on the results found in the above tables, an interesting observation can be summarized. It is clear that no single strategy has domination over others in terms of test data size. However, concerning test data generation time, MTTG is dominating in all the cases. On the other hand, WHITCH and TConfig appear to be a caterer for smaller configuration where 't' is below 4. In addition to that, MTTG and GTway appear to be more effective for complex configurations. In terms of test data generation time, Table 3b shows the effectiveness of MTTG. In that scenario, GTway takes about 20 hours where MTTG takes less than 1 minute. Thus, concerning complex configuration MTTG is highly acceptable than all other strategies.

6   Conclusion

We propose MTTG (Multi-Tuple Test Generator) which is an effective test data generation strategy. The performance of the MTTG has been compared with other strategies in terms of test data size and time complexity. It is to remember that, the NP-hard problem prevented any strategy from outperforming others in terms of both efficiency and complexity. Thus our approaches involves in generating test data in most of the cases so that it can be acceptable in all aspect. In some cases, the testing professional often knows the importance of a particular parameter over others. Thus, it might be important to implement different interactions among different parameters. As an example, if A, B, C are three parameters containing 3 values each in a configuration, and parameter C is less important to consider then, a 3-way interaction might be require to apply between A and B where, A and C or B and C might require only a 2-way interaction.

References

1. Lions, J.L.: Ariane 5 Failure: Full Report. http://sunnyday.mit.edu/accidents/Ariane5accidentreport.html (accessed February 11, 2015)
2. Patrick, M., Alexander, R., Oriol, M., Clark, J.A.: Subdomain-based test data generation. The Journal of Systems and Software, 1–15, November 2014. Elsevier
3. Lei, Y., Kacker, R., Kuhn, D.R., Okun, V., Lawrence, J.: IPOG: a general strategy for t-way software testing. In: 14th Annual IEEE International Conference and Workshops on the Engineering and Computer-Based Systems (2007)
4. Cui, Y., Li, L., Yao, S.: A new strategy for pairwise test case generation. In: 3rd International Symposium on Intelligent Information Technology Application (2009)
5. Chen, X., Gu, Q., Qi, J., Chen, D.: Applying particle swarm optimization to pairwise testing. In: 34th Annual IEEE Computer Software And Application Conference (2010)
6. Younis, M.I., Zamli, K.Z., Isa, N.A.M.: Algebraic strategy to generate pairwise test set for prime number parameters and variables. In: IEEE International Conference on Computer and Information Technology (2008)

7. Younis, M.I., Zamli, K.Z., Mat Isa, N.A.: IRPS – an efficient test data generation strategy for pairwise testing. In: Lovrek, I., Howlett, R.J., Jain, L.C. (eds.) KES 2008, Part I. LNCS (LNAI), vol. 5177, pp. 493–500. Springer, Heidelberg (2008)

8. Klaib, M.F.J., Muthuraman, S., Ahmad, N., Sidek, R.: A tree based strategy for test data generation and cost calculation for uniform and non-uniform parametric values. In: 10th IEEE International Conference on Computer and Information Technology (2010)

9. Shitao, W., Hao, W.: A novel algorithm for multipath test data generation. In: 4th International Conference on Digital Manufacturing & Automation (2013)

10. Cohen, D.M., Dalal, S.R., Kajla, A., Patton, G.C.: The automatic efficient test generator (AETG) system. In: 5th International Symposium on Software Reliability Engineering (1994)

11. Bach, J.: Allpairs Test Case Generation Tool. http://tejasconsulting.com/open-testware/feature/allpairs.html (access September 27, 2009)

12. Cohen, D.M., Dalal, S.R., Fredman, M.L., Patton, G.C.: The AETG System: An Approach to Testing Based on Combinatorial design. IEEE Transactions on Software Engineering (1997)

13. Lei, Y., Tai, K.C.: In-parameter-order: a test generation strategy for pairwise testing. In: 3rd IEEE Intl. High- Assurance Systems Engineering Symposium (1998)

14. Shiba, T., Tsuchiya, T., Kikuno, T.: Using artificial life techniques to generate test cases for combinatorial testing. In: 28th Annual International Computer Software and Applications Conference (2004)

15. Harman, M., Jones, B.F.: Search based software engineering. Information and Software Technology (2001)

16. Klaib, M.F.J., Zamli, K.Z., Isa, N.A.M., Younis, M.I., Abdullah, R.: G2Way – a backtracking strategy for pairwise test data generation. In: 15th IEEE Asia-Pacific Software Engineering Conference (2008)

17. Kennedy, J., Eberhart, R.: Particle swarm optimization. In: IEEE international Conference on Neural Networks (1995)

18. TConfig: http://www.site.uottawa.ca/~awilliam/ (access September 27, 2010)

19. TVG: http://sourceforge.net/projects/tvg (access September 27 2010)

20. Jenny: http://www.burtleburtle.net/bob/math/ (access September 27, 2010)

21. Yan, J., Zhang, J.: A Backtracking Search Tool for Constructing Combinatorial Test Suites. Journal of Systems and Software – Elsevier (2008)

22. Chateauneuf, M., Kreher, D.: On the State of Strength-Three Covering Arrays. Journal of Combinatorial Designs (2002)

23. Colbourn, C.J., Martirosyan, S.S., Mullen, G.L., Shasha, D., Sherwood, G.B., Yucas, J.L.: Products of Mixed Covering Arrays of Strength Two. Journal of Combinatorial Designs (2005)

24. Williams, A.W.: Determination of test configurations for pair-wise interaction coverage. In: Proc. of the 13th International Conference on Testing of Communicating Systems (2000)

25. Hartman, A., Raskin, L.: Combinatorial Test Services (2004). https://www.research.ibm.com/haifa/projects/verification/mdt/papers/CTSUserDocumentation.pdf (accessed March 2015)

26. Bach, J.: ALLPAIRS Test Generation Tool, Version 1.2.1 (2004). http://www.satisfice.com/tools.shtml (accessed March 2015)

27. Ellims, M., Ince, D., Petre, M.: AETG vs. Man: an Assessment of the Effectiveness of Combinatorial Test Data Generation. UK, in Technical Report, Department of Computing, Faculty of Mathematics and Computing, Open University (2008)

28. Cohen, M.B., Dwyer, M.B., Shi, J.: Exploiting constraint solving history to construct interaction test suites. In: Proc. of the Testing: Academic and Industrial Conference Practice and Research Techniques - MUTATION, 2007. IEEE Computer Society, UK (2007)

29. Yu-Wen, T., Aldiwan, W.S.: Automating test case generation for the new generation mission software system. In: Proc. of the IEEE Aerospace Conference (2000)

30. Cohen, M.B.: Designing Test Suites for Software Interaction Testing. Computer Science. New Zealand, University of Auckland (2004)

31. Forbes, M., Lawrence, J., Lei, Y., Kacker, R.N., Kuhn, D.R.: Refining the In-Parameter-Order Strategy for Constructing Covering Arrays. NIST Journal of Research (2008)

32. Hartman, A., Raskin, L.: Problems and Algorithms for Covering Arrays. Discrete Mathematics-Elsevier (2004)

33. Zamli, K.Z., Klaib, M.F.J., Younis, M.I., Isa, N.A.M., Abdullah, R.: Design and implementation of a t-way test data generation strategy with automated execution tool support. Information Sciences, Elsevier (2009)

34. Ahmed, B.S., Zamli, K.Z.: PSTG: A T-Way Strategy Adopting Particle Swarm Optimization. Mathematical/Analytical Modelling and Computer Simulation (AMS) (2010)

35. Khatun, S., Rabbi, K.F., Yaakub, C.Y., Klaib, M.F.J., Masroor Ahmed, M.: PS2Way: an efficient pairwise search approach for test data generation. In: Zain, J.M., Wan Mohd, WMb, El-Qawasmeh, E. (eds.) ICSECS 2011, Part III. CCIS, vol. 181, pp. 99–108. Springer, Heidelberg (2011)

36. Rabbi, K.F., Khatun, S., Yaakub, C.Y., Klaib, M.F.J.: EasyA: easy and effective way to generate pairwise test data. In: 2011 Third International Conference on Computational Intelligence, Communication Systems and Networks (2011)

A Secure Cross-Domain SIP Solution for Mobile Ad Hoc Network Using Dynamic Clustering

Ala' Aburumman[1], Wei Jye Seo[1], Rafiqul Islam[2],
Muhammad Khurram Khan[3], and Kim-Kwang Raymond Choo[1(✉)]

[1] School of Information Technology & Mathematical Sciences,
University of South Australia, Adelaide, Australia
{abuaa001,seowy002}@mymail.unisa.edu.au,
raymond.choo@fulbrightmail.org
[2] School of Computing & Mathematics, Charles Sturt University, Bathurst, Australia
mislam@csu.edu.au
[3] Center of Excellence in Information Assurance (CoEIA), King Saud University,
Riyadh, Kingdom of Saudi Arabia
mkhurram@ksu.edu.sa

Abstract. With the increasingly popularity of mobile devices (e.g. iPhones and iPads), Mobile Ad hoc Networks (MANETs) have emerged as a topical research area in recent years, and adapting and implementing voice protocols over MANETs is a popular area of inquiry. Successful implementation of voice over MANETs would present a more efficient and cheaper way of communication. In this paper, we propose a cross-domain Session Initiation Protocol (SIP), a widely used voice over Internet Protocol (VoIP) protocol, solution for MANETs using dynamic clustering by extending the scheme of Aburumman and Choo. Our enhanced solution allows us to scale across domains, and deal with outbound requests using the reputation method. Advantages of this solution include avoiding the shortcomings associated with centralized approaches, such as a single point of failure. To demonstrate the utility of the solution, we simulate and evaluate the proposed solution under different conditions and using metrics such as trust level, overhead, network delay, success ratio, and network management packet.

Keywords: Mobile Ad hoc Networks (MANETs) · Session initiation protocol · Security · Privacy · Wireless ad hoc networks · Voice over IP (VoIP) · VoIP over manets · Cross-domain · Dynamic clustering SIP · Network Simulator 3 (NS3)

1 Introduction

Wireless devices are an integral role in our daily communications, supporting applications such as Radio Frequency Identification (RFID) and Voice over Internet Protocol (VoIP). VoIP, for example, can be used to deliver voice and video contents over the internet in real-time, instead of the Public Switched Telephone Network (PSTN) [17][18]. In the past decade, there have been significant advances in the

© Institute for Computer Sciences, Social Informatics and Telecommunications Engineering 2015
B. Thuraisingham et al. (Eds.): SecureComm 2015, LNICST 164, pp. 649–664, 2015.
DOI: 10.1007/978-3-319-28865-9_43

wireless arena; consequently, we have witnessed an increase in consumer adoption of wireless technologies. The two most popular signalling protocols for an IP-based network are the H.323- defined by the ITU, and the Session Initiation Protocol (SIP) - defined in RFC3261 [4]. Increasingly, SIP is becoming more popular than H.323, mainly due to SIP's flexibility and relative simplicity [1][2]. Due to the popularity of 802.11/Wi-Fi enabled devices with more powerful built-in capabilities, such as smart mobile devices (e.g. iOS and Android devices) [19], Ad hoc networks can be used to support VoIP and other applications. For example, students physically present on the same campus can communicate with each other using MANET-based VoIP services [2]. However, implementing VoIP services over MANETs remains a challenge due to the inherent characteristics of MANETs (e.g. self-configuration of IP addresses).

One potential solution is to modify VoIP signalling services in order to support decentralized infrastructure-less networks. The challenge, however, is to modify existing SIP services for deployment in a peer-to-peer (P2P) communication environment without compromising on availability, flexibility and efficiency (e.g. accepted call ratio) [1] [3].

In this paper, we propose a Cross-Domain SIP solution for MANETs using dynamic clustering to provide scalability, reliability and availability. In the proposed solution, we extend the cluster-based logical overlay network from our previous work [16] by introducing new functionalities to the proposed entities with an enhanced reputation equation. The solution would allow SIP users to communicate with each other either directly or to request for contact information from the logical SIP servers distributed among the network; thus, solving the bottleneck issue due to a standalone SIP server serving numerous client requests. In addition, our proposed solution employs security mechanism on different levels (i.e. servers and clients). As found in literature, this is one of few publications to date that supports the secure use of SIP over MANETs. This is, probably, due to the fact that SIP has its own architecture, which is more suitable for networks with a predefined infrastructure.

This paper is organized as follows: Section 2 reviews the background and related work. Sections 3 and 4 describe our proposed cross-domain SIP solution for MANETs, and our implementation, respectively. We discuss the findings from our implementation in Section 5. Finally, Section 6 concludes this paper.

2   Background and Related Work

2.1   Background

SIP is a signalling protocol for initiating, managing and terminating the multimedia sessions for voice and video across packet switched networks. The main components of SIP are shown in Fig. 1 and explained below.

SIP main components are:

- User Agents (UAs) are a SIP endpoint entities that interact with other SIP components and used to either generate requests and send them to servers (i.e. User Agent Client - UAC) or receive requests, process them and generate responses (i.e. User Agent Server - UAS).

- Servers (Proxy, Registrar and Redirect) they hold a predefined set of rules to handle requests and response generated by UAs and they play the role of mediator to communicate with each other or with the UA providing service to enforce those rules.
- Location Service/Server is used to store the addresses registered by the registrar.
- Gateway is used to translate SIP to other protocols, if to be used by different type of network (e.g. PSTN [4][5].

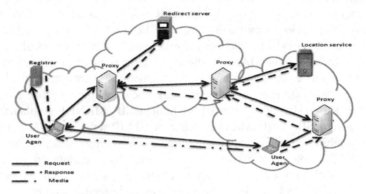

Fig. 1. SIP Overly Network architecture.

An Address of Record (AoR), a SIP User Resource Identifier (URI), allows one to call other SIP users. The AoR will point to a domain with a location service, which maps the URI to one where the user might be available.

Similar to other protocols on the IP stack, SIP may suffer from various vulnerabilities. Despite the range of security mechanisms proposed for SIP-based applications [4][6], securing SIP-based applications remain an active research challenge.

Wireless ad hoc networks are collections of autonomous nodes. These nodes form a temporary network without the need for a centralized administration. A key difference between a wireless ad hoc network and a traditional wired networks is that in the former, changes in the network needed to be tracked due to the absence of an administrator point [2][3]. This complicates the establishment of a secure VOIP session. SIP would be more practical solution for secure SIP (rather than another signaling protocol) deployment in a real-world implementation, since it is the dominating signaling protocol for VoIP service.

2.2   Related Work

By implementing all the necessary functionalities of a SIP, Leggio et al. [7] proposed a decentralized ad-hoc network framework. This approach elects a registrar to control manage while other newcomers who joined the network are being bounded with the registrar. It is possible to have SIP services with the decentralized approach; however, the issues of fault-tolerance and scalability remain.

Bai a et al. [8] use a test-bed infrastructure to form a distributed wireless multimedia network based on SIP protocol that allow text, voice and video communication to both wired and wireless devices. Utilizing Authentication, Authorization, and Accounting (AAA) server and SIP server, Bai approach still require a centralized controlled authentication which is not application in an Ad hoc network and other decentralized environment.

Focusing on the two different MANET environments, which are standalone MANETs and Multihop Cellular Networks (MCNs), the research detailed in [9] aims to address the service provisioning aspects in both environment. The research proposed a business model that defines the relationship and interfaces of MANET and the service provision in the MANET. The approach is tailored for closed environment setting with the voice service and security mechanisms that are agreed in advance.

By using an emulator architecture and local multipath for SIP services, Kogoshima, Kasamatsu and Takami [10] built a SIP_MANET emulator, which is evaluated using a SIP_VoIP call. The simulation of SIP service in MANET suggested a high probability of preserving the required path by implementing an enhanced adaptive AODV routing protocol. The simulation was conducted in a test bed environment with limited nodes. Other important factors, such as performance analysis, scalability, and security, were not addressed in their research.

As security concerns are increasingly important in SIP services, including those for Ad hoc networks, Alshingiti [11] suggested the combination of cryptographically generated addresses (CGA) with the social network paradigm for authentication and message integrity. Although this approach did not cost traffic overhead in terms of the registration process, it significantly increases the traffic on the call establishment and termination process. Scalability of the SIP services in MANET in this approach was also not considered.

Leggio et al. [12] proposed a fully distributed location service to locating SIP users in as small scaled network to avoid a single point of failure. This is done using by embedding a sundet of SIP proxy and registrar server functionality in all nodes.

In our previous work [13], we presented a secure nomination–based solution to implement SIP functionality in Ad hoc networks by combining Distributed SIP Location Service with two security techniques, namely; the Digest Authentication Access (DAA) and Simple/ Multipurpose Internet Mail Extensions(S/MIME). Both DAA and S/MIME are used to provide secure log in service for users and data exchanged between proxies, respectively. In the proposed solution, a node is elected to be a proxy server (PS) that handles SIP functionality and another node, Change D'affair (CD), is elected to be a backup for the server. The proxy is set to be the first node in the network, and then it will broadcast an election message to select a CD to be the next proxy after the PS delivers the task to the elected CD.

Abdullah et al. [14] proposed a secure cluster-based SIP service over Ad hoc network to protect the adapted SIP service from several types of attacks. This research eliminates the shortcomings of centralized approaches such as single point of failure, as well as reducing the overhead presented in fully distributed approaches.

Almobaideen et al. [15] proposed an adapted and semi distributed SIP protocol that works using clustered MANETs (referred to as FCSIP). In FCSIP, a new role for SIP server was introduced, where the SIP server also acts as a cluster-head to be the discovery servers to allow SIP agents to get information about other clients in the SIP cluster. It was claimed that such implementation would perform better than the fully-distributed SIP protocol over MANETs.

In [16], we presented a solution addressing the scalability limitation in a domain-based distribution of SIP services. We used a dynamic clustering to maximize the usage of resources to facilitate the deployment of SIP over MANETs. Our simulation results demonstrated that scalability of SIP service is increased, while minimizing the overheads by eliminating or dividing the workload among servers (i.e. cluster heads). However, security was not considered in this work.

It is clear from the literature that improving the scalability and security of SIP services on MANETs is an ongoing research challenge. This is not surprising as SIP relies on the resources of server functions, and unfortunately in a MANET environment, servers play a limiting role. As the size of the network increases, the load on the servers increases; consequently, this affects the level of reliability and availability. The dynamic, unpredictable and self-configuring nature of MANETs also complicates efforts to maximize the scalability and security of SIP services over MANETs.

In this paper, we aim to contribute to addressing the literature gap. More specifically, we extend our previous solution in [16] in order to enhance the scalability and security of implementing SIP over MANETs.

3   Our Proposed Solution

This section describes our proposed cross-domain SIP solution for MANETs using dynamic clustering proposed in our previous work [16], which allows calls to be established between peer-nodes ubiquitously using infrastructure-less environment. It is assumed that the SIP application can perform at least one-hop message broadcasting.

In the proposed solution, we introduce the functionality of redirect servers inherited from the SIP standard protocol for Backup Servers (BS). The BS will be directing the outbound requests; requests from nodes in neighboring domains. SIP entities comprise SIP User Agent (UA) and SIP Proxy (a combination of SIP Registrar and SIP Discovery Server - SIP DS), and are implemented on the protocol stack. Nodes can also function as Registrar or as DS to register other SIP UAs or provide address-of-record (AoR) resolution respectively.

Cluster-based solutions can address various limitations associated with Ad hoc networks, such as in routing, traffic coordination and fault-tolerance. Our proposed solution, therefore, builds logical clusters over the SIP network at the application level. In our approach, the SIP network's clusters are formed based on the positions of the nodes within the network and the neighborhood degree. Such an approach allows us to eliminate the need for additional message types, as we are able to reuse SIP messages by inserting additional headers (and indicating the nature of the exchanged message). The clusters consist of Cluster Head (CH).

We assume that the network is subject to various types of attacks. For example, external attackers could seek to flood the network with messages, which affects the availability of the SIP network (e.g. poisoning information to SIP users so that the SIP network is unable to establish calls). We also assume that SIP users will pre-share or establish their security associations with each other (e.g. they have exchanged their security keys offline or via other secure means), and all SIP users are capable of using basic security algorithms, such as Message Authentication Code (MAC) cryptographic algorithm.

The aim of our solution is to support both standard and ad-hoc SIP operations with the following design goals:

- Provide a scalable SIP service over MANET, within the constraint of the existing network;
- Enable Ad hoc node peers to establish calls over the decentralized SP-based Ad hoc network environment;
- Overcome existing limitations of relying on static, fixed, and centralized entities;
- Prevent unnecessary expensive overheads (e.g. eliminating the need to distribute all SIP functionalities over the entire network) without affecting scalability or resulting in higher energy and bandwidth consumption; and
- Provide a compatible solution complying with the standard SIP.

Next, we will outline the modifications required to deploy the SIP standard components in MANETs to implement our proposed solution.

3.1   Proposed Server Functionality

The Primary Server (PS) is a node elected to act as a SIP Proxy and Registrar server to transmit and receive peer-to-peer (P2P) connection requests for the nodes in the cluster that it manages.

This server maintains three different tables containing node data, namely: tables for local node, global node and server. The PS has other duties, such as servicing special invite requests of new nodes and merging and splitting the cluster based on the node count.

The Backup Server (BS) is a backup node with the capability to redirect outbound requests that will take over or be promoted to act as the PS, if the PS goes offline, as well as supporting the PS with load balancing functionality. The BS keeps an identical set of the tables containing node data.

3.2   Proposed New Clustering Mechanism

For the SIP service to be able to be utilized by MANETs, we need SIP servers for the initialization and teardown of the P2P sessions as well as AoR resolution. Nodes in MANETs typically have relatively little CPU power and battery life; therefore, limiting the number of users in this service before latency issue occurs. To address this limitation, we propose a clustering mechanism to dynamically elect or retire servers to load balance based on a pre-determined threshold. Once the latter is reached, a function will be automatically activated to ensure a balanced and uniform service level.

The proposed clustering mechanism assigns one server to a specified set of nodes referred to as a cluster head. Each cluster has a maximum and a minimum saturation limit of nodes, which is used to trigger the respective SPLIT and MERGE functions in the cluster forming a dynamic clustering mechanism. In a cluster SPLIT Function, the BS node becomes the PS in the new cluster taking approximately half of the nodes and then performing an election to select a BS. Conversely, MERGE function triggers once a cluster falls below the minimum saturation limit, the PS of that cluster will send merge requests to other clusters to amalgamate into an efficient cluster size – see [16].

3.3   Server's AoR Entities

Address-of-records (AoR) are extended for the servers to have a global and local view of the (inbound and outbound) network, which are referred to Global Node Table (GNT) and Local Node Table (LNT), respectively. The GNT contains a list of all registered nodes in the domain, and each node can only be updated by their respective PS or BS. The table is distributed and installed on all in-domain active servers (i.e. participating clusters). This is a slight variation from our work in [16], as the BS will have a field to register outbound extended-domain. Alien-domain records will be able to redirect requests to either neighboring domains (e.g. different divisions in the same university) or Alien domains (e.g. other universities). To differentiate between these two domain types, an enhanced reputation mechanism will be used to deal with such requests and decision will be made by the BS server and recorded on both PS and BS's AoR (see Section 3.4)

The LNT holds the records of the local in-cluster nodes installed on every server, which include information such as the Name, Status, Priority and Offline duration for all nodes in the cluster. This table is stored on both PS and BS to keep track of all nodes in the cluster. This arrangement also provides redundancy, in case the table in one of the servers is corrupted.

The Server Table contains information about the cluster servers such as Type, Public keys, Cluster ID, Server name and Priority. The priority field of the server cannot, however, be updated by itself – this field can only be updated by the in-domain active servers (cluster heads).

3.4   Reputation-Based Election

In this section, we will use two levels of reputation-based Elections for both inbound and outbound requests. For inbound requests, a reputation-based technique is used to select a PS or BS in order to ensure that the chosen server is a trusted entity [12]. However, in such an approach, the preference of a server needs to be updated each time they are elected; hence, affecting the stable operation of the network. To avoid this limitation, we adapted our priority algorithm in [16] which takes into account the amount of time that a server has been operational when increasing its priority. This is to ensure that reliable servers are selected in preference to others.

For outbound requests, another reputation-based technique is used to authenticate PSs in other domains. This is done using a ranking system that uses a counter of valid digital signatures to be calculated on each PS along the way. The combination algorithm is based on extended-domain digital signatures (PSDS) and Alien digital signatures (PSds) and will be recorded, updated and saved in the AOR and used on each server along the way. The final decision to authenticate this request will be made by the BS at the receiving end (i.e. the value will have to pass a minimum pre-determined threshold in order to be allowed to proceed and for the invitation to be forwarded to the intended recipient).

Our proposed priority algorithm is as follows:

$$AUTH = PSDS + PSds/2 + TLAoR > X \qquad (1)$$

In the algorithm (see Equation 1), AUTH denotes the Reputation Point Count and TLAoR denotes the Trust Level of the PSs, initialized as Zero. All servers receiving the requests will include their digital signature on outbound forwarded requests to 'earn' more points. Invalid signatures will be counted as Zero. This algorithm gives more weight to PSDS, assuming that most of these domains are an extension of the same service as mentioned earlier (e.g. a division within a university). Those requests that have not passed the minimum pre-determined threshold will need to send more requests (referred to as the warm-up period).

The priority algorithm computes the reputation of selected functioning servers, which is used to determine their eligibility and authenticity as PS. To be able to scale better and achieve a higher priority score, servers will have to serve longer in the network.

Our priority algorithm sets AUTH in AoR to Zero, if PS is inactive for a significant period of time (T) using a dynamic time counter every time the record is updated. T is a dynamic decreasing timer calculated based on how active the PS involved is (Number of valid digital signatures) and the status of the outbound requests (extended or Alien).

4   Implementation

In this section, we will briefly summarize the steps involved in initiating SIP-service over MANETs in the domain level.

4.1   Service Initiation and In-domain Clustering

In the startup phase, the node initiating the service; Cluster Head and Proxy Server (CH and PS, respectively), will advertise to all other nodes that are in range of the service. The first interested and eligible node will be assigned to act as the BS.

Should the PS decides to exit the service (e.g. due to insufficient battery power or mobility), the BS will be promoted to be the new PS by the departing PS. On the other hand, if the PS or BS is to exit the service, a LEAVE message will be sent allowing to promote an eligible node to replace it.

In case of undeclared leave from both functioning servers PS or BS, either server with no backup will either elect or take over and promote eligible node to replace it.

The handover process should not affect any client node cluster affiliation or the progress of already initialized SIP P2P communications, although nodes sending messages to the server may experience minor delays.

Dynamic clustering is also employed as described in Section 3.2 and involves Merge and/or Join functions, which will be triggered based on pre-determined thresholds. This would allow the optimization of the network and better scalability.

4.2   Cross-Domain Communication

We classify domains as either extended or Alien; the former is an extension of the same service, e.g. divisions in the same university, while the latter is an external or anonymous domain. The key difference between the two is the level of trust which will be built through the PS in each domain.

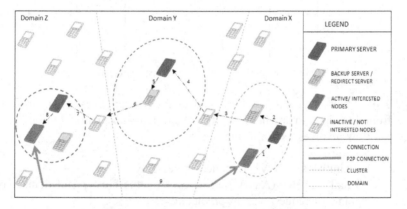

Fig. 2. A cross-domain SIP solution for MANETs

We assume that domains are built using our own solution, such as [16].   We introduce a new BS functionality in order for the BS to act as redirect servers. This would allow the BS to redirect outbound requests, and calculate AUTH. Its reputation builds over time and the local decision whether to either invitations to clients in the cluster or require more authentication points are required (see Equation (1)).

Once domains have been built and communication within clusters in the domains is up and running, subsequent requests from other domains (outbound requests) will be handled as follow:

1.   PS authenticates the request using public keys of the initiating PS.
2.   Once authenticated, PS will then sign the requests using its private key and forward them to the redirect server (BS). Points will also be gained by the PS.

3. BS authenticates this request using the sender PS's public key. Once authenticated, the AUTH field will be updated in its AOR against the PS who initiated the request. This will trigger the dynamic timer, T.
4. BS forwards the requests to the next functioning PS where the same process will be repeated until the request reaches its intended recipient.
5. Once the PS who holds the record in the location service table of the client who is the intended recipient of the invitation receives the request, will forward the request to its functioning BS without signing the request.
6. BS will then make a decision based on the AUTH field of the request initiator PS.
7. If the request is authenticated, ACK will be sent back to the caller allowing P2P communication between both parties to be established (see Fig. 2).

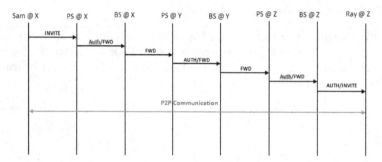

Fig. 3. Call flow through SIP proxy server and backup server

Fig. 3 illustrates a typical call flow, and in this example, user Sam initiatives a request from domain X to another user, Ray, from domain Z, passing through domain Y. The call flow involves the following steps:

1. Sam initiates an INVITE request to call Ray.
2. PS authenticates (Auth) Sam as part of this cluster and domain before signing the request with its private key.
3. PS forwards the message to its functioning BS.
4. BS at domain X labels this request as outbound and forwards it to the next available PS, and in this context, PS at domain Y.
5. PS at domain Y will authenticate the PS at X using its public key and forward it to its BS.
6. BS at domain Y will update its AUTH field using equation (1) and forward the request to the next available PS, and in this context, PS at domain Z.
7. PS at domain Z receives the request and authenticates (Auth) Ray as part of this cluster and domain and forwards the INVITE to its BS.
8. BS at domain Z will then update its AUTH field in its AoR and make a decision on either to forward the request to Ray or not. The decision is made based on the threshold calculated against the points resulted from Equation (1).

9. Once the threshold is achieved and the decision has been made by BS at domain Z, BS forwards the INVITE request to Ray at domain Z.
10. Once an INVITE received by Ray at domain Z, the P2P communication channel will be established between both parties.

Note that if the INVITE requests routes through additional PSs and the involved PS stay online longer, the reputation of the PS involved will be increased. This will result in more eligible or 'trustworthy' PS, and consequently, increasing the scalability of the network. This concept is analogous to passport and visa, where requests are similar to passports, and the more visas the passport holder receives, the more 'international exposure' the individual is (in our context, cross-domain).

5 Discussion

We evaluate our implementation outlined in Section 4 using the following parameters:

- Overhead: The average number of SIP messages received per second.
- Success Ratio: The average rate of invitations successfully delivered to the intended recipient over time.
- Scalability: The performance of the implementation when the number of nodes and area increases.
- Stability: The effect on the service request time when the number of nodes increases.
- Time: The amount of time in seconds for the running of the network. For each second of run-time, the power of the nodes is decreased by one unit to take into consideration that the simulation time is not equivalent to one second in real-time network.
- Power: The measurement of power consumed in each node.
- Mobility: The movement of the node and its effect on the node.

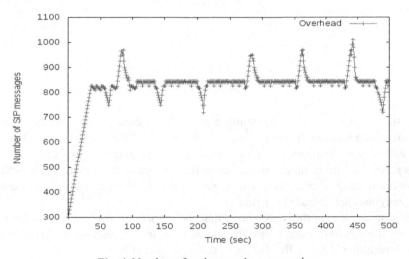

Fig. 4. Number of nodes per cluster over time

We conducted 100 simulations under different conditions, and computed the average of the findings, also taking into consideration that all the nodes are changing position (i.e. mobility) with time.

Fig. 4 presents the findings of the effect of the number of packets measured in kilobits over the lifetime of the network. As observed in the simulation of the implementation, at the startup of the scenario, the number of SIP management messages increases significantly until it reaches a stable position that ranges between 700 and 1000 messages across the network. This is due to the fact that at the initiation of the simulation, the discovery messages dominate the computational resources. Once the network reaches an 'acquainted' state (i.e. where PSs are familiar with neighboring clusters and domains), the network stabilizes and behaves normally according to the proposed solution. It is also observed that the network might face some what is shown in the figure as peaks and drops. The peaks are justified as an impact of authenticating a new domain which adds up a significant number of nodes to the network allowing the number of SIP messages through the redirect servers to increase, conversely, the drops are justified by un-authenticating a domain which significantly decreases the number of nodes, hence an overall decrease of the number of SIP messages through redirect servers.

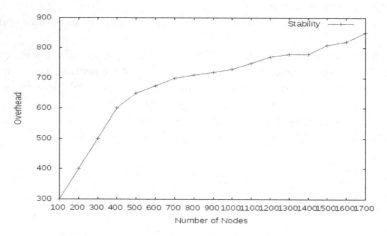

Fig. 5. Stability

As shown in Fig. 5, as the number of nodes increases, the overhead in our implementation remains relatively low – in the range of 100 to 500 nodes. Once the simulations hit the ballpark range of 600 to 1500, the overhead gradually increases with a reasonable delay time. This is due to the restriction that our proposed solution had on the number of messages. This ensures that the success rate is consistent and the system does not degrade over time.

It is also evident in the simulations that the impact on the network is kept to a minimal; the dynamic multi-clustering mechanism in our proposed solution divides the load, resulting in a fair distribution of the load carried by each cluster.

However, once the simulations are 1500 or more, the overhead increases rapidly which produces a significant delay time. This may cause messages to be dropped. This is due to the large number of inbound and outbound messages influenced by the large number of nodes. This limitation will be the subject of future investigation.

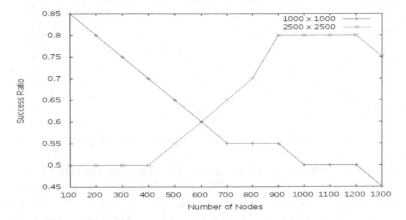

Fig. 6. Scalability (number of nodes against the simulation time)

As shown in Fig. 6, our cross-domain approach has significantly increased the number of participating nodes; addressing one of existing challenging issues. We were able to achieve this by employing a new functionality of the redirect servers and by dividing the network into clusters and domains to evenly share the network load using dynamic clustering across domains in the same domain. The approach is simulated in different terrain areas to achieve an optimized solution. Our simulations suggested that the average success ratio is inversely proportional to the number of nodes for a smaller terrain area for the network layout. On the other hand, our simulations suggested a gradual increase of the average success ratio as the number of nodes increases in a bigger terrain area, from an average starting point of 50% to an average of slightly above 80%. This is due to the impact of the increased number of available routes, which reduces disconnections among cluster and domains. We also remark that the domain can choose not to authenticate and register other domains based on the AUTH equation as the domain may not be stable or is known to be compromised.

As shown in Fig. 7, our cross-domain approach has also been simulated using four different terrain areas. We achieved an average success ratio of 65%-60% for the condensed scenario (i.e. between 500 and 1,800 modes), and 50%-45% for the scattered scenario for the 1,000 m^2 terrain area. For the 1,500 m^2 terrain area, we achieved an average success ratio of 60%-50% for the condensed scenario and 45%-35% for the scattered scenario. In the 2,000 m^2 terrain area, the average success ratio is 50%-45% for the condensed scenario and 35%-30% for the scattered scenario; and for the 2,500 m^2 terrain area, the average success ratio is 45%-35% for the condensed scenario and 30%-25% for the scattered scenario.

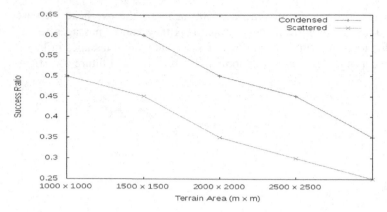

Fig. 7. The impact of terrain area on the success ratio

The simulations indicated that a condensed network results in better performance. This is, probably, due to a higher probability of finding routes and a lower probability of disconnections (i.e. gap between connections). As the number of nodes increases, the success ratio decreases as the increased number of SIP messages would cause a high overhead. Consequently, this leads to a significant delay, which causes the packets to be dropped.

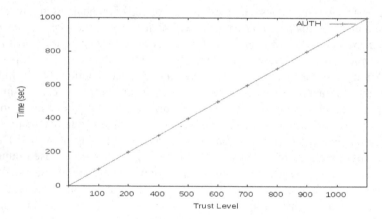

Fig. 8. Reputation

Fig. 8 shows a linear relationship between reputation and time resulting from implementing the equation (1) which ensures a growth of the trust level over time, and points rewarded ensures the most stable servers are preferred and maintain a global list of the authenticated registered entities (i.e. based on number of times the local and global entities were selected).

Table 1. Comparative summary

	Kagoshi ma et al. [10]	Leggio et al. [12]	Abdullah et. al. [14]	Almobaide en et al. [15]	Aburum man et al. [16]	Our Solution
Priority	Dynamic	Static	N/A	N/A	Dynamic	Dynamic
Scalability	Up to 10 nodes	Up to 100 nodes	Up to 50 Nodes	Up to 100 Nodes	Up to 350 Nodes	Up to 1500 Nodes
Average number of management packets	*Gradual Increase	*Rapid Increase	*Rapid Increase	*Gradual Increase	Gradual Increase	Gradual Increase
Stability	Stable	Limited	Stable	Limited		Flexible
Overhead	Low	Varies	High	Average		Average

*The results may vary depending on the conditions of the network, which relies on the applied parameters for the simulated network.

We proposed a solution that is able to enhance and overcome issues previously identified in [13], [14] and [16]. In other words, we were able to address the shortcomings associated with scalability without compromising on reliability and security.

Existing approaches (see Table 1) do not generally address security and stability [10], security and scalability [12, 15], and scalability and overhead [14]. Our proposed solution attempts to address these issues; using an improved priority mechanism, we enhance the trust level associated with the functionalities of SIP entities and consequently, enhance the overall security and availability. This allows one to virtually organize and administrate the network in a dynamic way, and across domains.

6   Concluding Remarks

In this paper, we proposed a cross-domain SIP solution for MANETs using dynamic clustering, which resulted in a stable, secure and scalable MANET service. Our proposed solution introduced new functionalities designed to scale across domains, providing an effective way to deal with outbound requests. We demonstrated the utility of our solution by simulating the implementation under different settings, and evaluated using different metrics and parameters.

Future work includes deploying the solution in a university campus involving student and staff mobile participants, which will allow us to evaluate and refine the design.

References

1. Garber, M.: Securing Session Initiation Protocol Over Ad Hoc Network, Master Thesis, Institute for Pervasive Computing, Zurich (2005)
2. Basagni, S., Conti, M., Giordano, S., Stojmenovic, I.: Mobile Ad Hoc Networking. IEEE Press and A John Wiley & Sons Inc. (2004)
3. Alonso, G., Remund, A., Stuedi, P., Bihr, M.: SIPHoc: efficient SIP middleware for ad hoc networks. In: Cerqueira, R., Campbell, R.H. (eds.) Middleware 2007. LNCS, vol. 4834, pp. 60–79. Springer, Heidelberg (2007)
4. Rosenberg, J., Schulzrinne, H., Camarillo, G., Johnston, A., Peterson, J., Sparks, R., Handley, M., Schooler, E.: SIP: session initiation protocol, RFC 3261, IETF (2002)
5. Sparks, R.: SIP Basics and Beyond, Estacado Systems. ACM Queue 5(2), 22–33 (2007)
6. Arkko, J., Torvinen, V., Camarillo, G., Niemi, A., Haukka, T.: Security Mechanism Agreement for the Session Initiation Protocol (SIP), RFC 3329, IETF (2003)
7. Leggio, S., Manner, J., Hulkkonen, A., Raatikainen, K.: Session initiation protocol deployment in ad-hoc networks: a decentralized approach. In: Proceedings of 2nd International Workshop on Wireless Ad-hoc Networks (IWWAN) (2005)
8. Bai, Y., Aminullah, S., Han, Q., Wang, D., Zhang, T., Qian, D.: A novel distributed wireless VoIP server based on SIP. In: Proceedings of International Conference on Multimedia and Ubiquitous Engineering (MUE 2007), pp. 958–962. IEEE (2007)
9. Bah, S.: SIP servlets-based service provisioning in MANETs, Concordia University (2010)
10. Kagoshima, T., Kasamatsu, D., Takami, K.: Architecture and emulator in ad hoc network for providing P2P type SIP_VoIP services. In: Proceedings of IEEE Region 10 Conference (TENCON 2011), pp. 164–168. IEEE (2011)
11. Alshingiti, M.: Security Enhancement for SIP in Ad Hoc Networks, Carleton University (2012)
12. Leggio, S., Miranda, H., Raatikainen, K., Rodrigues, L.: SIPCache: a distributed SIP location service for mobile ad-hoc networks. In: Proceedings of Annual International Conference on Mobile and Ubiquitous Systems: Networking & Services (MobiQuitous 2006), pp. 1–4. IEEE (2006)
13. Aburumman, A., Choo, K.-K.R., Lee, I.: Nomination-based session initiation protocol service for mobile ad hoc networks. In: Proceedings of 22nd National Conference of the Australian Society for Operations Research (ASOR 2013), pp. 149–155. The Australian Society for Operations Research (2013)
14. Abdullah, L., Almomani, I., Aburumman, A.: Secure cluster-based SIP service over Ad hoc networks. In: Proceedings of IEEE Jordan Conference on Applied Electrical Engineering and Computing Technologies (AEECT 2013), pp. 1–7. IEEE (2013)
15. Almobaideen, W., Kubba, N., Awajan, A.W.: FCSIP: fuzzy and cluster based SIP protocol for MANET. In: Proceedings of International Conference on Next Generation Mobile Apps, Services and Technologies (NGMAST 2014), pp. 169–174. IEEE (2014)
16. Aburumman, A., Choo, K.-K.R.: A domain-based multi-cluster SIP solution for mobile ad hoc network. In: Proceedings of International ICST Conference on Security and Privacy in Communication Networks (SecureComm 2014). Springer (2015)
17. Azfar, A., Choo, K.-K.R., Liu, L.: Android mobile VoIP apps: A survey and examination of their security and privacy, Electronic Commerce Research (In press)
18. Azfar, A., Choo, K.-K.R., Liu, L.: A study of ten popular Android mobile VoIP applications: are the communications encrypted? In: Proceedings of Annual Hawaii International Conference on System Sciences (HICSS 2014), pp. 4858–4867. IEEE (2014)
19. Imgraben, J., Engelbrecht, A., Choo, K.-K.R.: Always connected, but are smart mobile users getting more security savvy? A survey of smart mobile device users, Behaviour & Information Technology 33(12), 1347–1360 (2014)

Community-Based Collaborative Intrusion Detection

Carlos Garcia Cordero[1]([✉]), Emmanouil Vasilomanolakis[1], Max Mühlhäuser[1], and Mathias Fischer[2]

[1] Telecooperation Group, Technische Universität Darmstadt / CASED, Darmstadt, Germany
`{carlos.garcia,manolis,max.muehlhaeuser}@cased.de`
[2] Networking and Security Group, International Computer Science Institute, Berkeley, USA
`mfischer@icsi.berkeley.edu`

Abstract. The IT infrastructure of today needs to be ready to defend against massive cyber-attacks which often originate from distributed attackers such as Botnets. Most Intrusion Detection Systems (IDSs), nonetheless, are still working in isolation and cannot effectively detect distributed attacks. Collaborative IDSs (CIDSs) have been proposed as a collaborative defense against the ever more sophisticated distributed attacks. However, collaboration by exchanging suspicious alarms among all interconnected sensors in CIDSs does not scale with the size of the IT infrastructure; hence, detection performance and communication over-head, required for collaboration, must be traded off. We propose to partition the set of considered sensors into subsets, or *communities*, as a lever for this trade off. The novelty of our approach is the application of ensemble based learning, a machine learning paradigm suitable for distributed intrusion detection. In our approach, community members exchange data features used to train models of normality, not bare alarms, thereby further reducing the communication overhead of our approach. Our experiments show that we can achieve detection rates close to those based on global information exchange with smaller subsets of collaborating sensors.

1 Introduction

The continuous growth and sophistication of cyber-attacks poses a serious threat to networked infrastructure. To contest this, Intrusion Detection Systems (IDSs) monitor a host or a network for signs of intrusions or security policy violations. Detecting intrusions within IDSs is typically performed through *misuse analysis* or *anomaly detection*. Misuse analysis assumes the availability of fingerprints of previously seen attacks, so that they can be detected upon their next occurrence. Anomaly detection establishes a model of normal system behavior. Each deviation from this model is an anomaly and thus a potential attack. Models of normal behavior can be manually provided or automatically learned [1]. IDSs

© Institute for Computer Sciences, Social Informatics and Telecommunications Engineering 2015
B. Thuraisingham et al. (Eds.): SecureComm 2015, LNICST 164, pp. 665–681, 2015.
DOI: 10.1007/978-3-319-28865-9_44

usually operate isolated from each other. There is no communication or inter-action between them and, as a result, isolated IDSs fail to detect distributed attacks as different monitoring points are not exchanging information.

To create a holistic view of the monitored network, collaboration between IDSs is required, which has led to the development of Collaborative IDSs (CIDSs) [2]. These systems consist of *sensors* and one or several *analysis units* that attempt to detect distributed attacks collaboratively. CIDSs can be either cen-tralized or distributed. In centralized CIDSs, sensors send their monitored infor-mation directly to a central analysis unit, while in distributed CIDSs sensors exchange data among each other and do a distributed analysis. Distributed CIDSs provide better scalability than centralized CIDSs while reducing the com-munication overhead. However, compared to centralized systems, this usually comes at the cost of a decreased detection precision, i.e., the ratio between true alarms (or *true positives*) and the total number of alarms (*true positives + false positives*), as there is no component in the system with global information.

CIDS exchange data either on the alarm or detection level. Information exchange on the alarm level, e.g., [3], encompasses the exchange of intrusion alarms for post processing. The main goal of this type of collaboration is to ease the manual task of analyzing all issued alarms by creating summaries and to discover related attacks. In contrast, collaboration on the detection level encom-passes the exchange of monitored information (or data features) to collabo-ratively create or improve mathematical models. These mathematical models aim to improve the detection accuracy and, thus, lower the number of False Alarms (FAs). However, to the best of our knowledge, there is no CIDS that currently supports data exchange on the detection level [2]. We recognize that on the detection level, however, ensemble learning can be applied as a distributed machine learning method [4]. Furthermore, ensemble learning has been demon-strated to be effective in the generic setting of improving anomaly detection [5].

In this paper, we propose a CIDS concept for learning models of normality to detect network anomalies. Our focus is not to introduce a full-fledged CIDS, but rather to demonstrate the applicability of ensemble learning on intrusion detec-tion in a distributed and collaborative setting. We propose the establishment of communities of sensors that exchange data to build anomaly detection models and detect anomalies collaboratively. A sensor is able to participate in multiple communities concurrently, which enables the applicability of ensemble learning techniques. Each sensor shares data with its communities, so that subsets of the entire dataset are created. This allows each community to create an alternative hypothesis from each subset. Each hypothesis represents a particular interpre-tation of normal behavior and all hypotheses can be used together to determine whether arbitrary network traffic is normal or not. We evaluate our novel CIDS concept with a modified version of the DARPA dataset [6] that reflects a dis-tributed monitoring setting. Our results indicate that a community-based CIDS approach performs better, in terms of detection accuracy and precision, than isolated IDSs in the task of learning models of normality.

The remainder of this paper is organized as follows: Section 2 introduces the related work on anomaly detection and CIDSs. Section 3 presents our community-based CIDS concept. Section 4 evaluates our community concept using anomaly detection. Finally, Section 5 concludes the paper and gives insights into future directions.

2   Related Work

In this section, we give a brief overview of related work for anomaly detection algorithms as well as distributed CIDSs.

2.1   Anomaly Network Intrusion Detection

Discovering anomalies in categorical data is of particular interest to anomaly-based IDSs as they heavily rely on the analysis of categorical attributes [7]. For example, IP addresses are normally represented as categorical rather than numerical attributes. This is an important issue to take into account as not every machine learning technique is able to work well with network data. There are, however, many machine learning algorithms that are well suited for this task.

Rule induction techniques are examples of algorithms suitable for handling categorical attributes. Mahoney and Chan published the Packet Header Anomaly Detector (PHAD) algorithm [8]. It focuses on finding rules describing the normal appearance of the Ethernet, IP, TCP, UDP, and ICMP protocols. Detection of anomalies in this context is limited to packets not adhering to one of the learned protocols. Learning Rules for Anomaly Detection (LERAD) [8], finds rules on its own through a stochastic sampling algorithm. Instead of modeling hand picked rules, LERAD is capable of finding a subset of effective conditional rules that describe normal network data.

Rule learning algorithms, such as LERAD, are prime candidates for building ensembles of learners. An ensemble is a collection of classifiers that come together to classify novel instances as a group. Ensemble learning is comprised of a set of techniques to join the decisions made by different classifiers. The two most common techniques are called Bagging and Boosting [9]. Bagging is the process of sampling, with replacement, instances from a large dataset to create subsets. These subsets are used by many classifiers to learn different models of normality (for anomaly detection). To classify a novel instance, each classifier makes a decision. Multiple techniques can be used to mix all the classification decisions into one final decision. A popular technique is to consider each classifier output as a vote and use the class with the most votes. In this paper, we use a technique where the decision of the classifier with the most confidence in classification is used. LERAD is able to output not only the class, but also the confidence of detection as an *anomaly score*. Therefore, for one particular novel instance, the LERAD classifier with the highest anomaly score is taken as the classification decision.

2.2 Distributed CIDSs

CIDSs can be classified, with respect to their communication architecture, as centralized, hierarchical or distributed [2]. In *centralized CIDSs*, e.g., [10], sensors deliver data to a central analysis unit responsible for performing data analytics. However, centralized CIDSs do not scale with an increasing number of sensors as each additional sensor increases the communication overhead of the central analysis unit. Additionally, the central unit represents a single point of failure. Hierarchical CIDSs employ a hierarchical tree structure of sensors, e.g., [11]. Within this hierarchy and starting from leaf positions, monitored data is correlated, preprocessed, and detection algorithms are employed until the data converges to a central analysis unit at the root of the tree. *Distributed CIDSs* follow a flat P2P architecture and disseminate the functionality of the central analysis unit across multiple sensors. Thus, each sensor also conducts data analysis, so that sensor data is correlated, aggregated, and analyzed in a completely distributed manner. Beside structured CIDS approaches, e.g., [12], several unstructured proposals have been made, e.g., [13,14]. However, all existing CIDS approaches operate on the alarm level for the exchange of information [2], while our approach of communities establishes collaboration on the detection level.

3 Community-Based Collaborative Intrusion Detection

In this section we give insights into our community-based CIDS. We provide a description of our concept followed by a formal model and a discussion on how the parameters of the formal model affect the properties of a CIDS. Subsequently, we describe our community formation algorithms and how the formed communities are used to perform intrusion detection.

3.1 Basic Concept

Sensors are grouped into communities to create samples of the network traffic all sensors are capable of observing. The samples are used to learn models of normality and perform anomaly detection. This idea is inspired by ensemble learning and guarantees the reduction of variance in the process of learning [9]. The overall outcome is an increased detection performance, in contrast to isolated sensors, and the reduction of communication overhead, in contrast to centralized systems.

In each community, one sensor becomes a *community head*. Community heads retrieve monitored data features from all other sensors in their community and perform intrusion detection. Upon detecting attacks, community heads forward alarms to a central administration interface where further correlation may take place. Selecting community heads can be done either stochastically or coupled to specific sensor properties such as their computational capabilities.

This paper focuses on the detection accuracy and precision a distributed CIDS can achieve. We leave out the practical realization of distributed community formation. However, sensors could be grouped together into a P2P network using Distributed Hash Tables (DHTs) or P2P-based gossiping techniques [15]. Afterwards, techniques like flooding can be applied on top of the overlay to establish communities in a distributed way.

3.2 Formal Model

Our community-based CIDS overlay can be modeled as a graph $G = (V, E)$ where the nodes V represent computer systems capable of communicating between each other through an overlay communication links E that exist between them. Let $S \subset V$ be the set of intrusion detection sensors capable of collaborating among each other to detect attacks. Additionally, let $u \in V$ be a central administration interface responsible for collecting the alarms issued by all IDSs $s \in S$ and for generating intrusion reports. A community is a subset $\mathcal{C} \subseteq S$ of sensors, with $n_c = |\mathcal{C}|$ members. The set of all communities is $\mathbb{C}$, and the total number of communities is $n_t = |\mathbb{C}|$. Each community $\mathcal{C}$ has one sensor $s_{\mathcal{C}}^\star \in \mathcal{C}$ chosen as the community head; responsible for performing data analysis and intrusion detection. Every other member $s \in \mathcal{C}$ is connected by an edge $e = (s, s_{\mathcal{C}}^\star) \in E$ to $s_{\mathcal{C}}^\star$. Each sensor s is responsible for sending all features extracted from the data they collect to $\{s_{\mathcal{C}}^\star | \forall \mathcal{C} \in \mathbb{C} : s \in \mathcal{C}\}$, i.e., all other community heads they are connected to. The community heads of all communities are summarized in the set $S^\star = \bigcup_{\mathcal{C} \in \mathbb{C}} s_{\mathcal{C}}^\star$. Each sensor $s \in S$ may be repeated up to n_s times between different communities.

Fig. 1 shows three different parametrization scenarios. The parameters specify how sensors s and community heads $s_{\mathcal{C}}^\star$ are grouped together. In Scenario 1, two communities are shown ($n_t = 2$). These communities have four sensors each ($n_c = 4$) and each sensor is allowed to be used only once ($n_s = 1$). Scenario 2 depicts three communities ($n_t = 3$), each having three members ($n_c = 3$), where the sensors are allowed to be repeated at most twice ($n_s = 2$). Lastly, Scenario 3 shows four communities ($n_t = 4$) with two members each ($n_c = 2$) where sensors cannot be repeated more than once ($n_s = 1$).

3.3 Parameters for Building Communities

When doing collaborative intrusion detection with communities, we recognize three dimensions that influence accuracy, scalability and communication overhead. First, we discuss the influence of the size of communities n_c and second, the number of communities n_t. These two parameters allow to model a centralized CIDS, a fully distributed CIDS, or communities. Third, we discuss the impact of the number of times n_s a single sensor can be part of different communities.

Number of Sensors per Community (n_c). The community size n_c significantly influences the detection accuracy. When $n_c = |S|$, there is one community with all sensors. The sensor head $s_{\mathcal{C}}^\star$ of this single community observes all data in the network and, thus, has full knowledge. This is equivalent to a centralized system that can access all data from one single location. In contrast, when $n_c = 1$, the scenario reflects $|S|$ isolated sensors learning without any data being

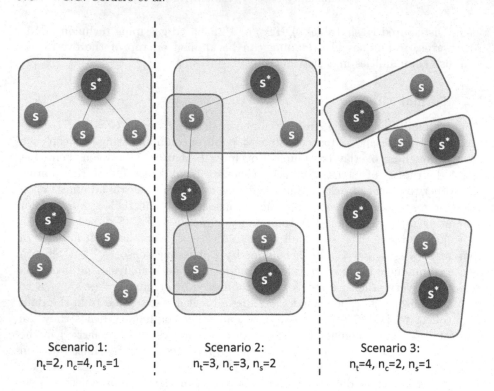

Fig. 1. Two communities (left), three communities (center), and four communities (right), with sensors s and community heads $s^\star$.

shared and no collaboration involved. In this scenario, each community has one sensor that must also be the community head. The size of n_c is bounded by $1 \leq n_c \leq |S|$.

The communication overhead affected by n_c can be expressed as the edges connecting the sensors $s \in \mathcal{S}$ to the community heads $s^\star \in \mathcal{S}^\star$; being inversely proportional to n_c. This overhead is calculated as $|S| - \frac{|S|}{n_c}$ and represents the number of edges required to interconnect all sensors to their respective community heads. Furthermore, with a small n_c, the system as a whole becomes more scalable as communities become responsible for analyzing less data. By increasing n_c, more information becomes available to each community head and a more accurate model can be derived; however, the communities become less scalable as more computational power and memory is required from every community head.

Number of Communities (n_t). The second parameter that has an influence on the detection accuracy and precision is the total number of communities n_t. When $n_t = 1$, only one community is established. This is equivalent to $n_c = |\mathcal{S}|$. On the other hand, when $n_t = |\mathcal{S}|$ and $n_s = 1$, all sensors are their own community and no collaboration is involved. This is analogous to the scenario where $n_c = 1$. This shows that both n_t and n_c are inversely related to each other. The number of communities n_t is bounded according to $1 \leq n_t \leq |\mathcal{S}|$.

The parameter n_t affects scalability only in combination with n_c. Having a high number of communities does not imply anything unless n_c is taken into account. The main scalability issue in any distributed environment is the amount of data that needs to be collected and processed. For instance, a large n_t and low n_c implies that there are many communities processing small amounts of data.

Sensor Repetitions in Multiple Communities (n_s). We define n_s as the upper bound of the total number of times a sensor can be repeated in different communities. This parameter leverages the impact one specific sensor can have when communities are established stochastically. It is bounded according to $1 \leq n_s \leq n_t$. A sensor cannot be repeated within a community; otherwise, it would introduce bias because of the redundant data being shared.

As this parameter increases, more data is allowed to be repeated among many communities. The availability of all data can be augmented by increasing n_s. However, as this parameter increases, the communication overhead increases as well because sensors must transmit the same information to multiple community heads. The parameter n_s also directly affects the size of each community. As n_s increases, the number of sensors $|\mathcal{C}|$ of each community is increased on average. More members equates to more communication overhead.

3.4   Community Formation

The construction of communities demands criteria for coupling together the set of sensors S into communities $\mathcal{C} \in \mathbb{C}$. The coupling depends on parameters that affect how these are formed, i.e., the community size n_c, the total number of communities n_t, and the maximum sensor repetitions within different communities n_s. The remainder of this section contains a detailed discussion of coupling criteria and the algorithms that implement these criteria.

Coupling Criteria. One important design question of our CIDS concept is how to assign sensors to communities, or, more precisely, how the data of all sensors is distributed for analysis. We base our ideas on the bagging ensemble technique. The bagging technique trains a classifier multiple times using different subsets of a dataset. Bagging reduces the variance of the detection accuracy [9]: it reduces the disagreement that might exist when communities are trained on different subsets of a dataset. To create different subsets of the data, data records are sampled with replacement from the entire dataset. To make a decision, every learner classifies the training dataset independently and a combination of all decisions is used to classify each individual training data.

Our proposed community-based CIDS behaves like an ensemble of learners. Each community $\mathcal{C} \in \mathbb{C}$ is a classifier that learns with the data supplied by its members $s \in \mathcal{C}$. Sensors can appear in different communities, which is analogous to sampling batches of data observed by different sensors with replacement. The community size n_c specifies how much will be sampled. The number of communities n_t specifies how many classifiers will be built. Bagging does not usually limit the sampling in any way, we introduce n_s, however, to limit the bias one single community may have in the whole system.

Ensemble methods traditionally split samples of the data randomly (with replacement) among the set of available learners. This is the motivation behind our stochastic creation of communities. We do recognize that in the context of network data more intelligent decisions can be used to split the data. For instance, network traffic can be split according to common network services, IP addresses or other network-related criteria. In this paper, we focus on stochastic community creation and leave other alternatives as future work. We are trying to demonstrate how ensemble methods are able to perform well in the task of anomaly detection when coupling criteria are as general as possible.

Community Construction Algorithms. Multiple strategies can be used to form communities by varying the parameters n_t, n_c and n_s. Each parameter can be fixed to a specific value for all communities to share or vary for each individual community. Because of this, we propose two different algorithms to build communities. Algorithm 1 fixes n_c to a particular value such that all communities exhibit the same size. The other two parameters, n_t and n_s, are left to vary for each community. In contrast, Algorithm 2 fixes the parameters n_s and tries to fix n_t whenever it is possible, while leaving n_c to vary for each community.

Algorithm 1. comm$_1(\mathcal{S}, n_c)$

---

1 $\mathbb{C} \leftarrow \{\emptyset\}, T \leftarrow \{\emptyset\}$
2 **for** $s \in S$ **do**
3   **if** $s \notin T$ **then**
4          $C \leftarrow \{s\}$
5          $T \leftarrow T \cup \{s\}$
6   **for** $|C| \leq n_c$ **do**
7              $s \leftarrow \text{rand}(S - C)$
8              $C \leftarrow C \cup \{s\}$
9              $T \leftarrow T \cup \{s\}$
10         $\mathbb{C} \leftarrow \mathbb{C} \cup \{C\}$
11   **return** $\mathbb{C}$

Given all sensors S and n_c as input, Algorithm 1 outputs a set of communities $\mathbb{C}$. This algorithm consists of two parts: In its first part (lines 2 - 5), the algorithm selects an initial sensor, not belonging to any other community, to start a new community. The list T is used to track sensors that already belong to a community. This restriction ensures that all sensors appear at least once among all communities while forming as few communities as possible. The second part of the algorithm (lines 6 - 9) adds random sensors to C from the set $S - C$ until $|C| = n_c$.

Given all sensors S, n_t and n_s as inputs, Algorithm 2 outputs a set of communities $\mathbb{C}$ where $|\mathbb{C}| = n_t$ and no sensor is repeated more than n_s times among all communities. In contrast to Algorithm 1, this algorithm creates communities of different sizes. Equally to the n_c parameter of Algorithm 1, n_t has the property of generalizing how the community members collaborate as described in Section 3.3.

Algorithm 2. comm$_2(S, n_t, n_s)$

---

1   **if** $n_s > n_t$ **then**
2     $\lfloor$ $n_s = n_t$
3   $C_1, C_2, \ldots, C_{n_t} \leftarrow \{\emptyset\}, \{\emptyset\}, \ldots, \{\emptyset\}$
4   $\mathbb{C} \leftarrow \{C_1, C_2, \ldots, C_{n_t}\}$
5   **for** $s \in S$ **do**
6     $x \leftarrow Uniform(1, n_s)$
7     $T \leftarrow \{\emptyset\}$
8   **for** 1 *to* x **do**
9       $C \leftarrow \mathrm{rand}(\mathbb{C} - T)$
10       $C \leftarrow C \cup \{s\}$
11       $T \leftarrow T \cup \{C\}$
12   return $\mathbb{C}$

Algorithm 2 follows the following strategy. Lines 3 and 4 initialize the set $\mathbb{C}$ with n_t empty communities. The first loop of the algorithm (line 5) iterates over each available sensor $s \in S$ to distribute it in the second loop (line 8). Each sensor s is placed, according to a uniform distribution in $[1, n_s]$, in multiple communities. It is possible that some communities are never chosen in line 9 and communities from the initial set $\mathbb{C}$ remain empty. These empty communities are discarded.

3.5 Community-Based Intrusion Detection

Each community $C \in \mathbb{C}$ represents an overlay where all sensors $s \in C$ are able to freely communicate with the community head, s_C^*. All sensors $s \in S$ extract features from the network they monitor and forward them to their respective community head where all these are bundled into one *aggregated training dataset*. Each s_C^* $\forall C \in \mathbb{C}$ learns a model of normality using its aggregated training dataset, performs anomaly detection, and sends all resulting alarms to the central administration interface u. The unit u receives the alarms of all $|S^*|$ community heads, sorts the alarms by anomaly score, and reports the top-most anomalous alarms according to a predefined threshold limited by the FAs.

After establishing a model of normality with the aggregated training dataset, the community heads perform anomaly detection using an *aggregated testing dataset* also gathered within the community. Sensors keep sending the same extracted data features used for creating the aggregated training dataset to the community head. However, the data features are now bundled into an aggregated testing dataset. The outcome of performing anomaly detection is the raising of alarms. Every community head sends these alarms to a central unit where alarm correlation and further analysis takes place.

4   Evaluation

This section presents the results of detecting attacks in a modified version of the DARPA dataset using our novel idea of communities (cf. Section 3) coupled with the anomaly detection algorithm LERAD (cf. Section 2). This evaluation demonstrates how communities outperform isolated sensors in the task of detecting intrusions using anomaly detection.

In our tests we compare the network intrusion detection capabilities of centralized, isolated, and community-based CIDSs. Community-based systems are a variant of centralized and isolated ones that represent a trade-off between scalability and accuracy. Each community analyzes the network traffic of multiple sensors and provide better scalability than centralized systems and better accuracy than isolated systems.

4.1   The DARPA Dataset

The dataset used for evaluation purposes is the DARPA dataset [6]. Regardless of this dataset being outdated and not representing modern traffic patterns, we argue that its usage does not disturb the evaluation results: The dataset is used to compare the performance of three different systems under the same conditions; all of them utilizing the same labeled data. Moreover, the general availability of this dataset and the precisely labeled traffic, without incorrect labels, makes this dataset more useful in this particular context than other alternatives such as the MAWILab [16] or the CDX [17] dataset.

For the evaluation of our approach, we modified the DARPA dataset to reflect the placement of multiple sensors at different points in the network rather than only at one. The description of how this is performed follows.

Modifications to the DARPA Dataset. The DARPA intrusion detection dataset [6] is a collection of network traffic obtained from a simulated military computer network with labeled attacks. In this evaluation, only the data records of incoming traffic are taken into account. There are a total of three weeks of training data and two weeks of testing data in the form of packet captures (pcap files). Only the third week of training data and both weeks of testing data are used. The training data does not contain attacks and is used to create models of normality. The testing data contains normal network traffic and 201 attacks ranging from denial of service to exploitation attempts. Due to the modifications described in the following paragraphs, 19 attacks are removed, i.e., traces of these attacks have been dropped as if no sensor was able to pick these up.

In the original dataset all network packets are captured by a single sensor at the ingress point of external traffic. For the purpose of testing the performance of multiple sensors analyzing the data independently of each other and within communities, the DARPA dataset is split according to the visible end-hosts in the local network. The incoming external traffic is split as if only end-hosts captured the traffic. Our modified DARPA dataset emulates multiple sensors, each monitoring a single computer system, gathering data independently of each other. As a consequence, the original testing and training network traffic is split according to the local IPs found in the training set as if captured by multiple sensors instead of only one.

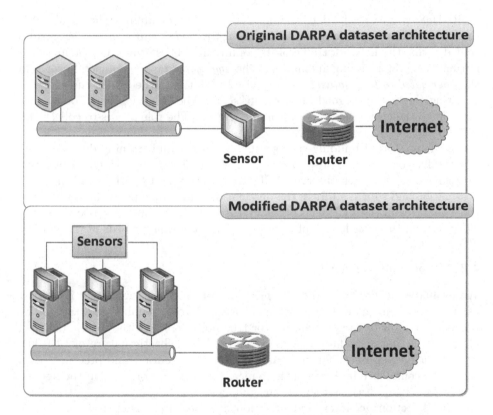

Fig. 2. Modifications made to the 1999 DARPA Dataset.

The DARPA modifications are illustrated in Fig. 2. The red sensor icons indicate the locations where network data is gathered. In the original DARPA dataset, one sensor, at the ingress point, collected all network traffic. Our modified DARPA dataset emulates multiple sensors, each monitoring a single computer system, gathering data independently of each other.

Splitting the original dataset caused two important changes in the resulting dataset. First, all packets targeting an IP address of a non-existent endpoint in the local network are discarded as if no sensor would have seen these. The discarded packets were mostly generated by services that probed a large range of arbitrary IP addresses. Second, we discarded all packets targeting a local IP address in the testing dataset targeted by incoming traffic that is not present in the training dataset. Many packets in the original testing dataset targeted local IP addresses not associated with normal traffic. Hence, for such traffic we cannot derive a model of normality. The end result was a training dataset containing 15 sensors (15 different IP addresses).

4.2   The LERAD Integration

LERAD [8] is used as the detection mechanism of all community heads $s^* \in S^*$. Each community head runs LERAD on its *aggregated training data* to learn rules that describe the network traffic of its community. These rules are the model of normality used for finding anomalies in the *aggregated testing dataset*. Records in the *aggregated testing dataset* are compared with the learned rules and the ones violating these are assigned an anomaly score. The rule violations, or alarms, are sent to the central administration interface u. The role of u is to collect and sort all alarms by anomaly score.

In the process of building the aggregated testing and training datasets, network traffic goes through pre-processing to extract 23 features which are effective for LERAD [8]. For each observed TCP stream we extract the date and time; the destination and source address; the destination and source port; the duration of the TCP stream; the TCP flags of the first, second to last and last packets of the TCP stream; the byte length of the stream; and the first 8 words of the stream.

4.3   Experimental Setup

We evaluate the *accuracy* and the *precision* of detection. Accuracy is defined as the total number of attacks detected over the total number of attacks. The precision equates to the true alarms (or true positives) over the total number of alarms (true alarms + false alarms). Due to the stochastic nature of LERAD, we run each experiment 500 times and average the accuracy and precision of all runs. The confidence intervals of these measurements are omitted in the figures, except for Figure 3(a), as they are insignificant.

The detection accuracy and precision are measured using the alarms the central administrator interface u receives from all community heads. In a preprocessing stage, duplicated alarms within a time-frame of 60 seconds are removed as, according to the original DARPA competition, alarms are deemed true if they detect an attack withing 60 seconds of its occurrence. We analyze each alarm, from highest to lowest anomaly score, assessing if the alarm is a true or false positive. This process continues until a predefined number of FAs is reached and all remaining alarms are discarded. In every experiment, we test the accuracy and precision with different numbers of random communities. Three cases can be distinguished given the size of the community:

Centralized System ($n_c = 15$): All sensors send the extracted features to a single community head.

Isolated System ($n_c = 1$): A community for each sensor ($|\mathbb{C}| = 15$) on its own without any cooperation.

Communities ($n_c = x \mid 1 < x < 15$): Variable number of communities.

On the one hand, the community of size 15 is expected to outperform all others, in terms of detection accuracy and precision, given that all the features extracted are available in one single location for analysis. On the other hand, it is expected that 15 single independent communities will perform the worst overall as there is no collaboration involved. In the following Subsection, we show that as communities include more sensors, the detection accuracy and precision is improved while at the same time leveraging the communication overhead. In addition, we show that under certain conditions the communities achieve a detection precision similar to the centralized system with a better detection accuracy.

4.4 Results

The analysis baseline is shown in Figure 3, where we compare the detection accuracy and precision of every possible community size n_c, as built by Algorithm 1. Figures 3(a) and 3(b) show the outcomes of our experiments varying the FA limit, i.e., changing the threshold for raising alarms. Each anomaly detection experiment is carried out until a predefined number of FAs are issued. At this point, the detection is stopped and the results are recorded. We measure the detection capabilities using 100, 150, 200 and 400 FAs. The testing data corresponds to two weeks (10 total days) of data; as such, 100 FAs equates to an average of 10 FAs per day, 150 to 15 FAs per day, and so on. The shaded area around the solid lines in Figure 3(a) show the confidence intervals of the measurements.

After 100 FAs are found in the sequential analysis of each alarm, from highest anomaly score to lowest, the accuracy and precision of the detections are reported. Figure 3(b) shows that as communities grow in size, the precision is improved. This translates to our hypothesis that the centralized system would have the highest accuracy and precision rates. As seen in both Figures 3(a) and 3(b), if the 100 FA restriction is relaxed, some community sizes are able to improve the detection accuracy in contrast to the centralized system (when $n_c = 15$). At 200 FAs, most community sizes have better detection accuracy than the centralized system. In addition, relaxing the FA restriction allows the detection precision to converge to the one of the centralized system. Lastly, at 400 FAs, a point is reached where every community is able to outperform, in terms of accuracy, both the individual approaches as well as the centralized system. It should be noted that above the 400 FA limitation, no significant changes are observed. However, as seen in Figure 3(b), the precision drops as the FAs are increased. With the 200 FAs limitation, communities with $n_c \in [9, 11]$, quickly approach the precision ratio of the centralized system.

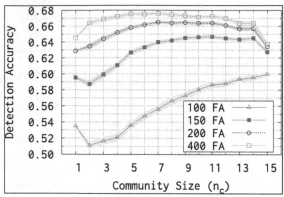

(a) Detection accuracy evaluated at different False Alarm (FA) rates.

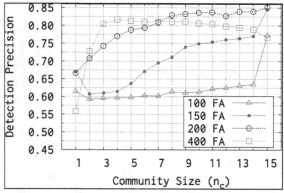

(b) Precision of detections at different False Alarms (FA).

Fig. 3. Detection accuracy and precision at different FAs when communities are built using Algorithm 1.

The number of repeating sensors (n_s) has also some interesting properties that impact the detection accuracy of fixed community sizes. We show the experiments of varying $n_s \in [1, 5]$ with Algorithm 2 in Figure 4(a). The graphs being plotted show the impact n_s has on the detection accuracy with respect to the number of communities n_t. As more sensor repetitions are allowed, the overall accuracy is improved. Here we also see the centralized system $(n_t = 1)$ still outperforming all others. Furthermore, Figure 4(b) strengthens our aforementioned statement that as n_t increases, the impact of n_s decreases.

To sum up, our results indicate a number of interesting facts. First, as expected, a centralized architecture outperforms all others when the threshold for raising alarms is set high, i.e., when the number of FAs is constrained to low values. Nevertheless, communities provide fair detection and precision ratio and

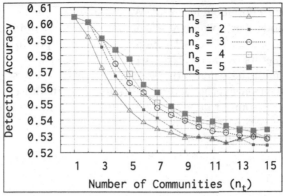

(a) Detection accuracy depending on the number of communities n_t evaluated using different repetitions n_s.

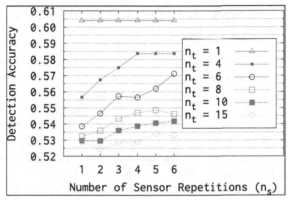

(b) Detection accuracy depending on the number of sensor repetitions n_s.

Fig. 4. Accuracy when the communities are built using Algorithm 2.

better communication overhead in comparison to a centralized system, while already outperforming individual IDSs at the lowest tolerated FA limit of 10 average alarms per day (100 FAs). Isolated sensors perform no collaboration and, in consequence, create less accurate models of normal traffic than the ones created by collaborating communities. Second, as the threshold for raising alarms is lowered (allowing 200 or more FAs), communities start to perform similarly to the centralized system; finally being able to outperform it (in terms of detection accuracy). This performance can be explained by the fact that, due to the stochastic nature of our algorithm, there is a point where communities are able to gather together enough sensors to generate accurate enough models of normality that explain general network traffic patterns. In addition, these results also comply with our initial argumentation that our community-based CIDS has properties similar to ensemble learning. We are able to improve performance by using different models of normality learned by different communities. Overall, our results in Figures 3(a) and 3(b) indicate that it is possible to find a combination of parameters n_t, n_c, n_s and a particular threshold for raising alarms that enables communities to perform close the a centralized system while reducing the communication overhead. For the particular instance of the modified DARPA dataset, we found that the best results are found when the community size $n_c = 9$, the repetitions $n_s = 3$, the total communities $n_t = 4$ and the FA threshold is set to allow 200 FAs.

5 Conclusion

The continuous sophistication of network attacks urges the development of novel IDSs and architectures. Collaborative IDSs (CIDSs) focus on techniques that group sensors and create a holistic view of the monitored network. In this paper, we presented a CIDS concept that applies the novel idea of communities of sensors that collaborate exchanging features of network traffic to create sufficiently accurate normality models for performing anomaly detection. We developed stochastic algorithms that group sensors into communities and demonstrate how these communities are able to leverage the detection capabilities and communication overhead of CIDSs. Our experimental results indicate that our community-based CIDS concept, performs better than isolated systems in terms of detection accuracy and precision. Furthermore, we demonstrated that communities can perform similarly to centralized systems even though less information is distributed to build normal models for anomaly detection and, as such, less communication overhead is involved. Lastly, we observed that if the threshold for raising alarms is lowered, communities are able to outperform the centralized system.

Future work will comprise additional criteria for community creation. For instance, we will investigate sensor coupling on the basis of exchanged fingerprints of locally monitored traffic, to interconnect sensors with similar traffic patterns. Moreover, we will focus on distributed algorithms for community formation.

References

1. Garcia-Teodoro, P., Diaz-Verdejo, J., Maciá-Fernández, G., Vázquez, E.: Anomaly-based network intrusion detection: Techniques, systems and challenges. Computers & Security 28(1–2), 18–28 (2009)
2. Vasilomanolakis, E., Karuppayah, S., Mühlhäuser, M., Fischer, M.: Taxonomy and Survey of Collaborative Intrusion Detection. ACM Computing Surveys 47(4), 33 (2015)
3. Chen, Y., Cai, M., Hwang, K., Kwok, Y.-K., Song, S.: Collaborative Internet Worm Containment. IEEE Security and Privacy Magazine 3(3), 25–33 (2005)
4. Peteiro-Barral, D., Guijarro-Berdiñas, B.: A survey of methods for distributed machine learning. Progress in Artificial Intelligence 2(1), 1–11 (2012)

5. Zhou, Z.-H.: When semi-supervised learning meets ensemble learning. Frontiers of Electrical and Electronic Engineering in China **6**(1), 6–16 (2011)
6. Lippmann, R., Haines, J.W., Fried, D.J., Korba, J., Das, K.: The 1999 DARPA off-line intrusion detection evaluation. Computer Networks **34**(4), 579–595 (2000)
7. Chandola, V., Banerjee, A., Kumar, V.: Anomaly detection: A Survey. ACM Computing Surveys **41**(3), 1–58 (2009)
8. Mahoney, M., Chan, P.: Learning rules for anomaly detection of hostile network traffic. In: IEEE International Conference on Data Mining. IEEE Comput. Soc, 2003, pp. 601–604 (2003)
9. Maclin, R., Opitz, D.: Popular ensemble methods: An empirical study. Journal Of Artificial Intelligence Research **11**, 169–198 (1999)
10. Kannadiga, P., Zulkernine, M.: DIDMA : a distributed intrusion detection system using mobile agents. In: International Conference on Software Engineering, Artificial Intelligence, Networking and Parallel/Distributed Computing, pp. 238–245. IEEE (2005)
11. Zhang, Z., Li, J., Manikopoulos, C.N., Jorgenson, J., Ucles, J.: HIDE : a hierarchical network intrusion detection system using statistical preprocessing and neural network classification. In: IEEE Workshop on Information Assurance and Security, pp. 85–90. IEEE (2001)
12. Marchetti, M., Messori, M., Colajanni, M.: Peer-to-peer architecture for collaborative intrusion and malware detection on a large scale. In: Samarati, P., Yung, M., Martinelli, F., Ardagna, C.A. (eds.) ISC 2009. LNCS, vol. 5735, pp. 475–490. Springer, Heidelberg (2009)
13. Locasto, M.E., Parekh, J.J., Keromytis, A.D., Stolfo, S.J.: Towards collaborative security and P2P intrusion detection. In: IEEE Workshop on Information Assurance and Security, pp. 333–339. IEEE (2005)
14. Duma, C., Karresand, M., Shahmehri, N., Caronni, G.: A trust-aware, P2P-based overlay for intrusion detection. In: International Conference on Database and Expert Systems Applications (DEXA 2006), pp. 692–697. IEEE (2006)
15. Ganesh, A.J., Kermarrec, A.-M., Massoulié, L.: Peer-to-peer membership management for gossip-based protocols. IEEE Transactions on Computers **52**(2), 139–149 (2003)
16. Fontugne, R., Borgnat, P., Abry, P., Fukuda, K.: MAWILab: combining diverseanomaly detectors for automated anomaly labeling and performance benchmarking. In: 6th International Conference on - Co-NEXT 2010, pp. 1–12. ACM (2010)
17. Sangster, B., Cook, T., Fanelli, R., Dean, E., Adams, W.J. Morrell, C., Conti, G.: Toward instrumenting network warfare competitions to generate labeled datasets. In: USENIX Security's Workshop on Cyber Security Experimentation and Test (CSET) (2009)

A Novel Clustering Algorithm for Database Anomaly Detection

Jinkun Geng[1(✉)], Daren Ye[1], Ping Luo[2], and Pin Lv[3]

[1] School of Software, Beihang University, Beijing 100191, China
steam1994@163.com
[2] Key Laboratory for Information System Security, Ministry of Education,
Tsinghua National Laboratory for Information Science and Technology(TNlist),
School of Software, Tsinghua University, Beijing 100084, China
luop@mail.tsinghua.edu.cn
[3] State Information Center, Beijing 100045, China

Abstract. As a main method in database intrusion detection, database anomaly detection should be able to detect users' operational behaviours for timely prevention of possible attacks and for guarantee of database security. Aiming at this, we apply cluster analysis techniques to anomaly detection and propose a novel density-based clustering algorithm called DBCAPSIC, which is adopted to clustering database users according to their behavior types and behavior frequencies. Privilege patterns are extracted from the clusters and serve as a reference in anomaly detection. The simulation experiment proves that the algorithm can recognize the anomalous operations with few mistakes.

Keywords: Database anomaly detection · Database security · Cluster analysis · Privilege pattern

1   Introduction

Computer science and network technology are developing rapidly, leading to data explosions in almost every field. Data has become an important asset today and database security is gaining more and more attention. [8-9] [14] As a crucial part in database security protection, database intrusion detection should be able to detect users' operational behaviours for timely prevention of possible attacks.

However, there is currently few intrusion detection researches focusing on database and the built-in security mechanisms are far from effective to detect and prevent anomalous behaviour of applications and intrusions from attackers [8-9].The existing intrusion detection systems are insufficient to make ideal intrusion detection for databases. Therefore, the study of intrusion detection aiming at databases, especially the anomaly detection, is of great significance both theoretically and practically.

Data mining techniques are widely adopted in the fields of business, medicine, education and engineering [10,19-23] because of the capability of discovering lots of useful knowledge automatically in the analysis of massive information. This inspire us to adopt some of the methods in our research.

© Institute for Computer Sciences, Social Informatics and Telecommunications Engineering 2015
B. Thuraisingham et al. (Eds.): SecureComm 2015, LNICST 164, pp. 682–696, 2015.
DOI: 10.1007/978-3-319-28865-9_45

In this paper, we focus on database anomaly detection and propose a "density-based clustering algorithm via pre-sampling and inferior centroid" (denoted as DBCAPSIC). We embed DBCAPSIC into the anomaly detection algorithm. With the privilege patterns extracted from clusters generated by DBCAPSIC, we can detect the real-time operations on the monitored DBMS and recognize the anomalous operations.

The rest of the paper is organized as follows: Section 2 introduces some preliminary concepts in the field of database intrusion detection. Section 3 first illustrates proposes the algorithm DBCAPSIC and states the anomaly detection method based on DBCAPSIC. Section 4 presents the experiment and analyses the experimental result. Section 5 concludes the whole paper.

2 Preliminaries

Before the description of the algorithm, we first provide some preliminary definitions in this section.

2.1 Definitions of Objects

Definition 1 The 2-tuple consisting of a database object and an operational behaviour type is defined as a behaviour pattern (BP),i.e.

$$BP = \{object, type\},$$

where *object* is a database object such as a table, a view and so on, and *type* is the type of the behaviour operated on *object*, such as *SELECT, UPDATE* and so on.

Definition 2 The 3-tuple consisting of a database object, an operational behaviour type and a frequency value of the behaviour is defined as a behaviour object (BO), i.e.

$$BO = \{object, type, frequency\},$$

where *frequency* is the times of the behaviour of *type* operated on *object* by a certain database user in a period of history. For example, if a user has made 3 *SELECT* operations on the table *discount*, then we get a *BO* like this:

$$\{discount, SELECT, 3\}.$$

Definition 3 The 2-tuple consisting of a database user and its corresponding behaviour object set (BOS) is defined as a user object (UO), i.e.

$$UO = \{user, BOS\},$$

where *user* the database user, usually represented by the user's account name, and *BOS* is the set of behaviour objects affiliated to the same user, i.e.

$$BOS = \{BO_1, BO_2, ..., BO_n\}.$$

For the convenience of the following narration, the definition of frequency function is given here.

Definition 4 The frequency function $F(user,BP)$ is defined as the operational times (frequency) of operated by *user* in a period of history.

Obviously for a certain behaviour object which is affiliated to *user*, let's say $BO_0 = \{object_0, type_0, frequency_0\}$, the following condition is satisfied that

$$frequency_0 = F(user, BP_0),$$

where $BP_0 = \{object_0, type_0\}$.

With the definition of frequency function we can have

$$BO_0 \Leftrightarrow \{BP_0, F(user, BP_0)\},$$

which is called the behaviour object's 2-tuple definition.

Furthermore, for the behaviour object set *BOS* affiliated to *user*, we can get the behaviour object set's 2-tuple definition:

$$BOS \Leftrightarrow \{BPS, FS\},$$

where $BPS = \{BP_1, BP_2, ..., BP_n\}$ and $FS = \{F(user, BP_1), F(user, BP_2), ...F(user, BP_n)\}$.

2.2   Definition of Measurements

Definition 5 Let UO_1 and UO_2 denote two user objects:

$$UO_1 = \{user_1, BOS_1\}, UO_2 = \{user_2, BOS_2\},$$

where BOS_1 and BOS_2 are represented with the 2-tuple definition, i.e.

$$BOS_1 = \{BPS_1, FS_1\}, BOS_2 = \{BPS_2, FS_2\}.$$

Then the similarity function is defined as

$$similarity(UO_1, UO_2) = \frac{\sum_{a \in BPS_1 \cap BPS_2} \min(\frac{F(user_1, a)}{F(user_2, a)}, \frac{F(user_2, a)}{F(user_1, a)})}{\max(|BPS_1|, |BPS_2|)},$$

where $|BPS|$ refers to the capacity of *BPS*.

Definition 6 The distance function is defined as

$$dist(UO_1, UO_2) = 1 - similarity(UO_1, UO_2),$$

From the definition, we know $0 \le dist \le 1$, and the more similar the two use objects are, the smaller the distance value is, and vice versa. Specially, when the distance value reaches 1, the two user objects have completely different *BPSs*, and they represent database users of different classes.

3   Anomaly Detection with DBCAPSIC

3.1   Basic Idea of DBCAPSIC

The algorithm DBCAPSIC learns from the idea of k-means-type algorithms and density-based clustering algorithms, and it avoids the user-defined cluster numbers and the random selection of starting points, thus overcoming classic k-means algorithm's susceptibility to initial conditions; Moreover, via "pre-sampling method", DBCAPSIC managed to reduce the time complexity to $O(n)$, and by introducing the concept of "inferior-centroid", it solves the "Clustering Failure" problem which common density-based clustering algorithms will meet on certain cases.

For the convenience of the following narration, here we provide definitions of density and radius.

Definition 7 For the data set denoted as $E = \{x_1, x_2, ..., x_n\}$, the elements' radius is defined as

$$radius = \frac{2}{n(n-1)} \sum_{i=1}^{n} \sum_{j=i+1}^{n} dist(x_i, x_j),$$

where n is the capacity of E, that is $n = |E|$.

Definition 8 The element's density is defined as

$$\forall x \in E, density(x) = \sum_{j=1}^{n} sign(radius - dist(x, x_j)), \text{where } sign(x) = \begin{cases} 1, x \geq 0 \\ 0, x < 0 \end{cases}.$$

3.2   Inferior-Centroid to Avoid "Clustering Failure"

The initial algorithm we adopted runs like this: firstly we calculate the distance of each pair of objects and then we get radius; with radius we can calculate the density of each object to construct density set, i.e.

$$densitySet = \{density(UO) | UO \in UOS\}.$$

We choose UO_m from UOS, which has the largest density in $densitySet$, as a centroid. With UO_m, we can find all objects within the radius of UO_m and remove their densities from $densitySet$. We will repeat the process until $densitySet$ becomes an empty set. Then we get the $centroidSet$. Next, we assign each object to its nearest centroid and get $clusterSet$. Finally we reset the centroid of each cluster to select the object with the largest density to represent the cluster.

During the process of clustering with the density-based algorithms, we discover the following problems: The first problem is the high time complexity which reaches $O(n^2)$ thus meeting a bottleneck when dealing with massive data. The second problem is the "Clustering Failure" —Some of the final clusters may contain user objects

686   J. Geng et al.

that are complete different, that is to say, different classes of *UO*s are assigned into the same cluster.

As for the first problem, we can use "pre-sampling method" to reduce the high time complexity. But for the second problem of "Clustering Failure" , we think it is the defect of common density-based algorithm.

The cause of "Clustering Failure" is because when we judge whether an object *UO* is "qualified" to be added into the cluster *cluster$_i$*, we just consider the similarity between *UO* and the current centroid *centroid$_i$* and ignore the similarity between *UO* and other objects that already have the "quality" to join *cluster$_i$*. Therefore, it may cause that objects that belong to the same cluster have low similarity or no similarity at all.

To avoid "Clustering Failure", we propose the definition of "inferior-centroid".

Definition 9 Inferior-centroid is the element in the cluster that is farthest from the centroid of the cluster, i.e. the object x is the inferior-centroid of *cluster iff*

$$x \in cluster, \text{ and } dist(centeroid, x) = \max\left(\left\{dist(centeroid, x_i) \mid x_i \in cluster\right\}\right).$$

3.3   Description of DBCAPSIC Algorithm

In DBCAPSIC, "pre-sampling method" is adopted to reduce the time complexity to a linear level and inferior-centroid is introduced to avoid "Clustering Failure".

The description of DBCAPSIC is shown in Algorithm 1.

Algorithm 1. DBCAPSIC Based on behaviour Type and behaviour Frequency

1.Input:
UOS---The database user object set ,i.e. $UOS = \{UO_1, UO_2, \cdots, UO_n\}$.

λ ---The artificially specified merge coefficient, which belongs to the interval [0,1].
2.Radius Calculation.
   2.1 Pre-Sampling. Make a simple random sampling of *UOS* and get the sample set *sUOS*, with the capacity of $\left\lceil \sqrt{n} \right\rceil$ ([ ] means to round down).

   2.2 Radius Estimation. The radius of *sUOS* ,denoted as *sradius* can be calculated and it serves as the approximated radius for *UOS*, i.e. $radius = sradius$.
3.Density Calculation.
$\forall UO \in sUOS$,calculate *density(UO)*, and $densitySet = \{density(UO) \mid UO \in sUOS\}$.

4.Center User Object Selection.
Initialize the center user object set *cUOS* and the inferior center user set *iUOS*, i.e. $cUOS = \varnothing$, $iUOS = \varnothing$.
While $densitySet \neq \varnothing$,execute the following sub-steps:
   4.1 Select the *UO* with the largest density, denoted as UO_m, then $cUOS = cUOS \cup \{UO_m\}$, $densitySet = densitySet - \{d_m\}$;the current center user object $cUO=UO_m$,the current inferior center user object *iUO* is null.

4.2 $\forall UO_i \in UOS$,

if $UO_i \in cUOS$ or $UO_i \in iUOS$, then traverse the next user object UO_{i+1};

else if $dist(cUO, UO_i) > radius$, turn to Step 4.3;

else we have $dist(cUO, UO_1) \leq radius$, then execute the following sub-sub-steps:

    4.2.1 If iUO is null, make UO_i the current inferior-centroid and put it into $iUOS$, i.e. $iUO = UO_i$ $iUOS = iUOS \cup \{UO_i\}$,

and remove its density from $densitySet$, i.e.

$$densitySet = densitySet - \left\{ density\left(UO_i\right)\right\},$$ then turn to Step 4.3.

    4.2.2 If iUO is not null, then judge whether it is satisfied that $dist(iUO, UO_i) \leq radius$ .If so, turn to Step 4.2.3, else turn to Step 4.3.

    4.2.3 If $dist(cUO, UO_i) > dist(cUO, iUO)$,then update the current inferior-centroid, i.e. $iUOS = iUOS - \{iUO\}$, $iUO = UO_i$ $iUOSet = iUOSet \cup \{iUO\}$,

then turn to Step 4.3;else directly turn to Step 4.3.

4.3 Repeat Step 4.1 and Step 4.2 until $densitySet = \varnothing$, then we get the center user object set $cUOS$ and the inferior center user set $iUOS$.

5.User Objects Clustering.

5.1 Combine the center user object set with the inferior center user object set, i.e. $cUOS = cUOS \cup iUOS$.

5.2 Initialize a cluster for each center user object in $cUOS$, then we get the cluster set, that is $clusterSet = \{cluster_1, cluster_2, ..., cluster_r\}$, where $r = |cUOSet|$ and $\forall cluster_i \in clusterSet, cluster_i = \varnothing$.

5.3 $\forall UO \in UOS$,traverse $cUOS$ and find a certain center user object cUO_j that satisfies $dist\left(UO, cUO_j\right) = \min\left(\left\{dist\left(UO, cUO\right) | cUO \in cUOS\right\}\right)$, cUO_j is the nearest center user to UO,then remove the UO from UOS and assign it into the cUO_j's cluster, i.e. $UOS = UOS - \{UO\}$, $cluster_j = cluster_j \cup \{UO\}$.

5.4 After Step 5.3 has finished, we get $UOS = \varnothing$, which means each user object has been assigned to a cluster, then we get the $clusterSet$ as the initial clustering result.

6.Cluster Merging.

6.1 Set the merge threshold, i.e. $MergeValue = \lambda \times radius$.

6.2 Select the two object cUO_1 and cUO_2 from $cUOS$ that have the largest similarity. If $dist(cUO_1, cUO_2) \geq MergeValue$, which means the two clusters are still not so similar to merge, then Step 6 has finished, turn to Step 7; else merge the two clusters and remove the two center user objects from $cUOS$, i.e. $cluster_3 = cluster_1 \cup cluster_2$, $clusterSet = clusterSet - \{cluster_1, cluster_2\}$,

$cUOS = cUOS - \{cUO_1, cUO_2\}$ .Then execute Step 6.3.

6.3 Select a new centroid for $cluster_3$. Make a random sampling of $cluster_3$ and get the sample set $scluster_3$ with the capacity of $\left[\sqrt{|cluster_3|}\right]$, calculate the average distance between objects in $scluster_3$ and make it the radius of $scluster_3$, named clt_radius, with it we can calculate the objects' density in $scluster_3$, choose the user object with largest density in $scluster_3$ as the approximate optimal center user object, named cUO_3, then cUO_3 is selected as the center user object of $cluster_3$, i.e. $clusterSet = clusterSet \cup \{cluster_3\}$, $cUOS = cUOS \cup \{cUO_3\}$, then return to Step 6.2.

7. Center User Object Adjusting.

7.1 Re-initialize $cUOS$, i.e. $cUOS = \varnothing$.

7.2 Pre-Sampling.

$\forall cluster_i \in clusterSet$, make a random sample of $cluster_i$, the sample set is $scluster_i$ with the capability of $\left[\sqrt{|cluster_i|}\right]$.

7.3 Cluster Radius Calculation.

For each $scluster_i$, calculate the approximated radius for $cluster_i$, i.e.

$$clt\_r_i = \frac{2}{n_i(n_i-1)}\sum_{j=1}^{n_i}\sum_{k=j+1}^{n_i} dist\left(UO_j, UO_k\right),$$

where $UO_j \in scluster_i, UO_k \in scluster_i$ and n_i is the capability of $scluster_i$, i.e. $n_i = |scluster_i| = \left[\sqrt{|cluster_i|}\right]$.

7.4 User Object Density Calculation.

$$\forall UO \in cluster_i, clt\_density(UO) = \sum_{j=1}^{n_i} sign\left(clt\_r_i - dist\left(UO, UO_j\right)\right).$$

7.5 $\forall cluster_i \in clusterSet$, choose the user object from its sample set $scluster_i$ with the maximum density, the user object is set as the final center user object of $cluster_i$, i.e. $cUO_i = UO_0$, $cUOS = cUOS \cup \{UO_0\}$.

8. Output;

The user object cluster set $clusterSet$ and the center user object set $cUOS$.

3.4   Analysis of DBCAPSIC

We adopt "pre-sampling method" in Step 2, Step 6.3 and Step 7.5 to get a linear time complexity (the time complexity is $O\left(\left[\sqrt{n}\right]^2\right) = O(n)$).

We will explain how the inferior-centroid is adopted to solve the problem of Clustering Failure".

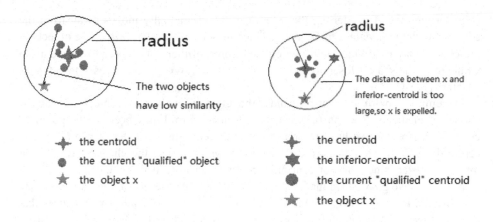

Fig. 1. Clustering without inferior-centroid   **Fig. 2.** Clustering with inferior-centroid

In Fig.1, without the inferior-centroid, when we judge whether the object x has the quality to join the current cluster, we just refer to the distance between x and centroid but ignore the distance between x and other "qualified" objects, thus may causing that the objects belonging the same cluster to have low similarity or no similarity at all.

In Fig.2, we introduce inferior-centroid to assist in judging whether x has the quality to join the current cluster. From Fig. 2 we can discover that although x still falls within the radius of the current centroid, but because the distance between x and the current inferior-centroid is so large that x is expelled from the cluster. Thus the problem of "Clustering Failure" is avoided.

After we have introduced the inferior-centroid to assist in judging, we may get clusters like Fig.3 and Fig.4.

Fig. 3. Cluster with one actual classes   **Fig. 4.** Cluster with two actual classes

In the process of clustering, the distance between the centroid and the inferior-centroid remains a small value (even 0 in extreme situations), then the centroid and the inferior-centroid are objects of great similarity, besides, the inferior-centroid is the farthest object away from the centroid in the cluster, therefore, it can be inferred that all objects in the cluster are very similar to each other. In this case, the cluster contains just one actual class. We denote it as "One-Class-Clusters" (Fig.3).

In the process of clustering, the inferior-centroid gradually moves away from the centroid with the update. Finally the distance may be close to *radius* . The objects in the cluster may be divided into two classes, some of them are closer to the centroid while the others are closer to the inferior-centroid. We denote it as "Two-Class-Cluster" (Fig.4).

In summary, with inferior-centroids, the clusters can have at most two actual classes of elements. We can find that the inferior-centroid may become the potential centroid. Therefore, we have reason to put both centroids and inferior-centroids into centroid set in the step "Centroids Selection", which means the clusters are all split into two clusters since inferior-centroids are regarded as centroids equally.

Now we have guaranteed that elements of different classes are assigned into different clusters. However, every "One-Class-Cluster" is also split into two clusters, that causes objects of the same classes may be also assigned into different classes. Since Clusters split from "One-Class-Clusters" usually have high similarity to each other and Clusters split from "Two-Class-Clusters" have low similarity to each other (The two clusters split from a "Two-Class-Clusters" each contain one class of objects). We then set a threshold λ to merge clusters split from "One-Class-Clusters" (See Step 6). λ should be set relatively high so that clusters split from "One-Class-Clusters" can be merged back into one cluster while clusters split from "Two-Class-Clusters"remain separate. After the clustering made by DBCAPSIC, we finally get clusters that represent each class of user objects.

3.5   Anomaly Detection

Through DBCAPSIC, we can get several user object clusters, each of which contains similar users, and we also get the center user object of each cluster. Because we think the *BPS* of the center user object represent the *BPSs* of user objects in the same cluster, we extract the *BPS* of the center user object from the cluster and use it as the privilege pattern (*PP*) for anomaly detection.

Definition 10 For a class of user objects, the 2-tuple consisting of a database user set and the behaviour pattern set(*BPS*) of the center user object of this class is defined as the privilege pattern (*PP*), i.e. $\forall cluster_i \in clusterSet$, correspondingly we have $cUO_i \in cUOS$, cUO_i is the center user object of $cluster_i$, thus the privilege pattern (*PP*) of $cluster_i$ is $PP_i = \{US_i, BPS_i\}$,where $US_i = \{UO.user \mid UO \in cluster_i\}$ and $BPS_i = cUO_i.BPS$.

We embed DBCAPSIC into anomaly detection. DBCAPSIC is adopted to make cluster analysis of database user objects (*UOs*) and mine out the privilege patterns (PP) for each class of users from the clusters. With these *PPs*, we can determine whether the operations under detection is anomalous or not.

The description of anomaly detection algorithm is shown in Algorithm 2.

Algorithm 2. Anomaly Detection Algorithm

1.Input:
HR ---Normal operational behaviour records collected in a long history period,
R ---Current operational behaviour records for anomaly detection.

2.*UOS* Construction.

  2.1 Initialize the user object set, i.e. $UOS = \varnothing$.

  2.2 Traverse the operational behaviour records in HR .

    2.2.1 As for the *ith* record $HRitem_i$, extract the user account name *user* , the database object *object* , and the behaviour type *type* .

    2.2.2 If $\exists UO \in UOS$, $UO = \{user, BOS\}$, then turn to Step 2.2.3; else generate a new user object, that is $newUO = \{user, newBOS\}$, where $newBOS = \{newBO\}$, $newBO = \{object, type, frequency\}$ and $frequency = 1$.

  Then add $newUO$ to UOS , i.e. $UOS = UOS \cup \{newUO\}$., and turn to Step 2.2.4.

    2.2.3 If $\exists BO \in BOS$, $BO = \{object, type, frequency\}$, then update its *frequency*, i.e. $BO.frequency = BO.frequency + 1$; else generate a new behaviour object, i.e. $newBO = \{object, type, frequency\}$, where $frequency = 1$.

  Then add $newBO$ to BOS , i.e. $BOS = BOS \cup \{newBO\}$, and turn to Step 2.2.4.

    2.2.4 If there still exists some record not traversed, then let $i = i + 1$ and return to step 2.2.1; else the traversal has finished and we get the user object set UOS .

3.*PPS* Construction.

  3.1 Use DBCAPSIC to make cluster analysis to get *clusterSet* and *cUOS* .

  3.2 $\forall cluster_i \in clusterSet$, correspondingly we have $cUO_i \in cUOS$, and cUO_i is the center user object of $cluster_i$ .With $cluster_i$ and cUO_i we can construct the privilege pattern PP_i , thus we get the privilege pattern set *PPS* , i.e.

$PPS = \{PP_1, PP_2, ..., PP_r\}$, where $r = |clusterSet|$.

4.Anomaly Detection.

$\forall Ritem \in R$,extract the account name $user_R$, the database object $object_R$ and the behaviour type $type_R$.

  4.1 If $\exists PP \in PPS$, $user_R \in PP.US$, then we need another judgment: If $\exists BP \in PP.BPS$, $BP = \{object_R, type_R\}$, then *Ritem* is marked as normal; else *Ritem* is marked as anomalous.

  4.2 Else *Ritem* is marked as anomalous.

4　Experiment and Analysis

4.1　Evaluation Setting

To evaluate the performance of anomaly detection, detection rate and false alarm rate are usually adopted as two evaluation indexes.

Let N denote the number of operational behaviour records detected in a period, I denote the total number of anomalous behaviour records among the whole records, C denote the number of behaviour records that are considered anomalous, and M is the number of anomalous behaviour records that are neglected.

Definition 11 The detection rate is defined as

$$\eta = \frac{I - M}{I} \times 100\% .$$

Definition 12 The false alarm rate is defined as

$$\mu = \frac{C + M - I}{N} \times 100\% .$$

From the definition we know that the higher the detection rate is and the lower the false alarm rate is, the more perfect the detection result is.

We target at the database of a simulated business system and collect the operational behaviour records with the database audit system (DAS) developed in our laboratory, The DAS capture the data packets and resolve from the packets the database user account name, the operational behaviour type, the database object, the source IP, the operational time and other useful information, which forms the operational behaviour records and can be used for intrusion detection.

We select 11 main tables as the database objects,that is

$$\left\{ \begin{array}{l} customer, company, discount, product, kind, sales, \\ sales\_item, shopcart, delivery, goodback, warehouse \end{array} \right\} .$$

The operational behaviour types are

$$\{INSERT, DELETE, UPDATE, SELECT, DROP, TRUNCATE\} .$$

The database users has 7 main classes:
Admin, Manager, SalesMan, StoreKeeper, TallyMan, HighCustomer, LowCustomer.
After the collection and process of the normal operations in a period, we comprise a data set with the capacity of 2000000.

The Anomaly Detection is based on the privilege pattern set (*PPS*) extracted from *clusterSet* and *cUOS* output from the DBCAPSIC.

In this paper the anomalous behaviours are divided into 3 types:

(1) An unknown user (illegal user) makes a database operation.

(2) A legal user makes a database operation where the operational behaviour type is within its privilege pattern but the operational object is out of its privilege pattern,

(3) A legal user makes a database operation where the operational object is within its privilege pattern but the behaviour type is out of its privilege pattern.

To validate the anomaly detection algorithm, we need to construct a record set that contains a large proportion of normal records and a small proportion of anomalous records. The record set serves as R in Algorithm 2 and we would like to find whether the anomaly detection algorithm is able to recognize the anomalous records in the set.

The description of the anomalous records construction is shown in Algorithm 3.

Algorithm 3: Anomalous Records Construction Algorithm

1. Input:
PPS --- The privilege pattern set extracted from *clusterSet* and *cUOS* ;
HRSet ---The set of normal operational records collected by the database audit system
    in a period.
2. Initialize the anomalous record set, i.e. $R_{anomalous} = \varnothing$.
3. $\forall HRitem \in HRSet$, extract from *HRitem* the account name *user* , the database object *object* and the operational behaviour type *type*. Traverse *PPS* and find the $PP \in PPS$ that meets *user* $\in PP.US$. Then randomly choose one way from Step 3.1, Step 3.2 and Step 3.3 to make transformation of *HRitem* .

    3.1 Select or construct an account name $user_{anomalous}$ that meets $user_{anomalous} \notin PP.US$, then construct the new behaviour record *Ritem* with $user_{anomalous}$, *object*, and *type*.
    3.2 Select or construct a database object $object_{anomalous,}$ that meets $\neg \exists BO \in PP.BOS, BO = \{object_{anomalous}, type\}$, then construct the new behaviour record *Ritem* with *user*, $object_{anomalous}$, and *type*.
    3.3 Select or construct a behaviour type $type_{anomalous,}$ that meets $\neg \exists BO \in PP.BOS, BO = \{object, type_{anomalous}\}$, then construct the new behaviour record *HRitem* with *user*, *object*, and $type_{anomalous}$.
4. $\forall HRitem \in HRSet$,we have made a transformation according to Step 3.1, Step 3.2 or Step 3.3 and get n anomalous records correspondingly. Add the n anomalous records to $R_{anomalous}$ thus we get the anomalous record set.
5. Output;
The anomalous record set $R_{anomalous}$.

With Algorithm 3, we generate some anomalous records and mix them with many normal records, constructing several record set with the capacity of 1000. We adopt the anomaly detection algorithm (Algorithm 2) to validate whether it can detect the anomaly record correctly.

4.2   Result and Analysis

In DBCAPSIC we set the merge coefficient $\lambda = 0.8$ and 7 clusters are generated by DBCAPSIC. Each cluster has one privilege pattern, 7 privilege patterns mined out from the 7 clusters respectively compromises the privilege pattern set.[1]

We generate some anomalous records based on Algorithm 3 and mix them with normal records, constructing several record sets with the capacity of 1000. We adopt the anomaly detection algorithm to validate whether it can detect the anomaly record correctly.

The result of the anomaly detection is shown in Tab.1.

From Tab.1 we can find that based on the privilege patterns extracted from clusters generated through DBCAPSIC we can detect the anomalous behaviour records effectively. The detection rate reaches 100% but there are still some false alarmed records(that is, some normal behaviour records are mistaken as anomalous ones). This is because we use the center user object's behaviour pattern set as the privilege pattern of the cluster it belongs to; but sometimes the center user object's behaviour patterns cannot cover all normal behaviour patterns of users in the cluster. It is because the center user does not make such operations or the operations has not been captured by the database audit system (the packet loss of the database audit system is not discussed here). Therefore, some normal operations will be mistaken it as anomalous ones.

Table 1. Experimental Result of Anomaly Detection

No.	Capacity	A.R.	D.R.	F.R.	I.R.	η	μ
1	1000	25	30	5	0	100%	0.50%
2	1000	25	26	1	0	100%	0.10%
3	1000	30	32	2	0	100%	0.20%
4	1000	30	30	0	0	100%	0.00%
5	1000	30	33	3	0	100%	0.30%

A.R.---The number of anomalous records.
D.R.---The number of records detected as anomalous ones.
F.R.---The number of records detected falsely as anomalous ones.
I.R.--- The number of anomalous records neglected.

However, if a normal operational behaviour is false alarmed,it can be corrected by human review, whereas if an anomalous behaviour is neglected, it may cause unexpected hazards afterwards, thus the neglected anomalous behaviour is more terrible than the false alarmed normal behaviour. It is plausible to eliminate neglected anomalous records at the expense of a little increase of false alarm rate.

---

[1] We cannot present the mined privilege patterns due to space limit, please refer to http://yunpan.cn/cw9LYX9FnTPLr (with the password :d7f3) for the full version of this paper.

5   Conclusion

Anomaly detection is an important aspect in database security and is attracting more and more attention recently. We adopt cluster analysis techniques in anomaly detection and propose a novel clustering algorithm called DBCAPSIC. With DBCAPSIC, we can mine out the privilege patterns for different classes of users from massive history operational records, and then we can detect the real-time operations made by various types of database users and discover the anomalous operations among them. The simulation experiment shows a relatively good performance of our method. This is of enormous practical value since it enriches methods for the database audit system in anomaly detection and improves the adaptability.of the database audit system under unsupervised conditions to discover intrusion behaviours. More effort is needed in future study to improve the representation of privilege pattern for each cluster so that the false alarm rate can be further reduced.

Acknowledgments. We thanks for the support from Nuclear Takamoto Significant Special and National Development and Reform Commission Information Security Special. We also thanks for the careful reviews and valuable suggestions from the anonymous reviewers.

References

1. Anderson, J.P.: Computer security threat monitoring and surveillance. Technical report, James P. Anderson Company, Fort Washington, Pennsylvania (1980)
2. Lee, W., Stolfo, S.J.: Data mining approaches for intrusion detection. In: Usenix Security (1998)
3. Denning, D.E.: An intrusion-detection model. IEEE Transactions on Software Engineering **2**, 222–232 (1987)
4. Sherif, J.S., Dearmond, T.G.: Intrusion detection: systems and models. In: 2012 IEEE 21st International Workshop on Enabling Technologies: Infrastructure for Collaborative Enterprises, pp. 115–115. IEEE Computer Society (2002)
5. Eskin, E., Miller, M., Zhong, Z.D., et al.: Adaptive model generation for intrusion detection systems (2000)
6. Ashoor, A.S., Gore, S.: Intrusion detection system (IDS): case study. In: Proceedings of 2011 International Conference on Advanced Materials Engineering (ICAME 2011) (2011)
7. Kokane, S., Jadhav, A., Mandhare, N., et al.: Intrusion Detection in RBAC Model
8. Zhang, J., Chen, X.: Research on Intrusion Detection of Database based on Rough Set. Physics Procedia **25**, 1637–1641 (2012)
9. Zhang, Y., Ye, X., Xie, F., et al.: A practical database intrusion detection system framework. In: Ninth IEEE International Conference on Computer and Information Technology, CIT 2009, vol. 1, pp. 342–347. IEEE (2009)
10. Pang-Ning, T., Steinbach, M., Kumar, V.: Introduction to data mining. Library of Congress (2006)
11. Campos, M.M., Milenova, B.L.: Creation and deployment of data mining-based intrusion detection systems in oracle database l0g. In: Proceedings of the Fourth International Conference on Machine Learning and Applications, 2005, p. 8. IEEE (2005)

12. Bloedorn, E., Christiansen, A.D., Hill, W., et al.: Data mining for network intrusion detection: How to get started. MITRE Technical Report (2001)
13. Feng, W., Zhang, Q., Hu, G., et al.: Mining network data for intrusion detection through combining SVMs with ant colony networks. Future Generation Computer Systems **37**, 127–140 (2014)
14. Kim, M.Y., Lee, D.H.: Data-mining based SQL injection attack detection using internal query trees. Expert Systems with Applications **41**(11), 5416–5430 (2014)
15. Pietraszek, T., Tanner, A.: Data mining and machine learning—towards reducing false positives in intrusion detection. Information Security Technical Report **10**(3), 169–183 (2005)
16. Khan, S.S., Ahmad, A.: Cluster center initialization algorithm for K-means clustering. Pattern Recognition Letters **25**(11), 1293–1302 (2004)
17. Mitra, P., Murthy, C.A., Pal, S.K.: Density-based multiscale data condensation. IEEE Transactions on Pattern Analysis and Machine Intelligence **24**(6), 734–747 (2002)
18. Macqueen, J., et al.: Some methods for classification and analysis of multivariate observations. In: Proceedings of the Fifth Berkeley Symposium on Mathematical Statistics and Probability, pp. 281–297 1967: Smith, T.F., Waterman, M.S.: Identification of Common Molecular Subsequences. J. Mol. Biol. **147**, 195–197 (1981)
19. Brossette, S.E., Ahymel, P.: Data mining and infection control. Clinics in Laboratory Medicine **28**(1) (2008)
20. Giudici, P.: Applied Data Mining: Statistical Methods for Business and Industry. Journal of the American Statistical Association **38**(475), 1317–1318 (2006)
21. Luan, J.: Data Mining and Knowledge Management in Higher Education -Potential Applications. Cluster Analysis (2002)
22. Zou, B., Ma, X., Kemme, B., Newton, G., Precup, D.: Data mining using relational database management systems. In: Ng, W.-K., Kitsuregawa, M., Li, J., Chang, K. (eds.) PAKDD 2006. LNCS (LNAI), vol. 3918, pp. 657–667. Springer, Heidelberg (2006)

Secrecy Rate Based User Selection Algorithms for Massive MIMO Wireless Networks

M. Arif Khan[✉] and Rafiqul Islam

School of Computing and Mathematics, Charles Sturt University,
Bathurst, NSW 2678, Australia
{mkhan,mislam}@csu.edu.au

Abstract. In this paper, we investigate user selection algorithms for massive MIMO downlink wireless channel using secrecy rates. Massive MIMO is new disruptive wireless communication technology that exploits the benefits of having large number of antennas at the base station (BS). Given the fact of large antenna dimensions at BS, still the number of devices/users in the system are larger than total antennas. Hence, selection of an optimal set of devices/users for efficient resource allocation is a critical issue. This paper investigates user selection algorithms in massive MIMO downlink/broadcast wireless system. Traditional selection algorithms are generally based on channel strength, channel angle information, algorithm complexity and capacity maximization. In this paper, we investigate selection algorithms based on secrecy rate which is important parameter for secure transmission and compare the performance of this new approach with existing algorithms.

Keywords: Conventional MIMO · Massive MIMO · Secure transmission · User selection · Secrecy rate · Active attack

1 Introduction

Security in any wireless communication is an utmost important issue due to the nature of wireless transmission. At the application layers, security is achieved through encrypting data before transmission. In most of the wireless networks, it is assumed that encrypting data at the application layer inherently incorporates the physical layer security as well. However, such encryption techniques do not consider the challenges and problems at the physical layer implementation. In [1], authors showed that using large number of antennas in a communication system makes it more robust and protective against passive eavesdropping attacks. It is also shown that with massive MIMO and passive eavesdropper, the situation of physical layer security (PLS) changes dramatically. This enhanced security is due to the fact that in conventional MIMO, the two rates of a legitimate device and an eavesdropper are of similar order of magnitude, whereas in massive MIMO these two rates have a considerable difference and hence the secrecy rate becomes an important measure. Massive MIMO also provides an advantage that

© Institute for Computer Sciences, Social Informatics and Telecommunications Engineering 2015
B. Thuraisingham et al. (Eds.): SecureComm 2015, LNICST 164, pp. 697–710, 2015.
DOI: 10.1007/978-3-319-28865-9_46

wireless channels of different devices/users are almost orthogonal to each other that helps the BS to align and beamform transmission signals to intended users more efficiently.

Massive MIMO is one of the major disruptive technologies for next generation 5G wireless networks where huge amount of devices will communicate with each other via internet [17]. Authors of [17] proposed that massive MIMO can be used to multiplex signals from several devices on each time-frequency resource and can be beamformed towards the intended users while minimizing the interference for other devices. It is anticipated that with a large number of devices communicating simultaneously; security, privacy and data integrity will become critical issues in designing future generation wireless networks. Authors of [18], present a new concept of embedded security at the physical layer by realizing that current security solutions fall short in terms of scalability with sheer number of devices connected in 5G systems. Their proposal is to exploit the reciprocity and fading of wireless channel information and to establish a common secret code between sender and transmitter from the channel information measurements. This information will not be accessible / decodable by the eavesdropper.

So the challenging task here is that when there are large number of devices contending for the resource from base stations, how to schedule a proper set of devices such that information to them can be transmitted securely? In massive MIMO system we have large number of antennas at the BS compared to conventional MIMO systems. Therefore, this new system can accommodate a large number of devices simultaneously. However, with the introduction of new wireless paradigms, such as Internet of Things (IoT), where each device is connected to the other device and access point (BS), proper device scheduling within given resources is an important issue. In conventional MIMO, efficient selection and scheduling of devices play a key role in the system throughput [9, 10, 11, 15]. However, in massive MIMO the research area of efficient and secure selection of devices is yet not fully explored. In this paper, we focus our attention to the problem of device selection and secure transmission of the information. We first discuss some already existing device selection algorithms for conventional MIMO that we can extend to massive MIMO systems. Then we propose a new device selection algorithm based on secrecy rate that can make sure that the information can be transmitted securely since it satisfies the condition of secrecy rate. Each device calculates its channel information and sends it back to the base station through an error free and minimum delay feedback channel. The base station calculates the secrecy rate for each device knowing that there is an eavesdropper and also knowing its channel information. BS then selects only those devices having data rates higher than the secrecy rate making sure that signal transmitted for a device is beamformed in its direction and the leakage signal towards eavesdropper is minimum. This algorithm performs reasonably well compared to other existing algorithms.

Rest of the paper is organized as follows. Section 2 describes Multiple Input Multiple Output (MIMO) systems. In this section, we describe both conventional and massive MIMO systems in detail. Section 3 presents system and wireless channel model used in this paper. Section 4 discusses user selection algorithms. In this section, we present both traditional and secrecy rate based user selection algorithms. Section 5 presents simulation results and discussion on the results. Finally, in Section 6 we conclude the paper.

2 Multiple Input Multiple Output (MIMO) Systems

In this section we introduce and discuss multi-user MIMO systems. Although, MIMO technologies are being used in the current wireless networks, its new and advance versions are still being introduced. We will highlight the importance and advantages of MIMO in wireless communication systems. We will also discuss conventional and massive MIMO and present the main differences in the two different yet similar technologies.

2.1 Conventional MIMO

In conventional MIMO systems, range of BS antennas, generally, is assumed between 2 to 8. Such MIMO systems promise high system throughput without increasing the transmit power or using large bandwidth since both are scarce resources. With the emergence of MIMO technology in mid 1990s, there has been a lot of interest in MIMO systems research and now is being used in most of the contemporary wireless communications. In addition to conventional time and frequency dimensions, MIMO leverages the benefits of spatial dimension [8, 9, 10, 11]. A typical conventional multi-user MIMO communication system is shown in Figure 1.

Efficient resource allocation and user selection is one of the important research areas of MIMO wireless systems. With the introduction of various new applications in wireless communication systems, the number of users (devices) has been increased exponentially as well. It became difficult for MIMO systems to serve all of these mobile devices / users simultaneously. Besides this, some users / devices / applications demand different resources than others. This has made user selection problem a trivial problem to solve for MIMO systems. In conventional MIMO, a number of researchers proposed user selection and scheduling algorithms based on various criterion such as channel strength, angle of separation among users, rate supported and complexity [9, 10, 11] few to name. We will further discuss different user selection algorithms in Section 4 of the paper.

2.2 Conventional MIMO Security Model

In conventional MIMO systems, secrecy capacity is defined as the system capacity that promises the integrity and confidentiality of the transmitted data. Most common MIMO security model is known as wiretap channel model where a transmitter sends some legitimate confidential information to one user for which it is intended whereas the other user is an eavesdropper [12]. In this paper, our discussion provides an insight on user (device) selection algorithms based on the

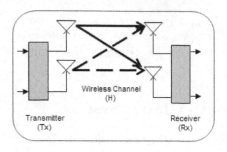 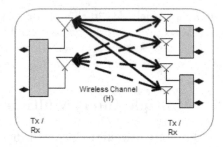

Fig. 1. A typical single user (left) and multi user (right) conventional MIMO wireless communication system.

secrecy rate that guarantees the promised data rate for intended user and makes the rate zero for an eavesdropper. The security model for a received signal, y_k, using MIMO system can be written as follows:

$$y_k = \mathbf{h}_k \mathbf{w}_k (\mathbf{s}_k + \mathbf{a}_k) + \sum_{j=1, j \neq k}^{M} \mathbf{h}_j \mathbf{w}_j (\mathbf{s}_j + \mathbf{a}_j) + n_k, \tag{1}$$

where $\mathbf{a}_k$ represents the attack vector from a non-legitimate user. It is worth noting that secrecy rate in conventional MIMO model is of similar magnitude as that of other rates, making it difficult to select an efficient user subset.

2.3   Massive MIMO

In massive MIMO (or large-scale MIMO) systems, number of antennas at the base station is in the range of hundred or more. This new MIMO paradigm has recently been proposed by *T. L. Marzetta* in his paper cited as [4] and later on many others such as [5, 6]. There has been a lot of interest in massive MIMO from academic and industrial communities. This is due to the reasons that massive MIMO potentially can fulfill the demand of big data services and the high bandwidth requirements in emerging Internet of Things (IoT) technologies. The author in [4] presented a multi-user MIMO system with an infinite number of base station antennas in a multi-cellular environment. We refer such a MIMO system as massive MIMO system here. In [6], authors discussed the potential advantages of massive MIMO system and highlighted that with the availability of large Degrees of Freedom (DoF), hardware-friendly signal shaping can be achieved for the better system performance. With the introduction of many signal streams in massive MIMO systems, security challenges grow as well. The system needs to integrate more efficient and effective encryption before transmitting the data to intended users.

3   System and Transmission Model

In this section, we present system and transmission model. We consider a single cell multiuser massive MIMO downlink (from BS to users) where base station (BS) transmits signals to multiple mobile terminals (MT) simultaneously as shown in Figure 2. These MTs can be either hand held devices or any other mobile device with the wireless communication capability. Let us assume that the BS has M transmit antennas and there are K number of MTs where each MT has a single receive antenna. This system model can easily be extended to MTs with multiple receive antennas, but for the sake of simplicity we assume MTs with a single receive antenna in this paper. Let us consider that the BS transmits a confidential data signal s_k to the kth MT. We can then denote the signal vector to all K MTs by $\mathbf{s}$ which is given as $\mathbf{s} = [s_1, s_2, \cdots, s_K]^T \in C^{(K \times 1)}$ where each signal vector is precoded using a beamforming matrix, $\mathbf{W} = [\mathbf{w}_1, \mathbf{w}_2, \cdots, \mathbf{w}_K] \in C^{(M \times K)}$ before transmission. Let us assume the total transmit power to be P and there is equal transmit power allocated to each MT, denoted by p and defined as $p = P/K$. Then the received signal at k^{th} MT denoted by y_k and at the eavesdropper denoted by $\mathbf{y}_e$ is given by:

$$y_k = \sqrt{p}\mathbf{h}_k\mathbf{w}_k s_k + \sum_{j=1, j \neq k}^{K} \sqrt{p}\mathbf{h}_j\mathbf{w}_j + n_k, \tag{2}$$

and

$$\mathbf{y}_e = \sqrt{p}\mathbf{HWs} + \mathbf{n}_e, \tag{3}$$

where $\mathbf{h}_k \in C^{1 \times M}$ represents the wireless channel vector of the kth MT with its elements being complex Gaussian random variables with zero mean and unit variance. Let us denote the rate of kth MT by R_k and is given as follows:

$$R_k = \log_2 \det \left(\mathbf{I}_M + p\mathbf{w}_k\mathbf{h}_k\mathbf{h}_k^H\mathbf{w}_k^H \right), \tag{4}$$

where $(.)^H$ represents Hermitian operator. Similarly, the capacity of an eavesdropper represented by C_e is given as follows:

$$C_e = \log_2 \det \left(\mathbf{I}_M + p\mathbf{w}_k\mathbf{h}_e\mathbf{h}_e^H\mathbf{w}_k^H \right). \tag{5}$$

Before transmission of the signal, it has to be precoded at the BS in order to minimize the interference for other users and also preventing for an eavesdropper. In conventional MIMO systems, typically Zero Forcing (ZF) and Minimum Mean Square Error (MMSE) based precoding schemes are used. However, due to huge computational complexity of these schemes for large dimensional arrays, typically of complexity order as $O(L^3)$ where L is the array size [13], we adopt the precoding approaches of simple ZF and conjugate beamforming (CB) as discussed in [19]. Therefore, the precoding vector for each user using ZF beamforming can be calculated as $\mathbf{w}_k = \mathbf{h}_k^H/\|\mathbf{h}_k\|$.

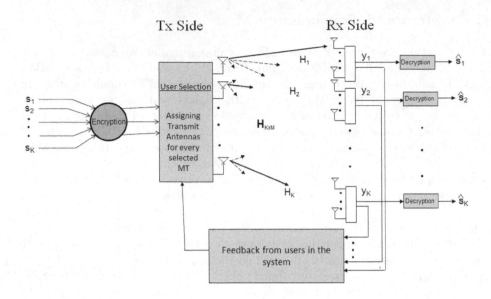

Fig. 2. Massive MIMO downlink / broadcast system used in this paper.

3.1 Feedback Model

In MIMO broadcast system, BS selects a set of devices based on certain information that it receives from devices. In most of the cases, this information is relevant to the wireless channel condition of the device. BS transmits a pilot signal for all active MTs in its vicinity. All MTs receive this pilot signal and send the information back to the BS via an error free low time delay feedback channel. It is assumed in the system model that this feedback has no error and eavesdropper or adversary user cannot tamper this information. However, this assumption may not be very realistic since active eavesdroppers can access this information and then can modify it to benefit the wireless transmission in their own favor. However, for the sake of simplicity, we assume that this feedback is error free and attackers cannot access this information. BS then uses this feedback in the selection process. We refer this channel information as the Channel State Information at Transmitter (CSIT) in the remaining paper. The feedback path is shown in Figure 2.

4 User Selection Algorithms

Although in massive MIMO systems, number of antennas at the BS are very large, we still consider that total number of users in the system are larger than total number of antennas at the BS. Therefore, BS needs to select a subset of users from all active users for transmission. Let us assume that the BS selects a subset S of users from K total active users such that $S \geq K$. BS then precodes the signals of these selected users before transmission by using the precoding matrix $\mathbf{W}$. There are a large number of user selection schemes available in conventional MIMO systems that can be used in massive MIMO systems as well. However, in this paper we discuss only three existing schemes. Our contributions in this paper are to extend these techniques from conventional MIMO to massive MIMO while considering the secure transmission in the selection process. Also we present a new user selection technique that is based on secrecy rate and we compare its performance with other existing schemes. In particular, user selection schemes that we present in this paper are: (i) Exhaustive Search (ES), (ii) Frobenius Norm based Selection (FNS), (iii) Round Robin Selection (RRS), and (iv) Secrecy Rate based Selection (SRS). The user selection techniques generally introduce extra computational complexity in the system, but on the other hand they also maximize the system performance which is essential for securing the data transmission at physical layer. Among all user selection techniques, ES is the best and optimal selection technique as discussed in Section 4.1. ES guarantees the maximum achievable system throughput, however, it also has very high search complexity. Also its search domain increases exponentially with the increase of users in the system. Therefore in practical systems, where number of users is generally very large, ES cannot be implemented. For example, in our system model we are required to select S users out of total K users with M number of antennas at the BS in such a way that for each user the secrecy rate condition is satisfied. Then the search domain for BS using ES selection technique becomes as follows:

$$D_S = \binom{K}{S} = \frac{K!}{S! \times (K - S)!} \tag{6}$$

Example: Let us consider that we have a conventional MIMO system where BS performs the user selection. We are interested to calculate the search complexity in this system for the BS. Let us assume that there are $K = 50$ active devices in the system and the BS has $M = 10$ antennas so that is why it can possibly select $S = 10$ maximum devices for transmission simultaneously. This is a common scenario in most of the current wireless communication systems. Then the search domain for this selection process using ES with Equation (6) will become as 1.0272×10^{10} combinations which is very large considering the real time communication scenario. Therefore, it is important that we find such selection schemes that have low complexity for practical considerations, yet provide an acceptable system performance. In the following we discuss each device/user selection scheme.

4.1 Exhaustive Selection (ES)

In general Exhaustive Selection (ES) process computes all possible combinations therefore it has the largest search space; as a result its complexity grows exponentially with the linear increase in dimensions. ES in particular is not suitable for massive MIMO systems with large number of devices in the system. But on

Table 1. FNS based selection algorithm

Initialization: $S = \emptyset$, BS transmits pilot signal.
Step 1: Let $\mathbf{H} \in C^{K \times M}$ be the channel matrix of all
active MTs and is defined as $\mathbf{H} = [\mathbf{h}_1, \mathbf{h}_2, \cdots, \mathbf{h}_K]$ where
$\mathbf{h}_k \in C^{1 \times M}$ is the channel vector of the kth MT
and $k = 1, 2, \cdots, K$.
Step 2: Compute $||\mathbf{h}||_F^2$ using Equation (7) for each MT.
Step 3: Each MT sends its $||\mathbf{h}||_F^2$ value as a scalar feedback
to the BS using error free feedback channel as shown in Figure 2.
Step 4: BS orders all received $||\mathbf{h}||_F^2$ such that
$$\left\|\overline{\mathbf{h}}_1\right\|_F^2 > \left\|\overline{\mathbf{h}}_2\right\|_F^2 > \cdots, \left\|\overline{\mathbf{h}}_K\right\|_F^2$$
where $\overline{\mathbf{h}}_k = \left\|\overline{\mathbf{h}}_K\right\|_F^2$ represents the ordered values.
Step 5: Construct at the BS: $\overline{\mathbf{H}} = [\overline{\mathbf{h}}_1, \overline{\mathbf{h}}_2, \cdots, \overline{\mathbf{h}}_K]$.
Step 6: Select S MTs from $\overline{\mathbf{H}}$ such that $S = \{m_1, m_2, \cdots, m_S\}$
is the set of MTs for transmission.
Step 7: Calculate the precoding matrix for S selected MTs
such that $\overline{\mathbf{W}} = [\overline{\mathbf{w}}_1, \overline{\mathbf{w}}_2, \cdots, \overline{\mathbf{w}}_S]$ where $\overline{\mathbf{w}}_k = \frac{\overline{\mathbf{h}}_k^H}{\|\overline{\mathbf{h}}_k\|}$.
Step 8: Calculate the rates of transmission for S MTs
using Equation (4).
Step 9: Terminate the algorithm.

---

the other hand it is an optimal selection scheme in the context of maximizing the system throughput. In this paper, we use ES only to benchmark the other schemes since this is the maximum throughput that can be achieved in a multi user / device MIMO communication system.

4.2 Frobenius Norm Based Selection (FNS)

In Frobenius Norm based Selection (FNS), each MT on receiving the pilot signal from BS, calculates the squared Frobenius norm of its wireless channel $\mathbf{h}$ with dimensions $1 \times M$ as follows [14]:

$$||\mathbf{h}||_F^2 = (\mathbf{h}^H \mathbf{h}). \tag{7}$$

Different variants of FNS algorithm are available in MIMO literature such as [9, 10, 15] few to mention here. FNS is attractive in practical implementations since it requires only scalar feedback to be transmitted back to the base station. In a large device regime, such as IoT, this algorithm can be a favorable choice. The complete FNS algorithm implemented at BS is given in Table 1.

4.3 Round Robin Selection (RRS)

Round Robin Selection (RRS) is the simplest and the fairest selection technique which does not require CSIT. In this technique a subset or group of MTs is selected with equal probability. In a single MT case, required transmit/ receive antennas are selected from total antennas randomly and the channel capacity is based on these selected antennas. In multi MTs, however, the subset of required MTs is selected randomly. The sum capacity of the system is based on these selected devices. The selection probability is kept uniform, so as to eliminate the fairness problem completely. The performance of this approach is very poor and it only sets the lower limit for performance. It has least computational complexity and also does not cause fairness problem but on the other hand results in the lowest sum capacity.

4.4   Secrecy Rate Based Selection (SRS)

In this selection algorithm, we make sure that a user / device receives guaranteed rate for transmission. In this proposed scheme, the BS selects a subset of devices in such a way that the secrecy rates of the selected MTs are greater than zero. A similar user selection algorithm for conventional MIMO downlink system is presented in [16]. Our proposed algorithm is different from the algorithm presented in [16] that it is for massive MIMO downlink systems and it is based on the selection process given in the following criteria [7].

$$R_k^{sec} = [R_k - C_e]^+ \tag{8}$$

where $[x]^+ = max\{0, x\}$, R_k and C_e are rates of kth MT and capacity of the eavesdropper respectively. In case, if BS does not find any user greater than the

Table 2. SRS based selection algorithm

Initialization: $S = \emptyset$, BS transmits pilot signal and
it knows the channel information of eavesdropper i.e. $\mathbf{H}_e$.
Step 1: Let $\mathbf{H} \in C^{K \times M}$ be the channel matrix of all
active MTs and is defined as $\mathbf{H} = [\mathbf{h}_1, \mathbf{h}_2, \cdots, \mathbf{h}_K]$ where
$\mathbf{h}_k \in C^{1 \times M}$ is the channel vector of the kth MT
and $k = 1, 2, \cdots, K$.
Step 2: Each MT measures its wireless channel $\mathbf{h}_k \in C^{1 \times M}$
and sends this information back to the base station.
Step 3: BS calculates the secrecy rate R_k^{sec} using
Equations (4, 5, 8).
Step 4: BS orders all secrecy rates R_k^{sec} such that
$\overline{R}_1^{sec} > \overline{R}_2^{sec} > \cdots, \overline{R}_K^{sec}$
where $\overline{R}_k^{sec}$ represents the ordered value of secrecy rate.
Step 5: Construct at the BS: $\overline{\mathbf{R}} = [\overline{R}_1^{sec}, \overline{R}_2^{sec}, \cdots, \overline{R}_K^{sec}]$.
Step 6: Select S MTs from $\overline{\mathbf{R}}$ such that $S = \{m_1, m_2, \cdots, m_S\}$
is the set of MTs for transmission.
Step 7: Calculate the precoding matrix for S selected MTs
such that $\overline{\mathbf{W}} = [\overline{\mathbf{w}}_1, \overline{\mathbf{w}}_2, \cdots, \overline{\mathbf{w}}_S]$ where $\overline{\mathbf{w}}_k = \frac{\overline{\mathbf{h}}_k^H}{\|\overline{\mathbf{h}}_k\|}$.
Step 8: Transmit S MTs with the calculated secrecy rates.
Step 9: Terminate the algorithm.

---

secrecy rate, it does not transmit any user during that particular time slot. The complete SRS algorithm implemented at the BS is given in Table 2.

5   Numerical Results and Discussions

In this section we present some numerical results and prepare discussion on these results. First experiment is based on the total system capacity where we compare the sum-capacity lower bound results of massive MIMO with conjugate beamforming and zero forcing precoding as described in [19]. This sets the benchmarks for other results. Figures 3 and 4 show these results. The system is operating at -6.0 dB SINR and number of users are varied as $K = [16, 32, 64, 128]$. It is interesting to note that both results have different operational insight for the system. Figure 3 shows expected growth in system capacity along with base station antennas and number of users in the system. However, in Figure 4 with ZF precoding the system performance does not increase as that of with CB precoding and it shows a number of interesting crossing points as for as system operation is concerned. For example, for considerable large number of base station antennas, system performance still remains below 0 bits/sec/Hz which suggests that ZF precoding is not optimal under such conditions. It is also interesting to note that ZF with large number of users and base station antennas does not perform well compared to less number of users and base station antennas, for example, see the

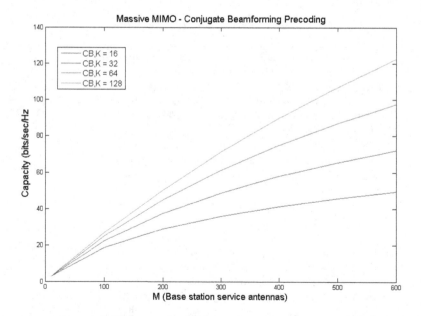

Fig. 3. Total capacity versus number of base station antennas for massive MIMO downlink with CB precoding.

curve with $K = 128$ users. One of the reasons for this poor performance could be that since ZF requires channel matrix inversion for nulling the interference, with large number of users and base station antennas this channel inversion may have some error and hence does not reduce the interference properly.

In figure 5, we show the sum rate per user with different user selection algorithms. The figure shows results of four different user selection algorithms. Black curve shows the sum rate when base station has perfect channel state information and we call this as perfect CSIT. This is the maximum data rate that base station can transmit theoretically since achieving perfect CSIT in practical systems is not feasible. The red curve shows Round Robin (RR) user selection algorithm when base station randomly selects M number of users and transmits them. In all the simulations we have $K = 100$ and $M = 50$. This result clearly shows inferior performance compared to other algorithms which shows that we need to apply some type of selection algorithm at the base station. However, one interesting feature of RR algorithm is that it is very simple to implement at the base station and does not require high computing resources. So in scenarios, where performance of the system does not matter very much, RR will be the algorithm of choice. Green curve in the figure shows Frobenius norm (FNS) user selection. In this algorithm as mentioned previously, base station calculates the Frobenius norm of all users and then selects M best users for transmission based on its channel norm. In blue curve, we show the result of eavesdropper capacity.

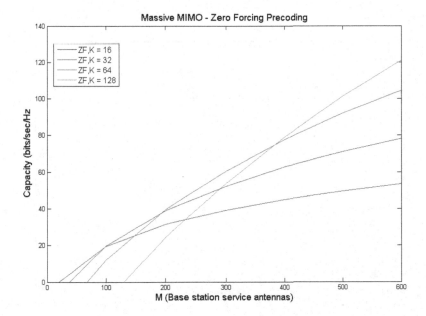

Fig. 4. Total capacity versus number of base station antennas for massive MIMO downlink with ZF precoding.

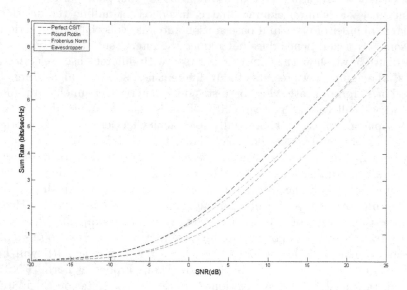

Fig. 5. Sum rate per user versus signal to noise ratio (SNR) with different user selection algorithms.

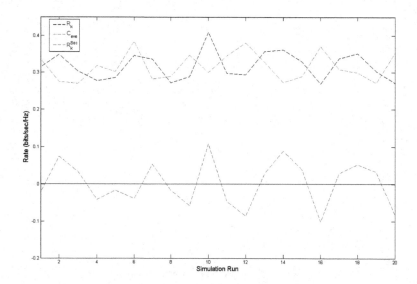

Fig. 6. Secrecy rate of a real user and eavesdropper comparison showing when user should be selected for transmission.

We assume that eavesdropper has perfect channel knowledge and it can achieve maximum capacity of single user equivalent. It is interesting to note that sum rates of FNS and eavesdropper cross each other at high SNR regime. In the proposed scheme if base station selects a user with its sum rate greater than eavesdropper rate then it is not possible for the eavesdropper to decode that users data.

Figure 6 shows an interesting implication that when a user must be selected for transmission securely. It shows the rate comparison of a single user with the rate of an eavesdropper and also shows the times when a real user is safe for selection without the ability of eavesdropper to decode its data. When the channel rate of a real user is higher than the data rate of eavesdropper, then it should be selected for transmission as shown in Equation (8). This result shows the evidence that it is not feasible for a user to be selected every time even though its channel may support a good data rate.

6 Conclusion

In this paper, we discussed the problem of user / device selection based on secrecy rate in massive MIMO downlink system. This is particular interesting for future 5G based systems where large number of users / devices are expected to share the available resources. Security, privacy and data integrity in such situations become even more important than in the systems today. Our results show that if a user / device is selected based on its secrecy rate, it has high probability of secure transmission. We have also shown the comparison of two precoding schemes for multi-user downlink scenarios. It is interesting to note that a user / device may not be suitable to transmit to every time if its data rate is less than the data rate of an eavesdropper. In future, we will extend these results with other layers and applications in the context of future wireless communication systems. Also we are interested in exploring the embedded security concept in future wireless networks.

References

1. Kapetanovic, D., Zheng, G., Rusek, F.: Physical Layer Security for Massive MIMO: An Overview on Passive Eavesdropping and Active Attacks (2015). http://arxiv.org/abs/org/pdf/1504.07154v1.pdf
2. Dean, T.R., Goldsmith, A.: Physical-Layer Cryptography through Massive MIMO (2013). http://arxiv.org/abs/org/abs/1310.1861
3. Mukherjee, A., Fakoorian, S.A.A., Huang, J., Swindlehurst, A.L.: Principles of Physical Layer Security in Multiuser Wireless Networks: A Survey (2014). http://arxiv.org/pdf/1011.3754v3.pdf
4. Marzetta, T.L.: Noncooperative Cellular Wireless with Unlimited Number of BS Antennas. IEEE Transaction on Wireless Communications 9(11), 3590–3600 (2010)
5. Rusek, F., Persson, D., Lau, B.K., Larsson, E.G., Marzetta, T.L., Edfors, O., Tufvesson, F.: Scaling Up MIMO: Opportunities and Challenges with Very Large Arrays. IEEE Signal Processing Magazine 30(1), 40–46 (2013)

6. Larsson, E.G., Edfors, O., Tufvesson, F., Marzetta, T.L.: Massive MIMO for Next Generation Wireless Systems. IEEE Communication Magazine **52**(2), 186–195 (2014)
7. Zhu, J., Schober, R., Bhargava, V.K.: Secure Transmission in Multi-Cell Massive MIMO Systems. IEEE Transaction on Wireless Communications **13**(9), 4766–4781 (2014)
8. Biglieri, B., Calderbank, R., Constantinides, A., Goldsmith, A., Paulraj, A., Poor, H.V.: MIMO Wireless Communications. Cambridge University Press (2007)
9. Tu, Z., Blum, R.S.: Multiuser Diversity for a Dirty Paper Approach. IEEE Communication Letters **7**(8), 370–372 (2003)
10. Yoo, T., Goldsmith, A.: On the Optimality of Multi-antenna Broadcast Scheduling using Zero-Forcing Beamforming. IEEE Journal on Selected Areas in Communications **24**(3), 528–541 (2006)
11. Dimic, G., Sidiropoulos, N.D.: On Downlink Beamforming with Greedy User Selection: Performance Analysis and a Simple New Algorithm. IEEE Transactions on Signal Processing **53**(10), 3857–3868 (2005)
12. Oggier, F., Hassibi, B.: The Secrecy Capacity of the MIMO Wiretap Channel. IEEE Transactions on Information Theory **57**(8), 4961–4972 (2011)
13. Roy, S.: Two-Layer Linear Processing for Massive MIMO on the TitanMIMO Platform. Nutaq white paper on MIMO Platform (2015). http://nutaq.com/en/library/whitepaper-news/new-paper-two-layer-linear-processing-massive-mimo-titanmimo-platform
14. Paulraj, A., Nabar, R., Gore, D.: Introduction to Space-Time Wireless Communications. Cambridge University Press (2008)
15. Khan, M.A., Vesilo, R., Collings, I.B.: Efficient user selection algorithms for wireless broadcast channels. In: The 2nd International Conference on Wireless Broadband and Ultra Wideband Communications (2007)
16. Yanase, M., Ohtsuki, T.: User Selection Scheme with Secrecy Capacity in MIMO Downlink Systems. Procedia Social and Behavioral Sciences **2**, 161–170 (2010)
17. Boccardi, F., Heath Jr., R.W., Lozano, A., Marzetta, T.L., Popovski, P.: Five Disruptive Technology Directions for 5G. IEEE Communication Magazine, 74–80, February 2014
18. Wunder, G., Boche, H., Strohmer, T., Jung, P.: Sparse Signal Processing Concepts for Efficient 5G System Design. IEEE Access **3**, 195–208 (2015)
19. Marzetta, T.L.: Massive MIMO: An introduction. Bell Labs Technical Journal **20**, 11–22 (2015)
20. Hong, Y.-W.P., Pang-Chang, L., Kuo, C.-C.J.: Enhancing Physical Layer Secrecy in Multiantenna Wireless Systems: An Overview of Signal Processing Approaches. IEEE Signal Processing Magazine **30**(5), 29–40 (2013)

Human Surveillance System for Security Application

Mozammel Chowdhury$^{(\boxtimes)}$, Junbin Gao, and Rafiqul Islam

School of Computing & Mathematics, Charles Sturt University, Bathurst, Australia
{mochowdhury,jbgao,mislam}@csu.edu.au

Abstract. Human surveillance is an important research activity for security concern. Due to the increasing demand of security in different domains, development of smart and efficient surveillance system has attracted immense interest in recent years. Most of the existing surveillance systems are based on monocular camera and limited by their fixed view angles and hence cannot provide sufficient three-dimensional depth information for person recognition and tracking. This paper proposes an efficient and cost-effective human surveillance system using stereo vision technique. The system uses a multi-view stereo camera pair for image capturing and analyzes the stereoscopic pictures to estimate the 3D depth information for accurate detection and tracking of the human objects. The system can provide automatic warning in case of unrecognized people and entrance in the restricted zones. Experimental results are arranged to demonstrate the robustness and efficiency of our proposed system. Our system is very inexpensive and computationally fast comparable to the existing state-of-the-art surveillance systems.

Keywords: Security · Surveillance system · Access control · Stereo vision · 3D depth information · Person detection and tracking

1 Introduction

Human surveillance is attracting more importance nowadays due to the increasing demand of security and defense in different environments including door access control, border surveillance, immigration control, monitoring employee activities, identifying suspicious people, theft and vandalism deterrence, preventing criminal acts and so on [1, 2].

Several techniques have been developed in last decades for automatic surveillance of people using CCTV cameras and sensors. According to the number of cameras used in these techniques, surveillance systems can be classified into two categories: monocular and multi-camera based system. Most of the conventional surveillance systems widely used for security applications in supermarkets, airports, stations, ATM booths and other public places, employ monocular or single camera [3-7]. They are limited by their fixed view angles, fixed resolutions and limited depth information. These limitations make it complex to estimate and recover the precise 3D information as well as motion behavior of human objects for accurate and robust tracking.

© Institute for Computer Sciences, Social Informatics and Telecommunications Engineering 2015
B. Thuraisingham et al. (Eds.): SecureComm 2015, LNICST 164, pp. 711–724, 2015.
DOI: 10.1007/978-3-319-28865-9_47

Due to the recent advancement in vision technology, multiple camera based surveillance systems have attained the superiority for tracking people with different view angles [8-10]. These systems are capable of viewing an object from multi-viewpoints and hence can deal better with occlusions. However, such systems are very expensive and difficult to set up due to the problems of establishing their geometric relationships or synchronizations since they require a large number of cameras [11].

In recent years, researchers have proposed stereo vision based surveillance systems for security applications [12-14]. Stereo vision has the advantage to estimate the 3D position of an object in a given coordinate system from two stereoscopic images [15]. Stereo vision based surveillance systems can easily segment an image into objects to distinguish people from their shadows and provide more accurate location information for their tracking. Most of these systems generally employ a static pan-tilt-zoom (PTZ) camera, whose pose can be fully controlled by pan, tilt and zoom parameters. The PTZ cameras are able to obtain multi-angle views and multi-resolution information However, the main disadvantage of these cameras is that they are unidirectional and their image resolution is poor [16, 20]. The existing stereo based surveillance systems are computationally expensive and hence they are not suitable for real time applications.

To overcome the aforesaid challenges in surveillance systems, we propose an efficient, computationally fast and cost-effective surveillance model for security applications. The system employs a low-cost stereo camera pair for image capturing and recovers the 3D depth information of the human object exploiting a fast stereo vision algorithm. The proposed system includes robust and efficient algorithms for human face identification, stereo correspondence matching, 3D depth extraction, and location estimation of the human objects for security monitoring.

The rest of the paper is structured as follows. Section 2 provides a brief discussion on most related works in this area. In Section 3, we present the architecture of our proposed surveillance system. Experimental results with real time image sequences are reported in Section 4. Finally, Section 5 concludes the paper and gives directions for future work.

2   Related Works

In the last few decades, lots of related research works have been performed by the researchers to develop smart and efficient human surveillance systems. In this section we attempt to review some of them which are more relevant.

Chen et al. [16] propose a vision system based on an omnidirectional camera and a PTZ camera. The omnidirectional camera monitors the surveillance object and the PTZ camera captures the image of the target object. These two cameras work in a master-salve mode. This surveillance system is employed mostly in indoor environment. Adorni et al. [17] propose a binocular vision system using two omnidirectional cameras which is generally used in robot vision. The system is capable of enlarging view fields. The main disadvantage of these vision systems is that the image resolution of the omnidirectional camera is poor. This drawback has great limitation towards their application in real time.

Munoz-Salinas *et al.* [18] propose an object tracking method which can combine color and depth information using dual static cameras. In another work [19], they use plan-view maps to represent stereo information more efficiently. The main drawbacks associated with these systems are that they cannot obtain multi-resolution and multi-visual-angle information.

Bimbo *et al.* [20] propose a novel framework exploiting two PTZ cameras aiming to relate the feet position of a person in the image of the master camera with the head position in the image of the slave camera. Benjamin *et al.* [21] present a multi camera based surveillance system that can automatically extract useful information from a given scene. It also alerts the user if the tracked object breaks certain defined regulations. Wang [22] illustrates an overview of the recent advances in the field of multi camera video surveillance. It compares the existing solutions and also describes the prevalent technical challenges.

Darrell *et al.* [23] propose a system for tracking people using stereo cameras. The stereo method is used to isolate people from other objects and background. They integrated color and face detection modules in the system. Bahadori and Iocchi [24] propose a semi-automatic surveillance system for museum environment using stereo vision. The system can detect the situations for providing warning messages to the surveillance personnel.

Manap *et al.* [25] propose a system for smart surveillance using stereo imaging. The system uses two smart IP cameras to obtain the position and location of objects. The position and location of the object are automatically extracted from two IP cameras and subsequently transmitted to an ACTi Pan-Tilt-Zoom (PTZ) camera, which then points and zooms to the exact position in space. This work involves video analytics for estimating the location of the object in a 3D environment and transmitting its positional coordinates to the PTZ camera.

Cui and Li [26] propose a surveillance system mainly used for indoor scene monitoring using binocular vision. The system uses two PTZ cameras and employs a rectification-disparity-based method to establish correspondence between two image sequences. The system utilizes depth information to deal with occlusion problem in object tracking.

However, these existing surveillance systems are commercially expensive and require high computation time. With a view to overcome the limitations of the existing systems, we attempt to propose an effective and inexpensive surveillance model using a fast stereo vision technique. The proposed system can measure the precise 3D position of the human object for accurate detection and tracking.

3   Proposed System Architecture

The proposed human surveillance system consists of the following components: (i) Pre-processing for image refinement, (ii) Face detection for person identification, (iii) Stereo correspondence matching for finding disparities in the image sequences,

(iv) Dense depth estimation for recovering the 3D position of the human object, and (v) Person tracking or localization. Fig.1 shows the general architecture of the proposed system.

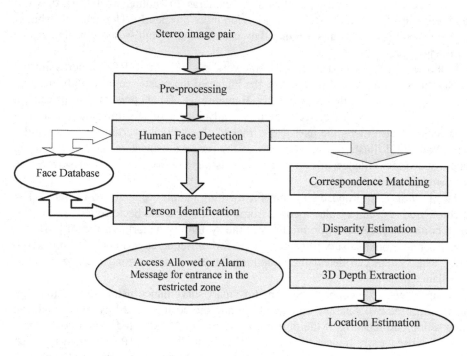

Fig. 1. Architecture of the proposed surveillance system.

3.1   Preprocessing of the Stereo Images

In real time stereo vision systems, there may be significant amount of noise in the captured image pair due to the differences in camera orientation and lighting condition. For this reason, we employ a fuzzy median filtering technique [27] for refining the stereoscopic images corrupted by noise. This filter employs fuzzy rules for deciding the gray level of the pixels within a window in the image. This is a variation of the Median filter and neighbourhood Averaging filter with fuzzy values.

3.2   Face Detection

Human face plays an important role in person recognition in vision-based surveillance system. Face detection is concerned with determining the part of an image which contains face. Different techniques [28-32] have been developed for face detection in last decades, which includes: geometric modeling, genetic approach, neural network, principal component analysis, color analysis and so on.

This paper proposes a fast and robust face detection technique based on skin color segmentation. For detecting the face area, the image is first enhanced using histogram equalization because, the face images may be of very poor contrast because of the limitation of lighting conditions. Then the face skeleton is detected from the largest connected area of the skin color segmented image. The method considers the frontal view of the face in color scale image. The overview of the proposed color histogram based face detection method is shown in Fig. 2.

The efficiency of color segmentation of a human face depends on the color space. While the input colour image is typically in RGB format, the RGB model is not used in the detection process because the RGB colour model is not a reliable model for detecting skin colour [29]. The RGB components are subject to luminance change and hence face detection may fail if the lighting condition changes from image to image. Consequently, we use HSV color model for fast and effective detection process.

Fig. 2. Block diagram of the face detection method.

In the HSV color model a color is described by three attributes Hue, Saturation and Value. Hue is the attribute of visual sensation that corresponds to color perception associated with the dominant colors, saturation implies the relative purity of the color content and value measures the brightness of a color. The HSV space classifies similar colors under similar hue orientations. The image content is converted from RGB to HSV color space using the following equations:

$$H = \cos^{-1}\left\{\frac{\frac{1}{2}[(R-G)+(R-B)]}{\sqrt{(R-G)^2+(R-B)(G-B)}}\right\} \tag{1}$$

Ranging $[0,2\pi]$, where $H = H_1$ if $B \leq G$; otherwise $H = 360° - H_1$;

$$S = \frac{\max(R,G,B) - \min(R,G,B)}{\max(R,G,B)} \tag{2}$$

$$V = \frac{\max(R,G,B)}{255} \tag{3}$$

Where R, G, B are the red, green and blue component values which exist in the range $[0,255]$.

Let a color image $I(x, y)$ consists of three color channels $I = (I_R, I_G, I_B)$, at (x, y) of size $M \times N$. First a hue histogram $H(i)$ is obtained by counting the number of pixels, given by the following equation:

$$H(i) = \frac{n(H(I_R, I_G, I_B) = i)}{M \times N} \tag{4}$$

Where n indicates the number of pixels with a hue value $H(I_R, I_G, I_B) = i$ and $M \times N$ is the total number of image locations. Fig. 3 shows a typical color image and its corresponding hue histogram.

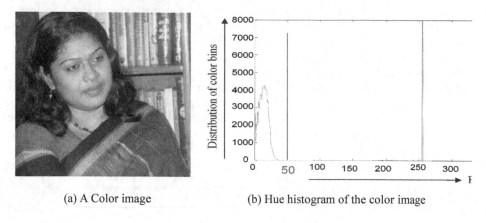

(a) A Color image   (b) Hue histogram of the color image

Fig. 3. Hue histogram of a typical color image.

3.3   Stereo Correspondence Matching

Stereo matching algorithms are used for correspondence matching of points or blocks between two image sequences to estimate the accurate depth and location of the human object. In stereo vision, two images of the same scene are taken from slightly different viewpoints using two cameras: left and right camera of same focal length and parameters, which are placed in the same lateral plane. Fig. 4 shows the process of capturing an object by two stereo cameras placed in different viewpoints separated by small distance.

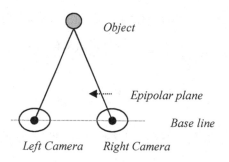

Fig. 4. Stereo vision process: an object is captured by two horizontally aligned cameras.

The main task in stereo vision is finding correspondence matching to estimate the dense disparity. In stereo imaging, for most pixels in the left image there is a corresponding pixel in the right image in the same horizontal line. The difference in the coordinates of the corresponding pixels is known as disparity, which can be expressed by the following equation:

$$d = x_L - x_R \tag{5}$$

Stereo algorithms are mainly classified into two categories: local and global methods [33]. The local algorithms [33-36], also referred to as window-based or area-based algorithms are typically faster and suitable for real time applications rather than global approaches [37- 40]. However, they have less accuracy compared to global methods. The local or window-based stereo algorithms traditionally estimate dense disparity by means of pixel correspondence matching through window cost computation using any one of the following statistical measures: sum of absolute differences (SAD), sum of square differences (SSD), or normalized cross correlation (NCC) [15, 34]. To determine the correspondence of a reference pixel in the left image, the window costs are calculated for all target pixels on the same epipolar line in the right image within a search range. The pixel in the right image that gives the best window cost i.e., the minimum SAD/SSD value or the maximum NCC value indicates the corresponding pixel of the reference pixel in the left image.

In this work, we consider the detected face area in the left image as a reference block and match with another target face block in the right image. The window cost $W_C(x, y, d)$ of a reference pixel at position (x, y) in the left image block with disparity d is computed with the following SAD measure, employing a window centered at position (x, y) in the left image block and another window centered at position $(x+d, y)$ in the corresponding right image block.

$$W_c^{SAD}(x, y, d) = \sum_{i=-m}^{m} \sum_{j=-n}^{n} \left| f_L(x+i, y+j) - f_R(x+i+d, y+j) \right| \tag{6}$$

Where $f_L(x, y)$ and $f_R(x, y)$ are the intensities of the pixels at position (x, y) in the left and right image blocks, respectively. $(2m+1)$ and $(2n+1)$ are the width and height of the rectangular window, respectively.

In this paper, we propose a fast algorithm based on local approach to compute the window costs for correspondence matching. To determine the correspondence of a pixel in the left image block, we just compute the window cost for candidate pixels in the right image block whose intensities are different within a certain threshold value (δ). To achieve a substantial gain in accuracy with less expense of computation time, our algorithm perform correspondence matching only on the diagonal pixels of the square windows rather than employing conventional matching upon all pixels in the windows. Empirically we find that this diagonal matching operation reduces significant computation time compared to the state-of-the-art stereo methods, which is a fruitful contribution towards the development of a fast and effective surveillance system.

The proposed fast correspondence matching or disparity estimation algorithm is depicted as follows:

Algorithm Proposed Stereo matching

---

1. For each candidate pixel (x,y) in the left image, search the corresponding pixel on same epipolar line in the right image within a search range employing a square diagonal window:

$$\text{for } d' = -d_{max} \text{ to } +d_{max} \text{ do}$$

$$\text{if } |f_L(x,y) - f_R(x+d',y)| < \text{threshold}(\delta) \text{ then}$$

$$\text{Calculate } W_C(x,y,d')$$

2. Find d such that, $d = \arg\min W_C(x,y,d')$
3. Repeat steps 1 and 2 to calculate disparities of all pixels in the left image.

3.4 Depth Extraction and Location Estimation

In stereo vision, the depth or 3D information of points in the images can be calculated from the estimated disparity map and the geometry of the camera settings. This process is illustrated in Fig. 5 where, L and R are two pinhole cameras with parallel optical axes; O_L and O_R are two center points of the left and right camera respectively with same focal length f. The baseline, which is the line connecting the two lens centers of the cameras is perpendicular to the optical axes. Let b is the baseline distance and x_L is the x-coordinate of the projected 3D point onto the left camera image plane and x_R is the x-coordinate of the projection onto the right image plane.

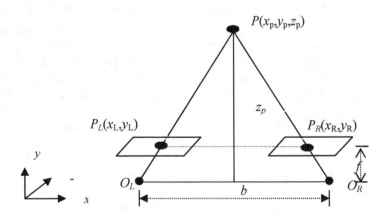

Fig. 5. Dense depth estimation in stereo image pair using triangulation

For a world 3D point $P(x_p, y_p, z_p)$, we can extract the dense depth information from the camera geometry as follows:

$$\frac{z_p}{b} = \frac{z_p - f}{b - (x_L - x_R)} \tag{7}$$

Thus the depth,

$$z_p = \frac{bf}{x_L - x_R} = \frac{bf}{d} \tag{8}$$

This is the distance of the target object from the stereo camera positions.

We can recover the 3D point P from its projections P_L and P_R. Therefore, we have:

$$x_p = \frac{bx_L}{x_L - x_R} = \frac{bx_L}{d} \tag{9}$$

$$y_p = \frac{by_L}{x_L - x_R} = \frac{by_L}{d} \tag{10}$$

Since the depth, z_p indicates a distance value (i.e. in mm or cm), we have to modify the equation (8) for its uniformity because, the parameters (b, f, d) in the equation possess different units. This modification is vital during measuring the distance of objects, otherwise it gives erroneous result. Accordingly, we can reform the equation (8) through converting the unit of the disparity value (d) by dividing it with the pixel size (normally in mm/pixel) of the camera. Thus the depth or distance of the target object becomes,

$$z_p = \frac{bf}{ds} \tag{11}$$

Where, s is the size of a pixel of the stereo camera. Thus, once we can estimate the 3D depth or distance value of the target, we can easily track or localize the human object.

4   Experimental Evaluation

The effectiveness and robustness of this approach is justified using different images captured by the stereo camera pair with different positions, expressions and lighting conditions. Experiments are carried out on a computer with 2.2 GHz Intel Core i5 processor and 4GB RAM. The algorithm has been implemented using Visual C++. We use two SONY VISCA cameras of same focal length and intrinsic parameters for stereo imaging.

The face images are analyzed to demonstrate the feasibility of the proposed detection method. When a complex image is subjected in the input, the face detection result highlights the facial part of the image. The face detection results with our proposed method are depicted in Fig. 6. Images of different persons are taken at different environments both in shiny and gloomy weather. To evaluate our proposed method we consider images with different expressions, pose, orientation, structural components and illumination. The system can also cope with the problem of partial occlusion. Our system demonstrates better performance in case of the frontal face images in simple background while provides worst results for the images in complex background. We perform experiments to compare our proposed algorithm with RGB and YIQ (Luminance, Hue, Saturation) based face detection methods. The results as shown in Table 1 and Table 2, confirms the robustness of our proposed face detection algorithm comparable to others methods.

Fig. 7 represents the stereo matching results with our proposed stereo algorithm. The algorithm computes the disparity values through matching the correspondence pixels within the selected blocks in the left and right image pair. The left and right image sequences are captured through the left and right camera respectively, placed in same epipolar axis. The correspondence matching is accomplished using SAD measures using a window of size 3×3 pixels. The disparities are computed with a search range of −10 to +10 pixels for a threshold level of 25. We estimate these parameters empirically in order to optimize quality of disparity results.

Experientially we find that computational cost increases with the enlargement of the window size. Fig. 8 represents a plot of computational time for different window size, which shows that a window of size 3×3 pixels is a good choice in respect to computational speed. We compare our algorithm with similar stereo methods in terms of execution time, as reported in Table 3. Experimental results confirm that our proposed disparity estimation algorithm outperforms with significant reduction of computation time compared to other existing methods.

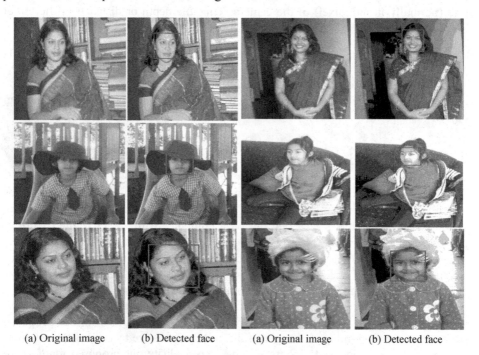

| (a) Original image | (b) Detected face | (a) Original image | (b) Detected face |

Fig. 6. Face detection process: (a) the original image, and (b) detected face image.

We estimate the distance or location of the human objects for five real image pairs using the obtained disparity values and known camera parameters. The focal length of the stereo cameras used in this simulation is 35 mm, pixel size is 0.1165 mm, and the baseline distance between two cameras is 20 cm. Table 4 shows the results of the location estimation process.

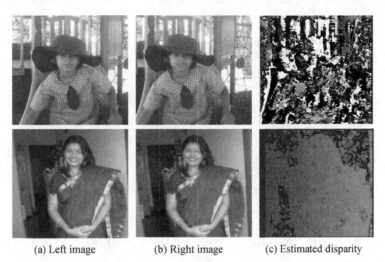

(a) Left image   (b) Right image   (c) Estimated disparity

Fig. 7. Stereo matching process: (a) Left image, (b) Right image, and (c) Disparity map.

Table 1. Performance of different detection methods in terms of detection accuracy (in %)

Type of Face image	No. of test image	Detection Accuracy (%)		
		RGB Color Based	YIQ Color Based	HSV Color Based (Proposed method)
Frontal	50	62.37	78.24	98.18
Tilted	50	58.42	74.65	95.34
Partial Occluded	20	56.72	72.29	91.56
Complex Background	30	50.35	67.17	86.72

Table 2. Performance of different detection methods in terms of computation time

Detection Method	Computation Time (second)
RGB Color Based	1.23
YIQ Color Based	0.87
Proposed Method	0.46

Table 3. Performance of different stereo methods in terms of computation time

Method	Computation Time (second)
Linear Stereo Matching [33]	15
Conventional Area Based [34]	1. 23
Large-scale Stereo Matching [36]	0.96

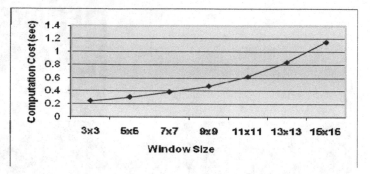

Fig. 8. Computational time versus Window Size.

Table 4. Results of Location estimation

Test	Actual Distance (cm)	Measured Distance (cm)	Error	Error (%)
Test 1	150	148.5821	-1.4179	0.94527
Test 2	200	197.2895	-2.7105	1.35525
Test 3	250	252.6481	2.6481	1.05924
Test 4	300	292.1137	-7.8863	2.62877
Test 5	350	343.7251	-6.2749	1.79283

5   Conclusion

Surveillance systems have gained importance due to the increase of safety and security of people. In this paper we propose an effective and inexpensive human surveillance system consisting of fast and robust algorithms for face detection, stereo correspondence matching, dense depth evaluation and human location estimation. The effectiveness of the proposed algorithms has been justified using real image sequences with complex and simple backgrounds. Experimental evaluation confirms that our algorithms perform superiority comparably to the state-of-the-art existing methods. Our next approach is to extend the algorithm for multi-face detection and location estimation.

References

1. Valera, M., Velastin, S.A.: Intelligent distributed surveillance systems: a review. In: Proceedings of Vision, Image and Signal Processing, pp. 192–204 (2005)
2. Irgan, K., Ünsalan, C., Baydere, S.: Low-cost prioritization of image blocks in wireless sensor networks for border surveillance. Journal of Networks and Computer Applications (JNCA) **38**, 54–64 (2014)

3. Kieran, D., Weir, J., Yan, W.: A framework for an event driven video surveillance system. Journal of Multimedia 6(1), 3–13 (2012)
4. Danielson, P.: Video surveillance for the rest of us: proliferation, privacy, and ethics education. In: Proc. of International Symposium on Technology and Society, vol. 1, no. 1, pp. 162–167 (2002)
5. Niu, W., Li, G., Tong, E., Yang, X., Chang, L., Shi, Z., Ci, S.: Interaction relationships of caches in agent-based HD video surveillance: Discovery and utilization. Journal of Networks and Computer Applications (JNCA) 37, 155–169 (2014)
6. Haritaoglu, I., Harwood, D., Davis, L.S.: W4: Real-Time Surveillance of People and Their Activities. IEEE Transactions on Pattern Analysis and Machine Intelligence 22(8), 809–830 (2000)
7. Pai, C., Tyan, H., Liang, Y., Liao, H., Chen, S.: Pedestrian detection and tracking at crossroads. Pattern Recognition 37, 1025–1034 (2004)
8. Wang, X.: Intelligent Multi-Camera Video Surveillance: A Review. Pattern Recognition Letters, 1–25 (2012)
9. Bodor, R., Morlok, R., Papanikolopoulos, N.: Dual camera system for multi-level activity recognition. In: Proc. of the IEEE/RJS International Conference on Intelligent Robots and Systems, vol. 1, pp. 643–648 (2004)
10. Yang, T., Li, S.Z., Pan, Q., Li, J.: Real-time Multiple Objects Tracking with Occlusion Handling in Dynamic Scenes. IEEE Computer Society Conference on Computer Vision and Pattern Recognition (CVPR) 1, 970–975 (2005)
11. Black, J., Ellis, T.: Multi-camera image measurement and correspondence. Measurement 32, 61–71 (2002)
12. Mittal, A., Davis, L.S., M2Tracker: A multiview approach to segmenting and tracking people in a cluttered scene using region-based stereo. In: Proc. of the 7th European Conf. on Computer Vision (ECCV 2002), pp. 18–36. Springer-Verlag (2002)
13. Darrell, T., Gordon, G., Harville, M., Wood-fill, J.: Integrated person tracking using stereo, color, and pattern detection. International Journal of Computer Vision 37(2), 175–185 (2000)
14. Ko, J., Lee, J.: Stereo Camera-based Intelligence Surveillance System. Journal of Automation and Control Engineering 3(3), 253–257 (2015)
15. Chowdhury, M.M., Bhuiyan, M.A.: Fast Window based Stereo Matching for 3D Scene Reconstruction. The International Arab Journal of Information Technology 10(4) (2013)
16. Chen, C., Yao, Y., Page, D., Abidi, B., Koschan, A., Abidi, M.: Heterogeneous fusion of omnidirectional and PTZ cameras for multiple object tracking. IEEE Transactions on Circuits and Systems for Video Technology 18(8), 1052–1063 (2008)
17. Adorni, G., Cagnoni, S., Mordonini, M., Sgorbissa, A.: Omnidirectional stereo systems for robot navigation. In: Proc. IEEE Workshop on Omnidirectional Vision and Camera Networks, pp. 79–89 (2003)
18. Munoz-Salinas, R., Aguirre, E., Garcia-Silvestre, M., Gonzalez, A.: A multiple object tracking approach that combines colour and depth information using a confidence measure. Pattern Recognition Letters 29, 1504–1514 (2008)
19. Munoz-Salinas, R.: A Bayesian plan-view map based approach for multiple-person detection and tracking. Pattern Recognition 41, 3665–3676 (2008)
20. Bimbo, A.D., Dini, F., Lisanti, G., Pernici, F.: Exploiting distinctive visual landmark maps in pan-tiltzoom camera networks. Computer Vision and Image Understanding 114, 611–623 (2010)

21. Justin, W.B., Benjamin, L.P., Kyle, K.E., Randy, L.M.: TENTACLE: Multi-Camera Immersive Surveillance System. Small Business Innovative Research (SBIR) Phase I Report, Air Force Research Laboratory (2011)
22. Wang, X.: Intelligent Multi-Camera Video Surveillance: A Review. Pattern Recognition Letters (2012), 1–25 (2012)
23. Darell, T., Gordon, G., Harville, M., Woodfill, J.: Integrated Person Tracking Using Stereo, Color, and Pattern Detection. Computer Vision and Pattern Recognition (1998)
24. Bahadori, S., Iocchi, L.: A stereo vision system for 3d reconstruction and semi-automatic surveillance of museum areas. In: Workshop of the Italian Association for Artificial Intelligence (AI*IA) (2003)
25. Manap, N., Caterina, G., Soraghan, J., Sidharth, V., Yao, H.: Smart surveillance system based on stereo matching algorithms with IP and PTZ cameras. In: 3DTV-CON 2010, pp. 65–68 (2010)
26. Cui, Z., Li, A.: A Novel Binocular Vision System for Surveillance Application. Journal of Multimedia **8**(4), 307–314 (2013)
27. Satter, A.K.M.Z., Chowdhury, M.M.H.: A Fuzzy Algorithm for De-Noising of Corrupted Images. International Journal of Computer Information Systems (IJCSI) **6**(4), 15–17 (2013)
28. Blanz, V., Vetter, T.: Face recognition based on fitting a 3-D morphable model. IEEE Trans. Pattern Anal. Mach. Intell. **25**(9), 1063–1074 (2003)
29. Uddin, J., Mondal, A.M., Chowdhury, M.M.H., Bhuiyan, M.A.: Face detection using genetic algorithm. In: Proceedings of 6th International Conference on Computer and Information Technology, Dhaka, Bangladesh, pp. 41–46, December 2003
30. Rowley, H., Shumeet, H.B., Kanade, T.: Neural Network-Based Face Detection. IEEE Transaction on Pattern Analysis and Machine Intelligence **20**(1), 23–37 (1998)
31. Gopalan, R., Jacobs, D.: Comparing and combining lighting insensitive approaches for face recognition. Computer Vision and Image Understanding **114**(1), 135–145 (2010)
32. Castillo, C.D., Jacobs, D.W.: Using stereo matching with general epipolar geometry for 2-D face recognition across pose. IEEE Trans. Pattern Anal. Mach. Intel. **31**(12), 2298–2304 (2009)
33. De-Maeztu, L., Mattoccia, S., Villanueva, A., Cabeza, R.: Linear stereo matching. In: IEEE International Conference on Computer Vision (ICCV 2011), pp. 1708–1715 (2011)
34. Di Stefano, L., Marchionni, M., Mattoccia, S.: A fast area-based stereo matching algorithm. Image and Vision Computing **22**(12), 983–1005 (2004)
35. Hosni, A., Bleyer, M., Rhemann, C., Gelautz, M., Rother, C.: Real-time local stereo matching using guided image filtering. In: Proc. IEEE-ICME, pp. 1–6 (2011)
36. Geiger, A., Roser, M., Urtasun, R.: Efficient large-scale stereo matching. In: Kimmel, R., Klette, R., Sugimoto, A. (eds.) ACCV 2010, Part I. LNCS, vol. 6492, pp. 25–38. Springer, Heidelberg (2011)
37. Yang, Q.: Stereo Matching Using Tree Filtering. IEEE Transactions on Pattern Analysis and Machine Intelligence **37**(4), 834–846 (2015)
38. Mei, X., Sun, X., Dong, W., Wang, H., Zhang, X.: Segment-tree based cost aggregation for stereo matching. In: CVPR, pp. 313–320 (2013)
39. Yang, Q.: A non-local cost aggregation method for stereo matching. In: CVPR, pp. 1402–1409, (2012)
40. Tatsunori, T., Yasuyuki, M., Takeshi, N.: Graph cut based continuous stereo matching using locally shared labels. In: CVPR 2014 (2014)

Security Considerations for Wireless Carrier Agonistic Bio-Monitoring Systems

Ben Townsend and Jemal Abawajy[✉]

Faculty of Science, Engineering and Built Environment, School of Information Technology,
Deakin University, Waurn Ponds Campus, Locked Bag 20000, Geelong, VIC 3220, Australia
jemal.abawajy@deakin.edu.au

Abstract. Advances in information and communications technology has led to a significant advances in noncontact portable devices capable of monitoring vital signals of patients. These wearable and implantable bio-monitoring systems allow collections of wearable sensors to be constructed as a Body Area Network (BAN) to record biological data for a subject. Such systems can be used to improve the quality of life and treatment outcomes for patients. One of the main uses for a bio-monitoring system is to record biological data values from a subject and provide them to a doctor or other medical professional. However, wearable bio-monitoring systems raise unique security considerations. In this paper, we discuss some of the security considerations that have arisen in our work around communications agnostic bio-monitoring, and how we have addressed these concerns. Furthermore, the issues related to the identifying and trusting sender and receiver entities are discussed.

Keywords: Bio-monitoring systems · Medical monitoring · Mobile communications · Information security · Information privacy · Telemetry · Medical telemetry

1   Introduction

It is a modern reality that portable medical monitoring systems are already with us, with such devices currently being used in hospitals using short range transmission infrastructure to allow patient sensors to communicate with ward-based central base-stations. Indeed, in both the academic and commercial worlds, there is much ongoing research into wearable bio-monitoring systems, looking at how we can build wearable networks of sensors and transmitters to monitor and care for patients while not physically confining them to a hospital ward. Such systems are intended to be used by patients in a hospital or in a remote location such as the home. They can provide monitoring for non-critical care patients or for those who require ongoing. Such systems are intended to be used by patients in a hospital or in a remote location such as the home. They can provide monitoring for non-critical care patients or for those who require ongoing monitoring during recovery from illness or operation. They can also be used for extended diagnosis-related data collection.

© Institute for Computer Sciences, Social Informatics and Telecommunications Engineering 2015
B. Thuraisingham et al. (Eds.): SecureComm 2015, LNICST 164, pp. 725–737, 2015.
DOI: 10.1007/978-3-319-28865-9_48

Bio-monitoring systems have been the subject of a significant amount of research over the past several years. These researches have produced wearable monitoring systems suitable for many applications such as:

- Athletes attempting to reach peak physical performance where monitoring determines biological and physiological status to define where they can focus training.
- Hospital patients who are mobile yet require ongoing monitoring can be allowed to wear a monitoring system and thus not be restricted to the hospital ward.
- Outpatients may require the collection of diagnostic data over a possibly extended period of time.
- The elderly or infirm who are not in a continuous care scenario but may need to be monitored in their homes, to preserve quality of life but ensure ongoing wellbeing.

The potential of wireless sensor networks for telemedicine and biometric monitoring, where sensors with communications capabilities interact to form a body area network for use in medical monitoring is well known. However, one of the concerns of the research into such systems is that the security of data is sometimes implied or assumed, but not explicitly considered as a requirement of the overall solution [3]. Because of the potential sensitivity and ethical concerns around the ability to access biological data measurements for a specific patient, any system transmitting and storing this data should enforce privacy and/or security mechanisms to prevent unauthorised access to the data. In this paper, we address this problem through the application of obfuscation of data and the ability to directly apply encryption to patient readings independently of the carrier that is used to transmit the data.

Our work relates to a communications carrier-agnostic bio-monitoring solution, where we allow the wearable monitoring system to seamlessly select and use the best available carrier to transmit bio-monitoring data and provide the best opportunity for the system to successfully send its data back to the doctor, As part of this research, we have had to consider the impacts that an agnostic approach has on the transmission of data, including how data is secured and how much data can be transmitted over each of the different carriers. Carrier agnosticism means that we cannot rely on the specific capabilities of any one carrier if such capability is not available across our suite of carriers. This includes assuming the presence of native carrier data encoding, identifying and trusting the senderand encrypting sensitive medical data. In developing the protocol, we have had to consider how to address limitations caused by our inability to rely on the capabilities of a specific carrier. In this paper, we discuss security considerations that have arisen in our work, and how we have addressed these concerns in the context of remaining carrier agnostic.

The rest of the paper is organized as follows. In Section 2, the background and related work are presented. In Section 3, security concerns for bio-monitoring data is presented. In Section 4, the issues related to the identifying and trusting sender and receiver entities are discussed. The conclusion is given in Section 5.

2   Background and Related Work

A bio-monitoring system is a system that converts information such as respiration, heart rate, temperature, brain activity, heart activity, or blood glucose levels into data that can be processed and recorded. These systems usually consists of set of sensors that collect data from the subject and communicate it to the gateway (e.g., smartphone) that transmits the collected data to a server or directly to the hospital [11].

Figure 1 is a general schematic of a wearable bio-monitoring system that uses mobile technologies with devices such as smartphones being used to co-ordinate the medical sensors and transmit sensor data to the medical professional. The systems are typically wholly body-portable – powered by batteries, worn or carried on the person, and disconnected from physical cables or power infrastructure. Measured data is sent through the wireless network to an acquisition point, which collects the data and transfers it to a database server. Using such a portable system, a patient in a non-critical-care situation can be monitored from the comfort of their own homes or at other remote locations, while on the move, at the shops or out for a walk.

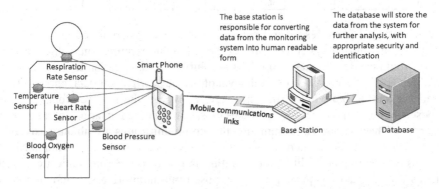

Fig. 1. A general wearable bio-monitoring system

There are a number of data types that we might conceivably record in a wearable bio-monitoring system. Budinger [2] discusses some of the data types we might want to encode as the output of a bio-monitoring system. Table 1 summarises the types, sizes, # Octets required to encode the data and min/max values for the sorts of medical data that we might have to record and transmit through the system. Data such as the above may be sampled, digitised and encoded quite readily. However, while these values are discrete and readily encoded, other values may be used in bio-monitoring. The recording of more extensive digitised data may require significant data capacity. As an example, the American Heart Association has stated that a single ECG (electrocardiogram) record showing heart activity could require up to 1.36 gigabytes of storage to allow it to be stored at a meaningful resolution [6].

Throughout the past ten years or so there has been a significant amount of research into wearable monitoring systems. Although many novel and unique systems have been suggested or developed to remotely monitor subjects, much research focus exists for the specific elements of the bio-monitoring system – the hardware, the sensors, the infrastructure and networking between the hardware which are used to make up a cohesive and wearable bio-monitoring system. However, security is not the main issue in the design of such systems.

Table 1. Medical data types

Type	Min	Max	Unit	Type	# Octets	Example
Temperature	0	~50	Degrees C	Binary	1	00100101
Heart Rate	0	~200	Beats per minute	Binary	1	00111100
Blood Pressure	0	~200	mmHg (x 2 measurements)	Binary	2.	01111000 01010000
Respiration rate	0	~50	Breaths per minute	Binary	1	00001110
Blood oxygen concentration	0	100	Percentage Oxygen Saturation (SpO$_2$)	Binary	1	01100100
Blood glucose concentration	0.0	~50.0	Mmol/L – a decimal value (to 1 decimal place)	Binary coded ASCII	3	8.2

Varshney [10] identifies several potential issues with existing and proposed wireless health monitoring systems, including the following requirements which, it is asserted, would need to be met by any viable solution for application to the real-world: (i) A high level of security; (ii) A high level of privacy for patient data; and (iii) Highly reliable and usable wireless infrastructure. However, the research focus of many proposed systems in the field concentrates on specific implementations of a BAN and its sensors. There is often an assumption that communications are ubiquitously available and that a pervasive Internet connection is always available. As communications are considered ubiquitous, little consideration is given to the communications backbone as a significant component of the proposed bio-monitoring solution, and issues such as security of data during transmission from the patient to the doctor seem to be assumed and/or implied.

Kwak et al [7] assert that there are three main areas of concern around healthcare monitoring systems. Of specific relevance to our work, they state that the areas of privacy and security are paramount in the implementation of any bio-monitoring system. We assert that a bio-monitoring system must consider the privacy and security of data as part of the fundamental system requirements. Kwak el al [7] state that most papers they reviewed take security against attack into account and that is highly relevant to medical systems. However, while the authors also identify privacy and obfuscation of data and the encryption of transmissions as requirements for bio-monitoring, these issues do not seem to be given the same levels of concern in the research we have reviewed. The presence of these capabilities seems to be assumed and not specifically implemented as part of the proposed systems. As our proposed communications protocol is carrier agnostic, these issues are concerns for us. We cannot rely on an assumption that our carrier will encrypt and/or ensure our data is private. To remain truly carrier agnostic, we must implement security and privacy ourselves.

Borec-Lubecke et al [12] discuss the looming use of the Internet of Things to assist in the monitoring of patients for healthcare purposes [12]. They identify the issues of data privacy and communication security as fundamental to the implementation of a functional eHealthcare solution. However, while identifying the issues, their paper does not propose any solutions to widespread transmission of patient data and/or records. Hanson et al [8] identify a number of the traits that a medical bio-monitoring system must possess or incorporate into its design, including security of access and configuration, privacy of information and encryption of data. Once again, privacy and encryption are key facts. Hanson also mentions configurability as a requirement of a solution and on this point we wholly agree. Our proposed communications protocol considers the need to reconfigure a monitoring system "over the air" while it is deployed in the field. In evaluating how this might be achieved, this has identified additional security and identification concerns that must be addressed in an operational real world solution.

Table 2. Fields in the message protocol

Field Nbr.	Field Name	Abbrev.
1	Start of Message Frame	SOMF
2	Message Protocol Format	MFMT
3	Message Type	MTYP
4	Application ID	APID
5	Sender Device ID	SDID
6	Recipient Device ID	RDID
7	Message ID	MSID
8	Message Structure	MSTR
9	Generation Timestamp	GENT
10	Validity Period	VAPD
11	User Data Segment Length	UDSL
12	User Data Segment Encryption ID	UDSE
13	Header Checksum	HCHK
14	User Data Segment Checksum	UCHK
15	Combined Message Checksum	MCHK
16	User Data Segment	UDSG

3   Security Concerns for Bio-monitoring Data

While a large binary data set such as an ECG may not be readily human readable, the data types shown in table 1 are quite easily interpretable. As with other transmissions, messages transmitted from a bio-monitoring system to a doctor may be intercepted by a third party during the transmission process. Where message data is not obfuscated and/or encrypted in such a way as to render the data incoherent to an external unauthorised attacker, patient data could be compromised. We would assert that the developers of bio-monitoring systems must consider the protection of information during transmission as a fundamental system requirement. The protection of data is especially important if we facilitate transmission of the data via an open network such as the Internet, where many devices may "see" a message between source and destination. To this end, both obfuscation and encryption of data should be considered an essential part of the overall capabilities of a bio-monitoring system.

3.1   Communications Protocol

In our research, we are creating a robust communications protocol to facilitate bio-monitoring communications via a carrier agnostic approach. Being carrier agnostic allows us to use carriers such as Internet, Packet Radio, Mobile Data, MMS and SMS. We have chosen a carrier agnostic approach due to the nature of medical monitoring and potential ramifications if the system cannot deliver a monitoring message for a critical medical situation. A remote wearable monitoring system must have every opportunity to "get the message through" to its base station. By supporting multiple carriers in the same monitoring system, our solution can select the best available communications method at the point of transmission and fail over between carriers as required. We have developed a simple communications protocol which consists of a header block and a user data segment,that can be transmitted via any of a number of possible carriers, including Internet, Mobile or Fixed Line Data call, SMS, Multimedia Message and Packet Radio. In being carrier agnostic however, we have had to facilitate a number of key features, including obfuscation of data, identification of sender and recipient, and encryption of the user data. The structure of our packet is shown In Table 2.

3.2   Obfuscation

In the context of a bio-monitoring system, the obfuscation of data removes the ability to associate data with the subject without the provision of a key to the data. As part of our research, we have created a communications protocol (see table 2 above) that can be used to transmit bio-monitoring data and associated header information. The communications packet header identifies the sender device, receiver device and the monitoring "application" in which a message is intended to be used. By remaining carrier agnostic, we cannot assume identification elements such as IP address or telephone number will exist in our message. However, we only identify devices in the header. No personally identifying details (such as patient ID, patient name etc) are incorporated into the message.

While the user data segment of our message may contain biological readings from a specific subject (amongst other possible uses for the data segment), the message itself contains no information that can associate a specific subject with their readings. To make the association between subject and biological readings transmitted in a message, the reader of the message needs to correlate the sender device ID (i.e. the ID of a specific bio-monitor) to a subject ID. This correlating data is stored at the base station used by the doctor, and is never transmitted over the network. As such, to perform this correlation implies access to data that is only available via direct access on the base station itself.

Because we divorce the data in the transmission from the identity of the subject, it is difficult for an attacker who intercepts a transmission to re-associate the data to a specific subject unless the attacker also gains access to the base station. To this end, we propose that the first security tool that any bio-monitoring system should implement is the effective obfuscation of the subject's data from its identification details. This can be further supplemented by the implementation of a rule that states that no personally identifying data is ever transmitted within a bio-monitoring application such that it could be intercepted and used to establish the link between the subject and their monitoring data.

3.3   Encryption of Data

Our communications protocol facilitates the control, management and transmission of data within a bio-monitoring system consisting of wearable bio-monitors and a central doctor's base station (for example at the hospital). In this system, the user data segment of our messages is used to transmit system data such as the biological readings of patients. Consider, for example, a hypothetical encoding scheme where user data segment is encoded with biological readings via a number of type/value pairs. In this instance the first octet defines the type and the next X octets define the data for that data type, repeated in each message as shown in Fig. 2.

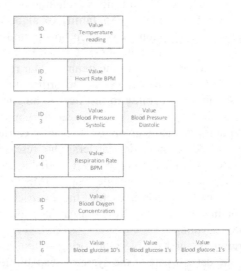

Fig. 2. Hypothetical Values and Octets of data in the User Data Segment

This data is obfuscated and cannot be related back to a specific subject without the index that shows which sender device ID relates to which patient. However, despite the obfuscation, if such data were encoded into a message without any form of encryption, in would in most cases be clearly readable by taking the data octets and decoding their binary values. The type/value pair encoding mechanism does provide a level of obfuscation to the data. To correctly interpret the data requires the attacker to "understand" what each type value means and what size the data for that type is. However, it could be argued that simple obfuscation of this nature is not enough to protect the data against a determined attempt to compromise the system and interpret the values.

Consider also an alternative scenario, where our user definable data segment may carry biological data encoded in a standards compliant packet of medical telemetry – for example using the IEEE 11073-20601 standard that has been defined specifically for this purpose. Where a standard's based format is used to transmit data, it is possible that the attacker could, through analysis, determine the standard in use and therefore have a ready "map" of the methods of encoding data within a message. It is as a result of these sorts of scenarios that we must consider whether the data we are transmitting requires encryption, over and above the obfuscation discussed previously. Our research makes use of a number of communications carriers, including public carriers such as the packet radio network and the Internet. This means that, in some cases, our transmissions may be broadcast and could be intercepted by anyone who is listening. For certain types of transmission, we may determine that our data should be protected over and above the capabilities of an obfuscated data set, and thus we must consider how we protect the data appropriately.

Where the need for encryption rather than obfuscation is identified, one might argue that many carriers provide encryption capabilities as a native part of their feature set. For example, GSM mobile communications including both mobile data and SMS have typically been encrypted using the A5 family of algorithms [1]. However, in recent years, A5 and other encryptions have been broken and there are a number of published solutions that allow decryption of GSM based mobile transmissions potentially in real time [1][5]. As noted earlier, the nature of our research is carrier agnostic, and this requires that we allow our system to utilise multiple communications mechanisms and thus maintain an ability to fail over to an alternate carrier when the preferred carrier is unavailable. As a result of the need to support multiple carriers, we cannot rely on encryption provided natively by a specific carrier unless the same capability exists across all of our potential carriers. Our research has identified that, where our data is to be transmittable via the best available carrier from a pool that might include Internet, Packet Radio, Mobile Data, MMS or SMS, we must accept that encryption does not exist natively in each of these carriers. As such, in taking the lowest common denominator of features from our carrier pool, we must not expect the carrier to provide the encryption.

Our solution therefore requires the bio-monitoring system implement the ability to apply encryption to the data as part of the system's capabilities and not rely on the carrier. While this is something we considered in our work through the necessity of our agnostic approach, we would strongly recommend the encryption of data transmissions be implemented as a native capability of any monitoring system over and above any capabilities offered by the carrier.

3.4   Appropriate Encryption

While encryption is a requirement of the bio-monitoring systems' transmissions, we must also consider that for some of our potential carriers the data capacity of a message may be limited. For example, in an ideal world we would use an unlimited Internet data stream, but in our system we may have to fall back to slow packet radio transmission at 9600 baud [4] (TAPR 1995) (TAPR 1995), or even use an SMS message with a mere 140 octets of data capacity [6]. Because we do not always have the luxury of an unlimited data stream, we must not only consider that encryption is essential. We must also consider whether the encryption to be applied is appropriate for the full gamut of prospective carriers in our system. In defining an appropriate encryption algorithm for use with our protocol, we believe that a number of factors must be considered:

- The encryption algorithm should require a (relatively) low overhead to store encrypted data. The number of additional octets of data required to encrypt the data should low when compared to the data content to be encrypted. Where we have length limited carriers, we do not want the encryption overhead to outweigh the volume of data in the message.
- The encryption algorithm should provide a level of data security that is commensurate with the requirements for data protection imposed by the application. For example, obfuscation of the data and the removal of personally identifying detail in all messages may reduce the need for complex, high overhead encryption. While monitoring data is personal and should be confidential, if it has no contextualisation to a specific subject in the case of interception of a specific message, do we need to make use of 1024 bit encryption that would take longer than the lifetime of the universe to break?
- Any encryption algorithm should ideally have a low processing overhead to encrypt or decrypt data. The remote monitoring system is likely to be battery operated may not have significant processing power.
- The time to encrypt or decrypt a message must allow us to treat messages urgently, so it is not acceptable to allow encryption to cause significant delays before the transmission can occur.

From the above set of constraints, it is apparent that the appropriate encryption needs to have a low processing overhead and a low data overhead (in terms of the additional octets that are required to encrypt the data). If we are using 1024 bit RSA encryption, for example, the overhead is such that we could not use SMS as one of our potential carriers (as the RSA encrypted data would exceed the 140 octets of the SMS payload). To facilitate the ability to encrypt user data, we have allowed our communications protocol to implement application specific encryption through the use of an application-defined encryption ID that is transmitted as part of the communications packet header. This single octet value allows the application using the protocol to select one of 255 possible encryption mechanisms that can be applied to the user data segment data. In this way, the application can define the types of encryption to be used based on the capabilities of the potential carriers in the system. For example, the ID may be used to identify different key sets for public key encryption, further securing the data by the use of multiple possible rolling keysets. Thus an encryption ID value of 1 may signify key set 1 is in use. An ID of 2 signifies keyset 2 in use etc. Alternatively, the encryption mode may change based on the carriers that are currently active. For example, where SMS is a potential carrier, only low overhead encryption may be used identified by a specific set of encryption ID's. Alternatively, if the carriers in use all have large possible data payloads (such as Internet, Packet Radio and Mobile Data Call), then higher overhead encryption may be defined on an application specific basis.

4   Identifying and Trusting Sender and Receiver

In a bio-monitoring system, it is highly likely that the component transceivers within the system will be known as part of the system configuration. This includes both the base station and any wearable monitors in use within a particular application. Because the component devices are known, this allows us to utilise device identification to assist us in trusting messages sent or received on the network. Because our communications are carrier agnostic, we cannot depend on any of the identification details that may be included in a carrier specific message (for example, IP address, telephone number etc). We must be cognizant of the fact that some of our potential carriers (such as packet radio) may not include a system level station ID as part of their message transmission. Therefore, as part of our protocol, we have implemented a number of identification fields to specifically identify one of the transceiver stations in the system. Four identification fields are part of our standard message header block, namely an Application ID, Sender Device ID, Recipient Device ID and Message ID.

The application ID is a single octet used to identify one of 255 possible applications that may use the same communications infrastructure. This is specifically relevant where one or more of our carriers are part of a broadcast infrastructure, for example over radio or Internet. In these cases, many participating (and nonparticipating) devices may "listen" to the same transmission, even if it is not addressed to them. The application ID allows segmented use of the communications infrastructure by defining different logical applications on the same infrastructure. Applications using our protocol must check the application ID matches their own application prior to actioning a message.

The sender device ID and receiver device ID are 24 bit numbers that identify a specific device within the application. While this may identify up to 16 million unique devices per application, it is unlikely that a single monitoring application would require this number of devices for an application. As there is no requirement that we sequentially allocate ID's to devices on an incremental basis, we are able to use the ID to establish a trust relationship. To do this, device ID's are allocated according to an algorithm. The algorithm can be application defined based on the requirements of the system using the agnostic-communications protocol. By using algorithmic allocation of ID's, only certain device ID's will be valid within the network. This will allow the application to implement checks to ensure that a device ID fits the allocation algorithm and may thus make it more difficult for a rogue device to easily obtain a valid ID and masquerade on the network to "listen" to the transmissions going back and forth.

The sender and receiver ID identify the source and destination of a message as part of the message header's addressing. This allows us to build an application where a message is only "read" by the device it is intended for. The receiver should check that its own ID value matches the receiver ID in the message. The sender ID allows us to define specific message types that will only be actioned when they come from a specific sender. For example, a message to change the configuration of a remote monitor may only be accepted if the sender ID is the same as that of the base station at the hospital.

Finally each message has its own internal identification, encoded in the message ID field. For our protocol, the message ID is a 24 bit number, and thus 16 million unique messages per sender and receiver pair can be identified using the message ID alone. The message ID is allocated by the sender of the message, using the next available ID from its pool of message ID's. Message ID's are used in conjunction with the application, sender and receiver ID's to provide a highly unique message identifier within the system. With 16 million (approx.) ID's available, we would assert that this is sufficient for a bio-monitoring application, as even sending 1 message per second, 24 hours per day, this would give us a monitoring period of 194.18 days before the pool was exhausted and had to cycle back to 1. If we reduce messages to 5 second intervals, we have over 900 days before the pool is exhausted.

To manage message addressing, we combine all of the identification fields together. The application, receiver, sender and message ID's provide a total of 10 octets or 80 bits of identification. To set the message ID, the sequence of messages between a sender and receiver pair is tracked by the sender. Thus, in application 1, for a combination of sender ID 1 and receiver ID 2, the message ID relates to the sequence of messages sent between this sender and receiver and is incremented for each message sent in that direction. When sending between sender ID 2 and receiver ID 1, the message ID relates to the sequence between sender 2 and receiver 1 and so tracks that series of communications in that direction. This will thus provide 16 million messages per sender/receiver pair. For example, see Table 3.

Table 3. The use of message ID between specific sender and receiver pairs

Transmission number	Sender ID	Receiver ID	Message ID
1	1	2	1
2	1	2	2
3	2	1	1
4	1	2	3
5	2	1	2

By combining the application, sender and receiver ID's, and the message ID in a sender/receiver directional pairing, we can ensure that messages come from a known and accepted source, that the message is being actioned by the correct device, and that the message was sent by a sender we will accept. By maintaining an application specific set of sender authorisations, we can also ensure we do not action specific types of message (for example, configuration messages) unless they come from a station that is authorized to make configuration changes (for example, the base station). By using the message ID in conjunction with the sender and receiver, we can also track the sequence of messages, and ensure we do not miss messages (for example, if the message ID between sender 1 and destination 2 suddenly jumps from message ID 10 to message 12, we can infer message ID 11 may have been lost).

5   Conclusion

Security of data, the need to obfuscate data and the ability to identify and trust a sender and receiver within a transmission can all be beneficial attributes to the successful implementation of a bio-monitoring system. Obfuscation prevents the transmitted data from being associated with a specific subject without additional data that is never transmitted over the network. In any system that transmits data over a public network, we should assume that the data may be intercepted and this, obfuscation should be the first line of defence for any biological monitoring data transmission. Encryption provides the ability to protect data from unauthorised access, even if that data has already been obfuscated. However, when using carriers with limited payload capacity it must be considered that encryption can have an additional bandwidth and encoding overhead, so we assert that the encryption used for the transmission of bio-monitoring data must be appropriate to the application. We identify a number of factors to inform the decision of what constitutes an appropriate data encryption mechanism. The use of message fields to uniquely identify the members of a bio-monitoring system facilitates a number of capabilities in the system. The use of algorithmic allocation of device ID's can make it more difficult for a rogue device to generate an ID masquerade as part of the network as any ID needs to match the allocation algorithm, which is not published by the network. The ability to specifically identify sender and receiver provides an ability to action messages only when they are received at the correct station, and allows us to restrict the use of certain message types (i.e. configuration messages) unless they are sent from an appropriate sender. We have found that all three elements are required to properly implement a carrier agnostic approach to bio-monitoring communications and must be considered as fundamental requirements of our system. However, given their benefits, we would assert that all of these features should be considered as security requirements of any medical bio-monitoring system.

References

1. Barkan, E., Biham, E., Keller, N.: Instant Ciphertext Only Cryptanalysis of GSM Encrypted Communication. Technion Technical Report, vol. CS-2006-2007 (2006)
2. Budinger, T.F.: Biomonitoring With Wireless Communications. Annual Review of Biomedical Engineering 5(1), 383–412 (2003)
3. Townsend, B., Abawajy, J., Kim, T.-h.: SMS-based Medical Diagnostic Telemetry Data Transmission Protocol for Medical Sensors. Sensors 11(4), 4231–4243 (2011)
4. ETSI: Digital cellular telecommunications system (Phase 2+); Technical realization of the Short Message Service (SMS) Point-to-Point (PP) (GSM 03.40), European Teleommuniations Standards Institute, Valbonne, France (1996a)
5. Guneysu, T., Kasper, T., Novotny, M., Paar, C., Rupp, A.: Cryptanalysis with Copacobana. IEEE Transactions on Computers 57(11), 16 (2008)
6. Iskandar, R., Simri W, I.W.: Compression of ECG Signal Using Neural Network Predictor and Huffman Coding. Proceeding Seminar Ilmiah Nasional KOMMIT 2010 30, 3 (2010)
7. Kwak, K.S.: Social Issues in Wireless Sensor Networks with Healthcare Perspective. The International Arab Journal of Information Technology 8(1), 7 (2011)
8. Hanson, M.A., Powell Jr, H.C., Barth, A.T., Ringgenberg, K., Calhoun, B.H., Aylor, J.H., Lach, J.: Body Area Sensor Networks: Challenges and Opportunities. Computer 0018–9162(9), 8 (2009)
9. TAPR 1995: Packet Radio: What? Why? How?, Tucson Amateur Packet Radio Corporation (2013). http://www.tapr.org/pr_intro.html (retrieved October 3, 2013)
10. Varshney, U.: Pervasive Healthcare and Wireless Health Monitoring. Mobile Network Applications 2007(12), 15 (2007)
11. Fang, X., et al.: An extensible embedded terminal platform for wireless telemonitoring. In: 2012 International Conference on Information and Automation (ICIA), pp. 668–673 (2012)
12. Boric-Lubecke, O., Gao, X., Yavari, E., Baboli, M., Singh, A., Lubecke, V,M.: E-healthcare: remote monitoring, privacy, and security. In: 2014 IEEE MTT-S International Conference on Microwave Symposium (IMS), pp. 1–3 (2014)

Author Index

Printed in the United States
By Bookmasters